COLE

MANAGEMENT
theory & practice

6e

Management Theory and Practice
6th Edition
Kris Cole

Publishing manager: Dorothy Chiu
Senior publishing editor: Sophie Kaliniecki
Developmental editors: Duncan Campbell-Avenell, Tharaha
Richards
Project editors: Michaela Skelly, Kate McGregor
Cover designer: Danielle Maccarone
Text designer: Norma Van Rees
Editor: Carolyn Beaumont
Permissions/Photo researcher: QBS Learning
Indexer: Julie King
Proofreader: Judith Bamber
Reprint: Magda Koralewska
Cenveo Publisher Services

Any URLs contained in this publication were checked for
currency during the production process. Note, however, that the
publisher cannot vouch for the ongoing currency of URLs.

For product information and technology assistance,
in Australia call **1300 790 853**;
in New Zealand call **0800 449 725**

For permission to use material from this text or product, please email
aust.permissions@cengage.com

National Library of Australia Cataloguing-in-Publication Data
Creator: Cole, Kris, author.
Title: Management Theory and Practice / Kris Cole.
Edition: Sixth edition.
ISBN: 9780170354059 (paperback)
Subjects: Supervision of employees.
 Personnel management.
Dewey Number: 658.302

Cengage Learning Australia
Level 7, 80 Dorcas Street
South Melbourne, Victoria Australia 3205

Cengage Learning New Zealand
Unit 4B Rosedale Office Park
331 Rosedale Road, Albany, North Shore 0632, NZ

For learning solutions, visit **cengage.com.au**

Printed in China by China Translation & Printing Services.
2 3 4 5 6 7 8 21 20 19 18 17

BRIEF CONTENTS

CONTENTS

Guide to the text

As you read this text, you will find a number of features in every chapter to enhance your study of management and help you understand how the theory is applied in the real world.

CHAPTER OPENING FEATURES

Chapter overviews establish learning objectives and provide a framework for revision and exam preparation.

Chapter opening scenarios set the chapter contents in a work context.

FEATURES WITHIN CHAPTERS

THEORY TO PRACTICE

Theory to practice boxes show how the chapter content applies to real-life workplace situations.

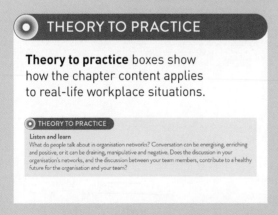

STRATEGIC PERSPECTIVE

The **strategic perspective** boxes provide a strategic overview of the theory to help you understand it in a wider context.

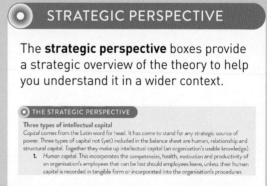

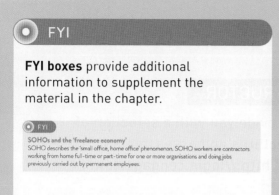

FYI boxes provide additional information to supplement the material in the chapter.

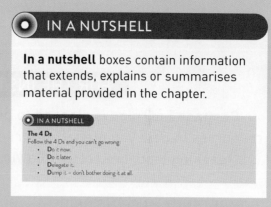

In a nutshell boxes contain information that extends, explains or summarises material provided in the chapter.

Action! boxes prompt you to CourseMate Express and give you guidance in how to use the digital resources that are included with this book.

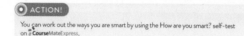

END-OF-CHAPTER FEATURES

At the end of each chapter you will find several tools to help you to review, practise and extend your knowledge of the key learning outcomes.

- **End-of-chapter** activities give you the opportunity to test your knowledge, apply your skills and consolidate your learning through the **Quick review**, **Build your skills** and **Workplace activities** sections.
- **Case studies** cover a variety of industries and sectors, encouraging you to integrate and apply the concepts discussed in the chapter to the workplace.

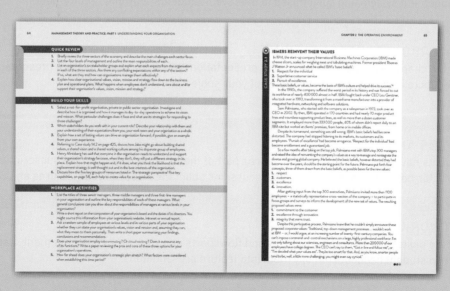

Guide to the online resources

FOR THE INSTRUCTOR

Cengage Learning is pleased to provide you with a selection of resources to help you prepare your lectures and assessments. These teaching tools are accessible via http://login.cengage.com .

COMPETENCY MAPPING GRID

The competency mapping grid shows you how the following qualifications are covered in this book:
- BSB42015 Certificate IV in Leadership and Management
- BSB51915 Diploma of Leadership and Management

LEARNER GUIDES

These assessments are cross-referenced to the text and include written assessments, project assessment, trainer interviews and checklists. Use them to test if your students are competent in the skills required by the training package.

INSTRUCTOR'S MANUAL

The Instructor's Manual includes:
- Case-study answers
- Group activities
- Metacognition questions

TEST BANK

Test Bank questions, which cover the learning objectives and key topics, have been prepared for your use. These are available in Word file format and can be uploaded directly into your learning management system and customised to meet your students' learning requirements.

POWERPOINT PRESENTATIONS

Use the chapter-by-chapter PowerPoint presentations to enhance your lecture presentations and handouts to reinforce the key principles of your subject.

VIDEOS AND VIDEO NOTES

Students have been provided with videos as part of their CourseMate Express subscription. Use the instructor notes provided to help lead discussions about the videos in your lectures and classes.

ARTWORK FROM THE TEXT

Add the digital files of graphs, pictures and flowcharts into your course management system, use them in student handouts or copy them into lecture presentations.

FOR THE STUDENT

New copies of this text come with an access code that gives you a 12-month subscription to the CourseMate Express website and Search me! Management. Visit http://login.cengagebrain.com and login using the code card.

The **CourseMate Express** website for students includes a suite of interactive resources designed to support your learning, revision and further research.

INCLUDES:

- Videos
- Simulations
- Self-tests, checklists and templates
- Revision quizzes
- Chapter endnotes
- Glossary and flashcards

Expand your knowledge with **Search me! Management.** Fast and convenient, this resource provides you with 24-hour access to full-text articles from hundreds of scholarly and popular journals and newspapers, including *The Australian* and *The New York Times*. Search me! allows you to explore topics further and find current references.

ABOUT THE AUTHOR

Kris Cole

Kris Cole is Australia's best-selling business author and a management consultant and keynote speaker. She is recognised internationally as a leading authority on performance and productivity management, leadership and effective communication.

Having held significant management and human resources positions in the engineering, oil, food and education industries and holding a Bachelor of Science (Honours) in Industrial Psychology, a Post-Graduate Diploma in Manufacturing Technology and a Graduate Certificate in Adult Education, Kris established her consulting company, Bax Associates, in 1983. She has created and led management training programs and assisted organisations in all sectors in Australia, New Zealand and South-East Asia to improve their workplace effectiveness, performance and productivity.

Kris has a practical approach and a clear grasp of bottom-line issues. Her books highlight current trends and best practices and are known for their clear writing style backed by solid knowledge and significant research. They offer practical ideas and everyday examples of how to lead, communicate, and work more effectively with colleagues and customers, identify and work to priorities, and thrive in a changing work environment.

Other books by Kris Cole include:

Business Administration and Supervision, Prentice Hall, Sydney, 2004.

Call Centre Communication: How to Make Each and Every Call a First-Rate Experience, East West Books (Madras) Pvt Ltd, 2003.

Crystal Clear Communication: Skills for Understanding and Being Understood, Prentice Hall, Sydney, 1st ed., 1993; 2nd ed., 2000. (Also available in Mandarin, German, Arabic, Tamil, Bahasa Indonesian and Farsi)

Leadership For Dummies, Wiley Publishing Australia, Brisbane, 2008.

Make Time Work for You, Tata McGraw Hill, New Delhi, 2001.

Making Time Work for You, Fishtail Publishing, Queensland, 2007. (Also available in Bahasa Malay)

The Complete Idiot's Guide to Clear Communication, Alpha Books, Pearson Education, 2002.

The Manager's Survival Guide, Tata McGraw Hill, New Delhi, 2001.

The Supervisor's Survival Guide, Woodslane, NSW, 2014.

Workplace Relations in Australia, Pearson Education, Sydney, 2007.

Matthew Coxhill

Matthew Coxhill is a critical thinker on sustainability and business and has worked and consulted in a variety of industries, from aquaculture to educational publishing. He has held management roles in Australia and overseas and presents internationally on management and sustainability challenges. Matthew is committed to facilitating behaviour change for sustainability and better management in business, using innovative ways to engage people in these issues. Matthew is a director of Fishtail Education, providing educational resources and training, as well as specialised consulting and troubleshooting, to a range of industries. He is a qualified Workplace Trainer and Assessor, holds a Bachelor of Science, a Masters in Peace and Conflict Studies, and is currently undertaking a PhD in Human Geography.

PREFACE

Readers may be divided into four classes:

1. Sponges, who absorb all that they read and return it in nearly the same state, only a little dirtied.

2. Sand-glasses, who retain nothing and are content to get through a book for the sake of getting through the time.

3. Strain-bags, who retain merely the dregs of what they read.

4. Mogul diamonds, equally rare and valuable, who profit by what they read, and enable others to profit by it also.

Samuel Taylor Coleridge, 'Definition of poetry', *The Broadview Anthology of British Literature*,
Broadview Press, 2010

Management as a discipline dates back to Frederick W Taylor's *Principles of Scientific Management*, published in 1911. In those days, organisations were shaped like pyramids, with deep layers of middle managers who passed information 'up the line' and orders 'down the line'. Workers did as they were told, kept their mouths shut and expected to work for the same organisation, doing much the same work, for most of their working lives.

Management today is entirely different. The industrial economy is gone and you are managing in a service economy that is moving rapidly towards a knowledge economy. The environment you are managing in is uncertain and unpredictable, and the organisation you are managing in has probably squashed its pyramid into only a few levels – it may not even be shaped like a pyramid any more. Organisations are more complex, business models are changing rapidly and stand-alone functions are being replaced by capabilities-based processes.

You are managing different types of employees with entirely different expectations from those of employees of 100 or even 50 years ago. You may not even watch the people reporting to you as they work, as did past generations of managers. In fact, you may not see those reporting to you for days or weeks at a time; and sometimes you may never even meet them face to face because they work on the other side of the world.

The world, Australian society, the Australian economy and the field of management are changing dramatically and much of what people automatically assumed management is about and how to manage has changed. The pressures on and expectations of today's managers are different and, not surprisingly, their duties and responsibilities are different and their typical working days are different.

How well equipped are you to manage in 21st century Australia? When you know the 'new rules' of adapting and innovating amid the uncertainties and unpredictability of the working environment, and have the 'new skills' of communicating, empowering, energising and supporting people, you can prosper and thrive.

Between the idea and the reality ... falls the shadow.

T S Eliot, in B C Southam, *A student's guide to the selected poems of T. S. Eliot*, Faber & Faber, 1994

Less poetically, this extensively revised and updated sixth edition of *Management Theory and Practice* attempts to throw light on the shadow and bridge the gap between theory and practice. It puts sound theory and breaking research into everyday language and into a context you can easily relate to and understand.

Management Theory and Practice can help you to develop the vocabulary you need to communicate effectively with your colleagues and team members and it provides models and frameworks you can use in various management situations. It can strengthen your 'hard skills', like managing poor performance, being more directive and solving problems permanently. It can also strengthen your so-called 'soft skills' (often the most difficult to learn).

Whether you are an aspiring manager, new to management or an old hand extending, refreshing or updating your skills, my goals in this edition (as in the previous editions) are three-fold:

1. To provide leading-edge information about the science and art of management so you can grasp the essential theoretical information and put it into practice in your own unique way.
2. To convey the information in a practical, everyday context so that it 'makes sense'.
3. To give you a reference to use for many years to come.

As Samuel Johnson said:

The next best thing to knowing something is knowing where to find it.

Samuel Johnson, in C Jackson Grayson, C O'dell, *If only we knew what we know*, Simon & Schuster, 2011

I love to hear from readers – comments, compliments and complaints are all welcome at KrisCole@bax.com.au.

Remember: Knowledge only becomes power when you use it. I wish each of you who use this text a good beginning. May you all be mogul diamonds!

Kris Cole

ACKNOWLEDGEMENTS

Ideas and material for this text come from many sources – from my own management experiences, from the experiences of practising managers and specialists, from the stimulating discussions on management development programs in which I have been involved in the private, public and not-for-profit sectors and at universities and TAFE colleges, and from the research and publications of numerous academics.

I would like particularly to thank the hundreds of course participants I have worked with whose ideas and experiences are included in this book.

I would like to thank Paul Petrulis and his colleagues at Cengage, Sophie Kaliniecki, Michaela Skelly, Kate McGregor and Duncan Campbell-Avenell, for the tremendous support they have provided for this sixth – and best-ever – edition of *Management Theory and Practice*. Never has it looked so good or been supported by such excellent teacher and student resources.

My heartfelt thanks to Matthew Coxhill, who has worked on this and earlier editions of this text in many capacities. Your experience and advice has been invaluable, Matthew.

Professor Gavin Andrews and Jess Smith generously provided insights, information and experience in leading knowledge workers; you can read about it in Case study 9.2: Management by filing cabinet, as well as in several Theory to practice boxes throughout the text.

Annette Guilfoile provided much useful information from her experience in leading off-shore teams.

Jim and Jan Williams shared their experience and best practice in operational planning and the day-to-day running of a small business.

Jane Bassam shared her experiences of setting up improvement teams using lean Six Sigma principles which you read about in Case study 19.1: Lean believers.

Jim Hayward offered an array of ideas, examples and information, particularly on risk management and project management. Gil Kearns shared her experience and knowledge in risk management and provided practical and useful information. Stephen Hartley and Tamea Turner shared their insights and experience on project management.

Tracy Randell and Sue McCormick shared their experience and knowledge in the rapidly changing field of recruitment.

Sallyann Shearer contributed her experience and insights on leading older employees. Pam Gerrard and Alexandrea Cannon provided thoughtful and helpful comments on Case study 26.1: Know-it-alls or Wisdom workers? Alexandrea Cannon and Carolyn Mitchell provided valuable information in the field of diversity and equal employment opportunities.

David Davenport offered a range of helpful suggestions, particularly regarding the Instructor's Manual and the additional resources we are now supplying.

Last but most certainly not least, it was a privilege to work once again with the best editor in the universe, Carolyn Beaumont.

Thank you all. And thank you readers and teachers. You make the book worthwhile.

Publisher's acknowledgements

The author and Cengage Learning would like to thank the following people for their feedback during the development of this edition.

Kelly Black	The Bremer Institute of TAFE
Peter Drapac	NBIA
Simone White	Chisholm Institute
Anna Russell	MARC School of Management
Robert Miles	International College of Management
Karen Artis	Sunshine Coast TAFE
Will Baker	BNIT
Tim Rule	Selmar Institute of Education
Karen Atkinson	AGB HR
Barbra May	Red Cross College
Karen Connaughton	Evocca College
Jim Hayward	Formerly of Mt Barker Institute
Elisa Uyen	The Pivot Institute
Shweta Singh	Formerly of Evocca College
Merran Renton	Bedford college

PART

1

UNDERSTANDING YOUR ORGANISATION

Tea ladies do the rounds. Smoking in the workplace is the norm. The standard working week is Monday to Friday, nine to five. No carer's, paternity or personal leave. Men do 'men's jobs' and are the breadwinners, and women do 'ladies' jobs' or stay at home. No computers? Sounds like ancient history? Ah, but that was the 1960s.

Life is different today. Whether we like it or not, the world is changing, the nature of work and working patterns are changing and organisations are changing. Is change positive, energising and uplifting, or is change challenging and stressful? The answer depends on whether the change is done to you, or by you.

In these first four chapters you discover the rapidly changing, shrinking yet expanding, turbulent and unpredictable external environment that your organisation operates in and the challenges this presents to employees, managers and organisations alike.

You find out how organisations are responding by changing their structures and their operations. You find out how the nature and types of relationships inside organisations are changing and how the relationships that organisations have with their customers and suppliers are changing. An organisation's values, vision, mission and strategy are explained, and you find out how to use them to manage your area of operations and lead your team.

You also find out how to understand the 'formal organisation' (your organisation as it appears on paper) and how to understand the 'informal organisation' (some would say the organisation as it really operates). This helps you interpret and understand your organisation's culture and norms, the relationships between people and groups and how power and influence operate.

This basic and essential understanding of organisations equips you to enter their world and quickly find your feet.

CHAPTER

1

THE CHANGING WORLD OF WORK

OVERVIEW

The economy, the marketplace, society, technology and the workforce are all transforming at dizzying speeds. The Australian workplace is changing too. You are managing in a new reality: A new economy, a changing society and an unpredictable environment. And the rules of the game are changing.

New ways of working and new groups of employees are being introduced in an effort to respond effectively to these changes. The people you're managing are demanding more flexibility, more involvement and more socially responsible ways of operating. In turn, new ways of managing and operating are replacing traditional practices.

The people you're managing are also more diverse than ever before. They're getting older, there are more women, more minorities, more people from other cultures with many whose first language is not English, and more people with disabilities. Then there are people you manage in name only: Contract workers, temporary staff and those in outsourced roles. Casual workers, part-timers and full-timers are also part of the mix. Each of these groups has different needs, motivations and expectations.

1. Are you aware of and prepared for the major trends facing you, including the forces driving our national economy and how they affect organisations?
2. Have you noticed how the nature of the jobs you manage is evolving?
3. Can you describe how the workforce itself is changing and the challenges these changes present to leader-managers?
4. Are you aware of the skills you need in order to manage in this changing world?

What does the future hold? The changing world of work (and living) and the challenges that managers face as a result are described in this chapter.

SCENARIO

The conference

Saul is preparing for the quarterly videoconference of call centre team leaders. The conference opens with the team leaders sharing news about motivational campaigns that bring results – the leaders are always looking for ways to energise and enthuse the call centre phone advisers in an industry notorious for high-labour turnover. Saul is looking forward to the conference because he usually picks up constructive ideas for his team and, at this conference, he's been invited to share one of his own successful campaigns.

Motivational campaigns are quite tricky to run, given that many team members work part time and some work from home. Many team leaders also have a pool of casual employees that they can call on to meet sudden surges in demand and they like to include them in the campaigns too. On top of that, many call centre teams are made up of people from wildly different age groups, many with different interests, making it difficult to come up with a campaign that can motivate everyone.

Saul is putting together his talking points to present his campaign, which is based on the sustainability program that his company recently introduced worldwide. He broadened the concept to sustainability in the home and produced a strong promotion for his advisers to help them appreciate the issues involved in sustainability and to get them engaged in the company's program. The advisers loved Saul's ideas and the call centre buzzed with excitement. Saul had everyone talking to each other as they compared notes and swapped plans. Better still, productivity rose by a massive 12% – no easy feat.

1. Get ready: The megatrends

> We cannot advance economically or socially by standing still – the Neanderthals and our cavemen ancestors are testimony of this.
>
> Phil Ruthven (IBISWorld chair), *Company Director* (June 2012)[1]

We're in a new age. For most of the last century, organisations operated in environments that evolved slowly and were reasonably predictable. Managers sent orders 'down the line' and workers sent information back 'up the line', just like in the military model developed by the ancient Romans.

Those 'good old days' of certainty, protectionism and an economy based on agriculture, mining and manufacturing have given way to open markets, fierce competition, new and complex business models and a global economy based on service, knowledge and information. Brains, not brawn, are now an organisation's, and an individual's, chief value.

 FYI

The 'good old days'?

There is always change. Had you lived at the start of the 20th century, not the 21st century, you would have witnessed dramatic change:

- Electricity transformed people's lives.
- Railways brought cities and the bush closer together.
- The agrarian economy gave way to the industrial economy.
- The telephone revolutionised communication.

>>

As the 20th century progressed, Australian life expectancy increased by 50%; household density halved and our house sizes quadrupled; divorce rates rose from near zero to over one-third of all marriages; medical science advanced in leaps and bounds; we gained clean water and sewage services, air travel, motor cars and the Internet. Our population increased 5-fold, our standard of living increased 6-fold and our gross domestic product (GDP), in real terms, increased 32-fold.

Our gross domestic product is currently the world's 28th largest and we have the second-highest quality of life and standard of living in the world, even though in population terms we fall at number 50.[2]

How will we fare over the next 100 years? We're positioned well, geographically at least. Our neighbours, the Asia Pacific (apart from Japan) and Indian sub-continent are growing three times as fast as the EU, Japan and North America. More than 80% of our trade and two thirds of inbound tourism and immigration come from our Asian neighbours.[3]

Australian society is changing as its people and the definition of the family unit continue to evolve. The capabilities of information, communications and other technologies continue to soar as the physical and economic environments become less stable and more uncertain. Figure 1.1 shows the kaleidoscope of changes we are experiencing.

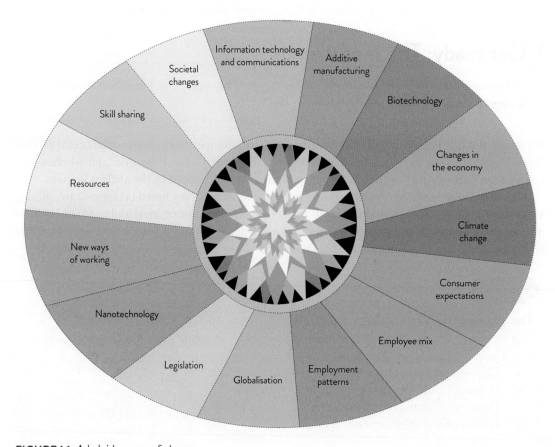

FIGURE 1.1 A kaleidoscope of change

This makes organisations more vulnerable and more difficult to guide than in the past. We know what we're leaving behind and we know what the major trends are, but we're still in a state of flux. The details of how these key trends are transforming organisations are emerging as organisations test out different structures, ways of working and ways of organising people and jobs to see what works best in this new age. (See page 80 for information on the changing structures of organisations.)

Meanwhile, you can expect discomfort, friction and stress as people struggle to come to terms with the changes around them, how these changes affect them personally and how they can make the most of the changes. It's no wonder that managers often feel beleaguered and bemused.

The acronym VUCA says it all: Volatility, Uncertainty, Complexity and Ambiguity. Each demands a different response from an organisation. Each affects both employers and employees. Here is a summary of the major trends that are causing organisations to fundamentally rethink their operating philosophies, strategies and tactics, to find new ways to measure return on investment and to place a value on the environment. Short-term thinking is out, innovation is in.

Climate change

An Australian Parliament Report on 'Human contribution to climate change' found, 'It is clear that the … net effect of human activities is a warming of the planet. The single most important influence is the increase in greenhouse gas concentrations due to fossil fuel combustion'.[4]

Devastating floods in Thailand in 2011 knocked out supply chains affecting a range of industries, including Toyota car manufacturing which forecast it could expect a loss reaching US$1.55 billion in earnings as a result of lost production due to lack of parts.[5] In 2012, Hurricane Sandy flooded New York and an electricity substation exploded, leaving lower Manhattan without electricity for four days, costing all (public and private) losses in New York US$19 billion. In New Jersey, which was worst hit, business losses were costed at US$8.3 billion.[6]

Typhoon Haiyan ravaged the Philippines in 2013, killing more than 6000 people and ruining entire communities. In 2014, fanned by high temperatures and strong winds, dozens of bushfires across South Australia and Victoria created their own weather systems, caused communities to evacuate, razed homes and killed countless wildlife and centuries-old heritage gum trees but, incredibly, only one person died.[7] The first half of 2014 also saw an earthquake in Chile, floods in Afghanistan and the UK, hailstorms and tornadoes in the USA and torrential rain in China. (See also page 719 for other recent natural disasters and the effects of climate change.)

Scientists agree that the planet is heating up, largely as a result of human activities. The severity of extreme and destructive weather events that threaten corporate profits and global prosperity are increasing.[8] Figure 1.2 shows five contributing factors to climate change.

As a result of climate change, we can expect to see rising sea levels and more frequent and more extreme climatic events such as droughts, floods and storms. These events have the potential to destroy infrastructure and ecosystems, disrupt agriculture, increase economic volatility and even render some regions of the country uninhabitable. As Australia's population and population density increase, so does the potential impact of disasters on the community.

Organisations must become smarter at predicting and planning to manage the risks of disruptions to their operations when their employees, markets, premises or suppliers are affected by climatic events. (Chapter 23 explains how to identify and manage risk.)

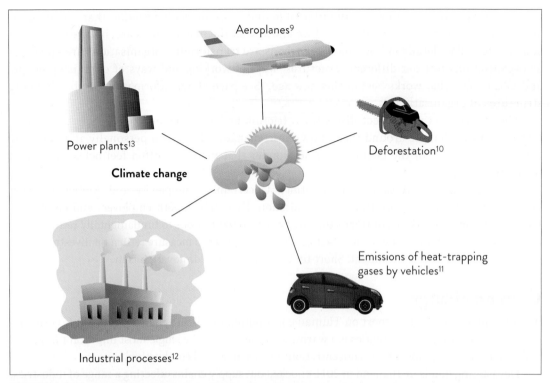

FIGURE 1.2 Five contributing factors to climate change

In adversity, however, there is also opportunity. For example:

- As the North Pole continues to melt, a microbrewery in Greenland is collecting 2000-year-old, super-pure ice blocks to make specialist beer.[14]
- Car manufacturers such as Toyota and Honda are gaining market share with the emission-reducing engine technology of their petrol–electric hybrid engines.

Organisations must also learn to adapt and benefit from climate change and share in the growing global market for environmental goods and services. 'Clean tech' is set to become a strategic priority for many companies. In Australia, potential winners from climate change include the alternative energy, engineering, recycling and sustainable property sectors; there are also opportunities for innovative financial services, chemical agriculture and some healthcare companies.

The environmental performance of a company is increasingly affecting share prices and many companies are already investing in improving their carbon footprint. (See 'A new way of assessing organisations' on page 26 to find out what organisations are doing to become more sustainable; see also Chapter 23, which provides more detail on managing for sustainability.)

Globalisation

Transportation and communications technology have drawn all areas of the world closer together. Deregulation has encouraged more trade between countries, expanding the marketplace. Breaking up and selling off national monopolies in areas such as air transport, the finance and insurance industries and telecommunications has enabled trading systems, which link the distribution and consumption of goods and services, finance and production, to span the globe.

Known as globalisation, the result has seen more and tougher competition. That's led to increasing pressure to customise products and services and improve efficiencies, productivity, quality and service. Markets are no longer bordered by national boundaries, which makes the world itself a single economic unit. In turn, that allows large corporations to become not just *multinational*, but *transnational* and increasingly outside the control of any one nation. Financing, product design, risk management, supply chains, support services and technology can be anywhere and everywhere. Management benchmarks can be set by any organisation of any size on any continent. An organisation's toughest competitor might no longer be down the road but on the other side of the world.

Companies are becoming more diverse in size and origin, and more Asian and less Western in orientation. Three of the four most populous countries in the world (China, India, Indonesia) and five of the 20 largest economies in the world (China, India, Indonesia, Japan, South Korea) are our neighbours. Economic power is shifting from West to East and from North to South as the world's economies realign themselves. Our businesses are now operating in an Asian, rather than an Australian context. Asia now accounts for 80% of our trade and two-thirds of our immigrants and in-bound tourists.[15]

As globalisation continues to grow and substantially shape all the other major trends, its impact on business ethics, currency rates and the financial markets, and on the way we do business and manage organisations, continues to increase. While globalisation allows poor countries to develop economically and raise their standard of living, and while it allows developed economies to purchase inexpensive goods and services, it also brings risks to individual organisations. For example:

- Dependence on overseas suppliers and contractors makes it easier for climatic events to wipe out part or all of an organisation's supply chain and a significant, possibly crippling, portion of its service providers.
- Epidemics and pandemics can more easily destroy or temporarily disable a significant part of an organisation's workforce.
- Organisations, which exploit workers in developing countries or behave irresponsibly towards the local environment, have faced public relations disasters and consumer boycotts.

Although emerging markets remain a growth engine of the global economy, critics of globalisation claim that multinational corporations in the West benefit at the expense of local cultures, local enterprises and the environment. This, in part, gives rise to the notion of corporate social responsibility and ethical investment funds. (See 'A new way of assessing organisations' on page 26.)

THE STRATEGIC PERSPECTIVE

Not new, just faster and deeper

During the Industrial Revolution, globalisation was known by the less glamorous term, 'international trade'. Even before industrialisation, there had been periods of relative openness in cross-border trade. During the Middle Ages, for example, the Silk Road across Central Asia connected China and Europe.

So globalisation of trade isn't new. However, the pace and extent of the current phase of globalisation is unprecedented. Pulitzer Prize-winning author, Thomas Friedman, cleverly described today's globalisation with the adjectives, 'farther, faster, cheaper and deeper', comparing it to previous waves of international trade.[16] In fact, many observers believe that the pace of globalisation has ushered the world into a new phase of economic development.[17]

The effects of globalisation are far-reaching:
- *Cultural.* Globalisation influences lifestyle factors such as dress, food, language and entertainment.
- *Environmental and biological.* Globalisation affects the environment as polluting industries move to developing countries. Polluting transportation and distribution networks moving people and products around the world to their markets can change natural habitats, spread disease and affect the health and diets of living organisms (domestic and wild) in many ways.

- *Political systems.* Globalisation could put pressure on authoritarian-style regimes to become more inclusive and democratic because the Internet, the media and people working for transnational corporations expose those regimes' citizens to more open cultures.
- *Social.* Globalisation increases the movement of people between countries and effects changes in society, for example in the nature of work, employment levels and prosperity.
- *Spatial.* Globalisation, and the changes it effects in society and the environment, influences the structure and layout of cities, the design of housing and the nature of working environments.

Information technology, communications technology, biotechnology and nanotechnology

Would it surprise you to learn that your (no doubt much-loved and essential) mobile phone (first introduced by IBM in 1993 and weighing nearly half a kilo) may well be extinct in the next few years?[18] Bitcoin is already shifting traditional centralised currencies to decentralised exchanges of 'money'. Wearable computing lets us find information, record and share data, and take videos and photos at the blink of an eye. Driverless cars are attracting significant investment from car manufacturers. Soon, we'll be receiving information through our contact lenses and using our skin as a touchpad and our brain to command various devices remotely.

Technology has advanced more in the past 30 years than it has in the past 2000 years, and it continues to make breathtaking leaps forward. Computer technology is so entrenched in our lives that, although computers have been around for only 40 years, if the world's microprocessors stopped working tomorrow, we would instantly be flung back 100 years.[19]

Advances in communications technology and the IT-related revolution, the central feature of which is the ability to manipulate, store and transmit large quantities of information at very low cost, have been the main enablers of the massive changes the world has experienced. 'Big data', or analytics, which analyses large data sets, has been around for some time but only recently has been able to provide information of value to an entire organisation. The insights it generates can change markets and organisations. It can be used to predict behaviour and trends with uncanny accuracy. It informs an organisation's decisions and is now an important platform for productivity growth, innovation and customer relations.

When IT is combined with traditional products, enabling them to send and receive data, the result is disruptive business models and transformed value chains, increased value through new efficiencies for customers, thanks to the built-in advanced analytics and algorithms, and increased revenue for the seller.[20]

Social media has exploded as a business opportunity since 2010. Cloud computing, only recently dismissed as not having any value for organisations, now enables a more flexible and efficient workforce.

Cyber security and data breaches notwithstanding, the Internet, intranets, groupware (or collaborative systems technology) and powerful databases allow organisations to operate wherever, whenever and with whomever they want. As they become more intelligent and intuitive, access to information becomes even easier, making better decision-making possible.

 FYI

The digital economy
Just about everyone participates in, and to some extent depends on, the digital economy, the network of economic and social activities enabled by the Internet and mobile and sensor networks. It includes computers, electronic banking and paying by credit card, game consoles, lecturers posting

>>

course outlines, study materials and videos online for students, mobile phones, online maps and photo and video sharing sites, sensor networks that monitor traffic flows and web searches.

Here are a couple of improvements you can expect to see in the near future:

- Improved high-definition video conferencing in a 3D environment that is almost the same as real-life face-to-face meetings.
- Haptic devices that can simulate the sense of touch.

High speed broadband, analytics and cognitive computing are all part of the digital economy. Superfast broadband is a necessity for any country claiming to be a developed and advancing economy because it makes life easier and better for individuals and households as well as businesses and government services. Superfast broadband is set to transform the operating landscape. Those businesses that do not embrace it are unlikely to survive.

According to the Australian government, a successful digital economy is essential to our economic growth and ability to maintain our standing in the world. It can transform many industries, including education and training, healthcare and social assistance, mining, professional, scientific and technical services, public administration, retail, outsourced home services and transport, postal and warehousing.[21]

Between the digital economy, superfast broadband and rapidly advancing technology, the game itself, not only its rules, are changing ever faster.

People can connect with others whenever they want, purchase from companies half a world away and sell their wares over the ether to someone they've never heard of in a country they've never been to. The Canadian educator, philosopher and scholar, Marshall McLuhan said in 1962, 'The new electronic interdependence re-creates the world in the image of a global village.'[22]

Rather than having to travel to work, technology now brings work (as well as education and entertainment) to employees. People no longer need to be in a specific place to share equipment and work together, as they did in the industrial era, because technology gives them the ability to work and cooperate with others wherever they can connect to the Internet. One person can belong to more than one team and more than one organisation at the same time.

This has changed the shape, style and function of workplaces. Teammates can be in other cities, countries or even hemispheres and may seldom or never meet each other outside the virtual world of videoconferences, teleconferences and collaborative technology. The managers who lead them may seldom or never meet the team members face to face, calling for a new set of management skills. (Chapter 14 explains how to lead and manage virtual teams.)

Information technology, biotechnology, communications technology and nanotechnology (*ultrasmall*, e.g. motors the size of a pinhead) lead to new products and new work methods, making some skills obsolete, creating need for other skills and enabling organisations to evolve new ways of working.

Breakthroughs in biotechnology and genetics also point to a radically changed world of increased possibilities. Biotechnology uses living organisms (such as algae, bacteria, yeast), their products or their component cells (such as enzymes), to improve our health and environment. Eventually, biotechnology is expected to lead to a sustainable 'bioeconomy', increasing food security, reducing the environmental impact of agriculture and fisheries and generating sustainable economic growth and jobs.[23]

These technologies continue to change the way we communicate, cooperate, innovate and manage teams and projects. Technologies influence how we use space, energy and materials. Technologies determine the way we store, retrieve and pass on knowledge.

Gotta keep up

Gordon Moore, the co-founder of Intel, the company that produced the first single-chip microprocessor, coined the term 'Moore's Law' in the 1970s, which tells us that the complexity of integrated circuits doubles every 24 months. That is, computing power doubles every two years. Today, most computer technicians say that it doubles every year, such is the rate of technological growth.[24]

This exponential growth has a tremendous impact on our lives, on the skills we need and on how fast our skills fade. And here's a career tip: If you want to keep up, learn all you can about big data, or analytics.

The knowledge and service economy

The slowest growing industries in Australia are agriculture, manufacturing, media and utilities. The fastest growing are finance, health, insurance, mining and professional and technical services. For every job lost in the declining industries, over six times as many jobs were created, most of them in the 'new' economy.[25]

Three interlinked factors are responsible for the emerging knowledge and service economy:

1. It is driven by consumer demand for high value-added, knowledge-intensive products and services.
2. It is enabled by technology.
3. It is accelerated by globalisation.

These factors, along with the reforms of the 1980s introduced by then Treasurer Paul Keating (including deregulation, privatisation and easier access to global money markets, which have now substantially been completed), have made Australia's knowledge and service economy possible. The new economy demands a host of changes inside organisations, from changing leadership styles to changing business models, organisation structures and organisation strategies. It has changed how people earn their livings, how and where they work, how organisations organise themselves and how companies and employees are valued. In short, the new economy rewrites the rules of business and changes the skill sets employees and managers need. In order to remain competitive, scores of labour-intensive manufacturing and production processes have moved to developing markets with cheaper labour. Routine and dangerous work is largely computerised and most of what is produced, whether it's a service or a product people can actually touch, is based on knowledge value rather than raw materials value (think of the fractions of a cent a microchip costs to make, for instance). The income and profits of large manufacturing companies, such as General Electric, IBM and Xerox, increasingly come from their service divisions.

The three industrial revolutions: From hammers and hard hats to computer screens

The mechanisation of the textile industry in Britain in the late 1700s kicked off the first industrial revolution. The second began in the early 1900s when Henry Ford mastered the moving assembly line and mass production. Digital manufacturing is now launching the third industrial revolution. (Digital manufacturing is popularly known as 3D printing, although 3D, and coming soon, 4D, really refers to additive, or digital, manufacturing with plastic.)

>>

No longer does material need to be bashed, bent or removed and wasted or recycled. Building up layer upon layer of material can make complex solid objects, from epoxy resin to ground glass, gold, nylon, stainless steel, wax and even stem cells and other living cells. Designs can be tweaked with a mouse and machines, once going, can be left virtually unattended.

Just as farriers' jobs all but disappeared with the advent of motorised vehicles, most unskilled manufacturing jobs will go, replaced by a few highly skilled manufacturing workers. Newly created jobs will go to designers, IT whizzes, logistics experts, office staff, marketers and other professionals. As a bonus, it looks as though digital manufacturing can lower the environmental impact of a range of goods by more than 40%.[26]

Until the 1980s, tangible assets (including money in the bank, plant and equipment, real estate and stock) made up about 80% of a company's worth and the knowledge of its employees made up the remaining 20%.[27] Today, it's intangible assets that count – including an organisation's:

* culture and capabilities (unique ways of doing things)
* goodwill and image in the marketplace
* intellectual capital (see 'The strategic perspective: Three types of intellectual capital')
* organisation structure
* strategies.

These intangible assets, also known as organisational capabilities, are really the outcome of investments in communication and people (staffing, training and other human resource management systems) and are the building blocks of corporate strategy (not the markets and products of old).

Their value has increased dramatically over the past 20 years and they now make up as much as 80% of a company's worth.[28] As a result, organisations are organising around core capabilities in order to manage value-creating processes more effectively. Because they are difficult for competitors to copy, organisational capabilities give a company its competitive edge.

● THE STRATEGIC PERSPECTIVE

Three types of intellectual capital

Capital comes from the Latin word for head. It has come to stand for any strategic source of power. Three types of capital not (yet) included in the balance sheet are human, relationship and structural capital. Together they make up intellectual capital (an organisation's usable knowledge).

1. *Human capital.* This incorporates the competencies, health, motivation and productivity of an organisation's employees that can be lost should employees leave, unless their human capital is recorded in tangible form or incorporated into the organisation's procedures and structure. Measures include attrition rates among top performers, employee engagement and innovation. For example, 3M has a goal that at least 25% of annual sales will come from products less than four years old.[29]

2. *Relationship capital.* This is the value of an organisation's relationships with customers, suppliers and outsourcing and financing partners. It is built over time and reflected by loyalty to the company and its products, producing, for example, cross-selling, ideas sharing, referrals and repeat business. Measures include brand value, customer retention rate and customer satisfaction measures. For example, when Boeing designed its 777 jet,

>>

suppliers, customers and users (e.g. frequent fliers and aircrew) were consulted and the result was almost universal acclaim.[30]

3. *Structural capital.* This could be described as the organisation's knowledge database. It is comprised of competitive intelligence, copyrights, customer files, databases, formulas, information systems, patents, policies, processes, software, trademarks, and so on, created by the organisation over time. All of these remain with the organisation when employees go home. Measures include effectiveness of processes (are they helping or hindering?), estimated cost to replace databases, suggestions made versus suggestions implemented, and time taken to develop new products and services and offer them to the marketplace ('time to market').

 FYI

The sectors of the economy

Economies are divided into groups of industries, or sectors, that you can think of as a continuum of distance from the natural environment. The further away from 'nature' the sectors are, the more 'advanced' the society is considered to be. On this basis, the Australian economy is considered to be an advanced economy. (Figure 1.3 provides a graphic representation of the four sectors of the economy.)

The *primary sector*, or agrarian economy, extracts or harvests products from the earth: Agriculture, farming, fishing, forestry, grazing, hunting and gathering, mining and quarrying. In these agricultural economies, which can generally be described as feudal societies, land is the key resource and control of land is the main source of wealth. At the end of the first decade of the 21st century, primary industries represented 7.6% of the Australian economy and accounted for nearly half (43.3%) of Australia's exports (38.6% were minerals and 4.7% were agriculture).[31] The primary sector's heyday lasted from 1788 to 1864 and our standard of living rose three-fold during that time.

The *secondary sector*, or industrial economy, processes primary sector raw materials into finished/manufactured goods and products through manufacturing, processing and construction; it includes car production, brewing and winemaking, the chemical, construction, engineering and manufacturing industries, food processing, energy production, shipbuilding and textile production. In industrial economies, natural resources and labour are the main resources, and control of capital (e.g. owning industrial machinery) is the source of wealth. In the early 20th century the desire by the poor majority of exploited workers to control the means of production, rather than it remaining in the hands of a few wealthy owners (capitalists), led to the rise of communism.

From 1864 to 1964, Australia was considered to be an industrial economy and our standard of living increased nearly four-fold. By 2010, the secondary sector accounted for only 15.6% of the economy and 33.3% of Australia's exports, and by 2012, manufacturing accounted for less than 9 cents of every dollar of value added in the Australian economy, manufacturing accounted for just 8% of employed people in Australia in 2012 and employed 10% of the workforce.[32]

The *tertiary sector*, or the service economy, provides services to the general population and to business. It includes administrative services, banking, distribution, entertainment, healthcare, law, media, restaurants, retail and wholesale (selling goods and products from the secondary sector), tourism and transportation. It is expected to last until the late 2040s, when the knowledge economy will hopefully take over. In most developed and developing countries, a growing proportion of the workforce works in the tertiary sector. About 70% of our economy and that of the Organisation for

>>

Economic Cooperation and Development (OECD) nations come from service industries, which make up three-quarters of the world's gross domestic product (GDP). More than 85% of our GDP comes from the service sector, which employs more than 85% of the workforce.

Although this sector doesn't produce any physical goods, it does create wealth – whatever consumers buy, either directly or indirectly, tangible or intangible, creates wealth. In fact, although the adjustment costs have been heavy, our current demand-driven, service-oriented economy has already made our standard of living 2.6 times higher than it was in the producer-driven, goods-oriented economy that came before it and it is expected to increase more than five times over the coming three decades.

The *quaternary sector*, or the knowledge economy, is information and finance-oriented. It includes 'intellectual activities' such as business and professional services, communications, consulting, culture, education, finance and insurance, government administration and defence, IT, libraries, property, and scientific research. In knowledge economies, knowledge, not just figuring out new things but also figuring out how to better use what people already know, is the key resource and control of information is the source of wealth.

In developed countries, knowledge is the main way forward to economic prosperity. Depending on the precise industries you include, these wealth creators accounted for nearly 50% of our economy and 48% of our GDP by 2010 and comprise the largest sector of Australian industry by far.[33] Our exports, traditionally resource-based, will increasingly include business services and health from the tertiary sector and education from the quaternary sector. Knowledge in the form of intellectual property has contributed over half of Australia's corporate value over the last 10 years. (See 'The strategic perspective: Intellectual property – a risky area' on page 740.)

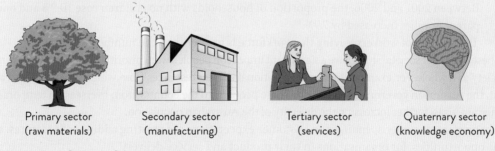

Primary sector (raw materials)   Secondary sector (manufacturing)   Tertiary sector (services)   Quaternary sector (knowledge economy)

FIGURE 1.3 Sectors of the economy

It may surprise many people, but we've enjoyed a huge rise in our standard of living with the decline of agriculture (once 50% of our GDP and now 2%) and manufacturing (once 29% of our GDP and now just over 7%). Some predict that those industries will experience a renaissance in the coming decades, although they won't dominate the economy. Agriculture will go 'corporate', capital intensive, largely foreign-owned and export to Asia. Manufacturing will no longer be craft- and engineering-skills based but digital and move to medium size companies.[34]

Worldwide, trade in services is growing faster than trade in goods. In the coming decades, we'll export more services than anything else, overtaking minerals – just as minerals overtook manufacturing, which overtook agriculture over the past 50 years.

Biotechnology, business services, education, environmental services, health, hospitality, household services, nanotechnology, property services – all the service and knowledge industries will grow and boost the economy. That's just as well because the industries in the 'old economy' will continue to shrink.

Resource scarcity

Non-renewable resources, for example, fossil fuels (such as coal, natural gas, petroleum) and some minerals (such as copper and gold) are becoming scarcer and more difficult to harvest and are likely to become more expensive. This will have flow-on effects, particularly in customer demands and prices, through organisations' supply chain. Companies that create products and services that eliminate wasted resources and keep them in use indefinitely will flourish.

Societal changes

The demographics of a society include statistics such as births, death and disease rates, distribution of wealth, marriages, population density, growth and distribution, and the percentage of people in the various age categories and religious groups. Many of these gauges are changing. We are becoming more diverse, getting older and living longer, marrying less and at older ages, and reproducing less. For example:

- Boys born in 1890 could expect to live 47.2 years; boys born in 2012 can expect to live 79.9 years. The life expectancy rates for girls born in those years are 50.8 and 84.3 years, respectively.
- The number of migrants coming to Australia (less people leaving the country) has grown from 348 600 in 2000–01 to 508 662 in 2012–3.[35]
- In 1901, 23% of Australia's population was born overseas; by 2008, 26% of Australians were born overseas and in 2006, 26% of people born in Australia had at least one parent born overseas.[36]
- In the past 10 years, the proportion of households with married couples has fallen from 60% to 47%.[37]
- In 2010, the median age of Australia's population was 36.9 years, 4.8 years older than in 1990.[38]
- Between 2001 and 2006, the proportion of households with no children rose 10.2% and one-parent families increased by 7.9%.[39]
- The number of workers leaving the workforce is greater than the number entering it.

These and other societal shifts have a significant impact on people's work priorities and motivations and on society as a whole. For example, to provide additional human resources from which organisations can recruit, the Australian government is allowing more people into the country from overseas on temporary and migrant visas, further increasing the diversity of the Australian population.

Changes in consumer spending and customer expectations are creating additional pressures, as well as opportunities, for organisations in their product and service delivery.

2. New ways of working

> Our [Australian] manufacturing industry ... all told, has shed 205 000 jobs [since 1989]. But over the same time, we have created 3.9 million new jobs (almost 19 times more jobs than those lost from manufacturing) at a rate of 13 640 a month.
>
> Phil Ruthven (IBISWorld chair), *Company Director* (August 2013)[40]

As the traditional male breadwinner arrangements have steadily declined since the 1960s and now both partners of couple families are likely to be employed, access to family-friendly leave provisions are important. People's working lives cover a wide range of hours and patterns, often related to their stage of life or family circumstances. Access to more paid leave entitlements and types of leave such as personal carer's leave and maternity/paternity/adoption leave has increased. What's a 'normal' job today? It's becoming harder to define.

Only 7% of employees still work from 9 am to 5 pm.[41] Some employees are 'time slaves', working long hours because of economic necessity or coercion; others are 'time lords', working long hours because they derive satisfaction, career and other benefits from doing so. Others are underemployed – they would like to and are able to work more hours than they currently work. Underemployment rose from 2.7% of the total labour force in 1979 to a high of 7.7% in 2009 and, since 2000, there have been more underemployed people in Australia than unemployed people.[42] (In May 2010, the underemployment rate was 7.2% while the unemployment rate was 5.2%.)[43]

As discussed earlier in this chapter, technology has rendered traditional work–home demarcations obsolete because people can work anywhere, any time. Thanks to information and communications technology, regional centres could blossom and we may see specialised centres with clusters of specialised producers or suppliers from multiple contributors in the way that Silicon Valley specialises in high technology.

The type of work is changing, too, as we continue to move into a service- and knowledge-based economy. Dangerous work and routine work (the mainstay of trade unions) are disappearing. Thanks to flattened organisation structures, many of the duties formerly carried out by middle managers now fall to leader-managers and, in turn, the work team members do many of their leader-manager's former duties. Goals are replacing job descriptions as job descriptions and organisation charts become less relevant and people and teams just 'get on with it'.

Today's workers might be casuals, contractors, part-timers or temporary employees, or any combination of these. They may have one or more jobs; they may be employees or self-employed.

The following sections examine three other key features of changing work patterns in the new economy:

- *Casualisation of the workforce.* Full-time, permanent jobs are being replaced by casual, part-time and temporary jobs.
- *Outsourcing and offshoring.* Work that is not integral to the organisation's core business is increasingly contracted out, or outsourced. When the jobs go overseas, this is known as offshoring.
- *Telecommuting (or teleworking).* Work is moving to the people, back into their homes (ironically, where it was prior to the Industrial Revolution).

These changes better suit a global, knowledge-driven economy, a hyper-competitive marketplace and consumer demand for inexpensive goods and services.

 FYI

SOHOs and the 'freelance economy'
SOHO describes the 'small office, home office' phenomenon. SOHO workers are contractors working from home full-time or part-time for one or more organisations and doing jobs previously carried out by permanent employees.

Casualising jobs

Casualisation of the job market refers to the discernible fall in the number of full-time jobs and the associated steady increase in casual, part-time and contracting jobs filled by agency workers, casual and temporary employees and independent contractors. This is common among developed countries, although it is by far the most marked in Australia. In fact, Australia has one of the most casualised workforces in the OECD.[44] (Interestingly, escalating casualisation like this is of great concern overseas, where more cooperative workplace relations are desired.)

There has been a gradual long-term trend away from full-time to part-time jobs, with part-timers increasing from 16% of the workforce in 1979 to 30.2% in 2013.[45] Casual employment has grown more slowly, from 17% of the workforce in 1992 to a peak of 21% in 2007, with 72% of casual employees working part-time hours. In 2007, 52% of casual employees reported they would prefer permanent work.[46]

Most large companies have trimmed down their permanent full-time workforce and now use temporary and casual employees. These employees enable companies to adjust their labour supply to meet the peaks and troughs of their business needs and access a range of specialist skills when required.

Employers call in casual and temporary employees only when the organisation needs them and pay them only for the hours they work. This allows employers to:

- minimise wage costs by decreasing employees' working hours
- roster on workers during peaks in activity
- save money by investing little or nothing in training and development activities for casuals.

The 'freelance economy', or 'Me Inc.'

The growth in casual, temporary and part-time jobs has given rise to what is sometimes called 'the freelance economy'. Sometimes called consultants and freelancers, self-employed business people account for about 10% of the labour force.[47] It's possible that by 2020, 40% to 50% of all income-producing work will be performed by these free agents. The term 'employee' may even fall out of use in the second half of the 21st century.

With the huge growth in professional, scientific and technical services, many of these jobs are 'high end' jobs: Six-month 'gigs' designed for CEOs, human resources and other managers, lawyers, and similar highly skilled specialists. They can be genuinely independent contractors who operate their own businesses and are engaged under a commercial contract, or they can be temporary employees engaged in short-term or fixed-term work, contracting their skills to one, two or three organisations at a time. Their livelihoods depend on their ability to sell their skills and value proposition.

● THE STRATEGIC PERSPECTIVE

Not a bed of roses

Casuals have no expectation of ongoing work and are not entitled to the benefits provided to permanent full-time and part-time employees, such as personal, long-service and annual leave, and superannuation. Because of their irregular work patterns, lack of job security and stability and their limited access to employer-provided training, casual workers are generally considered disadvantaged, compared with permanent employees.

Despite casual loading (an amount paid above the normal hourly rate), which is generally 25% to compensate casual employees for not receiving the entitlements of permanent employees, casual workers generally earn less than permanent staff. They typically work fewer hours and casual jobs tend to be in the lower-paid industries and occupations.

The downside

The downside of casualisation for organisations is that the benefits of increased flexibility and lower labour costs may be offset by casual workers feeling less committed, less engaged, less productive and less innovative – often a poor return on the cost savings made from drawing skills from a large temporary pool of 'free agents'.

Dissatisfied and untrained part-time and casual workers, especially when they're a large or strategically significant part of an organisation's workforce – for example, workers who deal directly with customers – can damage an organisation's service levels and reputation. Unless they're well managed, it's easy for casual (and part-time) workers to feel out of touch, unappreciated and ignored by their leader-managers and others they work with. Disengaged employees who are not aligned and engaged with the values and vision of an organisation and who have not personally invested in the results of the team they're attached to, can become underperformers and a strain on the other team members.

Outsourcing

Contracting out non-essential and secondary functions to independent providers, or contractors, allows organisations to concentrate on their core functions and benefit from both the efficiencies of outsourcers' expertise and the reduced labour and overhead costs of the providers. Another attraction is that should a provider be unsuited to a role, the organisation can cancel the contract and find another provider. When the arrangement works well, contractors can be responsible for a large percentage of the value added to a product or service.

Commonly outsourced functions include administrative work such as invoicing, human resources (including training, payroll and recruitment and selection), IT, maintenance and other types of specialist work.

THE STRATEGIC PERSPECTIVE

The reason for offshoring and smart working

As the Australian economy continues to become knowledge-based and the cost of living continues to rise, Australian workers without the education, skills and training to do knowledge work are increasingly left behind. Employers can't afford to pay them cost-of-living wages and still produce a service or product at a price consumers are willing to pay, so their jobs go to technology (routine computer processing and robots) or to labour forces in less-developed countries where wages are lower. Organisations also routinely outsource knowledge work to rapidly developing economies with lower labour rates and advanced technological capabilities, such as India and Eastern Europe countries.

FYI

Shamrock organisations

The three-leaved shamrock symbolises the three main groups of employees found in most modern Australian organisations: Core workers, contractors and flexible workers. The core workers perform the critical jobs of the organisation, those the organisation cannot afford to contract out; they are predicted to eventually make up less than one-quarter of an organisation's employees.

These core workers – indispensable managers, highly qualified professionals and technical specialists – will work long and hard hours and will be well remunerated in return.

Contractors, performing important administrative, marketing, training, accounting and other types of specialist work to support the core workers, will eventually be responsible for up to 80% of the value that is added to a product or service.

The flexible workforce is made up of the temporary, part-time and casual workers that the organisation needs to work on one-off projects and to fill in during busy times.[48]

The countertrend

Outsourcing is losing its attractiveness for a number of reasons:

- Continuing concerns about protecting intellectual property.
- Ethical concerns (is it 'un-Australian' to send our jobs offshore?) are increasing as politicians and organisations suffer negative public relations 'hits'.
- Humanitarian concerns are increasing (e.g. Bangladesh's Rana Plaza factory collapse in 2013, killing 1129 people producing a range of clothing for Western companies; in India, children as young as 10 years old hand-stitching footballs for 12 cents a ball for up to 12 hours a day, 7 days a week).[49]

- Organisations are striving to become more sustainable and reduce the risks that arise from long supply chains that are difficult, costly, slow and risky to manage.
- Technology is allowing cheaper production 'at home'.
- The cost of 'cheap labour' in developing countries, particularly China and India (where wages have risen 20% a year for the past decade or so) is increasing.
- The need to innovate products rapidly to keep up with the competition makes it easier to tweak specifications with a supplier down the road than with a supplier thousands of kilometres away.
- Transportation costs are increasing.
- Quality is difficult to assure.

As a result, many large corporations are considering 're-shoring' – bringing manufacturing and services 'back home'.

'Re-shoring' is predicted to result in producing goods closer to the market and the rise of regional trade patterns, enabled by additive manufacturing (dubbed the third industrial revolution), which will eventually replace the traditional subtractive manufacturing. Additive manufacturing allows goods to be easily customised and made at or close to where they're bought; for example, cars are now made in just a few hundred factories around the world but, thanks to additive manufacturing, may well be made in every metropolitan area in the not-too-distant future.[50]

Ideopoli: The path to wealth

As Australia moves further into the knowledge economy, we are likely to see the growth of the ideopolis, a knowledge-intensive city that drives growth in the wider region. Ideopoli are formed when a critical mass of a city's population and business is based on knowledge. Boston, Munich, London and Edinburgh are considered to be ideopoli and, luckily for them, an ideopolis is always wealthier than a city not based on knowledge. Basing an organisation in an ideopolis gives it access to large numbers of skilled workers and tacit knowledge, a diverse industry base with specialist niches and universities with industry collaboration and economies of scale.

Telecommuting

When employees travelled to work and leader-managers could see their employees, at least they knew they were 'at work'. Thanks to the advances in communications technology such as collaboration technology, real-time online chats and videoconferencing, it's now common for people to wander into the spare bedroom or home office to go to work, or hop into a vehicle and work at the premises of their customers or suppliers, seldom or never seeing their leader-managers face to face.

Temporary and permanent work teams comprised entirely of telecommuters, often in different cities, on different continents and in different hemispheres, are becoming more common. By 2014, 16.4% of Australian employees were doing some work from home.[51] By 2050, it's possible Australia could see one in four people working at least partially from home, which could reinvigorate rural communities, providing a workforce for city-based businesses.

Telecommuting can increase productivity, lower organisational, employee and environmental costs and make employees happy, giving organisations an edge in attracting and retaining talented, motivated employees. Research also indicates that remote workers are more available and more responsive than office-based workers and are seen to be better communicators and take on more responsibility. They also report reduced stress and increased job satisfaction.[52]

Happy employees and increased productivity sound good, although telecommuting requires a bit of work up front. (See 'In a Nutshell: Difficulties with telecommuting', on page 412. For more information leading and managing offsite employees, see Chapter 14 and page 965, 'The strategic perspective: Looking after home workers' for more information about managing the health and safety risks for home workers.)

⬤ THE STRATEGIC PERSPECTIVE

Why is telecommuting so popular?

Employees appreciate telecommuting. In fact, many younger workers see working flexibly as a right rather than a privilege. Telecommuting offers:

- additional independence and flexibility and the freedom to set up their work spaces to suit their own tastes and work habits
- more family time, me time and free time
- no office politics
- savings on clothes, commuting costs, lunch, and so on
- savings in time, expense and stress from not commuting
- the ability to work as, how and when it suits them.

Telecommuting is great, too, for people who are housebound; for example, people who have caring responsibilities or have a disability that makes leaving home difficult.

Organisations like telecommuting because it provides:

- continuity of operations, since operations are less affected by situations such as epidemics, extreme climatic events, personal (sick) leave, transport strikes and weather emergencies
- increased productivity, since telecommuters tend to be 15–50% more productive than onsite workers.[53] They also spend less time on intra-office distractions, interruptions and politics and more time working and with customers
- lower costs due to, for example, fewer offices to maintain in increasingly costly city office space (lower costs of real estate and overheads), fewer workers compensation claims (about one-third of claims result from incidents travelling to or from work) and reduced absenteeism (people are more likely to work at home when they or their children are ill)
- the ability to tap remote, often cheaper labour pools.

Society likes telecommuting, too, because it reduces pollution due to less use of fossil fuels, and reduces pressure on cities due to less traffic congestion and fewer car accidents.

There are a lot of ways to telecommute:

- full-time teleworkers working from home all the time
- mobile teleworkers working mainly on the road, travelling or attending meetings
- regular telecommuters working from home one or more days a week, according to a schedule agreed with their leader-managers
- self-employed contractors working mainly from home
- sporadic telecommuters occasionally working from home, for example when their children are sick.

For more information on teleworking and National Telework Week, go to the website: http://www.telework.gov.au/.

The message for leader-managers

Each of these new ways of working has major implications for leader-managers:

* How do you know that employees you seldom see are pulling their weight?
* How do you manage people whose output is often intangible?
* How do you engage and motivate teams made up of vastly different groups of employees, each with different needs and expectations?

The quick, but not simple, answer is by:

* building effective working relationships, based on open communication and trust
* making sure everyone understands their role and the part others play in achieving the team's goals
* providing the resources people need to do their jobs and removing obstacles that get in their way (difficulties that slow them down or frustrate them, or that make their work unnecessarily difficult or awkward)
* setting clear goals and managing by results and deliverables.

(See chapters 8, 11 and 14, which examine these management practices in more detail.)

◉ THE STRATEGIC PERSPECTIVE

The manager's changing environment

Every decade, it seems, has its defining characteristics. Here are the main features that have shaped management over the past 100 years:

* *1920s:* Assembly lines, mechanisation and paternalism are the order of the day, with a counter-trend in Mary Parker Follett's call for participative management – 'power with' not 'power over'.[54] However, the call is ignored for decades. The stock market mushrooms.
* *1930s:* The human relations movement begins, led by Elton Mayo and made famous by the Hawthorne experiments (see 'In a Nutshell: Better lighting or the Hawthorne effect?' on page 1017). The Great Depression hits, resulting in massive lay-offs. Trade unions challenge management control.
* *1940s:* Abraham Maslow provides a framework for gaining employee commitment through the hierarchy of needs. Women temporarily take non-traditional roles as the men go off to war. Production rises rapidly.[55]
* *1950s:* Middle managers gain power; the 'organisation man' becomes the model. Peter Drucker emphasises management by objectives over human relations. Statistical quality control becomes widespread and the PERT diagram is introduced. Corporate growth and confidence soar.[56]
* *1960s:* Douglas McGregor advocates a 'softer' management style with Theory X and Theory Y.[57] Group facilitation and sensitivity training waxes and wanes as Frederick Herzberg advises that fully using people's skills, not sensitivity training, boosts job satisfaction and productivity.[58]
* *1970s:* A rapid rise in oil prices produces a recession and slows GDP growth. Productivity and corporate profits begin to decline. Henry Mintzberg finds that managers rely heavily on intuition and personal contacts.[59] Quality of work life, social responsibility, the environment and women's issues gain attention in a conservative male bastion of 'managerial mystique'. Service management and quality circles become widespread as industrial strife and conflict escalate. The service industry leads modest employment growth.

- *1980s:* The pace of change increases and economic rationalism emerges, reversing the more equitable distribution of wealth that society had come to expect since the end of World War II. Large-scale lay-offs ignite the extensive use of temporary and contract workers. Conspicuous consumption, electronic spreadsheets, entrepreneurialism, information technology and personal computers flourish. Increasing attention is paid to customers, diversity and equality of employment opportunities. Open-plan offices are introduced and total quality management and lean just-in-time manufacturing flourish. ISO standards and benchmarking are introduced. Mergers and acquisitions make change management skills essential. The service sector of the economy grows.

- *1990s:* Downsizing breaks the psychological contract of steady employment in return for reasonable productivity, resulting in increased responsibilities, job empowerment and leaner, flatter organisations in the face of job insecurity and outsourcing. Some organisations go beyond 'lean and mean' into 'anorexic and angry', producing jaded and overworked employees. The service sector replaces the manufacturing sector as the main producer of GDP. The importance of learning organisations, process re-engineering, strategic alliances and supply-chain management grows. The triple bottom line combines financial and operating measures and begins to shift management's attention to ethics and corporate governance. The first virtual organisations appear.

- *2000s:* An increasingly casualised workforce, continuing job insecurity, organisation change and outsourcing persist as the service, information and knowledge economies take hold. Adding value, attracting and keeping valuable employees in the face of a looming labour shortage, leadership, vision and flexible working all become critical. Society expects more *honourable behaviour* from managers and companies to demonstrate their contribution to society as well as their ability to increase shareholder value.

- *2010s:* Disastrous droughts, earthquakes, floods and tsunamis put life as we know it on hold for many people and organisations. Deforestation, desertification, pest infestations and pollution march on, the economies of many OECD countries are in the doldrums and the population continues to age, draining the workforce of experienced people. The marketplace continues to shrink and virtual organisations, virtual teams and virtual working make their way into the commonplace. Work is becoming more informal and less routine as role descriptions become more open and flexible. The lines between personal, professional, social and family continue to blur and fade as technology becomes more sophisticated. Managers at every level continue to face situations they and other managers have never before faced, making flexibility, the ability to learn and a host of other conceptual, personal, interpersonal and technical skills essential for success. Shareholder value is no longer seen as a goal but a result of creating something worthwhile.

3. A new workforce

We all want more women to stay in the workforce after they take a break to have children, but the way to do it is through encouraging employers and employees to work together for arrangements that suit them both.

Kate Carnell, CEO, Australian Chamber of Commerce and Industry, Media release, 16 February 2015[60]

The old Australian workforce of mostly full-time white male employees has become a part-time, casualised and decidedly heterogeneous workforce. Here are the main changes:

* Younger generations with higher expectations of their jobs, their employers and their leader-managers, are entering the workforce and making more demands than older generations of employees; many younger workers want to work for leader-managers they respect in organisations that are 'green' and socially responsible. (See page 870 for further discussion about the expectations of different generations.)
* Casualisation and the legacy of downsizing have left many workers feeling dissatisfied with their employers and with their jobs.
* The employee mix is becoming more diverse.
* The skills that make people employable are mental rather than physical, and wider and deeper than ever before.
* The workforce is becoming smaller and older.

THEORY TO PRACTICE

Workplace hubs: The trend to watch

Approximately 70% of the employees of TELUS, a Canadian telecommunications provider, work virtually, the rest full-time in a company building. Employees join together for a purpose rather than to carry out a function, such as sales or finance, or to work in a department. This means that people who serve the same client can sit together at the company's Toronto hub, regardless of their functional expertise. When employees are working remotely, they can connect virtually with colleagues across the country. Since introducing these working arrangements, productivity has risen by 5%, which the company attributes to less lost work time and the improved communications between employees that hub working allows.

Workplace hubs are the current (third) wave of virtual working, where freelancers and corporate remote workers (untethered workers) come together to work in shared spaces, or hubs. More social than working from home or in a rented office, hub working is often based around 'communities' of workers engaged in similar work (such as architecture, digital business services or product innovation) and offers valuable collaboration, learning and networking opportunities.[61]

The shift to knowledge work and the shortage of skilled employees makes employees harder to come by than in the past, which increases their bargaining power. Today's employees want a greater say in how their work is assigned, assessed and rewarded. When knowledge becomes the important resource, people become more valuable because production and potential profits reside within people. Organisations can't own employees in the way they can own their other assets.

Whether they are casuals, contractors, part-timers, permanent full-time employees or agency-based temporary fill-in staff (temps), and whether they work onsite or offsite, people aren't 'workers' as much as individuals, professionals, specialists, leaders, executives or service providers, each with different expectations of their leader-manager and the organisation, and with different levels of commitment to the organisation.

This has far-reaching effects on the way organisations operate internally and manage people. Managing employees who are more skilled and better educated, more dissenting and more demanding, more willing to challenge authority and the hierarchy, and more insistent on being engaged and doing worthwhile work for worthy organisations, requires a higher level of skill, different attitudes from in the past and new organisational policies. Whether they work offsite or onsite, the 'flexible workforce' of casual, contractor, part-time and temporary workers needs to be paid, led and organised differently from their permanent full-time colleagues and, importantly, encouraged to feel part of the organisation and engaged with its mission, values and vision.

Employees are beginning to use their bargaining power to create the job content, working conditions and work patterns they want (e.g. more flexibility about where and when they do their work). As they bring more of their knowledge and creativity to work, whether they work at home or their employer's premises, their work becomes a more important part of their lives. As a result, people expect their work to be meaningful. Work is no longer separate from life or simply what people do to pay the bills. When organisations don't provide their human assets with what they want, these assets move on.

New ways of leading, managing and rewarding employees are necessary. The old authoritarian command and control style of management no longer works. Management must now be based on participation and a shared vision and values. Today's successful leader-managers are coaches and performance enablers who help employees achieve to their capacity.

A changing employee mix

The range of people who make up the employment pool is changing. For example, more women are entering the workforce and many of them are in their 40s, whereas 10 years ago they were in their 20s.[62] As discussed in Chapter 26, there are more distinct generations in the workforce than ever before; there are more employees from minority groups, more employees with disabilities and more permanent and temporary migrants, many from other cultures and with English as a second language. Each of these distinct groups has different:

* attitudes towards work
* expectations from work
* factors that motivate and engage them
* reasons for working
* reward and feedback expectations
* values and beliefs
* ways of working.

These various groups can find ways to work together. Leader-managers can help people integrate into their workforce and assimilate into and feel part of their organisation's culture so that they can contribute fully. As discussed above, managers leading distinct groups of employees can engage them and 'incentivise' them according to their requirements and offer them enough value from working with you that they don't move on with the next change in wind direction. Managers also can help everyone in a particular team develop the skills, knowledge and attributes that the organisation requires of them.

A more disgruntled workforce

The 1980s and 1990s saw many Australian businesses reduce labour costs (wages and salaries being among the largest expenses in most organisations). Australian organisations dramatically cut back employee numbers and reduced the layers of management. Prior to 1990, mostly blue-collar jobs were eliminated, but since then white-collar and managerial jobs have been cut back.

Severe downsizing brought with it a host of unfortunate repercussions:

* broken trust between management and the workforce due to breaking the psychological contract to provide long-term employment, career training and development in return for loyal and dependable service

- increased workloads, with some employees doing the jobs of two and even more employees, causing them to work long hours yet never feel on top of their jobs. The resulting stress, caused by overload, can, in some people, lead to bullying, illness and other unwanted outcomes
- less commitment to the organisation
- less job security
- loss of experienced and knowledgeable employees to turn to for assistance, increasing the workload and pressures on those left behind, particularly when older, more experienced and more 'expensive' employees were let go and younger, less experienced but 'cheaper' employees were retained, as was often the case
- loss to the organisation of the strong networks, valuable relationships and the knowledge of what works and what doesn't, along with the redundant employees
- reduced levels of morale, motivation and job satisfaction.

Casualisation of the workforce also poses problems, as discussed on page 16.

Unhappy employees are dangerous employees, particularly in knowledge and service organisations, because they feel less loyalty and are more willing to leave. High attrition substantially increases an organisation's costs and prevents it from fully benefiting from word-of-mouth recommendations from past employees whose goodwill is lost. Past employees are an important avenue of recruitment in a tight labour market.

A shrinking, greying workforce

Australia's population is relatively old by world standards. The number of people over the age of 65 is projected to double to about 24% by 2051 and, as the bulk of the working population retires, there are not enough younger people entering the workforce to take their places.[63]

Organisations are already finding it difficult to retain the employees they need, and it's going to get worse. Half the workforce is already over 45 years of age and needs active encouragement to stay in work. Between now and 2020, 200000 employees in Australia are expected to retire and more than one million new jobs are expected to be created; yet for every seven Baby Boomers approaching retirement, only one new entrant is expected to enter the workforce.[64] With the number of workers leaving the workforce outnumbering those entering it, the labour shortage promises to be severe, making recruitment difficult and retention imperative.

THE STRATEGIC PERSPECTIVE

Needed: Strategic answers to a severe labour shortage

More flexible work patterns and innovative ways to recruit, engage, energise and retain employees must be found. As well as making greater use of people on temporary work visas and migrants, organisations must draw on the underutilised pool of females as well as people with disabilities.

Here are some other tricky questions that organisations are grappling with:

- As older workers with experience retire in larger and larger numbers, who can provide the stability and continuity organisations need? Who can be the role models, mentors and coaches? Who can show people 'the ropes' and the 'tricks of the trade'? How can organisations encourage the best people to stay and share their knowledge as well as contribute in their usual way?

>>

- How can organisations actively retain older workers and attract others to join to fill the employee shortfall? What as yet untapped groups of employees can organisations employ to fill the shortfall?
- How can organisations make the necessary adaptations to their culture as the smaller groups of Generation Y and Z, each with different needs and expectations of their employer and work, replace the Baby Boomers?
- How can organisations retain the employees they want to keep when other organisations are trying to entice them away?
- When organisations can't find the people they need, what is their Plan B?
- What non-traditional employment pools can organisations draw on to find the people they need and how can they attract them? (Organisations can no longer afford to sit back, advertise a vacancy and wait for a response.)

Each organisation must answer these questions differently in the light of its customer expectations, market, strategy and vision. The solutions must be flexible enough to suit the range of people the organisation employs and must work for both the role and the employee since not all options are feasible for all roles. The sooner these questions are answered, the better. Organisations that leave it too long will be left behind.

How can organisations keep older workers and attract younger workers? Many are already experimenting with a range of options to find those that best suit their culture, strategy and vision, including:

- altered work duties and responsibilities
- career breaks to allow older employees to assess whether they want to retire
- closing off early exit routes and early retirement schemes
- delayed retirement
- flexible working arrangements
- interesting and challenging work performed in the preferred hours and location
- job sharing
- part-time work in the same job, in a different job or on a project team
- phased retirement schemes, gradually reducing the number of days worked
- sabbatical leave
- working from home all or part of the time
- working one month a quarter.

Such measures help at the tip of the iceberg, but only at the tip. Organisations must also develop and act on an **employer value proposition (EVP)** and **employer brand** to attract and retain the employees they need at all levels. Equally importantly, organisations must attract, develop and retain high-quality managers, who can create an environment that employees are loath to leave. (Chapters 10 and 25 deal with attracting and retaining employees and EVP.)

A more skilled and educated workforce

The economy's move from growing and making to thinking and helping has called forth a smarter, multiskilled workforce. Jobs are no longer narrowly defined and procedures spelled out – they are broad and flexible. People who can only follow instructions and procedures are being left behind as the ability to think and innovate becomes more critical.

Today's valuable employees are flexible, more in control of their jobs and able to work without supervision. They take responsibility for the quality of their work, so there is less need to direct them, plan their work, organise them or 'keep an eye' on them; this transforms your job as a leader-manager.

The demand for higher quality products and services is turning what looks like routine work into work that requires thought and judgement. Employers expect every employee to look for better ways of producing goods and offering services. Employees' energy, commitment, competence and ability to make judgements and to innovate are attributes that add value, since the physical material accounts for a fraction of the cost of many outputs, whether products or services. Excellent interpersonal skills and high levels of emotional intelligence are, more than ever, key workplace assets.

Knowledge workers

About 30% of Australian workers are classified as skill level 1 (managers and professionals).[65] These people are part of the knowledge worker workforce – as a leader-manager, you're a knowledge worker yourself. These are the people who work with their brains and with technology, creating and manipulating information, knowledge and ideas, providing services and making contributions that, in most cases, don't have a tangible outcome. Even the 'new' industrial workers are now knowledge-based – for instance, the latest car models have more built-in computing power than some of the first satellites, and to build and maintain them requires a high degree of technical knowledge and expertise.

The contributions of knowledge workers are making today's world go round. Tertiary-educated people and others who have kept their training up to date to maintain their 'employability' are in demand. Lifelong learning is compulsory.

Brainpower, not muscle power, is the order of the day. A person's employment prospects depend on ideas, information and intelligence. These 'three Is' describe the essence of knowledge-intensive organisations and knowledge and information workers. These workers can operate anywhere – at home, in an office or a laboratory, in Albury-Wodonga, Beijing or Calcutta – because they carry their brainpower with them.

In organisations in knowledge-intensive industries, such as accountancy, advertising, contract R&D, engineering, film, law, management consulting, pharmaceuticals, public relations and software, knowledge workers, or 'gold-collar workers' as they are sometimes called, often make up 70–90% of all the employees, dominating their organisations numerically and culturally.[66] (See page 407 for information on leading knowledge workers.)

A new way of assessing organisations

Business ethics, corporate social responsibility (CSR) and the notion of corporate citizenship reflect the fact that organisations have fundamental responsibilities to stakeholders other than their shareholders. These responsibilities go beyond mere compliance with local, state and federal government legislation and regulations. Measured by the triple bottom line, an organisation's responsibility to the economy, the environment and society is now an important aspect of its employer brand and EVP. The triple bottom line is:

* *People* (human capital). How the organisation's practices towards employees and the community benefit those constituencies rather than exploit or endanger them.
* *Planet* (natural capital). How sustainable the organisation's environmental practices are, how much they benefit (or at least do no harm to) the environment and whether the organisation is trying to reduce its carbon footprint through judicious consumption of energy and non-renewable resources, reducing waste and rendering waste less toxic before disposing of it.

- *Profit* (the bottom line). How much the organisation contributes to the economy.

CSR is becoming more important for three main reasons:

- Many consumers prefer to purchase from socially responsible organisations.
- Many employees prefer to join socially responsible organisations.
- Many investors prefer to invest in socially responsible organisations.

The growing preference is to deal with and work for 'green' organisations that operate in eco-friendly ways and behave responsibly when they enter developing economies to market their goods, outsource or purchase supplies. People increasingly expect organisations to contribute positively to, rather than undermine or have a zero impact on, society and the environment as they go about their business. The other main benefits resulting from CSR are:

- enhanced corporate and brand image
- improved financial performance
- increased staff motivation
- reduced costs through environmental best practice
- reduced risk exposure.

A reputation for good corporate citizenship can be an important way to set an organisation apart from its competitors and build a loyal customer and employee base. Conversely, irresponsible operations can effectively put an organisation's social licence to operate at risk, as breaches quickly filter through to consumers and government policy-makers.

Triple bottom line reporting is currently voluntary, although it is increasingly seen as mandatory for global companies and companies aspiring to become global. (Chapter 23 explains how to create sustainable workplaces.)

 THE STRATEGIC PERSPECTIVE

Measuring CSR

Westpac is one of Australia's leaders in the field of CSR, ranking first on many local and global indices that measure companies' corporate social responsibility and sustainability. These indices include Reputex, the Dow Jones Sustainability Index and Australia's Corporate Responsibility Index.

According to research by the federal government, 29% of Australian companies publish a sustainability report but only six of these companies have their reports audited. Australian companies have adopted sustainability reporting more slowly than have companies overseas. For example, 80% of Japanese companies and 75% of British companies publish sustainability reports.[67]

FYI

Who cares wins

Three prestigious organisations have found that meeting all the stakeholders' needs benefits the shareholders, too. An 11-year Harvard University study found that 'stakeholder balanced' companies showed four times the growth rate and eight times the employment growth of companies that were shareholder-only focused.[68] AMP Capital Investors agrees that strong financial performance can be directly linked to corporate social responsibility. Its research found that over four- and 10-year periods, companies with a higher CSR rating outperformed the Australian Securities Exchange Index by more than 3% a year.[69]

4. Wanted: Highly skilled leader-managers

> This is the age of intellectual capital, and the most valuable parts of jobs are the human tasks:
> sensing, judging, creating, building relationships.
>
> Thomas A Stewart (business editor), *Fortune* (17 March 1997)[70]

Management is becoming more demanding and challenging. You need different and broader skills than leader-managers of the past, particularly leadership and 'soft' skills such as the ability to listen and achieve consensus and to set a personal example. Flexibility, and the ability to cope with uncertainty and to think strategically will help you thrive in their changing environment.

More than ever, as a leader-manager you need strong 'right brain' skills for understanding yourself and working effectively with others. You also need strong 'left brain' skills for planning, solving problems, managing resources, working with technology, identifying and managing risks, and so on.

As specialisations grow and narrow, generalist leader-managers become more valuable. Yet even generalist management skills and knowledge are becoming outdated faster than ever, so, like all knowledge workers, continually developing, updating and refining your skills is important.

Today's leader-managers can master their complex, fast-changing, unfamiliar competitive environment and improve their relationships with Australia's new Asian customers. Managers have stepped away from the 20th century and its traditions, as you can see in Figure 1.4. They are building stronger bonds with their long-standing suppliers, partners, owners, colleagues and workforces, at the same time pursuing fresh initiatives.

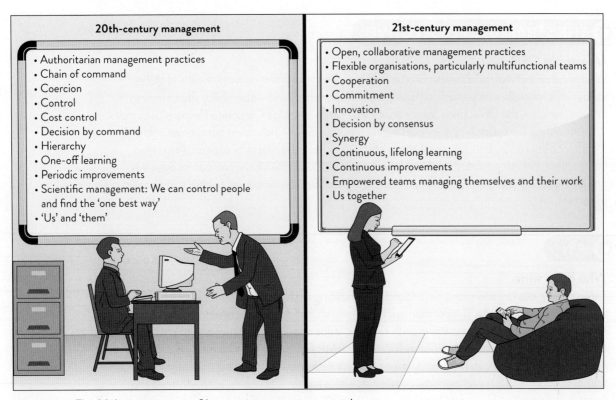

FIGURE 1.4 The 20th-century versus 21st-century management trend

In the 21st century, managers are enhancing the competencies that they have traditionally used. These competencies lie in the following three skill groups:

1. conceptual skills
2. personal and interpersonal skills
3. technical skills related to the job and to information and communications technologies.

Conceptual skills

Can you help your organisation meet the challenges of globalisation and a changing economy, environmental and other risks, technological advances and a shrinking, more educated and demanding workforce? Can you manage remote workers and introduce change? For Australia to remain prosperous and retain its high standard of living, managers at all levels in all sectors of the economy can develop an understanding of, and manage these issues and rise to these challenges. Failure to make the most of the continually changing environment will be fatal.

The conceptual skills of leadership authenticity, ethics and values help you manage relationships to ensure that you and your team meet or exceed customer expectations, are open to new ideas and ways of working, and can see the opportunities that surround you. Openness to change and the ability to adapt to new situations and changing work conditions, the initiative to identify opportunities not obvious to others, creativity, problem-solving and the ability to translate ideas into action, are all increasingly important.

With good conceptual skills, you can:

- anticipate future problems and implement preventive action
- coordinate the many activities you and your team engage in
- get to the heart of a problem and take appropriate action so you don't waste your time treating 'symptoms'
- think through plans, ideas and decisions and recognise their possible implications and effects on others
- understand the systems and procedures that flow through your organisation
- understand how a change in one section or system could affect other sections or systems.

These are foundation skills of the 21st-century leader-manager. They enable you to understand and apply your organisation's policies on health, safety and welfare, and diversity, for example, and to understand and uphold your organisation's values and strategies, such as its employer value proposition. They help you understand how each part of your organisation interrelates with and contributes to the success of the whole; how sound management is critical to the overall success of your organisation; and how mutually rewarding relationships with customers and suppliers companies are essential for success. Seeing the 'strategic perspective' helps you understand the role your organisation plays in the economic, environmental and social life of its community, the nation and the world.

Thinking skills help you evaluate the sea of information available to you. We're awash with information and can access anything and anybody, anywhere, any time. The ability to see through the 'clutter' – mere information that is not knowledge – and find information that is useful and serves your purpose, prevents information overload.

Personal and interpersonal skills

You may know someone who lacks personal and interpersonal skills – it's the person who opens their mouth only to insert both feet; the person who rubs people up the wrong way and can be counted on to say the wrong thing at the wrong time to the wrong person; the person who thinks only of himself or herself, managing to inconvenience, irritate and frustrate others by their actions and inactions. Personal and interpersonal skills are career essentials.

Today's managers understand how to work with a range of people and cultures, how to network and build relationships. This begins with self-awareness – understanding and mastering yourself so you can choose your thoughts, emotions, actions and reactions, take responsibility and have confidence in your own vision and goals. Self-awareness, combined with emotional intelligence, helps you accept that everyone is different, with different skills, abilities, beliefs, values and desires. Knowing that, you can empathise with attitudes and viewpoints different from your own which, in turn, helps you communicate effectively and work well with others. Your ability to work with, lead, persuade and inspire others, to understand where they're 'coming from', to speak your mind clearly and respectfully, to coach and develop team members, and to identify, recruit and retain the right staff, are all based on your self-awareness and ability to communicate.

Asia – Asia Pacific and the Indian subcontinent – is the fastest-growing of the world's eight regions and more than 75% of Australia's trade in goods and services is with Asia.[71] It's therefore important to understand your own culture and other cultures and to be able to work cross-culturally. The collaboration skills that help you work in and lead teams, including non-traditional teams, such as virtual teams, are increasingly valuable. (Chapter 25 has information on leading a diverse workforce and Chapters 13 and 14 explain how to lead traditional and non-traditional teams.)

IN A NUTSHELL

The core interpersonal skills

Here is a run-down on the most important interpersonal skills to develop:

- *Ability to be a team player and work effectively with others.* Work cooperatively and effectively with your work team, managers and people from other departments in your organisation and, increasingly, with people from outside your organisation – contractors, customers, the public, suppliers and temporary employees.
- Assertiveness *and empathy.* Know how to state your own requirements clearly and precisely, as well as to understand a situation from other people's points of view.
- *Clear communication.* Managers spend more than 75% of their time communicating so develop excellent communication skills.[72] Your best ideas and the most necessary instructions are worthless unless you can convey them so that others understand them.
- *Encouraging and motivating.* The ability to bring out the best in others and inspire them to perform well and productively is an asset no modern leader-manager can be without.
- *Integrity.* Acting honestly and ethically, and according to your values and principles, earns you the respect of others and increases your personal influence and power base. Integrity allows you to 'practise what you preach' or 'walk your talk' and gives you the courage of your convictions. It allows you to 'say what you mean and mean what you say', without deceit, deception or game playing. Your integrity allows others to know they can trust you to take the 'right' action and make the 'right' decision and, because of that, they willingly follow your lead.
- *Respect for others.* It is difficult to imagine an effective leader-manager who doesn't respect others and value their feelings, ideas, aspirations and contributions. Because the brain's mirror neurons trigger matching responses to other people's behaviour towards us, managers who respect others are respected in return; this is known as the boomerang principle.

Technical skills

You don't have to be expert in the work that your team members do, but you can develop an understanding of the nature of the jobs and the processes, methods, procedures and administration systems your team members use.

Keep up to date with information and communications technology. The ability to create, manipulate and understand spreadsheets and use other types of IT to organise data and research information, and apply IT as a management tool to plan and monitor your own work and the work of your team, is now a base-line skill, expected of all leader-managers.

As globalisation continues and managing and participating in teams becomes more virtual, understanding and using collaboration and communications tools is becoming more important. Given the rapid advances in IT and communications technology, keeping yourself and your team up to date is an ongoing challenge.

● ACTION!

Are you a 21st century manager? You can find out with the interactive self-test of the same name on *CourseMateExpress*.

CourseMateExpress

Go to http://login.cengagebrain.com to access CourseMate Express, your online study tool for *Management Theory & Practice*. CourseMate Express brings chapter concepts to life with interactive learning, and study and exam preparation tools:

* Test your skills in different aspects of management with interactive self-tests and simulations.
* Watch videos that show how real managers operate in real businesses.
* Test your understanding of the changing world of management by taking the revision quiz.

QUICK REVIEW

1. Summarise the major trends discussed in this chapter and describe how they affect organisations and its leader-managers.
2. Describe how the way Australians work is changing and the implications this has for leader-managers.
3. Discuss the ways in which the Australian workforce is changing, the reasons for these changes, the challenges these changes present to leader-managers and the skills leader-managers can develop to deal with them effectively.
4. Outline the managerial skills you believe to be most important now and over the next few years.

BUILD YOUR SKILLS

1. What new skills can you develop as Australia moves further into the knowledge economy? What are some strategies you can use to acquire and strengthen your skills? How can you know if you are succeeding and building these skills quickly enough?
2. What skills, qualities and aptitudes should you look for in employees in a knowledge economy?
3. Referring to the information in the chapter concerning the current trends in organisations' external environments and any other information about trends you may be aware of, discuss what a typical organisation or workplace from your industry might look like in 2030. What might it be

like to work in? Where might its employees be located? What might make it valuable and what could reduce its value?

4. Do you know people who work from home? If so, interview them to find out what challenges and opportunities working from home presents, and how they perceive and manage their relationship with their leader-manager. Present your findings and conclusions to the class.

5. Do you know people who are casual or temporary employees? If so, interview them to find out what challenges and opportunities this way of working presents and whether or not, and why, they feel like a valued part of their organisation(s). Present your findings and conclusions to the class.

WORKPLACE ACTIVITIES

1. Which of the trends discussed in this chapter have affected your workplace? Explain how they have affected your workplace and how you and your organisation have responded and are continuing to respond.

2. Referring to the information on globalisation's far-reaching effects (cultural, environmental, biological and so on) on page 6, discuss how you expect each of these ramifications to affect your workplace or college.

3. What have you recently done to 'spread knowledge around' in your organisation or work group? How can sharing knowledge help an organisation?

4. According to the Corporate Responsibility Index, a meaningful code of ethics, cooperative employee relations, social and environmental audits and reporting, philanthropy, employee volunteering and community forums are all ways for organisations to nurture corporate social responsibility. Prepare a short report describing how your organisation employs or could usefully employ any of these, or other, strategies.

CASE STUDY 1.1

SITTING AND THINKING, OR JUST SITTING? MANAGING KNOWLEDGE WORKERS

Bethany is troubled. This is a new job with a specialist outsourcer and her first as a team leader – a double whammy, but a job she felt quite confident applying for. After completing her journalism course, working for two years with a regional newspaper as a general reporter, settling down with her partner and having a baby, she felt it was time for a change and was delighted to be offered the position.

She knows she is ultimately responsible for her team's results and is determined to do a good job. At the moment, she's struggling to find a way to relax and let the team get on with their work. They're smart people, very experienced, and yet, given the nature of their work, substantive results for their efforts sometimes aren't apparent for a week or two. To complicate matters, she doesn't see her team members for days at a time, since they can work where and when it suits them. As technical writers and translators for complicated equipment manuals, their work habits aren't really the point. She's comfortable with that, as it isn't so different from the newspaper, where people came and went all the time, too.

A few team members who live nearby make a point of coming into the office every week or so. Others have taken to phoning her every few days to let her know how they're getting on, and a couple send quick emails or text messages to let her know of any breakthroughs or setbacks. There are a few she's never met because they live in the 'middle of nowhere' and stay there, and a couple of others live overseas. Apparently, they moved when their partners relocated and the organisation didn't want to let them go, given their specialised skills and their experience, and so arranged for them to continue working remotely.

As a part-timer herself who often works from home, Bethany supposes they're working too, but it's hard to know. Even those who come into the office sometimes look like they're just 'sitting' there – hopefully sitting and thinking, not just sitting! These are honourable, professional people, she reminds herself. Maybe their dedication isn't so much to the company or the clients as to their profession, but she wants to believe she can rely on them.

What she's really concerned about, as she thinks it through, is that some or all of the projects she is responsible for bringing to fruition on time might have fallen into a hole. She doesn't want to be left explaining to her boss any missed deadlines and her failure to keep on top of things.

Questions

1. How can Bethany tell whether people on her team are working? Does it matter? For instance, does it matter whether people work for the number of hours they are contracted to work or only that they achieve their goals?
2. What protocols could Bethany put in place to ensure that everyone on the team meets their goals? What does Bethany need to be careful of?
3. What skills and work habits do you suggest Bethany develop to help her meet the demands of her role?

CHAPTER

2

THE OPERATING ENVIRONMENT

OVERVIEW

Amidst the vast changes described in Chapter 1, some aspects of an organisation's environment haven't changed. Your management takes place in the same sectors as always – the private, the public and the not-for-profit sectors. You can manage from the top, the middle or the first line, or at leader-manager, level. You still have stakeholders around you, each with (sometimes conflicting) expectations of how the organisation should perform.

As always, at the core of every organisation remains a set of values that guides its operations: a vision, a mission and strategies that give purpose, meaning and direction to the operations of an organisation. These guide the essential activities of the organisation, such as attracting, engaging and retaining employees and providing them with worthwhile goals to move the organisation towards its vision.

In addition, stakeholders have strengthened their expectations that organisations today be 'good neighbours'. That is, that they be responsible and active members of the community and society in general.

1. Do you know which of the three sectors of the economy an organisation is part of?
2. Can you describe the roles and responsibilities of the four levels of management?
3. Can you list the six stakeholder groups every organisation answers to?
4. Can you explain the importance of values, vision, mission and strategy in guiding an organisation and its employees?

This chapter helps you understand, support and work with these four aspects of your organisation's operating environment.

SCENARIO

The strategic planning meeting

Charlotte is a new, part-time paid leader-manager working on funding with a community arts organisation. One of her first tasks was updating an induction guide for volunteers in the organisation and she included them with the organisation's funding sources, particularly bequests, an important source of funding in recent years. This will help the volunteers handle queries from members of the public who wish to donate funds to the organisation.

Charlotte's updated volunteers' guide is to be shown at today's strategic planning meeting. With only two employees, one person seconded part-time from the local council and 12 volunteers, everyone has time to contribute ideas to the meeting. The strategic planning meeting strengthens morale and develops team-member relationships as everyone works together to decide new goals and to agree on the strategies to achieve those goals.

An external facilitator starts the meeting with a short creativity exercise as a warm-up. The serious work of the meeting starts with a review of the organisation's values, vision and mission. Charlotte agrees with her colleagues that these core values are working well and that they be maintained because stakeholders are familiar with them.

Next, it's time to explore what future changes or trends might affect the organisation, particularly regarding funding. Charlotte is invited to present her updated volunteers' guide in order to demonstrate how personal initiative can help plan the future. Now the meeting's mood moves to the importance of the individual.

The facilitator introduces a SWOT analysis (strengths, weaknesses, opportunities and threats) and opens discussion on constraints that influence the way the participants perform their jobs and achieve their goals. Strategic goals are agreed and participants are assigned responsibilities for championing each strategic goal, adding timelines for their achievement.

Charlotte puts up her hand to develop a new funding initiative. None of Charlotte's 'hand-up' tasks are difficult. However, the strategic planning meeting has enabled Charlotte to show her new co-workers that she is a leader-manager who fits with this organisation.

1. The three sectors

> My role, and the role of senior executives, is to make our people as successful as they possibly can be.
>
> Nev Power (CEO, Fortescue Metals), quoted in Burrell, *The Deal* (August 2012)[1]

Which are you more familiar with: working in private enterprise, working for the government or working in not-for-profit organisations? Each of these sectors of the Australian economy needs top-quality leader-managers.

The challenge for the not-for-profit sector is to compete effectively for funding and skilled and motivated volunteers and paid employees. The private sector must learn to thrive in a global environment and a changing marketplace. The public sector must learn to deal with budget cuts, deregulation and *privatisation* (i.e. transferring ownership of a statutory organisation to the public sector). That's a pretty big ask for each sector.

The not-for-profit sector

Non-commercial, non-government organisations make up the large and diverse not-for-profit (NFP) sector. The sector's activities and services cover animal welfare, arts and culture, business and professional associations and unions, education and research, environment, health, human rights, religion, social services and sport and recreation. Together, they account for about 600 000 organisations in Australia, mostly small and dependent on voluntary members.[2]

In Australia, 380 000 NFPs are incorporated in some form and 41 000 of them are deemed by the Australian Bureau of Statistics (ABS) to be economically significant. NFPs employ about 8% of the workforce – approximately one million people (41% of whom are permanent full-time employees) while their 4.6 million volunteers contribute $14.6 billion in unpaid work. Most NFP organisations are democratically controlled and have a controlling body, often called a board of directors, which is usually made up of volunteers.[3]

The NFP sector forms an important part of the Australian economy, contributing around $55 billion annually to Australia's GDP, making it similar in size to government administration and defence, transport and storage and the wholesale trade sectors, and larger than the agriculture industry. More important than its economic contributions, though, are the NFP sector's cultural, environmental and social contributions.[4]

Money isn't the goal for not-for-profits, as it is in private enterprise; rather, their goal is the achievement of social objectives. Nevertheless, NFPs are concerned with money. They have to be. Money is the means to the end. NFPs must continually raise funds in a competitive marketplace, often in competition with private providers and other NFPs. And to get that money, NFPs must perform.

Their measures of success, therefore, revolve around controlling costs through efficient operations and the quantity and quality of the services they provide. They can measure their success directly (e.g. the number or percentage of people receiving a service) or indirectly (e.g. the impact of a service, such as the reduced number of people going through the court system or the increased number of people completing tertiary education). The days of big business, the government and even the wider community writing a cheque and turning their backs are over.

Corporate philanthropy is giving way to a partnership model. Business wants a return on its donations. Governments pit NFPs against each other in a race for outcomes and efficiency, and those at the bottom of the ladder are dropped from the next round of funding. In short, funders, whether governments, organisations or private individuals, want to know what NFPs do and how they do it, and they discontinue funding when professionalism and results don't eventuate.

Many NFPs have begun to partner with for-profit organisations to provide services and the *public private partnership* (PPP) business model has become more prevalent in this sector. As a result, today's NFPs are outcome driven as well as mission driven.

Many NFPs are taking the lead in organisation design, leadership and management style and performance management. Perhaps more than in any other sector, the leader-managers and key officers of not-for-profit organisations must know how to attract, empower and retain workers, and they must be able to make the most of workers' skills and energies. After all, many of the workers are volunteers who can easily leave when they feel they are not appreciated or not contributing in a meaningful way.

The private sector

The majority of Australian employees and employers are in the private sector, businesses whose owners expect to earn a profit by providing goods or services. Many of their measures of success, or key performance indicators, therefore, revolve around financial indicators. Increasingly, they also include social and environmental measures (see page 26 for information on new ways of assessing organisations). These businesses come in many sizes, from one-person businesses to organisations employing thousands of people.

Corporations

A corporation, or company, exists independently of its owners (the shareholders) and the people it employs. A corporation is an 'artificial person' (hence the expression 'the body corporate'). This means that the corporation continues even though its managers and employees come and go. Companies can behave as a natural person and hold property, issue shares, sue and be sued in the corporate name, and so on. About 3% of Australia's corporations are owned by overseas investors.[5] The Australian Investments and Securities Commission (ASIC) regulates all corporations.

There are two kinds of corporations: proprietary limited companies and public companies. Unlike sole traders and partnerships, both can issue shares to raise capital for the operation and expansion of the business. Should a company fail, the shareholders' responsibility, or *liability*, for paying its debts is limited to the amount (if any) of their respective shares.

Proprietary limited companies

Proprietary limited companies (private companies in Queensland) are registered under the provisions of the various Companies Acts. They can have no more than 50 owners (excluding employee shareholders). The right to transfer shares is restricted and a proprietary company cannot invite the general public to purchase its shares. These companies must have the words 'Proprietary Limited' or their abbreviation (Pty Ltd or P/L) after their business name.

Smaller proprietary limited companies tend not to have a board of directors, although many have an informal board, sometimes called a 'kitchen cabinet', made up of friends with business acumen and expertise who act as advisers and sounding boards.

Public companies

A public company, or listed company, must include the word 'Limited' or its abbreviation (Ltd) after its business name. These are the companies listed on the stock exchange and any individual or company can loan them money, or invest in them, by purchasing their shares. Public companies must have a minimum of one company secretary and three directors to represent the shareholders and there is no limit on the number of shareholders.

The mantra of 'big business' has long been 'shareholder returns' as in 'We *must* give our shareholders a good return on their money' with 'or else they'll sell up' left unsaid. But there is no legal obligation on company directors to aim exclusively to maximise shareholder value.

In fact, they can choose any strategy they like and some do. The penny has dropped and some company directors have realised that the short-term thinking of the stock market has restricted the ability of companies to be vehicles for long-term employment, economic advancements, retirement security, and in general, to contribute to the well-being of the world and the communities they reside in and sell to.

A new phenomenon called B corporations, or B corps, has entered the public playing field this century. These are companies that have stated their commitment to environmental and social goals, as well as profit goals, and they are regularly audited against those achievements.

There are now more than 1000 B corps in 35 countries and 121 industries subscribing to the movement called conscious capitalism, founded by Raj Sisodia of Harvard University and John

Mackey of Whole Foods (see 'The strategic perspective: A community of stores' on page 375). Companies like Ben & Jerry's ice cream, online retailer Zappos, The Container Store and The Hub Australia work for the benefit of all stakeholders, not just shareholders, and reportedly earn superior returns.

Convinced that shareholders will continue to support them, 'A list' Unilever has also stated that its 'paramount goals are to satisfy the demands of consumers and customers and serve the needs of the communities where we operate'.[6] The times are changing.

Money makes the world go round

One thousand corporations account for half of the total market value of the world's 60 000 public companies.[7] Australia's 200 largest companies, listed in the ASX 200, are valued at $1.05 trillion. This is almost 80% of the total value of all ASX-listed enterprises.[8] There is a vast concentration of economic power in these large companies.

Yet the number of public companies around the world has dropped sharply in recent years, most markedly in Europe and the USA, where numbers are down 23% and almost 50% respectively since 1997. Business, it seems, wants to do business its own way and not pander to the short-termism of shareholders (not a recipe for long-term success) or the demands of public scrutiny and costly regulation. The original function of the stock exchange, to raise capital, has become the reverse — to retire capital as founders and venture capitalists sell up to realise their investments. The smart money is on the fading away of public companies.[9]

Meanwhile, family businesses account for nearly 70% of the private sector in Australia and employ around 50 % of our workforce. Franchises, often family businesses, are another type of private enterprise.

One of Australia's most popular business models, franchises quickly spread from McDonald's fast food franchises in the 1970s to the retail and service industries. They are now worth $144 130 billion to the economy and employ more than 460 000 people.[10] While they have a lower failure rate than independent small business, perhaps because of their proven business models and the systems, training and support they offer franchisees, the model doesn't guarantee success, as the closure of the Borders and Angus & Robertson bookstore chains in 2011 witnessed.[11]

Sole traders

Sole traders are companies with a single owner who usually manages the business, although sometimes a paid manager is employed. Sole traders can trade under their own name or can register a business name with their state or territory fair trading department (or equivalent). Sole traderships are the simplest and most inexpensive businesses to set up and have the fewest reporting requirements. They tend to be small because of the difficulty in raising large amounts of capital for expansion.

The sole trader takes on all the responsibilities and financial risks of running the business. Although all the profits belong to the sole trader, when the business ceases trading, the owner is also responsible for paying any debts.

Partnerships

In a partnership, two or more people (or companies) own the business. Partnerships are useful when a sole trader can't cope single-handedly with the amount of work available, when more money is required to expand the business or when the original sole trader lacks all the skills needed to manage a growing business successfully. When many partners are involved, the business is often referred to as a firm.

The partners usually share the day-to-day management of the business and all the profits of the business. Like sole traders, partners have unlimited liability. In the event of the firm failing or becoming insolvent, the partners are totally responsible for paying all the firm's liabilities (debts).

Unless a partnership agreement states otherwise, the law assumes that the partners split the profits and contribute to the payment of business debts equally.

THE STRATEGIC PERSPECTIVE

The changing mix

The private sector is by far the largest in Australia with listed companies currently making up 32% of Australian enterprises, other private companies 30% and foreign companies 18%. The remaining 20% is largely the general government, at 16%, with government business enterprises at a small 4%. Together, they have revenue of $4 trillion.

Once much larger, the public sector has shrunk due to privatisation at federal and state levels (e.g. the Commonwealth and SA banks, Qantas and state railways and tramways, defence manufacturing, electricity and water utilities, and Telstra).

Although they employ significantly fewer people due to outsourcing and the move to virtual organisations, large private companies (those with over $100 million in revenue) currently account for just over 50% of Australia's total revenue.

But the mix continues to change. By 2050, private companies and small-to-medium enterprises (those with up to $100 million in revenue) will have grown in economic importance. Several factors account for this, two in particular: the trend to outsourcing by households and businesses, which is creating new entrepreneurial opportunities; and all the new industries (over 100 so far) that are emerging as the digital economy takes hold. And the stand-alone small business? These are set to give way to franchises that can provide the economies of scale and intellectual property (systems and procedures, etc.) needed to operate in the digital economy. (See 'FYI: The digital economy' on page 8, for more information on the digital age.) [12]

The public sector

Australia has a multi-tiered form of government that, directly and indirectly, governs the country. Known as the public sector, it protects the country, educates its residents and provides public and community services according to the policies and directives of the elected government.

The Commonwealth government governs the country as a whole, taking responsibility for matters of national concern such as defence, health, foreign policy and social services. State and territory governments manage the affairs of individual states and territories and, within each, there are local and city councils, as well as a range of statutory semi-autonomous bodies.

The structure of the various forms of public sector organisations is determined, in the first instance, by the *Commonwealth of Australia Constitution Act 1900 (UK)*, the set of rules by which the country has been governed since Federation, when Australia became independent of the United

Kingdom in 1901. The federal or relevant state parliament sets out the structure of statutory bodies in a charter, leaving the fine detail to the appointed senior managers.

Government departments

The activities of government are divided into functions, each with its own department. The head of each department is a public servant, employed by the government and responsible for structuring, leading and managing the department to achieve the government's objectives.

With the intention of transforming the public sector into a more economical, modern and responsive service to better meet the increased expectations of its clients and provide better value for money, the government began reforming the highly centralised, prescribed and regulated activities of the public sector in 1998. Most departments have been downsized and restructured in line with the private sector business model, moving, for example, to a workplace bargaining system, developing corporate values, vision and mission statements and managing performance in ways similar to the private sector.

Statutory authorities

Sometimes referred to as a *quango* (quasi-autonomous government organisation), a statutory authority is a government agency established by a statute, or Act of Parliament. Statutory authorities generally tend to have more independence than government departments. While most are subject to some form of ministerial control, the degree of control depends on the amount of freedom, or autonomy, the establishing government thought they would need to function effectively.

The way statutory authorities are structured and operate normally falls somewhere between that of government departments and large private sector organisations. In some cases, for example the Commonwealth Bank, Qantas, Telstra and state water and electricity authorities, they have been privatised (made public companies) or semi-privatised. When this happens, the state or federal government usually starts out as a major shareholder in the newly privatised organisation.

2. The four levels of management

> Australia is now at the forefront of governance changes that are taking place worldwide. We have traditionally punched above our weight in terms of governance and financial reform, and now Australian boards are right up there with the world's best.
>
> David Crawford, *Company Director*, Australian Institute of Company Directors (2014)[13]

Although the traditional pyramid is giving way to other forms of organisation and organisations have become 'flatter', you can still find the four levels of management, shown in Figure 2.1, in most organisations. (Page 79 has information on the new ways organisations are restructuring their operations and Chapter 1 explains why they are restructuring.)

Because of the way the working environment and the capabilities that make organisations successful are changing, today's management and non-management employees alike need different skill sets than those of even 20 years ago. In particular, the ability to develop effective working relationships with a wide range of colleagues, customers and suppliers, and skills for communication, networking and teamworking are must-haves. (Chapter 5 discusses how to build a strong communication foundation; Chapter 8 explains how to build effective working relationships and networks.)

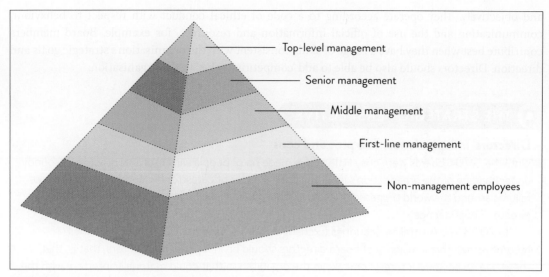

FIGURE 2.1 Traditional pyramid of management levels

Top-level management

The chief executive officer or permanent head of a government department, and the board of directors make up an organisation's top-level management. This highest management level is responsible for setting the 'tone' of an organisation: its ethics and standards, values and culture. It is also responsible for hiring and retaining employees, for ensuring that effective policies are developed for managing them and for their diversity and health, safety and welfare. Top-level management also oversees the appointment and development of senior leader-managers and monitors their activities.

Small-to-medium enterprises generally have up to five board members and larger organisations usually have seven to nine board members; the average number of board members of Australia's largest 200 companies is 7.15.[14] The board guides the organisation by establishing broad policies and goals. It works with senior managers to determine the organisation's vision, mission, strategies and policies, enables the acquisition of the resources needed to carry them out and monitors and guides the operations of the enterprise on behalf of the shareholders.

Board members can be executive directors or non-executive directors. Executive directors work full-time in the company, usually as senior managers, although some may be worker representatives, while non-executive directors are involved with the company only part-time, through the board. When all the directors work in the company, the board is known as an inside board, or executive board. A non-executive or external board is made up of directors who are not employed by the company full-time and hold no other roles in the company.

The advantages of an inside board are that its members know the company, its markets, its operations and its problems intimately. Yet this can sometimes mean that they are 'too close to the forest to see the trees'. External directors may see matters more objectively and bring fresh points of view and a range of experience and perspectives to bear on problems, decisions, strategies and policies. Not surprisingly, most Australian companies aim for the benefits of both executive and non-executive boards by appointing mixed boards made up of both insiders (executive directors) and outsiders (non-executive directors).

Board members should not have any conflicts of interest, that is, they must be free of internal or external influence (real or perceived) so that they can govern the organisation independently and objectively. They operate according to a code of ethical conduct with respect to behaviour, communication and the use of official information and resources, for example. Board members contribute best when they have a range of skills consistent with the organisation's strategic goals and direction. Directors should also be able to add 'competitive value' to the organisation.

⊙ THE STRATEGIC PERSPECTIVE

Directors' independence: The pros and cons

Until the 1970s, boards were cosy little affairs made up of people with useful contacts or a sound understanding of the organisation's industry. Then a series of catastrophic corporate governance failures around the world triggered regulatory strengthening, including new requirements for director independence.

In 2003, the Australian Securities Exchange (ASX) Corporate Governance Council recommended that a majority of board directors should be independent directors, that is, that they have no personal interests or stake in the organisation that could materially interfere with the impartial exercise of their judgement. Known as the 'Conflict Rule', in practice this means that directors should not hold more than 5% of the company's stock and should not have worked in an executive capacity in the company or an associated company for at least three years.

But this is advice only and some believe it is at times best ignored in the case of individual directors; the important thing, they say, is the sum of the parts in terms of diversity, effectiveness, experience, independence and skills of the board as a whole. Directors with no prior experience with a company or its industry can't have the depth of knowledge they need to make sound decisions, however well intentioned they may be.

A recent report by Macquarie Equities showed that companies whose directors are substantial shareholders outperformed the market. Suncorp recently announced that its directors must own at least $200 000 in company stock because directors with 'skin in the game' are more motivated to improve company performance. AMP also encourages directors to hold ordinary shares, although it discourages identical incentives to non-executive directors and senior managers in order to keep directors' allegiances to the shareholders, not management.

Ah, but could shareholding tempt directors into unethical behaviour? A large shareholding could lead to a material conflict of interest for a director who is, for example, responsible for signing off on financial statements or making strategic decisions.

The jury, it seems, is still out and the consensus is that the right balance is needed between independence and impartiality on the one hand and vested interest on the other.[15]

Governance

The board of directors doesn't *run* the organisation; it *governs* it by overseeing and advising senior management and ensuring they manage the organisation in a prudent way. Governance refers to the way organisations are managed and controlled. Good governance means that a board uses due care and diligence to carry out its responsibilities, acting independently and objectively, without domination by one individual or faction. Effective governance provides reasonable assurance to stakeholders that the organisation is achieving its goals in an acceptable and responsible way and ensures the enterprise is ready, willing and able to prosper in the long term.

IN A NUTSHELL

Some key board responsibilities

The best practice boards fulfil these duties:

- Appoint senior managers and auditors.
- Approve, scrutinise and monitor budgets (including executive pay), key decisions, performance, plans, risks and controls, and strategies.
- Avoid overemphasising short-term goals.
- Clearly define board and senior management responsibilities to avoid confusion.
- Decide how to distribute the organisation's profits: Some are returned to the shareholders; some are used to purchase plant and equipment or to acquire another organisation; some are invested in intangibles, such as training, research and development, and brand building.
- Ensure compliance with policies, laws and regulations.
- Ensure risk is identified and managed properly.
- Ensure succession planning for senior managers and other key managers and employees.
- Ensure the organisation meets its obligations to its stakeholders (see Section 3 in this chapter).
- Keep abreast of trends, threats and opportunities, and ensure the organisation responds appropriately and proactively.
- Manage communication with stakeholders.
- Monitor the overall performance of the organisation and the performance and behaviour of the senior management team.
- Oversee external communications (e.g. with shareholders).
- Set the strategic direction for key business drivers.
- Take professional advice.

Corporate governance

In corporations the directors' *fiduciary duty* is considered to be their obligation to act solely in the interests of the owners, or shareholders. This includes avoiding conflicts of interest and other matters that may lead to corporate governance issues being raised. Directors are expected to create wealth by contributing to shareholder value, raising the share price, being profitable, paying out large dividends and generally making the business attractive to investors.

However, corporations should take more into account than short-term share prices in order to run their businesses properly. When you consider the excesses of the 1980s, the business scandals in Australia and overseas in the late 1990s and early 2000s and the global financial crisis that struck in 2008, all related to corporate governance, you can understand why corporate governance is a hot issue.

FYI

SarbOx governs the governors

In April 2005, one of the biggest industrial failures in the United Kingdom took place. The MG Rover plant, the last British automotive manufacturing plant in England, closed down. More than 5000 jobs were lost in an already economically disadvantaged region, indirectly affecting countless suppliers and subsidiary industries. The four owners, known as the 'Phoenix Four', and the managing director left the company with £42 million in compensation, an amount that would have paid the redundancies of the rest of the workforce. The employees received no redundancy payments, no period of notice and no payment in lieu of notice. (After a seven-year battle, the workers received £3 each.)[16]

In 2002, the United States of America sought to reverse the trend of executive audacity and dubious ethics with the *Sarbanes–Oxley Act*. This highly prescriptive US federal government Act increased corporate governance requirements, particularly regarding audits, financial reports and directors' liability. SarbOx, as it is known, affects all Australian subsidiaries of US-owned companies. Meanwhile, Australians and Europeans are searching for less prescriptive ways to encourage more accountable and responsible corporate governance. (See 'Australia's answer' in 'The strategic perspective: Directors' independence' on page 42.)

Sadly, SarbOx seems to have failed because many of the directors and executives of the very financial institutions that brought on the global financial crisis in 2008, also walked away with huge bonuses and payouts.

Public sector boards

The key role of the boards of government enterprises is to help an organisation achieve its charter. Board of government enterprises differ from boards of private sector companies in other ways, too, for example:

- They don't have the same disclosure requirements.
- They have different stakeholders and they can suffer from stakeholder interference (the government minister is a stakeholder).
- They often don't have the power to hire and fire the CEO or appoint directors.
- They're usually paid less.

In addition, management prerogative is diminished by a range of public service policies and guidelines on matters such as entertainment, forced redundancies and relocations, as well as overseas travel, making it difficult to manage the enterprise commercially. And disgruntled special-interest groups can always pop through the ministerial back door to get their way.

Unlike the private sector, the overriding driver for the public sector isn't profit and, ultimately, the government calls the shots. For this reason, Nick Greiner, New South Wales premier and treasurer from 1988 to 1992 and now a company director, suggests the boards of government-owned enterprises and quangos be called 'advisory boards' or 'councils', so that it is clear that these boards are there to give input, while the government makes the decisions.[17]

● THE STRATEGIC PERSPECTIVE

A matter of trust

A review of Global, UK and US surveys on business ethics by the Institute of Business Ethics found that only one in four members of the general pubic trusts business leaders to correct business issues of ethics and 'general malfeasance' (unlawful conduct and malpractice). The review also found that 42% of 'informed' members of the public globally believed that there was not enough government regulation of business. The least trusted were banks and media companies.

In the USA, 45% of companies claimed to have lost business to unethical competitors in 2013. In the UK, 63% of managers said they had been asked to do something contrary to their own ethical code at some point in their career and 51% said they had been expected to behave at work in a way that made them feel morally uncomfortable at some point in their career, with 10% leaving their jobs as a result.[18]

Senior management

Senior management is the next level of management. Senior managers, sometimes called executives, develop long-term 'roadmaps' of values, vision, mission, strategies, plans and policies to guide the organisation and add value for its stakeholders.

It is their responsibility to see that the organisation achieves the goals established by the board and follows the agreed roadmap.

THE STRATEGIC PERSPECTIVE

Ethics isn't simple

Ethical behaviour is becoming simultaneously more important and more difficult to manage for four reasons:

1. The devolution of decision-making down the flattened hierarchy means that more employees at lower levels are making judgements that have ethical consequences.
2. Globalisation means that (a) the consequences of one poor decision can reach further than ever before, and (b) what is considered 'okay' in one region may be considered 'not okay' in another.
3. Outsourcing means that organisations are increasingly dependent on 'outsiders' to adhere to their codes of conduct and apply their stated values in their work.
4. The privatisation of public sector enterprises is blurring the line between the 'public good' and profit.

(You can explore a range of ethics advice, issues, resources, tools and ethical dilemmas at the website, The Institute of Business Ethics, http://www.ibe.org.uk.)

Middle management

Middle management comprises the level(s) between senior management and first-line management. They are the bridge connecting senior management's vision and strategies to the work priorities and aspirations of lower level staff by developing the tactics, specific policies and shorter-term plans to guide the organisation's day-to-day activities.

Large organisations can have several layers of middle managers while others have two or three. Generally, though, de-layering, downsizing and restructuring are decreasing the number of middle management jobs and increasing the number of first-line leader-manager jobs. Communications and information technology can replace middle managers as transfer and control points for information and can undertake many of middle management's traditional duties, such as monitoring performance, providing instant feedback and even creating reports. Other (formerly) middle management responsibilities have moved to first-line leader-managers.

FYI

Needed: Leader-managers

Managers represent 13% of the Australian workforce and have been in growing demand since 2009. Continued growth is expected to be in the region of 6.4%. The need for team leaders, or first-line leader-managers, is expected to grow strongly, particularly in accounting, construction, health, office work and private sector information technology.

In Australia, 35% of the country's 1.48 million managers are female; 50% are over the age of 45; and 40% work in regional areas. [19]

First-line management

First-line leader-managers work in shorter time frames than more senior managers, typically in weeks or months rather than quarters and years. They are the indispensable link between non-management employees and the rest of management. Because they are the only managers who have direct and daily contact with the workforce, their role is unique and one of the most important in any organisation.

They are ideally positioned to influence the output, morale, motivation, service levels and cost-effectiveness of the employees they supervise. To many employees, they personify the organisation as a whole. They serve as a focal point for attitudes and values and are role models of how to behave towards customers, the organisation and the job itself.

First-line leader-managers translate the enterprise's vision and goals to employees and explain employees' feelings and views to more senior management. Unfortunately, this can sometimes lead to a 'pig-in-the-middle' feeling because first-line managers can easily see, and often identify with, both sides of an issue.

This closeness can also lead to loyalty problems. On the one hand, first-line leader-managers work very closely with non-management employees and, in many cases, were part of this group before their promotion to management.

They may continue to identify with the workforce and more senior managers may mentally continue to place them there, too. Certainly, in some organisations first-line managers are 'glorified workers', expected to carry out the same tasks as the people they supervise with their management duties an added-on extra.

Not too many years ago, managers at this level were known as 'supervisors'. They are now known by such varied titles as coordinators, first-line managers, front-line managers, section heads, team leaders, or simply managers.

3. The six stakeholders

> While one should never underestimate the ability of risk-besotted financiers to wreak havoc, the real threat to capitalism isn't unfettered financial cunning. It is, instead, the unwillingness of executives to confront the changing expectations of their stakeholders.
>
> Gary Hamel (US management expert), *The Wall Street Journal* (2012)[20]

Whichever sector and level they work in, managers need to understand not just their day-to-day duties and responsibilities but also their wider responsibilities. Who do you think managers are primarily accountable to? Their own managers? Their organisation's owners? The general public? Those they lead? And what are managers' wider responsibilities? To deliver profits to shareholders? To reduce costs? To nurture an organisation so it can survive in the long term? To provide meaningful work? To contribute to society? To do no harm to the environment?

 FYI

'A new industrial philosophy'

General Robert Wood Johnson, who guided Johnson & Johnson from a small, family-owned business to a worldwide enterprise, had a progressive view of a corporation's responsibilities. In a pamphlet called 'Try Reality', written in 1935, he advocated what he termed 'a new industrial philosophy', which he defined as an organisation's responsibility to customers, employees, the community and shareholders. He believed that putting customers first would serve the business well — and it has.[21] (See, 'The importance of values in a crisis' on page 52.)

Ethics, corporate social responsibility and governance are increasingly important ingredients in an organisation's success. All managers need to understand and adhere to their organisation's policies concerning matters such as:

- bribery, corruption, facilitation payments and money laundering
- conflicts of interest
- entertainment and gifts
- harassment and discrimination
- privacy, security, and data and intellectual property protection
- supply-chain management
- whistle-blowing
- work–life balance.[22]

Organisations and employees at all levels are increasingly seen as having responsibilities to the six groups of people shown in Figure 2.2.

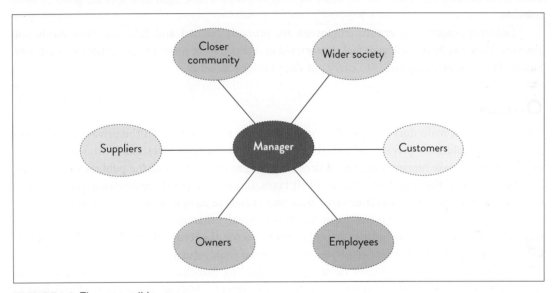

FIGURE 2.2 The responsible manager

The community and the wider society

Organisations have more than a responsibility to adhere to the laws and regulations of the governments of the countries in which they operate. They are increasingly expected to contribute to, or at least not harm, the environment and the economies in which they operate and to give something back to the communities in which their employees and customers live, and in which they make their money or provide their services.

Organisations meet these expectations in a variety of ways, such as implementing sustainable operations, providing time off for employees to undertake community service work, sponsoring local sports teams and environmental projects and partnering with or supporting charities.

Customers and/or clients

First-line managers ensure that those products or services are produced or provided within the established guidelines. This includes always striving to improve their products or services and the ways they are produced so that they continually represent better value for customers and, in turn, enhance the organisation's reputation.

Ann Sherry, who became the businesswoman behind Carnival cruises, has said, 'Too many managers believe that all they need to do is run their business. However, external factors are constantly encroaching on business and have the capacity to cost companies large amounts of money.'[23]

Employees

As discussed in Chapter 1, people's expectations of work and the workplace itself have changed. Today's organisations have a variety of policies that help meet employees' needs and all managers need to understand, support and carry out those policies.

Effectively, it is the responsibility of first-line leader-managers to treat employees fairly and to safeguard their health, safety and well-being, job satisfaction and morale. Leader-managers can also build good working environments by ensuring that employees have clear and specific goals to work towards.

Leader-managers can ensure employees are properly trained and fully use their skills and abilities. They can help employees feel appreciated and that they're receiving organisational support. Finally, they can help employees to carry out their duties efficiently.

Owners

An organisation's main duty is generally considered to be to its owners. In the private sector, these are the shareholders – private individuals as well as institutional investors – who invest in an organisation to make money. You can think of taxpayers as the 'owners' of the public sector because it is they who fund the operations through their taxes. In a not-for-profit organisation, you can think of those individuals and organisations that contribute funds to its operations as the 'owners'.

Owners want to know that the organisation is prudently managing their investments and they want a fair return for their investments. In the private sector, the return is profit. For public and not-for-profit organisations, an effective service is considered a fair return.

Top-level and senior managers determine the guiding principles and strategies they believe can provide owners with the best return on their investments. Middle managers work out how to realise these principles and strategies and first-line managers ensure these are followed so that the organisation's product or service is produced and delivered efficiently. (See Section 4 in this chapter, for more information on developing an organisation's vision and strategy.)

Suppliers

Senior managers establish the desired outcomes and set the guidelines for working with suppliers that middle and first-line managers execute, in part by developing and maintaining cooperative relationships with people from supplier organisations.

Believing that strength comes from mutually beneficial relationships, many organisations aim to forge genuine trading partnerships with their suppliers of goods and services. As more organisations outsource services, such as accounting, training, computing, maintenance and so on, many organisations also try to ensure their contractors 'buy into' their core values and principles so that they can help the organisation achieve its vision.

4. The roadmap

Wall Street is in the business of making money between now and next Tuesday. We're in the business of building an organisation, an institution that we hope will be here 50 years from now. Strategic planning is an important part of running any business and the more so for businesses that are operating in multiple states and countries.

James Sinega (co-founder, CostCo), cited by Cebon in Featherstone, 'Plotting the future', *Company Director* (March 2014)[24]

It takes careful thought and planning to manage an organisation that achieves worthy goals in a worthy way. A vague aspiration, such as 'Let's make great shirts' or 'Let's help people find jobs' may be a place to start, but it's only the first step.

Whatever the sector, the people employed in an organisation need a clear understanding of specifically:

- what the organisation aims to achieve
- what needs to be done to achieve it
- how employees should behave as they work towards achieving it.

To answer these questions, they also need to know:

- what makes the organisation distinct
- how to define and measure results
- what the organisation's core competencies are and how those competencies contribute to results
- why customers choose them and not another organisation.

With those questions answered, the senior managers can prepare a set of values, a vision statement and a mission statement. Together, values, vision and mission:

- enhance an organisation's reputation and help it attract like-minded employees
- position the organisation in the consumer and employee marketplace
- provide a framework for the organisation's strategy, business plans and day-to-day operations
- send a clear message to all stakeholders about what the organisation stands for, what it aims to achieve and, in broad terms, how it plans to attain its aims.

Based on its values, vision and mission, senior managers develop a strategy, or approach, to steer the organisation towards its destination. A strategy needs to be flexible but specific enough to help the organisation and its employees navigate the diversions, opportunities and problems they meet on the way.

A clear strategy ensures each part of the organisation works in harmony with all other parts to achieve its aims by:

- acting as a reference point for decision-making
- guiding employees' day-to-day activities
- helping employees concentrate on what's important.

Figure 2.3 shows the range of board involvement in developing the organisation's roadmap of values, vision, mission and strategy. In small organisations and not-for-profit organisations, the board is likely to be fairly hands-on due to limited resources. In large organisations, the board reviews the values, vision, mission and strategy to ensure that the culture, incentives, organisation structure, people, risk appetite, succession plans, systems and so on, can support the organisation's roadmap.

Source: Based on forthcoming published research by Dr Peter Cebon, University of Melbourne[25]. Used by permission.

FIGURE 2.3 Board involvement in the roadmap

THE STRATEGIC PERSPECTIVE

Who makes a strategy succeed?

Although senior managers are generally considered responsible for creating the values, vision, mission and strategy for board approval, many organisations involve employees at all levels in developing them. The e-technology consulting company, EDS, for example, involves thousands of employees in developing its strategy.

According to McGill University's Henry Mintzberg, whoever sets the strategy, it is the middle and first-line leader-managers who decide which ideas to push and which to let languish.[26] These leader-managers establish the 'rules' and set a daily example for how to adhere to the values, and how to carry out the strategy in pursuit of the organisation's vision. Salespeople decide what to sell, to whom and how. Individual employees portray whether and how much they support the values, vision and strategies in their day-to-day behaviours. As a result, some strategies are modified and others abandoned. Intel's middle managers, for example, pushed the company towards microprocessors when its senior executives were still concentrating on memory chips.

Once agreed, the roadmap is communicated throughout the organisation under the guidance of senior management. The board, usually through the chairperson, communicates the roadmap to large shareholders, such as retail shareholders and superannuation funds, while senior management communicates the shorter-term strategy and results to these groups.

There are no hard and fast rules about how to write an organisation's roadmap. In fact, there are many contradictory definitions of the term floating about. Some organisations combine their vision and mission, some have a six-word strategy and some organisations have a six-page strategy.

The point is not to get hung up on definitions but to ensure the organisation and its employees understand clearly:

- what the organisation stands for (values)
- what it wants to achieve (vision and mission)
- how it intends to achieve it (strategy).

Values: What we believe in

Iconic investor Warren Buffett told his employees, 'If you lose money for the company, I will be understanding. If you lose one shred of the company's reputation, I will be ruthless.'[27] An organisation's values describe what it believes is important and how it intends to operate. These values form the basis of the organisation's culture, guide its operations and show its employees how they are expected to behave every day. All employees have a duty to abide by and promote their organisation's values.

Equally importantly, values are what people fall back on when they're unsure what to do. In fact, 65% of first-line leader-managers and 84% of directors refer to their organisation's values statement when making decisions.[28]

Many organisations in all sectors also use values to drive cultural change and improve the services they offer. One way to use values this way is to rate managers and employees in their formal performance reviews on how well their actions uphold the organisation's values.

● THEORY TO PRACTICE

Values in action

As you read through the values statements of these six well-known and successful organisations, consider how living these values every day, as you go about your work, could guide your actions:

ANZ Bank's values are:

- Accountability: Own your actions.
- Collaboration: Work as one.
- Excellence: Be your best.
- Integrity: Do what is right.
- Respect: Value every voice.[29]

The Australian Army's values are:

- Courage
- Initiative
- Teamwork
- Respect.

In July 2013, the Chief of Army, Lieutenant General David Morrison, AO, announced the addition of the the army's fourth value: Respect.[30]

BHP Billiton defines its values like this:

- Sustainability: Putting health and safety first, being environmentally responsible and supporting our communities.
- Integrity: Doing what is right and doing what we say we will do.

»

- Respect: Embracing openness, trust, teamwork, diversity and relationships that are mutually beneficial.
- Performance: Achieving superior business results by stretching our capabilities.
- Simplicity: Focusing our efforts on the things that matter most.
- Accountability: Defining and accepting responsibility and delivering on our commitments.[31]

Bulla Dairy Foods has built its values alongside its heritage, with the company run by the same three families for five generations:

- Family values: The Bulla Family encompasses all staff and their family, owners, customers and suppliers.
- Trust and teamwork: We work towards common goals with a spirit of respect and confidence in each other. Trust is fundamental to the teamwork that makes Bulla a success.
- Communication: Everyone in the Bulla Family has a voice.
- Growth: Maintaining traditional strengths while embracing innovation, change and growth has always been a part of Bulla's success. Being part of the Bulla Family is an opportunity to grow with the business.
- Family Life: We strive to create an environment that promotes flexibility and understanding around work–life balance because we believe the Bulla Family extends beyond the workplace. [32]

Telstra uses bold to emphasise the core words in its values:

- Show we **care**
- Work better **together**
- **Trust** each other to deliver
- Make the complex **simple**
- Find our **courage**.[33]

Wesfarmers' values are:

- Integrity
- Openness
- Accountability
- Boldness.[34]

The importance of values in a crisis

In 1982, a number of mysterious deaths in Chicago were linked to a painkiller called Extra-strength Tylenol, made by Johnson & Johnson. Containers had been removed from shelves, cyanide added and the containers replaced on the shelves.

Johnson & Johnson's values are set out in a one-page statement called 'Our Credo', written in 1943 by Robert Wood Johnson and updated in 1979 and 1987 (but remaining essentially the same).[35] 'Our Credo' clearly puts saving lives before profits and it was integral in steering the company successfully through the 1982 crisis.

The company immediately assumed responsibility and communicated fully with the public, advising consumers not to use the product. It ceased production, stopped advertising and recalled more than US$100 million worth of Tylenol capsules from the shelves. This prompt and honest action ensured that damage to the business was short term and, despite the incident, Tylenol is still one of the company's most successful products.[36]

● THEORY TO PRACTICE

How values drive Infosys

Infosys provides a range of sophisticated and innovative IT and consultancy services. Founded by N R Narayana Murthy in his bedroom in Mumbai in 1981, with six software engineers and a working capital of US$250, Infosys is now a global business. Ranked number one in the Euromoney Best Managed Companies in Asia survey of 2013, Infosys has 158 000 employees worldwide and an annual turnover of nearly US$9 billion.

After discussing several possible visions, including 'India's largest employer' and 'the biggest software firm in the country', 'India's most respected company' was chosen. When he retired from Infosys in August 2011, Murthy wrote in his farewell letter to shareholders, 'Posterity will not excuse you if you did not dream big. You owe it to your customers, your colleagues, your investors, and the society. Every major civilisation, every great advance in science and technology, and every great company is built on a big dream.'

The company still operates to its original values:

- Client value: To surpass client expectations consistently
- Excellence: To strive relentlessly, constantly improve ourselves, our team, and our services and products to become the best
- Fairness: To be objective and transaction-oriented, and thereby earn trust and respect
- Integrity and transparency: To be ethical, sincere and open in all our transactions
- Leadership by example: To set standards in our business and transactions, and be an exemplar for the industry and ourselves.

Founder Murthy says this set of uncompromising values helped overcome Western prejudices and concerns about doing business with anonymous overseas business partners. His attitude: Adopt the values or leave the company.

Managing director and CEO of Australia and New Zealand, Jackie Korhonen, measures how well her operations measure up to the Infosys values. For example: 'We want our clients to be delighted and confident; we measure that in how likely they are to return to do business with us year after year, and their willingness to trust us with their most strategic work.'

Its strict 'no bribes' policy meant it took more than 20 visits to the Department of Electronics in Delhi just to gain permission to import a mini supercomputer and a year to get a phone line.

And the Infosys roadmap? It covers the next 200 years and involves growth through multiple business cycles (the normal ups and downs of business).[37]

Vision: Where we're heading

You can think of an organisation's vision as its purpose, noble cause or *raison d'être*. It provides further guidance for its operations and employees' actions. The best vision statements are short and snappy, easily remembered, and inspiring to employees. Henry Ford's early vision was to 'democratise the automobile'. There's no point in being modest – visions should stretch people – but they should be realistic, because when they're too distant, they're demotivating.

Amazon's vision is 'to be the world's most consumer-centric company'. It drives the way the company does business. Founder Jeff Bezos said, 'When [executives of other companies] are in the shower in the morning, they're thinking about how they're going to get ahead of one of their top competitors. Here in the shower, we're thinking about how we are going to invent something on behalf of a customer.'[38]

Here are some more vision statements:

- Bulla Dairy Foods:
  At Bulla Dairy Foods we produce and market the finest quality foods that delight our consumers by fulfilling their needs. We are committed to ongoing sustainable success to enhance the prosperity and growth of all in the Bulla Family.[42]
- The Girl Scouts:
  All girls and young women are valued and take action to change the world.[43]
- Google:
  To organise the world's information and make it universally accessible and useful.[44]
- Harley-Davidson:
  We fulfil dreams of personal freedom.[45]
- Kmart Australia:
  To ensure it is where families come first for lowest prices on everyday items.[46]

Clear, compelling and credible visions achieve six goals. They:

- clearly express what the organisation truly wants to achieve
- guide the behaviour of employees and volunteers
- help the organisation assess its progress
- help the organisation respond to change
- provide a starting point for moving forward
- unify employees by providing a shared ultimate goal to work towards.

● THEORY TO PRACTICE

How a vision saved Apple

Steve Jobs was a visionary genius, but his poor workplace relationships are legendary and he was eventually ousted from his own company in 1985. He said of his replacement, John Scully, 'What can I say? I hired the wrong guy. He destroyed everything I spent 10 years working for, starting with me.' Three CEOs later, Apple had 4% of the PC market, annual losses of more than US$1 billion and was a few months away from bankruptcy. The board tried to sell the company but no one wanted it.

Jobs returned in 1997 with a clear and compelling vision: 'We're no longer about competing with Microsoft. We're about beautiful, ground-breaking products no one has ever thought of. We're about awesome design and building emotional experiences.'

Apple went from a market capitalisation of US$3 billion in 1997 to US$350 billion in 2011, more than Microsoft and Dell combined, making Apple the second most valuable company in the world. Shares rose from US$4 to more than US$400. As Steve Jobs said, 'You can't talk about profit; you have to talk about emotional experiences.'[47]

● ACTION!

How well do you understand how an organisation's vision is intended to guide its operations and the behaviour of its employees? Find out with the interactive self-test: What's our vision? on ✸CourseMateExpress.

Mission: Our map

While the vision expresses an organisation's noble cause (and seldom changes), the mission sets out 'what we seek to achieve' (and changes and adapts as the world and the marketplaces change). The mission is more specific than the vision and reflects the organisation's standards in areas central to its vision (e.g. customer service, employee relations, product or service quality and reliability, as well as profitability).

Like visions, missions need to be clear, concise and memorable in order to motivate employees, guide their actions and inform their decisions. It's important to make sure that everyone in your team understands what the values, vision and mission mean for the organisation as a whole, for the team as a whole, and for them personally.

THE STRATEGIC PERSPECTIVE

Don't just frame and hang

Devising a meaningful set of values, a compelling vision and a clear mission is only the beginning. Organisations that frame them and leave them hanging on a wall, but do nothing to 'live the dream', only breed cynicism.

Enron, once the 17th largest company in the USA, went bankrupt in 2001 and is now infamous for shady dealings and fraudulent accounting.[48] The corporate values listed in its 2000 Annual Report were communication, excellence, integrity and respect. Clearly, these values did not reflect the way the company operated.

Values, vision and mission must be a daily part of employees' working lives.

Here are some mission statements:

- Bulla Dairy Foods:
  By using innovation in all that we do, we will safely manufacture high quality foods at low cost and market those foods so that we become the consumers' first choice for quality and value.[49]
- The Girl Scouts:
  To enable girls and young women to develop their fullest potential as responsible citizens of the world.[50]
- Harley-Davidson:
  Customers for life ... Harley-Davidson values the deep emotional connection that is created with our customers through our products, services and experiences. We are fuelled by the brand loyalty and trust that our customers place in us to deliver premium quality and the promise of a fulfilling lifetime ownership experience. We exemplify this commitment by embracing a culture of personal responsibility and stewardship for quality in everything we do.[51]
- LinkedIn:
  To connect the world's professionals to enable them to be more productive and successful.[52]

Aligning goals and values

When employees' goals and values are not the same as their organisation's goals and values, they find it difficult to work well in the organisation and even to remain in it.

How can the organisation describe and communicate its vision, goals and strategies to employees in a way that builds loyalty and earns their support? How can it make people feel part of and committed to a larger, worthwhile whole? What formal and informal communication channels can it establish to ensure that key messages reach people?

Keeping employees informed about key events in their organisation can help them understand their company and feel an important part of it. Corporate videos in a YouTube-style format, formal briefing meetings and papers, in-house magazines and newsletters, internal vacancy notices, intranet sites that are friendly, informative and interactive, noticeboards, senior managers' blogs and tweets, training programs and business conferences, and values and vision ambassadors, can all play an important role in aligning individual and organisational values. All managers, at every level, play a key role in talking about and supporting these mechanisms and making them work.

Top-down communication alone isn't enough. Interactive communication is important, too, because to increase **employee engagement** people need to feel that their voice is heard and that what they say matters. They want to know that their organisation considers them important enough not just to keep them informed about what is going on, but also to find out what they are thinking.

Values and visions, if only by implication

While not every organisation has put their values, vision and mission in writing, all organisations have them, if only by implication. Even when not written down, they exist and guide the organisation's decisions, directions and operations. You can infer them from employees' and managers' behaviour and actions and the way they organise their activities.

Strategy: The road we'll take

With the values, vision and mission in place, managers can develop a strategy containing more detailed information about how to achieve the organisation's aims. How far out strategies extend are different for every organisation. The 200-year roadmap of Infosys notwithstanding, most organisations used to look about 10 years ahead (For the Infosys roadmap, see 'Theory to practice: How values drive Infosys' on page 53).

As the operating environment began to change rapidly in the late 20th century, many organisations dropped this back to three to five years; some say that these days, planning for more than a year ahead is optimistic, given the rate of change we continue to experience. (Chapter 1 explains more about the rate of change and what it means for leader-managers.) Meanwhile, strategies for start-ups and companies testing new business models are more of a rolling hypothesis until they find their feet.

Capabilities-based organisations are becoming a key building block of organisation strategy (see pages 80 and 81). Some organisations break their strategy down into *strategic imperatives,* giving each function or capability a strategic imperative to guide the development of its business plans and goals. (See 'In a Nutshell: Begin with the strategic perspective' on page 737.)

From the strategy, even more detailed *business plans* and *operational plans* are developed, which in turn feed down into team and individual performance plans. (An explanation of business plans follows, operational plans are explained on page 492; team performance plans are explained on page 376; and individual performance plans are discussed on pages 323 and 443.)

Strategy is about what makes the organisation unique within the marketplace. Don't confuse strategy with aspirations, goals or vision. Nor is strategy an action, such as a merger or outsourcing. Strategy is not financial performance or operational effectiveness, either; these, like shareholder value, are results. Strategy is also different from tactics: strategy envisions and plans over time, while tactics react *now*.

◉ THE STRATEGIC PERSPECTIVE

The difference between strategy and tactics

Here is an example of strategy: In the 1980s, Procter & Gamble (P&G) incorporated entering the bleach business into their *strategy*. They developed a colour-safe, low-temperature bleach — a differentiated and superior product to Clorox bleach, their main competitor.

P&G's *business plan* was to test market it in the East coast, in Portland, Maine, hoping to 'fly under the radar' since the headquarters of Clorox bleach was on the West coast of the USA, in Oakland, California. P&G arranged full retail distribution, heavy product sampling and couponing (Americans love their coupons), and major TV advertising in order to create high consumer awareness that would entice them to try their new product.

Here's where it gets interesting. Clorox's *tactical response* was to deliver to the front door of every household in Portland a free gallon (nearly 4 litres) of Clorox bleach and a coupon for their next purchase of Clorox bleach. That sent a clear message to P&G: Don't even think about entering the bleach market.

P&G had already bought the advertising space and spent most of its launch budget on sampling and couponing. But no one in Portland, Maine, was going to need bleach for many months.

When Clorox decided to enter the laundry detergent market a few years later, P&G sent them a similarly clear and direct message and they, too, withdrew their product.

The moral of the story: You need a good strategy, but tactics win you the game or lose it.[53]

Two ways to develop a strategy

An organisation's strategy should be based on its competitive edge, its strategically valuable capabilities that enable it to perform more competitively or better than its rivals. These might be intangible assets, tangible assets or a combination of both. (See page 11 for a discussion on intangible and tangible assets.) Whatever strategically valuable capabilities the strategy is based on, it should be controlled by the organisation (not its employees, suppliers or customers). It should be difficult to copy and superior to any competitor's similar resource. It should depreciate slowly and not be easily substituted.

Organisations have two choices when deciding what to offer and how to offer it. One is to stick with the traditional business model and leverage your key capabilities to find ways to execute your business model better and offer better value to your customers. This is the way most organisations have traditionally developed their strategies (see 'Theory to practice: Strategies in action' and the 'The strategic perspective: Five key capabilities' on page 58).

A completely different way to develop and execute a strategy, made possible by today's information technology combined with creative brains, is to 'break the mould' and develop a completely new business model, or way of doing business. For example, a completely different way of travelling in a city from Point A to Point B, breaking the traditional taxi and chauffeur-driven hire car service business model. Airbnb is a completely different way to find and book accommodation when you're travelling, breaking the traditional hotel accommodation business model.

● THEORY TO PRACTICE

Strategies in action

To continue to grow its core Australian and New Zealand businesses, the Coca-Cola Amatil company's strategy is to:

- Continue to strengthen market leadership position with innovative new products and packages.
- Accelerate the cold drink cooler placement program to drive greater availability and sales of cold beverages.
- Deliver efficiency gains by leveraging the investments made over the past few years on state-of-the-art production and IT infrastructure.[54]

● THE STRATEGIC PERSPECTIVE

Five key capabilities

Five critical capabilities support an organisation's vision, mission and strategy, combining to create the value of an organisation:

1. *Culture and values*: 'The way we do things', which include leadership styles, problem-solving and communication methods and styles, responsibility and accountability, and trust.
2. *Skills*: Include training for the future as well as the present in, for example, conceptual thinking skills, leadership, and interpersonal, strategic and technical skills.
3. *Staff*: Includes the organisation's recruitment, selection, reward and retention processes and policies. Staff also includes the organisation's succession plans and capabilities, as well as the attitudes, motivation, innovativeness and productivity of its employees and directors.
4. *Structure*: Includes the design and physical layout of the organisation and its financial and budgeting arrangements.
5. *Systems*: Includes administration, cost control, customer service and delivery, information and knowledge management and training systems, sales, wastage and other operating systems and processes.

Figure 2.4 shows how the strategic plan relates to the organisation's external and internal environments. From it, you can see the damage that would be caused if just one area resisted the selected strategy.

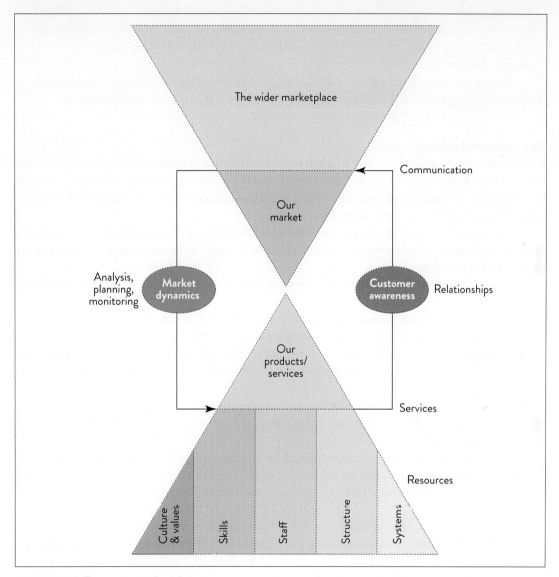

FIGURE 2.4 The strategic plan in context

SWOT analysis

A SWOT analysis can provide a solid basis for developing both strategies and plans. You can use a SWOT analysis to look for ways to improve your department or team, too.

It's a systematic way to identify your internal strengths (S) and weaknesses (W) and the opportunities (O) and threats (T) in your external environment. You end up with a list of the many factors that could help or hinder the organisation, department, team or the plan you have devised. (You can find out how to conduct a SWOT analysis on page 738.)

THE STRATEGIC PERSPECTIVE

Game-changing technology

Technology and the digital economy have become strategic issues for most enterprises. Both have the potential to destroy, create or reshape business models, industries and marketplaces with breathtaking speed. Just think how online shopping has affected the operations of traditional retailers.

Threats and opportunities abound as technology redefines industry boundaries, creates new or unlikely competitors, and enables organisations to reinvent themselves in global markets.

Key issues and strategic goals

Based on the SWOT analysis, the five to seven key issues (positive or negative) facing the organisation are identified. Beginning with the highest priority issue facing the organisation, ways to address that issue are discussed and agreed (bearing in mind the values, vision and mission, not just the strength, weakness, opportunity or threat under discussion).

Once the best ways to deal with the important issues facing the organisation are agreed, a series of challenging, clear, compelling and measurable strategic goals, or strategic imperatives, are developed. For example:

- *Administration*: Standardise the financial reporting and accounting systems across all sites by 30 April 2019.
- *Employees*: Achieve an employee retention rate of 90% by 30 June 2019.
- *Innovation*: Achieve 40% of sales from new products by 2019.
- *Operations*: Open six factories in three politically and economically stable neighbouring countries by 30 June 2020; develop and implement a self-financing equipment upgrade plan by 1 July 2019.
- *Safety*: Achieve an injury-free factory environment by 1 July 2018.
- *Sales*: Achieve $1 billion annual sales and a profit of $60 million by the end of the 2018 financial year.

Notice that these goals begin with verbs such as 'standardise', 'achieve' and 'open' and end with the date by which the goal should be achieved. Notice also that they are written in positive, not negative, language. Finally, notice that these goals are measurable, or their attainment can be proved in some other way.

Strategic goals should also be ambitious, flexible and consistent with the rest of the organisation's values, vision and mission. They should be easy to understand and inviting to achieve. Clear strategic goals like these are the basis for developing detailed business and operational plans to move the organisation forward towards its vision and mission.

It's easy to end up with dozens of strategic goals, but it isn't necessary, or possible, to accomplish all of them. The top six or eight to concentrate on are generally selected so as not to dilute everyone's efforts.

Gap analysis

All organisations have a strategy, whether they know it or not. Unconscious strategies often become clear only with hindsight, as organisations continually improvise, react and learn from mistakes, developing a strategy along the way. Discussing, agreeing and planning a conscious strategy, and communicating it so that people can support it and direct their efforts and resources towards it, is generally more successful than letting an unconscious strategy emerge of its own accord.

Assuming an organisation is consciously and systematically developing a strategy, three essential questions to finalise the strategy can now be asked:

1. *Where are we now?* How does the organisation currently compare against the strategic goals set to mitigate weaknesses and threats and capitalise on strengths, opportunities and other key success factors?
2. *Where do we want to be?* These are your strategic goals. Comparing where we are now with where we want to be gives you a gap.
3. *How will we get there?* What needs to happen for the organisation to close the gap and move towards its vision? From the many potentially helpful actions, the key action areas (e.g. funding growth, marketing initiatives, new product or service development, staff training) are identified and organisation-wide strategic plans developed. From there, business plans covering business units are developed and then operational plans for individual areas or departments are developed. Three more questions need to be answered during the third part of the gap analysis:

1. Should we go for *inorganic growth* (through acquisitions or mergers) or *organic growth* (by expanding the core business to serve more markets or increase market share)?
2. Should we move towards horizontal or vertical integration?
3. Which would best help us achieve our goals: A virtual organisation, an actual organisation or a mixture of both?

● THEORY TO PRACTICE

Horizontal or vertical integration?

Horizontally integrated organisations seek complementary products or complementary uses for their products and facilities. For example:

- A bed linen manufacturer might begin designing and producing beds.
- A chain of optometrists might build on its market image of healthcare and find an additional complementary use for its retail outlets by including hearing care in its services.
- A clothing designer might produce belts, eyeglass frames, homewares (e.g. glasses, plates, towels), perfumes, scarves and shoes.

Vertically integrated organisations secure control of critical 'upstream' suppliers and 'downstream' buyers of its products and services. They own and often manage their upstream (or backward) suppliers in order to create a consistent quality and secure supply of raw materials, as well as to set up subsidiaries downstream (or forward) to distribute and market their products or services, or they use those products or services themselves. For example:

- A movie studio might own a theatre chain.
- A company producing breakfast cereals might decide to farm its own crops and/or produce its own packaging.
- A retail pharmacy chain might invest in a research and development facility to create its own medicines and purchase a factory to manufacture them.

● FYI

Vertically self-sufficient

The Ford Motor Corporation was so vertically integrated by the late 1920s that it was completely self-sufficient. Ford controlled rubber plantations in Brazil, a fleet of ships, a railroad, 16 coal mines and thousands of acres of timberland and iron-ore mines in Michigan and Minnesota in the USA.[55]

● THEORY TO PRACTICE

A virtual harvest

The Harvest Company, a third-generation, Australian-owned family business, supplies supermarkets with fresh products gathered mainly from small family farmers. Most of these farmers had to learn new skills, hire managers and develop systems to meet quality and other supply chain demands as their businesses grew rapidly.

The growers themselves pick, pack, quality assess and deliver their products direct to the supermarket. The Harvest Company doesn't even see the produce before it arrives on the shelves. It arranges the contracts and manages the supply chain. Its business is totally intertwined with its suppliers, making them mutually reliant partners.

In virtual organisations, the real skill is in optimising a value chain of partners. Amazon, Apple, Dell and Nike, outsource virtually everything (get the pun?). Apple, for example, designs computers in California and manufactures them in South-East Asia. Dell outsources everything except marketing. Nike outsources everything except design and marketing. A small team of hard-working, top-level senior managers and specialists oversees the various operations and links them all together.

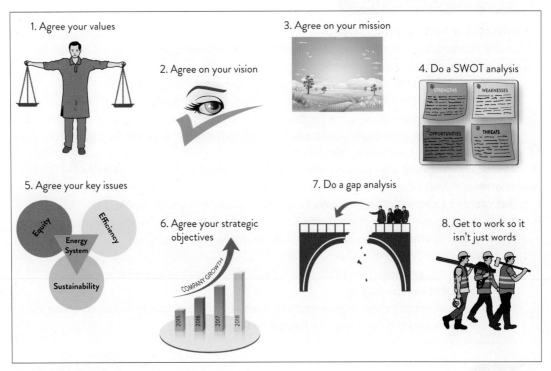

FIGURE 2.5 Developing a strategy

Business plans: How we'll navigate the road

Business plans show how the organisation's strategy is to be achieved. Depending on the organisation and how dynamic and volatile its environment, business plans can look ahead six months, or two or three years, although the pace of change means that long-term planning, which assumes a certainty that no longer exists in many industries, is fast being replaced by continuous replanning, making business planning a continuously evolving process.

● THE STRATEGIC PERSPECTIVE

Three ways to create more value for stakeholders

Stakeholders are important. Here are three ways to create more value for them:

1. *Behaviour and culture*: Ensure that the attitudes and behaviours of employees support the organisation's values and vision. For example, develop a learning culture or participative leadership, provide training and development, or build strong, productive teams.
2. *Future scanning*: Define factors critical to future success. For example, use competitive strategy trend analysis or scenario planning, or identify a range of potential outcomes as a basis for strategy.
3. *Operating methods*: Design more reliable, more efficient, cheaper or quicker ways of doing things. For example, apply benchmarking, continuous improvements, empowerment, process re-engineering, time savings or total quality management.

⫶CourseMateExpress

Go to http://login.cengagebrain.com to access CourseMate Express, your online study tool for *Management Theory & Practice*. CourseMate Express brings chapter concepts to life with interactive learning, and study and exam preparation tools:

- Test your skills in different aspects of management with interactive self-tests and simulations.
- Watch videos that show how real managers operate in real businesses.
- Test your understanding of the changing world of management by taking the revision quiz.

QUICK REVIEW

1. Briefly review the three sectors of the economy and describe the main challenges each sector faces.
2. List the four levels of management and outline the main responsibilities of each.
3. List an organisation's six stakeholder groups and explain what each expects from the organisation in each of the three sectors. Are there any conflicting expectations within any of the sectors? If so, what are they and how can organisations manage them effectively?
4. Explain how clear organisational values, vision, mission and strategy flow down to the business plan and operational plans. What happens when employees don't understand, care about and/or support their organisation's values, vision, mission and strategy?

BUILD YOUR SKILLS

1. Select a not-for-profit organisation, private or public sector organisation. Investigate and describe how it is organised and how it manages its day-to-day operations to achieve its vision and mission. What particular challenges does it face and what are its strategies for responding to those challenges?
2. Which stakeholders do you work with in your current role? Describe your relationship with them and your understanding of their expectations from you, your work team and your organisation as a whole.
3. Explain how a set of lasting values can drive an organisation forward; if possible, give an example from your own experience.
4. Referring to Case study 14.2 on page 425, discuss how Jake might go about building shared values, a shared vision and a shared working culture among his disparate group of employees.
5. Henry Mintzberg has said that everyone in the organisation needs to understand and support their organisation's strategy because, when they don't, they will put a different strategy in its place. Explain how that might happen and, if it does, what you think the likelihood is that the replacement strategy is well thought out and in the best interests of the organisation.
6. Discuss how the five key groups of resources listed in 'The strategic perspective' Five key capabilities, on page 58, each help to create value for an organisation.

WORKPLACE ACTIVITIES

1. List the titles of three senior managers, three middle managers and three first-line managers in your organisation and outline the key responsibilities of each of these managers. What general conclusions can you draw about the responsibilities of managers at various levels in your organisation?
2. Write a short report on the composition of your organisation's board and the duties of its directors. You might source this information from your organisation's website, intranet or annual report.
3. Ask a random sample of employees at various levels and in various parts of your organisation whether they can state your organisation's values, vision and mission and, assuming they can, what they mean to them personally. Then write a short paper summarising your findings, conclusions and recommendations.
4. Does your organisation employ telecommuting? Or virtual working? Does it outsource any of its functions? Write a paper reviewing the pros and cons of these three options for your organisation's operations.
5. How far ahead does your organisation's strategic plan stretch? What factors were considered when establishing this time period?

CASE STUDY 2.1

IBMERS REINVENT THEIR VALUES

In 1914, the start-up company International Business Machines Corporation (IBM) made cheese slicers, scales for weighing meat and tabulating machines. Former president Thomas J Watson Jr announced what he called IBM's 'basic beliefs':

1. Respect for the individual
2. Superlative customer service
3. Pursuit of excellence.

These basic beliefs, or values, became the basis of IBM's culture and helped drive its success.[56]

In the 1990s, the company suffered the worst period in its history and was forced to cut its workforce of nearly 400 000 almost in half. IBM fought back under CEO Lou Gerstner, who took over in 1993, transforming it from a mainframe manufacturer into a provider of integrated hardware, networking and software solutions.

Sam Palmisano, who started with the company as a salesperson in 1973, took over as CEO in 2002. By then, IBM operated in 170 countries and had nearly 70 major product lines and countless supporting product lines, as well as more than a dozen customer segments. It employed more than 333 000 people, 40% of whom didn't report daily to an IBM site but worked at clients' premises, from home or in mobile offices.

Despite its turnaround, something was still wrong. IBM's basic beliefs had become distorted. The company had stopped listening to its markets, its customers and its employees. 'Pursuit of excellence' had become arrogance. 'Respect for the individual' had become entitlement and a guaranteed job.

So a few months after taking on the top job, Palmisano met with IBM's top 300 managers and raised the idea of reinventing the company's values as a way to manage and reintegrate the diverse and growing global company. He believed the basic beliefs, however distorted they had become over the years, should be the starting point for the future. Palmisano put forth four concepts, three of them drawn from the basic beliefs, as possible bases for the new values:

1. respect
2. customers
3. excellence
4. innovation.

After getting input from the top 300 executives, Palmisano invited more than 1100 employees – a statistically representative cross-section of the company – to participate in focus groups and surveys to inform the development of the new set of values. The resulting proposed values were:

1. commitment to the customer
2. excellence through innovation
3. integrity that earns trust.

Despite this participative process, Palmisano knew that he couldn't simply announce these proposed corporate values: 'Traditional, top-down management processes ... wouldn't work at IBM – or, I would argue, at an increasing number of twenty-first-century companies. You can't impose command-and-control mechanisms on a large, highly professional workforce. I'm not only talking about our scientists, engineers and consultants. More than 200 000 of our employees have college degrees. The CEO can't say to them, "Get in line and follow me", or "I've decided what your values are". They're too smart for that. And, as you know, smarter people tend to be, well, a little more challenging; you might even say cynical.'

CASE STUDY 2.1

In July 2003, Palmisano opened the values creation process to all employees. Using a specially tailored 'jamalyzer' software tool, a three-day debate on the company's values began. Known as ValuesJam, it took place on the company's intranet, opening unstructured employee discussions around four topics:

1. *Company values*: Do company values exist? If so, what is involved in establishing them? … What would a company look like that truly lived its beliefs? Is it important for IBM to agree on a set of lasting values that drives everything it does?

2. *A first draft*: What values are essential to what IBM needs to become? Consider this list of the three proposed values. How might these values change the way we act or the decisions we make? Is there some important aspect or nuance that is missing?

3. *A company's impact*: If our company disappeared tonight, how different would the world be tomorrow? Is there something about our company that makes a unique contribution to the world?

4. *The gold standard*: When is IBM at its best? When have you been proudest to be an IBMer? … What do we need to do – or change – to be the gold standard going forward?

Most of the comments on Day 1 were cynical and scathing:

- 'The only value in IBM is stock price.'
- 'Company values (ya right).'
- 'I feel we talk a lot about trust and taking risks. But at the same time, we have endless audits, mistakes are punished and not seen as a welcome part of learning and managers (and others) are constantly checked.'

The comments were so bad that at least one senior manager wanted to pull the plug on ValuesJam.

But on Day 2, the counter-critics weighed in. Positive comments became more frequent and criticism became more constructive. By the end of Day 3, more than 50 000 employees had logged on and posted nearly 10 000 comments. IBM analysts sifted through over one million words and isolated key themes such as 'a silo mentality pits one business unit against another'.

The final set of values emerged and were published on IBM's intranet in November 2003:

1. dedication to every client's success
2. innovation that matters, for our company and for the world
3. trust and personal responsibility in all relationships.

In the next 10 days, Palmisano received more than a thousand emails and many more comments were posted on the intranet. The language was often sharp, saying just where IBM's operations fell short of, or clashed with, these ideals.[57]

Questions

1. What could lead to a company's strong values becoming distorted? How can managers guard against this happening?

2. If announcing the values to the rest of the company was good enough for Tom Watson Jr, why wasn't it good enough for Sam Palmisano? Explain your thinking.

3. Do you think something similar to ValuesJam would work in your own company? Why or why not?

4. When the emails and postings pointed out the contrast between IBM's new values and its operations, did this indicate that the exercise had been a failure or that people cared about the company? Explain your thinking.

CHAPTER

3

THE FORMAL ORGANISATION

OVERVIEW

Since ancient Roman times, the usual way to organise people has been to put them into a pyramid-shaped organisation, with a few people at the top calling all the shots. However, massive change 'without' requires massive change within. Organisations are changing the way they operate internally because the world around them is changing – so much so that organisation design is now a matter of high priority in many organisations. The traditional pyramid has been relentlessly eroded as, in an effort to keep pace with or even one step ahead of their competitors, organisations are testing other ways to structure themselves.

In fact, organisations have undergone more radical restructuring since 1985 than at any other time since the modern organisation evolved in the 1920s. This was when capabilities-based competition became the new source of competitive advantage which requires flat and fluid structures (see Section 1 of this chapter: Designing the (changing) organisation). Business complexity is increasing. The employee mix continues to change, golbalisation marches on and labour-intensive manufacturing continues to give way to knowledge- and service-based organisations. Outsourcing has become an accepted part of getting work done. All these, too, call for different types of organisation structures, enabled by advances in communications and information technology. (See Chapter 1 for more information on the changing workplace.)

What will replace the crumbling command-and-control hierarchy that suited the industrial era as Australia continues its journey into a service and knowledge economy?

1. Do you know the general principles by which organisations link employees and functions or processes, and the main ways organisations are altering these links?
2. Are you familiar with the traditional ways to structure organisations and how these are changing?
3. Are you ready for the new types of organisations you are likely to find?

This chapter helps you find your way around organisations without getting lost.

Finding their way around

Human resources (HR) officer Macayle Mataac sat at her desk working out how best to induct this year's work-experience students to the Electricity Corporation. She began brainstorming a list of all the information she could give them and then organised it into a logical sequence.

When they report to me on their first day, I'll explain how an Act of Parliament set up the Corporation in 1926 and how we were privatised in 1997 as part of government policy. That was when we split our vertically integrated structure into four distinct businesses to generate, transmit, distribute and retail electricity.

I'll outline the corporation's charter and talk about our mission and goals and strategy. I'll explain our key policies – and challenges – regarding customer service, the environment, equal opportunity employment and health, safety and welfare. And I'll present a series of organisation charts to show them how much we've changed over recent years, even since I've been here.

After that, I'll walk them through the current organisation chart so they can see how the different business divisions of the Corporation relate to each other. I'll talk a bit about the variety of employment options we have, ranging from full-time core employees to part-time, casual and temporary employees, self-employed contractors and employed-by-others contractors. I'll explain how a lot of our employees work from home, some sometimes, some always. And I'll explain how in some parts of the organisation, the 'office' has become a drop-in centre for people, whose base of work is elsewhere, to catch up with each other and exchange information. Then I'll throw the discussion open for questions. I'm sure they'll ask what we're doing about work–life balance, sustainability and other interesting topics.

I might close by taking them through a few examples of employees whose careers have taken some interesting paths within the corporation – it won't hurt to start these students thinking over the wealth of options open to them in their working lives. Then I'll ask them to think about what experience they particularly want to gain while they're with us. We're set for a couple of interesting inaugural hours.

1. Designing the (changing) organisation

The pyramid, the chief organisational principle of the modern organisation, turns a business into a traffic jam.

Ricardo Semler (majority owner of Semco SA), *Maverick! The Success Story Behind the World's Most Unusual Workplace*, Random House (1993)[1]

Have you ever thought about how your organisation is arranged? The way people and functions or processes are linked together is critical for success and employee productivity and satisfaction. Poorly designed organisations have problems:

- lack of flexibility and responsiveness to change
- lack of innovation
- lack of trust and cooperation
- slow decision-making and poor-quality decisions
- time wasted on 'administrivia' – unnecessary and trivial administrative issues
- unclear reporting lines and relationships
- unclear roles, goals and responsibilities.

Good organisation design doesn't just prevent problems. It also influences the type of employees and technologies an organisation needs. For example:

- Hierarchical organisations with highly compartmentalised activities need specialist employees willing to carry out a narrow range of highly prescribed tasks and sophisticated ways to monitor and control work and workflow.
- Organisations with flat, open structures and clusters of team-based employees with broad job responsibilities need multiskilled employees, support systems to store and retrieve information and knowledge, and, when the organisation is virtual or partially virtual, collaborative systems technologies that facilitate teamwork and open communication.

The way an organisation is designed also influences how it operates. For example:

- Tall, vertical organisation structures, or hierarchies, with lots of levels, slow down communication and decision-making and encourage power-based relationships and organisational politics.
- Flat structures encourage accountability, participation, teamwork and more rapid and responsive communication and decision-making.

So which is it to be? Tall or flat? Or maybe round?

The general principles of organisation design

Whatever the design selected, good organisation designs share a number of characteristics:

- The design creates feasible job roles in which employees are neither overworked nor underworked and that contain realistic groupings of skills and an interesting range of tasks.
- Duplication of effort is minimised or eliminated so that activities are completed only once.
- Leader-managers don't have so much of their 'own work' that they lack time to coach, offer feedback, mentor employees, and so on.
- The design is not overly complex and it supports the organisation's strategy and main goals. The design centres on core activities, it suits the organisation's general environment, including its customers, employees and marketplace and it is flexible enough to accommodate change.
- Overall policy and strategy development are centralised.
- Services and 'back office' functions are performed for as wide a base as possible to achieve economies of scale.

Four broad principles have traditionally guided the way organisations link their functions. These principles continue to apply, but as you see in the following four sections, one of them is changing.

Group size

People feel most comfortable and work best in worksites (e.g. a factory, a head office or a regional operations centre) when there are fewer than 150 people. This size allows people to get to know each other, learn a bit about each other's families, chat about where their kids go to school and so on. When worksites get bigger than this, the number of people employees know suddenly shrinks to around 60 to 70 people, taking the worksite from friendly to a more formal atmosphere with far less personal interaction (which some people prefer).

The Ringelmann effect

A classic study of the effect of group size on how much effort people put into a 'tug of war' (pulling on a rope) uncovered the 'social loafing' effect. The result: when a group gets big enough, it's easy to 'hide' and not pull your weight.[2]

Line and staff positions

People in line positions produce goods or provide services. In manufacturing firms, they make the product; in hospitals, they deliver healthcare; in restaurants, they serve the customers. People in staff positions serve or advise people in line positions. Accountants, cleaners, human resource and training staff, industrial engineers, most office workers, risk managers and safety officers are usually in staff positions.

People in line positions don't normally report to people in staff positions, although we often see a dotted line between them to indicate a staff employee advises or assists a line employee.

Does it seem that line positions are more important to an organisation and that staff positions would be the ones targeted for outsourcing? Sometimes. But then again, think of Nike, and also the PC industry: They contract out line work because the staff, not the line positions, are the critical positions that add the real value to the organisation. Other organisations are beginning to adopt this model, too.

⊙ THEORY TO PRACTICE

Mambo's 21st-century business model

Founded in 1984, iconic Australian brand Mambo was in trouble by 2008. Its old business model of designing funky surf and street clothing, taking orders from distributors and arranging production in China, left it strapped for cash and stunted its potential growth. A new, sustainable business model based on its design strengths brought it back from the brink.

Mambo now licenses to other manufacturers and earns a percentage of their sales in return for the manufacturer using its brands and designs, its style guides and some marketing support. The company can now accurately forecast cash flow, profit and loss – essentially removing its business risk. Margins are lower but Mambo makes more money due to hugely increased sales volumes across 20 product categories; in fact, turnover has increased ten-fold. The new licensing business model also allows it to expand globally.

At Mambo's Manly beach office, the company's 15 employees (eight of them are artists) and its trademarks and intellectual property are the prime assets of this $100 million a year turnover business.[3]

Span of management

The span of management (or span of control) is the number of people a person supervises. It's important to get this right because supervising too many people can lead to *undersupervision* and supervising too few people can lead to *oversupervision*.

The number of people a leader-manager can effectively supervise depends on several factors:

* ability of the employees to work without supervision
* amount of 'own work' the manager has to do in addition to leadership activities
* complexity of the jobs
* degree of independence or interdependence in the work
* location of those being supervised – scattered or all in one place
* number of different jobs done by those being supervised
* skills of the leader-manager
* strictness of quality standards.

Flatter organisation structures mean that the span of management is becoming wider, requiring different leadership and management skills.

Unity of command

Convention has it that an employee should report only to one person. This is called unity of command and is based on the thinking that having more than one boss can create a situation of potential conflict and confusion.

As you may have guessed from the military-style language, this principle flourished in the days of hierarchy and bureaucracy. Today, however, organisations need to be flexible and responsive to their environments and this principle is losing its hold on organisation designers.

Temporary teams, for example, often form to undertake special projects and then disband, contractors and part-time workers are often brought in to work in one or more areas and employees are often temporarily seconded to other areas. Matrix organisations (also discussed in this chapter) are purposely designed with people reporting to two or more managers. (For more information on the various groups of employees, see page 14; for information on leading today's non-traditional teams, see Chapter 14.)

Organisation structure

Organisation designers work out which type of structure would best suit an organisation's operations and external environment. (See page 49 for information on an organisation's values, vision, mission and strategy.) They think about the organisation's size and its activities. They look for ways to best link internal relationships between people and functions (administration, customer service, distribution, and so on) or processes (welcoming hotel customers and checking them in, providing a product or service and collecting payment, managing rental accommodation on behalf of property owners, and so on). This allows the organisation to make the best use of its internal resources, particularly people, so they can work with minimum cost and fuss and maximum effectiveness and satisfaction.

You can think of the resulting organisation structure as the organisation's 'framework' that ties together its various activities. This is the *formal organisation*, drawn as an organisation chart.

The power of the 'right' organisation structure

Alfred P Sloan Jr, then a senior manager with General Motors (GM), 'invented' the divisionalised-by-product organisation structure to bring GM's large and sprawling group of companies under control. He centralised policy and financial control and set up operating divisions organised by products and brands, with responsibility for day-to-day operations. The new organisation structure worked — GM finally overtook Ford to become the world's largest car maker in 1931.

Organisation charts

Organisation charts map the links between employees and functions in organisations, illustrating the officially recognised lines of authority, communication, relationships and responsibility. They are typically a series of boxes representing individual jobs or groups of jobs, grouped into functions or process flows. Boxes for positions on the same authority level are shown on the same horizontal level (space allowing). The boxes are linked by lines, showing reporting relationships. Then there are dotted lines that show sources of advice and service, or partial reporting relationships. Organisation charts also show you the levels in the organisation's hierarchy, as well as the spans of control of the various managers.

Organisation charts can highlight problems of duplication of effort, span of management and unity of command in a function, process or team. This alerts you to the need to adjust the organisation design. Organisation charts also help employees understand the organisation as a whole. The charts show how employees fit into the rest of the organisation and into their department.

Organisations that keep up-to-date organisation charts tend to be well structured, possibly because the charts keep people aware of the structure and make it easier to make changes when they are needed.

2. Designing organisations the traditional way

I don't actually think that the stereotype of a businessperson treading all over people to get to the top, generally speaking, works. I think if you treat people well, people will come back and come back for more.

Richard Branson (founder, Virgin group), with Anderson, 'Life at 30,000 feet', TED (March 2007)[4]

Also developed by the Romans more than 2000 years ago, bureaucracies compartmentalise work and break it down into simple, discrete steps to try to obtain the advantages of economies of scale. This makes bureaucracies well suited to making and moving progress. They work well with large groups of relatively uneducated people, as was the case in the early part of the Industrial Revolution. They are suited to large organisations operating in predictable and stable external environments.

These large, 'tall' centralised organisations encourage consistency, reliability and uniformity through controls, checks and balances. The different levels denote an individual's formal status, or rank, in the organisation. Vertical relationships give everyone a clear boss and bosses have a clearly defined group of subordinates.

It isn't surprising, then, that bureaucracies were still popular towards the end of the 20th century in both the public and private sectors when they continued to suit the external environment. Figure 3.1 shows an organisation chart for a bureaucracy.

Bureaucracies have three central features:

1. Organised into functions: They are organised around functions, or specialist groups such as accounting, engineering, human resource management and marketing that are often referred to as 'silos'.
2. Vertical relationships with knowledge concentrated at the top: Your level in the organisation chart denotes your formal status and level of authority and responsibility. Everyone has a clear boss and bosses have a clearly defined group of subordinates. Your manager closely directs your work and authoritarian leadership (the management) dominates, because managers 'know more' and telling people what to do is viewed as the most efficient way to get results.
3. Rules and regulations: Work is divided into small, discrete, independent tasks with clear procedures, or one best way of carrying them out, as much as possible. Individuals, rather than teams, are accountable for their performance. Employees and managers concentrate on how well individual tasks are carried out rather than on how they fit together to create value.

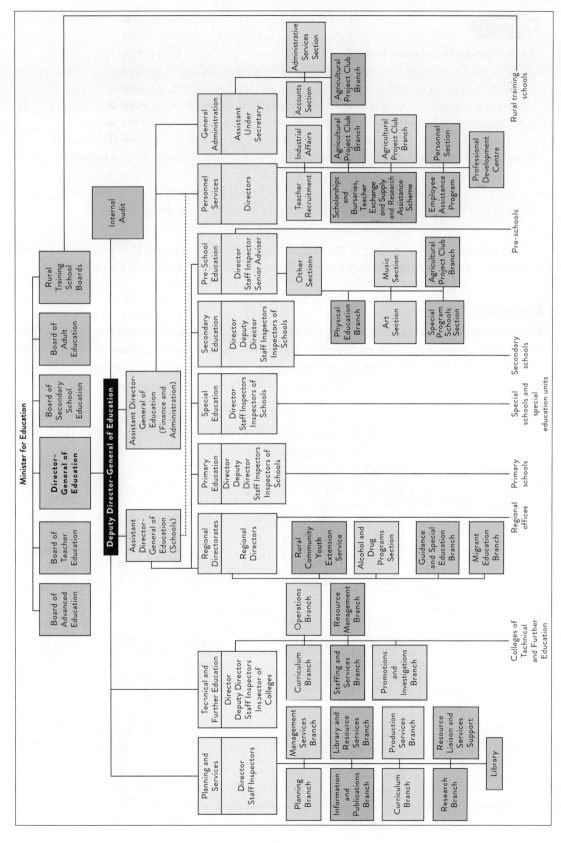

FIGURE 3.1 Organisation chart for the education department of a state government

How bureaucracies were named

In 1665, the French economy was in turmoil and King Louis XIV appointed Jean-Baptiste Colbert as his comptroller general of finance. Colbert prosecuted corrupt officials and reorganised commerce and industry according to economic principles known as mercantilism, demanding that officials abide by certain rules and apply them uniformly to everyone.

Then, in 1751, Jean Claude Marie Vincent de Gournay became France's administrator of commerce. He was outraged by the multitude of government regulations that he believed suppressed business activity. The government, he said, was run by insensitive creators and enforcers of rules who neither understood nor cared about the consequences of their actions. He coined the term *bureaucratie*, which translates as 'government by desks'.[5]

What follows is a quick tour of the typical organisational structures that prevailed until the 1990s. When a structure is right for its time and place, it's great. When it isn't, it's a disaster.

By function

Mass production allows organisations to achieve economies of scale by centralising key functions. Centralised organisations also work well in companies seeking to create value from economies of scope. Figure 3.2 shows a typical functional organisation with one person responsible for each function. The organisation chart is drawn horizontally. Functional managers, each responsible for

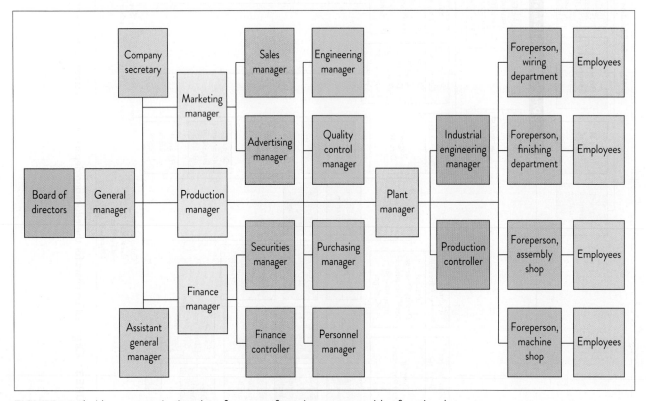

FIGURE 3.2 A sideways organisation chart for a manufacturing company with a functional structure

their particular function, report to a general manager. For example, the finance manager is responsible for all activities related to finance throughout the entire organisation.

Functional structures can work reasonably well in smaller organisations, but as an organisation grows and becomes more complex, functional structures tend to become bureaucratic, creating problems of accountability and slowing decision-making.

Because people are responsible for their tasks and to the function of those tasks, no one is responsible for meeting customer needs, so the customer can fall into second place. Sometimes that's fine. Walmart's customers, for example, are more concerned with price than flashy stores. So to keep prices down, operating functions, such as merchandising and distribution, are centralised. They then receive the bulk of funding, creating economies of scale and scope that can be passed on to customers through the lower prices the customers want.[6]

A corporate affair

Corporate affairs has moved from backstage to the footlights and is now considered a function in large organisations. That's not surprising when you think that a storm in a teacup can become a PR tornado in a few short hours. With a background in media relations or public affairs, corporate affairs managers generally report to the CEO and are responsible for everything to do with internal and external communication, government relations and public policy.

By customer or market type

As enterprises diversified their offerings and moved into new markets, new models that structured business units around customer type, geographic markets and products emerged. These lost some economies of scale but their greater flexibility allowed them to adapt to local conditions.

In customer-type organisations, a separate division looks after each group of customers. Figure 3.3 illustrates a company with an upside down organisation chart in which head office retains control of essential staff functions (distribution, finance and research and development).

Customer-type structures can work well in large organisations that offer a range of products or services to different groups of customers, especially where different manufacturing or processing techniques are used.

Sideways, upside down or inside out?

Organisation charts are usually drawn vertically, with the most senior people at the top and the most junior employees at the bottom. In the 1980s, people played around with drawing them sideways (as in Figure 3.2), with the senior people at the left and the junior people at the right, in an attempt to move away from obvious hierarchical relationships. Going one better, some then drew 'upside down' organisation charts (as in Figure 3.3), symbolising that the senior managers are all here to support the workers.

Of course, no one really fell for it. A hierarchy is still a hierarchy, however it's drawn. But perhaps the new ways of drawing the charts were an early recognition that the hierarchy was on its way out.

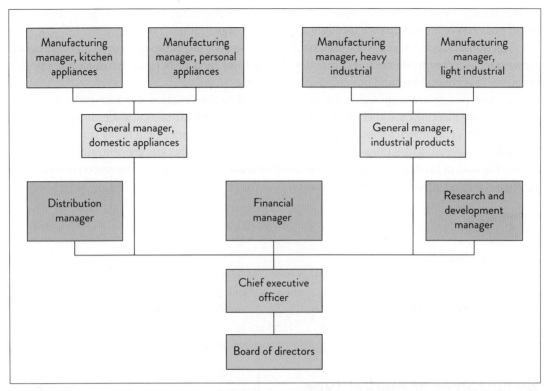

FIGURE 3.3 An upside down organisation chart by customer type

By geographic location

When an organisation has manufacturing plants in one or more states or countries and sales branches in several major cities, organising by geographic location can make sense. This structure also allows organisations such as Nestlé to customise its offerings to local preferences and regulations. Figure 3.4 shows a larger company with the same product lines as in the product organisation chart shown in Figure 3.4, but organised along geographic lines.

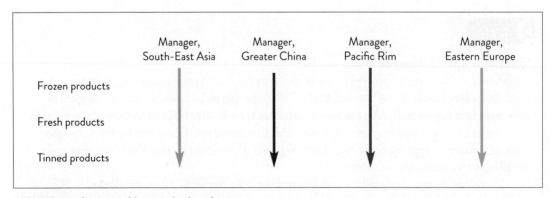

FIGURE 3.4 A geographic organisation chart

By product type

Organisations that arrange their operations by product have one division or department for each major product or service group. Figure 3.5 shows an organisation divided into three main product groups: frozen products, fresh products and tinned products.

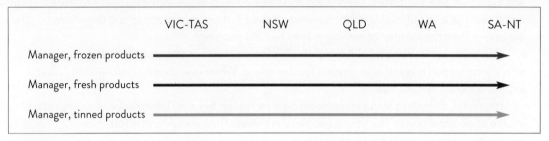

FIGURE 3.5 A product group organisation chart

Organising by products can work well when the organisation is not big and not widely spread out geographically and when the technology or brands are the organisation's key drivers of value. Most organisations that are spread out geographically opt to organise along geographic lines. Organising by product type also encourages more entrepreneurial behaviour than the above three structures.

Figure 3.6 shows another way to organise by product type. Here, each division has responsibility for its own finance, production, distribution and marketing.

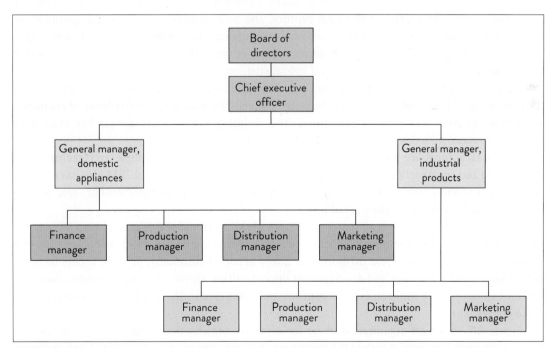

FIGURE 3.6 Structure by product, with each divisional general manager having control of each function

The demise of the hierarchy?

Downsizing during the 1980s and 1990s reduced the number of jobs and removed layers from the organisation hierarchy, resulting in smaller and flatter organisations, loss of knowledge and expertise, and disgruntled, overloaded and stressed employees with less loyalty to their employer. The levels of management have now halved in most organisations and they have about one third the number of managers they had 20 years ago.

Information, the lifeblood of hierarchies, has lost its power in today's 'information age', where information is available to anyone for the asking. When everyone has information, what is left if the hierarchy collapses?

It's always difficult to stop people hoarding information because information is an important source of personal power. But young people won't invest their energy and effort in an organisation where people hoard information.

Organisations increasingly need to make a conscious effort to make information available and become more open, inclusive and flexible. 'Democratic' companies with a flatter structure and more information flow, such as Semco and Apple, are making a start.[7]

Matrix structure

The traditional organisation structures discussed above dominated organisations while the marketplace was relatively stable. As competition, customer demands and business complexity intensified in the last quarter of the 20th century, and as a spate of mergers and acquisitions in the late 1990s ushered in yet another wave of restructuring, these models became less effective. Organisations began experimenting with other ways to organise themselves. Two early models that are still around are the matrix structure and hybrid structures.

Many multinational companies adopted a matrix organisation structure in an attempt to retain the economies of scale and efficiencies of bureaucratic centralisation and the flexibility of customer, geographic location and product structures. The resulting organisation design has employees reporting to more than one manager for different aspects of their jobs.

Matrix structures are popular in project-based organisations, for example architecture, civil engineering and construction companies, where projects run for long periods. IBM also has a matrix organisation where customer teams in industry-based 'verticals', coordinate product and service delivery from 'horizontal' product-based units.[8]

Matrix structures can spread scarce professional skills around the organisation and tap into the skills and experience of people in other countries. Working on several projects with several managers can be enjoyable and invigorating, give a sense of autonomy, provide access to more networks and offer learning and development opportunities. However, matrix organisations are difficult to coordinate and can lead to conflict and delay due to the need to try to keep two or more bosses happy.

Figure 3.7 shows an organisation chart for a matrix organisation structured around project teams, with team members in each of the projects reporting to two people – their functional manager (vertically) and their project manager (horizontally).

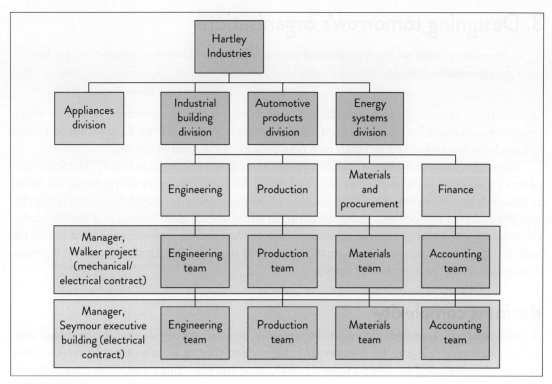

FIGURE 3.7 Matrix organisation chart

Hybrid structures

In the 1990s, process re-engineering introduced another way to structure organisations: organising around core processes. This was a popular alternative to the confusing matrix structures. Few companies at that time adopted a pure core-process design, but rather overlaid a core process on a functional structure or a functional structure over a process structure.

For example, a company might organise its manufacturing operations around processes and arrange the rest of the organisation according to functions. Google is organised around expert knowledge. In Google's case, technical research and development, which feeds into the rest of the organisation, is designed around product type. Microsoft has announced it intends to abandon its product type structure, with separate business units organised around Windows, servers, MSN, mobile and Xbox product lines, in favour of a Google-type hybrid based on expert knowledge.[9]

Other organisations retain features such as formal lines of communication, responsibility and authority and formal rules for promotion, while eliminating some of the other features of the classic bureaucracy so that they can operate in a more 'open' way.

⊙ THEORY TO PRACTICE

Another way to organise

There is one organisation that has thrived for more than 80 years, spans more than 170 countries and has more than two million members who join because they want to. It has virtually no hierarchy and its headquarters employs fewer than 100 people. Thousands of small, self-organising groups elect, not appoint, their leaders. The organisation does not operate according to budgets. It does have a mission but no detailed strategy or operational plans and yet it delivers a complex service to millions of people worldwide. The organisation? Alcoholics Anonymous.

3. Designing tomorrow's organisations

In companies whose wealth is intellectual capital, networks, rather than hierarchies, are the right organisational design.

Thomas A Stewart, *Intellectual Capital, Fortune* (2010)[10]

Organisations increasingly bear only limited resemblance to the organisations described above. Levels of management have halved or even reduced by two thirds. Knowledge-based work, performed by knowledge workers who direct their own performance, is the order of the day.

This is all because of the rate of change. Organisations have been forced to modify their structures far more frequently, many as often as every two years. But traditional ways of organising are failing in today's business environment for a number of reasons: vastly increased business complexity, capabilities-based competition, changing customer expectations, globalisation and the knowledge and information worker of the new economy.[11] Each of these factors intensifies the need to link the relationships between people and functions horizontally rather than vertically. (Chapter 1 has more information about the new world of work.)

Business complexity

Organisations have gone from complicated to complex, containing many diverse and interdependent parts as illustrated in Figure 3.8. Some organisations are turning to team-based operations, making the skill of putting successful teams together and leading and managing those teams critical. Rather than being a precise organisational structure, team-based organisations are more a philosophy that underpins structures such as matrix and capabilities-based structures. This makes a manager's job more difficult because:

- it's difficult to predict what will happen when various parts of the business interact
- seemingly simple changes have unexpected consequences
- it's difficult to understand all parts of the organisation
- rare events are occurring more often than we think and can be more significant than we expect.[12]

Autonomy, collaboration, innovation, interdependence, job empowerment, self-management, shared accountability for performance, shared leadership and mutual trust characterise multidisciplinary teams. These teams can't work well in authoritarian, hierarchical silo-type structures.

FIGURE 3.8 Complex organisations

Strategic capabilities

Changes to an organisation's strategy once occurred only periodically, in response to a major, often technology-based, innovation: think of horses and buggies to trains, and then to vehicles; or wood to coal and then to oil. By the end of the 20th century, companies sought to gain a competitive edge by strategically focusing on market position, based on brand value, cost or economies of scale or scope. The recognition that capabilities create value and competitive advantage now makes process management, or a capabilities-based organisation increasingly important to success. For example:

* Airbus, Apple and Google excel at technology.
* Amazon, Dell and Walmart excel at logistics.
* BHP Billiton excels at mining.
* Nestlé, Proctor & Gamble and Ralph Lauren excel at brand marketing.

Capabilities-based organisations

Traditional organisation designs don't suit an operating environment based on processes – the 'flow' of work. However, with work flow, or capabilities, increasingly becoming a key competitive advantage, enterprises in a variety of industries and in all sectors are identifying their core capabilities and restructuring their operations around them.

While more traditionally organised operations are likely to know their precise costs, value of sales, and so on, they often don't know how frequently they fill orders correctly or how long it takes to get a new product to market profitably. Capabilities-based organisations do. They measure their success on process goals rather than on a function's efficiency. This improves productivity and profitability as well as customer and employee satisfaction.

Processes aren't a series of discrete tasks but a flow of activities that is managed 'end-to-end' across functions, so it isn't the quality of individual task completion but the quality of the entire flow that matters, with the 'hands-off' or 'white space' between activities being just as important as the 'hands-on' or 'dark space' of each task.

Processes and capabilities

Capabilities are based on unique abilities, such as a reliable process, close relationships with customers and suppliers or corporate culture. They are made up of sets of *processes* and *subprocesses* that span functions and business units and that require cross-functional teamwork and strategic investment in support systems.

For example, a grocery store might combine a series of processes that effectively link shoppers with the store's website. This makes online shopping easy and efficient and offers reliable and efficient delivery, based on the subprocesses of product picking and packing, route mapping and delivery, as well as customer after-service. Together, they create a *core capability* (a capability critical to its success) of offering an excellent online shopping experience, which is markedly better than that of the store's competitors, and which is difficult for them to copy.

Process-based organisations concentrate on teamwork and customers. Being more flexible and responsive than traditional organisations, they handle change better. Figure 3.9 shows how a capabilities-based organisation might be structured. (See also the information on Core process redesign on page 571.)

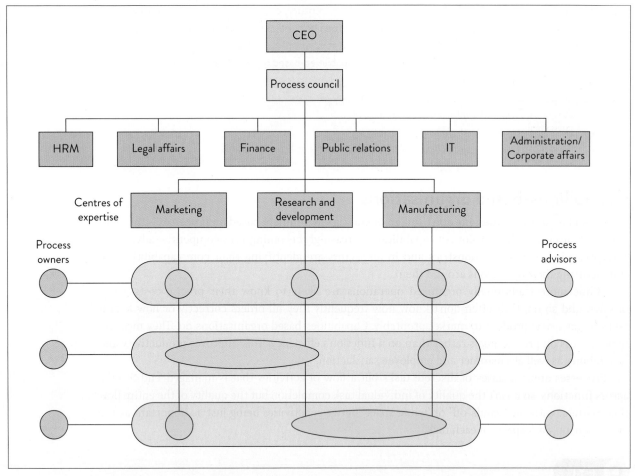

Source: Adapted from Tomislav Hernaus, Process-based organisation design model: Theoretical review and model conceptualisation, Working paper No. 08-06, University of Zagreb, faculty of economics and business, Croatia, 2008.[13]

FIGURE 3.9 A capabilities-based organisation structure

Each core process, from beginning to end, is the responsibility of a senior manager, or 'process owner', who has enough influence to obtain the resources needed to make the process flow smoothly. Process advisers support the process owners and centres of expertise, which create, gather and spread knowledge and provide specialist advice to each process. A process council coordinates the core processes and support units, which provide staff support to the various processes.

This makes four levels of hierarchy: The board of directors, senior managers (the CEO, process council and process owners), middle managers (responsible for processes and subprocesses) and team members who carry out the processes (the 'dark space') and coordinate the 'white space' between activities.

Why the traditional structures no longer work

The functionally organised traditional organisation structure, with its vertical, command-and-control relationships and rules and regulations, is completely unsuited to capabilities-driven organisations. Having 20 or more layers and narrow spans of control (i.e. five or six people reporting to an individual manager) encourages micromanaging, impedes workflow and makes decision-making too slow to respond to rapid change.

The efficient execution of processes (as opposed to discrete tasks) needs flexibility and local decision-making by knowledgeable employees who work together to optimise the process as a whole. It does not need centralised, slow decision-making. Employees need to be relatively autonomous and able to adjust complex processes to meet customer needs. They need information they have not traditionally had access to, as well as a strategic understanding of the organisation's strategy and goals. Employees like these don't respond well to the roles and rules of bureaucracy.

Horizontal processes, which emphasise the relationships between functions, break down 'silos'. The interdependence of tasks for which responsibilities are shared, makes employees interdependent, too. To coordinate their efforts across functions, employees need strong horizontal relationships, teamwork and a large dollop of empowerment. Status, so important in hierarchies, is far less relevant than the value each employee can add to a process.

Today's customers often want a complete package, of goods or services, which were historically provided by separate divisions or functions. But effectively providing a product or service 'suite' calls for horizontal integration.

The 'HQ' mentality of the centralised hierarchy doesn't work in a global economy, either. As organisations disperse their functions around the globe – design to one country, assembly to another and people servicing their customers from call centres in yet another – organisations need flat, fluid structures to link their varied groups of employees and their internal and outsourced functions.

Australian enterprises today are increasingly knowledge-based and employees increasingly work from home some or all of the time, as well as in locations removed from their parent organisation and even their leader-manager (virtual working and hub working). People working with information and ideas who direct and discipline their own performance, based on feedback from colleagues and customers, don't respond well to authority, to rules and all the other characteristics of bureaucracies.

● THE STRATEGIC PERSPECTIVE

Disruptive business models

If you are in a traditional business and are not seeing digital disruption, then it is ... likely that you are not looking hard enough.

A new business enters the market with a completely different – disruptive – business model. You can't predict what, when or how because that would be more of an 'extension' or an 'innovation' than a 'disruption'.

It may be a new way of doing business, such as CatchOfTheDay with a new model for selling online, which won it market leadership. Or it may be a product that eats into your own product sales, like the way e-cigarettes ate into the traditional cigarette market. [14]

You need to be adaptable and imaginative to respond fast enough to jump the S-curve and avoid a steady decline.

Major trends in organisation design

The major trends in organisation design for today's organisations are looking increasingly different to the traditional pyramidal structures described in Section 2. In the present operating environment, silos need to be broken or at least to be permeable in order to reduce bureaucracy, increase flexibility and eliminate non-value adding work. The enhanced coordination made possible by the teamwork and strong horizontal relationships that can then occur, drives everyone's attention to the customer. This increases customer satisfaction and further enables organisational flexibility and responsiveness.

As the more traditional structures continue to give way to new structures, employees at every level are likely to experience many psychological 'rubbing points'. Employees and managers alike need different mindsets and skill sets. Employees need to have a more strategic understanding of the organisation's vision and goals and solid interpersonal skills. Leader-managers need to develop a range of interpersonal, conceptual, strategic and leadership skills, as discussed on page 28.

Let's look at the major trends in organisation design.

From actual to virtual

As organisations increasingly outsource their assets and non-core functions and activities, they are moving to a virtual structure. They may continue to be represented by a pyramid shape, as shown in Figure 3.10. Or to be shown in other forms, such as a doughnut, with a core of strategic decision-makers surrounded by contractors and outsourced workers. Or perhaps as an atom, with a nucleus of essential core employees surrounded by electrons of contractors and protons of outsourced providers, as shown in Figure 3.11.

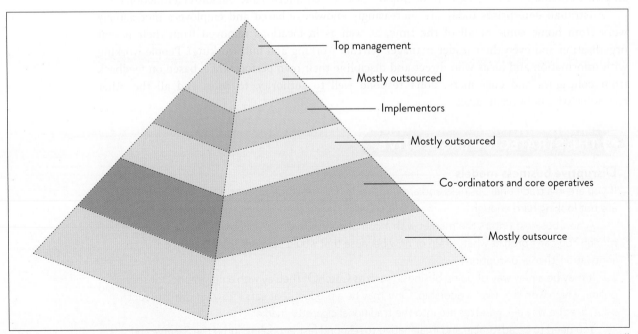

Top management

Mostly outsourced

Implementors

Mostly outsourced

Co-ordinators and core operatives

Mostly outsource

Source: Adapted from 'A snapshot of Australia's future to 2050' by Phil Ruthven. Copyright © 2012 by IBISWorld. Used by permission.[16]

FIGURE 3.10 The virtual pyramid

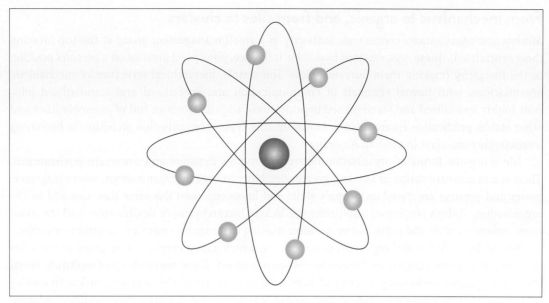

FIGURE 3.11 The atomic organisation

From big to small, and centralised to decentralised

The complex organisations of the past are expensive and can outweigh economies of scale. Organisations have responded by 'deconglomerating' and slimming down divisions and departments as they outsourced non-essential work and saved many of the costs of employment (e.g. employee tax, insurance, office space and superannuation). The 'big businesses' of tomorrow may be even smaller than businesses are today, at least in terms of employees: Twitter employs fewer than 1000 people yet has more than US$1 billion in earnings. Wikipedia has 65 employees and Pinterest fewer than 50.[15]

Many organisations have moved towards a flexible, decentralised organisation with simpler structures that emphasise autonomy and efficiency. Authority and decision-making are placed as close as possible to 'the action' in order to encourage the prompt decisions needed in a rapidly changing environment. Many of these flexible, decentralised organisations have become virtual, collaborative structures focused on capabilities and processes and they involve networks of outsourcers and suppliers, all adding value.

From pyramids to pancakes

Thanks to extensive downsizing and delayering, which has stripped out many middle management roles, the tall hierarchies of the past are largely gone. Five levels is now more the norm and with fewer levels, leader-managers have wider spans of control, with as many as 10 or 12 people reporting to them.

Whether partially centralised or decentralised, today's flatter, leaner, meaner, nimble organisations push decision-making and responsibility downward, opening up lines of communication and allowing information to circulate around the organisation more freely. Flatter organisations also tend to be less rigid and have fewer rules and regulations. This gives people at each level more autonomy and the greater creative latitude, decision-making authority and broader responsibilities that many people want, and this encourages flexibility and innovation. Greater empowerment means, in theory, greater job satisfaction.

From mechanistic to organic, and from silos to clusters

Mechanistic organisations concentrate authority in a small management group at the top (making them centralised). These organisations base their influence, power and prestige on a person's position in the hierarchy (making them bureaucracies). The simple, hierarchical structure of mechanistic organisations, with formal channels of communication and specialised and standardised jobs, suits highly specialised and standardised organisations, such as factories full of assembly lines and other stable, predictable environments. However, this type of organisation structure is becoming increasingly redundant in modern Australia.

More organic forms of organisation better suit today's dynamic and uncertain environment. There is less standardisation of jobs and greater flexibility in organic organisations, where influence, power and prestige are based on people's skills and knowledge and the value they can add to the organisation. Today's employees also prefer the lack of hierarchy, more flexible roles and the more open communication and participative decision-making that organic organisation structures offer.

Silo-style, or functional organisation structures, which group employees in terms of the roles they perform, are moving to capabilities-based organisations. These are made up of multifunctional clusters of people performing a range of roles that span many of the organisation's activities or functions. This increases job interest and provides more varied opportunities, which employees appreciate.

The growth of corporate responsibility

Corporate social responsibility (CSR), a one-size-fits-all approach to responsible operations, evolved to corporate responsibility (CR), identifying stakeholders' biggest concerns and addressing them. But even following the CR approach, most companies still try to reduce negative impacts rather than maximise opportunities for doing good. In many companies, CR is an add-on rather than 'the way we do business'.

Some businesses are further evolving into conscious capitalism and exist not just to make money. They also intend to have a positive impact on their communities and the world at large. They want to build brands that have substance and meaning and they want to put their values into action.

Sound too good to be true? Check these out:

1. the Container Store, which puts people (employees, customers and suppliers) first, paying employees nearly twice the industry average and training them 20 times more than the industry average (http://standfor.containerstore.com > Our foundation principles)
2. construction-toy company, GoldieBlox, whose goal is 'to get girls building' (http://www.goldieblox.com > About)
3. Toms shoes, which gives one pair of shoes and one pair of eyeglasses to a child in need, for every pair shoes or eyeglasses purchased (http://www.toms.com > About > Company Information)
4. Unilever's Sustainable Living Plan, which has, at the centre of its corporate strategy: Double the profits, halve the impact (http://www.unilever.com.au > Sustainable Living > Plan)
5. WHOLE Foods, whose business revolves around its core values (http://www.wholefoodsmarket.com/mission > Our core values).

From purely profit driven to holistic

Despite huge bottom-line pressures to perform financially, many organisations are trying to become more 'humane', socially responsible workplaces. They are encouraging employees to balance work responsibilities with responsibilities in other spheres of their lives and taking environmental and social concerns, not just profit, into account.

Based on the principles of corporate responsibility and conscious capitalism, *holistic organisations,* which are fulfilling to work for and add meaning to employees' lives, extend their focus from 'results only' to 'results plus employee and society's wellbeing'. These organisations expect higher productivity and increased shareholder value from their employees in return.

● ACTION!

How holistic is your organisation? Find out with the interactive self-test on  **Course**MateExpress.

CourseMateExpress

Go to http://login.cengagebrain.com to access CourseMate Express, your online study tool for *Management Theory & Practice.* CourseMate Express brings chapter concepts to life with interactive learning, and study and exam preparation tools:

- Test your skills in different aspects of management with interactive self-tests and simulations.
- Watch videos that show how real managers operate in real businesses.
- Test your understanding of the changing world of management by taking the revision quiz.

QUICK REVIEW

1. Provide an overview of the general design principles that organisations follow, and the purpose of these principles.
2. Describe the traditional organisation structures and the strengths and weaknesses of each.
3. Review the changing trends in organisation design and the factors underlying these trends.

BUILD YOUR SKILLS

1. Explain how a suitable organisation structure can be a powerful competitive advantage.
2. Interview someone who has experienced an organisational restructure first hand. Find out all you can about the positives and negatives of this experience, for the employees as well as for the organisation as a whole, trying to understand what helped to make these experiences positive or negative. Draw some general conclusions about the best way to help your work team maintain its morale and productivity during and immediately after an organisational restructure.
3. Describe the organisation framework you believe is best suited to the present day for the industry you work in, or aspire to work in, and explain your reasoning.
4. What would be the dangers in transforming the Australian Taxation Office into an organic, matrix-type organisation? Would these dangers be outweighed by the advantages? Why or why not?
5. Referring to the information on the sectors of the economy in Chapter 1, which economy or economies do you think virtual organisations suit? What about functional organisations?

WORKPLACE ACTIVITIES

1. Paint a 'word picture' of your organisation's structure. Discuss its features in relation to traditional and emerging organisation structures. Explain whether, and why, you believe your organisation's structure is 'up to date' and how well its structure is suited to its current environment.
2. What changes in organisation design can you predict for your organisation over the next few years? Why do you believe these changes will take place? Interview your HR manager if you need to.
3. Obtain an organisation chart for your organisation and describe the organisation structure. Discuss how this structure affects internal relationships and your organisation's ways of working.

CASE STUDY 3.1

LANCY'S LABORATORIES

Paul Lancy started his dental laboratory in 1992 as a sole trader, making dentures, dental implants and crowns. Due to the high quality of his work, his laboratory grew quickly and, in 1996, his brother Peter qualified and joined him as his partner. At Peter's urging, they began concentrating on customer service and the lab's business mushroomed to the point where they hired six additional technicians, a lab assistant and an office administrator. They also began doing facial reconstructive implants for the cranio-facial unit at City Hospital.

By 2004, Paul and Peter employed nine technicians, two full-time and one part-time lab assistants and two office administrators. On the advice of their accountant, Lancy's Laboratories became a proprietary limited company. They also began an apprenticeship scheme to ensure a continual flow of qualified technicians so that the business could continue to expand. As time went on, the brothers embraced the move towards partnering, developing strong and mutually beneficial links with their suppliers, which further strengthened the business.

In 2011, Lancy's forged links with laboratories overseas, developing a network of specialist manufacturers of dental and facial prostheses. For example, now their lab could email a three-dimensional image of a jaw to a company in Sweden, which would design and make a near-perfect implant and deliver it to Lancy's for finishing, all within five working days.

The lab had always been a relaxed and enjoyable place to work and, in 2015, Paul and Peter modernised laboratories and upgraded the premises. Last Monday, one of Lancy's most experienced and valued technicians, John Booth, approached Paul saying that his mother had been taken seriously ill and she would need continual home care for several months at least. Could he take leave for this, he wanted to know, or would he need to resign?

This started Paul and Peter thinking. Although it was highly specialised work, John could do quite a lot of his job from home, as long as he took his equipment with him. In fact, since everyone had their own dedicated equipment, perhaps others would be interested in working from home too. Some of the more technically advanced techniques, using specialised lab-based equipment, would still need to be done in the lab but clearly this didn't apply to all the work.

What about the office support people? Perhaps some of them might appreciate the opportunity to work from home one or two days a week. Thanks to a telephone switching system, Paul and Peter already had a home-based contact person available 24 hours a day for the benefit of Lancy's overseas partner labs and this was working out really well. What other new working arrangements might add value to their business, their customers and their trading partners?

Questions

1. What options do Paul and Peter have as they consider adopting flexible working arrangements?
2. What are the potential benefits and disadvantages to incorporating flexible working arrangements?
3. If you were advising Paul and Peter on organisation design, what general principles and organisation design concepts would you recommend, and why?
4. How would you expect a revised organisation structure to influence morale and efficiency in the lab? How might it affect relationships with partner labs, suppliers and customers, and among Lancy's employees?

CHAPTER

THE INFORMAL ORGANISATION

Wherever people come together, they develop specific ways of working, referred to as the organisation's culture. This is the mix of invisible rules and rituals that regulate activities and dictate what behaviours, what ways of communicating and even what ways of dressing are acceptable. And an organisation's culture also includes what is unwelcome. It's important to understand the culture – and subcultures – of your workplace and conform to them.

Wherever people come together, a power hierarchy also develops. Individuals jostle for their place in the pecking order and for power and influence. Organisational culture, politics and power affect everyone.

Conforming to the culture, subcultures and norms of your workplace helps you achieve your individual goals and also your team's goals. Understanding and working within the official hierarchy of your organisation is important (as explained in Chapter 3). Understanding and working within the unofficial hierarchies, the 'relational' networks and the 'political' structures of your organisation, can make or break your career. To exist successfully and comfortably within your organisation's culture, you need to know 'who's who', who can support you, who can advise you, who can 'make things happen' for you and who are the career-makers and career-breakers in your organisation.

1. Do you know how to recognise and interpret the webs of human relationships in an organisation and how they influence each other?
2. Are you able to diagnose your organisation's culture, subculture and norms and explain why they are critical to your success, and the success of your organisation and your team?
3. Can you interpret and influence the quality of the relationships inside your organisation and work team?
4. Do you know how to recognise and acquire power and influence in your organisation?

This chapter shows you how to weave your way through the complex and tricky maze of the informal organisation – its culture and its unofficial hierarchy.

SCENARIO

Sussing out the team

Arana walks into his new department. He's been a line manager before but this is his first role at one of the company's subsidiaries. As per his plan, he asks everyone to grab a coffee and join him in his office. He begins by saying a few words about himself in order to establish his technical expertise as well as the fact that he has led successful teams at the company's head office. (He thinks it won't hurt his new team members to know that he knows important people at head office, and has access to information and more than a few scarce resources.)

To get the team talking, he asks each person in turn for a quick rundown on his or her responsibilities and current projects, explaining he'll meet with everyone individually over the next few days. Then he throws the meeting open for questions.

What Arana is really interested in is who pipes up first and what questions and comments they have. He watches the team members carefully to see how they interact with one another. In his experience, this is an important clue to how well a team works together and, therefore, how much work he has ahead of him to develop the team climate and culture he's looking for.

1. Uncovering the relationships

> Every company has two organisational structures: the formal one is written on the charts; the other is the everyday relationships of the men and women in the organisation.
>
> Harold S Geneen (former president, ITT), *Managing* (1984)[1]

Organisation charts reflect the official organisation structure, or formal organisation. As important as the officially recognised lines of authority, communication, relationships and responsibility are to the way a workplace functions, they are only part of the picture.

The other part of the picture is the network of people working together (or not) to achieve a shared purpose. It's the (unpredictable) people involved in using the (reasonably predictable) technology, and following the (reasonably predictable) work systems and procedures of their organisation, who make organisations unpredictable and difficult to control.

Human networks

The webs of human relationships and the unofficial power hierarchy inside organisations are collectively known as the *informal organisation*.[2] This determines how the organisation really works and includes the following:

- *Career advice network*: People who others turn to for career guidance.
- *Expert network*: People who others turn to for advice and expertise.
- *Innovation network*: Where ideas are kicked around.
- *Learning network*: People who others work with to improve existing processes and methods.
- *Social network*: Made up of people who spend out-of-work time together.
- *Work network*: Made up of day-to-day assignment contacts.

These networks are far more than the sum of the individual employees who are part of them. They each have their own customs, energy and 'knowledge'.

When seen like this, organisations are complex, ever-evolving organic systems. The more the people within them trust each other and the more attuned to sharing and learning the organisation culture is, the more people can talk freely, explore ideas and develop their own views. This is how tacit knowledge becomes fresh learning and invention, and this is what a 'healthy' organisation is all about. (See page 222 for more information on networking.)

> **⊙ THEORY TO PRACTICE**
>
> **Listen and learn**
> What do people talk about in organisation networks? Conversation can be energising, enriching and positive, or it can be draining, manipulative and negative. Does the discussion in your organisation's networks, and the discussion between your team members, contribute to a healthy future for the organisation and your team?

Systematic chaos

When setting up responsibilities, systems and procedures, measures of success, and so on, management traditionally has worked on one part of an organisation at a time. Then came *systems theory*. A *system* is a collection of elements that together create a complex, meaningful whole. When you remove or change one part of a system, the entire system changes. A pile of sand is not a system – when you remove a grain of sand, you've still got a pile of sand. Bodies, cars, ecosystems and the environment, as well as societies, are systems – when you remove the kidneys, the body doesn't work; remove the battery, the car doesn't work. When you remove the species, the environment doesn't work. Each part, or *subsystem* as it's called, plays a special role outside of the system. The whole system is far more than the sum of its parts.

Organisations are systems, too. When you change the way you provide a service, it affects the whole organisation. When you change an office layout, the way people in the office (a subsystem) work together changes, which can affect the whole organisation.

Systems have a *structure* and *behaviour* that uses *processes* to transform *inputs* (e.g. information and materials) into *outputs* (e.g. products or services) and *outcomes* (e.g. profit and customer satisfaction). Systems can also share feedback to improve performance. Feedback can come from inside the system (e.g. the people working in it, and results attained) or from outside the system (e.g. from customers and the community).

Thinking about your organisation as a system made up of interwoven subsystems (functions, departments, teams and processes) helps you see it from a broader perspective and find and interpret patterns and events. It helps you understand how the various parts of the organisation are interrelated and how each affects, and is affected by, all the others. This, in turn, helps you coordinate work so that the organisation as a whole runs smoothly and efficiently.

Chaos theory is an extension of systems theory. Chaos theory concentrates on unpredictable, complex systems and offers helpful information about organisational systems:

* Organisations are not machines that can be controlled by rules and procedures.
* Small, even seemingly insignificant actions and events can have large and unpredictable consequences (or no consequences at all).
* Systems are always changing.
* Too much control kills creativity, innovation and productivity.
* You cannot predict the behaviour of a system from the behaviour of its parts because the whole is more than the sum of its parts.

FYI

The butterfly effect

In 1960, a meteorologist named Edward Norton Lorenz was using a computer to model and predict weather. When he double-checked a sequence, he used three decimal places instead of the original six. You wouldn't think such a tiny fraction would make a difference, but it did – it made a huge difference.

A miniscule action, comparable to a butterfly flapping its wings, can produce a big change over time and alter the behaviour of an entire system. In turn, an action comparable to a cyclone may have no effect on a system, while the absence of a cyclone may have a huge impact.[3]

2. Diagnosing organisation culture

Culture is the integrated systems of beliefs, values, paradigms, structures, processes and symbols that influence the behaviour of groups of people.

DEEWR, 'Australian cultural imprints at work: 2010 and beyond' (March 2011)[4]

Every organisation has a culture – it's impossible not to have one. No matter how awesome an organisation's values, how phenomenal its vision and mission, and how splendid its strategy, when it doesn't have a strong culture and operating system to pull it all together and make it happen, it is doomed to fail. Because it is difficult to reproduce, an organisation's culture is a core capability, which can be a distinctive competitive advantage.

Organisation culture – the shared attitudes, behaviours, beliefs, understandings and values by which employees operate – is the glue that holds people, teams and functions together. It is made up of employees' shared assumptions, expectations, mindsets and ways of working. It is also an essential part of an organisation's employer value proposition and its employer brand. Organisation culture influences an organisation's ability to recruit, retain, engage and motivate employees.

Based in part on the organisation's symbols and systems, in part on the messages leader-managers send and the behaviours and thinking processes they model, and in part on the norms that develop as people work together, an organisation's culture is like a blueprint of how it operates internally and how it relates to its external environment. Figure 4.1 summarises the components of an organisation's culture.

THE STRATEGIC PERSPECTIVE

Corporate culture – the invisible force that shapes behaviour

Consider the culture of Virgin Group Ltd. Staff behave professionally, dress comfortably and casually, have fun, shun bureaucracy, take responsibility, work with passion. Virgin is a culture in which people are proud to play a part.

One way Virgin builds and maintains its culture is by recruiting people who already fit its culture. Some of the interviews of promising candidates are conducted by staff members who themselves embody the Virgin culture and whose role it is to assess 'cultural fit'. When a candidate doesn't 'fit', that candidate isn't hired.[5]

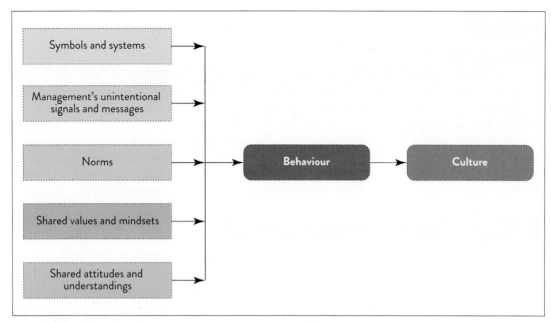

FIGURE 4.1 The constituents of culture

Organisation culture dictates how an organisation performs. Good cultures are immeasurably valuable to organisations. They energise employees and drive engagement and productivity. Poor organisation cultures drain energy and drag down engagement and performance, undermining long-term success. This makes culture one of an organisation's most powerful tools. In fact, the 'right' culture is increasingly essential to ensuring an organisation's long-term viability; it can make – or break – an organisation.

It is easier to experience an organisation's culture and a team's subculture and norms, than to describe it. This is because the rules or codes of behaviour that influence employees to behave in certain ways are usually implicit, or not stated. Yet these unstated 'rules' affect how an organisation goes about its business:

- how carefully and quickly people make and execute decisions
- how much people collaborate with each other to produce a better product or service
- how seriously people view their accountabilities
- how thoroughly people do their work.

When employees feel 'at home' in a high-performance culture – when their values, mindsets and ways of operating are a good fit with the culture – the path to high performance is smooth.

THE STRATEGIC PERSPECTIVE

The lost decade

Consider the history of Microsoft at the start of the 21st century. In 2000, it was the world's most valuable company; Apple didn't even make the list. Between 2000 and 2012, Microsoft's share price remained steady while Apple's grew nearly 20 times. In the same period, Microsoft's market capitalisation was US$510 billion versus Apple's US$4.8 billion. (The larger the market capitalisation, the less risky the business.)

>>

By 2012, the situation had reversed: Microsoft had dropped to the world's third most valuable company, with a market capitalisation of US$249 billion. Apple had become the world's most valuable company, with a market capitalisation of US$541 billion.

Some say Microsoft's lack of innovation was responsible for this stunning reversal. It just kept bringing out flashier models of the same old product. A new CEO took over from Bill Gates in 2000. Within a year, Microsoft lost more than half of its value and the stock options that had made many of its employees wealthier than wealthy had tanked.

From the start of the 21st century, the route to wealth was to climb the corporate ladder rather than concentrate on contributing to the business. Competition within Microsoft led to an endless series of internal battles. (See 'The strategic perspective: Rank and yank – point and counterpoint' on page 433.) By 2002, red tape, meetings, memos, power plays and bickering killed off, derailed or delayed innovations such as e-book and smartphone technology. By 2014, Apple's iPhone earned more than all of Microsoft.[6]

The lesson: Establish and encourage a culture that supports your organisation's and team's vision and goals. For example, when you need innovation and entrepreneurialism in your organisation, reward the risk takers and the 'wave makers'. When you want team players, don't pit people against each other.

Four organisation cultures

Charles Handy identifies four main types of organisation culture: person, power, role and task. Think of these as underpinning the elements of culture shown in Figure 4.1.

In *person cultures*, formal reporting lines take second place to informal power. This is a rare type of culture that occurs when non-management employees are highly valued for their particular professional skills such as in law or architectural firms.

Small, entrepreneurial companies typically have *power cultures*, although other types of organisations have power cultures, too. One individual or a small group dominates, controlling the organisation through power. This can be fine in start-up companies, but when an enterprise doesn't move on to another culture when the time comes, the organisation is likely to stagnate.

Functional organisations often have *role cultures* that, in mature organisations, including the public sector, can be efficient. Their main drawback is the 'silo mentality' that usually arises, where each function is a fiefdom in itself, leading to slow and inefficient work flows, a proliferation of rules and other elements of traditional bureaucracies, where customer needs trail in the wake of 'turf wars'. (See page 83.)

A *task culture* is often found in matrix organisations where the completion of a project or process takes precedence. Sharing ideas, internal flexibility and mobility of employees characterise task cultures.[7]

Subcultures

Inside every organisation there are subgroups made up of departments, work groups and networks. Each has its own subculture or operating code: its own common dress, 'hangouts', language, performance expectations and rituals. American journalist Paula Bernstein described it like this, 'A corporation does seem like a family. Not necessarily that one big, happy family they like to boast about ... but just like every family, a hotbed of passion, rivalry, and dreams that build or destroy careers.'[8]

Get to know the subgroups in your organisation, what functions they perform, which are the least and most influential, the least and most knowledgeable, and so on. Who are their informal leaders? Who is in the 'inner circle' and who is excluded from it? Finding out what makes one group different from another means that you can work with members of different subcultures more effectively. It means you can observe their unwritten rules and adjust your own behaviour and style to 'fit in'.

By and large, the CEO and senior managers, by their behaviours and actions, set the overall culture of an organisation. Employees interpret what they should and shouldn't do from what leader-managers do and don't do (not what they say). This applies to work team subcultures, too. People take their cues from the team leader.

> **◉ ACTION!**
>
> What's your team culture like? Is it empowering? Is it work-focused? Is it service-oriented or safety oriented? Or is it a toxic culture based on self-protection? Find out with the interactive self-test: What's your team culture like?, on **⸙CourseMate**Express.

Norms

Every team develops its own unique ways of how members work individually and together, solve problems and air disagreements, based on the wider organisation's culture and the experiences group members have together. Gradually, a team's accepted behaviour patterns and ways of working together become clearer and more recognisable and, eventually, they become established habits. Known as norms, they are the unwritten traditions and codes of behaviour, the (usually) unspoken 'rules' of 'how we do things around here'.

Fit in or pay the price

A work group's norms and culture shape, and even dictate, its members' behaviour – everyone wants to be accepted and liked. When people don't fit in by doing what is expected, the rest of the group snubs them. To avoid this, most new employees spend a lot of effort and energy trying to figure out the organisation's and team's culture and norms by analysing the organisation's corporate values and symbols, observing the people around them and working out their team's work habits and traditions.

When new team members struggle to understand the culture and norms that now surround them, they often unwittingly disrupt those norms and set the team back. (See page 386 to find out how this occurs.) It makes sense to save new team members any misunderstanding or embarrassment by taking the time to explain the team's culture and norms to them as soon as they start their new jobs. (Chapters 13 and 14 have more information on building your team's culture and norms and page 833 explains how to help new team members fit into your team quickly.)

Culture and norms trump vision and strategy every time, so it's important to ensure your team's culture and norms support your organisation's values, vision and strategy. And be sure that your team's culture and norms include rewarding those who achieve goals and rewards those who work well together. When you find your team's codes of behaviour holding the team back from achieving its task, meet the team members involved and discuss this openly to agree better ways of working together. (See page 384 to find out how team building does this.)

Here are some ways you can build a strong team culture and norms that support your organisation's values and goals:

- Be positive.
- Generate pride in the organisation and show how individual team members and the team as a whole contribute to it.
- Make it clear what you stand for.
- Make your team's purpose and goals clear to everyone.
- Pay attention to details.
- Walk your talk.

When you don't support your team and organisation in this way, be prepared to pay the price of a negative team culture and norms that deliver poor results.

● THEORY TO PRACTICE

The batik shirt

Paul Biddle works with a British government body called the Stabilisation Unit, helping to establish peace and security in countries affected by conflict and instability. He needs to apply his management skills in extremely challenging, hostile and sometimes life-threatening situations. Thorough preparation and cultural insight, he believes, are keys to success in such difficult circumstances.

While researching Indonesian culture before deployment to Java, he discovered that all Indonesians, even those in uniform, traditionally abandon normal work attire every Friday and don a batik shirt showing the region they hail from. One of the first things he did when he arrived in Indonesia was purchase a bright batik shirt. A few days later, an important meeting with local officials fell on a Friday and he wore the shirt. The batik shirt broke down the barriers that normally take at least six months to crumble. 'Just a little thing like that ... opened all the doors.'[9]

---

3. Working with group dynamics

> Coming together is a beginning; keeping together is progress; working together is success.
>
> Henry Ford (Ford Motor Company), in Andersen, '21 Quotes from Henry Ford on business, leadership and life', *Forbes*, 2013.[10]

The way people develop and manage their relationships inside an organisation, and within a team, and with their external suppliers and customers is an important feature of culture and norms (and therefore another key element of an organisation's success). These relationships, based on the way people interact with each other, are known as group dynamics.

A team's dynamics shape how its members go about doing the team's work, together and individually. Along with its culture and norms, a team's dynamics is another key determinant of its productivity and results. The main elements and influences on group dynamics are discussed in the following sections.

Cohesion

The members of a *cohesive* team stick together like glue and have a strong sense of 'us'. A cohesive team is referred to by its members as 'us' because of the 'attractiveness' of the group to its members. Since members of cohesive groups are more likely to work well together to achieve their tasks, try to build up your team's cohesiveness. Help members to develop a sense of team identity and pride along with a productive culture and norms. Provide opportunities for team members to get to know each other as diverse individuals, and respect what each member brings to the team.

But beware! A highly cohesive team, particularly one with poor group decision-making processes, is prone to groupthink. This occurs when members of a team get along so well that they are loath to contradict what appears to be the wish or belief of the majority. This holds back the team's performance and even encourages the group to make dangerous decisions. (When you think the team you are leading may be suffering from groupthink, you need to act. You can find out more about groupthink on page 539 and how to take steps to minimise it.)

Communication patterns

Do group members speak formally or informally with each other? What tone of voice do they use with each other? What does their body language say? Are their communications clear? What channels of communication do they use? Who talks to whom? When? Where? For how long? Who is left out? Do people really listen to each other?

Communication patterns like these influence your team's efficiency, productivity and morale. They can help you work out the informal status and power of group members, how effectively your group is using the skills of its members to get the job done and your group's working climate and cohesion.

⊙ THEORY TO PRACTICE

How do you communicate?
Do team members seem hesitant and tongue-tied around you? Perhaps they see you as domineering or remote. Share some information about yourself and your life outside work, and find out about theirs. You don't need to pry or become 'best friends' – just develop some bonds between yourself and team members to forge a strong team.

Decision-making

Groups are constantly making decisions. What are these decisions about? How are they made? Does everyone have a say or do only a few people express opinions? Is silence taken for agreement? Are issues discussed so that consensus is reached or does one person or a subgroup make most of the important decisions?

The more you need your team to participate in and support decisions that affect them and the team's operations, the more important it is to ensure that everyone in the team understands and follows effective decision-making procedures.

Group roles

Everyone wants to have a role in the group, whether it's as a spokesperson, an expert or a clown. One person might generate enthusiasm and start the ball rolling on new initiatives. Someone else might be able to relieve tension with an appropriate joke. Another might be the one to bring people up to speed when they've been away on leave or travelling. (See page 382 to find out about people's roles in teams.)

People take on roles that meet their own needs. Some of the roles people take it upon themselves to fill are helpful, or *functional*, while others are unhelpful, or *dysfunctional*, to the efficient functioning of a team. And some roles can be either functional or dysfunctional, depending on how they're 'played'. For instance, a *clown* can be disruptive or can relieve tension; a *gatekeeper* can shut people out or see that everyone has a say; *a devil's advocate* can pour water on good ideas or point out potential problems and how to fix them.

How helpful or unhelpful is the behaviour of your team members to the way the team functions? Does what they say and do help or hinder the other team members to do their best? When you know who plays which roles, you can act to encourage helpful role behaviours and discourage unhelpful role behaviours. You can find this out with the template, Functional and dysfunctional roles, on **CourseMateExpress**.

Observe your team to get a feeling for who performs which roles, and which roles help and which hinder the way the team works together to achieve its tasks. Do you sense any friction over who holds certain roles? How strong is that friction? The roles that team members take up (and those they avoid) say a lot about the team's dynamics.

Strengthen the way your team operates by helping people become aware of the roles they play and the effects these roles have on the team task and its process. As people become more sensitive to, and aware of, how they can help their team to function more effectively, their skills improve. Their roles can be divided into task and process roles. In practice, many serve both task and process functions. (Also see the Action! box you have just read and try the exercise.)

Informal leaders

Someone in your work team is probably an informal leader, the person others go to with ideas, questions or complaints, for advice, assistance or just a chat. Is it the person who gets the best results, who serves customers best, or who has the most expertise or technical knowledge? Or is it the most articulate and dissatisfied group member spearheading a group of discontented workers, perhaps?

Having an informal leader in your work team doesn't necessarily mean that you aren't leading properly. It may mean that the informal leader is meeting certain team and individual needs that you, the formal leader, cannot or should not meet.

Team members look to informal leaders (as much as they do to their official team leader) to see how they should and should not do things. The cues informal leaders send about how fast to work, how to dress, how much to cooperate with management, and how courteous to be to customers and suppliers and so on, are stronger than official policy or procedures on these matters. This makes the role of informal leader important in establishing and maintaining group norms. These people 'set the pace' and this 'pace' can be in your favour or in direct opposition to what you're trying to accomplish. Don't try to eliminate any informal leaders in your work group, but ensure that they are working with you and not against you.

The standing of informal leaders is precarious, especially when the composition of the work group changes frequently or when the work location, product or task changes. As a group's needs change, so too does its choice of informal leader.

Participation

Who are the high and the low participators in your team's activities and work? How are the high and the low participators treated? Is anyone left out and, if so, why? Who generates enthusiasm and 'keeps the ball rolling'? Who contributes ideas and suggestions? Who is the first to notice something going wrong and bring it to the team's attention? This gives you clues to the team's priorities and what it values.

Power and influence

Who influences whom and how? Who has the power to 'tell' others what to do? Who is listened to when they speak? Is anyone ignored or continually interrupted? Who do others copy? Who do others admire? When those wielding informal power and influence are doing so in ways inconsistent with the team's goals, trouble is brewing! (We discuss power and influence further on page 102.)

Work climate

Groups working in a supportive and relaxed atmosphere generally find it easy and enjoyable to complete their tasks and achieve their goals. Here are some signs of a positive working climate, one that is considerate, tolerant and trusting:

* Team members feel free to express themselves and share their feelings.
* Team members support each other.
* Team members contribute to the group goals in the best way they can.
* There is a sense of enjoyment as the team gets on with the job at hand.

Work climates can also be controlling, punishing and rigid, making task achievement difficult. You influence the climate of your work team, for better or worse, by the example and standards you set.

● THEORY TO PRACTICE

Group dynamics at work

A manager from South Australia relates the following story, which illustrates how group dynamics can work against you through no fault of your own:

'Several years ago, I became CEO of a regional quango [a quasi-autonomous government organisation], with six staff,' he said.

'It took quite some time to find out that the three male staff had all applied for my position. I was the outsider.

'One of the unsuccessful applicants left soon after I took up the position.

'Another was a most effective white-anter and moving him on was one of the toughest tasks I ever accomplished.

'The third unsuccessful applicant became my 2IC [second-in-command].

'Then our office manager left her husband and moved in with him and I certainly knew where her loyalties lay.

'Oh, it was a very good position to leave.'

Influences on group dynamics

Group dynamics are influenced by five groups of factors: What's happening in the surrounding environment, what's happening within the group itself, each group member's skills and personalities, the team's job or task and the leader-manager.

Together, these factors determine how your team organises itself and how well it functions. Monitor your teams members and try to ensure that each contributes positively to your team's operations. Be particularly watchful for a change in any one of these five factors because it could lead to a shift in the dynamics of the group as a whole.

The environment

The environment determines what a team can and cannot do in a broad sense. It includes the organisation's culture, the closeness and type of other teams, the organisation's formal and informal rewards systems, the type of organisation structure, the power structure within the organisation, the resources (e.g. information, space, time, tools) available and the quality and type of leadership. These aspects of the environment establish the boundaries within which teams must operate, shaping the dynamics that are possible within teams.

The group as a whole

Team size is important: five or 15 people work better together and enjoy the experience more than people in larger teams. Communication is less complicated. It's easier for members to get to know each other. And members can help one another more easily. The turnover of membership (how rapidly people leave and enter the group) also matters because new team members are likely to change the group's dynamics.

The extent to which team members have similar backgrounds, education, experiences and training is called the team's *homogeneity*. This also affects dynamics because an homogeneous team, while it can be cohesive and supportive, often has difficulty in adapting to change and in being creative. Homogeneous teams are also more prone to groupthink.

While team members should be of like mind in their understanding of their purposes, goals, roles and procedures, strong teams are heterogeneous, or diverse, in their approaches and ways of thinking. With good group dynamics and a positive culture, this diversity leads to insight, creativity and strength. With poor group dynamics and a poor culture, diversity leads to tension, conflict and mistrust. (See page 846 for more information on the benefits of diversity.)

Individual group members

Each team member's abilities, attitudes, emotional intelligence, experience, personality, role perceptions, skills and values – all the things that make people unique – determine what team members are able and willing to contribute. Add to that their level of motivation, the way they interact with other group members and the degree to which they accept group norms and the organisation's values and goals, and you can easily understand how much the a team's dynamics depend on the skills of its individual members.

The job

Three groups of factors concerning the job affect a team's dynamics by encouraging or limiting the freedom of its members to make decisions concerning their work and the amount of interaction that is possible between them:

1. Job design and the technology used
2. Layout of the department and individual workstations
3. Type of work involved.

The leader-manager

Effective leadership is a vital ingredient of every team's success. Employees take their cue from their leader-manager regarding such matters as the pace of work and what is, and isn't, important (customer service, quality, timekeeping). The leader-manager also establishes the working climate for the team.

Without a leader who 'paints the picture' and shows the way, a team is left floundering and looking to its informal leader for its cues. When that happens, it's the luck of the draw whether the team performs well.

ACTION!

What are they dynamics of your work group like? Are they helpful or unhelpful? The checklist for group dynamics on *CourseMateExpress* can help you find out.

4. Recognising and using power and influence

> Power does not consist in striking with force or with frequency, but in striking true.
>
> Honoré de Balzac (French novelist), *The Physiology of Marriage*, 1829, translated by the Gutenberg Project, 2010.[11]

Power and influence help you create productive relationships, engage and motivate employees, gain support, inspire others and persuade people. Formal, or official, power gives you some authority over the behaviour of others. Power and influence can often 'get you what you want' without resorting to coercion, manipulation or threats.

Influence is based on your personal authority, or personal power. The chief executive's personal assistant may have little formal power but tremendous influence. Others in the organisation, often at middle and junior levels, may have influence because of their expertise in certain key areas or because of their close contact with people who have power and influence.

Are you politically astute enough to know who has power and influence in your organisation and include them in your networks? To find out who actually has the power and influence, you need to be able to read between the lines of your formal organisation chart and 'see' the invisible connections:

*   What are the important networks and cliques and who is in them?
*   Who are the informal, unofficial leaders?
*   Who can convince others when no one else can?
*   Who generates ideas?
*   Whose opinion counts?
*   Who recruited whom?
*   Who socialises with whom?
*   Who trained whom?

Power and influence rarely lie with just one person. More often they rest with a group of people, a coalition, who respect each other and share similar ideas, values and experiences. These people combine their power and influence to achieve a shared vision for their organisation.

The six sources of power and influence you can draw on are examined in the following sections.

Position power

Three of the six sources of power are based on your position power, or formal authority. Position power comes from your official place in the organisation structure, and the resources you officially control. In the past, leader-managers relied heavily on this formal power, but this reliance has shrivelled in recent years.

Legitimate power refers to your right to issue orders and instructions and someone else's duty to carry them out. When team members feel they 'should' do something because 'the boss says so', they are responding to legitimate power.

Coercive power is based on fear. It rests on your ability to discipline. When employees do something in order to avoid an unpleasant outcome, for example to avoid criticism or to avoid you withholding overtime or cutting back their working hours (and therefore earnings), they are responding to coercive power.

Reward power is based on your ability to distribute something of value, such as overtime, interesting work assignments, pay increases, positive performance appraisals and promotion. When followers do as you ask in the hope of getting something in return, they are responding to reward power.

Personal power

At the start of this section, Honoré de Balzac was, perhaps, commenting on the difference between position power and personal power when he said, 'Power is not revealed by striking hard or often, but by striking true.' Personal power describes a person's unofficial power, or influence. The final three sources of workplace power are based on personal power, and this you must earn.

Expert power comes from special skills and knowledge, usually gained through study and experience, and your 'track record'. Expertise attracts both admiration and respect. Consistency and dependability strengthen your expert power, as does respect for what you stand for.

You derive much of your authority as a leader-manager from your experience, job knowledge and training. When employees do as you ask because they assume you know best, your expert power is influencing them. You ideally have some expertise in the technology and work of your group. Knowledge of the organisation as a system and how it operates (its culture, subcultures and networks) is also part of job knowledge. Knowing what needs to be done and where, when, why and how to do it also earns you a great deal of personal respect and influence.

Proximity power comes from the interesting information and knowledge you have and can share with others. This might include explaining the reasons behind a decision or passing on information about behind-the-scenes goings on in the organisation.

When people do as you ask or suggest because you know or have access to someone important, your proximity power is influencing them. Proximity power lends itself to 'trade-offs' of favours, information or resources, and the more scarce those items are, the greater your proximity power.

Referent power is also known as 'charismatic power'. It is that special something that attracts followers, based on the goodwill, liking and respect that you have earned. Your referent power comes in part from your ability to build cooperative and supportive working relationships; rapport, mutual respect, friendship and your package of people skills all play a part in building this aspect of referent power.

Integrity is the other main contributor to referent power. Acting consistently to a clear set of personal guidelines and standards that complement and support the organisation's standards, and not deviating from them, is very powerful and attractive to others. When employees do as you ask because they want to support you or cooperate with you, your referent power is influencing them.

People need autonomy, a feeling of choice, in order to be motivated. Position power generally removes that autonomy. This makes personal power the more important and reliable power base of today's leader-managers. People don't grant you respect because of the position you hold; you earn respect and influence through your personal knowledge and qualities. Attributes such as honesty, integrity, self-respect and respect for others, strength of personal vision and values and trustworthiness are particularly important in building personal power. (See chapters 7 and 8 to find out more about building your personal power.)

THE STRATEGIC PERSPECTIVE

Behavioural science, power and influence

According to Robert Cialdini PhD, a specialist in persuasion and compliance, persuasive managers share four distinctive patterns of behaviour:

1. They encourage people to make public commitments because they are more durable than private commitments.
2. They establish their authority because people defer to experts.
3. They find common interests with colleagues, learn what people are good at and praise liberally because people who feel liked and understood are more open to persuasion and influence.
4. They grant favours or give small gifts to establish an emotional debt.[12]

ACTION!

How well are you building your personal power? The checklist of the same name on CourseMateExpress can help you work this out.

CourseMateExpress

Go to http://login.cengagebrain.com to access CourseMate Express, your online study tool for *Management Theory & Practice*. CourseMate Express brings chapter concepts to life with interactive learning, and study and exam preparation tools:

- Test your skills in different aspects of management with interactive self-tests and simulations.
- Watch videos that show how real managers operate in real businesses.
- Test your understanding of the changing world of management by taking the revision quiz.

QUICK REVIEW

1. How does thinking about organisations as chaotic systems, which are made up of ever-evolving networks of human relationships, help managers organise an enterprise's operations and work teams and introduce change more effectively? Use this model to explain the operations of your own organisation.
2. Define organisation culture and explain how an organisation's culture and subcultures relate to employee attraction and retention and to its overall success.

3. Make a list of words that describe a work group with poor group dynamics; make a list of words that describe a work group with good group dynamics. Describe what you think it would be like to work in each of the work groups and the degree to which each would be likely to reach its goals.

4. Describe the six types and sources of organisational power and influence and discuss the relative strength of each.

BUILD YOUR SKILLS

1. How can the way an organisation's internal networks operate help or hinder its achievement of a goal?

2. What is systems theory and how does it differ from thinking about an organisation in terms of one function or process at a time? Can you give an example of how making a change in one part of an organisation can affect another part of the organisation in unexpected ways?

3. Explain how an organisation's culture can help or hinder its effectiveness and give an example from your own experience.

4. Discuss how a work team's subculture and norms can help or hinder its effectiveness and give an example from your own experience.

5. Referring to Case study 9.2 on page 284, how would you describe the culture of this work team?

6. Who are the informal leaders of your class, your study group and your work team? How do you know this? Considering both their personal qualities and the function they perform in the group, why do you believe they have become the informal leaders?

7. Who wields power and influence in your class, your study group and your work team? Which type of power and influence do they have and how do you believe they acquired it?

WORKPLACE ACTIVITIES

1. Thinking about your own organisation, which is more important to the way employees do their jobs, achieve their goals and implement changes and new ideas: The formal organisation or the informal organisation? Provide examples to illustrate your reasoning.

2. From your experience, describe what it is like to enter a new organisation and join a new work team, particularly understanding the expected behaviours.

3. Analyse the culture and norms of your work group by thinking through the following questions:
    a. Do people arrive at and leave work and take breaks strictly on time or are attitudes to time more relaxed?
    b. Do people socialise with each other?
    c. How do people treat each other? External customers? Internal customers?
    d. How do employees speak about the organisation and its management? Their customers?
    e. How formally or informally do people dress?
    f. How much attention to detail do people pay?
    g. How much fun do people have while they're working?
    h. How much do people focus on quality and customer satisfaction?
    i. How would you describe people's personal work areas and their wider work environment (e.g. cosy, friendly, business-like, clear desks, messy desks)?
    j. How would you describe the management style of the organisation?
    k. Is the working atmosphere relaxed, formal or tense?

l. What are the attitudes and practices regarding health, safety and the environment?

m. What are the systems and procedures like? For example, are they hierarchy driven, protocol driven, customer driven or production driven? Do they emphasise checks and controls, innovation or freedom to act?

n. What behaviours are rewarded and respected? What behaviours are 'punished' or frowned upon?

o. What do people do at breaks and for lunch?

p. What is the work ethic? For example, is it a 'She'll be right!' or a 'Get it right!' approach? How hard do employees work?

q. What priorities do people select?

r. What style of language do people use (e.g. formal, informal, lots of jargon or technical terms)?

s. What symbols does your organisation use to express itself, its values and the way it operates?

t. Where, how and by whom are decisions made?

u. On balance, do these attitudes and behaviours support or work against the team, the team leader, the organisation and its other stakeholders? What can you do to improve the balance?

v. Which is stronger in your workplace – power or influence? Give some examples to illustrate your answer.

CASE STUDY 4.1

HOW A BANK TRANSFORMED ITS CULTURE

When organisations get it right, their employees can be an important source of competitive advantage. Ah – but how to win back their trust and loyalty after years of deep downsizing in an intensely competitive environment? Culture is the key. Here's how Money Bank, a solid performer in financial terms, attacked the gargantuan task of transforming its culture to make the most of its employees and reach the heights of superior performance.

Based on the philosophy that when people are happy and productive, they create more value for shareholders and customers alike, the bank's first task was to win the hearts and minds of the people inside the organisation. It began by surveying its employees and benchmarking a number of key measures with other high-performing organisations. It found that while some positive values, such as a results orientation, had become part of the culture, the bank needed to do more to engage its employees and reduce the bureaucracy, hierarchy and silo mentality.

So Money Bank set about becoming 'the human bank' and established a three-fold strategy:

* *Build our culture* to create the foundations for sustainable leadership and long-term success through culture.
* *Build on our success* by further strengthening our brand, leadership and revenue.
* *Build our performance* by delivering improved financial performance and shareholder value.

Culture-building concentrated on creating a fundamentally different experience for the bank's key stakeholders: The broader community and the bank's customers, employees and shareholders. A dedicated culture team headed up three major initiatives:

* personal and emotional development workshops in which participants examine the thoughts and values that drive their behaviour
* process-improvement projects to support cultural transformation

● ● ● ○

- cultural consulting providing diagnostic and consulting services to assist business units and teams to identify their current cultural climate, assess it against key principles, improve their culture and measure their progress.

It worked. Money Bank's financial results improved and it was recognised as an employer of choice. Internal surveys of employee satisfaction rose from 50% to 85% over the next seven years and overall knowledge of Money Bank's values nearly doubled.[13]

Questions

1. It is generally accepted that the first step in maximising performance and gaining the people advantage is through an organisation's culture. Why is this the case?
2. Money Bank took a carefully thought out approach to transform its culture. Discuss the key steps in its approach and the role each played.
3. Here are some important factors in successful cultural transformation. Read them through and discuss what each of them means to you in practical terms:
   - a compelling aspiration and meaningful values
   - aligning mindsets and behaviours with the organisation's underlying processes and systems
   - being prepared to take risks and to learn from mistakes
   - matching the organisation's people to its culture so there is a strong fit
   - recognition that transformation is a journey, not a one-off program
   - strong ownership of and commitment to change from the CEO and the executive management team.

PART

2

MANAGING YOURSELF

Are you a practising or aspiring leader-manager? Whether it's a rock band or a team of rocket scientists, an organisation employing thousands of people, a virtual team scattered around the world or a work team of five, when people come together to achieve their individual and shared goals, they need someone who can provide direction, guidance and a sense of purpose. They need someone who is willing and confident enough to take overall responsibility for their activities and achievements. They need someone who can inspire them, empower them and show them the way.

To be this person, you must first understand and manage yourself. Only then can you successfully lead people and manage operations. Only then can you add real value to your organisation and to the team that looks to you for leadership.

People who possess these core competencies seem to attract opportunities. They are noticed and given the chance to contribute. With them, you're well on your way to building a successful career, a successful organisation and, ultimately, a successful country.

In the next four chapters, you find out how to set priorities so that you can concentrate your efforts and attention on what matters most in order to achieve meaningful results. You learn how to figure out what makes you 'tick' and what type of working environment you need in order to contribute optimally. You find out how to set meaningful and realistic life and career goals based on your values and interests and how to think your way into achieving them.

You find out how to communicate clearly, tactfully and thoughtfully and how to communicate in writing in a business-like way so that you don't let yourself or your organisation down.

The social and emotional intelligence you need to work effectively with others is explained because strong people skills propel your career forward like no other skill set can.

You find out how to gain recognition for your contributions and skills, how to present your ideas and persuade others and how to build a well-earned reputation for getting things done, honouring your commitments and making a difference.

CHAPTER

5

ESTABLISHING AND MANAGING PRIORITIES

OVERVIEW

In 1971, Henry Mintzberg, professor of management at Canada's prestigious McGill University, conducted a seminal study into how managers actually spend their time. He found that most managers work at an 'unrelenting pace' and their activities are brief and unrelated. How brief is brief? In 1971, managers spent, on average, less than 10 minutes on each task.[1]

Mintzberg recently repeated the study and the news is not good. Today's leader-managers spend less than five minutes on each task. The tasks leader-managers spend their time on continue to be unrelated. They hop from one activity to another, constantly switching mental gears and reorienting themselves to new and different tasks, and as we see below, this is not an efficient way to work.

But there's more. Managers average less than 30 minutes uninterrupted time every two days. This requires considerable mental flexibility and a tolerance for leaving work unfinished, at least temporarily.

Managers' days, it seems, are difficult to plan precisely. It's incredibly easy to become caught up in the day-to-day and lose sight of the bigger picture. We call the ability to stay involved in the day-to-day, and at the same time to rise above it, as being 'on the balcony and in the dance'. This is something all leader-managers need to do to be effective.

Some managers work so hard on 'the dance' that they fail to take the time to stand 'on the balcony' to see their job as a whole, reflect on their performance and undertake activities that are vital to their longer term success.

1. Can you see your role from the balcony clearly enough to establish and work to your priorities?
2. Can you dance your role well by organising yourself and scheduling your work?
3. Can you manage your career and prepare a professional development plan that identifies and develops the skills and abilities you need to succeed, and know when to make a move when the time is right?

This chapter helps you identify how you work best. You find out how to establish your career and work goals and plan your days accordingly. In today's hectic world, this is more important than ever.

Seeds of doubt

As Jane takes her seat on the bus, her thoughts return to her hectic workdays. 'I know my job and I'm a good team leader. So why can't I ever finish my 'To do' list? I juggle so many tasks that I hardly know which ones are on time and to budget. It's a miracle that I manage to achieve anything at all! And yet I work like a dog.

'I wake up worrying about things I need to do, decisions I need to make, comments people have made. Sam seems to think that I'm more short-tempered than usual, and so do the kids. It's just that I worry a lot. I need to sort out another line manager about a small but irritating matter and I hate conflict. And my boss doesn't seem to value my opinions. Sometimes I think I'm losing the support of the other managers, but I can't think why. Really and truly, am I as good a leader-manager as I've always thought? Or am I kidding myself?

'If only there were a few people whose brains I could pick. I'd like some objective information about how I'm perceived in the organisation, what I'm doing well and, even more importantly, how I could fine-tune my approach to become more effective.

'Maybe I haven't become involved enough in corporate politics and I'm paying the price; maybe my "image" isn't right; maybe I haven't developed a strong enough network of supporters ...

'What I need is a fairy godmother – someone who can help me figure out which direction my career should take, explain how people make things happen and get results here and in other organisations, and open a few doors for me. All I want is to be a better team leader and for people to know I'm a good team leader, and to build a worthwhile career that makes me feel good about myself, not like the loser I sometimes feel now.'

At that, the bus jerks to a stop outside her workplace. 'Into the fray I go,' she sighs.

1. Standing on the balcony: Establishing your priorities and goals

One worthwhile task carried to a successful conclusion is better than fifty half-finished tasks.

Bertie Charles Forbes (founder, *Forbes* magazine), quoted in *Forbes* (1975)[2]

The human brain craves structure and an overview, at home and at work. Standing on the balcony gives you that structure. From the balcony, you can see your job purpose, key result areas (KRAs) and measures of success (MOS). This doesn't just soothe your brain, it also highlights your important goals and priorities, guides your decisions and helps you decide how to use your time and organise your days. It gives your job purpose and prevents it from seeming like an endless series of tasks, each as important or as meaningless as the other.

A clear job purpose statement, KRAs and SMART targets provide role clarity. These comprise the balcony overview that helps you manage your work priorities and increase your productivity. They tell you precisely what you are expected to achieve, by when you need to achieve it and why achieving it is important. They also help you set priorities, establish a work schedule, focus your efforts and monitor your performance.

Your job purpose, KRAs and measures of success should support the organisation's vision and mission. This produces an 'aligned' organisation, one in which everyone is working towards the same ends – and this provides a powerful competitive edge.

It helps you personally, too. When you're constantly 'on the dance floor', immersed in your daily tasks, you concentrate on what you need to do and try to do a good job. But understanding how your work fits into the organisation, how it links with its strategy and why you are doing it, gives your performance an 'edge' and your career can accelerate rapidly.

Job purpose

A clear job purpose provides an important overview of your job by showing why the job exists and, therefore, what is important. This puts your role and responsibilities into context. A concise job purpose statement acts as your personal job vision or mission statement and provides overall guidance on how to do your job, showing you where to concentrate your efforts and mental energy. Really, you can't do a good job without one.

Job purpose statements answer the questions 'What do I do?' and 'Why do I do it?' or 'To what end do I do it?'

 THEORY TO PRACTICE

Job purpose

A job purpose statement should be written in one short and snappy sentence. For example:
- Retail store manager: To achieve or exceed sales and other targets in a way that delights my customers, my staff and myself.
- Assembly-line team leader: To help my team produce quality products within time and cost budgets so that the organisation's reputation is enhanced in the marketplace both as a quality producer and a quality employer.

Key result areas

Key result areas describe your main areas of accountability and responsibility. They are not individual tasks and they are not goals. Rather, they group together tasks that help achieve results in a specific area. Most jobs have five to nine KRAs.

A retail store manager might have the following KRAs:
- Administration
- Continuous improvement
- Customer relations
- Housekeeping
- Leadership
- Sales budgets
- Stock.

An assembly-line team leader might have these KRAs:

* Continuous improvement
* Health and safety
* Workplace relations
* Leadership
* Machine utilisation
* Output: Quality, quantity, cost, timeliness
* Staffing.

Notice two important aspects of these KRAs:

1. Each is written using one to five words and without verbs; this is because they single out areas of accountability.
2. There is no 'pecking order' – each KRA is as important as every other. You might spend a lot more time on one KRA than another, but they're both important. When you fail to achieve results in any one key area, your entire job suffers.

To achieve results in each KRA, you complete tasks (e.g. assign work, coach team members, develop and implement improvements to procedures, hold meetings, monitor results, update your team). Carrying out a series of tasks well achieves results in a key result area.

This is how KRAs put your tasks – even your small, seemingly insignificant daily activities – into context and give them meaning. And here's the important rule to remember: Every task you do should in some way contribute to achieving results in a key result area. Otherwise, why are you doing it?

Measures of success

Once you know your job's overall purpose and key areas of responsibility, you can set measures of success (also called key performance indicators and measures of performance). Measures of success help you in two ways: They establish a performance standard, giving you something specific to aim for; and they help you track your progress and monitor your performance.

For each KRA, choose two or three targets that measure that KRA's most important aspects and in some way contribute to the overall goals of your department or organisation. Make each one 'SMART':

* **S**pecific, which usually means measurable, time-framed and concise
* **M**otivating, in order to drive performance
* **A**mbitious, or achievable yet challenging
* **R**elated to the overall department and enterprise goals so they can drive performance
* **T**rackable, or easily monitored.

Ideally, establish your success measures jointly with your manager (often during a performance review or a planning meeting). Together, identify, agree and write down what you are aiming to accomplish, by when and to what standards.

Specific and concise

A target that is specific and concise is a clear target. Because a specific and concise target is usually measurable and time-limited, no one needs to wonder whether or not the target has been met, or even what that means.

You probably don't want to wait for your manager to tell you whether you are doing a good job. You want to monitor your performance yourself. Specific targets that are measurable, time-framed and trackable allow you to do this. The more frequently you can measure your performance, the more your motivation and productivity are likely to increase, provided your targets are achievable (yet challenging).

Measurable measures of success tend to fall into five main areas:

1. Cost.
2. Quality.
3. Quantity.
4. Safety.
5. Time.

Use these categories to help you write your own measures of success.

Reject measures where a change in performance does not cause you (or your team) to act differently, that are difficult to interpret, that do not illustrate progress towards achieving an important objective, that replicate other measures or that are too difficult or expensive to measure.

Difficult-to-measure targets

As the service and knowledge economies grow, organisations increasingly link measures of success to their vision and values. It isn't always easy to set measurable, time-framed targets for adhering to corporate values and honouring and reinforcing the vision, but that doesn't mean you shouldn't try.

For example, how do you specify and measure important management responsibilities like 'leadership' or 'ethical behaviour'? For matters like these, use your imagination and knowledge of the job and its requirements to determine targets. For example, one of your KRAs might be leadership; you might choose to monitor such factors by whether you have developed a successor or by how thoroughly and how quickly you induct new employees into the department and train them or you might work out a measure that indicates how well the employees reporting to you work as a team. You could attach timelines and ways to measure, or assess, your success for each of these factors.

Motivating

A target that links into your interests and abilities is motivating. It can power your performance and productivity. When the targets are also measurable and time-framed, you also have the ability to track your success. You always know how well you're doing and where you need to make some adjustments to improve.

Beware, though. Goals should guide you, not constrain you. They should not become ends in themselves, either, but rather encourage behaviours in harmony with your job purpose and your organisation's values and vision.

Ambitious yet achievable

Make your measures of success ambitious. When you think about the accomplishments you're most proud of, they probably took effort, stretched you and extended your skills. When a task is too easy you don't put much effort into it, yet when it's too hard and seems impossibly out of reach you probably don't put in much effort either. The lesson: Set targets that stretch you, but don't break you.

Related to department and enterprise goals

Make sure your measures of success contribute to overall organisational and departmental goals as well as to your own job purpose. This also makes them meaningful. Success measures like this drive your performance and make rising to the challenge of meeting them motivating and satisfying. Just make sure they relate only to those parts of your job that are actually under your control.

Trackable

Trackable targets offer a measuring stick that allows you judge for yourself how well you are doing.

Lead and lag indicators

Try to select measures of success that verify how you *are doing* (lead indicators), not how you *have done* (lag indicators). Lag indicators are historical measures that tell you whether you succeeded. They are the scorecards of cost of production reports, financial reports, human resources monitoring systems, market-share reports, mystery shopper surveys, profit results and sales results. Lag indicators don't show you where you're going but only where you've been.

Lag indicators are the 'scoreboards', lead indicators the 'ball'. Lead indicators measure what *is* happening as it occurs. They are the best measures to track because they provide an early warning when plans are not going as expected. When results are below expectations, lead indicators help you take corrective action quickly, before problems become more serious.

By the time a below-target performance appears in a lag indicator, it has probably become a problem. All you can do is try to put the problem right and make sure something similar doesn't happen again. Retrospective corrective action is more difficult and less effective than the timely corrective action that lead indicators make possible.

● IN A NUTSHELL

Terms for targets

Use positive terms so you can concentrate on what you *want* (not what you *don't want*), as shown in Table 5.1.

TABLE 5.1 Positive terminology helps reach targets faster

Term	Examples
Absolute obligations	All site personnel and visitors to wear hard hats and safety boots at all times.
	All kitchen workers and visitors to wear hair nets in the kitchen area.
	No smoking within 300 metres of the premises at any time.
Averages	Achieve 90% of customer queries answered fully within three working days.
	Average 40 transactions per day per operator completed and entered into the system.
	Complete 500 documents each week/every day/each hour.
Frequency of occurrence	Check stock every three months.
	Contact 10% of key customers randomly every month to monitor satisfaction rates.
	Take product weight samples hourly.
Percentages	Achieve 95% of deliveries on time.
	Increase attendance rates by 3% over the next three months to 92%.
	Greet 90% of customers within 12 seconds.
Time limits	Investigate all accidents and near misses within two working days.
	Answer all telephone calls within four rings.
	Take drinks orders within 10 minutes of patrons taking their seats.

Lead indicators can point to the type of corrective action to take or the area in which to take it. They also highlight when plans and activities are going particularly well so that you can work out how to retain or repeat those conditions.

State-of-the-art, systems-generated monitoring systems provide as many lead indicators as possible.

⬤ THEORY TO PRACTICE

See what's important from the balcony – or fail the dance

One of Blake's favourite conference venues was a large resort and conference centre near Perth. Over many visits, he had come to know and respect Richard, the manager. Blake marvelled at the fact that, although the centre was large and the manager's duties many and varied, nothing ever seemed to faze Richard. He'd walk around calmly, overseeing and observing, stopping to chat with guests and staff members alike. Tasks seemed to be accomplished effortlessly and on time. The staff were clearly devoted to Richard and year after year the same faces welcomed Blake back.

One day, Blake arrived to find that Richard had been promoted to an even larger resort and had been replaced by two managers. He also found that the conference room hadn't been set up as he'd requested, morning tea and afternoon tea didn't arrive on time, lunch was late and dinner took far too long to serve, badly delaying their evening session.

The two managers rushed around with a look of panic on their faces, never stopping to ask Blake whether everything was all right. He noted that one of them brought the morning tea himself, hot and flustered and shirt-tail hanging out, after Blake had rung reception to ask where it was, 20 minutes after it was due.

The only staff member Blake recognised on this trip was the evening cleaner. 'What happened?' he asked. 'Everyone's gone, the new staff look miserable, nothing happens smoothly the way it used to – the place has fallen apart!'

'Tell me about it,' she said. 'The only reason I'm still here is I can't find another job! These two clowns have no idea.'

What was the difference? On the surface, the two new managers actually seemed to work harder than Richard. Sadly, effort and results don't always equate.

Standing on the balcony allowed Richard to see the 'strategic perspective' and target his efforts on the most important goals. What he did fulfilled his job purpose and contributed to his key result areas. Standing on the balcony made Richard a graceful dancer.

The two new managers were breathless dancers, inviting one crisis after another. They stabbed blind-folded at the piñata, rushing around doing everyone's job but their own and failing to attend to the important matters for which they were responsible. They worked hard, exhausted themselves and accomplished next to nothing. They couldn't 'get their act together' because they had no balcony overview. As a result, they failed to establish and work towards their priorities and goals.

Decide what to do and when to do it

Your days are probably so busy that you find it impossible to do everything, and one of the worst ways to use your time is to do something well that you didn't need to do at all. Your goal is to concentrate your efforts on value-adding activities, activities that meet these three criteria:

1. Your customer (whether internal or external) needs and appreciates it.
2. Your actions must transform the product or service in some way.
3. You do it correctly the first time.

Apart from support activities, those that enable another value-adding activity to take place, any other activity is a waste and should be eliminated.

So how do you decide what to do straight away, what to defer, what to delegate and what to dump? Your effectiveness is as much a factor of what you *don't* do as what you do. This is where the 4 Ds come in (see 'In a Nutshell', below).

The only way you can establish priorities and know what to do and when, is by referring to your overall job purpose and key result areas. This helps you to distinguish between what's important (and therefore should be attended to), and what's superfluous and unimportant (which can be delegated, worked on when time permits or ignored entirely). Then you can develop a work schedule that concentrates on your high-priority activities – those that contribute *directly* to your overall job goals. Try to routinise everything you can to give you more brain power for your more difficult tasks.

IN A NUTSHELL

The 4 Ds
Follow the 4 Ds and you can't go wrong:
- **D**o it now.
- **D**o it later.
- **D**elegate it.
- **D**ump it – don't bother doing it at all.

Important or only urgent?

Importance is your first consideration when establishing priorities. *Urgency* is your second consideration. *Must* it be done now or can it wait? As shown in Figure 5.1, these factors give you four ways to consider tasks and whether, and when, to do them.

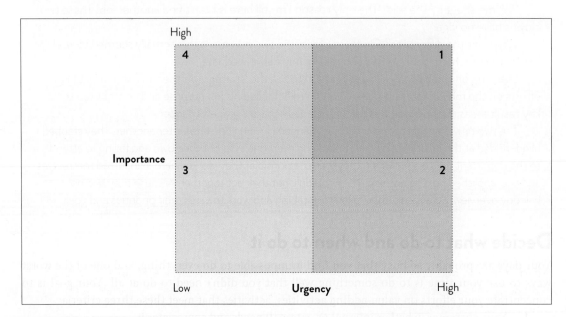

FIGURE 5.1 The establishing priorities model

Important but not urgent activities

Your view from the balcony shows you which tasks are important. Important tasks are usually directed at longer term contributions to goals in your key result areas; they are the essential matters you must attend to. When you attend to them in a timely manner, you're dancing smartly and smoothly; when you don't, bad things happen.

Some of your work tasks in the top left square in Figure 5.1 (important but not urgent) might be:

- building effective working relationships with your team, as well as with other managers, customers and suppliers
- conducting safety audits
- finding ways to improve operations
- learning new skills
- planning routine maintenance
- solving problems
- training and coaching staff.

Important and urgent activities

Many activities in the top right square in Figure 5.1, such as customer queries or requests for important information needed quickly, begin their lives as both important and urgent activities and should be attended to straight away. Many others, however, become urgent through neglect: It's tempting to put important but not urgent tasks, like learning a new skill or conducting that safety audit, in the 'pending' file because there is no immediate consequence to not doing them. The truth is, most important but non-urgent activities that you do not attend to in a timely fashion eventually become urgent and you're forced to do them *now!* – whether or not it's convenient to do so.

Convenience aside, whenever you tackle an important, urgent activity, you risk rushing and making mistakes. Whenever an important and urgent activity arises, take care to compose yourself first, so that there isn't an air of panic about you.

Unimportant but urgent activities

How often have you jumped to answer a ringing telephone only to find it was a wrong number, or a relatively unimportant matter that took you away from a more important task? Urgent and unimportant tasks in the bottom right square in Figure 5.1 might include dealing with routine 'administrivia', some interruptions, some meetings and some telephone calls. They often have a short-term flavour. You can often delegate them or do them later yourself (although why would you do them when they don't contribute to your KRAs?). Some unimportant yet urgent activities don't really need to be done at all.

When you complete a task just because it's there, because you enjoy it, because it provides a convenient excuse for putting off other, more important or more difficult work, or because it's marginally worth doing, the result is the same. You fall victim to the 'tyranny of the urgent'. You've succumbed to Gresham's law: 'The urgent drives out the important.'[3]

When that happens a lot, you end up lurching from crisis to crisis while important tasks slide until they, too, become urgent crises. This makes for an uncoordinated, frenetic dance.

Unimportant and non-urgent activities

Apart from the odd break, ask yourself why you're wasting your valuable time on activities in the bottom left square of Figure 5.1 that don't really need to be done. Excessively 'prettying up' unimportant documents and playing computer games, 'pouncing' on emails the second they arrive, some on-the-job socialising, some phone calls, unnecessary paperwork – these can be excuses for not getting on with 'real work'.

Evaluate your tasks: 'That can wait, this needs doing'

Get in the habit of using your balcony perspective to evaluate every task's degree of urgency and importance as it comes in so that you can deal with it appropriately, as shown in Figure 5.2.

Many tasks that you think are urgent probably aren't and can wait; other tasks might be 'nice but not necessary' – don't let them rule your life. To find out whether a task really does have some time pressure or deadline attached, or is necessary, ask yourself:

* What would happen (really) if I didn't do this right now?
* Could or should someone else do it rather than me?

Answering these questions helps you quickly assess how much value a task or an activity adds to your job. You can decide whether you should delegate it or do it yourself now, later or not at all. That way, you concentrate on work that directly contributes to your key result areas and goals, automatically channelling your efforts into high-priority matters. These two questions put you in charge of your job and help you achieve your work priorities. (Just make sure your deferred tasks aren't holding anyone else up. Delegate or attend to any that are.)

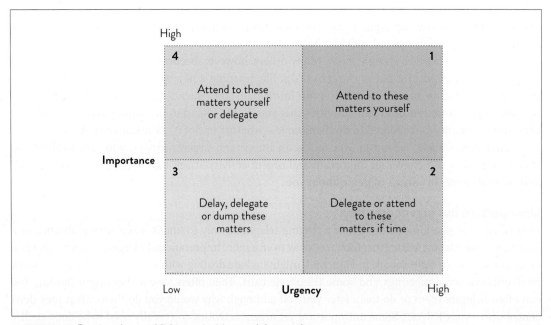

FIGURE 5.2 Putting the establishing priorities model to work

Types of tasks

No one can complete only important tasks, and ignore all the unimportant tasks. Attending to the occasional unimportant, non-urgent task can offer a needed break. Sometimes, you need to deal with a question or problem that won't, strictly speaking, move you any closer to reaching your targets but may assist someone else to achieve their goals. There are also tasks you need to do, such as routine administration, to 'keep the system working'.

The trick to the best possible achievement of your job goals is to find the balance between these three types of work:

1. *Manager-imposed work* is work that your manager asks you to do. Clearly, you can't ignore it. When your manager assigns you a lot of work, though, ask yourself why? Is it because you haven't shown that you can schedule your own work and determine priorities yourself? What kind of work is your manager assigning you? When it's unrelated to any of your key result

areas, think about discussing this, especially when the work interferes with your ability to complete tasks that do contribute to your key result areas.

2. *System-imposed work* is required by the 'system' (e.g. routine administrative tasks such as filling out expense sheets and customer reports, or taking a turn at tidying up the kitchen area). This work must be done, but when it takes up a large chunk of your time and stops you from completing your 'real work', think about how you could do these system-imposed tasks more efficiently.

3. *Imposed work* can be divided into two types: Discretionary and other-imposed. *Discretionary work* is work you choose to do, whether it's work that achieves results in your KRAs or 'busy work' that doesn't. *Other-imposed work* includes tasks that your team members delegate 'upwards' to you, as well as other people's work, for example work of other managers or your own manager, that lands on your desk. Other-imposed work is known as 'fleas': Fleas hop from other people's backs (where they belong) onto yours.[4]

Perhaps some of your staff or others you work with are unclear about your role and ask for your help with matters that relate to their KRAs rather than yours. Work like this can keep you from important work of your own and is usually better, and more properly, done by the people responsible for it. Spend some time on tasks to which you can uniquely add value. Otherwise, when people need help, show them how to do it. Don't do it for them.

● IN A NUTSHELL

Teach people to solve their own problems

When people approach you to resolve their problems, pretend you're playing tennis and return the serve. Ask:
- What do you recommend?
- What do you think we could do?
- What have you tried?

When they seem hesitant, help them think it through. Ask:
- What outcome do you want?
- What can help you achieve that?
- What do you need to do to make that happen?

● THEORY TO PRACTICE

Too much non-essential work?

If your manager or the system continually imposes work on you that doesn't contribute to your job purpose and KRAs, discuss the situation with your manager with a view to achieving one of three things:
- Adjusting your KRAs
- Channelling the work to a more appropriate person
- Fixing the system.

Use the balcony overview to improve your performance

Although your job purpose and key result areas are unlikely to change substantially, you may want to change a few measures of success every 12 months or so to give your efforts a slightly different focus. This helps you steadily improve your performance.

For example, you might be experiencing higher staff turnover than other comparable departments in your organisation and want to reduce it; you could set a success measure in your 'leadership' KRA of 'reaching a 90% staff retention rate by the end of the third quarter'. When you achieve that and hold the improvement for another two quarters, you might decide to concentrate on developing a successor and replace the success measure relating to staff retention with 'develop a successor by the end of the calendar year'. When you've done that, you would select another success measure that would help you improve your results further. This is how to make continuous improvements to your job performance.

Chapters 11 and 13 explain how to use this balcony overview to build the performance of your work team and team members.

⦿ THEORY TO PRACTICE

The price of nice

Malcolm manages the internal auditing section for a large firm. He is highly skilled at his work but he always seems to be rushing around trying to do several things at once. The result is that he completes few things on time or even well.

His leader-manager, Denise, recently pointed this out to Malcolm and suggested that part of the problem was his exceptional computer skills and sound business acumen. People from all over the firm constantly asked him for advice and opinions. Denise explained that she understood that Malcolm was happy to help and that the business benefited overall, but she needed him to be aware that, in spending so much time helping out other people, his own work was suffering. Denise suggested that this, combined with poor priority setting, was the source of Malcolm's apparently excessive workload and mediocre results.

Malcolm realised he'd better get on top of his job. He began using the A-B-C priority system (see page 10) to help him concentrate his efforts on his own priorities and to carefully think about requests for help in terms of his key result areas. He didn't want to let people down so, instead of doing things like complicated computer analyses for them, he began to show them how to do the analyses, providing written instructions, which he printed off from the program's help function, when necessary. He also began asking people questions to give them points to consider so they could work out the answers themselves.

At first, people were taken aback, but then they appreciated the skills Malcolm was teaching them. For Malcolm's part, between the hours he saved by not doing other people's work for them and channelling his efforts and energies to his own work priorities, he was soon back on top of his job.

⦿ FYI

The 80:20 principle

Vilfredo Pareto, a late 19th-century Italian mathematical economist and sociologist, developed the 80:20 principle, now often referred to as the Pareto principle, which states that a small proportion of effort, people or time (20%) accounts for a large proportion of the results (80%).[5] For example, 20% of salespeople in a sales team generate 80% of the sales; 20% of the customers yield 80% of the profits; and 20% of the employees cause 80% of the problems.

Are 20% of your efforts giving you 80% of your good results? Do 20% of your interruptions account for 80% of your wasted time? Are 80% of your efforts not providing many benefits in terms of achieving meaningful results?

Monitor your performance

The balcony helps you keep an eye on your overall performance and how well you're in sync with the other dancers. That's important because, no matter how skilled you are, one of Murphy's best-known laws of management is going to kick in: In any field of endeavour, anything that can go wrong, will go wrong.

Budgets change. Resources fail or are reallocated. Work conditions vary. However, when you are working to clear and specific measures of success for the key result areas of your job, monitoring is easy. You can identify variations in the quality of your work, spot tasks and processes going wrong and make the necessary adjustments.

Use the process shown in Figure 5.3 to monitor results. It involves three steps, although you use the third step only when your performance is below or well above expectations:

1. *Measure*: Keep the information you need cheap and easy to collect. You can keep the information you gather about your actual performance to a minimum but make sure that what you keep is key information. What you looking for are quick, clear, low-cost lead indicators that track how you are going.
2. *Compare*: How do your results compare with your success measures?
3. *Act*: Decide what action you need to take. When your performance is short of expectations, take corrective action. When it has exceeded expectations, find out why and take steps to ensure your stellar performance continues.

As Figure 5.3 indicates, monitoring is a continual cycle. (See page 505 for more information on how to monitor.)

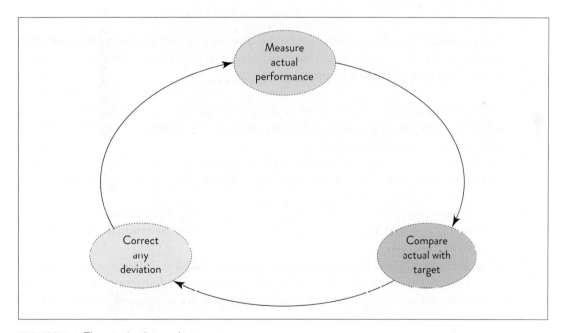

FIGURE 5.3 The monitoring cycle

Use a time log to check how well you manage your priorities

Keeping a time log for two or three days gives you an objective balcony overview of how well you are managing your job. It helps you make sure you don't let urgent, unimportant matters get in the way of important tasks when you're on the dance floor.

Time logs often show a lot of wasted time and frightening amounts of time spent on unnecessary and low-priority, unimportant activities that contribute little or nothing to people's key result areas. Equally sobering, a time log may well show that you aren't attending to some of the important tasks you should be doing.

● ACTION!

Try keeping the Time log template on *CourseMateExpress* for two or three days. Then analyse how you used your time in relation to the importance and urgency of each activity. You might be surprised at how you spend your time!

Here are seven questions to ask yourself about the way you work:

1. Which activities and tasks contribute to a key result area? In other words, which are *important* (squares 1 and 4 in Figure 5.1)? What percentage of my day do I spend on activities that directly contribute to achieving results in a KRA? (The more the better.)

2. What *urgent* activities and tasks do I take on (squares 1 and 2 in Figure 5.1)? Why do I do them? Does something or someone else cause me to? Or do I set out to do them? (The answers tell you whether you or circumstances are in charge of your job.) What percentage of my day do I spend on urgent activities? (Unless your job is to manage crises, doing too many urgent tasks indicates a 'crisis management' style, which is stressful and undermines your performance.)

3. Do I do a lot of *urgent, important* tasks (square 1 in Figure 5.1)? Why do I leave them to the last minute? Could I complete them more effectively by doing them earlier, before they become urgent? Does this indicate I work in crisis management mode? (Perhaps you need to learn to plan your work and stop procrastinating.)

4. Do I do any tasks that are *urgent but not important* (square 2 in Figure 5.1)? Could I delegate any of them? How do they end up on my desk when they do not contribute to one of my KRAs? (Perhaps you need to learn to delegate and to say 'No' to easy work and other people's work, and identify and work on high-priority matters.)

5. Do I do any tasks that are *not important* and *not urgent* (square 3 in Figure 5.1)? If so, why do I bother with them? (Working on your own priorities rather than 'easy work' and other people's work is the way out of this trap.)

6. Do I do many *non-urgent but important* tasks (square 4 in Figure 5.1)? (The more, the better, because this is a sign that you're in control of your job and concentrating on important, value-adding work.)

7. What is the overall balance between *urgent* (squares 1 and 2 in Figure 5.1) and *important* (squares 1 and 4 in Figure 5.1) tasks? (While individual jobs vary, doing too many urgent tasks can be stressful and a sign of poor work scheduling, poor prioritising and poor productivity management.)

'To do' or not 'To do'?
Which of these principles can best help you work more effectively?
- Set priorities based on important tasks, those that make maximum contribution to achieving results in your KRAs.
- Delay, delegate or dump anything that doesn't directly contribute to achieving goals in a KRA.
- Delegate work that you can safely leave to somebody else so you can concentrate on the most important aspects of your job that only you can do. This upskills others as a bonus.
- Don't let urgent, unimportant tasks override non-urgent but important matters.
- Set worthwhile (stretching yet realistic) SMART success measures and deadlines.

Work effectively and efficiently

The price you pay when you lack the balcony overview can spin your wheels: Are you working too hard, achieving little and paying the price in feelings of failure and stress? Clearly, working efficiently on the wrong or unnecessary tasks (unimportant tasks) is a waste of effort and time.

Standing on the balcony – using your job purpose and key result areas – helps you set priorities and work on the *right tasks*. This means you work *effectively*. Now it's time to dance.

To dance smartly, you need to work *efficiently*: To do things right – in the easiest, fastest, least costly, safest, smoothest and most reliable and streamlined way possible.

● THE STRATEGIC PERSPECTIVE

Just working, or working and achieving?
Do you work hard, and perhaps even efficiently, without getting results? That's just working. But it's results, not activity, that count. And to get results, you need to be both effective and efficient. When you're effective, you work on the right tasks – activities that bring results in your key result areas. When you're efficient, you work in a smooth, streamlined manner. Aim to be both effective and efficient, to do more of the right tasks in less time – that's how to increase your personal productivity.

2. Dancing smartly: Scheduling your work and organising yourself

> Never confuse activity with results.
>
> Lou Gerstner (CEO, IBM), quoted in Sellers, 'Can this man save IBM?', *Fortune* (19 April 1993)[6]

Now that you have your balcony overview, you know how smoothly (or feverishly) you're dancing. Which is it for you?
- Are you often distracted from what you're working on by a crisis or an emergency?
- Do you often finish something just hours or even minutes before it's due?
- Do you often lose something important on your desk?
- Do people complain that you unload last-minute jobs on them?
- Do people write 'Since you haven't responded, I assume ...'?
- Do you put things off until they become emergencies?
- Have you not looked at some of the papers or files on your desk for a week or more?

Answering 'Yes' to three or more of these questions suggests you need to find out how to dance smarter, not harder. Dancing smartly takes a bit of practice and commitment.

Keep a 'To do' list

How you choose to spend your working days may not be obvious or even deliberate, but you do have choices. Tending to tasks as they crop up, or attending to tasks as the mood strikes you, is a choice. Not a good choice, but a choice nevertheless.

A better choice is to invest 15 minutes up front developing a daily or weekly 'To do' list. No matter how good your memory is, you're probably far too busy to remember everything you need to do, and the sense of order and peace of mind a 'To do' list provides more than compensates for the time it takes to write it. You also have a sense of accomplishment as you cross off or delete items on your list as you complete them.

THE STRATEGIC PERSPECTIVE

Harried managers

You can easily spot leader-managers who fail to plan their work based on their priorities: They rush around, often trying to do several tasks at once, but actually achieve very little by the end of the day. They attend to whatever floats across their field of vision, whatever seems the most urgent at the time, or whatever 'makes the most noise'. Having fallen into the 'activity trap' and the 'tyranny of the urgent'[7], they go home, and when asked what they did that day, they can't really say. They feel harassed and stressed and worry about all the tasks they have left undone. Their jobs control them, not the other way around. They may work hard, but they don't achieve results.

A 'To do' list keeps what you need to do to achieve your goals 'front of mind', no matter how hectic your day becomes. This means you can work *proactively*, not *reactively*, which puts you in charge and lifts your self-esteem.

Here are some specific ways you can use your 'To do' list to help you:

* to establish priorities
* to group like tasks together, and do them together in blocks of time (which helps you work smoothly)
* to note down promises and commitments you've made so you don't forget them
* to plan your day or your week
* to remind you to do things
* to remind you to follow up on commitments others have made to you, tasks you've delegated or assigned to others and part-completed work, and to follow through on commitments you've made to others.

Make your 'To do' list work for you

List the tasks you need to complete, grouping them into four or five categories that represent major task groups (e.g. follow-up, meetings, projects and ongoing, telephone, miscellaneous). Add new tasks as they arise and cross tasks off or delete tasks as you complete them. (If you're using a paper-based 'To do' list, turn the page and begin afresh when your list gets too messy. Transfer undone tasks to the new page and put the date at the top for future reference.)

Grouping like tasks together into categories gives you a clear overview of what you need to accomplish and helps you tackle tasks in blocks of time. For example, completing several phone calls in a block of time, writing emails and letters in another block of time and reading your incoming mail in a third block of time gives a flow to your work and means that you don't have to stop and mentally readjust as you do when you hop from one type of activity to another.

Depending on your job, you probably need to review and update your 'To do' list at the end of each working day or week so that you can 'hit the road running' at the beginning of the next day or week.

Make sure that what you plan to achieve is realistic by keeping the anticipated time frames, available resources and your overall targets in the back of your mind. Try to balance competing work demands and build in a cushion of time to allow for unforeseen events, such as equipment breakdowns, impromptu meetings and technology problems.

When you are responsible for achieving results in a project environment – in other words, when it will be a lengthy period and many steps before your end results are accomplished – you may want to use a scheduling device, such as the Gantt chart or critical path analysis (discussed on pages 507 and 508). These also provide a quick and easy way to visually monitor your progress.

If you choose a paper-based 'To do' list, use a spiral-bound notebook, adding items as they come up and crossing items off when you complete them. When you find yourself transferring an item on your 'To do' list three or more times, or when it's been on your digital list for two or more weeks, it's a clear warning signal. Ask yourself why you haven't completed it. Are you procrastinating? If so, there's no time like the present, as the saying goes – do it now and get it over with. Or perhaps it's a low-priority task that you can delegate or drop from your list. Perhaps it's a big job and dividing it into smaller parts can get you started.

● THEORY TO PRACTICE

How to start the new day
Don't start your day checking emails or attending meetings. Instead, greet your team members and think about the tasks you need to complete and your team members need to complete.

Then pick a task you've been avoiding, maybe because it's difficult or dull, and do it. You'll feel good because it's behind you, done and dusted. Then you can get on with more enjoyable, important work.

Use the A-B-C method to work to priorities

Which items on your 'To do' list do you work on first? The easiest ones, or those you can 'knock off' most quickly? Maybe that's a good choice – provided they're important; when they're unimportant, it's a poor choice. Working on the easiest and/or quickest items on your 'To do' list all day may provide the satisfaction of deleting several items, but when the tasks that are left behind are the ones that move you most towards achieving a meaningful goal in a key result area, you haven't really achieved much.

The A-B-C method prevents this by setting priorities so that you can work on tasks in their order of importance. Here's how it works.

Pop up to the balcony when you're fresh and thinking clearly. Consider each item's urgency and importance. Think about what you want to achieve by the end of the day and by the end of the week and, with this in mind, identify the most important tasks, those that most directly contribute to achieving results in your key result areas. Assign them an 'A' priority. Any items that are both urgent and important are 'A' priorities too.

Which tasks contribute least to your KRAs and can therefore wait until you have enough time to do them? Assign these unimportant, non-urgent tasks a 'C' priority. The rest are 'B' priorities.

Try to get through as much of your 'To do' list each day as you can, concentrating on your 'A' priorities. That way, when you don't complete every item, it's the least important that are left. Don't ignore the 'Bs' and 'Cs', though, because many of them become urgent 'As' when you don't get on with them.

● THEORY TO PRACTICE

Step onto the balcony to decide how to deal with incoming work

When work comes in, even work that is seemingly 'urgent', ask yourself these four questions:

1. Does it contribute to achieving results in any of my key result areas? When the answer is yes, it's important, so schedule it in.
2. Could someone else do it? When the answer is yes, delegate it.
3. Must it be done now or can it be done later? When later is fine, delay it until it's convenient to attend to it.
4. What would happen if it weren't done at all? You may not need to do it.

This gets you off the treadmill of attending to whatever crops up by letting you consciously choose to do the most important tasks.

Clear your desk

Do you ever spend time looking for items that you know are 'right here, somewhere'? That's a sign you need to clear your desk and tidy your drawers. Too much clutter wastes your time, is emotionally draining and prevents you from concentrating.

Your desk is not storage space. There should be only three or four things on your desk: Your computer, the job you're currently working on, your telephone, and, if it's paper not electronic, your 'To do' list. This means that no other items can compete for your attention and break your concentration.

Clear your work area: Give everything its own 'home' and make a habit of putting items away so you know where to find them when you need them. Establish sensible electronic and paper filing systems and use them. Carefully name the files of information you decide to keep so that you can retrieve them easily later. The few minutes you spend putting items away and filing them makes it quicker and easier to find what you're looking for than searching a messy desk.

Spend 10 minutes at the end of the week to tidy and organise your desk. Evaluate any unfiled paperwork and electronic correspondence: Can you discard or delete it? Delegate it? File it? This way, when you arrive on Monday morning, only what's most important is on your desk waiting for you.

It's as the philosopher Ralph Waldo Emerson said: 'Finish every day and be done with it … You have done what you could; some blunders and absurdities no doubt crept in; forget them as soon as you can. Tomorrow is a new day; you shall begin it … serenely, and with too high a spirit to be cumbered with your old nonsense.'[8]

● IN A NUTSHELL

Pause and notice

Lots of jobs require people to fight countless distractions while struggling to stay focused. To combat that, before you launch into an activity, take a moment. Noticing what you are about to do rather than rushing in reminds you to appreciate and concentrate on the task at hand. For instance, when you sit at your desk in the morning, pause before turning on the computer. Take a deep breath and think about what you are about to do. The extra focus this brings may help you accomplish tasks more carefully and productively.

Restrict interruptions

If you're interrupted every five minutes or so, it may seem like you get your real work done in the intermissions between interruptions. If only it were that simple.[9]

Once you've dealt with an interruption, it can take another 25 minutes to re-establish where you were and regain your concentration … unless your brilliant train of thought has been permanently derailed. Much of the time, you never return to the original activity. On top of that, all those interruptions leave you feeling tired and lethargic, reduce your creativity and keep you out of your 'flow', as it's sometimes known, or 'flow zone' as we often say.[10] That's why management guru Peter Drucker reckons that 90 minutes uninterrupted time equals four hours of interrupted time.[11]

Limit human interruptions

You've probably tried the open-door policy and never had a moment's peace. To avoid interruptions and get on with some work that needs full concentration you've probably tried 'quiet time', 'time out' or even 'power periods'. That's fine, until someone needs you and they daren't disturb you because you're in 'quiet time', and their work suffers as a result.

With your team, draw up a scale of interruptions for them to use with each other and with you. The scale might be like this:

- Interrupt for important matters that require someone's specific input.
- When you need a quick 'Yes' or 'No' answer and maybe a few words of discussion, save up, say, five, and see the person then.
- When someone else would do as well as you, for example to talk something through or to provide some information that someone else or the files could provide, please go to that person or the files.

You can still use 'quiet times' – just keep them to an hour or less and, when appropriate, spread them across the entire department. That way, everyone gets some time to work on serious issues when they know they won't be interrupted. Rotate one team member (including yourself) to be available to field incoming calls and take messages. If there's a genuine emergency (unlikely), they can interrupt the person concerned.

So that your team members don't feel deprived of your presence, schedule regular one-on-one 'catch-up' meetings with them. Ask them to create a running list of discussion points, a summary of what they've achieved since the last meeting, and any problems they're dealing with and how they're dealing with them. Keep a paper or electronic file or list for each of your team members to remind you of what you want to follow up with them in the 'catch-up' meeting.

As with any new ways of working, sticking to them takes steadfast determination. Especially in the early days, don't permit 'backsliding' to the old ways.

Here are some other ways to discourage those productivity killing interruptions:

- Beat the traffic and get in half an hour earlier to work in blissful quiet.
- Cut interruptions short with a mental or written list of 'important' phone calls you need to make: 'Sorry, it's important that I phone this person now.'
- Don't sit facing the door or walkway; sit at right angles – this makes it more difficult for people to catch your eye and 'drop in' for a chat. Because your back isn't to them, your computer screen isn't either, and no one can come upon you unawares and make you jump through the ceiling when you're deep in thought.[12]
- Research shows that 40% of most people's interruptions are self-generated; in other words, you're nearly as likely to interrupt yourself as someone else is. Don't. When you're working on

something and a stray thought reminds you that you need to phone someone or check up on some information, don't stop and do it then. Write it down on your 'To do' list and get back to what you were doing.

* Steer the interrupter in another direction: 'The best person to help you with this is ...' or 'Could you send me that in an email, please, so I can think it through when I have more time?'
* Try keeping your pen in hand, poised for action, or standing up, or looking at your watch, to discourage an interrupter from settling in.
* When you want to concentrate, switch your phone to voicemail or ask someone to field your calls for 30 minutes or so.

When you need to deal with an interruption, make a note of what you need to do next on the task you are working on so you don't have to spend too much time reorienting yourself when you eventually return to it: Type it in a different colour on your word processor or write it in pencil or on a post-it note placed in the document in the exact spot you left off. Then take a deep breath and give the interrupter your full attention.

Limit technological interruptions

Think about the mental clutter and the time you (and perhaps your team members) lose as you deal with information of limited or no real value: Tsunamis of emails, instant messages, RSS alerts, blogs and Tweets written by bosses, colleagues or people at rival companies, discussion forums on your areas of interest, the latest banal Tweet of someone in your network, the corporate Intranet. Do you know anyone who would not agree that half of the information they receive is irrelevant and they never use most of what they keep?

Remove your name from distribution lists and RSS feeds that send information you seldom have time to read or no longer require. Automatically direct some incoming emails to folders and scan the rest for priority and subject titles. Read only the most important and delete the unimportant and unwanted ones unopened. Read the rest when you want a break, have a few spare minutes or hit a pocket of down time or a period of low energy.

Be bold. Ignore useless and irrelevant information. Switch off every alert for incoming communications and check them only when it's convenient to do so. Check those wonders of modern technology when you need a break so they don't end up your master rather than your servant. When you need to get work done, use Internet blocking software (e.g. Freedom or Training Wheels) to shut down access to the Internet for as long as you tell it to.

Tame the telephone

Don't be tempted to control incoming calls by leaving your voicemail constantly switched on. That's disrespectful to other people and wastes their time. You can use voicemail in blocks of time, though, to give you some uninterrupted working or thinking time. Leave a message saying when you are available to take calls and invite callers to leave their details. Resist the temptation to listen in each time the voicemail picks up. Return the calls so you don't get a reputation for being rude, unreliable or disorganised. You could also route your calls to the switchboard or a team member to give you blocks of uninterrupted time.

When someone calls you at a bad time, say so and arrange a time that is convenient for you both to talk, agreeing who will phone whom. This is especially useful to discourage known 'talkers': Explain that you're in the middle of something right now and offer to phone them back. Do so 15 minutes or so before the end of their day, or when you know they need to leave for a meeting soon.

To prevent lengthy calls, stand up. Your voice takes on a more 'urgent' tone, encouraging callers to be more 'to the point'. Standing also boosts your circulation and reduces fatigue. To politely end calls, say something like: 'I've just noticed it's 2.15 and I have to leave for a meeting in 10 minutes' or 'Just one more thing before we're finished ...'

Don't multitask while you're on the telephone. An alert caller can usually detect this and your split attention is bound to make you miss something important. When a clicking keyboard or random 'Uh-huhs' indicates someone is multitasking while they're talking to you, mention that it sounds like they're quite busy and ask whether they would prefer you to phone later.

Make several outgoing calls together and respect a person's time by asking whether they're free to talk. When someone isn't there, leave a message asking them to call back and saying when they can catch you at your desk. When you need some information, suggest what they do if you're not in when they call back: 'If I'm not in, please ask John to leave the figures with Deb.' (And let Deb know.)

When the person you need to phone is a known 'talkaholic', begin by saying something like 'Hi, I've got three quick questions for you,' or 'Hi, I'm in a bit of a rush but I wanted to give you the information you're looking for.'

When someone wants to put you on hold, say 'Fine, and please take down my number. I'm expecting a call and I may need to hang up.'

Avoid telephone tag by scheduling a time to talk next. When the person you need to speak with isn't in, ask when the best time to reach them would be or see whether someone else can help you.

Rather than relying on your memory, use a software program or the reverse side of your paper 'To do' list to make notes about what you want to speak to people about and the telephone messages you have left for others. Cross people's names off when they return your call and follow up anyone who doesn't get back to you. Make summaries of telephone conversations, too (remembering to note the date if you're using a paper-based system or if your software doesn't do this automatically).

Don't procrastinate

For some people, procrastination is a way of life. For some it strikes only at certain times, such as when it comes time to attack a task they don't particularly enjoy. For others, it appears in a particular area of their life, such as studying or solving tricky longstanding problems – worth doing, but often 'better' tasks that need to be done can muscle in.

If procrastination is one of your problems, here are some ideas to help you stop putting things off and get them done.

Break down 'big tasks'

By saying to yourself: 'I won't be able to finish this, so I'll do it later,' you guarantee that you won't finish anything. Don't be discouraged by big tasks and projects that require a lot of time and effort – nothing is particularly hard when you divide it into smaller jobs.

The 'Swiss cheese approach' is to break big tasks down into smaller, do-able chunks, and do them one bit at a time, in the 5- or 10-minute blocks between interruptions.[13] After a series of smaller 'attacks', all you usually need is one final 'assault' to pull everything together. Voila! Another big task has been completed.

Feel the fear and do it anyway

When fear of failure is stopping you from getting started, think 'chance to learn' instead. Embrace the opportunity – the only failure is not having a go. Or maybe it's fear of success that's making you dally and delay. If so, give yourself permission to succeed.

If it's a big task, is it fear of finishing? Some people drag their feet when they're coming to the end of a major task. They know they'll miss working on it and will have to get started on something else.

FYI

It's an age thing
There seems to be a relationship between age and procrastination. Procrastination seems to peak in our mid-20s, decrease over the next 40 years and increase again in our 60s.[14]

Find a reason

Examine your excuses and get realistic. 'I don't feel like it' isn't good enough. Motivate yourself with a good reason to do it. What's in it for you when you finish it? When you can't find a positive reason, try looking for a negative one: What will happen if you don't do it? When there's no good negative reason either, maybe it shouldn't be on your 'To do' list at all. Maybe you can pass it on to someone else or give it back to its proper owner.

Make a start

In physics, 'static friction' means that it's harder to move a stationary object than one that's already moving. The same applies to procrastination – once you make a start, the inertia of no movement disappears. Putting it off won't make it go away or make it any easier. However, taking the first step makes taking the following steps easier. It's easier to revise than create, so just begin: Call it a 'pilot' or test run, if that makes you feel better.

When making a start is too daunting, devote just 5 or 10 minutes to the task. Then decide whether to spend another 5 or 10 minutes. A journey starts with a small step, and once you've begun, the work often starts to roll.

Adopt 'Do it now!' as your motto, at least regarding important tasks.

THEORY TO PRACTICE

The magic question
When you're feeling harassed and harried and everything seems to be getting on top of you, ask yourself: 'What's the most effective use of my time right now?' When several things are demanding your attention at the same time, this simple question can be a great help in establishing priorities and keeping you out of the activity trap. It helps you decide what to do, not leave it to chance – to whatever is at the top of your in-tray or to the person at the other end of a ringing phone or the other side of an open door.

Make the most of your prime time

Everyone has their own energy cycle – periods when they are full of bounce and energy, periods when they are a bit flat, and periods in between. Use your peak energy periods for activities requiring careful thought and effort and try to avoid interruptions during this time.

When are you at your best? In the morning? Schedule work that takes the most thought, effort or energy then and avoid routine work, such as checking emails, until you've accomplished one or two important tasks.

Perhaps you 'come good' later in the day. That's when to schedule in some uninterrupted 'quiet time' to tackle a few important jobs. When you need to attend an important meeting first thing in the morning, have clothes, paperwork and so on ready the night before.

Minimise multitasking

Splitting your attention between several tasks, particularly tasks that require concentration or tasks that are similar to each other, creates a mental traffic jam in the prefrontal cortex of your brain, reducing your productivity by up to 40%.[15] The more work you have on the go at the same time, the more your brain struggles to keep tabs on all of it and the more you limit your available brainpower for each task.

Too much multitasking increases stress and can even reduce your memory and ability to concentrate for lengthy periods. Because so much is buzzing in your head, multitasking can also disrupt your sleep.

The truth is, you can concentrate on only one task at a time, and when you try to concentrate on more than one, you work more slowly and make more mistakes. That's inefficient, makes easy work hard and adds to your stress.

Rather than mess up several tasks at once with multitasking, work on one activity at a time and pay attention to what you're doing so you don't have to go back and fix mistakes. Try to complete it before moving on to the next task. Never multitask when you need to absorb and retain information, because when you multitask the brain only pops the information into your short-term memory.

When you must multitask, work on tasks that are so simple you could practically do them in your sleep. That allows your subconscious brain to take over and do them for you – provided the tasks are dissimilar to each other. When they're too similar – for example, reading and listening to sing-along music are both word-oriented – forget multitasking.

◉ ACTION!

Are you dancing SMARTly? You can find out with the interactive self-test: Dancing SMARTly, on  **CourseMate**Express.

3. Managing your career and professional development

In the business world, everyone is paid in two coins: Cash and Experience. Take the experience first. The cash will come later.

Harold S Geneen (former CEO, ITT), *Managing*, Doubleday (1984)[16]

It wasn't all that long ago that organisations planned and managed employees' careers for them. But no more. Do you know that the Generation Y-ers, born between 1981 and 1995, can expect to hold 20 to 25 jobs over the course of a 50-year career, with an average job tenure of 2.5 years?[17] As you may remember from Chapter 1, we have entered a new economy, and increasing numbers of employees fall into the self-employed 'Me Inc.'[18] category and hold down a portfolio of 'jobs' or contracts. Scary? Think of it more as the chance to be in charge of your own destiny.

You create and manage you own career, and, given the high movement of people between and within employers, the question to keep at the back of your mind is: 'What is the next role I am seeking either inside or outside my organisation?' With that in mind, you can strengthen the skills and experience foundations for your next move through training, assignments and developing the right networks. (For more on networking, see page 222.)

To run a successful career today, you need a range of new-economy skills, including:

- customer service
- effective follow-up
- goal setting
- the ability to innovate
- integrity-based self-promotion
- sales and digital marketing
- strategic planning and thinking
- teamworking
- initiative and enterprise
- self-management
- strong interpersonal skills
- cultural intelligence.

Some 38% of managers frequently look back over their career wishing they had developed new skills.[19] Don't let this happen to you. Manage your career so that it doesn't go the way of newspaper typesetters, telephone switchboard operators and typewriter engineers.

Management expert Peter Drucker offers three pieces of advice about managing your career in the new economy. It is up to employees, he says, to manage their careers and themselves, to develop themselves and to place themselves where they can make the greatest contribution.[20]

Robert Kaplan, professor of management practice at Harvard University, offers similar advice: Know what success means for you, take responsibility for managing your career, know yourself – your strengths, weaknesses and passions – identify and excel at the tasks critical to success in your job, and demonstrate character and leadership.[21]

The meaning of 'career'
The word 'career' derives from the French word for racecourse, *carrière*, which itself came from the Latin word, *carrus*, for wagon. In 16th-century England, career meant a short gallop at high speed, or a cavalry charge. The word acquired its current meaning, of a professional life, in the 19th century.

Your career vision: Money, meaning, or both?

You can earn your living in three ways. One is through a *vocation*, or calling; another is through a *career*, or line of work; the third is through *just a job*, working for whoever is employing you at the moment. Which way do you want to earn your living? When it's to be through a career or a vocation, your work needs to align with your values, interests and what you're good at.

Part of your life plan is a career plan that helps you live and work according to your values. This is how your work can bring you both money and meaning. (See pages 186 and 187 for an explanation of how to identify your values and set personal goals, and how to develop a life plan in keeping with them.)

Take the time to define what success means to you. Unless you know what you want, what you enjoy doing, what you're good at, what contribution you want to make and where you want to make it, and the skills and abilities you need to succeed, you can't manage your career. You're taking a chance that you can stumble into a job you love doing and which you're willing to do to the best of your ability.

Think about your skills and aptitudes, the types of activities you enjoy, the roles you want to undertake and the impact you want to make, rather than the jobs you want to do. There are two reasons for this:

1. Organisations are changing their structures and the types of jobs they offer more frequently. Targeting specific jobs may leave you stranded. Targeting roles that can energise you, make good use of your skills and aptitudes, and satisfy you by allowing you to have the type of influence and achieve the types of results that are important to you, offers a variety of opportunities.

2. The life spans of organisations are shortening – companies are coming and going more quickly. Of the 500 companies in the original Fortune 500 index in 1955 (the US' 500 largest companies), for example, only 61 are still in business. Only one company from the original Dow Jones Industrial Average of 1896 – General Electric – is still on that list, the others having changed names, merged with other businesses or split into component businesses.[22] The life span of your career could well be longer than your organisation's life span.[23]

Know yourself

To begin planning and managing your career and professional development, you need to know yourself: Your strengths and weaknesses, the ways in which you're smart, the skill gaps you need to fill, and the type of working environment and challenges that help you work best. You also need meaningful career goals regarding the role you want to play and the impact you want to make. This may sound like a lot of work, but it isn't when you think it through in the following stages.

Work to your strengths

You probably know what you're *not* good at, but do you know what you *are* good at? What do you have a 'flair' for? What skills and knowledge have you picked up or worked hard to attain? What activities do you most enjoy?

Everyone performs best when working from their strengths, not just avoiding their weaknesses. When you know your strengths, you can plan to develop them so you don't, at best, keep running in place and, at worst, get left behind by others who outperform you.

Ask 10 people who know you well – current and former work colleagues, family, friends, teachers and so on (the more diverse the better) – to describe your strengths. Ask in person or by email: 'What do you think I'm good at and can you give me one or two specific examples of how I have used this ability to help you or to make a contribution?' The answers will surprise you because a lot of what you do well is second nature, skills and abilities you use so automatically that you don't even realise you have them.

Here's what to do once you know your strengths:

*   Identify areas where you have *no* strengths, talent or skill – these are areas to stay away from. Don't waste time developing them, either, as you have little chance of becoming even mediocre.

*   Keep developing and improving your strengths.

*   Look for gaps in your skills and knowledge, where you need to acquire new skills and knowledge or further strengthen existing skills and knowledge.

*   Monitor your behaviour so that you avoid the trap of overusing your strengths. For example, if you're a good listener, make sure you don't listen when you should be talking. If being results-oriented is one of your strengths, think about whether you're oversupervising your team or being too task-oriented at the expense of considering people.

*   Put yourself in roles where your strengths can help you produce results.

- Recognise, and take steps to remedy, your bad habits. These may be actions or behaviours you do or fail to do that limit your effectiveness and performance.
- Redesign your job to include more of what you're good at and delegate tasks that leave you numb and that you find difficult. Make appropriate changes to the way you work, the composition of your team to cover your weaknesses and the way you spend your time.

FYI

Feedback analysis

Peter Drucker used a 14th-century technique called *feedback analysis*, which you might want to try, too. Whenever he had an important decision to make, or did something important, he noted down what he expected to happen. Nine to 12 months later, he compared his actual results with his expected results. He did this for 20 years and said he learned many surprising things, including the types of people he works best with.[24]

IN A NUTSHELL

How to compensate for areas in which you have no aptitude

If you have no aptitude for a particular task, then consider how you can deal with that:
- Cover your weaknesses by building a well-balanced team.
- Keep out of situations in which your weaknesses are likely to be continually exposed and your self-confidence eroded.
- When you are given a task that requires a strength in which you are underdeveloped, pick the brains of a colleague or delegate the job to someone you can trust. Better still, work with that colleague so you can learn from them as you complete the task.

You can't always avoid situations that challenge your underdeveloped areas; sometimes you must cope as best you can and learn to improve.

ACTION!

What are your strengths? If you're not really sure, complete the Strengths audit checklist on CourseMateExpress to find out. Then you'll know what roles to put your hand up for.

Know the ways in which you're smart

People's minds work in different ways. Howard Gardner, professor of education at Harvard University, identifies nine types of intelligence.[25] How does your smart-self operate? Is it:

1. *Body smart*: People with bodily kinaesthetic intelligence like to move and use their bodies in hands-on tasks.
2. *Music smart*: People with musical intelligence work well with melody, music and rhythms.
3. *Nature smart*: People with naturalist intelligence are keen observers of the natural order of things and are good at considering the broader principles in nature.

4. *People smart*: People with interpersonal intelligence enjoy participating and working cooperatively with others.

5. *Philosophically smart*: People with existential intelligence like to think matters through philosophically and from the strategic perspective.

6. *Picture and space smart*: People with spatial intelligence are good at watching and observing and working pictures and other images and representations such as flow charts and maps.

7. *Reasoning and number smart*: People with logical-mathematical intelligence (the traditional 'IQ') are good at classifying information, using abstract thought, and finding basic principles and patterns.

8. *Self smart*: People with intrapersonal intelligence enjoy thinking through ideas and working on their own.

9. *Word smart*: People with linguistic intelligence are good with words.

These nine 'smarts' are different ways of relating to the world and we all have them to some extent, in our unique combination. The ways in which you're smart affect what you're interested in and the types of tasks you excel in. When you know the ways in which you are smart, you have more of a clue to your strengths. (When you know what types of intelligences those people you work with have, you know how to work well with them, too.)

◉ ACTION!

You can work out the ways you are smart by using the How are you smart? self-test on **CourseMate**Express.

Know how you work best

Once you know what you're good at and smart about, you need to know how you work best, with others and with information. Then you can seek out career situations where you feel comfortable and can perform effectively. You also need to work out how you prefer *not* to work, because working in ways that don't suit you almost guarantees poor performance.

People work and perform differently. Here are some questions about working styles. Look for your own working styles and circle them (and think about the working styles of those you work with so you know how better to work with them).

- Are you a *decision-maker* or an *adviser*? Advisers don't excel under the burden and pressure of making decisions, while decision-makers, although decisive, often need advisers to help them think decisions through.
- Are you *practical*, down-to-earth and *present-oriented*, or *creative* and *future-oriented*?
- Do you pay attention to *facts* and *details* or do you prefer the *strategic perspective* and looking for *implications* and *possibilities*?
- Do you perform best in a *large* or a *small organisation*? Are you more comfortable in *hierarchies* or in *informal, relaxed structures*?
- Do you prefer to work *with people* or *alone*? If you like working with people, in what relationship are you most comfortable — mutual interdependency in a *team* situation, as a *leader-manager*, as a *colleague* or as a *follower*? Or do you prefer to be near people but working *independently*?

- Do you work best with *things* or *ideas*?
- How do you best grasp information and learn – by *doing*, *listening*, *reading*, *talking* it through or by *writing* it down?
- What kind of work environment do you perform best in – a highly structured, orderly and *predictable* one, or a hectic and *unpredictable* one? And are you happier in an *action-oriented* environment or an *information-oriented* environment?
- What sort of job structures do you work best in; for instance, *formalised and prescribed* or *flexible and ever-changing*?
- What sorts of time frames (for instance, *tight*, *flexible* or *generous*) and results (*stretching* or *achievable*, *longer-term* or *shorter-term*) help you work best?

Work to improve yourself and the way you perform, but don't try to change yourself because you're unlikely to succeed. Try to avoid work and environments where you know you won't be able to perform well. (To find out more ways to understand yourself, see page 209.)

However you work, make sure you have a balance between work and the rest of your life, whether it's through work–life balance or work–life blending. When you don't, you risk burnout (see page 1022).

Your career plan

Once you know yourself and how you work best, you're in a good position to take charge of your career and professional development. Decide the direction you want your career to take and list the options open to you, remembering that you can accomplish a goal many ways.

What types of tasks do you want more of? Less of? What do you want to stay the same? What do you hope to be doing in three years' time? In five years? The answers help you target specific roles inside and outside your organisation. Set goals that stretch but don't strain, establish some career milestones and target dates to aim for, and make a commitment.

Think about your personal needs and situation as well your personality type and preferred ways of working. For instance:

- How much *security and stability* do you need? Jobs with high security, such as accounting, law and medicine have high barriers to entry because they rely on specialised technical knowledge or qualification. This means that when only a few people can do them, the jobs are not likely to be outsourced. Low security jobs include customer service and support, IT and manufacturing).
- How much *personal contact* to you need? Do you enjoy interacting with others and forging strong relationships or are you more of a loner? If you enjoy interacting with others, do you prefer interaction based on, for instance, helping and advising, mutual respect and cooperation or just passing the time pleasantly?
- What *type of boss* do you prefer? One who gives you the goal and leaves you alone to get on with it, or at the other end of the scale, a boss who does your thinking for you? Perhaps you're looking for a boss you can learn from, a boss who will lavish praise on your efforts and achievements, or a boss who respects your personal life and encourages work–life balance.
- Do you prefer to stay in one place or get out and about? Different jobs call for different levels of environmental *flexibility*.
- How much *potential for fulfilment* are you looking for? At the other end of the scale, do you just want to work for the money only?

The answers to these questions are likely to change at different points in your career and life stage.

ACTION!

What sort of career and job are you interested in and suited to? Fill out the Career preferences assessment template on ·CourseMateExpress to find out.

Think of your career path as a lattice rather than a ladder. It may include a promotion or two (or even three). It may include one or more sideways moves in order to gain skills and experience in a range of jobs and tasks or to increase job interest. It may need a 'downward' move to learn something that is important to you, or involve jobs with different working hours or responsibilities to give you more personal time. You may want to incorporate working on special projects, standing in for someone on leave, contributing to committees or moving into an entirely different field. You may decide to stay in your current role when it provides you with the level of interest and challenge you want, or to develop your current job by adding to your duties and passing on duties that you've mastered and no longer motivate you to others.

Try to gain broad experience, technically and working in cross-cultural teams and in unfamiliar cultural contexts. Hone your ability to work with others in collaborative learning relationships.

Let your networks know what types of roles you're interested in. Follow relevant Tweets, join relevant Facebook groups and develop networks in industries you're interested in moving into; you can find people through social media and invite them for a coffee, join the industry organisation or engage with them in some other way. Then target a few organisations you're interested in and connect with people who work in them. Based on the 'six degrees of separation' principle, it won't take you long to arrange an introduction to people with authority to recruit people for roles you're interested in.

THE STRATEGIC PERSPECTIVE

Tenure thinking versus assignment thinking

In stark contrast to the 'job for life' thinking that prevailed from the 1920s to the 1990s, many managers are beginning to think of themselves as filling an assignment. When it's over, they move on. This assignment mindset began in project-oriented industries, such as agriculture, the arts, construction, consulting and sports. In these industries, people often joined for the duration of a project and then moved on to a different assignment.

Organisations may try to maintain the comforting tenure myth; after all, letting employees know that their jobs are finite may make them feel unimportant and damage the organisation's recruiting efforts. But the fact is, a growing number of leader-manager roles last three to five years. Then, for financial or strategic reasons, they come to an end. Consider building assignment thinking into your career plan.

Plan your professional development

Just as managing your career is up to you, so is keeping up to date – in your field, your industry, with management techniques and with technology. Adding to, developing and sharpening your skills and knowledge, and gaining experience in a variety of areas keeps you employable and increases your earning potential.

A career vision that plots the types of roles you want to undertake and the difference you want to make gives you a map to refer to as you journey through your career. It guides you to think about the additional skills, knowledge and experience you need to gain in order to achieve your career goals and decide how best to build your skills.

To create a sustainable career, strengthen your current value as well as your future value. Your *current value* is what you create for the organisation in your current role; your *future value* is based on qualities and skills like your ability to adapt to change, to creatively and innovatively solve problems, to learn quickly and to lead, and your willingness to tackle tough assignments, as well as the perceptions others have of you.

Include a variety of portable, adaptable skills in your professional development plan. Make sure your plan caters for adding to and building on your knowledge and strengths, filling skills, knowledge and experience gaps, and gradually rearranging or building up your job to make best use of, and further develop, your skills and strengths. Notice how others manage their careers. Find ways to make the most of your passions and extend your experience through assignments, professional associations, project work, volunteer work, and so on.

IN A NUTSHELL

Seven ways to assess your competencies

Competencies are the personal and technical knowledge, skills and attributes you need to carry out your day-to-day job tasks and duties effectively and efficiently and to move into future roles. To determine your development needs, assess your competencies:

1. Against your organisation's competency standards for your position level or the position you aspire to. You can also find competency standards at Innovation & Business Skills Australia (IBSA), or at your industry body.
2. Against the requirements listed in your performance plan or position description.
3. By comparing your results to your measures of success.
4. By observing others.
5. By feedback from your manager, colleagues, clients (internal or external) and your team.
6. From performance reviews.
7. Through personal reflection.

By now, you may have quite a long list of personal development needs. Which are most important for you to develop over the next 12 months to achieve and maintain a competitive edge and protect your employability? Select two or three high-priority development areas on which you would like to concentrate.

Once you have identified and prioritised your development needs, set some short- to medium-term goals and look for opportunities to build your skills and maintain continuous learning. Accept roles that are a good fit for your values, interests, personality, working style, lifestyle and attributes, and that can extend your knowledge, skills and experience.

Your initial learning and training cannot see you through the rest of your career; skills depreciate and need to be upgraded and replaced. There are many ways to build your knowledge and skills.

IN A NUTSHELL

Lots of ways to learn

You can build your knowledge and skills through:

- action learning, job exchange and job rotation, special and project assignments, temporary assignments and work experience
- asking questions
- asking other people for their thoughts on how you could improve your performance
- being coached and mentored
- delegation from your manager
- formal and informal learning programs: In-house, off-the-job or public
- internal and external training workshops, seminars and conferences
- general networking (for more on building effective networks, see page 222)
- joining a professional association or industry group to extend your networks and support groups, and reading its journal to keep your thinking and knowledge up to date
- joining physical and virtual learning communities and knowledge exchanges
- learning from your manager, your peers, your reports and others you admire, especially those whose strengths are different from your own
- online tutorials
- part-time tertiary study, day-release courses or self-paced learning
- participation in committees and advisory groups
- personal study (e.g. reading, e-learning)
- shadowing and acting roles
- volunteer and committee work.

Think about keeping a learning journal; reflecting on what you've learned, formally or informally, helps the learning 'stick'. You can just keep general summary notes or follow the format of the learning cycle in Figure 5.4. Keep a good record of the professional development activities you undertake and your significant development experiences (e.g. participation in committees and on project teams, shadowing and acting roles, and so on). It's a good idea to file samples of your work, too (avoiding strategic documents or trade secrets, of course). This could be useful when you're looking for your next job. Keep a 'smile file', too, with emails and thank you notes from bosses, customers and others complimenting your work, glowing performance appraisals and so on. (See page 886 for more information on learning and how to learn from mistakes.)

THE STRATEGIC PERSPECTIVE

Staying employable in a global market

Looking over your shoulder for career competition from people or technology doesn't do you much good in today's globalised, technological world – your competition may be in another hemisphere, totally out of sight, or just a glimmer in an innovator's eye. Here are five essential ways to nurture your career:

1. Be innovative: Technology can never replace innovative people.
2. Become a genuine leader: The ability to communicate a vision, set the pace and find willing followers practically guarantees lasting employment.

3. Keep learning.
4. Learn to be a skilful communicator.
5. Learn to work cooperatively and supportively with others: The adage 'no man is an island' couldn't be more appropriate.[26]

Learn as you work

Life can be so hectic it can be hard to take time to reflect. Yet taking time to reflect helps your career as well as your job. Reflection keeps you conscious of what you learn even from mundane, everyday activities and routine procedures.

Think of all the activities and tasks you have worked on in the past 24 hours: You may have calmed down a customer, developed or implemented a new procedure, problem-solved with a supplier, studied for an exam, trained an employee, worked on a project, written a report. You probably did some of these very well, some not as well as you could or should have, others in an acceptable or average manner.

You are undertaking activities and tasks all the time. You could do just about all of them differently and often better, so it pays to take the time to think through what you have done to see what you can learn. This helps you complete the task better next time, continually improving your performance. As Elbert Hubbard, the 19th-century writer, pointed out, 'The recipe for perpetual ignorance is to be satisfied with your opinions and content with your knowledge.'[27]

Develop a habit of thinking through the learning cycle shown in Figure 5.4. This simple reflecting process helps individuals, groups and entire organisations continually improve their performance by learning from their experience.

To apply the learning cycle, first select an *experience* – something you've done. It doesn't matter whether you were successful or unsuccessful; you can still learn from it. Then *review* that experience: What did you say? What did you do? How did others react? What actually happened? What was your thinking at the time? Try to review it as if you were seeing it replayed on a cinema screen, or 'feel' yourself doing it in your mind's eye.

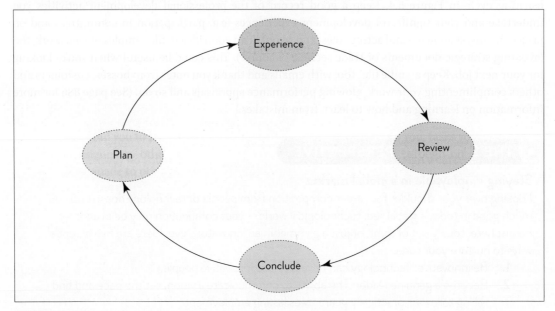

FIGURE 5.4 The learning cycle

Next, draw some *conclusions* about your performance. Be objective. What worked and what didn't work? What did you do well? What did you do poorly? What could you have done differently? Was your thinking correct? From these conclusions, *plan* what you can do the next time you're in a similar situation to improve your performance. Then practise what you've planned to build the skills and make them part of you. Look for learning opportunities in mistakes and setbacks, too.

Seek feedback

One of the most powerful ways to check your own performance is to ask others how they think you're doing. Colleagues, clients, your work team, your manager and people in your networks are all potential sources of valuable insights and information. Others can often see the details and effects of your actions and behaviour more clearly than you can, and make valuable improvement suggestions.

Think of feedback as information on how you're doing and how others see you. Make gathering this information an ongoing process because, as your career progresses, new challenges and different demands present themselves, and feedback helps you to improve.

You usually need to ask for feedback, and when you do people see you as genuinely wanting to improve your performance and build your skills. Here are some ways to ask for feedback:

* Can you see a better way to channel my efforts?
* Do you know of any other strategies I could use to achieve this goal?
* This is what I had intended; could I have reached that outcome more effectively?
* What could I do differently to be more effective in this area?
* What other ways of doing this do you think I could usefully explore?

Be open and receptive to what you hear, and show that you are. Don't deny, defend or excuse yourself, or blame others, all of which could draw you into an argument, stealing your chance to learn and improve and making the other person reluctant to give you feedback in the future. The person giving you feedback is probably trying to help you and it can be awkward or difficult for them too. Listen without commenting, and when you're tempted to brush feedback away, remember the words of Socrates: 'Thank not those faithful who praise all thy words and actions, but those who kindly reprove thy faults.'

Some feedback is bound to be accurate and useful, some of it less so. But all feedback is food for thought, and when similar information is given repeatedly, pay attention.

Sometimes, feedback is not delivered skilfully and it may even sound more like criticism than help. But don't discount it just because of the poor skills of the person providing it, because you don't like what you're hearing or because it doesn't immediately make sense. When you're doubtful, consider the possible motive of the person giving you the feedback. Consider all feedback carefully to see what you can learn. You're not obliged to take the advice when you don't want to.

Make sure you understand the feedback. When necessary, separate any emotional elements from the facts so you can respond to the useful information. Restate the feedback in your own words to check you understand it, and ask questions when you need to. For example:

* 'If I understand correctly ...?'
* 'When you said X, could you give me an example of that so I can completely understand what you mean?'
* 'You said the report was incomplete. What could I add to it to make it more complete?'

Thank the person providing the improvement information. Say something like: 'I appreciate your telling me and ...', 'I agree and ...' or simply 'Thank you for your feedback,' and commit to some change or at least to think through what they've said carefully.

IN A NUTSHELL

Receiving feedback

When someone is offering you feedback:

- Listen.
- Check that you've understood.
- Acknowledge positive feedback politely. Say 'thank you' – don't act embarrassed or change the subject.
- Don't argue, explain, defend or justify.
- Don't 'give as good as you've got'.
- Take the feedback on board and think about it.
- Thank the speaker for bringing the matter to your attention.
- Make any changes you feel are needed.

FYI

Feeling attacked?

If someone gives you negative feedback in public, move the discussion to somewhere private before continuing. Summarise your understanding of what they're saying and ask for improvement suggestions when you're still not clear. What does the person want you to do differently or suggest you do now or from now on? If the feedback is worded aggressively, avoid a disagreement. Move the discussion forward by focusing on what you can do in the future.

Find a mentor

Wouldn't it be nice to have a knowledgeable and experienced person to 'show you the ropes', teach you, encourage you, help you learn from your mistakes, advise you on career options and fill you in on organisational politics? People who do this are called mentors. They are usually older, more experienced people who take an interest in you and your career. They are not necessarily your direct manager or even from your department; they may work in your organisation or be a member of one of your professional networks. Whoever they are, they are people who can provide help, advice and support as you travel along your career path.

FYI

Some well-known mentors

In *The Odyssey*, Homer tells us about Odysseus, who was leaving for the siege of Troy in 1194 BC. He wanted to see that his son, Telemachus, would be well looked after. So he asked a friend to care for the boy and teach him, advise him and be his friend. The name of Telemachus' guide was Mentor.

Here are some real-life mentors:

- Aristotle, the Greek philosopher, mentored Alexander the Great.
- Socrates mentored Plato.
- Julius Caesar mentored Mark Antony.
- Thomas Edison mentored Henry Ford.

- Dr Taiichi Ohno, a developer of lean production, mentored Fujio Cho, who became CEO and president of the Toyota Motor Corporation.
- Freddie Laker, the British budget airline pioneer, mentored Richard Branson.
- Josef Korbel, the dean of international studies at the University of Denver, mentored his daughter, Madeleine Albright, and his star student, Condoleezza Rice (the first and second female US secretaries of state).
- The late Maya Angelou, the black writer and activist, mentored Oprah Winfrey.
- Warren Buffet mentored Bill Gates.
- Ravi Shankar, the Indian composer and sitar player, mentored George Harrison from The Beatles when Harrison began experimenting with the sitar and other aspects of Indian culture.

Some mentors are experts in their field and help you grow mostly in that particular area. Others are more like 'wise counsellors' who share the wisdom and understanding that the experience of years brings.

Although mentoring is formalised in some organisations, it is more often an informal, voluntary process. Mentors usually choose the people they help, so when you notice a more senior manager spending time with you and offering advice, listen carefully. (You can find out more about mentoring on page 905.)

⊙ THEORY TO PRACTICE

Finding a mentor

Would you benefit from a mentor but don't have one? You could be proactive and make the first approach. Look for someone who:

- has the life and work experience and skills necessary to help you deal with issues that concern you
- is a good listener – you don't want them to solve problems for you but help you uncover your own solutions
- is candid, so you get both the positive and the constructive feedback you need
- is well respected
- you can trust to keep your conversations confidential.

When you approach someone to be your mentor, make clear what help you think you need, and put limits on how much of the mentor's time you expect. Don't rush up and say, 'Will you be my mentor?'

Get a coach

Although people tend to use the two terms interchangeably, mentors tend to help you with your long-term career, often helping you achieve your personal goals as well as your professional goals, while coaches concentrate on helping you improve your current job performance.

There are two types of coaches:

1. People who are particularly good at a skill and help others develop that skill.
2. People who are not necessarily experts in a particular area but use a coaching process to help the people they coach uncover and develop their talents and skills.

Coaches can be from inside the organisation (internal coaches) or brought in from outside (external coaches). (You can read more about coaching on page 905.)

Think through your roles

Everyone plays different roles in different situations, acting out the parts required. Sometimes you're a leader, sometimes a learner, sometimes a caring friend, sometimes a fun friend. Playing a role doesn't mean that you are acting or in any way behaving falsely. Rather, it means you are behaving according to a set of concepts that defines, for you, how to behave in a particular situation. This personal set of concepts is called role perception.

Chapter 7 helps you to consider and set goals for some of your personal and professional roles: Boss, colleague, community volunteer, friend, parent, partner and supplier, to name just a few. You have a role perception of how you should act and behave, the sorts of attitudes you should hold, how you should dress and so on in each of those roles.

You develop your role perceptions by watching and reading about others (role models) in similar situations. The family you grew up in, your friends and the organisation in which you work all contribute to your role perceptions.

Many of the ways you perform a role are *functional.* They help your group or the people you're with to function more effectively. Some of your role behaviours, however, may be *dysfunctional.* That is, they make it harder for people around you to work effectively. How do you know whether you're helping or hindering? Feedback from others and feedback analysis are two excellent ways to determine how helpfully you play your roles and where you need to adjust your behaviour. (See page 98 for information on the functional and dysfunctional roles you can find in your work team.)

You fine tune your role perception to conform to the role expectations held by the people around you, to how they believe people should behave in a particular role. In some organisations, for example, managers dress very informally, while in others the expected dress is 'smart casual' or a business suit. Some organisations expect managers to be strictly task-oriented, while other organisations value putting people first. Your perception of acceptable managerial behaviour might alter when you move to an organisation with a different culture and working climate, and you might change some of your behaviours as a result.

Earn a professional reputation

Just as an organisation's reputation is priceless, so is yours. When you've earned a professional reputation, people listen when you speak and seek out your opinions and advice.

Your workplace reputation is built on how you walk, talk, dress and act, and on the results you consistently achieve. It's built on how you write, present ideas and behave in meetings, and on the character and leadership you demonstrate. It's the ribbon that wraps around your competencies and the value you add to the organisation.

Most organisations have a characteristic 'type'; people share similar ways of dressing and behaving. Who is promoted in your organisation? Whose ideas are implemented? Who is offered the interesting assignments? What skills, traits and 'style' do these people have in common?

Simply doing your job well isn't quite enough to forge a career, particularly in large organisations. Think about the image you want to project and make sure everything you do, say and write, including on social media, projects the image you want.

Show respect to people you come into contact with and remember your manners. Simple courtesies like saying 'Please' and 'Thank you' and knowing someone's name or asking after their family build a professional reputation. Manners help people work together effectively and engender cooperation and commitment. Ensure people can count on you for reliable and straightforward communications balanced with tact and consideration for others.

Try to be in the right place at the right time and build actual and virtual relationships with people who can help you in your career and who you can also assist. Demonstrate, by word and deed, your loyalty and commitment to your job, your department, your organisation and your customers.

Do more than you're asked for and deliver results and complete projects successfully. Have plans to streamline workflow and improve results, and discuss them with others. Build a team of high performers by training your team and team members well and supporting their efforts. Generate enthusiasm, build their confidence and self-esteem, and set and achieve high performance standards. Give credit where it is due and, without 'blowing your own trumpet', ensure that others know about your and your team's achievements, avoiding empty publicity that you cannot back up with solid achievement.

Look and act the part by maintaining a positive and professional attitude and dressing in the manner considered appropriate in your organisation for your job or the job to which you aspire. Blend your personal style with your organisation's culture so it is clear to others that you belong in your job.

Take care with how you present yourself online. Remember what you post is instant and permanent; even when you delete it, chances are someone saw it. What you write on social media needs to reflect your organisation's values and mission as well as your own. (If you can't do that honestly, you're in the wrong organisation.)

Keep up a professional profile on LinkedIn and similar sites and use privacy settings to keep private matters private. Think about separate accounts for family and friends and another for colleagues and other professionals. Be aware that when you post frequently, you can create an image that you're not working.

In short, to paraphrase Albert Einstein, 'Try not to become a man of success, but rather try to become a person of value.'[28]

And let's leave the final word to the early 20th-century playwright and entrepreneur, Wilson Mizner: 'Always be nice to people on the way up because you'll meet them on the way down.'[29]

Move on or fade out

In a working life that may last 50 years, you need to know how and when to change the work you do. The S-curve of change, where after a peak an organism or an organisation either declines or makes a leap to a new level, also applies to careers. At some point, it's either time to move on or fade out.

When deciding whether to move on, think about the balance between what you've contributed to your role (e.g. the improvements you've initiated) and what you've gained from it (contacts, employability, experience, skills). Think about whether you can continue to contribute to the role and whether you can still learn and develop in the role.

When you move too soon, you miss vital career experiences, learning, and personal and professional development that you need to succeed in your next role. In an ideal world, you move on once you have consolidated your contribution and your learning.

When you leave making a change too late, you risk 'rusting' – becoming complacent, working on autopilot and making mistakes. You risk curtailing your growth, learning and innovation, and you could end up occupying a role to which someone with a fresh approach might be able to add more value.

When considering your options, look for an organisation, a department or a team that trains employees and for a boss with a reputation for coaching and developing staff. Make sure the organisation has values similar to your own so you can work effectively.

● ACTION!

You can find out more about organisational values on page 51. To find out what you personally value, take Chapter 7's checklist: What do I value most? on ⫷CourseMateExpress.

When it's time to move on, tell your boss first. See out your notice period and complete all work as far as possible. Write a handover for your replacement, thank your colleagues and enjoy your last few weeks – but don't use them as a chance to slack off. Leave on good terms to protect your reputation and stay in touch.

Clarify your job purpose, key result areas and measures of success in your new role. Then aim to spend some time figuring out:

* how best to divide and allocate your time to different activities
* mastering new skills
* understanding what others expect from you
* your critical tasks and priorities and what you need to do to excel at them.

When you've done that, consolidate your learning and your performance before taking the role to a different level where you can make a unique contribution. That done, it may be time to move on again.

⫷CourseMateExpress

Go to http://login.cengagebrain.com to access CourseMate Express, your online study tool for *Management Theory & Practice*. CourseMate Express brings chapter concepts to life with interactive learning, and study and exam preparation tools:

* Test your skills in different aspects of management with interactive self-tests and simulations.
* Watch videos that show how real managers operate in real businesses.
* Test your understanding of the changing world of management by taking the revision quiz.

QUICK REVIEW

1. Explain how standing on the 'balcony' helps you 'dance smoothly' in your job and how you can use the information the view from the balcony gives you.
2. Explain how using the establishing priorities model shown in Figures 5.1 and 5.2 helps you prioritise your work so that you complete the most important tasks and activities.
3. List the three main techniques you use to complete your work as a student or an employee efficiently.
4. What does knowing the ways you work best, and knowing and working to your strengths and the ways you are smart, mean? Why are these important to know?
5. Discuss the pros and cons of managing your career thoughtfully and purposely versus letting it evolve.

BUILD YOUR SKILLS

1. Which squares did Richard mostly operate in? (See 'Theory to practice: See what's important from the balcony – or fail the dance' on page 115 and Figure 5.2 on page 118.) Which square or squares did his replacement managers seem to operate in? Explain your thinking.
2. How do you work best? How can understanding the way you work help you make more effective use of your strengths and compensate for your weaknesses? How can it affect the way you organise your job and progress your career?
3. You have decided you want to move into a different role within a year. List the steps you will take.
4. Find someone you know who either is a mentor or has been mentored. How do they describe the relationship? How did mentoring or being mentored come about for them? What do they see as the benefits of mentoring? Are there any disadvantages? Is all lost if a person doesn't find a mentor?
5. What role do you aspire to next? List the skills you need to develop in order to move into this role and prepare a plan to develop them over a timeframe that is suitable for you.
6. Referring to the opening scenario of Chapter 7, David's dilemma, on page 186, what advice would you offer David in managing his career?

WORKPLACE ACTIVITIES

1. Discuss three strategies you use to establish and work to your priorities and five strategies you use to organise yourself at work.
2. Print out the Time log on CourseMate Express and complete it for three days. Use it to a) analyse how well you are currently using your time to achieve your work priorities, and b) develop a plan for making better use of your time in order to improve your achievements in the key result areas of your job.
3. Briefly explain the 80:20 rule, or Pareto principle, and use it to analyse how you have spent your time at work or your study time over the past week. Then develop a schedule to improve your use of work or study time.

CASE STUDY 5.1

EXCITING TIMES?

Murray is watching the CEO's video address to employees around the Pacific Rim. 'We are facing challenging and exciting times,' the CEO is saying. 'Challenging, because our industry is in one of its periodic slumps and it's imperative we find, and make, a number of innovative improvements in all areas of our business. Exciting, because the company is developing a new computerised stock and invoicing system for use throughout the region.

'We all need to work smarter, not harder, by taking stock of the way we do our jobs and finding ways to do them better.' Then the CEO refers loosely to *Alice's Adventures in Wonderland*: how, in today's environment, if we're standing still, we're actually going backwards.

Murray knows that their competition is constantly seeking ways to improve and, if they don't improve too, they'll be left spluttering in the competition's dust. And he'd recently been reminded about working smarter, not harder, when he attended the company's time management course. The trainer said they all worked hard (and didn't he know it) and that she would help them identify how they could make their lives easier by working smarter. His mind wanders to the key result areas and measures of success he developed for himself on the course. He discussed them with his manager and, with a few minor adjustments, the manager agreed with them. Now that he knew precisely what he was supposed to be doing, Murray could see he had been wasting a lot of his efforts and energy on low-priority areas. The time log he kept prior to the course proved it.

Murray's mind wanders back to the new computer system the CEO is explaining and he decides to put some of the time he saves from working smarter (but not harder) to good use mastering it.

'Yes, these are exciting times,' the CEO is saying. 'I want you all to succeed in your jobs and take our business on to bigger and better things. I want you to be proud of your contributions and the company you work for, and the excellent service we provide our customers. I know you all work hard already and I appreciate your efforts. I mean it when I say that I want you to constantly search for better ways of doing things so that you can work smarter, not harder. Thank you for your attention. I look forward to a challenging and exciting year with you all.'

'Yes,' Murray thinks, 'it's shaping up to be both of those!'

Questions

1. Has Murray approached 'working smarter' sensibly? Now that he has worked out his key result areas and measures of success, what should his next steps be?
2. How could Murray increase his work efficiency in order to gain the time he needs to learn the new computer system?

CASE STUDY 5.2

ON THE MOVE

Now that senior management has shown its faith in her abilities by promoting her to lead the front-of-house team at the theatre, Jocelyn is determined to be the best line manager she can be. She knows her mentor from the personnel department, Sue, must have had a lot to do with her promotion. Sue recruited her to the theatre complex three years ago and seems to have taken a personal interest in her since then.

Sue is always friendly, never failing to take a few minutes to chat about the goings-on in the complex, plans for upcoming events, personnel moves between the departments,

● ● ●

and so on. Several times she requested that Jocelyn be put on working committees looking into various aspects of customer service and productivity. This gave Jocelyn a broad understanding of the workings of the complex and exposed her to people from every department at all levels. Sue also arranged for her to undertake a few project assignments in different areas of the theatre, and nominated her to be on the high-profile enterprise bargaining working group.

Jocelyn made the most of these opportunities, learning everything she could and contributing as fully as she felt able to. She tried to 'dress the part' when she was on these special committees and teams; in fact, she took her cues from the way Sue dressed. She was friendly and cheerful with everyone and made a conscious effort to keep up her contacts with people after the committees disbanded.

In this way, Jocelyn had gradually become known throughout the theatre complex as a cheerful, dedicated and hard-working employee who added value wherever she went. Her manager appreciated Jocelyn's efforts too. Jocelyn always presented information in writing, with plenty of facts and statistics, as she sensed her manager preferred information in writing with no holding back on the details. Jocelyn also made an effort to suggest good ideas and tried hard to motivate and energise the rest of the team.

When the time came for Jocelyn's manager to move on from supervising the front of house, there were ringing endorsements all round of Sue's recommendation that Jocelyn take on the role.

Questions

1. Analyse Sue's influence as Jocelyn's mentor.
2. Discuss Jocelyn's skills at building effective working relationships, strengthening her experience, skills and knowledge, and building her professional reputation.
3. Now that Jocelyn has been promoted to a team leadership position, what do you recommend she do in order to quickly understand the demands of her new role and ensure she meets them?

CHAPTER

6

BUILDING A STRONG COMMUNICATION FOUNDATION

OVERVIEW

Today's leader-managers need excellent people skills based on a foundation of strong communication skills. In fact, communication is a key employability skill. For good or ill, the way people communicate sets the scene for productive work or makes productive work exceptionally difficult.

As a leader-manager, you can expect to spend the bulk of your time in one of the four communication modes: Listening, reading, speaking or writing. Most of your verbal communication is unplanned, which means you need to think on your feet about what you want to say and how best to say it.

Poor communication is the most quoted cause of frustration and poor performance in organisations and is at the bottom of most misunderstandings, mistakes and problems, minor and major. In fact, poor communication causes more havoc in work groups, teams and organisations than any other issue. Conversely, good communication can unite a group of employees and help them work as a team, and it can weld the various parts of an organisation together into an enterprising, efficient and effective whole.

1. Can you recognise and overcome the main communication barriers that cause communications to fail?
2. Can you gather information effectively?
3. Can you give information effectively?
4. Do your body language and other non-verbal communications send the messages you intend?
5. Can you communicate clearly and persuasively in writing, following standard business protocols?

This chapter gives you the solid foundation you need to apply your personal skills as a leader-manager.

Talk, talk, talk

Mila studies the time log she has been keeping for the past week and is astonished to see that she spends about 80% of each work day 'communicating'. She communicates with her staff, her manager and other team leaders, with people in other sections and departments of the organisation, as well as with people outside the organisation. She communicates on the telephone, in virtual and actual meetings, in individual discussions and in interviews. She communicates in writing through emails and texts, reports and proposals and through social media … the list is endless.

Next, she turns her attention to the checklists she has been keeping of complaints and rework from her section. It looks as though communication problems may well be at the bottom of many of those, too.

Faced with the difficulties caused by poor communications and the massive amount of time she spends each day simply getting messages across to people and understanding the messages of others, Mila decides she needs to become better at this business of communication.

1. Overcoming communication barriers

> Communication is the conduit of leadership from the Prime Minister down to the leading hand of a small group of council workers fixing the roads. Leadership uncommunicated is leadership unrequited!
>
> General Peter Cosgrove (appointed Australia's Governor-General, 2014) 'Boyer Lecture No 3' (2009)[1]

To communicate effectively, someone – a *sender* – needs to express an idea so that someone else – a *receiver* – understands the idea in the same way. For that to happen, both sender and receiver need to weave through a multitude of communication barriers that, when not successfully navigated, can disrupt the flow of information and waste goodwill, money and time.

Most barriers can't be removed, so you need to accept them and learn to deal with them as best you can. Consistently failing to recognise and overcome, or at least put to one side, the many possible communication barriers causes tempers to fray, teamwork to break down and output to fall.

With every message you communicate, whether electronically or on paper, non-verbally or verbally, actually or virtually, you have three hurdles to overcome:

1. Physical and environmental barriers.
2. Barriers within receivers who sift, sort and often distort a message based on their existing beliefs and mindsets, their previous experience, and their understanding and interpretation of the signals.
3. Barriers within yourself.

How effectively you communicate depends on how successfully you and the receiver can overcome these barriers. Here are the top 10 communication barriers you can expect to face daily.

Environmental barriers

Even when you're in the same room, distractions, interruptions and noise can get in the way of communication, stealing your attention and making communication all but impossible.

When the communicators are not face to face, misunderstandings can occur even more easily because people can't see the expressions, gestures and other signals that help them interpret the meaning of a message. Distance also makes it more difficult to ask questions, check out meanings, convey confusion and establish rapport.

Incongruity

Imagine your boss says 'You did a great job there!' in a sarcastic tone of voice or while avoiding looking at you. What message would you take from this? A mismatch between someone's words and their actions or body language is called *communication incongruity*. Most people believe a person's body language and other silent signals over their words.

● IN A NUTSHELL

Six types of communication

Defining the six types of communication in Table 6.1 helps distinguish who is communicating with whom.

TABLE 6.1 Six types of successful communication in organisations

Term	Participants
Interorganisational	Communication between organisations (e.g. discussions with customers, outsourcers and suppliers)
Intraorganisational	Communication within an organisation (e.g. meetings or discussions between departments)
Intergroup	Communication between groups within an organisation
Intragroup	Communication within a work group or team
Interpersonal	Communication between individuals
Intrapersonal	Communication with yourself (e.g. to try to remember something or think something through)

Individual factors

Consider people's abilities and situations when communicating with them. For example, you may need to face a person who is hard of hearing and speak up or speak more clearly; sit down to match the height level of someone seated in a wheelchair; or speak clearly and a bit more slowly to someone with English as a second language and support your message with a diagram. Accommodations like these reduce barriers and smooth the passage of your message.

People from different age groups often have different values and world views from each other. 'Generation gaps' can make it difficult for people to empathise with and understand each other's point of view, which increases the chance of miscommunication. Similar gaps can exist when people from different cultures or backgrounds come together. (For more information on working with and leading people from different generations and cultures, see Chapter 26.)

Language

Complicated or unfamiliar words, complex sentence structures and long sentences can be obstacles to effective communication. Jargon (specialised technical terms or phrases) and slang can block communication when receivers don't know their meaning.

Some words are emotive, some are critical or negative, some are pompous and others are vague. Many words have several meanings, while others have different connotations or are open to different interpretations. Think of the many possible meanings of and responses to the words 'nuclear', 'order' and 'police'. The different emotions and images stirred by people's perceptions of words affect how they interpret a message containing those words. How many meanings of the word 'manage' can you think of? (The *Oxford American Writer's Thesaurus* lists more than 60 different meanings and shades of meaning.)[2]

Listening

People can usually sense when others aren't giving them their full attention, which is why poor listening creates its own barriers to communication. When you continue to jot notes or scan documents when a team member comes in with some information or a question, you're sending the message 'I'm not listening properly because I don't consider you or your message worth my full attention'. (See 'Gathering good information' and 'Giving good information' later in this chapter to find out how to listen well and encourage others to do so.)

● THEORY TO PRACTICE

Constant communication

If you want to succeed, then keep communicating. Table 6.2 shows you the many ways.

TABLE 6.2 Three types of message sending

Written	Verbal	Electronic
Articles and journals	Formal group meetings	Collaboration technology
Letters	Impromptu face-to-face meetings	Emails, texts and Tweets
Organisation policies	Phone conversations	Internet and Intranet announcements and messages
Proposals	Recorded messages	VoIP (Voice over Internet Protocol), such as Skype
Reports	Scheduled face-to-face meetings and interviews	Virtual meetings
Signage	Voicemails	

When you consider all the possible barriers to effective communication and all the varied ways people communicate, it is amazing that any communication gets through correctly.

Message complexity and quantity

The information leader-managers need to give can be complex, making understanding and recall difficult. Sometimes the sheer volume of information causes overload. When that happens, most of a message is lost and only the negative, first or last part of the message lingers in the receiver's memory.

Perceptions, prejudice and stereotyping

People evaluate and draw conclusions about what they hear and see in relation to their own backgrounds, beliefs, perceptions and previous experiences. Neuroscientists have shown that the human brain is designed to either ignore information that doesn't conform to a person's beliefs and expectations, or to twist the information to make it fit in with a person's beliefs and expectations. In short: It's natural for people to hear what they expect to hear, see what they expect to see, and think what they have always thought – whatever *you* may say.

For example, when employees think of management as the 'enemy', they are predisposed to disagree with whatever managers say. On the other hand, when they view managers as experts, they listen more closely and receptively. When managers think employees are lazy and irresponsible that is what they see and hear; when managers think employees are hard-working and do their best that, too, is what they see and hear.

Your own beliefs, expectations and prejudices not only filter and alter the communications you receive, they also 'leak' out to others when you communicate with them. For example, when you decide who or what is at fault for a missed deadline or a customer complaint before hearing all the facts, your closed mind cuts off any genuine communication on the subject and you can never hear what really happened.

People tend to rise or sink to meet others' expectations. When you think you know what a person is going to think, do or say because you've 'met their type before', or because people 'of that sort' are all the same, you communicate those attitudes and beliefs in subtle ways and you see the behaviour you expect to see, whether it's really there or not.

Stereotyping and prejudice can result in two effects that affect your ability to relate to and communicate with people and to the way work teams perform:

1. The halo/horns effect, which causes people's positive or negative opinions of someone in one area to carry over to their opinion of the person in other, unrelated, areas.
2. The Pygmalion effect or self-fulfilling prophecy, which causes people to 'live up to' or 'live down to' another's expectations.

Self-image

Your *self-image* is how you see yourself: bumbling or professional, strong or weak, eloquent or inarticulate, friendly or shy, anxious or confident. Your self-image is reflected in what you say and do and colours all your communications, as a receiver and as a sender. A poor self-image is a significant barrier to effective communication.

Status

Status, or a person's position in terms of influence and power in an organisation, can also block clear communication by preventing people from speaking freely to those 'up' or 'down' the 'ladder', offering necessary feedback and delivering 'bad news'. Some employees, for example, may be reluctant to express their concerns, ideas or thoughts clearly and openly when 'the boss' is around.

Time and timing

In today's slimmed-down organisations, people often don't have the time to communicate thoroughly and ensure they've made themselves clear. In their rush, they might give an incomplete, unclear, curt or poorly planned message. When you're pushed for time, it's easy to ignore the consequences of a message not being received and acted on properly and to forget how worthwhile it is to take the extra few moments to communicate well.

Poor timing can also cause communication failure. For example, you wouldn't explain a detailed new procedure to an employee who is just about to rush home and begin annual leave. You can overcome badly timed communications by asking for, or working out for yourself, specific times when your message would be most welcome or effective. Considering the consequences of rushed messages and poor timing, it's worth taking a moment to think through what you want to say and to select the best time.

THE STRATEGIC PERSPECTIVE

The growing challenge of communication

Paradoxically, a number of trends are making organisational communication simultaneously more difficult and more important. The number of full-time employees has decreased as many organisations have downsized, while the number of contractors and part-time workers has increased. Moves towards trading partnerships mean that relationships with customers and suppliers are more important, and community expectations are increasingly reflecting corporate responsibility and triple bottom line thinking. Never has it been more important for organisations to improve the quality of their communications, both internally and externally.

IN A NUTSHELL

Your role in effective communication

You are the link in the communication chain between your own and other departments in the organisation and between management and employees, making excellent communication skills indispensable. Your particular communication responsibilities relating to your work team include:

* Communicating the needs and requirements of your work team to more senior management.
* Ensuring that each team member understands their own, each other's and the department's objectives (explained in Chapter 11).
* Ensuring that each team member understands what the organisation stands for, where it is heading and how they contribute to its overall goals and mission (see page 49).
* Ensuring that everyone is able to carry out their duties by encouraging a learning culture and meeting team member's learning needs (explained in Chapter 27).
* Ensuring that everyone understands their department's and the organisation's policies, procedures and regulations.
* Establishing a climate where everyone feels free to ask questions, contribute ideas and challenge the status quo (explained in chapters 13 and 14).
* Explaining the organisation's changing requirements of its employees (explained in Chapter 22).

ACTION!

You can see how many communication barriers you bump up against by completing the Communication barriers checklist on **CourseMateExpress**.

2. Gathering good information

Nature has given to men one tongue, but two ears, that we may hear from others twice as much as we speak.

Epictetus (Greek stoic), Schweig (ed), *Fragments*[3]

Think of successful communication as a process of gathering and giving good information in order to achieve a goal. You need a goal (even when it's only to 'pass the time of day'). You need to know what's on people's minds; and people need to know what's on your mind. You need to be able to express your thoughts clearly and considerately.

Gathering good information is about asking smart questions, listening and sorting through the information you're collecting: Is it an assumption? A fact? An inference? An opinion? Temporarily set to one side your own opinions, feelings and thoughts – not always easy, especially when you disagree or feel strongly about a topic.

You use four important senses to gather information efficiently:

1. Your *ears*, as you listen carefully to the other person's words
2. Your *eyes*, as you observe the other person's unspoken signals
3. Your *head*, as you think about what the other person is saying (and not saying) and what might lie behind it
4. Your *heart*, as you put yourself in the other person's place to understand how they might feel.

Gathering information before giving it puts you in a position of strength because once you find out what other people already know, think and believe, it's much easier to give them your information or ideas in a way that blends with and adds to their beliefs and knowledge. This makes your information more persuasive and helps people grasp and remember it more easily.

Questioning

When you're genuinely trying to understand what the other person is saying and meaning, asking the right question tends to come naturally – with a bit of practice.

When you're asking questions to uncover information, facts and opinions, avoid making people feel like you're interrogating them. Ask your questions in a neutral tone of voice using neutral words, and show you're listening with attentive body language and occasional summaries to signal you're following.

You can find a list of the types of questions and when to ask them on page 940. Meanwhile, here's a rundown on the main types of questions.

 IN A NUTSHELL

Use your EARS!
Absorb and comprehend the information you're hearing by using the EARS technique:
*   **E**xplore by asking questions
*   **A**ffirm to show you're listening (e.g. nod, murmur 'uh-huh', make eye contact)
*   **R**ecap your understanding
*   **S**ilence – listen some more.

General questions

General questions are good for introducing a topic or highlighting the one you want to pursue further. They're usually open questions: 'Would you bring me up to date with the Cengage account please?'

Closed and open questions

Closed questions can provide facts: 'Will you have that finished by the time you leave for the day?' and 'Did you say they'd send the report in this week or next week?' However, they don't provide much else. When you want to uncover more information, ask an open question.

Open questions encourage elaboration and help you draw out the 'full story': 'What did you learn from working on that project?' and 'What problems did you run into?' and 'What's that new client like?' Open questions can be statements, too: 'Tell me about your new client,' or 'Tell me about your meeting with Jim.'

Open questions encourage people to give more than a 'yes' or 'no' answer and leave the way open for a range of responses, helping you explore and understand the topic at hand.

Both open and closed questions often begin with Who, What, Where, When or How. Avoid questions beginning with Why because they can sound critical and make the other person feel defensive.

 IN A NUTSHELL

Questions to avoid

Questions can elicit such valuable information. But they can also be a pit of snakes. Avoid these types of questions:

- *Coercive questions* narrow or limit the possible answers and can trap the responder into giving the answers you want: 'Don't you think ...?' or '... right?' or 'Wouldn't you prefer ...?'
- *'Gotcha' questions* (seemingly innocently) show up the other person's weaknesses or mistakes: 'Didn't you say ...?' (and look how wrong you were.)
- *Imperative questions* are really demands: 'Have you done anything about ...?' 'When are you planning to ...?'
- *Leading questions* imply the answer you're looking for: 'You won't have any problems with that, will you?' 'Are you just about ready to leave for the meeting?'
- *Multiple questions* ask several questions in succession, leaving the responder confused about which to answer: 'How did you get on with that assignment? Was everyone helpful? Did they give you the information you needed? Did you have any problems? Or did it go smoothly?' (A string of questions like this often ends up with a lame, closed question, which the confused responder answers, giving you little to no information.)
- *Sarcastic questions* mask what you really want to say, but the 'sting in the tail' gives it away: 'Did you have trouble with your car again?' (to someone late for work or a meeting, when what you really mean is 'Why are you late again?')
- *Screened questions* ask for the other person's opinion in the hope that it is the same as yours: 'What do you think we should do first?' 'What are your plans?'
- *Set-up questions* set people up only for you to whack them down: 'Do you agree that time-keeping is important?' ('Yes, of course') 'Then can you please arrive on time in future?' (This example uses two leading questions.)[4]

Clarifying questions

When you are unsure about what someone is saying, ask a clarifying question: 'Les, when you said you're behind schedule, can I check how much behind schedule you are?' 'Carole, when you said you didn't think Mary was the right person for this assignment, can I ask in which particular way or ways you think Mary is unsuited?' Most people want to make themselves clear and appreciate your efforts to understand.

Clarifying questions can help you clear up cloudy information. For example:

- *Hazy generalisations* such as 'Everyone knows …' ('Who is "everyone"?') or 'They all say …' ('Who are "they"?')
- *Meaningless comparisons* such as 'That's the biggest botch-up I've ever seen!' ('Can you run through precisely what is wrong with it?')
- *Vague comments* or *ambiguous words* such as 'I want a more interesting assignment.' ('What would a more interesting assignment involve?' or 'What would make an assignment more interesting for you?')

Probing questions

Probing questions help you delve deeper into a topic. They encourage the responder to flesh out the details: 'Sam, you mentioned you were having problems with finding that information. What avenues have you tried already?'

Unspoken questions

You're probably familiar with the raised eyebrow, the slight leaning forward, the 'Uhmmm?', which say 'Tell me more'. A short silence is another invitation to continue. So is repeating the last few words the other person has just said, or a key phrase they've used.

Listening

Some managers, especially inexperienced managers, think that talking, rather than listening, is the way to go. Having not yet learned the power of listening, they mistakenly think that being the person doing the talking puts them in charge. But they're wrong. Most experienced leader-managers spend more time gathering information than giving it (about 30% of their day talking and 60% listening).[5]

ACTION!

How good are your listening skills? You can find out with the checklist: Do you listen well? on *CourseMateExpress*.

Listen attentively

You can't build a relationship with people without listening to them. Genuine listening is one of the finest compliments you can pay someone. When you listen to others, others listen to you, you learn more and make fewer mistakes. Listening is about trying to understand how other people see situations and events, what the real meaning of their message is and what lies behind it. This can be hard work.

Consider this: When you listen hard and concentrate, with your eyes and heart and mind as well as your ears, your blood pressure, body temperature and pulse rate all increase; these same physiological changes occur when you run a marathon.

Listening well doesn't just take energy. It also takes effort, patience and practice and a genuine desire to build empathy and understanding. True listening may not be easy, but the results are well worth it.

Show you're listening

Nobody likes talking to brick walls. When you are really listening, your body language shows the speaker that you're paying attention, encouraging them to give even more information.

Looking at the speaker and repeating or rephrasing key words or phrases the speaker has used, and nodding your head in appropriate places, show you're following the speaker. Leaning slightly forward and making soft 'uh-huh' sounds are two more ways to show you're listening. Known as acknowledgement listening, this helps you listen better and encourages the speaker to continue without disrupting their flow.

Concentrate on what you're hearing

Since we can think three to four times faster than people speak, it's tempting to let your thoughts wander. Instead, use that 'free mental time' to look at the speaker, observe their body language and concentrate on what you're hearing. When you let your eyes wander around the room, or stare at the floor or out of the window, your mind wanders, too, and you miss the opportunity to pick up more about the meaning behind the words.

When you're not sure you fully understand what someone is saying, ask some questions. Clarify generalisations, jargon, meaningless comparisons and vagueness to make sure you understand the speaker. Help people to be specific and encourage them to fill you in on the details and other information you need.

As Figure 6.1 shows, you can listen for key ideas and supporting information, such as facts, feelings, intentions and opinions. Listen 'between the lines' for what might lie beneath a speaker's words, too. This helps you analyse what you're hearing.

For example, an employee may tell you she has been offered a 'better job', yet after discussing it, you learn that the job she is considering is at a similar level of responsibility, with only slightly higher pay. The real difference seems to be that the new job offers her more scope to try out new ideas and this may lead you to conclude that by offering more creative opportunities, you could retain a valuable employee.

Jotting down notes of key points can help you concentrate and understand more fully. This is because most people take in information best through their eyes (70–90% of everything that gets into the brain enters through the eyes[6] while as little as 10% goes in through the ears. Mental or written notes in words, symbols or drawings keep your mind 'on track' and help you summarise what the speaker is saying and remember the main points of the message. (Don't write down all the details, though – this stops you from listening.)

Summarise often

To truly communicate, you need to 'send back' what you've heard – but count silently to three first, to make sure the other person has really finished speaking.

Recapping, or summarising what the speaker has said, is a great way to confirm your understanding and keep the discussion flowing smoothly. You can repeat a key word or phrase or put the gist of what the speaker has said in your own words, without agreeing or disagreeing with it, and without adding your own experiences, feelings, ideas or thoughts.

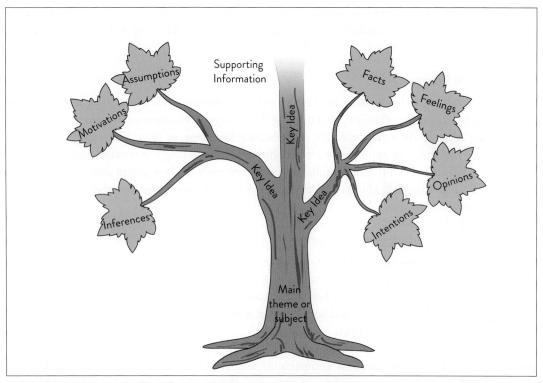

FIGURE 6.1 How to listen effectively

Summarising is perfect when you want to:

- disagree, but first, show you have heard and understood the speaker's viewpoint by summarising it
- find out what somebody really means but don't want to ask outright
- provide feedback about whether, or how fully, you have understood.

Summarising your understanding of the discussion every once in a while also:

- encourages the speaker to continue
- helps draw out the full story
- helps you concentrate on what the speaker is saying without letting your own thoughts get in the way
- prevents or minimises misunderstanding by giving the speaker a chance to correct or clarify any points you haven't fully understood.

◉ ACTION!

Do you think you listen well? Really? See if you fall prey to any of the Poor listening habits listed in the checklist of the same name on **⁊CourseMateExpress**.

Reflective listening

You can take summarising a stage further, to reflective listening (also known as *active listening*). When someone is talking about a personal matter or problem, and you can hear emotion in their voice, you can summarise either their meaning or feelings, or both. This has six main benefits. It:

1. Defuses emotion by showing the other person that you have heard what they said.
2. Helps people explore their feelings and thoughts.

   3. Helps you 'read between the lines'.
   4. Helps you understand and empathise, even when you don't agree with the speaker.
   5. Reassures the speaker that you are listening with an open mind.
   6. Shows that you are listening and trying to understand, which provides an incentive to continue communicating with you, now and in the future.

Briefly summarise the speaker's meaning and/or feelings with a statement, rather than a question. You can either repeat a key word or phrase or put it into your own words (keeping the meaning the same). When you haven't got it exactly right, the speaker can easily correct you.

When the speaker expresses several feelings, reflect the last one because that's usually the most accurate. Use objective words and a neutral tone of voice to avoid sounding judgemental or disapproving, and 'soften' your summary with phrases such as:

   • 'You feel ...'
   • 'You think ...'
   • 'It seems to you ...'
   • 'You sound as though ...'
   • 'You look ...'
   • 'It must be ...'
   • 'If I were you, I'd feel like ...'

When summarising or giving a reflective listening response, pause to let the speaker think about what you've said. Don't rush to fill a thoughtful silence with chatter.

● THEORY TO PRACTICE

Reflective listening responses: Feelings and meanings

When one of your team members reacts with frustration, how do you respond? Here are some suggestions for you to try in the right-hand column of Table 6.3.

TABLE 6.3 Strong words need reflective listening

Speaker	Listener
'I'm so fed up I could scream! I'll never get through all this in time.'	'It sounds like you're feeling snowed under.' (feelings) or 'You've got a lot to do and it seems like you'll never get it finished.' (meaning)
'Don't you have anything better to do than pick on me?'	'It sounds like you think I'm being unfair to you.' (feelings) or 'You'd prefer to do it the usual way.' (meaning)
'That way is no good – I'll do it my way!'	'You seem annoyed that I'm suggesting a different way to do that.' (feelings) or 'You feel a different approach won't work.' (meaning)
'Work, work, work and never a word of thanks. They treat us like cattle around here!'	'It's discouraging when no one seems to recognise all the hard work you put in.' (feelings and meaning)
'I'm loving my job; it's worked out better than I ever hoped it would.'	'You must be feeling really pleased with the way things have turned out.' (feelings) or 'Sounds like you're really glad you made the move.' (meaning)

Analysing information

Use the four Fs to help you think information through. Facts are facts, and managers deal with fewer of them than you might think. Many an expensive and embarrassing decision has been made by treating underlying assumptions, information and opinions as facts and many a conflict has flared for the same reason.

A lot of information people present is *fantasy*, or their opinion; you may want to take it into consideration, but don't treat it as fact. *Folklore* is based on hearsay, gossip or the rumour mill. As you probably know, most of it is fiction and should be treated as such (although it doesn't hurt to be tuned in).

Feelings have a place in organisations – after all, organisations are made up of people and people have feelings. Some feelings are useful: Intuition – hunches and gut feelings – can offer useful information, and with the world becoming more confusing and complex, your sixth sense can be important. People's emotions, whether they are happy, sad, angry, motivated or uneasy, provide useful information, too. You also need to take feelings of the ego kind into account, although these are far less helpful than intuition or emotions. If you've ever seen someone backed into a corner and forced to save face or act macho, you've seen unhelpful ego feelings at work.

Also consider what motivations, or intentions, might be behind people's communications. When in doubt, ask the other person to make their thinking process clear: 'What leads you to conclude that?'

IN A NUTSHELL

The four Fs and six tips for using them

Good communication can be further improved by using the four Fs:
- **F**act: Is this an indisputable fact that everyone would accept?
- **F**antasy: Is this someone's opinion?
- **F**olklore: Is this hearsay, gossip or rumour?
- **F**eelings: Is this someone's intuition, ego or emotion?

And when you speak, use these six tips to make sure you are clear that what you're saying is true and to think through what others say:

1. Get in the habit of checking to make sure any ideas, information or opinions you are accepting or putting forward as facts really are facts.
2. When you offer an opinion, state that it is your opinion so it doesn't come across as a fact.
3. Don't spread folklore (but listen to it for the insights it can provide).
4. Acknowledge and deal with feelings; listen to hunches and guard against ego-driven communications.
5. When someone is telling you something, listen carefully and ask questions to distinguish between fact, fantasy, folklore and feelings.
6. When in doubt, ask the other person to make their thinking process clear: 'What other factors have you considered?' 'Where did you get that information?' Think about what might be their motive for saying that.

3. Giving good information

To speak, and to speak well, are two things. A fool may talk, but a wise man speaks.

Ben Jonson (dramatist), *Discoveries Made upon Men and Matter and Some Poems* (1892)[7]

Have you communicated once you've told someone something? Maybe you have, maybe you haven't. Talking doesn't always make for successful communication. The truth is that what you mean to say isn't what matters. What matters is the message others receive. When the two are the same, *intended* communication takes place. When the message received is not the same as the message you tried to send, *unintended* communication, or *miscommunication*, occurs.

Once you have gathered information from the receiver and know what you want to communicate you can present your message clearly and persuasively, tailoring it to blend with what the receiver already knows, thinks and believes. This helps the receiver decode, or interpret, your message more easily and in the way you intended (see Figure 6.2).

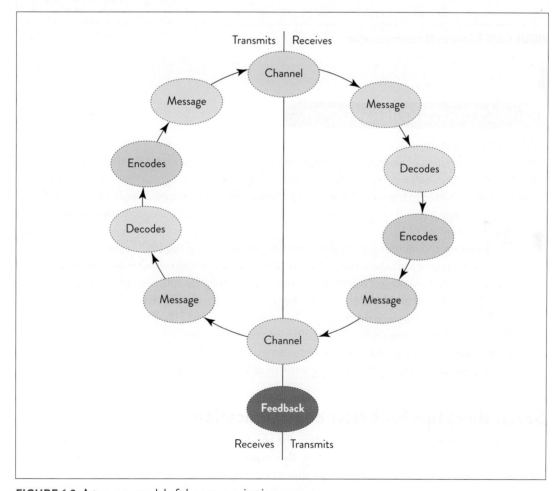

FIGURE 6.2 A two-way model of the communication process

As Figure 6.3 shows, your facial expressions, gestures, tone of voice, and often drawings and other symbols, are also part of your messages.

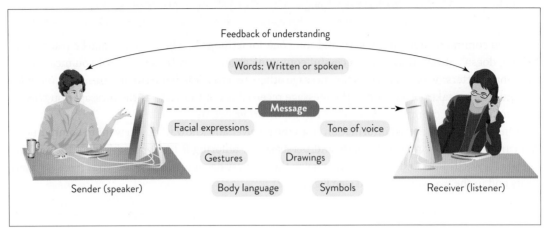

FIGURE 6.3 Elements of communication

THE STRATEGIC PERSPECTIVE

Choosing channels

An international study of workplace communication found that the average Australian manager spends 135 minutes a day in face-to-face meetings, longer than managers in any of the other five countries covered in the study (Hong Kong, New Zealand, Singapore, the UK and the USA). Australian managers spend 122 minutes a day on email, second only to Singaporean managers who spend an average of 133 minutes.

For delivering and receiving general information, about 40% of the 1400 senior and middle managers surveyed used email and about the same percentage chose meetings. How do managers prefer to communicate important messages? Two-thirds opted for a face-to-face meeting, 21% preferred email and only 6% preferred the telephone. The managers were even more in favour of face-to-face meetings for delivering good news (71%) and bad news (81%).

The study did give some credence to the horror stories occasionally reported in the media about employees receiving notice of their redundancy by email. The study showed that 10% of managers surveyed actually opted for using email to deliver bad news.[8]

Seven short tips for better communication

There's no such thing as a casual conversation for any leader-manager – employees repeat, dissect and interpret everything leader-managers say. This is just as true of the CEO's words spoken to the entire organisation as your words spoken to one or two employees at the water cooler.

Be positive

Which would you rather hear: The killer phrases on the left of Table 6.4, or the igniter phrases on the right?

TABLE 6.4 Positive words make positive results

Killer phrases	Igniter phrases
'That won't work.'	'That might work if ...'
'That's wrong.'	'You're making great progress; try it like this – you'll find it easier.'
'Just put it over there for now.'	'You're finished? That's great! Thanks very much!'
'Where'd you get that idea?'	'That's an interesting idea – I wonder how we could make it work.'
'We haven't got the time.'	'Time might be a problem – let's see how we could get around it.'
'We've never done it like that.'	'Let's give it a go and see whether it makes the job easier or faster.'
'It isn't in the budget.'	'Let's test it out, and if it works well we can find a way to get the funds.'

Chunk it and repeat it

Give information in small chunks because people can only remember about seven pieces of information at a time. This makes frequent communications on single topics generally more effective than one big 'hit' of information.

Repetition helps your messages sink in. There are lots of subtle but effective ways to repeat a message. For example, you can use more than one channel of communication, such as confirming a telephone call with an email, or you can use different words, different expressions or different examples. Choose the number and type of repetitions to suit the other person's background and experience and the complexity and nature of the message.

Manage your expectations

When you treat people in a way that shows you expect the best of them, thanks to the Pygmalion effect, they generally give their best. (On the other hand, when you indicate, even subtly, that you don't expect much from someone, you generally get that, too, because you have created a self-fulfilling prophecy.)

Select the location

When possible, talk somewhere that encourages open communication. Talking over problems in a quiet area, free from noise and distractions, is much easier than trying to discuss difficulties in a noisy office, in the hustle and bustle of a busy shop floor or 'on the run'. Try talking in the lunch area or going for a short walk to make communication flow more easily. You may not always be able to choose the best spot to talk, but try to choose a suitable location whenever you can.

Think it through first

Have you ever opened your mouth only to insert a foot? Once you've said something badly – used a poor choice of words, given a bad example, delivered an order instead of making a request – you can't take it back. The more important or complex your message is, the more you benefit from thinking it through first.

Think about what you want to say and how to say it. Think about the words you want to use. Speak (and write) to be understood, not to impress. Use plain English to avoid the jargon barrier. Simple, clear language goes a long way towards achieving understanding.

● IN A NUTSHELL

The six Cs of communication
These six keywords add up to clear communication. Try them:
1. Is it clear?
2. Is it complete?
3. Is it concise?
4. Is it concrete?
5. Is it correct?
6. Is it courteous?

Use empathy

Native Americans have a saying that explains empathy: To truly understand another, we must walk a mile in their moccasins. And before we can walk in another's moccasins, we must first take off our own.

To put yourself in another's shoes means understanding how that person feels. This doesn't mean you have to agree. Your goal is to see a situation as the other person sees it. Ask yourself: 'What must it be like for this person? What might be their feelings, opinions, desires, concerns and attitudes? How would I feel if I were in their position?'

Empathy helps you understand the possible effects that your communication could have. Empathy helps you coach, offer feedback and provide other information so it is well received, understood and acted on.

● ACTION!

How well do you communicate? Take the interactive self-test of the same name on CourseMateExpress and find out.

Watch and ask for feedback

Because face-to-face communication permits immediate feedback, it's usually a more reliable way to transmit ideas and information. This is why so much business communication is spoken (and often followed up in writing for confirmation or for future reference).

Talking directly with people allows you to ask questions and clear up any misunderstandings. The opportunity to observe body language can give you clues about how well someone has understood your message and can help you understand what the other person is saying. Look for non-verbal signs of agreement, disagreement, confusion, hesitation, lack of understanding or surprise. Listen to people's tone of voice, which can indicate their degree of agreement, commitment and understanding and can reveal otherwise hidden thoughts.

Encourage questions and comments. Questions can clear up confusion and help you assess whether you have communicated clearly. Establishing an atmosphere that encourages two-way communication helps people to add to, build on or disagree with your ideas, and present alternative ideas. Since unspoken opposition and concerns usually grow and cultivate resentment, it's better to discuss them early on and reach an understanding.

> ### ◉ THEORY TO PRACTICE
>
> **Encouraging questions and understanding**
> The way you ask questions is important. When you ask a closed question, such as 'Do you understand?', the response is likely to be 'Yes' to avoid looking stupid. It's better to use an open questions to encourage a full response. Say something like 'What else can I tell you?' The response lets you hear for yourself whether you have communicated successfully.
>
> When someone hasn't understood fully, take responsibility for not communicating fully or clearly. Rephrase your message; saying something in a different way often helps get your message across. Try giving an example, building on existing knowledge or giving a demonstration, or asking what in particular you need to clear up.

Assertiveness

Would others agree that you 'mean what you say', 'say what you mean' and 'walk your talk'? Assertiveness is a style of communicating and relating to others that enhances mutual respect and leads to clear, open, direct and honest communication, both verbally and through body language.

Assertiveness is based on a strong set of personal skills and grounded in your beliefs about yourself and others. To be truly assertive, you need the mindsets discussed on page 190. In particular, you need:

* an internal locus of control
* clear and strong values that include openness and honesty
* high self-esteem
* mental models that include self-respect and respect for others
* positive self-talk.

Being assertive can be useful in this situations, for example:

* accepting a compliment
* asking for a favour
* expressing annoyance
* initiating a conversation
* making a request
* offering a compliment
* responding to criticism
* saying positive things about yourself
* turning down requests.

Three styles of communicating

There are, in fact, three broad styles of relating with others, as shown in Figure 6.4. They are aggressive, passive (also called *submissive*) and assertive.

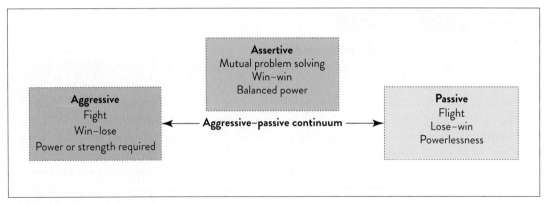

FIGURE 6.4 Styles of communication

Aggressive and passive styles are part of the fight, flight or freeze response that originates in a primitive part of the brain called the *amygdala*. All animals, including human beings, are born with the fight, flight or freeze response that instructs them to take one of three actions. They can stand their ground and fight, which leads to aggressive behaviour. They can flee (to turn and run) or they can freeze (when there is no hope or when flight is impossible). Both fleeing and freezing lead to passive behaviour.

When the fight, flight or freeze response kicks in, blood moves from the brain into the muscles (preventing the ability to think clearly) and adrenalin courses through the body to provide the energy needed to fight or flee. When neither is possible, massive amounts of brain chemicals, hormones and pain killers are released into the bloodstream so that we 'relax' and freeze, or stop moving.

Humans still have this ancient fight, flight or freeze response, although few face the life-threatening situations for which it was originally useful. Nevertheless, these passive and aggressive instincts can show up in the ways people communicate and in the types of relationships they develop.

People behaving aggressively are primarily concerned with achieving an outcome that satisfies them. This is called a win–lose position: *I win and you lose.* On the other hand, someone behaving passively is more concerned with making the other person happy. This is called a lose–win position: *I lose and you win.*

Assertiveness is a completely different style of behaviour and communication. Unlike aggression and submission, assertiveness is not instinctive. It doesn't kick in automatically, in as little as 1/20th of a second.[9] Rather, it consists of a learned set of skills. When people behave assertively, they work towards an outcome or solution that satisfies both or all parties. This is called a win–win position: *I win and you win too.*

 **IN A NUTSHELL**

Recognising aggressive, passive and assertive behaviour

Aggressive behaviour includes:

- blaming, criticising, name-calling
- demanding or threatening (rather than requesting)
- expressing opinions as facts
- failing to respect other people

>>

- generally behaving as if 'I'm better than you'
- making hostile remarks (e.g. derogatory, racist or sexist remarks)
- speaking in a dominating or domineering manner
- using sarcasm to drive home a point.

Non-verbally, you see:
- a jutting chin
- a set jaw
- clenched or thumping fists
- finger stabbing
- glaring eyes
- invading other people's personal spaces
- using what others might call 'standover tactics'.

Passive behaviour includes:
- apologising for what you say ('Sorry, can I just say ...')
- dismissing your own needs as unimportant ('What would *you* prefer?')
- failing to respect yourself
- frequently justifying yourself or your statements
- putting yourself down ('I'm hopeless')
- seeking permission for your thoughts or actions
- seldom expressing your feelings, opinions and preferences, or expressing them in an indirect way (e.g. through hints)
- talking in a hesitant, rambling, singsong or whining manner in a dull, monotone or soft voice
- undervaluing yourself and your opinions ('It's only my opinion, but ...').

Non-verbally, you see:
- downcast, evasive eyes
- 'ghost' smiles when expressing anger or being criticised
- tense body posture accompanied by hand wringing, hunched shoulders, nervous movements, shrugs and shuffling feet.

Assertive behaviour includes:
- being accepting and tolerant of others
- distinguishing between fact and opinion
- expressing feelings, needs and opinions in a way that doesn't punish or threaten others or ignore or discount others' feelings or wishes
- making statements that are clear and to the point, and that indicate respect for yourself as well as for others
- offering suggestions rather than giving 'advice' or orders, or making demands
- searching for ways to get around problems and differences of opinion.

Non-verbally, you see:
- appearing comfortable, relaxed, flexible and open
- appropriate eye contact that is neither too little (passive) nor a 'stare-down' (aggressive)
- congruent facial expressions and other body language that accurately reflect your feelings and your message
- open hand movements, emphasising key points.

4. Managing your body language

Eyes are vocal, tears have tongues. And there are words not made with lungs.

Richard Crashaw (Poet), *Upon the Death of a Gentleman* (1872)[10]

How you say something is usually more important than the words themselves. People receive information, often subconsciously, through non-verbal signals: a nod, silence, a smile, and even the way someone is dressed. In fact, most people believe their eyes, a person's *non-verbal communication*, over the words their ears hear.

Your gestures, tone of voice, the way you stand and your facial expression all add to (or detract from) your words. You communicate symbolically, too; for example, through drawings and gestures (thumbs-up for 'great'), the clothes you wear and accessories you carry, and the objects on your desk. Every part of this communication must be congruent for you and your message to be believable.

● THE STRATEGIC PERSPECTIVE

How important are words?

Only a small portion of communication is achieved through the spoken or written word. A classic study by Albert Mehrabian, Professor of Psychology at the University of California, Los Angeles, showed that in a conversation between two people, only 7% of the message is likely to come from the words that are spoken. The remaining 93% of the message that is received and understood comes from body language (55%) and tone of voice (38%).[11] Of course, these figures can't hold true in every communication situation, but they make an important general point about the importance of body language and tone of voice.

This is not to say that words are unimportant. Which would you rather hear: 'Your face makes time stand still' or 'Your face could stop a clock'? Or 'You look like the first day of spring' or 'You look like the last day of a long, hard winter'? Yes, words count, too.

Symbolic communication

Symbolic communication, such as the size of someone's office and the type of furnishings in it, are status symbols in some organisations. The clothing people wear is often a sign of rank or of the kind of work they perform. Clothing and personal grooming signal the way we expect others to treat us.

Body language

Body language 'speaks' volumes. For example, your posture tells others how confident you are and signals your status in relation to your companions and your 'ownership' of your surroundings. The pitch, speed, tone and volume of your voice subtly communicate the importance of your message and your degree of commitment to it.

Monitor other people's body language, too, particularly any abrupt changes, as these could indicate agreement, disagreement or other emotions. Do people step back from you, which could mean you are invading their personal space? Are they listening to you attentively? Or fidgeting so much that you would be better continuing the conversation another time?

Personal space

Do you know that you have your own personal, invisible space bubble? When people enter it, you feel uncomfortable. With close friends and family, your personal space zone can shrink to as small as 15–45 centimetres; at work most people prefer others to keep to an arm's length distance. With people you don't know well, or dislike, your bubble expands even further.

◉ IN A NUTSHELL

Body language is SO CLEAR

Here's how to make sure your body language supports your communications:

S is for the way you sit, stand and use space. Rather than facing the other person, which puts a discussion into conflict mode, or towering over the person, which is threatening, you can sit or stand next to the person or at right angles and, as far as possible, on the same level. When you're on the same level, it's easier to see things 'eye to eye'. Watch your use of space, too. In business situations, sit or stand about an arm's length away from others and avoid trespassing into their personal space (e.g. their desk) with your belongings or using someone else's equipment as if it were your own.

Open up. Keep an open body posture and use open gestures. Most people interpret crossed arms and legs, hunched shoulders, or averted face, eyes or body as closed and defensive, nervous and uncertain, or insincere.

C is for how exclusively you concentrate your attention on the other person. Centre your attention on the person and put any other thoughts to one side.

L is for how you lean to show attention and apply or reduce pressure. Lean slightly forward to show interest and attention. Lean a bit further forward to encourage people to provide more information. Lean slightly back to take the pressure off in a tense situation.

E is for eye contact – not too much, which is overpowering, and not too little, which indicates lack of attention, lack of self-confidence or shiftiness.

A is for being at ease. Avoid fiddling, fidgeting and other nervous mannerisms that say 'I'm not interested', 'I'm bored and want to get out of here', 'I'm nervous and uncomfortable' or 'I'm flustered'. Be relaxed and balanced, distributing your weight equally to both feet and sitting or standing straight (but not stiff).

R is for subtly reflecting the other person's body posture, type of language (formal or informal, colloquial or proper) and voice tone. This smooths communication by increasing harmony and rapport and helps people feel more comfortable with you.[12]

You can observe differences in personal space zones between country and city dwellers: Country dwellers tend to prefer bigger space zones than city dwellers. People from different cultures also have characteristic personal space zones. The personal space zones of people who live in high density cities, for example, tends to be smaller than those of people who are used to wide open spaces in the countryside.

Getting too close to people can make you seem pushy, while leaving too much distance can make you appear stand-offish. Keep your distance to the correct zone so that you don't invade anyone's personal space, making them feel ill at ease and uncomfortable around you.

5. Putting it in writing

The difficulty of literature is not to write, but to write what you mean.

Robert Louis Stevenson (Scottish author), *Virginibus Puerisque and Other Papers* (1907)[13]

Spoken words aren't suited to every occasion, and electronic communications, letters, proposals, reports, submissions and tender documents are a daily part of most leader-managers' jobs.

When you need to put something in writing, take measures to overcome the following shortcomings of written communications:

* It can be delayed or lost (even electronic communications).
* Putting something in writing is not as personal as a face-to-face, or even a telephone, conversation.
* The end result may be poorly written, difficult to read and open to misinterpretation.
* There is no guarantee when they will be read or even that they will be read.
* There is no guarantee that they will be understood and acted on as you expect.

● IN A NUTSHELL

When to put it in writing

There are lots of reasons to 'Put it in writing.' Here are some:

* You can overcome problems of distance, making written communications less costly than face-to-face meetings.
* It can be efficient when you need to convey the same information to large numbers of people and ensure that everyone receives the same message.
* It's perfect when you want a record for future reference. This is particularly important with complex material and when introducing new systems or procedures. People can study what you have written, take it in at their own pace and refer to it later.
* A written record is permanent and, because most people remember more through their eyes than through their ears, putting it in writing can make a more lasting impression.
* It helps you deliver a precise, carefully thought-out message. You can write, edit and rewrite your words until they say just what you want them to say, clearly and accurately. You can include diagrams, graphs, maps and other pictorial aids to help get your message across, too.
* You want to reinforce or confirm an earlier verbal message.
* Written messages carry an air of authority. People are more ready to believe the written word.

Be clear about your aim

Before writing anything, decide precisely what you want to achieve. Is it to encourage someone to take action? To help someone make a decision? To inform? Persuade? When your purpose is fuzzy, your writing will be fuzzy, too. Think about:

* What is the main point of this document?
* Who is receiving it?
* Why is it important to them?
* What do I want them to do after reading it?
* What do they need to know in order to do it?

- What do they already know and believe about the subject?
- How should I write it? With authority, as a subject matter expert, or am I communicating with peers? Am I cautioning someone or offering friendly advice? This helps you decide what 'tone' to adopt.

Organise your thoughts

With a clear aim, it's easy to organise your thoughts. Use the six 'trigger questions': What? Who? When? Where? Why? How? Jot down a few words under each heading.

Next, think through what else to include. When you're having trouble, try imagining you're an expert on the subject and being interviewed: What would you be asked and how would you respond? Or draft a summary of the highlights and 'call to action'. Or jot down notes about how you would explain your subject over the phone to someone, or in person.

Then put your material into a logical sequence. You can start from the beginning, for example, or begin with an overview or executive summary. Think about which approach would get your message across best. Here are some other ways to organise and structure your information:

- Causal: The facts and their results, or the problem and its causes.
- Differing viewpoints: Outline one way of looking at the subject, then another way.
- Principle: From the theory to the practice.
- Problem: From the problem to the solution.
- Process or sequence: From the raw material to the finished product, from the beginning to the end.
- Relative importance: From the most to least important.
- Space: Geographical, or from a central point outwards.
- Time: past to the present to the future.

● THEORY TO PRACTICE

Writing traps and how to avoid them

Have you fallen into any of the common writing traps in Table 6.5? If you have, take note of the suggested solutions.

TABLE 6.5 Writing around the problem

Writing trap	Antidote
Avoiding making direct statements in case you're held accountable.	People hold you accountable anyway, so you might as well use clear, precise, positive words and phrases.
Being more concerned with proving yourself right and the reader wrong.	Instead of handing out blame, look for a solution acceptable to yourself and your reader.
Boring your readers to sleep.	Write with a particular reader in mind and in a conversational tone.
Brushing aside complaints, making demands rather than requests and generally writing in a way that shows you think you are better than the person you are writing to.	Courtesy is far more professional and business-like than impoliteness and arrogance.

>>

TABLE 6.5 Writing around the problem (Continued)

Writing trap	Antidote
Continually excusing and explaining.	People generally don't care. Offer an apology and a solution to correct the situation; concentrate on what can be done to put matters right.
Insisting on so much precision that only a statistician can understand what you have written.	Explain facts and figures to avoid misunderstandings and remember that it isn't always necessary to include every detail.
Mistaking brevity and terseness for conciseness.	Warmth, friendliness and courtesy do not detract from professionalism.
Switching from one thought to another as you write, as they pop into your head.	Jot down the points you want to make so you can number them to structure your information into a logical flow.
Thinking bulk or length equals importance and displays intelligence.	Pare down overly wordy writing by cutting out unnecessary words and phrases. Write to express, not to impress.
Using too much jargon and leaving the reader wondering what you're on about.	Explain any technical terms or use terms you're sure your readers know.
Writing in an unnatural, unnecessarily formal and flowery style.	Think practical, not poetical, and write more as you speak.
Writing in clichés and platitudes.	Concentrate on what you want to communicate, not flowery phrases.

Group your ideas

Like a good story or presentation, written communications need a beginning, a middle and an end. The beginning introduces the subject, the middle contains the information that you want to convey and the end summarises what you have said and points towards the next steps.

Aim for each sentence to contain one idea and each paragraph to contain a group of related ideas.

● ACTION!

You can find a *Getting ready to write* template to help you clarify your aim and organise your thoughts on  CourseMateExpress.

Use plain English to meet your goals

Time is tight in most organisations. This makes it more important than ever that people write in clear, plain English. Write so that people can:

- read it easily
- understand it immediately
- act on it quickly.

Keep it short and simple

Unnecessary words in a sentence are like unnecessary ingredients in a cake. The first table in 'Theory to practice: Unnecessary and flowery words and phrases', shows how to trim flowery, unnecessarily long and trite phrases from your writing. The second table shows how to avoid déjà vu by pruning unnecessary words.

Good writing follows the ABCs: It is *accurate*, *brief* and *clear*. People can easily read and understand clear writing, while brevity adds punch and force. Say what you want to say in as few words as possible. Then stop.

This is not to say that you should write only in short sentences or avoid details or explanations. Use just enough words to communicate your message while avoiding extra words and sentences that don't contribute any meaning or add any information. Aim to average between 18 and 25 words per sentence and make every word count.

● THEORY TO PRACTICE

Unnecessary and flowery words and phrases

Flowery words might feel nice but they cloud the message you are trying to get across to your reader. Try the simple alternatives in Table 6.6.

TABLE 6.6 Wasting words when brief is better

Wordy	Better
a large number of	many
according to our records	we find
are of the opinion	believe
at the present time	now
consensus of opinion	consensus
despite the fact that	although
during the month of April	in April
during which time	while
for the reason that	because, since
give a description	describe
give consideration to	consider
has no confidence in	doubts
in addition to	also
in excess of	more than
in order that	so
in the absence of	without
in the event that	if
in the majority of instances	mostly

>>

TABLE 6.6 Wasting words when brief is better (Continued)

Wordy	Better
in the near future	soon
in view of the fact that	because
is sorry for	regrets
make application to	apply
on a regular basis	regularly
prior to	before
pursuant to your request	as you asked
reached an agreement	agreed
subsequent to	after
until such time	until
with reference to	about
with the exception of	except

Wasting words also occurs when you insert unnecessary words. See the left-hand column in Table 6.7.

TABLE 6.7 Why say it twice?

Redundant	Concise
absolutely necessary	necessary
advance warning	warning
as of now	now
at a price of $60	$60
basic fundamentals	fundamentals
during the course of	during
each and every one of us	each of us
enclosed herewith	enclosed
end result	result
first and foremost	first
I am in the process of preparing	I am preparing
it is blue in colour	it is blue
my personal opinion	my opinion
one of the main factors is, of course, the question of quality	one of the main factors is quality
other alternatives	alternatives
postponed until later	postponed
take into consideration	consider
we can supply them in the following colours: blue, red, green ...	we can supply them in blue, red, green ...
we seldom ever make this mistake	we seldom make this mistake

Use short words

When you need a long word, use it. Otherwise, go for familiar, precise, short words. These have greater impact and readability. Only use a long word when it:

- adds richness or special meaning or is more exact than a short word (e.g. 'courier' is more precise than 'send')
- is economical, replacing a lot of small words (e.g. 'destination' is more economical than 'the place to which they are going')
- is more familiar to the reader than a short word (e.g. 'sponsorship' is more familiar to most people than 'aegis')
- is unique and can't be replaced by a short word (e.g. inventory, appreciation, communicate).

● THEORY TO PRACTICE

Lose the long word – use the short word

Keeping words short and to the point keeps your message clear, as you can see in Table 6.8.

TABLE 6.8 The long and the short of good writing

Long	Short	Long	Short
abbreviate	shorten	incorporate	include
abundance	a lot	indication	sign
accomplish	do	initiate	begin, start
administer	give	majority of	most
aggregate	total	manufacture	make
alternative	choice	participate	share, join
anticipate	expect	primarily	mostly
application	use	regulation	rule
apportion	assign, divide	reiterate	repeat
approximately	about	remunerate	pay
assistance	help	requirement	need
commencement	start	residence	home
consequence	result	similar	alike
demonstrate	show	subsequent	later
difficult	hard	terminate	end
endeavour	try	ultimate	final
frequently	often	utilise	use
fundamental	basic	visualise	see

Write naturally

It's easier and more effective to write the way you speak, using words that come naturally to you. Don't try to sound like something you're not or be unnecessarily formal. If you would normally say, 'We took the long way round', don't write 'We arrived via a circuitous route'. Ornate, elaborate, overblown words and phrases are off-putting and cloud your meaning.

When you sit down to write, speak your thoughts mentally (or even aloud) as you put them on paper. Then go back and check the spelling and grammar. That way, you write more freely and naturally and your writing is more alive, more interesting and easier to understand and act on.

But don't be glib

Business writing needs to be in full sentences and include vowels and correct punctuation. Writing as though you are texting – in phrases rather than sentences, shortening words by leaving out vowels and spelling them as they sound – is not acceptable in a business environment.

Overly casual writing lacks professionalism and sincerity and invites derision and mistrust. For business, write in standard English, avoid slang words and expressions and avoid being overly familiar with your readers.

● IN A NUTSHELL

The seven steps to good business writing

Just remember that the standard of your writing reflects the standard of the way you do business. Here are seven steps to writing success:

1. Be clear about your purpose: Think about your reader and what they already know and believe. What else do you want your reader to know, and why? What do you want your reader to do, and why? How do you want your reader to feel, and why?

2. Plan your message: Jot down the key points you want to make. Then put them in a logical sequence and gather any facts you need to include to demonstrate your case: 'I think we should ...' is weak, but 'We're currently spending $X on Y and by implementing my proposal we would save $X a quarter' is strong and persuasive.

3. Give your reader a reason to read your document: Have a specific reader in mind and write to that person. Use the WIFM factor to help you: What's in It For Me? Ask this question from the reader's point of view.

4. Draft your document: Use normal language and aim for a readable, natural flow of ideas. Explain your main idea in the first paragraph and include any diagrams and graphs that would help to illustrate your points.

5. Edit: Read through your document to ensure it accurately, briefly and clearly says what you want to say. Change any obscure words to familiar words, long words to short words, complex sentences into shorter, simpler ones. Prune unnecessary words and remove any waffle and trite phrases. Check grammar, punctuation and spelling.

6. Produce the final draft: Check it for readability. Are your headings clear? Does the information flow smoothly? Are there logical transitions between major points? How does the layout look? A poor layout costs you 'eye appeal' and looks unprofessional. Are margins big enough? Is there enough space between paragraphs and enough white space so that the page or screen doesn't look crowded? Are paragraphs and sentences as short as possible?

7. Check it carefully: Whenever you can, leave it for a day or two before the final check. Don't just glance over the document but re-read it thoroughly; you can even read it out loud to highlight any problem sentences and awkward wording. Does it still make sense?

Be positive and precise

Most people don't like being told what is *not* the case or what they should *not* do. People want to know what *is* the case and what they *should* do. Avoiding negative statements and words improves your writing style and helps people remember your message more accurately.

For example, instead of saying, 'We will not be able to fill your order this month because we are out of stock', leave out the negative and include specific information. Say, 'We will fill your order early next month, as soon as replacement stock arrives.'

Write actively, not passively

'The moon was jumped over by the cow' is a passive sentence. As you can see, it's boring. 'The cow jumped over the moon' is active and strong. Active writing is generally a better style and easier to read. Placing the *actor* (in this example, the cow) in front of the *action* (jumped) makes the flow of the sentence active, clear and powerful.

Occasionally, for reasons of tact, you may decide to write in the passive voice. For example, it is more diplomatic to say: 'We believe there was an error in your last invoice' than 'You invoiced us incorrectly'.

Write for your reader

Use words and terms your readers can readily understand, interpret and visualise, and avoid technical terms when writing to people with a non-technical background. To meet your readers' needs and word your message persuasively, think about what your readers are concerned about, what matters most to them, what opinions they may already hold on your topic, and what background information they probably have.

Check spelling and grammar

Use a dictionary or the spell-check function on your word processor to check the spelling of an unfamiliar word, or use another word that you know how to spell. Be careful of words that are often misspelled and those that are often misused. Some examples are given in Theory to practice: Frequently misspelled words.

● THEORY TO PRACTICE

Frequently misspelled words

It's easy to spell a word incorrectly. Table 6.9 has examples of words that are particularly easy to type wrongly. Watch out for these and don't be shy to use the spell-check function on your computer.

TABLE 6.9 Spell-checking your way to success

Correct	Incorrect
acceptable	acceptiable
accidentally	accidently
calendar	calander or calender
committed	commited

>>

TABLE 6.9 Spell-checking your way to success (Continued)

Correct	Incorrect
license (verb)	licence
occasionally	occasionaly
occurrence	occurance or occurrance
publicly	publically
receive/receipt	recieve/reciept
separate	seperate

Just as bad as misspelling is the habit some people have of misusing words, often choosing a word similar to the correct word, as you can see in Table 6.10.

Frequently misused words

TABLE 6.10 Frequently misused words

Often misused	Correct use
accept, except	I will accept all ideas except rude ones.
affect, effect	Their pleas did not affect my decision but my decision did effect a better solution.
imply, infer	Did you imply that he is wrong or did I incorrectly infer it?
moral, morale	The moral of the story is to keep employee morale high.
personal, personnel	It's improper to get too personal with the personnel.
stationary, stationery	The wagon bringing the stationery supplies is stationary in the corridor.
their, there, they're	Their files are over there where they're meeting.
to, too, two	I, too, think that two is too many to have.
your, you're	You're wearing your shirt inside out.

Watch your apostrophes, too. Use an *apostrophe s* (...'s) for one of two reasons:

1. To indicate possession: This is Deb's diary. That is Dave's desk.
2. As a contraction, when the apostrophe takes the place of a letter: Where is Deb's diary? (possession) becomes *Where's Deb's diary?* It's (It is) over there on Dave's desk. Where's (where is) my diary? Your diary's (diary is) there. You're (you are) right next to it. That's (that is) Dave's desk over there.

When you want to pluralise a word, you don't need an apostrophe: *There are three computers on three different desks.*

A confusing exception to these rules is the possessive 'its': *The computer lost its memory when it crashed during the storm.* Here 'its' is not a contraction, so an apostrophe is not needed. 'Its' only needs an apostrophe when it is the contraction for 'it is': *The computer lost its memory and it's a major inconvenience.*

Grammar is sometimes more difficult to get correct, although most word-processing programs have a grammar checking function that can be useful. You can ask someone to look over your writing for errors, too. Basic errors of spelling and grammar seriously erode your professionalism.

Set out documents professionally

A document, letter or book filled with long paragraphs, tiny margins and small print brings out the groan-response in most people and the temptation to shuffle it to the bottom of the pile. When your documents look reader friendly and inviting to read, people are more likely to read them. Follow your organisation's protocol for setting out business documents, but generally:

* Break up the text with headings.
* Leave as much white space as possible.
* Leave margins of at least 5 cm.
* Use a font size of 12 points or larger.

CourseMateExpress

Go to http://login.cengagebrain.com to access CourseMate Express, your online study tool for *Management Theory & Practice.* CourseMate Express brings chapter concepts to life with interactive learning, and study and exam preparation tools:

* Test your skills in different aspects of management with interactive self-tests and simulations.
* Watch videos that show how real managers operate in real businesses.
* Test your understanding of the changing world of management by taking the revision quiz.

QUICK REVIEW

1. Briefly review the main barriers to effective communication and give examples from your own experience of them. In hindsight, were there any signals that could have alerted you to the presence of those barriers? Had you heeded them, what action could you have taken to remove them or reduce their effects?
2. What does gathering good information entail? Give an example from your own experience.
3. Summarise the techniques for giving good information and, from your experience, give an example of each.
4. Explain how being aware of body language has helped you communicate more effectively, whether you are giving information or receiving it.
5. Describe the characteristics of a professional written business communication and provide an example of a business letter, proposal or report you have written.

BUILD YOUR SKILLS

1. Does effective communication mean you must agree with what the other person is saying or, conversely, that they must agree with what you are saying? Explain your reasoning and illustrate it with examples.

2. Think of an instance when you made an assumption without asking for clarification and the outcome of the communication was less than ideal. Write down at least five questions you could have asked during the communication that would have corrected your assumptions.

3. Review the differences between assertive, aggressive and passive behaviour and illustrate your explanation with examples from your experience, either your own behaviour or what you have observed in others. Do you think it's possible to manage people effectively without the ability to be assertive? Why or why not? Give an example from your own experience to illustrate your answer.

4. Find a group of people talking together that you can observe quietly from a short distance away. Ignore what they are saying; instead, observe their body language. Who seems to be the leader of the group? Who likes whom? Does anyone feel uncomfortable or left out? Is anyone impatient or bored? Is anyone angry? Are they good friends or just acquaintances? Give reasons for each answer.

5. Investigate the grammar options on the word-processing system you use, particularly the readability indices. Find out what each of them measures and what a 'readable' score is.

WORKPLACE ACTIVITIES

1. Keep a log of your communications for one day, noting any barriers that were present, what they were and the action you took to remove them or reduce their effect.

2. Describe a time when you needed to ask a lot of questions and listen carefully to understand what someone was telling you. Discuss what, if anything, made it difficult for you to listen and how you overcame this and other barriers. Provide examples of the sorts of questions you asked.

3. Describe a time when you planned and presented complex information successfully.

4. Select a document of 500–750 words you have written recently and edit it, aiming to make it clearer and easier to read by following the guidelines outlined in this chapter.

5. Select one of your organisation's policies – for example a human resource policy such as diversity, flexible working or sustainability – and write a series of two-paragraph summaries of the policy for the following groups of stakeholders: white-collar workers, blue-collar workers, employees who speak English as a second language, leader-managers, senior managers, local community residents and shareholders and potential investors. What factors are you taking into account as you write each of these summaries? When they're written, check them for accuracy, brevity, clarity, readability and layout.

CASE STUDY 6.1

SIMON SPEAKS

Simon was recently appointed to the position of area manager for a chain of eye-care stores. Each store, depending on its size, has one or more qualified optometrists who conduct eye tests, and two or more trained optometric assistants who help clients to select flattering spectacle frames, show them how to use and care for contact lenses, carry out minor repairs to spectacles, and so on. The assistants also do most of the administrative work in the stores, such as booking client appointments and handling billing.

When Simon took on the role, he was told that his primary goal was to ensure that the staff in each store worked as a team, concentrating on customer service and profitability. Simon took up his position enthusiastically.

He visited each store, called the staff together, introduced himself and gave a 'pep talk' on the importance of customer service and teamwork. 'We're in the business of really adding value for our customers,' he said. 'You can look on your jobs as filling in time during your shift, or you can see yourselves as part of a great team, helping to improve the quality of our customers' lives.' Simon always closed his talk with the example of a football team working together to score goals and how each member of the team, playing their assigned position, is important to the success of the whole team.

Simon also took the opportunity to inform the optometric assistants that they would need to be more vigilant in following up overdue accounts. 'I intend to introduce a seven-day account period in order to help our cash flow,' he explained. 'At the end of the day, we have a business to run and our shareholders expect us to make a good profit. We all need to do our bit in this and I expect you to do yours.'

After his talk, Simon met with each staff member individually. He asked what they liked and disliked about their jobs, whether they felt everyone in the store was 'pulling their weight', whether staffing levels were right or they were employing too many people, whether any systems could be tightened up to reduce costs. He asked whether they could speed up their service to customers by agreeing an average length of time to spend with each one, so they could serve more customers in a day. Simon concluded each interview with the statement: 'I'd like you to feel free to tell me anything you can about the way this store is *really* running. I'm all ears.'

After completing the store visits, Simon based himself in his office and hasn't been seen in the stores since. He began a concerted campaign to reduce costs, sending memos instructing staff to make sure that customers paid their bills on time and telephoning stores when the amount of outstanding accounts reached a certain level. He instigated a survey to find out the length of time each optometric assistant spent with each customer. He issued a lengthy memo on what staff should be doing to improve the quality of their customer service.

Rumours begin circulating about Simon. 'He's all talk,' people were saying. 'He says one thing and means another.' 'He talks teamwork but he really wants to cut back on staff.' 'He talks big about customer service, but he expects us to spend less time with our customers and hound the pensioners for money!'

Questions

1. Did the questions Simon asked the staff in their interviews reflect his stated commitment to teamwork and customer service? Why, or why not?
2. Was Simon's 'pep talk' reflected in his subsequent dealings with employees?
3. What problems do you see in Simon's communications with the store staff?

CASE STUDY 6.2

SANDRA'S SOLUTION: PUTTING IT IN WRITING

'Sandra, would you mind coming in here for a moment? I want to talk about the SOPs (standard operating procedures). I'm concerned because I don't think they're being followed correctly.'

'Sure, Lien. What is it you're worried about?'

'Well, I have four items here that were completed today. They clearly show that the SOPs weren't adhered to. I'm worried not only from a quality point of view but also from a safety aspect. I'd hate to see anyone get hurt.'

'Yes, I know what you're getting at. The staff often take shortcuts. The problem is, sometimes it doesn't matter and sometimes it does; they don't seem to be taking that into account.'

'Mmm. Yes, well, the SOPs have been very carefully worked out and I really need everyone to follow all of them all of the time. What do you think we can do about this?'

'Well, as it happens, we had a meeting and thrashed it all out only last week. Or at least I thought we'd thrashed it out. I don't want to call another meeting because we're running to tight deadlines over the next few weeks. How would it be if I drafted up a memo reminding everyone to follow procedures?'

'That's one option. Do you think it would work?'

'Well, no, I guess not. If the meeting didn't work, I don't suppose a memo would do much.' Pause. 'Maybe the problem is the procedures are just too complicated for people to get straight. Now that I think about it, that did come up at the meeting. Hmm. What if I rewrote the SOPs in key-point form so they could be referred to and followed at a glance? We could post them by the work stations. That might just do the trick.'

'Thanks, Sandra. That sounds like a good idea. How long do you think it would take you?'

'Oh, not long. I know most of them off by heart anyway and I'll just double-check the manual to make sure I don't leave anything out. I think if I get stuck into it, I could have them ready by tomorrow.'

'Great! Why don't you write them up and I'll see you tomorrow at coffee to see how you're getting on. I'll take a look at them before you post them, if you like.'

'Yes, okay, great. See you tomorrow.'

Questions

1. Do you agree with Sandra that the memo wouldn't work? Why, or why not?
2. How would having the standard operating procedures as a reference in key-point format help the situation?
3. If Lien's boss asked her for a short report summarising the problems with following standard operating procedures, how could she structure it? Prepare an outline showing the main sections.
4. Analyse the conversation between Lien and Sandra and list the elements that made it effective.

STRENGTHENING YOUR PERSONAL SKILLS

Do you know people who are great to be around because they're positive and make you feel good about yourself? Who are confident and assured, who respect others and who people respect in return? Who have a clear sense of who they are, what they stand for and what they believe in? People who know what they want from life and know where they're headed and who can deal calmly with the ups and downs along the way?

These are personal skills that are vital to every leader-manager's success, from their first appointment to a leader-manager role, all the way to the top.

1. Do you know what's important to you, what you want from life and how to achieve it?
2. Do you have a mindset that empowers you to act, makes things better and achieve the goals that are important to you?
3. Do you have the emotional intelligence and resilience you need to succeed?
4. Are you comfortable making presentations to small groups and can you do them well?

This chapter explains the principal resources you need to strengthen your personal skills and succeed in your personal and working life.

David's dilemma

David is at a career crossroads. His position is being outsourced and made redundant. He has been offered a sideways move within the organisation, but in a different location less convenient to his home. It's a safe and easy option, although not particularly appealing. He considers his other options: Become a contractor himself, with all the attendant risks and expenses (and the benefits, too) of being his own boss, setting his own hours and so on. Risky, and not particularly appealing, either.

He can brush up his résumé and launch a job search: Check out the job sites and speak to people in his professional networks to let them know he's available. Something suitable is bound to turn up.

'What's my ideal job right now,' he muses? 'Do I even want another job? Maybe I should take a few months off and travel. Or go back to full-time study with a bit of casual working.'

There are many options and a lot to think about, he realises. He 'slips, slops, slaps', picks up his journal and a pencil, and heads off to the surf for a bit of soul searching.

1. Setting personal goals

> Everything that is properly business we must keep carefully separate from life. Business requires earnestness and method; life must have a freer handling.
>
> Goethe (German author), *The Sorrows of Young Werther and Other Tales* (1882)[1]

You've probably heard words to this effect: When you don't know where you're going, any road will do. Put another way, you can either purposefully guide your life and your career, or you can accept whatever comes along.

Before you can guide your life, you need to know what you value and what you want to achieve. Then you can decide how best to work towards your goals and update and refine your plan.

Your values and interests

Values give you deep roots. Do you have a strong sense of your own values and your organisation's values? People are happiest, do their best and achieve the most when they spend their time, at work and at home, on activities that are in line with their values.

Values are deeply and strongly held beliefs and principles. They express what you believe is right and wrong, good and bad, should and shouldn't be. They are so much a part of you that you may not even be conscious of what your values are.

People's values usually firm up when they are in their early 20s and remain stable throughout their lives. They provide an 'inner compass' that guides your actions and decisions whether you are aware of their guidance or not.

Just as living according to your values leads to a satisfying life, choosing a career that links with your main values can give you genuine job satisfaction. A satisfying job must also link with your deep interests. (See page 131 for information on managing your career.)

ACTION!

What do you hold dear? What do you want from life? What is important to you? To identify your own values, complete the checklist: What do I value most? on **CourseMateExpress**.

Your life plan

Follow these four steps to bring your thoughts to fruition:

1. Think about your various life roles: colleague, friend, leader-manager, parent, partner, sibling, student, and so on. Think about your major life areas: your career, your family, your mental and physical health, your place in your community and so on. What are you aiming at in each of these roles and areas? What sort of person do you wish to be in each of them? What contributions do you want to make?

    Spend some time alone with a pencil and notepad thinking around these questions. Some people like to imagine their 75th birthday party and what the 'significant others' in their life might say about them. Others like to sit quietly and write down the words and phrases that describe them, or that they would like to describe them. Other people make 'spidergrams', or mind maps. Do what feels right for you.

2. Look back over your thoughts. What are the common themes? Set some specific goals in the main areas of your life. Keep asking 'How can I know I've succeeded in this?' until you arrive at a clear goal that you can 'see' yourself achieving.

3. Then ask yourself: 'What needs to happen before I can achieve this goal?' Break your goals down into shorter-term targets that you can realistically expect to achieve in, say, the next three to six months and write them down. These are your milestones – concentrate on these and use them to assess your progress towards each goal.

4. Now list the first two or three steps you need to take towards achieving your targets. Remember:

This is your vision of your future. Invest time in it because your life plan gives overall direction and guidance to your life and power to your leadership (see page 136, which explains how to plan your career).

> ### ● THEORY TO PRACTICE
>
> **How to set a great goal**
> Setting goals is one of the best life lessons you can master. Here's how you start:
> *   Set a few goals and state them simply, so that you can keep them in mind.
> *   Make them specific, so you know precisely what you want to achieve.
> *   Make them achievable and, at the same time, a little bit 'stretching'.
> *   State them in positive terms – say what you do want, not what you don't want.
> *   Set a target date for achieving each goal.

Work–life balance

As Goethe explained at the opening of this section, the lines between 'business' and 'life' can become blurred. While 'business' does require 'earnestness and method', 'life' must have have 'freer handling'. Personal and work lives are merging as workloads increase and Australians work longer hours and take work home. On top of that, many employees feel pressured to show they're adding value and are on a career track.

But we need to be sensible about this. All work and no play doesn't just make Jack a dull boy; it also leads to cynicism, interpersonal conflict, low productivity, substance abuse and tiredness – all these are symptoms of working too hard and feeling constantly under pressure.

Balancing your various life roles with your workplace roles (Steps 1–4) is not only in your employer's interests because people work better and more productively when they lead balanced lives, it is in your interests, too. Work–life balance increases your job satisfaction and improves your family life and physical and psychological health.

Most Australians would probably agree that a full, healthy and happy life – a well-balanced life – is a successful life. But it doesn't happen by itself. It takes planning and scheduling.

You may not be able to find the time for everything, but you can probably find the time for everything that is meaningful to you. Go for 'quality time', not 'quantity time'. What matters isn't how long you spend in each life area, goal or role; it's how you use your time to make the most of them.

Remember to schedule some 'me time', in which you need not respond to the demands of your other life roles. This is time just for you and your mental and physical health; it might be bushwalking, gardening, jogging, learning a language, playing a sport or taking a painting class – whatever helps you unwind and relax. Activities like this keep your batteries charged, not just for your job but for your entire life.

2. Think like a leader

A man cannot be comfortable without his own approval.

Mark Twain (author), *What is Man* (2014)[2]

What do you believe, deep down, about yourself, other people and the world around you? Unquestioned and strongly held beliefs are known as mindsets or paradigms. They are your mental models of the world and how it operates, and they guide your thoughts and your behaviour. More than that, your beliefs are self-fulfilling prophecies. They attract outcomes and 'evidence' that confirms them.

Once the brain takes in information, it proceeds to discard most of it and uses what is left to create a 'parallel world' of its own.[3] This means that we each have our own reality; and everyone's 'world' is different.

● THEORY TO PRACTICE

Self-fulfilling beliefs

Manager X believes, deep down inside, that employees are irresponsible, lazy and untrustworthy. He treats employees differently from Manager Y, who believes the opposite – that employees are hard working, responsible and trustworthy. Driven by their paradigms, these two leader-managers develop different working relationships with their employees and, in turn, those relationships confirm their deep-seated beliefs about employees.

Your mindsets form during childhood as your parents, siblings, friends and early experiences influence your development. As you continue to live your life, you expand your mindsets and adjust them according to your experiences and what your culture and society teach you.

Your mindsets are so much a part of you that they direct your behaviour, usually without your being aware of it. Nevertheless, they are a key component of your personal skills. Since they colour everything you say and do, it's worth taking the time to reflect on your mindsets so that you can ensure they are up to date and based on facts.

You are what your thoughts make you. Successful leader-managers share remarkably similar mindsets that combine with their values and personal goals. Four important managerial mindsets – respect yourself, set high standards, see positives and possibilities, and pay attention – are listed in the next section.

> ### ⊙ THE STRATEGIC PERSPECTIVE
>
> **How paradigms can work against you**
> Organisations can have paradigms, too. Ford famously refused to add the chrome and fancy bodywork to its cars, allowing Chrysler to steal Ford's number one spot with its 'Yank Tanks'. Eventually the entire US car industry followed suit and then refused to believe consumers wanted smaller, simpler and more economical cars, leaving the door open for the Japanese car industry to usurp its market dominance.

Respect yourself

How do you feel about yourself? Do you value yourself as a worthwhile individual? Are you self-confident and self-assured? Do you respect yourself?

Your self-esteem describes your mindset about yourself. People with low self-esteem feel unworthy and uncomfortable within themselves. They lack self-confidence, which makes it difficult for them to reach decisions, state what's on their mind and tackle difficult issues.

High self-esteem gives you the confidence to deal with difficult issues and difficult people, to keep going when the going gets tough and to state your opinions and desires clearly. Whether it's high or low, your self-esteem is a self-fulfilling prophecy.

In case you're wondering whether holding yourself in high regard might make you seem arrogant, remember these four phrases:

1. I'm okay, you're okay.
2. I'm okay, you're not okay.
3. I'm not okay, you're okay.
4. I'm not okay, you're not okay.[4]

The first phrase describes people who hold themselves, as well as others, in high regard; these people are generally assertive. The second phrase describes people who are arrogant, because while they hold themselves in high regard, they do not hold others in high regard. These people are generally considered to be aggressive. The third phrase describes people who respect others, but not themselves, and are generally passive. It is said, only half-jokingly, that the fourth phrase describes many people who populate our prisons – it is a 'get nowhere' position, characterised by a lack of respect for oneself as well as for others. This scenario plays out (often unconsciously) as: 'I don't respect others, so it's okay to steal from them or murder them. Sure, I may get caught and go to jail, but that's probably all I deserve anyway.' (See pages 167 and 233 to find out more about assertive, aggressive and passive behaviour.)

The bottom line is that as long as you hold others, as well as yourself, in high regard, you are unlikely to behave in an arrogant or aggressive manner.

FYI

The impostor syndrome

Film stars, pop stars and sports stars suffer from it. So do managers. So do you, if you ever feel you don't belong where you are, that you're winging it, that you are going to be found out to be a fraud and a sham and that you don't have the smarts or the talent to be in the position you're in.

And you wouldn't be alone. Up to 70% of professionals suffer from the imposter syndrome.[5] The higher they rise, the more like imposters they feel. It's something to do with 'the more you know, the more you know how much you don't know', so it's a natural symptom of gaining expertise.

A realistically high sense of self-esteem helps you work through the impostor syndrome.

Build your confidence with self-talk

Psychologists have estimated that people talk to themselves at least 50000 times a day.[6] So whether you are aware of it or not, you are constantly talking to yourself. You probably even hold little conversations with yourself: 'Should I or shouldn't I?'

Your conversations and instructions to yourself often take place in the blink of an eye, far too quickly for you to be conscious of them. But they hit home just the same and your subconscious makes sure you follow your instructions. Henry Ford, founder of Ford Motor Corporation, believed that whether you think you can do something, or whether you think you can't do it, you'd be right either way.[7] Some people are their own best friends, others their own biggest critics. Your self-talk reflects your self-esteem and guides your behaviour, which boomerangs back to reinforce your beliefs about yourself. High self-esteem leads to positive, empowering self-talk, which strengthens your self-esteem; low self-esteem leads to negative, limiting self-talk which crushes your self-esteem. Whatever its message, the most important voice you ever hear is your own.

THEORY TO PRACTICE

Examples of hurtful and helpful self-talk

Consider the examples of self-talk in Table 7.1 and think about how each could deflate or bolster a person's self-esteem. Do you recognise any of the examples as similar to your own self-talk?

TABLE 7.1 Are you hurtful or helpful to your self-esteem?

Hurtful self-talk	Helpful self-talk
I always get things wrong.	Next time I'll put more effort into it.
I can never understand topics like this.	I plan to concentrate to make sure I understand this topic and stick with it until I master it.
I'm always awkward around people I don't know.	I will make an effort to be really friendly.
I'm terrible at things like this.	I haven't learned to do this well yet, but I'm getting better.
Isn't that just like me to do something stupid?	That isn't like me – I usually do things better than that.
It's too complicated for me.	I can work this through logically and carefully.
What a clod I am.	I need to watch where I'm going.

Consider two leader-managers: the first believes she makes mistakes, doesn't communicate well with others and has few skills to offer. These self-limiting beliefs lead her to behave quite differently, and get quite different results, from the second leader-manager who believes she is a skilled and effective leader-manager who communicates well and makes good decisions easily.

Whether or not the beliefs of these two leader-managers accurately reflect reality, they do reflect their self-esteem and act as self-fulfilling prophecies, because each unconsciously finds ways to make their beliefs about themselves come true.

Imagine now that these leader-managers are asked to make a presentation at a meeting. The first, believing she is a poor communicator and makes many mistakes, is nervous. Imagine her self-talk: 'Oh no, I'll make a terrible presentation! I'll forget what I'm going to say. No one will pay any attention to me and I'll look like a fool.' This negative self-talk embeds itself in her subconscious and instructs her to fail. This poor manager unwittingly follows the very instructions she gave herself: To fail.

In contrast, the second leader-manager is more likely to give a good presentation because she believes in her own abilities. Her self-talk might be more like: 'Well, this is my first presentation. I'd better think it through carefully so that it makes sense and practise it thoroughly so that I deliver it well. People usually listen to me and this is really no different from a conversation with several people.' Her subconscious acts on its instructions and she successfully delivers her presentation.

● THE STRATEGIC PERSPECTIVE

Feel it, think it, see it, do it!

Have you ever 'known' you were going to fail a test or miss kicking a goal? Even if you were mentally and physically able to succeed at the task, your own thoughts would probably have prevented you from doing so.

Elite athletes, sportspeople, businesspeople and many others repeatedly rehearse a first-class performance in their mind's eye before the actual event. This *visualisation* greatly increases their chances of achieving excellence.

Think about an upcoming important event: Do you imagine yourself falling flat or sailing smoothly *through*? What does this tell you about your self-talk and your ability to visualise success?

Control yourself

People with low self-esteem generally have an external locus of control – other people and events control their behaviour, actions and reactions. For example, people with an external locus of control tend to:

- allow others to make them angry
- be rude right back when someone is rude to them
- do tasks because they have to
- let someone else's bad mood bring their mood down, too
- react without thinking.

People with high self-esteem generally have an internal locus of control, making them masters of their own behaviour, communications and responses to others. They, not other people or outside events, choose their behaviour. People with an internal locus of control tend to:

- act with integrity, according to their own values, and can ignore peer pressure
- choose whether, how and when to respond to rude or otherwise difficult people
- do tasks, even those they dislike, because they want to
- remain calm, cool and collected, even when people around them panic.

Develop an internal locus of control by learning to take a few deep breaths and thinking before responding. Ask yourself: 'What do I really want to do here?' Maintain your professionalism, regardless of how people around you are behaving.

High self-esteem, positive self-talk and an internal locus of control are important personal skills not just for when you're leading and managing, but in all aspects of life. With high self-esteem and an internal locus of control, you appear more mature, self-contained and in charge. Others naturally trust you and look to you for guidance and leadership.

Build self-esteem in others

Think of the best boss or the best teacher you've worked with. Did they bring out the best in you? Did they help you achieve beyond what you thought you were capable of? Did they stretch you and extend your skills, talents and self-confidence?

Help people feel good about themselves through coaching, encouragement, positive praise and by placing them in jobs that stretch them and develop their skills. In this way, you can surround yourself with high-performing 'winners' and build a team that achieves results.

Set high standards

Is your approach more like 'She'll be right' or 'Get it right'? Set high standards. Expect the best for yourself, from yourself, and from the people around you. Whatever you attempt, aim to do it to the best of your ability and expect others to do their best, too.

Thanks to the self-fulfilling prophecy, this mindset brings out the best in everyone. Since people enjoy stretching themselves, learning and working at their potential, most employees are glad of the opportunity to work with leader-managers who expect the best.

Set goals, establish priorities and act on them

When you expect the best, you establish priorities, set realistic yet challenging goals and take responsibility for doing what is required to achieve them. Rather than complaining, daydreaming or seeing only problems and difficulties, this mindset guides you to keep working towards making things happen.

What is the difference between a dream and a goal? A dream is a 'wish' while a goal is a plan to achieve followed by action. The more concrete steps you take towards a goal, the more easily you achieve it. Is earning a diploma a high priority for you? Then you need to pass exams; to pass exams, you need to attend class, pay attention, take notes, study them, buy the textbook, read it, take more notes and revise them several times. These are all actions that help you pass exams and take you down the path to your qualification. Wanting to earn a diploma but doing nothing to pass exams practically guarantees failure.

Concentrating on your goals, combined with taking responsibility and action, helps you to achieve them, especially when progress is slow or you run into difficulties. A mindset of consistently working towards your goals also ensures you look for ways around problems, rather than giving up and giving in to them.

Set goals and establish priorities for yourself as well as for your work team and individual team members. Establishing a clear vision and goals that employees can understand, share and feel good about contributing to is a critical part of your personal skill set, as is setting the pace for how action-oriented and goal-focused your work team is.

THEORY TO PRACTICE

Examples of blaming statements and statements that take responsibility

Table 7.2 has some examples of statements that blame and statements that take responsibility. Which do you use?

TABLE 7.2 The blame game versus taking responsibility

Blaming statements	Taking responsibility statements
Why doesn't my manager recognise how good I am?	What can I do to prove my value to my manager?
Why doesn't my manager spend more time with me?	What can I do to build a better relationship with my manager?
Why don't my employees do as I tell them?	I'll work out a different way to explain what I want so they 'hear' it.
When are my team going to get motivated?	I need to take time to find out how they're feeling about their work and adjust everyone's roles so they're more in tune with their needs.
When will all this pressure let up?	I need to establish my priorities and learn to let go of what I can't control and what is low priority.

See positives and possibilities

Do you optimistically see the glass as 'half full' or pessimistically as 'half empty'? Or perhaps you see it realistically, as twice as big as it needs to be! Successful leader-managers have a mindset that says 'Maybe the glass is a bit bigger than it needs to be, but it's nearly full – let's figure out how to fill it to the top!'

A positive 'can do' approach makes your days and everyone else's that much brighter, thanks to the boomerang principle. When you smile at someone, they smile back. Try giving a compliment to someone and watch what happens. A positive outlook is refreshing and energising. It attracts people to you and it rubs off on others.

A large body of research shows that people with a positive approach are happier, healthier and live longer than gloomy people. For instance, the Mayo Clinic reports that an optimistic attitude can extend your life by up to 20% (and for most Australians that's more than 10 years). Pessimists are two to eight times more at risk of cancer, depression and heart attack than optimists.[8]

With a positive outlook, you can concentrate on what you can do now, and how, when problems loom, not on what you can't do and why. For example:

*   Help employees improve their performances by concentrating on what you want to happen, not on what you don't want to happen.
*   Look for ways around, over and through obstacles, rather than give up.

See mistakes as learning opportunities

You may know someone who denies a problem exists, even when something has clearly gone wrong, or who blames other people or circumstances when a situation isn't working out perfectly. Or perhaps you know someone who is paralysed by guilt when they do something wrong and dare not take further action in case of making another mistake.

Mistakes are inevitable, natural and normal; learning from them, however, is optional. Successful people profit from their mistakes and try again in a different way. Acknowledging and learning from your mistakes helps you get better all the time and moves you out of the past and feeling bad, and into the future, where you find ways to improve and develop your skills. It makes you the sort of person others want to be around and take their lead from. (You can find out more about profiting from mistakes on page 887.)

◉ THE STRATEGIC PERSPECTIVE

Flat world thinking

Ancient Greek mathematicians proved the Earth was round. People in Christopher Columbus' era knew quite well the earth wasn't flat. And Christopher Columbus didn't really 'discover' America (Native Americans and Vikings beat him to it).[9] Never mind. The story that Cristóbal Colón, to give Columbus his correct name, rejected the mental model of a flat earth with waterfalls at the edges, which enabled him to cross the Atlantic Ocean, discover a 'new world' and have a national holiday named after him in the USA, is a nice one. It allows us to talk about 'flat world thinking' and the importance of breaking old mindsets.

'Flat world thinking' blinds us to opportunities and threats and limits possibilities. Especially in times of rapid change, it's important to challenge your mental models and conventional wisdom so you don't get stuck in a time warp. How up to date are your mental models and mindsets?

Pay attention

Avoid 'autopilot'. Pay attention to detail, to finding out the facts before making a decision or acting. Pay attention to everything you're doing as you do it. Psychologists call this *mindfulness* and it does four things:

1. It helps you spot backtracking, bottlenecks, hiccups and wasted effort and resources so you can improve systems and procedures. (See page 565 for more information on making continuous improvements.)
2. It helps you spot ways to do tasks more easily, economically, reliably, safely or quickly.
3. It keeps you involved, interested and out of 'ruts'.
4. It prevents mistakes.

3. Nurturing your emotional intelligence

> In the confrontation between the stream and the rock, the stream always wins – not through strength, but through persistence.
>
> Buddha (founder, Buddhism) Finlay, *The Vault of Motivational Quotes* (2013)[10]

Emotions are impulses to action in response to life situations. The degree to which you have mastered your emotions – not to snuff them out or keep them buried but to acknowledge them and choose how and when to act on them – describes your emotional intelligence (EI).

There are three components to emotional intelligence:

1. *Perceiving*: The ability to recognise different feelings (such as angry, happy, nervous, surprise) in yourself and others.
2. *Understanding*: The ability to identify the causes and consequences of those different feelings.
3. *Regulating emotions*: How well you manage what you and others feel.

FYI

Emotional intelligence

'Emotional intelligence' (EI) is a term coined in 1989 by P Salovey and J D Mayer of Yale University and New Hampshire University in the USA.[11] It was more lately popularised by Daniel Goleman of Harvard University.[12]

EI is an outgrowth of the concept of *social intelligence* identified by E L Thorndike of Columbia University in 1920.[13] Social intelligence includes *interpersonal intelligence*, the ability to understand other people – what motivates them, how they work, how to work cooperatively with them, and so on – and *intrapersonal intelligence*, the ability to understand oneself. Thus, EI includes skills that drive people's responses to both the external world and their internal world.

People with high EI can monitor their own and other people's emotions and use that information to guide their thinking and actions. Their *personal competence*, made up of self-awareness, self-regulation and motivation, enables them to manage themselves. Their *social competence*, made up of empathy and social skills, enables them to handle relationships and interactions with others.

By developing your EI in these areas, you can become more productive and successful, both personally and professionally, and you can help others become more productive and successful, too (see 'In a Nutshell: The inner strengths of emotional intelligence', below for more on EI).

Is it worth the effort? It depends on your job. EI helps job performance in high emotional labour jobs, such as those in customer service, counselling, leading-managing, sales and other roles that call for the job holder to work closely and cooperatively with others. But in jobs where people don't work closely with others, such as accountants, engineers, scientists and other jobs that deal mostly with data, ideas and things, emotional intelligence actually detracts from job performance.[14]

IN A NUTSHELL

The inner strengths of emotional intelligence

The following abilities of emotionally intelligent people are learned skills:

- *Self-aware*, which means they know their own drives, emotions, goals, strengths, values and weaknesses and can understand the link between their emotions, thoughts and actions. This gives them self-confidence, a desire for constructive feedback and the ability to cope with stress, adversity and hardship.
- *Self-regulating*, which means they can control or redirect unwanted emotions and impulses. This makes them resilient, comfortable with ambiguity and change, and gives them integrity, resourcefulness and trustworthiness.
- *Motivated*, wanting to do things well and able to delay gratification in order to succeed, which gives them energy and passion for their work and for new challenges.
- *Empathic*, which helps them understand their impact on others and attract, develop and retain talented employees, and gives them cross-cultural sensitivity.
- *Socially skilled*, which allows them to manage relationships and conflict productively and to network well, and makes them persuasive and effective in building teams and leading change.

EI helps you to close the gap between *intent* (what you want to do) and *action* (what you actually do). For example, you may want to be a considerate leader-manager; high EI helps you overcome the frustrations and time scarcity of leading and managing so that you can pause and take the time to act considerately towards others, while low EI allows you to become caught up in the daily rush and pressures and speak curtly to people out of frustration.

⊙ ACTION!

How strong is your EI? You can find out by doing the interactive self-test: Emotional intelligence on CourseMateExpress.

Build your resilience

Do you know that Winston Churchill lost every public election until he became Prime Minister at age 62? Or that Henry Ford went bankrupt five times? Or that Vincent Van Gogh sold only one painting during his lifetime? They had resilience.

Closely related to EI and the mindsets, psychological resilience is also a learned set of skills. Resilience is mental toughness. It's the ability to adapt and find your way around, over or through adversity. It isn't about toughing it out and just plodding on, making lemonade out of lemons or about brushing problems or difficulties aside; it's about keeping going in smart and imaginative ways and being resourceful and rolling with the punches *while* you adapt and keep going.

Resilient people have the confidence and inner strength to deal with whatever life throws at them. Naturally, they get dismayed when the going gets tough, but they can rein in their emotions in order to keep going and concentrate on working towards making the situation better or living through it.

People who lack resilience have a defeatist and pessimistic attitude. They fall apart under stress and don't bounce back quickly from difficult situations; they dwell on problems, feel victimised and become overwhelmed easily.

⊙ THEORY TO PRACTICE

How to increase your resilience

After a while, even die-hard pessimists find they're more able to bounce back from setbacks better when they develop the following skills:

- Build strong networks of family, friends and colleagues who can listen to your concerns and offer advice and support. Ask for help when you need it and offer it to others.
- Count your blessings, even when you have to hunt for them.
- Figure out what you need to perform at your best and in which areas you have particular skills and abilities. Concentrate on developing your skills in those areas. (Page 131 explains how to identify how you work best and work to you strengths.)
- Get in the habit of interpreting negative events as temporary. You want to think to yourself: 'This is one situation and it isn't going to last forever. I can get through it one step at a time.'
- Go with the flow, especially when it comes to change. Know which battles are worth fighting and are winnable and which are not.

>>

- Know what your priorities are and work towards accomplishing them every day. (Page 110 explains how to establish and work towards your priorities.)
- Learn from the past. Figure out how you have dealt with similar situations – even when you dealt with them poorly, you have information about what not to do again.
- Look after yourself, emotionally and physically. Participate in activities you enjoy, eat healthy food, take time to rejuvenate.
- Look on the bright side. You can't change events but you can control the way you think about events beyond your control and set your sights on a positive outcome. 'Travelling hopefully' helps you avoid 'catastrophic thinking' (the tendency to assume the worst) and helps you maintain your performance in difficult circumstances (known as 'consistent competence under stress').
- Monitor your self-talk and build your self-confidence and self-esteem so you know you can get through setbacks.
- Stay flexible. Keep working towards whatever it is you want to achieve, and should you find that's no longer possible, adjust your goals and get to work on the new ones.
- Take purposeful action. You can't wish away or ignore problems and difficulties but you can hop up onto the balcony to see them in the bigger context, decide what needs to be done, and do it. Improve the situation when you can, prevent it from happening again, or take action to make it less bad if it does happen again.
- Use humour to help you get through the difficult patches. This doesn't mean ignoring them, but laughter is a great healer.

Manage your stress

Efficiency increases when stress increases, but only up to a point. For most people stress levels of 50–70% of their ability to cope are tolerable; when stress levels rise to 90% or more and remain there for some time, performance falls off dramatically, as shown in Figure 7.1.

So while you need some stress to perform well, too much stress at too high a level is certainly unhealthy and can be life-threatening. Burnout is an early sign of poorly managed stress. Over time, stress accumulates and causes identifiable and increasingly severe physical, emotional and behavioural responses related to the fight, flight or freeze response. The body goes on 'full alert', which it can't do indefinitely without damaging itself. [15]

Physical responses to stress include increased blood pressure, heart rate and muscle tension and loss of appetite. When the physical responses aren't dealt with, *emotional symptoms* follow, for example, apathy, depression, mood swings, negativism, resignation and tension. People who fail to deal with stress at this point then display *behavioural responses,* for example, becoming short-tempered and easily upset over trifles, procrastination, difficulty in concentrating, organising themselves and making decisions.

Here are six quick ways to avoid burnout:

1. Avoid working unnecessarily long hours.
2. Build your self-esteem so that you feel more resilient.
3. Develop and maintain interests outside work, including exercise, which lifts energy levels and produces feel-good endorphins that reduce stress.
4. Keep your expectations about what you can achieve at work realistic.
5. Say 'No' when you need to, so you don't heap too much on your plate.
6. Slow down, take regular short (10-minute) breaks throughout the day, and take a full lunch break.[16]

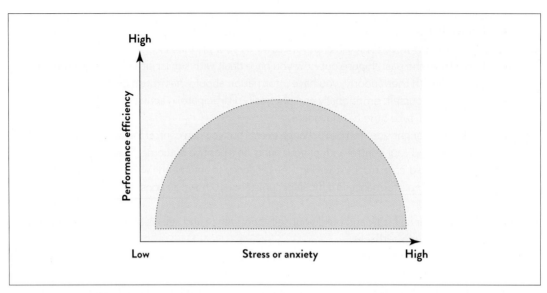

FIGURE 7.1 The Yerkes–Dodson Curve

Some stress helps you concentrate better, use your time better and think clearly and creatively. Too much stress disables your performance, efficiency and health. Should stress become a more serious problem, follow these four steps:

1. Learn to recognise your own physical, emotional and behavioural responses to stress. These alert you to the presence of a stressor so you can deal with it.

2. Identify the stressor, or source of stress. It (or they) may be at home (e.g. death of a family member or close friend, going on holiday, illness or personal injury), in your job (e.g. demanding deadlines, major change in working hours or conditions, the perceived actions of bosses, colleagues or customers, a promotion or lack of a promotion), in your finances (e.g. difficulty paying bills, making a major purchase), in your environment (e.g. noise, pollution, rising prices, traffic) or within yourself (e.g. ageing, outstanding personal achievement, a sense of inadequacy).

3. Reduce or eliminate the stressor or deal with it differently. When you can't prevent or reduce the stressor, perhaps by modifying the environment, change the way you perceive it and alter your self-talk.

4. If you continue to experience distress, act to reduce the stressor's negative effects. Alcohol, drugs, food, cigarettes, or other short-term coping mechanisms, might provide some temporary relief, but in the long run they are worse than doing nothing; they merely cover up the distress and fail to deal with its source or your responses to it. Experiment with various stress-management activities, such as exercise, meditation, relaxation training, self-talk and yoga to help alleviate the symptoms of stress. Otherwise, you are at risk of serious health problems in the future.

Causes of stress and stress-prone people

The specific sources of stress are different for everyone. What one person deals with as invigorating *eustress*, another takes on as its flipside – debilitating *distress*.

Since everyone has different genes, backgrounds, life experiences and learned skills to cope with stress, people have varying abilities to deal with it. Some people, known as *Type A* people, respond more strongly to stress than others, who are known as *Type B* people.

Type A people talk, move and even eat quickly, anger easily, are very competitive, are impatient and always in a hurry (e.g. they hate to wait in queues). They try to do several tasks at once and often have few interests outside work. Type A people are more tense and even have more car accidents than Type B people.

In contrast, *Type B* people are relaxed and easy going in their pursuit of their life and daily goals. They are casual about appointments and seldom feel rushed, even when under pressure. They have a variety of interests, yet do one activity at a time. While Type As often bottle up their stress and try to cope with it alone, Type Bs tend to talk it out with others (an excellent way to manage stress).

Think of Type A and B personalities as opposite ends of a continuum, with most people falling somewhere between the two extremes. At one end are the Type As who might clench the steering wheel with white-knuckled fists, eyes bulging and fuming in a traffic jam. At the other end are the Type Bs who, in the same traffic jam, sit calmly, thinking through the day's events, listening to music or cleaning their fingernails.

External events, people and situations (e.g. a traffic jam, conflict, feeling rushed, lack of job challenge resulting in boredom, major changes in family arrangements, organisation restructure, technological change, working long hours) can trigger stress. So can internal events; your own behaviour, feelings and thoughts about people, situations and events can exacerbate or calm these external events. 'Grrrr! Another traffic jam. It's going to make me late!' (stress) or 'Hmm, heavy traffic again today' (no stress).

4. Making successful presentations

Be sincere; be brief; be seated.

Franklin D Roosevelt (US president during the Great Depression and WWII), in Soper, *Basic Public Speaking* (1963)[17]

Since Aristotle wrote *The Art of Rhetoric* in the 4th century BC, people have strived to make effective presentations. And without a doubt, preparing and delivering presentations is an important management skill. Unfortunately, speaking in public rates high on most people's list of fears. Why? Nerves! Nerves are caused by lack of knowledge, lack of preparation and lack of confidence. You can overcome all three when you know your material thoroughly, prepare carefully and put in plenty of practise.

Here are four of the main groups you are likely to find yourself making presentations to:

1. Customers and suppliers (e.g. to explain your organisation's or team's offerings or needs)
2. Industry groups and conferences (e.g. to represent your organisation and offer your experiences and insights)
3. Other managers (e.g. to present proposals or your team's results)
4. Your work team (e.g. to announce an important corporate decision, event or change).

While presentations vary in their degree of formality and the size of the audience, preparing and delivering any presentation follows the same process, summarised 'In a Nutshell: Eight steps to proficient presentations'.

Step 1: Determine your purpose

Why are you making this presentation? Do you want to, for instance, offer your audience some insights, knowledge or skills, persuade your audience to accept your ideas or provide information?

Have a precise goal in mind and write it down: *After hearing my presentation, I want my audience to …*

Based on this, decide what your main message is: *My main message is …*

Write that down, too, in six or fewer words, and keep both clearly visible as you prepare your talk.

Step 2: Analyse your audience

Successful communication in any form begins with understanding the person or people you are communicating with and tailoring your information accordingly. Who are you making the presentation to? Why are they listening to it? What is their background knowledge of, and previous experience with the subject? Are they likely to be sympathetic to your message, neutral or hostile to it? Tap into their needs and concerns – what do they want and need to hear in order to understand your message?

When you don't know your audience personally, get a feel for their demographics – their age, cultural and language backgrounds, literacy skills, numeracy skills and so on – and let this guide what you say, how you structure and explain your information, the examples you provide and your support material.

This is also the time to confirm logistics; for example, how much time you have to speak, the room set-up and the time of day.

● ACTION!

The next time you are tasked with making a presentation, use the Audience analysis template on CourseMateExpress to guide you through analysing your audience.

Step 3: Decide what to cover

Bearing in mind your audience, your goal and your main message, take a piece of paper and brainstorm the points you could make and the supporting evidence you could use. Jot down your ideas as they occur to you. There's no need to write in full sentences; key words or phrases are enough.

Now look over your ideas. Cross out any that aren't necessary, keeping only the most relevant. Keep it short and simple. To help decide what to cut out, consider:

- *Must know*: What *must* the audience know about your topic in order for you to achieve your objectives?
- *Should know*: Ideally, what *should* the audience know about your topic?
- *Could know*: What is the non-essential but 'nice-to-know' information you *could* provide?

Include the 'must know' information and work your way through the 'should know' and then the 'could know' information, based on how much time you have available for your talk. Three to five main points with supporting information and examples are generally enough, since too much information overwhelms your audience and prevents them remembering it.

Step 4: Develop an outline

You now have several ideas or key words that you haven't crossed out. Number them into a logical sequence, bearing in mind the audience's attitude and current knowledge and understanding of your topic. Look for an order that flows well, with one point leading easily into the next. Remember, you're working still on an outline in this step, using key words and ideas.

Next, think about how you can help your audience to grasp your ideas. Maybe handouts, models or samples of what you are speaking about could help your points hit home. Here are some other ways to make your points memorable to your audience:

- analogies
- anecdotes or story-type examples
- case studies or stories
- charts, graphs and so on
- computer simulations
- demonstrations
- diagrams, flow charts
- facts and figures
- groups or pairs to practise a skill or discuss a topic
- lists
- metaphors
- rhetorical questions
- role-play or other simulations
- small group discussions.

Flip charts, PowerPoint or Prezi slides with video and audio recordings and whiteboards are other tools to help you drive your points home (but don't over-do the technical wizardry).

Step 5: Write your talk

Some people prefer to write their presentation out in full, using complete sentences. Those who are more practised at making presentations generally prefer to stick with a key-point outline using only words or phrases. This ensures a natural delivery style – no one wants to bore their audience by reading their presentation word for word.

Once you've organised the main *body* of your presentation, develop a short *introduction* to make the audience sit up and listen. What will grab their attention? Is there a startling fact or piece of information you can begin with? Or a relevant anecdote that will lead nicely into your topic? You could state the dilemma or problem and how you recommend solving it.

Your introduction should also establish your objectives. When you make a training presentation, review your objectives and what you plan to cover at the beginning and give your audience an opportunity to add topics or remove unnecessary ones.

Finally, write a short *conclusion* summarising your main points and pointing to the next steps. Try to tie your closing comments back to your introduction. Finally, thank people for their attention and, if appropriate, invite questions.

Work towards creating a user-friendly set of speaking notes to guide you through your talk. Use a large font or large handwriting so you can glance down and find key points easily. You may want to draw a line between key points if you're using A4 sheets of paper, or you can use a separate index card for each key point. Develop some techniques to help you navigate through your speaking notes quickly and easily; for example, if you can draw, images are great memory joggers and different-coloured highlighter pens can signal important points or words. Always number your pages or index cards in case you drop them.

Think about questions you could be asked so that you won't be caught by surprise and at a loss for words.

 IN A NUTSHELL

Don't 'slide' your audience to sleep

You are the presentation, not your technology. Whether you use PowerPoint or Prezi, never, *ever*, stand there reading one slide after another. Your audience can read too, and more quickly than you can read slides out loud, so they'll be annoyed at your holding them up.

Your slides are not your speaking notes or even a memory crutch. They should highlight your points and help your audience follow along, enhancing your presentation, not delivering it for you. Technology should add value to your presentation – not the other way around.

Here are some other tips to make sure technology enhances your presentation:

- Avoid fancy transitions and slide effects (building up slides word by word with text flying in, noises, meaningless cartoons and so on); they are distracting and detract from your message. Let what you say, and the way you say it, hold people's attention, not gimmicks.
- Bullet points are best – avoid sentences and paragraphs.
- Leave the lights on. Dimming the lights cues your audience to switch off and doze.
- Don't turn your back on your audience to read the slide to them or to check which slide is showing. (Use the computer screen in front of you.)
- Keep to one key idea per slide and limit the number of words per slide to about six.
- Use a big bold font, high in contrast to the background.
- Use clear headings.

You don't want your audience reading through your slides and jumping ahead rather than listening to you, so avoid distributing copies of your slides to the audience before your presentation. An exception is a highly technical presentation when audience members can benefit from using copies of your slides to assist in note-taking.

Step 6: Practise your presentation

As they say, 'It's all in the delivery.' The more times you run through your presentation, the more confidence you gain and the better you can deliver it when the time comes. A common problem, generally caused by nerves, is speaking too quickly; avoid this by practising out loud – often – to get the right rhythm and speed imbedded into your brain.

Rather than practising for hours the night before your presentation, practise often in the days or weeks leading up to it. Practise in short sessions, running through the presentation fully each time. Stand up for your out-loud practise at least once, timing yourself to make sure you don't commit the cardinal speaker's sin of running over time.

Your practising has two goals:

1. Not to memorise your material but to know what you are going to say so thoroughly that an occasional glance at your notes is all you need to stay on track.

2. To become comfortable with a delivery style that includes facial expressions and gesturing that reinforce your message, looking up to smile and make eye contact with the audience, pauses to convey control speaking clearly, and a varied speed and tone that conveys conviction.

⦿ THEORY TO PRACTICE

Tips for making presentations

Relax and send some oxygen to your brain by taking a few deep breaths before you begin. As you practise and during your presentation, remember:

- Avoid filler words and non-words such as 'uhm', 'yeah, yeah' and 'ya know'.
- Be confident, natural and relaxed.
- Gesture to emphasise key points. Don't distract the audience by being as stiff as a soldier at attention or a fidgeting bundle of nerves.
- Before you begin, take a deep breath and smile at your audience. Thank the person who introduced you.
- Make eye contact with as many people as you can. Let your eyes meet the eyes of audience members for at least five seconds, or for a complete thought. This makes you look confident, establishes rapport, provides you with some feedback and personalises your information.
- Move around a bit to release tension, but avoid rocking, shuffling or pacing back and forth.
- Project your voice strongly and clearly so your audience can hear you, and speak clearly. People won't bother straining to hear or understand you for very long.
- Relax and be yourself.
- Refer to your notes when you need them, but avoid reading out your presentation word for word.
- Speak in a conversational tone of voice that shows enthusiasm and commitment to your topic. A low-level, monotone or lifeless voice is guaranteed to put even the kindest audience to sleep.

Step 7: Deliver your presentation

Here is where all your hard work pays off. Don't worry about being nervous – that's normal. Channel your adrenalin from stage fright into enthusiasm so that you can deliver your talk with passion and commitment.

Think of your presentation as an expanded conversation with a few friends and remember that the audience is on your side – no one wants to sit through a horrible presentation. Concentrate on your audience and on making sure they understand your message.

Your presentation is really about the audience, not you, so relax and enjoy it. Keep breathing, tune your brain into listening to what you're saying and concentrate on communicating with your audience. This drains self-consciousness and nerves and helps you deliver a natural and powerful presentation. Have a glass of water nearby and take a sip when you feel you need to slow down.

Keep your eyes on your audience, not on your notes or other speaking aids, so you can watch for non-verbal signals that indicate you may need to explain further, slow down or speed up your delivery.

When you're asked a question, paraphrase it in case some people didn't hear. Look around the audience as you answer because others may be wondering the same thing. If the question seems negative, hostile or designed to trap you, rephrase it more objectively. Treat all questions and questioners respectfully.

Step 8: Plan to keep improving

Afterwards, take a quiet moment to mentally replay your presentation. What worked well? Where did you run into problems?

Ask audience members, your manager, the conference organiser and others involved in the presentation for their reactions and improvement suggestions. When the audience provides written feedback, read it through carefully. Then jot down a few useful notes to make your next presentation even better.

CourseMateExpress

Go to http://login.cengagebrain.com to access CourseMate Express, your online study tool for *Management Theory & Practice*. CourseMate Express brings chapter concepts to life with interactive learning, and study and exam preparation tools:

* Test your skills in different aspects of management with interactive self-tests and simulations.
* Watch videos that show how real managers operate in real businesses.
* Test your understanding of the changing world of management by taking the revision quiz.

QUICK REVIEW

1. What are the benefits of knowing what you value and what you want from your career and your private life?
2. Summarise the managerial mindsets explained in this chapter and discuss how you have observed them operating in yourself or by inference in other people's behaviour.
3. Explain the concepts of emotional intelligence and resilience and why they are important skills to develop, both professionally and personally.

4. Prepare a 5- to 10-minute talk on how to make an effective presentation using the first six steps outlined in this chapter. You can deliver your presentation to your class, if you draw the short straw, or to your family or pet (see Step 7 in the previous section). Which steps did you find most difficult? Which did you find easy?

BUILD YOUR SKILLS

1. Investigate your organisation's policies and mechanisms for helping employees to achieve work–life balance and prepare a short report. Search on the Internet for ways organisations encourage work–life balance and for measures individuals can take to improve their own work–life balance.
2. Select a person you believe to be an excellent leader-manager, sportsperson or athlete. Conduct an interview to find out about their mindsets regarding their self-esteem, performance standards (self and others), optimistic or pessimistic attitudes, and mindfulness during their management, sporting or athletic activities.
3. Who do you know with high emotional intelligence? Observe their behaviour, particularly under difficult conditions, and note the particular skills you observe them using.
4. Pay careful attention to the next few presentations you attend and note the techniques the speakers use to make them effective, as well as any distractions or other aspects of the presentations that could be amended to make them even more effective.

WORKPLACE ACTIVITIES

1. Complete the values survey on CourseMateExpress. What are your top 10 values? How do your values influence your decisions, how you spend your leisure time and how you approach your job?
2. Ask your manager and/or a few colleagues for some feedback on how they view your emotional intelligence. Note any areas that you are strong in and any areas that you could strengthen. What are some specific measures you can take to strengthen your emotional intelligence?
3. Draw a map of the stressors in the various facets of your life and circle the top three. (Remember that stress may come at the interface of various facets of your life as each competes for your time and attention.) Develop a plan for dealing with them more effectively so that you can savour life and prevent illness in the future.

CASE STUDY 7.1

DES' MENTAL APPROACH

Des and his baggy brown trousers, crumpled shirt and tie that has seen better days are a familiar sight around head office. He has been the oil company's technical trainer since Noah was a lad, training the newly hired field representatives when they come to head office for their induction and touring the country running various training programs for franchisees' staff members.

In the staff kitchen, Des bumps into Lisa, the company's recruitment consultant, and takes the opportunity to tell her exactly what he thinks of the past few groups of newly hired field representatives. 'They just aren't up to scratch,' he says. 'They're not interested in the material they need to learn, they don't pay attention in class, they're totally irresponsible and just plain thick. I hope the new group that starts next week will be better than your last couple of groups.'

'Irresponsible?' asks Lisa.

'Yes, for instance at lunchtimes I always have to round them up to get started again, even though I warn them I won't. Even coffee breaks, for heaven's sakes – I need to herd them up after coffee, too. And thick. They don't pick up the material I teach them, they just don't seem bright enough or interested enough and they're too lazy to apply themselves. They just aren't up to standard and you need to fix it or you'll find you'll be losing your contract with us.'

'Des, I'm really shocked to hear that because I've been totally happy with the people we've selected for you. I wonder – would it be possible for me to sit in on one of your training sessions with them?'

'Absolutely! I have them Wednesday through Friday next week and you're welcome to pop in any time.'

'Thank you so much,' says Lisa. 'I appreciate that. I'd love to join you for your opening session on Wednesday – what time do you kick off?'

'Nine o'clock. See you then.'

On Wednesday morning, Des tells everyone to take their seats and begins by laying down a few rules. 'Right,' he says, 'you people are going to have to work hard and apply yourselves because this technical material is difficult. In fact, a lot of new hires never come to grips with it, so some of you probably won't either. Just pay attention and do your best. Another thing: Timekeeping. I'm sick of people waltzing in late from breaks and lunch and having to round people up. I want you here and ready to start at the appointed times. Now, switch off your mobiles and pass them to the front to me – I won't tolerate phones going off and SMS-ing in my class.'

'Ah,' thinks Lisa, 'I think I know what the problem may be . . .'

Questions

1. What specific conclusions can you make about Des' mindset from the case study? How might it prevent him being an effective trainer?
2. How would you describe the way Des went about informing Lisa of his dissatisfaction with the field representative recruits? What advice would you offer him?
3. What does Lisa's response to Des' feedback tell you about her emotional intelligence?
4. Re-word Des' opening comments to make them more palatable to a roomful of new employees.
5. Referring to the subsections 'Earn a professional reputation' and 'Move on or fade out' in Chapter 5 if you need to, what career advice can you offer Des?

CASE STUDY 7.2

THE CHRISTMAS PARTY

The annual Christmas party for the Goodman Wire Company is, as usual, a family affair, with partners and children of employees invited. At the end of the party, Father Christmas appears with bags of goodies for the children and presents for the partners.

Ben Goodman, the owner and manager, traditionally says a few words on the occasion. Then, after a polite round of applause and the wishing of 'Happy Christmas' all round, the party comes to an end. Everything is the same this year until Ben rises and makes the following remarks:

Fellow employees and friends: This year is the 30th anniversary of the founding of the Goodman Wire Company. Some years have been good, some trying. But, in all, they have been good years for most of us.

This has been a difficult year financially. Sales and profits have eroded and expenses and costs have pushed steadily upwards. All this has had a dampening effect on profits and consequently we are not in as strong a position as we have been in the past. The only hope I can see for continued strong growth and a financially sound business is for us to cut expenses. This means we have to reduce labour costs, along with any other expenses we can control.

I know that many of you are restless. Some of your children are hard to manage at this hour and you want to be on your way, but I do want to take this opportunity to say a few words to you. This business is our entire life. We all have to nurture it, like we do our children, because we want to see it develop and grow.

I know that most of you have heard on the grapevine that business has been decreasing and that profits and bonuses will suffer this year. Part of this rumour is true. I am very concerned about those who will remain with me through the future years. I want to see your children develop into strong and loyal young people. I want to see them married and establishing homes of their own.

New ideas call for new wage and productivity agreements and I hope that in the coming months we can generate better agreements in the true spirit of workplace bargaining.

In summary, this has been a memorable year and I am happy to give each employee a bonus remembrance.

'Finally, let me wish you all a Merry Christmas!'

With that, Ben calls out names and the employees and partners come forward to receive their cheques and gifts. They find that their bonuses have increased significantly over last year's. When the party breaks up, some families head towards their cars. A good many, however, gather in small groups, talking. 'What does the old fella mean?' 'Is he firing some of us?' are the types of questions they are asking each other.

Questions

1. Ben Goodman's intention is to reassure his employees that their jobs are safe and that the company is sound, provided some necessary changes are made. What evidence is there for this in his speech?
2. Ben is warning his employees about the hard times and redundancies to come. What evidence is there for this in his speech?
3. Why is it important that Ben gives a good presentation here? Are all management presentations this important?
4. What do you think are Ben's objectives for his message? Write a short sentence describing them. From your reading of the Case study, conduct a short analysis of Ben's audience.
5. Develop a key-point outline for Ben's speech that would help him to achieve the objectives you specified in Question 4.

CHAPTER

8

BUILDING EFFECTIVE WORKING RELATIONSHIPS

OVERVIEW

Most people need to work with others to achieve results. The good working relationships you have with your work team, your own leader-manager and with people across and outside your organisation – your customers, suppliers and other stakeholders – help you to reach your goals. More than that, good relationships at work mean more than satisfied and engaged employees; people are naturally social creatures, and friendships and positive interactions with others are important for our psyches.

Good working relationships are critical to organisational success, too. Research has found that the single most important factor in extraordinary workplaces that are exemplars of productivity is the quality of working relationships – how people relate to each other as friends, colleagues and co-workers:

> The quality of working relationships represents the central pivot on which excellent workplaces are founded, underpinned by such key variables as good workplace leadership, clear values, having a say and being safe ... In excellent workplaces, the existence of mutual trust and respect is overwhelming. We became convinced that central to excellent workplaces is an understanding that to produce quality work in Australia, one must have quality relationships.[1]

For quality relationships to flourish, people need to understand themselves and others. This requires well-developed interpersonal skills and the ability to build trust and confidence and to understand and navigate the sometimes stormy seas of organisational politics. It requires wide-ranging support networks for people to draw on and provide advice and assistance. And it requires clear and open communication and the willingness to recognise and deal with conflict and differences of opinion.

1. How well do you understand yourself and others?
2. Can you build and sustain people's confidence and trust?
3. Can you establish, contribute to and benefit from professional networks?
4. Can you make organisational politics work for you and your work team to get your ideas implemented and achieve work priorities and goals?
5. Are you able to turn conflicts into agreements?

This chapter helps you build the relationships you need to work effectively as a leader-manager.

SCENARIO

Glenys designs her future

Everyone knows that Les plans to retire sometime during the next 18 months, and Glenys decides that she wants to be offered his position as section manager. She has experienced no real problems on the many occasions she has acted in Les' position when he was away on leave, so she has no doubts about her ability to do the job from a technical point of view. But she suspects that she needs to develop more solid working relationships with her would-be staff and with the managers she hopes to make her peers.

She begins by reading up on the skills and techniques that forge effective working relationships. She finds several articles and blogs on these topics and learns that effective working relationships are based on understanding oneself and others, and on a collection of attitudes that underpin interpersonal skills.

The information she learns and puts into practice really does seem to make it easier to get along with people – staff and management alike. Of course, it isn't easy and she often feels uncomfortable but, as she read, people can't improve their skills unless they take risks and try out new things.

Everyone seems impressed with the changes in Glenys and in her overall performance and it comes as no surprise when she is appointed to succeed Les. Although she realises she still has a lot to learn, she finds, to her delight, that she is able to handle her new responsibilities. She is even able to get funds for extra staff and equipment – not an easy achievement! It seems to Glenys that all her hard work is paying off.

1. Understanding yourself and others

> The basic truth: Improved productivity in Australian workplaces is the outcome of the quality of working relationships on the job.
>
> Professor Daryll Hull (Macquarie University), *Simply the Best* (2004)[2]

Bad news or not, without self-knowledge, you can't improve or become wiser; you are doomed to self-delusion. Without self-awareness, understanding others is next to impossible, too. 'Know thyself' is even inscribed on the Temple of Apollo at Delphi, in Greece; it is believed that 'knowing thyself' is the basis of wisdom and the basis of leadership.

To be an effective leader-manager, you need to understand yourself: Your values and the motives that drive your behaviour, your strengths and your limitations (discussed on page 111). You need to be aware of your mindsets and develop empowering mindsets (discussed on page 188). This boosts your emotional intelligence and resilience (discussed on page 196) and your ability to achieve goals (your personal goals and your work-related goals) and helps you build a successful career (see discussion on page 131). Self-knowledge also opens the door to understanding others, making it easier to develop effective working relationships and bring out the best in people.

ACTION!

You can pinpoint what's important to you by completing the checklist *What do I value most?* on CourseMateExpress. It is part of the student resources for Chapter 7.

The Johari Window

The novelist Aldous Huxley said, 'To see ourselves as others see us is a most salutary gift. Hardly less important is the capacity to see others as they see themselves.'[3] Are you self-aware and open, or secretive, self-absorbed and blind to your effect on others?

The Johari Window can help you increase your self-awareness in this area. It looks at two dimensions to understanding yourself:

1. Aspects of your behaviour and style that are *known* or *not known* to you.
2. Aspects of your behaviour and style that are *known* or *not known* to others.

Combining these two dimensions reveals four areas of self-awareness, shown in Figure 8.1. The top left square is your public self, or the *arena*. It contains information about you that you and others know, such as your name, your job and your experience in the organisation.

The top right square in Figure 8.1 is your *blind* area. It contains information about yourself that others can see but of which you are unaware. For example, Kay is curious and keen to learn, yet is unaware that the way she asks questions often irritates people and makes them feel like she is cross-examining them.

The *closed* area in the bottom left square of Figure 8.1 contains information you know about yourself but which others do not; it might be secret information or merely information you never thought to or chose to reveal. For example, John's boss keeps him standing during informal meetings, which annoys John, but he says nothing; until John tells his boss that he would prefer to sit, this information will remain in his closed area. Sometimes there is a good reason for privacy. Sometimes, opening up and telling others would improve communication, trust and teamwork.

The final area in the bottom right square of Figure 8.1 is the *unknown* area. This contains information that is unknown to others and to yourself. This is the vast area of the unconscious.

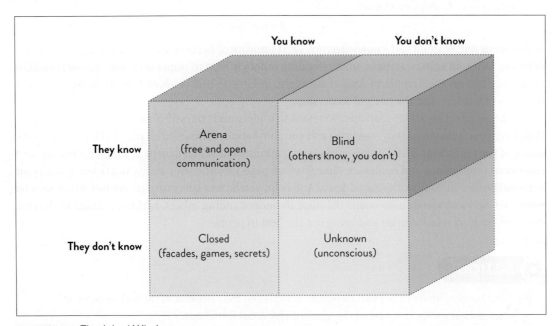

FIGURE 8.1 The Johari Window

The cubes in Figure 8.1 are shown equal in size, but for most people this is not the case. The relative size of each cube is different for everyone. Imagine, for example, expanding the *closed* area upwards, shrinking the open *arena*; people with a large closed area are seen as puzzling, secretive and difficult to communicate with and build relationships with. Now imagine increasing the *arena* to the right, shrinking the *blind* area and indicating a greater degree of self-knowledge, and down, shrinking the *closed* area and indicating fewer 'secrets'. People enjoy working with people with a large *arena* because a large *arena* helps them communicate openly, work well with others and develop honest and trusting relationships.

> ● THEORY TO PRACTICE
>
> **Putting the Johari Window to work**
> To promote effective working relationships, increase the size of your arena and shrink your *blind* area. You can do this through self-reflection and by asking for, listening to and acting on feedback from others (see page 141) and by being aware of the public aspects of yourself, such as your facial expressions and body language, and their impact on others. Disclosing more of yourself to people you trust also increases your *arena* by shrinking your *closed* area.

Espoused theories versus theories-in-use

Knowing your values (see page 186), acting on them and making decisions based on them, builds your integrity and self-respect and earns the respect of others.

Ah, but does it? Newspapers frequently carry stories about people who act on their values of self-interest and 'winning' at all costs. You may even know a manager who values self-preservation or self-promotion more than anything else. This is still value-directed behaviour, isn't it?

Then we have people who say one thing and do another. A manager might say: 'I believe in participation and I really value the contributions of my work team.' This is known as *espoused theory* – what people *say*.[4]

The way people *behave* is their *theory-in-use*. When that same manager fails to listen to team members' ideas or suggestions, the theory-in-use might be something like this: 'People don't have any ideas worth listening to or valuable contributions to make.'

Are these managers hypocrites? Possibly. More often, a theory-in-use that contradicts an espoused theory is due to one of three reasons:

1. *A person's theory-in-use hasn't yet caught up with his or her espoused theory*: For example, a manager believes in his head that people are reliable and he talks about how much he trusts his team members (espoused theory) but believes the opposite in his heart, leading him continually to check up on their work (theory-in-practice).

2. *A person feels pressured to conform to a set of values that is not his or her own*: For example, a manager who values independence and works in an organisation that values teamwork feels obliged to give 'lip-service' to teamwork but continues to praise and reward individual results.

3. *Another value, or theory-in-use, overrides the value in question, or the espoused theory*: For example, a manager who values participation and works in an organisation that punishes mistakes daren't risk involving her team because she values staying out of trouble and keeping her job more.

Whatever the reason, sometimes people's espoused theories (what they say) and their theories-in-use (what they actually do) disagree. When people say one thing and do another, they are difficult to work with. This is often part of their blind spot (others see their inconsistency but they don't). People who have a large gap between their espoused theories and their theories-in-use lose credibility with their work teams and colleagues, harming their working relationships.[5]

To manage effectively, you need *congruence*, or agreement, between your espoused theories and your theories-in-use. This is often called 'walking your talk'.

Personality styles

Accepting that everyone has their own strengths, values and ways of working increases your flexibility and willingness to work differently with different people. Although people are extremely complex, you can learn to spot basic characteristics so that you can work more effectively with a range of people.

Part of what makes life interesting is individual differences and it's these differences that help you and your team achieve results. The sections below describe different ways to think about people's personalities, including your own. Each approach is valuable in its own way, with each offering different strengths, shortcomings, qualities and quirks. As you read through the following ways to think about people's personalities, think about which types of personalities apply to you and the people you work with.

Extrovert or introvert?

Dr Carl Jung, building on the work of Sigmund Freud, pioneered the study of personality types in the early 1900s. People, he said, face the world in two basic ways: as extroverts or as introverts. Most people fall somewhere between the two types, leaning more towards the extrovert or more towards the introvert end of the spectrum.

Between 50 and 74% of the population are *extroverts*.[6] They relate best to the external world of people and things and tend to be 'doers'. Extroverts love mixing with others and feel lost when by themselves. When persuading or explaining something to extroverts, show them how what you are saying fits in with other people's thinking and what others are doing, and how they can put it to immediate use.

Introverts make up the remaining 26 to 50% of the population.[7] They are the thinkers, who prefer the inner world of concepts and ideas and are happiest when they are by themselves, doing their own thing. Although not necessarily shy, they do not seek out social or group activities. To communicate best with introverts, find out what ideas are important to them and try to fit your suggestions and instructions into that framework.

Feeler, intuitor, sensor or thinker?

Jung also concluded that people receive and deal with information in four ways: feeling, intuiting, sensing and thinking. For most people, one of those four ways dominates, two are partially developed, and one is underdeveloped.

Feelers see the world, problems and decisions – and other people – based more on their personal values and gut reactions than a technical weighing up of facts, pros and cons. They are warm and outgoing and, because they are sensitive to people's feelings, moods and reactions, they work well in groups. Feelers make good counsellors and public relations people. They can build teams, organise people and harness their enthusiasm. When you're working with feelers, make your values explicit, so they understand 'where you're coming from', and take care to make them feel supported and accepted.

Intuitors are imaginative and are good at playing around with ideas and theories; they see the strategic perspective easily but often miss the details. Their hunches are often correct. At work, intuitors are strongest at long-term planning and creative tasks. Explain your vision and ultimate goals, and then let their creative minds work out how to help you achieve them.

Sensors are down-to-earth, energetic and hard working, preferring action to words or ideas. They are practical people with a lot of common sense and are the first to roll up their sleeves and say, 'Let's get on with it' – often before thinking a problem through. 'Try it, then fix it' is their motto because they are impatient and like to get work done. At work, sensors are usually well organised and adept at converting ideas into action, 'getting the ball rolling', negotiating, setting things up and troubleshooting. When you're working with sensors, speak clearly and in practical terms and get to the point quickly, avoiding too much detail or 'fancy theory'.

Thinkers are strong on clear, logical reasoning. They are methodical and enjoy analysing problems but are less effective when it comes to implementing solutions. You can often find thinkers working with facts and figures, in systems analysis or in research. Give them facts and sound, rational information to help them overcome their natural scepticism.

People- or task-focused?

Another basic difference between people is whether they focus first and foremost on the *task* at hand or on the *people* doing the task. Those who put the task first probably care about people too – they just concentrate on the job at hand. When you're chatting to or meeting with task-oriented people, skip or minimise the 'small talk' and get down to business.

People-focused people usually care about the task too – they just consider the people aspects of a task first. When talking with people-oriented people, discuss how a decision affects people, who needs to be informed or consulted about a problem or decision and other people issues.

⦿ THEORY TO PRACTICE

The value of a cuppa
Jim Hayward, CPA, a former TAFE teacher and now a company director and consultant in South Australia, describes the value of a cuppa like this:

'As a young man I didn't drink tea or coffee. That was a disadvantage in my first management appointment in Ceduna. Andrew, my "2IC" always treated me very formally. There was no relationship. We had one very tough week when I decided I did need a coffee. With cuppa in hand, I walked into his office … and we talked.

'I soon learnt the value of walking around with half a cuppa, when I could very easily talk with my three staff. But without a cuppa, it all became very formal – hard to build trust that way.'

Conscientious thinker, dominant director, interacting socialiser or steady relater?

Psychologists have expanded greatly on Jung's findings. One way of understanding people combines the extroversion–introversion and people–task continuums discussed above to give four different personality types: conscientious thinkers, dominant directors, interacting socialisers and steady relaters. One type or temperament is no better or worse than any other – they are just different.

Conscientious thinkers are introverts who pay attention to the task and produce high-quality work. They look after the details, check things carefully, keep to time and produce accurate, comprehensive information. They have a strong need for achievement and 'getting things right'. They are deliberate, well-organised people who are good at analysing problems and thinking them through. They enjoy study and analysis, weighing up both sides of an issue and examining alternatives carefully. Their approach to work is accurate, diligent, exacting, objective, orderly, systematic and thorough. Conscientious thinkers are serious and well-organised perfectionists but they can also be stuffy, fussy, judgemental, critical and slow at making decisions. A team with too many conscientious thinkers would suffer 'paralysis by analysis'.

Don't ask the conscientious thinkers to turn in a rushed, 'close enough is good enough' job and don't ever present sloppy work to them. When you need to criticise a conscientious thinker, do so gently and tactfully. Explain decisions, problems and situations fully and carefully and include the details they crave. When you need to make changes, for example to the departmental layout, a job assignment or a procedure, spell them out clearly, allow time for questions and give them time to adjust. Don't try to rush conscientious thinkers.

Dominant directors are extroverts who focus on the task. They provide energy, 'get the ball rolling' and make decisions. They are competitive, direct, outgoing and results-oriented. They are often ambitious, willing to speak up, make decisions easily, 'set the pace' and use their initiative. Strong-willed and practical, dominant directors often have a strong need for power, preferring to be in charge. They resist authority from others, often challenging the status quo. Dominant directors get to the point quickly – so quickly they can seem blunt, impatient and pushy. They are fast-paced, want things done *right now* and dislike sloppy results. But too many dominant directors in a team would be so busy fighting between themselves for control that they wouldn't get much work done.

To work effectively with dominant directors, communicate clearly and accurately and get to the point quickly. Turn in quality work that is practical and results-oriented. Don't try their patience with abstract theories and concepts or too much attention to people issues, which they view as 'fluffy'. Treat dominant directors with the respect they believe they deserve and let them think they're in charge (even when they aren't).

Interacting socialisers are extroverts who focus on people – they like people and like to have people around them, and they enjoy working with and helping others and trying out new and better ways of doing things. They add enthusiasm, spirit and a sense of fun to the team and are impulsive, optimistic, persuasive, sociable and talkative. Interacting socialisers are good at influencing people and creating a motivating environment. They are creative, energetic and open with their feelings. They thrive on change, ideas and new trends and they need their achievements and contributions recognised. But interacting socialisers are often disorganised and inattentive to detail, excitable, manipulative, undisciplined and vain. A team might never get anything done with too many of these energetic, talkative people!

To develop good working relationships with interacting socialisers, keep details and detailed work well away from them. Focus on the strategic perspective and vision and let them talk, participate, motivate and create an enjoyable atmosphere. Treat them as friends.

Steady relaters are people-oriented introverts who pay attention to people and relationships in order to complete the task. Willing, reliable, cooperative, easy going, consistent, helpful and relaxed, steady relaters may not be balls of fire but they are valuable team players. Quiet and often unassertive, they are comfortable taking a back seat. They dislike conflict, changes in direction or goals and sudden surprises. They prefer their known and stable routine to the untried and untested. Good thinkers and patient listeners, the stable, quiet manner of steady relaters makes them good at calming down upset people. Others sometimes see them as insecure conformists who are awkward, indecisive, possessive and unsure. Too many steady relaters could cause a team to stagnate and fail to improve.

To discover a steady relater's thoughts or opinions, ask a lot of open questions and listen carefully. Don't overlook them or take their contributions, hard work and loyalty for granted.

Analyst, empathist, legalist or realist?

You probably have a few *analysts* in your team. These are the people who work best on their own. Their ability to think conceptually, intuitively, logically and theoretically makes them valuable for their creativity and good ideas. They're competent, competitive and serious self-starters who often seem to be married to their jobs.

Keep detail, routine and practical matters away from analysts. Tell them what you want and then stand back and let them work out what to do. Give them ways of tracking their progress and ask for their thoughts, especially when you're short of good ideas.

No doubt you have a few *empathists* on your team, too. They're warm, communicative people who strive for meaning and harmony. Like analysts, they're intuitive but pay attention to their feelings as much or more than to logic. They're natural coaches, encouragers, helpers and supporters.

Give these empathic team members encouragement, 'face time' and personal instruction. See that they know the importance of the job they're doing and that you value their contributions. When you need to offer feedback, do so carefully and constructively so they don't interpret it as criticism or as a personal attack. Give empathists autonomy and a chance to learn, and don't burden them with detail.

You're bound to have quite a few accurate, conservative, loyal, practical, responsible, serious and steady people on your team, people who tend to be cautious, seek security and avoid change. Known as *legalists*, you can count on them to work well with details and work best in structured, predictable situations where they reliably apply rules and procedures, follow regulations and keep to the routines.

Give legalists the detail they need to do their work and formal recognition for their contribution and effort. Be punctual and thorough when dealing with legalists and don't spring surprises on them. Since they dislike change, explain any required changes fully and carefully.

You probably have nearly as many *realists* as legalists on your team. They're the hands-on, practical, technical people – the action-oriented trouble-shooters. Often flamboyant, fun loving, impulsive and spontaneous, they thrive on excitement. They're flexible, good at coping with change and open-minded and tolerant.

Coach realists on self-organisation and time management and give them hands-on, well-planned training. They need plenty of freedom and enough variety so they don't get bored and 'muck around'. Help them practise and perfect their skills and count on them to rise to the challenge in a crisis. Enjoy their company.

(To find out about working with people from other cultures, see page 858.)

● IN A NUTSHELL

Stay flexible!
From the preceding section, it should be clear that treating everyone the same is a mistake. Adjust the way you assign and delegate work, ask for help or information and thank people for it, give information and present your ideas to suit each individual you work with.

2. Building trust and confidence

Example is not the main thing in influencing others. It is the only thing.

Albert Schweitzer (German theologian, physician, philosopher) *Brothers in Spirit* (2007)[8]

Without trust, good working relationships cannot develop. Customer loyalty, employee attraction, retention and morale, leadership effectiveness, profitability and gaining the benefits of diversity – all depend on trust. According to leadership scholar Warren Bennis, trust 'is the lubrication that makes it possible for organisations to work'.[9]

Departments and teams can't work without trust, either. Team members must trust each other, their leader-managers and their organisations to perform at their best. As empowerment, cross-functional teams, self-managed teams, virtual teams and telecommuting spread, not only must employees trust managers and the organisation to treat them fairly, but managers must also trust employees to do their jobs responsibly and correctly. Trust is truly a two-way street.

Because you depend on the goodwill of people above, below and at your level in the organisational hierarchy to achieve results, you need to build trust and confidence across, down and up the organisation. The way to build trust is to balance the attention you pay to the task at hand with the attention you pay to people – the two are inextricably linked.

● THE STRATEGIC PERSPECTIVE

Trust pays

Trust is important. But how important is it? Broken trust may harm morale, loyalty and productivity, but does it show up on the bottom line?

Research shows it does. For example, a survey of 6500 employees at 75 North American Holiday Inn hotels, using questionnaires in six languages and oral surveys for illiterate employees, asked for a response to statements such as 'My manager delivers on promises' and 'My manager practises what he preaches'. Researchers then correlated the responses with customer satisfaction surveys, personnel records and financial records.

The results were conclusive. Hotels with employees who strongly trusted their managers were substantially more profitable than hotels with employees who trusted their managers an 'average' amount or less. The link was so strong that a one-eighth point improvement in trust increased a hotel's profitability by 2.5% of revenue, which translated to a profit increase of more than $250 000 per hotel per year.[10]

Trust is an absolute. You either trust someone, or you don't. Trust is fragile: It takes time to develop but seconds to destroy and, once lost, it is difficult to earn back. An organisation's formal rules and policies can't build trust; only its culture, values and the integrity with which people work can breed and sustain trust.

Think of trust as 'relationship capital'. Like real capital, it takes time to amass and effort to preserve. When you keep drawing on it without replenishing it, your account quickly empties. Trust is deposited in your relationship accounts through genuineness, empathy, integrity and time; when you don't deposit enough, you can't draw on it.

> ● **IN A NUTSHELL**
>
> **How to keep trust**
>
> Here are six actions that can cost you trust, with suggestions for guarding against them:
>
> 1. Creating the impression of change for the sake of change: Explain clearly what a change is intended to achieve, why it is needed and what you expect from your staff; keep communicating.
> 2. Failing to ensure people know where they stand: Make your expectations clear and apply your values and ethics consistently.
> 3. Falling for fads: Employees are sceptical of managers who constantly tout new techniques and implement them half-heartedly. Explore and experiment, but don't dabble.
> 4. Playing favourites: Don't spend more time chatting with one employee than another. Don't give most of the interesting assignments to one employee. Don't say 'Yes, great idea' to one employee but not to another, or in any other way show favouritism.
> 5. Reneging on your commitments: When you make a promise, keep it. For example, when you promise an employee he can take time off in lieu of working overtime on a project, honour that commitment when the time comes.
> 6. Shifting sands: Unclear and changing priorities, rules and standards that you adhere to one day but not the next, show you have a lack of values, vision and goals and shout 'inconsistency and hypocrisy'. Know your overall team purpose, and your organisation's vision and goals, concentrate on them and abide by the rules and standards you have set.

Earn trust

Trust and credibility go hand in hand, and underpinning both is honesty. People are only willing to follow leaders they believe look after their rights and their best interests. When people believe this, they are willing to follow those leaders to the degree to which they rate their competence, honesty and ability to inspire.[11] You communicate these qualities through your confidence and enthusiasm.

There are five components of trust:

1. Competence: Interpersonal and technical knowledge and skills.
2. Consistency: Good judgement, predictability and reliability.
3. Integrity: Honesty and truthfulness (considered the most important).
4. Loyalty: Willingness to protect people and save face for them.
5. Openness: Willingness to share ideas and information freely.[12]

Leader-managers who earn trust create an atmosphere and expectation of trust so that people behave accordingly, and they actively cultivate trust so that people feel safe. They trust others, which allows them to empower people, and use consultative and participative leadership styles. Here are some other characteristics of leader-managers who earn trust:

- They admit when they get it wrong, enabling others to do the same and learn from their mistakes.
- They are passionate about what is important to them, motivating people and making it easy for people to follow them.
- They confront people without being confrontational, for example, by tactfully tackling under-performance when necessary.
- They consider the impact of their actions or inactions on others.

- They give credit when tasks succeed and accept responsibility when they don't.
- They keep confidences, so people can confide in them and tell them the truth.
- They pursue team or organisational goals rather than personal goals.
- They speak clearly and in a straightforward manner, without hidden agendas, so that people know where they stand.
- They stay true to their values and principles, which makes them consistent and reliable.
- They use power positively, to do the right thing, not to massage their egos.

The late Maya Angelou summed it up nicely when she said, 'I've learned that people will forget what you said; people will forget what you did; but people will never forget how you made them feel.'[13]

● THEORY TO PRACTICE

Jim Dawson, transformational leader

Jim Dawson joined Zebco, a company that makes fishing tackle, at a time when high-quality yet inexpensive Asian imports began to flood the US market, threatening the company's viability. Because workplace relations between employees and management were poor, it was difficult to make the necessary increases in productivity that might save the company from going out of business.

As an 'outsider', Dawson knew that trust would be an important issue in rebuilding workplace relations. He chose two highly visible and symbolic actions to reduce 'class differences' between workers and management. He discontinued the reserved parking spaces for management and instituted the President's Club – anyone with 100% attendance won a reserved parking space. And he walked into the factory one morning and smashed the time clock with a crowbar.

Productivity increased three-fold. Today, Zebco is the world's largest fishing tackle company.[14]

● ACTION!

How trustworthy are you? Take the interactive self-test of the same name on CourseMateExpress and find out.

Don't blame – take responsibility

Imagine a manager who blames circumstances, the economy or other people when results are disappointing or a project doesn't go according to plan. Imagine a manager who rants and raves when people make mistakes rather than putting matters right or showing them how to avoid similar mistakes in the future. These managers would find establishing effective working relationships hard going and they probably wouldn't last long in their roles. Here's a motto they could usefully adopt: 'Don't just see problems. Solve them.'

Taking responsibility for fixing mistakes, putting plans back on track and solving problems helps you to develop and maintain effective working relationships. When people face problems and mistakes head on and do what they can to fix them, they are a pleasure to work with. Taking responsibility builds your personal power (see page 103 to find out more about how to do this) and increases your overall effectiveness.

People who take responsibility don't do these three things:

1. Blame themselves, others or circumstances for problems and mistakes.
2. Ignore problems and mistakes, hoping they'll go away.
3. Make excuses for problems and mistakes.

● THEORY TO PRACTICE

Build trust first
Before people decide what they think of your message, they decide what they think of you. Two characteristics weigh heavily when people form an opinion of others: *trustworthiness* and *competence*. These characteristics answer two important questions:

1. What are this person's intentions towards me?
2. Is this person capable of acting on those intentions?

Without trustworthiness, even the most competent people are treated with envy or resentment. But warmth without competence elicits pity.

So what to do? According to a growing body of research, projecting strength and competence before establishing trust risks a host of unwanted responses, including fear, which ultimately drags down productivity.

It's best to establish trust first; this is where the important qualities of employee engagement and influence begin. Even a few non-verbal signals, such as a nod, a smile and an open gesture, show you're pleased to see someone and are paying attention to them. A foundation of trust, supported by competence, leads to cooperation, flexibility, information sharing, innovation and openness, and makes planning, coordinating and executing easier.[15]

Treat people 'right' – show respect

Do you treat everyone with respect, regardless of their position or personal characteristics? Or do you grace just a select few with your consideration and high regard based, perhaps, on their seniority or on whether you 'like' them?

People who build and keep effective working relationships don't treat people differently based on what they do, where they're from or who they are. They treat internal customers and suppliers as valued colleagues, and contractors and external customers and suppliers as valued contacts – regardless of their size or the amount of business they do with them. (Chapter 20 explains how to develop effective relationships with customers and suppliers.)

Empathy, integrity and respect are essential ingredients of effective working relationships. According to the principle of *psychological reciprocity*, which reminds us that *mirror neurons* in the brain are designed to encourage people to treat others the way others treat them, behaving respectfully and with empathy and integrity towards people encourages them to treat you the same way.

A mindset that accepts and respects people for what they are also helps you work effectively with people from different cultures and social backgrounds and people with special needs. (See Chapter 26 for more information on working with a diverse range of people.)

● IN A NUTSHELL

The politeness principle
To build effective working relationships, follow these three maxims:

1. Don't impose.
2. Give the receiver options.
3. Make the receiver feel good.[16]

Do the 'right thing'

People watch what you do and they make assumptions about the kind of person you are and what you value based on their observations. People notice what you pay attention to, what you reward and what you discourage, and the way you treat people every day. People notice whether you say 'good morning' when you arrive at work and 'goodbye' before you leave the office. They notice when you return their emails promptly. They notice whether you wait to sit when you enter someone's workspace until you know they're ready to talk. People notice whether you bypass rules, cancel meetings without explanation and 'walk your talk'.

When you have high self-esteem, you automatically want to do the 'right thing' because you owe it to yourself and to others. Even when the 'right thing' is awkward, inconvenient or uncomfortable, your high standards encourage you to make the 'right' decision and take the 'right' action. Doing the 'right thing' involves behaving ethically and with integrity and begins with self-awareness and knowledge of your core values (explained on page 186).

How do you know what is the 'right thing' to do? Try the 'mirror test': Ask 'What kind of person do I want to see in the mirror when I shave ... or put on my lipstick in the morning?'[17] You can also ask yourself whether a decision, idea, plan or strategy is morally defensible? Whether reasonable people would agree with it? And whether it would compromise your integrity, your reputation, your profession or your organisation's reputation? When the answers are doubtful, the right answer is probably, 'No'. Here are some more questions:

- Is it legal?
- If someone did it to me, would I consider it fair?
- Would I be comfortable for it to appear on the front page of the newspaper?
- Would I like my mother to see me do it?

Think about the effects of your actions and decisions, too. For example, consider how your decisions or actions affect those you work with internally and externally (e.g. your work team, your customers and your suppliers) and how they affect the wider community, the environment and other stakeholders. Straightforward? No. Easy? No. That's what management is all about – balancing the complex and the contrary.

THEORY TO PRACTICE

Being 'the boss' doesn't mean you can avoid having to explain yourself

The more you communicate your goals and intentions, the more you build understanding and trust and therefore, effective working relationships. Rather than assume people know or understand your motivations and aims, tell them. Especially tell them when there is a chance that they could misinterpret your meaning. For example, you may have a difficult message to convey or you may have made a decision that can't please everyone. You can help people understand your intentions in three ways:

1. *Talk specifically about what's important to you*: the goals, purpose and values that guide your actions and decisions and the experiences that forged them. Explain both the business and personal reasons behind decisions.
2. *Through integrity*: keep your word and make sure what you do (your theory in practice) reflects what you say (your espoused theory).
3. *Through consistency*: This comes naturally when you behave with integrity and follow your values and beliefs. When there are differences, explain them.

THEORY TO PRACTICE

The psychological contract and mutual rewards

The package of unwritten and usually unspoken expectations between employers and employees, or the psychological contract, generally refers to intangible expectations regarding loyalty, salaries keeping pace with market rates, work performed in certain ways, and so on. When all parties honour the contract, it works well. Violating the contract erodes trust, and relationships suffer as a result.

Make sure that your psychological contract with your team is a healthy one that respects individuals and their contributions, that it ensures that relationships are cooperative and mutually rewarding, and that it includes all the stakeholders. You may also want it to include such expectations as employees turning up on time and sharing knowledge and information freely. You may want employees to treat customers and each other with respect, and have fun and enjoy each other's company while working towards achieving their goals. In return, you might allow, for example, flexibility in timekeeping to accommodate personal needs when required, provide formal and informal training and development, keep employees informed about matters that affect them and provide informal cakes and teas to celebrate team achievements. Unspoken agreements like this lead to cooperation and mutually rewarding behaviours.

Behave ethically and with integrity

Have you ever been placed in a situation where you were tempted to take the easiest course of action even though it was not the most ethical action, particularly when you took a longer-term perspective or the needs of other people or the organisation into account? Managers often face difficult choices. Doing the 'right thing', choosing the ethical option or behaving according to your own or your organisation's set of values can sometimes be a difficult choice. What guides you in situations like this?

Acting with *integrity* means acting according to your own personal set of values and principles, which are different for everyone. Behaving *ethically* means behaving according to a set of standards that are the same for everyone, at least for everyone in the same culture. Acting with integrity and behaving ethically builds your credibility.

FYI

Code of ethics keeps everybody happy

Companies are increasingly adopting a code of ethics; for example, 96% of the FTSE100 in 2013 compared with 73% in 2001 had a code of ethics.[18] Many professions and organisations have developed their own ethical standards and codes of behaviour, too. A *code of ethics* spells out an organisation's or a profession's operating guidelines, setting out the obligations and expectations from the point of view of a range of stakeholders. In so doing, it acts as a decision-making guide for the organisation's employees or profession's members. A *code of conduct* outlines the types of behaviour that are acceptable and those that are unacceptable.

When managers and corporate culture lack the strength and resilience to observe the expected standards of ethical behaviour, we end up with disasters.

Most cultures share many ethical standards, for example, not killing people, and not stealing from people. Other ethical standards are more culturally based, for example, in some societies it is expected that managers hire their relatives, even when the relatives are not particularly well suited to the job. Family responsibilities come first. Australians expect managers to hire the person best suited to the job and not show favouritism towards relatives or friends. 'Smoothing the way' is *baksheesh* in some cultures but bribery in others. Caring for the environment might be mandatory in one culture and a luxury in another.

Having said that, you can think of management ethics as standards that are right or moral and that every manager should follow. Working ethically often involves managing competing tensions between an organisation's stakeholders. The ability to be assertive underpins your ability to behave ethically and with integrity. It helps you to state your needs, wants and opinions clearly and respectfully and to work with others to establish goals, agree responsibilities, identify and resolve problems and improve work performance. Stating your own point of view while respecting the rights of others earns you respect and a reputation for having the courage of your convictions.

● THEORY TO PRACTICE

The code of conduct for the Australian Institute of Management

Australian Institute of Management members have a code of conduct that represents most codes used in business today:

1. At all times discharge allotted and accepted responsibilities as a manager with integrity and observe those standards prescribed in the Guides to Good Management Practice determined from time to time by the Australian Institute of Management.
2. Not misuse authority or office for personal gain.
3. Comply with the laws of Australia and operate within the spirit of those laws.
4. So order personal conduct as to uphold and not to injure the standing and reputation of the Australian Institute of Management.[19]

Check out the website of the Institute at http://www.aim.com.au and see its code of conduct regarding 'The Manager – the Person', 'The Manager and the Organisation' and 'The Manager and the Community'. These set out the standards of ethical conduct expected of the institute's members and how to apply these behaviours in the workplace and in daily life. It calls on managers to exercise integrity in everything they do, to adhere to rigorous personal values in resolving potential conflicts of interest and to be accountable for their actions.

3. Establishing and sustaining networks

> Though most people recognise that networking is important to career advancement and success, few fully understand that a lack of access to influential networks can become a barrier to even the most talented employees.
>
> Laura Sabattini (US talent management strategist) *6 Unwritten Rules to Advancement in the Workplace* (2008)[20]

Networks are relationships of people who share similar aspirations and interests. Networking helps you expand and share your information, knowledge, perspectives and skills and extend your sphere of influence. The wider the variety of people your networks include, the wider the range of advice, help, information and support you can draw on.

Networking is becoming more important as organisation structures become flatter and the power that was invested in the hierarchy moves to people with strong and cordial networks – these connected individuals are now an organisation's information brokers and persuaders.

Here's how the Australian Institute of Management defines networking: 'Connecting with others without the need for immediate gain. It is a proactive investment in the future aimed at building a relationship with another well before assistance is sought.'[21]

Networking is not about seeing and being seen, or petty politicking. Think of networks as strategic alliances and the people in your networks as allies. Access to the advice, contacts, emotional support, resources and technical and task assistance they provide helps you contribute to your organisation and team. And helps you to achieve your professional and personal goals more easily, effectively and quickly than you could on your own.

● IN A NUTSHELL

Four characteristics of effective networks

Networking is a critical skill for managers and one of the key behaviours of effective leader-managers. Effective networks have some or all of these four characteristics – diversity, quality, size and strong bonds:

1. The more varied your networks, in terms of people's backgrounds, interests and skills, the more powerful they can be in supplying a wide range of information and ideas. Don't just network with people who are similar to yourself or with whom you spend most time – mix it up!

2. Network with the best. Network with skilled, smart and influential people who have strong networks themselves.

3. Large networks have more potential for supporting you, so include lots of people from outside your organisation as well as from inside it.

4. Mature networks that have been nurtured over time have strong rapport between members, which increases their willingness to support each other.[22]

You benefit from networking in three ways: operationally, personally and strategically. Make building networks part of your personal development plan.

- *Operational networks* help you manage internal responsibilities. Networks, made up of reports, peers and more senior managers, as well as key customers, distributors and suppliers, help you do your job by ensuring coordination and cooperation. Your role and responsibilities largely determine the people you include in them.
- *Personal networks* are made up mostly of a range of people outside the organisation who add to your personal and professional development.
- *Strategic networks* build business acumen and help you figure out future priorities and challenges that the organisation (and therefore you) needs to contend with.[23]

Your current and former bosses, colleagues and teachers can all be valuable to include in your professional circles. Friends, relatives, neighbours and acquaintances from professional and other groups can help you build knowledge, develop your ideas and broaden your perspectives. Include some customers, competitors, consultants and suppliers, too. Page 102 lists the six types of informal networks you can link into in most organisations. Some organisations have introduced Corporate Social Networking (CSN), a type of corporate LinkedIn, to help employees connect and share information and ideas. They can also include blogs, threaded discussion boards, Wikis and other web tools.

Add value to your networks without being asked, or you won't be in them for long. Find out what is important to people you network with, what they're thinking about and the challenges they face so you know how you can assist them. Mutual understanding helps you and the people in your networks achieve goals, develop and learn. Keep contact information up to date so that you can find each other when you need to do so. Build mutual respect and trust with everyone, concentrating your efforts on the people you plan to call on and support the most.

● IN A NUTSHELL

Some ways to network

You can network anywhere. All it takes is a smiling face, a stack of business cards and some information that is useful to someone else who may pass on some of their information to you. You can do this by:

- Attending seminars and conferences
- Being a friendly face and lending a helping hand to people who join your organisation, professional association and other networks; and being open to the fresh insights these people can offer you as you help them to assimilate and adjust
- Being active in service clubs, social clubs, industry groups and associations related to your work and interests
- Being thoughtful and staying in touch with phone calls and emails or by sending a relevant article, newspaper clipping, website link or a thank-you note or letter of support to someone who has contributed something worthwhile
- Eating lunch with different people two or three days a week; in company cafeterias, sit at a long table to increase your chances of meeting people you don't know yet
- Generally getting 'out and about' and putting yourself, your industry and your organisation forward in a good light, or writing a short article for a company blog or newsletter
- Interacting formally and informally with people inside and outside your organisation
- Participating in company events and making a point of speaking to a few people you don't know
- Maintaining professional profiles on social and business networking sites and using them to extend your networks.

---

4. Navigating organisational politics

A drop of honey catches more flies than a gallon of gall. So with men. If you would win a man to your cause, first convince him that you are his sincere friend. Therein is a drop of honey which catches his heart, which, say what he will, is the highroad to his reason.

Abraham Lincoln (US President) 'Temperance Address' (1842)[24]

It's been called the 'shadow organisation', the political side of organisations that consists of the unspoken alliances and coalitions of influence, and the often hidden norms and networks of relationships. Politics is a reality in every organisation.

Awareness of, and sensitivity to, this shadow organisation – who is what to whom, what people want and need and why, and the patterns of loyalty criss-crossing the organisation – is known as *political intelligence*. It gives you the ability to read and understand the undercurrents of relationships and build good working relationships with the people around you, without being seen as 'self-serving' or labelled as 'political'.

Should you involve yourself in your organisation's politics? Plato thinks you should. He said that one of the penalties for refusing to participate in politics is that you end up being governed by your inferiors. He was thinking of the state more than organisations, but the outcome is probably the same. Certainly, some people could use the energy they expend on politicking much more productively. Fortunately, though, politicking without the underlying management and technical skills, abilities and values to support it can seldom sustain a career. When backed by sound management and technical skills, however, political intelligence increases your personal effectiveness.

Organisational politics is not about 'protecting your turf' or pursuing personal advantage (or it shouldn't be). It's about forming alliances with like-minded people across the organisation, and with influential customers, suppliers and other stakeholders to help achieve team and organisational objectives. It's about managing your image in a positive way (discussed on page 144), fitting in with and contributing to the organisation's culture, and recognising and building networks and alliances with people who have power and influence (discussed on page 102).

Politics is about identifying your supporters and opponents and knowing how deep their support and opposition is. It's about saying 'thank you' for people's support and helping others (letting 'one hand wash the other'). It's about sharing the credit, making people feel good and building personal relationships throughout the organisation. Politics is about thinking several 'moves' ahead, finding out who to stay away from and whose opinions to listen to most carefully.

Provided you follow these four 'prime directives', strong political alliances can help you shape key priorities in the organisation and line up supporters to promote change and support your ideas and proposals:

1. First and foremost, don't make enemies and don't burn bridges. Don't whine or complain, intimidate people, make other people look bad or criticise anyone except in terms of the organisation's interests.
2. Don't assume anything you say stays secret. Think about what you say; don't discuss personal problems.
3. Be worth being around. Be assertive (but not tough or aggressive) when you need to and otherwise be pleasant, laugh and smile.
4. Play the political game in a professional, ethical way at all times.

Promote your ideas

You need more than a good idea for it to be implemented. In fact, in most organisations there's a bit of an art to promoting your ideas and getting them accepted. You need political know-how.

You need to know 'who's who' in terms of influence in the organisation (see page 102) and how to persuade people by linking your idea and its benefits to their goals. You need to know what people want and why they want it, and how to help overcome any objections they may have to your ideas. To succeed at that, you need to be up to date with your organisation's networks.

Think your idea through

First, give your ideas time to mature in your own mind. Rather than rushing off with a proposal when you have a brainwave, think about the specific outcomes and benefits your idea can achieve. Look at what you're trying to achieve from other departments' and key players' points of view. Who is likely to resist your ideas? How can your idea help them meet their goals? Think like the decision-maker(s). What do they want? What do they want to know?

Then float your idea by a few people whose opinions you trust; find one or two colleagues you can use as sounding boards to assess the viability of your ideas and gather suggestions on how to improve them. (If you're so positive about an idea that you can't see any potential resistance to it, ask what objections people might have to your idea.)

THEORY TO PRACTICE

Some points to ponder

When developing your idea, think about:

* How your idea fits in with or conflicts with other people's and teams' main goals and how the success or failure of your idea would be advantageous or detrimental to these people and groups
* Which people and groups might help or hinder the implementation of your idea – senior managers, other managers at your own level, other departments, your work team and so on
* Who might block your idea, why they might block it and what you can do to bring potential blockers on side
* Who might support your idea, why they might support it and how you can bring these potential supporters on side
* Who your idea affects and how it affects them (e.g. your idea might lower a person's or a team's visibility, importance or influence, or it might make more work for a person or group)
* Whose opinions you trust and whose support you need the most to have your idea accepted and implemented.

Lay the groundwork

Once you've discussed your idea with a few allies, thought about its ramifications across the organisation and adjusted it to make it more palatable all round, you can gradually build a coalition of supporters. Who is most likely to support you and who should you get onside before formally putting forward your recommendations?

Think about the best way and order in which to approach them. Who should you speak to face to face and who would prefer an email or a short memo? How should you communicate with each of these people to be the most persuasive? For example, who should you enthuse with the 'big sky' overview and who should you entice with the finer details? Who should you stress results with and who should you stress the people aspects with? (The first section of this chapter sheds light on this.)

Make your approach one of sharing your idea and involving others in shaping and strengthening the idea into its final form. Ask for people's views on your idea and listen to what they say, particularly when they have reservations with your thinking. Pay attention to their body language, tone of voice and other clues to gauge how much they really support, or don't support, your idea.

Expect some opposition. With every proposal, some people and teams stand to lose, just as some stand to gain. Don't take opposition personally and avoid becoming defensive – people naturally try to protect themselves and stay in their comfort zone. Think of resistance as a file to help you smooth off your idea's rough edges. Ask questions and try to see doubts from the resistors' points of view. People are more likely to open up to your ideas when you acknowledge their opinions. When 'my idea' becomes 'our idea', people respond more positively. Show people how you have incorporated their input to help them feel some ownership of the idea.

As you sound out the idea to a wider audience across the organisation, keep track of the responses, concerns and questions so you can prepare more thoroughly for your final presentation. Running your ideas by several people first also provides a 'comfort level' down the track.

● THEORY TO PRACTICE

Selling your idea to your team and colleagues

The decision-makers aren't the only ones you need to convince. Your colleagues, team and other stakeholders may not be the ones to give your idea the go-ahead, but you probably need to sell it to them just the same. Get their input and build in their ideas – right from the beginning.

Consider your idea from their viewpoints, both its advantages and its disadvantages. Write the advantages and disadvantages down and identify one or two of the most important benefits and one or two of the most important drawbacks. Then rework your proposal to minimise the drawbacks (or at least make them more manageable) and increase the benefits. Try to include a WIFM (what's in it for me) for everyone.

Try saying 'What would you think of doing it this way?' rather than 'This is how we should do it.' The former seeks their input and gives them a say. Make sure they understand that doubts and constructive thoughts are what you're after.

Present your idea

It goes without saying that your idea needs to be well thought out, practical and cost-effective. It's usually the best-packaged idea that wins approval, not necessarily the best idea.

Your first step is to frame your idea so that it meets the organisation's main aims and strategy. For example, when cost containment is an important theme in the organisation, show how your idea limits or reduces costs. When building a cooperative, professional culture is the current priority, show how your idea helps build that culture. Clearly state the business benefits (e.g. the bottom line, effect on morale, public image). When people know you're motivated by the benefits to the organisation, they're more likely to support you than when they think you're out to feather your own nest.

Your proposal must do more than address the organisation's needs, though. This means you need to sell not just its logical component, by supplying the objective information the decision-makers need, but also the emotional component, by subtly showing how it benefits the main decision-makers and the people it most directly affects.

So present facts and numbers by all means, but remember that people's hearts, as well as their heads, must support ideas. Saying 'because' after a statement greatly increases your chances of a 'Yes' because accurate facts and figures appeal to a person's sense of logic and reason – that's the head. Use the heart to strengthen your arguments further by aligning your ideas with the decision-makers' values and aspirations.

Position your idea so that it is 'our idea', the 'our' being influential key players, including experts and the decision-makers' peers, who have given you a positive response. The clearer it is that many people have been involved with and support your idea, the harder it is to reject it. When you can, link your idea with what the decision-makers have gone on record as saying they want or value, because people want to be consistent with what they have said or done in the past.

One bite at a time
According to recent research, it's better to dole out your evidence one point at a time rather than all at once because it leads people to conclude the evidence is stronger.[25]

Take into account how your idea will be evaluated and who the decision-makers might consult so you can link your idea into their priorities, too. Do the decision-makers have any positive or negative emotional attachments you may be asking them to accept or agree with? Have they had any previous positive or negative experiences with something similar? If it's positive, how can you link your idea to it? If negative, how can you show your idea is different from their past experience?

Know the financial cost and the risks of implementing your idea and how the risks can be addressed. Know the consequences of *not* implementing your ideas and be ready to present them. Should the mood of the decision-makers be 'Let's wait and see', you'll be armed with what the cost of waiting is.

Make it easy for the decision-makers by making your recommendation or proposed actions easily understood. Think about how your idea can roll out when it is accepted: once that first step is completed, what comes next? When there are a number of steps, use a table to show who does what by when. Once your idea is up and running, how do you plan to make sure it doesn't collapse? (That's your 'keep it in place' strategy.)

Finally, show that you have considered the pros and cons of your idea and weighed them carefully; have your answers ready for probing questions about the pitfalls of your idea.

When deciding how to best present your idea, think about the decision-makers' preferred modes of dealing with information (e.g. considering the overall picture or knowing all the details, as discussed in Section 1 of this chapter, 'Understanding yourself and others'). When you present your idea in writing, explain it clearly and persuasively and set it out well (see Chapter 6). When you present your idea verbally, present information in chunks that the decision-makers can easily 'digest' and slowly enough that they can follow your argument. When you rush or when your proposal is complicated, they may reject your idea rather than work hard to understand it (see page 199 for more information on making presentations.)

Work well with your boss

Your most important working relationship is probably the one you have with your manager. Although it can take time and energy, developing and nurturing it (yes, it's your responsibility, too) almost certainly increases your job effectiveness and avoids a host of problems and frustrations, and may open the door to interesting projects and career moves.

You need a good understanding of both yourself and your manager, particularly regarding strengths, weaknesses, working style and foremost concerns and goals. Find out what concerns and problems are uppermost in your boss' mind, what your boss' organisational and personal objectives are and what pressures are on your boss from his/her boss and colleagues. Use your empathy and pay attention to behavioural clues.

Find out how often your boss wants you to report progress and general information and in what format – for example, all the details or just the end result, in writing or verbally. Does your boss prefer formal meetings or informal discussions? Does your boss prefer information to be presented with diagrams, illustrative examples or statistics? Do you know how to avoid wasting your boss' time? This way you can fit in with your manager's working style and provide more effective (and appreciated) support. Otherwise, you're flying blind and misunderstandings are inevitable.

Find out about your boss' background and interests, management style and values, what your boss appreciates most in team members, and how your boss fits into the organisation's unofficial power structure. You can find some of this information online and from the grapevine and some through careful listening during general conversations with your boss. The more you know about your manager's 'world', the more effectively you can work together.

Anticipate your manager's concerns and address them ahead of time, or as they surface, without being asked to do so. Volunteer to take on tasks you know your manager would rather not handle. Fit in with your boss' routines and make your priorities reflect and support those of your boss. Here are some questions that help you understand your boss' world:

* How did my boss come into her current job?
* How well does my boss get on with his boss?
* What are my boss' career aspirations?
* What does my boss do outside of work?
* What was my boss' previous position?
* What does my boss value in the job?

⊙ THEORY TO PRACTICE

Find out the basics

Here are four key questions to discuss with your boss:

1. What are my key result areas and main goals?
2. How can we best measure my performance?
3. What operating guidelines do you want me to work within?
4. How can I support you do your job better?

Maybe you already know the answers to these questions. If so, what does that tell you about your relationship with your boss and your organisation's culture?

Make it easy for your boss to give you feedback. Ask questions when you need to, listen to any tips your manager passes on about how you can do your job better and put those tips into practice. When your boss praises you, don't feign modesty – say 'Thank you' with confidence.

Schedule regular meetings to update your manager on your work, what you've accomplished, what improvements you and your team have made, what problems you have resolved and are working on, and generally how the task is going. Be prepared, don't ramble. Be objective and factual to avoid bragging. Anticipate problems and solve them before they grow. Report any problems you can't fix early on and have the facts with you. Pass on any interesting information you've heard that might affect or interest your boss.

See yourself as your manager's partner in achieving results. Just as you depend on your manager for help, guidance, resources and information, your manager depends on you for support and cooperation. Do what you're asked. When you disagree, explain why and offer an alternative. Accept your manager's decisions and ideas and work to make them succeed.

Don't expect your manager to be perfect – no one is. Find out what your manager expects of you and find ways to let your manager know what your own needs and expectations are. If you're unhappy with your boss' management style, suggest ways you could work better together, explaining what you would like (not what you don't like) in objective, uncritical terms. Focus on the future and what you'd like to happen.

Don't take yourself too seriously. Your manager is an individual, not a job title. Show interest in your manager as a person and share a smile.

How to disagree with your boss

Here's how to open a discussion when you and your boss don't see eye to eye:

1. Pick a good time and place to discuss the situation, a time when your boss is most likely to be receptive and when you're not angry, emotional or upset.
2. Find out what your boss thinks and any background information you may not know.
3. Offer your views; put them in positive terms and frame them as suggestions for your boss to consider and word your comments so you don't appear to be dogmatic or aggressive, (e.g. 'I agree with … On the other hand, I think we may get a better result by …').

Here are some other pointers:

- Aim to see the situation from your boss' perspective as well as from your own.
- Choose your 'battles' wisely so you aren't seen as argumentative or disagreeable.
- Don't get personal: Stay factual, objective and professional, respectful and thoughtful.
- Identify what you agree on.
- Show how your ideas benefit the boss and the team.
- Speak about common interests and needs.
- Unless you are speaking on behalf of others with their agreement, say 'I' rather than 'we'.
- Your goal isn't to 'win' but to agree a course of action that benefits the team and the organisation.

Your position is stronger when you have built a good working relationship, consistently made your boss look good, have shown your are committed to the overall success of your team and organisation and when you're straightforward and don't play games.

Reporting to more than one boss

Convention has it that an employee should report to only one person. Called unity of command, this is based on the thinking that having more than one boss can create conflict and confusion. This principle flourished in the days of hierarchy and bureaucracy but is eroding in today's organisations in which flexibility and responsiveness to the environment are critical.

Temporary teams, for example, often form to undertake special projects and then disband; contractors and part-time workers are often brought in to work in one or more areas or in matrix teams. Employees are often temporarily seconded to other areas; and some organisations have opted for matrix organisation structures.

Reporting to several managers, each making requests of you, each with their own agenda and priorities, can be tricky. You're in danger of:

- Competing demands on your time: Which boss' work gets priority? This can be very tricky when each boss thinks their work deserves precedence.
- Conflicting messages: Different bosses have different expectations and communication styles and they can unintentionally undermine each others' messages.
- Work overload: This occurs especially when each boss treats you as if you work only for her or him.

To protect yourself, work out who your primary boss is. This is the person you formally report to, who does your final performance review and who makes decisions about your pay. Make sure you have regular, at least monthly, meetings with this boss and ask for his or her help in mentoring or coaching you to work well with your other bosses.

Be open about your workload so all your bosses know your commitments. Share your electronic calendar with them and block off specific times for working on different projects and assignments so they know when not to interrupt you. Provide each with a document updating your progress on all of your projects and other work. However briefly, check in with each boss face-to-face or virtually once a week to maintain your good working relationships.

When you have several bosses, it's probably fair to ask each to adjust to your preferred working style so you don't have to keep chopping and changing, which is stressful in itself. Let them know whether you prefer to receive questions and requests via email, meetings or in some other way. Agree on mutual expectations regarding response time for queries, regularity of meetings and regularity and format of update briefings. Try to agree on one way that works for everyone.

As with working for one boss, be clear about your deadlines and deliverables (as explained on page 110), focus on results and keep communication flowing.

Reporting to a remote manager

What if your manager is in Singapore and you're in Sydney? Because you can't see each other 'in the flesh' it's easy for each of you to miss the signals of energy, mood, personality and so on. When you report to a manager in a different location, it's critical that you communicate efficiently and build trust quickly.

As with any manager, agree on your job purpose, your key result areas (KRAs) and your SMART targets and find out your manager's preferred working style so that you can fit in with it. What is the best time of day to contact her or him? What is the preferred method of contact? Do they prefer progress reports in virtual person, or in writing? How much detail should be included? Does the boss prefer to take queries or receive results feedback as they occur, or in regular batches?

One of your initial goals should be getting to know your boss; when you can't meet face-to-face, make good use of virtual meetings and the telephone. Small talk is important, so avoid the temptation to move straight into task talk.

Provide regular progress reports and updates, with the frequency depending on you and your manager's agreed plan. Involve your manager in what he or she should be involved in (but avoid information overload). Make sure you aren't forgotten by establishing subtle routines; for example, phone at a certain time every day with a quick update or email a lunch-time status report in addition to your other regular reports.

Schedule regular virtual meetings with an informal agenda and prepare the agenda to go to your boss in advance. This is your opportunity to summarise what you've achieved since your last virtual meeting. Ask any questions you have now and finish with an outline of the next steps you are taking to achieve your mutual goal.

Confirm your commitments in a follow-up email, including date and time of your next scheduled virtual meeting. Design the email's content so that you can print it off to use as a checklist, or to list goals and create work schedules and plans to achieve them.

Eight ways to nurture effective working relationships

Strong and professional relationships with your work colleagues can improve your position in their organisation and improve their positions as well.

1. Even when you can spare only five-minute breaks, devote a portion of your day to building good working relationships. Ask a colleague for advice, be generous with another, check Twitter or LinkedIn, tell a joke, share a laugh, show appreciation of your team.
2. Fit in with people's preferred working styles and personality styles (explained on pages 135 and 212).
3. Give colleagues a newspaper or journal article on a subject that interests them.
4. Have lunch with colleagues to get to know them.
5. Include people in relevant emails.
6. Invite a new team member or colleague from another area to join you for a quick coffee.
7. Make a point to drop by your colleagues' workspaces, especially when they aren't on your regular path.
8. Pay attention to how people use language and personal space and adjust your own style to be more similar.

5. Turning conflicts into agreements

People who fight fire with fire usually end up with ashes.

Abigail van Buren (US agony aunt) *It's the Customer, Stupid!* (2011)[26]

Who do you know who has never had a conflict with anyone? No one? That's not surprising. Courteous and clear communication helps avoid some conflicts. Other conflicts, though, are inevitable because people are bound to have different opinions and want different outcomes. Some differences are merely minor irritations that people can quickly and easily forget, while others are more serious and can do lasting damage when not handled promptly and skilfully.

Think of conflict as verbally and/or non-verbally expressed disagreements between individuals or groups. It can occur between two individuals – between a manager and an employee or between a customer and an employee, for example – or between team members. It can occur between an individual and a group, between groups in the same organisation or between organisations. Conflict can even exist within an individual; for example, when one part of you wants to stay in bed and sleep, while another part of you knows you should get up and go to work.

Direct or indirect aggression, such as backbiting, gossiping, malicious compliance, passive compliance and scapegoating are all consequences and signs of underlying, unresolved conflict. Unresolved conflicts can poison the atmosphere of a workplace. The responsibility for seeing that doesn't happen usually falls to the team's leader-manager.

You may be called upon to resolve conflict between work teams within the organisation and, occasionally, between an employee and the organisation. As organisations strengthen relationships with contractors, customers, outsourcers and other suppliers, you may need to manage apparent conflicts with them, too. You may also have to resolve conflicts with other managers in the organisation when the needs of your respective departments seem to be at odds. Clear thinking and the ability to communicate clearly and sensitively can help you reach solutions that are acceptable and beneficial to everyone in all of these situations.

Conflict can be useful

Conflict can lead to clashes of will and the formation of 'camps' (taking up strong stances), 'either/or' thinking, power struggles, quarrels, resentment and self-righteousness. It can be destructive, disagreeable, disruptive and stressful, leading to anxiety, anger and frustration, harming morale and productivity and weakening the teams and the organisation.

But that doesn't mean that the absence of conflict is good. Lack of conflict can indicate stagnant relationships or that people aren't sufficiently interested in an issue or each other to bother resolving their differences. At least when people argue, it shows that they care about the issue and each other.

In fact, some conflict is healthy, and it can be productive. So conflict itself isn't a problem. How people resolve it can be a real problem. When people's energies are pointed in the right direction – the team's purpose or organisation's vision – conflict can:

* Allow people to discover the best way to resolve a situation
* Bring hidden feelings into the open so people can deal with them constructively
* Develop confidence in and even enhance a relationship
* Move a relationship out of a rut
* Result in better ways of working.

Assertiveness and conflict

When what you want differs from what someone else wants, how do you approach it? Do you want to have your way no matter what? Would you do just about anything rather than have an open disagreement over it? Or do you want to figure out how you can both be satisfied?

The first way describes an aggressive, competitive, win–lose approach to conflict: 'I win–you lose', 'me versus you' or 'us versus them'. When you adopt an aggressive win–lose approach, you're sure to meet compliance, hostility and resentment rather than cooperation and goodwill. You need to rely on threats and your formal authority to deal with the situation and the outcome is never fully satisfactory.

The second stance is passive; it describes an avoiding, submissive or accommodating lose–win approach: 'I lose–you win.' When you take a passive approach – 'don't make waves', 'peace at any price', 'sweep it under the carpet' – you're likely to find that people take advantage of your good nature and difficult issues remain unresolved; resentment can build up to such an extent that an aggressive 'explosion' occurs.

The third describes an assertive, collaborative, win–win approach: 'Let's see how we can both win.' The focus is 'us together' versus 'the problem'. When you confront and deal with conflict openly and constructively, seeking a 'win–win' result that satisfies all or both parties, you keep exploring options until you find the one that is most acceptable to all parties. This style helps turn conflicts into agreements, or at least into satisfactory outcomes.

Causes of conflict

See if you recognise any of these top 10 sources of conflict:

1. Barriers, such as preconceived opinions, prejudice and selective hearing (explained on page 151).
2. Competition for limited resources.
3. Content matters such as who said what about plans, policies and priorities.
4. Differences in expectations, goals, needs and wants.
5. Differences in values.

6. Emotional issues, such as fear of what people might lose (including 'face').
7. Perception, for example, who has authority? Who knows best? Whose job is it?
8. Personality clashes.
9. Poor communication such as an inability to listen reflectively, lack of assertiveness, lack of empathy and poor summarising skills.
10. Role pressures.

When you are aware of these common causes of conflict you can avoid unnecessary problems. Keep an eye open for tension brewing around you and do what you can to address it.

Common responses to conflict

The only internal responses to conflict available to a person lacking assertiveness skills are 'fight' (aggression), 'flight' or 'freeze', (submission) all of which are stressful. Stress responses to conflict include breathlessness, 'butterflies' in the stomach, clenched fists, a clenched jaw, grinding teeth, a thumping heart and tightening of the vocal chords (resulting in a higher than usual, or shrill, voice or the need for repeated throat clearing). When conflict is unresolved or unsatisfactorily resolved, long-term stress responses such as problems associated with tension or substance abuse, and domestic problems can result. (See page 197 for more information on the fight, flight or freeze response, and on stress and stress management.)

People who have learned to deal with conflict successfully, either by watching others deal effectively with conflict or through formal or self-guided training, are better able to respond assertively, avoiding much of the stress that conflict can cause.

> ● IN A NUTSHELL
>
> ### Hurting and helping responses to conflict
> How you survive conflict depends on how negative or positive you can be. Table 8.1 contrasts the two types of responses.
>
> **TABLE 8.1** Conflict resolution: Hurting versus helping
>
> | Hurting responses | Helping responses |
> |---|---|
> | Apologising inappropriately | Clearly stating your position and goals |
> | Being negative | Staying positive and showing mutual respect |
> | Changing the subject | Isolating what you disagree about and what you agree about |
> | 'Either/or' thinking, unwillingness to explore options or compromise | Knowing what you want and your own limits and being willing to 'move' on some points |
> | Getting angry | Keeping calm |
> | Giving up and giving in – playing the martyr, pretending to agree | Agreeing shared goals and outcomes |
> | Lack of empathy | Empathy |
> | Personal attacks | Willingness to listen and respond objectively and non-judgementally, appointing a 'referee' if necessary |
> | Refusing to see the other's point of view | Trying to understand the other's point of view |

TABLE 8.1 Conflict resolution: Hurting versus helping (Continued)

Hurting responses	Helping responses
Trying to turn the conflict into a joke	A genuine desire to resolve the conflict, remaining respectful and polite while working towards a resolution
Win–lose or lose–win mindset	Win–win mindset

Hurting responses can create deadlocks, prevent mutual understanding, and leave losers resentful and even inclined to sabotage. Helping responses can unlock creativity, build stronger relationships and achieve mutually satisfying outcomes.

How conflict grows

Each conflict is different. Having said this, most conflict passes through the predictable phases, as shown in Figure 8.2. These stages are shown against a curved line. Think of this line as a hillside and think of the conflict as a ball. As a ball moves down a hill, it gains momentum and becomes increasingly difficult to stop. Like the ball, conflict gains momentum as it progresses through the

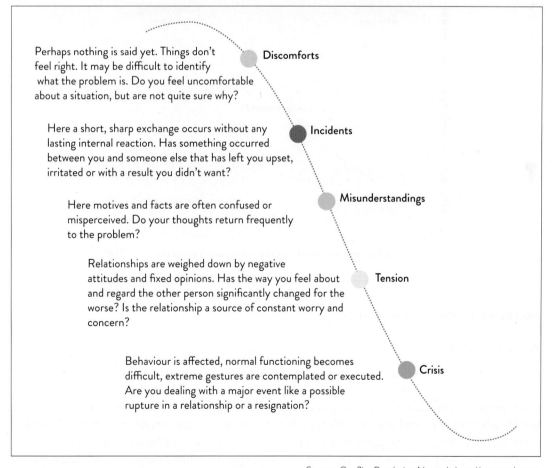

Perhaps nothing is said yet. Things don't feel right. It may be difficult to identify what the problem is. Do you feel uncomfortable about a situation, but are not quite sure why?
Discomforts

Here a short, sharp exchange occurs without any lasting internal reaction. Has something occurred between you and someone else that has left you upset, irritated or with a result you didn't want?
Incidents

Here motives and facts are often confused or misperceived. Do your thoughts return frequently to the problem?
Misunderstandings

Relationships are weighed down by negative attitudes and fixed opinions. Has the way you feel about and regard the other person significantly changed for the worse? Is the relationship a source of constant worry and concern?
Tension

Behaviour is affected, normal functioning becomes difficult, extreme gestures are contemplated or executed. Are you dealing with a major event like a possible rupture in a relationship or a resignation?
Crisis

Source: Conflict Resolution Network, http://www.crnhq.org.

FIGURE 8.2 Stages of conflict[27]

stages and becomes increasingly difficult to deal with. This makes it important to stay alert to signs of potential or underlying conflict and address it early.

When you ignore conflict, it can become increasingly serious until it reaches a crisis. When a 'scene' is not possible, one or both of the parties may 'vote with their feet', for example by resigning. Or the people involved may become depressed, impatient, intolerant, irritable, moody or sulky – costly in terms of morale, productivity and team harmony.

Five ways to manage conflict

The conflict modes shown in Figure 8.3 illustrates the five approaches people can take to conflict. The model is based on a person's or group's intentions along two dimensions: How much effort or energy they put into satisfying their *own concerns* and how much energy they devote to cooperation and satisfying the *concerns of the other party*. Each style is appropriate in some situations and inappropriate in others, so you need to be able to use each of them as well as know when to use them.

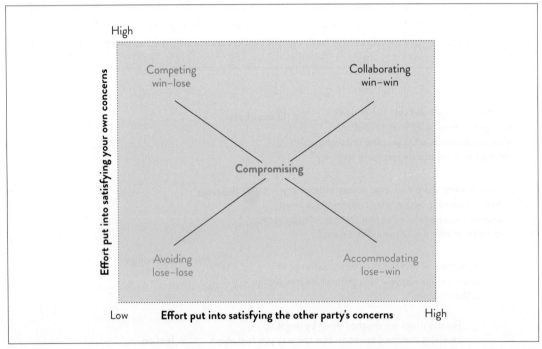

Source: Adapted from K Thomas, R Kilmann, *Conflict Mode Instrument*[28]

FIGURE 8.3 Conflict-management styles

Accommodate

Accommodating takes cooperation to its extreme – you put the other party's wishes before your own. The message is 'I give up' or 'Go ahead – walk all over me' or 'I don't care – do what you want'. It is often passive or submissive and might take the form of agreeing to someone's request when you would rather not or resentfully carrying out someone's request. Accommodating can also be selfless generosity or charity, or yielding to another's point of view against your better judgement.

Even when they are sure they are right, some people don't like taking a stand. Some leader-managers might be uncomfortable about using their power or afraid of losing the goodwill or cooperation of their staff and think it safer to 'give in'. The danger of too much accommodating or inappropriately accommodating is that others seldom take accommodators or their ideas seriously.

You might sometimes *choose* to accommodate and when that's a choice, rather than an automatic reaction, it's assertive. Accommodation can be a good choice when:

- the relationship or building the relationship is more important than the issue
- you have no hope of having your wishes met and accommodating minimises your losses and maintains a climate of cooperation with the other party
- your 'stake' in the conflict or issue isn't high.

Avoid

When you avoid conflict, you pursue neither your own concerns nor those of the other person. Instead, you 'let sleeping dogs lie', pretending that the conflict isn't there or hoping it will go away. Automatically avoiding issues when you shouldn't leads to displacing your feelings (the proverbial 'kicking the dog'), and general discontent and resentment, which in turn leads to griping and gossiping.

Avoiding the conflict might be a good – assertive – choice when neither the relationship nor the issue is important to you. Many potential conflict situations are just not worth the time and effort of taking a stand and sometimes it isn't really your place to become involved. Avoiding can also have its uses, particularly when you want to:

- collect more information before taking action
- diplomatically sidestep an issue
- postpone discussion until a better time
- withdraw from a threatening situation
- wait, to let people 'cool down'.

Collaborate

Collaborating is cooperative, and almost always assertive. The opposite of avoiding, it involves establishing an atmosphere of constructive cooperation and working with the other party to find an outcome that satisfies you both. It might take the form of exploring a disagreement to learn each other's concerns, needs, wants perceptions and positions, and then working together to come up with a satisfactory resolution. This is not easy and it takes time, effort and skill in communication and problem-solving, and the willingness to remain objective and impersonal while searching for a solution.

This 'let's fix it together' approach is particularly useful in situations where both the issue and the relationship are important to you and you want an outcome that satisfies both parties. Use it when you need all parties to be committed to the solution and when you need a creative solution, too.

⊙ THEORY TO PRACTICE

Agreement management
Think of conflict management as agreement management. How can you reach a mutual understanding? What goals do you share? How can you move towards the same side? How can you best reach agreement on this issue? How can you prevent similar problems or misunderstandings from occurring again?

Compete

Competing is uncooperative and aggressive when you automatically pursue your own concerns at the expense of the other person. This win–lose method of managing conflict relies on power (e.g. the ability to argue forcefully, pull rank or use financial incentives) to impose a solution on the other party. The usual response is antagonism, hostility, lack of cooperation and resentment.

'Do it my way' is the message of the competer, so it isn't surprising that 'yes men' and 'yes women' often surround managers who continually compete in conflict situations. People consider such managers hard to get on with as they don't know when to admit they are wrong. Not surprisingly, habitual competers find it difficult to form effective working relationships.

This is not to say, however, that competing is never an appropriate response to conflict. When decisiveness and speed are essential, as they are in emergencies, and when the issue is more important than the relationship, consciously taking a 'do it my way' approach might be the best option, at least in the short term; for example, when:

- nothing else has worked and 'no' isn't an option
- safety issues are at stake
- you need to make a difficult or unpopular decision
- you're in conflict with parties who refuse to cooperate and who are trying to take advantage of you.

When you assertively choose a competitive stance, be aware that you are likely to damage the relationship. Behaving assertively, not aggressively, and explaining your reasons, can help lessen the negative responses a competing style brings out.

Compromise

Compromising is the middle ground between accommodating and competing, where you give up more than in competing but less than in accommodating to arrive at a solution partially acceptable to both parties. 'Splitting the difference' or 'making a deal' is quicker and easier than collaborating. However, while it addresses issues more directly than avoiding them, it doesn't explore the issues in as much depth as collaborating.

Sometimes, settling for a workable compromise is the best you can do, so you might assertively choose to collaborate. Some other occasions to consider looking for a compromise are when:

- collaboration or competition has failed
- time is running out
- you need a temporary, short-term solution to a conflict while collaborative discussions continue
- you want a quick solution and are willing to live with the fact that neither party is fully satisfied.

IN A NUTSHELL

Win–lose, win–win and lose–win attitudes

The goal is to achieve a win–win outcome. The challenge is to work out how to achieve it. Table 8.2 can show you how.

TABLE 8.2 How to be a win–win leader-manager

Win–lose leader-managers	Lose–win leader-managers	Win–win leader-managers
I'll 'attack' you personally if I have to.	Let's not argue.	Let's deal with this objectively.
I must win this battle.	Have it your way.	Let's solve our problem.
I want a quick fix.	I want a quick fix.	We both need to be satisfied long term.
I want total victory.	You win.	Let's see if we can both be satisfied.
Me against you.	You against me.	We're in this together.
My goals are most important.	Your goals are more important than mine.	Let's see if we can meet your goals, too. What are our common goals?
My way or the highway.	Yours is the way to go.	How can we resolve this?
This is a fight.	Let's not fight.	Let's deal with this amicably.
This is how it is.	We'll do it your way.	Here's my point of view; what's yours?
We're on opposite sides.	We're on opposite sides.	We're on the same side.

THEORY TO PRACTICE

To speak or not to speak?

Is it wise to say something or not? When deciding, think about your goals, the issue and your relationship with the other person. How important to you is each? Say something when both your goals and the relationship are important to you. Say something when the issue alone is extremely important to you. Save your breath when neither is that important.

Four steps for reaching agreement

You can reach agreement, even in the most difficult situations. These four steps will help get you there.

1. Open a discussion

Make sure you have enough time to discuss the issue. Begin with a framing statement: a short, clear statement that 'sets the scene' and explains what you want to discuss. Make it clear that your aim is to reach an agreement that satisfies everyone. (You can find out more about framing statements on page 468.)

2. Give useful information

Helping the other party see the situation from your point of view can increase their willingness to collaborate. State it clearly, accurately and objectively, and stick to behaviour descriptions so the other person doesn't feel under attack. Explain the tangible, or real, effects the conflict or issue has on you using neutral, non-emotive language, or 'I' language. State your point of view assertively and congruently – look as though you mean what you say. See 'Theory to Practice 'I' language versus 'you' language', to see the different effects. Which would you rather hear?

THEORY TO PRACTICE

'I' language versus 'you' language
Table 8.3 contrasts the difference in expressing how a situation makes you feel, rather than directing the problem at the other person.

TABLE 8.3 How 'I' language helps solve conflict

'I' language	'You' language
I can't think when you raise your voice.	Don't shout.
I feel I'm being pushed into a corner here. I need some time to think it through.	You can't force me to …
Let me show you a better way to do that.	You did that the wrong way.
I'm not following you.	You're confusing me.
I need you to be on time.	You're late again.
I see it differently.	You're wrong.
I'm annoyed because …	You've annoyed me.

3. Gather useful information

Listen to the other person's point of view. Use empathy and reflective listening to make sure you fully understand them. Ask clarifying questions and summarise to check your understanding whenever you can, especially when the other person is using jargon or speaking indirectly or vaguely. Avoid becoming defensive, taking a hard-line approach, attacking the other person or telling the person what to do, which would escalate the conflict. Remember, you only have to understand the other person's viewpoint, not necessarily agree with it. Don't move on to Step 4 until you are sure you understand each other's points of view. You often begin to see a problem differently as you discuss it.

Discussing and listening to each other's views, *self-disclosure*, or explaining how the subject of a conflict makes you feel, can help to bring your discussion back into perspective. It can also result in similar responses from the other party, leading to greater understanding of the issues involved in the conflict. (See 'Theory to Practice: Self-disclosure' for some examples of self-disclosure.) Calm discussion can keep each person on the discussion if it tends to stray and keep you cool if the discussion threatens to become heated.

The same is true for *relationship statements*, or saying what you think or feel about the person with whom you have a conflict. For example, you might say, 'I'm really uncomfortable discussing this with you (self-disclosure using 'I' language) because I'm worried that it will damage the good working relationship we have and which I'd really like to see continue (relationship statement using 'I' language).'

If a discussion becomes heated: Stop! Ask for some time out. For example, say, 'I'd like a minute or two to digest what you've said. How about a short break?' or 'I'd like to take a break now; can we meet again this afternoon?' Better still, suggest a break when you feel yourself tensing up or becoming angry – before tempers flare.

THEORY TO PRACTICE

Self-disclosure

Self-disclosure means letting people know what's going on for you. Table 8.4 shows how expressing feelings can help in the conflict resolution process. Choose one of these three categories and use the self-disclosures appropriate for you.

TABLE 8.4 Stating your feelings can assist in conflict resolution

Your situation	Your self-disclosure
How you are feeling	'I feel angry and disappointed to have to bring this up again. However ...'
	'I feel uncomfortable discussing this with you right now.'
	'I'm at a loss to know where we should go from here.'
How you are thinking	'As I see it, there are two options open to us right now ...'
	'I think it would be a good idea to take a break and continue our conversation this afternoon.'
	'I think we've made excellent progress.'
	'Our next step appears to be ...'
How you are reacting to something	'I really appreciate that. Thank you.'
	'I'm confused – would you go over that again?'
	'I'm too upset to discuss this right now. Can we meet this afternoon?'
	'It seems to me we're going round in circles.'

Self-disclosure sometimes requires courage, trust and a willingness to take a risk to build a better working relationship.

4. Problem-solve

When both parties understand each other's views, you can turn to problem-solving. Here are the steps:

1. Summarise the problem: What is the issue? What are the facts? What are the feelings and concerns of each party? Define the problem in terms of conflicting needs, not as a conflict between competing solutions. Make sure you agree on your differences.
2. Search for mutually acceptable solutions: Think of as many ways to resolve the conflict as you can; the more solutions you have to choose from, the more likely you are to resolve your

conflict successfully. It can be difficult to come up with a good solution right away, so be patient. (Chapter 18 has more information on problem-solving and generating solutions.)

3. Evaluate the possible solutions: It generally becomes apparent when to move on to this step. Are there any reasons that a solution might not work? Might a solution be too hard to carry out or implement? Is each solution fair to each party? Remember, you are trying to reach a good, workable solution, not just any solution.

4. Decide together: Shared commitment is essential. Choose the solution that is most acceptable to both parties and plan how to implement and evaluate its effectiveness together. Don't make the mistake of trying to persuade or push a solution onto the other party. When people don't freely choose a solution, they're unlikely to abide by the decision or implement it fully. If the chosen solution doesn't work, meet and begin the problem-solving process again at Step 1.

THE STRATEGIC PERSPECTIVE

Take the opportunity to learn

After you've resolved a conflict, review it and learn from it:

- What caused it? Have you removed the cause so it won't occur again?
- What helped you resolve it? What obstacles were in the way?
- What signs were there that the conflict was brewing? Would identifying and addressing them earlier have helped? What could you have done? What should you bear in mind for the future?

IN A NUTSHELL

Tips to reach agreements

When you reach the stage of agreement to end a conflict, try these handy tips:

- Act, don't react: Pause and think, 'What outcome am I after and how can I best achieve that outcome?'
- Adopt a problem-solving approach: See the disagreement as a problem to solve rather than a battle to win.
- Agree on the content: State your position and your understanding of the other party's position clearly to make sure you are both talking about the same issue.
- Agree on the process: Right at the beginning, agree how to approach the discussions.
- Bring in a trusted third party: Mediators can often clarify the issues and help both parties see them and deal with the conflict objectively.
- Don't assume you have all the facts: Find out what other facts the other person has and what 'facts' you may have wrong.
- Don't assume you know what the other person wants or needs: Find out by asking questions and listening.
- Emphasise the relationship: When you clearly state that you want a continuing good relationship, it's easier to work towards that end.
- Interpret demands as opportunities: Thinking of demands as a way to spot more ways of resolving the problem lessens possible resistance.

>>

- Keep a long-term view in mind: This helps to keep what you say in perspective.
- Keep all verbal 'weapons' out of reach: Hiding behind an outdated or irrelevant corporate 'policy', point scoring, pulling rank or threatening only adds fuel to the fire.
- Keep early discussions informal: It's easier to 'toughen up' than to 'soften down'.
- Limit each discussion to a few issues: This helps to ensure that the 'mountain' doesn't appear insurmountable.
- Listen carefully and summarise frequently: This ensures that the other person knows you have heard and understood their point of view. Recap the other's point of view, especially before disagreeing.
- Look for and foster flexibility and creativity: How can you both get what you want? Don't limit yourself by grasping the first solution that comes to mind.
- Recognise that you're as likely to be biased as the other person: Respect each other's points of view, even when you don't agree.
- Respect the other party: Put-downs and personal attacks damage the relationship and lessen the likelihood of a successful resolution. Don't back the other person into a corner.
- Search for common ground: Once you have identified an outcome you both want, or want to avoid, you can begin working with, not against, each other. Find your common ground and work out how to reach it.
- Stick to the facts: Becoming personal really heats up a conflict.
- Test your assumptions: Identify any assumptions clearly and verify them. Making assumptions about what the other party does or doesn't know or want can be a recipe for going around in circles.
- Try tackling the easier problems first: This doesn't mean you're avoiding the tough problems. The progress you make solving easier problems can encourage you to find solutions to the tougher problems.

CourseMateExpress

Go to http://login.cengagebrain.com to access CourseMate Express, your online study tool for *Management Theory & Practice*. CourseMate Express brings chapter concepts to life with interactive learning, and study and exam preparation tools:

- Test your skills in different aspects of management with interactive self-tests and simulations.
- Watch videos that show how real managers operate in real businesses.
- Test your understanding of the changing world of management by taking the revision quiz.

QUICK REVIEW

1. Explain why people need to understand themselves before they can understand others, and review some of the ways people can understand themselves and think about others in order to work more effectively with them.
2. Explain how earning trust, taking responsibility, treating people with respect and behaving ethically and with integrity are linked and how they help develop effective working relationships.
3. The ability to network is becoming a key skill of employees at every level in the organisation. Discuss.
4. Why do managers need to be able to engage in organisational politics? At what point do you think politicking becomes counterproductive?
5. Discuss the types of conflict that you are likely to meet and explain the most effective way to deal with them.

BUILD YOUR SKILLS

1. Referring to the Aldous Huxley quote on page 210, discuss this advice in terms of establishing effective working relationships.
2. Explain why the ability to network may be more important for employees at all levels in the organisation today than it was 40 years ago.
3. Do you think the ability to understand and employ organisational politics is more or less important today than it was 40 years ago? Why?
4. Explain why assertion can be mistaken for aggression if the asserting person isn't careful to respect the other person's rights, as well as protecting his or her own. Give an example to illustrate your explanation.
5. If you have studied Chapter 7, discuss the mindsets that help managers establish and maintain effective working relationships with their staff, their colleagues and their customers.

WORKPLACE ACTIVITIES

1. List the people you work most closely with, including your reports, your manager, peers and internal customers and suppliers. Develop a matrix and, working through Section 1 of this chapter, 'Understanding yourself and others', note each person's characteristics.
2. Which manager in your organisation do you trust most? Brainstorm the characteristics and behaviours of this person that you believe earns this trust.
3. Give an example of a psychological contract at your workplace and explain how understanding and honouring it helps people's working relationships. What is your role, as a manager, in establishing and maintaining the psychological contract?
4. Find out whether your organisation has a written code of conduct or ethics policy and an anonymous mechanism for reporting misconduct, fraudulent practices or dishonesty at work. If it does, review and summarise them.
5. What are your personal and professional networks and how do the networks you belong to help you to do your job well and manage your career? Provide two or three specific examples.

6. Who in your organisation is able to 'make things happen' and obtain approval for their proposals? To what extent is this person's political intelligence helpful? Give one or two examples of how you have achieved outcomes you may not otherwise have achieved had it not been for political astuteness.

7. Describe a recent workplace conflict you have witnessed or been a party to and discuss its cause. Was the conflict useful or destructive? How did the parties deal with the conflict and how satisfactorily was it resolved?

CASE STUDY 8.1

DELUSIONS OF GRANDEUR?

David finally gets the break he has been hoping for. He is appointed team leader of the technical trainers of his company's learning and development unit. Now he really has a chance to show management what he is made of! His career is about to begin.

First, he intends to make some important changes in the way the team operates. He calls a team meeting and announces that, from now on, everyone is to adhere strictly to the standard working hours stated in their job contracts. Also, he intends to check everyone's expenses quite carefully when they return from their frequent interstate training trips. Under no circumstances does he intend to let his budget blow out.

The trainers point out that their frequent travel is often done outside working hours and a lot of their preparation for training is undertaken in their personal time. They see some of the 'relaxed' timekeeping when back at head office as *quid pro quo* – normal give and take. David replies that, on the contrary, this is a normal part of the job and they'd better start getting used to it. Seeing which way the wind is blowing, the trainers keep the rest of their thoughts to themselves.

The next item on David's agenda is the training program he ran last week. The training manuals and training aids didn't turn up. 'Sheila was supposed to send them and, as usual, she messed up. I intend to find a replacement for her as soon as possible. I won't have my unit looking unprofessional in front of the trainees.'

Later, in the canteen, the trainers have quite a few words to say among themselves. 'Fancy him checking up on our expenses – he's the one who over claims, not us!' They all agree on that point. 'David always says one thing and does another. And if he thinks I'm doing any travel or preparation in my own time, he's got another think coming!' Once again, there is agreement all round.

'What really gets me,' says Margot, 'is that the only way David seems to feel good about himself is by putting others down. He even does it in training sessions. He's always flying off the handle, too. I've seen him rip into trainees when they don't understand what he shows them first time around. All the trainees hate him – what in the world could management have been thinking when they made him team leader?'

'Perhaps they just wanted him out of the training room,' suggests Andy, only half-jokingly. 'Great! So now he can take all his inadequacies out on us.'

'Poor Sheila. She never makes mistakes on our programs – only David's. That's because he leaves her such poor instructions about what he wants. I wonder how we can help her?'

● ● ●

'He won't listen to us. He always has to be the one with the answers and the good ideas. We might as well forget about suggesting anything or pointing anything out to him. I'm off to polish up my résumé and reach out to my networks!'

'Me too! He's such an aggressive little fella! I don't want to stay around here any longer than I have to.'

With that, the technical trainers amble back to their workstations.

Questions

1. Where is David going wrong in his working relationships with his team?
2. What advice can you give David to help him develop more effective working relationships with them?
3. Thinking about the Johari Window, what might some of David's blind spots be? If you were going to help David understand some of his blind spots, how would you go about it? Explain the general approach you would take and write down your opening comments.
4. Is David building trust with his team or is he draining his account? Explain your thinking.
5. David seems to be heading for conflict with his team. What do you suspect is his natural style for handling conflict? How would you advise David to handle any conflict between himself and his team? What skills would he need to use to notice that conflict is looming?

A 'TIMID MANAGER'

Annya is leaving next month to take up a new position and Zed is clearly the best suited employee in terms of skills, knowledge and experience to replace her as the service centre manager. Yet one thing worries Russell, the customer service manager, as he contemplates the decision: Can Zed develop effective working relationships with his team and their customers? Can he deliver the difficult messages that managers often need to deliver and still maintain staff and customer goodwill and confidence?

As Russell reflects on the service centre's performance over the past 10 months, he realises it has had its fair share of 'uneasiness' and even conflict. Certainly, Annya's management style was rather aggressive, and the recent technological changes probably didn't help, either. And, according to a few comments that Annya had made to him as they discussed her handover process, there were one or two 'bad apples' in the centre who loved a good argument, especially when it involved 'riding' the boss.

Zed has always struck Russell as rather timid, although that doesn't mean that he is. Perhaps he could stand up to these difficulties as well as anyone; perhaps he could do it without the aggression Annya sometimes displayed. Perhaps he could re-build a few crumbling bridges. What to do … ? A mistake could mean disaster in such a key part of the business.

'Can I coach Zed to build trust and resolve conflict amenably or get him some training?' wonders Russell. 'I could support him through the first few months until he finds his feet, but perhaps I shouldn't take the risk,' he thinks. Yet Zed is, in all other respects, by far the best choice for the job.

Questions

1. Russell is confident that Zed is technically competent; what can he do to find out whether Zed has the skills to develop effective working relationships and to handle the conflict and discontent in the service centre that Annya has referred to?

2. Assuming that Zed needs coaching and training in developing effective working relationships and managing conflict, what skills would you advise him to concentrate on?

3. If Russell is correct in his guess that Zed is timid, what conflict-management style would he be most likely to adopt? What would be the repercussions of this style?

PART 3

LEADING OTHERS

'What's the biggest challenge in your job?' a senior manager asked a newly appointed manager.

'Well, this job would be a hell of a lot easier if you took the people out of it!'

Ah, the people. Every organisation can buy the same computer systems, the same furniture, the same everything. It's the way the people inside those organisations use those resources that makes the difference between success and failure.

Leadership is a big test. It is perhaps the most critical and most elusive skill set of all. It's no secret that people join organisations but leave managers.

Leader-managers may manage functions, operations or capabilities. They also manage themselves. But the best leader-managers *lead* people rather than *manage* them.

With the possible exception of managing knowledge workers, you are expected to understand the technical aspects of the jobs you supervise. Indeed, it's likely that you once performed the jobs you now supervise. Your role as a leader-manager also includes assigning and delegating work in a way that allows employees to stretch and extend their skills. Your role includes building and fostering diverse, intergenerational and multicultural work teams.

Those employees come from a wide range of employee groups in most organisations, including full-timers, part-timers, casuals, contractors and temporary employees, as well as employees you seldom or never spend time with face to face. You need to know how to bring out their best skills and abilities, as well as how to turn around sub-par performances.

This part of the book explains the skills of leading and managing your 'people', your team members. It helps you understand and build a work group that is a innovative and energised, and creates competitive advantage for your organisation. When it comes to leading people, you can expect challenges, surprises and self-development opportunities. So, here starts the never-ending journey of leading others.

CHAPTER

9

UNDERSTANDING LEADERSHIP

OVERVIEW

The Japanese say that leadership is like air: Necessary for life but impossible to see and touch.

As a leader-manager, you have a significant influence on your work group's performance. Therefore, you have a direct effect on your organisation's success. As a high-calibre leader-manager, you harness people's energies, you coach, guide and support them in their efforts and you see that they have what they need to do their jobs to the best of their ability.

As a leader-manager you express goals clearly and precisely in a way that encourages people to work willingly and cooperatively towards achieving their goals. More than this, you supply the vision, the overall sense of purpose, that inspires people and gives their work special significance. You don't *tell* people what to do. You *guide* them.

Leaders with these skills do not grow on trees – which is why these leaders are so valuable to organisations. In the long term, successful leadership is worth more to your organisation than modern technology, new buildings and a favourable quarterly result.

The challenges that today's dynamic environment presents make effective leadership essential. In fact, leadership is now a core competency that all managers must possess.

1. Can you distinguish between the main approaches to leadership and extract useful information and tips for yourself from those approaches?
2. Do you recognise when you should be leading and when you should be managing?
3. Can you predict how Australian leadership will develop in the 21st century and which of your skills you can strengthen?

This chapter explains different ways to view leadership and how you can put different approaches into practice, now and in the future.

Sandra's china and glassware team

Sandra manages the china and glassware department of a large city store. She has five staff members reporting to her:

- Bill, 22, a management trainee attached to her department for three months
- Ummi, 35, with three years' experience, is the most senior sales assistant in the department
- Labib, 17, has been with the store for six months, four of those months in Sandra's department
- Adila, 16, straight from school, has had three weeks in the department
- Marie, a part-timer in her mid 50s, has worked in china and glassware for nearly a year.

We join Sandra on a Monday morning late in October as she parks her car and walks towards the store. 'I must organise something really special for my team before the Christmas rush starts; they have a long, hard period coming up. Of course, Adila is new, but she seems all right – as long as you tell her every little detail of what you want done. But that's to be expected …

'Labib's coming along well, but I must impress on him the need for the "daily dust" in his area – customers don't want to handle dusty glasses! For the most part, though, you tell him what you want done and why you want it done and he's just fine.

'Ummi is more than fine – all she needs is a little help here, a small suggestion there, and everything happens like magic. Best move I could have made, delegating the display work to her – it seems to have given her a new lease on life.

'Bill's coming along well now, too. He even comes up with the odd good idea; he's a fast learner – just explain what you're doing and he catches on quickly. He likes to discuss his ideas.

'And then we have Marie, a real brick. You can always count on Marie to raise spirits and liven everyone up.

'Which reminds me, I must call a meeting over lunch to discuss how we can use the extra floor space we've been allocated for the Christmas period. I'll begin by thanking them for their hard work – our sales are up 8% and it's largely because of this increase that senior management has given us that extra space.

'Oh, and I must thank Marie for staying behind yesterday to clear up that backlog of credit slips …'

1. Understanding leadership

Absorb what is useful. Discard what is not. Add what is uniquely your own.

Bruce Lee (martial artist) *Wisdom for the Way* (2009)[1]

Effective leadership rests on three pillars: leadership skills, mindsets and temperament (or personality). You can learn leadership skills such as how to build strong, high-performing teams, how to ensure a safe and healthy workplace, and how to introduce and manage change, solve problems and make decisions. You can adopt and develop leadership mindsets (see more about mindsets on page 188). The temperament, or personality part is trickier because this is driven by a combination of your genes, your life experiences and your upbringing (see more on personality on page 212).

Whether or not you were born with a personality inclined to leadership, you can still learn to become a better leader. Knowledge about leadership has grown over the years through careful observation and research. Many ideas about leadership reach similar conclusions by different paths.

What is known about leadership today may not be the whole story, but you can improve your leadership skills by applying what *is* known. Your task is to choose what's important for you from the information available. Then you can build your understanding of what you can do to successfully lead others.

There are four schools of thought on how to approach leadership:

* Trait approach
* Behavioural approach
* Situational approach
* Transactional approach.

We look at these four approaches next and as you read through them, try to relate them to leaders you know, and think about which approaches you could best apply.

Trait approach

The top three traits most commonly found in effective leaders are:

1. *Initiative*, which entails independence and inventiveness and the capacity to see what needs to be done, combined with the willingness and ability to do it without being asked.
2. *Intelligence*, which should be above average (but not of genius level) and should include particularly good skills in solving abstract and complex problems.
3. *Self-assurance*, which involves self-esteem and setting challenging personal goals.

Sounds simple, doesn't it? But … these traits do not always hold true. Researchers who analysed the results of more than 100 leadership studies found that, of the many traits identified for successful leaders, only 5% of them were reported in four or more of the studies.[2]

The trait approach is generally considered an oversimplification of a very complex subject, for four main reasons:

1. The 'top three traits' of initiative, intelligence and self-assurance, while important, are not sufficient in themselves to make an effective leader.
2. Many leadership traits are so ill defined as to be useless in practice.
3. No one can have all the leadership traits identified by the research.
4. There are too many exceptions: Many successful leaders do not display so-called 'necessary' leadership traits.

Despite the lack of hard data to support the trait approach to leadership, it has wide, popular appeal. Is this because people intuitively know there is 'something to it'?

The trait approach not only makes intuitive sense, it may make scientific sense, too. Evolutionary psychologists have long looked at how the brain is 'hard wired': People have individual differences and are born with many character traits and predispositions that harden as we age into adulthood. Some personality traits, the evolutionary psychologists believe, are inborn in the form of deep-rooted inclinations; some people may be born to lead and others are born not to lead. Perhaps the trait approach just hasn't defined its terms well enough yet.

So let's review two important leadership traits:

1. Desire to lead.
2. Mental toughness.

Then we'll look at five theories associated with personal traits:

1. Charismatic leadership.
2. Empathic leadership.
3. Servant leadership.
4. Narcissistic leadership.
5. Transformational leadership.

Desire to lead

Reluctant leaders are invariably poor leaders. To be a good leader, you first need to *want* to lead.[3] People can be trained to manage but they can't be trained in the passion to lead.

IN A NUTSHELL

Some definitions of leadership

At a training program on leadership held at Uluru, more than 200 managers from across Australia developed the following definitions of leadership. Leaders:

* articulate and embody a vision and goals and enable others to share and achieve them.
* communicate and achieve goals and plans effectively.
* get results by establishing a vision and a strategy, and coaching, communicating, delegating and motivating people to achieve that vision.
* have the courage of their convictions and are fair and just in achieving their goals.
* help others to achieve a shared goal without relying on position or power.
* use an elusive quality that inspires others to perform, as well as a set of skills that help them persuade others to accept directions and goals willingly.[4]

Definitions of leadership abound and most agree that leaders are people who can influence the behaviour of others to achieve a goal. However, there is not one definition that covers all situations. The definition you adopt has to be 'right' for you.

Mental toughness

Mental toughness has long been linked with athletes and is now being linked with successful leadership. Mental toughness is stamina, or 'staying power'. Here are its main features:[5]

* *Chilling out*: Switching on and off as needed; the ability to relax, recover and recharge your batteries, to leave work behind and find balance in your life.
* *Competitiveness*: Raising your game when you need to get the result, no matter what.
* *Control*: Regaining psychological control following unexpected, uncontrollable events; staying calm and keeping a lid on your nerves.
* *Drive*: Having the desire and will to succeed.
* *Focus*: Compartmentalising and concentrating fully on the task at hand, despite personal or other distractions.
* *Resilience*: Recovering from setbacks and using them as opportunities to come back stronger.
* *Resolve*: Accepting that pressure comes with the territory and not being fazed by it; the ability to grit your teeth, push through the physical and emotional pain barrier, and keep going when the going gets tough
* *Self-belief*: Having faith in your abilities.

What this says is that you don't have to be tough all the time. You just need to know when to be tough. (See page 194 for more information on emotional intelligence and resilience.)

Charismatic leadership

People with charisma are charming and powerful. They inspire and motivate people by reaching them on an emotional level by tapping into their hopes and ideals. Charismatic leaders provide a sense of purpose, inspiring their followers to achieve great results. They scan and read their environment, picking up people's concerns and moods. They hone their actions and words to suit different situations. They are excellent, often 'theatrical', communicators with high verbal and visual skills, using storytelling, symbolism and metaphor to create a desired effect.

Charismatic leaders have that 'special quality' – charm and a powerful personality – that attracts followers like magnets. Their charisma is actually made up of many traits, including clear and inspirational communication, self-confidence, self-awareness and the ability to set challenging goals. They can inspire and encourage their followers to do their best and hold high performance expectations of their followers.

Charismatic leaders give their teams (or groups of followers) a unique identity. They bestow a distinct sense of belonging and build their team's image, particularly in the minds of the team members, as being superior to the others. The downside is that the the group success may depend on the leader – the glue that holds the group together.

THE STRATEGIC PERSPECTIVE

Using charisma, for better or worse

There have always been larger-than-life leaders, some of whom made the world a better place, some a worse place. For every Mahatma Gandhi, Steve Jobs, Nelson Mandela and Mother Teresa, there is an Adolf Hitler, a Pol Pot, a Saddam Hussein and a Joseph Stalin. As positive or negative leaders, each one oozed charisma, created motivating, energetic environments. Each communicated a clear vision and was willing to pursue risky endeavours.

Charismatic leaders such as these find it easy to lead people – and sometimes they lead people astray. When well intentioned, charismatic leaders can elevate and transform a team, a company or even a country. When self-driven and Machiavellian, they can bring people, companies or countries to the abyss.

Business plays a big role in our society and the media places business leaders in the limelight. Perhaps not surprisingly, then, some of today's business leaders are like the charismatic leaders described above. Maybe that's not a bad thing. Organisations need a special type of leadership, especially at senior levels, to lead them through today's dramatic changes. (See Chapter 1 for more discussion on today's changing world.)

Skilful charismatic leadership is arguably better for short-term projects, too, especially projects requiring energy and talent. Charismatic leaders are also useful in the early stages of an enterprise and when an enterprise needs to be transformed. (See, for example, the Theory to practice: How a vision saved Apple, on page 54.)

Charisma is a personality trait and real leadership isn't about personality. Luckily, charisma is not essential to effective leadership. And certainly, relying on charisma alone, without the foundation of leadership skills and mindsets, would lead to horrible outcomes. Perhaps transformational leadership (discussed later in this chapter) is a better way to turn around organisations (and countries).

THEORY TO PRACTICE

Becoming more charismatic

Charisma is based on three qualities, what Aristotle called:

1. *Logos*: Strong, well-reasoned rhetoric.
2. *Ethos*: Personal and moral credibility.
3. *Pathos*: The ability to rouse emotion and passion in others.[6]

Some people are naturally charismatic, but charisma can also be learned (albeit perhaps not easily). Here are some ways to develop charisma in your leadership role:

- Be passionate about what you do.
- Do more to motivate your team.
- Learn to become comfortable with taking risks and standing up for your convictions.
- Learn to stage events that send powerful messages.
- Learn to think more critically about the status quo and its shortcomings.
- Make your goals and future vision attractive and attainable and communicate them clearly.
- Take courses to improve your speaking skills.

Empathic leadership

Sir Edward 'Weary' Dunlop developed his approach to empathic leadership in Japanese prisoner of war camps where he cared for debilitated men who were building the Thai–Burma railway during World War II. Dunlop identified 11 desirable aspects of leadership:

1. Ability to communicate.
2. Courage.
3. Decisiveness.
4. Initiative.
5. Integrity.
6. Judgement.
7. Knowledge.
8. Loyalty.
9. Motivation.
10. Responsibility.
11. Selflessness.[7]

Weary Dunlop was thinking of military leadership. Might these characteristics also help business leaders, not-for-profit leaders and public service leaders, too?

Servant leadership

Similar to empathic leadership (and forming a bridge to behavioural leadership because it combines personality traits with actions) is servant leadership. In essence, servant leaders help followers to grow and reach their potential in their jobs. They release people's capabilities and bring out their best. Servant leadership is unselfish and is not built around a person's ego or desire for fame and glory, but based on a genuine desire to help people achieve their potential.

Genuine caring

At the heart of leadership is what in Greek is called *agapé* and in Latin is called *caritas* – a genuine caring about other people that puts aside self-interest so that you consider people's feelings while making balanced decisions.

Here are some of the main attributes of servant leaders, who adopt the principles of stewardship: being responsible for the long-term welfare of others. They:

- are committed to the truth regardless of the cost.
- are decisive and flexible; having weighed up the alternatives they commit to a path of action unreservedly while remaining open to new information.
- are not concerned with protecting their own position but with doing what is 'right' according to their own values and standards.
- are persuasive and convincing.
- are prepared to learn from others.
- develop strong, empowering and energising visions on which their followers can concentrate their efforts and they live their vision in their daily actions.
- have and display compassion and empathy.
- have foresight and the ability to predict a likely outcome based on intuition, judgement and perception.
- listen carefully and non-judgementally to others' thoughts and opinions, and think about what they have heard.
- make informed decisions based not on short-term benefits for a few but on long-term repercussions, which often requires courage and self-denial, since sometimes the best decisions are unpopular.
- protect those who cannot protect themselves.
- reconcile conflicting ideas.
- right wrongs.
- think conceptually, describing the picture that is in their mind in words and feelings so that others can share it.

This certainly sounds like a 21st-century leadership style to aspire to. We can all exercise these qualities, although they're probably easier to describe than to practise.

An early servant leader

Are you familiar with the legend of King Arthur of Camelot? The previous king had died and a successor was to be chosen. But how?

Some versions have it that a sword was embedded in a huge stone, so far that only the hilt was exposed. It was declared that he who could draw the sword would be crowned king. Many tried and failed. They pulled and pulled at the sword but it stuck fast.

>>

Arthur, who was at the time not known to be of royal blood, was acting as a servant in a contest between knights. The knight he was assisting broke his sword and Arthur went in search of another one for him. He remembered the sword in the stone and ran to it. He grasped it to take back to the knight he was serving.

The sword slipped easily from the stone and Arthur was proclaimed king. His unselfish act in seeking to serve another gained him a kingdom. Unselfish acts of service have been rewarded through the ages. The most common reward is self-satisfaction, but other more material rewards often result too.

● THE STRATEGIC PERSPECTIVE

Leaders at all levels

Leaders are now found at all levels of an organisation, not just at the top. Often, they don't have a formal title or position of power to support them but rely on their personal power to get the job done. (See page 102 to find out more about the types of power.)

There are three types of leaders in organisations:

1. *Executive leaders*: The top-level managers who mentor local line leaders, steward cultural change and manage the strategic aspects of an organisation.
2. *Internal networkers*: People with no formal authority who move inside the organisation to spread new ideas and practices and generate commitment.
3. *Local line leaders*: Leaders (e.g. business unit managers and team leaders) who introduce and implement new ideas.[8]

Narcissistic leadership

Despite their charm, charismatic leaders are often more concerned with themselves than with others. Indeed, many are narcissistic leaders – the opposite of well-balanced, humble people. Some narcissistic leaders are also charismatic, and some are transformational leaders who act confidently and optimistically, clearly articulate a grand and appealing vision and help people achieve it, and are excellent and often theatrical communicators.

People like Napoleon Bonaparte, Andrew Carnegie, Thomas Edison, Henry Ford, Mahatma Gandhi, Bill Gates and Jack Welch (former chair and CEO of General Electric), inspire people and shape the future. They are creative strategists who have the strength of will to push through massive transformations and the charm to convince others to help them do it. The world needs people like this. They can 'rally the troops' (Winston Churchill) and engage people's hearts and minds (John F Kennedy) to achieve great things.[9]

The downside is that these leaders can become emotionally isolated, distrustful of others and prone to feelings of grandiosity. They can become self-involved and unpredictable. Their self-belief is so high they can believe they're invincible, leading to flagrant risk-taking against all advice. Take Joseph Stalin and Adolph Hitler, for example. Not all narcissistic leaders are this extreme, it's true. But those whose leadership becomes overwhelmingly about themselves, will most often fail in the long term.

The case for bureaucracies

The 19th-century German political economist Max Weber spotted the dangers of larger-than-life leaders and recommended leader-proof organisations: Bureaucracies. In bureaucracies, people are bound by strict rules and regulations which prevent them from making their own rules to suit themselves and becoming 'bigger than life'.

Narcissistic leaders hear only what they want to hear. They prefer to indoctrinate rather than teach (making them terrible coaches and mentors), dominate meetings and cannot tolerate criticism or dissent. Their self-absorption and need for admiration is legendary and they cut down anyone who challenges them, including promising subordinates. They lack empathy, are hyper-competitive and are not restrained by conscience.

Perhaps the real Achilles heel of narcissistic leaders is that their failures tend to become more pronounced the more successful they become. The good news is that narcissistic leaders can protect their Achilles heel in three ways: aligning those around them to their vision, finding a trusted confidant to keep them grounded in reality, and developing self-awareness.

Brilliant or average, honest or corrupt, wise or foolish, narcissistic leaders share boldness and an unshakable conviction of their abilities and the value of their vision.

THEORY TO PRACTICE

A breathtaking business failure

Headed by charismatic, determined, unscrupulous leaders, Enron is one of history's most spectacular business failures. Its former chief financial officer, Andrew Fastow, and chief executive, Jeff Skilling, were imprisoned and its chairman, Kenneth Lay, died while on trial. All three displayed classic narcissistic behaviours: immune to consequences, an inability to consider the needs of others, manipulation of the environment for personal gain, and the sense they can do no wrong.[10]

Working for a narcissistic leader

If you work for a narcissistic leader, empathise with their feelings, praise their achievements and look elsewhere for your own self-esteem. Show your willingness to protect their image and refrain from the type of honest feedback that threatens their inflated self-image. Offer ideas and let them take the credit. When you believe they're wrong, show how a different approach would be in their best interest.

Transformational leadership

Despite the limitations of charismatic leadership as a formula for success, the cult of the heroic leader remains strong. Transformational leaders are similar to charismatic leaders.[11] Indeed, transformational leaders often have charisma but it's a charisma based on high ideals, for example, Mahatma Gandhi and Lee Iacocca on the positive side, Osama bin Laden and the Reverend Jim Jones (who led the mass suicides in Jonestown in the USA) on the negative. The main difference is that transformational leaders want to transform their organisations or society, while charismatic leaders transfix.

Transformational leaders look beyond present constraints, striking out in new directions, taking risks, and influencing beliefs and values. Transformational leaders and their followers share a purpose, motives and values. The three most significant functions of transformational leaders are:

1. They develop a clear and compelling vision that all employees understand and can commit to.
2. They guide their organisation through revitalising change, redesigning it from top to bottom, with a goal of making it more effective, efficient and responsive, and better able to meet the changing requirements of the marketplace and society.
3. They drum up enthusiasm for these changes throughout the organisation.

Transformational leaders seem to share a number of important core traits: well-developed conceptual abilities, a strong goal orientation and high levels of energy, personal integrity and trustworthiness. Like charismatic leaders, they are excellent communicators and master motivators. They are strategic thinkers who take the strategic perspective and set clear visions, missions and goals. (See pages 53 and 55 for information on visions and missions.) They have the courage of their convictions, and their drive and enthusiasm set the pace for others to follow.

● THEORY TO PRACTICE

Ann Sherry, transformational leader

Who would want to take over a cruise company whose reputation was still suffering from the tragic and highly publicised death of a young woman on one of its cruises five years previously? Ann Sherry was game.

She began by setting a stretch goal: To have more than one million passengers a year travelling with the company. The staff thought she was mad.

Since Sherry took on the job of running the Carnival Australia cruising company seven years ago, the company has grown 20% each year and passenger numbers have increased ninefold, from 100 000 to 900 000 a year. A systematic analysis of the market helped Sherry establish two key elements of her strategy: building relationships with key stakeholders, including customers, the government, the media and suppliers; and improving the quality of the ships as well as destinations, entertainment, food and beverages.

Sherry is no stranger to creating transformational change. While running the office of child care for the Victorian government, she established after-school child-care programs and from the (federal) Office of the Status of Women, she was instrumental in extending mandatory superannuation to part-time and casual employees. She also obtained inaugural funding for the Breast Cancer Foundation at a time when that disease received virtually no funding, despite being the largest killer of women in Australia.

As a general manager, human resources, in the then very-blokey culture of one of Australia's major banks, Sherry demonstrated the bottom line benefits of introducing paid maternity leave, recruited several other women to senior roles in key functional areas and provided training in sexual harassment for every executive – all part of the strategy to transform the bank into an employer of choice.[12] From early in her leadership career, Sherry demonstrated her ability to create transformational change.

The behavioural approach

Proactive, smart, self-assured … looking at the traits of effective leaders doesn't really help anyone learn to be a better leader. Leaders should be smart, yes; but how do you *do* smart? The trait approach looks at what effective leaders *are*. The behavioural approach sees leadership as a set of behaviours and looks at what effective leaders *do*. Effective leaders do things that poor leaders do not, which means you can learn to be a better leader by adopting the behaviours of good leaders – not copying them, but doing them in your own way, filtered through your own personality, experiences and knowledge.

This section begins with the commonly referred to styles of leadership and then moves on to four other ways of considering the behaviour of leaders:

1. Continuum of leadership styles.
2. Consideration and structure.
3. Managerial grid.
4. Theory X and Theory Y.

Each offers useful insights and practical ways of thinking about leadership. (A fifth behavioural approach to leadership, functional leadership, is discussed on page 383.)

Leadership styles

In 1939, a group of researchers isolated three main types of leadership, particularly in relation to decision-making:

1. Autocratic.
2. Democratic.
3. Laissez-faire.

These researchers believed the most effective leadership style was democratic because it brought out conscientiousness, friendliness and originality in followers. Autocratic leadership, they said, led to revolution, while laissez-faire, or 'do nothing', leadership wasn't motivating enough to bring out the best in followers.[13]

However, as we see in the next section, it may be safer to say that each style has its uses, depending on the situation. This means you need to choose your leadership style to reflect the needs and objectives of the group.

Autocratic and dictatorial leaders

Autocratic leaders, also known as authoritarian leaders, use power and strong control. They are task-centred leaders who avoid employee participation and keep information and decision-making to themselves. They issue orders with no questions allowed and no explanations given. This tends to make followers dependent upon them for decisions and directions, and can result in the group feeling 'lost' in the leader's absence.

This style of management has been described as 'a loose grip around the throat'.[14] We might describe that as a more extreme version of authoritarian leadership: dictatorial leadership. Dictatorial leaders are negative leaders who rule through force. Holding threats of punishment over the heads of people to compel them to perform may get results in some work situations but generally the resulting quality and quantity of work do not remain high for very long. Instead, dictatorial leadership usually creates unrest and dissatisfaction. Employees eventually 'rebel' by doing the bare minimum of work or transferring to another job. As US president Dwight D Eisenhower observed: 'You do not lead by hitting people over the head. That's assault, not leadership.'[15]

Democratic leaders

While authoritarian leaders are task-centred, democratic leaders are people-centred. Sometimes called *participative leaders*, they encourage involvement, ask for employees' opinions and suggestions, and involve them in solving work-related problems. Because employees are well informed and used to solving problems themselves, they can function effectively when their leader is absent.

◉ IN A NUTSHELL

When to be hands-off and when to be hands-on
A team can move along mostly in a hands-off mode when everything and everybody is working satisfactorily. But when the situation changes, and that can happen without warning, then it's time for strong hands-on leadership. Table 9.1 compares the differences.

TABLE 9.1 Hands-on leadership can steer an organisation back on track

Laissez-faire 'hands-off' leadership is fine when:	Teams need a strong 'hands-on' leader when:
Everything is going well.	There is a crisis.
Followers understand the task clearly.	The goal is unclear.
Followers are committed to the task.	Followers are unskilled or inexperienced.
Followers are skilled and experienced.	Followers are confused or uncertain.
Followers are working well together.	Followers are not working well together as a team.
Time is not an issue.	Time is tight.

Laissez-faire leaders

Laissez-faire leaders, also called *non-directive* and *free-rein leaders*, do not appear to lead at all. They provide the group with information and possibly some general direction and then let them get on with the job with little or no interference.

This delegative type of leadership can be effective when the work group is highly skilled and motivated and the work is complex or unstructured, as may be the case when managing professionally qualified employees and knowledge workers. However, when established standards and goals must be met regularly, this is probably not the most suitable style of leadership.

The continuum of leadership styles

The continuum of leadership styles describes leadership behaviour as ranging from leader-centred strategies to employee-centred strategies (as shown in Figure 9.1).[16] In this model, authoritarian leaders are at the left end of the continuum, laissez-faire leaders at the right end and democratic leaders somewhere in the middle.

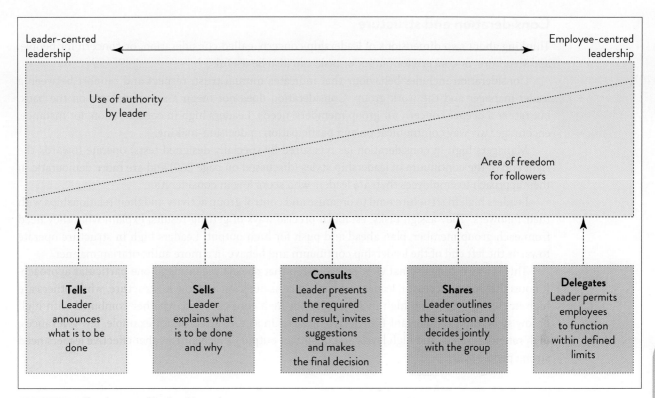

FIGURE 9.1 Continuum of leadership styles

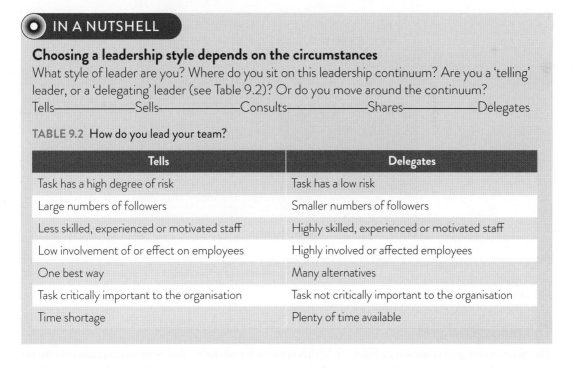

IN A NUTSHELL

Choosing a leadership style depends on the circumstances

What style of leader are you? Where do you sit on this leadership continuum? Are you a 'telling' leader, or a 'delegating' leader (see Table 9.2)? Or do you move around the continuum?

Tells————Sells————Consults————Shares————Delegates

TABLE 9.2 How do you lead your team?

Tells	Delegates
Task has a high degree of risk	Task has a low risk
Large numbers of followers	Smaller numbers of followers
Less skilled, experienced or motivated staff	Highly skilled, experienced or motivated staff
Low involvement of or effect on employees	Highly involved or affected employees
One best way	Many alternatives
Task critically important to the organisation	Task not critically important to the organisation
Time shortage	Plenty of time available

Consideration and structure

Thinking about two dimensions of leadership concern, called consideration, or concern for people, and structure, or concern for output or task, can also be useful.[17]

Consideration includes behaviour that indicates mutual trust, respect and rapport between a leader-manager and the work group. Consideration does not mean a superficial pat on the back, but rather a deeper concern for group members' needs. Leaders high in consideration, for instance, encourage two-way communication and participation in decision-making.

Managers high in consideration (as measured by specially designed tests) operate towards the right end of the continuum of leadership styles (discussed on page 260) and are more democratic in their approach to employees than are leaders who score low in consideration.

Leaders high in structure tend to organise and control group activity and their relationships with their followers. They assign tasks, establish precise ways of getting results, explain what they need from each group member, plan ahead and push for high output. Leaders high in structure operate towards the left end of the leadership continuum and behave in a more authoritarian manner.

This is a two-dimensional view of leadership that doesn't recommend one particular approach. It notes that some successful leaders are high in consideration and low in structure, while others are high in consideration and high in structure. But high consideration, whether combined with high or low structure, is important for effective leadership as measured by, for example, few grievances, high retention levels, and high levels and quality of output. This confirms that effective leaders need strong people skills.

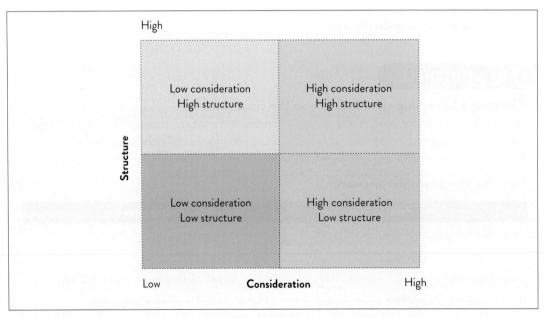

Source: Adapted from Rensis Likert, *New Patterns of Management*, McGraw-Hill, 1961

FIGURE 9.2 The consideration and structure model

The managerial grid

The managerial grid is shown in Figure 9.3. This approach concludes that leaders can concentrate on one of two key factors – *people* or *output*. These two factors form the axes of the managerial grid, on which five possible leadership styles are positioned. A specially developed questionnaire ranks how much attention a leader pays to each of the two factors on a scale of one (1) for low and nine (9) for high. For example, the first item of the following list shows the two factors (people:output) scored 1:1, a low score of one (1) for people and a low score of one (1) for output.

- *Impoverished leadership* (1:1): Leaders show little concern for either people or output. They are leaders in name only and make little effort to encourage their work group towards high performance. People often describe them as laissez-faire leaders.
- *Task leadership* (9:1): Here the leader's main concern is accomplishing the task, getting the job done. They show little concern for the needs and welfare of employees and people often describe them as authoritarian or dictatorial.
- *Middle-of-the-road leadership* (5:5): These leaders show some concern for both employee satisfaction and job performance, but only enough to get by.
- *Country-club leadership* (1:9): The country-club leader's main concern is employee satisfaction and maintaining a comfortable work tempo, a friendly atmosphere and good working relations. Like the impoverished leaders, they are sometimes described as laissez-faire.
- *Team leadership* (9:9): Leaders with a team style of leadership involve all the members of the work group in planning and making decisions. They aim at a creative approach to getting the job done, listen to and encourage people, and seek agreement, commitment and understanding. The team management style is similar to the democratic, or participative, leadership style.[18]

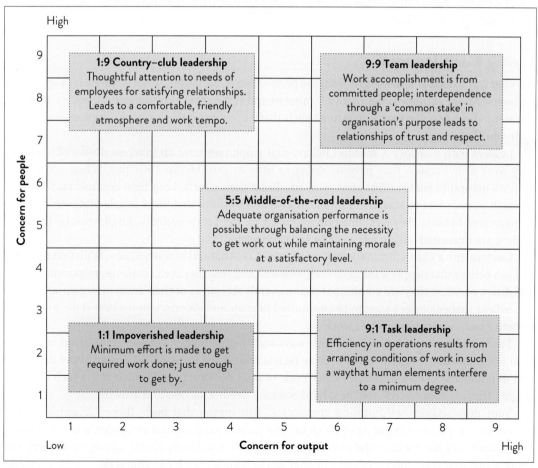

FIGURE 9.3 The managerial grid

It was once believed that a 9:9 team leadership style was the most appropriate in all situations. However, we now know that this is not the case. Sometimes task leadership works better; for instance, when supervising repetitive work being done by inexperienced, unskilled or unmotivated employees, as indicated 'In a Nutshell: Choosing a leadership style depends on the circumstances', on page 261. Similarly, 1:9 country-club leadership, akin to sharing and delegating, often works well with highly experienced, skilled and motivated staff. It is safe to say, however, that the impoverished 1:1 leadership style is unlikely to work in any situation.

THE STRATEGIC PERSPECTIVE

Leadership, not leaders

In their extensive Australian research of Australian corporations, Graham Hubbard and colleagues found that the best leaders in Australia are different from the best leaders in the USA. Where American leaders challenge people to achieve big, hairy audacious goals, Australian leaders are better served by the leader-as-coach model and by engaging employees in their organisation's vision and mission. Australia's best leaders are inspiring, passionate and supportive, making statements such as 'We can do this', 'I will help you succeed' and 'I will catch you if necessary'.

They also found that the CEOs of Australia's top 11 companies all came from within the business and stayed, on average, 10 years in the job. They were then succeeded by a different type of leader with a different set of skills, who could, by virtue of their differences, take the organisation to a new level.[19]

Theory X and Theory Y

Another way to look at leadership is from the perspective of the leader. What is the leader's opinion of followers? At one extreme is the Theory X mindset and at the other extreme is the Theory Y mindset. These mindsets describe two contrasting beliefs that leaders can hold about how employees approach their jobs.[20]

Leaders with a Theory X mindset believe that employees have an inherent dislike of work and they work only because they have to, doing as little as possible for their pay. When you believe that, it's natural to continually coerce workers, direct their efforts, keep tight controls on them and threaten punishment to keep them in line. It's natural to think that most people prefer this type of management because they lack ambition and want to avoid responsibility. Employees, to Theory X leaders, are interested only in job security and good wages.

Leaders with a *Theory Y* mindset believe that work is as natural as rest and play. With that mindset, you can believe that people want to do their jobs well and that they seek challenge, responsibility and self-direction when they are committed to the overall objectives of their team or organisation. You can believe that employees want to be committed to goals and visions, to learn new skills, and to use initiative and imagination in their work.

Leaders advertise their beliefs in subtle ways and, sooner or later, followers to respond in the way their leaders predict. Negative labels such as 'he is lazy' and 'she is stupid' are powerful and damaging and trap managers and teams in a vicious cycle of poor performance. Positive labels such as 'she is bright', 'they are cooperative' and 'he is hard-working' predict success and growth.

Your mindsets are self-fulfilling prophecies. This means that both Theory X and Theory Y leaders are correct. People live up or down to their leader's expectations and predictions, depending on whether they are positive (the halo effect) or negative (the horns effect). Changing the way you think about your team members and why they work changes your leadership style.

THEORY TO PRACTICE

Tough love

Do you think a Theory X approach leads managers to use a dictatorial style of leadership? Not always. A Theory X country-club leader might think: 'I'll be really nice to employees to con them into helping out when I need it.' Or Theory X leaders might 'help' their team members to the point where they practically do their jobs for them because they believe that the team members are incapable of high performance and that it's too risky to let them work on their own, without their help.

Does Theory Y leadership sound like laissez-faire or country-club leadership to you? Not necessarily. Because they hold employees in high regard, Theory Y leaders often set high standards for them to meet. After all, they are perfectly capable, intelligent, responsible and hard-working, so there is no reason why they should not meet high standards. In this sense, Theory Y leaders can be 9:9 leaders. They are also participative, democratic leaders.

THE STRATEGIC PERSPECTIVE

All kinds of leaders

There are all kinds of leaders. Here are some examples:

* Gough Whitlam (Australia's 21st prime minister): *Charismatic*, leading by personal magnetism. We look to charismatic leaders when we need goals and inspiration.
* John Howard (Australia's 25th prime minister): *Stern*, leading based on the strength and certainty of their convictions, and by reminding people of their duties and responsibilities. We look to stern leaders when we need direction.
* Linda Burney (first Aboriginal person elected to the NSW Parliament and, at one stage acting leader of the Opposition): *Coaches*, who develop people for the future. We look to coaches when faced with big challenges.
* Greg Combet (former politician, trade unionist) and Sue Vardon (23 years as a chief executive in federal and state government agencies): *Pacesetters*, who show the way by leading from the front. We look to pacesetters when the going gets tough.
* Nelson Mandela (South African anti-Apartheid leader) and Mother Teresa (missionary to the poor of India): *Noble*, leading by example and moral authority. We look to noble leaders when we're disillusioned.
* Bishop Desmond Tutu (South African social rights activist, Anglican bishop): *Affiliative*, creating emotional bonds and goodwill. We look to affiliative leaders when we need support and encouragement.

The situational approach

Looking at how successful leaders behave can be instructive. But behavioural theories aren't very useful in explaining *when,* or in *what situations,* leaders should behave in certain ways. Sometimes, for example, directing behaviour – 'bossing people around' – is effective. And sometimes it isn't. When should you choose an authoritarian leadership style and when should you choose a participative leadership style? Should you ever choose a country-club leadership style?

The situational approach adds another piece to the leadership puzzle. Situational leadership explains that effective leaders sometimes behave in an authoritarian manner, sometimes in a participative manner and sometimes in a laissez-faire manner. The situation dictates the leadership style that works best. This means that, to be an effective leader, you need to be able to use all the leadership styles and know when to use them. This increases the range of situations in which you can lead effectively.

Leaders who are not familiar with situational leadership ideas, or who are not flexible enough to adapt their leadership style to suit the circumstances, can lead effectively in some situations but are doomed to lead poorly in others. The following three models of situational leadership examined in this section can help you decide which leadership style to choose:

1. Contingency approach.
2. Elements of leadership approach.
3. Task-readiness approach.

● THE STRATEGIC PERSPECTIVE

'Horses for courses'

You've heard the saying 'Horses for courses'? It applies to leadership as well as other spheres of life. Some situations call for leaders high in dominance, while others need leaders high in empathy and tact. Still others need leaders with finely honed negotiation skills. There are as many types of leaders as there are leadership situations. What unites successful leaders is not their particular sets of skills as much as the fact that their personality profiles meet the demands of the situation, that they *want* to lead and that they have and use the skills the situation calls for.

The contingency approach

The contingency approach says that the style of leadership that works best depends on the situation, or the environment in which you are leading. Three factors determine the appropriate leadership style in any given situation:

1. *Leader–member relations*: How much the followers trust, respect and have confidence in their leader, which can be subjectively assessed as high (good) or low (poor).
2. *Position power*: How much power and influence go with the leader's job – the power to hire, fire, reward and punish, which can be high (strong position power) or low (weak position power). (See page 102 for an explanation of power and influence).
3. *Task structure*: Whether established procedures must be followed (high structure) or whether employees have discretion in carrying out the task (low structure).[21]

An autocratic, telling style of leadership – one that emphasises a high concern with task – seems to work best in situations that are either favourable or unfavourable for the leader. For example, when there is high structure and little scope for followers to decide what to do, or low structure and the many options leave followers reeling, leaders should give clear instructions: What to do (and sometimes why), and when, where and how to do it. In moderate situations, a more democratic, people-centred approach is more successful.

The most favourable, or easiest, situation for a leader is one characterised by:

• good leader–member relations
• strong position power
• a highly structured task.

In contrast, the least favourable situation for a leader is characterised by:

* poor leader–member relations
* weak position power
* low task structure.

The elements of leadership approach

The second situational approach is the elements of leadership. This approach incorporates the continuum of leadership styles (discussed on page 266) and adds three situational dimensions to take into account when deciding which leadership style to use.

Here are three situational guidelines to help you select the most appropriate leadership style:

1. *Consider the employees*: For example, what style of leadership is the work team used to and comfortable with? How much independence and responsibility do they want? How many followers are there? How competent and willing are they? Are they directly affected by a decision or involved in its execution? How experienced are they at working together? How confident are they? Do they understand and identify with the organisation's goals?

    When people are used to, and expect, participative leadership and are skilled and motivated, you are unlikely to gain their loyalty and cooperation with an autocratic leadership style – go for participative leadership. Similarly, when a work team is used to highly directive leadership, a sudden change to democratic, consultative leadership would almost certainly fall flat – be more directive, at least initially.

2. *Consider the task*: For example, is there one best way to do it or are there several ways? How routine or complex is it? How critically important to the organisation is the task or decision? Is a high degree of risk involved? Is time short?

    A small, highly skilled team performing a flexible task in a changing environment generally responds best to democratic, people-centred leadership. On the other hand, when time is critical, or when a large work group is carrying out precisely specified, routine work, you can probably achieve better results by using more directive behaviour. (Remember that directive behaviour needn't be rude or harsh; it can be polite and helpful.)

    When the issue or task at hand is highly critical or sensitive and team members are skilled and willing, due diligence requires you to keep a reasonable amount of authority by consulting (not sharing or delegating authority).

3. *Consider the leader*: Don't forget yourself in this. What style of leadership are you most comfortable with? What styles of leadership have you experienced yourself? Who are your role models? How confident are you about using each of the leadership styles? What is the expected leadership style in your organisation – its cultural norm of leadership? What are your organisation's values, traditions and policies? How dispersed are its work units?

    Whichever style of leadership you choose, you need to feel comfortable with it. Some people find it next to impossible to use an autocratic, telling style convincingly, while others feel uncomfortable using a delegating or sharing style. [22]

The task-readiness approach

The concept of considering employees, the task and the leader, which we have just discussed, was used to develop the task-readiness approach to selecting a leadership style. The task-readiness approach's two dimensions of leadership behaviour are:

1. *Directive behaviour*: How much task focus and supervision a leader provides.
2. *Relationship behaviour*: How much support and encouragement a leader provides.

Directive behaviour includes developing plans, programs and schedules related to employees' work, directing the way in which employees are to carry out tasks, maintaining close and frequent supervision of the task, providing job training and setting objectives.

Relationship behaviour looks at how much a leader shares with employees such tasks as developing plans, programming and scheduling employees' work and setting objectives. It also relates to how much the leader shares problem-solving and decision-making about how to carry out the task, and how much coaching, counselling and encouragement the leader provides.

Using this model, four styles of leadership are possible, as shown below. Notice that these four leadership styles are similar to the styles described in the continuum of leadership behaviour. Both were developed around the same time.[23]

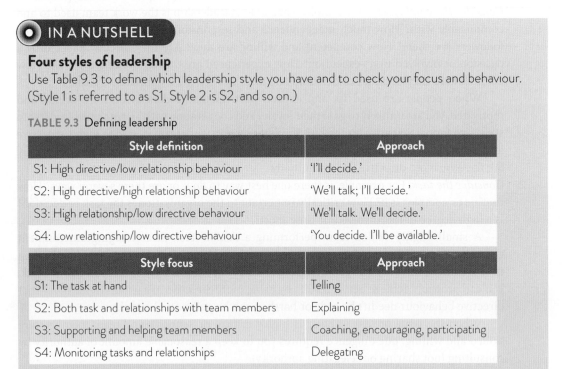

IN A NUTSHELL

Four styles of leadership

Use Table 9.3 to define which leadership style you have and to check your focus and behaviour. (Style 1 is referred to as S1, Style 2 is S2, and so on.)

TABLE 9.3 Defining leadership

Style definition	Approach
S1: High directive/low relationship behaviour	'I'll decide.'
S2: High directive/high relationship behaviour	'We'll talk; I'll decide.'
S3: High relationship/low directive behaviour	'We'll talk. We'll decide.'
S4: Low relationship/low directive behaviour	'You decide. I'll be available.'

Style focus	Approach
S1: The task at hand	Telling
S2: Both task and relationships with team members	Explaining
S3: Supporting and helping team members	Coaching, encouraging, participating
S4: Monitoring tasks and relationships	Delegating

Task-readiness level

How do you know which of the four leadership styles to use? The idea is to vary your leadership style according to each employee's 'readiness' to do a particular task, referred to as their task-readiness level.

Two factors make up an employee's task-readiness level:

1. *Competence, or ability* to do a particular task: A combination of skills, knowledge and experience in doing a particular task.
2. *Willingness* to take responsibility for doing the task: A combination of motivation and self-confidence.

The concept of task-readiness level relates to each task an employee does, not to an employee's overall competence for the job as a whole. This means that a person's readiness level might be high on some tasks and low on others. Therefore, you need to use different leadership styles with the employee depending on the task. Readiness levels are referred to as R1, R2 and so on.

- *RI*: Low competence and low willingness to do a task unsupervised. This person needs direction, so an S1 or telling style of leadership is called for.
- *R2*: Growing competence and willingness. This calls for an S2 or explaining style of leadership.
- *R3*: Satisfactory competency but low willingness based on lack of confidence or lack of motivation. This person needs support, so an S3 or encouraging or participating style of leadership is needed.
- *R4*: High levels of competence and willingness. This calls for an S4 or delegating, 'hands off' style of leadership.

Figure 9.4 shows ways of recognising employees at different levels of task readiness.

Readiness level 1

I don't know how.
I can't do it.
I did my best, but ...
I've never done this before.

Readiness level 2

Show me.
I'll have a go!
I'm not sure.
I don't know how but
I'll give it a try.

Readiness level 4

I've already done it.
Leave it to me.
No worries!
Here, let me help with that.

Readiness level 3 (developing)

How does this look?
Can I run this by you?
I'm not sure if I can.

Readiness level 3 (regressing)

I'll do it later.
It's someone else's turn.
What? Me again!
Been there, done that.

FIGURE 9.4 Assessing task-readiness level

Use Figure 9.5 to help you decide which leadership style to use with each of your team members for their various duties. First, consider the task-readiness level of an employee in relation to the particular task and assign a readiness level from 1 (low) to 4 (high). Now draw a line vertically up to intersect the bell curve in one of the four leadership styles (S1, S2, S3 or S4). This indicates the most suitable leadership style for this staff member in relation to that particular task. (You can also apply the concept of task-readiness level to a work group to get a feel for the overall leadership style you should use with them.)

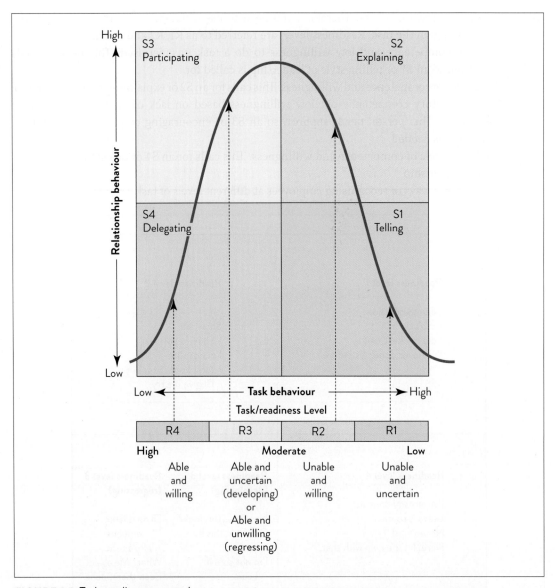

FIGURE 9.5 Task-readiness approach

Using the task-readiness approach, you can see that your behaviour towards employees should change as they develop skills, experience and confidence. That's why leaders need flexibility in their styles of leadership.

● THEORY TO PRACTICE

Putting task-readiness theory to use
You may need to use a directing, or telling, style with employees who are very skilled and experienced in most areas of their job, for example, when you delegate a task to them or train them to undertake new work.

>>

Explain that you're going to use the directing style: 'Since you've never done this before, it might be helpful for me to give you some direction to get you started.'

Remember to adjust your style as the employee makes progress. Look, listen and ask how they feel they're going, and begin to reduce directive behaviour and increase relationship behaviour as the employee's task-readiness level increases at the new task.

Continue doing this until the employee reaches a moderate level of readiness. As the employee begins to move to an above-average job-readiness level, decrease both directive and relationship behaviour. As task-readiness levels increase still further, reduce close supervision and increase delegating behaviour as an indication of your trust and confidence.

Regression

This isn't the end of the story. As experienced leader-managers know, employees sometimes 'go off the boil' or 'lose the plot'. A once-skilled and motivated employee, due to boredom, poor working relationships within the team, or a poor working environment, can turn into a disgruntled, uncooperative bludger who *knows* how to do the job but no longer *wants* to do it; or the productivity of a valued employee, distracted by problems at home, drops away.

Whatever the reason, people occasionally move backwards (regress) from being a skilled and willing employee (readiness level 4) to a competent but unwilling employee (readiness level 3). Figure 9.4 shows some ways to recognise a regressed employee.

Look at Figure 9.5 and locate R3 on the task-readiness scale. Follow the line up to see what leadership style to use with R3 regressing employees. You can see that regressed employees need low-task, high-relationship behaviour. Telling them what to do or providing further training is a waste of time because they already *know* what to do. High-task behaviour is not the answer (although it is usually the first refuge of inexperienced or poor leader-managers).

An R3 regressing employee needs supportive, participative, relationship-building behaviour. Sit down and chat. Ask questions to find out what the problem is. Try to see the situation from the dissatisfied employee's point of view. You might find that boredom has set in and a new challenge is required, or that the employee feels unappreciated and neglected. Or you might find that faulty tools or equipment or poor work systems are such a hindrance that the employee has given up trying.

It could even be that you're such a pitiful leader that the employee baulks at the thought of doing a good job to make you look good! You can't act effectively until you find out what is causing the problem. (Chapter 11 helps you analyse the reasons that employees regress.)

The transactional approach

If you like a nice, clear chain of command, think rewards and punishments motivate people, and want the people in your team to do what you say, you'll like the transactional approach to leadership. First described by Max Weber, it's about *quid pro quo*: Rewards and punishments depend on performance. Yes, the same Max Weber who thought bureaucracies were the ideal way to organise an enterprise and well-positioned to prevent narcissistic leaders from rising to power. (See page 72 for more on bureaucracies.)

Although people tend to sneer at bureaucracies as being hampered by red tape and lack of innovation, many organisations continue to reward employees for good performance (for instance, a bonus or a commission) and punish them in some way for poor performance (even if only with a poor performance review or an undesirable job assignment). And in fairness, this approach works well enough in situations where work is repetitive, problems are simple and judgement isn't required. However, it's generally considered a poor way to lead and manage today unless it's combined with other (more sophisticated) forms of leadership and motivation.

For transactional leadership to work, you need to make clear what you expect from the people who report to you (goals, measures of success) and the rewards they get when they achieve this. You need to provide the resources employees need to achieve their goals, monitor employees' performance (management by exception is generally fine), identify performance gaps and coach as necessary. When people perform above expectation, you need to provide praise and other rewards; when people perform below expectation, you apply corrective action.

The transactional approach links with the path-goal approach to leadership and the expectancy theory of motivation (see page 310).

You have a variety of leadership styles to select from, depending on how you choose to exercise transactional leadership and the type of work employees are engaged in. Here are examples of leadership styles you can use:

* *Achievement-oriented*: Setting challenging work and personal development goals and setting high standards and expectations works best with complex tasks.
* *Directive*: Telling or explaining what needs to be done, providing coaching and guidance and so on works well with complex, unstructured tasks when followers are inexperienced.
* *Participative*: This works well when followers are experienced and knowledgeable, provided you need and heed their advice.
* *Supportive* (or *high consideration* leadership): Creating a friendly working environment, making jobs as interesting as possible, raising followers' self-esteem, showing concern for employees' welfare, and so on works best as a reward when work is boring, hazardous or stressful.

Path-goal leadership

The path-goal approach to leadership is a type of transactional leadership in that leaders specify the path (or the goal), remove the stumbling stones along the path and provide followers with rewards as they move down the path towards the goal.[24]

You can set the path clearly or vaguely, remove only the biggest roadblocks or scour the path for pebbles, give mild encouragement or lavish followers with praise – the choice is yours depending on the situation, the needs and expectations of followers, your own inclinations and the leadership culture of your organisation. Similarly, the choice is yours as to whether and how much to involve the followers in establishing the goals and identifying and removing the obstacles to achieving them, and whether to use the lower order or higher order needs described on page 301 as rewards.

● THEORY TO PRACTICE

Which style of leadership is best?
These approaches show that one style of leadership is no 'better' or 'worse' than any of the others. The art is to be able to use each of them when you need to, at the right time and in the right place. In the end, a leader may be 'best right now' but there is no 'best' for all situations.

2. Leading or managing?

Managers are people who do things right and leaders are people who do the right things.

Warren Bennis and Joan Goldsmith, *Learning to Lead*, 2003[25]

Management as a profession dates back to the late 1800s and grew quickly in the early 1900s, matured, and, some would say, stagnated in the classic S-curve (the S-curve of change is shown in Figure 22.1 on page 685).

Designed for the industrial era in order to get semi- and unskilled labour to perform repetitive activities efficiently and reliably and to coordinate their efforts so that complex goods and services could be produced cheaply and in large quantities, classic management gave us the classic bureaucracy, hierarchies, precisely circumscribed jobs, and lots of rules and procedures. Its goal was to produce order and consistency and maintain the status quo.

As covered in Chapter 1, we've moved on from the industrial era. Most jobs in today's Australia aren't repetitive and prescribed. Today's leader-managers work in a different economy, a different marketplace and face different problems. Today's organisations need employees with imagination, and who are engaged, flexible and innovative – nothing like the employees needed in the industrial era. Today's organisations are about brains, not brawn, and today's rapidly changing circumstances call for a different sort of management.

Management is still about allocating resources, increasing efficiencies, dealing with budgets and numbers, and optimising processes and structures. Managers produce order and consistency and maintain the status quo.

Leadership is different. It is as old as humankind and is about vision and inspiration. Leaders produce change. The difference between leading and managing is the difference between *'path finding'* and *'path minding'*.[26]

IN A NUTSHELL

Leading versus managing

What is the difference between leading and managing? Table 9.4 defines what leaders do in the left-hand column and then matches them with what managers do in the right-hand column.

TABLE 9.4 Leaders and managers

Leaders	Managers
Align people	Organise people
Ask what and why	Ask how and when
Bring new perspectives and challenge the status quo	Protect the status quo
Create change	Work to established procedures
Create ideas and innovate	Control and administer, promote stability
Encourage experimentation	Give direction, use formal authority
Empower and support	Use formal authority
Focus on people	Focus on results

>>

TABLE 9.4 Leaders and managers (Continued)

Leaders	Managers
Focus on the longer term	Focus on the short term
Give purpose and meaning	Plan and coordinate
Help people develop	Solve problems
Involve	Delegate
Lead by example, inspire	'Do as I say'
Push out the boundaries	Work within the boundaries
Set direction and live values, vision and mission	Adhere to direction
Tap into people's strengths	Monitor
Use interpersonal skills	Focus on the task

So, what do we want today – leaders or managers? It can be a fun debate, but one that has tended to turn leaders into heroes and managers into prigs and given rise to a cult of hero-leaders. Today's leader is (or should be) a leader-manager, just as today's manager is (or should be) a leader-manager. If anything, leading and managing is a continuum. 'People skills' (building teams, building trust and confidence, coaching, communicating, displaying self-awareness, motivating people, turning conflicts into agreements, using emotional intelligence, and so on) fall towards the leading end of the continuum; the technical skills of management (assigning work, making decisions, managing risks, monitoring results, planning, and so on) fall towards the managing end.

The reality is, the two are part of the same whole. Modern leader-managers can't lead without managing or manage without leading. Managers who manage without leading are insipid, uninspiring and ineffective, and leaders who don't manage become detached and out of touch with what's going on.[27]

Here's the bottom line: Whatever your title, when you're required to get results in the 21st century, you need both leadership and management skills. Then you can be a leader-manager. Let's leave the last word to Professor Bob Sutton: 'To do the right thing, a leader needs to understand what it takes to do things right, and to make sure they actually get done.'[28]

3. The 21st-century Aussie leader-manager

Australia is a country of 'Fair Dinkum', 'Fair Go' and 'Bullshit Detectors.'

Aust. Government, DEEWR, 'Australian Cultural Imprints at Work: 2010 and Beyond' (March 2011)[29]

Although we've been examining various ways of thinking about leadership, we've just seen that leadership is really inseparable from managing. So let's take a look at what it means to be a 21st century leader-manager.

To recap the discussion in this chapter so far: In factories where strict rules and regulations apply, and rewards based on simple productivity measures work, the 'old-fashioned' leadership styles of commander, controller, decision-maker and dictator can get results. But as discussed in Chapter 1, the world is changing fast, and as Australia moves from the industrial economy to the knowledge and service economies and organisations evolve in response, these old leadership models are becoming increasingly ineffective. (See 'In a Nutshell: Less path minding and more path finding', opposite).

Service and knowledge workers don't respond to firmness and inflexibility. Leadership based on authority, dominance and power doesn't work; leadership based on influence and persuasiveness does. Leading and managing today is about communicating principles, not setting rules. It is about being a guide, not a teller, and a facilitator of high productivity. The 21st century leader-manager responds quickly and appropriately to change and helps others do the same. (For more about helping people be productive, leading knowledge workers and leading change, see chapters 11, 14 and 22.)

Followers expect their leader-managers to be participative and democratic, and to empower, inspire, motivate and support them. This means you need to know how to create a sense of purpose, earn loyalty, dedication and commitment, and lead the way by example (these topics are discussed in chapters 7, 8, 10 and 11). You need to know how to innovate and maintain an unwavering customer focus (discussed in Chapter 20).

You need to build teams made up of a diverse group of people (see chapters 13, 14 and 26 for more), help them find innovative ways to improve their productivity, empower them to make the decisions they are trained and equipped to make, identify develop and draw on individual team members' talents, reward their efforts in the right ways, and resolve conflicts (see chapters 8, 10, 11, 18 and 19 for more).

You need to stay tuned into the ways the digital, globalised future is changing your industry, your organisation and your own work, and be open to new information and ideas. And while no one is perfect, you need to work on your personal growth: Your emotional intelligence, resilience and self-awareness. Take time to reflect: What are you doing that's working? What do you need to correct? You need always to behave ethically and with integrity and manage your stress well enough to lead under pressure (see chapters 7 and 8). This is known as *authentic leadership*.

Your leadership style needs to reflect you, your unique skills, personality and values. Certainly, you should learn from others and from the different ideas about leadership we've examined in this chapter, but you also need to be comfortable that the way you lead reflects who you really are; that's what makes you an authentic leader. Quite a tall order.

● IN A NUTSHELL

Less path minding and more path finding

As discussed in chapters 1 and 3, the world and organisations are in a state of flux. A number of forces require a different style of leading and managing, including:

- A workforce of multiple generations working together, each working for different reasons and having different motivations and attitudes to work and the workplace, needs empathic and perceptive leader-managers.
- Flattened organisation structures need locally led creativity and innovation, decision-making, ethics, judgement, and other leadership skills.
- Globalisation exposes every organisational weakness. We need strong and dynamic leader-managers with their eyes on the horizon to create strong and dynamic organisations.
- Organisational success depends less on *what* people do than on *how* they do it. People, not equipment, make the difference and people need leader-managers who can bring out their best.
- Technology can simplify and even take over many of the planning, scheduling, monitoring and reporting functions that managers used to do.

»

- The greater number and magnitude of risks to prepare for calls for leader-managers who can grasp the strategic perspective.
- The necessity to engage employees to attract and retain those you need call for leaders who align people to a shared purpose and enable them to achieve it.
- The need to work successfully with suppliers, as even specialist expertise and technical and knowledge work is increasingly outsourced, calls for leaders with self-awareness and strong interpersonal skills who can successfully build relationships with diverse groups of people.
- Today's leader-managers have more responsibility and wider spans of management, requiring strong time management, prioritising and self-organisation skills.

No one can be expected to know everything, to stay on top of everything or to be all things to all people. This means you need to continually examine and refine your leadership skills and understand yourself realistically – your strengths and limitations, your preferences, your blind spots (for more on these characteristics, see pages 133 and 210).

Leaders, bosses and bastards

Australian leaders care for their followers and the welfare of their followers, according to an Australian government DEEWR study (see Figure 9.6).[30] They build cordial working relationships with them, empathise with them and build their self-esteem. Striking the right balance between firmness and decisiveness on the one hand and flexibility on the other, determining the right level of personal involvement and providing the right amount of public and private acknowledgement, are also hallmarks of Australian leaders. People gladly follow leaders like this.

Australian leaders also strike the right balance between 'close support' and 'support from a distance' and the support they provide ensures their followers don't fail, which allows them to stretch themselves. (We Australians have 'a strong aversion to failing', it seems.) Not surprisingly, to be an Australian leader, you must also be authentic.

Bosses, on the other hand, remain somewhat distant and are concerned more with the task at hand. There are two kinds of bosses – 'good bosses' and 'bad bosses', the latter often referred to as 'bastards'.

Good bosses do many things a leader does. They often act like the 'captain-coach' and don't put up barriers between themselves and their followers. They are well accepted, sometimes even more so than leaders. When they build trust and show genuine concern for their followers, they are seen as leaders, provided they are 'fair-dinkum' – true to both themselves and the task and knowing when to distance themselves from their followers for the good of the task.

Bad bosses, on the other hand, often 'take credit where it is not due, sacrifice others in their own interests and use followers to their own advantage.' They tend to be results-driven at the expense of people and are unlikely to develop into true leaders.

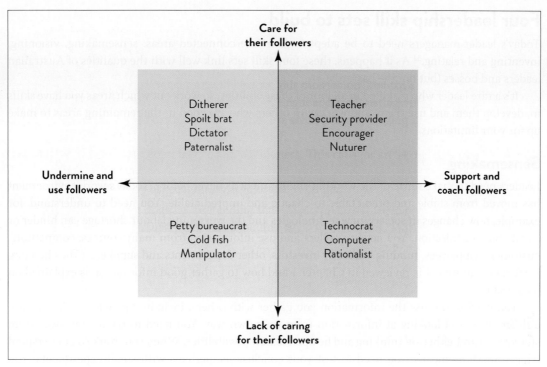

Source: Adapted from 'Australian cultural imprints at work: 2010 and beyond', Australian Government, Department of Education, Employment and Workplace Relations (DEEWR), March 2011[31]

FIGURE 9.6 Four Australian leadership styles

IN A NUTSHELL

The 21st-century leader-manager

The 21st-century boss may as well be a century away from the late 20th-century boss, their methods are so far apart. Table 9.5 shows the differences.

TABLE 9.5 How bosses have changed

Yesterday's boss	Today's boss
Organised people	Aligns people
Protected the status quo	Brings new perspectives and challenges the status quo
Promoted stability	Creates change and innovates
Did things right	Does the right things
Focused on results	Focuses on people
Used formal authority	Uses interpersonal skills
Gave direction	Encourages experimentation
Examined and inspected	Enables and empowers
Planned and coordinated	Gives purpose and meaning
Controlled	Supports, coaches and develops people
Gave directions	Leads by example and inspires

Four leadership skill sets to build

Today's leader-managers need to be adept in four interconnected areas: sensemaking, visioning, inventing and relating.[32] As it happens, these four skill sets link well with the qualities of Australian leaders and bosses (but not the bastards).

It's a rare leader who is skilled in all four of these abilities, so work out which areas you have skills in, develop them and use them, and work with others who are good in the remaining areas to make up for your limitations.

Sensemaking

Leaders need to make sense of the working environment as never before. Today's work environment has moved from stable and predictable to chaotic and unpredictable. You need to understand, for example, how changes in society, new technologies and the worsening labour shortage can hinder or assist your organisation. You need to collect and use information from many sources: competitors, customers, employees, funding bodies or investors, other departments and suppliers. (The changing working environment is reviewed in Chapter 1 and how to gather good information is explained on page 158.)

You need to discuss the information you gather with others, including people you know have a different way of looking at information from your own way. You need to try to stay away from stereotypes and 'either/or' thinking and be open to new possibilities. When you think you understand what something means, you need to test your conclusions, perhaps with small experiments. You need to hone in on what's important to your operations and explain it to others so they can plan how best to deal with the important issues. In healthy organisations, sensemaking is continuous. (These matters are discussed in chapters 6, 18, 20, 26 and 27.)

Visioning

In an ever-changing world, today's leader-managers need to be able to create a compelling and reassuring picture of the future for employees to work towards. Sensemaking helps you figure out what is going on, while visioning helps you decide how to use this understanding to create and describe a desirable future. You need to explain your vision and what it can achieve in a way that inspires others, using stories, metaphors and images. As part of this process, you need to 'walk your talk' and embody the core values and ideas contained in the vision. (These skills are discussed in chapters 8, 11, 13, 14 and 22.)

Inventing

Visions themselves aren't worth the paper they're written on until we start making progress towards them. Inventing is about executing and implementing a vision, but it also has the dimension of creatively developing new ways to achieve the vision. To work towards a vision, we can't keep doing what we've always done. We need to find new ways to work together and new ways to organise. Innovation and continuous improvement are part of this process, too, because fine-tuning how tasks are carried out is always important.

To succeed in the inventing area, you need to understand that just because something has always been done a certain way, a different way may be better today. You need to look for, and encourage others to look for, better, cheaper, easier, faster and safer ways to work towards their goals, and experiment with different ways of organising work and linking people. (Visions are discussed in Chapter 2, structuring organisations in Chapter 3, innovation in Chapter 19 and leading change in Chapter 22.)

Relating

Today, it's nearly impossible for a leader-manager to succeed without effective working relationships. You need to spend time with a variety of people, within and across the organisation, and with stakeholders outside it, encouraging them to speak up, listening with an open mind and trying to understand their various perspectives. What do they care about? How do they interpret what's going on?

You need to stay 'tuned in' and explain your own point of view, and before expressing your own opinions and ideas, you need to think about how others might react to them and how best to explain them. You also need to build and maintain effective networks to help you think through difficult issues, support your initiatives and in other ways help you accomplish your goals. (These skills are discussed in chapters 2, 4, 6 and 8.)

⊙ THE STRATEGIC PERSPECTIVE

Ape leadership

In chimpanzee troops, the leader sits at the centre. About every 30 seconds, all the other apes orient themselves to him. They take their cues from him. When he's stressed or nervous, so are they. When he's calm, so are they.

We take our cues from our leaders, too. Like the chimp troops, we need our leaders to remain calm, even in times of difficulty. Remaining calm doesn't mean doing nothing, though; you still need to be decisive and set clear directions, particularly in the face of crisis, threat or uncertainty.

⊙ ACTION!

How skilled are you in these four skill sets? You can find out by taking the interactive self-test: Where are your opportunities to develop your leadership abilities? on ⚲**CourseMateExpress**.

Tips for new leaders

From the moment you take up a leadership role, people are watching you. You are leading by example, and the only question is: Is it the example you want to set?

It isn't your job to set out to impress your new team. Your job is to get to know them and find out how you can help them do their jobs well. That impresses not only your new team but also your own manager when you hit the numbers.

Australians don't like a 'task master' boss, one who is autocratic, results-driven and provides little feedback. People whinge and ultimately do the bare minimum, and 'the numbers' crash. Concentrate on your team and its work (as explained in chapters 11 and 13) and 'the numbers' look after themselves.

Good leadership, for Australians, is based on quality relationships, and Australians are either 'full on' or 'full off' in terms of engagement and motivation; this means that the little things really count, like saying 'G'day' and using a person's name. Open communication, without compromising confidentiality, is seen as a sign of trust and inclusion, and contributes to followers' self-esteem. In contrast 'mushroom management' – keeping people in the dark – is definitely not appreciated in Australia. Make sure you include all team members when you share information, too – not just a favoured few. And tell the truth – remember those finely tuned 'bullshit detectors'.

Stay visible and talk – and listen – to people face-to-face; leader-managers don't retreat behind their desk and fire off emails. Keep your problems – work and personal – to yourself. Spend time building relationships with your team and across the organisation, and don't pretend you have all the answers. Jot down a few notes to make sure your memory isn't selective and be alert for feedback, especially the non-verbal kind that can tell you what team members and colleagues *really* think of you.

Today's employees aren't too fazed by your place in the hierarchy, but they'll work for you as best they can when they respect you for your personal qualities, know what you stand for and know they can rely on you to 'do the right thing'. But you need to prove yourself first, to earn peoples' trust and respect by demonstrating your character first, and later, your competence. (See chapters 7 and 8.)

Australians want positive feedback and recognition, but give it sincerely and keep it low-key ('employee of the month' schemes may work in the United States but tend to flop in Australia). We also respond best to clear and precise operating guidelines and are powerfully motivated by a clear vision and purpose (as described in chapters 2 and 11).[33]

As a leader-manager, you're no longer a 'me', working on getting great results as an individual performer (even though that might be what got you the job). Your job is now 'we' – getting great results from others by harnessing the power of collective effort. Build a culture that strives for high productivity and quality and one that is enjoyable and personally rewarding for team members to work in.

Since you're only as good as your followers' performance, individually and as a team, set high standards and insist on peoples' best efforts – no one will thank you for mediocrity. That doesn't mean micromanaging, but finding out what people need, procuring it for them, and standing back while they get on with it, ready to help when they need it.

When the results are good, step back and let your team share in the glory. (Remember, though, that the buck stops with you and you may occasionally need to take the blame for team mistakes.)[34]

Your role is probably more than helping your team succeed, though. It's probably also helping your organisation succeed, by recommending and initiating changes that help your team and your organisation do even better in the future.

Now that you're no longer 'one of the gang', you may want to make a few verbal contracts with your former workmates to establish ground rules for working together and identify potential problems and how to avoid them. Lead the conversation to cement your new relationship. If a team member/friend asks for special treatment, consider whether you'd provide it to other team members. When the answer is No, the answer is No. You will face difficult decisions and doing what is needed sometimes makes you unpopular.

Find a mentor to talk through difficulties with, someone whose mistakes you can learn from so that you make fewer of your own. Build your support networks and ask for help when you need it.

Learn to work well with your new boss (see how you do that on page 228) and agree your measures of success so you can spend your time working to priorities – which means you may not always need to be available to your team. Sometimes you need to say 'Sorry, I don't have five minutes now. Can we catch up at 4 o'clock?'

Maintain a 'tidy' workplace, one that operates safely at all times and respects people as individuals, for the contributions they make and for what makes them special. Not everyone has to love everyone, but each team member should understand what the others do, value their contributions and treat each other with professional respect and common courtesy.

Make time to step back and reflect on how you're going – an hour a week as you sit on the train or chew on a solitary sandwich is fine; every day is better. What are you doing that's working? What isn't working? What can you do better? (See Figure 26.1: The learning cycle, on page 866.) Should 'the imposter syndrome' strike, remember: You got the job because you deserve it (see more on this syndrome on page 192).

Robert Frost wrote, 'Education is hanging around until you've caught on.'[35] The same might be said of leadership.

The final word

As enterprises have become leaner and more fluid, and organisations evolve and integrate their functions along the lines of core processes, work more closely with their suppliers and customers and form strategic alliances with other enterprises to offer shared services, leading and managing is becoming harder all the time. It's imperative to keep on learning. To take a line from Curtis Mayfield, you also need to 'keep on keeping on'.

FYI

Words of wisdom

In his inauguration speech, US president, John F Kennedy said: Ask not what your country can do for you but what you can do for your country.[36]

The same might be said about true leaders. They don't ask 'What can my followers do for me?' but 'What can I do for my followers?'

Leadership is personal. Build your own leadership model and add to it as you grow into the role and develop your skills in your own way. Borrowed behaviours don't look authentic; something that is perfectly natural for one leader can easily look fake and forced when adopted by another leader. A leader's actions need to be true to themselves and in harmony with their own personal style. This is authentic leadership.

Here are some concepts to apply in your own unique way:

* Build employee engagement to drive productivity and customer loyalty.
* Build pride in good performance and achievements.
* Lead by conversation, not dictation.
* Make clear the behaviours and attitudes you expect people to exhibit.
* Show that you appreciate people's efforts.
* Show that you expect team members to learn and share what they've learned.

Pick two or three of these that best match your values and style and make them synonymous with 'Brand You'.

Leading is about more than knowing and doing. Leadership really begins inside, with your mindsets and world views (see page 190). More than anything, to be a leader, you need to think like a leader.

Leadership is a lifelong journey.

ACTION!

You can rate your ability as a leader by taking the interactive self-test: How do you measure up? on CourseMateExpress.

CourseMateExpress

Go to http://login.cengagebrain.com to access CourseMate Express, your online study tool for *Management Theory & Practice*. CourseMate Express brings chapter concepts to life with interactive learning, and study and exam preparation tools:

- Test your skills in different aspects of management with interactive self-tests and simulations.
- Watch videos that show how real managers operate in real businesses.
- Test your understanding of the changing world of management by taking the revision quiz.

QUICK REVIEW

1. Summarise the trait, behavioural and situational approaches to leadership and highlight the main differences between them. Which of the three approaches are you more drawn to?
2. What do you see as the main differences between leading and managing? Discuss the job of a manager from a leadership point of view, and from a managing point of view.
3. Compare and contrast Theory X leadership with Theory Y leadership and explain how the two styles are self-fulfilling prophecies. Which do you believe is a more appropriate form of leadership in the 21st century and why?

BUILD YOUR SKILLS

1. What is a leader? Illustrate your answer using each part of the following definition: 'A leader articulates and embodies a vision and goals and enables others to share and achieve them.'
2. How do you define leadership? Why are good leaders vital to modern organisations?
3. Give an example of each of the four styles of leadership from your own experience.
4. Referring to the situational approach to three styles of leadership, illustrate why different styles of leadership are appropriate in different situations using examples from your own experience.
5. Royal Australian Navy Commander Thomas Phillips has the following to say about leadership. Does this apply to your workplace? Why or why not?

   The most successful captains are the ones who change their style for the moment. Sometimes, it's this completely direct leadership, no questions asked. Because of the hazardous environment, you need to give an order and get a direct response. There's no teamwork, it's completely directive leadership. When you're looking at long-term planning you need a far more consultative approach, and the trick is being able to shift between the spectrum at the right times.[37]

6. 'Leaders can lead only when the followers are willing to follow.' Discuss the implications of this statement for leader-managers.
7. 'Manage yourself. Lead others.' Discuss what this means to you.
8. Can you see any parallels between authentic leadership and authentic parenting or authentic friendship? What might they have in common?

9. Peter Cosgrove said the following in his third Boyer Lecture. What actions can you as a leader take to avoid patchy leadership like this?

Overall, I think it is fair to say that while the sort of leadership on offer in Australia is pretty good, it can be 'patchy' – that is, spasmodic in practice. Sometimes leaders stop leading and sort of go on a leadership holiday and sometimes their leadership descends in quality so that the team wish they would go on holiday.[38]

WORKPLACE ACTIVITIES

1. Select one of the approaches to leadership discussed in this chapter and explain how you can use it to improve your own leadership in your workplace.
2. Analyse your work situation. What does it tell you about the leadership style you should adopt?
3. Select and apply a situational leadership theory to four common situations in your workplace.
4. How do you rank your own task-readiness levels for the main tasks you perform in the workplace? How do you rank your staff's task-readiness levels for the key tasks they perform? Are you using appropriate leadership styles according to the task-readiness approach to leadership?

BOB'S ORGANIC OZZIE BURGERS

As managing director of Bob's Organic Ozzie Burgers, Bob Johnson is always on the lookout for potential high-quality franchisees. The business has grown from the original outlet, opened in 2008, to a franchise with 17 outlets in two states, and there are plans for further expansion. The Ozzie Burger outlet is known as the leader in its field, and no small part of its success is due to the shrewd and capable management of Bob, his small management team and his excellent supplier chain and operating systems. He is also very fussy about his franchisees, who must be proven leaders able to maintain the company's standards.

Bob's latest aspiring franchisee is a young man named Robert Nicosea, whose father has recently been made redundant and is willing to use his payout to back Robert in his bid for a Bob's Organic Ozzie Burger franchise.

Robert's experience is not too exciting: work in a supermarket as a checker, summer work during the school holidays as a construction labourer and work as an assistant in an accounting firm. This is not an impressive record, but what strikes Bob is Robert's burning desire to get ahead – to succeed and to make something of himself.

Robert's job in the supermarket was head checker, responsible for training and supervising 11 other checkout staff. The job also entailed checking each register to ensure that the tapes and the money tallied. When Bob telephoned the store manager for a reference check, she gave a glowing account of Robert's job performance.

Robert is also the leader and informal spokesperson for his local fishing club and president of his town's youth group. At his first interview with Bob, Robert exhibits an almost contagious enthusiasm for honest work, his belief in others and a desire to succeed.

Bob asks Robert why he wants to take on the responsibility of running his own small business and why he thinks he is a good leader. Robert thinks for a moment, then replies: 'First of all, I know I can do the job. I've had experience in food handling in a supermarket and I know figures and bookwork. Also, I think I know how to handle employees. I believe that people like to see their boss exercise strong control. They like a manager who is not afraid to make decisions and who makes them quickly. They like a boss who runs a tight ship. And I

CASE STUDY 9.1

think that all of these qualities apply to me. I'm not afraid to make a decision. And I certainly don't mind giving instructions. Furthermore, when an employee isn't performing, I don't mind pointing that out and explaining how they can do better. And I don't believe in "suitcase management" – carrying people who aren't pulling their weight.'

He pauses, then goes on. 'I honestly believe that I'm a born leader. I've always wanted to tell others what to do. Even when I was little, I always wanted to lead the rest of the kids on my street and be the captain of the teams I was in at school.

'Bob, I know that I can be one of your most successful franchisees. I'm sure that I can run one of your food centres well and build a profitable business. I'm a hard worker. I don't mind long hours, hard work and tough goals. Give me a chance and I will prove to you that I can get results.'

Bob thanks Robert for meeting with him. The two shake hands and Robert departs.

Questions

1. What leadership qualities do you see in Robert Nicosea? Are they qualities that would be effective in a fast-food outlet? In running a small business?

2. Choose two leadership theories presented in this chapter and use them to analyse Robert's leadership style as he described it.

CASE STUDY 9.2

MANAGEMENT BY FILING CABINET

How would you like to work for one of the most cited, distinguished and influential psychiatrists in the world? Daunting? Not when it's Professor of Psychiatry Gavin Andrews, AO, MD, FRCPsych, FRANZCP, the research director of the Clinical Research Unit for Anxiety and Depression of the University of New South Wales at St Vincent's Hospital in Sydney.

His team includes two other MDs who rotate through the team as part of the hospital's psychiatry training unit; a chief psychologist and a team of clinical psychologists who work with patients combining face-to-face consultations with remote therapy over the Internet; a trial manager and a team of research fellows and research assistants, some of whom also have patient contact as well as research responsibilities. Non-medical staff – an administration assistant, an IT whiz and a project manager complete the team of 18. A sprinkling of overseas team members and Australians who have worked overseas bring a variety of approaches and perspectives to the team.

Leading a team of knowledge workers is 'clean sailing' once you get the right people and the right culture, Professor Andrews says. 'The thing to do is hire stars and let them get on with it. It soon becomes self-perpetuating – the rumour gets around: "This is a great place to work." You become a magnet employer and the best people come to you.'

The team is set up so that members bounce ideas off each other, support each other and train each other, which builds a culture of collaboration, innovation and team working. The professor keeps that culture going, building camaraderie and gently monitoring performance and quality in several ways, as described below.

Tuesday team lunches: The medical and non-medical staff, including the professor, take it in turn to bring in lunch for the rest of the team. 'Last week, it was make-your-own wraps with a variety of fillings, but the point is, these lunches encourage off-beat discussion and immersion in a stream of different ideas. After half an hour, I tap the table and kick off a more formal discussion. I take about five minutes talking about policy, plans going forward and what I've been up to; then we go around the table and everyone updates the rest of us on their week.'

The quality book: 'At the end of the meeting the chief psychologist goes around with a book that lists people's KRAs [key result areas], about four each, and people sign off on each one that there are no quality or safety issues in their areas of responsibility. When someone says "Ah, well actually ..." they have a chat and decide how to handle the situation based on our two prime directives:

1. Get people better.
2. No one comes to harm.

'That go-around only takes about five minutes at the end of our meeting, so we're pretty much done and dusted in an hour.'

The one-hour rule: 'Of course, if anyone is worried about something before Tuesday rolls around, the rule is – and they do this within one hour of becoming concerned about something – they come to me or another clinician and appropriate action is taken *instantly*. That might be, for instance, phoning the police to say someone is threatening self-harm.'

Wednesday presentations: Each Wednesday, between 1 pm and 1.30 pm or 2 pm, the professor's Anxiety and Depression team meets with the Schizophrenic team and someone gives a formal presentation about a paper recently published or about to be published. (Both teams are prolific writers of scientific papers for peer-reviewed journals.) This exposes everyone to different methodologies and ways of thinking. 'Cross-fertilisation of approaches and ideas is extremely important to our work,' the professor explains.

Wednesday ideas meetings: Come 4 pm, the professor's team meets to fly ideas, free associate, get feedback – whatever they want. People simply put their name on the board when they have something to discuss with the rest of the team. 'Last week I put my name up there. I am about to do a series of big talks around the country to teachers and educators and I wanted feedback on my presentation. As a result, I re-vamped quite a lot of it. These meetings are another way we build a culture of coming up with ideas.'

Induction for acculturation and comfort: 'When someone joins the team, I spend a lot of time sitting on the filing cabinet next to their desk; fortunately, we have low filing cabinets. We chat about what they're doing, how things are going, and so on. After two or three weeks, they usually let me know they're too busy with work to chat. Then I know they're comfortable with their roles and acculturated to our ways, and they know I'm there when they need me.'[39]

To find out about the unit, check out ABC-TV's *Catalyst* program with Dr Norman Swan talking to the professor on the team's work, at https://www.youtube.com/watch?v=SP7_FYybMSY and link into the unit's website at https://thiswayup.org.au/clinic/.

Questions

1. Based on the material in this case study and the 'Theory to practice: Leading knowledge workers', on page 408, relate three of the approaches to leadership considered in Section 1 of this chapter to Professor Andrews' leadership, giving examples to support your thinking.
2. Is the professor's leadership style more similar to the 'old fashioned' leadership styles or to the 21st-century Aussie leader-manager considered in Section 3 of this chapter? Provide examples that illustrate your opinion.
3. Which of the quadrants in Figure 9.6: Four Australian leadership styles, would you place Professor Andrews in and why?

CHAPTER

UNDERSTANDING MOTIVATION, ENGAGEMENT AND RETENTION

An organisation can't operate effectively when it has trouble attracting, motivating and retaining the people it needs – the top-performing 'stars' as well as the solid, everyday reliable performers. To succeed, organisations need employees at every level who are willing to invest their energy, effort and ideas in their work and who identify with the organisation's vision and values.

Most employees, when they join an organisation, sign some sort of job contract that details the hours of work, the rate of pay and other benefits, and the job they are to do. The contract doesn't say how hard they must work, how much cooperation and effort they must invest in their job, how much they must identify with and feel loyalty towards the organisation or how long they must remain in the job. In short, a job contract gives no guarantees about an employee's motivation, engagement or retention.

The fact is, people choose how hard they work. As the saying goes, 'Ya gotta wanta'. People can do their jobs with gusto or indifference, with zest or apathy, with passion or lethargy, and the results are poles apart. That's why at some point every manager has pondered the perennial question: How can I motivate my staff? And there is no one answer; what motivates one person doesn't necessarily motivate another.

And just when everyone is working energetically and well, a valuable employee resigns, taking their experience and tacit knowledge about the job, the people they work with and the organisation with them, and putting the team's ability to meet its goals at risk.

1. Do you know the difference between motivation and engagement, why they matter and what engages employees?
2. Do you know what motivates people and how to appeal to their key needs?
3. Can you list a variety of specific actions that you can take to boost people's motivation?
4. Do you understand your role in retaining employees?

This chapter explains how to motivate, engage and retain demanding employees in the face of a growing labour shortage.

A motivating situation

Sara, Leslie, Frances and Norm are enjoying a cup of coffee after the monthly leader-managers' meeting. The message the general manager delivered was brief but very clear: Sales are declining, costs are rising, productivity is deteriorating, labour turnover has soared through the roof and the right people to replace them are as rare as hen's teeth. Worst of all, the company is not keeping up with the innovations of the opposition in an industry where, only a few years ago, it was the acknowledged leader. 'What we need,' said the general manager, 'is for you team leaders to get out and motivate yourselves and your people to get this company on the go again.'

'It's all right for you,' Sara says to Leslie, the sales manager, 'all you have to do is run a sales competition with a weekend on the Gold Coast for the winner. Money and bribery – that's what motivation and retention are all about.'

'I wish it were that easy,' replies Leslie. 'The main challenge I have motivating staff is that my people operate quite independently of me. I don't see some of my salespeople for three or four weeks at a time. They're generally self-motivated, especially when they're making sales, but when they come face-to-face with a customer complaint, then not even money motivates them. Plus, my people are highly visible, which makes them "easy pickings" for the competition, and people these days are just as happy to move on as to stay. No, I think that people are easier to motivate and keep with you when you have them under constant observation so you can see any change in their attitude and do something about it right away.'

'I think it's keeping busy that motivates people,' replies Sara. 'My staff are happiest when the office is hectic. They know exactly what I need from them, and when they're busy doing it, they're happy, and when they're happy, they stay. That's why the easiest people to motivate and keep are those in the assembly area. Results are easy to measure, and when you can easily see how well you're performing, you work hard, and when you're getting good results, why would you leave?'

'That isn't quite right,' replies Norm. 'My people are semi-skilled and do a monotonous job. The only way to motivate them is with fear – a sort of spear-and-stick approach. The boss wants us to motivate people, so I'll sack a few whose work isn't as good as the rest to scare the others into trying harder. Then the boss will be on my back about labour turnover and I'll be scrounging around for replacements – talk about being between a rock and a hard place.'

'My problem of motivation is quite different from the rest of you and nothing that you have suggested can help motivate my people, still less keep them,' says Frances, from the research and development section. 'My team are highly qualified and work independently of each other most of the time. Personal achievement motivates them and they're off the second another company offers them more interesting work, better facilities or better technology.

'As for motivating ourselves, that might be all right for you younger managers who are after promotion and who have mortgages to pay. My motivation comes from looking forward to surviving long enough to retire and collect what's left of my superannuation.'

1. Motivating and engaging employees

You can buy a person's time. You can buy their physical presence at a given place. You can even buy a measured number of their skilled muscular motions per hour. But you cannot buy their enthusiasm or loyalty, the devotion of their hearts, their minds and souls. You must earn these.

Clarence Francis (US businessman), in Bickham, *Liberating the Human Spirit in the Workplace* (1996)[1]

More than ever, an organisation's success depends on the commitment and productivity of its employees, which rest on motivation and engagement. Motivation comes from within and creates a desire to do your job well and a willingness to invest your effort and energy in your work. Engagement is how committed you feel to the organisation as a whole, not just to your job. Both make you willing to put extra effort into your work – extra time, energy and brain power. And both are key to retaining the employees that organisations need.

Organisations set the scene for engagement at a broad policy and strategic level, while individual leader-managers set the scene for motivation in their relationships with employees and the work they assign them.

 THEORY TO PRACTICE

Loyalty lives

Apple's cult following means it has no shortage of job applicants and the retention rate in its Australian retail stores is nearly 90% – almost unheard of in the retail industry. The Apple culture turns every job into a mission, allowing Apple to pay its employees a modest hourly wage and no commission. Yet they remain fiercely loyal.[2]

The bottom line benefits of engagement

Engaged employees have 20% higher performance and are at 87% less risk of leaving the organisation.[3] They are also more loyal and enjoy better health and personal wellbeing than unengaged employees. Other studies have also found that engaged employees' enhanced feelings of self-worth reduce attrition and absenteeism and that engaged employees perform 20% better than satisfied but not engaged employees. Organisations with engaged employees are significantly more profitable and have higher customer ratings and fewer safety incidents than those with actively disengaged employees, and they benefit from increased agility and improved efficiency in driving change initiatives.[4] This affects the organisation's bottom line, particularly organisations that depend on their employees' goodwill and innovativeness to succeed.

The higher the ratio of engaged to disengaged employees, the better an organisation's performance.[5] But be careful. Strongly engaged employees are at risk of burning out.[6]

 IN A NUTSHELL

Measuring motivation and engagement

It isn't difficult to assess how motivated and engaged employees are. You need to measure the following for groups of employees and compare the measures with other similar organisations and organisations in your area, and monitor the trends over time. Table 10.1 shows you how.

TABLE 10.1 Motivated employees engage with the job

Measuring motivation	Measuring engagement
absenteeism/attendance	attrition/retention
attrition/retention	costs per hire
presenteeism	revenue generated per employee compared with competitors
	productivity improvement rates per employee
	time to fill high revenue-generating positions

THEORY TO PRACTICE

Engagement pays

Brands like Baileys, Bundaberg Rum, Guinness, Johnnie Walker and Smirnoff have made Diageo the world's leading premium drinks producer. Four of the company's five values are closely linked to driving engagement:

- Be the best
- Freedom to succeed
- Proud of what we do
- Value each other.

Diageo measures employee engagement through six questions in its annual employee survey. Giving the most positive response to all six questions labels an employee as super-engaged, the level the company is targeting. Quarterly surveys of three or four questions on topical issues around employee satisfaction measure progress by framing the questions in terms of whether they're doing better compared to a year ago.

The phrase 'Know me, focus on me and value me' guides managers' conversations with employees when setting objectives and discussing career aspirations and development plans. The senior leadership team has a monthly agenda item on employee engagement and the team holds regular meetings with groups of 20–25 employees so they can ask questions and say what's on their minds.

Results have been impressive. The percentage of super-engaged employees doubled from 25% to 50% in three years and voluntary turnover dropped from 18.4% to 13.5% in 12 months, providing a measurable saving in recruitment costs.[7]

Organisational foundations of engagement

Engagement is rational as well as emotional. It revolves around commitment to your:

- day-to-day work
- direct manager
- organisation
- work team and colleagues.

Organisations invite engagement in three areas, which you can think of as the three Cs: connection, contribution and credibility.

Connection

Understanding and relating to your organisation's goals and vision, and how your work contributes to them, combined with a sense of community and camaraderie within the organisation (liking the people you work with), creates bonds between employees and their organisation. Actively informing employees about what is happening in the organisation, as well as seeking their ideas for improvement through effective upward feedback channels, deepens the connection between employees and the organisation. Employees need to feel trusted and respected as individuals, so discussing their interests outside work as well as their work goals and career aspirations increases the connection still further.

Contribution

The right employees need to be placed in the right jobs – jobs that use their strengths. And those jobs must be well designed and provide meaningful work that contributes to the organisation's performance. People need to know precisely what is expected of them and that they are receiving an appropriate level of rewards and recognition for their contribution (and the best performers don't work just for money). People also need the resources, tools and training to do their jobs well and to know that poor performance is addressed, because it's frustrating for high performers to see poor performance ignored (and even rewarded).

For many employees, autonomy and flexibility in their roles, clear career paths, a chance to learn and grow in their job, and opportunities to develop skills and knowledge also build engagement.

Credibility

Employees regard organisations that have a reputation for integrity as worthy of their commitment and contribution, and corporate social responsibility, employer brand and employer value proposition are increasingly seen as important elements of engagement.

As discussed in Chapter 9, high-quality leader-managers who show they are committed to the organisation and who acknowledge and appreciate employees' efforts and contributions, demonstrate honesty and integrity. They handle difficult situations well, inspire commitment, treat employees as individuals and show loyalty to their work teams (engagement needs to flow both ways). This is critical to employee engagement. Even when the news is not good, employees expect managers to be honest – this stops the rumour mill and earns employees' trust.

When countless moments of truth, or interactions, between employees, their manager, other managers and the organisation itself add up to an intrinsically rewarding work experience, employees feel appreciated, respected and valued. In this environment, employees bond with the organisation and perform to the best of their ability.

YouTube-style formats are taking over from the 'talking head' corporate videos. Deloitte in the UK has even launched its own TV channel on which employees can watch corporate videos or download them to their iPods.

Expect to see more of this as Generation Y, which has grown up with these technologies, continues to join the workforce.

Individual factors of engagement

Engagement isn't just about the organisation and its managers. Age and personality can affect how engaged employees are likely to become. For example, younger employees may be positive when they first join an organisation but can quickly become disengaged, and outgoing and adaptable people find it easier to engage and remain engaged.

Engagement levels also vary according to seniority, occupation and length of service in an organisation, although not by sector. On the whole, more senior employees, hands-on employees and operational employees are all more likely to be engaged, while professionals and support staff are more likely to have the lowest levels of engagement, although this varies between organisations.[9]

Ultimately, engagement is a choice and depends upon what individual employees deem worthy of investing themselves in. This highlights the importance of correct job placement, not just between the employee and the job, but also between the employee and the organisation and its employer brand and employer value proposition.

THE STRATEGIC PERSPECTIVE

Engaged employees
What engages employees depends on where they live: their national culture, the stage of economic development and the market conditions. These all influence employee expectations and perceptions of the workplace. Here are some of the main engagers of employees around the world:

- being able to provide good customer service (UK)
- opportunities for personal growth and promotion (India)
- pay and benefits (China)
- respect (USA, UK, Asia)
- the people you work with (Germany)
- type of work (India, France).[10]

Three levels of engagement

Engaged employees work with passion and pride. They identify with and are committed to their organisation's values and vision and voluntarily perform at levels that exceed their stated job requirements to help their organisation succeed. They see a direct connection between their efforts and the organisation's results and enjoy their jobs and the organisation they work for so much that they're advocates and recruiters for the organisation: 'Come work with us – it's terrific here!' 'Buy our products and use our services – they're great!' (A 2013 Gallup poll found that worldwide, only 13% of employees are engaged at work.)[11]

At the other end of the scale are *actively disengaged employees*, who are only staying for the pay and may even be actively looking for a job elsewhere. They are so unhappy in their work that they undermine what their engaged colleagues accomplish and speak poorly of the organisation to anyone willing to listen. These employees are a huge drain on economies around the world. Gallup estimates, for example, that active disengagement costs Australia about $54.8 billion (or US$51.3 billion) a year, the USA US$450 to $550 billion a year, Germany US$151 to $186 billion a year and the UK US$83 to $112 billion a year.[12]

In between are *satisfied but not engaged employees*. They might be quite content doing their jobs and put time – but not energy or passion – into their work. When something better comes along, it's easy for them to leave for greener pastures. (Figure 10.1 illustrates these three levels.)

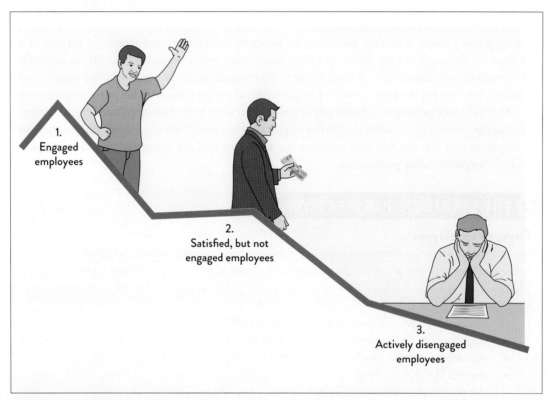

FIGURE 10.1 Levels of engagement

ACTION!

How engaged are you? Find out (if you don't already know) by taking the interactive self-test of the same name on *CourseMateExpress*.

Good news

In Australia and New Zealand, 24% of employees are engaged while 60% are not engaged and 16% actively disengaged. The resulting ratio of engaged to actively disengaged employees, 1.5:1, is one of the highest among all global regions and similar to results from the USA and Canada (1.6:1). Australia is among the global leaders in the ratio of motivated and productive (engaged) employees versus the negative and disruptive (actively disengaged) employees in its workplaces.

Most of our employees (60%) fall into the 'satisfied but not engaged' category, meaning they lack the psychological commitment to maximise their efforts on behalf of their organisations. Here's how to get even better:

* Align the organisation's leaders to its values and vision.
* Align every employee's role with the organisation's mission.
* Monitor employees' psychological safety.[13]

THEORY TO PRACTICE

An engaging culture

You probably know which is the most sought-after employer – Google. But another highly sought-after employer is NetApp, an IT infrastructure company that primarily provides data management solutions to organisations. In an industry where continual forward movement is mandatory, engaged employees are a must.

Although NetApp doesn't have the beanbags, death benefits or free gourmet cafeteria of Google, it's a 'fun' place to work and offers good career pathways, a great culture and open communication. NetApp's culture is collaborative and involved. For instance, staff are included in go-to market strategies and decisions about who NetApp should partner with.

NetApp's Australian offices are open plan, and more important than their track record are people's cultural fit and what they can bring to the culture. Recruits from around the world attend the New Hire School in NetApp's US headquarters where they meet the executive team for most of the first day.

Benefits include a competitive remuneration package incorporating share options and bonus schemes, a fifth week to do community service on top of four weeks' annual leave, and good training. (And don't forget the fun.)

Despite the shortage of people with IT skills and an economy in which many tech companies are struggling to survive the global recession, NetApp's Australian and New Zealand operations have tripled in size.[14]

How to be an engaging leader-manager

Engaging leader-managers share many characteristics. But perhaps surprisingly, personality is not one of them. Some are energetic extroverts, others shy and quiet; some are creative, others highly practical and still others intellectual. Their behaviour towards their teams, however, is very consistent.

Leader-managers who engage employees are described as protectors, steadfast, able to keep calm in busy and confusing environments and willing to stick their necks out. They listen to employees, value them as people and involve them. They're approachable, honest and open, supportive and encouraging and they develop people's skills and 'keep things interesting'. The quality of their relationships with employees invites engagement. (See Chapter 9 for more about the pivotal nature of effective working relationships and Chapter 8 to find out how to build them.)

Engaging leader-managers are good two-way communicators and give frequent positive, constructive and corrective feedback, using an encouraging, informal, coaching style (see page 447 for more on feedback and page 905 for more on coaching). They respect and take an interest in people as individuals and develop and nurture their skills. At the same time, they have high standards, set clear goals and expectations, and address performance problems quickly, firmly and fairly. When they need to resort to dismissal in order to protect their teams and their team's performance, they do so with empathy and follow 'proper procedures'.

Engaging leader-managers see the strategic perspective and take immediate action when plans go wrong. They motivate employees and give them autonomy while making it clear they are there to support them when necessary. When employees need help, they guide them to solve problems, rather than hand them a solution on a plate.

Engaging leader-managers build strong teams where members work well together, 'share ups and downs' and help each other out. They are clear about the contribution of individual team members to the team as a whole and present their team in a positive light to the rest of the organisation. They encourage ideas and suggestions and are willing to make changes to improve workflow and work methods.

● THEORY TO PRACTICE

Lisa Paul, an engaging leader

Lisa Paul bases her leadership style on Australian research conducted by John Evans who found that employees have two requirements of their leaders:

1. They want them to articulate the organisation's strategic direction.
2. They want them to care about them.

Paul put that into practice when she was appointed head of the Commonwealth Department of Education and Training in 2004.

When she oversaw a significant budget cut of 20% over three years, she communicated extensively and gave staff every chance to express their views and concerns and ask questions. Despite the cutbacks, staff engagement was, and remains, high.

When the department commissioned research that compared companies performing highly and poorly on factors such as engagement and wellbeing, the difference was astounding. The higher-performing workplaces were 12% more productive, had 23% less staff turnover and their average profit margin ratio was 10% higher – that's about $40 000 for each employee.[15]

Here are some other behaviours that engaging leader-managers share. They:

* agree clear goals
* allocate resources fairly
* encourage work–life balance
* engage in fair and open decision-making
* provide employees with development and learning opportunities
* provide leadership people can respect
* provide worthwhile, meaningful work that fits into the organisation's and employee's value systems and that matches employees' skills, strengths and interests.

Disorganised, egotistical, pessimistic micromanagers all need to learn to change their ways. But there is hope for them. Engaging managers aren't engaging from their first appointment. Their ability to engage employees grows over time, along with their confidence and self-awareness (as discussed on page 209).[16]

THE STRATEGIC PERSPECTIVE

Engagement is not a panacea

Engagement alone can't make a business profitable or creative, or provide a fantastic customer service experience. When jobs are badly designed or people don't know clearly what's expected of them, or the technology people work with is hopelessly slow and out-of-date, or when you're asking people to do a lot with less (fewer people or resources), you're just driving them into the ground.

THEORY TO PRACTICE

A surprisingly quick fix

Global Italian eyewear firm, Luxottica, owner of the Australian chains Bright Eyes, Budget Eyewear, Laubman & Pank, OPSM and Sunglass Hut, had a problem. In Australia, Luxottica's satisfied customers and its dissatisfied employees were viewing the company in vastly different ways. After years of poor management and a series of 'merger' takeovers, morale was poor – to the extent that only 56% of its staff bothered to respond to a survey designed to gauge their alignment to the company goals, values and leadership. One-on-one interviews indicated that employees lacked a basic understanding of the company's business strategy and the significance of their contribution in achieving it. Turnover was high (27% a year), making recruitment expensive and damaging the bottom line as well as overall performance.

To combat this, Luxottica quadrupled its learning and development (L&D) expenditure and launched a three-year 'People Plan' to improve both employee engagement and retention by 5%. Based on four months of focus groups with leader-managers, the plan was constructed around five major themes: core business process, corporate culture, leadership and communication, learning and development, and staff benefits. A series of 'roadshows' was rolled out to 970 stores across Australia and New Zealand.

The corporate structure was reduced from 34 layers to a mere five. Leadership profiles were rewritten to highlight the importance of challenging expectations, encouraging staff to help shape the company's future, delivering great results, engaging and empowering people, having a sense of fun and putting customers first.

Luxottica well and truly exceeded its original goal of 5% improvement in engagement and retention. Eighteen months into its three-year plan, retention was up 8%, engagement was up 15%, recruitment costs dropped by 30% and the parent company now regards its Australian arm as an incubator of new ideas. Employee engagement can work fast when it's introduced well.[17]

2. Understanding motivation

> In order that people may be happy in their work, these three things are needed: they must be fit for it; they must not do too much of it; and they must have a sense of success in it.
>
> John Ruskin (19th-century social reformer), *Pre-Raphaelitism* (1880)[18]

Many would say that a leader-manager's role is to:
- help people do their jobs to a standard of excellence
- build healthy teams
- develop leaders for the future of the organisation.

Promoting a climate that motivates people to do the best job possible fulfils all three of these important responsibilities.

Doing that little bit extra, looking after the tools and equipment of the organisation, guarding its proprietary information and sharing important knowledge with colleagues – in short, doing the thousand and one little extras that make a workplace productive and efficient and ensure its future – takes motivation.

So what is motivation? Motivation isn't about lighting a fire *under* a person – it's about lighting a fire *within*. Motivation is like an internal engine that gets a person 'moving'. You can start the engine or stall it, encourage employees to do their best or dampen their enthusiasm. Knowing how to start the engine makes you a valuable asset to any organisation.

 FYI

Finding the gold within

Andrew Carnegie, the renowned steel magnate of the 1930s, was at one time the wealthiest man in America. At one point he had 43 millionaires working for him. These employees weren't millionaires when they began working for Carnegie. They became millionaires while working for him. When asked how he had developed them to become so valuable, he replied, 'Men are developed the same way gold is mined. When gold is mined, several tons of dirt must be moved to get one ounce of gold. But one doesn't go into the mine looking for dirt. One goes in looking for the gold.'[19]

Charles Schwab was the first person to earn more than US$1 million a year in Andrew Carnegie's steel mills. When asked what equipped him to earn US$3000 a day – was it his vast knowledge of steel? – he replied, 'Nonsense! Lots of people work here who know lots more about steel than I do. I can inspire people. I consider my ability to arouse enthusiasm among employees the greatest asset I possess.'[20]

What motivates?

People often have pet theories about what motivates other people, based on their experience and on what motivates them. Three of the most common explanations of motivation are 'fear', 'laziness' and 'money'. Do these really motivate people? Let's see.

Fear?

In his book, *Who Killed Channel 9?*, founding executive producer of Channel 9's *60 Minutes*, Gerald Stone, wrote of the late media owner, Kerry Packer's management style: 'Packer ... occasionally referred to a sad flaw in his character, a trait he was ashamed of in himself. "I don't know any other way to manage people than through fear ...".'[21]

Is fear a good motivator? Threats of losing your job or being reprimanded may light a fire under you for a while, but generally the effect doesn't last long or work very well. This is especially true in areas where jobs are plentiful, such as in Australia.

The positive motivation of gaining something you want works better than the negative motivation of fear and threats. If you're tempted to motivate through fear, remember these consequences:

*   Fear sets off an automatic adrenalin response in the body that triggers the ancient fight, flight or freeze response – employees instinctively want to hit managers who manage through fear, run from them or do nothing, or at least as little as possible, lest they do something else 'wrong'.
*   Fear loses its power as people become accustomed to the threats.
*   To motivate employees by fear, you must supervise them often and closely; it's hard work.

Laziness?

There are no unmotivated people, only unmotivated employees. This popular saying is so often true. Have you ever watched people rushing off home at the end of their shift? How many anglers do you know who leap out of bed at 3am to go on a fishing trip? Or perhaps you know skiers who are happy standing in freezing temperatures waiting for the chair lift, anticipating the run down the mountain? People are motivated to do things when they receive something they want in return.

Most people aren't inherently lazy. You probably don't like being lethargic and bored. Neither do most employees. People welcome leader-managers who can help them enjoy their jobs and get satisfaction from them. So you don't have to worry about transforming lazy, unmotivated employees into industrious 'workaholics'. You just need to channel their existing energies into desirable work performance.

Your brain's reward network

By mapping the human brain with advanced technology such as fMRI and using advanced statistical techniques, neuroscientists have found a number of brain networks and subnetworks that guide our perceptions and behaviour.[22] One of them, the *reward network*, activates in response to enjoyment. What has that to do with motivation? Plenty.

Immaterial rewards work just as well as material ones, often even better. (And they're less expensive.) Here are a few non-material rewards you can use to motivate:

- *A culture of fairness*, such as equitable, fair and transparent decision-making versus treating people differently for no clear reason; open communication versus withholding information; and including versus excluding people.
- *Intrinsically interesting work*, such as solving interesting problems.
- *Long-term goals (versus interim targets)*, which are specific enough to reach for but not so specific that they curb curiosity and flexible thinking (see the discussion on job purpose in Chapter 11 and team purpose in Chapter 13).
- *The opportunity to learn*.
- *Social approval*.

Money?

Economic rationalists tell us that human behaviour is mindful and logical. Employees calculate how much effort to put into a job based on how much money they receive in return for their efforts. It sounds sensible, but then again, we know that people are ruled by their hearts as much as their heads.

For repetitive or routine jobs, financial incentives, or pay for performance, can work. But that's mostly old economy, 20th-century jobs, where both white- and blue-collar jobs followed established steps. These jobs are now often automated or outsourced, which is good, because these jobs are pretty dull and unsatisfying. That's why you have to coax people into doing them with external rewards and threaten them with external punishment – the good old 'carrot and stick'. Even when money boosts productivity in those monotonous tasks, once the goal is achieved and the money is in your hand, productivity tends to fall.

Most jobs in Australia today are knowledge and service jobs calling for creative and emotional work and brain power. Financial incentives can actually disincentivise, or reduce performance.

Heuristic tasks, where you have to work out what to do each time because each situation is different and calls for a novel solution, can't be automated or outsourced and, because they're generally more enjoyable and satisfying, they need intrinsic motivation.

Not convinced? Study after study shows that money does not motivate, at least not for long. People will forgo moving to a job that pays substantially more in order to remain working in a place where they enjoy the work and can use and develop their skills and talents and work with others in an atmosphere of mutual respect.

Think about it: Your manager walks up to you and says, 'My friend, in recognition of your excellent performance and because we think you're a terrific person, we have decided to double your pay.' Naturally you would be pleased, and perhaps, in gratitude, work really hard for three, four or even five weeks. However, if you're like most people, you would quickly learn how to spend your increased earnings and come to take them for granted. They would then cease to motivate you (although the fear of losing them might motivate you for a little while longer).

As explained later in this chapter, money for most people is what is known as a hygiene factor that helps satisfy their lower order, or physiological and security needs. There are exceptions, of course. Some people really do go to work just for the money. They may need it badly or they may consciously choose a high-paying but not necessarily satisfying job for some other reason. For example, they may be getting most of their psychological, higher order needs met away from the workplace. Or they may want to earn money to give their children a good life and educate them.

Money (in the form of a bonus, performance incentive or pay rise), when it is clearly paid to reward good performance, can motivate. In this case, though, it isn't so much the money itself that motivates but rather what it symbolises – recognition of good performance.

⬤ THEORY TO PRACTICE

Using money to motivate

People no longer trade their time for money; they're more interested in work that rewards in other ways. Nevertheless, pay-for-performance incentives can help attract and retain employees, particularly those with a 'drive to acquire' (see below). Here are some guidelines for using monetary incentives to motivate:

- Establish a clear link between the targets and the organisation's goals to ensure that people's efforts benefit the entire organisation.
- Establish clear and demanding, but not impossible-to-attain, easily measured targets.
- Make it possible to earn 10% to 15% on top of the total remuneration package so that the extra effort is worthwhile.
- Place the incentives on top of a high base pay – don't use incentive payments as a way to transfer business risk to individual employees.
- Reward effort as well as performance to accommodate the degree of difficulty of a task.

Saying that fear, laziness and money motivate people is known as a *fundamental attribution error*, or the tendency to put observed behaviours down to someone's personality, ignoring situational explanations for the behaviour. So next time you're tempted to say 'That's just how they are', consider what in the situation may be causing the behaviour:

- How do others behave in that situation? If most others behave similarly, you can bet it's the situation, not a personality that's driving the behaviour.

- How would you behave in that situation?
- Look for hidden causes of the behaviour, like group dynamics, the incentive structure or unchallenging work. (Chapter 11 describes other causes to look for.)

THE STRATEGIC PERSPECTIVE

Extrinsic versus intrinsic motivation

Modern management practice is based on a set of principles, many of whose origins date back more than 100 years: hierarchy, planning and control, specialisation, standardisation and using external, or *extrinsic*, rewards to motivate. Generations of managers have mined these principles and many seem to have reached their natural end.

When you're tempted to bribe people to be productive, consider:

- Wikipedia, the world's largest encyclopaedia, written by volunteers.
- Habitat for Humanity, a not-for-profit organisation that builds homes for low-income families around the world, through volunteer labour and donations.
- Linux, the operating system voluntarily coded by once-upon-a-time hackers.

All three are examples of non-hierarchical communities of self-managed volunteers working without job descriptions for internal, or *intrinsic*, rewards such as a sense of shared purpose and emotional satisfaction.

In the long run, fear and force are outdated and unsuccessful motivators. Other motivation methods that may have worked in the past, particularly money and competition, are also less effective than they once were for most employees.

Climate, culture and content

Since laziness isn't a widespread problem and fear and money don't motivate, what does? Research consistently identifies intangible factors as motivators – the higher order, psychological needs identified by Maslow, Herzberg and other researchers (discussed further on in this chapter). This means work climate, culture and the job itself are much more effective ways to motivate people.

But it doesn't mean that motivation is simple. As a maintenance manager remarked: 'People can be a source of joy or an absolute misery.' Motivating others is one of the biggest challenges that leader-managers face.

Chapter 4 examines climate and culture. Job content is the third important piece of the motivation puzzle. Monotonous, boring jobs drain interest and motivation and are a source of stress. Even when the surroundings and co-workers are congenial, dull jobs can cause problems. Humans, like most living things – even amoebas – constantly seek stimulation, and when they aren't stimulated, they can fall into repetitive, harmful patterns of behaviour.

Environmental stimulation and job challenge fine-tune the brain, which is why job rotation and job design increase job satisfaction and motivation as well as productivity. Job design refers to a job's content, or its specific duties, accountabilities and tasks. Well-designed jobs give employees autonomy, responsibility and the chance to work in teams. They provide variety, interest and challenge as well as opportunities to learn and grow, use skills and contribute ideas. (See page 234 for more information on job design.)

Hopeless and futile labour

Do you know the story of Sisyphus? The gods condemned him to ceaseless effort rolling a rock up to the top of the mountain, whence it would fall back down. They believed that there is no more dreadful punishment than hopeless and futile labour.

The founder of cybernetics, Norbert Wiener summed it up when he said, 'If the human being is condemned and restricted to perform the same functions over and over again, he will not even be a good ant, not to mention a good human being.'[23]

How to uncover people's key needs

To 'light the fire within', you need to find the answers to these three questions:
1. What are people's basic needs?
2. What do people need from their work?
3. What happens when people's needs are not met?

Values, beliefs and needs

Values, beliefs and needs are powerful motivators for most people. Values express what a person holds dear and believes is right and wrong, good and bad, important and unimportant. Each person's values and belief systems – about themselves, others and the world around them – are unique to that person, based on their upbringing and life experiences.

Although we're all different, we are also alike in many ways. Psychologists believe that everyone shares the same basic needs (although in different strengths and combinations) and that these needs join a person's values and beliefs to motivate and guide their behaviour. Figure 10.2 gives some examples.

 ACTION!

What do you value? You can find out more about your own values and belief systems by completing the checklist: What do I value most? on ⌘**CourseMateExpress** in the activities for Chapter 7.

● THE STRATEGIC PERSPECTIVE

How needs drive behaviour

An action is the basic unit of behaviour. When you feel hungry, you are motivated to eat. You might go out and buy some food for a quick snack, you might cook a big meal, you might even go out and steal some food if you were hungry enough. Sometimes consciously, but usually unconsciously, you do what seems most likely to get you what you want with the most positive, or fewest negative, consequences.

This means that everything people do, they do for a reason, whether they are aware of the reason or not. When people are hungry, they eat. When people are lonely, they try to make friends. When people need the respect or approval of others, they behave in ways they think will earn them respect or approval (see Figure 10.2).

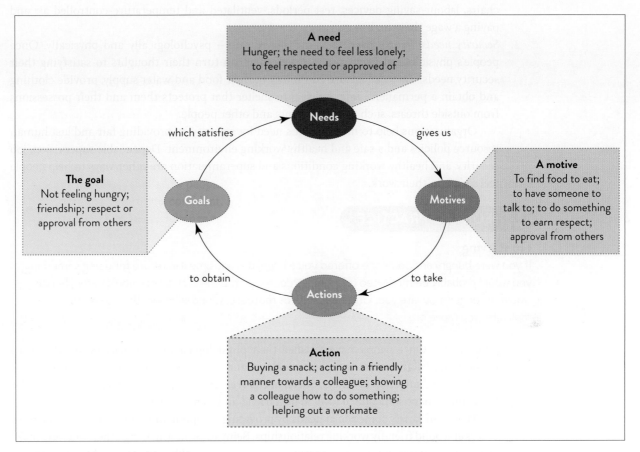

FIGURE 10.2 How needs drive goals

Following are four ways of looking at motivation that are particularly helpful in explaining the basic needs that most people share. These needs motivate everyone to varying degrees, although for most people they are buried in the unconscious and they are not aware of them in their day-to-day lives. As you did with the approaches to leadership explained in Chapter 9, read through these ideas about motivation, and work with those that makes most sense to you.

Maslow's hierarchy of needs

Mahatma Gandhi spoke of people's basic needs when he said: ' ... those hungry millions who have no luster in their eyes and whose only God is their bread.'[24]

Human beings have certain physiological and psychological needs, which Abraham Maslow grouped into categories and arranged into a hierarchy. Maslow's hierarchy of needs, illustrated in Figure 10.3, shows Maslow's six levels of needs, with the most basic, or lower order, physiological needs at the bottom. Once a need is reasonably well satisfied, it loses its ability to motivate and the need at the next level up emerges and begins to motivate.[25]

1. *Physiological needs*: People cannot live without air, food, sleep and water. When any of these necessities are in short supply, they become urgent and people spend most of their time and energy trying to obtain them. Other basic physiological needs are shelter, sex and a comfortable temperature.

   Organisations help to meet employees' physiological needs by providing basic working conditions such as a safe and secure building, ergonomically designed work stations and chairs, labour-saving devices, rest periods, ventilated and temperature-controlled air and paying a wage they can live on.

2. *Security needs*: People need to know they're safe – psychologically and physically. Once people's physiological needs are satisfied, they can turn their thoughts to satisfying their security needs. They can ensure continuity in their food and water supply, provide clothing and obtain a permanent, safe and secure shelter that protects them and their possessions from outside threats, such as the elements and other people.

Organisations help to meet people's need for security by providing fair and just human resource policies and a safe and healthy working environment. Dependable supervision, job security, and healthy working conditions and superannuation are other ways to help people feel secure in their work.

⊙ THEORY TO PRACTICE

I'm starving

If you were hungry and someone offered you a large, delicious meal in return for doing something, you would probably be motivated to do it in order to get the meal. But once you'd eaten, hunger would no longer motivate you. Unsatisfied needs motivate. Once satisfied, they cease to motivate. You move on.

3. *Social needs*: Once people have satisfied their physiological and security needs, they turn to social needs. They want to feel they 'belong' and begin to seek the company, acceptance, friendship and affection of others. Social needs are expressed, for example, in the need to be loved and to have someone to love, to be a friend and to have friends.

Work can satisfy some social needs by providing an opportunity to be in the company of others and build friendly working relationships. Being informed, helping others out, organised employee activities, supportive supervision and trust can all help meet people's social needs.

4. *Esteem needs*: Some esteem needs are satisfied internally. For example, through autonomy, achievement, self-confidence and self-respect. Other esteem needs are satisfied externally, through appreciation and respect from others and from status and recognition.

Work is an important way for many people to satisfy both their internal and external esteem needs. Appreciation and recognition for work, delegated authority, merit awards, opportunity for advancement, participation in decisions, status symbols, job title and responsibility can all meet esteem needs.

⊙ THEORY TO PRACTICE

Saying thank you

You can say thank you in many ways, ranging from letting someone leave work early to having your boss recognise an employee with a phone call. Or you can drop by in person, to simply say: 'Thank you for your effort with X – it really made a difference.'

When recognising employees, match your thank-you strategy and its delivery to the person. For example, shy people may not feel comfortable being recognised in front of a large group so do this in private.

5. *Self-actualisation needs*: This is the need for creativity, learning, self-improvement and personal growth – the need to use your abilities and skills to the full and to reach your

potential. At this level, you aren't spurred on by a sense of deficiency (must find food, must make friends) but to explore and become more of what you can be.

People at this level react against situations that prevent them from doing so. For example, people who find their job dull and boring often try to make it interesting and challenging. When this is not possible, they often look outside work for opportunities to develop and grow as a person.

Provide challenging work that allows creativity, freedom to make work-related decisions and opportunities for personal growth. And assign work that gives people the opportunity to use their skills and learn new ones. All these can be important ways to satisfy self-actualisation needs and are under your control.

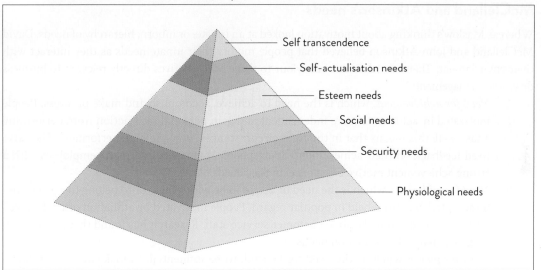

Adapted from the ideas of A Maslow, 'A Theory of Human Motivation', *Psychological Review*, Vol. 50. No. 4, 1943, p370[27].

FIGURE 10.3 Maslow's hierarchy of needs

6. *Transcendence needs*: In later years, Maslow added this sixth level to his hierarchy. Transcendence includes profound experiences of feeling part of the greater whole as well as the need to serve and to help others achieve, find self-fulfilment and realise their potential.[26]

Having 'grown' and self-actualised, you're ready to 'give back'; coaching, mentoring and passing on your skills and knowledge to others in the workplace and in your professional circles can satisfy this ultimate desire.

Although people are never fully satisfied at any level, some satisfaction at the lower levels is necessary before most people seek to satisfy the upper-level, or higher order, needs.

THEORY TO PRACTICE

Going backwards
People can move up and down the hierarchy. For example:

- A young couple who has just taken on a large mortgage might have security as a primary motivator and step away from socialising with friends in their spare time in order to save money.
- As they near the age of retirement, many employees become concerned with security again.
- Someone with a satisfying job, a group of friends they enjoy spending time with, and sufficient income who then suddenly loses their job might also revert to security as a key motivator.

Sound common sense?

Maslow's theory is known as an 'armchair theory'. This means that he sat in a chair, thought about people and what motivates them and developed his theory. Although it isn't research based, it's been around for a long time, since 1954 in fact, which indicates that it makes sense to most leader-managers.

McClelland and Atkinson's needs

Whereas Maslow's thinking about motivation looked at an innate, or inborn, hierarchy of needs, David McClelland and John Atkinson believed that people modify their innate needs as they interact with their environment. Their model relates behaviour to three basic motives directly relevant to business drive and management:[28]

1. *Need for achievement*, which is the need to achieve, accomplish and make progress. People motivated by achievement are independent and gain personal satisfaction from performing a task well; this means that in the right circumstances, they are high performers. They also need feedback on their achievement. Sportspeople, managers and many employees with a strong achievement motive often excel in their fields.

2. *Need for affiliation*, which is the need or desire to be with others or to belong to a group and be accepted, liked and held in popular regard. People motivated by affiliation often deal well with the public and make good customer service staff. Research has found that many Asian managers have high affiliation needs.

3. *Need for power*, which is the need for control, to be influential, to make an impact. Some individuals have an intense desire to be in charge and in a position of authority, for their ideas to prevail, and for personal status and prestige. Research has found that many managers in Western cultures have a high need for power.

Everyone has each of these three needs to some extent. The strength of each need relative to the others gives people their own unique 'needs profile', which affects their behaviour and working/ management style. Your task, as a leader-manager, is to find out the needs profile of each of your team members and meet it in ways that are within your control.

 IN A NUTSHELL

It's up to you

Try to match people with jobs that offer the greatest opportunity for satisfying their particular needs and that make the best use of their particular skills and abilities. Then make sure that they understand precisely what is required of them. Try to ensure they realise that they will receive rewards they value through good job performance. Always recognise employees' efforts.

● THEORY TO PRACTICE

Seven proven ways to motivate employees

Motivation and positivity go together. Try these positive motivating moves:

1. *Allow personal freedom* with as few rules as possible and the opportunity for high earnings; being in charge and controlling one's own destiny motivate people who savour a high-risk, high-rewards environment.

2. *Build a culture of camaraderie and collaboration* that values teamwork, openness and friendship to motivate people who enjoy the opportunity to work with people they trust and like and help satisfy employees' social, recognition and esteem needs. Structure your team in a way that invites an exchange of ideas, interdependence and mutual support. Australia's basic mateship system encourages people to help one another, so ensure employees feel able to ask for and offer help and assistance.

3. *Build a sense of pride* in the organisation's and your work team's mission, accomplishments and values; this motivates and engages most people.

4. *Build* self-esteem *and confidence* because only people with high self-esteem and confidence can perform at their best. This is one of the unrecognised keys to motivation. (For more information on the importance of self-esteem, see page 167.)

5. *Make everyone a winner* because nothing succeeds like success. Give every employee the opportunity to be successful, or at least make a significant contribution to the team's success. Give credit to everyone involved in success.

6. *Offer well-designed jobs* with clear standards, measures of success and easy ways to track results. Worthwhile, interesting and challenging work motivates people who are into learning and developing their skills and abilities and who want to make a meaningful contribution and knowing what is expected, why it matters and how they are doing.

7. *Show appreciation and celebrate,* because recognising and celebrating accomplishments motivates people who want a fun, supportive and interactive environment. Recognising people for the quality of their individual performance and the value they add to the work team motivates people who enjoy achieving goals and earning the respect of others.

Herzberg's two-factors of motivation

In 1959, Frederick Herzberg adapted Maslow's thoughts on motivation to a work setting. His model has also stood the test of time. While Maslow saw motivation operating across a single continuum of needs from physiological to self-transcendence and McClelland and Atkinson saw motivation as a balance of three primary needs, Herzberg divided people's needs into two groups of factors operating along two independent continuums. He called them *hygiene factors* and motivation factors.[29]

The first group of factors, the *hygiene factors,* do not motivate, but they can dampen enthusiasm. They operate across a scale from dissatisfaction to no dissatisfaction, or 'neutral'. As Figure 10.4 shows, hygiene factors relate to the environment in which people do their jobs. When hygiene factors fail to meet employees' expectations, employees are dissatisfied. When an organisation meets its employees' hygiene needs, employees are in neutral and ready to be motivated by the second class of factors, the *motivation factors.*

The *motivation factors* operate across a continuum from not motivated (no job satisfaction) to highly motivated (job satisfaction). From Figure 10.4 you can see that the work itself, not the environment in which it's done, provides job satisfaction and motivation.

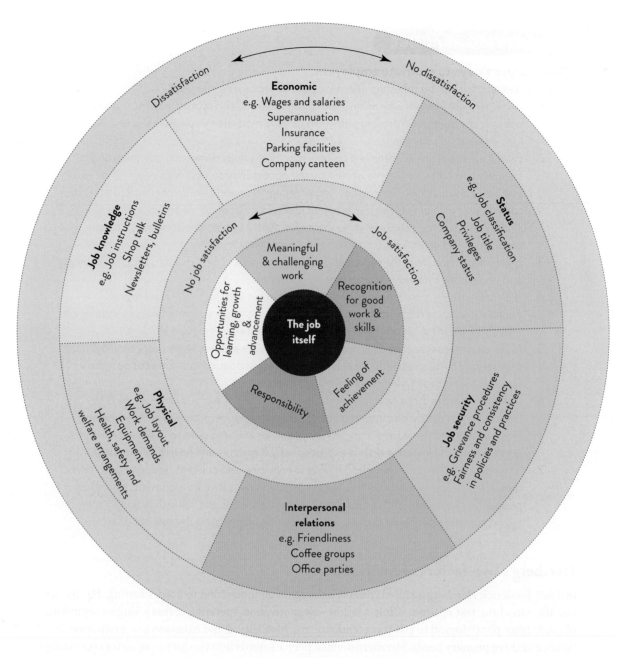

Source: Adapted from the ideas of Frederick Herzberg, *One more time: How do you motivate employees?* Harvard Business Review Case Services. 1987.

FIGURE 10.4 Herzberg's two-factors of motivation needs

Once people consider their working terms and conditions (hygiene factors) to be adequate, they can find motivation if doing their jobs gives them satisfaction by providing meaningful and challenging work, a sense of accomplishment, recognition and responsibility, and opportunities to continue to learn and advance – or some combination of these factors. This illustrates the importance of job design and job placement.

THEORY TO PRACTICE

Hygiene or motivator?

To remember the difference between hygiene factors and motivators, think of hygiene factors as physical and motivators as psychological. When an employer fails to satisfy employees' hygiene needs, dissatisfaction results and motivation cannot occur. Satisfying people's hygiene needs does not motivate them but puts them in 'neutral', ready to find motivation in a satisfying job and a competent leader-manager.

As you can see from Figure 10.5, there is a close relationship between Maslow's and Herzberg's ideas about motivation. Herzberg's hygiene factors relate roughly to the lower three levels of Maslow's hierarchy (physiological, security and social needs) and the motivators relate to the top levels (esteem, self-actualisation and self-transcendence needs).

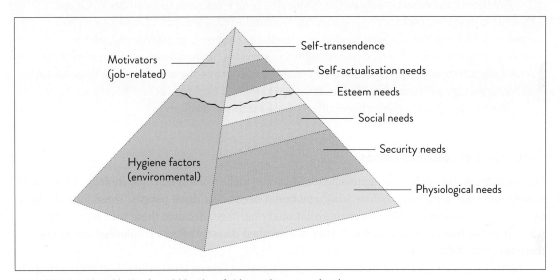

FIGURE 10.5 How Maslow's and Herzberg's ideas relate to each other

THE STRATEGIC PERSPECTIVE

Why hygiene factors matter

It's only when hygiene factors fail to meet employees' expectations that they grab their attention. Dissatisfaction with the working environment comes to dominate the behaviour, not only of individual employees but also of whole work groups, and even an organisation when the problem is organisation-wide.

Organisations must continually strive to be competitive in the hygiene areas (e.g. comfortable and attractive office furnishings, good pay and benefits, suitable working conditions, training) so they can attract, motivate and retain quality staff.

Organisations generally attend to the hygiene factors, but it's mostly up to individual leader-managers to provide the intangible motivation factors: Interesting and challenging jobs with clear goals that allow a sense of responsibility and achievement, appreciation for one's contributions, opportunities for learning and so on. In truth, acceptable hygiene factors are fairly easy to provide, although they cost money. The motivation factors don't cost money but they do require excellent leader-managers.

THE STRATEGIC PERSPECTIVE

Perquisites: Golden handcuffs, hygiene factors or motivators?

Kicked off by Google, the 'perk wars' heated up when Facebook poached the late Josef Desimone, one of Google's star chefs, and executive Sheryl Sandberg, now Facebook's chief operating officer. Pets to work? Game-maker Zynga offers pet insurance, too. Video streamer Netflix lets employees take as much time off as they like and customise their remuneration mix of cash and stock. Still losing employees, Google raised everyone's salaries by 10%, putting them well above average and since then, found it easier to attract and retain 'talent'.

Are these inducements really golden handcuffs, tying employees to a company? Or are they more than that, perhaps proving how highly valued employees are? Google says its free meals aren't so much about good food as 'manufactured moments of serendipity', where chance conversations in the food queue might spark an idea. To increase the likelihood of these potentially lucrative interactions, Google measures the length of the queues: below three minutes isn't long enough and more than 10 minutes is too long.[30]

What do you think – golden handcuffs, hygiene factors or motivators?

Four basic emotional needs

Research from the fields of neuroscience, biology and evolutionary psychology, along with motivational research, identify four basic emotional needs that drive people. These four needs, or drives, are the product of our common evolutionary heritage. Because these four needs are hard-wired into the human brain, how well they are satisfied directly affects employees' emotions and, therefore, their behaviour.

Further research to determine the actions managers can take to satisfy those four areas of need to increase employees' motivation found that an organisation's ability to meet the four needs explains, on average, about 60% of employees' variance on the motivational indicators of engagement, satisfaction and commitment. (In contrast, the researchers believe the three ways of looking at motivation just discussed cover about 30% of employees' motivational variance.) The four needs are:

1. *The drive to acquire*: People are driven to acquire items that bolster their sense of wellbeing – physical goods like clothing, housing and money, experiences like entertainment and travel, and indicators of status such as a promotion and a private office. (People compare these items to what others have, and this explains why people always seem to want more.)

   The organisation's reward system is perfect for satisfying this need, provided it discriminates between good and poor performers, ties rewards to performance and offers the best performers opportunities for advancement.

2. *The drive to bond*: Human beings need to connect not only with their parents and kinship group, as do many animals, but also with larger collectives such as organisations, associations and nations. Motivation receives an enormous boost when employees feel proud of belonging to an organisation and it plummets when the organisation betrays them. (This need also explains why people can find it difficult to break out of their functional 'silos', despite organisations' attempts to connect 'silos'. (Silos are explained on page 86.)

An organisational culture that engenders a strong sense of 'us' and a team spirit, collaboration, friendship, openness and pride is the best way to satisfy the bonding need.

3. *The drive to comprehend*: People need to make sense of the world around them and contribute to it, which explains why learning and working out answers engages and energises employees. Challenging jobs that encourage employees to grow and learn motivate and retain employees, while dead-end, monotonous jobs demoralise and encourage attrition.

    Job design is the key to satisfying this need – challenging, interesting, meaningful jobs.

4. *The drive to defend*: As part of the fight, flight or freeze response, people naturally defend themselves, their family and friends, their property, and their accomplishments, beliefs and ideas against external threats. This extends to the desire for clear goals, procedural justice and processes that allow people to express their ideas and opinions. Fulfilling this drive leads to feeling secure and confident. Not fulfilling it leads to resentment and fear. (This explains people's resistance to change and their dismay at the prospects of mergers and acquisitions.)

    Fair, transparent, trustworthy procedures for allocating resources, dealing with grievances, making decisions and managing performance, and policies and programs for enhancing work–life balance and employee welfare satisfy this need.[31]

As with McClelland's ideas about motivation, people have each of these needs in different proportions. The drives are independent and therefore each must be satisfied. For example, you can't pay employees a lot (drive to acquire) and ignore their need to bond. The research showed that the organisation *as well as* individual leader-managers need to address all four of these drives. The research also showed that individual leader-managers influenced overall motivation as much as did organisational policy.

Employees may or may not be familiar with motivational theory but they instinctively realise that many aspects linked to engagement and motivation are out of their boss' hands because they are a matter of organisational policy. However, employees also realise that many factors are squarely in their boss' hands. For example, you can reward employees with praise, recognition and interesting assignments. You can encourage teamwork and make jobs more meaningful and interesting, and you can manage with a participative approach and with fairness, establish key result areas and set clear measures of success.

Motivating around the world
Contributing to the community or society motivates Australians. The 'impossible dream' – achieving despite adversity – drives Americans. Germans are motivated by achieving technical excellence, Japanese by the search for perfection and Italians by recognition of style or design.[32]

3. Encouraging and discouraging motivation

If you want to build a ship, don't drum up people to collect wood and assign them tasks and work. Rather, teach them to long for the endless immensity of the sea.

Attributed to Antoine de Saint-Exupery (French author, aviator), Quoted in Krause, *Sell or Sink* (2011)[33]

Fabulous hygiene factors, including money, are sometimes called *push factors* because the fear of losing them pushes, or forces, an employee into doing the job. Push factors are negative and external to people, which makes them weak. As you probably know from your own experience, doing a job for fear of what you stand to lose if you don't do it usually means doing only the bare minimum. Push factors aren't good motivators.

The higher order, psychological needs are good motivators. These are called *pull factors* – people want to move towards them, not away from them. Because pull factors are intrinsic, they attract people's best efforts the way a magnet attracts iron. The interesting nature of the work itself draws out people's energy – they can't help but do a good job. Once again, we see the importance of correct job placement – giving people jobs they find interesting and rewarding in themselves, jobs that meet their higher order needs and motivate them to do a good job.

● IN A NUTSHELL

Appealing to higher order needs

Here are some ways that help motivate people:
- Assign complete units of work when possible.
- Communicate team results and organisation news and results.
- Encourage participation.
- Get to know employees as individuals.
- Give feedback on performance.
- Increase people's accountability for their own work.
- Induct new employees thoroughly.
- Offer sincere praise and recognition.
- Train, coach and develop employees' skills.

Vroom's expectancy questions

You probably know from your own experience that your level of motivation can range on a scale from none to very high. According to Victor Vroom, how highly people are motivated depends on three things:[34]

1. *How strongly people believe they can succeed*: For example, a salesperson who believes his chances of making a sale to a prospect are extremely low would probably not feel motivated to spend a great deal of time and effort on that prospect, but would instead look for prospects more likely to buy and focus his efforts on them. If you were asked to write a 5000-word essay on the relationship between chaos theory and quantum physics, you might not be too motivated to write it unless you happened to have a good understanding of those subjects or a keen interest in finding out about them.

   In short, people don't feel motivated when they think a goal is too hard to achieve. Funnily enough, the opposite is true, too: People don't feel motivated when they think that achieving the goal is an absolute certainty.

2. *Whether people believe that they will receive something they value in return for their efforts*: If you were offered $50000 to write an essay on chaos theory and quantum physics, you might be more prepared to put a bit of effort into it. Or perhaps an adventure trip overseas in return for a well-written and well-presented essay would be a better motivator for you.

3. *Whether people believe that what they receive in return for their effort is equitable, or worth the effort*: You might not knock yourself out to write that essay for five cents or even $5; maybe even $50000 or an adventure holiday would make the angst of writing that essay worthwhile.

In short, when faced with a task, some questions run quickly through people's minds:

* *How hard will I have to work?* This is known as *expectancy*, and is based on the belief, or expectation, that your efforts will yield success.
* *What's in it for me if I do it?* This is known as *instrumentality*, or the belief that your performance success is linked to rewards.
* *Will this reward be worth it?* This is called the *valence*, which is the value, or importance, you place on the reward.

Expectancy theory reminds you that to motivate people you must first help them believe that they can succeed and then let them know they will receive something they want in return for succeeding.

When motivation needs are not met

Do you know anyone for whom 'life begins at five o'clock'? Or anyone who hates their job and turns up only for the money? Their days drag; they are miserable. They probably do as little as possible and may even have become dissatisfied troublemakers. How sad. Being unhappy at work adds up to being unhappy for a large chunk of their lives.

If only their leader-managers could find a way to place these people in jobs that they could enjoy and would give them some satisfaction. If only their leader-managers could make them feel their jobs were worthwhile and valued and their efforts appreciated. If only their leader-managers could find out what they wanted from their jobs and try to provide it. If only their leader-managers knew something about motivation. If only.

While a job can't meet all of people's needs, it should meet many of them. When jobs don't satisfy enough of people's needs or satisfy them well enough, their needs don't disappear or take a back seat – people still try to meet them in one of two ways:

1. *They try to satisfy their needs off the job*: Consider Ken, who likes to organise people and is good at it. His job provides no scope to use his organising abilities, so Ken satisfies his desire to organise (which in turn helps meet his needs for responsibility) by running a local youth group. This may work out well for Ken, but employees who find it necessary to meet many of their needs outside work usually end up withdrawing from their job and becoming unengaged 'nine-to-fivers', doing only the bare minimum.
2. *They become frustrated and express their frustration on the job*: Linda, like Ken, is an organiser whose job provides no outlet for her skills. She has become the informal leader of a group of disgruntled workers and a thorn in the side of her leader-manager. Rebelling, withdrawing their cooperation and engaging in subtle acts of sabotage and malicious compliance are other undesirable ways people try to meet their needs when their jobs fail them.

When employees keep asking for more

Unmotivated, unengaged employees seldom demand more responsibility, more respect or greater challenge. The same goes for motivated and engaged employees: Have you ever heard of a workplace bargaining meeting where the employee representatives demanded more opportunity to use their creativity or track their results so they could feel a greater sense of achievement? Unlikely. People generally focus on the hygiene factors (Herzberg) or the physiological and safety needs (Maslow): They ask for more pay, better superannuation plans, better lighting or air conditioning, and so on.

This is especially true when jobs fail to satisfy people's higher order needs. Under these circumstances, when you 'give people what they ask for' and they still complain and lack motivation, it may be that what they asked for was not what they really wanted – achievement, camaraderie, challenge, respect, responsibility, and so on. Attempts to satisfy higher order needs with better hygiene factors that target lower order needs fail because satisfactory hygiene factors only put people in 'neutral', so that they can be motivated when their higher order needs are satisfied. Hygiene factors don't motivate people – motivation factors do.

● THEORY TO PRACTICE

The WIFT factor
When you assign a task to an employee, think of the WIFT factor: What's in it for them? Which group of needs would appeal to them most? Achievement? Esteem? Self-actualisation? Social? What can I supply in return for good performance? Further training? More challenge? Recognition?

The bottom line

Virgin Group founder Richard Branson says motivating your employees is simple: 'Respect, reward and empower your staff and they'll do the same for your business'.[35] Branson's way to motivate may be basic, but it seems to be successful. And certainly, from the ideas about motivation we have considered, it is clear that people have similar needs, summarised in Figure 10.6. Yet everyone has them in different combinations and expresses them differently. Everyone also has their own ideas of how they want their needs met. To complicate matters further, different motivational need groupings come to the fore at different times in people's lives and careers.

So what motivates Bruce does not necessarily motivate Sheila. Bruce may value recognition from his manager (esteem) and friendly relationships with his colleagues (social), whereas Sheila may value job training (self-actualisation) and a space in the company car park (esteem). Or perhaps Sheila and Bruce are both motivated by a need for power, but Bruce expresses it as a desire to dominate and control others, while for Sheila it appears as a desire for independence and decision-making in her work.

Similarly, what motivates Bruce for one month, for one year or even for one decade may not motivate him for the next month, year or decade, because people's needs change over time.

Since the strongest motivation comes from within, there is no standard package for motivation other than this one: *Establish what people want from their work, then see that they get it in return for good performance.* Don't fall into the trap of assuming that you know what people want from their jobs. And remember, as a need becomes satisfied, it tends to lose its importance as a motivator and another need replaces it, even if it's only 'more' of the same – a bigger bonus, a better office, more training or more responsibility.

To put the motivation theories to work, then, you first need to get to know as much as you can about the people you work with. This helps you identify and satisfy their needs in ways that are important to them in return for high productivity and performance.

● ACTION!

How well do you motivate people? Complete the checklist: What do people want from their work on **CourseMateExpress** to find out.

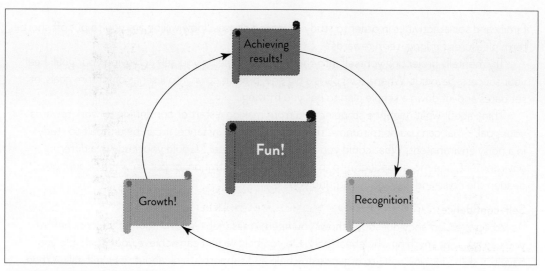

FIGURE 10.6 The motivating circle

Staying motivated yourself

It's hard to ask your team to be motivated when you're not. Whether it's to do a task you dislike or start a conversation you're not looking forward to, or you just need 'energising', leader-managers need to be able to motivate themselves.

You need three things to be motivated:

1. The desire to reach a worthwhile goal.
2. The commitment to put in the effort.
3. The self-confidence to take action.

Desire

Whether it's large or small, you need a clear goal to hold in your mind's eye. How will you, and perhaps others, too, benefit when you achieve it? Here are some questions to ask yourself to help you locate your desire when you're lacking motivation:

- What positive outcome is there in accomplishing this?
- What will be my reward for achieving this?
- What will happen if I don't do it?
- Why is it important that I do this?

When you're searching for the motivation to tackle a task you dislike, try listing the major push factors associated with the task. How can you turn them into pull factors? Try changing your language. Instead of saying: 'I *have* to do this (groan)', try saying 'I *want* to do this because …' *Having* to do something usually leads to half-hearted attempts, while *wanting* to do something produces whole-hearted efforts and a better result.

Commitment

Are you committed enough to willingly put in the time and effort required to achieve your goal and to forgo something else in order to achieve it? For example, part-time study while working at a full-time job takes a lot of commitment. You may need to pass up many enjoyable personal, family and social activities in order to study or attend classes. How willing are you to put off short-term pleasures for long-term rewards?

Try mentally projecting yourself into the future and seeing yourself achieving your goal. Feel your success. Savour it. When your goal is a big one, break it down into a series of interim goals, or set dates and jot down a simple plan to get you moving.

Think about what might be stopping you from making a start or continuing to work towards your goal. What can you do to remove those barriers? For instance, it can be difficult to study in a noisy environment. What could you do to make it quieter? Could you study in a different environment, one more conducive to thought and concentration, or put on some headphones to deaden the noise and distractions around you?

Self-confidence

As Vroom's expectancy questions show, you need a reasonable expectation of success before you can attempt anything wholeheartedly. Do you believe you can achieve your goal? Do you have the skills? Do you need to organise any help and support? Think about your self-talk. When you're giving yourself limiting, negative messages that you can't succeed, change them.

4. Retaining employees

> The brain is a wonderful organ. It starts working the moment you get up in the morning and it does not stop until you get into the office.[36]
>
> Robert Frost (poet), quoted in S Rathus, *Psychology* (2013)

Actually, that's not quite right – the brain never stops working, even when you're asleep. And when you're in the office, too! But what is the brain working on? That's what matters. Is it working on the job at hand or on plans for the weekend?

No longer is it only presenteeism and poor productivity that managers need to worry about. Today's employees demand more from their employers and when employers don't deliver, they are happy to walk, or at the very least, rein in their efforts while they look for a new role.

When an employee leaves, you're faced with finding someone willing and able to fill your vacancy, bringing the replacement 'up to speed' and stabilising working relationships within your team and with customers and suppliers.

There are two types of voluntary employee turnover:

1. *Push turnover*: When the organisation is so bad it pushes people out.
2. *Pull turnover*: When the organisation is good but another organisation pulls the employee out. The less engaged employees are, and the weaker the employer value proposition (EVP) is, the more likely this is to happen; conversely, organisations with a stronger employer brand and EVP find it easy to attract employees and 'pull' them from other organisations.

◉ THEORY TO PRACTICE

How SAS encourages work–life balance

SAS Institute is the largest private software company in the world. As CEO of SAS, Jim Goodnight said of his employees: '95 percent of my assets drive out the gate every evening. It's my job to maintain a working environment that keeps those people coming back every morning.'[37]

SAS has a Work–Life Department that tracks what benefits employees want and whether those benefits can provide a good return on investment. Some of the benefits SAS offers are onsite medical facilities for employees and their families, a Montessori day-care centre, welcoming children in the company cafeteria so families can eat lunch together, onsite basketball courts, a swimming pool and exercise room, and massages, dry-cleaning and haircuts offered onsite at reduced costs.

The company believes that its range of work–life balance initiatives provides a net gain to the company in terms of productivity, loyalty and retention. It seems to be correct: SAS has an incredibly low employee turnover – 3.5% in an industry average of nearly 20%. It's financially successful, too. In 2013, the company had its 38th straight year of revenue growth and in 2014 it ranked number two on the Fortune 100 Best Companies to Work For list, its 17th year on the list.

Employee turnover

Employee turnover is costly (between $10 000 and $50 000 and rising), and time-consuming, but how much employee turnover is too much?[38] How much is healthy? The generally accepted benchmark is to be in the 25th percentile for your industry in voluntary separations. This means that about 75% of similar organisations have a turnover rate higher than yours, which puts your organisation in the preferred top 25% of organisations to work for. Many organisations analyse the turnover figures separately for different areas of the business, which gives more meaningful measures.

To keep the people you need, make sure you know what motivates and engages each of them and what they each need to be most productive. For example, you should know what team members like most and least about their work, how they prefer to be managed, how much and what type of recognition they need in return for a job well done, and what they want to learn to make their jobs more satisfying.

Don't make the mistake of thinking employee retention is 'HR's problem' – it isn't. The main reason employees leave organisations is because of a poor relationship with their direct leader-manager. Your ability to retain staff could well be a career maker – or career breaker. Managers with a high turnover of employees may soon be too costly for organisations to keep on, no matter how strong their other skills.

Exit interviews

Two factors increase the importance of monitoring how regularly and why people resign:

1. Employee turnover is expensive.
2. It is often difficult to find suitable replacements.

That's where exit interviews come in. When an employee resigns, an exit interview provides an opportunity to find out the source of dissatisfaction, if any, and perhaps take action to prevent others leaving for similar reasons.

When an employee is terminated or retrenched, an exit interview provides an opportunity for the employee and the organisation to part formally and for the organisation to correct any misunderstandings that may have occurred. Any counselling or other form of support that might be needed can also be offered at this time.

Just finding out why people leave isn't enough, of course. You need to take action based on the information collected.

Formal exit interviews

Employees who are leaving an organisation may hesitate to tell their leader-manager the real reasons they are leaving but may be willing to tell someone else. For that reason, someone from the human resources (HR) department or a neutral third party generally conducts exit interviews, which generally last from 15 to 30 minutes, and keeps records of them for future collation and analysis.

Alternatively, some organisations replace the traditional interview with an online exit survey, which can be less threatening for the departing employee and provides information that is easier to analyse. The aggregated findings are reported anonymously, further increasing the likelihood that departing employees will 'tell all'.

⊙ THEORY TO PRACTICE

Some exit interview questions

Try all or any of these questions when interviewing an employee leaving the organisation:

- Can you explain what led to your decision to leave us?
- Could your work environment have been improved in any way?
- Do you feel you had enough training and support?
- If circumstances change, would you consider returning?
- We're not offering to do this, but if we were able to match (the new salary or other reason given for leaving), would you stay? If not, why not? If we could 'fix this' (whatever is mentioned), would you stay? (Keep asking until you get a 'yes' response – this tells you the *genuine* reason for leaving, not the 'polite' reason. You are not offering to match the salary or other things mentioned as an enticement for the employee to stay. You are asking a hypothetical , or 'what if?' question. This hypothetical series of questions helps you determine the real or most important reason/s the employee is leaving.)
- What are you intending to do?
- What are you most looking forward to in your new role?
- What did you enjoy most about working here? What did you enjoy least?
- What policies and practices do we follow that you feel are praiseworthy? Are there any you think we should scrap or change?
- Is there anything else you would like to mention at this time?

Thank the employee for their time and their honesty.

Informal exit interviews

If you have a small business with not many employees, the informal exit interview may suit you; or even in a larger business where there are no formal procedures for interviewing departing employees, you don't want to waste your networking and trust-building opportunity – conduct your own exit interview. (Beware of 'hearing what you want to hear', as you may not be 100% impartial.)

Your first priority is to gather information that can help you improve your leadership and improve your team and the way it works. You also want to emphasise the potential ongoing nature of the relationship – in Australia's small employment market and with the 'tour of duty' concept becoming ever-more popular (see chapters 1 and 8), you may well find yourself working with former team members in a different capacity in another organisation.

When someone leaves your team, ask him or her these five important questions:

1. What outstanding promises or commitments have you made?
2. What parts of your work are more in your head than written down?
3. What does your replacement need to know to get off to a good start?
4. What will you miss most about working here?
5. What will you miss least about working here?

Keep a database of former employees (including those outside your work team) and maintain contacts via email, LinkedIn, and so on.

 THE STRATEGIC PERSPECTIVE

Fix the problems, keep the employees

A US technology company studied exit interviews in an effort to reduce its 51% annual turnover of call centre staff. They found the main reasons people left were due to issues with coaching, compensation, flexibility and the nature of the job itself. Those problems were fixed and turnover fell to 25% in two years.[39]

Key retention factors

Many types of employees – casual, full-time, part-time and temporary employees, contractors and teleworkers – make up modern organisations. Many groups of employees – people born overseas, people of varying abilities and from various groups in society, and people from three generations – make up most modern organisations, too.

The vital question for organisations and individual leader-managers is how to provide the types of jobs and working environments that appeal to disparate employees. How can you meet, at the same time and in the same workplace, the differing needs and expectations that these groups and types of employees have? When you don't, you can't expect them to become and remain engaged, energised and willing to invest their energies in the organisation's outcomes.

Fortunately, we know what the key factors are in retaining Australian employees:

* a culture of clear values
* effective leadership
* having a say
* mutual trust and respect
* the quality of working relationships – how people relate to each other as friends and colleagues.[40]

Although a company's policies and its reputation as a good place to work are important because they attract people to the company in the first place, employees' relationships with their managers largely determine how long they remain. That makes each employee's relationship with their direct leader-manager and colleagues the single most critical element in retaining people. When you're not the sort of leader-manager people want to work for, you struggle to retain valuable, motivated, productive employees.

 THEORY TO PRACTICE

Culture and people, not money, engage and retain employees

When employees don't like the culture, the company and what it stands for, or the people they work with, they leave. There are endless ways to retain employees without adding huge costs to your bottom line. Here are some ideas:

* Be an organisation and a work team that people are proud to work for (e.g. by achieving results, being socially responsible and supporting your local community).
* Build social communities to develop bonds among employees: investment clubs, jogging clubs and other social activities can improve retention levels, even in notoriously mobile industries and occupations.

>>

- Frame customers' letters that praise employees' work and hang them in a prominent place.
- Give employees a say in matters that affect them.
- Keep employees informed about the organisation's performance and other matters.
- Offer flexible working arrangements, help with child care and elder care, and other modern, life-friendly practices.
- Organise an informal lunch (or breakfast) with the CEO, so the CEO and employees can brief each other on the organisation's and the department's recent successes.
- Provide plenty of feedback and learning opportunities.
- Say 'happy birthday' and 'thank you' for jobs well done, ask how people's children are, and how their new house is; in short, develop relationships that recognise people as individuals as well as employees.
- Send a letter to employees' homes on the anniversary of their joining the company to thank them for their support and saying that you appreciate their hard work.

It isn't rocket science, is it?

Look after high flight-risk employees

Employees in the 20- to 30-year-old age group, who can change employer with less risk to their personal circumstances because they have few major commitments in their lives and can easily find another job, are almost twice as mobile (i.e. twice as likely to resign) as employees over the age of 30. Those with the skills, knowledge and attributes other organisations want are particularly at risk and it's difficult to find and train a replacement for them.

Dr Kim Rickard of the Australian Association of Professional Engineers, Scientists and Managers says that graduates are often thrown in at the deep end with little support or even proper induction. Younger people, she says, need to see how they are contributing to the organisation and growing professionally. They should be helped to understand the organisation's strategic priorities to provide a context for their work, and given a chance to network with their fellow graduates and take on project responsibilities with appropriate supervision and mentoring.[41]

A diverse and friendly work group, coaching and development, effective and transparent career and performance-management systems, feeling valued, generous health and wellbeing policies (including arrangements for flexible working), lots of feedback, meeting career expectations, modern communications and information technology, performance incentives (tangible as well as psychological) and social responsibility are all important aspects of the EVP, particularly for younger employees. Find out what they want from work and try to provide it, and honour the promises made at the recruitment stage. (See page 870 for more information on leading and retaining different generations.)

Your top performers are also high-flight risks, especially when your organisation is cutting back on staff and/or freezing pay to improve the bottom line. (Sadly, the disengaged and less productive employees are less likely to leave in these circumstances.) In addition to the above, make sure your top performers understand where the organisation is heading and how they fit in.

CourseMateExpress

Go to http://login.cengagebrain.com to access CourseMate Express, your online study tool for *Management Theory & Practice*. CourseMate Express brings chapter concepts to life with interactive learning, and study and exam preparation tools:

- Test your skills in different aspects of management with interactive self-tests and simulations.
- Watch videos that show how real managers operate in real businesses.
- Test your understanding of the changing world of management by taking the revision quiz.

QUICK REVIEW

1. What is the difference between employee motivation and engagement? Briefly describe your role as a leader-manager in each.
2. Briefly explain, compare and contrast the four ways of thinking about employees' needs discussed under the heading 'How to uncover people's key needs' on page 300 and explain how Vroom's expectancy questions can help you use these four approaches to motivation.
3. Select three effective methods of motivating people that you have witnessed or experienced and explain them in terms of one or more of the approaches to motivation discussed in this chapter.
4. Explain the leader-manager's role in retaining employees and outline two reasons why retention is important.

BUILD YOUR SKILLS

1. Discuss how social media can engender employee engagement and how your own organisation triggers engagement.
2. What do you think the quotation from Gandhi on page 301 is referring to? Discuss it in relation to Maslow's hierarchy of needs. Contrast it with this statement: 'A person does not live by bread alone.' Can they both be correct?
3. Based on Maslow's and Herzberg's ideas about motivation, and thinking about the higher order needs and the lower order needs, what do you think are the primary motivators of employees in Australia? Would the same things motivate employees in a country devastated by floods, earthquakes or a tsunami? What about workers in growing economies like India or China, where people might be very wealthy, middle class or so poor they can barely subsist?
4. Atkinson and McClelland identified three areas of need that are at least partially learned and other researchers have identified four needs or drives they believe are instinctive. Briefly describe each of these seven needs and give an example of how you would recognise each need in an employee – what behavioural or other clues would you look for?
5. Imagine three managers, one with a high need for achievement, another with a high need for affiliation and the third with a high need for power. How would each of them lead and manage their teams when they were at their best as managers? When they were at their worst as managers?
6. Give an example from your own experience that explains and illustrates Vroom's expectancy questions about motivation.
7. 'Managers don't motivate people. People motivate themselves when the conditions are right.' What are the necessary conditions for motivation to occur?
8. Explain how the specific ways in which an organisation manages its people affect how easily it can recruit and retain high-calibre staff.

WORKPLACE ACTIVITIES

1. Briefly define employee motivation and engagement and discuss how motivated and engaged the employees in your work group are, and why you believe this is the case.
2. List the employees in your work group. What do you believe motivates each of them and why? You may want to draw a bar chart to illustrate the motivators of each employee in proportion to each other.
3. How well designed are the jobs in your work team? How can well-designed jobs motivate employees and encourage good performance? How does job placement factor into this equation?
4. List three specific ways you can apply Vroom's expectancy questions at your workplace.
5. How critical is each team member to the success of your team and your organisation? What is the impact if you lose team members? How ready are the key employees for promotion or a move to a new and challenging role? If they are ready now and no positions are available, what can you do to keep them? If you do lose them, who is ready to replace them in your team or who could you make ready? A staffing strategy like this is an important responsibility of all leader-managers.

CASE STUDY 10.1

CRISIS IN THE KITCHEN

Gregory Kean was Manly Bistro's top apprentice six years ago and has always been a fast learner and an ambitious and willing worker. Because of his work ethic, his clear thinking and his organising abilities, the owner promoted Gregory to the position of head chef with a kitchen team of five. On his promotion, Gregory became more determined than ever to show his capabilities. His level of motivation was high and he decided to make a clean sweep of the kitchen and really smarten the place up.

The previous chef had run the kitchen in a relaxed, informal manner and, for the most part, everyone did their work well. However, as far as Gregory could see, the previous head chef didn't really 'manage' at all – meals just 'happened'.

So in went Gregory, ensuring breaks weren't extended, handing out jobs at the beginning of each shift, tightening up systems and procedures, checking people followed them, continually monitoring everyone's work and generally ruling with the proverbial iron hand.

Now, four months later, the sous-chef has quit, the general kitchen hand is openly looking for another job and the team is no longer functioning as a unit. The four who are left seem to have withdrawn their cooperation, use no initiative and do only what Gregory tells them to do.

The owner decides it is time to have a chat to get to the bottom of what can only be described as a crisis in the kitchen.

Questions
1. What, specifically, do you think led to this crisis?
2. Using the information in Chapter 9 on leadership, what leadership style would you say Gregory is using? Is this style appropriate? Give evidence for your answer.
3. Which of the ways of thinking about motivation could Gregory use to help him correct the situation? Explain how your suggestion could help him and how it reinforces the ideas about situational leadership approach discussed in Chapter 9.
4. Gregory concentrated on task matters rather than people matters. Many new leader-managers do this. Why can this be a mistake?

CASE STUDY 10.2

THE TRANSFER PROBLEM

According to his previous manager, Dana had always been a conscientious and accurate worker with a pleasant and willing attitude. Yet, ever since his transfer to Andrea's team four months ago, his error rate has been above average, he seems sullen and he generally exhibits a 'couldn't care less' attitude. Andrea is at a loss to know what to do. She has spoken to Dana about his performance twice. After the first discussion, his performance improved slightly, only to fall off again about two weeks later. The second time they discussed the problem, his performance improved dramatically and remained excellent for about three weeks. Now it is back to its previous low level.

Andrea goes to the employee relations officer (ERO) for advice on how best to deal with Dana. As far as the ERO can determine, Dana's duties in Andrea's area and in his previous area are similar, although in his current role, because of the additional 'due diligence', or prudential requirements, in Andrea's team, he has less discretion in decision-making and somewhat less freedom regarding how the work is actually carried out. The only other difference, and this so far is just guesswork, is that in his old department Dana had built up a reputation of 'knowing what he was doing' and was regarded by the other members of the work group as something of an 'expert'. The bottom line is this: Even though Dana is clearly capable of meeting the requirements of his present job, he just doesn't seem to want to.

Questions

1. What motivational needs seem to be missing in Dana's new work team? What could Andrea do to meet them?
2. If you were Andrea, what would be your next move?

CHAPTER

INCREASING PERFORMANCE AND PRODUCTIVITY

OVERVIEW

The more productive we are as a nation, the better our standard of living and the better we can respond to everything from an ageing population to climate change. Many factors come together to improve (or reduce) productivity:

* Government actions, through economic reform, the infrastructure provided (e.g. Internet connectivity, roads, transportation), and policies (e.g. investment in the education and training system, policies that encourage innovation).
* Corporate action, through investment (e.g. in employee training, research and development, technology) and the culture organisations develop (e.g. of innovation and quality).
* Individual action, through individuals' health, knowledge and skills to, for example, block distractions, delegate effectively, organise their workspaces, work to a 'To do' list and not multitask. (Working smarter raises productivity; so does working the same hours for less money or more hours for the same money – but people generally aren't too happy about doing that.)

Australia has experienced a productivity slump over the past decade. Our productivity is significantly below the productivity of other leading countries and our long-term productivity growth is well below the OECD average.[1] We need to fix it.

Productivity refers to quantity. It measures output against costs. Performance includes quality – how well work is done. Increasing both performance and productivity begins with making sure the five critical factors, or keys, which make peak performance possible, are in place. When they aren't, no amount of performance counselling can induce people to meet their job goals.

1. Do you know how to ensure that employees know '*what to*' do?
2. Can you use the tools of job design, job placement and motivation in a way that encourage people to '*want to*' do a good job?
3. Can you help employees acquire the skills and experience they need to know '*how to*' do a good job and help them further by building their confidence and providing a learning environment?
4. Can you provide a working environment that gives employees the '*chance to*' do their jobs well?
5. Can you manage to be the sort of leader who encourages employees to want to be '*led to*' do a good job?

These are the five keys that unlock peak performance and high productivity, making it possible for employees to meet their measures of success, keep up their good work and improve on it. Who is primarily responsible for putting these five keys in place? You guessed it – you are – the leader-manager. When you ensure each of the five keys are right, you unleash people's willingness and ability to do their best and you, your team and its individual members are virtually assured success.

322

Starting from scratch

Because of his track record in managing similar assignments on time and within budget, Damien has been given the responsibility of leading a strategically important and highly visible project. He has worked out a rough plan of the logistics and thought about the skills and knowledge he needs in the team itself. That done, he set to work putting the team together.

Having finalised his choices, Damien is now making plans for bringing people on board and getting them up to speed quickly. He chose most of the team members for their expertise in their fields, fully aware that quite a few lacked experience of working in the type of tightly knit team this project calls for. He makes a note to contact a couple of trainers he's worked with in the past to discuss the team's need for some workshops on communication and team-working skills.

Next, he schedules an inaugural briefing meeting to introduce the team members to each other and outline the scope of the project and his logistics. 'I'll get them working together to map out the milestones the team as a whole needs to achieve to bring the project in on time and ask them to each begin developing their own deliverables,' he mumbles to no one in particular. 'Then I'll meet with them individually to agree the details of each person's contribution before bringing the team together again to structure their project plan more tightly.

'That way, they all know what to do, as a team and as individuals. Because this is the first major project for most of them, I know they're all keen and want to participate, and technically, they all know how to do the jobs I'm bringing them in for. Their confidence will grow once they've had some interpersonal skills development. That leaves making sure they have the resources and tools they need to do their jobs ... the old '*chance to*.' He flips the page of his notebook and begins brainstorming.

1. The '*what to*' key

> Productivity growth is the only sustainable source of improvements in a community's or a nation's material well-being and that of its citizens.
>
> Saul Eslake and Marcus Walsh, 'Australia's Productivity', Grattan Institute Report (February 2011)[2]

The '*what to*' key provides a structure, or job framework, for employees, so they aren't left guessing what they should be doing. This framework also helps employees to understand their role in the team's and the organisation's success and provides the overview that the human brain craves when it is undertaking a task. The '*what to*' key is the first of the five keys that lead upwards to peak performance, as shown in Figure 11.1.

There are three aspects of the '*what to*' key, shown in Figure 11.2:

1. The job framework, which is made up of job purpose, key result areas (KRAs) and measures of success (MOS). (Chapter 5 explains these in relation to your own job.)
2. Non-task goals, which are often to do with individual employee behaviour standards in the job environment.
3. The hot-stove principle, which are regulations that apply to everyone, for example customer service standards and safety precautions.

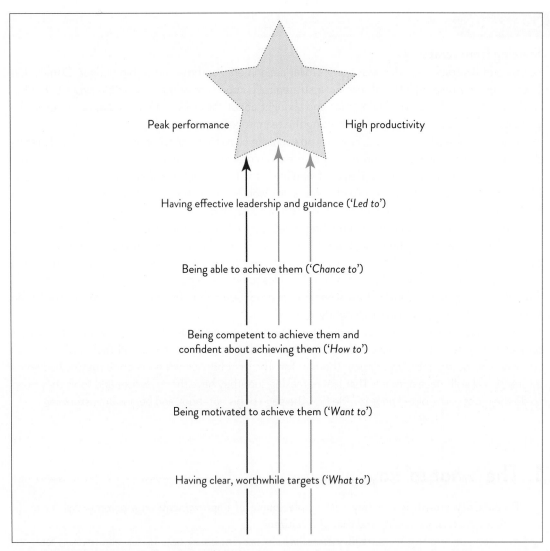

FIGURE 11.1 The path to peak performance and high performance

Job purpose

When people know clearly and specifically what you expect of them, they have role clarity. Clear roles and responsibilities give people a target to aim their efforts at and strive to achieve, and encourage people to monitor their own performance.

Each employee should understand the organisation's values, vision, mission and goals and have a broad understanding of the strategy, or overall approach, it intends to use to reach them (explained on page 49). Discuss this strategic perspective with them in a way that emphasises their personal role and their team's role in helping the organisation reach its aspirations.

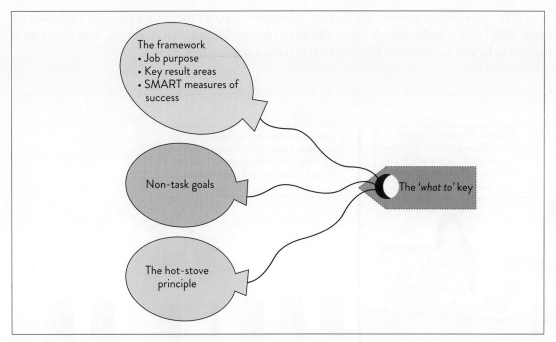

FIGURE 11.2 The three elements of the '*what to*' key

Highlight any other aspects of the organisation's overall operations that are of particular interest to each employee, for example:

- Employees interested in community: Explain how the organisation's vision and values support local involvement and how reaching its goals allows the organisation's participation in the community.
- Employees interested in sustainability: Explain that the organisation meet its sustainability targets while achieving its goals.
- Employees interested in flexible working: Explain that the organisation offers flexibility in return for high productivity and how flexibility helps people contribute to the organisation's vision and goals.

Now you're ready to write the employee's job purpose statement. A job purpose statement is the job-holder's personal mission statement. When you ask people to write the overall purpose of their job in one succinct sentence, their job becomes more than just a series of tasks. Employees can see that their job is worthwhile and therefore worth doing well. The job purpose statement also gives employees overall guidance about the way to approach their job and describes the difference between doing a job well and excelling. (Chapter 5 explains how to write your own job purpose statement.)

A job purpose statement generally follows this formula:

'To do … (describe the job), so that … (describe the outcome).'

To kick-start a high-performance culture, ask every person in your work team to write his or her own job purpose statement like those shown in Figure 11.3, and share it with the rest of the work team. When new employees join your work group, help them to develop their own job purpose statement.

Make sure that employees' job purpose statements support the team's purpose (discussed on page 376) and the organisation's vision and goals. And make sure they're not too long – you want people to be able to remember them and 'carry them around in their heads'.

FIGURE 11.3 Two job purposes

Key result areas

Key result areas (KRAs) describe a job-holder's main areas of accountability and responsibility. KRAs put tasks into context. They are not tasks or goals, but groups of tasks that together achieve results in important areas (see Figure 11.4). (Page 111 discusses how most jobs have five to nine KRAs. Fewer than five can indicate an 'underemployed' employee, while more than five can indicate an overstretched employee.)

There is no 'ranking' of KRAs in terms of order of importance – each is as important as every other, even though employees may spend different proportions of their time on each one.

If someone has fewer than five KRAs, make sure that some of those listed aren't too big and don't describe more than one KRA. With fewer than five KRAs, break them down into separate KRAs. If someone lists more than nine, they have probably broken down one or more KRAs incorrectly. For example, an employee might divide a KRA of 'output' into 'quality' and 'productivity', when both should come under the umbrella of 'output'.

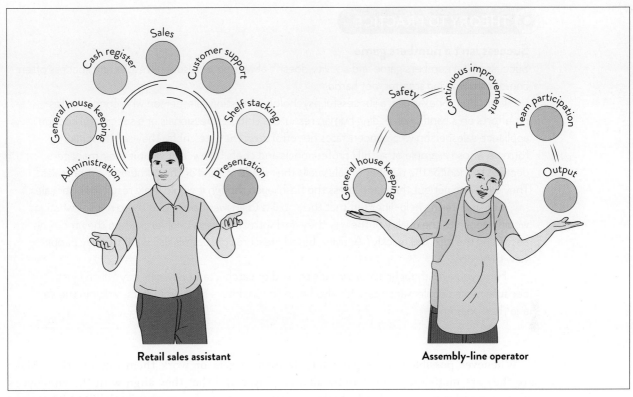

FIGURE 11.4 Two sets of KRAs

Measures of success

You've probably heard the truism 'What gets measured gets done'. Measures of success, also known as key performance indicators (KPIs), help people concentrate on what's important.

Measures of success strengthen the job framework by establishing the *performance standard*, or the end result the job-holder is seeking. This gives job-holders targets to aim at ways to check how well they are reaching their goals, which in turn fosters individual accountability for productivity and results. The best measures of success also allow people to feel that they are part of an exciting project and allow them control over how they achieve the target. (And we know that the more control people have over their jobs, the higher their job satisfaction.)

There are many ways to measure people's success at achieving their goals. To avoid spending too much time measuring results, measure one or two important indicators of performance – preferably lead indicators – in each KRA (see page 114 for information on lead and lag indicators). To help you decide which MOS to select, measure the most important or critical outcomes of each KRA. Think about the expectations of your stakeholders and service partners, the outcomes that illustrate movement towards your organisation's business goals and strategies, and the outcomes that will contribute to the overall goals of the team.

Reject any measures that would not alert the job-holder to do something differently if the measure were not met and that would be difficult, expensive or time-consuming to collect. Reject any 'short-term thinking' measures that interfere with longer-term strategic goals (as in the examples in the following' 'Theory to practice: Success isn't a numbers game', on the next page). Also reject any that measure activity only – you don't want to confuse 'busy-ness' with achieving goals.

◉ THEORY TO PRACTICE

Success isn't a numbers game

Success isn't a numbers game and activity doesn't always equal results – results and success often come from working smarter, not harder.

Consider, for example, a successful psychological testing salesperson who concentrates his efforts on a handful of leading human resources (HR) professionals or a successful kitchen appliance salesperson who concentrates her efforts on the elite chefs. They sell to opinion-formers whose example other HR professionals and chefs follow. But what if their managers decided to monitor the number of sales calls they made instead of the number of overall sales? They'd have to get out there and 'press the flesh' even though it would likely result in fewer sales.

Consider telling help-line staff that their goal is to answer calls within three rings – what would happen to the quality of the way they deal with customers' problems when they focus on answering the next call quickly? Activity-based measures of success can warp the way people view their jobs.

Have you ever thought about why it's so hard to catch a taxi on a rainy day? It isn't just because more people want a taxi. It's also because the drivers hit their targets earlier in the day and then go home.[3]

Whenever possible, let people set their own targets or work them out together. Make sure they are motivating to the individual employee and that they align with the employee's experience and competence levels. Make sure the measures of success meet the SMART targets criteria:

* **S**pecific (which usually means measurable and time-framed) and concise
* **M**otivating in order to drive performance
* **A**mbitious (achievable yet challenging)
* **R**elated to the overall department and enterprise goals and therefore meaningful
* **T**rackable, or easily monitored.

Specific: Measurable, time-framed and concise

An example of a poor MOS is 'reduce returns to a minimum' because it is negative and not specific. How would you know whether or not the employee succeeded? Consider the following:

* Four purchases were returned last month because of cosmetic flaws to the product's surface.
* Six purchases were returned last month because they were unsuited to the purpose for which they were purchased.
* Three purchases were returned last month because they failed to work.
* Total returns fell by 14% last month.

Did the employee succeed? There is no way of knowing because the success measure is not specific: It's neither measurable nor time-framed. There is no 'finishing line'. What is a 'minimum' number of returns? What number of returns is acceptable? By when should this minimum acceptable number be reached?

Now consider this success measure: Decrease the number of returns to 2% or less of sales per month by:

- discussing the intended use of the product with the customer to ensure the suitability of the product purchased
- inspecting and testing all purchases with the customer to ensure that the finish is acceptable and the product works before completing the sale.

Both you and the job-holder now know whether the goal was achieved and you can both track progress as the month progresses, allowing the employee to take any necessary corrective action quickly. The job-holder has a specific goal to work towards (the outcome – to decrease returns to 2% of sales or less per month). This particular MOS indicates clearly not just *what* the employee should achieve (the *outcome*) but also *how* the employee can achieve it (*activities*). However, while every MOS should measure outcomes, not every MOS need indicate how a task is to be done.

Keep the targets as concise as possible so they're easily remembered.

Motivating

There's no point setting goals that employees aren't motivated to achieve. To make sure goals are meaningful and motivating, link SMART targets to:

- the job holder's job purpose
- the team's purpose (see page 376)
- the organisation's values, vision or goals.

Ambitious

Make sure the targets you set are achievable. It's fine to challenge people but setting them up to fail by asking them to aim for an unreachable target de-motivates them in the long run. (See expectancy theory on page 310 for more information on why people need to believe they can reach their goals.)

Impossible goals don't motivate people to achieve outstanding performance; challengingly achievable goals do. The best way to improve productivity is to combine small individual wins with incremental process improvements (i.e. continual small improvements to the way work is carried out, as explained on page 565).

Our mental traffic system

One of the brain's many automatic programs is called the *control network*. Its task to help us pay attention, block out distractions and impulses, and focus our efforts on our goals when we need to – even when we'd rather do something else. Amazingly, it does this by moving blood away from regions motivating our immediate desires to regions that help us achieve our longer-term objectives, in the same way managers continually reallocate resources to meet the changing needs of the enterprise.

Directing our mental energy like this places quite a burden on our control network. You can lighten the load by removing distractions when you need to concentrate – silencing the pings that alert you to incoming emails and texts, putting on earphones to dampen extraneous noise, avoiding multitasking, and keeping the goals you're working towards to a manageable few, for example. Teach team members to do this, too. Overworking ultimately reduces your productivity and the productivity of your employees.[4]

Related to the organisation's goals

Every measure of success you agree with team members should help them succeed in their own KRAs as well as move the team and the organisation towards their goals.

Trackable

Selecting lead indicators that work as a signal to employees about how they're going with a task, and that alert them to make any necessary changes to the way they're operating, helps lift both motivation and productivity. (Pages 353 and 361 explain how to monitor performance and page 447 explains how to provide feedback on performance.)

● ACTION!

How well can you write SMART targets? Find out with the checklist of the same name on **CourseMateExpress** to find out.

Measures of success for broad, ambiguous jobs

It's easy enough to set SMART outcome-based success measures for clearly defined, routine, assembly line-type work, but perhaps not quite as easy for knowledge and service work and the broad and complex roles that organisations are creating as they build more flexibility into their job designs to reflect increasing business complexity. Quality is often more important than quantity in these jobs: Someone can serve 50 customers in a day and leave them all dissatisfied, or serve 35 and leave them all completely satisfied and intending to come back. Important behaviours such as mentoring others or energising the team don't fit easily into productivity equations, either.

Consider, for example, a human resource officer (HRO) who is responsible for designing and introducing a performance management system to the organisation. To create success measures, you could list the milestones, or deliverables, needed to complete this project, each meeting the SMART criteria; you might agree, for example, that researching and reporting back on possible systems, with a recommendation, be completed by a certain date, a draft design be piloted with a representative cross-section of employees and managers by a certain date, and a final version submitted for discussion and approval by another date. Success could be measured against these deliverables.

You might also consider the strategic fit of the performance management system with the organisation's overall vision and goals and the degree to which it is accepted and used throughout the organisation. Because these two criteria are difficult to measure, you would use careful judgement to assess effectiveness.

The trick is to define the behaviours and results, or outcomes, that are most critical to productivity and work out how to measure them, not just day-to-day but over the medium and the long term.

● THE STRATEGIC PERSPECTIVE

What is productivity?

Productivity is a measure of outputs (goods, ideas and services) in return for inputs (labour, time, money, land, electricity, raw materials and other resources). Nations, organisations and people become more productive in one of two ways by:

1. Producing or creating more value with the same resources.
2. Producing the same or creating the same value with fewer resources.

$$\text{Productivity} = \frac{\text{Outputs}}{\text{Inputs}}$$

Improving performance with measures of success

Treat any shortfall in meeting an MOS as an opportunity to improve, rather than a problem, and work with the employee to help them reach the target. Discuss the reasons for the shortfall using the five keys as a guide; for example, something in the *'chance to'* key might be blocking success or you may need to provide some coaching to strengthen the employee's skills or confidence.

Although an employee's job purpose and key result areas are unlikely to change substantially, you may want to periodically change some of the measures of success you monitor. For example, you could drop a measure of success for one activity an employee consistently completes well and agree a new SMART measure of success to boost performance in another area. You could do this during the performance appraisal/performance planning and review meeting, or at any time between formal performance reviews when you want to shift an employee's attention to an improvement area.

For example, you may have noticed that, although a retail sales assistant is knowledgeable about the stock and her performance is excellent in many areas, she doesn't deal with customer queries very well. You feel she's a bit abrupt and decide to coach her on questioning customers about their needs and wants and explaining the products that best meet them. Together you estimate that currently about 40% of her responses to queries result in a sale. You agree that she will try the techniques you coach her in and track the customer queries she deals with over the next month, aiming to convert 70% of queries to a sale, which is closer to the average you expect. You arrange to check back to see how she's going in one week's time and provide any further coaching or support she may need. (See page 192 for more information on coaching employees.) Naturally, you won't expect her to jump from a 40% success rate to a 70% success rate in one week because she'll need to gain experience and confidence; but you would expect to see progressive improvement.

In general, it's a good idea to meet with each employee every 6 to 12 months to formally acknowledge their efforts and agree a few new measures of success to replace those that are met consistently. This gives everyone a slightly different focus and ensures continuous improvement.

(For more information on SMART targets, see page 112.)

 IN A NUTSHELL

Putting the five keys to work

Your job is to help people deliver the results you need at the level of productivity you need. When they struggle and performance counselling doesn't work (see Chapter 16) try to move them to a role that better suits their capabilities so they can deliver a great performance.

Non-task goals

Employees also need to meet non-task goals. Non-task goals are concerned with the way people work. Here are some examples:

- Be cooperative, friendly and helpful to colleagues and customers.
- Clean up after yourself in our shared kitchen area.
- Find ways to improve the way you and the team work (discussed in Chapter 19).
- Help out your teammates when you have a few spare minutes.
- Keep your work area tidy.
- Make our customers glad they deal with us.
- Share your knowledge.
- Try to finish one task before moving on to another.

Although some of these expectations are written down formally (e.g. in the role description or job contract), many are left as unspoken group norms that employees must infer, or pick up, for themselves. Team problems can develop when team members fail to meet unspoken expectations and, when that happens, it's important to meet with the team or the individual employee and discuss your expectations openly.

Discuss these expectations with new members who join your team in their first day or two. This helps them fit in more quickly and prevents bad habits forming. When you openly discuss expectations, you can be certain everyone understands them and can work towards achieving them. Make sure employees are fully aware of how they benefit from reaching their success measures.

The hot-stove principle

The hot-stove principle is about important bottom-line rules and regulations that apply to everyone and involve matters such as customer service, housekeeping, safety, standard operating procedures and working with others.[5] Figure 11.5 shows how the hot-stove principle works.

Just as you can see from a distance whether a stove is hot and will burn you if you touch it, everyone should know your bottom-line rules in *advance* and know they will be 'burned' if they break or bend them. Just as when you touch a hot stove you are burned straightaway, the consequence of breaking or bending a bottom-line rule should be *immediate*: If someone breaks a hot-stove rule, discuss it with the person at once (in private) to make sure it doesn't happen again. A hot stove is *impartial*: Everyone who touches it is burned. Hot stoves are *consistent* – they always burn people who touch them: Don't 'play favourites' – bottom-line rules apply to everyone, all the time.

You can find out how well you can apply the hot-stove principle to build performance by taking the checklist: Using the hot-stove principle on **CourseMateExpress**.

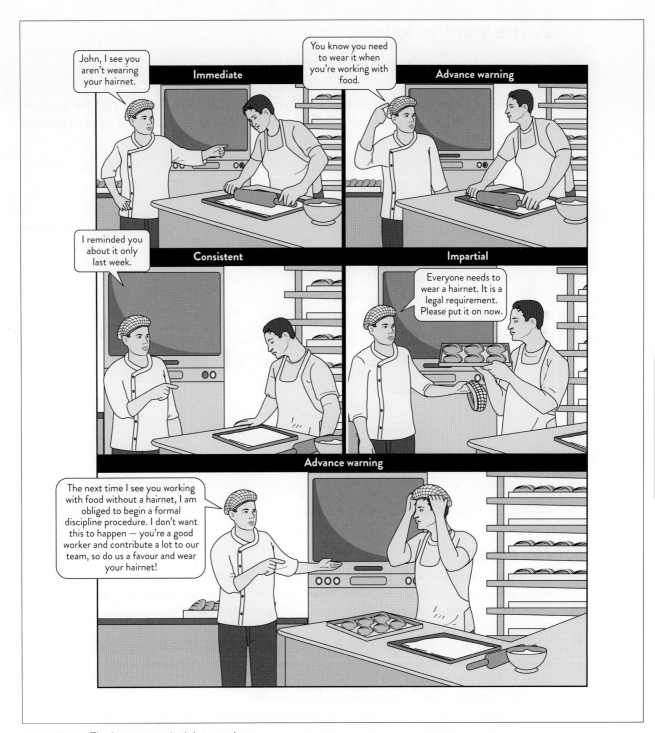

FIGURE 11.5 The hot-stove principle at work

2. The 'want to' key

If you want people to do a good job, give them a good job to do.

Henry Mintzberg (management academic), *The nature of managerial work* (1973)[6]

People can work hard when they '*have to*', but they work harder when they '*want to*'. For people to '*want to*' do a good job, three elements need to be in place. Figure 11.6 shows the three elements of the '*want to*' key:

1. Job design.
2. Job placement.
3. Motivation.

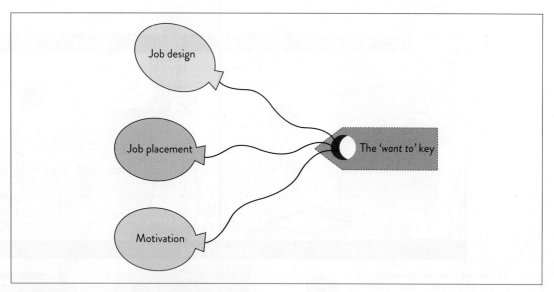

FIGURE 11.6 The three elements of the '*want to*' key

Job design

The '*want to*' key links with the '*what to*' key because, in order to be motivated to perform well, employees must know their job is worth doing well. The '*want to*' key helps you to further motivate employees by offering well-designed jobs and putting people in jobs that match their interests and abilities – job placement).

Good job design and correct job placement directly relate to motivation, performance and productivity. When individuals or whole teams aren't performing well, check whether they're really suited to their jobs and how well designed their jobs are.

The principles of job design are that each job should:

* allow the job-holder to complete a whole job or piece of work wherever possible
* allow the job-holder to have as much control over the work and work methods as technology allows
* contain a variety of tasks and activities requiring different levels of experience and training, and a minimum of repetitive, monotonous tasks
* contain variety in work pace and work methods
* contribute significantly to the organisation
* give the job-holder access to the resources needed to do the job

* have clear roles and responsibilities and a clear set of easily measured objectives that the job-holder can monitor
* offer a reasonable workload in terms of deadlines and demands (neither too much nor too little).

Job content often grows over time, sometimes haphazardly and often informally, which is why you should periodically examine the content of each job in your team to ensure each one makes the best use of people and resources.

⊙ ACTION!

Find out how well your job is designed with the interactive self-test, How well is your job designed? on 🔺CourseMateExpress.

⊙ THE STRATEGIC PERSPECTIVE

Meaningful work

'Meaningful work' is a concept that was unheard of only a few generations ago. Yet today it's important, at least in affluent societies. What is meaningful to one person may not be meaningful to another and what someone finds meaningful at the age of 23 may not be what they find meaningful at the age of 53.

Meaningful work relies on balancing three sets of motives:
* *Moral motives*: The idea that the 'ends' of the work are worthwhile.
* *Compensation motives*: The ability to use one's skills and abilities, authority, money, responsibility, status.
* *Craft motives*: The desire to do a good job for its own sake.

It's up to individuals to find work that is meaningful for them. However, employers have a role in enabling the search for meaningful work by providing high-quality jobs – jobs with autonomy, security and variety, and a reasonable balance between effort and reward and skill levels and job demands.[7]

The three Es

A 'good job' often involves the three Es: enlargement, enrichment and empowerment.

* Job enlargement means expanding a job *horizontally*, giving the job-holder more duties at the same level of responsibility. Cross-skilling and multiskilling are forms of job enlargement; when the additional duties are at a higher level of responsibility, multiskilling is also a form of job enrichment.
* Job enrichment means expanding a job *vertically*, increasing the depth of an employee's responsibilities through upskilling.
* Job empowerment is an expanded form of job enrichment. Empowered employees and teams take on many responsibilities previously carried out by first-line and middle managers, particularly the ability to make on-the-spot decisions. But you just can't foist those responsibilities onto employees; empowerment grows as a result of a management style and an organisation's culture and climate.

When jobs are enlarged or enriched and employees empowered, the employees usually need training to expand their skills. Particularly with empowerment, training must include interpersonal skills, how to lead and participate in meetings, and problem-solving and decision-making skills and techniques. Just adding new duties and responsibilities to employees' workloads as a hierarchy flattens out isn't job enlargement, enrichment or empowerment – it's just more work.

The benefits of the three Es include:

* increased motivation
* increased organisational flexibility and responsiveness
* increased responsibility and job interest
* improved job design
* improved job performance and productivity
* strengthened customer and supplier relationships.

Empowerment often has the added benefit of enabling organisations to restructure their internal relationships and ways of working to increase efficiency and competitiveness and move towards a capabilities-based organisation (explained on page 81).

While not every employee wants a job that excites and challenges them, the commitment, loyalty, productivity and motivation of most employees can be increased with good job design combined with correct job placement, frequent feedback and visible results from their efforts.

Job placement

Everyone is good at something. What are your team members best at? When you know that, you can assign the right work to the right people. You won't be putting 'square pegs in round holes', as the saying goes. Correct job placement means putting square pegs in square holes: Placing people in jobs they enjoy and to which they are temperamentally suited. This is essential to employee retention, motivation and productivity. It means that employees can work at jobs they enjoy and with people they like, and feel confident about what they do. Correct job placement gives employees the opportunity to contribute fully, develop their skills and derive satisfaction from doing their jobs well.

Clearly, jobs need to suit employees' skill and experience levels. Just as important, however, is that jobs suit employees' motivational needs, temperaments and work-style preferences. For example:

* Some people are happy working on their own, while others want to be part of a friendly, cooperative team.
* Some people enjoy detailed work, while others prefer to take a 'broad brush' approach.
* Some people like a chance to move about, while others prefer to stay in one place.
* Some people need a lot of variety in their work, while others prefer a routine or predictable work environment.

Good job placement allows people to have a sense of achievement in doing the work itself and a sense of using, stretching and expanding their skills. Giving employees the opportunity to work to their strengths – at work they enjoy and are good at – means they are six times more likely to be engaged in their jobs and more than three times as likely to report having an excellent quality of life than employees who are poorly placed in their jobs.[8]

Fortunately, you have a great deal of control over job placement. Naturally there are aspects of everyone's job that they'd rather not have to do, but try to minimise this as much as possible. Remember, what one person finds difficult or dull, another finds interesting. You may find that redesigning some jobs to make them more challenging and more satisfying or to provide employees with opportunities to develop their skills, or transferring an employee from a job that requires working in isolation to one that allows working with a group, improves the morale, motivation, satisfaction and productivity of your work team. (For more information on matching people to jobs to build performance and productivity, see pages 212 and 807.) The important thing to remember is that people only do their best work when it closely matches their underlying interests and abilities.

⊙ THE STRATEGIC PERSPECTIVE

The right people, not the best people

Australia's Top 11 companies select the right people, not necessarily the 'best' people.[9] They pick people who are right for their culture and their strategy and who are enrolled for 'the cause' – and these organisations have queues of people wanting to work for them.

They promote from within and spend a lot of money on in-house customised training and development. They set measures of success and provide honest feedback on performance. This makes them tough to work for because they're tough on poor performers. When people don't do a good job, they're told so and they're helped to achieve their targets. Only when that doesn't work are they 'managed out' of the organisation.

Motivation

There is fable about three labourers. One says, 'I'm breaking rocks.' Another says, 'I'm building a wall.' The third says, 'I'm building a cathedral.'[10] Which of those three do you think would be most motivated to do a great job? One form of motivation is to know why you are working hard. Worthwhile work encourages people to do their best.

Without motivated employees, performance and productivity can never be more than mediocre. People need to be satisfied with their pay and working conditions. But when these are the only rewards people get, they respond by doing only the bare minimum, enough to get by. Hygiene factors alone can't build better performance and productivity.

For this, you need to provide psychological rewards. Employees need to know that they are doing a worthwhile job and reaching their goals (which links back into the '*what to*' key). They need to know you appreciate them and they need to feel proud of the contribution they are making. They need to use their talents and develop their potential, and to be treated with respect. (For more information on how to motivate people, see Chapter 10.)

3. The '*how to*' key

> Productivity performance, if not continuously improved, raises the risk profile of the economy.
>
> Peter Harris (chair, Australian Productivity Commission), Media release (13 June 2013) [11]

When people know '*what to*' do and '*want to*' do it, can you set them to work? Not unless they also know '*how to*' do the job. Figure 11.7 shows the three elements of the '*how to*' key:

1. Training.
2. Experience.
3. A learning environment.

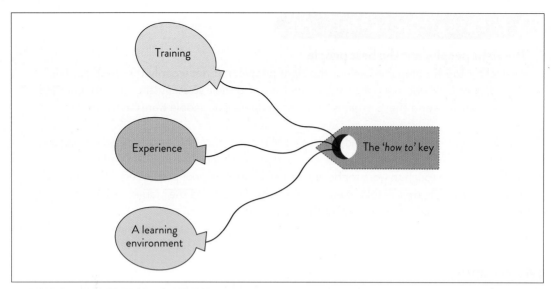

FIGURE 11.7 The three elements of the 'how to' key

Training and experience

People attain competence, or job skills and knowledge, through training and experience. You need to train employees to do their jobs and give them time to build their skills and gain confidence. Pages 905 and 917 explain how to coach people to improve or develop their skills and how to show them the correct and safe way to do a job, step by step.

Training and coaching provide ideal opportunities to let employees know that what they do makes a difference. This is an important element in establishing positive attitudes, motivation and the desire to perform well, which strengthens the 'what to' and 'want to' keys.

A learning environment

The third element of the 'how to' key is an environment that encourages learning and improving. Learning, sharing knowledge and continually finding better ways to work builds teams and organisations. Training and continual learning are investments in one's own future as well as the organisation's future. (Chapter 27 explains how to build a learning environment.)

⊙ THEORY TO PRACTICE

How the US Marines build performance

Many organisations depend on their rank and file to make products or provide services that delight their customers. Their influence on their organisation's success is huge. Yet these front-line employees are generally unskilled and low-paid. Their work can be boring and repetitive and chances for advancement limited. What else is there to work for but money?

There may be many differences between your organisation and the US Marines, but there may also be lessons to learn. How does your organisation compare to the US Marines?

>>

- The service's most experienced and talented people conduct the induction of rank-and-file US Marines. To enthuse the inductees, they spend a lot of time early on inculcating the values of the Marine Corps – honour, courage and commitment. The trainers don't spend much time communicating procedures and policies. Instead, they foster collective pride in the Marine vision and legacy.

   Do you provide a brief introduction to your company or show a short video? Or do you bring your vision and values into the heart of your induction? Do you involve your most talented and best managers in training new people and let recruits see them as role models and draw on their experience? Do you strengthen collective pride by continuing to focus on values after training ends?

- The Marines don't distinguish between followers and potential leaders but train everyone to lead. This builds collective pride, morale and mutual trust. They assign inexperienced officers to highly experienced and successful non-commissioned officers to work as a team and learn from each other. The young officers keep the experienced older ones fresh and, in return, learn from the older officers' experience.

   Do you prepare all your employees for leadership? Do older, more experienced employees mentor those who are new and inexperienced?

- The Marines build teams that draw their motivation from their mission and goals. Members work together as peers and hold one another accountable for the team's performance and results. No one individual can win or lose – they're in it together. Only the group can succeed or fail.

   Do you build empowered teams whose members depend on each other to succeed? Are your teams accountable to the leader and to each other?

- The Marines use self-discipline to build pride – not negative discipline but sticking to the rules and being one's own tough boss. Self-discipline and pride in your work build motivation and results.

   Do people monitor their own performance in your organisation and continually try to improve it? Do they know the rules and follow them without being reminded?

4. The 'chance to' key

Nobody trips over mountains. It's the small pebble that causes us to stumble. Pass all the small pebbles in your path and you will find you have crossed the mountain.

Anon.[12]

When employees know 'what to' do and 'how to' do it, and 'want to' do it well, what can cause poor performance? This is where the 'chance to' key comes in. It helps you to create an environment for success by ensuring that the necessary tools, equipment, materials, work methods, systems and procedures, and other important factors in the job environment, such as teamwork, time and information, contribute to productivity by making it easy for people to do their jobs well.

Surprisingly often, the reverse is true – these factors get in the way of people doing a good job. They slowly 'grind them down' and sap their motivation to perform.

Figure 11.8 shows the five elements of the 'chance to' key:

1. Tools and equipment.
2. Work systems and procedures.
3. Time, information and other resources.
4. Team support.
5. 'Acts of God' and personal problems.

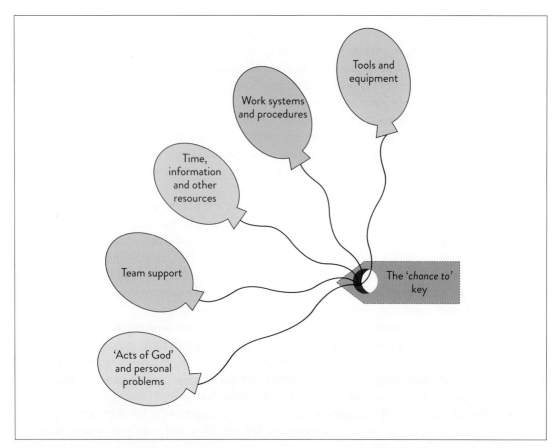

FIGURE 11.8 The five elements of the 'chance to' key

Tools and equipment

Faulty, inadequate or badly designed and maintained equipment, machinery and tools are a more common cause of poor performance than you might think.

When everyone has limited time and many tasks to carry out, it's easy to let the important but not urgent tasks slip – tasks like carrying out routine maintenance. And as equipment, machinery and tools gradually become less efficient, often in incremental steps that people don't detect, they make it more and more difficult to get a job done well.

Similarly, without investing in updated equipment, machinery and tools, perhaps due to budget constraints, it becomes harder and harder for employees to remain as productive as the competition, and productivity falls behind, even when people's performance stays the same.

Work systems and procedures

Cumbersome work systems and procedures don't just discourage people from doing a good job – they can actually prevent them from doing a good job. Because procedures usually develop over time as additions and changes are made ad hoc, unwieldy work methods can mushroom unnoticed. This is an all-too-common cause of less-than-optimal performance and productivity.

Get together periodically with your work team or individual team members and examine how they work. Look for unnecessary steps and backtracking, bottlenecks, hiccups and hassles that make employees' lives difficult. Look for ways to streamline systems and procedures and redesign any awkward steps or processes so that employees can complete them more smoothly, more easily, more quickly or more economically.

Making sure that all work systems and procedures help employees do a good job rather than hinder their efforts makes a huge contribution to building performance and productivity. (Check out Chapter 19, which explains how to use flow charts and other techniques to help analyse and improve work systems and procedures.)

Time, information and other resources

When employees say they feel overloaded with work, they may have a valid point. Most organisations run 'lean and mean'. While reducing staffing levels can reduce overheads, it can also mean that people sometimes just don't have the time to do a job properly or to pass on complete information. Too many trivial tasks, duplication of work and inefficient procedures are other causes of running out of time to do everything that needs to be done and pass on needed information. People can be so busy 'keeping their heads above water' that they let important but non-essential tasks slide into oblivion. In the long run, quality and service suffer.

Doing jobs a second or third time because they weren't done correctly in the first place doesn't just cause annoyance and require effort. It also eats up huge chunks of time. Imagine saving 13 hours per person per week by eliminating duplication. This one good habit alone – doing a task right first time – is guaranteed to help people reach their targets consistently.

Time and information are intangible yet critical resources. Another habit to build among your team is passing on needed information and helpful knowledge. Don't underestimate the importance of other resources like working-space environments, frequently replenished stationery and other supplies, access to a quiet place to meet and discuss work matters or to work on an important task uninterrupted, and access to up-to-date technology that increases efficiency.

Team support

It's unusual to find peak-performing employees in a team that doesn't have a high-performance culture – one in which challenging goals are set and people are expected, and expect, to achieve them. The leader coaches and helps employees perform to the best of their abilities, and people learn from their experience and help each other out. Productive teams are made up of people with high self-esteem who work together to achieve more than they could working on their own.

When team members don't understand what everyone else is trying to achieve, when they don't share common goals and purposes, when they don't support and value each other's efforts, work becomes unnecessarily difficult. When working relationships in the team are poor, work becomes unnecessarily unpleasant. These are major barriers to work performance and productivity.

Support teamwork through team building and team maintenance and build an enjoyable, collaborative working climate so that your team members remain willing to put in the effort required to do their jobs well. When people are having fun, they work harder, stay longer and are more engaged in their work.

'Acts of God' and personal problems

The 85:15 rule says that, provided people know clearly what is expected of them and are trained to do it well, you can find 85% of the causes of poor performance and low productivity in the work environment – the four aspects of the *'chance to'* key described above. 'Acts of God' and personal factors account for only the remaining 15% of poor performance.[13]

'Acts of God' are events you can't do anything about. When your factory or office floods or loses its electricity, or a debilitating virus keeps a significant number of your work group home due to illness, it is difficult or impossible to get production or services out on time.

Personal factors include the occasional 'bad hair' day, domestic problems that are so pressing it is difficult to concentrate properly on work and severe personal problems such as alcohol or drug abuse. They can also include happy events, like being so excited about your upcoming wedding that you find it difficult to concentrate fully on your work.

It makes sense to concentrate your efforts on improving productivity and performance where they are most likely to pay off – in the work environment.

● THEORY TO PRACTICE

Around sound learning

Linn Products in Glasgow, Scotland, makes high-end audio equipment for the royal household – as well as less distinguished households. A multiskilled workforce makes each of the company's complex products entirely by hand, giving each employee a feeling of responsibility for their work. Since the people who build the products often service them later, interacting with customers and seeing how happy – or unhappy – they are, they can see the connection between what they do and how the product performs.

'So they're learning a lot more than just how to assemble a product,' says founder and chairperson Ivor Tiefenbrun. 'They start to spot connections that no engineer, service technician or assembly-line worker ever would and bring skills developed in one area to bear on what they do somewhere else. As a result, they can contribute to product quality with improvements and innovation.'[14]

5. The *'led to'* key

> The quality of leadership and management skills can have significant direct effects on productivity.
>
> Peter Gahan (Centre for Workplace Leadership), 'Why Australian workplaces need much better leaders'(20 February 2014)[15]

You set the pace for peak performance and high productivity. Your sound leadership that sets clear goals and a good example, inspires people with a compelling vision and coaches them to bring out their best, provides the final touch to building performance and productivity. Even when the other four keys are in place, poor leadership can spoil everything.

Do you practise what you preach, lead by example, and empower and help employees to do their jobs well? (Chapters 5, 6, 7, 8 and 9 discuss some of these aspects of leadership, and you can find more information on how to think like a leader on page 188.) Six important characteristics of effective leaders that help build performance and productivity, shown in Figure 11.9, are reviewed on the following pages:

1. Ambitious goals.
2. Focus.
3. High standards.
4. Interpersonal skills.
5. Action orientation.
6. Self-esteem.

Ambitious goals

People with high standards and positive expectations set stretching (yet achievable) goals. By aiming high, you can achieve more than by aiming low. And keeping goals to a manageable number, as explained in the 'FYI: Our mental traffic system', on page 329, means that people aren't over worked.

Focus

To meet the high standards and achieve the challenging goals you set for yourself and others, you need to keep your eyes on the ball – it's much easier to achieve goals when you keep them clearly in mind. Removing distractions allows you to concentrate, too.

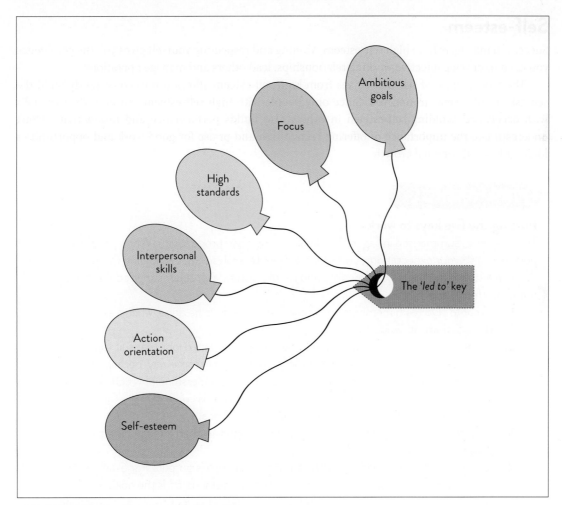

FIGURE 11.9 The six elements of the '*led to*' key

High standards

Mediocrity is a choice. So is excellence.[16] This saying illustrates the importance of setting high standards and expecting the best – for yourself and from yourself and others – makes it easier to build performance and productivity.

Interpersonal skills

To successfully build performance and productivity, you need well-developed interpersonal skills. Communicating and working effectively with others give you the influence you need to encourage and guide people to lift their performance.

Action orientation

Managers with a record for building performance and productivity are invariably proactive – they take responsibility for making things happen. Don't sit back and wait, blame others or find excuses for not achieving your goals or meeting high standards.

Self-esteem

Successful managers have high self-esteem. Valuing and respecting yourself gives you the confidence you need to develop effective working relationships, lead others and manage operations.

The secure sense of self that comes from high self-esteem allows you to consistently build the self-esteem of people around you. Since only people with high self-esteem can perform their jobs with excellence, building self-esteem in others also builds performance and productivity. Don't underestimate the importance of offering recognition and praise for good work and opportunities for learning and personal growth.

● IN A NUTSHELL

Putting the five keys to work

The five keys , summarised in Figure 11.1, help you increase productivity. When people aren't performing to your expectations, you can use them to analyse what is holding them back. You can also use the five keys to identify and rectify potential problems that could affect your team's performance.

1. *'What to'*: Do team members understand what needs to be done, what is expected of them and why it's important?
2. *'Want to'*: Have you placed team members in well-designed jobs that suit their skills and interests? Is poor current performance rewarding in some way, perhaps even more rewarding than better performance? Does everyone understand how achieving the expected goals benefits them? (Remember that rewards come in many forms, not just money, and that the strongest rewards are psychological.)
3. *'How to'*: Have team members been properly trained and had enough time to build experience and confidence?
4. *'Chance to'*: Might something be interfering with people's output? For example, are machines running properly? Are raw materials up to standard? Is the quantity of work unusually high? Is one team member's absence or lack of training or experience putting pressure on the rest of the team? Are there any bottlenecks you can remove or cumbersome procedures you can smooth out? Might internal power struggles be hindering the group's effectiveness?
5. *'Led to'*: Is your leadership everything that it should be?

CourseMateExpress

Go to http://login.cengagebrain.com to access CourseMate Express, your online study tool for *Management Theory & Practice*. CourseMate Express brings chapter concepts to life with interactive learning, and study and exam preparation tools:

- Test your skills in different aspects of management with interactive self-tests and simulations.
- Watch videos that show how real managers operate in real businesses.
- Test your understanding of the changing world of management by taking the revision quiz.

QUICK REVIEW

1. Briefly explain the job framework and how it provides role clarity. Is it possible for an employee to perform well without role clarity, other than by chance?
2. Explain the three elements of the '*want to*' key and how each contributes to people's ability and willingness to do their job well.
3. How do the elements of the '*how to*' key contribute to job performance and incremental improvement?
4. How can factors outside an employee's control prevent them from doing their job well, even an employee who knows '*what to*' do and '*how to*' do it well and who '*wants to*' do it well?
5. How does leadership affect productivity? Briefly explain six actions effective leaders can take to build performance and productivity.

BUILD YOUR SKILLS

1. Review each of the five keys to high productivity and peak performance, giving an example of each from your own experience. What happens when a leader-manager fails to manage one of these keys properly? Select one 'deficient' key to illustrate your point.
2. Relate the five keys to Vroom's expectancy questions about motivation discussed on page 310.
3. Discuss why people need a vision or job purpose statement for their job, and the role that clear targets play in motivating people and helping them monitor their own performance and build their productivity.
4. Study Chapter 1 and Chapter 3 and explain why job enlargement, enrichment and empowerment will become more common, and why you should become familiar with the principles of job design and job redesign and the five keys to unlocking productivity and performance.
5. Referring to chapters 2 and 13, briefly explain corporate values, vision and mission and how they link to a team's purpose, goals and objectives and to an individual job-holder's job purpose, key result areas and measures of success.

WORKPLACE ACTIVITIES

1. What non-task goals does your work team have? Is everyone aware of them?
2. Give an example of how you have applied the hot-stove principle to ensure that people in your work team follow rules correctly and consistently.
3. Assess your own job and the jobs in your work team against the criteria outlined in the chapter. How well designed are these jobs? How well placed are you and your team members in your jobs?
4. When did you last check that the tools and equipment in your department were well designed, properly maintained and suited to the job at hand? Does your team have the resources it needs, or quick and easy access to them? (If you're not sure, all you have to do is ask them.)
5. Are any systems or procedures in your workplace outdated, poorly integrated or just plain cumbersome? How do systems and procedures like these sap people's motivation and their desire and ability to be fully productive? Provide an example to illustrate your thinking.

CASE STUDY 11.1

NEW EQUIPMENT AT THE DRYCLEANERS

Just about everyone knows Margaret, who has worked for many years at the drycleaners in a country town. She knows all her customers by name and always has a cheerful greeting and a few comments about local events as she organises their cleaning for them. It would not be an exaggeration to say that smiling, cheerful, friendly and super-efficient Margaret is responsible for much of the business enjoyed by the drycleaners.

One day, a new cash register is delivered. 'This is a wonderful piece of equipment,' says the representative who brings it in. 'You can record everything you need to know with it, as well as make change! Here, let me show you.'

With that, he proceeds to give Margaret a two-hour lesson on how to use the new cash register. Access to the machine begins with entering the customer's telephone number. Then the garment type, colour and fabric are coded in using a special keypad on the left-hand side of the machine. This is quite complicated, given the variety of possibilities, but when Margaret expresses dismay, the rep assures her that she's sure to get the hang of it quickly.

The machine automatically prices each garment as its details are entered. Drop-off time is recorded automatically and the operator enters the desired pick-up day and time (morning or afternoon), along with any special instructions. These are coded using a different keypad at the right-hand side of the machine. The usual amount-tendered/change-owing function is also part of the machine, located on the central keypad.

Poor Margaret! After two hours of training, her head is spinning. After two weeks of fumbling with the new cash register, she is no closer to mastering it. She is so busy working out what to do on the machine and fixing mistakes (unfortunately, there is no quick and easy way to delete incorrect entries) that she no longer has time to chat to her customers. The new process takes a lot longer than the old one, which means that customers are kept waiting and tempers fray. Margaret is embarrassed at her inefficiency – the whole thing is a nightmare. After six weeks, Margaret decides to retire.

Six months later, a succession of six new employees have been hired and trained. All six have struggled and quit. Business is falling as long-time loyal customers take their dry-cleaning elsewhere.

● ● ●

Questions

1. Use the five keys to analyse what is going wrong at the drycleaners.
2. Based on your analysis, what do you recommend the owners of the dry-cleaning business do to rectify the situation?

CASE STUDY 11.2

EDDIE'S EXHAUSTS

Eddie's Exhausts is a national chain of car exhaust specialists. Its motto is: 'Travel clean, travel quiet'. The chain has recently experienced a drop in business that the general manager believes reflects a general air of caution in the economy. In an effort to improve profits, he allows natural attrition to reduce the staffing levels in each of the stores in the chain. The stores are now running at about 60% of their usual staff numbers.

In an attempt to attract more customers, management begins a campaign of Superior Customer Service, based on improved levels of housekeeping, staff presentation (e.g. uniforms), upgraded customer waiting rooms and improved telephone techniques. Store staff are now required to answer the telephone within three rings, saying, 'Welcome to Eddie's Exhausts. We'll help you travel clean and quiet. This is [staff member's name] speaking; how may I help you?'

Store staff are pleased with the company's upgrading of customer waiting areas and their uniforms, and are more than willing to meet the improved housekeeping requirements. Because they are well aware that they can win a great deal of their business over the telephone, they know how important telephone technique is and are already making every effort to be as professional as possible in this area.

The phones are located behind the customer service counter in the stores' showroom. In the past, there had usually been someone behind the counter tending to paperwork and housekeeping and ready to deal with walk-in customers and to answer the telephone. Now, everyone is out in the fitting bay most of the time, fitting exhausts.

In most stores the fitting bay is located next to the customer reception area. When putting in the exhausts, the staff use dollies to wheel themselves under a vehicle or they hoist the car into the air over the recessed working area, depending on how the store is equipped. Either way, access and egress are awkward.

It comes to the general manager's attention that few stores are actually answering the telephone within three rings and with the required greeting. He hires 'mystery shoppers' to telephone each of the stores randomly and note down which stores are answering correctly and which are not. This list is then given to the area managers in each state.

Most of the area managers telephone the stores that are not meeting the required telephone standards and tell the staff to 'get it right' from now on. The trouble is: Things aren't improving. The general manager is furious as he considers telephone technique to be of primary importance in attracting customers.

Questions

1. Using the information provided in this chapter as a guide, what do you believe is the main problem with the telephone answering technique of store staff?
2. What do you recommend management do to address this problem?
3. Do you believe that the area managers could have handled the problem better? What could they have done differently or in addition to the actions they took?

CHAPTER

12

ASSIGING WORK AND DELEGATING DUTIES

OVERVIEW

Everyone who leads and manages people needs to know how to allocate work and delegate duties. Deciding who should receive an assignment, and explaining it and making sure the person delegated to do the work does it well, isn't as simple as selecting the first employee who passes by, handing over the work and forgetting about it.

Telling, or even asking, someone to do something isn't enough, although certainly most people respond more willingly to a request than to an order. Although the circumstances and the recipients determine the most effective way to assign work, your ultimate goal is cooperation, not mere compliance. When employees cooperate with you, they carry out the assignment to the best of their ability; those who are complying do only as you ask, no more and no less.

The words you use, your tone of voice and your body language reflect your respect for yourself and the person you are directing, which in turn affects the way employees hear and respond to your assignments.

The other side of the coin is that receiving work instructions and accepting delegated duties aren't necessarily as straightforward as listening to what's wanted and then rushing off to do it.

1. Can you explain the differences between the leadership style called delegating and delegating work, and between delegating work and assigning work?
2. Can you assign work in a way that achieves cooperation and commitment and avoids coercion and compliance?
3. Do you know what to delegate and how to delegate to ensure that the job is done well?
4. Do you know how to receive assignments and what to do when you disagree with an instruction?

This chapter explains what you need to do when you are on the giving end and the receiving end of assignments.

The end of the financial year

The end of the financial year is always a tough time. Stocktaking is a major task. Numerous reports need to be prepared and the auditors are always sniffing about checking on things. Everyone feels under pressure and overworked.

Derek Walsh, the warehouse manager, is in charge of the stocktake. He understands the importance of an accurate count and takes the responsibility very seriously. Everyone is involved, from senior management to factory hands, and Derek is number one on stocktake day.

Derek is finishing his email with instructions for carrying out the count. He wonders whether he should change his style when telling the managing director how to do the count from the way he tells the people who work for him in the warehouse.

1. Defining our terms

> No person will make a great business who wants to do it all himself or get all the credit.
>
> Andrew Carnegie (US industrialist), in Whitten, *Managing software development projects* (1995)[1]

In today's participative organisations, the need to give work instructions can lead to confusion and misunderstanding. Yesterday's manager was the supreme order-giver. Is a manager who gives orders today a relic from the past? Or a strong, decisive leader?

People sometimes criticise the laissez-faire style of leadership as 'do-nothing' leadership. Is the manager who gives few work directions a 'do-nothing' leader? Or a strong, empowering manager?

The dilemma of assigning work is not just a question of leadership style. Some leaders fear it is a way to lose the valued friendship, cooperation and support of their work team.

In all this confusion, it's no wonder that people sometimes back away from the concept of assigning and delegating work. Let's begin by defining the meanings of assigning work and delegating:

- *Assigning* work means directing people to carry out duties and tasks that are part of their job.
- *Delegating* work means giving people the authority to carry out tasks that are normally your responsibility.

Assigning work

Assigning work does not mean issuing orders in a dictatorial way. That sort of autocratic approach makes most 21st-century Aussie leader-managers feel uncomfortable. The last thing you want to be is a power-mad manager who barks out commands without thought or respect. Giving orders that leave no room for discussion and giving unnecessary orders are two quick ways to lose people's goodwill and support.

In this chapter, the concept of assigning work is not being used in a harsh, commanding context, but rather in the sense of allocating duties to a team or team member. Does this detract from empowerment? In its strictest sense, full empowerment means that members of a work team have a great deal of autonomy and share out duties among themselves. The members of synergistic, high-performing teams are competent and willing and don't need to be told what to do very often, either.

Try to avoid telling people how to carry out tasks or complete an assignment. Instead, explain the desired outcomes, the deadlines, constraints, resources available and so on, and work with the team or individual to decide how best to proceed. Guide people and use questions to help team members work things out for themselves. When you need to explain how something should be done, instruct people following the steps explained on page 917.

Delegating tasks

If you have completed Chapter 9, you probably remember a leadership style called delegating. You can use a delegating leadership style only with employees who are fully trained and competent, willing and confident.

In this chapter, the term 'delegate' isn't used in the strict sense required by the leadership style of the same name. It is used in the sense of a leader-manager of a work team assigning one of their own duties or responsibilities to a direct report. This may be someone who is already competent and willing to do the job; or it may be someone who does not yet know how to do it and needs training.

● IN A NUTSHELL

The three Ms of assigning and delegating work
Every task or duty you assign or delegate should meet the three-M criteria:
1. Manageable.
2. Measurable.
3. Motivational.

2. Assigning work

> When I was first put in charge of a team 19 years ago, I had to come to terms with the fact that I was no longer a lone professional doing my own job. I had to manage in such a way that other people would be the ones making things happen, not me. With every year, the lesson has intensified.
>
> Olli-Pekka Kallasvuo (former chairman, Nokia), 'Humility', *Harvard Business Review* (January 2007)[2]

When employees are uncertain of the reasons behind assignments or don't agree with them, they find it difficult to carry them out. Begin by establishing the specific outcome you're after and the task you want done. Explain why the task is important and where it fits into the work of the department and the organisation. Seeing tasks in their wider context gives people a better understanding of what is required, and why, and increases commitment.

Use the following headings to explain *what* needs to be done in terms of:

* safety
* quality
* quantity
* time.

When an employee is unfamiliar with the task, and when you need to give direct and explicit work instructions, you may need to explain how to do the work. (Page 917 explains how to walk employees through a task, step by step.) When an employee is clear about what needs to be done, and why, establish measures of success and check that the employee fully understands the assignment. When necessary, go over the task and your expectations two or three times or, better still, ask the employee to explain it back to you. Give the employee ample opportunity to ask questions so that you can clear up any areas of uncertainty or doubt.

We know that people perform best when working in their strengths areas, so select someone with both the ability and the desire to carry out the task. (Page 212 and page 807 explain more about matching people to tasks.) A good match between the person and the task is known as a good *job fit*. For example:

- When a task is repetitive, think about who is best suited to doing it.
- When a task requires a fine eye for detail, consider who in your team enjoys detailed work.
- When a task requires working with others cooperatively, select someone who is good at that.
- When the unexpected might occur, pick someone who can handle surprises well.

Think about your timing, too. It is unwise, for example, to assign work when you're angry. Other examples of poor timing are giving assignments when employees are about to go to lunch or knock off for the day, or when the assignment comes on top of an incident that has lowered the morale of the group. Try to anticipate the employee's reactions and plan your explanations and timing so that the assignment is willingly accepted.

Monitor the employee's progress so that should things start to go wrong, you have time to rectify the situation. Don't forget to thank the employee and give timely and specific feedback on his or her efforts. (Page 447 has information on how to provide feedback and page 327 has information on establishing measures of success.)

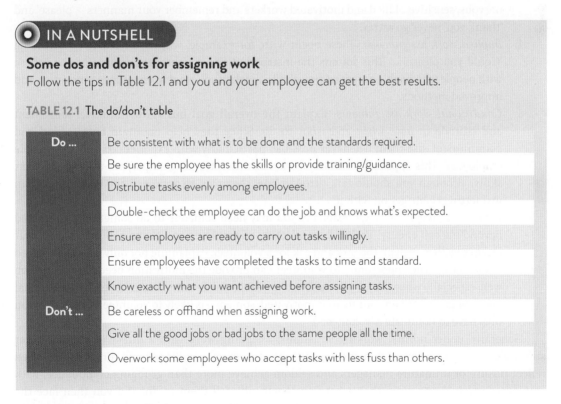

IN A NUTSHELL

Some dos and don'ts for assigning work
Follow the tips in Table 12.1 and you and your employee can get the best results.

TABLE 12.1 The do/don't table

Do ...	Be consistent with what is to be done and the standards required.
	Be sure the employee has the skills or provide training/guidance.
	Distribute tasks evenly among employees.
	Double-check the employee can do the job and knows what's expected.
	Ensure employees are ready to carry out tasks willingly.
	Ensure employees have completed the tasks to time and standard.
	Know exactly what you want achieved before assigning tasks.
Don't ...	Be careless or offhand when assigning work.
	Give all the good jobs or bad jobs to the same people all the time.
	Overwork some employees who accept tasks with less fuss than others.

Six ways to assign work

The way you assign work depends on the situation and the employee. Emergencies and dangerous situations, for example, require prompt action. You need to be clear and decisive and you may not even have time to explain. At the other end of the scale are situations where there are many options and plenty of time. Here, you can afford to take a more relaxed approach.

Your reports may have different skill levels and expectations of their jobs, too. Those who are highly motivated and self-directed generally respond best when you state the end result and let them decide the best way to achieve it. People who are just learning a job need clear, step-by-step direction. Those lacking motivation need ultra-clear success measures and frequent 'check-ins'.

1. *Direct orders*: Give a direct order, and even call on your formal authority, when giving instructions that must be followed without question, leaving no room for discussion. They are useful when time or outcomes are critical, such as with health and safety matters; for example, you might say: 'You *must* close the machine guard *fully* before proceeding' or 'Always put on a hairnet and wash your hands before handling food'. When an employee is engaged in an unsafe work practice, you must take prompt action and you may need to resort to giving a direct order. You may occasionally come across employees who, because of past experiences or their attitude to the job, respond only to direct orders.

2. *Explicit assignments*: These state clearly the result that's required and describe precisely *who* is to do *what*, *when* it is to be done, *how* it is to be done and *where* it is to be done. Use explicit instructions with people with limited experience or abilities and with people who lack commitment to the job.

3. *Requests*: These begin with, for example, 'Would you …' or 'Will you …'. Use them with nervous, sensitive, skilled and motivated workers and remember your manners – 'please' and 'thank you' never go astray.

4. *Implied work assignments*: These begin with, for example, with 'We need to …' or asking 'Could you please …' This softens the instruction and encourages cooperation. Use these with people who readily accept responsibility or when you want to encourage innovation and improved methods.

5. *Conditional work assignments*: Explain the overall goal but allow initiative, judgement and latitude in *how*, *when* and *what* to do. Since they help maintain cooperation and commitment, use them whenever possible, particularly with experienced and responsible employees. This approach can also work well when training employees to upgrade their skills, although you should talk through how they plan to approach the task rather than just letting them 'get on with it'.

6. *Undirected assignments*: Occasionally you may need someone to do something 'above and beyond the call of duty'. Rather than selecting an employee and giving a direction, call your group together, explain the task and ask for a volunteer, explaining not only *what* is required but also *why*. The opportunity to volunteer can provide the motivation needed to do the job well, especially when the job allows the volunteer to satisfy one of his or her own motivational needs or goals. (When your team is motivated, someone is likely to volunteer; otherwise, you may have to nominate a 'volunteer'.)

Generally, under normal working situations, assigning work with a direct or explicit order stifles ideas, initiative, innovation and suggestions. Too many commands and direct orders often reflect unsure or immature managers and seldom achieve more than grudging compliance, with employees rarely doing more than what you specifically tell them to do, and you then face the problem of supervising reluctant staff. So try to take another approach. When you assign work in a directive or explicit way only occasionally, employees know it's for a good reason and respond better.

The exception is with people who have low levels of task readiness. They are unlikely to be able to carry out requests, implied, conditional and undirected assignments successfully, because they lack either the skills or the willingness, so these approaches can be dangerous with inexperienced or unreliable staff. You should also avoid these other four approaches when you are not able to give a specific objective or sufficient background information.

The other four ways of assigning work are particularly useful in complex situations and when employees are capable and willing, as they allow some discretion and initiative in carrying out the request. Many employees are capable of modifying or improving an assignments, too. In fact, people generally need to put their own stamp on the way they complete tasks, and the other four ways of assigning work allow this latitude. Giving employees the opportunity to express their opinion and become creatively involved in the way they carry out a task also helps overcome resistance and encourages people to put their skills and experience to use.

◉ THEORY TO PRACTICE

Three vital 'To dos'
Clear and courteous communication can help get the message across.
1. Be concise, because irrelevant details cloud your work assignments and invite employees to 'tune out'.
2. Instead of asking, 'Do you have any questions?', pause, smile and say something like: 'What else can I tell you?' or 'Did I explain that clearly enough?'
3. Sit next to employees as you explain assignments. This literally puts you on the same side and emphasises that you're working together to achieve important goals.

Five levels of monitoring
You can select from five levels of monitoring, depending on the employee's skill level, experience and willingness to do the task:
1. *Just do it!* When employees are both skilled and motivated, you can safely assign them the work and let them get on with it, provided you have warning signals in place to alert you to any potential problems.
2. *Keep me informed*: Ask employees who are dependable, but slightly less skilled, experienced or willing to carry on with the task, to update you with certain key information or at milestones so you can satisfy yourself that things are progressing well.
3. *Check back first*: Ask employees with even less experience or willingness to check back with you before proceeding at certain critical control points so that you can assure yourself that the work is being done correctly.
4. *Let's talk it through first*: Ask employees who are trained but inexperienced in the task to decide what to do when a problem or something unexpected arises and then come and talk it through with you before acting. This is an expanded version of level three and lets you review how the employee is thinking about approaching the task. It gives you a chance to coach and develop the employee's skills.
5. *I'll walk you through it*: Use the training approach discussed on page 917 for employees new to a task.

⬤ THE STRATEGIC PERSPECTIVE

Keeping the bad news quiet

Most managers overestimate their openness to receiving bad news and, at the same time, underestimate the extent to which the power difference between themselves and their reports discourages employees from alerting them to adverse situations. Many managers often unconsciously signal they don't want to hear bad news by, for example, changing the subject or avoiding discussion. On top of this, employees tend to hold back from announcing bad news. This impedes the flow of information that is so necessary to effective working relationships, preventing and dealing with problems in a timely manner and running effective operations.[3]

When an employee seems reluctant to carry out directions

If an employee is hesitating about taking on an assignment, you can first consider the assignment. Was it reasonable? Was it clear? Does the employee have the skills, ability and time to carry it out correctly? Is it work the employee enjoys doing, or at least doesn't dislike doing? Perhaps the task you assigned is unpleasant or interferes with something in the employee's work or private life.

When you can't understand why an employee isn't cooperating, ask. Maybe the employee has a good reason or has misunderstood. Maybe something you said annoyed the employee or was misinterpreted. Ask questions (in a non-threatening way) so you can see the situation from the employee's point of view. Find out what the employee needs in order to begin the assignment – something in the five keys is sure to be missing (see Chapter 11). When you need to, review what you require, the importance of the task and why you're assigning the work to that employee.

In the unlikely event you make no progress and the employee still seems reluctant to begin the assigned work, what should you do? You could try modifying the assignment, and talk again later, privately and constructively, keeping a cooperative, win–win approach uppermost in your mind.

Ultimately, your job is to help people accomplish their work and, to succeed in this, you need to work with, not against, them. Once the immediate situation has settled, think through what happened carefully, so that you can learn from it and ensure that a similar situation does not occur in the future.

The north-bound-bus approach

When your work assignments are reasonable, particularly regarding a change in policy or procedures, try the the north-bound-bus approach. When you board a bus going north, you go north, too. When you don't want to go north, the best thing to do is to get off that bus and find another one.

Organisations and work teams often alter course to head in a new direction. They might introduce a new customer service philosophy, establish new procedures and work methods based on a new technology, or reorganise and change established reporting structures. Symbolically, they are now heading 'north'.

Some employees may have trouble accepting the new direction. When, after you have followed the advice on introducing and managing change in Chapter 22, an employee still refuses to 'head north' with everyone else, the north-bound-bus approach may be a last resort. Clearly, like invoking your organisation's formal discipline procedure, this is a method to adopt only when other approaches have failed.

When the task is done incorrectly

Everyone misunderstands sometimes. When an employee who has not carried out an assignment to your satisfaction says, 'I didn't know that was what you wanted', apologise for not making yourself clear and make an effort to communicate better next time.

When you're sure you have communicated clearly, use Figure 12.1 to select the best course of action. Each quadrant suggests a possible cause of poor performance and a recommended approach to rectify it. In the first quadrant, the employee is willing but has insufficient job knowledge or skill, so training may be the answer. In the second, the employee is willing and has sufficient knowledge or skills, so you need to look to the environment or the 'chance to' key (see page 339) for a clue. Perhaps the employee has insufficient resources (tools, equipment, time or information) or is constrained by cumbersome systems.

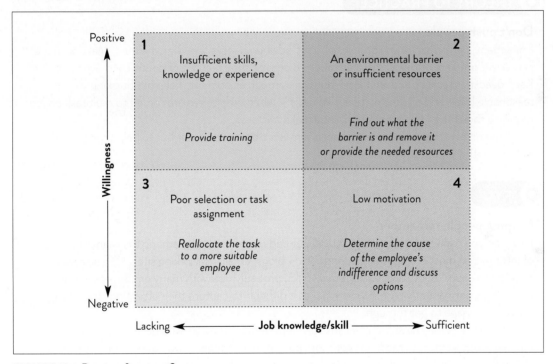

FIGURE 12.1 Poor performance?

In the third quadrant, the employee lacks not only skills and knowledge but also willingness. This suggests that you should examine your selection procedures or task assignment (to stop this happening in the future) and consider assigning the employee other, more suitable work. In the fourth quadrant, the employee has sufficient job knowledge but lacks willingness, so the problem is a motivational one and you need to discuss options with the employee. (See pages 459 and 912 for more information on correcting underperformance and coaching employees.)

Who should assign work to your employees?

The principle of unity of command states that employees should receive their assignments from only one person.[4] This prevents employees from feeling conflicted and confused about whose directions should have priority. As a general guideline, therefore, try to ensure that you are the only person who assigns work to your employees.

A matrix organisation is a relatively new form of organisational structure that seems to go against this principle. Instead of the predictability of one boss, employees must learn to cope with the ambiguity and potential conflicting priorities that come with reporting to two or more managers. This need not necessarily go against the unity of command principle provided each manager manages clearly defined, and different, aspects of a person's job.

When this is not the case, confusion and conflict are likely to arise. However, unless they are comfortable dealing with the uncertainty involved in reporting to more than one person and are able to invest their personal energy, enthusiasm and creativity in dealing with multiple projects and challenges, many people find responding to more than one manager a difficult task.

 THEORY TO PRACTICE

Don't push people

Enjoyment, performance and productivity suffer when people feel overwhelmed. Make sure the people reporting to you don't have so much to do that they feel out of control and overstretched. Keep deadlines realistic and limit interruptions as much as possible. Keep multitasking to reasonable levels and to simple, repetitive tasks – when employees are forced to multitask on jobs requiring thought and concentration, they make mistakes.

Your job isn't to push people to make them work harder or faster but to help them do their work smoothly and to a high standard.

 FYI

Helping people remember

How can you make your information stand out and be remembered among the many streams of information most employees contend with – blogs, email, networking sites, RSS streams, smartphone apps, texts, tweets, voicemails? You probably deal with many employees whose attention is permanently partial, which makes it difficult to capture their attention long enough for your message to get through.

Researchers may have found an answer: Repetition. Managers who deliberately repeat their messages using different mediums get more buy-in than managers who don't. Using multiple channels (e.g. combining emails, personal discussion and shared files) gives messages more weight and helps them sink in.[5]

3. Delegating tasks

The great and terrible irony of modern business is that so many managers feel overburdened with responsibility while so many employees feel unchallenged and unfulfilled in their jobs.

Ken Iverson (mathematician, author), *Plain Talk* (1997)[6]

It's silly to feel overworked when your followers feel underworked. Delegation is the answer – giving someone else the authority to carry out a specific task and the responsibility for carrying it out, while you retain the accountability for its correct execution. (You can delegate authority and responsibility, but you cannot delegate accountability.)

Don't be one of those 'lazy delegators' who shovel off work to others because they're too lazy to do it themselves, because they don't want to do it or because they can't be bothered to do it themselves. They often use the 'I'm time poor' excuse or simply say to someone else, 'Please do this', with no explanation when they should be doing it themselves. They're the people who often fill their time with 'busy work', instead of real work that adds value. They can often be seen rushing around looking busy and important when they're actually doing very little. No, don't be one of those lazy delegators.

Be a 'leader delegator'. These are the people who give someone a task because it will enhance that person's skills, experience and opportunity as well as allowing them to get on with value-adding leading and managing work that only they can do. This section explains how to be an achieving leader delegator.

What happens when you don't delegate?

Can you imagine a football coach suiting up, jogging out onto the field and grabbing the ball? When you find yourself using any of the excuses in the 'In a Nutshell: Common excuses for not delegating', think again. These excuses just prevent you from increasing employee productivity and usefulness, developing and extending employees' skills and job interest, and freeing up some of your own time to do other things.

Have you ever thought to yourself 'It's quicker and easier to do it myself and anyway, I haven't got time to train someone to do it' or 'I enjoy doing this task far too much to hand it over to someone else?' Or maybe you've said, 'I don't dare let any of my people take this on. They may make a mistake and I'll be the one on the firing line for it.' Or maybe you've thought, 'No way can I delegate this. It's far too important and I can't afford to lose control'. If so, you may be surprised to learn that these are common excuses for not delegating work to the people meant to be doing it. And these excuses do not hold up to scrutiny.

When you don't delegate, you end up doing everything yourself. You become caught up in day-to-day tasks and don't have the time to devote to the *real* job of managing – communicating, planning, thinking, and so on. Your desk overflows, your team's work slows and team members become confused because you've been too busy rushing around doing 'odd jobs' to organise work and resources properly. You stay behind and work late, trying frantically to catch up and do some 'real work'.

 **ACTION!**

Do you fall for any of these excuses in the *Why don't I delegate?* checklist on ⚡**CourseMateExpress**?

The importance of delegation

How did John D Rockefeller, an office boy earning US$16 a month in 1855, become one of the richest men in the world? By surrounding himself with the best people he could find and delegating to them. That's how to get a life beyond work, too. Rockefeller summed it up simply for us like this: 'I never, from the time I first entered an office, let business engross all my time and attention.'[7]

Yes, it can be risky and somewhat alarming to let go of a task you're responsible for and place it in the hands of someone else. Nevertheless, you're unlikely to succeed as a leader-manager unless you take that risk.

Here are some good reasons to delegate. Delegation:

* attracts motivated employees to your department because they know they can learn from you
* can free you from details, giving you time to monitor the bigger picture and be sure that your department is operating smoothly, that output is integrated and synchronised, and that you are attaining your key objectives effectively and efficiently
* can help you take control of your time and concentrate on what's most important in your job
* gives you time to look ahead – time to plan your work and your department's work more effectively
* helps train people who can step into your role, putting you in a position for promotion or assignment to other interesting duties
* is good for the bottom line because jobs are completed at a less expensive level
* lets you relax when you go on holiday, knowing your team can carry on in your absence.

From the employees' point of view, delegating indicates faith and trust in them. It can enrich their jobs and it's a great way to develop, train and coach people. Sharing your knowledge and skills with employees and giving them additional responsibilities can also be a great motivator.

Tasks to delegate and tasks to keep

Wise leader-managers make a point of not doing work that people in their team could do or would like to learn to do. Actor John Cleese, a popular public speaker on matters other than acting, once told an interviewer that '… the ideal leader was the one trying to make himself dispensable … helping the people around him acquire as many of his skills as possible so that he could let everyone else do the work and just keep an eye on things'.[8] That way you have time to sit back, and think and plan.

However, some tasks are clearly not suitable for delegation:

* boring jobs and unpleasant or otherwise disagreeable tasks that you don't like to do yourself
* high-risk and high-cost tasks
* matters dealing with organisational policy or security
* planning and monitoring activities
* sensitive or confidential matters such as pay or performance counselling
* something that needs to be done quickly
* tasks that are well beyond employees' training or experience – setting people up to fail is the worst possible kind of management.

Most other tasks are suitable for delegation:

* any tasks that you don't add any value to by doing yourself
* recurring and routine duties
* tasks that would train, develop and stretch employees
* tasks that don't require your personal input
* tasks that need to be done but you can't squeeze into your schedule, such as small projects, data collection, portions of larger projects and research
* tasks that require special skills or aptitudes that you may not have but team members have
* tasks that would make employees' jobs more interesting in some way.

THEORY TO PRACTICE

Deadlines work, but not just any deadline

Researchers found that the way managers set deadlines affects their timely performance. With long or complex tasks, interim deadlines or milestones work best.

They also found that deadlines you let people set themselves seem less important than those you set.[9]

Make sure that when a task is done on the agreed date, you follow it up immediately. When you let work that an employee has rushed to hand in on time sit on your desk for days or weeks with no action, don't be surprised when they feel annoyed and resentful and don't believe your next 'due date'.

With employees who tend to procrastinate, set a 'start date' as well as a completion date.

Five steps to effective delegation

Last-minute delegation and crisis delegation are doomed to failure. Delegating well takes planning and thought. Delegation saves you time in the long run but it does take time to set up properly. Like assigning work, delegation involves matching tasks to people, providing the right information and necessary training, and following up correctly.

1. Decide what to delegate

Use the work delegation plan shown in Figure 12.2 or the Work delegation plan template on CourseMate Express, to help you decide which tasks you could or should be delegating. Think about your recurring and routine tasks, tasks that would increase or develop an employee's skills or knowledge, your occasional duties or tasks and tasks that you do that are in one of your team member's areas of interest or expertise. When new work comes in, ask yourself whether you could delegate it.

Recurring and routine tasks	Who can do it now?	Who could be trained to do it?
Tasks that would increase or develop an employee's skills or knowledge	Who can do it now?	Who could be trained to do it?
Occasional duties or tasks	Who can do it now?	Who could be trained to do it?
Tasks I do that are in someone's area of expertise or interest	Who can do it now?	Who could be trained to do it?

FIGURE 12.2 Work delegation plan

2. Select the delegate

Then think about who in your team can already do these tasks, who could be trained to do them and who would enjoy or benefit from learning how to do it. Select suitable delegates based on whether they:

* are already able and willing to take on the responsibility for doing the task
* have a flair for the task (see, for example, 'The Strategic perspective: Multiple intelligences', on page 134)
* have shown interest in a particular type of work and delegating it can help them decide whether they really enjoy it
* need to develop particular skills for future assignments or promotion
* want to learn the task in order to develop or extend their skills
* would appreciate learning the task because it adds interest or challenge to their job or because they enjoy that type of work.

Avoid the urge to delegate only to your most skilled or promising employees – everyone can benefit from the experience and knowledge that delegation provides.

 **ACTION!**

Keep the delegation plan template on ⫶CourseMateExpress handy and use it every few months to make sure you're using recurring, routine, occasional and new tasks to develop team members' skills and to maintain their job interests.

3. Delegate

Don't leave employees wondering why you have selected them, whether the job is really important, by when or how often the task is to be done, the standard or end result you expect, what resources the employee can draw on or whether there are any constraints such as time or money. Delegate using these headings:

* Why the task is important
* Why you are delegating *this* task to *this* person
* Quality
* Quantity
* Safety
* Time.

Explaining why you are asking this particular person to do a task means you aren't just *using* the skills and knowledge of the employee – you are also *recognising* them. One of the keys to effective delegation is reframing a task you can't realistically manage or don't have time to handle so that delegates don't feel you've dumped it on them but feel excited about taking it on.

Go through the task with the delegate, filling in knowledge or skills gaps with training or coaching. Discuss how the delegate intends to approach the task and any problems they might run into and how they could deal with them. Don't insist that it be done the way you used to do it or would have done it. In other words, delegate according to the results desired, not according to the methods to use, unless these are very clear-cut and specific and really are the best way to approach the task.

Be clear that you are there to help or give advice, or to help the delegate think through the task should any difficulties arise. 'I'm sure I can figure it out' or 'I think I understand' are code for 'I don't know what you want but I'm not about to say so' and a clear signal to explain more or ask what other information the employee needs. When delegated tasks are complicated or you're not sure the employee is completely clear about what you want, ask questions about how they could approach it, or ask for a written summary to make sure everything has sunk in.

Discuss how you will monitor the task to ensure that it is being completed correctly. Decide what to monitor. What is important: Costs? Production? Quality? Sales? Use lead indicators whenever you can and monitor only what is important – probably the critical measures of success.

Set up a systematic method of measuring progress against measures of success or milestones to alert you and the delegate to deviations from the requirements. When the delegate is highly skilled and motivated, you can use management by exception – the delegate monitors progress and comes to you only when there is a deviation. Or you can arrange the system so that the actual results go directly to both you and the employee for comparison with the desired results. (The results should never go only to you because this makes employees overly dependent on you for feedback on performance, reducing their motivation.)

Once you have delegated, don't hound the delegate, trying to keep on top of every detail. Release the task to the delegate and monitor only the critical control points you have agreed. Don't take the task back and do it for the delegate at the first sign of a problem.

The US president, Theodore 'Teddy' Roosevelt, knew how to stay out of the way. He put it like this: 'The best executive is the one who has sense enough to pick good men to do what he wants done, and self-restraint enough to keep from meddling with them while they do it.'[10]

4. Inform others as necessary

When employees need to liaise with others to carry out a delegated task or duty, let those people know they can expect to be dealing with your delegate on this matter in the future. Let them know, too, that you have complete confidence in their ability to do the job well.

5. Monitor results

You can't afford to delegate a task and hope for the best. Keep tabs on it to ensure that the employee is carrying it out safely and efficiently and progressing satisfactorily towards the goal. When things are going wrong, you need to know in plenty of time so you can take, or guide the delegate to take, swift corrective action.

From time to time discuss with the delegate how they are enjoying the task, what they are learning and how they can use the skills they are acquiring in other aspects of their job. Give feedback on how you see the delegate's results, how it helps you and perhaps others, and thank them for their help.

IN A NUTSHELL

Delegate thoroughly

Don't be under any illusions about delegation. It is not a quick and easy way to offload your work to someone else – that's for lazy delegators. Always make sure that people understand clearly what you want them to do, why it's important, how it fits into the bigger picture and how results are to be monitored. Match the delegate's skills, abilities and interests to the delegated duty as much as you can. Train delegates who don't yet know how to do the task properly (explained on page 917). And see that delegates have the resources they need to do the job correctly in terms of time, information, equipment and so on (explained on page 339).

Delegate, allowing for errors

Remember that reaching a goal is not the only important outcome of delegation. Allowing people to learn is also important, even when at first they don't accomplish the task as quickly, efficiently or effectively as you could.

When you delegate, you also offer the right to learn by mistakes. When a delegate makes a mistake or does something incorrectly, or when there is a better, easier or faster way to approach the delegated task, use it as an opportunity for training, coaching and guidance. Help the delegate fix any mistakes quickly and limit the fallout; then discuss what you will both do differently next time – you have as much to learn as they do. (To find out more about coaching employees and offering corrective feedback, see page 451 and Chapter 27.)

 IN A NUTSHELL

Five mistakes in delegating
Five of the most common delegation mistakes managers make are:
1. Delegating the best jobs to the team member they like best.
2. Failing to thank employees when they complete a delegated task enthusiastically or well.
3. Forgetting that they can't delegate accountability.
4. Not delegating to people who have excellent skills and commitment for fear of being shown up.
5. Not fully handing the job over to the person they've delegated it to.

Delegate, don't abdicate

Leaving employees floundering and expecting them to 'get on with it' is not delegation – it's 'sink or swim'. Far from training staff or 'testing' their skills, it's setting them up to fail and likely to shatter their confidence. Failing to ensure a delegate is approaching a task properly or failing to monitor progress is not delegation – it's abdication.

Dealing with unenthusiastic reactions to delegation

Not all employees receive a delegated task eagerly. One might say, 'I already do enough' and this might be true – the person might be overworked; on the other hand, the person or the department might be poorly organised. Another employee might complain, 'I never know what I'm expected to do!' This may be a sign that you need to be more comprehensive or clear with your information or that the employee lacks confidence or is concerned about your reaction to mistakes.

When an employee complains, 'You knock yourself out and never a word of thanks!', you may need to review the information on motivation (Chapter 10) and learn to give positive feedback (Chapter 15). Someone else might say, 'Tell me exactly what you want me to do.' Perhaps you have always thought for them and told them exactly what you wanted them to do, step by step, or perhaps they don't want to take on this task at all and this is their way of telling you.

'I can't do it!' might mean 'I lack confidence and need a bit of help' while 'Why should I bother?' or 'Why should I be doing your job for you?' might mean 'You don't reward me enough' or 'There's no point in my doing it – I'm going nowhere in this job anyway!' It might even mean 'Why should I help you out? You never do anything for me.'

Deal with negative reactions like these tactfully. Use your reflective listening skills and ask questions to fully understand the employee's objection to taking on the delegated task. The responses may be valid or they may signal a deeper morale and motivation problem.

FYI

Upwards delegation

Some employees have a habit of subtly shifting their responsibilities upwards to their manager. This 'upwards delegation' can take many forms. A team member may ask for your help or say they've run into a problem. When you say 'Leave it with me' and do the job yourself, you soon find yourself solving your employees' problems and doing their work for them instead of managing your department. Accepting tasks your employees delegate up to you eats away at your time and results in dependent employees who don't think for themselves or act without your permission.

When an employee approaches you for help, be courteous, listen to the problem and help those who really need help. Here are some strategies to deal with those employees who are trying (perhaps without even being aware of it) to get you to do their thinking or their work for them:

- Ask them to explain their problem or dilemma in one thorough, objective statement.
- Ask them to suggest some solutions and help them select the best one.
- Ask them to think it through and return tomorrow with a list of recommended actions or a 'plan of attack'.
- Ask what the logical first step to take is, satisfy yourself it's reasonable, and suggest they take it and let you know how they get on.
- Ask what they consider is the key issue and how they can deal with it.
- Ask what they have done already and what they could do next.
- Ask whether they have come across anything similar before and how they dealt with it.
- Ask whether they need any more information and how they can get it.

Let 'upwards delegators' know that you have every confidence in their ability and provide whatever support they genuinely need.

4. Receiving assignments

> Never tell people how to do things. Tell them what to do and they will surprise you with their ingenuity.
>
> George S Patton Jr (US general, WWII), *War as I Knew It* (1975)[11]

Don't be shy about asking questions when you are on the receiving end of work assignments or delegated duties. It's important to thoroughly understand what your manager expects and any challenges and constraints you need to take into account in order to minimise the risk of misunderstanding and underperforming.

Assumptions can be dangerous, so clarify all areas on which you have any doubt: Guidelines on timing, quality and quantity, and restrictions on money, time or other resources. You don't need to ask your boss to do the job for you or to explain it step by step, but specific operating parameters ensure that you are both on the same wavelength. When you need to enlist the cooperation of others or temporarily acquire any special authority, confirm your manager has made the necessary arrangements.

Find out what priority the task has, to both your manager and the organisation. Be positive in your attitude and show through your words and actions that you are willing to complete the assignment. When your manager is inclined to 'shift the goalposts' or change priorities, confirm your assignment in writing; should something go wrong, you at least have a record of what you were trying to achieve and your operating parameters.

Disagreeing with a directive or assignment

Occasionally, you may be required to relay to your work team information or a changed procedure that you do not agree with or you believe will draw an adverse reaction from your team.

An easy response to such a situation would be to side with the employees and accuse senior management of being 'out of touch' or unaware of the repercussions, and to pass on the information or change of procedure with a comment like, 'I know it's crazy and won't work but that's the way they want it done.' A negative attitude like this only makes it harder to enlist the cooperation of your team.

Look at the situation from the strategic perspective and try to understand the overall reasons behind the change in policy or procedure. Remember that sometimes tough decisions must be made even though they are likely to be unpopular. When you pass the information on to your team, explain the reasons behind them as fully as possible. Remember that you are part of the management team and must be a supportive member of that team.

Your manager may also ask you to take on an assignment or delegated duty that you have reservations about or would rather not do for some reason. Meet with your manager to talk through your concerns. If you still have misgivings, state your opinions thoughtfully, calmly and clearly. Cite any relevant examples, facts or figures to illustrate your points. Try to be constructive, not negative, in your remarks. In other words, don't just say 'It will never work' or 'I can't help you with that' but explain why you think the way you do and suggest some alternative approaches.

If, at the end of the discussion, your manager still requires you to complete the assignment, do so, provided there is no breach of the law or corporate policy involved. When you believe that rules are being breached, raise the matter again with your manager or, as a last resort, with your manager's manager.

CourseMateExpress

Go to http://login.cengagebrain.com to access CourseMate Express, your online study tool for *Management Theory & Practice*. CourseMate Express brings chapter concepts to life with interactive learning, and study and exam preparation tools:

- Test your skills in different aspects of management with interactive self-tests and simulations.
- Watch videos that show how real managers operate in real businesses.
- Test your understanding of the changing world of management by taking the revision quiz.

QUICK REVIEW

1. What is the difference between assigning work, delegating work and the leadership style called delegation?
2. List and briefly explain the six ways to assign work, when to use each and what can happen when you assign work in the wrong way.
3. List and give an example of each of the five levels of monitoring you can use after you have assigned or delegated work.
4. Explain how you would handle an employee who is reluctant to carry out a directive.
5. How important is it for team leaders to know and understand the different strengths, working styles, work preferences, motivators and expectations of team members when assigning and delegating work?
6. List the information you need to know when receiving an assignment.

BUILD YOUR SKILLS

1. How should you handle the situation of an employee making a mistake or having trouble carrying out an assignment or a delegated duty? Discuss the four possible causes of an employee carrying out an assignment incorrectly and the remedies each cause suggests.
2. Explain how you would respond to an employee who says 'I'm too busy to take on this task' and to an employee who asks for help with a problem.
3. Although delegation is a good time-management tool, managers should take care not to overuse it. Do you agree? Why or why not? What do you think are the dangers of delegating boring work?
4. What should you do when you disagree with an assignment or change in policy or procedure? Develop some action guidelines based on the information provided in this chapter.
5. Refer to the opening scenario: 'Decisions ... decisions ... ' on page 518 of Chapter 18. Khalid has a number of decisions to make. Referring to Figure 5.1 on page 116, which quadrant is each decision in? Based on the information in this chapter, how do you recommend he deal with each of the following?
    *   Decision 1: Ventilation in the gym
    *   Decision 2: Mattie Smith, the receptionist
    *   Decision 3: General manager's email
    *   Decision 4: Note to ring home
    *   Decision 5: Problems with the pool filtration system
    *   Decision 6: Candidate waiting for an interview

WORKPLACE ACTIVITIES

1. Interview a manager you know to be an effective delegator to find out which duties she or he delegates and how delegation has helped. Has the manager run into any problems when delegating duties? What general advice can the manager offer about delegation?
2. Use the work delegation plan in Figure 12.2 on page 359, or the 'Work delegation plan' template on CourseMate Express to identify which of your tasks you could delegate and to whom. Select one to delegate and do so, following the steps outlined in this chapter.

CASE STUDY 12.1

THE UNTIMELY OVERTIME

When a special order for the following day comes in, Ann Turnbull asks everyone to work overtime that night. All agree except Tony Small. Tony claims he has prior arrangements for that evening and isn't interested in the overtime anyway.

'Besides,' he says, 'our workplace agreement says that we should have 24 hours' notice of being required to work extra hours.'

Ann explains that this is an emergency, the order is for a valued customer and she couldn't have given prior notice, but Tony remains unmoved. Ann allows herself to be provoked into insisting he works the overtime or risk dismissal.

When the normal finishing time comes, everyone starts work on the special order except Tony, who leaves in full view of the rest of the team, saying in a loud voice, 'You can't make me work overtime if I don't want to.'

Questions

1. Apart from meeting the deadline on the order, what other problems does Ann Turnbull probably face?
2. What action should Ann take when Tony arrives for work the next day?
3. How should Ann have handled Tony's refusal to work overtime?

CASE STUDY 12.2

A POOR APPOINTMENT

Charlie Simmons' resignation from the position of administration manager came as a shock. Charlie had run 'his office' for the past 10 years and was not expected to retire for another eight, so nothing had been done about developing a successor for his position. His staff accepted his rather stern but avuncular leadership style out of respect for his long years of experience and knowledge of the organisation and because they enjoyed their work and their workmates.

But they have mixed feelings about Mary Williams' appointment to Charlie's position. Although Mary has been with the organisation for only 18 months, she is by far the best qualified person for the job, especially in view of management's decision to bring into head office many administrative functions that were previously done in branch offices. Mary is responsible for introducing an upgraded computer system – a major project in itself and something she had experience with in her last role. The new system makes it unnecessary to recruit additional staff to help with the extra duties and may even allow Mary to downsize the office.

Mary takes over her new position and begins to adjust the workflow of the office in preparation for bringing in the additional work and introducing the new system. To avoid confusion about what is expected of individual staff members, Mary plans to tell each of them how the changes will affect his or her job and give everyone written details of the standard operating procedures (SOPs) to follow from now on.

With so many changes occurring, management sees the opportunity of introducing some other new ideas, too, and gives these to Mary to implement urgently. Mary feels that many of these schemes are not practical. However, when the staff complain that the schemes are unworkable, her only explanation is 'This is what they want us to do'.

It isn't long before work in Mary's section falls behind its implementation schedule. Staff are frustrated with trying to make the new system work and complain that some of the new standard operating procedures (SOPs) appear to be in direct conflict with each other. Standards and reliability of information from the office are falling, deadlines are whooshing by unmet and morale is at an all-time low. The senior management team is beginning to have second thoughts about Mary's appointment.

Questions

1. What do you think is the basic problem in this office? What are the main contributors to the current situation?

2. What steps would you advise Mary to take to rectify the situation? What support does she need from senior management and how could she get it?

3. What approach would you recommend Mary take in giving and passing on assignments and directives? Why?

4. How could Mary have handled her misgivings about some of management's ideas more effectively?

CHAPTER

BUILDING PRODUCTIVE WORK TEAMS

OVERVIEW

What does it feel like to be a member of your work team? For example, are your team members open or guarded, supportive or undermining, tolerant or judgemental, trusting or suspicious? Do they aim to fix problems or fix blame? Do they take responsibility or pass the buck? This depends on your organisation's culture, on how interpersonally skilled you and your team members are and how skilfully you build and support your team.

Managing in today's streamlined, informal team-based organisations is different from managing in the conformist hierarchical organisations of the past. If you aren't already, you will probably soon be leading a team whose members need to work together, rather than as independent performers, to achieve challenging goals. The ability to nurture high-performing teams and empower them to innovate and work productively is a prized skill in modern workplaces.

Understanding what goes on in teams and what it means to be a team helps you encourage and assist your work group to become a cohesive, highly productive team. Recognising the behaviours that effective team members display and how teams develop, set goals, make decisions, motivate their members, celebrate and reward success, and manage change are all part of building effective work teams.

1. Can you explain the highlights and lowlights of teams and the types of teams that you're likely to work with?
2. Do you know how to establish a performance plan for the team and for individual team members?
3. Can you help your team concentrate its efforts on its purpose and goals and help its members work effectively together?
4. Do you know how to build and sustain a high-performing team?
5. Do you know how to support your team in your daily activities?

In this chapter, you discover the real power of teams and how to build them and lead them to achieve meaningful, worthwhile results in an innovative, enjoyable way.

Trouble in the team

John is feeling dispirited about the team he leads and voices his concerns to Joan, another team leader on the same floor. 'I'm at the end of my rope, Joan. My team has a terrible attitude – they drive me to distraction with their constant whingeing, whingeing, whingeing. It's their attitude – their attitudes are all wrong. They think they're here for a picnic.'

'In what way, John?'

'Well, for instance, when I hold a group meeting, which is about once a fortnight, we always spend the first 20 minutes listening to everybody's complaints. They just don't settle down until they've had their moaning session ... And it's always such petty stuff.

'And they never help each other out. Like, you know, when someone is overloaded, which often happens, no one lends them a hand without being told to. No, no, they'd rather have their long lunch breaks. That's the other thing – they've got no sense of responsibility. They think they're here just for fun and games. It would never occur to any of them to suggest ways to overcome problems or remove bottlenecks in the workflow.'

'I can see why you're concerned. What have you done so far to try to swing things round a bit?'

'I'm a bit stumped, really, Joan. I don't know what I can do. Some days, the chit-chat gets so loud you can hardly hear yourself think. So they must have a bit of team spirit, I guess. But when it gets out of hand, I have to tell them to pipe down.'

'Does talking stop them from working?'

'Well, no, of course not, but I don't think it's the image we want when people pass by.'

'It does sound like you may have a problem there, John. Let's fix a time for a chat about building productive teams.'

1. Understanding teams

> We're a pack animal. From earliest times, we have used the strength of the group to overcome the weakness of the individual. And that applies as much to business as to sport.
>
> Tracey Edwards, round-the-world yachtswoman, 'UK: Teaming with talent', *Management Today* (1999)[1]

It's natural to join with others. People can achieve more together than they can achieve alone and most people also enjoy being part of a team, particularly a successful team. Think of how much satisfaction people get from participating in and contributing to a winning sports team or a successful community project team, for example, and how much time and effort they are willing to put into those teams as a result. Teams can be enjoyable and motivating.

A group of individuals or a team?

In 2009, Australia's retired Chief of the Defence Force, General Peter Cosgrove, delivered the ABC's Boyer Lectures. He had this to say about leadership: Most groups of people form into teams in order to strive for goals which are beyond the reach of an individual. The operative word of the previous sentence was strive.[2]

People come together in differing ways. As Figure 13.1 shows, a collection of individuals with no sense of identity or team spirit can be at one end of the scale and at the other end is an interdependent team whose members share common goals, a sense of purpose and an identity.

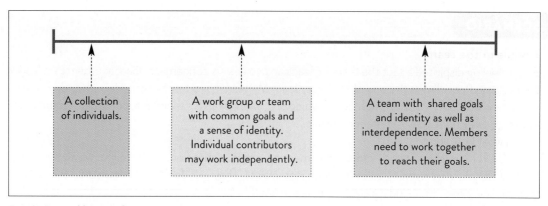

FIGURE 13.1 Me or we?

A group of people working together in the same area or for the same leader-manager isn't necessarily a team. A work group becomes a work team when its members need to pool their efforts to achieve shared goals following a shared strategy. Teams share values and a vision that all members understand and are committed to. Members are collectively responsible for the end results and blend their complementary skills to achieve them.

⊙ THE STRATEGIC PERSPECTIVE

What's the best size for a team?

Teams really began with the dawn of humankind. Stone Age families of four to seven people lived and worked together. Eventually, they congregated into larger associations of four to six families.

Effective teams today mirror those numbers. Small teams have five to seven people, large teams up to 25 people. Teams with more people don't work as well because the members have trouble communicating and developing sufficiently effective working relationships. When teams have more than 10 members, sub-teams generally form; this may be fine or not, depending on the type of task they engage in and how much coordination of team member's work is needed.

While research on optimal team size is not conclusive and high-performing teams depend on more than size, five to 12 is often cited as a good range but it all depends on the task. When a team needs to be highly motivated and well coordinated, for example, the ideal size seems to be six.

The good ...

Well-led teams can achieve cost savings and remarkable gains in innovation, productivity and responsiveness to customer needs. Some organisations that have introduced team-based operations report up to 40% gains in productivity, improved customer responsiveness, and manufacturing and design flaws cut by half.[3] Other organisations have reported massive cost savings because of recommendations by problem-solving teams and quality improvement teams. Teams can also increase efficiency in other ways and reduce costs due to fewer layers of management.

Teams are an excellent way to benefit from people's skills and knowledge. They can increase morale and and job satisfaction by providing people with more control over their jobs and the fulfilment of working collaboratively with others.

● THE STRATEGIC PERSPECTIVE

From lines to cells and back again

One well-known example of self-managed teams is Volvo, which introduced them in its car factories in Kalmar and Uddevalla in Sweden. Work became more interesting but also more costly. Eventually, Volvo closed down these experimental plants and concentrated production at Gothenburg using the traditional assembly line. Clearly, teams are not the best answer in all situations.

But in some situations teams work well. Linn Products in Glasgow, Scotland, has closed its assembly lines in favour of manufacturing cells. Each of its products is assembled and tested by hand, by a single employee.

Productivity increased (from 22.5 to 17 minutes to make a turntable, for instance) and customer responsiveness soared. Everyone in the plant can build every product, enabling manufacturing to meet customer orders on the day they come in.

Using people at the highest possible level creates wealth and value. One hundred years ago, expensive machines were the scarcest resource on the manufacturing line and people's jobs became less skilled, so it was smart to use cheap labour. But today, as Linn's executive chairperson Ivor Tiefenbrun explains: '... automation is cheap and available and skilled people are once again the scarce resource. The challenge is to do justice to the skills and imagination of your employees. We redesigned our manufacturing process so that, rather than use people at the lowest level to feed the machines, we have robots supplying people, allowing them to work at the highest possible level.'[4]

... the bad and the ugly

There are downsides to teams, too. Not everyone has the skills or disposition to participate fully and effectively in a team. And maintaining high levels of cooperation and creativity takes skill and effort on everyone's part.

It isn't easy to introduce teams into the workplace or to find people with the skills to lead and support them. Failing to address poor performance or disruptive team members and allowing groupthink or dysfunctional conflict to develop are just four threats to effective teams brought about by poor leadership.

Many organisations have rushed into creating teams for the wrong kinds of jobs or have created the wrong kinds of teams. Not all jobs and activities are best handled by teams, and teams are often introduced when they aren't really needed or when another solution, such as automation, would be more effective. Some types of teams are better suited to certain activities than others. For example, when self-managed teams are called for, but the concept seems too 'radical' for the organisation and quality improvement teams are introduced instead, management is left wondering why the expected results have not materialised.

When organisations introduce teams in isolation, as a quick fix or as a half-hearted experiment, team members are not given sufficient training and support; they generally lack clear objectives and the team can meet endlessly trying to figure out what it's supposed to do and how it's supposed to do it. Not surprisingly, poorly introduced teams usually fail to achieve the expected results.

THEORY TO PRACTICE

To team or not to team?

When are teams the best option? And when are they not needed?

When the members can produce something together that they cannot produce individually, real teams are needed. Real teams are needed when the combined abilities, experience, knowledge and skills of team members contribute in different ways and at different times to team direction-setting, innovation, leadership, problem-solving and results.

Teams are not needed when the leader really does know best and when people can work independently to achieve goals.

Ten types of teams

Teams vary in their leadership, longevity and purpose. Some teams cover several functions; others perform only one function. Some teams are permanent. Others are temporary. Some have leader-managers to guide them. Others have a team facilitator who is also a member of the team – and other teams manage themselves. The number and type of teams an organisation has depends on what the organisation does, its culture and size and the expertise of its work force.

1. Functional teams

Shannon is an accounting clerk in a large organisation. Her workstation is on the third floor, where all the finance people work. On the next floor is human resources, and on the next is sales and marketing. She only sees employees from these and other functions in the lift and at the occasional training workshop. Her work group, and the other functional work groups in her organisation, are teams only in a loose sense.

Functional teams like Shannon's carry out specific organisational functions and include members from several vertical levels of hierarchy. (See Figure 3.2 on page 74.)

2. Management teams

Don is the marketing manager in the same company Shannon works in. He leads the marketing team and is also part of the senior management team which meets monthly to review the company's performance, discuss corporate initiatives and proposals, coordinate work across the organisation and update each other on their respective function's progress against targets. This is the only time the senior management team meets and works together as a team.

3. Matrix teams

Lisa is an ergonomics engineer who works on three of the company's design teams, two based at head office and one a virtual team made up of employees from several offices. Each of these teams reports to a product manager and is responsible for either improving an existing product or developing a new product, depending on its brief. Because of her specialised knowledge, she contributes valuable advice on making the company's products safe and user-friendly. When she isn't meeting with a team, she is researching and developing designs, or consulting with other team members or outside experts.

In matrix organisations, employees are members of two or more teams, each made up of members from different functions. Members of matrix teams report to a different leader-manager for each aspect of their job (see Figure 3.7 on page 79. You can find more information on matrix organisations on page 78.)

FYI

The original team
Originally, a 'team' was two or more animals harnessed together to drag around a heavy object such as a plough.

4. Merged teams

Carolyn is the human resources manager of two recently merged banks. Her top two priorities currently are overseeing a temporary team responsible for combining the best of the two banks' policies (including the 'bring-your-own-device' policy, dress code and grooming policy, and leave policy) and working with the CEO and the other senior managers to firm up the organisation design and team composition.

Acquisitions, mergers and takeovers are common. Employees from once-competing organisations are asked to work together cooperatively for the good of the newly combined company. This presents special challenges as people mourn the loss of the old, struggle to come to terms with the new, and cope with new ways of working and a host of new people, cultures, procedures and systems. (For more information on leading merged teams, see pages 403 and 222.)

5. Mixed teams

Henri often works from a hub, or co-working site, where other 'road warriors' from his organisation regularly congregate to share ideas and meet to work on specific problems or client queries. He enjoys the freedom and flexibility of working with a range of specialists, some of whom are full-time and others part-time employees and some are contractors, with the odd casual freelancer brought in as necessary.

Full-time, part-time and casual employees, temporary employees and contractors, and off-site employees make up mixed teams like Henri's. While most of Henri's team members are off-site workers, most organisations have on-site mixed teams, too. Leading teams of various groups of workers presents special challenges. (For more on mixed teams, see page 405.)

6. Multifunctional or cross-functional teams

The three teams Lisa, the ergonomics engineer who works in the matrix organisation discussed above, belongs to are all cross-functional in that they are made up of specialists from across the organisation's functions.

Matrix teams are also multifunctional teams. Project teams and other temporary teams usually are, too. In teams like these, most of the members are from about the same hierarchical level. They may be responsible for delivering an entire product or service, from design to manufacturing, marketing, delivery and after-sales service, or they may be organised into customer account teams that handle every aspect of a customer's work. (For more information on leading teams like this, see page 415.)

7. Problem-solving and innovation teams

Junti has recently been seconded to a temporary, part-time innovation team along with six other leader-managers, each from functions whose work flows overlap. They have been tasked with devising streamlined workflows and opening communication channels between their functions. They have been asked to particularly consider the 'white space', or 'hands-off' work as well as the 'dark space' or 'hands-on' work. (See page 81 to to find out more about 'hands-off' and 'hands-on' work.)

Problem-solving and innovation teams (sometimes called task forces) are generally temporary teams who meet to solve a specific problem, often through innovation, and then disband. Quality circles were an early form of this type of team; they are still present today but usually are named differently, often with a 'corporate branding' flavour. They typically meet for a few hours a week to identify, analyse and rectify problems, particularly problems of workflows and systems.

8. Project teams and committees

Gil has been asked to head up a project team to review her organisation's IT and communications requirements. Although the team won't begin its work for two months, giving Gil time to second the members she needs and finalise the project charter, she has joined Junti's innovation team in order to get a feel for the sort of technology that may be helpful as the organisation moves towards becoming a capabilities-based organisation.

Project teams are generally temporary teams brought together to undertake a specific, usually large, assignment, such as introducing new technology throughout an organisation, launching a new product or managing the construction of a large building or residential development. Team members are generally chosen from across the organisation for their knowledge and experience in the project area and may be assigned to the project full-time or work on it along with their normal duties. Once the project is completed, the team disbands. Increasingly, members of project teams come from all over the world and work together virtually using collaborative systems technology.

Other teams, often called committees, are permanent, and undertake ongoing tasks. Their members often rotate in and out. Health and safety committees, internal communications committees and risk management committees are examples of this type of team. (For more information on leading project teams, see page 315.)

9. Self-managed teams

Clayton's team manages its own budgets, plans and schedules its work and assigns tasks to team members, and organises the resources it needs. It also improves work systems and workflows as needed and selects its own team members. Decisions are reached by consensus and team members evaluate each other's performance. Officially, leadership rotates among team members, although in practice, leadership moves between members informally, according to team needs, with the most knowledgeable or experienced team member 'stepping up'. (When the team first formed, an experienced leader-manager was appointed to help the team learn how to manage itself and coach them in the interpersonal and technical skills they needed.)

In self-managed, or self-directed, teams like this, team members take on many of the responsibilities of their former leader-managers and because of their broad responsibilities, they are usually kept informed about their company's financial affairs and how it is faring in the marketplace. Empowered teams like this can achieve impressive results. (Or fall flat, when the organisation doesn't provide the training and support they need.)

10. Virtual teams

Lisa's virtual team does everything her two other teams do. Sophisticated information technology makes it easy to communicate and work on documents together in real time. Although Lisa's virtual team is temporary, there are other, permanent, virtual teams in her organisation, too. Some of those teams are made up entirely of employees from different locations while others have members from other organisations as well, usually suppliers and joint partners – some of them in different states and even different countries. Depending on team members' locations, they sometimes meet in person as well as via videoconferences, teleconferences and computer link-ups. (For more information on leading virtual teams, see page 416.)

THE STRATEGIC PERSPECTIVE

A community of stores

Whole Foods Market is a US supermarket chain with 360 stores in North America and the UK that sells natural and organic foods. In 1980, founder and CEO John Mackey (and the co-founder of conscious capitalism) set out to create an organisation based on love instead of fear. He envisaged the company as a community of people working together to create value for other people. The basic organisational unit of Whole Foods is small teams that manage departments such as fresh produce, prepared foods and seafood. Store managers consult teams on store-level decisions and teams have a large degree of autonomy, deciding what to stock and vetoing new hires, for example. Bonuses are paid to teams, not individuals, and teams have access to comprehensive financial information, including how much people are paid.[5]

Members make teams

To be an effective team member of any type of team, people need sound communication and interpersonal skills, emotional intelligence and self-understanding as well as training and supportive leadership to work well together as a unit. The members of matrix, multifunctional, project, and self-managed teams generally need extra training in these areas to develop the team-working skills they require, as do the members of virtual teams, who often need training in the technology of their team as well. These arrangements can be costly and time-consuming but without them frustrations can mount and anticipated results can turn to smoke.

Members of merged and mixed teams often benefit from team building, while members of problem-solving and innovation teams need specialised training in problem identification and resolution and in statistical and other total quality management tools such as cause-and-effect diagrams, brainstorming and flow charting.

THE STRATEGIC PERSPECTIVE

Getting the rewards right

It can be challenging to work out how to remunerate and reward teams most effectively. Should members be paid individually or as a group? Paying people individually does little to encourage teamwork, yet paying the team as a whole can frustrate star performers. For a team to be a truly interdependent team, you need to replace individually based monitoring and reward systems with team-based monitoring and reward systems. Building a culture that applauds team performance rather than individual contributions is critical, too.

2. Fixing the goalposts

Our chief want is someone who will inspire us to be what we know we could be.

Ralph Waldo Emerson (writer), *Letters and social aims* (1884)[6]

When you think of organisations made up of exceptional teams, where high performance is a daily event, which ones spring to mind? A Formula One racing team? Or perhaps Amazon or Google, or a skilled restaurant service team, or an operating team in a hospital? People can't achieve much without the assistance, cooperation and support of others, and outstanding teams have learned to overcome obstacles that block other teams and find and fix the causes of poor performance. How do they do it?

Team purpose

Your team as a whole needs a short, clear statement of intent so that everyone understands what they are jointly working towards. A team purpose statement does this. A good example is the team purpose statement for DePuy, the Johnson & Johnson division that designs and manufactures orthopaedic implants: 'Restoring the joy of motion'.[7]

A team purpose statement like this defines the team by describing clearly why it exists. It keeps everyone moving in the same direction and shows team members how their individual efforts contribute to it. The team purpose acts as a team vision and a touchstone for decision-making and it guides members' day-to-day behaviour. It should relate to the wider context of the organisation's goals. Two other examples of team purpose statements are shown in Figure 13.2.

Involve the whole team in crafting its purpose statement. Think about displaying it somewhere visible. When this isn't possible, post it at each meeting and suggest team members use the statement as a banner screensaver.

Here are three ways to keep your organisation's vision and team purpose alive:

1. Acknowledge and reward team members who support the vision and team purpose.
2. Align your performance goals and measures with the vision and your team purpose.
3. Refer to the vision and team purpose when reaching decisions.

● THE STRATEGIC PERSPECTIVE

Three strategic team questions
Asking these three questions will keep you on track:
1. What is our team purpose?
2. What are we best capable of?
3. Is there a good fit between our team purpose and our capabilities?

Role clarification

Role clarification means making your expectations of the team and its members clear. You do this by agreeing your team purpose, individual team member's job purposes, key result areas (KRAs), measures of success (MOS), non-task goals and 'bottom-line rules' (see page 323 for more on this).

1 An assembly-line team

An assembly-line team To enhance our company's reputation in the marketplace by working cooperatively together to produce a top-quality product that meets or exceeds our measures of success, continually refining our approach to increase our efficiencies and reduce waste and costs.

2 A retail sales team

GOOD DAY

A retail sales team To organise and present our merchandise in an attractive and relaxing environment and serve our customers in a friendly, enjoyable, knowledgeable and helpful way, so that we win their repeat business and meet or exceed our key performance targets.

FIGURE 13.2 Two team purpose statements

On the task side, role clarification ensures that everyone understands precisely what is expected of them in their job and as a team member, and that they understand how everyone else in the team contributes to the team purpose. On the process side, role clarification helps the team to openly discuss and agree on the behaviours expected of all team members. You can do this through formal and informal individual and team discussions and in specially convened team-building workshops (explained below).

Measures of success

SMART measures of success were explained in relation to individual jobs on pages 112 and 327. Teams also have SMART measures of success. For example, a work team might be responsible for attaining the SMART target of 'designing, testing and implementing a streamlined workflow by the end of the next quarter'. To achieve this, it draws up a list of milestones or tasks that it needs to accomplish, each meeting the SMART criteria, and assigns these tasks, or deliverables, to individual team members. The team can measure its success by whether or not it meets its SMART targets, or outcomes, and individual team members can measure their success by whether or not they met their deliverables.

The beauty of outcome-based success measures is that team members can work anywhere, at any time, using whatever methods they want. You don't need to watch them work – just check in with team members to find out whether they're on track or whether they have run into problems and need assistance. This makes outcome-based success measures ideal for teleworkers and other off-site employees such as sales and service employees, and members of project and virtual teams. Expect to see more teams working this way as more organisations become capabilities based.

In addition to measuring whether team members meet their deliverables, you can also gauge the effectiveness of their contributions by looking at team members' abilities to 'add value' to a project or the team through their expertise, the ideas they help to generate, and the quality and timeliness of their contributions. Although subjective, these success criteria are at least clear and open.

As with individual performers, you can use measures of success to continually improve a team's performance. For example, your team might have had a spate of near misses and you are concerned that an accident is waiting to happen. To concentrate everyone's attention on health and safety, you might introduce a team goal, such as 'to reduce incidents by 70% next year'. When this is achieved, you could set a target of 'an incident-free quarter'. Once safety is back under control, you can shift the team's attention to a different improvement goal with another measure of success.

Now your team has a performance plan to build its performance. Here is a caveat to setting ambitious success measures: They should reflect what you believe is possible and what ought to happen, not what you would like to happen in your wildest dreams. They should also help achieve the organisation's vision and objectives.

Monitoring performance

With both task and process expectations agreed and understood by everyone, it's easy to monitor performance and support team members in meeting these expectations. Monitoring performance also helps you to spot any training needs and manage performance by giving you a basis to discuss and uncover the reasons for performance not meeting expectations. (Chapter 11 explains how to uncover reasons for poor performance and productivity. Page 353 explains how to monitor performance and page 447 explains how to provide feedback on performance.)

> ### ◉ IN A NUTSHELL
>
> **Australian team leaders**
> No matter how much you apply the principles of effective leadership, the individual human factor – how you choose to lead – is essential. Here is how five Australian leader-managers might describe their roles:
> * 'In this job, you have to remove the hurdles, the things that stop people from doing the good job they want to do, the things that frustrate them – the hassles. That's my job: To make people's jobs hassle-free.'

>>

- 'I think it's important to emphasise the positive. To "catch people doing something right", as they say.'
- 'I work to build a team that works well together and helps each other out. I want them to respect each other, trust each other and innovate. And I want them to have fun while they do it!'
- 'When someone makes a mistake, I treat it as a learning experience. We figure out what went wrong so it won't happen again. Then we see what else we can learn from it. After all, no one intentionally makes a mistake, right?'
- 'I work *with* my team. We work together to get the job done – solve problems, make decisions and so on. I oversee the process but, basically, the way I see it is: "We're all in this together."'

3. Getting the team task and process right

A large organisation is a collection of local communities. Individual and institutional growth are maximised when those communities are self-governing.

Mary Parker Follet (pioneer theorist in management), *Creative experience* (1924)[8]

To forge a group of diverse individuals into a team that works together to achieve a common goal isn't easy, but it is rewarding. To create an environment where team members participate in team activities, communicate openly and meaningfully with each other, work together to identify and resolve work problems and problems with the way they work together, and find ways to keep improving the ways they achieve their goals, you need to find the delicate balance between two aspects of team working: The team task and the team process.

Figure 13.3 shows that leaders and teams need to balance their efforts and attention between task and process. Too much concentration on one or the other causes a team to flounder.

◉ IN A NUTSHELL

Task and process

Task refers to the goals the team is working to achieve. Task is the *what*. Make sure the team and job purpose statements, KRAs and measures of success are crystal clear to each team member.

The way the team approaches its task is referred to as its *process*. Process is the *how* – how team members are communicating and working, individually and together, to achieve results.

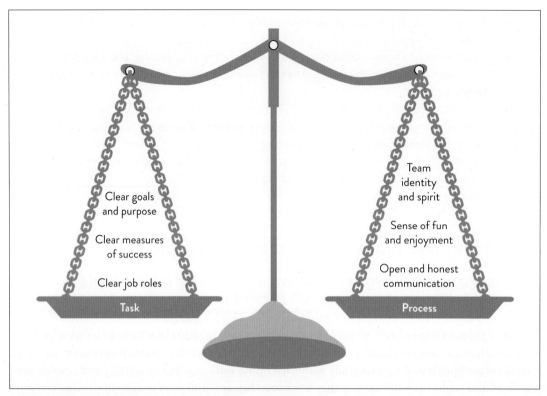

FIGURE 13.3 Task and process issues in a team

What about crises?

Should you still balance task with process when a crisis occurs? No. In times of crisis, for instance when there is a backlog of work to get through, when you're suddenly short-staffed and deadlines are looming, or the building is on fire, you almost certainly need to focus primarily on task issues – on what needs to be done. When the situation has calmed down, you can turn your attention to people and process issues to restore the balance.

When the crisis is more emotional and affects team members, such as downsizing or a PR disaster, you may need to be extra-supportive to team members to allay their concerns and accept that a small, short-term loss of productivity is inevitable.

Should you balance task with process when things are going really well? No. Now is the time to relax a bit, congratulate the team, celebrate and enjoy your success.

The balance between task and process isn't always constant or evenly split.

The task

Task is the *what* – what we do. You can increase task commitment by involving your team in planning, decision-making and other operational aspects of their work. To further boost teamwork, hold continuous improvement meetings, in which you identify and address issues and problems that prevent team members from working easily and smoothly to achieve their goals.

The process

Process is the *how* – how we go about achieving our task. Ironically, when you pay too much attention to the task and ignore the way the team works together, the task itself ends up suffering. A team's process – how people work together – has a dramatic influence on its task achievement; it is the all-important lubricant that keeps the team wheel turning.

How clearly and openly team members communicate with each other, how enjoyably and supportively they work together, and how much they trust each other, set the stage for how fruitfully they exchange ideas and information and how well they achieve their task. Staying alert to team processes like these helps you recognise and diagnose problems early and deal with them effectively.

The specific communication patterns that characterise high-performing teams are observable, quantifiable and measurable.[9] Interestingly, they are better predictors of team success than the actual content of the communications and are as significant to a team's success as individual intelligence, personality, skill and the substance of discussions combined – particularly when the communications take place outside of formal meetings.

In successful teams, members all talk to each other, not just to the team leader, and talk and listen in roughly equal amounts. When addressing the entire team, they keep their contributions short, and when speaking one-to-one, they face each other and speak and gesture with energy. Social exchanges, as opposed to task discussions, account for at least half of all communications between individual team members.

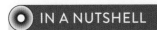

IN A NUTSHELL

What counts in team talk

Here's what characterise the communications of successful teams:

- *Energy*: Measured by the nature and number of exchanges among team members, even short 'G'days' or nods of the head. Lots of interactions make for a high energy, high performing team. (Face-to-face exchanges, followed by telephone and videoconferencing are best; email and texting contribute least to a team's success.)
- *Engagement*: Measured by who talks to whom. All members having a roughly equal number of high energy discussions with all other team members predicts a successful team.
- Exploration: Measured by how often team members speak to people outside the team and bring back ideas, information and fresh perspectives. Members of productive teams connect often with members of other teams.

Isn't it nice when science agrees with common sense? But here's something surprising: In team meetings, team members talk to each other individually about half the time and to the team as a whole the other half. So maybe short whispered exchanges between team members at meetings isn't as bad as a team's leader-manager might think it is.[10]

Guide and shape your team's communication patterns; set an example by talking to team members face-to-face (or on the phone or via video chat in virtual teams) as often as you can. Adjust the layout of the workplace so conversation between members is possible. Address these issues with your team and revisit them periodically:

- How can we measure our team's success in working together to achieve results?
- How do we want to celebrate our successes?

- How do we want to communicate with each other?
- How do we want to pass on information to each other?
- How do we want to work, together and individually?
- How often do we want to meet?
- What makes it worthwhile for each of us to be a member of this team?
- What must we each do to achieve the team goals?

Write the answers down and give a copy to each team member to guide them in their daily activities. (For more information on what goes on inside a team, its culture, norms and group dynamics, see pages 95 and 97. For information on leading multicultural teams and team members from different generations, see pages 858 and 870.)

● THEORY TO PRACTICE

A challenging team task in a volatile environment

When the British government sent a team of specialists to Haiti to oversee the reconstruction of two prisons to replace those that had been destroyed in the 2010 earthquake, they arrived not knowing what construction materials would be available (the country's cement factories were destroyed in the earthquake), whether any labour would be available or what other construction was under way that might take priority. The political-social environment was unstable and unpredictable and, on top of this, the team had to contend with Haiti's slow and unwieldy bureaucratic culture.

Working with the culture rather than trying to fight it, the team turned down the offer of a house and made its operational HQ a tent in the heart of the makeshift government camp, showing solidarity with local officials whose offices had been destroyed. They followed the local protocol of putting absolutely everything, even small requests for a meeting, formally in writing. This helped the team win trust and credibility early on and they were rewarded with temporary status as members of the Haitian police force, giving them the authority they needed to move ahead quickly with their project.

In just a few months, construction of the two prisons was under way and policies and procedures were in place to run them to international standards.

According to team member Paul Biddle, several factors helped the team succeed. They set small, realistic targets and held daily 'warts and all' debriefs to review progress, celebrate achievements and plan for the next day. To ensure team members didn't crumble under the stress of working in such a high-pressure environment, they agreed small rules such as 'no one drinks alone', male team members would shave and wear a fresh shirt each day, and the team would have at least one day off a week. They took their time off together in activities such as watching a film, driving up to the mountains and walking on the beach, which allowed people to keep an eye on each other's stress levels.[11]

Task and process roles in teams

Team members characteristically behave and communicate in predictable ways, with predictable effects, called roles. Team member's roles can be *functional* (helpful) or *dysfunctional* (unhelpful).

For example, the informal leader in your team can work with you or against you. The *clown* can be disruptive or can relieve tension. The *gatekeeper* can shut people out or make sure everyone has a say. The *devil's advocate* can pour water on good ideas or point out potential problems and how to fix them. (Page 98 explains more about team members' roles.)

Strengthen the way your team operates by helping people become aware of the roles they play and the effects these roles have on the team's task and process. Team members' skills improve when they become more sensitive to, and aware of, how they can help their team to function more effectively.

Use your mirror neurons ... and smile

Mirror neurons are located throughout the human brain. Their job is to help people detect another person's emotions and empathise with them, and to instruct them to mimic, or *mirror*, what the other person does as a way of reflecting empathy. There is, for instance, a specific subset of mirror neurons whose only job is to detect other people's smiles and laughter and prompt smiles and laughter in return.

Your behaviour and emotions create similar responses in your team members – when you feel positive, so do they; when you feel despondent and worried, so do they. Protect your managerial career by being positive and friendly, laughing and setting an easy-going tone, and build your team's cohesion, morale and productivity in the process. Now that's a win–win.[12]

Three areas of team needs

To be an effective leader-manager, you need to satisfy three distinct areas of need:

1. *Individual needs:* The need for individuals to feel satisfied with their work – developing and motivating individuals.
2. *Task needs:* The need to succeed in reaching set goals – achieving the task.
3. *Team needs:* The need for the group to work as a team – building the team.[13]

This is called functional leadership or *action-centred leadership*. As shown in Figure 13.4, ignoring any one area of need adversely affects the other areas.

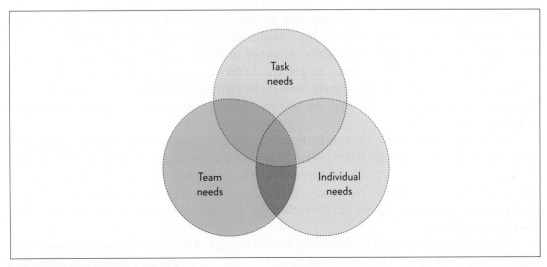

FIGURE 13.4 Overlapping needs

Jackpot leadership

Because these three areas of need overlap, it is sometimes possible to satisfy two or even all three areas of need with just one action. Training, for example, satisfies all three areas: It helps to ensure that the task is performed well; it satisfies individuals' needs to increase their skills and knowledge; and it helps provide the team with a useful member.

> **( ) ACTION!**
>
> To find out how you stack up as a functional leader, and to discover any areas you need to pay more attention to, log on to **CourseMateExpress** to complete the checklist: How are your functional leadership skills.

4. Building and maintaining your team

> You are only as good as the people around you. You should hire people that think differently to you and have different skills. If you develop a crack team then you can do anything and once you have the team, you have to provide them with clear direction and let them get on with it.
>
> Ann Sherry (CEO, Carnival Australia), in Skotnicki, 'Leaving all in her wake', *Management Today* (2014)[14]

When your team members speak about their team, do they say 'they' and 'them', or 'we' and 'us'? The former indicates they don't feel part of things; the latter is what you want to hear. Teams, like people, have learning curves. The better team members know each other, how each other works, their individual experience, knowledge, skills and traits, and how to put them to best use, the better they can perform.

The more clearly people understand their own and each other's job purpose and key result areas – their roles and goals – the better they can work together and support each other's task achievement. When they understand each other's contributions and how their work is interdependent, they and the team as a whole have a sense of accountability for the team's actions, decisions and performance, and a sense of 'us'.

Try asking job-holders to write their own job purpose statements (they may want to refer to their role description or similar for this), read them to the rest of the team and then help each other refine them. This ensures that everyone in the team understands and appreciates everyone else's role and contributions. People who do the same jobs may decide to combine their job purpose statements or to keep their own, slightly different statements to reflect their key concerns; either way is fine. (To find out how to write individual team member's job purpose statements, see page 324.)

Periodically, teams need to revisit both their main goals and the way they are going about achieving them with a view to making refinements and improvements (or getting the team back on track, as the case may be). This is generally done in a two- to three-day offsite team-building workshop led by an experienced facilitator who guides the team to examine and clarify its purpose and goals (task issues) and explore and strengthen the way team members work together to achieve them (process issues).

The shared experiences of a team-building session strengthen the ties between team members by helping them to see each other in a different light and appreciate each other's differences, similarities and contributions. The store of shared experiences helps to establish or strengthen the team's culture and translates into improved working relationships. It leads to a cohesive team – less 'they' and 'them', and more 'we' and 'us'.

◉ IN A NUTSHELL

A typical team-building meeting

On the task side, the team explores and defines its purpose and goals. Team members also explain their own job purpose, key result areas and measures of success so that everyone understands everyone else's roles, responsibilities and contributions. This helps team members take responsibility for their own work and makes them more able to assist each other, increasing the likelihood that the team achieves the desired results.

On the process side, specially designed and facilitated activities help the team explore the way members currently work together, identify areas for improvement and agree specific actions to help them work together more effectively. This may involve developing communication guidelines, learning how to give and receive feedback more effectively, and agreeing ways to obtain and share information, for example.

While team building can be conducted once every 12 or 24 months, ongoing team maintenance is also essential for teams to work effectively. Every time you or a team member assists the team to clarify or work towards its agreed purpose, or to improve the way people are working together, team maintenance occurs. Every time you make an announcement or the team celebrates achieving a goal, a major milestone or a member's birthday, team maintenance occurs. Every time team members spend some time enjoying each other's company and sharing a laugh, team maintenance occurs.

A team's daily interactions help it sustain the progress it makes during more formal team-building meetings. You can't afford to ignore team maintenance when you're leading a successful team.

Team composition

The good news is that people have different personalities and ways of working. That's good news because the most effective teams are made up of different types of people with different attributes, whose skills and working styles complement each other so that each contributes in their own special way. In fact, individual differences are essential for a team to perform effectively. The more diverse the team, the better they reach decisions, solve problems and innovate. (For more on diversity in teams, see pages 212 and 846.)

Members of strong teams understand that everyone is different and that these differences strengthen their team. They don't personalise their disagreements but communicate honestly and deal openly with different viewpoints because they're all working towards the same outcomes. they may argue as they move towards their goals, but that's because they're intent on reaching the goal – together. Apple co-founder Steve Jobs used The Beatles as an example: 'My model for business is The Beatles: They were four guys that kept each other's negative tendencies in check; they balanced each other. And the total was greater than the sum of the parts. Great things in business are never done by one person. They are done by a team of people.'[15]

That's the good.

Here's the bad: Individual differences also have the potential to create conflict. Some people are scornful of those who are different from them.

Your job is to see to it that team members make the most of their differences. Create an environment of respect for different ways of working and for the different backgrounds and experiences each member brings to the team. When you recruit, make sure you don't just replicate current team members' personality styles and ways of working. (See page 846 for information on how diversity strengthens a team and page 209 for more information on different ways of working.)

Stages of team growth

Just as people go through a life cycle from infancy through childhood, adolescence and adulthood to old age, teams also grow, develop and change. Just as an adult behaves differently from a child and has the capacity to cope with more complex tasks, members of mature teams behave differently from members of newly formed teams and are able to complete complex tasks more easily.

A team's maturity has nothing to do with how long it has been a team or the ages of its members; it relates to how effectively team members work together (process) and how well they fulfil their job purpose to achieve their team goals (task). Members of mature teams understand and contribute fully towards achieving the team's goals and work cooperatively together.

When you understand the stages of a team's growth, you can do a lot to help your team move through the growth stages to reach the mature, 'performing' stage.

A team's life cycle has five predictable stages: forming, storming, norming, performing and adjourning.[17] These stages of team development are not always distinct but often merge into each other. Although the stages are described in a linear sequence below, teams move back and forth between the stages as new members join, new challenges emerge and changes are introduced. Growing teams is a complex process.

THE STRATEGIC PERSPECTIVE

The continuum of team effectiveness

At one end of the continuum of leadership effectiveness are very successful teams. At the other end are unsuccessful teams. Funnily enough, teams tend to be on one side or the other of the continuum – there are not many middle-ground teams.

What makes the biggest difference between a successful team and an unsuccessful team? Two answers:

1. The leader.
2. How much the organisation provides the support that its teams need to be successful.[16]

Forming

Teams form when 'strangers' come together to carry out a task or an activity. They have little common understanding about the team's aims, and individual roles and responsibilities are unclear. Team members must sort out exactly what their purpose is, what their relationships to each other are, where each fits into the team's 'pecking order' and what each can contribute.

Task issues take a back seat to personal feelings: Anxiety and apprehension, and wondering what the group and its leader are really like and how to behave. People are careful, cautious and conscious of themselves and each other. They watch for clues about appropriate behaviour. Polite, impersonal discussions revolve around 'why are we here?' and getting acquainted. In a group's infancy, people's need for approval is strong and group identity is low or absent.

Newly formed teams depend on their leader for guidance and direction, so take a strong leadership role. Inform people what you expect of them, how you want team members to work together and how formally or informally you want them to behave. Give plenty of information about the team's purpose, its objectives, its customers and so on. Use the directing behaviour of situational leadership or the telling behaviour outlined in the continuum of leadership styles (explained on pages 260 and 267).

Storming

The storming phase describes the conflict and in-fighting that surface as people explore their differences in aims, values and working styles. Team members are tense as they vie to establish their 'turf' – for informal leadership and other roles. Cliques may form, power struggles may develop and your leadership may be challenged.

Productivity remains low as the team deals with the difficulties of establishing common goals, working principles and procedures. Because of the many interactions between its members, a team learns through trial and error even more than individuals do, however well trained and professional the members are. Make it safe for them to experiment and try new ways so that they can recognise their mistakes and learn from them.

Storming teams often seem to be 'stuck' in some way. This may be due to internal conflicts about what the group should do or how it should be done or to a 'crisis of energy', where team members seem to lack their earlier spark and enthusiasm and seem reluctant to 'get stuck into it'. Disillusionment and frustration with the team and its capabilities may surface.

Young teams need strong leadership that provides clear boundaries, direction and guidelines. No matter how bad the storming gets, help team members to concentrate on their goals rather than becoming distracted by relationship issues. Keep team members together and talking until they feel comfortable with each other and their goals and procedures. This can take months.

Use the situational leadership coaching style or the continuum of leadership selling style (explained on pages 265 and 260) and continue to show confidence in the team.

Norming

Sadly, some teams stay stuck in storming. Others emerge into the norming phase of adolescence. Codes of behaviour and team customs are established both formally and informally as the team resolves how it functions day to day and how it makes decisions. This is the time to ensure that appropriate team norms develop. Norms such as 'We insist on high quality', 'We put customers first', 'We listen to each other's views' and 'We turn up on time' are essential before a team can reach the next stage, performing. (You can find out more about norms on page 96.)

During the norming phase, team members settle into working rhythms, patterns and relationships. They begin making progress on the task and start to have fun with each other, providing a renewed sense of hope. Don't be alarmed if a short period of 'play' and celebration of their new-found working arrangements temporarily overrides task matters.

Team members get down to work more seriously as the norming phase progresses. They respond well to the leader and become more skilled in working with each other. Accountability is shared so that team members don't think 'That's not my problem' but 'That's our problem, how can we fix it?' Everyone's roles and responsibilities are now clear and accepted as members come to understand and appreciate each other's differences and talents.

Team members know where they stand in relation to the other members and have a clear idea of their role and the contributions they can make. Trust and openness between team members grows and commitment to the team strengthens. 'Me' gives way to 'we' and a team identity emerges towards the end of the norming phase.

Team members begin to depend less on the leader, although they continue to need your guidance and confirmation that work is progressing in the right direction. Become a facilitator and an enabler, participating in situational leadership terms and sharing in the continuum of leadership terms (explained on pages 260 and 267).

Performing

Performing teams are creative, harmonious and productive. They are clear about the task and why it is important, and members work independently or in any combination to achieve more together than they can individually, drawing on each other's unique strengths and knowing how to compensate for each other's weaknesses. Productivity is high on the task side, and satisfaction, loyalty and cohesion are high on the process side.

Performing teams achieve their goals, and continually seek ways to improve and resolve any internal disputes openly and effectively. Members gain a sense of meaning from what they're doing and achieving. Open communication, close teamwork, flexibility, innovation, resourcefulness and trust are evident. You can practically feel the team spirit. Membership of a performing team brings out the best in all its members and members expect the best of each other.

High-performing teams are a team leader's dream come true because they don't need much direction. Their high autonomy means you can become a colleague and a resource to help the team achieve its goals. Use the delegation 'hands-off' leadership style of situational leadership and the continuum of leadership styles (explained on page 260 and 267) and stand back to let the team itself set, monitor and achieve its goals.

● THEORY TO PRACTICE

Preventing team regression
A new member joining a team can dent the feelings of camaraderie and team spirit that arose as the team developed and alter the internal dynamics of the team, causing it to regress to an earlier stage. To get the team working well again, become more 'hands on' for a while. This restores the team's growth, carrying the new member along in the process.

Adjourning

Adjourning, or *mourning*, is the final stage of some teams. Temporary teams disband, worksites close down, a team or part of a team merges with another team, or the organisation makes a team redundant and contracts its work out. This leaves a hole or sense of emptiness in team members' lives, with feelings of loss and sadness and promises to get together in the future.

Some sort of official closing celebration or 'ceremony' can help a team through this difficult phase – perhaps a shared meal or an informal get-together.

● IN A NUTSHELL

The stages in team development

Table 13.1 shows the five stages of a team's development in a nutshell:

TABLE 13.1 A team's five-stage life cycle

Stage 1 Forming	
Key issues	Leader should show confidence.
Key questions	What can I offer this group?
	Who am I in this group?
	Who is in this group?
	Do I want to be in this group?
	What are our goals and objectives?
Process issues	The team depends on the leader to set ground rules.
Task issues	The team depends on the leader to provide structure and guidance.
	Team members become familiar with the team purpose, objectives and tasks.

Stage 2 Storming	
Key issues	Conflict or crisis of energy may make the group seem 'stuck'.
	The team may become disillusioned.
	Leader should show confidence.
Key questions	How are decisions to be made?
	How much power and influence do I have?
	What are the coalitions in this team?
	Who has the formal/informal power?
	Who's in charge?
Process issues	Conflict, hidden or out in the open, regarding leadership, power and authority roles may arise.
Task issues	The team works out how best to work together and individually to achieve its goals.

>>

TABLE 13.1 A team's five-stage life cycle (Continued)

Stage 3 Norming	
Key issues	Leader should ensure appropriate norms develop.
	The team may abandon the task and 'play' a while, enjoying their cohesiveness.
Key questions	How should this team operate?
	What are our policies, rules and procedures?
	What are the ways to behave in this group?
Process issues	Cohesion and team identity emerge.
	Openness and trust begin to develop.
	Ideas, information and feelings start to be shared.
	Team members strive for harmony.
Task issues	Data and information begin to flow.
	The team makes visible progress in achieving its goals and team purpose.

Stage 4 Performing	
Key issues	How can we best achieve our goals and work together?
	Leader should take a back seat and act as coach and facilitator.
Key questions	Are we getting the best results possible?
	How can I best contribute to the team's task?
	How can we improve our effectiveness and efficiency?
	What is the best way to do my job well?
Process issues	Interdependence is evident – team members can work singly, in any combination of subgroups or in the whole team.
Task issues	Team members continuously improve systems and the way they work, together and individually, and identify and solve problems.
	Team members collaborate effectively and work 'in harmony'.
	Task goals are clear to everyone.
	Let's get on with the job and do it well!
	Strong commitment to the team and its tasks is evident.

Stage 5 Adjourning	
Key issues	How do we achieve formal closure and goodbyes?
Key questions	How will I feel when I (or others) leave or when we disband?
	What are the consequences of leaving or disbanding?
Process issues	Team members feel both sadness and excitement about 'going it alone'.
	Team members feel impending loss or anxiety about what comes next.
Task issues	Final winding up ensures that achievements and learning won't be lost.

THEORY TO PRACTICE

The relationship between leadership styles and team growth

The stages of team growth model was developed around the same time as the continuum of leadership styles and situational leadership models. In each of these models, the principle is the same: As the team develops and becomes more skilled, the relationships between the members and between the members and the leader change. The leader moves from a directing style through to coaching, then participating and finally delegating.

ACTION!

To assess your team's current stage of growth and decide whether your leadership style is appropriate, log on to CourseMateExpress and complete the checklist: How mature is your team?

IN A NUTSHELL

Ten tips to help teams grow and keep growing

Here are ten ways to help teams grow into high-performers and to lift a team out of a slump:

1. *Balance team membership* with a range of backgrounds, experience, personalities and skills, and make the most of its diversity.
2. *Invite participation* in decisions that affect the team; for example, involve your team in deciding what materials and equipment it needs and the best way to complete a job.
3. *Communicate,* for example, hold monthly update meetings about the organisation's activities and successes, customers and new initiatives to ensure a steady flow of information.
4. *Keep innovating and improving team procedures.* People get bored when they're stuck in ruts and frustrated when the hassles, bottlenecks and extra, unnecessary steps that make their jobs harder aren't fixed.
5. *Publicise the team's successes.* Make sure the rest of the organisation hears about how well your team is doing.
6. *Revisit the team purpose and processes frequently.* The team purpose may change in the light of changing organisational priorities; even when it doesn't change, the review serves as a useful reminder. Set new goals to challenge the team so that members don't become stale, and periodically review and update the team's process guidelines.
7. *Reward extra effort.* When team members go 'beyond the call of duty' and put in extra time and effort or achieve something special, make sure they benefit in some special way.
8. *Rotate assignments.* When there's a chance that people's tasks could become monotonous once mastered, cross-train team members and rotate tasks to keep interest and morale high.
9. *Support the team.* Clearly define the team's goals and other expectations. Recognise and celebrate team success. Make sure people have ways to evaluate the team's progress in both its task achievement and the way they're working together.
10. *Train team members.* Involve the team in deciding their own training needs and how best to train new team members.

Changes in team membership

Team members leaving or new members joining can disrupt a team's productivity, which often falls as members adjust their relationships and roles. Now is the time to put extra effort into rebuilding your team. Use your understanding of the team life cycle and of group dynamics to help your team remain productive.

Departing members

Each time someone leaves, a kind of 'grieving process' and a sense of impending loss occurs, and the team often takes a step backwards as it attempts to regain its sense of self and former efficiency levels. As soon as you know that a team member is leaving, bring the team together to discuss the departure and the reasons for it. Members may be proud of a teammate's promotion, sad about the loss or anxious about an increased workload. Be open and willing to listen and provide the support the team needs to rebuild itself.

Examine how the departure might affect each team member's productivity and the productivity of the team as a whole and how to lessen the negative effects of the departure. Discuss what projects or tasks might be at risk and how to keep the team's output on track. Talk about when and how the team member can be replaced and how to induct the new member into the team.

New team members

Each time a member joins a team, modified versions of forming, storming and norming begin all over again. Loyalties and alliances may shift as the new member settles in and learns the routines and rhythms of the team, which may be interrupted, at least temporarily. Group norms and morale may be threatened or changed. Dynamics often change irrevocably (Chapter 4 examines group dynamics and norms).

As the team moves forward into norming, allow it to explore its new identity. Ensure the goals remain clear and that new team members have plenty of feedback on their performance and how they're fitting in. As the team moves into performing, step back into your former role of support (page 833 explains more about how to induct new team members).

Temporary members

Casual and temporary workers and contract workers often join teams to help out with the day-to-day work or to add their specialist expertise. They need guidance, too.

They need to be engaged to make the most of their potential value and feel that they are part of the host organisation. This often means giving them a shortened version of the same induction and assimilation process that permanent employees receive. Your goal is to integrate them into the workplace and the team, so discuss the organisation's values, vision and mission and the team's purpose. Make their role clear, too; discuss the value you expect them to add to the team – their own job purpose – and how they'll know they've succeeded – their key result areas and measures of success.

Provide any supplies temporary team members need such as hardware, software and network access, and provide any other tools, equipment or background information they need to succeed. Make sure the permanent team members understand the contribution the temporary members are there to make and encourage them to welcome them and treat them as a valued part of the organisation. While they're with you, include temporary team members in corporate communications, newsletters, company events and so on so they feel part of the team.

5. Supporting your team

The most successful leader in business ... is the man who gives his subordinates only general guidelines and instils confidence in them and helps them do good work.

Akio Morita (co-founder, Sony Corp), *Made in Japan* (1986)[18]

Even the most skilled, motivated and engaged team members can't keep up peak performance and productivity when their leader fails to support them, whether as individuals or the team as a whole.

◉ IN A NUTSHELL

Coach your team to win

You can support your team members every day in countless ways:

- building and maintaining your team
- carrying out your various managerial roles
- championing your team (especially important for teams whose work the rest of the organisation doesn't fully understand and off-site teams)
- coaching and training (see Chapter 27)
- helping the team understand and deal with bad news (see Chapter 22)
- instilling effective team processes
- obtaining the resources the team needs, such as providing assistance from experts and temporary help, funding, information, materials, space, time, and tools and equipment (see chapters 11 and 17)
- providing a clear vision and goals (see chapters 2 and 11)
- providing feedback (see Chapter 15) and development opportunities (see chapters 12 and 25).

Your managerial roles

Managers draw on a number of personas, called *managerial roles*, as they carry out their duties. These managerial roles draw heavily on a leader-manager's personal skills and are a good way of describing and understanding how they spend their time and support their teams. The amount of emphasis you give to each role depends, of course, on your organisation and your job duties.

Managers play 10 roles that fall into three groups. Three *interpersonal roles* arise from your formal authority and involve leadership, communication and official management duties. These interpersonal roles lead to three types of *informational roles* that serve to keep people informed on matters that affect them. These in turn lead to four *decisional roles* that call for you to exercise judgement in dealing with problems, allocating resources and dealing with others.[19]

These roles were identified in the early 1970s, long before computers became commonplace and certainly long before the explosion of information availability. Only a couple of decades ago, managers were disseminators of information; now, in the 'Age of Google', managers' informational roles include helping people make sense of all the information swirling around.

● IN A NUTSHELL

Managerial roles

Table 13.2 sums up the three groups of roles that managers fulfil.

TABLE 13.2 **The 10 managerial roles divide into three groups**

Group 1 Interpersonal roles	
Figurehead role	Acting in an official capacity (e.g. signing documents).
Leader role	Leading effectively (see Chapter 9).
Liaison role	Communicating inside and outside the organisation.

Group 2 Informational roles	
Monitor role	Collecting information in order to remain 'in the picture' and detect changes or problems.
Disseminator role	Distributing information from both internal and external sources to more senior management, employees and colleagues.
Spokesperson role	Representing the organisation to external people and groups; representing employees to management, and vice versa.

Group 3 Decisional roles	
Entrepreneur role	Initiating changes and improvements, discovering problems, innovating solutions.
Disturbance-handler role	Dealing with conflict, grievances and unexpected problems that arise, even with the most careful planning.
Resource-allocator role	Deciding who does what, when and with which resources; scheduling time, tasks, materials and resources.
Negotiator role	Making agreements with groups or individuals, inside and outside the organisation.

Build your team's emotional intelligence

Emotional intelligence (EI) unlocks effective working relationships, creativity and innovation. The ability to be aware of and take into account the emotions of team members, the mood of the team itself, and the mood of other groups and individuals outside the team that the team interacts with is not due simply to the sum of the team members' emotional intelligence, but their emotional intelligence as a collective. (See page 194 to find out more about EI.)

There are three critical ingredients of a team's emotional intelligence, each built on the one preceding it:[20]

1. *Trust*: Recognising team members' care and concern for each other and faith in each other's honesty and ability to do what they commit to. Give team members time to build bonds and establish areas of commonality, and make expectations and goals realistic.

2. *Shared identity*: Understanding that each member needs the team and the team needs each member to accomplish its collective task; and that, together, they are special and create something special. Ensure everyone in the team understands how they and the others contribute.

3. *Confidence*: Knowing that not only can team members achieve the task but also they can achieve it better together than they can separately.

● THE STRATEGIC PERSPECTIVE

How trust develops

Trust develops in three stages:

1. *Deterrence-based trust*: At first, team members do things because they fear punishment if they don't do them.
2. *Knowledge-based trust*: This develops when team members know each other well enough to predict each other's behaviour with confidence.
3. *Identification-based trust*: Trust built on empathy and shared values emerges as members begin to identify with the team and with each other.[21]

This shows how important a team's process is to building trust.

Here are some specific actions you can take to develop your team's emotional intelligence:

*   Don't let factions develop.
*   Don't let people drive through a proposal – see that the team reaches genuine consensus.
*   Encourage members to speak out when they disagree with something relating to team goals and decisions.
*   Find shorthand ways of expressing the team's emotions and fun ways to relieve stress.
*   Ensure that members support a course of action once the team has agreed to it.
*   Make the team feel like winners. For example, acknowledge success and the importance of the team's purpose, by noting how the team members have successfully solved similar problems in the past and by keeping their attention on matters they can control.
*   Provide a clear team purpose.
*   Question any decisions that are made quickly.
*   Respect everyone's contributions.

Teams in crisis

Customers' security is compromised, your organisation is going through a financial crisis, layoffs, lawsuits, mergers or a PR crisis, rumours about downsizing abound … Whatever the cause, you're sure to find yourself leading a team through stormy waters sooner or later and helping members stay afloat.

When the going gets tough, your team looks to you more than ever. Now is not the time to be hands-off.

First, get your what, where, who, why and how facts straight. Find out as much as you can about how the organisation plans to deal with the difficulties, how long before life is expected to return to normal and what you and your team members should say if the media approaches them (the answer is probably 'No comment').

Put yourself in your team's shoes and think about what questions and concerns will be uppermost in their minds and how you can best respond. Think also about their unasked questions and how to best address them. Think through what you and your team can do to help the organisation's image in relation to its stakeholders and what you and your team can do to stay productive.

When you can, alert your team of the storm in advance, preferably in person. But should you become aware of an imminent storm during holiday periods or late Friday night, gather your facts and send a group email or phone your team members individually. Now is a good time to advise them how to respond to any media queries and, crucially, to warn everyone to say nothing on social media about the situation.

When you're leading a virtual or dispersed team (one with teleworkers and/or off-site workers, for example) establish a time and place where you can all meet (somewhere private) even if only virtually. That personal touch can be ultra-important when the situation is dire. After that, you can hold teleconference or videoconference updates and meet again personally when there is sensitive or significant information to impart.

Perhaps the storm is distant and there is just conjecture so far. Your goal is to prevent the rumour mill magnifying the turbulence and draining productivity. Meet with your team and tell them the facts as you know them, when you expect an official announcement or when you will update them again. Assure your team that you will keep them fully in the picture as best you can. Request they refrain from speculating amongst themselves (although they will anyway) and ask them to come to you with any questions or concerns.

◉ THE STRATEGIC PERSPECTIVE

Crisis or challenge?

Organisations are born and grow. Management systems are introduced to guide them. Crisis and renewal follow in cycles, with companies inventing new ways of operating to respond to the unexpected calamities. This clears dead wood and prevents bushfires. It's natural, normal and healthy, even though it may look like a catastrophe at the time. [22]

Why is it, then, that people tend to see such surprises and crises as signs of poor planning and clumsy leadership?

Be a strong leader and tell the truth

While senior management is focused mostly on customers, the public and other stakeholders, your job is to make sure your team doesn't lose faith in the organisation – or themselves. A crisis is tough on your staff, too, and some may even want to abandon ship or turn against your organisation because they've lost faith in it. Be resilient yourself and help your team be resilient. You can do a lot to allay their fears by being a strong leader, looking after task, team and individual needs (explained on page 383), and giving them faith that you can all come out of this together. People are counting on your cool, calm, confident and consistent leadership.

Be honest, though. Don't spin or even worse, lie; the truth eventually comes out and your team will never trust you again. Don't withdraw either, because saying nothing feeds the rumour mill and has a terrible effect on your team. Get out and about, communicate openly and honestly, and do as much as you can to reduce speculation and fear. Even when you can't share all the details, give as much information as you can, as quickly as you can.

Be aware of the silent messages you're sending out too – huddling with your manager or your peers, closing the door to your office for a phone call … This adds to the tension and speculation and creates feelings of insecurity, destroying productivity and fostering uneasy and negative team dynamics. You want to create stability.

When you're not sure what is okay to share, ask your boss or discuss with your colleagues what they're sharing. (You don't want to be the one to spill the beans but you don't want to withhold information unnecessarily.) When you don't know an answer to a question or you can't share the information at the moment, say so and promise to fill people in as soon as you can.

Depending on the severity of the crisis and how much team members are affected, you may need daily update meetings, perhaps a 'team huddle' each morning; when your team is dispersed or virtual, try a daily teleconference or videoconference update. Use this time to let your team members ask you questions, too. Keep your team aligned to the organisation's vision and values and your team purpose (see 'The importance of values in a crisis', on page 52). Listen to their concerns, feelings and suggestions and respond as honestly as you can.

Discuss with your team how to and what to communicate with your external suppliers or customers; they need reassurance. Your organisation's senior managers or crisis manager will guide you, as will your organisation's values, vision and mission. This may add to everyone's work, so help your team stay organised and set priorities appropriately.

Stay productive

Don't forget the task. People still need clarity on roles and responsibilities, which may need to be adjusted during the storm. Set a goal towards winning through the adversity, discuss how best to keep productivity on track and agree on a 'storm plan' to get you through. Staying organised and productive also helps your team feel in control and helps assure them you'll weather the storm together.

Stay productive yourself; dropping the ball signals to the team that it's okay for them to drop the ball, too. Make a 'To do' list of high priority items and work through them. Budget for the extra time you're spending on communication with your team in your high-priority list.

Look after yourself. Plan your exercise and go for a walk at lunchtime and get some fresh air and thinking time; this is often when good ideas and breakthrough insights hit, so make that a high priority. Look after yourself in other ways. Your own stress levels are likely to rise; and remember – your team is looking to you for guidance and take their signals from you. Remember the chimps (see the Strategic perspective: Ape leadership on page 279).

When the stormy waters have settled, look for the learnings and discuss them with your team.

IN A NUTSHELL

When the crisis is your team's making

What do you do when your team accidentally creates a crisis? It can happen, no matter how careful you and your team members are. Here's what you do:
- Keep calm. Get the facts.
- Ask the hard questions. Listen to the answers.
- Identify and evaluate the options.
- Decide what to do.

ACTION!

To find out how you measure up, log on to ⨏CourseMateExpress and complete the checklist, How well do you support your team?

CourseMateExpress

Go to http://login.cengagebrain.com to access CourseMate Express, your online study tool for *Management Theory & Practice*. CourseMate Express brings chapter concepts to life with interactive learning, and study and exam preparation tools:

- Test your skills in different aspects of management with interactive self-tests and simulations.
- Watch videos that show how real managers operate in real businesses.
- Test your understanding of the changing world of management by taking the revision quiz.

QUICK REVIEW

1. What characterises a true team?
2. List and define the elements of a performance plan. How can you use it to build a team's performance?
3. What is the difference between task and process? Is one more important than the other?
4. Explain the developmental stages of a team and the way team leadership needs to change as the team develops.
5. What is the difference between team building and team maintenance? What are some ways you can maintain and support a team?
6. List your top three priorities as a leader-manager when your team is going through a crisis.

BUILD YOUR SKILLS

1. What was the most enjoyable team you have ever been a part of? Describe the team's characteristics. What goals did it set out to accomplish? Were they quantifiable, time-framed, visible, worthwhile, challenging and shared by the whole team? How well were the goals achieved? How did members work together? What were the task and process roles of each team member? What sort of task and process feedback was available?
2. Discuss the types of teams you might find yourself leading.
3. Referring to Chapter 4 if you need to, explain how poor team dynamics and processes could cause a team to fail at its task.
4. Give an example of when you have worked collaboratively with others in a team situation and state at least six specific skills you used.
5. Describe the four personality types needed in any team and discuss the results of an imbalance among team members. Refer to page 212 if you need to.
6. The stages of team growth model was developed in the 1960s, when white, male Anglo-Europeans made up the bulk of organisations. Do you think the model applies to today's diverse teams? Would a team comprised of female and Asian members, for example, come together to undertake a project and storm away until a pecking order and team 'rules' were normed? What about a team of knowledge workers?
7. When a new team member is highly skilled at his or her job, would you expect any change to the way the team functions? Why or why not?
8. Referring to the opening scenario in this chapter, how do you analyse John's leadership? What would you advise John to do to build the morale and productivity of his work team?

WORKPLACE ACTIVITIES

1. Which type of team is your own work team? Does it have a clear performance plan? Describe the team purpose and its process, or the way in which team members work together. What stage of development would you say the team has reached? What is your evidence for this?

2. Refer to the description of the four personality types needed in any team on page 212. Identify the people in your work team according to these four groupings. How do they contribute to the team's effective functioning? What would the team be like without them? Are any of the four types missing? If so, what is the effect of this? What could you do to better balance your team's composition?

3. Observe your work team and list the task behaviours you notice. Then list the process and team maintenance behaviours. What behaviours most aid task achievement? In what ways did the task succeed or suffer because certain task or process behaviours were or were not used?

4. List some of the ways in which you support your work team, including individual, task and team support.

5. Analyse your level of team leadership skills and write a plan to increase your effectiveness as a team leader.

CASE STUDY 13.1

TED'S TRAUMA

Ted Richardson heads up a team of 14 software engineers who work on as many as five design projects at any one time. The team is highly skilled and experienced and its members work in various subgroupings and alone, depending on the task at hand. They have been together for 26 months and their team spirit is generally high.

Jim Johnson, one of the longer-serving members of the group, was an especially good employee. In fact, Ted recommended him to lead another major project and his recommendation was accepted. Although everyone was sorry to see Jim leave, they were happy about his promotion.

Ted is still angry as he relates the following story to his family at dinner:

'When Jim left, we hired a new employee named Neem Verma. After the initial "getting-to-know-you" phase, things seemed to be settling back to normal, if still a bit tense. This is Neem's first design job, so she's a bit green but smart as a whip. We've fallen a bit behind our schedules, with Jim leaving and bringing Neem up to speed and so on, and this week we missed an important milestone. Accusations have been flying and the team seems to be blaming Neem, although a couple of the women came to her defence. So a few of the blokes accused the women of sticking together and not putting the blame where it lay.

'I called an impromptu team meeting and tried to re-focus everyone on our projects. We had a quick go-round to hear where we were up to and how soon everyone thought they'd be back on track. That worked to some extent, but I could see they were still upset. No one likes missing deadlines.

'So amidst a bit of grumbling, everyone went back to work, but afterwards, a few of them told me that they couldn't work under such tension and would be "up and off" if I didn't do something. All this disruption because I recommended one of our most skilled team members for a promotion.'

Ted lapses into silence, wondering what his best course of action would be. How could things have gone so wrong so suddenly?

Questions

1. What do you think is happening in Ted's team? Is the trouble Neem's fault?
2. What should Ted have done when Neem first joined the team?
3. What specific steps can Ted take to help the team through this crisis?
4. Ted may be tempted not to recommend any other team members for other projects. Would that be a mistake? Why or why not?

CASE STUDY 13.2

A CRISIS IN PRIDE

Black Saturday, 7 February 2009: Fuelled by extreme weather, a series of bushfires swept through country Victoria, levelling hundreds of homes, nearly destroying several communities and killing 143 people. It was Victoria's highest-ever loss of life due to bushfires. The Country Fire Authority (CFA) faced a Royal Commission and a class action for failing to issue adequate warnings about the fire.

CFA employees and volunteers alike were in shock, many just 'going through the motions'. Hardest hit were head office staff, who had lost all confidence. At least the field brigades could see they were valued in their local communities, which buffered their spirits somewhat.

'The effects of our performance in that disaster left us in some crisis as an organisation,' said Mike Bourke, who had been brought in as CEO seven months after the fires to turn the still-struggling organisation around. 'People were shocked, fatigued, stressed, demoralised and many felt totally gutted.'

In the interim, the board had stepped in to fill the leadership gaps and support the besieged organisation. It managed the welfare program for its 60 000 people, 97.5% of whom were volunteers. It communicated with various stakeholders, set up a fires' board sub-committee to provide information to the Royal Commission, and began restructuring the CFA.

When Bourke took up his position, he set about strengthening the CFA's communication capabilities so that it could communicate more openly and effectively with the media, its own members and the public about its initiatives. Perhaps most difficult of all was admitting that, however hard their people had worked, the CFA had made mistakes on the day. This management of the crisis, under Bourke's leadership, made it possible for the organisation finally to begin its recovery.

The other significant milestone was the Royal Commission's report. It was constructive and resources were made available to implement its recommendations, boosting the organisation's faith in its future.

Although the effects of Black Saturday are still being felt by many of the people affected, the CFA has emerged with a sense of pride and a clear purpose – to work together with communities to keep Victorians safe from fire and other emergencies – as well as a strategy to achieve it. The CFA's organisational change program targets three areas: Prevention and preparedness, response and recovery, and building a modern and sustainable organisation. Bourke considers the CFA now to be a stronger and better-managed organisation that is developing its leaders and supporting its volunteers better than it did in the past.

Lessons learned from the crisis included highlighting the need for a strong business continuity plan, the need to invest time in building good relationships with key stakeholders, the mistake of being inwardly focused during a crisis, and the need to go out quickly and often to the community brigades that had dealt with the brunt of the fires. In addition, holding their own internal independent review of their performance on Black Saturday would have helped the organisation implement changes while still waiting for the Royal Commission's report. [23]

Questions

1. List the factors you consider to have been pivotal in turning the CFA around and explain the significance of each.
2. Discuss the motivation levels and sense of self-worth of employees and volunteers before Black Saturday and in its aftermath.
3. How can acting on the lessons learned help the organisation in a future similar circumstance?

LEADING TODAY'S TEAMS

The astounding advances in information and communications technology, combined with globalisation, mean that the types of teams discussed in this chapter are springing up everywhere. The new work patterns reviewed in Chapter 1 give rise to mixed teams of casual, contract, full-time, off-site, part-time and temporary employees.

Acquisitions, mergers and restructuring give rise to combined teams made up of people from different work cultures who are used to different work practices and who may even have once been competitors. Business complexity calls for capabilities-based organisations and permanent and temporary project teams whose members are highly specialised and often scattered across the world. When teams are virtual or partially virtual and their members speak different languages and come from different cultures, never mind different time zones, complications magnify.

You can find actual project teams, matrix project teams, mixed project teams and virtual project teams. In fact, any of these teams can be permanent or temporary, and virtual, actual or a mixture of virtual and actual.

Teams like these present special challenges. They need different types of leadership and cultural and emotional intelligence in team leaders and members alike. They call for different types of organisational policies and procedures, different ways of communicating, different ways of building trust and working relationships, and different ways of engaging, motivating and managing their members. This can test both leader-managers and team members when they have been used to sharing a workspace and seeing each other every day.

1. Do you know how to support the productivity of merged teams and teams made up of a variety of team members such as casual and contractor workers, part-timers and full-timers, knowledge workers and off-site team members?
2. Do you know how to support the performance of project teams and virtual teams whose members you may seldom or never see face to face?
3. Do you know how to use technology to overcome distance between team members?

This chapter explains how to develop and lead a non-traditional team so that its members perform well, even when they're scattered across the city, the country or the globe.

The Irish connection

Jake is sitting at his desk preparing for a web meeting with his design team, most of whom are in various locations around the world, when Nella, one of his few office-based team members, pops her head around his door: 'Got a minute?' Nella has just returned from Ireland, where she has been liaising with some of their key suppliers. At the same time, she took the opportunity to meet Rory, one of her design team counterparts, 'in the flesh'.

'Oh! Welcome back, good to see you,' says Jake. 'It sounds like you had a successful trip. How's the jet lag?'

'Not bad, thanks – I slept a lot over the weekend, though. Kept dreaming about surfing a sea of Guinness and riding a wave into an Irish pub! Anyway, we're squared away with the suppliers. They all know exactly what we need and are confident they can supply on time. But what I really want to tell you is what Rory said. I nearly fell over!'

Jake widens his eyes expectantly. 'He told me I actually seem quite nice, much nicer than he thought I'd be. When I asked what he meant, he said he'd formed the impression that I was quite blunt and rude. It seems my emails are a bit "business-like" and "to the point". I explained that my typing skills aren't all that flash and that's why I keep my emails short. Fancy that, eh?'

'Well, at least you know for next time to tell people up-front that your skills don't lie in keyboarding but in surfboarding and design. Are you all set for the conference? We're on in 10 minutes. There's one thing I want to bring you up to speed with before we start ...'

1. Developing productive merged and mixed teams

> From a company's point of view, the cost of having someone work partially or wholly at home is tiny compared with the cost of providing them with a desk.
>
> Jakob Nielsen (IT usability expert), in Rigby, 'Homing in', *Management Today* (2005)[1]

You may already have been part of and even led a merged or mixed team; if you haven't, that's likely to happen soon. You probably know people who work from home some or all of the time. Maybe casual employees, contractors or volunteers help out your work team during busy periods. Perhaps your organisation was taken over by or merged with another, or your organisation downsized and restructured and you found yourself working with a new set of colleagues and survivors. That is the future and it has arrived.

As Figure 14.1 shows, managing any team, traditional or non-traditional, requires similar actions. However, each type of non-traditional team also poses its own leadership challenges and requires additional skills, over and above the challenges and skills needed for leading and managing traditional teams.

Merged teams

Mergers are common and organisations regularly restructure, so you may well find yourself leading a newly combined team. When you do, you have a lot of 'baggage' to deal with.

Not surprisingly, members of newly merged teams feel uncertain, uncomfortable and often suspicious and fearful for their future. When new members join an existing team in its own territory, the 'home team' may see the newcomers as interlopers and seek to protect their 'turf'. The newcomers or those taken over may grieve for the loss of their old team or organisation and resent those they perceive to hold the power.

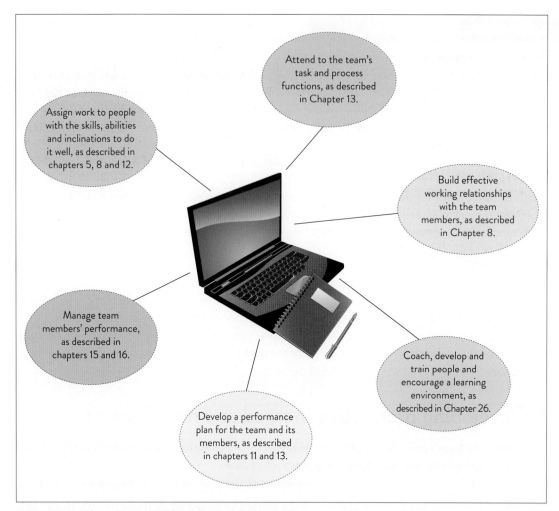

Attend to the team's task and process functions, as described in Chapter 13.

Assign work to people with the skills, abilities and inclinations to do it well, as described in chapters 5, 8 and 12.

Build effective working relationships with the team members, as described in Chapter 8.

Manage team members' performance, as described in chapters 15 and 16.

Coach, develop and train people and encourage a learning environment, as described in Chapter 26.

Develop a performance plan for the team and its members, as described in chapters 11 and 13.

FIGURE 14.1 Managing traditional and non-traditional teams

When the merged team results from a merger or an acquisition, one of your first duties is to align the members towards the new organisation's values and vision (see page 51). Because the members of the merged team come from different cultures (see page 93) and work in different ways, plan to put in a lot of effort to gain agreement on team processes (see page 381), establish a team purpose and shared goals (see page 376), and build a culture that works towards achieving them. Another priority is developing team norms quickly, so that the new team can leave storming behind and progress as quickly as possible to the performing stage (see page 386). The sooner the team is comfortable with its identity and goals, the sooner everyone can get down to business.

Leaders of merged teams have three options when the team comes together: Make one culture dominate the other to obliterate it. Merge the cultures, or create an entirely new culture. Whichever you choose, establish the new culture as quickly as you can. Find ways to bring the merged members together. For example, you could launch short-term projects and ask one or two members from each of the two merged teams to get together and examine how each team met internal or external customer expectations and combine the processes to create a new and better one.

Communication is essential. Keep the lines open between employees and yourself and act as an information channel from the organisation as a whole. The more you communicate, the more you defuse the rumour mill. Listen as well as talk, and deal with issues quickly. Answer people's questions as fully as you can. Before they start to worry about their customers or how their databases will be combined, they're wondering how they, personally, are affected. How will their jobs change? Do they have to learn new procedures or processes, or how to use new equipment? The longer you take to answer these questions, the more quickly you can expect productivity to plummet. (Chapter 22 explains how to introduce and promote change and the importance of answering questions.)

THEORY TO PRACTICE

Quirky St George meets corporate Westpac

Merging these two very different banks with very different cultures – one of the largest mergers in Australian history – was no easy task. Maintaining staff engagement during the eight months between the announcement, the shareholder vote and the actual merger was an 'Olympics of communication' that included a dedicated intranet page to allow employees to ask the merger committee questions and fortnightly 'pulse check surveys' via emails with 700 randomly selected staff to help sense the mood and effectively target communications.

To fulfil the mission of being Australia's leading financial services organisation, a multibrand strategy was pursued and the two different brands and cultures were retained. Employee engagement actually rose 2% during the merger and voluntary resignation rates fell to below 9%, 3% lower than before the merger was announced.[2]

THE STRATEGIC PERSPECTIVE

Culture counts

Mergers and acquisitions (M&As) are a temptingly fast way to add products and customers. (The other way is organic, or do-it-yourself, growth, generally through innovation in products and marketing.) Sadly, most M&As fail to add shareholder value and most perform well below their industry average. Unfocused leadership, petty politicking, poor communication and the loss of valuable employees are the more likely outcomes. The outcome is similar for internal reorganisations resulting in merged teams: Too often, the expected productivity improvements fail to materialise.

Many researchers believe that a large part of the reason that most mergers fail to achieve their anticipated value is that their people-related aspects in two spheres are not mastered: Integrating different corporate and departmental cultures and maintaining and leveraging customer–supplier relationships. Both are notoriously difficult, yet the strategy for mastering both is the same: *Communicate*. Communicate your commitment to your employees, customers and suppliers and make sure they know you haven't abandoned them so that they don't abandon you. And keep the communication channels open.

Mixed teams

The standard model of work has disappeared – only 7% of employees work the traditional 'nine to five' and work days have become working lives.[3] Today's teams are made up of a variety of groups of employees, including casual, contract, full-time, part-time and temporary employees, knowledge workers, telecommuters and volunteers. Their members are also from a variety of backgrounds, from up to four generations, and of varying abilities and educational and expertise levels.

Each of these groups of employees has different expectations of their leader and of their work and are motivated and engaged by different factors. Whatever their differing expectations, however, they probably all want to feel they are making a worthwhile contribution to the work of the team and the organisation. Your team purpose and a sound performance plan for the team and its members (job purpose, key result areas and measures of success, described on page 377) are your best tools for ensuring that each team member feels wanted and needed and knows what to do. Use the relevant elements of your organisation's values and vision and employer brand to engage them.

When many members of a mixed team don't see each other every day, it can be hard for them to feel like a team and develop the ties that create high performance. To overcome this, create opportunities for get-togethers, both social and work-related. Encourage members to communicate with each other and share information, ideas and 'tricks of the trade'. Invite everyone to team meetings and include everyone in team celebrations. Building relationships and creating bonds between team members strengthens their commitment to their team and their desire to perform.

THEORY TO PRACTICE

Different yet similar
Most teams need people who have different views and backgrounds for the creativity, expertise, innovation and insight they can provide. Yet collaboration is easier when team members perceive themselves as being alike. Therefore, stress similarities between your diverse team members, not differences.

Casuals, contractors and part-time team members

These people are destined to make up an ever-growing part of your work team. Avoid the trap of thinking that these employees aren't fully committed to the team or their jobs – they want to be and can be when you encourage it – and you need them in the current labour shortage.

To bring out their best, communicate often to keep them 'in the loop' on both task and process matters, and see that casuals and part-time employees have a chance to build working relationships across the rest of the organisation, as well as with their team. This ultimately increases the value they can add to your team. Manage their performance by results, not time spent.

The team takes its cues from you, so set the example of including everyone in the team's activities and treating everyone as a valuable and valued contributor. Include casual and part-time employees and long-term and regular contractors in team meetings and social activities. Demonstrate that all employees are necessary to achieve the outcome – people may have different roles and different working hours, but they each contribute.

Make sure these employees (and any others who are not on site regularly) know where to find any information and supplies they need. They also need to understand the workflow through the team and their own and their teammates' contributions to the team's work. This helps them prioritise because, for example, they know which of their tasks would hold up others if they didn't complete them on time.

 FYI

Contract workers' parental rights
Long-term casual employees and casual employees whose jobs are ongoing and who care for children under school age are entitled to make formal requests for flexible working arrangements.

Contractors, sometimes referred to as consultants and freelancers, generally operate their own business and contract to perform work without having the legal status of an employee.[4] They may contract only to your organisation or to several. Think of them as specialist service providers, give them goals and measures of success to work to, and establish a good working relationship with them, even when it is to be a short one. Your team and your organisation benefit from the goodwill this generates.

Since contractors probably have wide experience that includes many organisations and ways of approaching problems and work, ask for their opinions and listen to what they have to say. When their assignment is complete, debrief them. Find out what they enjoyed about working with your team and what changes, if any, they would make to improve the workflow and procedures. When they are particularly skilled and fit into your team well, you may want to find out whether they would be willing to work with you in the future.

IN A NUTSHELL

Bringing temps on board

Due to seasonal working requirements and the peaks and troughs in demand in some businesses, such as hospitality, many teams have migrating membership, with members joining and leaving according to the needs of the team.

When bringing casual and contract workers on board, review your team purpose and how their duties contribute to it, and explain what their own measures of success are. Make them feel welcome and help them settle in. Towards the middle or end of their first week, catch up to find out how they're going and whether they have special skills or talents you're not using and should be. When they need to improve aspects of their work, that is the time to explain what you expect.

Knowledge workers

Knowledge-intensive companies are the fastest growing and most successful in the world, so get used to leading teams of knowledge workers – they are destined to become the backbone of the Australian economy. In fact, these highly skilled and specialised workers already comprise nearly 40% of the workforce.[5] (Chapter 1 explains why.)

When you're leading knowledge workers, you're leading people at least as gifted as you are and whose primary tool of trade is deep specialist knowledge. They're generally engaged in complex tasks with high levels of uncertainty and value chains that extend beyond the team and even beyond the organisation. They're resourceful and have a large tacit knowledge base and good connections.

Knowledge workers tend to feel more 'entitled' and be more demanding and dissenting than traditional workers, so be ready for difficult questions. They'll argue with you when they're convinced they're right and they're likely to be idiosyncratic and need individual treatment.

All of this can make knowledge workers tricky to manage, especially for managers who are into 'time spent' and 'overseeing' people while they work. Added to this, although you may manage them, you may not fully understand their work. How do you know whether they're just sitting, or sitting thinking? How do you know whether they're producing, since their work is often intangible and invisible?

Knowledge workers want competent and credible leader-managers who convey a vision and build a culture that supports its execution. Use your personal power, passion and vision to lead. Position power leaves knowledge workers cold. You need to know who you are, be confident in your abilities and say what you mean, because knowledge workers have good antennae for 'spin'. They respond to you only when they respect you.

Most knowledge workers are well aware of their worth in the marketplace, so make sure they recognise they need the organisation for the structure and support it offers, just as the organisation needs them. Encourage team spirit and pride in the organisation to engage and retain them; knowledge workers often have a high need to know they are contributing to a larger whole and doing meaningful work for an organisation they respect.

 THEORY TO PRACTICE

Leading knowledge workers

Anxiety and depression specialist, Professor Gavin Andrews, MD, AO, leads a team of 18 knowledge workers, mostly clinical psychologists, research scientists and MDs (see Case study 9.2 on page 284.) Here's how some of his team members describe him:

- 'He's very much a hands-off leader. He's there when you need him but he certainly isn't a micro-manager.'
- 'He's dynamic and, well, a little bit eccentric. He's unique and he's impressive.'
- 'He's very business oriented and hi-tech – no mean feat for someone in his early 80s.'
- 'We're really empowered and engaged and know that we can go to him when we need a decision. He's very accessible; yeah, we go to him – not the other way around.'
- 'This is going to sound strange, but Gavin and everyone else on the team signs in when we get to work and out when we leave. It isn't to count hours or anything; it's so we know who's around in an emergency. I was a bit shocked by this – I thought it was really old fashioned but now I see what a simple and useful tool it is.'
- 'In one word: Creative. I don't think a week goes by when he hasn't had an original idea.'

Stretch and inspire them

Knowledge workers have a low boredom threshold, so assign tasks that stretch and test their talents. Provide strategic direction to prevent them going off at a tangent and following a path that intrigues them but is unrelated to the team's or the organisation's strategy.

Help them keep up to date in their fields by assigning work and projects that meet their needs for extending their skills and doing interesting work. Assist with their ongoing professional and personal development and develop a team learning culture. Let them network with their peers, because knowledge workers work best when in contact with others in their field; for them, networking is a source of continual improvement, inspiration and new ideas.

FYI

Keep an eye on the future

Hire knowledge workers who have the potential to keep up, not just those who meet today's requirements. Be prepared to invest in training them and provide opportunities to develop their technical and interpersonal skills.

Give them autonomy

Never micro-manage a knowledge worker. Instead, set measurable goals, or deliverables, and explain the constraints and timelines. Organise the communications and information technology, equipment, information, time, funds and other resources they need, smooth out bottlenecks and provide a quiet space to think without distractions. Then give knowledge workers the freedom to get on with it. Know you're leading them well when you hear them say you're not getting in the way too much!

Provide help and mentoring, not instructions. Shelter them from hierarchy and red tape and remove hassles and 'administrivia' that prevent them doing what they do best.

Be accessible. Meet for progress reports and be their chief coach and supporter rather than a traditional boss. In fact, think of your relationship to them as an inverted pyramid and yourself as a servant leader (see page 254). Measure the value knowledge workers add by what they achieve rather than by the tasks they do, how long they spend doing them or where they do them. It's quality, not quantity, that counts.

Even when knowledge workers exude an attitude of competence and confidence, they need to be reassured that they add value. Recognise their good work, but don't over-do it; they often value recognition from respected peers and clients more.

Make sure your team of knowledge workers is diverse – they need the friction of different ideas and the mental stimulation of different ways of thinking to be most productive.

● IN A NUTSHELL

Managing knowledge workers

Professional workers are proud of what they do, want to do it well and want to enjoy doing it. They thrive on assignments that allow them to learn and grow professionally. They work best when they are given the goal and the boundaries and left to work out the best way to achieve the objectives. They resent close supervision and monotonous and routine work. They are specialists who are often more loyal to their specialism than to their employer. When you manage them well, engage them and motivate them, you can keep them with you. When you manage them poorly, they go elsewhere.

Telecommuters and off-site team members

When you first manage off-site employees, you may worry about whether they're working remotely or not remotely working. How do you know when someone has done something of value? How do you know whether people are floundering when you can't see them?

On the other side of the coin, your off-site workers probably worry about whether you know how hard they're working. You need to trust each other – you that they're working and they that you appreciate their work and know they are adding value to the organisation.

British journalist Katharine Whitehorn summed up the office versus home experience with this quip: 'I yield to no one in my admiration for the office as a social centre, but it's no place to actually get any work done.'[6] For leader-managers as well as off-site employees, the goal is to get the work done.

Managing off-site workers means transferring most of your hands-on management to the employees themselves; this makes frequent communication, feedback and trust essential. Since you can't 'manage by eyeball', become comfortable with managing by results (if you're not already). Use outcome-based success measures to assess off-site workers' contributions. As long as they produce the results you expect, it doesn't matter whether they spend the odd half hour in the garden, surfing the waves or at the gym.

Of greater concern than whether telecommuters are working is how much they work. Some have problems switching off and work longer hours than may be healthy. People are rarely so ill they can't crawl across the hallway to go to work, and when a sick child keeps them home, they can still work.

◉ THEORY TO PRACTICE

Telecommuting isn't for everyone

Not everyone makes a good telecommuter. For many people, telecommuting means fewer distractions, a more productive atmosphere and avoiding long commutes. For others, it means the hell of isolation and no support.

Look for people with excellent communication skills – written, interpersonal, keyboarding and so on. Look for people who are confident in making work-related decisions, reliable at meeting deadlines, have basic computer maintenance skills and are able to solve basic technical problems in the absence of on-premises IT support. Look for people who are well organised, and who can work independently and be self-disciplined and self-reliant.

When the social nature of the workplace is a favourite part of a person's job, when they don't have an office space that can remain organised and free from distractions and when they need external validation for good work, teleworking probably isn't for them. Beware of people who are known to take work home and work long hours – working from home may make 'workaholism' worse.

Be aware of the difficulties of working off site, especially for those taking up the option for the first time. Plan how to help them adapt to the new style of work and new ways of communicating. For example, provide them with training and coaching in how to manage their time, communicate with far-flung and office-based colleagues and customers, set up a safe and ergonomically viable home office, separate work from private life, inject some social contact into their working day, and so on. Provide the tools and training they need to produce and communicate. (See 'The strategic perspective: Looking after home workers' on page 967 for more information about managing the health and safety risks for home workers.)

◉ ACTION!

Are you ready to telecommute? How do you know whether an employee is suitable for telecommuting? Log on to ⚡CourseMateExpress, where the interactive self-test: Is it safe to telecommute?, can help you decide.

Build the sense of 'us'

When people work autonomously, their sense of responsibility grows, and with it, their sense of independence, lessening their sense of connection to their organisation. So take particular care to keep that connection alive.

Build a strong culture that telecommuters and *road warriors* – delivery people, maintenance engineers, police officers, sales representatives – identify with and instil it in them whenever they are on site. Make an effort to build and maintain their morale and team identity because common beliefs, rituals and values are more difficult to establish at a distance.

You probably need to train the members of your mixed team to work effectively together. For instance, on-site workers can be reluctant to telephone ('disturb' or 'bother') a telecommuting colleague even during working hours because they're 'at home' and don't want to intrude. They need to understand that phoning is fine, just as stopping by someone's desk to ask a question is fine.

When you can, periodically bring everyone together for a meeting (and an informal coffee or meal) to help them maintain and strengthen relationships, provide adequate psychological interaction and facilitate information-sharing. Review the team's progress and successes, discuss goals for the next period, find out whether any members are experiencing any difficulties and bring everyone up to date on important organisation happenings.

Don't forget to invite off-site employees to on-site meetings. When they can't attend in person, they can still participate by speaker phone or webconferencing. When you do this, make sure the team members present don't forget about their virtual colleagues – when they talk quickly to each other rather than into the telephone microphone, for instance, their absent teammates may not hear and feel left out.

Deal with any misunderstandings quickly. In an office, where you see each other, it's easy and more automatic to discuss problems. This is harder for remote workers. Help team members share ideas and information, frustrations and triumphs. Even when your meetings are virtual because of distance, post the agenda before the meeting in your virtual team room (described below), prepare for the meeting and follow it up as you would any other meeting. (See page 948 for information on how to lead virtual meetings.)

◉ THE STRATEGIC PERSPECTIVE

Family-friendly virtuality

Telecommuting and virtual teams are becoming an important way of achieving work–life balance and work–life blending, and building family-friendly and flexible working practices into jobs. The benefits to organisations of employees working at least part of the time from home are well documented and include employee motivation, lower overheads and improved productivity and staff retention, leading to increased competitive advantage.

Signal your understanding

Show you understand off-site workers' problems, such as the lack of toilets, the lack of exercise they may get, loneliness from spending a lot of time on their own, the stress of driving and the temptation to eat quick and easy but unhealthy and fattening junk food. Give them a website showing the location of public toilets in their areas, http://www.toiletmap.gov.au. Provide short workshops explaining the benefits of healthy eating and exercise and showing them simple ways to stay fit and eat healthily on the road and at home. Showing you understand what your off-site workers deal with increases your credibility and builds loyalty.

Offset their loneliness with phone calls and webconferencing. Phone texting doesn't provide the same psychological satisfaction a real 'chat' does. Even though your remote team members can't see it, keep your door open by responding quickly to queries and returning messages promptly (at least that day or, better still, within half a day). You don't want them to think they're all alone, with no support. Non-replies and delayed replies communicate disrespect.

Establish policies and procedures for issues that on-site employees normally take for granted – for example, how to obtain general office supplies and materials, what couriers to use and whether there are there any specific times everyone should be available for telephone calls and meetings.

When telecommuters work different hours, agree in advance the best times to contact each other. Agree other matters, such as response times to answer emails, queries and telephone messages. (This is discussed under the heading Virtual teams on page 416.)

IN A NUTSHELL

Difficulties with telecommuting

If working from home seems to suit your team, here is some handy information for you and them to consider:

- *Adaptation difficulties*: Some people find it difficult to adapt to working from home. They find it lonely and miss the structure of regular office routines and they miss the buzz of people around them and the satisfaction of teamworking.

  Workplace hubs, well-appointed bases for mobile workers set up by organisations for their own mobile employees or independent hubs that cater for freelancers, can lessen the loneliness, and as a bonus allow the natural collaboration and innovation modern organisations depend on. (There is even an online magazine devoted to hubs: http://www.deskmag.com.)

- *Administration*: Administration work can pile up and it can be difficult to participate in meetings and decisions.

- *Balancing work and personal life*: Some telecommuters have problems knowing when, and how, to switch off and 'shut the office door' and get on with their personal life, while others are too easily distracted by the temptations of home.

- *Culture*: It can be difficult to design a team structure and build a culture that supports telecommuting.

- *Initial set-up costs*: Providing the technology and connecting telephone and high speed broadband lines is not cheap when large numbers of employees are involved. Some employers provide an allowance to furnish the home office, which adds to the expense. Measures to ensure that digital mobile devices and intranet connections in home offices do not pose IT security risks are also needed.

- *Management issues*: Managers need to learn new skills and methods of working and leading, particularly in building relationships with and supervising telecommuters, and ensuring their health and safety when working remotely.

- *Practical hurdles*: Remuneration, for example, can be tricky. Take the case of a virtual team whose members work in SOHOs in Hong Kong, India, Orange and Sydney. Each of these cities has different costs of living and people living there are on different salary scales, yet they're each doing the same job. 'Perks' can be problematic, too. When your main office offers a gym or subsidised canteen, how can you compensate home-based workers? Technology can also be tricky: computer software and hardware must be standardised, and people trained and provided with full technical support.

Concentrate on results

When home workers do routine work such as call centre operations or data entry, technology easily quantifies their productivity. Until you're comfortable that they're producing the results you need, you can use computer-monitoring programs to track whether people are working and provide summaries of, for example, what websites they're using and for how long. This way, you can keep an eye on their activities without being invasive. (Naturally, you should only track business-related activities and inform employees they're being monitored.)

You can also monitor how your knowledge workers use their computers and use a shared calendar to track projects and scheduled meetings. Email, instant messaging and quick phone calls keep you in touch and webconferences give you 'virtual face time'. With video chats, you can see whether your knowledge worker is walking in the park (where she may be thinking through a thorny problem) while smartphone monitoring software can tell you where she is now and where she's been by tracking GPS locations.

But really, especially when home workers are knowledge workers, what matters is their results. Whether it took them five inspirational minutes or 50 hard-slog hours to achieve the result is inconsequential.

It's better to base clear individual goals on outcomes, and not worry about time spent at a desk or on a telephone. Develop a solid performance management system to ensure that everyone knows exactly what is expected of them and how their contributions are measured. Agree how often and in what format you want progress reports. Make regular contact and make it easy for people to flag when they are struggling with something and need support. Remember that finding the right balance between autonomy and direction varies for each person.

● THEORY TO PRACTICE

The British Automobile Association model
Britain's Automobile Association has created virtual call centres, with operators working from home. Leaders manage 20 to 25 people and visit them at home once or twice a month. They are on the employees' 'turf', which significantly changes the dynamics of the relationships. For example, when an operator is experiencing a personal problem such as the breakdown of a relationship, it might not become known in the workplace, or could be skirted over. It's different when you're in the person's home, though. Leader-managers need to understand how to deal with some difficult situations they might otherwise not encounter.

Keep them safe

You are responsible for ensuring that off-site team members work safely, so you need to satisfy yourself that their working environment is set up ergonomically and safely. Train them to identify and manage risks and provide them with the same safety and emergency equipment found at their main workplace: fire extinguishers, first aid kits, personal protective equipment and other equipment they need to do their work in a healthy and safe way.

Train telecommuters to set up their office ergonomically and efficiently (see 'In a Nutshell: The five Ss of lean Six Sigma' on page 568 and 'The strategic perspective: Looking after home workers' on page 967). Consider visiting telecommuters' home workplaces to conduct your own safety audit. When it isn't feasible to complete a safety audit in person, obtain enough information about their home working environment to enable you to jointly assess risks and control hazards (as described on page 983).

Discuss emergency plans too – you hope they won't be needed but you need to have them in place. Review these arrangements at least annually to make sure your agreed safety measures are working.

● ACTION!

You can find a template for a Telecommuter's safety audit on ⁊CourseMateExpress that you or your off-site team members can use to identify, monitor and remove or mitigate the hazards in their working environment.

Keep in touch

Often, your main role as the leader-manager of home workers is to keep in touch, have a friendly chat, pass the time of day and generally help them to feel like a valuable part of a worthwhile team.

It's easy to let 'out of sight' become 'out of mind' (this applies to part-time and casual team members, too). Nothing drains motivation faster than feeling forgotten, 'out of the loop', undervalued and unimportant. Keep off-site team members informed and involved through formal and informal contact, for example, newsletters, your organisation's Intranet, regular (at least weekly) telephone calls, e-cards, instant messaging, meeting with remote workers when they're in the office, personal notes, teleconferencing, videoconferencing and spending time with remote workers in the field. Find out how they're doing and what they might need from you. Let them know how the team's progress against goals is going and pass on any news. Regular check-ins also let you give remote workers as rapid and as equal a say as office-based workers, which is very empowering.

While the task and the job they do are important, don't forget the personal side – ask after telecommuters' families, find out how their weekend was, include them in the office 'happenings'. Let your on-site team know what their off-site colleagues are up to, too, and make sure they understand how their off-site teammates contribute to achieving the team's goals.

 FYI

Three types of teams, three-time management solutions
In collaborative teams, people need to work together to manage their time well and the way to effectively manage collective time needs to be based on the way the team works.

When team members work across time zones and feel pressured to be available around the clock to meet tight time lines or client expectations (or even just because they can, thanks to technology) provide predictability. Agree times and even a day when everyone knows that they and the whole team are 'off' – not working and not available.

When teams are expected to work long hours, perhaps in periods of peak demand, provide extra time off in lieu to recognise their efforts.

When teams work in a hectic, interruption-filled environment with constant distractions, for instance in open-plan offices or where meetings abound, provide a 'quiet time' when people can concentrate and complete their work, so they don't have to take it home or leave it unfinished.[7]

2. Developing productive project and virtual teams

Among the principal challenges in leveraging remote teams is finding managers with the right mix of skills, temperament and other attributes necessary to direct, monitor and motivate workers they may rarely, if ever, meet in person.

Allan Schweyer, 'Managing the virtual global workforce', *HC Online* (17 October 2006)[8]

Does your organisation assign employees to temporary project teams, either full-time for the duration of a project or part-time while they continue to work on their other duties? Do you know anyone who works with people in different cities or countries some or all of the time? Project teams may or may not be virtual and virtual teams may or may not be temporary, but one thing they certainly aren't is yesterday's type of team.

Yes, you still need to manage task and process matters of both these teams. On the task side, you still need to clearly state the team purpose and shared goals and establish clear individual roles and responsibilities by implementing a performance plan centring on outcome-based success measures (as described in chapters 11 and 13). And you still need to manage performance through coaching, training, and formal and informal feedback (as described in chapters 15, 16 and 27).

On the process side, you still need to develop open communications and build relationships and trust; as with any team, the culture, dynamics and norms (explained in Chapter 4) make or break the success of project and virtual teams. But getting the team norms and dynamics right and building a strong, high-performance culture is tricky at the best of times and even more tricky with today's teams. Begin by establishing a team operating agreement as explained on page 669.

These and other customary team management activities are only part of what it takes to lead today's teams.

Project and temporary teams

Project teams are formed to complete a specific assignment such as:

* Managing a large engineering project (e.g. building the Sydney Harbour Bridge, converting Adelaide Oval into a multi-sport facility, designing and building the Snowy Mountain Dam).
* Solving a problem (e.g. attracting more overseas visitors to the Flinders Ranges, making a city more pedestrian friendly, improving traffic flow in Sydney during rush hours).
* Creating an innovative product, process or service (e.g. completing the protocols for a royal visit, designing a faster, more fuel-efficient passenger aircraft, developing a sensational customer-greeting experience that speeds up their check-in).

Depending on the size of the assignment or project, the team leader is generally full-time. Members are chosen for their different specialisms (making the team cross-functional, or multifunctional) and may either be seconded full-time or part-time in addition to their normal duties (making the team a temporary matrix team). Some project teams have a mixture of full-time and part-time members; others have core team members supplemented with part-time and advisory members brought in to assist as needed. For large projects, the team is divided into subteams, sometimes many of them.

Project team members might be from the same organisation or from two or more organisations. Team members could include, for instance, customers and service partners, contractors and freelancers, permanent staff, volunteers, or any combination of these. When the work of the team is complex and the project large, team members may come from all over the world to form a virtual team.

When team members work part-time on a temporary or project team and belong to another team as well, try to ensure that split loyalties do not develop. For example:

* Agree in advance how much time the members can commit to your team.
* Explain to your team members and their other managers how much they and the organisation stand to gain from their participation on your team.
* Keep the team member's other leaders informed about your temporary team's progress and the progress of their member 'on loan' to you so they aren't tempted to keep pulling them off their duties on your team for other work.

Most project teams disband once the assignment is completed, although some may be semi-permanent, with a few core members and other members who participate at certain times or for particular purposes, for example to help out during busy seasons or other periods of high workload (as in the teams in Case study 14.1 at the end of this chapter). In capabilities-based organisations, teams are often permanent, working together to design and bring to market ever-better products, produce specialised products or provide particular services, or service particular customers or customer groups.

THEORY TO PRACTICE

Diversity in teams

Like knowledge workers, project teams need the collaborative tension that comes from a diverse membership. That's easy to provide. Project teams are made up of cross-functional specialists who are likely to think in different languages and follow different customs – the languages and working practices of their own specialisations. When the project team is also virtual and made up of people from other countries, they may literally think in different languages and follow different cultural customs, too.

>>

Add to the mix people from different backgrounds, experience, lifestyles and personality styles, and you've got the diversity you need. Watch out though: While this diversity provides strength, it can lead to misunderstanding and conflict. (For more information on how to make the most of differences in teams, see pages 212, 846 and 855.)

People have not only to learn new skills but also to unlearn traditional roles and behaviours when they join non-traditional teams and often need extra training, especially in organisations with a tradition of poor cooperation between functions. Rather than train the team before it actually forms, because people do not know what they need to learn, spread training in teamworking skills over a period of time (rather than in one hit) so that team members can absorb more information, try it out, perfect it and then learn some more. (Chapter 21 explains how to manage the task side of project teams and support the team's process.)

⊙ IN A NUTSHELL

Leading successful project teams

Leader-managers have a strong influence on the success of project and temporary teams. Here are some of the things the most successful of them do:

- Act as coaches, facilitators, networkers and protectors to team members.
- Emphasise continuous improvement and innovation, experimentation and risk taking.
- Emphasise openness and honesty in communication and avoid hidden agendas.
- Encourage informal meetings for gathering and sharing ideas.
- Ensure the decision-making processes that affect the team are transparent.
- Gain team member's personal and emotional commitment to the team.
- Hold frequent formal meetings.
- Invest in developing member's interpersonal skills.
- Make resources and information available to team members.
- Pay attention to team building and team process issues.

Virtual teams

Thanks to advances in telecommunications technologies and access to high-speed Internet, the global virtual workforce already numbers in the hundreds of millions and is growing at many more times the rate of the traditional workforce.[9] Experts predict that within a few years, more than 1.3 billion people will be working virtually.[10] If you have a global mindset and cultural intelligence, and are good at relationship management, learning to lead virtual teams is a smart career move. (Leading virtually is different from traditional team leadership and needs to be learned.)

Virtual teams can be permanent or temporary and, when temporary, work together long-term or short-term. Their members may seldom or never meet face to face. They may be home-based or office-based employees at various locations, contractors, or a mixture of all of these. They may be in different cities, time zones or hemispheres and have different ways of doing business. Your team may be their only team and they may work in it full-time or part-time, or they may also belong to other virtual or actual teams.

As with telecommuters and other off-site workers, you are the all-important link between the organisation and your virtual team members. Build a sense of team, organisation identity and loyalty by passing on company news and information and making it accessible to team members. Try to make it possible for them to plug into the organisation's formal and informal networks – they need to be, and feel like, effective members of the corporate team, as well as your team.

Virtual teamworking works

Although managers often fear that teamwork deteriorates in a virtual work environment, the experience of most organisations is the opposite. Teams actually become more effective, partly because distance forces them to become more organised about their meetings, processes, procedures and other important matters.

The challenges revolve around communication. It is particularly important to make sure that meetings actually do happen and are rich in opportunities for members to interact and be stimulated and motivated, and that the lines of communication stay open outside scheduled meetings.[11]

Build virtual trust

Building and maintaining trust with people you seldom (or never) see can be a tough task. Establishing trust is easier when 20–40% of the team members already know each other and when team members have been trained in effective team working and have worked in effective teams. When this is not the case, provide training in areas like building effective working relationships, clear communication and resolving conflicts. These 'soft skills' are critical your team's success.

It's easier to hide problems, sweep misunderstandings under the carpet and make wrong assumptions in virtual teams than in actual teams, which means that problems and conflicts can magnify and fester. Problems can escalate quickly over distance and it isn't as easy to step in and take over, so, while providing autonomy, stay close and make sure you know what's going on at all times; stay in regular contact and over- rather than under-communicate.

When team members are in different countries, virtual teams may also have cultural and language differences to overcome, and when they specialise in different areas, they may need to overcome the different thinking and working habits of their various specialisations, too. All this can be disastrous unless the team acknowledges potential problems, discusses how to prevent them and develops norms of open communication and trust. This begins with you – the leader – and it begins in the team's first few meetings.

Your first contacts set the tone for trust, and the pattern set at the outset quickly hardens. In fact, trust is established (or not) quickly – during a virtual team's first few meetings. To set the scene for better working relationships, establish an understanding about 'how we work together' and spend time allowing team members to get to know each other and become familiar with each other's communication styles and ways of working.

THE STRATEGIC PERSPECTIVE

Virtual trust

In virtual teams, the three stages of trust discussed on page 395, deterrence-based trust, knowledge-based trust and identification-based trust, exist. But instead of evolving slowly over time as it does in actual teams, trust tends to be established – or not – right at the beginning.

>>

And the type of trust established at the start usually sticks. This makes the first few interactions of team members decisive in establishing which kind of trust becomes the norm for your virtual team.

Avoid introductory messages that imply a lack of trust. This sets the scene for a virtual team plagued by low morale and poor performance and you're stuck with deterrence-based trust. Instead:

1. Begin interactions with a set of social, getting-to-know-each-other messages and ask members to introduce themselves and provide some personal and professional background information before turning to the work at hand, to establish knowledge-based and identification-based trust.

2. Make clear each team member's role and function in the team, to further establish identification-based trust.

3. Develop an action-oriented, enthusiastic team culture.

◉ THEORY TO PRACTICE

Deliver the deliverables

When team members are spread around the world, the team can operate around the clock – while some team members sleep, others work. You often don't know whether or when people are working; as with telecommuters, all you have to go by is the results people produce.

Matt Mullenweg, creator of WordPress, had the right idea when he said 'I don't care if you sleep late or if you pick up a child at school in the afternoon. I don't care if you spend the afternoon on the golf course and then work from 2 to 5 am. What do you actually produce?'[12]

Support your team

Once the team is working well towards its task, continue to support its task achievement, the team as a whole, and individual team members. On the task side, monitor team member's results and the team's results as it progresses through its milestones. Help team members keep to their agreed timelines and deliverables and address any problems of underperformance quickly before they mushroom and affect the entire project. Keep your feedback constructive and assist any team members who need to get back on track. (Page 383 explains how to look after the task, team and individual needs of your team; Chapter 16 explains how to manage underperformance and the information applies to virtual as well as actual team members.)

Keep everyone up to date on the team's progress by posting regular progress reports in the team room. Give lots of positive, enthusiastic feedback to the team as a whole through the team room, your leader's blog and to individual team members.

On the process side, monitor the team's dynamics and help it grow into a high-performing team (explained on page 384). Remember that, as the team leader, one of your key result areas is relationship management – managing the relationships within the team and building your own relationship with each team member.

When you can't meet face to face very often or at all, build a team scrapbook as the months go by and publish it every 12 months. Include, for instance, team news and accomplishments to build a sense of pride, some interesting information about the team's suppliers, customers and other stakeholders, and a photo of each team member with a paragraph about them to reinforce common ground.

Make good use of the holidays

Celebrating holidays together helps build the shared identity, community and enthusiasm that virtual teams, just like other teams, need. When holidays roll around, encourage team members to discuss and select ways to celebrate virtually. When some team members are from other cultures, join in with their celebrations. When giving a small gift is appropriate, think about a gift card to a café that you know has an outlet near each team member; make the amount big enough for two and ask them to share a photo of them and their guest enjoying their gift.

Consider creating team Christmas, Diwali, Eid ul-Fitr, Hanukkah, Naw-Ruz and Vesak cards for customers and suppliers that team members can sign on line and include their photo.

Communicate

Speak to members individually between your regular team meetings to maintain their sense of connection. Communicate the team's progress, news and general information in person, as well as posting it in your meeting room. Make your information both constructive and positive: 'We had a great week. One thing to keep on top of is …' or 'One thing to remember for next time is …'. Deliver small chunks of information over time rather than in one big occasional hit. Use multiple channels – instant messaging, your leader's blog, online chats, telephone calls, texting – to increase the likelihood that your message is received and understood, and because different formats appeal to different people.

At all costs, avoid contacting team members directly only when there's a problem. Team members need to feel comfortable airing alternative viewpoints and opinions, challenging each other and disagreeing with each other. Build norms of open and honest communication so that team members aren't afraid to share bad news.

Beware emails. Your own collaboration tools are a better bet than email when team members need to communicate in writing or send each other documents. Email has poor documentation and filing features, making it hard to find information quickly, and emails sent through external servers are a security risk and a spam nuisance. (Spam accounts for up to 80% of all emails.)[13] A virus or worm could not only compromise your team member's ability to work but also temporarily disable your organisation's communications system.

High-quality virtual face time

Virtual meetings are a great way to build rapport and trust with your remote team members. To make sure your contact is expected, let your team member choose the time so you don't unintentionally pick a time when they get their best problem-solving or work needing intense concentration done, or when they're rushing to meet a deadline. When you can't video-chat, use the phone and listen carefully for unspoken indications of enthusiasm or frustration. While you don't want to force friendship on them, begin your one-on-one with questions like 'How will you be celebrating the holiday?' and 'How is your family?' before moving on to task questions like 'How is everything going?' and 'Is there anything I can help you with?' Your team member should feel supported, motivated and ready to move forward after your chat.

Virtual communication

In virtual teams, pay special attention to making regular contact since it doesn't occur automatically. In fact, the more dispersed team members are, the more you need to communicate, even when it's just to say hello and ask how everything is going, and to listen – to concerns, inspirations, setbacks, thoughts. Frequent contact builds bridges that can span vast distances and provide the essential contact that builds team member's loyalty and ties to the team.

When you communicate, resist the urge to get straight down to business, which could be interpreted as impatience or criticism. Spend time keeping up to date with matters of personal importance to your team members.

Be careful with jokes and humour, because they can be misinterpreted from a distance and in the absence of the usual body language clues that inform communications; emoticons help, but only to a point.

Put as much energy into developing communication channels and building the culture as you do into getting the technology right, and be prepared to work extra hard on communication in virtual teams. Over-communicate rather than under-communicate.

Working across different time zones means when you're at work, your team may not be and vice versa. Set clear guidelines around your availability out of (your) hours. For instance, you may say 'You can call me *any* time. When I'm not available, my phone will be switched off, so never worry that you're interrupting me. If my phone is switched off, just leave a message and I'll phone you back as soon as I can'.

3. Using technology to overcome distance

A man is not idle because he is absorbed in thought. There is visible labour and there is invisible labour.

Victor Hugo (French author), *Les Misérables* (2012)[14]

Technology helps your telecommuters and 'road warriors' keep in touch and work remotely, and lets your virtual team do just about everything an actual team can do. Team members can drop short notes on each other's desks, have serendipitious interactions and share triumphs and successes with texting and instant messaging, meet virtually as an entire team, in subgroups or in pairs with teleconferences and web meetings, share data and documents and work on them together in real time using collaborative systems.

You can integrate all your team's communications – email, fax, instant messaging, video and voice – over an Internet protocol (IP) network, making it possible to manage all your communications from a single web workspace. Groupware – online workspaces, real-time application sharing, shared calendars and tasks lists, and so on – helps remote teammates work together creatively, flexibly and quickly. Chat systems messaging let team members see when teammates are available.

Make sure every team member has precisely the same version of the same technology to allow full and easy collaboration. For example, when team members use different versions of even something seemingly simple, like instant messaging, they can't all contact each other and cliques can form.

Sophisticated technology isn't enough – people need to know how and when to use it. When you or any of your team members are not familiar with the advanced technologies you're using and when you upgrade, arrange training. Figuring it out as you go and using the long route rather than efficient short cuts is frustrating and time-wasting.

Establish ground rules for using your team technology and use the technology effectively. Develop a set of code subject titles and a system to flag a message's importance, topic and urgency. Consider how to prioritise messages, how quickly to act on requests and respond to messages, when to copy others or the entire team, how quickly to post responses to threaded discussions, when it's okay and not okay to contact team members using text and instant messaging. Agree how often people should check their messages and various sections of their actual or virtual team room, and guidelines for placing information on the bulletin board. This also serves to overcome differences in individual communication styles, heading off potential problems. Technology is there to aid people's work, not interrupt it.

When some of the team is working while others sleep, team members should check the relevant sections of the team room when beginning their work day to make sure they're on the same page and decide whether to adjust the day's schedule and alter their priorities to fit in with other team members. This is particularly important when they need to work closely with each other.

● IN A NUTSHELL

Collaboration and conferencing

The Internet protocol (IP) network's continually developing facilities allow ease of collaboration and conferencing between team members. Many collaboration and conferencing tools are available via hosted services on the web and many organisations have their own in-house collaboration and conferencing tools that they host on their Intranets.

Collaboration systems let you assign tasks to different team members and let members report back on their progress, track the progress of the team and individuals, use a shared calendar (to show important dates and deadlines, meeting dates, team member birthdays and so on), and let freelance and contract employees track the number of hours they work on a project.

Conferencing systems include features such as application sharing, instant messaging, flash animation, pointer and annotation, screen drawing tools, shared files, and streaming audio and video. Depending on your software, it can also give you the ability to run great virtual team meetings. (Page 948 explains how to lead virtual meetings – teleconferences, videoconferences and web meetings.)

Your virtual team room

An informative, interactive, 'sticky', password-accessed virtual team room that team members visit daily to see what's new and report their own progress, ask questions, share information and join threaded problem-solving and ideas-generating discussions is valuable for on-site project teams and essential for virtual teams. Because it's virtual, your team room is 'open' 24 hours a day, seven days a week. It should include everything the team needs to progress its work, together and individually, neatly categorised, easily navigated and always current.

A good virtual teamroom builds a sense of team, trust and effective working relationships between team members. It gives team members a place to meet, discuss problems, share ideas and monitor progress. It also provides a valuable knowledge base for now and for the future, contributes to innovation and continuous learning and helps to build a learning team culture and a learning organisation, one in which individual employees continually create, acquire and transfer knowledge through the organisation, enabling the organisation itself to learn and improve as its employees learn and share what they have learned.

As team leader, you would normally manage the virtual team room, keep it up to date and moderate discussion threads. Create sections within the team room for each aspect of the team's work, for example:

- *A home page* that welcomes team members to their team room; you can place team members' photos and names in a circle around the team purpose statement. (Team members can use it to identify each other until they get to know each other – 'This is Tomo at 10 o'clock'.)

- *Action plans, schedules and responsibilities*, where team members can tick steps off as they complete them and add footnotes or comments they believe are important.
- *Best practice summaries* that document what team members have found to be best practice relating to the team's work.
- *Bulletin board*, the virtual version of the café bar or kitchen, where members can share ideas, news and views.
- *Discussion threads*, listed by topic, where members can post notes about problems they're grappling with to see whether other team members can help, work on designs, options and problems together, and so on. The discussion initiator usually summarises the comments weekly, or more often when it generates a lot of comments, highlighting areas of agreement and disagreement.
- *Files* of documents the team creates and decisions the team makes.
- *Leader's blog*, giving you an opportunity to pass on task and team information, update the team on organisational news and information, and share your thoughts.
- *Meeting centre*, with notices of virtual meetings, meeting agendas, minutes and actions arising, background information for meetings, links to any relevant threaded discussions, and so on.

  Ask members to post their progress and to check each other's progress before meetings so that you can use the meeting time to discuss problems, make plans and handle other matters that are more effectively done through conversation than in writing.
- *Members' page*, with information about each team member, including contact information, professional summary (areas of expertise, experience and so on), personal profile (such as hobbies and interests) and a chart of their responsibilities and deliverables.
- *Progress reports*, continuously updated, on various aspects of the team's work.
- *Scrapbook*, for team and team member news and accomplishments and interesting or informative titbits about the team's suppliers and customers.
- *Team charter, goals and timelines*, showing the goals and the milestones the team plans to achieve, updated to show what has been completed and what is yet to be completed.
- *Working documents*, organised by topic and into clearly numbered versions, so team members don't mistakenly work on the wrong version.

CourseMateExpress

Go to http://login.cengagebrain.com to access CourseMate Express, your online study tool for *Management Theory & Practice*. CourseMate Express brings chapter concepts to life with interactive learning, and study and exam preparation tools:

- Test your skills in different aspects of management with interactive self-tests and simulations.
- Watch videos that show how real managers operate in real businesses.
- Test your understanding of the changing world of management by taking the revision quiz.

QUICK REVIEW

1. List and describe the types of teams and team members you are increasingly likely to lead and the special considerations you need to be aware of when leading each of them.
2. Explain why you need to take particular care to develop a high-performance team culture and norms and to build trust in today's mixed and merged teams, and list some of the ways you can do this.
3. Explain why you need to take particular care to develop a high-performance team culture and norms and to build trust in temporary project teams and virtual teams, and discuss some of the ways you can do this.
4. How does technology help you run today's teams efficiently and effectively?

BUILD YOUR SKILLS

1. Interview two or three leaders of mixed teams and find out what techniques they use to overcome the problems inherent in such teams; for example, how do they measure and build their teams' performance and keep in touch with team members?
2. Referring to 'Theory to practice: Leading knowledge workers' on page 408 and to Case study 9.2 on page 284, how would you describe Professor Andrews' leadership style? In what ways does the Professor depict the qualities needed for leading knowledge teams described in this chapter?
3. Do you know anyone who leads or works in a virtual team? If so, ask them about the technologies they use and the advantages and disadvantages of virtual teams from their point of view. Ask whether they have any tips on leading or participating in a virtual team.
4. Describe the purpose and content of a virtual team room in terms of both process and task.
5. Investigate the collaboration technology currently available and predicted to become available in the near future and prepare a short report on how you would use it to lead a mixed, project or virtual team.
6. Read Case study 21.2 on page 681 and answer Question 3.

WORKPLACE ACTIVITIES

1. Do people in your organisation work from home all or part of the time? Do salespeople, service people or tradespeople spend more time on the road and with customers than in the office? They still need to be part of a team. How is your organisation managing this?
2. Does your organisation allow occasional or regular telecommuting? If so, what arrangements does it make for setting up home offices? Do you ever, or have you ever, worked from home? What are the benefits and drawbacks of regular telecommuting? In your opinion, what does it take to be an effective and contented home worker?
3. If you have participated in or led any temporary knowledge, project or virtual teams, select one and describe how the team developed, using the stages of team growth described on page 386. Discuss the leader's role and the team members' roles in the team's development and the factors that helped and hindered the team to achieve its goals. What lessons did you learn for the next time you work with a temporary or virtual team?
4. What technologies are you familiar with that can be useful to mixed and virtual teams?

CASE STUDY 14.1

THE EASTERFEST TEMPORARY TEAM

Each year since 1997, Toowoomba, in south-east Queensland, hosts Easterfest, a local community celebration that supports the child sponsorship organisation Compassion and draws millions of dollars into the local economy.

Isaac Moody was 19 when he took over Easterfest. As CEO, he managed fewer than a dozen paid staff and recruits and managed the Easterfest volunteer crew of more than 1000 people. Two weeks before and one week after Easterfest, volunteers worked up to 18-hour days – free.

Here's how Moody ran the show: The CEO assembles the volunteers, develops a culture and working environment and sets up working and human resources (HR) systems in just three days. (As the years pass, Easterfest develops an amazing 80% crew retention rate.)

Moody recognises that a successful festival relies on the volunteer workers and their team effort. He says cracking a whip doesn't work. Volunteers just leave and it's too late to find replacements if crew members get in a huff and quit. He sells the volunteers a vision and watches them become inspired.

'Our volunteers,' he says, 'realise there's a purpose beyond just picking up that rubbish or doing whatever their task is.' Picking up rubbish becomes a drag after several hours, but Moody's volunteers know they are contributing to developing a strong, family-friendly community as well as contributing their time and energy to a good cause, Compassion, and they know their efforts are appreciated.

Considering the volunteers to be vital assets to Easterfest, Moody develops resources to manage them. He recognises that jobs can be dull and hours long, so they have outlets for people to express their frustration with other people and with their tasks. 'We incorporate pressure valves like an open-door policy so team members can quickly access managers to sort out issues' he says. 'But we also have a call centre with staff trained to solve problems, so if people are frustrated, they don't take it out on their fellow crew.'

Easterfest even has a whole team called 'crew support'. Their purpose is to see that every crew member feels appreciated for giving their time. Under Moody's plan, a volunteer might be working when another volunteer comes along and says, 'Hey, thanks for the helping hand, have an Easter egg.'

Moody believes it's a small token, but 'when it's unexpected, it really makes them feel appreciated and wanted.

'I think the more you appreciate and make people feel welcome, because they are really contributing, the better their performance becomes – even when their jobs are boring and tiring.'

Easterfest became one of many not-for-profit organisations that rely completely on the contributions of volunteers for its success. Moody's secret? Appreciation, inspiration and structure.[15] (In 2011, Isaac Moody handed over the management of Easterfest, at that stage one of Australia's most successful volunteer-staffed events.)

Questions

1. Is Easterfest's culture of appreciation, inspiration and structure more important in volunteer teams or do you believe these principles apply to all teams?
2. How would the success of Easterfest be affected if one of those three elements (appreciation, inspiration or structure) failed for some reason?
3. What lessons does this case study hold for leaders of temporary teams?

NEWCASTLE NERDS

Slowly and steadily, Jake built up his computing business to include technical support and procurement for small businesses and website design and maintenance for SMEs.

Three years and three employees later, and buoyed by his success and his loyal customer base, Jake decided to expand further and bought another small computing business that subcontracted maintenance work mostly from larger government bodies and NGOs. Jake felt that its client base would provide access to new business opportunities and that the skills of its employees would complement his own employees' skills.

The three employees of his acquisition joined his other three employees in new premises. Jake thought that the move to new accommodation would give them a chance to 'begin anew' together and in a sense he was right. His new team got to know each other during the move, although it soon became clear that his 'acquired' employees had a somewhat different work ethic. In particular, they seemed reluctant to work weekends and what they considered to be 'out of hours'. This concerned Jake but he was unsure how to address it and, in any case, he was busy overseeing the additional business the acquisition brought.

Eight months after Jake's acquisition, the opportunity presented itself to merge his business with a similar business run by an old friend from his TAFE days. They felt that their combined client lists and business activities would give them the momentum they needed to take the business to a higher level and provide enough market share to become a significant force in the city. They rebranded the new company as Newcastle Computech and Jake's premises became its base.

Newcastle Computech prospered, gaining clients and recruiting additional employees and contractors as needed. The first 18 months flew by and now the company has a large and varied client list, 23 employees, including three part-timers, and a small group of contractors it regularly outsources work to, two of whom are based in Mission Beach, further up the coast. At any given time, about half of the employees are likely to be out of the office either working from home or at a client's premises.

It's Friday afternoon and Jake leans back in his chair and looks around. He's just finished reading an article in the trade journal about building a business that stressed the importance of shared values, a shared vision and a shared working culture when building a business. He'd never thought about these matters, but off the top of his head he'd have to say that although everyone works well enough together at a professional level, he and the others probably have different views about vision and values. The employees from the two original companies tend to keep together, especially since the merger, and each group works a bit differently and, he suspects, thinks of Newcastle Computech's clients and their relationships to them in different ways.

According to the article, shared values give everyone clarity about what is expected of them and define what they can and cannot do – they cannot violate the values. A shared vision keeps everyone moving in the same direction and, like the values, guides their actions. A shared culture helps everyone work better together and sets them apart in the marketplace.

'We're a group of computer experts,' he thinks. 'We're fantastic at what we do and we love our work. But to really take the business to the next stage, we're supposed to become a team and look at things the same way. Fine. But how? And how necessary is it, really?'

● ● ●

Questions

1. What issues does Jake face with employees?
2. Do you agree that Newcastle Computech needs to establish a shared set of values and a vision for the future of the business to take it to the next level? Why or why not? (Refer to pages 51 and 53 if you need information about corporate values and vision.)
3. Develop a plan to help Jake build his mixed, merged, semi-virtual team into a cohesive unit and build the type of culture it needs. (Refer to page 93 if you need information on corporate culture.)

15

PROVIDING FORMAL AND INFORMAL PERFORMANCE FEEDBACK

OVERVIEW

How often do you know that you like something or someone without having gone through any deliberate, systematic assessment? Most people evaluate and form opinions about people, products and ideas every day, often unconsciously. So it's natural for managers to evaluate employees (and vice versa). Managers usually know who the good workers are and who the not-so-good ones are, and so do their teammates.

The people who report to you deserve your feedback on their performance and it's too important to leave to chance. Whether it's informal or formal, your performance feedback and performance planning can build employee performance and motivation.

Yet the thought of offering formal and informal feedback on performance can fill a leader-manager with dread. The unpleasant confrontations, damaged working relationships and demoralised, hurt or angry employees that can result from poorly conducted formal performance discussions or careless, off-the-cuff remarks are the stuff nightmares are made of.

1. Do you know the benefits and drawbacks of performance discussions and the types of formal performance review systems most commonly found in organisations?
2. Can you plan for and lead an effective formal performance discussion?
3. Can you explain the importance of informal feedback and deliver it well?
4. Do you know your role when you're on the receiving end of a performance discussion?

This chapter explains how to plan and conduct encouraging, honest and supportive formal and informal performance discussions that benefit working relationships and increase the value of the employees to the organisation.

Performance review time

Here we go again, thinks Mark as he opens the email asking him to complete the annual (lengthy) performance discussion with each team member, holding a (lengthy) conversation about it with each one. The email links to the organisation's performance management system, with blank discussion documents to download and explanations and instructions for completing them. All employees receive a similar email, so they can prepare, too.

He sighs and files the email in his staff-pending folder, quickly diarises a timetable to complete the forms and invites each employee to a performance discussion meeting using the Intranet's meeting arranger. One more item to add to his already bursting file of tasks to do.

Formal performance discussions are supposed to be good for morale, but Mark isn't so sure. It seems to result in people wandering around with hurt and sullen expressions, not happy ones. The human resources (HR) manager claims that these discussions are a crucial part of the organisation's strategic people management plan and must be completed on time. They help formulate training and career development plans, predict staff requirements and structure the annual salary review.

Mark sighs again. How am I supposed to tell Philippa, who thinks she's 'tops', that her work is only average? And how can I tell Ken, who has been here for years, that, although his work is fine, his sullen and uncooperative attitude gets on my nerves? And what about Lena, the new one – so pleasant and she tries so hard – if I give her the poor rating she deserves, she may get discouraged and give up. And Tom – he's already at the top of the pay scale. If I give him the excellent rating he deserves and no pay rise, won't that demotivate him? Oh, these performance discussions – I wish someone would tell me how I'm supposed to manage them.

1. Understanding the benefits, drawbacks and types of formal performance discussion systems

Never mind who you praise but be very careful who you blame.

Sir Edmund Gosse (writer), *Gossip in the library*, (1913)[1]

Formal performance reviews and forward planning are part of the ongoing workplace communication that helps employees perform well. They are an excellent way to highlight the link between the organisation's strategic goals, operational objectives and individual goals. And because people want to be appreciated and developed, frequent performance discussions also help retain staff.

They open up communication channels and strengthen working relationships, replace managers' quick, unsystematic, unconscious evaluations of employees with a balanced consideration of their performance, and provide a sound basis for dealing fairly and impartially with employees. Considering how much they can help managers, organisations and employees, formal performance discussions are well worth the time and effort you need to put into them to make them effective.

THE STRATEGIC PERSPECTIVE

Performance management

Performance management aligns individual employees' goals and measures of success with the organisation's strategic and business plans. Formal performance discussions and informal performance feedback are two important elements of the performance management process. Two other elements of performance management are performance counselling and coaching.

Benefits to employees

Well led formal performance discussions give employees time out from the day-to-day hustle and bustle of their jobs to consider their performance and discuss it with their managers. Discussing how they see their roles provides an important overview and context for their efforts and ensures that employees and managers hold the same realistic expectations of each other. Performance discussions also provide a chance to get things out in the open and discuss any small but nagging doubts, irritations or questions.

Performance discussions provide the opportunity most employees need and want for regular, comprehensive feedback on how their leader-manager perceives their performance. Discussing how the previous review period has gone, setting objectives for the upcoming period and discussing how employees can build on their strengths, further develop their skills and learn new skills, helps them add value to the organisation. It also increases employees' employability and job satisfaction through continued learning and development. Figure 15.1 lists additional employee benefits of formal performance discussions.

Benefits to managers

Formally assessing and discussing your team members' performance allows you to stand back from your daily routine and look clearly and objectively at each person's performance, potential, career aspirations, and training and development needs. It helps you monitor individual skills and past performance, set future performance objectives and motivate employees, and gives you an opportunity to show your interest in employees, their jobs and their training and development. Regular performance discussions also help you monitor team and individual competencies to confirm that the team as a whole is able to achieve its goals. Figure 15.1 shows other ways that managers can benefit from formal performance discussions.

Benefits to organisations

Organisations need an objective way to calculate merit-based pay, pay for skills and general pay increases. When vacancies and other opportunities arise, many organisations look internally to find people suitable for promotions, special assignments and transfers and use performance reviews to assist in placing people in jobs that suit their capabilities. Organisations also use performance discussions to help shift their organisational culture by encouraging and acknowledging behaviours that reflect their values. Perhaps most important of all, formal performance discussions link individual performance with organisational values, strategies and goals. Figure 15.1 shows other ways organisations benefit from formal performance discussions.

● IN A NUTSHELL

Terminology

Termination of employment is a permanent separation from the organisation, usually a result of poor job performance or a serious offence by the employee. Objective performance discussions documenting the employee's performance over a period of time and records of performance counselling interviews can show that dismissal was fair and justified. (Terminating employment is explained on page 477.)

Economic or business reasons may make demotions, redundancies or retrenchments necessary. Formal performance discussions can help management reach an impartial and fair decision about who to demote, retrench or make redundant.

A demotion is a reassignment to a job of lower rank and pay, usually resulting from factors beyond an employee's control. Recessions, changing technology or changes to production or service requirements can cause restructuring and redundancies, with some demotions occurring among the remaining employees. It is unwise to demote a person for disciplinary reasons, although demotion for continued substandard performance could be an alternative to dismissal.

Redundancies occur when positions are no longer required in an organisation. This may be due to job redesign, organisational restructuring or outsourcing. In such cases, the position disappears and therefore the employee is no longer required.

Retrenchments, or lay-offs, are caused by a lack of sufficient work to keep people fully occupied.

The three main uses of formal performance discussions

Although they sometimes end up this way, performance discussions are not intended to punish for misdeeds or provide a 'short, sharp kick'. They are intended to do three things:

1. *Look backwards* to discuss job-holders' performances during the period under review. What did they do particularly well? What needs improving? What special skills or helpful behaviours do they have and do any need strengthening? What mistakes did they make and what can be learned from them? This gives you an ideal opportunity to recognise good work, uncover problems, increase an employee's motivation and clarify any areas of misunderstanding.

2. *Plan improvements*: To make sure high performance and productivity are possible, take the opportunity to review each of the five keys – '*what to*', '*want to*', '*how to*', '*chance to*' and '*led to*' (explained in Chapter 11) to make sure they are operating optimally. Discuss how to alter the job to make it easier, quicker or more economical to carry out. What problems has the employee run into? What prevents even better job performance? How can the job be streamlined and hassles eliminated? This can prevent misdiagnosing performance shortfalls, encourage innovation, solve problems, improve your department's and the organisation's operations, and show employees that you value their opinion – provided you act on what you learn.

3. *Look to the future*: Align individual goals with the overall goals of the organisation and the department and discuss employee aspirations. What results do you expect for the forthcoming period and what new goals can the employee work towards? What training and development would the employee benefit from? What additional or delegated duties would provide increased job development or job satisfaction? What directions would the employee like their job and their career to take? What other jobs in the organisation interest the employee?

Both parties need to think through these three topics in advance and be prepared to discuss them openly and honestly.

Three other uses of formal performance discussions

You should also discuss a *newly hired employee's performance* during probation as the final and most important stage in the selection process. By the end of the probationary period, you should be confident that the recruit meets or exceeds performance expectations. When this is not the case, discuss your misgivings openly with the employee and HR manager when there is one. You want to determine whether the employee and the organisation are best served by further training the employee for the position, transferring the employee to a more suitable position or discontinuing the hiring process.

Benefits to employees
- Air any irritations and clear up any uncertainties or concerns so they can be dealt with.
- Ask for assistance in improving or extending their performance.
- Establish clear work expectations and goals for the next period.
- Explain and have their work, training and career goals taken into consideration.
- Formally summarise and gain feedback and recognition for their performance and achievements over the previous period.
- Gain a better understanding of their strengths and development needs.
- Gain a recorded commitment from their manager that certain actions will occur, for example in training, development and support.
- Help employees plan and prioritise their work.
- Identify and meet training and development needs.
- Meet employees' desire to know how their manager views their performance.
- Protect employees from arbitrary decisions.
- Provide a 'balcony overview' (see Chapter 8) of their roles.
- Understand how they contribute to the goals of the work area and organisation.

Benefits to managers
- Help employees concentrate on their goals.
- A way to formally acknowledge and recognise employee talents and achievements.
- Find ways to further improve current performance by highlighting areas where the employee needs training, further development or coaching.
- Improved morale through constructive feedback and providing clear direction and expectations.
- Open communication channels and gain understanding of career aspirations, strengthen working relationships, agree areas of strength and improvement goals and opportunities.

Benefits to organisations
- A permanent written record to support decisions regarding promotions, transfers, dismissals, retrenchments, salary and wage changes, training, etc.
- Collate organisational training and development needs.
- Ensure that employees are not poorly placed or misplaced in jobs and use employees' skills where they are most needed in the organisation.
- Establish potential career paths for employees.
- Establish succession plans.
- Fill vacancies internally.
- Identify, develop and nurture particularly talented people.
- Identify employees to retrench and make redundant downturns and restructuring.
- Improved organisation performance through enhanced communication.
- Link individual performance and behaviours with organisational values and strategy.
- Monitor the effectiveness of selection or promotion procedures.
- Shift organisational culture.
- Structure pay and bonus reviews.

FIGURE 15.1 Uses of formal performance discussions

Some organisations include a *pay and bonus review* in performance reviews while others keep these completely separate. Some organisations also include an assessment of the employee's *suitability for promotion* to use in their career and succession planning processes.

Problems with formal performance discussions

Some problems are inherent in any performance discussion system. Different managers are likely to rate differently – some leniently, others severely, for example. Some appraisers let the halo/horns effect corrupt their assessments and others base their assessments on arbitrary, imprecise and subjective 'evidence'. Some managers bring their own biases and prejudices into the assessment, consciously or unconsciously stereotyping their assessments based, for example, on age, dress, gender, personality or race. To some extent, good training and a culture that values honest and helpful feedback can overcome these inbuilt problems.

Two other problems are: Not applying the formal discussion process to everyone, including those at the top of the organisation, which invites cynicism; and developing a technically brilliant but overly cumbersome and complicated system that is difficult and time-consuming to use, which invites people to avoid using it or to use it poorly. Everyone's performance should be discussed using a well-designed, straight-forward system.

The most popular ways to formally discuss performance

Formal performance discussions are usually conducted on a six- or 12-month cycle or, in the case of some operator and customer service jobs, even more frequently. The employee's immediate manager conducts them and, in many organisations, that manager's manager reviews them. Results are often collated and analysed for use with succession, training and other HR plans for the organisation.

The particular skills and abilities assessed depend on the job and the organisation's employee profile. Some typical areas for assessment include:

- ability to achieve results
- ability to develop productive working relationships
- ability to make decisions
- ability to work as a member of a team
- attendance and punctuality
- business acumen
- commitment to safety
- communication skills
- customer focus
- dependability
- future potential/ability to work in other areas
- how well the employee upholds the organisation's values
- job knowledge
- personal drive and integrity
- quality/accuracy of work
- quantity of output
- technical and job-related skills
- training and development needs.

The following methods are described below. Each falls prey to the problems discussed on page 432:

- Balanced scorecard
- Comparison or forced ranking
- Critical incident
- Essay
- Management by objectives
- Peer review
- Performance diary
- Rating scale
- Role description
- The 360-degree feedback.

Balanced scorecard method

With the balanced scorecard method, you rate employees against a list of values, attributes and qualities the organisation believes is critical to success. These may include, for example, cooperativeness, innovation, openness to new ideas, strategic thinking and working as part of a team.

Think about the behaviour linked with the attributes, qualities and values being assessed. For example, 'cooperative' – what does a cooperative person do? Cooperative people help teammates, help others learn, go the extra distance. 'Initiative' – what do people with initiative do? They set their own goals, find ways around problems and work without supervision.

Using behavioural examples to explain your ratings increases their objectivity; this is known as a *behaviourally anchored rating scale*.

Comparison or forced ranking method

The comparison, or ranking, method compares each job-holder with the others in the team or department against set criteria, ending up with, for example, the most/least productive employees, the highest/lowest quality producers, and so on. Because it is difficult to compare every individual with every other one, some ranking methods place employees only into the top third, middle third or lowest third instead of ranking each individually. Some organisations use a quota-based system known as *forced ranking* and *stacked ranking*, which forces employees' performance into a normal distribution, or 'bell', curve.

The variables being assessed are usually independent of each other, so an employee could rank, for example, in the top third of employees for planning and organising work and in the bottom third for accuracy of work. The collated results give organisations a quick, if rough, assessment of employees' value to the organisation, a way to determine pay increases (the top employees receive, for example, a 5% increase, the average employees 2%) and a way to identify underperforming employees.

● THE STRATEGIC PERSPECTIVE

'Rank and yank' – point and counterpoint

General Electric introduced forced curved ranking, or 'rank and yank', in the 1980s. The then CEO Jack Welch claimed this method boosted GE's revenues from US$70 billion in 1995 to US$130 billion in 2000. As a result of GE's success, other large companies adopted versions of the system. 'Rank and yank' sees managers compare each employee's performance on a bell curve. The top 20% are 'A players', the next 70% 'B players' and the bottom 10% are 'C players'. If the performance of the C players doesn't improve, they are dismissed – even when they are performing satisfactorily.

>>

When Bill Gates stepped down as CEO of Microsoft, the culture quickly became the politics of promotion and survival rather than creativity and innovation. (See 'The strategic perspective: The lost decade' on page 94, for more on this subject.) At the heart of this toxic culture was a stacked rating system. Every six months, each unit had to declare a certain percentage of employees as 'top' performers, then 'good' performers, then 'average', 'below average' and finally, 'poor' performers. The rewards were promotions and bonuses. Bad luck to those 'good' performers whose bosses needed one more 'average' performer.

'Rank and yank' pits one employee against another, destroys morale and trust and discourages collaboration and teamwork. Why would anyone want to work with a 'star' who would outshine them in the rankings? Why wouldn't you compete with your colleagues rather than the competition and curry favour with the boss?[2]

Critical-incident method

Critical-incident, or behavioural, performance discussions are based on a record of important – critical – incidents, both positive and negative, that have occurred during the review period. You maintain a record and employees often keep their own records as well. A shortcoming of this method is that people often record only negative incidents, seeing positive incidents as merely normal job performance.

Essay method

With the essay method, you write a few paragraphs about each employee, usually according to set guidelines. This takes thought and care and can be quite time-consuming. Some managers can write more convincingly than others, which means that employees whose managers are not good writers may suffer by comparison with those rated by managers who write well.

Management by objectives method

The management by objectives (MBO) method compares an employee's results for the period under review against clear and agreed SMART targets; you then agree goals for the next review period. Putting the focus on *what* is done rather than *how* it is done makes the MBO method ideal to use with knowledge workers, teleworkers and other off-site workers and people on project teams.

⊙ THEORY TO PRACTICE

Management by objectives
Here's how MBO works: Your department's goal might be to reduce expenses by 3% and increase output by 2% during the forthcoming quarter. The administration assistant might suggest a personal target of producing 35 documents a day by the end of the next quarter and to begin at once to use recycled paper for all drafts and to print on both sides. If you and the admin assistant agree that this is reasonable, it becomes one of the admin assistant's targets. In a similar fashion, you would agree personal targets with each team member that contribute to reducing expenses and increasing output to reach the department's overall goals.

Peer review method

Some organisations include peer reviews as part of their performance evaluations. Team members review each other's performance against key criteria such as job knowledge, the ability to work as a member of and contribute to the team, to innovate and solve problems. This can be effective in productive teams where members work well together and value each other's contributions in achieving work-related objectives. When teamwork is not critical, peer reviews offer few benefits.

Performance diary method

Sometimes called full-time performance review, employees and managers both make notes on performance-related matters throughout the review period. This means that when they review past performance, both are well prepared with a full record of achievements and development areas. This method links well with most other review methods, particularly the balanced scorecard, critical incident and MBO methods.

Rating scale method

With the rating-scale method, you rate specific job-related skills and abilities of each employee according to a defined scale, as shown in Figure 15.2. This is an easy method to use and allows quick comparison between employees.

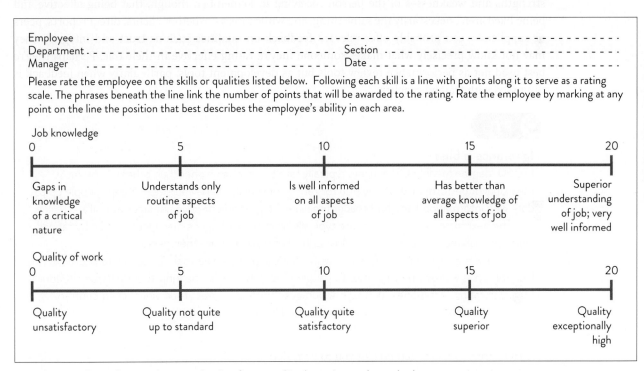

FIGURE 15.2 Part of an employee evaluation form used in the rating-scale method

Role description method

An accurate, up-to-date job or role description that includes competencies and measurable standards of performance is the key to this method of performance review. In its simplest form, the role description method provides a list of duties that the job-holder performs and you tick those the job-holder performs adequately and put a cross against those needing improvement. This method is quick and easy and highlights training needs. It's particularly effective for routine jobs such as administrative or assembly work.

The 360-degree feedback method

Multi-rater feedback, or 360-degree feedback, are often used to appraise managers and members of high-performing work teams and project teams. This feedback provides anonymous information to job-holders from 8–12 people who interact with them: direct reports, internal customers, their own manager, peers and sometimes external customers and suppliers. The person being rated also completes the feedback form for later comparison – this is how I think I perform and this is how others think I perform.

Because 360-degree feedback often measures subjective attributes rather than performance against objectives, it is more useful as a development tool than an assessment of whether an employee is meeting basic job requirements. It can provide valuable insights into how job-holders' behaviour affects others and can help them assess and improve their operating styles. This information can also be useful for succession planning and establishing and reinforcing the organisation's culture and values.

To be effective, 360-degree feedback needs to be completed in a spirit of generosity and honesty so that the feedback isn't more about the neuroses of the person giving the feedback than the strengths and weaknesses of the person receiving it. Remember, though, that being effective and being liked aren't necessarily the same thing, and while raters – whether clients, direct reports, peers or suppliers – can probably offer relevant feedback on qualities such as trust and integrity, they may not know precisely what makes someone they're rating effective in their role. Perhaps they're best used not as performance review tools but as development tools, particularly when feedback is discussed with trained coaches.

 FYI

Ignorance is bliss

In 360-degree feedback, managers typically rate themselves higher than others do on most measures of performance. This is true for ratings of specific behaviours (e.g. 'Keeps people up to date with information') and for broader measures (e.g. 'Is an effective manager overall').

The next most positive ratings are typically from the manager's manager followed by ratings from the manager's direct reports. Most critical of managers are their peers.

Patrick Barwise and Sean Meehan write that the gap between self-evaluation and evaluation from others is widest when it comes to gauging receptiveness to hearing about difficult situations (e.g. with ratings categories such as 'Encourages others to express their views, even contrary ones' and 'Listens willingly to concerns expressed by others').[3]

Here are two more methods for you to consider:

1. Mixed method.
2. Best method.

Mixed method

Many organisations try to gain the advantages of all these methods by using a combination of them – the mixed method. Performance discussion documents are divided into several sections, each consisting of one or more of the above methods. In striving to retain a wide variety of features and benefits, however, document designers can fall into the trap of creating lengthy, complicated forms that take too long to complete and may become ends in themselves.

Best method

The best method is one that:

- encourages open discussion and builds understanding between employees and their managers
- helps job-holders improve their performance and find ways to meet their personal goals
- managers and employees understand and use willingly
- sheds light on organisational difficulties and problems and helps to fix them.

Whatever method of assessing and providing formal feedback on performance your organisation uses, the resulting document can be an important reference for translating organisational goals into personal work goals and performance agreements and encouraging employees to take responsibility for meeting those goals.

2. Planning and leading formal performance discussions

It is an immutable law of business that words are words, explanations are explanations, promises are promises – but only performance is reality.

Harold S Geneen (ITT), in Levine, *The Power of Persuasion*, Wiley (2003) [4]

To lead effective performance discussions, you need to combine your communication and interpersonal skills with a systematic approach. This approach consists of three parts:

1. Preparation for the meeting
2. The meeting itself
3. Follow-up to the meeting.

Figure 15.3 shows the overall cycle of individual performance discussions in the wider context of the organisation's goals.

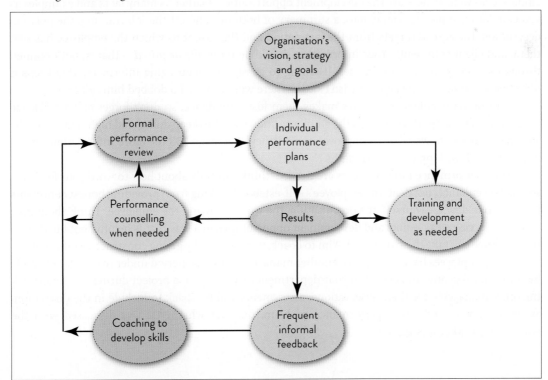

FIGURE 15.3 The cycle of performance discussions

Preparation for the meeting

Employees have only one formal performance discussion meeting – their own – and it is important to them. Careful preparation by both of you is essential.

Where is the best place to meet? This may not be your office if it's a busy one. Meeting in a neutral area, such as a conference room, can help reduce employees' anxiety and make the discussion more constructive. Make sure you have privacy so that you can't be overheard. Put a 'do not disturb' sign on the door if necessary, silence any auditory alerts on your computer, divert your phone or switch on voicemail and turn your mobile phone off to prevent interruptions. Allow about an hour for the meeting.

Think about what you can do to establish a comfortable atmosphere to make the meeting less threatening. For instance, you could sit in chairs by a low coffee table rather than face each other from opposite sides of a desk. Make sure you have chairs of similar height and arrange the blinds so that light doesn't shine in the employee's face.

One or two weeks before the meeting, schedule a date, time and place to meet. Advise employees how long you expect the meeting to last and how you plan to conduct the meeting. Provide a copy of the discussion document or explain how to find it on your organisation's Intranet. Ask the employees to consider:

* the period since their last formal performance discussion (e.g. successes, the most and least enjoyable parts of the job, any problems, their causes and how they could be resolved)
* what could be done to make their work easier, smoother or more, efficient, whether any bottlenecks hold them up, and so on (see page 342)
* the future (work goals for the forthcoming period, any help they need, career aspirations, and training and development that might be useful).

Think about your opening comments and what you are going to say and why. What does the employee do well? Where are the development opportunities? Gather as many facts and examples as you can; for example, personnel files, a summary of both on- and off-the-job training, the position description, the agreed targets from the last period and the extent to which the employee has met them, and client comments. Your information should be *naturally acquired* – that is, not obtained through snooping, from third parties, listening to gossip or encouraging informers. This keeps it objective and it means the employee isn't sitting there wondering who dobbed him or her in.

Focusing on people's weaknesses makes them lose confidence, so don't forget to acknowledge areas of satisfactory performance so the employee knows what to keep doing, and highlight strengths so the employee knows what to improve even further. (See page 133 for more information on the importance of working to your strengths.)

When performance improvements are needed, think carefully about how to word your feedback so that you enhance, not dent, the employee's self-esteem. Shirking from providing honest comments lets everyone down – yourself, the organisation, the work team and the employee. Think about how you can describe weak points and development opportunities in a way that is helpful, not hurtful, so the employee can take them on board. Aim to coach, not criticise, by giving constructive information.

When employees have reported to another manager during the period under review, for example because they recently transferred to your department or worked on a project during the period, ask the other manager(s) for their observations, assessments and feedback to include in the discussion. When comments indicate a performance problem, find out whether it was discussed with the employee and what was agreed.

> **◉ IN A NUTSHELL**
>
> **Information needed from formal performance discussion meetings**
> What you need to know from employees:
> - ambitions and aspirations
> - attitudes and feelings about their job
> - expectations of the job, work, rewards, etc.
> - how you can be of more help as a leader-manager
> - main problems faced
> - opportunities for continuous improvements
> - self-assessment of performance
> - successes during the review period
> - views on any job changes.
>
> What employees need to know from you:
> - clarification of job, targets, responsibilities
> - constructive help with any difficulties or problem areas
> - departmental or team objectives and how the employee contributes
> - recognition of good work.
>
> What you agree together:
> - action plan for future development
> - an overall assessment of performance
> - performance plan and targets for the next review period
> - what help and support you will provide.

The meeting itself

The meeting itself has the following stages, which cover the past to the future:
- Creating the right climate
- Performance review and planning
- Final summary.

There should be no surprises in a performance discussion meeting – think of it as a dotting of the i's and a crossing of the t's. When an employee has performed better or less well than expected in some areas, or is generally improving or declining, you should have mentioned it long before now in an informal feedback meeting (discussed below). This is not the time to begin documenting performance shortfalls or counselling an employee about poor performance. (Chapter 16 explains how to counsel employees who are underperforming.) When discussing areas of disappointing performance, keep your input constructive in order to maintain or enhance the employee's self-esteem and discuss what assistance and support you can provide.

Creating the right climate

Performance discussions can be intimidating and employees can have feelings that range from defensiveness to eagerness to indifference, from looking forward to the meeting to feeling anxious about it. Create a non-threatening atmosphere to make the meeting as relaxed, constructive and pleasant as possible. Throughout the discussion, make sure your verbal and non-verbal messages say the same thing.

Put employees at ease so they are willing to talk freely. Set the scene by reviewing the purpose of the interview, stressing that you want it to be a two-way discussion about the employee's contributions and an opportunity to plan his or her future development and job and career goals. Outline your plan for how the interview will proceed.

Performance review and planning

Formal performance discussions generally begin by looking backward over the previous period and then move on to discussing how the job or workflow can be improved to increase efficiency. This is followed by looking forward and planning for the future in terms of goals and targets, job progression, and training and development goals.

Aim for an open and honest exchange of views, conversational in tone. Try to do most of the listening and let the employee do most of the talking.

 IN A NUTSHELL

What performance reviews are not

A performance discussion is not an argument. It is not patronising ('Let me point out to you some of your shortcomings') or a game of cat and mouse ('You tell me how you think you did and I'll tell you what I think').

Neither is a performance discussion a performance counselling meeting. When performance is below standard, address it straightaway – don't wait until the formal performance discussion to address the matter. When you need to address performance shortfalls during an appraisal, switch to problem-solving. Most people want to do a good job, and when you handle the discussion well you can jointly explore the causes of poor performance and the steps that you can each take to improve it.

Looking backward: Performance review

Begin by asking what the employee believes they have contributed to the organisation or the team since your last discussion. Then compare the targets with actual performance, highlighting and appreciating areas of sustained good and excellent performance and areas in which the employee has made improvements. Review the employee's progress since the last discussion to reinforce what went well and agree how to remedy any difficulties. Follow the Bat–Mice acronym for giving feedback summarised in Figure 15.4 on page 442. To reinforce a learning culture, ask what the employees have learned during the period under review and how they've put it to use.

 THEORY TO PRACTICE

Tread softly and concentrate on your goals

Back in the hunter-gatherer days, people literally couldn't survive outside the 'work group'. Today, criticism at work strikes at the same psychological fears of abandonment and exclusion. That's why people tend to hear negative information the loudest, even when the majority of comments are positive: blood pressure rises, hearts race, muscles tense.

Our brains have separate circuits to handle negative information and events and these circuits are more sensitive than the circuits that handle positive information and events. People notice negatives in others and themselves more readily than positive information and are hypersensitive to criticism, even hearing criticism when it really isn't there.

Here's the antidote: When you need to offer a corrective or constructive comment, frame it to emphasise inclusion. Starting off with a question, for example, helps the employee feel

>>

included: 'How do you think you're going? What are your goals for ...?' When you make your corrective or constructive comment, move straight into what you want. Use phrases like 'From now on', 'In future' or 'How can we improve this?' This is a way of saying: 'Let's not dwell on the past, it's done', 'Let's get it right from now on', 'We're in this together'. That makes a performance improvement more likely.

Listen to the employee's point of view using the EARS formula, shown 'In a Nutshell: Use your EARS!' in Chapter 6 on page 156. This reduces defensiveness, increases your understanding and ability to empathise, and sets the scene for collaborative problem-solving. (To find out more about how to listen well, see page 158.)

Looking at now: Making improvements

Ask employees whether they have experienced any problems since their last performance discussion and how they resolved them or whether they're ongoing (see page 156 for more information on asking questions). Fully explore the *'chance to'* key explained on page 339 to find ways work could be carried out more easily, safely, quickly, reliably or cheaply and to remove obstacles to successful performance. This is a perfect opportunity to uncover and resolve problems and make continuous improvements.

When there are opportunities to improve performance, employees generally respond better when you help them to figure out how to themselves. Table 15.1 shows you the difference.

TABLE 15.1 Use open questions

Closed question	Open question
Can I help you?	How can I help you?
Do you want to give it more thought?	What other thoughts do you have?
Is there a better way to do this?	How else could you do this?

THEORY TO PRACTICE

Hone your messages

Do you want your feedback to to make a difference? Table 15.2 shows you how to turn positive general feedback into positive specific feedback and how to turn unhelpful negative general feedback into corrective feedback and, better still, constructive feedback.

TABLE 15.2 Negative versus positive feedback

Negative feedback	Positive feedback
Unhelpful (negative general feedback)	**(positive general feedback)**
'You're unreliable.'	'You're a fantastic team member.'
Better (corrective feedback)	**(but still a bit general)**
'I need prior warning if your project is late'	'I can always count on you to meet your deadlines.'
Better still (constructive feedback)	**(specific positive feedback)**
'When you were late with that project, how do you think it affected the rest of the team?'	'I very much appreciated the way you pulled out all the stops to complete the XYZ project on time.'

The way you provide feedback is critical. Here's how to provide effective feedback – make it:

Balanced Give both positive and constructive feedback that builds self-esteem.

Actionable Feedback should be about something the person is responsible for. Give examples.

Timely Now or later? When will be the most receptive/productive time to arrange a discussion?

Meaningful Keep your feedback to the point and based on facts, not hearsay. If you're not sure of the facts, find out. Be clear about the standards required and specific about performance shortfalls or what the employee did well. Provide only as much information as the employee can assimilate and act on.

'I' language Say 'I' rather than 'you' to keep defensiveness, resistance and arguments to a minimum and to stop your praise from sounding like insincere flattery: 'I appreciate that you did such-and-such because …' is useful, positive and specific. 'You're a good worker' is too general to be useful and can sound patronising. 'I need' rather than 'You must' is less pushy and more confident. Avoid stating your opinion as if it were a fact.

Constructive Aim to be helpful, not hurtful. Even negative feedback can be put into a positive context. Use objective, neutral words to avoid confrontations and to prevent your feedback from being taken personally.

Empathic Be considerate and relate your comments to the employee's point of view. Make it clear that it is not a criticism or reflection on the employee as a person.

FIGURE 15.4 The Bat–Mice feedback acronym

Looking forward: Performance planning

Don't concentrate so much on the past that you short-change the future. Agree future measures of success and timeframes for their achievement. Nobody is quite sure who said this first, but thousands of managers over the years have repeated the saying, 'What gets measured gets done.'

It's true. Clear targets help people do their jobs well by helping them concentrate their attention and energy on important matters. That's why it is necessary to review them even when they haven't changed much from the last period. Make clear how they fit into the organisation's vision, strategy and goals and place them in the context of the job-holder's job purpose and key result areas.

Keep targets flexible enough to accommodate changes in the marketplace and your operating environment. You may even need to alter targets that have been in effect for a long time when work conditions, different materials or processes, or other factors demand it. You may also need to change targets to reflect changing priorities or to develop employees' skills and extend and broaden their motivation and contribution to the organisation.

Targets should be SMART: Specific, Motivating (in order to drive performance), Ambitious (achievable yet challenging), Related to the team's and organisation's goals, and Trackable. Discuss how the employee's success is to be monitored. Go for as many lead indicators as you can so that both you and the job-holder know how things are going. (See pages 113 and 327 for more information on SMART targets and using lead and lag indicators to measure success.) Write down the measures of success, along with any agreed-upon actions; both you and the employee should keep a copy.

When agreeing success measures for the next period, remember that people often set themselves overly ambitious targets and you might need to help them adjust the targets to more realistic levels.

Looking further forward: Development planning

Most systems also call for a development plan for the job-holder. Depending on your organisation's system, this may include a training or development plan, career aspirations and a list of other internal roles that interest the job-holder.

Get employees talking about themselves and their work-related likes and dislikes. Find out their short- and long-term career aspirations (remembering lateral moves as well as upward moves) and the learning and development opportunities that interest them most. Ask what assignments, projects and work they've found most enjoyable, what accomplishments over the last period they've felt good about and what makes for a great day at work. Ask what's most important to them and how they view themselves in relation to their team and the organisation and how they believe they can make the best contributions. Think about any trends in the organisation and industry and how they may affect employees.

Based on this information, draw up a development plan identifying any skills the employee needs to learn or strengthen. Set some development priorities by selecting two or three skills to concentrate on, based on what is most achievable and what would be most useful to the organisation and identify the best approach (e.g. adding responsibilities to the current job, coaching, delegation, professional reading, shadowing someone, special assignments, training programs). Discuss the next steps in implementing the plan, and diarise to check in with the employee every few months to find out how his or her development plan is progressing and what help, if any, you can provide. (See Chapter 27 for more information on encouraging learning and creating development plans and learning opportunities.)

As well as developing and retaining valuable employees, realistic development plans help match employees' skills and talents to the needs of the organisation and help employees ready themselves for changes and trends in their working environment. You benefit, too, by attracting the best people to work for you because of your reputation as a manager who builds people's skills and cares enough about them to help them build their careers.

(Don't worry that training employees hastens their departure. The reverse is more likely true: People who grow in an organisation stay because they know they and their potential are valued. Failing to develop employees, place them in jobs they enjoy or provide the opportunities they want hastens their departure.)

And what about me?

It's a good idea to ask for some feedback for yourself, too. You may get useful ideas that help you improve your own job performance, and gain the employees' respect for your openness and willingness to listen and learn. A simple question like 'What can I do to make your job easier?' can start the ball rolling. Here are some other questions to try:

* Am I involved enough, or too much, in your work?
* Could I do anything to help you balance your personal and work commitments?
* Do I encourage learning?
* Do I explain the strategic direction of the organisation clearly enough?
* Do I listen to your ideas?
* Do I promote a team spirit?
* Do I provide enough information on what's happening in the rest of the organisation?
* Do I seek your input frequently enough?
* Do I set a good example and promote and display the organisation's values and vision?
* Do I show you that I'm interested in your success here?
* Do I treat you fairly?
* How could I communicate what I expect from you more clearly?
* How could I encourage more creativity and innovation?
* How could I make you feel more comfortable asking me questions and discussing work-related concerns with me?
* What do I do that helps you in your job?
* What do you wish I would do differently?

Encouraging and listening to feedback demonstrates the behaviour you expect.

Final summary

Before closing the meeting, find out whether the employee has any questions or anything to add. Answer questions as fully, tactfully and truthfully as possible. Ensure the employee understands the performance agreement and has realistic expectations of career and pay prospects for the next period. Confirm the main points covered and the actions and priorities agreed and diarise a short follow-up meeting in about six weeks to discuss progress against targets and agreed actions.

Then conclude the discussion constructively. Employees should leave feeling confident that you have appreciated their strong points and contributions to the department.

THEORY TO PRACTICE

A typical agenda for a performance discussion meeting

Try this timetable at your next formal performance discussion:

1. Put the employee at ease. He or she should be able to feel relaxed and speak freely. Do this by explaining how you are going to guide the meeting (allow 2 minutes).
2. Review the discussion form and listen to the employee's thoughts. Explain your perspective. Discuss specific behavioural examples (only examples that you have seen or heard) or refer to objective, measurable standards, such as agreed targets met or not met (allow 15 minutes).
3. Look for ways to make continuous improvements and improve the employee's job (allow 10 minutes).
4. Agree on SMART goals and targets to drive performance for the next period (allow 10 minutes).
5. Agree on development goals and a development plan (allow 5 minutes).
6. Finish by asking the employee to provide feedback for yourself (allow 10 minutes).
7. End the meeting by inviting the employee to ask questions. Review the actions you have mutually agreed to take and be sure to end on a positive note (allow 3 minutes).

IN A NUTSHELL

Five ways to help performance reviews go well

Your employee deserves to have the best possible performance review. Here are five ways to help make that possible:

1. Have a sound and accurate knowledge of the employee's deliverables and work performance.
2. Accept the employee as a person, distinct from their performance.
3. Be positive and constructive and find ways to make the employee's job easier, improve performance further, and develop skills and job interest.
4. Gain the employee's active participation in the discussion.
5. Thoroughly prepare for the discussion and encourage the employee to do the same.

Follow-up the meeting

In order to keep any promises or agreements you have made, put automatic reminders in your electronic task list. Show a continuing interest in the employee's performance and career. Keep up the two-way communication with regular informal feedback.

Treat all performance discussions as confidential. Store all documents securely. Don't leave them lying on your desk.

ACTION!

Complete the interactive self-test, How did I do? on **CourseMateExpress** to gauge how well you have conducted the performance discussion.

Feedback traps to avoid

Giving formal and informal performance feedback poorly not only lets you down as a manager but lets the organisation and employees down, too. Here are some ways to avoid the common mistakes.

Develop self-awareness so that you're alert to any personal biases and blind spots that could affect your judgement. Don't allow whether or not you personally like an employee, or how easy or difficult a person is to manage, to compromise your objectivity. Concentrate on a person's work performance, not their personality, by distinguishing between personality traits and performance criteria.

Don't rely on hunches or intuition. Compare previously agreed targets against actual performance. Don't overemphasise uncharacteristic performance – when someone has done something unusually well or unusually poorly, don't let it eclipse their more typical job performance or behaviour.

Recognise good performance and address any areas of concern. Remaining impartial and objective helps you overcome any feelings of awkwardness at having to 'judge' employees. Don't gloss over any mistakes or areas needing improvement.

Don't use different standards to rate employees doing the same job. For example, don't rate a low-performing but highly motivated employee higher than an employee who is performing the job adequately but unenthusiastically. Keep your rating standards fair and consistent and directed at results or work performance.

Don't confuse length of service with job performance. Being with the organisation for a long time doesn't guarantee high performance. Conversely, being new to a job doesn't automatically mean someone is unable to do it well.

No matter how busy you are or how efficient you want to be, avoid the 'assembly line' approach (holding one interview after another). Rushing the meeting can result in 'telling' rather than 'discussing'.

● IN A NUTSHELL

Five traps to avoid

A performance review that goes wrong can be a disaster for your employee and also affect the work he or she does for your organisation. Be careful not to fall into these traps:

1. *Halo/horns effect.* Allowing your assessment of one area of an employee's performance to influence how you assess the other areas greatly reduces its accuracy and objectivity. Rate each aspect of performance independently of the others.

2. *Positive, negative or centralising.* This is a tendency to be too lenient, too strict or too average in ranking employees. Assess each aspect of an employee's performance individually and objectively.

3. *Psychoanalysing.* Labelling people or their behaviour is dangerous and is usually incorrect and offensive to the person being 'analysed'. Don't worry about 'why' someone does something; all you're concerned with is job performance.

4. *Recency.* Allowing recent events to overshadow older ones and overemphasising non-typical or most recent incidents, either good or bad, can artificially sway your evaluation, limiting its fairness and accuracy. Base your discussion of job performance over the whole period under review, not just a small part of it or what has occurred most recently.

5. *Stereotyping.* Assuming that people who belong to certain groups (Generation Ys, men, women, people from specific ethnic groups, etc.) are identical can prevent you from seeing their performance realistically and objectively. Be sensitive to cultural differences, but treat each job-holder individually and on their merits.

3. Providing informal feedback on performance

Employees rarely need to be reminded of their mistakes. However, they do need to be told how important and valuable they are.

Olivia McIvor (corporate culture adviser), *The Business of Kindness* (2006)[5]

People need, and deserve, to know how they are doing and that their efforts are noticed and appreciated. They also need, and deserve, to know whether they could improve in some way and, if so, how. And they need, and deserve, to receive this information promptly; one annual or six-monthly formal performance discussion isn't enough. You need a continuing dialogue to keep up the momentum of your formal discussions.

Being miserly with feedback leaves employees floundering; eventually, they give up trying and just 'go through the motions'. That's performance *mis*-management! When employees do a good job – tell them. When there is an opportunity to improve an aspect of their work – tell them.

Regular informal feedback, in words and actions, about how employees are going builds motivation and morale and demonstrates your interest in them and their job performance. It keeps everyone's attention on what is important, builds good work habits and ensures that work standards are maintained. The more often you give feedback, the more expected and valued it is and the better it works.

If your workload or personality doesn't lend itself to lots of informal feedback, schedule regular short sessions with each team member. One well-conducted 10-minute feedback conversation a fortnight or a month can keep spirits and performance high. Keep brief notes that identify areas of excellent performance, coaching or development opportunities, or demonstration of your organisation's values, to draw on when it comes to the formal review and regular catch-up meetings.

When you give feedback, think of yourself as a mirror that helps people see themselves objectively. Focus on visible behaviour, not personality, the results you expect and how employees are meeting their targets. (See 'FYI: Cultural feedback' on page 864.)

The ultimate goal of feedback is to help people monitor their own performance so they can give feedback to themselves.

Think of 'feedback' as 'information'

Here's the rub: As soon as you say 'feedback', most people think 'negative' and 'criticism'. That's unfortunate. From now on, when you hear 'feedback', think 'information' – information that helps people perform better, learn and build their skills and value as employees.

The right kind and amount of information at the right time maintains high productivity and lifts average and low productivity. It helps people feel noticed, supported, valued and encouraged. It develops individuals and teams, builds a positive working climate and develops an open, honest communication culture. The more you offer informative feedback, the more employees come to expect it and appreciate it.

Types of feedback

Constructive feedback, given to help employees further improve already acceptable performance or work out for themselves how to improve their permanence, is explained below and discussed further in Chapter 27, while corrective feedback, given to assist underperforming employees bring their performance up to the required standard, is explained on page 470. The section below examines the informal, everyday feedback you give to boost motivation and keep performance moving forward.

As demonstrated by the 'In a Nutshell' below, there are three types of feedback: Positive, negative and none at all. Positive and negative feedback can be general or specific.

THEORY TO PRACTICE

Examples of feedback

Constructive feedback is the most effective but any type of positive feedback will always beat the negative varieties, as Table 15.3 shows.

TABLE 15.3 Defining feedback

Manager says	Type of feedback
'It's great to have you on the team.'	Positive general
'You met all your targets again this week. I really appreciate your hard work and the contribution you make to our success as a department.'	Positive specific
'You'll need to try harder.'	Negative general
'You're doing that the wrong way.'	Negative specific
'Here, let me show you an easier way to do that.'	Constructive
Walking past an employee's work station and ignoring her.	No feedback at all
Continually ignoring targets being met or not being met.	No feedback at all

 IN A NUTSHELL

The three types of feedback

Feedback can be divided into positive and negative feedback and no feedback at all. Table 15.4 shows you the effects of specific and general feedback.

TABLE 15.4 The right feedback

	Specific	General
Positive feedback	Behaviour that is reinforced with positive specific feedback is repeated. Use it when people do something you want them to keep doing, such as meeting or exceeding a performance target, making a new team member feel welcome, or keeping their work area tidy. Use it to ensure that people continue to meet performance standards and to increase employees' skills and willingness. Say *what* you appreciate as well as *why* you appreciate it: 'Thanks, that was great – particularly the way you presented the data in graphs – it made it much easier to understand.'	This is feedback you give employees just for being themselves. A cheerful 'Hello', a friendly smile, or a 'Thanks, that's great', develops productive working relationships. General positive feedback makes people feel good and raises their self-confidence and self-esteem. It's excellent for general motivation and morale and for maintaining a constructive working climate. Combine it with positive specific feedback and negative specific feedback so it doesn't lose its effect and you're seen just as a jolly person, not as a helpful leader-manager.

>>

TABLE 15.4 The right feedback (Continued)

	Specific	General
Negative feedback	Specific negative feedback provides clear information regarding a particular action or result. Because it is specific, it can help reduce or eliminate the behaviour in question and improve results. The best specific negative feedback is <u>corrective</u> or <u>constructive</u> – it says precisely *what* is wrong and suggests an improvement or explains *what* is wrong and *why* it matters: 'Thanks, this looks really good. The layout is fantastic – it's clear and easy to read. I think a great final touch would be to display the data in graph form. Would you have a go at that?' Feedback like this strengthens relationships and helps people perform tasks better.	Criticism, put-downs and sarcasm make people feel unimportant and unappreciated and lower morale and self-esteem. Messages like 'You again. What is it *this* time?' can be verbal or conveyed with just a look or a sigh. Avoid this type of feedback at all costs. There is never a good reason to use it.
No feedback	A feedback vacuum implies that neither the employees nor their performance matter. Continually ignoring employees or walking by their desks each morning without saying 'Good morning!' shrivels performance, motivation and even self-esteem. Lack of feedback extinguishes good performance and invites poor performance.	

Constructive information

Ignored problems tend to grow worse, so address them in an impartial, non-threatening way. Remember, though, that however helpfully you do this, constructive information can still sting. So unless it involves the whole team, give it in private and think first how best to phrase it. You may think you're simply pointing out a problem or offering advice but off-hand comments can be misunderstood. You don't want your words or tone of voice to crush someone's confidence or enthusiasm; you want to help people improve their performance.

Negative information is more palatable when it is supported by facts and directed at behaviour and not at the person. Stick to facts and factual descriptions of behaviour, something job-holders do or say, and work performance, particularly outcomes or targets they are not meeting, and be careful to distinguish between a fact and your opinion.

Only give feedback on aspects of employees' performance that they can control; that is, behaviours they can change or skills they can improve or develop. Aim at changes in behaviour that can bring a measurable difference in results that both you and others can see. Deal with one issue at a time because too much information at once is difficult to absorb. Include the three pieces of information shown in Figure 15.5.

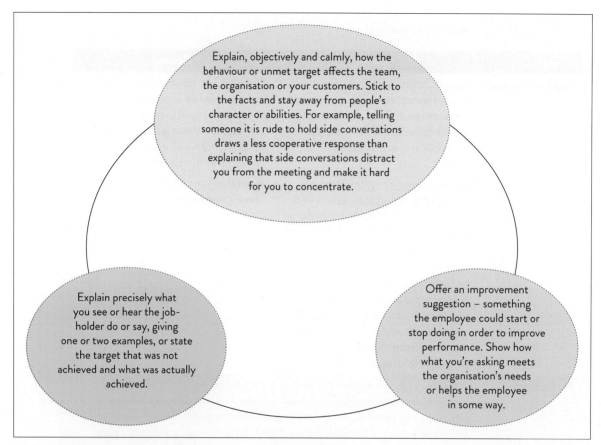

FIGURE 15.5 Constructive information

THE STRATEGIC PERSPECTIVE

Destructive information

A long chain of criticism is hard to take and hard to digest; it sets up barriers of suspicion and resentment and damages your relationship with employees. When you make people feel bad about their performance, the stress hormones (adrenaline and cortisol) can increase so much that creativity, memory, planning, thinking, and other mental functions shut down and performance worsens – the opposite of what you want. The employee's attention fixates on the threat you pose, not their performance. (In fact, when research scientists want to study the highest levels of stress hormones, they give their subjects intense face-to-face criticism, causing these hormones to surge and the heart rate to spike by 30 to 40 beats per minute.)[6]

You can't make people do better by making them feel bad. Giving feedback in a critical, confrontational or impolite way invites a self-protective response and creates bad feelings and poor performance. Make your comments clear, objectively describe the behaviour or unmet target that concerns you, and convey the information in a positive, helpful way. In short: Say what you mean, but don't be mean.

There are helpful and unhelpful ways to present the same information, so think about the words you use when offering feedback. Table 15.5 shows you how.

TABLE 15.5 Choose the better feedback option

Poor ways to begin feedback	Better ways to begin feedback
'You don't seem to be able to …'	'I see you're having trouble …'
'You're not doing that properly …'	'I'd like to run through how I'd like you to do this.'
'You didn't …'	'You'll find it easier to …'
'You shouldn't …'	'It's faster to …'
'You always …You never …'	'Next time … From now on …'

Notice that in these examples most of the 'you's' are changed to 'I's'. This turns your information from a critical 'push' to a helpful 'pull'.

There are other ways to begin feedback tactfully. For example:

- Saying 'could' instead of 'should' creates less guilt about something the employee did that can't be changed and gives the employee a choice for next time: 'You could have begun collecting the data last week so that you didn't have to rush through preparing your quotation.'
- Saying 'not wise' rather than 'bad' means you're not commenting on the employee's character but on the natural consequences of their actions: 'The decision to wait to collect the data until the week the quotation was due was not wise. Not only did you need to rush the preparation of the quotation, which I'm sure affected its quality, but the last-minute rushing affected the rest of the team.'
- Referring to a mistake as a 'valuable lesson' means that employees can learn from their actions: 'Waiting to collect the data until the week the quotation was due was a valuable lesson for next time.'
- Say: 'You did a great job, and …' rather than 'You did a great job, but …' because people know when they hear 'but' that bad news is about to follow. 'You did a great job, and one thing you could do to improve it is …' is much more effective.

Research shows that your manner in delivering feedback is critically important. People who receive constructive or corrective performance feedback accompanied by the positive emotional signals of nods and smiles feel better about their performance than people who are given positive performance feedback delivered in a critical manner, with frowns and narrowed eyes. Why is it important that people feel as good as possible about your feedback? Because when people feel better, they perform better. You can, and should, set high standards, but do so in ways that foster a positive mood in your teams.

 **IN A NUTSHELL**

Offering feedback and raising concerns

The 'Keep – Stop – Start' method is another good way to offer feedback:

- Keep doing these helpful things.
- Stop doing these unhelpful things.
- Start doing these things.

»

And then there's the 'More – Less – Keep' method:
* More of this (actions which may be lacking or you would like to see more of).
* Less of this.
* Keep these effective behaviours and practices.

Be specific so that your comments aren't misinterpreted. When you have a concern, try these two ways to express your concern and the solution. Just fill in the details where the ellipses are marked:
* 'When you ... (describe the action), it's a problem because ... (describe the effect). Could I ask that you ... (describe the solution)?'

Or
* 'It would really help me achieve ... (describe the goal), if you could ... (describe the solution) instead of ... (describe the current action).'

The sandwich technique

You may have heard of the 'sandwich technique' for giving feedback, where you 'sandwich' a negative piece of feedback between two positive pieces of feedback. It can work, provided you don't train employees to wait for 'the bad news' every time they hear some 'good news'.

For the sandwich technique to be effective, use it with bigger matters. In other words, don't say 'You handled that well but you forgot to ... But keep up the good work.' That's too small a matter. For small matters, coaching is more effective: 'Everything worked well there, except for this ... Next time, try doing ... instead. I think you'll find it a lot easier and you'll get a better result.'

For bigger matters, you could say, 'Sam, you're doing a great job. There is one thing I'd like to see you doing and it's this ... Sam, when you do this, you'll be meeting all your key responsibilities.'

You can find out more about how to coach on page 912.

The hot-stove principle

The 'hot stove' is a particular type of specific negative feedback that you probably need to use only occasionally, and only with three types of employees:
* Employees who are 'testing' rules to see how far they can go.
* Newer employees who inadvertently break a rule.
* Skilled and experienced employees who 'know better'.

As explained on page 332, the hot-stove principle is particularly useful for safety and other straightforward infringements of the organisation's rules and policies. However, make sure you don't use this technique when performance drops for reasons outside the employee's control at the workplace or because of a personal problem (see the *'chance to'* key on page 339). To do so under such circumstances would be harsh, aggressive and unfair.

● IN A NUTSHELL

How to turn criticism into information

You can't force people to change. You can only bring something to their attention and point out what they can do to improve their performance. Think of feedback as sharing ideas and information rather than giving orders or advice. Think about how you would feel being given the same information. Work out how to make the information useful to the receiver and choose your words to show that you are both on the same side. Choose your time, too. Don't wait too long, but make sure the job-holder has the time to listen and is in the right frame of mind.

>>

- Ask, don't tell.
- Avoid vague statements and generalisations; when you use words like 'always' or 'never', you may be exaggerating.
- Describe behaviour and offer your observations rather than judge the person and make inferences.
- Don't fix blame, fix the problem. Ask: 'How can we ...?' or 'What can we do to ...?'
- Focus on the future and on solutions and goals (what you *do* want), not on the past or on problems or mistakes (what you *don't* want). Paint the picture of the end result you're after.
- Think before you act or speak.

Offer improvement suggestions:

- 'I'll know you're doing a good job when ...'
- 'From now on ...'
- 'Here's another thought ...'
- 'Next time ...'
- 'That disappointed me because ...'
- 'That was good and you could also ...'
- 'That was great and another thing you could do is ...'
- 'Try it this way ...'
- 'Would you please ...'

When you have trouble turning critical remarks into constructive remarks, ask yourself how the employee would describe his or her behaviours and results.

Positive information

Once upon a time, most managers thought like this: 'When my people don't hear from me, they know they're doing all right and still have a job. They hear from me soon enough when they're not getting it right, though.'

Most people don't equate silence with approval – even employees whose work is always good need to hear it from you. Since each role is critical to success (if it isn't, why is it being done?), each job-holder expects you to monitor his or her contributions and provide feedback. Don't ignore performance that meets expectation. When your team or department is running smoothly, recognise and encourage work well done.

Praise and 'thank yous' build productivity and general positive recognition is fine. Specific positive feedback is stronger, though; most employees would rather hear how good their work is than what nice people they are.

Offer positive specific feedback for behaviours that fall short of expectations, too. Sometimes people try hard but events outside their control prevent them from fully reaching their targets. Similarly, when people try hard while they are still learning or building skills and experience and don't quite reach their targets, keep their motivation high by thanking them for their commitment to the goal. This reinforces the behaviour you want so that it continues. Acknowledge and appreciate extra effort and behaviour that supports the organisation's values, too.

Saying thanks is great and, when you can, an unexpected movie voucher or box of chocolates does wonders for morale, too. When you thank a member of another team for something they've done, do so in person when you can, and thank them again by email so you can cc their boss; you'll have a fan for life. Building a culture of appreciation builds performance.

> ◉ **THEORY TO PRACTICE**

Go for balanced, intermittent feedback

Monitor your feedback to make sure it is balanced, because overusing any one type of feedback soon makes it meaningless. Even constant 'Good on ya's' wear thin.

To build or activate new behaviours (e.g. with new recruits or transfers or when training existing staff in something new) use a lot of positive specific feedback. Gradually reduce it to maintain behaviours once they are established. Once people are doing a good job, the most effective feedback is *intermittent* (irregular or random), positive and specific.

4. Receiving feedback

There are two things people want more than sex and money: Recognition and praise.

Mary Kay Ash (cosmetics entrepreneur), quoted in Eckert, 'The two most important words' (Apri 2013)[7]

It's worrying having to guess how your boss thinks you're doing. Most people need guidance to figure out how to improve their performance and steer their careers. These are two good reasons to look forward to your own performance discussion. Here are some tips to follow.

If you haven't already done so, organise your job into key result areas (KRAs) and measures of success (MOS) or key performance indicators and confirm them with your manager to ensure that you both assesses your performance on the same objective, measurable criteria. (See page 111 and 112 to find out more about KRAs and MOS.) Discuss which of your responsibilities are most important, too. This gives you a clear basis for your performance discussion.

Between discussions, keep notes of your successes and achievements; in case your manager has a short memory, you can jog it. Similarly, note any difficulties and review the five keys (explained in Chapter 11) to identify their causes so you can take, and note, remedial action.

Think about any issues you want to raise and how best to introduce them. What problems bother you that your manager might be able to assist with? Which problems, when resolved, would provide a key to solving others? Which problems, left alone, promise to grow worse? Which problems need help or support from others to fix? From what training and development opportunities would you benefit? What direction would you like to see your career take? (See page 131 to find out how to plan your career.)

Approach the performance discussion in a positive frame of mind and with the aim of gathering ideas on how to improve your performance, develop your skills further and enhance your contribution to the organisation. Don't make your manager fight every point; be open to advice and listen carefully to any suggestions and constructive feedback. Take a deep breath, listen and learn, and don't become defensive. When you're not clear about the feedback your manager gives you, ask for examples in a way that shows you want to understand.

When your manager asks for your feedback, concentrate on job-related areas where you interact with your manager. Acknowledge the ways your manager assists you to achieve your objectives. Try the Keep – Stop – Start or the More – Less – Same approach described above.

Don't shy away from asking for help or for changes in your working relationship that could help you achieve your goals more effectively (e.g. more cheaply, easily, quickly). Think about how to raise these issues sensitively and tactfully.

Page 141 gives information on seeking informal feedback.

CourseMateExpress

Go to http://login.cengagebrain.com to access CourseMate Express, your online study tool for *Management Theory & Practice*. CourseMate Express brings chapter concepts to life with interactive learning, and study and exam preparation tools:

- Test your skills in different aspects of management with interactive self-tests and simulations.
- Watch videos that show how real managers operate in real businesses.
- Test your understanding of the changing world of management by taking the revision quiz.

QUICK REVIEW

1. List at least five ways that organisations and managers use formal performance discussions and briefly describe the main methods that are commonly used, stating whether each is best suited to particular types of jobs.
2. What role do informal and formal performance discussions play in performance management?
3. Briefly describe the three main parts of a formal performance discussion, stating what should be covered during each part and what is off limits.
4. Summarise the principles of giving feedback and explain how formal and informal feedback can encourage good performance and turn around poor performance.

BUILD YOUR SKILLS

1. List and describe what you believe are the main hazards managers should watch for in assessing employees' performance, and discuss how each of these can be overcome.
2. Discuss five practices that managers should follow when holding formal performance discussions.
3. Referring to the Scenario at the beginning of this chapter, what are some ways Mark could motivate Tom and show that he values him without giving him a pay rise? How would you persuade Mark of the benefits in conducting well-planned performance reviews?
4. Turn the following critical comments into coaching comments:
   a. 'You should ...'
   b. 'Why can't you ...?'
   c. 'You'll have to ...'
   d. 'I've told you before not to ...'
   e. 'You never ...'
   f. 'You don't understand.'
   g. '... but ...'
5. Janeth consistently turns in quality work but, unfortunately, equally consistently, it is a day or two late. This creates a bottleneck as others rely on her work and can't carry on without it. You know that nothing in the work environment is holding her up. Apart from this, Janeth is a consistently good employee. What could you say to address this problem? Write down something you would feel comfortable saying that follows the suggestions in this chapter.
6. You have spoken to Janeth about her work coming in late and causing hold-ups for others and she has made an effort to complete her work on time. Instead of being late 90% of the time, she is late about 50% of the time. Write down feedback that you would feel comfortable giving to Janeth and that follows the suggestions in this chapter.

WORKPLACE ACTIVITIES

1. Describe your organisation's formal performance review and planning system and how your organisation uses it to manage its human resources from a strategic perspective.

2. List and explain the steps you went through before conducting a recent performance discussion, including your planning before the meeting and your actions after it.

3. Have you ever had a formal performance discussion? Discuss the system that was used, your feelings during the meeting, and whether and how it helped build your performance and morale. In your experience, what makes for an effective performance discussion?

CASE STUDY 15.1

THE PERFECT OPPORTUNITY

Peter is thinking about the forthcoming performance discussion with Samantha. For several months now he has been concerned about her ability to perform her job to the required standards, in terms of both quality and quantity of service. When he assigns her fewer tables to serve, her attention to detail, correct order delivery and customer service are first class. But when he assigns her the number of tables he expects her to serve, and that the others cope with adequately, her service level drops.

She doesn't seem to be able to get the balance right, despite his feedback and coaching. Peter decides that the formal performance discussion next week is the perfect opportunity to warn her that her job is on the line unless her performance improves.

At the meeting, Peter explains to Samantha that her performance is unsatisfactory and outlines why, giving her several examples from the last few weeks, which, he is careful to point out, are representative of the way she has worked since joining the restaurant service team four months ago. He also explains that, as good as her service is when she serves fewer tables, he can't afford to keep her on unless she can find a way to deliver great service to the required number of customers.

Samantha seems to be truly shocked. While she knows that her productivity is lower than some of the others, she clearly hasn't realised how serious the problem is. She says that she is trying as hard as she can and she really needs her job. She also indicates that she feels she has made progress over the last two or three months. With this, she bursts into tears, leaving Peter at a loss to know what to do.

Questions

1. Was the formal performance discussion the perfect opportunity to begin the termination of employment process? Why or why not?
2. What mistakes did Peter make with Samantha's performance discussion?
3. What should Peter have done before the meeting? What should he do now? Should he have dealt with Samantha's performance shortfall before?

CASE STUDY 15.2

THE EVALUATION CONFERENCE

Harry Chan is the uncontested chief at the bank. He is articulate, conservative, pleasant and well groomed, and he wants his staff to fit into the same mould. He isn't always successful, however, even though he uses every opportunity to try to get the message across.

In his performance conference with Bob Regan, for example, he brings up the subject of how a bank employee should look and act. The conversation goes as follows:

Chan: 'Come in, Bob, and let's get this show on the road.'

Regan: 'Sorry I'm late, Mr Chan, but a customer wanted to change an account.'

Chan: 'I'm glad you brought up changes, because I'd like to see you change somewhat. Your looks don't say "You can trust me" to a customer.'

Regan: 'Pardon?'

Chan: 'Well, take that stubbly beard you wear. Our customers don't like to deal with employees with fuzz on their face.'

Regan: 'I've never had a complaint and ...'

Chan: 'And another thing, your general demeanour is far too glib. You ought to be more subdued in the way you approach people. This isn't a fairground, you know.'

Regan: 'Mr Chan, I've been working in banks for seven years and I've never had a customer refuse to see me. On the contrary, I have a good many who wait for me. In fact, as far as I can tell, my beard and manner have never interfered with services to our customers. I really can't agree ...'

Chan: 'This review session is for you to find out what I think, not for me to find out what you think. I think you present the wrong image and I want you to change it.'

Regan: 'What about my job performance, Mr Chan? Is my work satisfactory?'

Chan: 'No real complaint in that department, Regan. You ought to know your job by now. Oh, there is one thing. I noticed that you took a loan application last week that was totally outside the criteria we use. You've placed the bank and the customer in an embarrassing situation. You'd better watch that.'

Regan: 'Mr Chan, I remember the case you are referring to. As a matter of fact, I knew it was marginal, but with the emphasis on equal treatment I thought we ought to look at it. In fact, when you consider that the husband's father co-signed the note, it meets our criteria.'

Chan: 'Hmm. Yes, well, that about wraps up the evaluation for this year. Send Rhonda in, will you? She's next.'

Questions

1. What mistakes did Harry Chan make in this evaluation?
2. How would you rate this evaluation conference? Why? How would you have handled it?

CHAPTER

16

MANAGING UNDERPERFORMANCE

OVERVIEW

Here's something to remember: Someone who works for you could get you fired – unless you protect your job, and your team members' jobs, by ensuring that all team members pull their weight and meet their goals. You do this in part by creating a working environment in which employees know clearly what is expected of them and that they want to do their jobs and they know how to do their jobs. You do this by providing a working environment and a high-performance culture that supports them in doing their jobs (as explained in Chapter 11).

Occasionally, however, an employee's performance is so poor that counselling is needed to bring it back up to expectations. Sometimes, counselling fails and you need to move or remove someone who consistently underperforms. Although most leader-managers would rather never to have to do this, dealing with 'the tough stuff' is part of managing performance that all leader-managers need to tackle at one time or another.

The bottom line is: Don't compromise your performance standards. Explain what they are and help employees to attain them.

1. Do you know how to think through poor performance before jumping into a performance counselling discussion?
2. Do you know how to plan and lead a performance counselling discussion that helps employees improve unsatisfactory performance?
3. Are you aware of the process for terminating someone's employment when performance counselling is unsuccessful?
4. Do you know how to support employees who have a personal problem?

This chapter explains how to deal with the tough stuff – how to turn poor performance around and what to do when you can't.

Revving up Jed

As Susan gets ready for work, she thinks about the performance improvement meeting she has scheduled for first thing this morning with Jed, her '2IC'. She appointed him about eight months ago, knowing that she would have to give him a lot of on-the-job training. She is convinced she did this well because until recently he has been doing a good job, steadily improving, as one would expect.

Lately, however, he seems to have lost some of his initial enthusiasm. For example, he is no longer at his desk, 'ready to roll', 15 minutes before starting time, although how could she, in all fairness, bring that up? No, it's more than that. The all-important weekly activity summary for the department that he is responsible for preparing was late twice in the past six weeks and there were two serious errors in last week's report. He has let other key tasks slide over the past six weeks, too, notably the forward-planning schedules, which were now three weeks behind.

Worst of all, one of the employees who reports to Jed came to her last week, complaining that the deadlines Jed is assigning to them don't allow time to complete the work properly. He seems to be leaving things to the last minute and, when the employee pointed this out to him, he told her to spend less time complaining and more time working. She feels quite offended by his attitude and wants to register a formal grievance.

As Susan reflects on Jed's performance, she decides to arrive at work a bit earlier and make a list of the points she wants to discuss with him. She knows he realises the importance of all these tasks and she knows he can do them satisfactorily. So why has his performance slipped? She also knows that he normally has good people skills, which is why the complaint from one of his team members surprised her. She should get to the bottom of this before the situation gets worse. She just hopes she hasn't left it too late.

1. Thinking through poor performance

> As all managers know from painful experience, when it comes to managing people, the 80:20 rule applies: The most intractable employees take up a disproportionate amount of one's time and energy.
>
> Nigel Nicholson (London Business School) 'How to motivate your problem people' (2003).[1]

When an employee's performance is unsatisfactory, you have a responsibility to recognise the problem and take corrective action. Most underperformance problems can be resolved when you address them promptly and correctly.

When you don't address underperformance promptly and properly, other team members may need to work extra hard to compensate; they'll be willing to do this for only so long – it's demoralising to work your socks off when someone next to you is skating through, getting away with the bare minimum. You also lose credibility and respect when you avoid performance issues and your team's morale is bound to suffer. As performance worsens and continues to cause problems, there is a danger that you become so annoyed you overreact and handle the situation poorly.

◉ IN A NUTSHELL

Poor excuses for managing poor performance poorly

Do you shy away from giving what you think of as negative feedback or criticism? You may be doing just that if you fail to address a performance problem based on any of these pretexts:

- I don't want to disrupt working relationships or seem harsh or unkind.
- I hope hints and sarcastic comments about someone's performance may do the trick.
- I prefer to put off giving performance feedback until the time is right – usually at the annual performance review or, better still, just before they go on holiday, so the employee has time to calm down.
- I'm uncomfortable with criticising someone and hope that if I wait long enough, the situation may resolve itself.
- I've let the situation go on for so long and I've become so angry that I'm sure I'll lose my temper.

If you subscribe to any of those excuses, forget them. Giving information on performance – positive, constructive and corrective – is your responsibility. Speak up when you see the need for improvement because when you let a problem slide, people think you're happy with their work and what they're doing is acceptable. At the same time, don't speak in haste. First, think through what you are going to say.

Don't assume it's the employee's fault

One of the biggest misconceptions people have about performance problems is that they are the result of individual failure. Most people aren't innately good, average or poor performers; rather, the quality of people's work depends, in large measure, on the context in which they are doing it. Do they clearly understand what they should do? Have they been trained correctly? Are they placed in the correct jobs, jobs that suit their skills, talents and interests? Do they have the information, time and tools they need to do their jobs well? Do they have a positive, productive relationship with their manager and other team members?

As you may remember from Chapter 11, the 85:15 rule tells us that, provided people know clearly what is expected of them and are trained to do it well, 85% of the causes of poor performance and low productivity can be found in the work environment. When you find them and fix them, you can get productivity back on track.

This is not to say that poor productivity never results from personal factors or factors outside anyone's control. Here are the main signs that indicate an employee's poor performance may fall into this 15% category (part of the 'chance to' key) or be the result of a regressed task-readiness level (part of the 'want to' key; see page 271 for information on regressed task-readiness and Chapter 11 for information on the five keys to increasing productivity):

- *Absenteeism*: A higher absenteeism rate than other employees, excessive sick leave, frequent unscheduled short-term absences or multiple instances of unauthorised leave, particularly when absences follow a pattern, such as after a day off or at the beginning of shifts or where improbable reasons for absences are given.
- *Difficulty with concentration*: Continually forgetting instructions, having to make a greater than normal effort to complete a task or taking too long to complete jobs.
- *On-the-job absenteeism*: Absenteeism (or presenteeism) while at work can result in erratic work quality, frequent trips to the rest area, long coffee breaks or more absences from the work station than the job requires.

- *Failure to observe the organisation's regulations, policies and procedures*: This applies when an organisation's standards are clear and the employee is aware of them.
- *Lowered job efficiency*: This can result in failing to follow safety or standard operating procedures, falling productivity or quality (e.g. due to excessive use of social media sites during work hours), lack of care for the customer's or the organisation's equipment, missed deadlines, mistakes due to inattention, poor judgement or wasting materials.
- *Poor relationships*: This can apply to managers, colleagues, suppliers or customers, which can result in, for example, avoiding workmates or the manager, overreacting to real or imagined criticism or wide mood swings.
- *Reporting-to-work problems*: Examples include arriving at or returning to work in an obviously abnormal condition, arriving late and/or leaving early.
- *Unacceptable conduct*: Examples include bullying, harassment or racial vilification of colleagues either in person or via social media, using social media sites to defame the organisation, to disclose confidential information or intellectual property or to publicise workplace disputes.

● THEORY TO PRACTICE

Dealing with employees who have regressed

At one time or another, every leader-manager has to deal with someone who used to be an excellent performer but has somehow 'fallen off the rails'. Here's what to do:

- *Acknowledge the change in performance*: 'Scott, you've always been one of our top performers. Lately, you seem to have problems.'
- *Uncover any problems*: 'Is anything the matter?'
- *Brainstorm solutions*: 'Let's put our heads together and see what we can do.'
- *Show your faith*: 'I really need you back up to speed and at your best again.'

Highly skilled employees probably know what's wrong and what to do about it. They just need your support.

Given that the above examples account for a minority of performance problems, it makes sense to concentrate your efforts on improving productivity and performance where they are most likely to pay off. Employees often struggle on despite environmental barriers getting in the way of good performance and productivity, trying to do the best they can despite them.

● ACTION!

Use the Analysing poor performance template on **⌁CourseMateExpress** to think through the main sources of an employee's poor performance.

● THE STRATEGIC PERSPECTIVE

Is your leadership the problem?

Here are some of the signs of poor leadership:

- *Being hands off*: Not knowing or caring much about what makes employees tick crushes motivation and invites poor performance. Roll up your sleeves and get to know the people reporting to you so you can assign the right jobs to the right people.

>>

- *Going around in circles*: Having the same, fruitless conversation with an employee is a clear sign you need a new approach. Discard your assumptions and analyse the problem with an open mind using the five keys.
- *Having monochrome vision*: When you see only the negatives in an employee, it's time to find some positive points. Finding even one redeeming feature can re-colour your relationship and help you connect better.
- *Jumping to conclusions*: Thinking you know all the answers to turning around an employee's poor performance is seldom helpful. Drop your blinkers and think about how the employee sees his or her performance and the reasons for it.
- *Kidding yourself*: When you think something is true, it's true – if only to you. Work with other people's realities, not just your own.
- *Taking the moral high ground*: When you've been thinking of the employee in the wrong and yourself in the right, it's time to decide whether or not you really want to improve the employee's performance or sit in judgement.
- *Telling and selling*: Continually trying to convince employees to 'mend their ways' seldom works. Figure out what the employee needs to be motivated and try to provide it; it's easier to change your approach and alter a job than to change an employee.[2]

A 'bad attitude' or a 'bad personality'?

Who is the most difficult person you ever worked with? What made them difficult? Chances are, you're describing their personality or a personal characteristic rather than their behaviour when you think of the difficulties in working with them. While that's natural, it isn't really helpful because it puts attention on who the person *is* rather than what the person *does*.

For example, people often talk about a person's 'attitude' as a shorthand way of describing characteristics they like or dislike. They may say, 'Keith has a good attitude … Kath has a bad attitude.' Although this may mean something to the person saying it, it's fairly meaningless to others – what 'attitude' means to one person is different from what it means to another. When you say to an employee, 'You've got the wrong attitude', they probably don't know what you're talking about. Few people intentionally go to work with the 'wrong attitude'.

Although 'attitudes', 'personalities' and 'personal characteristics' are a perennial nightmare, when you make the person the problem, you have only two alternatives: termination or transfer (handballing the 'problem' to someone else).

Avoid the 'A' and 'P' words and stick to behaviour because people can change the way they act. Before raising the issue, ask yourself these three questions:

1. Have you reinforced the unwanted conduct in some way? Perhaps the way you respond to the behaviour invites the employee to continue it. For example, ignoring tardiness sends a message that it's ok to be late.
2. Is the employee doing the best he or she can under difficult circumstances in the work environment or in his or her personal life? For example, maybe your own behaviour makes 'serial complainers' feel they must create a 'fuss' in order to be heard, or maybe whatever they complain about really does need to be fixed and they're right to complain.
3. What makes the behaviour difficult for you? Perhaps it reminds you of a similarly difficult family member – or even yourself! Consider whether the behaviour would be a problem for other managers; when it isn't, the problem may be yours, not the employee's.

When you decide that the problem rests with the employee and not yourself, raise it in relation to how the conduct affects the employee's performance or his or her workmates or the team's results. Stick to specifics, remain clear, constructive and neutral and provide examples so the employee understands your point. Be prepared to suggest ways to improve, too, along the lines of 'When you do this, it has this effect on the team/on me/on your work. This is what I need from you instead, which will help me/us (in this specific way).'

⊙ **THEORY TO PRACTICE**

The 'entitlement culture'
People often speak about the 'entitlement culture'. They are referring people who think work is all about them and their needs, not performance, productivity or customers. When this applies to any of your team members, talk candidly with the employees to help them realise that this is the real world and that their approach must change. Help them see how their work contributes to the team and the organisation and, when it isn't done correctly or on time, how it adversely affects their teammates and the way people think about them.

Think through the five keys

To find and fix the cause of underperformance, meet with the employee (or the team, when it's a team performance issue) and explore the possible reasons for it, using the five keys to guide you. Don't attempt to psychoanalyse an employee; the only causes of poor work performance you need to diagnose are in the five keys.

Work through the five keys, asking questions like these:

1. *'What to'*: Is there a clear and realistic standard of performance? Is the employee aware of it? Is the employee aware that she or he is not meeting it?
2. *'Want to'*: Is the job well designed? Is the employee temperamentally suited to doing it?
3. *'How to'*: Has the employee been fully trained in the job and done it enough to have built up the necessary experience and confidence?
4. *'Chance to'*: Is there anything in the environment, such as poor tools, insufficient information or time, substandard or unsuitable materials, awkward procedures, or poor team culture or group dynamics, that makes good performance difficult?
5. *'Led to'*: Am I providing the right kind of leadership and setting the right examples? Do I think like a leader and act like a leader?

When you have a 'No' or a 'Possibly not' answer to any of these questions, it becomes clear what needs to happen to lift the employee's performance (see Chapter 11 for more information on these keys).

⊙ **THEORY TO PRACTICE**

Adjust people's roles
When other aspects of an employee's work are good, the employee may not be temperamentally suited to the task being done poorly or not have any aptitude for it. Think about assigning that part of their job they perform poorly to someone else who is better suited to it or has more interest in doing it. Job content need never be permanent – in fact, it's a good idea to shift tasks around periodically to increase employees' job interest and further develop their skills.

Role conflict

Sometimes a difference in perception or wanting to do two conflicting activities lies at the heart of underperformance. This is known as role conflict and there are two types that can cause performance problems – interpersonal and intrapersonal.

Interpersonal role conflict occurs when others' ideas of how a job-holder should behave or what a job-holder should do differ from the job-holder's own ideas. An example of this type of role conflict is the school-leaver who begins her first job wearing clothing or a hairstyle that conforms to her school peer group rather than to the role expectations of her organisation. A more serious example is the employee for whom wearing standard safety protection gear is not part of his role perception.

Determine when it is important that the role perception of an employee and the role expectations of the organisation match. In the wearing of safety gear, it is clearly important that they do, so it's important to bring the employee's role perception into line with the organisation's role expectations. Sometimes, however, matching role perceptions and role expectations makes little difference to how well employees do their jobs.

Intrapersonal role conflict occurs when two or more of a person's several roles conflict with each other. Take Leslie, for example. She is a single parent with three children still at school and is the sole provider for her family. She has no income other than her earnings from work outside the home. She is also secretary of the local school's parents' association, which meets every month, and she actively follows the leisure and sporting activities of her children. During busy periods, Leslie's manager wants her to work overtime almost every night of the week. Leslie is very keen to have the extra income but she feels she is letting her children down, as they have to prepare their own evening meal and occupy themselves without her guidance. Stay sensitive to role conflicts like this and help your team members balance their work and personal life roles.

● THEORY TO PRACTICE

What's the fuss about?

Role expectations can be complicated when front-line staff deal with the public or external customers. Once upon a time, for example, there was an uproar when some front-line male staff began wearing earrings and, later, when some front-line staff began wearing eyebrow studs and nose studs. Was this appropriate attire and did it offend customers' role expectations and tarnish the image of their organisations? Some organisations attempted to introduce a 'dress code' or other policies to manage the dilemma. But the fuss was short-lived. Few people today notice or care who is wearing what type of body adornment.

2. Counselling unsatisfactory performance

Persons appear to us according to the light we throw upon them from our own minds.

Laura Ingalls Wilder (novelist), in Hines (ed), *Laura Ingalls Wilder, Farm Journalist: Writings from the Ozarks* (1922).[3]

The longer you delay addressing a performance gap, the bigger the issue becomes and the more difficult it may be for the employee to break a bad habit. It's important to discuss performance problems when they become apparent. That doesn't mean jumping into a discussion without preparing for it or beginning a discussion in the heat of the moment, without the benefit of facts and a clear performance gap. On the contrary, you should plan each discussion carefully.

Think about how best to meet your two overall goals when discussing underperformance:

1. To maintain or enhance the employee's self-esteem.
2. To help the employee accept and correct the performance shortfall.

Think about what to do should the discussion go in a different direction from what you planned. Think about the best time to meet and how to present the situation without shattering the employee's dignity or confidence.

Lead the discussion fairly and without hostility, and in private. See that you won't be interrupted and assemble concrete evidence or examples of the performance shortfall, or performance gap, and any other information you need (discussed below).

Figure 16.1 summarises the six systematic steps for improving an employee's work performance. When the situation calls for a formal performance counselling process to begin, inform the human resources (HR) department and enlist its help according to your organisation's protocol. But don't abdicate the problem to the HR people or expect them to fix it for you.

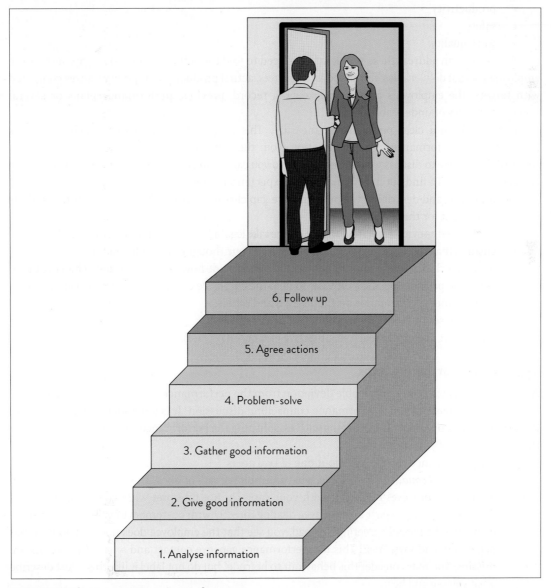

6. Follow up

5. Agree actions

4. Problem-solve

3. Gather good information

2. Give good information

1. Analyse information

FIGURE 16.1 Six steps to improving performance

IN A NUTSHELL

Mutual responsibilities

Just as organisations have responsibilities to their employees, employees have responsibilities to their employers. These revolve around carrying out their duties correctly, honestly, safely and to the best of their ability and training.

Step 1: Analyse your information

Common performance shortfalls involve the following:

* attendance and timekeeping
* behaviour towards colleagues, customers, managers or suppliers
* care of tools and equipment
* productivity
* safety
* work quality.

Before you can address these problems, you need to find the actual performance gap, such as the employee's actual deliverables compared with targets, actual production or quality figures compared with targets, the employee's actual time-keeping record, previous performance plans or several specific examples of undesirable conduct.

First, establish a clear performance measure. This is the standard against which you assess the employee's performance. A clear deviation from the standard, the performance gap, gives you something concrete to discuss with the employee so you can establish the reasons for the gap and agree corrective action. (To find out how to make your expectations about performance clear, see page 323.)

Documenting and describing the performance gap clearly in specific behavioural or measurable terms is important for these reasons. It:

* can be used as evidence should the employee take legal action (e.g. unfair or unlawful dismissal).
* ensures that you have analysed and organised your thoughts and information.
* helps you clarify your counselling objectives and decide how best to go about achieving them.
* helps you provide specific examples to help the employee understand the detrimental effects of their underperformance on themselves and others.
* helps you set the scene for a productive discussion.
* makes sure the gap is 'real' (i.e. objective and based on fact).

Types of performance gaps

A clear and measurable or quantifiable deviation from the performance standard – the performance gap – forms the basis of your performance counselling discussion. It is a mandatory starting point. Performance improvement always begins with establishing the performance gap – it's your insurance that you are sure of your facts.

A clear performance gap can be about one of two areas:

1. *Work-related conduct*, for example, what an employee says or does. This means that you should see it with your eyes or hear it with your ears. Do not interpret what you see or hear. For example, you may expect an employee dealing directly with customers to greet them with eye contact and a friendly greeting. Instead, you see that the employee does not look up from her paperwork and says, 'Yes?' This is a performance gap: eye contact and a friendly greeting are missing. You may consider this behaviour to be 'rude', but do not label it like this – just describe what you see and hear.

2. *A work target (or deliverable) that is not being met.* This target should be SMART (**S**pecific, **M**otivating, **A**mbitious yet achievable, **R**elated to the organisation's and team's goals, and **T**rackable). For example, you may expect employees to acknowledge and greet customers within 16 seconds. Taking longer than this, perhaps by leaving the customer waiting while they finish paperwork, is a performance gap.

Typical performance gaps are shown in Table 16.1 in 'Theory to practice: Examples of performance gaps' which looks at unwanted conduct and targets not met.

THEORY TO PRACTICE

Examples of performance gaps

Ensuring that a performance gap relates to a specific work-related behaviour or a clear work target means you can give the employee clear and factual performance information without becoming personal or critical.

It allows you to remind the employee what 'right' looks like and present the performance information objectively. This reduces the employee's defensiveness and sets the tone for constructive and cooperative problem-solving.

Table 16.1 looks at performance gaps related to conduct and also to targets not met.

TABLE 16.1 Performance gaps

Conduct	Targets not met
Keeping three out of five customers waiting for more than three minutes without acknowledging them	Arriving 10–15 minutes late two to three times a week for the past three weeks
Speaking briefly and curtly to 90% of customers or colleagues, especially during busy times	Producing the last three reports two days late
Once or twice a week, for the last two weeks, taking a break instead of helping team members complete their work	Producing an average of 80% accuracy in documents for the past two weeks, missing the 95% target
Having to be reminded two or three times a day to complete routine work	Not answering the telephone within four rings and not identifying the department and saying your name

When dealing with performance gaps, consider, too, the employee's task-readiness level and the leadership style it suggests (explained on page 267) and think about your opening comments, too – how you can best 'frame' the discussion explained on page 468.

Your goals

Don't go into the discussion thinking you know 'why' someone is underperforming or what to do about it (unless it's completely obvious). Begin with a clear performance gap and state your desire to explore the reasons for it.

Your goals are to ensure that the underperforming employee clearly understands:

* the standard of performance required (the measure of success)
* the precise performance gap and why it matters
* that you are prepared to help the employee reach that standard

- that nothing less than meeting the performance standard will do
- that the choice of whether or not the employee improves his or her performance is the employee's
- the consequences of continued poor performance.

For more on this type of conversation, see 'Theory to practice: Tread softly and concentrate on your goals', on page 468.

Step 2: Give good information

Set the scene by beginning your discussion with a framing statement that makes it clear your primary concern is satisfactory work performance. A framing statement is a short, clear sentence (or two) to introduce the discussion. It explains what you want to talk about and how, which gives you and the employee a mental target to aim for. Just as a frame encloses and draws attention to a picture, your framing statement encloses the conversation to come and draws attention to the main topic of the conversation.

● IN A NUTSHELL

Types of framing statements

Your framing statement might be designed to:

- *Set limits on what will, and won't, be discussed*: Today, we won't be talking about your overall job performance, which is excellent, but only about the progress on the customer service project.
- *Review the key events that have a bearing on the conversation*: We have spoken twice over the past month about your targets not being achieved, and your targets were not reached again last week.
- *State your expectations from the discussion*: We've had several conversations concerning your level of customer service being generally below expectation; today I want to discuss actions we both need to take to turn this around and what must happen if we can't.
- *Outline how you want the discussion to proceed*: Before talking about your productivity, I suggest we first review the required standards. Then I'd like to move on to the possible reasons why you are not meeting your targets consistently. How does that sound to you?
- *Outline the result you're looking for*: James, I want you to be a top loans officer and I'd like to discuss some ideas that may help you.
- *Summarise the information you plan to discuss*: During this meeting, I would like to review your safety record and formulate an action plan for improving it.
- *State the problem and summarise the facts*: Sam, we need to talk about your timekeeping. My records show that you've been late to work three times and back late from lunch four times this past month. I've been keeping track because timekeeping is important to me and I'd like to discuss with you now any problems or difficulties that could be causing this and agree what we can do about it.

After your framing statement, describe the performance gap clearly and explain why it's important that the employee meets it. Separate the person from the problem so you can offer this information in a way that builds the employee's self-esteem and makes it clear you are interested only in improving performance. Use language that shows you are taking a 'we' approach – that is, looking at and trying to sort out the problem together.

This way, you can be 'hard' on the problem while 'soft' on the person. You want to be clear, but not combative, about the performance you require. Don't dance around it and don't act overly optimistic or the employee may leave the meeting thinking everything is okay. Convey the seriousness of your feedback and the ramifications should the employee not improve; the employee should understand that this is an opportunity to get his or her work (back) up to standard in order to continue to be employed with you.

Three ways to give this information are:

1. 'I' messages.
2. Describe – explain – suggest (or specify).
3. Describe – explain – specify – consequences.

As you provide this information, watch the employee's reactions. How is the employee receiving what you're saying? Is the employee actually listening?

Some employees don't really want to hear that their performance could be improved. Don't be put off by their discomfort. Acknowledge your suspicions: 'I sense some resistance. Am I right?'

Put yourself in the employee's shoes so that you can remain empathic and put your message across without being too intimidating. Observe the employee's personal limits: If the employee is not handling the discussion well, arrange to meet later; for example, after a short break, later the same day or the next day.

Here are two ways to describe an employee's unsatisfactory performance:

1. Pat, your work is slipshod and going to pot. You'll have to improve. And make sure you're in on time in the mornings, too – there's no room on my team for slackers.
2. Pat, as you know, your output was down by 8% over the last period and you were late four times this month. This isn't like you and I'm concerned about what is happening.

The first statement is non-specific and accusing and likely to cause defensiveness, while the second one is more constructive and opens the door to joint and productive problem-solving. Which would you rather hear?

 FYI

Working with hostile employees

'Passive-aggressive' is a term coined during World War II by US Army psychiatrist Colonel William Menniger to describe 'disguised hostility'.[4] For example, someone who works for you does not keep an agreement, which makes you look bad; or they make sarcastic, barbed comments as 'a joke'; or they continually let you down with a 'good excuse' or misunderstand you and, as a result, they don't do what's required. In short, they work against you in a roundabout way.

When this is the problem, deal with the recurring behaviour, not their various 'reasons' and 'excuses' for each incident.

'I' messages

An 'I' message is a clean, clear way to give good information. 'I' messages make it less likely for underperforming employees to counterattack or become defensive. Rather, they help them hear your message and agree to improve their performance or work with you to try to improve it.

An 'I' message has three parts:

1. Clearly describe the performance gap. Be specific, factual and concise; for example, 'When you are 10 minutes late …' is specific, while 'When you dawdle …' is fuzzy. Don't guess; for example, 'You left work 15 minutes early' is a factual observed behaviour, while 'You don't seem to care about your job these days' is speculation. Avoid absolutes such as 'never', 'always' or 'constantly' and judgemental words such as 'lackadaisical', 'careless' or 'rude'.

2. Describe your own feelings regarding the underperformance – not what you think about it, but how you feel about it. For example, when an employee continually arrives at work 10 or 15 minutes late, you might feel angry, annoyed or irritated, or you might feel worried about the effect it has on the rest of the team. (This is called *self-disclosure* and it makes your message powerful.)

3. Explain why the performance shortfall matters. What are the consequences of the underperformance? What effect does the performance shortfall have on you, the work team, the organisation and the employee?

● IN A NUTSHELL

'I' messages

'I' messages are ideal when you want to communicate clearly and make sure your point hits home. Table 16.2 shows the three parts of an 'I' message.

TABLE 16.2 How 'I' messages can work for you

The three parts of an 'I' message	Conduct
1a. What you saw or heard	'When you speak before I'm finished …'
or	**Target not met**
1b. What you think the facts are	'My records show that you have been absent for six Mondays out of the last 15 …'
and	**Your response**
2. How you feel about it	'I am/get/feel … angry/annoyed/concerned/ irritated/uncomfortable'
and	**Tangible effects**
3. Why it matters	'This means … or …' 'Because …'

You can use these three parts of an 'I' message in any order. For example:

- 'John, it annoys me when you speak before I'm finished because I lose my train of thought.'
- 'Carol, I'm concerned about your absences on Mondays, both because of the effect this may have on your own work and also because it may affect the team. Are you aware you've been absent for six Mondays out of the past 15?'

For straightforward performance gaps, where the solution is obvious, use corrective feedback to state precisely what you want to happen instead of what is happening. For example, you could say, 'Jo, you're not wearing your safety goggles again. This really upsets me. I need you to always wear them when you come into this area. Can you do that for me?'

When the solution is not obvious, indicate that you need to work out how to resolve the problem together. For example, you could say, 'Jo, your last three reports have been up to a week late and that worries me because you're normally so dependable. Can you tell me what it is that's been holding you up?' or 'This is a real problem for me and we need to figure out what needs to happen so your reports can be on time again.' This moves you from giving good information (Step 2) to gathering good information (Step 3).

You can also use 'I' messages to turn positive general feedback into positive specific feedback, which ensures that the behaviour continues (see 'In a Nutshell: The three types of feedback' on page 448).

● IN A NUTSHELL

Summary of 'I' messages

'I' messages help you to be *clear* by saying what you mean, *honest* by saying what you feel and *direct* by saying what you want.

When describing a performance gap:
- Be brief.
- Be specific.
- Describe what you saw or heard the person do or say or the specific target not met.
- Speak to the right person.
- State genuine concerns or real issues.
- Stay objective.
- Stick to the facts.

When describing your feelings:
- Be non-judgemental.
- Don't attach blame.
- Say what you feel, not what you think.

When explaining the consequences of the performance gap:
- Be honest.
- Be specific.

DES: Describe – Explain – Suggest (or Specify)©

The Describe – Explain – Suggest (or Specify) model is another way to follow up your framing statement. First, *describe* the performance gap using neutral, objective language. Then *explain* why performing to the required standard is important or the effects of poor performance. The explanation may involve, for example, how poor performance affects other team members or other stakeholders, or how it affects product or service quality.

When the performance shortfall is straightforward, *suggest* what you would like the underperforming employee to do instead. When it is more complex, *specify* the performance goal you want met and move on to discuss what might be preventing the job-holder from meeting it, and what could be done, with your help if necessary, to help the job-holder meet it.

DESC: Describe – Explain – Specify – Consequences©

This model is slightly stronger than the Describe – Explain – Suggest (or Specify) model. Again, you *describe* the conduct or target not met; *explain* why it matters or the effects it has on efficiency, service, workmates, and so on; *specify* the performance goal and the time frame in which it must be achieved. Finally, state the *consequences* of not meeting the performance goal in the time frame (e.g. loss of job).

Stay on track

What do you do when an employee doesn't accept that a performance gap exists or that it presents a problem? Or when an employee produces one excuse after another? Or tries to change the subject? Keep calm and concentrate on the performance gap. Until the employee accepts there is a performance problem, it can't be fixed.

Make sure you have provided a clear and measurable target and clear evidence or examples of current performance; particularly when the performance problem concerns conduct, be ready to offer several recent examples. Try stating the problem as a goal and discuss ways the employee can achieve it, with your assistance if necessary.

Don't be sidetracked: Calmly repeat your main message (the performance gap and why it's a problem) as often as you need to and make it clear that you intend to help the employee reach the expected standard. Repeating your position is known as *echoing*; it prevents people from sidetracking a conversation, ignoring your message or 'talking you around'.

 THEORY TO PRACTICE

Echoing

This conversation echoes, or repeats, the point you're making, which prevents the conversation being sidetracked:

Manager: 'Sam I noticed you were 20 minutes late this morning. That's the third time this month and we've spoken about this before. I really need you here on time.'

Sam: 'Oh, it's my car. It's still giving me trouble.'

Manager: 'Well, I still need you here on time.'

Sam: 'Yes, well, I'll be getting it serviced next week.'

Manager: 'And have you made arrangements to get in on time until then?'

Four possible reactions

How might the employee react? Here are four possibilities:

1. The employee might simply say something like: 'Okay, sorry, I hadn't realised. I'll make sure to do that in future.' This takes you directly to a brief Step 5.

2. From the employee's response, it's clear that the problem is complex and you need to spend time thoroughly exploring the problem using the five keys (Steps 3 and 4).

3. The employee may come up with a string of excuses (and you're sure they're excuses), produce 'red herrings' or try to sidetrack the discussion ('Jane does it, too'). This is the time to use the *fogging* technique: Just as fog on the road forces you to put the brakes on, verbal fogging puts the brakes on irrelevant comments. Without agreeing, disagreeing or justifying, acknowledge that there may be some truth in what the employee says without commenting on it further. This cuts off the topic and closes that aspect of the conversation. For example, to close the 'Jane does it too' topic, you would say something like 'We're not discussing Jane. We're discussing your performance', and restate the performance gap.

4. The employee may deny or not accept that there is a problem. Keep giving good information (Step 2) by providing specific examples and evidence or comparing the actual performance figures with the performance targets. If this fails, reiterate how the employee's conduct, or failure to achieve targets, is adversely affecting the team or the department.

   If that fails, switch to the *change/time/consequence formula*: 'If not this *change* by this *time*, this is the *consequence*.' The consequence is usually a formal discipline interview or termination of employment. Say something like: 'Carl, I need to be able to rely on you to produce at 95% accuracy or better. If you continue to miss accuracy targets, I must begin a formal dismissal process. I hope that won't be necessary. Let's meet on Friday to review your figures. If they haven't improved, I have to give you a formal warning. Carl, you could lose your job because of this. If you need some help from me or if there's something I should know, now is the time to tell me.' This gives the employee a choice of continued poor performance (and possible loss of employment) or improved performance.

   This approach works with knowledge workers, too. Let's say Carl is behind on the interim targets that need to be met to provide his deliverable for a project on time. You've discussed this with him and could not find a good reason for the delays. Moreover, Carl doesn't think the delays are a problem and, having done your utmost, you have reached the point where you believe Carl is not suited to the work he has been assigned. You could say something like: 'Carl, I need to be sure you can provide your deliverable on time. If I don't see any progress in catching up by Wednesday week, I have to give you a formal warning. Let's meet then at 11 o'clock and take a look at where you are. Without progress, Carl, I might have to take you off the project. If you need some help from me or if there's something I should know, now is the time to tell me.' The ball is in Carl's court.

◉ THEORY TO PRACTICE

Gathering good information with fogging

Avoid sidestepping, or fogging up the issue:

Manager: 'Beth, I'd like to discuss your accuracy figures on routine documents. As you know, we target 95% accuracy and you've been working to 80% this week. I'm worried about this and I want to find out what might be holding you back so we can do whatever we need to do to help you reach the target. Do you have any idea what might have caused this drop in accuracy?'

Beth: 'It isn't my fault. None of the others are meeting their targets either. Why are you picking on me?'

Manager: 'I don't want to discuss the others' targets with you, just your targets. Do you feel I'm picking on you?' (Asking someone to provide more details when they've criticised you is known as *negative inquiry*.)'

Step 3: Gather good information

Don't be tempted to end the discussion once you've described the performance gap and explained that it needs to be fixed. Unless the employee says 'Oh, I hadn't realised – I'll fix it straightaway', switch to reflective listening and hear the employee's thoughts. Ask questions when you need to so you can see the situation as the employee sees it. Remember, this doesn't mean you have to agree; you just need to understand the employee's perspective (see 'In a Nutshell: Use your EARS!' on page 156.)

It's essential that employees have an opportunity to explain their viewpoint and to feel they've been given a fair hearing; this is known as procedural justice and would be taken into consideration should the performance counselling process end in termination of employment and the employee claims unfair dismissal (see 'In a Nutshell: Procedural justice' on page 998). In any case, railroading employees seldom results in long-term performance improvement.

● THEORY TO PRACTICE

Recalcitrant employees
When employees are totally uncooperative, ask them to write short weekly reports under the following headings:
- What have I achieved this week?
- What went right?
- What went wrong?
- Do I need any help?

These reports should take less than 15 minutes to write and less than five minutes to read.

Step 4: Problem-solve

When you've each expressed your points of view and the employee accepts that the performance gap needs to be fixed, you can turn to problem-solving, structuring your discussion around the five keys to determine the source of the problem. What's preventing the employee from reaching the required standard? Perhaps there are circumstances beyond the employee's control that are easily fixed.

Once you know the source of the problem, you and the employee can work out how to fix it. (It is usually best to help the employee to come up with the solution.) You may need to provide further training or coaching of some sort; you may need to redesign the job so that it provides the employee with more challenges, delegate one or two extra duties to develop the employee and increase motivation or lighten the employee's too-heavy workload; you may need to streamline or rearrange poorly designed work systems, or provide more accurate or timely information. Or the actions needed may be up to the employee to take. As with any problem-solving, the more solutions you consider, the better the chosen course of action is likely to be. (See page 526 for information on how to solve problems.) Do whatever you reasonably can to help the employee reach the required standard.

Step 5: Agree actions

Summarise what you have agreed – who is to do what and when, and how to monitor the performance improvement. For example, Sam and his manager (in 'Theory to Practice: Echoing' on page 472) might agree that Sam record the time he arrives at work for the next week and meet with his manager to review his timekeeping halfway through the week and again at the end of the week. Or the manager might know that Sam is a dependable employee and decide to allow him some leeway in his arrival times for the next week (only), provided he completes his work. This might mean Sam works a bit later at the end of the day or through part of his breaks if necessary.

When the employee seems uncommitted or unmotivated to improve, run through your expectations one more time before parting. Be specific and direct, and specify performance targets and time frames, and why it's essential the targets are met. Explain the consequences of not improving using the *change/time/consequence formula* described earlier. Put the performance plan in writing and have the employee sign off on it; this shows that you are serious about wanting to see an improvement. When people make a commitment to improve, they are more likely to stick to it. Keep a copy of the performance plan in the employee's file.

Part on a positive note. Remind the employee about what he or she does well and why you value the employee. It's important to maintain the employee's self-esteem and provide an incentive to improve this aspect of the employee's performance. You might want to stand up and make fleeting physical contact – squeeze the employee's elbow or shake hands.[5] This does wonders for an employee who is feeling a bit bruised and battered.

Step 6: Follow up

Simply holding a performance counselling discussion isn't the end of the story – you need a feedback system. Beth and her manager (in 'Theory to practice: Gathering good information with fogging' on page 473), might agree to meet halfway through next week to go over her accuracy figures, for example.

Both you and the employee should monitor the employee's performance to ensure that the employee achieves the agreed improvement. Remember, though, that Rome wasn't built in a day and neither is excellent performance. Don't wait for perfect performance. When you see some improvement, offer specific positive feedback so the employee knows you've noticed. Otherwise, the employee is likely to think that performance doesn't matter after all and their performance may well drop off again as a result. Positive support and encouragement, showing that you have noticed and appreciate the improvement, keeps performance moving in the right direction.

You can't force anyone to change. People change when it suits them and when there's a benefit in it for them. When an employee doesn't make the expected improvement, go back to Step 4 and look harder for the cause of the performance gap. When this happens several times with the same performance gap, you may consider implementing the dismissal procedure (discussed below) or transferring the employee to a job better suited to their skills and abilities.

ACTION!

Do you have the skills you need to successfully help an employee improve their poor performance? Find out with the checklist of the same name on  CourseMateExpress.

Document your discussions

Record, objectively and precisely, the following:

- date, time and location of each performance discussion
- names of any other persons present (such as someone from the HR department or a union or employee representative)
- performance gap, how long it has existed, where and how often it occurs and any other evidence for the gap
- specific performance target
- performance plan that resulted from your discussion
- subsequent performance, which is indispensable in case the performance doesn't improve and you need to dismiss the employee.

File your records in the employee's personal file, place a copy in your work diary and, when appropriate, send a copy to the HR department.

Manage all performance, not just poor performance

Consider three levels of performance: high, good and underperformance. Most employees perform in all three categories. Some employees are generally high performers but occasionally underperform. Others are generally good performers who are high performers sometimes and underperformers at other times; others underperform frequently with occasional good and even high performance.

Deal with chronic underperformance so it doesn't become 'toxic'. Work at raising good performance to high performance. Value high performance so it isn't taken for granted.

What can go wrong?

To manage underperformance effectively you need skill, patience and practice plus a genuine desire to help the employee to correct poor performance. Remain objective and factual and don't let the discussion degenerate into a demoralising argument that destroys cooperation and goodwill. Don't fall into the trap of attacking the person instead of the problem, or conducting the interview in a punitive or malicious way. Remaining constructive is the key.

When an employee becomes emotional, empathise with the employee's feelings or at least acknowledge them ('I can see I've upset you'). Give the employee some time to regain his or her composure and then proceed gradually or postpone the discussion. Do not cancel the discussion or ignore the issues. Rekindle the employee's confidence before the meeting ends.

One final point: Don't spend all your time on problem staff. When you fail to support your good people, they won't support you.

Use the Performance counselling discussions template on **CourseMate**Express to assist you in preparing for a performance counselling discussion with one of your team members when necessary.

Absenteeism counselling

Here is a sample outline for counselling an employee with excessive absenteeism.

At the initial discussion:

- Discuss the importance of dependable and regular attendance and review the organisation's leave procedures.
- Express concern about the continued absences and the effect on the employee's work and/or the work team.
- Inquire about any work-related or other factors contributing to the absences.
- Find out whether the employee needs any employee assistance programs the organisation provides.
- Use reflective listening responses (explained on page 160) to encourage the employee to talk.

>>

- Make sure you agree on an action plan.
- Minute the meeting and send the employee a copy.

You need a formal interview when the absences continue:

- Review the details of unauthorised absences and the action plan previously agreed.
- Make it clear that the employee's attendance record continues to be unsatisfactory and specify the improvements required.
- Find out whether the employee requires any assistance.

Should attendance not improve, hold a third meeting, according to your organisation's procedures. This begins the formal discipline process; normally one or two further formal meetings result in dismissal.

Minute each meeting and file them according to your organisation's policy; for example, place the original in the employee's file and give a copy to the employee and the HR department.

 **IN A NUTSHELL**

The hot stove

It isn't always necessary to have a lengthy discussion with an employee about a performance shortfall, especially when the employee is clearly capable of performing at the required level and when the required action is clear. Apply the hot-stove principle – point out the error straightaway and remind the employee of the required conduct or performance (see Figure 11.5 on page 333).

3. Terminating employment

> An employer can only dismiss an employee if it would not be considered harsh, unjust or unreasonable.
>
> 'Terminating staff', NSW Government, Office of Industrial Relations[6]

Dismissing employees is always unpleasant, but there are four reasons it might be necessary:

1. Their performance continually fails to meet the required standard over a reasonable period of time.
2. They do something seriously wrong (for example, theft), which can result in summary, or instant dismissal.
3. Their job has been included in the redundancy list.
4. There is insufficient work to keep them employed, making it necessary to place them on the retrenchment list.

Before moving on to termination of employment for the first two reasons, bear in mind the following general principles.

General principles

Follow your organisation's protocol to ensure you treat the employee fairly and follow procedural justice (explained on page 473). Because termination of employment is a serious business, many organisations take the precaution of requiring managers to talk it over with their own manager before beginning the termination process. Others require the manager's manager to be involved in each step along the way. Organisations with HR departments sometimes require a senior HR officer or manager to become involved at the verbal warning or first written warning stage. These sensible precautions safeguard the organisation as well as the employee. Be sure that you know, and follow, your organisation's procedures.

Employees may request a support person, for example their union or employee representative, attend any or all of these interviews. Agree to this and consider inviting your manager or someone from the HR department to attend, too, to 'keep the numbers even'.

When you need to terminate someone's employment, think through the logistics first. Should the employee leave the premises immediately? If not, when? What items belonging to the organisation might the employee have that need to be returned (for instance, company car, computer files or documents, laptop, mobile phone) and how should this be done? Should you back up the employee's computer files before breaking the news?

Experts recommend avoiding termination discussions on Fridays and before holidays. Arrange to have an HR representative with you to provide information about final payments and to ensure that the meeting follows the organisation's guidelines.

Before you meet with the employee, think through what you want to say, not to work out what's easiest for you but to plan how you can make the bad news more palatable for the employee while still being honest, tactful and sticking to the facts. Picture the (now former) employee walking out of the room – what do you want him or her to be thinking?

Always dismiss people in private and in person. (Sadly, it is not an urban myth that some organisations have terminated employees by email and SMS. This is inexcusable.) Get right to the point by stating that the news is not good (e.g. 'I have some unpleasant news'). Should the employee become emotional, let them 'vent'; telling people to calm down or to be reasonable only fuels the emotional fire. (When you are in any way concerned about an employee's possible reaction, take precautions, such as placing yourself between the employee and the door or asking security to stand by.)

Offer any assistance you can, following your organisation's policies and procedures. When appropriate, offer to provide contacts that might help the employee find another position. Just because someone's employment with you was not successful does not mean he or she cannot be a success elsewhere.

Once the details of the employee's departure have been worked through with the employee, and without going into details, let your team know their colleague is leaving.

Forgive yourself for being the bearer of bad news. The news causes distress, not you. (Or in the case of termination for poor performance or misconduct, the employee has caused the distress, not you.)

Termination for poor performance or misconduct

You know from Chapter 10 that managers don't motivate people – people motivate themselves. Acknowledge the fact that there are some employees who can't do that, for whatever reason, and who would be happier in a different working environment. The decision to perform to standard is theirs alone (provided you have provided the necessary training, resources and other support they need).

You also know from chapters 10 and 11 that employees are sometimes placed in jobs they are unsuited to. When alternative positions in the organisation aren't available and it seems fairly certain the expected performance standards can never be reached, these employees would almost certainly be better off in a job that better matches their skills and aptitudes. Consider how the employee came to be in the 'wrong slot' so that you can avoid similar mistakes in the future.

IN A NUTSHELL

Lawful and unlawful reasons for terminating employment

You can terminate employment based on the following:

- An employee's failure to conduct himself or herself in a manner appropriate to the job (see the section on summary dismissal on page 481).
- Inability or continued failure to do the job adequately (provided you have discussed the problem with the employee, offered remedial training and given the employee an opportunity to improve).
- Redundancy as a result of the introduction of new technology or organisational changes and the inability of the organisation to transfer the employee to another part of its operations.
- Retrenchment due to the operational requirements of the business.

You cannot terminate a worker's employment based on the following:

- Absence from work due to carer or parental leave.
- Acting, having acted or seeking to act as an employee representative or other trade union activities.
- Discriminatory reasons: age, breastfeeding, carer status, colour, criminal record (except in some circumstances), disability, ethnicity, family responsibilities, gender, gender identity, intersex status, marital status, medical grounds, national extraction, nationality, physical or mental disability, political opinion, pregnancy, race, religion, sexual preference or social origin.
- Filing a complaint or participating in proceedings against an employer involving alleged violation of laws or regulations.
- Membership or non-membership of a union.
- Participation in union activities outside working hours, or with the consent of the employer within working hours.
- Temporary absence from work because of genuine illness or injury, provided the employee has given appropriate advice and the period of absence is not unreasonable in the circumstances.
- Time off work while on workers compensation.

Except in the event of summary dismissal, employees must be notified, preferably in writing, that they are at risk of dismissal if there is no improvement in their conduct or job performance. Employees must be given an opportunity to respond and a reasonable chance to rectify the problem. Employees can have another person present to assist in the discussions, but not a lawyer acting in a professional capacity.

For more information on unfair and unlawful dismissal, contact the Fair Work Commission or go to their website: http://www.fwa.gov.au.

When you must dismiss someone for poor performance, do it right or risk unfair dismissal. It is essential to adopt the performance counselling procedure described above, document it fully and follow the warning procedure set out in your organisation's workplace agreement. Follow the guidelines precisely, taking the advice of your HR department when possible, or your manager. Your organisation's guidelines probably incorporate the three-step procedure detailed below. This procedure dovetails with the performance counselling procedure and legal requirements.

Be cautious: Be consistent in your warnings and don't make idle threats. Be specific and definite in your details to avoid confusion. Stick to the facts, to avoid getting into personalities, subjective observation and 'psychoanalysing'.

1. Verbal warning

When an employee's work performance is measurably or demonstrably below an acceptable level, the initial warning should take the form of a performance counselling meeting, described earlier. You should have already held one or more performance improvement discussions before beginning termination proceedings. For this meeting, have the notes from the previous meeting(s) to hand. Choose your tone and words carefully so you are objective and non-threatening and direct the conversation to the employee's work performance and the need to reach the required standards.

Give the employee an opportunity to explain his or her underperformance and request assistance. The performance plan you agree should allow a reasonable amount of time for the performance improvement to occur and include any help, such as training, the employee needs. How long is a reasonable amount of time? Long enough to realistically allow the employee to perform to expectations. During the meeting, ensure the employee understands that the consequence of continued poor performance is dismissal.

Some organisations require this first warning to be in writing. If yours does not, note the details of the discussion in your diary and in the employee's personal file. Document it fully and carefully, as described on page 475, because these notes could be used as legal evidence should the employee lodge an unfair dismissal complaint.

2. Written warning

When the agreed performance improvement does not occur within the agreed time, hold another performance counselling meeting. Give the employee a chance to respond and listen carefully to the employee's views.

When you decide to proceed with the dismissal process, give the second, written, warning to the employee and ask the employee to sign a copy for your own records. The warning should refer to the date of the previous verbal warning and other performance counselling discussions, and specify the performance gap and the time by which the improved performance should occur. The letter should be on your organisation's letterhead or specially designed form. Make a copy for your own records and another copy for your HR department if there is one.

3. Final written warning

When the employee's performance does not improve, repeat the procedure outlined in Step 2, double-checking the five keys. This is the employee's last chance to explain or improve his or her underperformance and save their job. Ensure that the employee is clear about the required performance ('*what to*'), understands that it is important to meet it ('*want to*'), has been trained correctly ('*how to*'), that nothing in the work environment is preventing acceptable performance ('*chance to*') and that you are providing appropriate leadership ('*led to*').

When the employee's performance remains below the required standard after the final written warning, termination of employment results. This is done in a formal interview.

● ACTION!

Should the worst come to the worst in a termination situation, you can find help online. You can access the Format for a written warning for poor performance template on *CourseMateExpress*. This is a last resort. We hope, by following the performance counselling procedures outlined in this chapter, you will not have to use that template.

How long does this process take?

The length of the dismissal process depends on the length of string. In other words, dismissal process can take days or weeks, depending on the nature of the performance shortfall. When an employee refuses to follow safety procedures or adhere to the organisation's code of conduct, for example, it need take only two or three days to complete the dismissal procedure. When complex remedial training or coaching is needed, the process may take several weeks to complete. The golden rule is that the length of time allowed for the performance improvement must be realistic.

Summary dismissal

Summary, or instant, dismissal is dismissal without notice or warning, or pay in lieu of warning, which can result from serious misconduct such as fraud, theft of or wilful damage to company or customer property, physical violence against other employees, customers or managers or others on company property or while on duty, substance abuse while on duty and blatantly unsafe conduct that endangers the employee, other employees or the public.

Many workplace agreements specify a 'cooling-off period' before dismissal, and legal precedent in Australia requires that you give the employee an opportunity to respond. You might, for example, send the employee off the premises immediately, asking him or her to return the next day to discuss the matter. After you have both had a chance to think, you may or may not decide to go ahead with the dismissal.

When an investigation takes longer than the day the employee is sent home, suspend the employee on full pay. Discuss the matter with your manager, someone in the HR department or your employer organisation and refer to your workplace agreement before taking any action.

THEORY TO PRACTICE

Is instant dismissal appropriate?

In most cases, it's better to investigate fully before dismissing. Here's how:

- Address whether there are any mitigating circumstances (e.g. the employee's personal situation) by making inquiries first.
- Determine yourself whether the misconduct is serious by objective (not subjective) standards.
- Discuss it with the employee and give the employee ample opportunity to explain the situation.
- Give the employee time to think.
- Make sure termination is proportionate to the misconduct.
- Speak to any witnesses.
- Take the employee's comments into account in your deliberations.
- Work out whether the employee's actions were provoked in any way (for instance by other employees or by management).

Follow your organisation's policy at all times.

4. Assisting employees with personal problems

Job loss, retrenchment or unexpected loss of income can cause financial and emotional distress and hardship. It is normal to experience a range of reactions, which may include shock, anger, guilt and a sense of powerlessness.

'Retrenchment or financial loss: Health issues', Better Health, Victorian Government[7]

There would be few leader-managers qualified to provide counselling on issues such as bulimia, financial problems, gambling, grief, post-traumatic stress, relationships, self-mutilation, substance abuse, terminal illness or work–family conflict (e.g. caring for a parent who has suffered a heart attack or stroke or a family member undergoing treatment for cancer). Yet many employees, being real people, come to work with these problems and these problems can affect their work and working relationships.

Employees with personal problems may experience reduced concentration, productivity or service levels and are at risk of making poor judgements and having more accidents; it's easy to imagine an employee thinking about a personal problem at the expense of some small but vital detail of their duties, which could be expensive in terms of quality or safety. People with personal problems may take time off more frequently than you would normally expect, too.

When you take an interest in your team members, you are likely to notice when something is wrong. The most obvious sign of a personal problem is a slip in work performance, which makes Step 3 in the performance counselling process – gathering good information – critical. There may be factors in an employee's underperformance that you are not yet aware of but that directly relate to a personal issue. The last thing an employee going through a difficult patch needs is for you to ladle on more pressure.

Even when performance doesn't suffer, changes in an employee's usual behaviour can signal personal difficulties; for example, when a normally cheerful employee becomes glum and quiet or when a normally shy and reserved employee becomes unusually boisterous or talkative. There are also some obvious things to look out for when you suspect drug or alcohol abuse (see 'FYI: Signs of drug misuse' on page 1030).

Offer assistance

It makes sense to offer assistance for a number of reasons. In terms of morale, nothing is worse than for a person to be in some sort of trouble and feel they're on their own. Employees with problems can do more harm than good when they are not helped; they are difficult to motivate and supervise and they can demoralise other employees.

And there is certainly a cost attached to losing an employee. Not only do you lose valuable experience but there is a significant replacement cost: time taken for interviewing, induction, job training and the cost of all those little errors that new recruits make while they learn the job.

There is also the intangible, but potentially large, reputation cost should an organisation become known for an uncaring attitude towards employees, making it difficult to attract the employees it needs; a company's reputation also affects buying behaviour. (See page 1015 for more information on employee welfare.)

When an employee experiences a personal problem, you may decide to provide a shoulder to cry on to let the employee talk it through or to act as a sounding board. No one expects you to be a professional counsellor. Personal counselling from a leader-manager's point of view is really a listening activity. Find out what you can do to ease the employee's work pressure; depending on the size of your organisation and its policies, you may be able to offer the employee time off with or without pay, for example. Don't expect the problems to be resolved quickly, though. Based on the employee's track record (including past performance reviews) and the value they add to the workplace, decide how long you can accommodate their reduced contribution.

When personal problems lead to underperformance, you should intervene following your organisation's performance management protocols, and offer any professional counselling your organisation provides at each performance counselling meeting. Many organisations provide employee assistance programs (EAPs); failing that, you or someone from the HR department can refer the employee to a person more qualified to deal with such problems, such as a professional counsellor. It is up to each employee whether to avail themselves of the offer of counselling (see page 1030 for more information on EAPs).

Employee assistance programs

Macy's, the famous US department store, is credited with establishing the first employee assistance program in 1917. In 1990, there were 500 EAPs operating in Australian organisations. By 2000, the number had grown to more than 3000.

Many organisations outsource EAPs to external providers who use psychologists, psychiatrists and social welfare workers to provide confidential, free, professional counselling. They offer a 'one-stop-shop' type of service and can provide early warning of emerging trends. Employees are asked to attend counselling when their performance becomes unacceptable or they can self-refer to these programs. About 80 of Australia's top 100 organisations offer formal outsourced counselling.[8]

Under many EAPs, the employer does not know who self-refers or for what type of problem. Because of the confidential nature of counselling, it is difficult to quantify the value of outsourced EAPs to the organisation in terms of costs and benefits.

Separating employees

Statistics show that 32% of Australian marriages end in divorce and one in every 15 employees goes through a separation every year.[9] The impact of separation is likely to be felt at most workplaces. However bravely affected employees attempt to 'soldier on', their performance is likely to be affected in some way. It has been estimated that up to four hours a week are lost by every employee struggling with separation.[10] This comes at a cost of more than $1 million per year for every 1000 employees.[11]

What to do if you suspect a serious psychological problem

Some mental illnesses can pose a threat to the sufferer as well as those around them when untreated or spasmodically treated. While it is not your job to diagnose or treat psychological disorders, remember that you are responsible for ensuring the safety of employees at work – the employee you think may be ill as well as those she or he comes into contact with.

When you believe an employee may be dangerous and needs professional help and are not sure whether it is safe for the employee to remain at work, work with your HR specialist to manage the situation. You might ask the employee whether he or she would consent to an independent medical assessment. If the employee agrees, ask for this consent to be confirmed in writing; if the employee refuses, check whether the employment contract, company policy, workplace agreement or award that applies contains a clause allowing the organisation to direct the employee to attend a medical assessment.

Where this is not the case, you could seek legal advice based on your concern for the employee's safety and the safety of other employees. It is preferable to use an experienced clinical psychologist or psychiatrist (rather than a general practitioner) to conduct the assessment; provide the specialist with detailed background information, including the reasons you suspect the possibility of psychological illness. Also provide a copy of the job or role description and a clear set of questions you want the medical practitioner to report on, particularly whether the employee is currently able to safely perform the duties listed in the job description.

When an employee is found to have a psychological illness, the practitioner can recommend that the employee return to work on alternative duties until the condition is resolved. Allowing a person to remain at work often aids recovery.

 FYI

The cost of mental illness

The cost to Australian business of mental illness is estimated at between $12 and $13 billion a year. Consider depression, just one of many mental illnesses. More than six million working days a year are lost because of depression. Symptoms include inability to concentrate, loss of interest and sadness. About 1.5 million Australians have anxiety disorders and depression, yet only 25% of them receive effective treatment; each employee whose depression is untreated costs their employer $9660.[12]

Address performance concerns

When you suspect or know that a personal problem lies at the heart of underperformance, discuss it with the employee, minimising the employee's stress as much as you can. Concentrate on how the employee's fitness for work concerns you and stress that your goal is to assist them to deal with their problem if possible and to help them return their performance to its previously high level.

First, outline the performance issue you've noticed. Then you might say something like:

* 'Are you able to discuss whatever is affecting your work performance?'
* 'Do you know what is preventing you from doing the good work we both know you usually do?'
* 'I'm wondering whether there is a deeper issue affecting your performance. Would you like to discuss it?'
* 'I sense that there is something here that does not "meet the eye" and, while I don't wish to intrude, I have taken the liberty of making a list of the employee assistance that the organisation makes available to employees. Assistance is completely confidential and whether or not you use it is entirely up to you.'

Don't probe into the employee's personal life, although when she or he volunteers information you can be willing to listen when you are comfortable doing so.

CourseMateExpress

Go to http://login.cengagebrain.com to access CourseMate Express, your online study tool for *Management Theory & Practice*. CourseMate Express brings chapter concepts to life with interactive learning, and study and exam preparation tools:

- Test your skills in different aspects of management with interactive self-tests and simulations.
- Watch videos that show how real managers operate in real businesses.
- Test your understanding of the changing world of management by taking the revision quiz.

QUICK REVIEW

1. What are your first steps when an employee's performance slips below the required standard?
2. What are the dangers of describing underperformance as a 'bad attitude'? What should you do when you believe an employee has the 'wrong' attitude? How should you describe these sorts of underperformance?
3. Describe the circumstances that make it necessary to terminate a person's employment and the process by which you should do this. What documentation is necessary?
4. What should you do when you think an employee may have a personal problem that is affecting his or her performance?

BUILD YOUR SKILLS

1. What should be your overall aims when counselling an underperforming employee? Describe the steps that you would work through to achieve these objectives and the skills you would draw on in each step.
2. What are Jed's performance gaps in the opening Scenario of this chapter? Write a framing statement that Susan could use to open her meeting with Jed.
3. Below are four examples of how a manager might begin a performance improvement discussion. Explain why they are unsatisfactory and suggest an alternative for each one.
   a. 'You've been coming in late. You've got a really bad attitude towards your work and it had better change.'
   b. 'You made a mess of that last job. Obviously, you're not competent or you've lost your drive.'
   c. 'I was talking. You're rude to interrupt me.'
   d. 'You're not doing a good enough job. You need to boost your confidence.'
4. Write a framing statement and an 'I' message, a Describe – Explain – Suggest (or Specify) message or a Describe – Indicate – Specify – Consequences message you could use to open a performance counselling session for each of the following situations when an employee:
   a. Argues with a colleague in front of the rest of the team at least once a fortnight about non-related work matters.
   b. Fails to wear a hairnet in the food preparation area unless he is reminded. This has been going on since he transferred to your section (from a non-food area) three weeks ago.
   c. Has a pattern of absence on Mondays and Fridays. In fact, in the last six months, she has been absent on six Fridays and four Mondays.

   d. Is a very low participator in your virtual project team meetings; in fact, he doesn't contribute unless asked a direct question.

   e. Shows work quality that is spasmodic. In the last six weeks her reject rate has been 30% above average and this is costly in terms of material wastage.

5. Draft a first written warning letter to an employee who has been late seven times over the past 12 shifts and has been unable to provide a satisfactory explanation for the lateness.

WORKPLACE ACTIVITIES

1. What are your organisation's policy and procedures regarding counselling underperforming employees? At what point does performance counselling end and dismissal proceedings begin?

2. What are your organisation's policy and procedures regarding termination of employment for continued poor performance and for summary dismissal?

3. What assistance does your organisation offer employees who are experiencing personal difficulties?

CASE STUDY 16.1

SHAUNA KUMAR VERSUS FRED KNOX

The day that Shauna Kumar has been dreading has arrived. She is to meet with her most experienced team member, Fred Knox, to discuss his unsatisfactory work conduct. Shauna has managed the IT section for the past three months and her appointment was a shock to most of the employees. Everyone expected the job to go to Fred, who has been with the organisation for more than eight years.

Fred always provided valuable assistance to the previous leader-manager through his knowledge of organisational procedures, his loyalty to the organisation and his responsible attitude. However, when it came to selecting the new leader-manager, it was felt that Fred would be unable to meet the changing needs of the job. Fred felt betrayed and some of the team felt betrayed on Fred's behalf.

Being aware of Fred's disappointment at not getting the job, Shauna dealt with him leniently since taking up her new position and made every effort to get him 'on side'. She hoped that time would heal Fred's discontent and that eventually he would give her the same support he gave her predecessor.

So far, things have not happened that way – hence this morning's meeting. Fred is displaying a 'don't care' attitude to the job and several times Shauna has found him talking to people in other sections while work piled up on his desk, causing the section to fall behind schedule and miss deadlines. Fred's explanation for these visits was that other people were asking for his help, and he appeared to be the only one in the place who knew what should be done and how to do it.

On two or three occasions, Shauna discovered Fred and two or three of his cohorts arriving back from lunch up to three-quarters of an hour late and showing obvious signs of having been drinking, which then affected that afternoon's work output. She informally warned Fred on two occasions that this conduct was a breach of the rules and hoped that this would be enough to settle the matter.

Unfortunately, it had no effect and the same thing happened three days ago. Shauna's manager became aware of it and the previous extended lunchtimes and discussed this with Shauna. When she explained her difficulties with Fred's disregard of her directions and the 'split' in the team over her appointment, her manager suggested she conduct a formal performance counselling interview with Fred before the end of the week and warn him that, unless there was an immediate change in his attitude, the formal termination of employment procedure would begin. Her manager also suggested Shauna look into holding a teambuilding session to heal the breach in the team.

Time is now up and Shauna is about to call Fred to her office to carry out her manager's instructions. She wonders whether she can get Fred to change, and what she should do if Fred threatens to resign.

Questions

1. Has Shauna handled Fred's conduct adequately? What could she have done differently?
2. Develop an outline that Shauna could follow to conduct the interview, highlighting the skills she needs to use.
3. What should Shauna be careful to avoid doing during the interview?

THE COOL DUDE

CASE STUDY 16.2

With four full-time and two part-time optometrists and three full-time, three part-time and two casual optometric assistants, the branch Lindy manages is the chain's largest. And it isn't without its headaches.

She is now sitting at her desk gob-smacked. When Jone joined them fresh from university a couple of weeks ago, his first (of many) requests was that they schedule no appointments for him until after 10.30 am because he 'isn't a morning person'. Somewhat taken aback, Lindy explained that most of the optometrists used the time between 8.30 and 9 am, when their first appointment would normally be scheduled, for administration.

She was aware that he strolled in most days between 9 and 9.30 am – he seemed to have charmed the optometric assistants because he seldom had an appointment before 9.45 am. He charms the customers, too. Ah, youth: good looks, muscles, cool dude dreadlocks …

The first time his turn for Saturday working rolled around, he announced that he couldn't possibly work that weekend because he had an out-of-town rugby match. Lindy agreed to schedule someone else on and asked him to give her a schedule of his other out-of-town matches so she could take them into account when putting together the rosters. Come to think of it, that was last week and she hadn't received it.

Today's stunner was Jone blithely waltzing into her office, announcing that he normally goes to Fiji for a few weeks every year to see his mother's family and, since he began studying optometry, he has been volunteering part-time at a local hospital to help out with eye care. Now that he is qualified, he plans to volunteer for a full three weeks at the hospital, full-time, after spending a week with his cousins. What he wants to know is how many spectacle frames with standard prescriptions the company could donate.

Lindy mumbled something about looking into it for him and, as gently as she could, pointed out that he wouldn't have accrued enough holiday to take four weeks off for nearly 12 months. 'Oh, no,' says Jone, 'this isn't holiday. I assumed you'd be sending me over as part of our corporate social responsibility. I can't afford to take holiday – I need the money!'

The problem is, Lindy thinks to herself as she ponders how best to deal with Jone's latest 'request', that qualified optometrists are rather thin on the ground. As it is, most of the chain's optometrists put in a good many hours of overtime each week just to keep up with appointments.

Questions

1. How would you advise Lindy to deal with Jone?
2. If Lindy decides to address Jone's requests, develop a frame and an 'I' message or other message that she could use to open the discussion.
3. What do you think Jone's reaction is likely to be? How should Lindy respond? Prepare a sample dialogue.

PART

4

MANAGING OPERATIONS

To manage daily operations, you need to know the answers to three questions:

1. What end result are we after and what interim results can tell us we're on the right path?
2. What steps are needed to traverse this path successfully?
3. Who should do what along that journey?

In this part, you find out how to develop, manage and monitor plans, quality and service levels that contribute to your organisation's strategic goals; how to identify and manage risks to operations, people and the environment; and how to introduce, monitor and foster change, both large and small. You find out how to resolve problems, make decisions and continually improve processes, products and services based on a systematic analysis of what is working well and what isn't. You find out how to provide your customers with what they want, how to manage projects and how to build sustainability into your operations.

As with any set of skills, you can learn them but you must also apply them. You may know in theory, for example, the seven steps to follow to solve a problem, but you must actually work through these steps for them to be of any use to you. You may know how to minimise risk or how to build a sustainable organisation, but you need to turn your knowledge into reality for it to be useful.

Applying any new skill can be difficult and even frustrating at first. But practice makes progress. By working with the skills explained in this part until you are familiar with them, you become a more effective leader-manager.

DEVELOPING, MANAGING AND MONITORING OPERATIONAL PLANS

OVERVIEW

You probably plan a lot without realising it. Can you imagine arranging to meet a group of friends for a picnic without first deciding who is to bring what food, who is to bring the barbecue, chairs and rugs, where you'll go and precisely when and where you'll all meet up? Or not agreeing an alternative plan in case it rains?

For the much more complex job of running an organisation, a department or a team, you need clearly established goals and measures of success and a detailed written plan to achieve them. Everyone needs to understand the plan – who is to do what, when – and be willing to work towards achieving it, so it is sensible to involve others in developing the plan, particularly those it affects and who will implement it. You may also need to gain approval for your plan from others in the organisation before setting it in motion.

Setting goals and thinking through how best to achieve them (yes, that's exactly what a plan is!) is worth the effort because it curtails chaos, missed deadlines, blown-out schedules, idle equipment and people scratching their heads wondering what to do. Organisations need plans to operate smoothly and employees need plans to feel comfortable and settled, knowing that things have been thought through and are under control.

From simple plans like holiday rosters, to daily and weekly plans for a work group, to complex production and business plans, from plans involving just one project to those for an entire enterprise, organisations need all sorts of plans for both day-to-day effectiveness and long-term success.

1. Can you explain why planning is needed and how your operational plans relate to strategic and business plans?
2. Can you prepare and present operational plans and estimate and secure the resources your plans need according to your organisation's guidelines and requirements?
3. Are you able to give your plans the best possible chance of success?
4. Do you know how to monitor your plans easily and effectively?

They say that the more you plan, the luckier you get. This chapter explains how to get lucky so you can avoid behaving like the one-legged duck – swimming hard but only in circles.

Plans within plans

Hamish sits back and draws a deep breath. This is big.

His boss has just left his office, having dropped the bombshell that Hamish's section, which manages accounts payable and receivable nationally, is to take on all national administration, which was outsourced and offshored several years ago. The workload is set to treble, although from what Hamish gathered, while there is a budget to expand their staffing and other resources, trebling them is not on the cards.

As section manager, Hamish is to play a key role in the project team that is to plan and execute the transfer of operations. The project scope includes planning for the section's technical, communications and human resource needs, refurbishing and expanding the office, and risk and stakeholder management, assessment and planning. As his boss left, she stressed that the project transfer team would need to 'think outside the box' in order to produce a viable plan within the time and budget constraints.

Hamish mulls over various scenarios in his mind. He'll need to reallocate duties and redesign some of the jobs, find and train additional staff, upgrade IT and communications systems, develop an office layout and design, purchase the necessary equipment – at this point, his mind starts spinning. He'll need a project team himself.

As soon as the official announcement is made, Hamish can brief his team on the finer points. He begins listing what he wants to tell them and thinking about how best to present the news. He'll need their help and support to form subcommittees to work out sub-plans within the larger project plan and he wants them to be fully on board and conversant with the plans so they roll out smoothly when the time comes.

1. Understanding the context and components of operational plans

If you are planning for one year, grow rice. If you are planning for 20 years, grow trees. If you are planning for centuries, grow men.

Chinese proverb

We don't know who first uttered this old Chinese proverb but thousands of management specialists have quoted it over the years. You've probably also heard the saying, 'The right hand doesn't know what the left hand is doing'. And you probably know someone who is too busy putting out 'bushfires' to develop an overall plan of 'fire prevention'.

These sayings carry the same basic message: The up-front time you invest in planning saves time in the long run by keeping an organisation running smoothly and preventing emergencies and crises. Up-front planning allows you to get on with important work and to be proactive rather than reactive. As the old Australian management proverb says, 'Those who plan can make things happen; those who don't plan have things happen to them.'

Like much important work, planning is mental work. It might look like you're sitting there doing nothing, but when you're planning you're actually being proactive and doing vital preliminary work. Thinking through how best to achieve a desired result is the first step towards taking charge of events and circumstances.

Plans are projected courses of action aimed at achieving goals. They provide clear milestones and sub-goals, or targets, and map the activities needed to reach them with a minimum of fuss. Plans can be long-term, like the *strategic plans* that guide entire organisations discussed on page 56, or they can be the shorter-term *operational plans* that guide the daily or weekly work of an individual, team or department that we examine in this chapter.

> **● IN A NUTSHELL**
>
> **Strategic plans and operational plans: What's the difference?**
> Think of strategic plans as the wheels that steer organisations in a chosen direction and operational plans as the rudders that guide organisations and fine-tune their direction.

The benefits of planning

Don't be tempted to put planning into the 'too hard' category or avoid it because you are so busy keeping up with the workload that you just don't have time to plan. And don't put off planning because you'd rather be 'out there', active and doing something. These are self-defeating excuses and actually make your job much more difficult.

In 1919, an American Reverend, H K Williams, voiced this saying in the magazine, Biblical World: 'When you fail to plan, you plan to fail'.[1] By 1940, Reverend Williams wisdom had become a modern proverb and even the famous *Newsweek* magazine had published it. And so they should have. What grand advice.

Plans are your foundations for the future. They give you a way to track progress and assess achievements, help you identify and concentrate on important issues, and remind you of what needs to be done and in what order. They help you coordinate people's efforts and skills, eliminate duplication of effort, minimise disruptions and put the necessary information, materials, people and tools in place. Plans free you from *crisis management* – responding quickly and under pressure – and help you reach your goal more easily.

Thinking things through in plenty of time reduces uncertainty and helps you anticipate and prepare for change. When you communicate plans well, everyone knows 'what, who, when, where, how and why', which gives their efforts purpose and direction; they can relax and perform better knowing that things are under control. Having a plan doesn't guarantee success, but it attracts more success more often than thoughtlessly jumping into action.

Whether first thing in the morning or late in the day, get in the habit of thinking about the upcoming day and what you need to achieve so you don't just charge in. Making planning part of your regular routine pays off. As the saying goes, 'It wasn't raining when Noah built the Ark.'

Developing operational plans that support strategic and business plans

An organisation's values, vision and strategic goals guide it in the same way that a team's purpose statement and measures of success guide the team. Similarly, an organisation's strategic and business plans explain how its vision flows through to functions and to teams, which develop their own goals and operational plans to help the organisation achieve its vision and realise its strategy. In this way, each team follows its plan, each aiming at reaching the same overall goal via a different path. (See page 51 for information about values and vision and page 376 for information about developing a team purpose statement and measures of success.)

● THEORY TO PRACTICE

How a vision drives operational plans

An organisation decides that achieving its vision depends in part on having an enticing employer brand in order to recruit the employees it needs when it needs them. As part of its strategy, it includes three strategic goals in its business plan to this end:

1. Best-in-the-industry leadership at all levels achieved within 18 months.
2. Top-quartile remuneration achieved within 24 months.
3. World-class health, safety and welfare systems achieved within 24 months.

These goals then flow on to the organisation's departments and teams, which build them into their goals and operational plans. The HR department, for example, sets several objectives, including:

- Design and test a leadership development and mentoring program within six months; develop a roll-out plan and begin leadership training within eight months (to meet the first strategic goal listed above).
- Develop and launch an internal health, safety and welfare campaign in three months to raise key safety benchmarks to the top industry quartile by year end (to meet the third goal listed above).
- Develop, test and begin publicising a strong employer brand and employer value proposition within six months (to help meet the strategy of building an enticing employer brand).

Other departments also set their own goals to work towards achieving the organisation's strategic goals. For example, to meet the third goal listed above, the production department sets these goals:

- Analyse accident and near-miss statistics and design and launch a campaign within three months to improve safe working practices, targeting the highest risk areas, to reach an accident-free target of 100 days by the end of the financial year.
- Eliminate notifiable incidents within 12 months.

Departments then develop operational plans that set out, step by step, who is to do what by when in order to achieve their goals.

From goals to plans

Remember: Goals are your glimpse of the future. They identify where you want to be, giving meaning and purpose to your actions and the actions of your team members. Like vision statements and team purpose statements, goals guide the choices you and your team make and help you to respond to change more easily because they give you a clear picture of where you want to be in the long term Pages 327 and 377 explain how to develop useful, SMART targets.

But don't sit around thinking too much about how you're going to get there. The American actor Will Rogers once observed: 'Even if you're on the right track, you'll get run over if you just sit there.'[2]

Break big goals down into shorter term, more specific objectives. Make them positive so that you know what you're aiming for (not trying to avoid), as well as trackable and measurable so that they can provide clear measuring posts as you proceed towards your goals. When objectives are still big or distant, chunk them down further into smaller, closer targets. Keep breaking down, or refining, your goals until you arrive at objectives and targets that are meaningful, believable and specific enough to provide a sense of direction and drive performance, and that help you fulfil your team purpose to help your organisation attain its strategic goals.

Now you're ready to develop an operational plan.

2. Preparing and presenting plans and estimating the necessary resources

> Our plans miscarry because they have no aim. When a man does not know what harbour he is making for, no wind is the right wind.
>
> Lucius Annaeus Seneca (Roman philosopher), *Letters from a Stoic*, Penguin (2004)[3]

While goals, objectives and targets focus on results, plans focus on activity – what people need to do in order to achieve the desired results. The operational plans that leader-managers develop are shorter term than the strategic and business plans they support; they generally look ahead one week to a few months. As plans become more short term, their precision increases.

Figure 17.1 shows a simple planning format that you can adapt to suit your needs, using the questions as triggers to help you fully think through your plan.

What results are we aiming for? (goals) or **What** do we need to do? (activities)	**Why** is this important? (strategic goal)	**When** or **by when** do we need to do it? (today, tomorrow, next month)	**Where** should we do it? (at the workplace, in the stockroom)	**How** should we do it? (steps to be taken)	**Who** is to do it? (list people by name)
Update our database	To enable us to access and retrieve current information on assistance programs in under three minutes in order to provide timely and helpful advice to the families and carers of people with Alzheimer's	By July 2017	Use the conference room as a project room	IT and marketing to work on project together	IT technical support adviser, marketing officer and client services manager

FIGURE 17.1 A basic planning format

 **ACTION!**

If you would like to develop your own operational plans, you can find a Basic planning format template on **CourseMateExpress**.

You can expect to work with three different types of operational plan:

1. *Recurring plans*, such as health and safety improvement plans, holiday rosters, training plans and work schedules.

2. *Specific operational plans*, such as project plans that are needed for once-only activities or special occurrences. These can be very complex and preparing them can be highly specialised, requiring computer programs and techniques such as PERT (program evaluation review technique) and other types of flow charts and network diagrams to schedule the specific steps, highlight critical tasks and task paths, and monitor progress.

   Special temporary project teams are often formed to prepare and carry out these specific plans, which can require a range of tasks – from those that are straightforward to those that are so complex that external consultants and contractors are brought in to assist. (Page 415 explains how to lead temporary project teams and Chapter 21 discusses how to manage projects.)

3. *Standing plans*, or standard operating procedures, which set out procedures to follow in specific situations, such as evacuation procedures in the case of fire and the process to follow in issuing a formal reprimand to an employee. Also known as programmed decisions (see page 519), these are established according to organisation policies and strategies.

● THEORY TO PRACTICE

The planning statement
A planning statement helps crystallise your thinking. Try the Verb–What–Why formula.
For example, your planning statement might be 'To develop and implement (verb) a plan to increase our department's output by 14% by the end of the financial quarter (what) in order to ensure we meet our growth objectives and help achieve our corporate vision (why).'

The planning process

Sometimes, once you've developed a plan, it's finished. More often, planning is iterative – always moving, always changing, always being revised and updated, making planning an ongoing process of adapting, adjusting and fine-tuning to meet changing circumstances or unexpected events, to take advantage of new ideas and technologies, or to incorporate new or modified customer needs or updated organisational or departmental goals. Achieving one plan can lead to launching another one.

Another Roman interested in management theory was Publilius Syrus (85–43BC), a Roman slave who was freed and educated by his master. According to Syrus: 'It is a bad plan that admits of no modification.'[4]

Unless a plan is really straightforward and people's input is completely unnecessary, or the plan is confidential because it involves, for example, yet-to-be-announced business initiatives, involve your team in developing plans and call in specialist staff to help when you need to. Involving people that the plan affects and who are to carry it out ensures they understand it and are committed to its success. Involving others generally results in a higher quality plan, too, because you're drawing on a range of skills, experience and knowledge.

3.   Sequence the activities in the order in which they should occur. Network diagrams such as flow charts, PERT diagrams and Gantt charts (discussed later) are useful tools for this because they provide a visual representation of your plan. Assign target dates to each activity. (Pages 585 and 659 discuss a range of tools and methods you can use.)

4.   Communicate your plan to those it involves or affects. Making people aware of your objectives and how you intend to achieve them means they are more able and more likely to help you.

5.   Implement your plan: Once you're happy that your plan is complete and you have communicated it well, put it into action. You might think about conducting a force field analysis first. When your plan is sensitive or critical to your department or the organisation, test it first, as explained on page 756.

6.   Check your progress to satisfy yourself that your plan is working. This is your insurance – you want to find out in plenty of time if the plan is failing so that you can take effective corrective action. (Monitoring is discussed in the final section of this chapter.)

⦿ THEORY TO PRACTICE

Be positive, precise and flexible

Because you're more likely to get what you concentrate on, express your goals, objectives and targets as positive outcomes (what you do want, not what you don't want); for example, 'a 97.5% satisfaction rate', not 'a 2.5% dissatisfaction rate'.

Aim at concise and precise plans that others can easily understand. Keep them flexible so you can adjust them should something go wrong and you can fine-tune them to changes in the operating environment. But flexibility doesn't mean vagueness. The more specific you make your targets and the more detailed your plans, the easier it is to deal with unexpected events.

Estimate the necessary resources

You now need to make sure you have or can obtain the capacity, knowledge and systems your plan needs to succeed. *Capacity* is mostly about the people you need to carry out the plan and deal with its results. For example, your plan may be to develop a new sales area; you need not only people to make the new contacts and work with them, but also enough people to provide the service or make the product, and to process the inquiries and sales that result.

You also need people with the *knowledge* to carry out the plan; in the previous example, you need people who know enough about the organisation's offering and values to develop the new sales area and answer the resulting inquiries. You also need to consider the ability of your existing *systems* to support your plan and whether they need to be expanded, increased or redesigned; your plan may require more work stations or more equipment, for example, or a new way of working with your internal or external suppliers. This is summarised in 'Theory to Practice: Working out the details'.

Although you can work out the details on your own, involving others gains both their ideas and their support. Consult your manager, your work group and other relevant stakeholders, or, more likely, a combination of all three.

THEORY TO PRACTICE

Working out the details

Work out the resources your plan needs to succeed, such as:

- *Equipment.* You may need to acquire, temporarily or permanently, additional equipment such as computer terminals.
- *Facilities.* You may need to arrange facilities such as transportation or computer software.
- *Funding.* You may need to arrange for additional funds to cater for extra staff, new or hired equipment, overtime and any unforeseen events that arise.
- *Materials.* Your plan may require additional materials, such as procedures manuals.
- *People.* You may need to bring in extra people to complete the plan; when your plan requires additional people, decide whether they should be casual, full-time, part-time, permanent or temporary employees or contractors, or whether you could second people from other parts of the organisation.
- *Space.* You may need more space to set the plan in motion or more work stations to accommodate the additional people you need.
- *Time.* When people are to undertake additional duties, you may need to free up some of their time from another project or duties.
- *Training.* People may need additional training to carry out the plan.
   Other resource issues to consider:
- Does your plan have enough support from management and key stakeholders? How can you increase their support?
- Does your plan make it necessary or possible to upgrade equipment or facilities?
- Does your plan support the organisation's strategic and business plans sufficiently?
- How can you allocate available human, physical and system resources most effectively and efficiently?
- How does your plan affect the resources you and your team have to hand?
- When your plan calls for you to do more or the same amount of work with fewer resources, for example with fewer people or in less time, carefully refine your work procedures and practices.

ACTION!

Do you want to make sure your 'ducks are in a row' when you next develop a plan? You can, with the interactive self-test: Have you organised your resources? on CourseMateExpress.

FYI

Estimating staffing requirements

Here is a straightforward way to work out how many people you need:

1. Determine your product or service requirements for the period of the plan – for example, to serve 2000 customers or to produce 2000 ceiling fans next month.
2. Calculate the number of hours needed to deliver the service or produce the products. The HR department or the industrial engineer in the fan factory may have these figures,

or you may need to rely on your experience. If it takes an average of 17 minutes to serve each customer and you expect to serve 2000 customers, multiply 2000 by 17 and then divide by 60 to find the number of hours.

3. Work out how many employees you need to provide the service or produce the product. Divide the number of hours required (from Step 2) by the number of hours each person will work during the period. For example, in Steps 1 and 2, your plan calls for serving 2000 customers next month at an average of 17 minutes per service interaction, requiring 567 hours. In Step 3, you divide this figure, 567, by the number of hours each employee will work over the month. This may be, for example, 20 days at eight hours a day, or 160 hours; divide 567 by 160 to get 3.54, so you need 3.54 service providers.

4. Consider any support or service staff these employees need, such as maintenance workers, canteen workers, personnel officers or administrative assistants. Add the number of support staff to the figure arrived at in Step 3.

5. Allow for employee absences. Your records might tell you that each service provider and support worker is absent for an average of two days per month. Multiply the number of employees calculated in Steps 3 and 4 by the average absenteeism rate (in this example 16 hours) and divide the result by the hours to be worked. This tells you the number of extra people you need.

   For example, in Step 3 you found that you needed 3.54 service providers; Step 4 might have shown that you need 1.5 support workers, totalling 5 employees. In Step 5 you found that the average absence for both support staff and service providers is 16 hours per month. Hence, $16 \times 5 \div 160 = 0.5$ extra employees.

   In this example, as the allowance for absences is quite small, there is probably no need to employ extra people unless the labour turnover is high. Therefore the labour requirement is 5 people. So you need a total of 5 service providers and support staff to serve the 2000 customers per month called for in your plan. (Chapter 25 explains how to recruit additional staff.)

Secure the necessary resources

Once your plan is ready and you know the resources it needs, you can plan to acquire them. When you need money for overtime, for purchasing equipment or materials, or for hiring facilities, equipment or additional personnel, find out how this fits into your department's or project's budget and whether funds have been set aside. Investigate several options and providers and select or recommend the most cost-effective option that meets your needs.

Follow your organisation's procedures for requesting funding and other resources. Depending on your organisation's protocol, this may involve briefing your manager, project manager or other nominated person, either verbally or in writing, about what you need and why you need it and estimating the costs involved. Support your estimates with actual quotes if possible and clearly outline the benefits you expect to gain from investing in additional resources.

Cost-benefit analysis

Are additional or improved resources worth the expense? Is a decision worth implementing or a change worth making? Is the solution to a problem worth the cost of fixing it? A cost-benefit analysis helps you answer questions like this. You quantify, in dollar terms, the benefits and the costs you expect from a purchase or course of action; when the benefits are worth more than the costs, you have a good indication it is worth going ahead.

Some costs, such as capital costs and contractor costs, are once-off while other costs, such as labour costs, are ongoing. These can be calculated quite easily. Other costs, such as the opportunities-lost costs of not going ahead, or environmental costs, are more difficult to quantify and you may need to be subjective, and prepared to defend your guesstimates. Some costs can increase or recur, too, as for example, when once-new machinery ages and needs increasing maintenance or when technology becomes outdated and needs upgrading. The benefits of less costly investments, for example improving a system, can deliver ongoing benefits once implemented, at no increase in costs.

Like costs, some benefits are easier to quantify than others, too; savings in energy, labour costs and time, for example are easier to put a dollar value on than benefits to the environment, health and safety or morale. Benefits often accrue over time and take a while to build up and some can reduce as when, for example, equipment ages and becomes less efficient.

The time it takes for the benefits to repay the costs is called the *payback period* and the point at which costs equal benefits is called the *break even point*. Many organisations look for paybacks on projects over a specific time, for example, three years.

You can plot your cost-benefits analysis as a graph by, for example plotting the costs and the benefits (in dollars) on the vertical axis and showing them over time on the horizontal axis, sometimes called the *return on investment*, or ROI. The break even point is where the two lines intersect, as shown in Figure 17.3: Cost-benefit analysis graph.

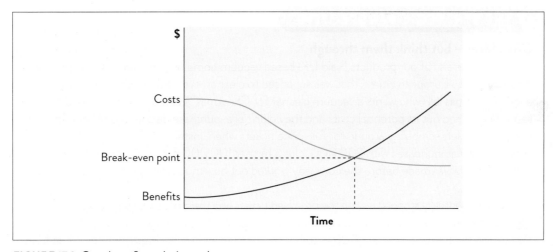

FIGURE 17.3 Cost-benefit analysis graph

Secure the right people

Most plans affect people – how people are deployed, the actual jobs or tasks they carry out, the skills they need, even their working relationships. (To find out how to support people while introducing change, see pages 694 and 701.)

Here are some other staffing issues to consider:

* Do you need any special expertise to help you implement the plan? If so, should you use internal or external people? If external, should you use contractors or consultants?

- Do you need more or fewer people?
- Do your current team members need any training? Who should design and deliver it? How long will it take? When should you do it? Who can cover for staff while they are in training? What will training and providing staff coverage cost? Which budget is to cover the costs? If it is your budget, do you have sufficient funds?
- If you need more staff, should they be temporary or permanent? If temporary, should you use contractors or outsource the work? How should you attract and train the additional staff you need and when should you begin? Are there enough people in the local area or would it be better to retrain existing staff from other areas of the organisation?
- Should you adjust the mix of casual, contract, full-time, home-based, onsite, part-time, permanent and temporary staff in your team?
- Should you reallocate or redistribute duties to implement the plan more readily?
- Should you work towards cross-skilling, multiskilling or upskilling?

Present your plans

Most organisations have formats they follow when setting out and presenting plans. When you're not sure what to do, get an example of a previous plan of a similar type and follow the layout used.

Your aim is to make the plan clear and easy to follow; usually, the more simply you present something, the easier it is to understand. (Refer to page 172 when you need to present a written plan to management and page 199 when you are presenting your plans orally.)

◉ THE STRATEGIC PERSPECTIVE

Great ideas – but think them through

'Spend £119 on any of our products,' said UK-based vacuum company, Hoover, 'and win two free return flights to European cities.' That was supposed to clear an over-full warehouse of products over a Christmas lull (who wants a vacuum cleaner for Christmas?) Good plan. But they didn't test it first to find out its potential costs and they didn't pre-purchase discounted tickets. The company was left scrabbling around for full-price tickets when, instead of the expected 50 000 applicants, it was inundated with 200 000, plus a further 100 000 for the second offer for free flights to the USA (made before the company worked out how much money the extra sales were costing them).

Hoover eventually stopped issuing the promised tickets and the BBC's *Watchdog* exposed the wrong-doing. The resulting nightmare included thousands of complaints, questions asked in Parliament, the formation of the 8000 member-strong Hoover Holiday Pressure Group, hundreds of customers taking Hoover to smalls claims courts up and down the country, the sacking of the entire board of directors, a loss of £48 million and the sale of Hoover to an Italian firm.[5]

3. Protecting your plans

Intellectuals solve problems. Geniuses prevent them.

Albert Einstein (Physicist), in Butler, *Navigating Today's Environment* (2010)[6]

You may have heard of the joiner's rule: Measure twice. Cut once. That's so Murphy's Law doesn't kick in: 'Anything that can go wrong, will go wrong'. Even worse is when O'Toole's Corollory kicks in: 'Murphy was an optimist'. That's why you always monitor your plan as it rolls out to make sure that it doesn't go woefully and irretrievably off track when the unexpected happens at the most inopportune time.

The more important it is that your plan works right from the start, the more important it is that you put on your doom-and-gloom spectacles and look for things that could go wrong. For highly critical plans, conduct a live trial run to identify hitches. If you're an optimist, make an extra effort to look for potential problems.

Here's how to prevent problems. Once you have formulated your plan, ask yourself these questions to assess your plan's viability:

* What could go wrong? Brainstorm the events, people and problems that could turn your plan into a fiasco. Select the most likely and those with the worst impact or repercussions to work on, and unless it's a risk management plan, ignore any that are well outside the range of reason.
* What would indicate it's about to happen? For each potential problem and adverse event you're working on, work out what would alert you that it's about to happen.
* What could prevent it from happening? Now think about how you could prevent each possible problem from occurring.
* What should be done if it does happen? When you can't prevent a problem or an adverse event, have a *contingency plan* ready to implement.

Working your way through those four questions means that you can arm yourself with a *preventive plan* to stop a problem from occurring and a contingency plan so you know what to do if it does occur (or an *adaptive plan* to live with it when you must). You can refine your contingency plans with an *interim* plan, which describes what to do if something does go wrong until you can fix it with a *corrective* plan, which outlines the steps to take to put it right.

When you involve your team in developing a plan, involve them in protecting it, too. (See page 744 for more information on risk analysis.)

FYI

Are you an optimist or a pessimist?

Optimists might live longer, happier lives, but they tend to fail to notice looming problems and potential pitfalls. This can reduce their effectiveness as managers. If you're an optimist, force yourself to write down everything that could go wrong with a plan. Then make the appropriate protective plans.

If you're a pessimist, you'll naturally be alert to what could go wrong and have a few solutions ready – just in case. Take time to look for the upside to things, too, so you don't worry yourself into an early grave.

IN A NUTSHELL

Protective plans

Different plans apply to different situations. Read through these plans and decide which one best suits your situation:

* Adaptive plan: Occasionally, you may set your sights unrealistically high during the planning phase, or an important variable may change, making adaptive action necessary. An adaptive plan tells you what to do to ensure that a problem or difficulty you cannot eliminate or minimise has negligible negative repercussions.

>>

- Contingency plan: This describes what to do should something go awry or your monitoring shows a negative trend or hints that something may be going wrong.
- Corrective plan: This tells you how to correct a problem that may occur by eliminating the unwanted event to get your plan back on track.
- Interim plan: This describes how to deal with unwanted events until you can find their cause and implement a corrective plan. However, like the Dutch boy with his finger in the dyke, it is merely a stop-gap action.
- Preventive plan: You might be able to avert potential problems entirely.

Force field analysis

Force field analysis is another way to spot people, problems and events that could prevent your plan from working – *resisting forces*. It also helps you identify factors working in your favour – *driving forces* (see Figure 17.4). Once you know what they are, you can look for ways to rectify, reduce or remove the resisting forces and make the most of the driving forces.

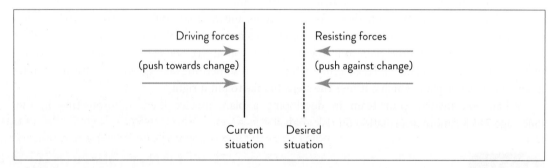

FIGURE 17.4 Force field analysis

Driving and resisting forces can come from many areas, including these illustrated in Table 17.1.

TABLE 17.1 Internal and External driving and resisting forces

Internal forces	External forces
Administrative practices	Changing government regulations
Financial and other resources	Changing marketplace conditions
Individual employees	Community pressures
Influential parties (e.g. management or unions)	Competition
Leadership styles	Customers
Organisation culture	Technology
Policies	The economic environment
Procedures	The domestic supply chain
Team culture	The international supply chain
Time and information	The labour supply shortages
Tools and equipment	The world's extreme climatic events

Force field analysis can also help you identify the implications of your plans and predict how they will affect people, systems, procedures and so on, both 'upstream' and 'downstream'.

● IN A NUTSHELL

How to conduct a force field analysis
Follow these steps and you can conduct a force field analysis:
1. Draw and label a vertical line to represent the current situation (the starting point of your plan). To the right of it, draw and label a dotted line to represent the desired situation.
2. To the left of the lines, brainstorm the driving forces that can help your plan succeed.
3. To the right of the lines, brainstorm the resisting forces that could work against your plan's success.
4. Decide which are the most important or significant driving and resisting forces. Circle or highlight these forces to work on in Step 5.
5. Decide how you can minimise or remove the resisting forces and make best use of or increase the driving forces.

---

4. Monitoring your plans

For if you stay there, disorders are seen as they arise, and you can soon remedy them; if you are not there, disorders become understood when they are great and there is no longer a remedy.

Niccolo Machiavelli (Italian Renaissance writer), *The Prince*, Mansfield (trans.), (1998)[7]

That's a long-winded way to say that when you keep your eye on your plan's progress, you can spot problems quickly and fix them. When you don't, problems grow and by the time you've noticed them, it's difficult or even too late to fix them.

That's why you need to monitor the progress of your plans. Keeping track of the right measures and milestones shows you how well your plan is unfolding. Think of monitoring as the partner of planning. It's the feedback that gives you an early warning of whether and where your plan is going off the rails so you can put it back on track.

Monitoring also lets you quickly adjust to changing conditions. It may reveal the need to alter the way you give directions, modify the plan, reschedule activities, use the available resources differently, or even change the monitoring methods themselves.

When monitoring, beware of *confirmation bias*. When you believe something or hope for something – in this case, hoping your plan works – it's easy to find the evidence you're looking for and ignore contrary evidence.

Four steps to monitoring

To ensure your plans succeed once you've launched them, follow these four steps:
1. Decide what you should monitor. Concentrate on what is most important to your plan's success, for example, delivering on time, improving quality, improving service levels, increasing output, increasing sales or reducing costs. Consider the danger points and what could cause the most damage if the plan went wrong. Think about your objectives and targets.

2. Establish specific measures to monitor. What counts most? In the customer service area, for example, measure the factors that are most important in satisfying your customers; perhaps it's cost, product reliability, quality or time – whatever your customers care about most. Measure what supports your organisation's values, vision and strategy; for example, in an organisation that values teamwork, it's counterproductive to measure only individual contributions.

So that you don't eat up valuable time by over-monitoring, look for the critical control points, the most important aspects of your plan, and monitor those. Look for measures that give you a lot of information easily and quickly. Whenever possible, measure lead indicators rather than lag indicators (explained on page 114).

3. Compare what is happening with what should be happening. Once you know what to measure, you can simply compare the actual with the planned.

4. Take remedial action when you need to. When what is happening isn't precisely what should be happening, remember that some amount of variation always occurs. Decide which variations are important enough to warrant taking corrective action. Implement your contingency plans as discussed earlier in this chapter or carry out a gap analysis (explained in 'FYI: Gap analysis') to determine the best course of action.

◉ IN A NUTSHELL

Some common success measures to monitor

Customer satisfaction is important. Be sure to satisfy your customers by watching what's important. Perhaps it's:

- complaint response time
- on-time delivery
- percentage of inquiries resolved.
  Financial success is important. To keep your business thriving, you can watch:
- market share
- profit
- return on assets and on investment.
  Growth, innovation and learning are important. Keep your business from stagnating by watching forward measures like these:
- number of new ideas generated and implemented
- percentage of revenue from new products and services
- research and development as a percentage of sales.
  Smooth operations are important. Keep your eye on what's important to your organisation's operations. Perhaps it's:
- billing accuracy
- employee productivity
- tender success rate.
  People commitment is important. Monitoring measures like these can help keep your employees' committed and meet your organisation's strategic goals:
- individual and group training needs met
- number of internal promotions
- number of training hours per employee per annum.

IN A NUTSHELL

What not to measure

You don't have to measure everything. Don't bother measuring results that:

- are difficult or expensive to measure
- are measured elsewhere
- aren't 'owned' by an individual or a team
- don't demonstrate progress towards achieving your plan
- would be difficult to interpret or understand
- wouldn't cause individuals or teams to act differently
- wouldn't identify problem areas.

FYI

Gap analysis

Comparing current results with your desired results is called a gap analysis (see Figure 17.5). It can help you decide how best to 'bridge the gap', or move from the current situation to the desired situation. The resulting plan aims to close the gap between 'where you are now' and 'where you want to be'.

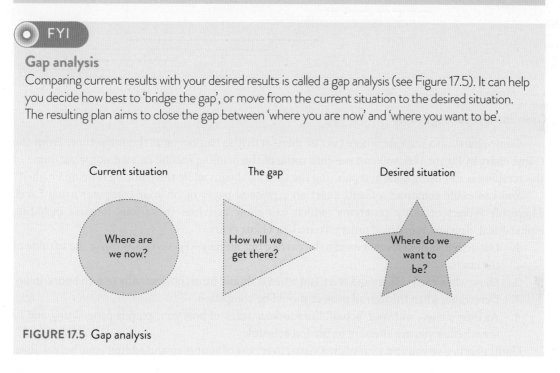

FIGURE 17.5 Gap analysis

Common monitoring tools

You probably deal with a variety of tools every day to both plan and monitor recurring and occasional activities. You may even design many of them yourself, perhaps with computer databases, project-management software and personal schedulers. Ways to monitor using statistics are discussed on page 585, including bar charts, control charts, histograms, Pareto charts, process capability charts, run charts and stratification charts. Four other common planning and monitoring tools are explained in the following sections: Gantt charts, network diagrams, financial tools and inventory controls. Then we take a look at the informal monitoring you can do.

Gantt charts

A Gantt chart is a horizontal bar chart designed to aid in operational planning and monitoring. It shows the anticipated start and finish dates for activities called for in a plan; as work starts and progresses, you fill in the actual line below the appropriate planned activity. This quickly shows whether your plan is on schedule.

Figure 17.6 shows a plan for painting a house. You can see that the plan calls for the scraping and sanding to be completed by midday Tuesday but the actual time required to scrape and sand was all day Monday and Tuesday.

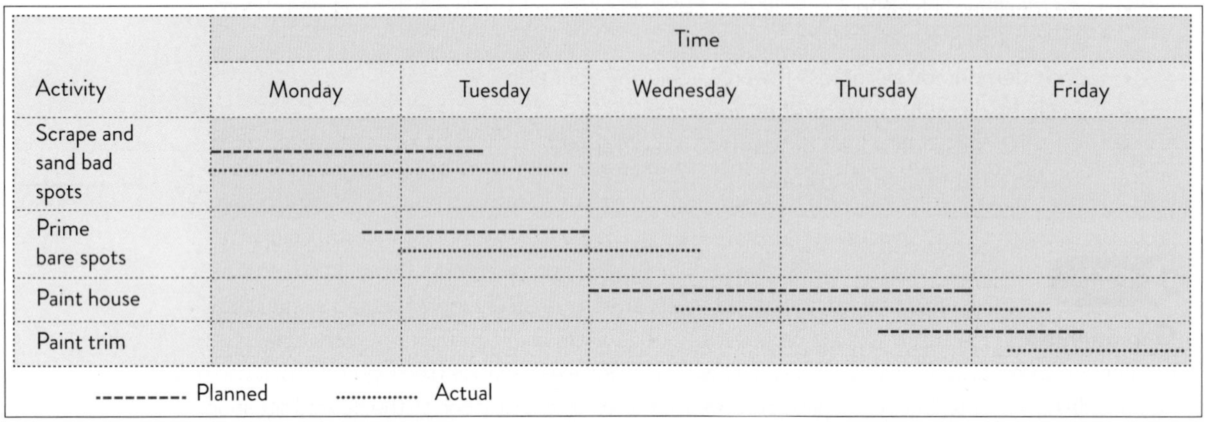

Activity	Time				
	Monday	Tuesday	Wednesday	Thursday	Friday
Scrape and sand bad spots					
Prime bare spots					
Paint house					
Paint trim					

-------- Planned   .... Actual

FIGURE 17.6 Gantt chart for painting a house

Gantt charts also indicate where two or more activities can occur at the same time. From the Gantt chart in Figure 17.6, you can see that some of the priming can be carried out while some of the scraping is still being done and painting the trim can begin while the painting is being finished.

You can easily construct a Gantt chart on a piece of paper or on your computer using Excel, Microsoft Project or other programs (which can show activities in various formats including alphabetical, date and numerical order). To make a Gantt chart:

1. List activities or tasks that need to be carried out, step by step, vertically down the left side of the chart.
2. Show when each task should start and when it should finish horizontally (e.g. in hours, days).
3. Determine when the overall project should be completed.
4. As time passes, add your 'actual' lines to keep track of how your plan is progressing and to see whether you are ahead of or behind schedule.

Gantt charts give you and your team a visual overview of your plan and adding your 'actual' lines helps you monitor the plan.

Network diagrams

Network diagrams and Gantt charts are powerful tools that help you schedule, manage and monitor the tasks that must be completed to achieve the goals of your plans and projects. Network diagrams help you identify the minimum time needed to complete a plan or project. Although they can be more difficult to interpret than Gantt charts, the benefit of network diagrams over Gantt charts is that they allow you to identify which tasks you can delay should you need to shift resources to catch up on other tasks.

Critical path analysis (CPA), or the critical path method (CPM), is a form of network diagram. CPAs show you how various activities relate to each other, which activities you cannot start until other activities are finished (known as *dependent* or *sequential activities*) and which activities you can work on in tandem with other activities (known as *parallel tasks* or *concurrent tasks*).

Specialised software helps you develop a CPA by:
- identifying the tasks that need to be carried out
- estimating how long each task should take
- scheduling when the tasks should occur.

Program evaluation and review technique (PERT) is another type of network diagram. A simplified PERT diagram is shown in Figure 17.7. Time flows from left to right; circles represent events or activities, such as the start or completion of a task; and lines represent the tasks themselves. Label each task line with the time it is expected to take, then add the times of task paths together to identify the critical path – the longest path through a plan or project. This critical path is the series of tasks that, if not completed on time, hold up the entire plan or project.

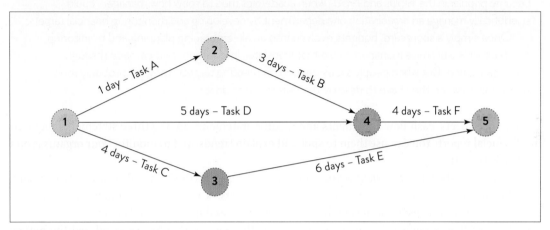

FIGURE 17.7 PERT chart

PERT charts take a slightly more sceptical view of time estimates made for each project stage than CPA, which helps to balance the optimistically short timelines people often estimate. You estimate the shortest possible time each task could take, the most likely length of time and the longest time each might take. Then you use the formula below to calculate the time to use for each project stage:

$$\text{Shortest time} + 4 \times \text{likely time} + \text{longest time} \div 6$$

 FYI

PERT charts and critical path analyses
PERT charts schedule, organise and coordinate the various tasks of a plan or project. The technique was developed by the US Navy in the 1950s to manage the Polaris submarine missile program.

The critical path method was developed for project management in the private sector at about the same time.

Financial tools

Budgets are targets expressed in financial terms that forecast income and expenses over a specific period, most commonly a quarter (three months). Advertising budgets, purchasing budgets, salary budgets, sales budgets and training budgets are common types of budgets you might deal with, trying to either reach budget (e.g. a sales budget) or stay within budget (e.g. a purchasing, training or travel budget).

Often created on a spreadsheet, budgets establish the goal and, at the end of the period, show you whether you've reached it. During the period, you can get interim budget reports to track your progress. When you fail to reach or stay within your budget, you need to find out why and fix the problem. For example, you may need to stop all non-essential spending, freeze recruitment or sell more. Budgets can also help you identify wasteful expenditure.

A dangerous promise?

An offshoot of management accounting, budgets are relatively modern in organisational terms. They became popular in the 1950s and 1960s when academics tried to show how managers could scientifically manage an organisation or a department by developing and monitoring financial targets.

Once simply a scorecard, budgets evolved into an all-embracing planning and monitoring mechanism – a promise managers make that translates into targets that cascade through the organisation. But when people's jobs depend on meeting targets, they will probably meet them – even when they have to destroy the enterprise to do it.[8]

Balance sheets, cash flow statements and income statements are the three statements required in a financial report. You can use them to spot and explain trends, and to monitor your organisation's financial strength.

The balance sheet (or *statement of financial position*) describes the financial position of a company on a specified date, showing what the business *owns* – its *assets* and *reserves* – and what it *owes* – its *liabilities*. It's like a snapshot of the company's affairs expressed in dollars and cents.

The cash flow statement summarises the money the organisation has received and the money paid out in its operating, investing and financing activities. It indicates the *liquidity* of an organisation (assets that can be easily converted into cash) by showing how much working capital (money) is available; the more cash an organisation can quickly raise, the more liquid it is.

The income statement, also called the *profit and loss (P&L) account*, describes the financial performance of a company by comparing the income from all sources with the expenses incurred to determine the net profit (or loss) made during the accounting period (e.g. one month, one quarter, one year). It shows you what is known as the 'bottom line' – did we make money or didn't we?

An organisation's accounting systems generate these and a variety of other financial reports, making it easy to compare planned with actual results.

THE STRATEGIC PERSPECTIVE

What's a company worth?

Microsoft and Cisco are two of the world's largest and most successful companies, but you'd never guess it from their balance sheets. Like many modern companies, neither owns much that can be measured, weighed or counted, but both have a huge intangible worth based on their cultures, employees and systems.

In today's world, in which organisations need a sound employer value proposition and a positive public relations image, marketing may be an important investment, not an expense, as it usually appears on the P&L account. Today, many companies need 'smart' employees to succeed – are they an expense, as they have traditionally been, or an asset? Is training them an expense, as it has traditionally been, or an asset?

New ways of doing business may require new ways of accounting for an organisation's success.

Inventory controls

Carrying excess stock is expensive, while holding too little stock can lead to delays, inefficiency and even lost business. Factories, stores, warehouses – any organisation or site that needs to keep track of goods coming in and going out, uses some type of inventory monitoring and control system. At their most basic, they set maximum and minimum stock levels for inventory items and detail the most economical quantity of each item to carry.

More sophisticated inventory systems can also help employees locate items, for example in transit or in a warehouse. The most modern systems also help organisations integrate inventory management across their functional subsystems and integrate the information with other control systems such as accounts receivable, financial control and sales information that includes customer purchasing patterns.

While many small businesses continue to track inventory manually, other small and many medium-sized businesses now use a computerised system to monitor and control inventories. These systems generally use bar code technology to track items in real time and use wireless technology to transmit information to a central computer system that automatically alerts staff to place an order, indicating how much to order; some systems even place orders automatically.

Just-in-time and similar methods aim for raw materials to arrive 'just in time' for use, minimising the need for expensive stock holdings and storage. Sophisticated computer techniques, such as *materials resources planning*, aid planning, coordinating and monitoring despatch, goods inwards, manufacturing and stores operations.

Vendor-managed systems use their customers' automated daily reports to replenish stocks as needed giving the customer the savings of just-in-time inventory management and the supplier the ability to more accurately anticipate production requirements; both customers and suppliers benefit from the stronger trading partnerships that can result.

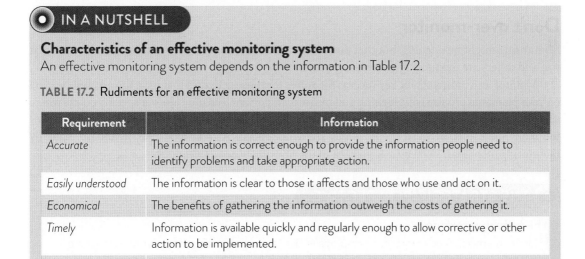

● IN A NUTSHELL

Characteristics of an effective monitoring system

An effective monitoring system depends on the information in Table 17.2.

TABLE 17.2 Rudiments for an effective monitoring system

Requirement	Information
Accurate	The information is correct enough to provide the information people need to identify problems and take appropriate action.
Easily understood	The information is clear to those it affects and those who use and act on it.
Economical	The benefits of gathering the information outweigh the costs of gathering it.
Timely	Information is available quickly and regularly enough to allow corrective or other action to be implemented.
Useful	It meets the needs of the organisation and the people using it.

Informal monitoring

Monitoring needn't be impersonal, official and onerous. Keeping your eyes open, 'managing by walking around', talking to people and listening to their comments are all good ways to keep your finger on the pulse. Your diary, personal organiser, task manager and 'to do' list are also effective monitoring tools.

Build in consultation mechanisms

When your plan involves people outside your team, build in consultative monitoring mechanisms – perhaps a 'half-time review' with stakeholders in the form of a meeting, a survey or informal discussions. This can provide information about how to improve your performance and the value you and your team add for your stakeholders.

When the benefits to your stakeholders aren't as great as you hoped, seek their input on how you and your team can better meet their expectations.

THEORY TO PRACTICE

How to develop an effective monitoring system

If you want to keep your monitoring system simple, here's how:

- Make it clear who is responsible for taking any corrective or other action that may be required.
- Make sure that people can produce, collect and use the monitoring feedback relatively quickly and easily. It must be worth the time and effort to collect and document it, and to analyse it or make use of it in some other way.
- Try to incorporate **management by exception**, where you are advised as soon as a critical activity deviates from the expected.
- When your monitoring system shows that things are going according to plan, remember to thank people for their efforts.

Don't over-monitor

Monitoring might be ongoing, but that doesn't mean it needs to take a lot of time. Coordinate what you and others are monitoring to avoid duplication.

Monitor lead indicators for key success measures for those activities that have the greatest bearing on your plans and productivity. Identify and measure important lead indicators at specific points where variations from plans indicate that performance is slipping or is in danger of doing so. Don't monitor too many indicators, or you'll spend all day studying reports. As a general rule, if you are regularly monitoring more than 15 measures, go back to the drawing board and simplify.

THE STRATEGIC PERSPECTIVE

The human interface

Improve teamwork and incorporate employees' desires to do a good job into your monitoring systems by letting them monitor and control their own performance whenever possible. Involve the people whose performance or activities you are monitoring as much as you can when establishing monitoring systems and procedures.

This also ensures that those responsible for implementing the plan, meeting the targets and using the monitoring information understand and accept the measures and are aware of why they are needed. No one likes to think they're being checked on without good cause.

CourseMateExpress

Go to http://login.cengagebrain.com to access CourseMate Express, your online study tool for *Management Theory & Practice*. CourseMate Express brings chapter concepts to life with interactive learning, and study and exam preparation tools:

- Test your skills in different aspects of management with interactive self-tests and simulations.
- Watch videos that show how real managers operate in real businesses.
- Test your understanding of the changing world of management by taking the revision quiz.

QUICK REVIEW

1. Briefly explain how planning and monitoring help organisations, managers and individual job-holders to achieve results.
2. List the types of plans that leader-managers need to understand and describe how operational plans fit into the wider activities of the organisation.
3. What distinguishes a good plan from a poor plan?
4. Why do plans sometimes fail? What actions can you take to safeguard the success of your plans?

BUILD YOUR SKILLS

1. It is often said that crisis management is a sign of poor planning. Do you agree? Explain why or why not, giving examples from your own experience. What advice would you offer a leader-manager who is caught up in dealing with crisis after crisis because of poor planning?
2. Should you stick firmly to your plans or consider them to be working documents that guide your actions?
3. How do you rate your planning and organising skills? Which, if any, do you believe you need to strengthen? How could you do this?
4. Describe a situation in which you invested the time and effort to develop a plan. Relate the plan you made to the six steps of the planning process described in this chapter. Was the time you spent in planning worth the effort? Why or why not? What conclusions can you draw about the usefulness of making plans?

WORKPLACE ACTIVITIES

1. Describe the planning skills you use in your current role and the type of plans you develop and follow. How do you monitor these plans?
2. What was the last activity you planned in detail at your workplace? Describe how you went about planning it and the steps you followed. How did you determine and secure the resources you needed to carry out your plan?
3. Describe a time when you worked with others to plan and organise activities and when you communicated with others to coordinate the implementation of the plan.

4. Describe a time when you worked with others to plan and organise a presentation, an event or something similar. What did you do that helped and hindered? What did others do? What lessons did you learn for next time?

5. Referring to Case study 22.1 on page 711, conduct a force field analysis of the forces working for and against successfully multiskilling non-salaried employees and achieving the benefits the organisation expects.

6. What monitoring tools do you and your work team use? Write a short essay describing these tools and how they alert you to problems, and explaining how they conform to the characteristics of an effective monitoring system described in this chapter. How do these monitoring tools help in the job?

CASE STUDY 17.1

THE HEARING-AID LAUNCH

Sahana is the marketing manager of Perfect Fit Hearing Aids, a large manufacturing and retailing company based in Melbourne. After several years of research and development their US parent company has designed one of the most advanced hearing aids on the market and assured them it would be ready for release in Australia well in time to launch at the Adelaide Convention Centre in 12 weeks.

Sahana has just returned to her office from meeting with the financial controller and the managing director to adjust the conference budget to accommodate the launch. With part of the funds coming from the parent company and the rest from the annual marketing and promotions budget, she intends to get maximum bang for her bucks.

'The timing couldn't have been better', she thinks, 'since product launches are most effectively done at these big conferences.' Good timing, too, because the conference team, which she is chairing, is holding its first meeting in 20 minutes. She sets to work adapting the planning statement to incorporate the product launch. This is important and she wants to make sure as many audiometrists as possible – no, make that *every* audiometrist at the conference, visits their stand to learn about their great new product.

Sahana opens the meeting by thanking everyone for coming, drawing their attention to the planning statement she has posted and saying a few words about how she is looking forward to working together to organise the most successful conference launch ever. Then they get down to work, brainstorming what needs to be done. In no special order, they quickly list the main activities:

- Develop a stand 'theme' for the space they've already booked in the main conference hall in conjunction with their external stand developers who will then design, build and erect the stand.
- Design, print and post industry and media invitations to the stand.
- Design and send email industry and media announcements about the launch.
- Create enticing draw prizes as a way to gather business cards and ensure audiometrists visit the stand.
- Decide how much hearing care equipment to have on the stand to adequately demonstrate the new hearing aid, book the freight company and liaise with the conference organisers and stand developers to ensure sufficient power points, extension cords, leads, etc. will be available at the stand for the equipment.

- Decide how many and which sales and technical staff should attend the conference and book the necessary accommodation and flights.
- Investigate, source and decide the giveaway and promotional materials for audiometrists' 'show bags', assemble the bags and send them to the conference.
- Monitor the arrival of locally produced publicity material and publicity material sent by the US parent company.
- Keep track of the money, honey.

'Well, that looks pretty complete. Let's leave this list up and if anyone thinks of anything else before the next meeting, please come in and add it. Now then, lets assign some responsibilities: Who wants to be in charge of the stand committee? Jim? Great, thanks', says Sahana writing his name next to it. 'Maybe we can combine the invitations and emails; who's up for that? Melanie, great thanks.' When they have worked their way through the list of activities, Sahana asks the committee leaders to come up with a plan of action with milestones and due dates by next Wednesday so she can put together a network diagram they can use to track their progress. 'Wonderful! Thank you so much everyone. We really got a lot done today. See you all same time, same place next Friday.'

Questions

1. How do you rate the conference team's initial planning efforts?
2. Can you suggest a planning statement the team can all work to?
3. How should the team monitor each activity and the budget to make sure everything will be ready in time to launch the new hearing aid at the national conference?
4. Prepare a simple Gantt chart illustrating the various activities, guestimating the timelines involved in each.

CASE STUDY 17.2

JOAN SIMON DISCOVERS THE NEED TO PLAN AHEAD AND KEEP TABS

Joan Simon has just been promoted to the position of sales manager in charge of eight sales representatives, two key account managers and three merchandisers.

As a key account manager before her promotion, all she needed to look after was herself – making sure she serviced her customers properly, that goods were delivered, that they sold well, that her customers were up to date on payments, and that they received the sales and merchandising support she deemed necessary. A simple spreadsheet system plus diligent use of her personal organiser had always sufficed.

But now that Joan is managing the whole team, she has the people to look after, as well as all the sales in the territory, product promotions, expenditure, business development and so on. The first thing she should do, she decides, is set up some planning and monitoring systems – systems that can quickly and easily give her the information she needs to manage the sales operation. How her predecessor had managed, she can't imagine – he must have kept track of everything in his head.

Her first move is to set up a spreadsheet for each sales representative and key account manager, showing their sales to date against their budgeted sales so that she can monitor their results against targets and see who might need a bit of help. While she's on a roll, she sets up a similar spreadsheet for each customer, showing their purchases month by month and year to date and comparing both figures against previous months and years.

Joan discovers that she receives a monthly debtor statement for each customer and, upon looking it over, she finds that a number of customers, both small and large, are more than 90 days in arrears. Since the company policy is 30 days credit for small customers and 60 days credit for larger-volume customers, she realises she needs to remind the reps to push for payment. She suspects that some of these customers, and even some of the sales reps, may have taken advantage of the change in personnel (i.e. her appointment) to allow their payments to drift. While she doesn't want to jeopardise the company's business relationship with these customers or her relationship with the sales reps – no rep likes reminding customers to pay, as she well knows – part of her responsibility as a manager is to ensure that their customers pay on time. And if one of those customers were to 'go under' with unpaid debts, no doubt management would be looking to her for an explanation.

With that gloomy thought in mind, Joan moves on to develop another spreadsheet to track her expenditure to ensure that it remains within budget and looks around to see where she should hang the large wall planner she has purchased to track her team's annual and personal leave.

When Joan meets with her manager at the end of the week to discuss how she's settling into her new role, he seems impressed with her planning and monitoring initiatives. Explaining that he's a big fan of management by exception, he says that when she compiles her monthly reports to him, she need only include information that is more than 10% above or below target, which essentially gives him a summary of what is going well and what isn't.

He advises her to apply management by exception principles with each of her staff and incorporate them into her department's weekly summaries for the management team so that she doesn't spend most of her valuable time pouring over results.

On her way home, it occurs to Joan that she should also plan the year's promotions for their customers. 'I should probably get the team to help plan those, since they're the ones who manage the promotions,' she thinks.

Questions

1. What risks did Joan's predecessor take in not using any planning and monitoring systems?
2. How do you rate Joan's efforts so far in establishing effective planning and monitoring systems for her department? What should her next steps be?
3. What formal and informal planning and monitoring systems do you think would be the most suitable for Joan's needs and why? Consider all the types of planning, including, for example, contingency and preventive planning.
4. Is Joan's idea of involving members of her team in planning the year's promotions for their customers a good one? Why or why not?

CHAPTER

18

SOLVING PROBLEMS AND MAKING DECISIONS

OVERVIEW

Some people call them 'challenges'; others call them 'headaches', 'inconveniences', 'issues', 'obstacles' and even 'opportunities'. But just as a rose by any other name is still a rose, no matter what you call it, you are going to face difficult situations that you need to handle and difficult choices you need to make.

When you know where problems can arise and are sensitive to early warning signs, you can deal with looming problems in a systematic, thoughtful way before they grow or cause too much harm. And when problems arise that you haven't spotted and squashed, you need to analyse and solve or resolve them before they do a lot of damage.

Someone once remarked that when everything is going according to plan, something somewhere is going massively wrong. One thing is certain: there will never be a world or a job without decisions to make and problems to solve. As the authority to solve problems and make decisions is pushed down flattened organisational hierarchies, as work teams become more involved, and as customer demands, market conditions and technology continually change, the need for sound problem-solving and decision-making skills at all levels continues to grow.

Every decision can't please everyone and many problems can't be fixed in a way that pleases everyone, either. The more complex the situation, the more this is so. But although there may not be a perfect solution or decision, it doesn't mean that any will do – all solutions and decisions should meet carefully thought-out objectives.

1. Are you aware of the range of decisions that managers and teams make and the common decision-making and problem-solving traps and how to avoid them?
2. Do you know how to apply a seven-step process for solving problems and making decisions?
3. Do you know what your decision-making style is, and are you familiar with which of the six ways to reach decisions never to use, which to use sometimes and which are usually a good choice?

This chapter shows you how to recognise and solve problems properly and how to make sound and timely decisions.

Decisions ... decisions ...

Khalid Bibi, the superintendent of the local council's Sports and Recreation Centre, is just returning from the weekly management meeting when he passes the chief aerobics instructor. She says that her team of casual instructors is becoming more vociferous in their complaints about the ventilation in the gym and the problem needs to be sorted out quickly. Then Mattie Smith, one of the best receptionists he has ever worked with, catches up with him to say that she has been offered another job with an increase in pay and responsibilities, and she wants to speak to him about opportunities at the council.

When he gets back to his desk, Khalid finds himself faced with a number of additional issues. An email from the general manager of the centre asks for his thoughts about whether, and how, to implement a proposed customer service program. There is a message from his partner requesting that he phone home immediately, and another from the maintenance contractor warning that problems seem to be developing with the pool filtration system. A quick check of the monthly costs analysis shows a trend towards increased chemical and cleaning costs for the pool and, to top it all off, there is a candidate for a job opening in the cleaning staff waiting to be interviewed.

Everything always seems to happen at once, thinks Khalid, as he considers which problems to tackle first and which can safely wait.

1. Understanding the range of problems and decisions and the traps to avoid

Better a good decision quickly than the best decision too late.

Harold S Geneen (past CEO of ITT), quoted in Spender, *Business Strategy* (2014)[1]

Leader-managers are called upon every day to make quick decisions and act to resolve immediate problems. Nearly as often, they face decisions and difficult, tricky problems that require thorough consultation, investigation and thought.

What's the best way to deal with pressing problems and with complex problems? What's the best way to reach a decision? Your skills in this area are certain to affect your career trajectory as well as your team's success.

Decide now or later ...

Problems don't improve with age. The best time to solve a problem is in its early stages, before it festers and seriously compromises operations. On page 115, you found out how to decide whether to do a task now, later or not at all by assessing its *importance* and *urgency*. You can do the same with problems and decisions.

When a problem or decision comes to your attention, consider how serious or potentially serious it is. Give those that are serious (important) and urgent a high priority. Give those that are serious (important) but not urgent a high priority too, because when you don't, they become urgent and you then need to work on them under pressure. Put any that might take care of themselves on the back burner to check on later.

Also ask yourself whether the situation merits your involvement. Delegate decisions that you don't need to be involved in and any that are urgent but not important. You probably don't need to waste your efforts on those that are neither important nor urgent.

... or pay the price

A number of unfortunate outcomes affect leader-managers and teams that don't follow systematic problem-solving procedures. Ironically, one of the worst results is a lack of time to solve problems properly because people are too busy putting out 'bushfires', dealing with crises and implementing 'quick fixes'. As a result, many 'solutions' that are applied are actually incomplete 'patches' – not solutions at all – which means that problems come back again and again and flow on to other parts of the organisation. Failing to solve the original problem then creates new problems.

Here's what to do to avoid this happening to you:

* Don't patch a problem: When you can't fix it properly, leave it until you can. Put important problems on your high priority list.
* Keep investigating a problem until you find its real cause: Gut-feeling diagnosis can be fine, as long as you supplement it with systematic analytical tools and techniques (some of which are explained below and some on page 585).
* Put the most urgent problems first: When you have a lot of problems, prioritise them and work on them in priority order.
* Remove the solution that doesn't work: When your first attempt doesn't fix the problem, remove the solution. Don't leave it in place. Once it's removed, try something else.[2]

IN A NUTSHELL

How to recognise and prevent problems

Be alert to something that:

* is supposed to happen but doesn't
* isn't supposed to happen but does
* is supposed to be somewhere but isn't
* isn't supposed to be somewhere but is
* is unexpectedly broken, spoiled or ruined.

Look for patterns and repetitions. Find out the cause and see what you can learn. The sooner problems are identified (and few jump up and announce themselves), the sooner you can make those decisions and remedy those problems.

Variations in complexity

Some decisions and problems are cut and dried: there's clearly one best action to take and it's obvious what that action is. That's when a programmed decision or an automatic response is needed. A standard operating procedure that provides a consistent solution means people don't need to waste time and energy figuring out what to do each time, which allows them to attend to more important matters. Standard responses also make dealing with routine matters easier, faster and more reliable.

At the other end of the complexity scale are problems and decisions that aren't linear and logical because they involve unpredictable events and ever-changing activities and relationships. How best to distribute work to the team? How best to divide scarce resources between users? How best to provide better services to customers and win their undying loyalty? How best to deal with a major environmental disaster or an epidemic that severely compromises your organisation's ability to operate?

In an increasingly complex and demanding business environment where predictability is far from common and no one can forecast the future with any degree of certainty, where logic leaves people scratching their heads and when the unexpected keeps happening, the importance of making wise non-programmed decisions is increasing.

The variations in complexity of problems and decisions call for different approaches, as summarised in Figure 18.1 and outlined here:

- *Simple situations*: Programmed decisions are ideal for 'simple' situations – situations that are predictable, when the cause and effect are clear, when the same patterns repeat over and over and when there are many *known knowns*. There is often one right – and obvious – answer. Best practice procedures, established policies and practices, programmed decisions and standard operating procedures are your best option. Communicate them clearly and directly.

  Or put a computer in charge. Computers can use decision rules and algorithms – a series of logical steps – to make and process many programmed decisions without any intervention by people. Although automation can be difficult to develop and the decision criteria may change, it is accurate and quick. Take, for example, automated inventory control and purchasing; once you have determined the minimum and maximum levels of stock to be carried and worked out the optimal order size, a computer keeps track of the use of each inventory item and automatically prepares and transmits an order when levels drop below a specified point.

- *Complicated situations*: When a situation is 'complicated' and there are one or several possible right answers, when there is a cause and effect that takes expertise or time and patience to see and when there are *known unknowns*, it's more appropriate to listen and discuss. Use an algorithm to find the cause of a problem and point to the correct action. (For example, the five keys in Chapter 11 comprise a performance algorithm that helps you think through how to build performance and productivity.) Work with experts and others to analyse, diagnose and probe the situation (but beware of analysis paralysis). Investigate several options before reaching a decision.

- *Complex situations*: When you find yourself dealing with a 'complex' problem or decision where there are *unknown unknowns*, when the whole is greater than the sum of its parts, the situation is dynamic and unpredictable, and there are no right answers, you need creativity and innovation. Probe the situation, look for patterns and let solutions emerge through investigation and discussion.

- *Chaotic situations*: At the far end of the scale are 'chaotic' situations that are constantly in flux and filled with *unknowables*, where there are no rules and no right answers and there isn't much time to think. Immediate action, communicated clearly and directly, is needed to establish control, and once taken, you can analyse its effectiveness and fine-tune your response, or come up with a more creative solution.

The seven-step model described in Section 2 of this chapter is ideal to use with the range of decisions and problems, from simple to complex.

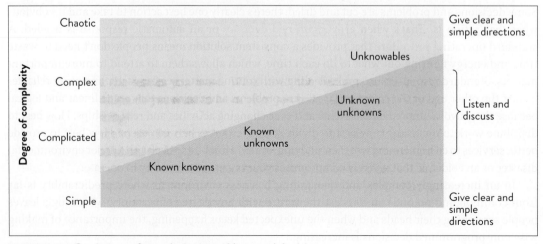

FIGURE 18.1 Gradations of complexity in problems and decisions

Automated decision-making

Cemex, a Mexican-headquartered global cement company, paints pipes in all its factories with the same colour code. Transferring employees don't need to figure out the way a factory is set up and don't make expensive or potentially dangerous mistakes.[3]

But with more complex decisions and problems, you need to put your brain into gear. The thornier the problem, the more you need to stand back and look at the underlying principals that are operating. Considering only surface, or superficial, parts of the problem prevents you from making a sound decision or finding a really workable solution to the problem.

The traps to avoid

When you decide to tackle problems or decisions, do so accurately and cleanly by deciding how much of your time and attention they deserve based on their importance and urgency. Then deal with them appropriately based on their complexity. Remember to take into account stakeholder feelings, opinions and situations, (explained on page 194) and your organisation's vision, values and strategy into account in deciding what to do, too (explained on page 51). Finally, don't be what Henry Ford considered to be a typical problem-solver, 'Most people spend more time and energy going around problems than in trying to solve them.'[4]

Here are the main traps to avoid. You can control the first four traps described below with determination and practice. The other nine 'brain traps' are less easily controlled because you need to recognise and override your brain's programming. Your emotional intelligence and resilience (described on page 194) can help you overcome these traps.

The reluctance, haste and hesitation traps

Perhaps you have met the conflict avoiders who hesitate to upset anyone, the worry warts who agonise over every decision no matter how small, or the escapists who shuffle their facts, feet, figures and papers, trying to fool themselves and others that they are 'working on it' rather than face the problem head-on. These are traps to avoid. As the German philosopher Johann Friedrich von Schiller once said, 'He who considers too much will perform little.'[5]

You may know people who are *too hasty* or *too slow* at reaching decisions and solving problems – two more traps to avoid. Quick decisions and problems solved with a snap of the fingers frequently fail to consider people's feelings or the facts, while hesitation and endless 'research' can cause unnecessary bottlenecks, delays and frustration, while opportunities slip past.

Guidelines for effective decision-making and problem-solving

Be very careful making decisions. Wrong decisions can be difficult to turn around:

- *Decide whether the problem or decision is a big one or a small one.* When you have a complicated or complex decision to make or problem to solve, carefully follow the seven-step procedure explained later in this chapter. When you have a simple decision to make or a simple problem to solve, don't spend hours agonising over it at the cost of more important matters.

>>

- *Don't be too impatient.* 'Decide in haste, repent at leisure' is a good rule to remember when making important decisions. On the other hand, don't wait for the perfect decision either.
- *Don't put off making a decision or solving a problem until it becomes a crisis.* Stand back and consider the situation and decide how much time you have. Then use that time to make the best decision you can. When you do have a crisis or a chaotic situation to resolve, remember that you are the leader and your team is looking to you for clear thinking and calm direction.
- *Concentrate on what you do want, not on what you don't want.* When all you can see is the problem, you can't find a way around it. Pause, establish your objectives and think about how to achieve them. It isn't always easy to find solutions, but that's part of your job. The best ideas sometimes take a while to surface.

The ignoring near misses trap

It's comforting, but wrong, to ignore everyday small failures that cause no immediate damage. Rather than turn a blind eye to near misses, treat them as problems to be investigated and solved before the failures become more serious.

Researchers investigating near misses in dozens of companies in a variety of industries have concluded that multiple narrow escapes preceded and foreshadowed every disaster and business crisis they studied. The problem is two-fold:

1. *Normalisation bias of deviance*: Over time, people become blind to problems, accepting them as normal
2. *Outcome bias*: When a glitch doesn't cause damage, people focus on the 'successful' outcome rather than the (often) pure good luck that allowed the narrow escape.[6]

THEORY TO PRACTICE

The well from hell and bad apples

Statistically speaking, when you give an accident enough opportunities to happen, it happens. Take, for example, the series of ignored near misses and poor decisions that resulted in incalculable damage to BP and the environment when, in April 2010, the Deepwater Horizon well blew out. The resulting fire killed 11 people, sank the rig and triggered a massive underwater spill that took months to contain.

Warning signs, rather than prompting investigations, were taken as an indication that safety and operating procedures worked (outcome bias) and the fact that many wells in the Gulf of Mexico suffered similar problems enticed BP employees to view the problems as routine (normalisation bias). In fact, there had been dozens of minor blowouts but disaster had always been averted by sheer luck such as a favourable wind direction and no one welding near the gas leak at the time of the blowout.

When Apple launched its iPhone 4 in June 2010, complaints about dropped calls and poor signal strength poured in almost immediately. When Apple blamed the users for holding the phone incorrectly (then CEO Steve Jobs described the dropped calls as a 'non issue'), customers complained loudly in social and mainstream media and filed class action lawsuits, including a suit alleging fraud by concealment, negligence, intentional misrepresentation and defective design.[7]

>>

Like the problems with BP's Deepwater Horizon well, the problems underlying Apple's crisis had long been present. The flaw allowing a drop in signal strength had been present in earlier iPhones, as well as in competitors' phones, for years and came to be seen as increasingly acceptable (normalisation bias), and the lack of outcry over shortcomings with previous models was seen as evidence of a clever strategy rather than good luck (outcome bias).[8]

Brain traps

Fortunately, you can overcome the cowardice, haste and hesitation traps, and the 'blind eye' trap due to normalisation of deviance and outcome bias, with training and experience and by using the seven steps outlined in Section 2. The next nine traps are more treacherous. They arise not because you haven't followed the seven steps or are cowardly, hasty, hesitant or blindly biased, but because your brain sabotages your decisions. The human brain is wired to go through unconscious routines, or *heuristics*, when dealing with complexity. These heuristics are meant to help people think problems and decisions through quickly and easily, but speed and ease aren't always a good thing.

Each of the following nine heuristics can work in isolation or in combination with the others. They lurk in every stage of the problem-solving, decision-making process, and high-risk decisions leave people particularly prone to them.

Forewarned is forearmed. The key to beating these tricks of the mind is to stay alert and recognise when you're succumbing to them.

The anchoring trap

It's easy to give too much weight to what you see or hear first and last, whether it's estimates, evidence, ideas, information or opinions. An off-the-cuff comment, prejudice, previous similar experiences and stereotypes can also act as anchors, even in the face of strong counter-evidence. Anchors influence the way you think about a problem or decision and can even set the terms on which a decision is made.

You can't avoid this trap, but you can reduce its impact. Be aware, and beware of your first and last impressions, and the first and last pieces of information you receive, and make an effort to give fair weight to what you learned in between. Take the trouble to view problems from different perspectives and don't automatically stick with whatever occurs to you first. Be open-minded and seek a variety of information and opinions. And hold your own opinions and ideas until last so that you don't unintentionally anchor your team members with your own views.

The confirmation bias trap

Your brain seeks evidence that confirms and supports your point of view or preferred decision and avoids information that contradicts it. This affects both where you go to collect information and how you interpret it, and it causes you to put too much weight on supporting evidence and too little on opposing evidence.

To avoid seeing only what you want to see, don't make a decision and then figure out how to justify it. Don't undermine the real facts with your own expectations or biases. Don't accept evidence that confirms your position without question. Be aware of your initial assumptions and admit that you may be inclined to think a certain way – then consciously open your mind to other ways. Treat all the evidence and information, both the pros and the cons, objectively. Ask someone to play devil's advocate and argue against your preferred decision. When asking others' opinions, avoid leading questions (questions that make plain the answer you want or expect).

The first devil's advocate

In the 16th century, the Catholic Church established the role of devil's advocate to criticise canonisation decisions.

Self-serving reasoning is a sub-set of confirmation bias. When you recall the recent scandals involving accounting firms and the even more recent banking and investment scandals that led to the global financial crisis, you can see self-serving reasoning at work. This trap is a subset of confirmation bias.

On the one hand, accountants are paid to provide an independent assessment of a client's financial situation. On the other hand, they also provided tax, technology and other consulting services to these same clients for large fees. How independent are their audits likely to be? Yet until recently, accounting firms fooled themselves, their clients and even the agencies that regulated them by reasoning that their professionalism overrode their desire to please their clients. Similarly, banks are obliged to safeguard the money their depositors invest with them, yet investment divisions of some banks produced and sold high-risk investments as completely safe, making lots of money in the short-term but losing everything in the not-so-long term.

It's natural to seek evidence that supports your inclination or point of view and to avoid information that contradicts it, especially when you are the beneficiary. To survive this trap, keep your thinking honest and consider different perspectives by running your reasoning by people who are unlikely to agree with you. Examine both contradictory and supporting evidence with equal rigour and examine your motives carefully.

The estimating and forecasting traps

When you have regular feedback on the accuracy of your estimates and forecasts (e.g. about distance, time, volume or weight) you learn to reckon and predict fairly accurately. With uncertain and unfamiliar events, however, this is more difficult.

Although your job no doubt often requires you to estimate and forecast, it may not provide enough feedback on your accuracy to allow you to develop and fine-tune your estimating and forecasting skills. The more uncertain or unusual the subject of your estimate or forecast, the more difficult your task is. It's easy to become overconfident or overcautious, or to rely too much on past events or dramatic events that have left a strong impression.

Be disciplined when you need to make forecasts or assess probabilities. Consider the extremes, examine all your assumptions and try not to be guided by impressions. Use accurate facts and figures when you can; when you can't, cross your fingers, know it's a long shot and be prepared to be wrong, cut your losses and change course.

The framing trap

The way you *frame*, or state, a problem or decision is important. It can highlight spent effort, money or time, for example, or lead towards confirming evidence. Your framing statement guides you down one path or another, towards the status quo or away from it, towards taking a risk or towards safety.

Wording your decision in terms of *potential gains* or *potential losses* makes a big difference because losses loom larger in our brains than gains – people are wired to notice dangerous things far more than things that make us feel happy or safe. Research shows that people avoid risks and choose the safer option when a decision is framed in terms of gains but when a decision is framed in terms of risk or loss, people risk a larger loss rather than accept a sure, smaller loss.[9] (In evolutionary terms, this made sense when life was riskier than it is today and even a small loss could mean your downfall. Today, it means that when we don't have the inclination or the time to work out the decision logically, we go with the mental programming that's served us well over 200 000 years. But it doesn't necessarily mean the resulting decision is a good decision.)

The point is this: Frames cause distortions. The more important the decision or problem, the more important it is to word it in different ways. Don't automatically accept the way problems or decisions are presented to you. Restate them in neutral ways that combine gains and losses and reflect different reference points. Ask yourself how your thinking would change if you word, or frame, the problem or decision differently. Think the decision through carefully.

The not cutting your losses trap

Have you ever made a mistake and stuck with it rather than cut your losses and change course? When your previous choice isn't working, set it aside. What's done is done. Don't base future actions on a misguided attempt to recover your investment in time or money, or trying to turn a poor decision into a good one.

Prolonging a mistake only compounds it. Look at the situation with new eyes and ask for objective opinions, especially from people who were not involved in the original decision. As one of the world's richest people, investor Warren Buffet, says: 'When you find yourself in a hole, the best thing you can do is stop digging.'[10]

Adopt what psychologists call a *promotion focus* by looking to the future and thinking about what you have to *gain* by cutting your losses, rather than looking backwards and seeing what you're *losing*.

The pattern recognition trap

The brain is hardwired to recognise patterns, integrating information from up to 30 different parts of the brain. When faced with a new situation, we make assumptions based on prior experiences and judgements. This usually works well but can also mislead us, particularly when we're dealing with seemingly familiar situations that turn out to be out-of-the-ordinary – we think we know what's going on, but we don't.

History doesn't always repeat itself, especially in today's fast-changing world. What worked well last year may not work this year. Conditions, technology, people and economic situations all change, and these changes influence what does and does not work.

So that blindly following past experience doesn't lead you down the wrong path by causing you to overlook or underestimate important differences, think about whether you're seeing patterns that you want to see because the resulting decision suits you. Then check whether your memories could be misleading you – what might be *different* about this situation to previous situations? When you've done it or something similar in a similar situation before and it worked, remember – there are no guarantees the same action will work this time. Involve people who could challenge your thinking and gather a range of opinions and ideas before acting.[11]

The representativeness trap

People tend to believe that they can safely act on their experience, even limited experience. Whether it's new leader-managers facing unfamiliar situations or old hands facing decisions or circumstances not often encountered, the belief that what has held true in the past will continue to hold true can lead to unwarranted confidence and misplaced assumptions. Given the rapidly changing operating environment, this heuristic is a bigger trap for the current generation of leader-managers than for previous generations.

The sticking with the status quo trap

It often seems easier to continue with things as they are. The conventional wisdom of 'Leave well enough alone' or 'Let's wait and see' warns against doing anything radical or different. Giving in to inertia and doing nothing when faced with tough choices can seem temptingly 'easy' and 'safe', while taking action requires courage. Also, the less action you take, the less responsibility you may feel and the less criticism you are open to. The pull of the status quo becomes even stronger when you are faced with several options.

Maintaining the status quo may be a good choice but don't do it just because it's easy and comfortable. Keep your objectives clearly in mind. Does the current situation serve your team members well or would another alternative serve them better? Ask yourself: 'Would I select the status quo if it were just another alternative?'

THE STRATEGIC PERSPECTIVE

Two brain boosters

When you're having trouble solving a problem, take some time to let your mind wander and daydream a bit. This activates problem-solving areas of the brain – the 'executive network' associated with high-level, complex problem-solving.[12]

Subconscious incubation works well, too. As you're falling asleep, think about a problem you are trying to solve or a decision you need to make. What do you know about it already? What do you need to know? What do you want the solution to offer? Then go to sleep and let your subconscious work on it. More often than not, you have your answer within a few nights of incubation – it pops into your mind upon wakening or during the next day.[13]

---

2. Using seven steps to solve problems and make decisions

> Anyone can hold the helm when the sea is calm.
>
> Publilius Syrus (freed Roman slave), *Senteniae* (1895)[14]

What thorny problems have you solved recently? What sensible decisions have you made? You may not always have been conscious of the method you used, but you probably followed similar steps to the seven steps explained below. Notice the three distinct mental processes that those seven steps, summarised in Figure 18.2, go through: analysing, imagining and evaluating.

As you apply these steps, remember that the more complex the problem you're dealing with, the more important it is to intervene at a higher level, where your actions can have an impact. From the highest to the lowest level, consider:

- Strategy or objectives: Are these appropriate?
- Systems: Is there something awkward or wrong with the procedures or with the allocation of responsibilities?
- Incentives and information: Do the rewards (psychological as well as monetary) support your objectives? Do you have enough information?
- Individual performance: Is the problem a 'people problem' that training or motivation could help?

For instance, training people won't help when the incentives to use the training are missing. Providing incentives can't help when the procedures are flawed. Designing great systems won't do much good when they're aimed at progressing a poor strategy.

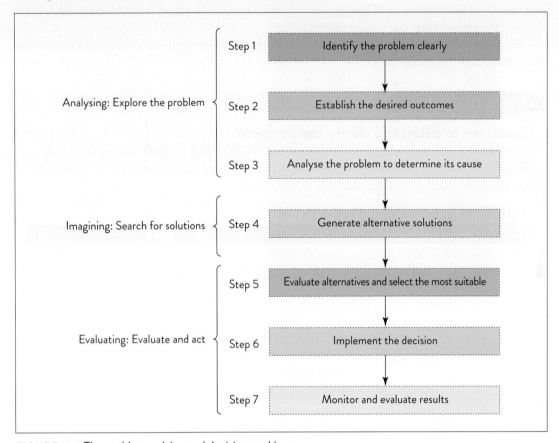

FIGURE 18.2 The problem-solving and decision-making process

Phase 1: Explore the problem

In Phase 1, you draw on your patience, clear and logical thinking, and a bit of intuitive insight to analyse the problem. You determine where you are now and why, and where you want to be, laying the groundwork for a successful outcome.

Step 1: Identify the problem clearly

Say, for example, that you notice your team's equipment seems to be breaking down more than usual, or someone comments that 'our equipment is less reliable than it used to be', or your work team has brainstormed a list of problems and decided to work on fixing the problem of equipment breakdowns first.

However, 'too many equipment breakdowns' doesn't describe the problem precisely enough to work on. After asking and answering a number of questions, your problem statement for 'too many equipment breakdowns' might become: 'For the past three quarters, 60% of portable equipment over two years old used in the vans and in home offices has been failing before its service warranty expires; in previous quarters, the failure rate was 40%.'

A clear problem statement like this tells you what to work on and why. No matter how pressing the need for a solution seems to be, don't move on to Step 2 until you have clearly described the problem you intend to solve. Here's what Albert Einstein says about the importance of knowing precisely what the problem is: 'If I were given one hour to save the planet, I would spend 59 minutes defining the problem and one minute resolving it.'[15]

Some questions to help you define problems clearly are shown in the 'In a Nutshell: Questions to detail and clarify the problem'.

IN A NUTSHELL

Questions to detail and clarify the problem

Here are two problems in the left-hand column of Table 18.1. Each is stated too vaguely to help the person solving the problem. Use the questions on the right to add details to the problems and help clarify the detail so that the problems can be solved.

TABLE 18.1 Using detail to clarify problems

General problem	Questions to ask
'Too many equipment breakdowns'	How many breakdowns?
	Which equipment?
	What is the nature of the breakdowns?
	When do they occur?
	What is happening when they occur?
	Who is involved?
	How regularly has the equipment been serviced?
	Has anything changed?
'Too many accidents'	What is the specific nature of the accidents?
	Where do they happen?
	When do they occur?
	Who is involved?
	Exactly how many accidents of each type are there and how does this compare with previous periods and similar workplaces?
	Has anything changed?

Step 2: Establish the desired outcomes

Next, think about the results you want. What must the decision or the solution to the problem achieve? What position do you want to be in after you have taken action? How can you tell whether your action is working?

A clear outcome to aim for concentrates your thinking and helps you in Step 5 (when you select the most suitable solution) and Step 7 (when you evaluate the effectiveness of your decision or action). Reaching a perfect decision or solution to a problem may not be possible, but at least when you have goals, you can aim at the best possible outcome. This helps you and your team concentrate on what you are trying to find answers to and keeps you on track.

Try making a 'how to …' statement to set goals. For example, how to:

- ensure availability of raw materials to the front line when they are needed without tying up extra working capital in stockholding
- get more storage space in the administration section
- increase battery sales in stores
- reduce the failure rate of portable equipment over two years old
- respond to 80% of inquiries for quotations within three working days
- serve customers more quickly during the lunch hour
- speed up the invoicing process at the checkout.

For complex or very important problems, divide your criteria into *musts* and *wants*: what must your decision do for you and, ideally, what would you also like it to do? Clearly establishing musts and wants puts you in a good position to select the best alternative when the time comes and to determine how well it is working.

 FYI

The beginner's mind

Shoshin is a Japanese word meaning 'beginner's mind', or an open, uncluttered mind, a ready mind. *Shoshin* is useful indeed when solving problems because sometimes years of experience can limit our thinking, causing us to miss better solutions. The Buddhist scholar, Shunryu Suzuki said: 'In the beginner's mind, there are many possibilities; in the expert's mind, there are few.'[16]

Try to force yourself to approach every problem from different points of view with a 'beginner's mind'.

Step 3: Analyse the problem to determine its cause

Now that you've defined the problem clearly and know what you want the solution to the problem to achieve, it's time to analyse the problem. 'Analyse' comes from the Greek verb meaning to undo or loosen, and that's what you do with problems – you pull them apart and break them down into their smallest elements.

Analysing problems helps you identify *symptoms*, which result from problems but are not the problem. Symptoms can alert you that a problem exists, but until you know its cause, you can't fix it. (Think of the analogy of taking an aspirin for a headache (trying to cure the symptom) when the real problem is eye strain and the cure is therefore eyeglasses.) 'Solving' symptoms leaves the real problem unsolved, to recur again and again, and often creates even more problems.

The only way to fix a problem is to find its cause and remove it; you do that by analysing the problem and untangling it from its symptoms. Once you've pinpointed the cause, you can look for a solution that removes it. When you can't remove the cause of the problem in order to fix it, look for a solution that minimises the cause.

THEORY TO PRACTISE

The cost of treating symptoms

As the US$200 million Mars Climate Orbiter headed toward Mars to study the Martian weather, climate, and water and carbon dioxide budget, it drifted slightly off course four times. Each time, managers treated the symptom with small trajectory adjustments but didn't investigate the reason for the drifting.

>>

> When it neared Mars, the spacecraft disintegrated rather than entering into orbit. That's when NASA looked for, and found, the cause of the problem: programmers had used Imperial rather than metric units in their software coding. The apparent success in treating the symptoms lulled some of the world's best brains into thinking they had rectified the problem.[17]

Remember the brain traps discussed earlier and guard against jumping to conclusions about the cause of a problem. Think the problem through and examine it from all angles – competitors, colleagues, customers, management, the public, suppliers, and so on. A thorough analysis saves you a lot of time and trouble in the long run because you won't waste time 'solving' symptoms. In fact, a clear and accurate analysis of a problem sometimes points directly to its solution.

Gather facts, ideas and the opinions of others that may help in your analysis. Test your theories before you act on them. You probably won't be able to get all the facts, but use those you have plus those you can get without too much trouble or expense.

⦿ IN A NUTSHELL

Analysing the problem
Table 18.2 shows you how to analyse and then solve a simple problem.

TABLE 18.2 Analysing the problem

Analysis	Problem
Step 1: Analyse the symptoms	*Home computer suddenly switches off*
Step 2: Identify possible causes	*Loose wire to terminal, or*
	Power failure, or
	Blown fuse
Step 3: Test these possible causes to see whether one is the cause of the problem	*Check the wires to the computer*
	Check the power by switching on a light
	Check the fuse board

Cause-and-effect diagrams

A cause-and-effect diagram, also known as an *Ishikawa diagram* (after its creator) and a *fishbone diagram* (because of its appearance), is a time-tested way to break down problems to determine their true cause. They are especially helpful with complicated problems that require you to sort out a maze of facts to isolate the most likely cause(s) of a problem.

Diagramming a problem allows you to 'see' it from its various aspects and identify its most important features. It's relatively quick to do and usually enjoyable. You can diagram a problem alone or with a small group of people. Either way, you use the technique of brainstorming (discussed on page 534).

To make a fishbone diagram, put the problem in the square at the 'head' of the fish. Then decide the possible categories of causes of the problem and show them as major 'bones' off the central 'spine' of the fish. It is usual to break a problem down into four components, but don't let this constrain you – use three or five categories when you need to. Do whatever best helps you analyse your specific problem. Always note who prepared the diagram and the date.

Figure 18.3 shows a cause-and-effect analysis for the problem of employee turnover. You can see that four possible causes of the problem are considered: employees, work environment, equipment and rewards. These possible causes may not suit every problem. See the 'In a Nutshell: Contributors to problems' on page 533, to choose from the diagnostic areas and create your own.

When you think of a possible cause of a problem that could go under more than one category on your diagram, don't worry – just put it down somewhere. The main thing is that you are looking at the problem from all angles, which is essential to a thorough problem analysis.

When you've finished brainstorming possible causes of the problem, stand back and consider them. Which seem most important to you? Circle those causes that seem most promising to investigate further.

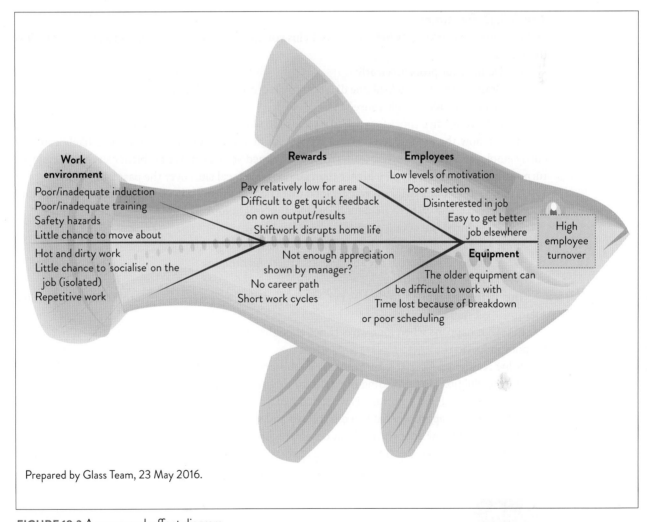

Work environment
Poor/inadequate induction
Poor/inadequate training
Safety hazards
Little chance to move about
Hot and dirty work
Little chance to 'socialise' on the job (isolated)
Repetitive work

Rewards
Pay relatively low for area
Difficult to get quick feedback on own output/results
Shiftwork disrupts home life
Not enough appreciation shown by manager?
No career path
Short work cycles

Employees
Low levels of motivation
Poor selection
Disinterested in job
Easy to get better job elsewhere

Equipment
The older equipment can be difficult to work with
Time lost because of breakdown or poor scheduling

High employee turnover

Prepared by Glass Team, 23 May 2016.

FIGURE 18.3 A cause-and-effect diagram

IN A NUTSHELL

Contributors to problems

Choose from this list or use other factors to analyse your problems systematically and comprehensively:

Clear goals	Job design	Rewards
Customers	Machinery, equipment, tools	Systems and procedures
Efficiency	Materials	Team culture
Employees	Methods	Time
General public	Money and funds	Training
Information	Policies	Work environment
Internal policies	Procedures	

Ask 'Why?' five times

Did you know that asking 'Why?' five times helps you to drill down to the cause of a problem? Follow these steps:

1. Define your problem clearly.
2. Brainstorm or use a fishbone diagram to determine possible causes.
3. Decide the most likely cause(s).
4. Ask 'Why?' five times for each likely cause to work out the real reason.

Here is how the technique of asking 'Why?' could work to determine the most likely cause of costly employee turnover in your team. You have defined your turnover problem clearly as employee turnover being consistently 20% higher than comparable local sites over the past 24 months.

From your fishbone diagram you decided that the two most likely causes are poor selection and poor induction. Your 'Why?' chain for poor selection might look like this:

Why? I've hired the wrong people.

Why? I'm not applying effective recruitment and selection techniques.

Why? I'm not confident in my ability to use these techniques.

Why? I need more training.

This is the logical end to this 'Why?' chain. Four 'Whys?' were enough to arrive at a possible solution – get more training.

But what happens when four whys is not enough? You need five whys. Here is the 'Why?' chain for poor induction:

Why? New employees aren't learning key skills and are not fitting in properly.

Why? Induction isn't providing the right information and motivation.

Why? It's too ad hoc – nothing is written down.

Why? I haven't approached it in a disciplined and systematic way.

Why? I don't know enough yet about developing induction programs.

As you can see, by the time you've reached the end of the 'Why?' chain, the solution often becomes clear.

FYI

Always ask 'Why?'

Asking 'Why?' even works with knowledge work: Why am I going to this meeting? Why am I reading this report? Why am I not able to move forward on this deliverable?

THEORY TO PRACTICE

Dangerous assumptions

It pays to think outside the box. Try these examples:

- Jeffrey Baumgartner reported that Polaroid designed digital film in the early 1990s but didn't bring its invention to market until 1996 because it couldn't figure out a way to bundle it with a printer. Falling for the 'sticking with the status quo' heuristic, the company assumed its customers wanted to see prints, missing the fact that customers would be more than happy to look at their photos on a computer screen.[18]

- New to Thailand and working with a company then called the Nation Publishing Group, which produced magazines and newspapers in Thai, English and Japanese, Jeffrey Baumgartner advised the company to change the title of a fortnightly English-language tabloid for teenagers it was about to produce called *Nation Junior*. Baumgartner argues that teens would not like the condescending word, 'junior' in the title. The company ignored Baumgartner's advice, based on his own culturally based assumptions, and the tabloid soon became its best-selling title.[19]

Phase 2: Search for solutions

In Phase 2, you need to let go of assumptions, longstanding beliefs and preconceived ideas and have the mental energy to look beyond the obvious in order to generate viable and novel solutions. It's time to use your creativity, innovativeness and imagination.

Step 4: Generate alternative solutions

The more possible solutions you have to choose from, the better your chances of fixing your problem properly. Here are three things to remember about finding suitable solutions:

1. The good ones seldom announce themselves: They can be elusive, and to find them you usually need to develop several possible solutions and keep an open mind to all of them. This is not as easy as it might sound. People often have fixed ideas about what caused a problem or how it should be solved. When that happens, jumping to conclusions and trying to solve a problem without considering other possibilities – and overlooking a better solution in the process – is a real danger.

2. The best solutions sometimes come not from logical thinking but from creative thinking: Seemingly 'wild' or 'crazy' solutions can lead to some great ideas. This makes it essential to keep Step 4, generating solutions, completely separate from Step 5, evaluating them.

3. Don't settle for the first solution that occurs to you – keep looking: You need plenty of options to select from. When you're tempted to choose the first (or last) action you think of, remember the anchoring heuristic. Brainstorming is a good way to tap into your creativity and develop lots of options.

And here are five guidelines to remember when it's time to come up with possible solutions:

1. Bring underlying assumptions out into the open: This ensures you're aware of them and can change them or drop them when they're unrealistic.

2. Review the strategic perspective: This helps you assess your options and check that the one you select is best for the organisation.

3. Don't waste effort, money and time by gathering data indiscriminately: We know that 90% of all the world's data has been produced over the past two years.[20] But data is not information. Seek information that is useful and relevant and find out only what you need to know. Consider 'soft' and limited information, too.

4. Get help when you need it: Ask other people what they think, especially informed people whose judgement you trust. When necessary, seek the help of experts.

5. Work on eliminating the cause of the problem: Don't just cover up its symptoms. Bandaid solutions seldom work and only serve to confuse matters.

Brainstorming

Done correctly, brainstorming boosts creativity and generates lots of ideas quickly. You can brainstorm alone or with a group of people; six to nine is a good number because smaller groups have trouble generating enough ideas and some participants can be left out in larger groups.

● IN A NUTSHELL

Ways to generate solutions

Look beyond the obvious. There is usually more than one 'right' answer.

- Brainstorm: Collect as many ideas as possible to provide a good starting point
- Chunk down: Break the problem down into smaller parts. Is it possible to fix part of the problem when you can't fix all of it?
- Chunk up: Look at the problem from a wider perspective
- More information: When answers elude you, do you need more information
- Ask yourself: What if we do not find a solution, what alternatives do we have?

When brainstorming in groups, seat people informally – in a circle of chairs, for example. Use a flip chart or whiteboard; butcher's paper or an electronic whiteboard are best because the ideas generated can be saved for future reference. Write up the ideas as people call them out without changing, editing or 'improving' the words. Everyone should be able to see the ideas list being generated so they can build on each other's ideas; write clearly and large enough for everyone to read the ideas easily.

Make sure the topic is specific and everyone understands both it and the goal of the brainstorming session (not just 'to brainstorm' but, for example, 'to brainstorm possible causes of a particular problem' or 'to brainstorm possible solutions for a particular problem'). Make sure everyone has a say; use the *round-robin method* (explanation following) when necessary.

Here are five more brainstorming guidelines:

1. *Don't expect to come up with a great idea every time*: When you have this expectation, the pressure can stifle your brain's ability to freewheel.

2. *Go for quantity*: Forget normal constraints and limitations. Be wild! Ideas can be 'sensibilised' later. Wait until Step 5, when you evaluate alternatives and select the most suitable, to consider quality.

3. *Have some fun*: Laughter and fun encourage creativity.

4. *Let your thoughts freewheel*: Let them hop easily from one line of thinking to another, so that a continual flow of ideas streams out. Don't constrain your thinking in any way.

5. *Suspend judgement*: New ideas are delicate and easily killed by a frown, a sneer or a wisecrack; don't worry about whether they are good or even workable. Aim to produce as many ideas as you can before evaluating them, because even the silliest idea can spark off a great one through a process known as *cross-fertilisation*.

There are two ways to generate ideas in a group brainstorming session. The first is to let everyone call out their ideas as they come to mind. This works well with enthusiastic and involved groups who are experienced at brainstorming. The second is known as the round-robin method. Here, each person calls out their idea in turn, one after the other, or says 'Pass' when they have nothing to contribute when their turn comes up. Keep going until everyone has 'passed' on the same round.

Whether brainstorming on your own or with a group, don't give up at the first sign of ideas running out. When you wait a minute or two, more ideas are sure to come. A good rule of thumb is to keep going through three 'dry periods' before stopping to evaluate the ideas.

THEORY TO PRACTICE

How four heavyweights make decisions

Amazon founder Jeff Bezos believes that informed decisions are so important he makes his senior executives read a six-page narratively structured memo (one written in full sentences and carefully thought through) for about 30 minutes, in silence, before meetings begin. This guarantees the group's attention and promotes clear thinking on the part of both the readers and the writers. Bezos also bears in mind how things may change and spurns the conventional wisdom about how things are typically done, preferring to reinvent everything, even small things.

Stephen Borg, global director of strategy and market development at electronics manufacturer AOPEN, emphasises consultation throughout the decision-making process and leaves difficult decisions until after his morning exercise, which gives him clarity and takes away some of the emotion.

Co-founder of travel search website Adioso, Tom Howard says he thinks about which of the alternatives can deliver the biggest upside and looks for the best outcome with the fewest downsides.[21]

Phase 3: Evaluate and act

In this final phase of problem-solving and decision-making, you evaluate the possibilities, select the one likely to work best and put it in place. Problem-solving has become decision-making. You need clear, logical thinking and the ability to implement your decision and follow it through.

Step 5: Evaluate alternatives and select the most suitable

Every potential solution you developed in Step 4 is likely to have some good points and some bad points. Evaluating them helps you select the one that can achieve the objectives you set in Step 2 in the best way possible.

FYI

Remember Buridan's ass

In the 1300s, French philosopher Jean Buridan wrote about a hungry donkey standing between two identical piles of hay. The donkey could find no logical reason to choose one over the other and starved to death.

The irony is that Aristotle came up with the paradox centuries earlier, using the example of a hungry and thirsty man dying because he could not decide whether to slake his hunger or his thirst first. In his commentaries on Aristotle, Buridan chose a dog. Buridan's critics parodied him by turning the dog into an ass, so Buridan's ass was named after a person who neither proposed the paradox nor picked the animal to illustrate it.

>>

> Nevertheless, Buridan's ass reminds us that we need to make a decision when the time comes. Doing nothing is a decision and that logic alone isn't the only way or the best way to make decisions.[22]

Remember Buridan's ass when choosing between alternatives. Here are some other factors to consider:

- Do you feel comfortable with this alternative?
- Does this alternative fit in with your organisation's values and policies?
- How does this alternative affect the task, the team and the rest of the organisation?
- How does this alternative affect your customers (both internal and external) and other stakeholders?
- How does this alternative affect the quality of your product or service?
- How readily would employees accept this solution?
- How well does this alternative achieve your objectives? Discard any that do not meet all of your 'must' criteria.
- How will you feel about this alternative in three days, three weeks or three month's time?
- What other parts of the organisation does this alternative affect? Check with other sections of the organisation, both 'upstream' and 'downstream', to make sure you have not neglected something and to build support. Bear in mind that some decisions create precedents that may involve the total organisation and not just your own section.
- What resources does this alternative need and what are the costs? When the costs outweigh the benefits, revise or discard it.
- Which people or groups stand to benefit and which stand to lose from your decision?
- Would putting this alternative into operation create any problems?
- What could go wrong with this solution? Would it be serious? Could you do something to stop it or to minimise its effects? When potential problems are serious or outweigh the potential benefits, revise or discard the alternative. (See page 534 to find out more about how to protect your plans and page 744 for more information on risk analysis.)

An increasingly critical factor to consider is the rapid changes in the marketplace, society, the economy, technology and the workplace (described in chapters 1 and 3).

Remember *Ockham's razor*, too: Go for the simplest alternative that will work or the one that makes the fewest untested assumptions. (And did you know that Buridan studied under William of Ockham, who developed that rule?) Other decision-making aids are cost–benefit analysis and force field analysis. (See pages 500 and 504.)

◉ THE STRATEGIC PERSPECTIVE

Facts, emotions or intuition?

The 17th-century scientist and philosopher Blaise Pascal said, 'The heart has its reasons of which reason knows nothing.'[23]

Author Lewis Carroll said, 'Use your head'.[24]

American writer Gore Vidal said, 'It is the spirit of the age to believe that any fact, no matter how suspect, is superior to any imaginative exercise, no matter how true.'[25]

Pascal seems to argue for emotions, Carroll for facts and Vidal for intuition. Which is better? Logic or emotion? What part does intuition play?

>>

Neuroscientists have discovered that a type of neuron, or brain cell, called a spindle cell is in part responsible for the phenomenon of intuition. The spindle cells are about four times larger than other brain cells and have extra long branches that make it easier to attach to other cells to link up and transmit thoughts and feelings. In less than one-twentieth of a second, your spindle cells trigger neural pathways whenever you need to choose the best alternative or response among many – even for a task as routine as prioritising your 'to do' list. They also help you gauge whether someone is trustworthy.[26]

The best solutions balance both logic and intuition. When it's all one or the other, implementing the solution may be difficult. (You use both logic and intuition in the seven steps to problem-solving and decision-making.)

Step 6: Implement the decision

Now it's time to implement your carefully thought-out solution. You have three important tasks:

1. Plan: Decide what must be done, by when and by whom. Use the who, how, what, where, why and when prompts to develop your plan (page 494 explains how to develop a plan).
2. Safeguard: Become a pessimist for a short while. What can go wrong? How would you know it is about to happen? What action could you take now to prevent it happening? What could you do to recover if it does happen? What can you monitor and how can you monitor it to ensure your decision is working? (Page 503 explains how to protect your plans.)
3. Communicate: How and to whom should you communicate your decision or solution? Include everyone who is involved or affected. How can you motivate people to accept your decision or solution and help make it work? Communicate promptly to gain people's support and answer any questions carefully and fully. When people don't support your decision, they can make you, as well as your solution, look pretty silly. (See Chapter 22 for information on how to introduce any changes your decision or solution might entail.)

Step 7: Monitor and evaluate results

This step is important because no matter how carefully you have thought through your implementation plan, unexpected events can interfere with its success. Monitoring is your insurance. This is not to say that you must be involved in every detail, but you should never implement a decision or solution and fail to track whether or not it's working out as expected.

Make routine checks, diarising them if necessary, so you can catch and fix small deviations before they grow into major problems. Be prepared to work with your chosen decision or solution to make it succeed. And be prepared to 'let it go' and try something else when it is not achieving its objectives. (To find out more about monitoring, see page 505.)

● IN A NUTSHELL

Monitoring and evaluating results

Here are some questions to consider once you have implemented your decision or solution:

- Have the desired outcomes been met? If not, why not?
- If not, can you turn the situation around? When you can't, remove your solution or decision and start again.
- When the plan is working, can you improve the results still further?

>>

- What can you and your team learn from anything that worked less well or better than expected?
- What can you do better next time? Examining disappointments and hiccups can highlight errors to avoid in the future.
- What did you do well that helped your plan succeed? Note these factors to draw on in the future, too.

Helping others solve problems

The maxim 'Bring me solutions not problems' doesn't mean you shouldn't be interested in problems. Management's aversion to hearing about problems also seems to have been a major contributor to the *Challenger* disaster (discussed in 'Theory to Practice: Seven avoidable deaths, an avoidable war and more' on page 540). As well, consider the BP Texas City Oil Refinery in 2005 when 15 workers died and more than 170 were injured.[27] And the chaotic opening of Heathrow Airport's Terminal 5 in 2008.[28] Sometimes, the person who spots the problem isn't responsible for solving it, bringing us to another maxim: Don't shoot the messenger.

When the person who spots the problem *is* responsible for solving it, help them, but don't do it for them. Page 119 explains that accepting other people's 'fleas' – solving their problems for them – is not the way to go. Help people benefit from your experience by showing them how to solve their own problems; otherwise, you could wind up being a full-time problem-solver and doing everyone's job except your own.

Show people how to apply the seven steps described above to their problems. Ask questions to help them think their problem through with a 'beginner's mind'. Help them pinpoint what they want to happen and to concentrate on solutions and on finding a way forward. Help them establish a goal and a timeline for solving their problem.

Should you hear 'Yes, but …' when you suggest a possible solution or offer advice, stop: your help is being butted away. Switch to asking questions, listening and summarising. When 'Yes, buts …' really mean someone doesn't want to solve their problem, just moan about it, it soon becomes clear.

● THE STRATEGIC PERSPECTIVE

You can't solve 'em all

Yes, you need to spot and attend to problems but there is no guarantee that you can fix them all to perfection. Sometimes, you just have to learn to live with them. The Leader-Manager's Prayer, adapted from the 'Serenity Prayer', used with success by Alcoholics Anonymous, may help you to remember this:

Grant me the serenity to accept the things I cannot change,
The courage to change the things I can,
And the wisdom to know the difference.[29]

● ACTION!

Use the Seven steps for problem-solving and decision-making template on ⨁**CourseMate**Express the next time you have an important problem to solve or an important decision to make.

3. Reaching sensible decisions

A decision is an action an executive must take when he has information so incomplete that the answer does not present itself.

Arthur William Radford (chairman, US Joint Chiefs of Staff), in Freund, *Lawyering*, Law Journal Press (1977)[30]

Three situations exist in which leader-managers are required to make sensible decisions:

1. In a crisis.
2. To solve a problem
3. When an opportunity arises.

Phase 3 of the problem-solving and decision-making process, evaluating and acting, is decision-making. This is where you select the most suitable alternative (discussed earlier in Step 5), implement it and monitor it (discussed in Step 6 and Step 7).

But how? Which of the decision-making methods available to you should you use? Which style of decision-making should you use? Should you involve your team and, if so, how much? What are the traps to be alert for so you don't kid yourself you've consulted others and gained their commitment when, in reality, you haven't?

Six ways to make decisions

You have six possible decision-making procedures to choose from, ranging from decisions that you reach yourself to those you agree with your team. We begin with two that are never useful, move on to two that are seldom useful and conclude with two that are usually useful.

Factional decisions

Factional decisions are those that a minority bulldozes through. The minority may be the people with the loudest voices or those with the most power or influence. Or they may be a few articulate people who are prepared to speak up.

The leader might announce the decision after consulting 'the clique', so it may look like a unilateral decision, but it is really a factional decision. Or 'the clique' might railroad a team into reaching the decision it wants, maybe even fooling the rest of the team into thinking they've had a voice and actually participated in the decision.

Either way, when you condone factional decision-making, you lose out on the potentially valuable input and insights of the whole team, especially when you listen to the same people all the time. When a decision is made by a select few, some team members are bound to feel left out and uncommitted to the decision.

Groupthink

Have you ever heard the saying 'There can be too much of a good thing'? Without a cohesive team whose individual members respect and support each other, it's hard to achieve great results. Yet too much unity can be counterproductive. When harmony and 'the team' come first, people can feel that the approval of their colleagues is more important than stating their reservations or an opposing viewpoint, even one that might add new information or provide a better perspective.

A team may think it's reaching a joint decision, but when individuals aren't prepared to speak up with an alternative point of view, groupthink is probably in play. Conforming to group norms overrides members' desire to develop new and better ways and innovative approaches, and anyone who dares to disagree is seen as a 'deviant' or 'traitor'.

As a result, the group ignores negative aspects of its decisions and fails to test its decisions against reality. Task-oriented and goal-driven groups are particularly vulnerable to groupthink when they are under pressure to make a good decision. As a result, a team can reach poor and even dangerous decisions, or develop policies or strategies that harm a department or an entire organisation.

● THEORY TO PRACTICE

Seven avoidable deaths, an avoidable war and more

On 28 January 1986 the space shuttle *Challenger* exploded 73 seconds after blasting off from the Kennedy Space Center in Florida. All seven crew members, including a civilian teacher, died.

Investigations later showed that the tragedy could have been avoided. The primary cause of the accident was found to be the failure of a rubber O-ring to seal the joint between two stages of the rocket, allowing hot gases to escape and explode in the flames of the 'burn'; up to 1100 people knew about the potential danger of the failure of the O-ring. Investigations also showed that the *Challenger* was launched when there was good reason to believe that the conditions weren't safe, and that a highly flawed decision process was a major contributor to the disaster.[31]

In 2004, a US Senate Intelligence Committee found that the US intelligence community overstated the threat Saddam Hussein posed to the USA and used inadequate information to justify the war in Iraq.

The findings stated: 'The group [the committee] concluded that the intelligence community suffered from "collective groupthink" which led to the presumption that Iraq had an active and growing weapons of mass destruction program. This groupthink caused the community to interpret ambiguous evidence such as the "procurement of dual use technology" to mean Iraq had an active weapons program … "It is clear that this groupthink also extended to our allies" and other nations, "all of whom did believe that Saddam Hussein did have an active WMD program".'[32]

The decision to invade Iraq in 2003 has been costly in terms of military and civilian deaths and casualties, the economy and the USA's diplomatic standing in the world.

Other examples of groupthink include the failure of the USA to anticipate the attack on Pearl Harbor during World War II, the Bay of Pigs failed invasion in 1961 (when the USA attacked Cuba hoping to overthrow Fidel Castro), the escalation of the Vietnam War in 1965, the Watergate scandal of the early 1970s and the failed hostage rescue in Iran in 1980. More recently, the false allegations of asylum seekers to Australia throwing children overboard, the collapse of Swissair in 2001, the bankruptcy of Enron in 2002 and of Lehman Brothers in 2008, and the explosion of the space shuttle *Columbia* in 2003 during re-entry are cited as examples of groupthink.

The main symptoms and consequences of groupthink are:

- *An illusion of invulnerability,* which creates excessive optimism and risk-taking, ignoring obvious danger and consequently failing to develop a contingency plan.
- *An unquestioned belief in the 'rightness' of the group,* inclining members to ignore the moral or ethical consequences of their decisions and to fail to ask experts outside the group for input.
- *Discounting or rationalising warnings or signs* that the team is operating under false assumptions, making a poor decision or developing a faulty plan, which prevents it from searching for more information or more alternatives.
- *Limiting discussion to only a few alternatives, possibilities or solutions,* looking mostly at its good points instead of gathering a wide range of information, thereby reaching quick agreement on a decision or course of action.

* *Not criticising or questioning each other's ideas and an absence of devil's advocates* to bring to the group's attention any information or evidence that does not conform to the group's expectations and stereotypes, or that might shatter its complacency about its correctness and effectiveness.
* *Rationalising, or 'explaining away', contrary information and decisions or plans not working as expected,* rather than reconsidering decisions, plans and strategies.
* *Shared stereotypes of 'enemies' outside the group,* leading to a reluctance to negotiate and to underestimating the enemies' ability to counter the group's plans or strategies.
* *Strong pressure on group members to conform to group norms* and adhere to the group's commitments, illusions and stereotypes, making members unwilling to state their true thoughts and feelings and to air any discomfort, doubts or uncertainties they have about the group's decisions or plans in order to avoid appearing 'disloyal' and to maintain an illusion of unanimity.

● THEORY TO PRACTICE

Not enough dissent

When Dick Fuld was promoted to chair and chief executive officer of failed financial services firm Lehman Brothers in 1994, its culture was argumentative, conflict-ridden and highly competitive. Although highly competitive himself, he made collaboration, loyalty, teamwork and unity priorities, turned the 1993 loss of $102 million into a profit of $4.2 billion by 2007, and was named the US's top CEO by *Institutional Investor* magazine in 2006.

In 2008, Lehman Brothers collapsed and filed for the largest bankruptcy in history, kicking off the global financial crisis. The culture had become a little too harmonious, it seems. In 2007 and 2008, many signals indicated the firm was headed for a crisis but those who saw them were too 'loyal' to risk pointing out the looming dangers.[33]

Avoiding groupthink

To avoid feeling like you and your team are in an echo chamber, take a lesson from Alfred Sloan, former chair of General Motors, who closed his meetings this way, 'Gentleman, I take it we are all in complete agreement on the decision here. I propose we postpone further discussion until our next meeting to give ourselves time to develop disagreement and perhaps gain some understanding of what the decision is all about.'[34]

A participative leadership style also discourages groupthink (authoritarian leadership encourages it). Here are some other ways to ensure that your team does not fall into the groupthink syndrome:

* Actively look for the weak points in your decision or chosen course of action.
* Assign at least one team member to play the role of 'devil's advocate' when evaluating alternatives.
* Be suspicious when agreement seems to come too quickly and too easily. Be sure that people have yielded to other opinions for objective and logically sound reasons and are not changing their minds simply to avoid conflict. Confirm that everyone genuinely accepts the decision or solution.
* Brief the group impartially and objectively, without advocating your own preferences.
* Develop the habit of open inquiry and careful consideration of alternatives; help the team to explore alternatives impartially and view honest differences as a healthy sign of progress.
* Have subgroups discuss and then report back.
* Invite and consider opposing opinions, objections and doubts.
* Invite experts within the organisation to share their thoughts and ideas and encourage them to air views contrary to team members' views.

- Know the warning signals that might indicate your decision is failing, keep alert for them, have a contingency plan ready and reconsider your decision when necessary.

◉ THE STRATEGIC PERSPECTIVE

A cultural tightrope

We are told that differences of opinion are fine in teams because it prevents groupthink. But in a multicultural context, disagreement can be awkward. In Indonesia, for example, confrontation is considered aggressive, disrespectful and rude, especially in a group forum. Even questions such as, 'What do you think?' can feel confrontational and like you're being put on the spot.

At the other end of the confrontation spectrum is France, where conflict is part of the culture. In school, children are taught to build up their *thesis* (one side of an argument) and then build the *antithesis* (the opposite side) before coming to a *systhesis* (conclusion). That is how the French conduct meetings, too. Conflict is seen as revealing hidden contradictions and stimulating new ways of thinking, reaching excellence and eliminating risk.

Unilateral decisions

Managers sometimes make a decision and announce it to the team. While this is appropriate in some circumstances – for example, in an emergency or when there is no other possible course of action – consultation and participation usually result in not only a better decision but also one that is backed by greater understanding and commitment.

Pretending to consult people before reaching a decision when you have already decided generally fools no one and invites cynicism and mistrust. Guard against this should you ever feel obliged to consult your team but really know the outcome you want.

Voting

People often think that voting is a quick way to reach agreement and the democratic way to do things. Voting is quick and certainly guarantees that a decision is reached. To the uninitiated, it can even look like consensus decision-making.

However, voting has three big drawbacks:

1. It accentuates the differences of opinion between people and produces 'winners' and 'losers', which can create a confrontational atmosphere and make some people uncomfortable – especially those in the minority.
2. It commits people publicly to a position, making it difficult for them to change their minds later without appearing weak and vacillating.
3. Those who 'lost' the vote usually feel bad about losing and may carry out the 'winning' decision with little commitment or enthusiasm and may even undermine it.

No matter how impatient you are to reach a decision, unless the vote is about something straightforward and in which people have no emotional or vested interest, it's usually better to work towards consensus than to take a formal vote.

Consultation

People work harder to ensure the success of a decision they have had a part in reaching than when they are merely complying with someone else's wishes. Ask team members for their ideas and opinions when a decision or solution to a problem affects them and when they are involved in implementing a decision or solution to a problem.

Participation

Do you think it's quicker and easier to make decisions yourself or that it's your job to make decisions yourself since you're the boss and accountable for the results? Think again. Research shows that teams make better decisions than even the brightest individual in the group, provided the group is harmonious and cohesive (but, of course, not too cohesive) and clear about its purpose and goals.

Consider how a group of people can inspire each other and build on each other's ideas, and how involving people – more brains, more experience, more information, more knowledge – can yield better results. And it gets better: as you probably know from your own experience, people are more committed to decisions they helped make and solutions they helped design because their involvement gives them a more complete understanding of why and how the decision or solution was reached. This in turn assists and encourages them to make the solution or decision succeed.

Does this mean that you should involve your team in every decision? No. Involving your team generally takes more time and more skill on your part, so don't involve them in making decisions or in solving problems that have no real effect on them or that they have no real interest in. When this is the case, make the decision yourself, and then announce or explain it.

When to involve your team

Here are four important guidelines for when to involve your group in problem-solving and decision-making:

1. The issue affects the group. The more the problem or decision affects the group, the more necessary it is to involve them.
2. The group members are able to, and want to, become involved. When people want to become involved, try to involve them, particularly when they have sufficient knowledge of, or expertise in, the issues involved. Even when they don't, though, remember that involving people can provide useful training and development.
3. The group will be involved in implementing the decision. Involve the team when it is expected to implement a solution or carry out a decision.
4. The decision needs to be accepted. The more you need people to accept the decision or solution, the more you should involve them.

Figure 18.4 summarises the five ways you can involve your work group. When solving any problem or making any decision with your team, make sure everyone understands the problem, goals and constraints in the same way.

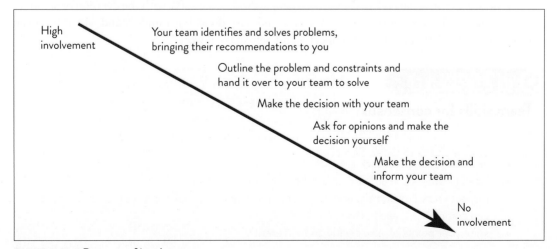

High involvement — Your team identifies and solves problems, bringing their recommendations to you

Outline the problem and constraints and hand it over to your team to solve

Make the decision with your team

Ask for opinions and make the decision yourself

Make the decision and inform your team

No involvement

FIGURE 18.4 Degrees of involvement

IN A NUTSHELL

Guidelines for involving your team

When you decide to involve your team, follow these guidelines:

- Don't force the group into agreeing with you.
- Don't let people become competitive.
- Don't make early, quick, easy agreements and compromises. These are often based on flawed assumptions resulting from groupthink.
- Don't vote. This divides people into winners and losers.
- Encourage people, particularly the quieter ones, to offer their ideas.
- Include the major stakeholders in the outcome of the problem or decision as well as anyone concerned with or affected by the solution or decision. Seek their information, ideas and suggestions and pay attention to what they say (see Chapter 8 for whom to involve).
- Keep everyone's attention on the objectives and on solving the problem or reaching the decision. Don't dwell on past mistakes.
- Take your time so that the group takes ownership of the whole process.
- Treat differences of opinion as a way to gather additional information, clarify issues and force the group to seek better information.

Consensus

Genuine participation results in consensus because, having discussed the goals of the decision or solution to a problem and how best to achieve them, everyone is aware of the issues and understands and supports the decision and resulting plan.

Although consensus requires skilled communication, meeting management and problem-solving and decision-making skills from both the leader and the group members, and although it is generally more time-consuming than unilateral decisions or voting, consensus usually results in better decisions and solutions and greater commitment. As an added bonus, the process of participating in and achieving consensus is usually both instructive and motivational for team members.

During discussions, everyone hears everyone else's point of view and explains their own. Team members explore differences of opinion and use diverging points of view to clarify issues, gather more information and polish their ideas. Gradually, consensus is achieved.

The beauty of consensus is that, even when people don't agree 100% with the decision or solution, everyone can say, 'It may not be exactly what I would have done, but I understand why it has been agreed and I agree with it enough to support it and help make it work.'

IN A NUTSHELL

Team skills for consensus

You and your team need to be able to:

- communicate empathically
- give and receive feedback
- listen to others and admit that another approach is better
- respect and value diversity and various points of view and look for ways that differences can complement each other
- state your points of view clearly and coherently

>>

- support and encourage team members
- understand and use the problem-solving and decision-making steps and tools
- use creativity techniques and think innovatively
- work in a collective spirit, putting the interests of the group before your own.

Achieving consensus

Reaching consensus takes time, skills and patience. It also takes practice because as groups become more experienced in participative methods, they usually get better at them. You need meeting management and participative leadership skills and you need to be able to help everyone think of their own point of view as one piece of the puzzle and understand that others have other pieces based on their experience, their field of expertise, and so on. Then you need to be able to lead a discussion that helps put all the pieces of the puzzle together.

You can encourage participation by inviting discussion once you have stated the purpose of the meeting and provided the necessary background information. Create an atmosphere that treats what everyone says as important and that values everyone's participation. Try to lead the discussion without entering into it so that you hear the team members' points of view. (See page 933 for information on how to plan and lead a meeting to achieve consensus.)

Four other factors help a meeting reach consensus:

1. Clarity about the issue under discussion and what the discussion is intended to achieve: to solve a problem, to come up with a range of options, to analyse and explore a problem, to determine its cause, to reach a decision, and so on
2. Ensuring participants understand and agree with the desired outcomes
3. Frequent summaries, particularly each time a major conclusion or decision is reached
4. Keeping the discussion to the stated topic: no 'rambling shop talk', sidetracking or digressing.

Discussion is a key ingredient of consensus yet, ironically, meeting participants often report a feeling of going 'round in circles' until a point is reached when 'suddenly' consensus is achieved and a decision made. Until members become used to it, this feeling can be frustrating and disheartening. Here are two clear signs that consensus is approaching:

1. People ask for specific information.
2. People begin their sentences with 'Yeah, …'

● ACTION!

Use the checklist Team skills for consensus in 🍃**CourseMateExpress** to check whether you and your team have the necessary skills to reach consensus.

The stepladder technique

The stepladder technique helps small groups avoid anchoring, confirmation bias and groupthink, and encourages everyone's full participation (four to six is a good number). It prevents decisions being hijacked by a few vocal or influential people and ensures everyone's ideas are considered equally. It's easy, interesting and quick and, better still, research shows that this technique yields better results than conventional group discussions.

Here are the five steps for using the stepladder technique:

1. Present the decision or problem and ask group members to form their own ideas about the decision or solving the problem.
2. Pair two members together and ask them to discuss their thoughts.

3. Add a third group member to the pair and ask the third member to present their ideas to the first two members *before* hearing the ideas they have already discussed.

4. Repeat Step 3 by adding a fourth member and so on, to the group, allowing time for discussion after each additional member has presented their thoughts.

5. Once everyone has been brought in and presented and discussed their ideas, the group is ready to reach a decision.[35]

Decision-making styles

Research shows that decision-making styles change over the course of successful leader-managers' careers.[36] What style of decision-maker are you at the moment?

Perhaps you're a *satisficer*. You are if you usually stop at the first answer. Satisficers want the key facts, leap into action and perhaps test it as they go along. *Optimisers*, on the other hand, like to mull over reams of data and keep looking until they've found 'the best answer'.

Then there are *single-focus* decision-makers who want to take one course of action and put their energy into making it work, and *multi-focused* decision-makers who prefer to pursue multiple courses of action and who adapt to changing circumstances.

That gives us four decision-making styles, as shown in Figure 18.5:

1. *Decisive*: These are the action-oriented, speedy decision makers. Once their decision is made and their plan in place, they stick to it and move on to the next decision. Time is precious to them and they value brevity, clarity, honesty and loyalty. They come across as task-oriented.

2. *Flexible*: Flexible decision-makers are speedy, too, but they're also adaptable. They get just enough information to reach a decision and quickly change course when they need to. They come across as sociable and responsive.

3. *Hierarchical*: If anyone is going to suffer analysis paralysis, it's the hierarchical decision-maker. They want their decisions to stand the test of time and expect others to join their search for the truth. They come across as intellectual.

4. *Integrative*: You can't rush these decision-makers, either, and they like lots of input, even from people whose views conflict with their own. But rather than looking for the one best solution, integrative decision-makers frame the situation broadly and reach decisions that have multiple courses of action. They come across as creative and participative.

	Single-focus	Multi-focus
Satisficer	Decisive	Flexible
Optimiser	Hierarchical	Integrative

FIGURE 18.5 Four decision-making styles

You need to make decisions in a way that reflects your circumstances, so you need to be able to use all four styles. Sometimes, there just isn't enough time to be an optimiser. Sometimes, the operating environment is so uncertain that you need to be multifocused, while in a stable operating environment you can be more single-focused in your decision-making style.

Interestingly, research suggests that successful managers adjust their decision-making style as they move up the hierarchy, and failing to do so can be disastrous in career terms. In general, most first-line leader-managers use a decisive decision-making style, middle and senior managers use an integrative style, and directors use a hierarchical style in public. You might want to remember this as your career progresses.

When managers mull matters over on their own, though, the most successful ones are integrative decision-makers throughout their careers, and many use increasingly more hierarchical (lots of data, one option) and less flexible decision-making as a secondary style as they move up the hierarchy.

When you have an emergency or too many decisions

Whatever decision-making style you use, don't rush. Few problems require immediate action. While decisiveness is an admirable leadership trait, you still need to take whatever time is available to consider your options.

Take a few deep breaths to help you relax and remind yourself that you can think your way through the problem. Gather facts and opinions, analyse the situation, challenge and check assumptions and generate and assess your options before leaping to a decision.

FYI

Keep your 'reptilian brain' under control

Your higher order thinking functions are located in your neocortex, or 'thinking brain'. But just when you need to use it, your lower brain, or 'reptilian brain', sometimes takes over and triggers the fight, flight or freeze response. You may not even know when your reptilian brain kicks in, but when it does, panic sets in and fear and aggression dominate your decision; your brain 'freezes' and can't work well enough to reach a sound decision.

This makes the seven-step process for solving problems and making decisions even more important: it keeps your primitive reptilian brain in check and forces you to use your more sophisticated thinking brain.

Some signs you need to improve your approach

When you and your team spend more time responding to problems and emergencies than preventing them, you may need to build your own and your team's skills in identifying and preventing potential problems and in planning ahead. When team members continually bring you their problems to solve and you spend more time fixing up their work than working on your own priorities, you may need to teach your team to solve their own problems (Page 119 explains how to do this).

When your plans tend to stray off course, you may not have spent enough time protecting your plans or monitoring them; or maybe you didn't develop a workable plan in the first place. When team members seldom or never come to you with concerns about something that 'might' happen or alert you to something that 'might' be a problem, it might be because you unwittingly discourage bad news and people are reluctant to be the bearer-of-bad-news messenger who is shot. Looking back and saying 'I had a feeling …' is another sign you may need to work on your problem-solving and decision-making skills.

THE STRATEGIC PERSPECTIVE

Ethical decision-making

You can probably think of examples when doing the right thing is a difficult choice. What guides your decisions in situations like this? Do you ask yourself questions such as:

- Is this action legal?
- Is this decision morally defensible?
- Could this decision compromise me or my reputation, personally or professionally?
- Would I be comfortable if the decision were announced on the front page of my newspaper?
- Would I approve if I were on the receiving end of this decision?
- Would reasonable people agree with it? Would my family agree with it?

When the answers to questions like these make you uncomfortable, then the decision is questionable and probably unethical. (For more on ethics, see page 221.)

When you've made a poor decision ...

The only way never to get anything wrong is to do nothing. You'd be safe – like a ship in a harbour – but, as American author John Augustus Shedd said, '... that's not what ships are built for.'[37] Doing nothing may be safe, but you won't make any improvements or learn anything, either.

Since no one can be 100% right all the time, you're bound to make a few poor decisions. This fact is compounded by the rapid rate of change: today's leader-managers are facing situations they've never faced before. This makes testing new approaches mandatory and making the odd mistake inevitable. (For more on learning from mistakes, see page 887.)

CourseMateExpress

Go to http://login.cengagebrain.com to access CourseMate Express, your online study tool for *Management Theory & Practice*. CourseMate Express brings chapter concepts to life with interactive learning, and study and exam preparation tools:

- Test your skills in different aspects of management with interactive self-tests and simulations.
- Watch videos that show how real managers operate in real businesses.
- Test your understanding of the changing world of management by taking the revision quiz.

QUICK REVIEW

1. Summarise the types of problems and decisions leader-managers face in terms of complexity and the best way to approach each.
2. List the more easily avoidable and less easily avoidable traps when solving problems and making decisions and summarise how to avoid them.
3. List and explain the seven steps to solving problems and making decisions and the role each step plays.
4. Summarise the six ways to make decisions described in this chapter.

BUILD YOUR SKILLS

1. Describe the three distinct mental processes involved in solving problems and making decisions and explain why each is important.
2. Why is it critical to focus on the cause of a problem rather than its symptoms?
3. How can you recognise groupthink? What steps can you take to avoid it?
4. Referring to the Scenario at the beginning of the chapter, how should Khalid tackle each problem and decision in order to avoid falling into the decision-making traps discussed in this chapter?
5. Imagine that you are going to rent or buy a home or a car. Develop a list of 'must' and 'want' criteria for it. How would this list help you in identifying possible homes or cars and making your decision?
6. Discuss the following quotation in relation to problem-solving: 'Every problem has in it the seeds of its own solution. If you don't have any problems, you don't get any seeds.' (Norman VIncent Peale, *The power of positive thinking*).[38]

WORKPLACE ACTIVITIES

1. List your last 10 workplace decisions and review the criteria you used to reach your decision. Which deserved a lot of time and which didn't? Which did you make as quickly as possible, which did you wait to make and which did you delegate? Explain your reasoning.
2. Give some examples of programmed and non-programmed decisions that you make.
3. Think of a current or recent problem you have experienced that had many possible causes. Analyse it using a cause-and-effect diagram to determine its most likely cause. Discuss how this technique can help you identify the cause of the problem and explain why knowing the cause of a problem helps you solve it.
4. Think back over the last few days and make a list of all the problems you solved and decisions you made (however major or minor). Select a suitable problem (i.e. a fairly substantial problem, one that was not a programmed decision and one where you wanted to fix the cause of the problem to stop it recurring) and apply to it the seven-step problem-solving and decision-making model described in this chapter.
5. Describe a time when you worked with others to solve a problem. What helped people work well together? What lessons did you learn for next time?

THE SOUTH SYDNEY FURNITURE COMPANY

CASE STUDY 18.1

The South Sydney Furniture Company is a medium-sized manufacturer of bedroom and dining-room suites. The company also produces a small line of occasional lounge-room pieces such as coffee tables and chairs.

Rather unexpectedly, the purchasing manager, Henry Parden, resigned to accept the position of purchasing manager with a manufacturer of upholstered furniture. To fill his position, the company hired Iona Kelford, an experienced purchasing officer from a local kitchen manufacturer. The management team of the South Sydney Furniture Company felt that her familiarity with furniture in general and with the purchasing function would enable her to assume Henry's duties easily and make a significant contribution to the purchasing department.

On Iona's first day, the general manager outlines her duties and shows her around the plant. He also introduces her to her assistant, Virginia Bellamy, and to the rest of the team. Iona sets to work, beginning with analysing how the purchasing section operates. She is rather dismayed. She finds that a supply of core stock (timber used as a base for veneers) sufficient to last for 16 months is on hand. In addition, two container loads of core stock have just been received and six more are on the way. All available space is being used to store this material and she doubts they have storage space for the additional stock. Although she and Virginia search the files, they are unable to find a purchase contract authorising the shipments. On Wednesday, two urgent calls from the assembly plant inform her that they are out of drawer pulls, hinges and braces for dining room suites for a large order. Unless they can obtain a supply immediately, they must stop production and delivery will be late, incurring penalties.

The next day, the accountant asks Iona to approve a bill from a paint and varnish supplier. On checking, she finds that, although the material has been received, no purchase order seems to have been issued. She learns that her predecessor's practice had been to allow the paint sales representative to inspect the company's stock and ship whatever supplies the representative thought appropriate. As a result, she estimates that the South Sydney Furniture Company has 18–20 months' supply of various types of fillers, paints and varnishes. Several times during her first week, team leaders from the plant bring Iona bills for brushes, sandpaper, and so on, saying that they have exhausted their supplies and have replenished them locally.

Questions

1. List the problems Iona faces and the decisions she must make. Are any suitable for programmed decisions? Should she involve other people in any of them? If so, who, why and to what extent?
2. If you were Iona, what immediate action would you take? Why?
3. What would be your short-term and long-term objectives?

CASE STUDY 18.2

NIPPED IN THE BUD

Alma and her team in finance and corporate services seem to have everything under control after completing the hectic budgeting period. They settle down to what they hope will be a routine month of financial analysis and reporting.

It is not to be. Early in the month, one of the customer service reports highlights what seems to be a significant increase in the number of customer complaints. Most concern the length of time customers are kept waiting and the lack of attentiveness from service staff. The complaints came over the telephone as well as in letters and emails.

Alma whisks the report down to Siva, who supervises the corporation's field customer service operations. They agree to 'nip this problem in the bud' and set about planning their approach.

Questions

1. Develop a step-by-step plan showing what Alma and Siva should do based on the seven-step problem-solving and decision-making process described in this chapter.
2. Which of the systematic techniques discussed in Chapter 19 and this chapter would you recommend Alma and Siva use at each stage of your plan?
3. Should Alma and Siva involve the service staff? If so, in what way and for what purpose? What level of input from field staff would you recommend and why? Should Alma and Siva involve anyone else?

19

SATISFYING THE QUALITY, INNOVATION AND CONTINUOUS IMPROVEMENT IMPERATIVES

Making improvements so that your team keeps getting better results is one of the most important things you can do. This approach for ever-improving quality and efficiency is the opposite of the 'If it ain't broke, don't fix it' approach, where you keep operations running smoothly and maintain the status quo. That approach only works in a world where nothing changes and when your systems and processes have reached the pinnacle of perfection. Neither can be true. Time passes, technology advances, a new competitor comes along and changes the rules ... there is no such thing as a steady state – you're either moving forward or falling behind.

What was once considered good in terms of quality and service (and, soon, sustainability) is now considered the bare minimum; what is considered good today is about to be surpassed, too.

So if it ain't broke–it soon will be, at least without constant improvements to products, services and ways of working. The 'leave well enough alone' approach may be comfortable and easy, but it spells trouble.

Continuous improvements to all parts of the organisation are essential and these often require creativity and innovation.

1. Do you know what quality is for your organisation, why quality is important and how to monitor the quality of your products or services?
2. Can you lead improvement efforts with your team?
3. Can you identify the barriers to creativity in yourself and your team and overcome them to become more creative and innovative?
4. Do you know how to use a range of qualitative and quantitative tools to gather and analyse relevant and reliable information?

This chapter shows you how to use a range of techniques to keep your team and your organisation moving forwards, rather than drifting backwards.

The quality improvement team

Jane gathers up her papers and prepares to meet her team of four travel consultants and a trainee administration assistant in the boardroom. They are about to continue with their series of weekly Customer Care Circles. She is pleased with the way they are responding to their latest challenge: learning and applying quality management tools and techniques to identify and resolve problems and improve their work systems. Their overall goal is to keep finding ways to make work flow more smoothly and serve their customers even better.

In the first meeting, they developed a list of 'circle rules' for the way they would work together. Guidelines like 'Turn up on time', 'Let everyone have their say', 'Share your ideas even when they sound crazy!' are on the list that they review briefly at the beginning of each meeting to set the scene. At the next meeting, they brainstormed a list of 'job hassles' and used the nominal group technique to prioritise them in the order they would work on them.

In their third meeting, the circle used the fishbone technique to analyse the problem they decided to work on first: delays in ticket issuing. This showed them that there was a lot more to this issue than first met the eye. In the fourth meeting, they finished 'fishboning' their problem and began to flow-chart the ticketing process – first the way it is currently done, then the ideal way to do it.

Their fifth meeting is due to start in 10 minutes and Jane doesn't want to be late. They plan to finish flow charting the current ticketing system and have a look at the check sheets that two of the consultants have been keeping since the last meeting. These are going to help them analyse the nature of delays so they can design and flow chart a more streamlined and effective ticketing system.

The circle is making good progress and a real team spirit and energy is developing. Although they are still analysing the problem, Jane feels that they will soon be ready to design and test a new, improved system. Whatever it is, she knows it will make everyone's life easier and allow them to offer a faster and more reliable service to their customers. She also knows that the business will benefit enormously from the improved teamwork that has already resulted from the Customer Care Circles.

1. Abiding by the quality imperative

> Quality is free. It's not a gift.
>
> Phil Crosby (quality analyst), *Quality is Free*, Mentor (1980)[1]

Hmm. What is quality, then? It's something you have to work to attain.

How do you measure quality in your job and at your workplace? How do you decide whether a product or service is a quality product or service? According to another pioneer in quality studies, Joseph Juran, 'Quality is whatever the customer says it is.'[2]

Here is another definition of quality, this one from Warren R Plunkett et al, 'Quality is now defined as ability of a product or service to meet or exceed customer expectations and needs.'[3]

It's safe to say that no one ever wanted poor-quality products, products unfit for their purpose or incompatible with products they already had, unfriendly service, or unreliable or dangerous products. But today, customers not only expect more in terms of service and quality than yesterday's customers, they can also compare products and even services from all over the world, and read online reviews by real customers and from experts at organisations such as http://www.choice.com.au.

Customers typically make decisions on who they will and won't deal with based on the quality and service they and their friends receive; even business-to-business (B2B) customers trust word of mouth and social media when making purchasing decisions.

What makes a product or service 'sensational', 'good', 'disappointing' or 'poor' is its quality. But there's a hitch: the definitions of 'quality service' and 'quality products' are constantly changing. Even when you get your quality spot on, over and over again, you need to keep 'raising the bar' to meet changing customer expectations. This means you need to keep adjusting the way you produce your products or service. This holds true for B2B transactions as well as business-to-consumer (B2C) and end user transactions.

Quality can make or break an organisation. It builds loyalty, attracts repeat business, generates word-of-mouth (free) business and boosts profits. Kaoru Ishikawa, another quality pioneer, believed that the drive for quality should flow through the entire organisation and that quality should be present in every part of a product's life cycle.[4] In today's highly competitive and global marketplace where sustainability of operations and products is becoming a necessity, this is more essential than in the past.

Quality: The Japanese miracle and the West's wake-up call

Continuous incremental improvements are a key feature of total quality management (TQM). Although TQM originated in the USA, few organisations paid attention to quality until World War II, when poor quality became a matter of life or death. Each manufacturing failure, however small, threatened the lives of thousands of soldiers and the freedom of millions of people. After the war, organisations seemed to forget about quality until the 1980s, when the West went into recession and, based largely on quality issues, nearly lost its manufacturing base to Japan.

Dr W Edwards Deming, Armand Feigenbaum and Joseph Juran, leaders in the early Total Quality Movement, used TQM techniques and approaches to help Japan rebuild after World War II. Japan moved from being a non-industrialised society with a low standard of living to one of the world's manufacturing giants and the undisputed leader in quality and service. In less than 40 years, Japan became one of the most economically developed and powerful nations on earth.

The costs of poor quality

You can see how expensive 'doing things wrong' is when you calculate the costs of:

* customer allowances and other tactics to offset customer dissatisfaction
* investigating and processing customer complaints, returns and warranty claims
* product recalls
* repairing or replacing damaged, faulty or lost goods
* scrap
* lost customers and lost sales.

Then there are the more hidden costs, to name a few:

* correcting billing and other errors
* expediting late deliveries
* field service expenses
* late paperwork
* overtime
* premium freight costs
* re-doing work or repeating a service.

When you 'do it right', those costs are not incurred. 'Doing it right' improves employee efficiency, minimises processing constraints, reduces rework and scrap, reduces costs and vastly improves customer satisfaction.

● THE STRATEGIC PERSPECTIVE

The cost of fixing mistakes
A problem that costs $1 to fix in advance can costs $20 to fix during a process and $50 to fix afterwards. Building quality into the system saves money.

The four cornerstones of quality

Four important principles of quality give organisations the ability to provide goods and services that meet or exceed customers' expectations throughout their life cycle:

1. A culture that says, 'Quality is the way we do business.'
2. Work systems and procedures designed to build in quality and eliminate waste.
3. Forging effective relationships with internal and external customers and suppliers so that *everyone works together* to supply quality goods and services.
4. Making continual systematic improvements to processes, products and services.

Quality culture

In organisations with a quality culture, employees walk, talk and think quality. They work with suppliers to streamline their work so that both benefit, and make a habit of systematic, continuous improvements, or enhancements, to processes, products and services.

There are no 'silos' in a quality culture – all functions in the organisation work together as service partners in one continuous customer–supplier chain (discussed on page 620; see also 'Theory to practice: Just a small mistake' on page 561, for an example of 'silo thinking'). Employees at all levels share the organisation's values, vision and commitment to its goals.

A quality culture like this takes commitment and time to build. Employees need to be trained, well-resourced and committed to quality; they need training in people skills such as teamwork and participating in meetings, and in quality management techniques to identify, analyse and solve problems and continually refine systems and procedures. They need to be motivated to work together to understand and meet customer needs. They need to be empowered and involved and they need to be innovative, so they can keep finding ways to not only 'do it right' but to 'do it better'.

To maintain a quality culture, you need the five keys (explained in Chapter 11) in place. Most of all you need open and supportive quality leadership; you need to 'beat the quality bandwagon' through constant communication about quality – through emails, tweets, newsletters, informal conversations and team meetings.

The effort is worth it. For every 5000 employees, moving from the bottom 20% to the top 20% of companies with a highly developed quality culture would save a company $71.5 million annually.[5]

● ACTION!

How strong is your workplace's quality culture? You can find out with the interactive self-test: How is your quality culture? on  CourseMateExpress.

● THE STRATEGIC PERSPECTIVE

The drivers of a quality culture

Here are four essential elements that develop a quality culture:

1. Leadership emphasis. Make quality a leadership priority with managers 'walking their quality talk' and emphasising the importance of quality in formal and informal employee feedback.
2. Message credibility: Deliver clear and consistent quality messages from respected sources that can appeal personally to employees.
3. Peer involvement: Encourage peers routinely to raise the topic of quality, to assist each other in improving quality and to hold one another accountable.
4. Employee ownership: Ensure employees understand how quality fits into their jobs, are empowered to make quality decisions and challenge anything that could reduce quality.[6]

● THEORY TO PRACTICE

A costly culture

A well-developed culture may not always be an asset to a company. It can be a liability too. Question: What could cause the world's third most admired company to fall to 33rd place in two years?

Answer: Covering up two serious safety issues.

It all came to a head in 2009 when a family was killed when the car it was test-driving 'accelerated unintentionally' to nearly 200 kph before it crashed. In his report in *Company Director* magazine, journalist John M Green detailed how, over the following two years, Toyota bore the cost of 12 million vehicle recalls worldwide (not for 'unintended acceleration' but for 'floor mat entrapment'. Toyota instructed employees not to put anything in writing about the company's cancelled instruction to make a design change which would have rectified that particular cause, one of two causes, of unintended acceleration.) Toyota failed to recall Corolla, Venza or Highlander models although they, too, had the floor-mat entrapment design flaw. No vehicles were ever recalled for the second, mechanical, cause of the acceleration problem.[7]

The company faced a penalty of US$1.2 billion and lost a further US$2 billion in sales. Toyota was blamed for 37 deaths and countless injuries. The US transportation secretary declared the company 'safety dead' and its market value dropped by US$30 billion, around 25%.

In 2013, Toyota settled a class action for US$1.6 billion. In 2014, the company admitted it lied when it told both the public and US safety regulators in 2009 that it had addressed the root cause of the problem by fixing floor mats that could trap the accelerator and agreed to a record US$1.2 billion settlement to end a four-year criminal investigation by the US government. This was the largest penalty imposed on a car company in history of the USA, which US Attorney General Eric Holder described as appropriate in terms of Toyota's deception. The company still faces hundreds of lawsuits for personal damages.[8]

What seems to be at the heart of the problem – covering up two deadly design flaws and lying about them – was that a culture of increasing sales and lowering costs engulfed the quality and safety culture the company had been known for. Two other cultural factors came into play, too. The belief that admitting to design problems would have brought shame on the company and its employees; and in a hierarchical organisation structure such as Toyota's, no employee is game to challenge superiors even when their superiors' behaviour is blatantly dangerous and illegal.[9]

Quality systems and processes

Quality systems formally control the processes and activities that influence the quality of the goods and services an organisation produces. Each organisation develops its own quality systems that reflect the nature and size of its operations.

A system that reliably and predictably delivers a quality product or service is *in control.* An *out-of-control* system is haphazard: sometimes it produces good quality and sometimes it doesn't.

The 'get the systems right' approach helps you design systems that reduce the chance of error and variation – the normal ups and downs in a process – so that you consistently produce the quality your customers want. The goal is to design the systems themselves in such a way that mistakes and defects are virtually impossible, eliminating the need for the traditional quality checking at the end of a process.

Quality systems eliminate duplication and unnecessary work and streamline the flow of work by reducing or eliminating activities that don't add value but needlessly take up effort, 'space' and time. They reduce frustration and help you guarantee quality, improve the way you gather and use information, increase flexibility, lower operating costs and reduce inventory and waste.

Variation

There are two types of variation: *assignable-cause variation* and *chance-cause variation*. You can use a control chart to distinguish between the two. You then identify and remove assignable-cause variations to bring processes into 'statistical control', meaning there is only chance-cause variation. Chance-cause variation explains why no process can ever be 100% perfect – things happen.

How are your quality systems? Do the systems and procedures at your workplace efficiently and reliably meet or exceed your customers' expectations and requirements? Every time? Have they been simplified and streamlined to avoid unnecessary activities and duplication of effort and make it possible for people to 'get it right first time'?

To build quality systems, concentrate on these five areas:

1. Suppliers: Ensure that their inputs (information, raw materials and so on) meet your needs reliably and consistently; think about mandating 'green' supplies that don't damage the environment.

2. Throughout each process: Where do things go wrong? Where are the bottlenecks? Where are the hassles? Where is effort duplicated or wasted? Where are materials wasted? How can you prevent this? How can you make each process more environmentally friendly?

3. Just before handover or delivery: Is the information, product or service packaged, or put together, in a way the customer appreciates? Does it contain everything the customer needs and wants? Is the packaging reusable or recyclable?

4. Post-sale or post-service support and follow-up: Are your customers happy three months later? How could you have made them happier?

5. End-of-life: How can the product be disposed of easily for upcycling or recycling?

When errors do occur, look for the causes in the right places – work systems and processes, not workers – and fix them quickly. Employees struggle to provide quality service and products unless their work systems and processes back them up. (Page 339 explains why inadequate and poorly maintained tools and equipment, substandard materials, poor or inappropriate training and production processes beyond the control of employees are the main causes of poor productivity and inconsistent quality and reliability.)

● THEORY TO PRACTICE

The importance of systems

Sally was pleased as punch. She'd just found a terrific pullover on sale in an up-market national retail chain. The sales assistant had been very pleasant and helpful, hanging the pullover in the changing room for her so she could look around the store with her hands free and walking her to the changing room when she was ready to try it on. She even waited nearby in case Sally needed any help.

When she took her pullover to the cash register, Sally noticed that the sales assistant became a bit flustered as she searched first for tissue paper to wrap the pullover in, then for a bag to place it in, then for the credit card machine. Clearly embarrassed at her seeming lack of efficiency, the sales assistant explained, 'I normally work in another shop and everything is different here. In my other shop, the credit card machine is to the left of the cash register and here it's to the right of it. The bags are just under the register, and here they're over there ...'

'Ah,' thought Sally, 'we need some consistent systems here, so staff can change shops and do their jobs without holding customers up and being embarrassed by looking like they don't know what they're doing. It would be so easy to fix – I wonder if they'd hire me as a consultant.'

Monitoring quality to find problems

Many factors affect quality: ageing machines, differences among components and raw materials, differences in employees' skills, and so on. Although there can't be 100% perfection because of the natural variation in all systems, the constant operations challenge is to reduce variation as much as possible, keep it within acceptable limits and make quality highly predictable.

Once upon a time, there was *quality control*. Quality control relied on inspectors to carry out quality checks. They used various techniques, ranging from visual observations to complex testing and measurement, to catch defects in work in progress and at final inspection. But unless they used a 100% monitoring system, which was costly and time-consuming, it was virtually impossible to spot all defects. The result was that poor-quality products could, and often did, reach the customer. Paradoxically, these traditional quality control approaches sometimes resulted in lowered quality standards because employees considered quality to be someone else's concern.

Then came *statistical process control* (SPC) which systematically monitored and measured conformance to specifications of manufactured items. Using SPC, employees – not experts and specialists – monitor the quality of their own work.

Control charts are one way to monitor quality. Figure 19.1 shows a control chart with measurements taken and recorded hourly. As long as the readings remain inside the *upper* and *lower control points*, the quality of the product is acceptable and the system is in control. When the readings stray outside these points, the process is considered out of control and action must be taken to find the cause of the variation and fix it in order to bring the system back into control. Be sure to put your chart details at the bottom of the chart, as in Figure 19.1 (Control charts and other ways to monitor using statistics, such as histograms, Pareto charts, process capability charts, run charts and stratification charts, are examined in the final section of this chapter.)

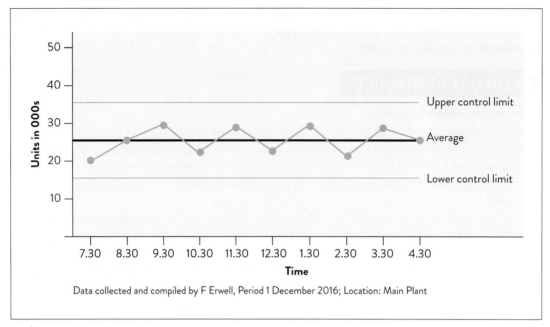

FIGURE 19.1 Control chart

Employees check key performance indicators either randomly or continually, and keep records plotting variations of output so they can spot problems early on. Whenever variation in key performance measures approaches or falls outside the upper or lower control points, employees fix the process. This might mean recalibrating a machine or resetting tools, for example, or assigning additional staff to the front counter to cover an unusually busy period. Later, they can analyse what caused the problem and take steps to prevent the same problem recurring.

When variations become too wide or too frequent, employees 'fix the process' using the statistical and systematic problem-analysis tools explained in Section 4 to identify and correct the causes of poor quality. While this doesn't guarantee perfect quality, it helps to identify and correct the causes of below-standard performance quickly and prevent substandard products from being used again in the production process or being dispatched to customers.

Involving employees in monitoring and improving the quality of their own output or service is one of the keys to effective quality management and achieves better outcomes than the more traditional 'inspection' quality control approaches.

Monitoring quality to make improvements

Quality isn't just about fixing problems. In a true quality culture, you're always looking for ways to improve what is already working just fine. We discuss this continuous improvement mindset further on page 563.

Australian and international quality standards

Having quality systems is so important that it is an internationally certifiable process that guides you to establish, supervise, maintain and improve your organisation's quality systems and processes. Most governments and major organisations around the world do business only with organisations that have been certified as conforming to the relevant quality standards.

The quality standards of the International Organization for Standardization (ISO) are developed by a panel of experts and reviewed and updated as necessary, at least every five years, to ensure they remain current, and more than 1000 new standards are introduced every year. The ISO has developed more than 18 500 standards, most of which are highly specific to a particular product, material or process. The two exceptions are:

1. The ISO 9001 series, which deals with implementing quality systems in order to meet customer requirements, enhance customer satisfaction and achieve continual improvements.
2. The ISO 14001 series, which deals with environmental management systems aimed at minimising harmful effects on the environment caused by an organisation's activities and achieving continual improvement in the organisation's environmental performance.

These are known as 'generic management system standards' because they can be applied in any organisation, regardless of its sector, size, product or service. Nearly 1 600 000 organisations in 163 countries and more than 20 000 organisations in Australia currently implement the ISO standards.[10]

FYI

The ISO acronym

Because the International Organization for Standardization can have different acronyms in different languages (e.g. IOS in English, OIN in French), it is known as ISO, derived from the Greek *isos*, meaning 'equal'. All over the world, whatever the language spoken, the short form of the organisation's name is always ISO.

The standards help organisations to assure quality during the many stages needed to supply a product or service. The benefits of standards include:

- economically incorporating desirable characteristics of products and services such as efficiency, environmental friendliness, interchangeability, reliability, safety and quality.
- facilitating trade between countries and making it fairer.
- making the development, manufacture and supply of products and services cleaner, safer and more efficient
- providing governments with a technical base for health, safety and environmental legislation
- safeguarding consumers and other users of products and services.
- spreading good management practices, innovation, solutions to common problems and technological advances that save organisations 'reinventing the wheel'.

When organisations are quality certified, their customers can be sure that they have quality systems in place that ensure they are capable of reliably producing a product or service that meets customer requirements. To become certified, an independent external body audits the organisation's quality systems and verifies that they conform to the requirements specified in the relevant standard(s).

The auditing body then issues a certificate, which it registers in its client register, making the organisation both 'certified' and 'registered'; the two terms can be used interchangeably, although the term most widely used is 'certified'. ('Accredited' has a different meaning. It refers to the fact that the auditing body has been certified, or accredited, as competent to carry out inspections and certifications in the specified sectors.)

IN A NUTSHELL

The process of becoming certified

To become certified, organisations must define, establish, explain and guide the way they design, develop, produce, install and service their products and services. This entails analysing the processes and activities they carry out and improving them to eliminate waste in materials and effort, and to minimise the likelihood of errors and *non-conformance* (any product or service that fails to meet the agreed quality standard). They must document these procedures explicitly, setting out in writing precisely how they achieve the specified quality throughout the entire manufacturing or service provision process (including design, inspection, measurement and testing).

Organisations must also document other procedures, including, for example, their procedures for dealing with customer complaints, maintaining machinery, purchasing, and training employees and contractors. They must keep quality records that monitor and report on their quality performance to show that they are using their quality systems and that they have minimised variations in systems and processes.

Other documents required include a quality policy that defines the organisation's approach to quality, a quality manual, work instructions that explain how each service or manufacturing process is to be performed, position descriptions and quality improvement plans that explain how the organisation intends to improve its quality. These documents and records provide proof that an organisation has quality systems in place and that it follows and improves them to guarantee quality and meet its customers' specifications and expectations.

The initial certification process usually takes 12–18 months. Once certification is awarded, regular 'check' audits, or surveillance audits, follow every six months, and a full and thorough audit is carried out every three years.

Although the process of becoming certified is neither easy nor cheap, it may be the price required to stay in business, since many organisations require their suppliers to be quality certified. (The costs include fees to the accrediting organisation and countless hours of internal staff time to develop, install and document the systems.)

Organisations undertaking certification benefit from a thorough 'spring cleaning' and rethinking of the way they do things, with a resulting lift in their quality levels. Certified companies also gain better market access, both domestically and overseas, improved customer satisfaction, improved quality and business performance, raised employee morale, and cost savings through reductions in materials handling, operating expenses, absenteeism and injuries. Some studies have estimated that the benefits of reducing costs through quality can amount to about 10% of sales.

Yet some companies say that certification hasn't really improved their business and they find it too costly to maintain for too few benefits; instead, they have kept their quality systems but given up their certified status. Good systems and, in particular, *traceability* (when a problem occurs you can trace back to find its source and fix it properly so it won't happen again) are what is required, they say, and a company doesn't need certification to have these.

Service and trading partnerships

Does your organisation have a cost-cutting mindset that forces its suppliers to the brink of bankruptcy and give contracts to the lowest bidder? Or is it loyal to its customers, demanding high standards and helping them find ways to achieve them?

The third cornerstone of quality is managing the entire supply chain, or *integrated value chain*. You work with your internal customers and suppliers, or service partners, to continually refine and improve the way you create and provide products and services. You do the same with your external customers and suppliers.

Working with your organisation's external customers and suppliers in a cooperative relationship so that everyone wins is often referred to as a trading partnership – collaborating with your customers and suppliers to grow your businesses together. This approach to supply-chain management reduces costs, provides better products and services and often opens up a whole new way of doing business.

For example, companies that excel at managing their integrated value chain incur roughly half the costs of companies that are only 'average' in their supply-chain management. Excellent value chain managers also turn over their assets more quickly and hold 20% to 40% lower inventories – yet they can still respond quickly to their customers. That's a big difference in a tough marketplace.[11]

Working with your suppliers and customers to create a smooth and efficient supply chain needs a different approach from the more traditional 'adversarial' relationship that existed between supplier and customer organisations. This often did long-term damage to the goodwill needed between customers and suppliers and ultimately harmed both businesses. What good does it do an organisation, for example, to beat down a supplier's price so low that the supplier goes out of business? The customer organisation is then faced with the problem of finding a new supplier that can meet its needs and the trials and tribulations of 'getting it right' with the new supplier.

To work effectively with your customers and suppliers, you need to commit to 'co-prosperity'. You need to understand how you each work and what you are each capable of. You need to work together to create compatible production philosophies and systems, build a common language, transfer knowledge and help each other improve. You need to give regular feedback on how well your trading partners are doing and meet regularly to share information. It isn't easy, but it is worth the effort. Organisations are increasingly relying on suppliers to reduce costs, improve quality and develop new processes and products. As professors Jeffrey Liker and Thomas Choi point out, 'The issue isn't whether companies should turn their arms-length relationships with suppliers into close partnerships, but how.'[12]

As the marketplace continues to be highly competitive and demanding, as global supply chains are hit by rising energy costs and as carbon costs increasingly need to be factored into supply-chain management, this area looks destined to become increasingly pivotal to an organisation's success. Fortunately, advances in technology are making it easier to streamline and optimise this complex and data-intensive activity.

⦿ THEORY TO PRACTICE

Just a small mistake

Every two months for several years, Jodie has been taking a veterinary prescription for her cat to her local chemist, who faxes it to their retail group's principal chemist, which has a lab in the back with the facilities to make up compounding medication. The following Wednesday, the medication is delivered to the local chemist for collection. At nearly $60 a batch, it isn't cheap, but Jodie loves her little moggie. Every morning she rubs a small amount onto her cat's ear to help her thyroid function properly.

Unlike most compound medications, this particular one should not be refrigerated. Over the years, however, it had been refrigerated twice at the local chemist. Although percentage-wise

>>

this is a tiny error as far as Jodie is concerned, it's a significant one in that refrigeration turns the medication hard, which means she can't use it as intended and she has the inconvenience of taking it back to the local chemist. Both times, she's been uncomfortable about complaining. The first time, the pharmacist hotly denied it had been refrigerated, and the second time, the retail assistant passed on the wrong message to the compounding chemist and the batch was sent back to Jodie unchanged; as a result, Jodie had to phone the compounding chemist herself and explain the problem.

When Jodie collected the second replacement batch, the pharmacist explained that when the compounds come in they are automatically put in the refrigerator. Several days may go by before someone happens to notice the error and often they're too busy to attend to it immediately and plan to do it later (which they often forget to do). Jodie formed the distinct impression that hers were far from two isolated incidents.

'Why doesn't the compounding chemist use a colour code or separate bags for compounds that do and don't need refrigeration?' she asked.

'Hah!' said one of the assistants nearby who had overheard the conversation. 'As if the compounding chemists would go out of their way to do anything to make life easier for us.'

Strategic alliances

When you think you've gone as far as you can with streamlining, there's always more. The next wave of streamlining processes is between non-competitive suppliers. US food producer General Mills, for example, is working with a non-competitive supplier to supermarkets, butter and margarine producer Land O'Lakes, to improve its delivery efficiencies and costs by distributing Land O'Lakes' products with its own. The arrangement is working so well that the companies are now integrating their order-taking and billing processes, too.[13]

Forming strategic alliances, also known as *business collaboration*, that combine strengths is cheaper and easier than buying a company with capabilities you need and merging it with yours. As with trading partnerships, it requires good personal relationships, mutual trust and a commitment to co-prosperity, plus plenty of planning and feedback to make it work. You need to know what each partner is able to deliver and to understand each other's objectives so that each organisation benefits.

You also need to manage potential risks. For example, it's important to understand where potential conflicts exist. These might be from different decision-making styles, different national or organisational cultures and ways of operating, different norms for social and business behaviour, the long-term aspirations of your alliance partner to enter your market and become a competitor, or competitors your alliance partner is aligned or otherwise involved with. When you understand potential risks like these, you can acknowledge and resolve differences and reduce and manage any remaining competitive and other risks effectively. (Page 239 explains how to manage conflict and you can find out about risk management in Chapter 23.)

Strategic alliances also offer important learning opportunities. You can learn, for example, how another organisation manages its research and development, how its information systems operate, how it manages overseas subsidiaries and how it determines remuneration packages. Some strategic alliance partners even set up internal seminars to share this information to further each other's development.

> ### ◉ IN A NUTSHELL
>
> **How to raise your quality**
> Raising standards of quality is not difficult. Try these tips for starters:
> - Know your customers and know what they want.
> - Develop products and services that meet their needs and keep improving those products and services to meet both the customers' and the organisation's changing needs.
> - Develop processes that can reliably produce the products and services and keep improving those processes.

Systematic continuous improvements

The fourth principle of quality is to continually improve your work systems. As media analyst Marshall McLuhan said, 'If it works, it's obsolete.'[14]

Sections 2 and 4 of this chapter explain how to make continuous, systematic improvements using analytical tools and techniques and Section 3 considers the creative and innovation abilities you need to make these improvements.

2. Abiding by the improvement imperative

> In a sense, every business today, not just the garment trade, is a 'fashion' business. To compete effectively, companies must innovate continually and in ever-shorter cycles.
>
> Professor Rosabeth Moss Kanter (Harvard Business School), *World Class* (1997)[15]

There are only two ways for a company to grow: *organically,* by winning greater market share; or through *mergers and acquisitions*. Mergers and acquisitions seem easy but they are frequently disappointing. Organic growth may be harder but it's usually cheaper and more rewarding financially and psychologically. In fact, organisations like BMW, General Electric, Nestlé and Samsung that grow organically have shareholder returns almost double those of organisations that grow through acquisitions.[16]

So how can you grow organically? By getting better at what you do. You can improve your processes, your products or services, and your business models, and you can do this in four ways:

1. Big step, or *breakthrough improvements*, such as a major reorganisation or a re-engineering project, which are usually costly.
2. Capital investment, which is expensive and one-off.
3. Cost reduction, such as large-scale redundancies, which works initially, but then what?
4. Little step, or *incremental improvements*, which slowly and surely sharpen and polish an organisation's systems and processes.

> ### ◉ THEORY TO PRACTICE
>
> **How General Electric manages innovation**
> General Electric concentrates on ideas that have the potential to produce at least US$100 million in organic growth over three years. All ideas are sent to a review board of senior managers who assess their potential and estimate the investment required. About 10 projects run concurrently, each sponsored by a senior manager. About half the projects relate to improving the way existing products are produced or delivered. The other half are breakthrough, big ideas.[17]

Most improvements come from making small adjustments and refinements to the way people do their work. Occasionally, a major redesign makes a 'great leap forward'. Both incremental (little step) and breakthrough (big step) improvements address the challenges of:

* achieving higher quality
* increasing efficiencies, saving time and reducing hassles through flexible and well-organised processes
* making the most effective use of people and information
* saving money through lower inventory and less waste.

The Alice factor

Many organisations must feel a bit like Alice in Wonderland when she said, 'It takes all the running you can do, to keep in the same place.'[18]

The fact is, when you're not getting better, you're getting worse. You don't need to look too far back to see that everything your organisation was doing is now outdated. Look forward: everything you're doing now is destined to become obsolete, too. The intensity of competition has more than doubled in the past 40 years, so it takes a lot of running to maintain your position and faster running to improve it.[19]

The operating environment is changing so rapidly and is so complex that while you continue to do what you've always done, the rest of the world moves on and leaves you behind. Henry Ford discovered this in the early days of building Ford motor cars, when he said, 'The competitor to be feared is the one who never bothers about you at all, but goes on making his own business better all the time.'[20]

In the past, infrastructure improvements such as the internal combustion engine and the telephone led to sharp bursts of innovation which then stabilised. The digital infrastructure shows no sign of stabilising, which means that organisations can't stop to draw breath but must continue to innovate to improve.

When you don't keep improving, your competitors eventually overtake you, no matter how good you are right now. The question is: do you wait until your organisation or your team's results start to wither or do you get to work on the next idea now?

Collaborative systems technology and social media allow people work together in real time, enabling learning and collaboration, rapid knowledge flows and finding answers fast. This means that cross-functional teamwork and quality-improvement projects, diversity, employee engagement, a learning environment and trading partnerships, are all becoming essential to moving forward.[21]

The continuous improvement mindset can even change the way organisations do business. For example, confident that they can quickly match the cost of external suppliers and pocket the margin they pay them, many organisations that successfully manage for quality are *insourcing* rather than outsourcing activities. Keeping activities in-house or bringing them back in-house also gives organisations greater control over their operations and the ability to spread overheads over a wider base.

Whatever the size of your organisation, the way you work needs to be constantly reviewed, strategies discussed, opinions shared and decisions questioned (see 'Theory to practice: Keep tie-breakers fresh' on page 635.)

THEORY TO PRACTICE

Innovative Lego

In 2004, the Danish Lego Group was nearly bankrupt. In 2005, the negative results turned into small positives. Between 2007 and 2011, its pre-tax profits increased by 400%, revenue was up 127%, net profit after tax was up 636% and profit per employee had risen from 9% to 47%. In 2012, pre-tax profits increased a further 36%.

Breakthrough and incremental innovation, led by a cross-functional team called the Executive Innovation Governance Group, turned the company around. This guiding group set innovation goals and strategy and coordinated eight distinct types of innovation efforts across four areas of the company: Concept Lab; Community, Education and Direct; Functional Groups; and Product and Marketing Development.

Located in its own building, Concept Lab works on breakthrough improvements, developing new products and play experiences. Community, Education and Direct undertakes both incremental and breakthrough improvements to support customer communities and learn about their needs. Functional Groups also innovate small- and big-step improvements, enabling business processes from supply chain to manufacturing to sales. Product and Marketing Development innovates more towards the incremental end of the scale, refining the next generation of existing products and play themes.[22]

THE STRATEGIC PERSPECTIVE

The Australian banana peel

Bionic ears, Hill's hoists, in-vitro fertilisation, penicillin, polymer banknotes, wine casks – all world-beating Aussie innovations. But according to the government, Australia's recent innovation performance has been 'uneven' and behind the rest of the world. As a result, we slipped from fifth place in the World Economic Forum's Global Competitiveness Index in 2002 to 21st place (out of 148) in 2013–14; scoring 4.6 out of a possible 7, our ranking for innovation is 22.

Too bad, because innovation pays. Apple, Google and Nintendo work hard to recruit and develop innovators and report impressive revenues per employee. IBM, even though it operates at a rate per employee that is 25% better than the average company, still needs 10 times more employees than Nintendo to generate the same revenue.[23]

Incremental improvements

Online retailer Amazon established a new way of doing business. It concentrates on making incremental improvements in every aspect of the business, from order taking to speed of delivery. Little things count, and incremental improvements are about little things – doing 100 things 1% better, not 1 thing 100% better. This slowly but surely adds up to big improvements in productivity and performance – essential in today's marketplace. In organisations with a quality culture, each incremental improvement averages a 10–15% improvement and many are made month after month, year after year.

Kai = change   Zen = good

The Japanese word for continuous incremental improvement is *kaizen* – change for the better. The kaizen approach is to keep examining everything you do to find ways to make small enhancements towards perfection. How can you do things a little bit better? How can you 'tweak' them, refine them, polish them?

Here are the seven key questions for continuous improvement:

1. How can we do this better?
2. How can we do this more easily?
3. How can we do this more economically?
4. How can we do this more reliably?
5. How can we do this more safely?
6. How can we do this more quickly?
7. How else can we do this?

You can ask these questions in three main areas, either to fix problems or to improve systems that are already working well:

1. Customer-oriented innovation, to be asked in all areas where you interact with your customers.
2. Process innovation, the 'bread and butter' of internal innovation.
3. Product and service innovation, the continual small improvements to products and services that keep an organisation successful.

(Page 441 explains how to use performance reviews to encourage continuous improvements.)

● THEORY TO PRACTICE

Innovation can save the day

Apple was struggling at the end of the 20th century but had increased its turnover twenty-fold within eight years of the new century.[24] Devices such as the popular iPod must always have a limited shelf life and are easily copied technology. Always creating new devices through innovation gives Apple a huge competitive advantage. Apple built iTunes, the iTunes Store and a multitude of applications, and has formed innovative partnerships with Nike (your shoes can talk to your iPod) and BMW, Mercedes and other car manufacturers (which integrate Apple devices into their cars).

Here are three other interesting innovative strategies:

1. Gillette recently gave away its new razor because it wanted people to buy its new razorblades, which is where the company makes its money.
2. Virgin Blue changed the airline industry in Australia by bringing in a new low-cost airline, forcing Qantas to follow suit with Jetstar and shaking up the industry.
3. Social media can act as a catalyst for innovation and help organisations unearth new and better ways of doing things. Virgin Media, for example, uses its network to troubleshoot in its customer service team and speed up response times. When customer service reps come across a problem they can't answer, they just post it on their network and ask for advice from someone who's found the answer already – simple but effective.

Innovative strategies like these change the whole way organisations approach their markets, whether with their services or products, their internal operations or how they work with their suppliers and customers. Innovation can even change business models.[25]

> **● IN A NUTSHELL**
>
> ### Dr Deming's 14 key points on quality management
>
> Dr William Edwards Deming, engineer and management consultant, wrote the following 14 principles that organisations with a quality culture follow when designing their operations and processes:
>
> 1. Adopt a philosophy that makes delays, mistakes, defective materials and defective interactions between people unacceptable.
> 2. Break down barriers between job functions and departments.
> 3. Build quality into the way we do things to eliminate the need for final checks and last-minute 'fixes'.
> 4. Continually strive to improve products and services.
> 5. Drive out fear so that everyone in the organisation can work effectively.
> 6. Eliminate numerical goals and slogans asking for improvement without explaining how.
> 7. Eliminate work standards that prescribe numerical quotas; focus on quality instead.
> 8. Find problems and eliminate them by improving the system (e.g. redesign the system; improve equipment, incoming materials, maintenance, management and training).
> 9. Implement a vigorous program of education and training throughout the organisation.
> 10. Implement the best methods of on-the-job training.
> 11. Measure quality and price together (e.g. don't award contracts based purely on the price tag).
> 12. Remove barriers that stand between people and their right to pride in their work.
> 13. Train managers to help improve quality and productivity.
> 14. Create a management structure that pushes, every day, on all these points.[26]

Lean

Total quality management is the philosophy that guides organisations to design quality into their operations. Lean is a methodology that encourages innovation and improvements to existing processes. It concentrates on reducing waste and improving cycle times, resulting in a streamlined process whereby each step adds value from the customer's perspective. Essentially, lean seeks to preserve or increase quality with less work, following three key principles, each based on traditional quality management principles:

1. Giving employees responsibility to increase efficiency and eliminate waste in their jobs through continuous improvement
2. Commitment to data-driven experiments (discussed in Section 4 of this chapter)
3. Relentless attention to detail.

Lean methodologies were pioneered by Toyota in Japan and have been called the most important invention in operations since Henry Ford improved the assembly line by adding conveyor belts. Lean has since been used by other manufacturers and in industries such as finance and health.

Although the lean approach isn't as rigorous and detailed as Six Sigma and re-engineering (discussed on page 572 and page 571), introducing lean principles can nevertheless generate worthwhile results, including reduced costs, cycle times, inventory, lead times, materials handling, obsolescence, scrap and work in progress, and improved productivity, quality and use of space.

Lean Six Sigma, a combination of lean and Six Sigma, has been popular in Australia. It requires less employee training than Six Sigma (but more than lean) while overcoming the statistically 'light' nature of lean, and results in quicker 'wins' than Six Sigma.

● IN A NUTSHELL

The five 'S's of lean Six Sigma

Try these to add to your team's daily operations:

1. Sort: Keep only necessary items.
2. Set in order: Arrange the work area to promote efficient work flow and have a place for everything.
3. Shine: Keep everything clean, neat and tidy.
4. Standardise: Maintain a consistently organised and tidy work area.
5. Sustain: Maintain and review the above to make sure it 'sticks'.

See how one company used the five 'S' plan to make huge cost savings, reduce injuries and improve morale and productivity in 'Theory to practice: Good housekeeping saves money and reduces injuries' on page 968.

● THEORY TO PRACTICE

A lean success story and a cautionary tale

Nestlé's savings from improved operational efficiencies allowed it to more than double its research and development spending, resulting in a breakthrough idea – Nespresso – and creating a new market for pre-portioned coffee systems.

Lean works, but don't get too carried away. Lean worked so well at a custom-made titanium bicycle factory that the eight weeks delivery time to customers was reduced to two days. And the customers hated it. It seems the process of acquiring a pricey cycle was nearly as important as the product itself. Some customers loudly complained that a true custom bike couldn't be built in two days; others complained that the two days didn't give them enough time to save up the US$5000 price tag. Still others complained that they didn't have time to enjoy musing about how to equip their new prestige bike.

The company listened to its customers and increased its lead time to three weeks, and customers were happier. So was the company – it took the $500 deposit, sat on it for 19 days, then built the bikes. Then the company introduced a special expedite service and charged an additional $500 on top of the $500 deposit for an 'extra fast delivery' of 10 to 12 days. Customers were delighted. The lesson: Remember to listen to what your customers want.[27]

Finding improvements

Innovation is essential in our rapidly changing global environment, but that doesn't mean it's easy. Rather than sudden inspiration, innovation is more usually a result of thinking and experimenting, trial and error.

Opportunities to improve are all around us when you look and listen. Listen to your customers, colleagues and other stakeholders. Analyse benchmark, complaint, lost time management reports, rework and other data. It generally works like this:

1. You identify a problem or an opportunity for improvement.
2. You generate some ways of improving the procedure, select a few to develop further and test them. (It's generally best to test early and often.)

3. You implement the improvement that works best.
4. You monitor the improvement to see that it's achieving its objectives; when it isn't, you remove it and go back to Step 2. (See Chapter 18 for more information on problem-solving and decision-making.)

These steps often loop back and forth, as ideas are refined and lessons learned. Whenever possible, involve your team and anyone else who will implement and use the improved procedure.

⦿ THEORY TO PRACTICE

Always consider risk and sustainability

It's a good idea to get in the habit of considering sustainability and risk issues in any improvement plan and liaise with relevant personnel when you need to. (See chapters 23 and 24 for more information on risk and sustainability.)

Eliminating waste

Waste is anything that doesn't add value, whether it's equipment, material, people or unnecessary steps in a process. There are seven types of waste:

1. Defects (because they result in rework and scrap).
2. Excessive inventory (because it ties up money and space).
3. Over-processing (because it results in useless work).
4. Overproduction (because it ties up money and space and creates unnecessary work).
5. Unnecessary transportation or movement of materials (because it results in useless work).
6. Unnecessary worker motion (because it results in wasted energy).
7. Waiting, including machine downtime and idleness, (because it results in wasted time).

    Look for small waste, not just big waste. For example, waste might be identified and eliminated in:

- unnecessary activities, for example, looking for equipment, information or materials, rework (doing something a second or third time), unnecessary component or tool changeovers or unnecessary walking
- in layout, for example, backtracking, distances travelled, unnecessary handling
- other areas, for example, damaged materials, faulty or poorly maintained tools and equipment, housekeeping, having incorrect information.

Improving systems

Process innovation is about improving work flows and internal efficiencies – finding ways to make systems add value more cheaply, easily, reliably, safely, and quickly. When deciding how to improve systems, break them into their component steps (you can use the job breakdown method explained on page 917 for this). Then ask what value each step adds; this tells you whether the step is needed and why it's needed. When you're not sure what value a step adds, ask:

- What would happen (really) if it didn't get done?
- When was it first done? Why? (It may have made sense once, but ...)
    For every step that adds value, ask questions like these. How can this step:
- add even more value to the product or for the customer?
- be done more cheaply?
- be done more easily?
- encourage innovation?

- improve communication?
- improve productivity?
- improve quality?
- improve service?
- increase employee motivation or morale?
- minimise or eliminate waste?
- speed or ease decision-making?
- speed up the process or service?

    Other questions to ask about each step in a process include:

- Could someone else (inside or outside the organisation) do it better? Cheaper? More easily? Faster?
- How can we achieve the same results with less effort or better results with the same effort?
- Is someone else doing it, too (duplication of effort)?

Quality improvement teams

Special project teams or natural work groups might be assigned a process to improve, or they might select their own issue to work on. The teams meet regularly, usually once a week for an hour, and use a clear, systematic process and the tools and techniques discussed in Section 4 of this chapter. (See chapters 14 and 21 to find out how to lead projects and project teams.)

Whether they're working on acquisition and suitability of materials, materials storage, product or service quality, rate of output or smoothness of operations or workflow, quality improvement teams generally attain similar results:

- enhanced working relationships
- greater job involvement and employee motivation
- greater safety awareness
- improved communication
- improved efficiencies
- improved problem-solving skills
- improved quality and customer service
- improved employee–management relationships
- more effective teamwork
- personal development for the members
- problem prevention
- reduced costs
- reduced errors
- reduced waste.

 FYI

Breakthrough or incremental?
A total of 30% of innovation in Australian business is breakthrough and 70% is incremental. Of the incremental, 45% is made up of product and service innovation and 55% of process innovation.[28]

Breakthrough improvements

In sport, rules can't be broken without a penalty. But Picasso broke the rules on how a face should look and Gaudi broke the rules on how a building should look. In business, it's good to break rules once in a while, too – especially self-imposed rules about how something should be done. That's what breakthrough improvements do.

There are two main ways to achieve breakthrough improvements: core process redesign (also known as *re-engineering* and *process re-engineering*) and Six Sigma (which is also used to achieve incremental improvements).

Core process redesign and Six Sigma attain breakthrough improvements through temporary cross-functional quality improvement teams using the systematic tools and techniques discussed in Section 4. Because their improvement projects generally relate to major improvements in key areas of the organisation, a management group usually selects the project, often targeting chronic problems. The teams aim to achieve a 50–90% improvement within 4–12 months, depending on the project scope.

Core process redesign

Core process redesign first appeared during the early 1990s. It uses the concept of an enterprise as part of a web of relationships and information systems to dramatically improve the integrated value chain. It potentially results in far more than incremental improvements because it totally rethinks the organisation's processes, systems and procedures from top to bottom, aiming at great leaps forward in all measures of operating efficiency.

Re-engineering is a back-to-the-drawing board approach to designing systems. Instead of doing what you've always done and refining the way you do it, you start with a blank piece of paper and ask, 'What is the best way to organise our activities?' (See also the information on capabilities-based organisations on page 80.)

Redesigning systems begins with identifying the customers, internal and external, of the organisation's key processes, and what those customers need and want. Then it works backwards, using technology and systematic analytical methods, to redesign – often radically – the work flows and operating procedures. The improvements in productivity and customer service that result can be dramatic.

Re-engineering aims to:

* increase productivity
* increase responsiveness
* reduce functionalism (silos)
* reduce non-value-adding activities
* reduce overhead costs
* reduce specialisation.

Unfortunately, in some organisations, process re-engineering became synonymous with mindless retrenchments, ill will and lowered morale among employees at all levels. When used correctly, however, core process redesign offers potentially significant gains in producing and offering products and services.

THE STRATEGIC PERSPECTIVE

Reasons for re-engineering failures

About 70% of re-engineering efforts fail to achieve impressive improvements, largely because the fundamentals are ignored. An organisation may fail strategically by neglecting to examine

>>

the vision and strategic plan and identify how to help each arm of the organisation work towards achieving them. It may fail to examine the markets and customers before redesigning the organisation to meet their needs and wants. It may see re-engineering as a tool to achieve predetermined objectives, such as a convenient way to reduce the workforce, close a factory or shut down a department, rather than a way to provide quality products and services by building quality into systems.

In addition, re-engineering projects often neglect to recognise that organisations are complex and convoluted networks of multiple connections and relationships. Redesigning deeply embedded systems generally fails because the old systems that re-engineering designs out 'mysteriously' keep reappearing. 'Clean sheets' just don't work in complex systems.

Six Sigma

A Motorola engineer coined the term 'Six Sigma' in 1986 when the company decided to measure defects not per thousand but per million and went on to document more than US$16 billion in savings as a result.[29] Hundreds of companies have now adopted Six Sigma and it became popular in Australia in the 2000s, when all the major banks (except ANZ), BHP Billiton, Boeing Satellite Systems and Telstra, among others, adopted it.[30]

Former General Electric chair and CEO Jack Welch described Six Sigma as the most important initiative the company had ever undertaken and 'part of the genetic code of our future leadership'. It became General Electric's central business strategy in 1995 and by 1998 had added an estimated US$600 million to General Electric's bottom line.[31]

Six Sigma is usually applied after re-engineering core processes. A rigorous process centred on data gathering and statistical analysis pinpoints where errors occur and eliminates them, seeking improvements in seven areas:

1. Design methods.
2. Investor relations.
3. Processes.
4. Products.
5. Services.
6. Suppliers.
7. Training and recruitment.

    Six Sigma typically results in:

- faster turnover of working capital
- fewer defects, rejects and errors and therefore less rework
- freeing up existing capacity and making new capacity unnecessary
- improved profitability
- improved response times
- increased employee empowerment, development, morale and motivation
- increased productivity
- increased reliability through decreased variation, achieving consistent, reliable quality
- increased sales
- optimised cycle time and equipment usage
- realising greater results from investments
- reduced capital spending

- reduced downtime
- reduced inventory levels
- reduced waste.

IN A NUTSHELL

D–M–A–I–C: The five steps to Six Sigma improvement

Try these steps, and use systematic analytical tools and techniques, to:

1. **D**efine customer value and opportunities for improvement or **D**efine the problem.
2. **M**easure current performance.
3. **A**nalyse current performance.
4. **I**mprove performance.
5. **C**ontrol performance and integrate it into day-to-day operations.

IN A NUTSHELL

The benefits of minimising variation

Sigma is a statistical measure of variation used to measure defects per million. The greater the sigma number, the fewer the defects, as you can see in Table 19.1. Most major companies have a defect rate of three sigma (about 66 000 defects per million) or four sigma (about 6000 defects per million). Organisations at the Six Sigma level are considered to be virtually defect-free, with only 3.4 defects per million, resulting in 99.9997% of products and services meeting quality standards or specifications. This translates into a huge leap forward in productivity, profits and customer satisfaction.

TABLE 19.1 The greater the sigma number, the fewer the defects

	4.3 sigma (99.7% perfection)	4.6 sigma (99.9% perfection)	6 sigma (99.9997% perfection)
Incorrect drug prescriptions a year	54 000	4000	1 every 25 years
Incorrect surgical operations a week	5000	1350	1 every 20 years
Lost mail per hour	54 000	4000	1
Newborn babies dropped by doctors and nurses annually	10 000	3000	10
Unsafe drinking water: hours a month	2	1	1 second every 16 years[32]

At first considered best suited to high-volume, highly standardised production for which consistent quality is crucial, Six Sigma is now generally acknowledged to be valuable for non-manufacturing processes, too, including accounts receivable, call centres, customer service and support, finance, insurance, marketing, research and development, sales, and supply-chain management.

Six Sigma training

Employees need training to use Six Sigma techniques, progressing through five levels: *white belts*, progressing to *yellow, green and black belts*, and finally, to the *master black belt* experts. Master black belts are qualified to teach analytical tools and techniques and coach black belts; they generally supervise multiple projects in parallel. Black belts have four to six months of training and work full-time, leading up to seven breakthrough improvement projects a year in temporary cross-functional teams.

Green belts have about six days of training and are the grassroots practitioners in the operational level of the business, working on both little-step and big-step improvements. They spend at least 50% of their time on their normal duties and the rest of their time working and driving projects in their functional areas. White and yellow belts are trained in the basic approach outlined in the 'In a Nutshell: D–M–A–I–C: The five steps to Six Sigma improvement' and undertake continuous incremental improvements, generally in their work teams.

In organisations committed to Six Sigma, all projects have a high profile and status – when you're trained to belt level, it's clear you're on the fast track.

● THEORY TO PRACTICE

Six stories of Six Sigma success

Six Sigma has been particularly successful in high-tech, mass market industries and other high-volume process areas such as back offices and call centres. For example:

1. Dell emphasises incremental improvements with its Six Sigma projects. It streamlined its accounts payable department with Six Sigma, saving an estimated US$2.4 million a year; a team leader in Dell's server factory replaced coloured paper with white paper to print out parts lists, saving US$23,000 a year.[33]

2. Dow Chemical has had 75 000 Six Sigma projects and trained more than 12 000 project leaders since they introduced the technique. The company claims more than $US10 billion EBIT (the difference between revenue and expenses), or more than a billion dollars in savings per year companywide. Between 2000 and 2002 for example, applying Six Sigma to environmental, health and safety services saved it US$130 million; the company was so impressed that it went on to apply Six Sigma to finance, information systems, HR processes, legal, marketing, public affairs and R&D. Since then, Dow has used Six Sigma to improve its operations (including health and safety), lower capital costs, identify and implement best practice, forecast capital spending, predict market opportunities and much more.[34]

3. Froedtert Hospital in Milwaukee in the US credits its Six Sigma standardising of intravenous drug procedures with there being only one incident of a patient being wrongly medicated. The hospital has also used Six Sigma to eliminate diverting emergency ambulances to other hospitals, reduce the length of patients' stay in the Emergency Department, optimise staffing levels and reduce patient waiting times.[35]

4. After 15 years of practising Six Sigma, IT software manufacturer Honeywell won an Australian Business Excellence Award. It continues to use Six Sigma as a critical strategy to accelerate improvements in processes, products and services, radically reduce administration and manufacturing costs and improve quality. Focusing on eliminating waste and reducing defects and variation, Honeywell has saved billions from tens of thousands of sustainable improvements across all areas of its activities and considers Six Sigma activities one of its principal growth and productivity drivers in all areas of its business. It expects its managers, supervisors and most professionals to become Six Sigma certified to at least the green belt level and gives new employees 12 months from their hire date to earn certification.[36]

>>

5. A project team at Raytheon Australia working on manufacturing helicopters for the Royal Australian Navy reduced unscheduled maintenance by 57%, reduced supply lead times by 35% and increased aircraft availability by 15%.[37]

6. Suncorp Metway trained 60 black belts and 200 green belts who worked on 120 projects between 2001 and 2005 and achieved, among other things, faster credit approvals, shorter queuing time for customers and tighter commercial lending practices.[38]

How are we doing?

You don't need extensive organisation-wide quality programs to make continuous improvements in your own job and in your own work team. Make sure everyone in your team understands the importance of both quality and continuous improvement and include both on your agenda for team meetings. Find out what changes team members think would improve quality and service and what bottlenecks and hurdles they continually encounter.

Three other ways you and your team can keep getting better without huge effort are after-action reviews, benchmarking and using measures of success.

After-action reviews

When did you last think back over something you did to see what went well and what you could have done better, with a view to improving your performance next time? Reflecting on what you've done and how you've done it to see what you can learn is a way to use the past to improve the future and undertake next week's or next month's tasks and projects more efficiently and successfully.

To debrief an activity, ask yourself and your team these questions when events are still fresh in everyone's minds:

- What did we set out to do (your goals and measures of success)?
- What did we do? What actually happened? Review what you did and how you did it.
- What worked well, what worked better than expected and what didn't work as well as we'd hoped? Discuss and agree, not to blame anyone but to learn from experience. (Mistakes happen. When you don't learn from them, you're likely to repeat them.)
- What should we do next time? Decide on actions for the future and how to implement them – both successful steps to repeat and improvements to make.

Think about making after-action reviews part of your routine team meetings and conducting one at the end of each day (on your own or with your team) and at the end of a project. Do it in the spirit of understanding, learning and improving. (For more about after-action reviews, see pages 140 and 886.)

THE STRATEGIC PERSPECTIVE

Just a fad?

Benchmarking, customer service, lean, process re-engineering, Six Sigma, total quality management ... Are these fads? No.

A competitor uses one of these techniques and gains a competitive advantage. So the rest use it too. Failing to use it is a disadvantage. Using it levels the playing field and the bar is raised. This

>>

is known as *competitive convergence*: a competitive advantage becomes mandatory and it is no longer a winning edge.

Organisations then need a new way to gain competitive advantage. The best way to achieve sustainable operational effectiveness as a competitive advantage is by preserving what is distinctive about an organisation – its culture.

Benchmarking

How do you know how you're doing in the areas of, for example, innovation, performance, productivity and quality? Benchmarking is a reliable way to find out.

To benchmark, you establish meaningful key performance measures for important aspects of your operations. These become the benchmarks that you use to measure and monitor your performance and to compare with other organisations. Be cautious: it's easy to measure irrelevant benchmarks and miss the key factors that really drive a successful organisation; the latter is what you want to benchmark.

You can use benchmark measures in three ways:

1. To monitor and continually improve your own department's or team's quality, progress and improvements over time to stay alert to problems; for example, when a quality benchmark measure suddenly drops, it can warn you of a problem in the system that you can study and rectify.
2. To compare your quality with that of other departments in your own organisation. An organisation with operations in Beijing, Chennai, Kuala Lumpur and Melbourne might benchmark key productivity and performance measures in each location and compare them with the others. If Melbourne has the most accident-free days, the others can study its work safety methods and adapt or copy them. If the Beijing factory has the highest number of orders delivered on time, the others can study and adopt its delivery methods.
3. To compare your own organisation's performance in key measures of quality and efficiency with the performance of other organisations in your own industry or in different industries. Best practice benchmarking allows you to compare your own performance with the world leaders' performance in a particular area that you are interested in. A finance department, for example, might set benchmarks for a number of key indicators of financial management, such as average length of time taken to invoice customers, errors per invoice, number of days for outstanding debts and interest earned on capital. It might find that a company in a different industry has reduced outstanding debts to 15 days and meet with that company to learn how it achieved this. Organisations can learn a lot from each other and benchmarking makes this possible.

When you benchmark, don't just collect data. Data is not the same as information and not all data is useful. Decide what information you need first; this tells you what numbers you need to gather. Benchmark often enough to keep abreast of what's really happening but not so often that measuring becomes an end in itself. At the other end of the extreme, annual or irregular benchmarking sends signals that what you're measuring isn't really important.

Be careful, too, about how you benchmark. For instance, it's virtually meaningless to benchmark customer satisfaction across an entire organisation. Company-wide figures may look good but hide the huge variation that can exist from location to location, customer group to customer group, product to product, or shift to shift. Your stores may score 9 out of 10 for happy customers, but what have you learned if one or two stores are consistently scoring 2s and bringing down the average of the stores consistently scoring 10? A global score of 9 doesn't give you the information you need to improve the business.

Remember, too, that while benchmarking can help you improve, innovation can take you further.

> ● **IN A NUTSHELL**
>
> **Benchmarking blues**
> Here's how to avoid the most common mistakes in benchmarking:
> * Keep your eye on the competition. The competitors are out there, always trying to woo your customers. Find out how your customers, and theirs, perceive both you and the competition.
> * Measure what's important, not what's easy to measure. What's important is what matters to your customers and what makes you special to them.
> * Update performance measures. Yesterday's sensational service is today's expected service, so it's important to keep your performance measures current.
> * Measure either continuously or periodically. It can be dangerous to generalise from one-off studies that measure quality at one point in time.
> * Resist superficial interpretations. Analyse the numbers in the light of your organisation's culture and circumstances and verify that you're comparing apples with apples.
> * Don't go mad with benchmarks, key performance indicators, metrics and scorecards. A 'dashboard' of a few clear targets communicates what's important while too many measures is a recipe for confusion. Less is more.

Measures of success

A third quick-and-easy way to kaizen is through the measures of success (MOS) you set for yourself, your team and individual team members. Once you are consistently achieving an MOS, replace it with another one that lifts your performance still further.

3. Encouraging creativity and innovation

He was a bold man, that first ate an oyster.

Jonathan Swift (author, satirist), in Ashbourne, 'Polite conversation' (1841)[39]

Whether small step or big step improvements, creativity and innovation require boldness, too. Perhaps that's because when something is new, it's usually odd, or even absurd. For most people, odd and absurd aren't good. Take these three examples:

1. It's one of those stories that could be created in Hollywood myth but it used to be said that the actress Lana Turner's grandfather owned shares in a small company that made a soft drink called Coca-Cola. He sold them because he didn't think the name would catch on and bought shares in another drinks company with a more sensible name: the Raspberry Cola Company.
2. In 1971, Daisuke Inoue invented and even sold a few karaoke machines.[40] Most people chuckled. Then a few people stopped chuckling and took out patents, and then quite a few followed and now millions of yen and dollars have been made on them.
3. Discussing his work that led to the unique adhesive of 'Post-It' notes, Spencer Silver later remarked that had he given thought to it, he wouldn't have done the experiment because the advice was you couldn't do it.[41]

Antibiotics from bread mould, light bulbs, the PC and refrigerators were all scoffed at. Wasabi-flavoured cough drops? Reckitt markets them as 'Streusels warm lozenges'. Marmite cashew nuts? Unilever markets them. An opera maestro and a rock band on the same stage? Pavarotti and U2 brought a new audience to each other's music. Ideas only seem strange, silly or absurd because they are creative – not thought of before.

Thinking of ways that haven't been thought of before to provide better products and services, operate more efficiently, reach goals more effectively, find new ways to earn revenue or engage employees … these are vital to an organisation's success and an individual leader-manager's success. Innovation is critical for the future; when you're innovative, you're valuable.

◉ THEORY TO PRACTICE

Innovation through integrated supply chains

Dutch company ASML, an imaging solutions provider for semi-conductor manufacturers, works closely with its customers and its own suppliers to develop the advanced micro-chips that the market demands. So closely, in fact, that three of its largest customers (Intel, Samsung and TSMC) are contributing €1.38 billion over five years to ASML's research and development program (R&D) to top up ASML's already-huge R&D budget of €78 000 per employee per annum (a sum more than most pharmaceutical or vehicle companies spend on R&D per employee).[42]

Innovation: The essential ingredient

Consider these companies: Apple, Blackberry, Boeing, Canon, Corning, Dow Chemical, Du Pont, Google, Intel, Johnson & Johnson, LG Electronics, Microsoft, Nike, 3M. What springs to mind? Innovative? Not surprising, as they're all in the Thomson Reuters annual Top 100 Global Innovators League Table for 2013.[43] Successful might also spring to mind. That's not surprising either. Innovation is increasingly a key driver of competitive advantage, and the pace of innovation seems to be increasing.

Innovation isn't just about new products or providing a better service. Working with non-competitive suppliers to jointly take orders, deliver products and invoice for them, as General Mills and Land O'Lakes are doing (discussed on page 562) is a whole new take on doing business. Scoopon is a new way to market goods and services.

A large-scale study of Australian managers found that innovation leaders are also leaders in cash flow, customer satisfaction, productivity, profitability, revenue growth and other indicators of business performance that lead to long-term success. The study concludes that 'innovation performance is strongly linked to business performance' and that innovation is critical for Australia's future economic success, given that Australian wages are higher than many overseas competitors (creating a cost disadvantage) and that many overseas competitors are eating into our service and quality advantages.[44]

Of course, not all innovations are instant successes or even successes:

- Apple has a 90% failure rate in creating products.
- Einstein published hundreds of papers, many of which received no citations at all (a key measure of 'sound science').
- Finnish company Rovio developed 51 games before scoring with one of the best sellers of all time, Angry Birds, which added about $10 billion to its value.
- The Virgin Group launched over 400 ventures but is known for only a few.[45]

Darwin noted that mutations (read innovations) happen all the time, but most don't work out – just like new ideas.

To innovate successfully, you need an 'innovation culture', one that encourages experimentation and learning and has strong relationships with customers and suppliers, and open communication.

Lengthy development times, remuneration not being tied to innovation outcomes and a risk-averse culture have been found to be the three biggest obstacles to innovation in Australia.[46]

When you innovate – use it

Don't be like Kodak, which invented digital photography in 1975 but did nothing with it until it was too late, and then marketed it only half-heartedly, believing that people would never give up their hard copies of photographs and that digital imaging would compete directly with their lucrative film sales. Kodak filed for bankruptcy in 2012.[47] (See 'The strategic perspective: Thanks for the memories' on page 524.)

Barriers to creativity

Everyone is creative to some extent but perhaps, like many people, your natural creativity has become rusty through neglect. You may recognise some of the barriers to creativity listed below. They close your mind to 'absurd' and 'odd' solutions and tempt you to stop at the first answer you think of rather than search for more and possibly better alternatives:

* fixed ideas, especially the belief that everything should be orderly and predictable
* habit
* laziness – finding original solutions generally requires effort
* not wanting to sound silly
* obsessing on problems rather than looking for ways to fix them
* the 'only one right answer' syndrome.

Fortunately, most people can learn to be more creative and to promote creativity in others.

The elements of creativity and innovation

Five characteristics are commonly found in creative people. Although many creative people possess two or even three of them, it's unusual for even the most creative person to possess all five or even four of them. These five characteristics are:

1. Determination: It usually takes persistence and effort to find good ideas, and creative people carry on despite frustrations. They have the drive to make up another list of alternative solutions when the first list produces nothing worthwhile. Creative people don't give up; they are willing to try, try and try again.

2. Fluency: Although not all of their ideas are useful, creative people are often able to come up with one new idea after another, seemingly without effort.

3. Helicopter thinking: Creative people are often able to see 'the strategic perspective', the wood as well as the trees. That helps them see the 'same old thing', whether it's a problem, an event or a person, in a new light.

4. Mental nimbleness: Many creative people can let their minds freewheel. The momentum this builds is contagious and builds enthusiasm – anything is possible!

5. Originality: Creative people are able to produce innovative, novel and unusual ideas.

Creative people are similar to knowledge workers in many respects: they are often able to produce more creatively when working in collaboration with other creative people; they detest 'bureaucratic obstructionism', hierarchy and routine; they respond better to intrinsic rewards and intellectual stimulation, loving challenge and craving the feeling of accomplishment that working creatively brings; and they want to be trained and kept up to date with cutting-edge technologies and knowledge.

 THEORY TO PRACTICE

How to lead and motivate creative people

Whether it's advertising, architecture, computer software design, entertainment, fashion, films, financial or legal services, media, music or publishing, creative people are the main 'raw material' for many of today's knowledge and service organisations. In manufacturing, too, 'making' often takes a back seat to creating and innovating as customers demand new features and good product design that uses less material and less energy. So you can expect to be leading creative people soon, if you aren't already.

Creative people enjoy their work and want to 'get it right' and they enjoy tough challenges. As with knowledge workers, it's important to provide SMART targets that engage their curiosity, but leave how to reach those targets up to them. It's not dissimilar to motivating anyone, when you think about it.

Seeing with new eyes

Having new eyes, or the beginner's mind discussed in the 'FYI: The beginner's mind', on page 529, means that when you see an everyday object, your mind doesn't automatically make the usual associations with it (pen → writing; hat → coat). Instead, you can make other, innovative, associations (pen → plant stake; hat → container).

 THEORY TO PRACTICE

Flooded with opportunity

Creative people see what everyone else sees, but they see it differently. Did you know that left and right shoes were only thought up just over a century ago? Here are some other examples of what you can see when your 'innovation specs' are on and your 'beginner's mind' is open:

* A drug intended to treat the chest pain caused by angina had surprising side effects and is now known as Viagra.[48]
* Japan Railways (JR) East is the largest rail carrier in the world. When crews tunnelled through Mount Tanigawa in 1978, water gushed out of the tunnel wall at the rate of 60 tonnes per second. As engineers drew up plans to drain it away, a maintenance worker stepped forward with a different idea. He noticed that tunnel workers were drinking the water because it tasted unusually good. He suggested that JR East bottle it and sell it as mineral water. Called Ohshimizu, it became so popular that JR East installed special vending machines on its 1000 platforms and introduced a home-delivery service. Since then, a range of other Ohshimizu products has gone to market, including Ohshimizu tea and Ohshimizu coffee.[49]
* Two Bell Laboratory technicians, trying to eliminate radio static, found to their horror that the bigger and better they made their equipment the louder the static became. They discovered the reason – they were picking up whispers from the Big Bang. It was 1931 and radio astronomy was born.[50]

>>

- Ernest Hamwi's Syrian Zalabia waffle stall wasn't selling much at the 1904 World's Fair, while the ice-cream stall beside him was doing so much business that it kept running out of plates and spoons. Hamwi twisted one of his waffles into a cone, passed it to the next stall, and the ice-cream cone was born.[51]
- Antoine Feuchtwanger's Bavarian sausage restaurant ran out of cutlery one busy day in 1880 and he had to serve the sausages in a bread roll. Snags in a roll are now a favourite in many countries, including Australia.[52]

Becoming more innovative

One of the most important things you can do to become more innovative is to recognise the barriers to creativity and innovation within yourself and break them down. Do you worry about being criticised for a new idea? Maybe you shouldn't. Is there a lot of pressure on your time? Take some time out to identify a problem and brainstorm some creative solutions to it. Do you usually go for the obvious solution or the one that has worked before? Look for another idea that might work even better.

Have a clear objective when you're searching for an innovative solution. The more precisely you know what you're trying to achieve and the more you know about the situation, the more easily your creative subconscious can get to work on it – even while you're asleep – and the more easily you can tell people what kind of help you need with your ideas, for instance, adding to them, building on them or finding flaws.

Wait until you have a long list of possibilities before evaluating them; suspend judgement and let ideas emerge and grow. Then wait some more – 'sleep on them' a bit and don't dismiss any without a good reason; 'It costs too much', 'The boss will never go for it', 'It's too big a change' or 'We've tried it before' are not sufficient reasons for abandoning a good idea.

Look for situations in which you seem to be the most creative and observe what you do. Watch creative people to see what good ideas you can pick up from their approach. Take a break when you feel 'stuck'. Pushing yourself stifles creativity; relaxing and daydreaming switch it on.

⦿ THE STRATEGIC PERSPECTIVE

Left brain, right brain

For most people, the left side of their brain is better at language, logic, numbers and reason; it's linear and rational, literal and objective. The left brain is used for arithmetic, organising, planning, reading and scheduling.

The right side of the brain is imaginative, intuitive and subjective. It specialises in colours, images, music and patterns, and is good at creating, developing and communicating ideas as well as seeing, and making sense of, the strategic perspective. Creativity uses the right side of the brain to think outside the 'logic box'.

No one uses only half of their brain and the division between the two halves of the brain isn't as dramatic as it sounds. We work best when both halves of the brain work together and there are bundles of nerves called the corpus collosum that help us do just that. For instance, the left half of the brain picks out the sounds that form words and how those words are put together while the

>>

right half picks up on the emotional features of the language – its rhythms and intonations, for example.

Until recently, organisations have valued left-brain thinking, encouraging people to accept the 'obvious', evaluate any out-of-the-ordinary idea quickly and negatively, fixate on the usual and accepted assumptions and solutions, give the expected answers and see events, problems and decisions in the usual, accepted ways.

It's different in many of today's capabilities-based organisations. Business complexity makes creative, innovative leader-managers and teams highly prized. You need both the linear, logical left brain to use many of the tools and techniques discussed in Section 4 of this chapter and you need your creative, intuitive right brain for others. And to light upon those innovative solutions – ah! – that takes both halves of your brain working together.

IN A NUTSHELL

Four steps to creative innovation

Follow these four steps when you need to bring your creativity to bear on a decision or problem:
1. **Prepare:** Explore the problem, discuss it with others, let your mind 'daydream' over it.
2. **Incubate:** Let your subconscious work on it as described in 'The Strategic perspective: Two brain boosters' on page 526.
3. **Illuminate:** You may get that sudden flash of inspiration. When you do, it's time for Step 4. (When you don't, keep on with the problem-solving and decision-making steps described on page 526.)
4. **Verify:** Not all all ideas work. Think them through to sort the good from the bad.

Creativity techniques

Innovation can pop into the prepared mind by chance, which is fantastic, but 'lucky breaks' and haphazard, unplanned innovation is not enough. We need sustained innovation and creative breakthroughs that lead to a continuous stream of improvements and brand new business models, marketing strategies, processes, products, services and technologies. We need to systematically seek out innovative and creative ideas.

There are lots of ways to get your creative right brain working. Try writing your name as you usually do. Then write it backwards. Then upside down. Then in mirror writing (right to left). Then with your left hand.

Here's another: write this question to yourself with your non-dominant hand: How's it going? Answer the question writing with your other (dominant) hand. Keep switching hands and hold a short conversation with yourself.

Check out <http:/www.mindtools.com> and click on the creativity tools tab to find some more useful ways to boost your creativity. You can also take a test on that site to see how creative you are.

Scenario planning (explained on page 742) can also help you generate innovative ideas.

THEORY TO PRACTICE

Work on it, dream on it

There are lots of strategies to encourage strategic innovation:

- Google has 20% time, where engineers get a day a week to work on whatever they want; it has led to products such as Google Now and Google's Transparency Report, AdSense (now bringing in about 25% of Google's revenue), Google Transit, Google Talk, Google News, Google News, Gmail and other innovations.[53]
- Australian software company Atlassian pioneered programming marathons, or 'hackathons', where every quarter, engineers have 24 hours to work on projects that intrigue them; hackathons have now been adopted by Google, LinkedIn, Lonely Planet, NASA, The World Bank and Yahoo!, among others.[54]
- LinkedIn also has InCubator, where every quarter, engineers put small teams together, pitch an idea to an executive team and if approved, have 30 to 90 days to develop it into a prototype, going through two rounds of judging to gain a further 30 days.[55]

You don't need to be a hi-tech company to let employees get together, cross-fertilise ideas and let their creativity run wild.[56]

Adapt other people's ideas

Don't be afraid to put other peoples' ideas to use: did you know Henry Ford first saw a production line in a meat packaging plant? He applied the principles to automobile manufacturing and as a result of his innovation, he is now credited with 'inventing' the assembly line.

That's why benchmarking is so popular, but you don't have to do it officially. Keep your eyes open, listen, look and learn from others in your organisation and professional and other networks. Good ideas can come from anywhere.

Ask crazy questions

Here are two examples of how effective short, simple, open questions can be:

- Once upon a time, a manager at the delivery giant UPS asked a crazy question: Can we lower fuel costs by avoiding left turns? Today, routing technologies and strategies, including avoiding left turns, reduce miles driven and wasteful idling, saving 31.8 million litres of fuel a year.
- Managers at Adidas and Nike asked whether it would be possible to dye clothes, a water-intensive process, without using water. Neither company now uses water in its dying processes.[57]

To get started, think through the five Ws and one H trigger questions (what? when? where? who? why? and how?) and then ask questions such as: What if we did it another way? What if someone else did it? What if we did it somewhere else?

Challenge your assumptions

Challenge your assumptions and self-imposed rules; you can become so used to seeing things the way they 'are' that you assume that's the way they'll always be. Just as fish probably aren't conscious of the water they swim in, people aren't conscious of the assumptions they operate within. Incorporate the elements of creativity listed above into your day-to-day behaviour and turn misfortune into good fortune and stumbling blocks into stepping stones by being open to new possibilities and seeing with 'new eyes'.

Study the unexpected

Examine the extremes to see what you can learn – high sales in one area, low sales in another, for example, or high output in one area, low in a comparable area. Study anomalies and surprises – results or behaviours you expect to see but don't. What you find out might lead to an insight that suggests an innovation or a completely new approach.

Think like other people

Study your products and services from other points of view – your colleagues, customers, suppliers, and other stakeholders. What would you want and expect if you were in their shoes? What suggestions might they offer you? What might frustrate them most about what you provide them? What might they appreciate the most and would like increased or improved further? How could you make their lives easier?

Whether your customers are external or internal, visit them. Talk about how they use your products, watch them as they use them to see what you can learn and watch them as they go about their daily activities. You may discover ways you can help them even more. (You can find out more about this on page 627.)

Think in other languages

Try thinking in other 'languages': make mental pictures or think in symbols instead of words. Use all your senses as you approach a problem. Find another way to describe the problem you're trying to solve, the improvement you're searching for, or the opportunity you're trying to make the most of. Look for another but similar issue or benefit to build on.

Build an innovative team culture

Encourage your team members to do these things too. Make sure they understand why creativity and innovation are important to the organisation's future success. Then motivate, inspire, encourage and empower them to think creatively and innovatively. Train them, let them experiment, and provide development opportunities inside and outside the organisation that foster cross-fertilisation and value curiosity and 'what if' questions. Try writing innovation into everyone's key result areas and reward innovators.

 IN A NUTSHELL

Creativity boosters for your team

Here are some ways to help your team think more innovatively:

- Accept mistakes as a detour to good ideas.
- Build a well-rounded, diverse team with different perspectives, backgrounds, expertise and thinking styles. Homogeneous teams may have less friction and reach solutions quickly but they suffer from a lack of creativity because everyone is so similar.
- Encourage collaboration and communication within the team and across the organisation.
- Give people autonomy over how to achieve goals. Choose the mountain, but let the team decide how to climb it.
- Greet new ideas with openness, not scepticism, and explore them.
- Match people to the right jobs. Take advantage of people's expertise, interests and training. Let people select the projects they want to work on to increase their motivation.

>>

- Provide both positive and constructive feedback. Without it, enthusiasm and creativity wilt.
- Provide enough resources – money, people, psychological safety, space, support, time, and so on, and opportunities for employees to interact with each other, face to face and electronically, to share ideas and learnings.
- Specify goals clearly. People need to know where they're headed.

4. Using systematic analytical tools and techniques

It is a capital mistake to theorise before one has data. Insensibly one begins to twist facts to suit theories, instead of theories to suit facts.

Arthur Conan Doyle (author, 'Sherlock Holmes' stories) *A Scandal in Bohemia* (1895)[58]

Real information and numbers, not guesswork, good luck, hunches, opinions, past experience or trial and error, are the most reliable ways to abide by the quality, innovation and continuous improvement imperatives. The tools and statistical techniques reviewed in this chapter (and summarised in Figure 19.2) give you and your work team objective and systematic ways to identify, analyse and resolve problems and to streamline and build quality into systems and processes. (Four of these techniques – ask 'Why' five times, brainstorming, and cause-and-effect diagrams and force field analysis – are explained on pages 530, 532, 534 and 504.) Together, these tools are an indispensable part of any quality, innovation and continuous improvement effort.

Although you can apply these tools and techniques on your own, they work best in a team environment because those involved in doing a job know it best and are more likely to develop workable solutions. Drawing on the skills, experience and ideas of a range of people also increases their commitment to the resulting improvement efforts. (Chapter 13 explains how to build your team's group dynamics and help its members work together effectively.)

These tools and techniques help you address today's key challenges of:
- achieving higher quality
- improving customer satisfaction
- increasing efficiencies, saving time and reducing hassles through flexible and well-organised processes
- making the most effective use of people and information
- making continuous improvements and innovations
- saving money through lower inventory levels and less waste
- solving a wide range of problems.

Where to begin?

You might have identified a specific problem or perhaps an unexpected success has occurred that you want to ensure continues to happen; or maybe you want to prevent an unexpected failure from happening again. Maybe there is a gap between a result you're getting and the result you want, or maybe there has been some sort of change in a customer or supplier – for example, in the people or the ways they do business – that you want to capitalise on or make sure doesn't adversely affect you. Perhaps you have so many 'headaches' that you need to prioritise them so you can work on the most important problems first.

Brainstorming is a common way to begin. A work team or quality improvement team brainstorms problems, bottlenecks, and so on to work on and then prioritises them using the *nominal group technique* (explained below). Or you might use check sheets, control charts or run charts to collect

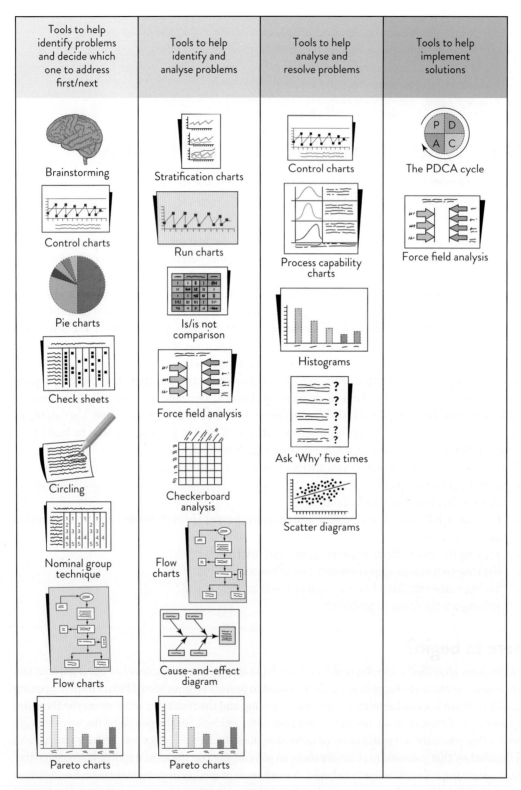

FIGURE 19.2 Using the systematic analytical tools and techniques

relevant information about current performance and trends in performance, and Pareto charts to identify the most important problem to work on first.

You then collect more information about the problem you have decided to work on, which you display and analyse using the tools and techniques discussed below, before developing and testing options to improve the situation and selecting and implementing the most effective. (You can find the seven steps to problem solving explained on page 526.)

Test and learn

Once you've developed options to test, test only one at a time; changing many variables at once is no good because you don't know which one worked if there's an improvement, and you don't know how the different variables affected each other. So the only way to find out what drives results, positive or negative, is to change one thing at a time. When there is no improvement, remove the change and either refine it or try another option.

Have a large enough test group to offer statistically significant results; this is known as the *scientific method*. When you can, have a *control group* or *control site*, where there is no change. This ensures that any change in your test group or test site wouldn't have happened anyway. For instance, if sales go up in your experimental, or test, group, that's great. But if they also go up in your control group, where nothing has changed, you can't claim your experiment was a success since sales would probably have risen without your intervention.

Once your improvement plan is implemented, use the P–D–C–A cycle (Plan–Do–Check–Act), customer feedback and other techniques to monitor its effectiveness and make further refinements as needed.

The P–D–C–A cycle helps you ensure improvements actually work. First, you Plan what you will do to improve a system or process and then you Do it. Next, you Check to make sure your plan is achieving the desired results; when it isn't, you remove your change and plan a different one. When it works, you Act to ensure the change 'sticks'. (Chapter 17 explains how to plan and check, or monitor your plan and Chapter 22 explains how to introduce change and make it 'stick'.)

● IN A NUTSHELL

An expanded P–D–C–A cycle
Kaoru Ishikawa expanded Walter Shewhart's P–D–C–A cycle into six steps:
1. Determine goals and targets.
2. Determine methods of reaching goals.
3. Engage in education and training.
4. Implement work.
5. Check the effects of implementation.
6. Take appropriate action.[59]

Nominal group technique

You may have noticed that it is often the person with the loudest voice in the group, the most articulate person or the most senior person who gets their way. The rest lose heart and interest because it seems their point of view is never 'heard'.

The nominal group technique is a way of making sure that this doesn't happen. It gives everyone an equal say in deciding which problems to work on and in what order, clearly showing the wishes of the group without the divisions caused by straightforward voting (discussed on page 542). Giving everyone a say increases interest and commitment.

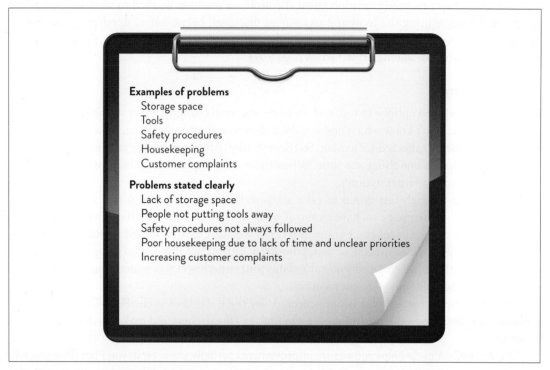

Examples of problems
  Storage space
  Tools
  Safety procedures
  Housekeeping
  Customer complaints

Problems stated clearly
  Lack of storage space
  People not putting tools away
  Safety procedures not always followed
  Poor housekeeping due to lack of time and unclear priorities
  Increasing customer complaints

FIGURE 19.3 Stating problems clearly

Here are the steps to using the nominal group technique:
1. Brainstorm problems that need to be resolved. A list of problems that a work group might brainstorm is shown at the top of Figure 19.3.
2. Word each problem clearly so that everyone has the same understanding of it. Examples are shown at the bottom of Figure 19.3. Double check that you have listed each problem only once and not repeated a problem using different words.
3. Assign a letter to each problem (see Figure 19.4).
4. Each team member then votes on which problem they believe is the most important. In Figure 19.4 there are five problems. Each member assigns a 5 to the problem they believe is the most important, a 4 to the next most important problem, and so on, ending with a 1 next to the least important problem. One team member's vote is shown in Figure 19.4.

  When you are discussing a large number of problems, follow the 'half plus one' rule. Instead of ranking each problem, rank only half plus one of the problems listed. For example, if 22 problems are listed, rank 12. Each member would assign a 12 to the problem they believe is most important, an 11 to the next most important, and so on.

  Another way to 'see' the opinions of the group, after brainstorming and recording ideas on a flip chart, is to give everyone coloured dots to rank problems. Then count the coloured dots beside each problem.
5. Tally the ratings. For example, the results from a team of five voting on how to rank problems to decide which to work on first might look like the ratings shown in Figure 19.4. Problem C, safety procedures not always followed, has the highest score. This team thinks that this is the

most important problem to work on first. They will work on Problem B, people not putting tools away, next, and so on.

Once you know where to begin, you can launch the problem-solving process described in Chapter 18.

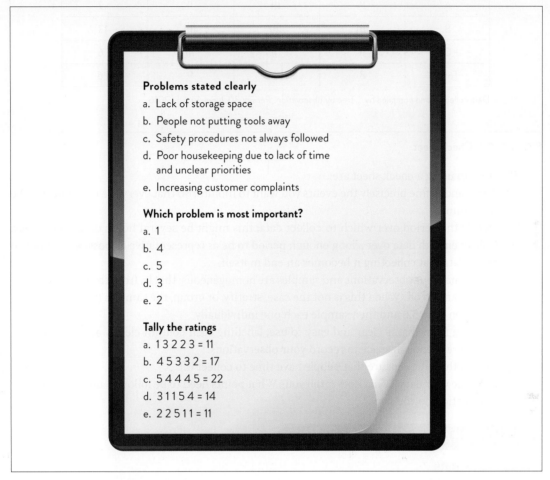

Problems stated clearly

a. Lack of storage space

b. People not putting tools away

c. Safety procedures not always followed

d. Poor housekeeping due to lack of time and unclear priorities

e. Increasing customer complaints

Which problem is most important?

a. 1

b. 4

c. 5

d. 3

e. 2

Tally the ratings

a. 1 3 2 2 3 = 11

b. 4 5 3 3 2 = 17

c. 5 4 4 4 5 = 22

d. 3 1 1 5 4 = 14

e. 2 2 5 1 1 = 11

FIGURE 19.4 Problems labelled and rated

Check sheets

Check sheets help you gather data based on sample observations so that you can detect and isolate patterns of non-conformance and variation – in other words, check sheets highlight where work is going wrong. They are a good starting point because they help you identify problems and build a picture of them, so you can see which occur most often, which occur when, and so on. They are a simple way to answer the question 'How often are certain events happening?' and begin the process of translating opinions into facts.

Figure 19.5 shows that problem A occurred seven times, problem B occurred 13 times and problem C occurred six times. It seems that attention should focus on problem B, particularly as the number of times each problem occurred each week is consistent. If one week stood out from the others as having far more or far fewer problems occurring, you would want to examine what happened during that week to see what you could learn from it.

Problem	Week			Total
	1	2	3	
A	II	III	II	7
B	IIII	IHHI	IIII	13
C	II	I	III	6
Total	8	9	9	26

Data collected and compiled by T Tree by observation. Period: 30 June–14 July 2016.

FIGURE 19.5 Check sheet

The steps to using a check sheet are:

1. Agree and define precisely the events you want to monitor so that everyone is looking for the same thing.
2. Decide the period over which to collect data; this might be several hours or several weeks. Collect enough data over a long enough period to be as representative as possible, but not so much data that collecting it becomes an end in itself.
3. Check that your observations and samples are homogeneous; that is, from the same machine, person, and so on. When this is not the case, stratify, or group, the samples (see stratification charts on page 52) and then sample each one individually.
4. Design a form that is clear and easy to use, labelling each column clearly and making sure that there is enough space to record your observations.
5. Collect the data. (Ensure that people have time to collect it.)
6. Examine your data. What does it tell you? What points need to be followed up? What further information do you need?

● THE STRATEGIC PERSPECTIVE

Meaningful data

Having tools doesn't necessarily mean that people use them well. Easily available information, thanks to technology, can result in an abundance of meaningless information. How can you best sift all the information at your fingertips? How can you assess what's important and what isn't?

Scottish historian Andrew Lang wisely said of a man he knew, 'He uses statistics as a drunken man uses lampposts – for support rather than illumination.'[60]

Think about your current position and what you want to achieve, the information you need and what you want to do with it (e.g. spot trends, isolate problem areas or pinpoint where and when certain events occur). Think about what data can provide the information you need, how to ensure the data is accurate, the size of sample you need, and any possible biases (e.g. from poorly gathered data – see 'Theory to practice: Tips on charting' on page 51). You need to gather good data for it to be useful. Then think about how best to arrange or display your data to make understanding it easier.

Circling

When you want to tighten up a very broad or complex issue, write it up on a flip chart and then circle the key words, as shown in Figure 19.6.

Each time you clarify, you sharpen your problem definition. When there is an 'and' in the description, check whether you're trying to solve two problems at once (as in this example). Split them and solve each separately.

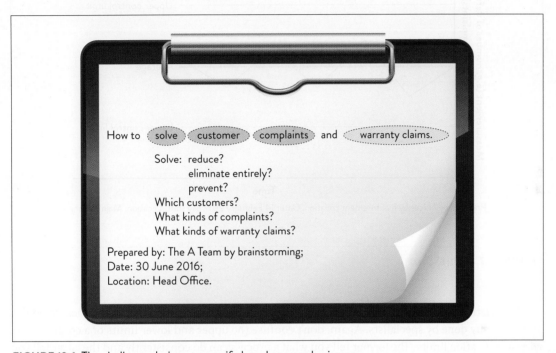

FIGURE 19.6 The circling technique to specify broad or complex issues

Control charts

A control chart is a type of run chart that shows the upper and lower statistically acceptable limits of results drawn on either side of the average (see Figure 19.7). Note that these are statistically acceptable limits that may or may not be the same as customer requirements or specifications. They may be tighter than the customer requires (are you putting too much effort into this?) or they may be looser than the customer wants (you'd better fix what you're doing or risk losing a customer).

Every process and system has natural variation, but too much variation results in unreliable quality and increased costs. Control charts show you how much variation exists in a process, whether this variation is random or follows a pattern, and whether or not the process is in statistical control. Thus, they indicate whether a problem exists and help you implement and monitor solutions. For example, control charts show you:

- how long it takes to complete a process (e.g. answer a customer query, make a sale, resolve a customer complaint, send out an invoice)
- how machine A's productivity and quality compares with machine B's

* the running speeds, temperature, pressures and other factors in a process
* when/how often delays are occurring.

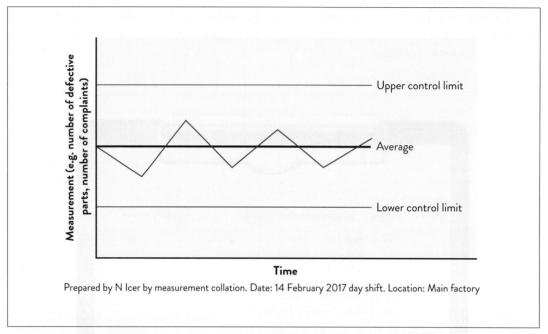

Prepared by N Icer by measurement collation. Date: 14 February 2017 day shift. Location: Main factory

FIGURE 19.7 Control chart

Calculating the upper and lower control limits requires the use of complex statistical formulas and is usually done by specialists. Again, don't confuse the upper and lower limits of a control chart with specification limits. The former tell you what a process can do consistently and the latter tell you what you or the customers think is needed.

Once the control limits are established, you can plot the sample averages onto a control chart and find out whether any of the points fall outside the control limits or form unlikely patterns. When either of these is the case your process is statistically 'out of control' and you need to examine and fix it. Find out what event or events caused the result to be outside the control limits (check out the 85:15 rule in the Glossary) and fix it so that it doesn't happen again.

When the averages fall within the control limits, your process is 'in control'. Although there is always some variation in any system, you can probably improve your system (in this case, make it more reliable and predictable) by bringing the control limits closer to the average.

Figure 19.8 gives some indications of processes that are 'out of control' and suggests questions you could ask.

You can also use control charts as a monitoring tool by taking samples at regular intervals and plotting them on the control chart. This ensures that the process doesn't change in important ways and remains reliable. It also highlights any non-conformance, or variations outside the control limits, that you need to investigate.

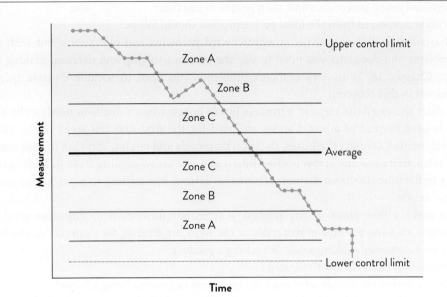

Data collected and complied by A Bundance, using 50% sampling. Date: 3 March 2016, night shift.
Location: Main factory

A process is 'out of control' when one or more of the following happens:
1. One or more points fall outside the control limits.
2. Two out of three successive points occur on the same side of the centre line in Zone A.
3. Four out of five successive points occur on the same side of the centre line in or outside Zone B.
4. Nine successive points occur on one side of the average line.
5. There are six consecutive points increasing or decreasing.
6. There are 14 points in a row alternating up and down
7. There are 15 points in a row within Zone C.

Questions to ask with an out-of-control process:
- Are the methods used changing?
- Are the raw materials, information or other process inputs different?
- Could the environment be affecting the process (temperature, humidity, etc)?
- Could the equipment need maintenance?
- Did the samples come from different methods, machines, shifts or operators?
- Have different measuring instruments been used that may not have the same degree of accuracy?
- Is everyone trained in how to carry out the process?
- What has changed in the process or the environment (e.g. maintenance procedures, training, overtime levels, raw materials)?

FIGURE 19.8 Out-of-control systems

Flow charts

A flow chart is a graphical representation of an algorithm, a detailed sequence of simple steps that helps you work through a situation to decide what to do. By helping you 'see' each step in a process and how it relates to the other steps, flow charts can also help you:
- analyse a process to find out where value is (or is not) added and identify duplication of effort, hassles and sources of problems

• design and refine procedures and train people to use them
• highlight deviations from the ideal path a process should follow.

Flow charts are good for relatively straightforward problems and operations, but with more complex problems and decisions you need to use the problem-solving and decision-making steps explained in Chapter 18. With very complex problems, you need to include creative thinking (discussed earlier in this chapter).

A flow chart shows all the steps of a process inside boxes; when a decision needs to be made, a diamond is used instead of a box. Circles are used for the first and last steps of the process being charted. Arrows connect the boxes, decision diamonds and circles, showing the sequence of activities. Each activity has one arrow leading into it and one arrow coming from it, leading to the next activity or decision. Decision diamonds have two arrows, one leading to a 'yes' action and the other to a 'no' action.

You can make a flow chart of any process – from administration to customer service to manufacturing – showing the flow of materials or the steps involved in, for example, producing an invoice, serving a customer, making a sale or making a product.

To develop a flow chart, follow these steps:

1. Gather together the people who work in the system or process being charted.
2. Discuss and agree the steps the process actually entails and, using the symbols shown in Figure 19.9, diagram the process as it is currently followed.
3. Agree how the process should ideally occur when everything is working right and diagram this.
4. Compare the two charts to find out where you can improve the process.

Make sure that everyone is clear about the process they are flow-charting, including where it begins and ends. See that every feedback loop in the chart has an escape.

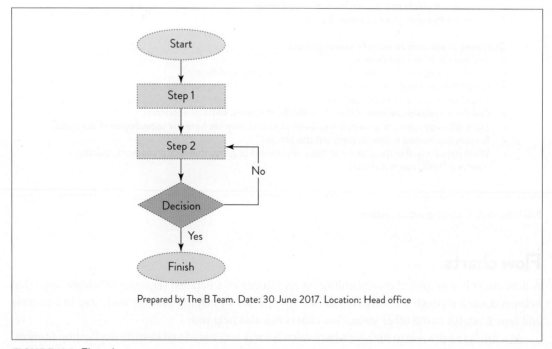

Prepared by The B Team. Date: 30 June 2017. Location: Head office

FIGURE 19.9 Flow chart

Pie charts

As Figure 19.10 shows, pie charts are circular graphs in which the entire circle represents 100% (not 360 degrees) of the data. You divide the circle, or pie, into percentage slices that clearly show the relative sizes (e.g. amounts, frequencies) of the data you are studying. This can point to where to begin your problem-solving efforts. Be sure to mark the subject matter clearly, showing the percentages within the slices and what each slice represents.

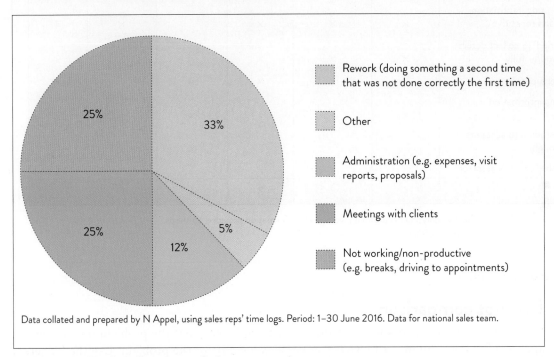

Data collated and prepared by N Appel, using sales reps' time logs. Period: 1–30 June 2016. Data for national sales team.

FIGURE 19.10 Pie chart: Time usage of sales representatives

Checkerboard analysis

Checkerboard analysis uses a matrix to analyse a problem. Elements of one key aspect of a problem are placed on one side and elements of another aspect across the top. Concentrate your analysis on where they intersect.

The example shown in Figure 19.11 is from a chain of wholesale shops that serve mainly trade account customers but also sell to the general public. The shops have experienced problems with delayed invoices sent from head office, particularly to general public customers. The preparation of these invoices is based on information sent in by the shops.

From the information shown in Figure 19.11, you would probably concentrate on the form itself and the number of interruptions occurring in the shops as the forms are being filled out. How could the form be improved? What could be done to reduce the errors caused by interruptions in the shops? This might lead you to consider changing the system of information gathering itself. You would probably also want to clarify why the shops are providing insufficient information and the cause of the processing difficulties at head office.

As former British prime minister Benjamin Disraeli was reported to have said: 'There are three kinds of lies: lies, damned lies and statistics.'[61]

Problem: How to speed up the invoicing process to non-account customers						
Problems within accounts ⟍ Problems at source	Insufficient information	Inaccurate information	Details incorrect	Processing difficulties at head office	Accounts staff not clear about procedure	Total
Form for collecting information confusing and repetitive	×	×	×		×	4
Staff too 'hurried' to collect details correctly and/or fully	×	×	×			3
Too many interruptions	×	×	×	×		4
Correct pricing information unavailable	×			×	×	3
Forms not passed on to accounts quickly enough				×		1
Forms not batched correctly at source				×		1
Total	4	3	3	4	2	

Data collated and compiled by J Cob by analysing head office invoices and information provided by shops.
Date: 1 July–31 July 2016. Location: Head office

FIGURE 19.11 Checkerboard analysis

Is/is not comparison

To do an is/is not comparison, write down what you *know* about the problem in one column and, in a second column, write what you know is *not* part of the problem. Use the 'Where?', 'When?', 'Who?', 'How often?', 'How much or how bad?' and 'What?' triggers to guide your thinking.

Once you have written down everything you know about the problem, compare the *Is* and the *Is not* columns, looking for differences and changes. This gives you points to follow up which could lead you to identify the source of the problem. An example is shown in 'Theory to practice: Is/is not comparison – Absenteeism among office staff'.

● THEORY TO PRACTICE

Is/is not comparison – Absenteeism among office staff
Table 19.2 shows an is/is not comparison of absenteeism among office staff to look for points to follow up in order to improve the situation. As always, show the details of who collected the data or conducted the analysis, the time period covered, and how, where and when this was done.

≫

TABLE 19.2 The Is/is not strategies chart

	Is	Is not	Points to follow up
Where?	General office	Accounts Public relations Sales and marketing Finance Human resources	Working conditions, hours of work, supervision: What is different about the general office?
When?	Most days	No obvious patterns (e.g. Fridays or Mondays)	Complete a check sheet to identify any hidden patterns.
Who?	Mostly newer staff	No absenteeism from longer serving staff	Make a histogram of age groups to check this. Check ages and profiles for 'job fit'. Check training and induction given to new recruits. Check their jobs for job interest: Are they different from jobs of longer serving staff?
How often?	About 17% on any given day		Benchmark with local organisations to see how bad this problem is for them.
How bad?	Problem may be increasing	Not getting better or staying the same	Check this year's absenteeism rates against those of previous years.
What?	Mostly one-day absences	Seldom longer than two days	

Prepared by: General Office team using internal records

Date: 21 July 2016 (covering 1 April–30 June 2016)

Location: Head Office

Pareto charts

Pareto charts are vertical bar charts that plot events or problems in descending order of quantity, showing you the relative importance of all the problems or events you are examining. This directs your attention and efforts to the truly important problems and helps you choose a starting point for problem-solving. Pareto charts can also help you to identify and describe a problem or its basic cause, plan to resolve it and monitor your success.

From the information shown in Figure 19.12, you would want to investigate the causes of raw materials run-outs to try to stop this occurring. Then you would want to find the causes and sources of faulty raw materials and discuss this with your suppliers; you might even consider changing to a more reliable supplier. Next, you would want to investigate the types and causes of machine breakdowns and see what you could do to stop or reduce them.

You can compile Pareto charts from check sheets or other forms of data collection. To construct a Pareto chart, follow these steps:

1. Select the problems to compare and rank.
2. Select the unit of measurement (e.g. cost, frequency, percentage) and the period to study (e.g. hours, days, weeks).

3. Gather the data.

4. Plot the data by listing the units of measurement vertically and each category (problem or event) from left to right horizontally in decreasing order. Mark the measurements and categories clearly. Combine the categories with the fewest items into one category called 'other', which goes at the extreme right as the last bar. (This final bar is often 'higher' than the bars to its immediate left because it contains several categories.)

5. Draw a vertical bar above each category with the height representing the unit of measurement in that classification.

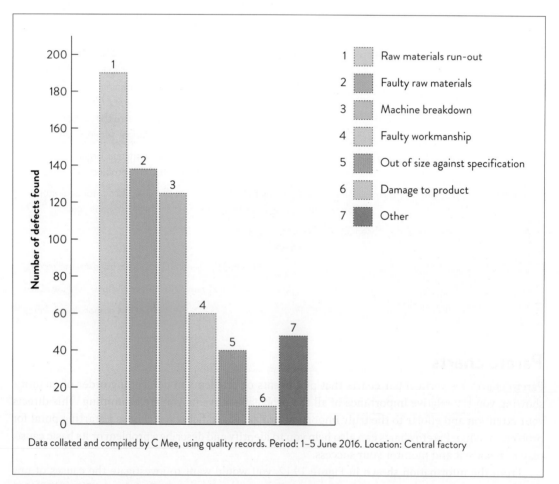

Data collated and compiled by C Mee, using quality records. Period: 1–5 June 2016. Location: Central factory

FIGURE 19.12 Pareto chart: Defects found at in-process inspection

Pareto charts can provide surprising insights. For example, the two charts in Figure 19.13 illustrate the importance of examining a problem from different perspectives: resolving the most frequently occurring problems first might not be the most cost-effective way to proceed.

Figure 19.14 shows that you sometimes need to use your imagination when measuring problems and information. Showing defects by type and by machine doesn't give you very much information, but showing defects by shift really gives you something to investigate.

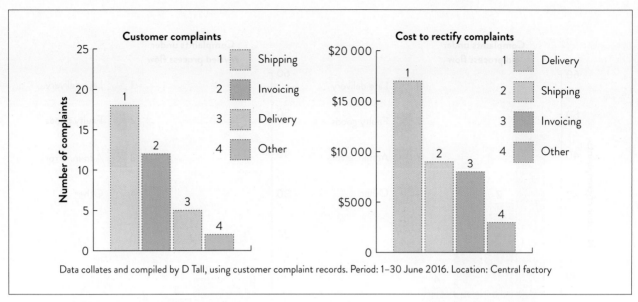

FIGURE 19.13 Using Pareto charts to identify the most important problems through different measurements

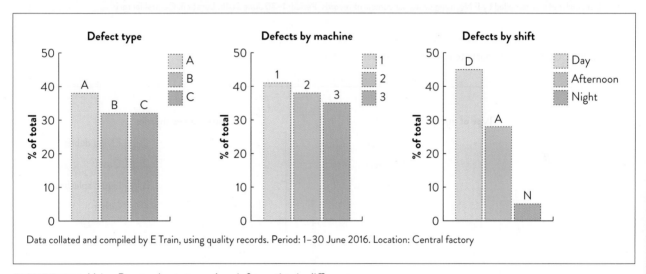

FIGURE 19.14 Using Pareto charts to analyse information in different ways

Figure 19.15 shows how you can use Pareto charts to measure the impact of change, with 'before' and 'after' comparisons. In the example shown, the number of complaints drops markedly after the introduction of a revised process flow.

Pareto charts can also help you to break down a problem, as shown in Figure 19.16. This can help to isolate the causes of problems from their symptoms.

Use your common sense when constructing and analysing Pareto charts. For example, it may pay to resolve a recurring complaint from a major customer before resolving numerous other complaints from small customers.

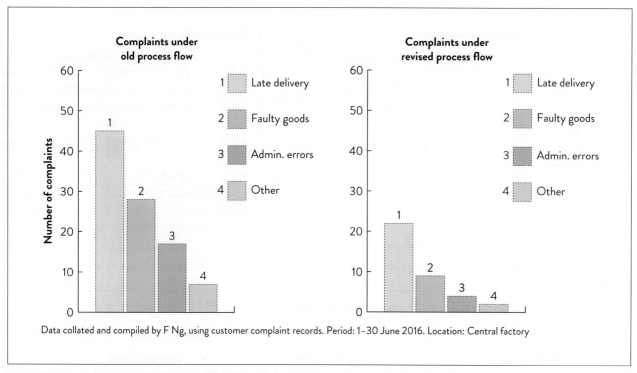

FIGURE 19.15 Using Pareto charts to measure the impact of change

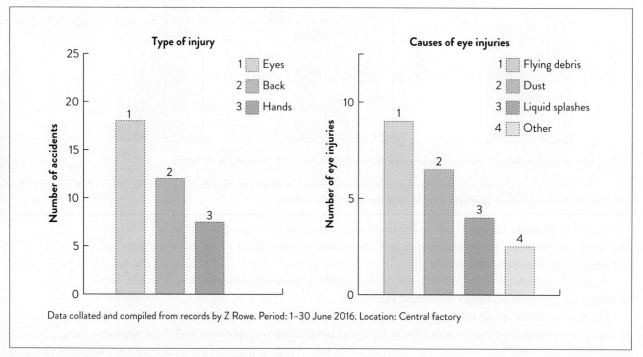

FIGURE 19.16 Using Pareto charts to break down a problem

Run charts

Run charts are a simple way to show trends in processes such as administrative errors, customer complaints, machine downtime, productivity, scrap or yields. Seeing how things vary over time (are they getting worse, staying the same or improving?) can help you to identify and describe a problem or monitor a process.

Run charts are simple to construct and interpret. To make a run chart, plot what you are measuring as points on a graph and then connect the points. Plot the measurements in the order that you made them, since you are tracking them over time (see Figure 19.17).

Pay attention to any wide variations because they might point to a problem in a process. Run charts can also highlight shifts in the average results. For example, when monitoring a system, an equal number of points should fall above and below the average. When this does not happen, it indicates that either an unusual 'event' or a change has occurred in the system, or the average has changed. When the shift is favourable, study it to find out why, so that you can make the change a permanent part of the system. When it is unfavourable, find out why it has occurred and eliminate the possibility of it happening again. Examine any steady increase or decrease in a trend, too; since you would not expect this to occur randomly, it can indicate an important change that you need to investigate.

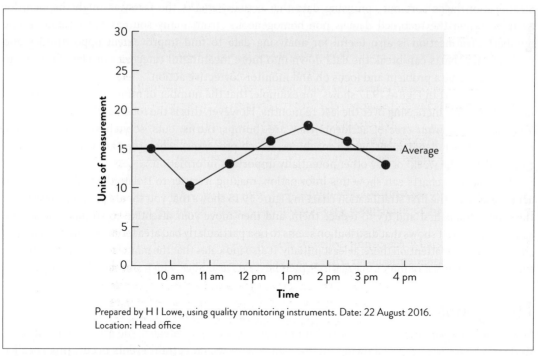

Prepared by H I Lowe, using quality monitoring instruments. Date: 22 August 2016.
Location: Head office

FIGURE 19.17 Run chart

◉ THEORY TO PRACTICE

Tips on charting

Here are some tips to help you get the most from your charts:
- Base the data you use on random representative samples taken from homogeneous groups and gather it consistently (in the same way each time) to ensure that it is not biased.
- Don't make decisions based on just one piece of evidence. Gather other information to ensure you have it right.

>>

- Get help from experts whenever you need it; that's what they're there for.
- Keep it simple. Use the simplest appropriate tool or technique possible and don't overcomplicate your graphs.
- Remember that the point of charts and graphs is not to collect and display just *any* numbers. The point is to collect and display *meaningful* numbers – information that helps you to analyse and improve your service or production processes.
- Show the following information on every chart and diagram: the name of the person or team who compiled it; the time span covered (e.g. time of day, shift); the date and where the data was collected; and who collected the data and how (e.g. by instruments, observation). Someone may need to refer to them in the future, so be meticulous in the way you label your charts.
- Use your common sense when interpreting graphs and charts.

Stratification charts

Stratification helps sort out confusing data that actually masks the facts, as might happen, for example, when the recorded data is non-homogeneous (from many sources but treated as one number). Stratification is also useful for analysing data to find improvement opportunities and stratification charts can break the data down into more meaningful categories or classifications to help you describe a problem and focus on and monitor corrective action.

The run chart in Figure 19.17 shows, for example, that the number of minor injuries in a factory has been steadily increasing over the last 12 months. However, this is the total of all minor accidents. You don't know *what type* of accidents they are (bumps, burns, cuts, scratches), *where* they are occurring (which department, which machines, which processes), when they are occurring (which shift or day of the week) or any other potentially important information.

Stratification charts can show this information, making it easier to isolate the real problem and act to resolve it. The first stratification chart in Figure 19.18 shows that you should probably investigate the cause of falls first and try to reduce them, and then move your attention to strains. The second stratification chart shows that distribution seems to be a particularly bad area for minor injuries and you should focus your attention there, at least initially. It also indicates that the main factory had a far higher than average number of minor injuries in September and December, which you should investigate.

Histograms

Histograms are bar charts that show the number of units in each category you are studying. It's best to display these bar graphs showing the frequency with which certain events occur; this is called *frequency distribution*. Whereas Pareto charts display characteristics of a product or service, called *attribute data* (e.g. complaints, defects, errors), histograms display the distribution of *measurement data* (e.g. dimensions, temperature). This can reveal the amount of variation in a process and help you discover and describe a problem and monitor its solution.

Figure 19.19 contains a typical histogram. It shows the greatest number of units in the centre with a roughly equal number of units on either side. A *normal distribution curve*, or bell shape, is statistically what you can expect from any process, because every process varies over time. Repeated samples of any process that is 'under control' follow this pattern.

When a histogram does not show this pattern, you need to investigate. Figure 19.20 shows an out-of-control process where the data is 'piled up' at points to the left of centre. A distribution like this is referred to as *skewed*.

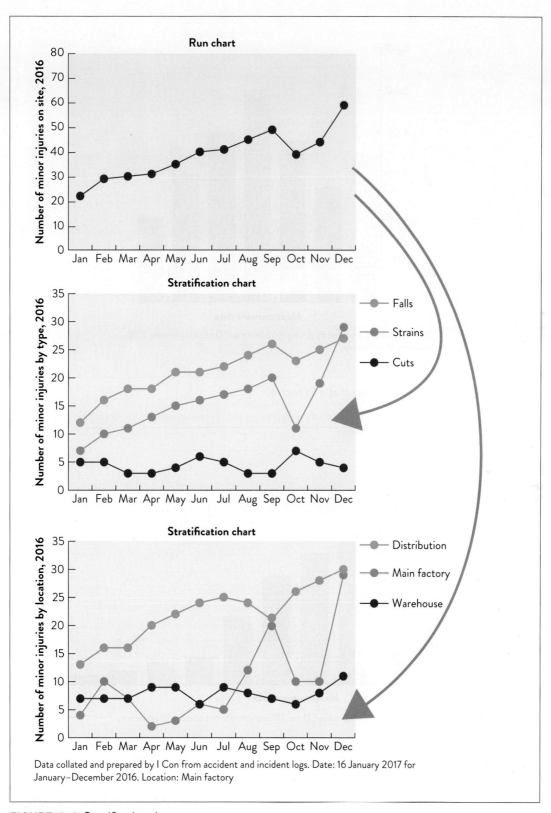

Data collated and prepared by I Con from accident and incident logs. Date: 16 January 2017 for January–December 2016. Location: Main factory

FIGURE 19.18 Stratification charts

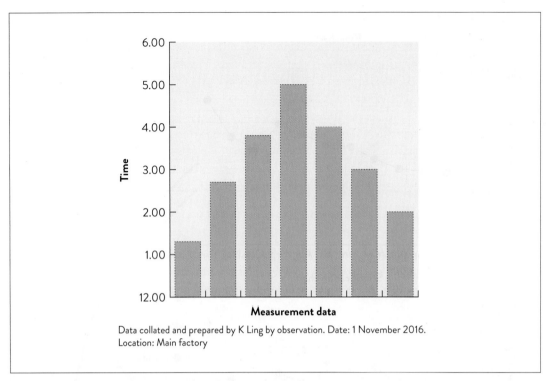

FIGURE 19.19 A histogram of a process that is 'in control'

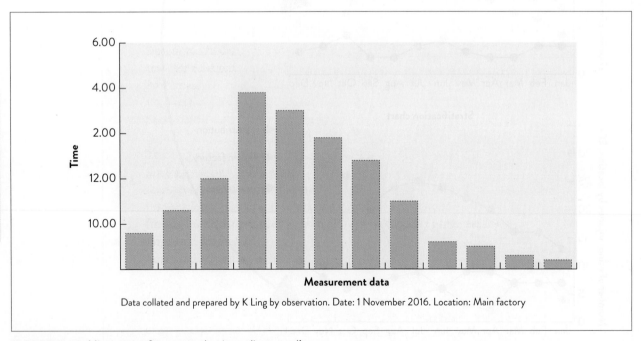

FIGURE 19.20 Histogram of a process that is not 'in control'

When examining histograms, look at the shape of the distribution for surprises. For example, a distribution that you would expect to be 'normal' (a centred curve) but is skewed. Are most measurements skewed on the 'high side' or the 'low side'? Look for whether the 'spread' of the curve (*variability*) falls within specifications; when it does not, how far outside the specifications is it? Analyse the process further to find out what you can do to bring it back to specifications.

 FYI

The number of classes based on the number of data points
Table 19.3 shows you how to calculate the number of classes according to the data points.

TABLE 19.3 Calculating classes

Number of data points	Number of classes
Under 50	15 to 7
51 to 100	16 to 10
101 to 250	17 to 12
Over 250	10 to 20

To construct a histogram, follow these steps:
1. Gather your data (*data set*) and count the number of *data points* in your data set.
2. Determine the *range* (R) value for the entire data set. This is the smallest data point subtracted from the largest.
3. Divide the range value into a certain number of *classes* (K), or *bars* on the chart.
4. Determine the class width (H) using the this formula:

$$H = \frac{R}{K}$$

5. Decide where each bar on the histogram should begin and end by determining the class *boundary*, or *end points*. Take the smallest measurement in the data set and use that number (or round it down to an appropriate lower number) as the lower end point for your first class boundary. Then add the class width to your lower end point and this number becomes your next lower class boundary, as shown in this example:

Smallest measurement in the data set = 7 = lower end point
class width = 0.20
7 + 0.20 = 7.20 = next lower end point
7.20 + 0.20 = 7.40 = next lower end point

Therefore, the first class (or bar on the histogram) would be 7 and would include all data points up to but not including 7.20. The next class would begin at 7.20 and include data points up to but not including 7.40. The third class would begin at 7.40 and stop just before data point 7.60, and so on. Keep adding the class width to the lowest class boundary until you obtain the correct number of classes containing the range of all your data points.

This process makes each class mutually exclusive – each data point fits into one and only one class (or bar) – and gives you an accurate histogram.

6. Construct a *frequency table* based on the number of classes, class width and class boundary, calculated above. This is actually a histogram in tabular form.

7. Construct a histogram based on the frequency table, as shown in Figure 19.21.

Use the histogram to diagnose variations and problems in a system. In the example shown in Figure 19.21, the data centres on 7.80 to 7.99, which is close to a normal curve. If the specification for the temperature were 5.5 to 8.5 with a target of 7, the histogram would show that the process was

Class	Class boundaries	Mid-point	Frequency (number of data points falling into this class)	Total
1	7.00–7.19	7.1	I	1
2	7.20–7.39	7.3	HH IIII	9
3	7.40–7.59	7.5	HH HH HH II	17
4	7.60–7.79	7.7	HH HH HH HH HH II	27
5	7.80–7.99	7.9	HH HH HH HH HH HH I	31
6	8.00–8.19	8.1	HH HH HH HH I	21
7	8.20–8.39	8.3	HH HH II	12
8	8.40–8.59	8.5	III	3
9	8.60–8.79	8.7	IIII	4
10	8.80–8.99	8.9		0

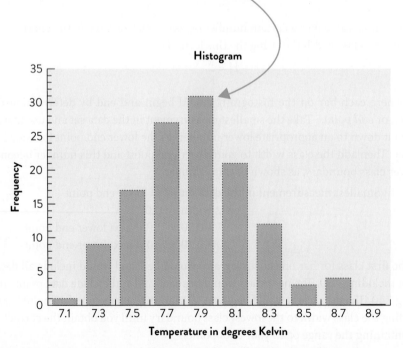

Data collated and prepared by L Ninio, based on thermostat readings. Date: 2 December 2016. Location: Main factory

FIGURE 19.21 Constructing a histogram from a frequency table

running high and producing too much unacceptable product. If, on the other hand, the temperature specification were 7 to 9 with a target of 8, the process would be in control.

When studying histograms, remember that some processes are naturally skewed – not all follow a natural bell-shaped curve. When a class suddenly stops at one point without a previous decline in number, check your data for accuracy; someone may have made a mistake. When a histogram shows two high points, check whether two or more sources provided the data; if so, go back and get homogeneous data.

Process capability charts

A system may be 'in control', but that doesn't mean it meets your needs; it only means it is consistent – it may be consistently bad. This is where process capability charts come in. They show you whether a process, given its natural variation (as established by control charts), is capable of meeting the specifications.

You can also use process capability charts to monitor a system and check that your improvements are working. Capable systems meet customer requirements every time because they are 'in control' and the controls match the specifications.

As Figure 19.22 shows, capability charts show graphically whether or not your system is meeting requirements by illustrating the distribution of your process in relation to its specification limits.

A *process capability index* is calculated from the upper and lower specification limits, the measured natural variation in the process and the standard deviation in the process. When the process variation exceeds the specification, you know that there are too many defects or that services are not being provided satisfactorily. Even when the process variation is within specification, defects could still occur if the process is not centred on the specified target.

Scatter diagrams

Does overtime affect quality? Does training improve results? Does placing an advertisement on the right-hand side of a page affect sales? Does reducing the temperature in a process affect a product's quality?

To know for sure, construct a scatter diagram. This reveals any relationships between one variable and another and possible cause-and-effect relationships. Scatter diagrams can't prove whether one variable causes another, but they clarify whether a relationship exists and how strong it is. In this way, scatter diagrams help you determine the basic cause(s) of a problem.

The horizontal axis measures one variable and the vertical axis the second variable. Figure 19.23 is a typical scatter diagram showing a positive relationship or correlation between two variables. Notice that the plotted points form a clustered pattern. The direction and tightness of the cluster indicate the strength of the relationship between the two variables. The tighter the cluster and the more it resembles a straight line, the stronger the relationship between the two variables. Figure 19.24 shows other scatter diagrams and how to interpret them.

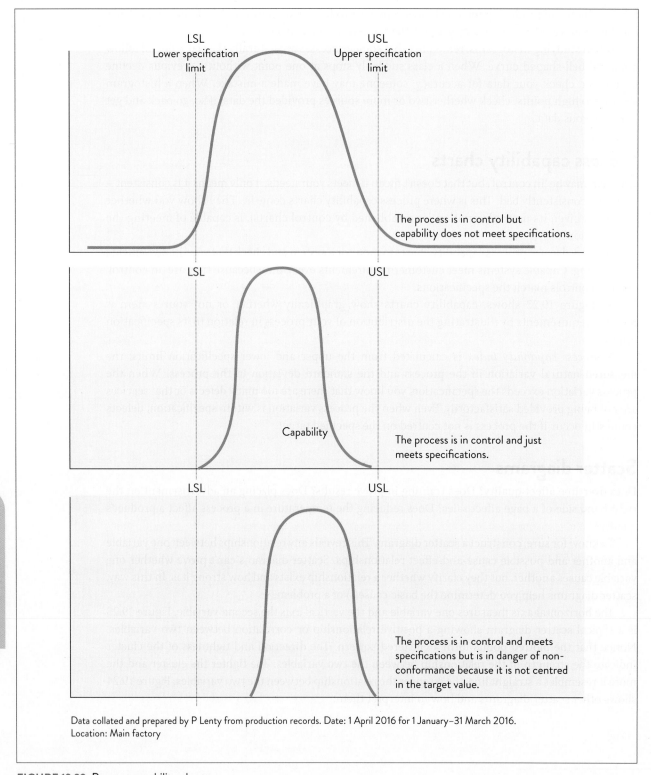

Data collated and prepared by P Lenty from production records. Date: 1 April 2016 for 1 January–31 March 2016.
Location: Main factory

FIGURE 19.22 Process capability charts

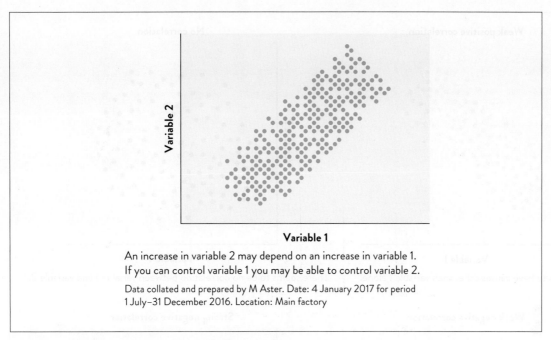

An increase in variable 2 may depend on an increase in variable 1.
If you can control variable 1 you may be able to control variable 2.

Data collated and prepared by M Aster. Date: 4 January 2017 for period
1 July–31 December 2016. Location: Main factory

FIGURE 19.23 Scatter diagram: Strong positive correlation

Here are the steps for making a scatter diagram (persons 4–49 have been omitted here for space reasons but you would fill them in on your diagram):

1. Collect 1 to 50 paired samples of data that you think may be related and construct a data sheet as shown in the example below (persons …

Person	Weight	Height
	kg	*cm*
1.	73	178
2.	65	155
3.	100	191
…		
…		
…		
50.	82	155

2. Draw the horizontal and vertical axes of the scatter diagram, with the values increasing as you move up on the vertical axis and to the right on the horizontal axis. Put the variable you are investigating as the possible 'cause' on the horizontal axis and the effect variable on the vertical axis.

Remember that negative relationships are as important as positive relationships, and that scatter diagrams show only relationships – they do not prove cause and effect.

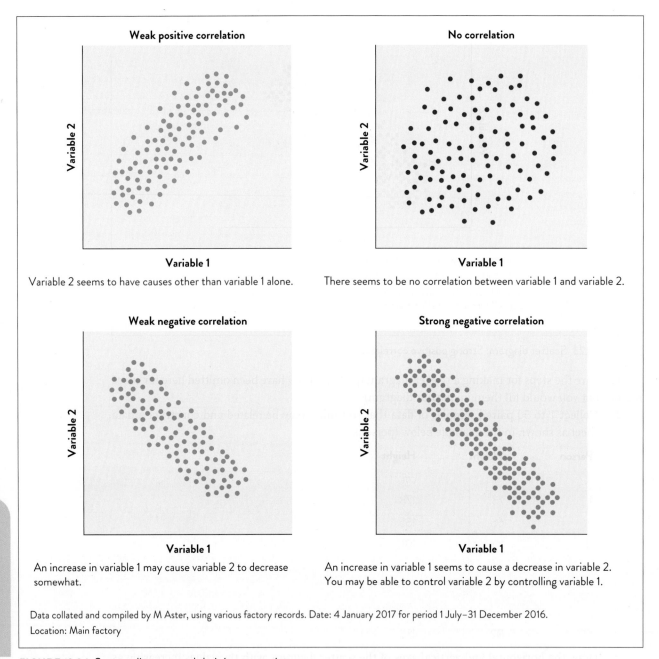

FIGURE 19.24 Scatter diagrams and their interpretations

CourseMateExpress

Go to http://login.cengagebrain.com to access CourseMate Express, your online study tool for *Management Theory & Practice*. CourseMate Express brings chapter concepts to life with interactive learning, and study and exam preparation tools:

- Test your skills in different aspects of management with interactive self-tests and simulations.
- Watch videos that show how real managers operate in real businesses.
- Test your understanding of the changing world of management by taking the revision quiz.

QUICK REVIEW

1. Briefly explain the following principles and how they help organisations provide quality products and services:
   a   examining and streamlining systems and practices
   b   forming teams and involving people at all levels to identify and solve problems and make continuous improvements to work systems
   c   monitoring quality and performance and comparing it with other organisations' or departments' quality and performance levels
   d   using solid statistical information to examine problems and measure performance
   e   working with your internal and external customers and suppliers to develop better ways of meeting customers' needs.
2. Explain the differences between breakthrough and incremental improvements and give an example of each from your own experience.
3. Explain how you can increase your own creativity and the creativity of your team.
4 Explain three easy techniques that take little training or time commitment and that team leaders can use to continuously improve the performance of their work teams and individual team members.
5. Explain how systematic analytical tools and techniques can help you identify, analyse and rectify problems and make the most of opportunities.

BUILD YOUR SKILLS

1. 'People are an essential element of quality and service.' Do you agree? Why or why not? What else do you believe is essential to providing a quality product or service?
2. Consider three examples of products you think are high quality at three price points: low, medium and high; why are they good quality? Consider three examples of high quality service; what makes them high quality? How does quality relate to price? Does high quality mean higher prices?
3. What are the last three improvements you have made to the way you do things, in either your private or working life?
4. What do you believe are the important ingredients of creativity and innovation? Brilliance? Luck? Perseverance? Using creativity techniques? Or other conditions and qualities? How much do you think organisation culture contributes to an employee's innovativeness?

5. Use an after-action review to analyse something you have recently done at work or in your studies; for example, preparing and delivering a presentation, studying for an exam, or researching and writing a report. Summarise your conclusions.

6. Data is made up of numbers. Some data is useful; some isn't. What are some ways you can ensure that the data you collect is useful?

7. Referring to Case Study 9.2 on page 284, discuss how this team's group dynamics, the way it is led and managed and the types of meetings held contribute to quality assurance, innovation and continuous improvement and support a quality culture.

WORKPLACE ACTIVITIES

1. What quality systems do you have at your workplace? How do they help you to reliably provide a quality product or service?

2. How does the culture of your work team and your workplace correspond to the quality culture described in this chapter?

3. Why do quality standards matter? Investigate and report on the Australian or international quality standards currently used in your organisation.

4. How is quality monitored at your workplace? Discuss this in relation to how quality monitoring has changed over the years.

CASE STUDY 19.1

LEAN BELIEVERS

Like most metropolitan hospitals across the country, Flinders Medical Centre (FMC), a public tertiary teaching and research hospital in South Australia, suffered from overcrowding in the Emergency Department (ED), delays in timely treatment and forced cancellations of elective surgery. Ambulances were being diverted, clinical outcomes were being compromised, and staff were unhappy. Despite regular hospital executive crisis meetings, internal and external reviews of safety in the Emergency Department, lots of attempted small fixes and the best efforts of everyone involved, nothing had helped.

FMC then looked internationally for ideas and ended up with a plan: go lean; set up improvement teams, each with a clinical leader and executive sponsor; set targets; reorganise the ED and set up a cross-functional Redesigning Care Team to oversee the process. This was followed by some fairly intensive training, including attending conferences, reading, self-guided learning, teaching each other what they'd learned and visiting manufacturing plants using lean methodologies. Team members kept learning logs and learned a lot by doing over the next two and a half years.

A host of improvements followed in all areas of the hospital, from the ED, to admissions, pharmacy, and central sterilising. Nearly everything that didn't move had the five Ss applied to it, workflows and patient flows were redesigned and systems developed to smooth patient flows and improve discharge procedures.

Written communications, team meetings and special meetings kept everyone up to date with progress and ongoing joint improvement team meetings ensured a consistent approach to problem solving and other methodologies.

Despite increasing numbers coming to the ED, waiting time has dropped, fewer elective surgeries need to be cancelled, and the number of ED patients seen within the recommended time has improved for all three triage categories.

Naturally, there were challenges, deciding what to work on and when to stop working on something, bringing cynics on board and embedding improvements to make them 'stick' among them. From their struggles and successes, FMC has learned a lot about the importance of:

- executive support
- an improvement team structure with the right people and tools and enough time to take on projects that would make an impact
- learning as you go
- targets
- early 'wins' and going for big impacts.

Lean has helped FMC tackle some tough challenges and become a safer, more quality and customer focused hospital.[62]

Questions

1. Explain why each of the lessons FMC has learned from its lean efforts are important; how do they translate to your organisation?
2. Develop an action plan for bringing cynics on side.
3. What specific tools and techniques would you use if you were assisting FMC's quality teams?

CASE STUDY 19.2

FEWER PROBLEMS, HAPPIER CUSTOMERS

With 14 400 employees in 30 countries and sales of US$4.2 billion, Fujitsu Services is one of the largest providers of IT services in Africa, Europe and the Middle East. When other companies began outsourcing their customer services and internal technical support, Fujitsu put its hand up. After all, its help desks had been successfully servicing its own customers and providing technical support for its own products for many years.

Companies generally pay outsourcers per complaint handled. This business model gives no incentive to reduce the number of complaints received and even discourages effective complaint resolution since fewer complaints mean lower revenue. Fujitsu approached the problem differently. It decided to eliminate the causes of the customers' complaints. This meant that instead of being paid for each call handled, it could bid for the business with a set fee based on the number of potential callers to the help desk – less than the current outsourcer's bid, yet still profitable for Fujitsu.

When Fujitsu took over the internal help desk contract for British airline BMI, it immediately analysed the types of calls coming in from BMI employees and examined the problems that gave rise to the calls. Then it tracked the time and effort required to fix them, and measured the impact on the client's business of failures or delays in fixing the problems.

More than half the calls were repeat complaints about recurring problems or repair delays. One of the most common reasons for calls – 26% of the total – was malfunctioning printers: check-in staff couldn't print boarding passes and baggage tags for passengers.

Clearly, solving the printer problem was critical to the airline's business as it could cause flights to miss their take-off slots.

While BMI's previous contractor approached the problem by trying to get service technicians to respond more quickly, Fujitsu looked for the most cost-effective way to keep the printers working properly. The option it chose was to convince BMI senior managers to spend money up-front on better quality printers. It worked: the number of calls about faulty printers dropped 80% in 18 months, resulting in major savings in flight operations that far exceeded the cost of the new printers; a happy customer. It also allowed the technician response time to fix printers that still failed to drop from 10 hours to three – a happy customer again. Continuing to identify and rectify the causes of the callers' problems, Fujitsu went on to reduce the total number of calls to the help desk by 40% within 18 months. A very happy customer.

Fujitsu applied the same approach to its other customers that awarded it help desk contracts, analysing and optimising their IT response systems and delivering far beyond their customers' expectations.

Fujitsu doesn't stop at fixing defects, giving its customers only what it promises; it also goes a step further to create additional value by offering information about potential problems the customer hasn't experienced yet but will, if not forewarned. More happy customers.

And the benefits flow both ways. While Fujitsu staff are working with customers to prevent current and potential problems, they learn about what problems the customers are trying to solve with their systems, which can lead to ideas for new products. The process builds customer loyalty and Fujitsu gains market intelligence and saves money by reducing calls to the help desks it is contracted to run. Fujitsu customers are so happy they give the company even more business.[63]

Questions

1. What tools and techniques would Fujitsu have used, and in what order, to determine which caller problems to work on first and how to resolve those problems? Refer to the problem-solving steps explained in Chapter 18 if you need to.
2. The way Fujitsu approached the help desk function was an innovation in itself, requiring a different mindset from other help desk outsourcers and resulting in delighted customers. Which of the four ways to improve organisations discussed in this chapter did Fujitsu take?
3. This case study is an example of trading partnerships. What element does trust play in the process?

CHAPTER

20

CARING FOR CUSTOMERS

OVERVIEW

Customers can't hold service in their hands and it has no shelf life. It is only as good as each customer perceives it to be right now. When a customer thinks you've done a bad job, you can't take it back – you can only try to make up for it. Customer service may be fleeting and insubstantial, but it can make or break an organisation.

Today's customers are more demanding than ever before. They're better informed and more knowledgeable. Customers have a choice and they know it; and when they don't get what they want, they are prepared to exercise their choice – with their feet, their tweets, on Facebook, their holiday and restaurant reviews, and so on. Customer service, once a 'nice add-on', is now mandatory.

Australia has moved from a supply-led service economy to a demand-led service economy and over 87% of Australians are now employed in service industries.[1] This makes organisations vulnerable in another way: although they set the standards, they depend on each employee and each contractor, every day, to meet those standards. Every day, in every organisation, there are tens of thousands of individual points at which customer service can break down.

1. Can you say precisely who your customers are, what determines what you offer them and why providing what they want pays off?
2. Are you able to identify what your customers want from you and provide it?
3. Can you manage your relationships with your customers effectively?
4. Do you know how to resolve customer difficulties and complaints in a way that maintains and even improves your relationship with the customer?

This chapter explains how to find out who your customers are, what your customers want and how to provide it in a way that delights them enough that they keep coming back – even when there are occasional hiccups.

SCENARIO

The local newsagency

Laura runs a small business from her home and was in the habit of popping into the newsagency in a near-by Adelaide Hills village at least once a week. It stocked a large range of office supplies and was well laid out and clean. Most weeks, her purchases ranged from $8 to $20.

Despite the fact that she was in there so frequently, the owner never appeared to recognise her. However, the owner was always business-like and efficient and always gave the correct change. Laura didn't particularly enjoy going there but there was no other newsagency close to home.

Then that changed. Another stationery newsagency opened in her own village, just two minutes from her home, so Laura called in the next time she needed stationery supplies. The woman greeted her and introduced herself as Chris, asking whether she could help Laura find anything in particular. 'No thanks, I'll just have a look around first,' Laura replied.

Laura concluded that, although the shop wasn't quite as well stocked as the other newsagency, it could adequately supply her stationery needs. She paid for what she wanted and thanked Chris, who cheerfully said, 'Thanks. See you next time!'

Laura now purchases all her stationery items from the new shop. She enjoys going in there and having a quick chat with Chris while she browses and picks up supplies. Laura's weekly spending is now between $12 and $27.

1. Reaping the rewards of caring for your customers

Take care of the customers and the profits will take care of themselves.

Soichiro Honda (founder, Honda Motor Company) in S Caulkin, 'Why winners stand to lose', *The Guardian* (4 March 2001)[2]

When you're serious about caring for your customers, you think of customer service as your business and the business of your team. This means taking four actions:

1. finding out who your customers are and what they expect from you
2. identifying and communicating precisely how to meet their needs and wants
3. making sure your work team's procedures and culture support the desired behaviours and service levels
4. using relevant, reliable and verifiable information and data, and systematic analytical tools and techniques, to measure and analyse the level of service customers actually receive, and seek to continually improve it.

This chapter examines the first three points above, and Section 4 of Chapter 19: 'Using systematic analytical tools and techniques', beginning on page 585, explains how to use verifiable evidence and customer feedback to monitor and continually improve the quality of the products or services you provide.

⊙ THE STRATEGIC PERSPECTIVE

Why customer service is critical

From the 1930s to the 1970s, *managerial capitalism*, the thinking that professional managers ought to run organisations, ruled the roost. Then *shareholder-value capitalism*, the idea that maximising profits and thus shareholder value, became the leading priority of most organisations. Evidence suggests, though, that making customers the leading priority makes organisations even

>>

more money. Are we entering a third era: *customer-driven capitalism*, an idea already adopted (very profitably) by companies such as Johnson & Johnson and Procter & Gamble, who both put customers ahead of shareholders in their mission statements?

In fact, shareholders benefited more under managerial capitalism, when compound annual real returns of the S&P, Standard and Poor's corporate rating index, were 7.6% a year. Under shareholder capitalism, they fell to 5.9%. Why? Perhaps because stock prices are driven by shareholder's expectations of growth, which can't be fed forever under shareholder capitalism.[3]

Customer-driven capitalism, though, can feed growth expectations. But that doesn't mean offering unprofitable goods and services. It means adjusting priorities. Procter & Gamble's Purpose states: 'We will provide branded products and services of superior quality and value that improve the lives of the world's consumers, now and for generations to come. As a result, consumers will reward us with leadership sales, profit and value creation, allowing our people, our shareholders and the communities in which we live and work, to prosper.'[4]

For companies like these, shareholder value is a by-product of their primary focus on customer satisfaction, not their top priority. Perhaps Peter Drucker was, once again, 'on the money' when he observed that the primary purpose of a business is to acquire and keep customers.[5]

This doesn't just apply to the private sector. Hospitals heal patients, colleges and schools teach students. When these organisations can't do that, they cease to exist. How organisations go about satisfying their customers is what separates failed organisations, surviving organisations and thriving organisations.

Who are your customers?

Shops and hotels have customers. Who else has customers? Does a mailroom assistant have customers? An orderly in a hospital? A trash collector? A volunteer for a charity? Do HR and IT teams have customers? What about finance and purchasing departments, or public servants – say, employees of the Tax Office or Centrelink?

Everyone has customers. Whatever sector they work in, whether they work directly with customers or behind the scenes, every employee has customers and every department has customers. Jan Carlzon, former CEO of Scandinavian Airline Associates, put it like this, 'If you're not serving a customer directly, you'd better be serving someone who is.'[6]

There are two kinds of customers in organisations:

1. External customers: Customers outside the organisation who purchase or use its products or services.
2. Internal customers: Customers inside the organisation who use or benefit from the work of other employees.

● THE STRATEGIC PERSPECTIVE

Know your primary customer

Customer is a loose term. You might think that a pharmaceutical company's customers are the people who purchase their drugs. But their most important customers are the medical doctors who prescribe them. Who are the customers of packaged consumer goods – the end users who purchase them? The stores who buy them? The purchasing departments of those stores?

>>

They're all customers. But when you don't know who your main customer group is, you can put your efforts into the wrong customer – at the expense of your most important customer. Your primary customer may not be the group that provides the most revenue but the group that unlocks the most value in your business. The more than 300 million individual users of LinkedIn don't provide any revenue but they make the network attractive to LinkedIn's revenue providers – recruiters, who provide 54% of LinkedIn's revenue, and advertisers, who provide 26%. That makes individual users LinkedIn's value creators and its primary customer group.[7]

Here are five quick and easy ways to improve your customer service:

1. Ask your customers: Their ideas aren't necessarily all great, but some of them will be very worthwhile.
2. Observe your customers: Iconic US jeans maker Levi Strauss saw customers ripping their jeans and brought out a line of ready-ripped jeans.
3. Analyse complaints: Use a check sheet or other quality improvement tool (explained on page 589) to find what customers can be bothered to complain about most and remove the cause of those complaints.
4. Eliminate: Eliminate the services and items that add no value or too little value for too few customers.
5. Ask your team: They're probably closer to customers and to ways to improve service by removing the hassles and bottlenecks (see page 339).

External customers

External customers may be individual customers, such as the shopper who purchases a box of cornflakes. Or they may be the organisations you supply, such as the supermarket chain that purchases the cornflakes in bulk or in pallets of pre-packaged retail boxes.

Both types of customer have a choice about where to spend their money. As summarised in Figure 20.1, you can think about, and deal with, your customers in the traditional way, or in the customer-focused way. Sam Walton who founded the US Walmart chain, said, 'There is only one boss. The customer. And he can fire everybody in the company, from the chairman on down, simply by spending his money somewhere else.'[8]

◉ THEORY TO PRACTICE

The customer is king – but only the right customer
Every month, the Royal Bank of Canada calculates the economic benefits and profitability of each of its 15 million customers. Knowing which customers are making money tells the bank who to target to become customers.[9]

This illustrates an important principle: Don't waste time and money pursuing and keeping unprofitable customers. Concentrate on the customers and market segments that can generate a good return on investment and treat them so well that they would never consider going elsewhere.

What are they worth?

Some customers are very profitable, some are moderately profitable, some are marginal and some cost you money. The lifetime value of existing and future customers is known as *lifetime customer value* (LCV). Calculating the sum of the value of the current and future customers of a business is one way to assess the business's value; many people believe that it is the only possible way to value many new Internet and e-commerce businesses. It is also a key success measure in many businesses in high-growth sectors as well as in more traditional industries.

LCV is important because it costs money to win a customer. It costs 1000 direct mailings to win one new customer and, on average, the cost of winning new customers is five times greater than the cost of retaining existing customers.[10] Since repeat business is free, you can think of happy customers who are 'regulars' as 'money in the bank'. Not for nothing do people say we should see our customers as appreciating assets, and appreciate those assets.

  FYI

What is success?

Judge your success using Table 20.1 which shows traditional versus customer-focused values:

TABLE 20.1 **The way to success**

Success	The traditional way	The customer-focused way
Value determined by	Balance sheet	Profitability of customer relationships
Success measured by	Market share	Lifetime value of customers
Keys to success	Mass marketing and production	Mass personalisation and customisation
Driving force	Production: We sell what we make	Customers: We provide customers with what they want
Business improvements	Through investment in plant and equipment	Through investment in customer knowledge and relationships

Here is a simple way to calculate LCV. Take the average purchase value of your average customer per week (or month). Multiply this by 48 (weeks) or 11 (months) to allow for holidays. Multiply this by the number of years you normally retain a customer. The answer gives you their lifetime value.

There are four ways to increase the lifetime value of your customers:
1. Extend the range of goods and services they buy from you.
2. Retain their business longer.
3. Sell them more expensive items than they are currently buying.
4. Sell them more of what they're already buying from you.

THEORY TO PRACTICE

Now that's service!

Kath was posted to Japan for two years. One of the first items she bought there was an answering machine for her apartment. A pleasant sales assistant from the department store helped her select the machine and explained how to set it up.

A few days later, the sales assistant telephoned Kath to make sure she had been able to install it correctly. 'I don't know. I think so. I haven't been out since I bought it, so I haven't tested it. I've had the most terrible cold ...'

>>

Later that afternoon, the sales assistant appeared on Kath's doorstep with apples, chocolates, cornflakes, milk and flowers. 'I thought since you haven't been out you might need some food and I brought some flowers to cheer you up.'

Guess where Kath shopped for the rest of her two years in Japan? Fortunately, it's just as easy to please customers as to annoy them.

Internal customers

External customers 'pay the rent', but internal customers help you collect it. They are your service partners, the employees and contractors who are part of the customer–supplier chain that makes and supplies the goods and services your organisation offers.

Seeing an organisation as a network of interdependent people, teams and departments working together to provide a quality service or product opens up the communication channels and develops a customer service culture. It builds bridges between design and manufacturing, administration, finance, purchasing and marketing, and integrates them into one mutually supporting chain, each playing an important part in adding value to the product or service.

In organisations with a customer service culture, departments don't battle with each other – they are partners. Production is a customer of purchasing, administration is a supplier to marketing, and so on. In this way, the entire organisation becomes a customer–supplier chain. Every department and every employee works together to satisfy the customer.

THE STRATEGIC PERSPECTIVE

Silos or bridges?

In many organisations, departments seem to operate in a vacuum. The left hand doesn't know what the right hand is doing:

- 'What! You needed this urgently? No one told me!'
- 'The salespeople keep sending in orders requiring uneconomic production runs. We just save them up until there's enough to make a run worthwhile.'
- 'How can I meet my deadlines when people don't give me the right information?'

Marketing seems to fight with production and production blames purchasing and supply for its problems. Sales battles with distribution. Departments operating in isolation, like separate silos, disrupt work, divert energy and efforts away from the real problems, and do nothing to satisfy customers. When departments work together and concentrate on what their customers expect, it's much easier to provide quality.

To forge strong customer–supplier chains, you need to know who your service partners are. To find them, ask yourself:

- What do I produce?
- Who receives it?
- If I didn't do my job or didn't do it well, who would be affected?
- Who depends on my work or information to do their job well?

These are your internal customers.

Next, ask yourself whose work or information you and your department depend on to do your jobs well. These are your internal suppliers.

Meet with these service partners to find out how you can work together more effectively and efficiently to provide a quality service or product that the customer needs and wants. Discuss what you're doing well and what you could improve. Listen to each other's insights and suggestions. Keep looking for ways to provide an ever-improving product or service.

FYI

Customer service charters

Many organisations have a customer service charter, which states who the organisation considers its customers to be and explains how it intends to serve them. Many charters even state what customers can expect from the organisation when they contact it by email, post or telephone or visit it in person, and explain how customers can offer the organisation feedback.

Check out these websites to see some customer service charters:

- Australian Red Cross' customer charter at http://www.redcross.org.au > Client service charter
- Australia Post's customer service charter at http://auspost.com.au > Customer service charter
- Virgin Australia's guest charter at http://www.virginaustralia.com/au/en > Guest charter (Customer service plan)

THEORY TO PRACTICE

Customer service: Above and beyond

At 9.30 pm on 26 November 2008, the first gunshots of terrorists storming the deluxe Taj Mumbai Palace hotel were heard. Examples of employees putting the comfort and security of terrified guests before their own safety abound – extraordinary, yet completely in line with the company culture and giving customer service a whole new meaning.

The Taj group expects employees to delight their guests and put them at the heart of all their actions and decisions. Employees are trained to deal with guests without consulting a leader-manager and encouraged to improvise in the guests' interests rather than 'by the book'. To this end, and based on the thinking that happy employees lead to happy customers, the company provides extensive training and recognition, particularly from direct leader-managers.

In addition, a Special Thanks and Recognition System (STARS) links customer delight to employee rewards. Each of the group's 108 hotels' general managers, HR manager, training manager and the department head concerned review compliments from guests and colleagues, and employee suggestions; they do this daily, showing the company is serious about service. Points are awarded for compliments that reflect exceptional performance and for worthwhile suggestions and are accumulated over 12 months, leading employees to reach one of five performance levels: the managing director's club, the chief operating officer's club, and the platinum, gold and silver levels. Employees who reach the last three levels are rewarded with gift vouchers and STARS lapel pins, shields and trophies. At the Taj Business Excellence Awards ceremony, an annual organisation-wide celebration, employees reaching the managing director's club are presented with crystal trophies, certificates and gift vouchers.

Knowing their contributions are valued and being empowered to put the customer first changes the way employees respond to situations.[11]

From the inside out: The service–profit chain

As summarised in Figure 20.1, providing a service external customers value starts inside the organisation, with satisfying your internal customers. This raises employee satisfaction, which fuels employee loyalty and productivity, which boosts service, which ultimately increases the satisfaction and loyalty of external customers.

The result is profits in the private sector and a fulfilled mission in public and not-for-profit sector organisations. This is known as the service–profit chain.[12]

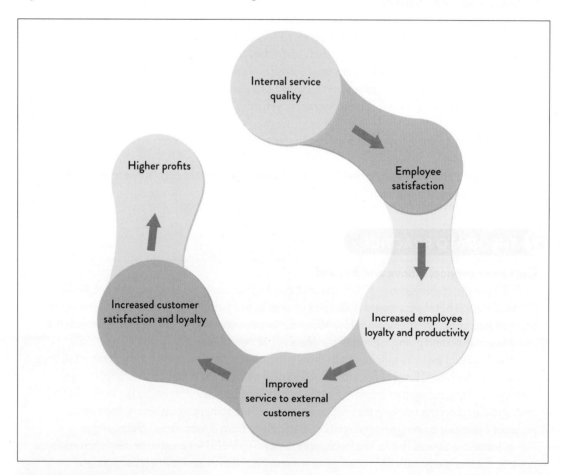

FIGURE 20.1 The service–profit chain

THEORY TO PRACTICE

Best practice leadership lifts results

Researchers from the University of New South Wales, the Australian National University, Macquarie University and the Copenhagen Business School recently studied what drives organisational performance in the service industry. They found that not-so-easy to measure attributes such as fairness, employee engagement, innovation and leadership make a quantifiable difference to profitability and productivity. High-performing workplaces, about 15% of the workplaces studied, were up to 12% more productive and three times more profitable than lower-performing workplaces.

>>

The leadership skills that seemed most important were involving people in decision-making processes, being receptive to and even welcoming criticism and feedback, practising (not just preaching) the organisation's values and having a clear team purpose.[13]

Companies known for their great customer service (as well as for their profitability) consider customer service a key measure of success. They tend to have extensive employee training and treat employees well, rewarding them with incentives, strong career development paths and other benefits.[14]

Satisfied employees satisfy customers

Satisfied customers begin with satisfied employees because customers mirror the satisfaction employees experience. But lest you think that service failures stem from individuals, remember that individual employees need the support of streamlined procedures that build in quality and service and make it automatic (as explained on page 102). They need a customer service team culture, training and a working environment that enables and encourages them to provide superior service to their internal customers.

So when customer satisfaction – external or internal – is lower than it could be, don't simply assume that employees are intentionally doing a poor job.

Examine the working environment to see whether it allows or even encourages poor quality or poor service by making it easy to make mistakes, or makes it easier to let quality and service standards slide than to maintain them. Include satisfying or delighting your customers in your team purpose and make sure everyone understands what that means. Recruit the right people – people who will 'do it right' even when no one is looking, people whose skills, abilities and drives are suited to their jobs and whose jobs can engage their loyalty and passion (this is explained on pages 287, 334 and 807).

Customer-driven, product-driven or cost-driven?

Identifying precisely who your customers are and exactly what they want from you, and working with your service partners to provide it, means you're *customer-driven*. Placing a high priority on identifying and meeting the needs of your external customers often requires a change in approach from the more traditional *product-driven* thinking which says, in effect, 'This is what we can produce. Do you want it or not?'

A product-driven organisation produces goods or services and then finds customers who want to buy them. It might say, 'We make cornflakes and we sell them in 500 gram retail packets supplied in pallets of 24 packs. Too bad if you want to buy 100 gram packets. We don't make them.'

In contrast, a customer-driven organisation would say, 'Did you say you'd like to buy our cornflakes in 100 gram retail packets? Let me find out how soon we can adjust our manufacturing process to accommodate you.'

Customer-driven organisations are also different from *cost-driven* organisations, which concentrate mainly on reducing the costs involved in producing a product or service. 'Beat our competitors on cost' is their motto. A cost-driven organisation would say something like, 'Sorry, we can't do 100 gram packets. It would be too expensive to install the machinery.'

Until about 2000, internal cost-cutting was a good move. But once everyone started doing it, another competitive advantage was needed and it's this: working with your customers to give them exactly what they want and to add significant value to their business. This requires considerable innovation, optimising supply chain costs and efficiencies by, for example, joining some operations and sharing proprietary data with your external customers and suppliers (as discussed on page 560), and flexible manufacturing and/or service provision – something low-cost producers in emerging countries can't easily do.

Whether your customers are internal or external, here are the four steps to becoming a customer-driven work team:

1. Identify your customers, listen to them and make meeting or exceeding their needs and wants your primary goal.
2. Develop work procedures that reliably satisfy your customers.
3. Build a culture that focuses team members on their customers and on providing what they want.
4. Use customer-friendly systems to build strong relationships with your service partners.

ACTION!

How solidly does your work team focus on your customers? Find out with the interactive self-test: How customer-driven is your team? on *CourseMateExpress and there's also a question template called Do you really know your customers' needs?

THE STRATEGIC PERSPECTIVE

Thanks for the memories

It built one of the world's first digital cameras in 1975 and introduced the first camcorder into the US market. Until the 1990s, it was one of the world's leading brands and boasted a 90% market share of the film industry and an 85% share of the camera market. Once the Apple of its day, thanks to its innovativeness, pioneering technology and advanced marketing practices, it filed for bankruptcy in 2012, the victim of its loyalty to its superseded technology. Who is it? You guessed it – Kodak. Rather than shift its attention, vision and resources to the up-and-coming digital imaging, it remained loyal to film.

Like the product-focused railroads that thought they were in the railroad business rather than the transportation business, product-focused Kodak thought it was in the film business rather than the business of capturing and sharing memories.

Contrast this with the specialty ceramics and glass manufacturer, Corning, established in 1851. Half of its revenues in 1908 came from making glass bulbs. Today, it works with customers to create, innovate and manufacture high-technology systems for consumer electronics, mobile emissions control, telecommunications and life sciences – products that didn't exist 10 years ago and which now account for most of its earnings.[15]

The lesson? Being customer-driven and innovative leads to longevity and success.

THEORY TO PRACTICE

Serving your customer's needs

Reasoning that construction companies care more about the productivity they can achieve from using tools than about owning them, Hilti, the Liechtenstein-based maker of high-end power tools, introduced a fleet management program. Construction companies, their main customer group, pay Hilti a monthly fee. In return, Hilti manages customers' vehicle fleets to suit each customer's business model and provides, services and repairs all tools. Hilti's slogan is: 'We manage your tools, so you can manage your business.'

This simplifies their customers' financial planning and reduces their administrative work and downtime. Customers also appreciate using high-quality tools.[16]

2. Meeting customer needs

Being good in business is the most fascinating kind of art.

Andy Warhol (pop artist), *Andy Warhol* (2001)[17]

Government agencies and employees need to know who their customers are and what they want, and then develop services and other ways to meet their needs. So do not-for-profit service providers, retailers, and suppliers of utilities and commercial goods and services. Even sports teams, orchestras and colleges need to identify and meet the needs of their various customer groups. And they all need to find a better way to do this than their competition and to keep improving their offerings.

The only reliable way to match your products or services to your customers' needs is to work with your customers to provide what is important to them. The process is similar to the problem-solving and decision-making process summarised in Figure 18.2: Exploring and understanding, searching for solutions, evaluating and agreeing on page 527. In fact, the more complex and sophisticated your offering, the more closely you should follow the seven steps described on those pages. When your offering is complex and sophisticated, you may need to work through several options with your customers and assist them to evaluate which best meets their needs.

⊙ THEORY TO PRACTICE

Customising to meet customer needs
Providing small-run, customised products that enhance your customers' businesses is another way to endear your company to its customers. BuS Elektronik in Germany custom-designs and makes small-and medium-sized electronic components and systems and their customers pay a premium for them. They give BuS free reign in designing products for them, knowing the solutions will simplify their complex assembly process and reduce labour inputs.[18]

In all your dealings with customers, remain aware of and uphold your *customers' rights.* For example, their right to be told the truth, to be provided with a service or product that does the job you present it as doing and their right to confidentiality of information.

⊙ IN A NUTSHELL

Dr Deming's message on total quality
Quality analyst Dr William Edwards Deming believed the following would lead to success:
* Find out about your customers and what they want.
* Study and improve your products and services until they cannot be beaten.
* Involve everyone throughout the organisation, at all levels and in all disciplines.[19]

Identify customer needs

Here are some questions that you and your team members can ask each other.
* Are we doing anything for our customers they'd rather we didn't or that they find irrelevant or unnecessary?
* Are we not doing anything for our customers that they wish we would?

- Do our internal and external suppliers provide us with what we need in the way we need it? What could they do better?
- How does the way we operate make it difficult/easy to work or do business with us?
- How well do we currently satisfy our customers in the areas they care about most?
- What are we doing that makes our customers' lives easier? Are we making their lives harder in any way?
- What can we learn from what the best companies are doing to delight their customers?
- What do our customers care about most? How do we know?
- What do our customers want from us? How do we know?
- What opportunities do we have to delight our customers? Are we making the most of them? Are we missing any opportunities?
- Who are our most important customers? Why? How do we know this?
- Who else benefits from our efforts? Who else uses the services or products we provide?
- Who exactly are our customers?
- Why does our department/team exist?

Have you heard about the large international airline that asked its staff to identify the 10 main needs of its customers?[20] When they compared their answers with a survey asking customers what they needed, they found that the staff had six out of the 10 top customer needs wrong. That tells us two important things:

1. It's easy to make assumptions, to see what you want or expect to see. You and your team may think you know what your customers want, but you never know for sure unless you ask them.
2. You could waste your time, energy and resources 'satisfying' customer needs that aren't important to them and alienate customers by ignoring needs that are important.

● ACTION!

Find the template Do you *really* know your customers' needs? on ⚡CourseMateExpress. You can use it to kick off your thinking about your customers really want. Listen for your team's perspectives and ideas.

● THE STRATEGIC PERSPECTIVE

Partnering pays

Two European companies imbed valuable information into their offerings that only they can provide, binding them more closely to their customers and giving them the edge over cost-driven producers.

Schmitz Cargobull, a German truck body and trailer maker, supplies its customers with a range of support services including telematics (sophisticated information technology) that track and transmit key information of any Schmitz Cargobull-produced trailer. Customers, drivers and freight agents can track, in real time, the location of a trailer, its maintenance history, the temperature of its cargo, and the weight it is carrying. The information also helps reduce the risk of breakdowns.

Thanks to the telematics and working closely with its customers, over three years, the production pace needed to meet customer demand dropped 90%, from 120 to 12 minutes. Its internal failure rate fell 91%, from 35 to 3 per semitrailer; and accidents with its trailers dropped 95%, from 85 to 5 per annum.

>>

In the oil and gas industry, fluctuating temperatures in pipelines cost money. It damages pipes, making the flow of oil more variable and reducing drilling efficiency, for example. By producing intelligent pipelines that monitor and level out temperatures throughout the pipeline, the subsea division of French company Technip increased its revenues by 35% in one year and had operating margins 50% higher than for the company overall.[21]

Ask the customer

Nestlé has a 'war room' where analysts monitor social media to find clues about consumer acceptance and use of its products. Some companies hold annual or biannual 'summits' where they host a sample of their customers and pick their brains for ways to better meet their needs. Other organisations run focus groups, where customers discuss their offerings.

Google analytics (big data) teams spend hours in their labs analysing customers' eye movements and other variables to assess their reactions to tiny changes in their products (display, maps, searches, and so on). It beta tested Gmail on more than 1000 technology opinion leaders for five years before its release. AGL, Australia Post, the Commonwealth Bank, Wesfarmers and Woolworths all process big data for customer analytics, marketing strategies, risk management, audit reports and supply-chain management.[22]

Less formally, you can simply ask your customers what they expect:

- Do you feel free to discuss your needs with us and do we listen to you enough?
- Do you find us easy, helpful and pleasant to work with?
- How would you describe the way we work with you?
- What value do we add to your part of the business?
- What would you like us to do more of? Less of? To keep doing as we're doing it?
  Listen for three important areas of information in your customers' answers:
- What they must have (their *needs*).
- What they would like to have (their *wants).*
- What would really thrill them (*delighters*).

● IN A NUTSHELL

Needs, wants and delighters

A *need* is what your customers require. A *want* is what your customers desire. A *delighter* goes surprisingly and wonderfully beyond your customers' wants, so much so that they'll probably tell others about it. Delighters multiply your customers' loyalty and goodwill towards your department, your organisation and their individual service providers.

When was the last time you sat down with one or more of your customers and discussed what they expect, want and need from you? Don't assume you know the answers. What they expected, needed and wanted last year or six months ago may have changed.

Ask and keep asking until you are certain that you fully understand their expectations. Keep records to highlight any changes or trends in your customers' expectations, preferences and satisfaction levels. The better you know your customers, the better you can serve and delight them.

What specific quality measures can you apply to your customers' needs? What time and cost specifications do you need to meet? When your customers' expectations are extensive, can you rank them in priority order? Of the possible ways you could provide the product or service that your customers want, which way would suit them best?

● THEORY TO PRACTICE

Not listening to customers causes epic crash

Do you remember Friendster, a pioneering social network site launched in 2002? It had thousands of customers and Google offered to buy it in 2003 for US$30 million – even though it was difficult to create groups of friends. Then one day, a Friendster worked out that creating a fictitious person with a name such as Adelaide High School Class of '90, for others to befriend, made it easier for people to connect.

The bosses of Friendster saw what was going on but rather than take the hint that their customers wanted easier ways to connect, they hunted down and destroyed the 'fakesters'. May 2011: End of Friendster. Welcome myspace and Facebook.[23]

Here are three easy ways and one high tech way to 'eavesdrop' on your customers' and check out their needs and wants:

- Call your organisation's customer service or help line: Present a problem and see how it's handled.
- Seek out the 'grass roots': Your organisation's receptionists, regular drivers from car hire firms, repair people, contractors – all sorts of people have insights to your organisation that they've gleaned while doing their jobs.
- Tune into online forums: What are customers and potential customers asking about, complaining about and talking about relating to your products and services? What can you learn about their needs, wants and delighters?
- Analyse big data: Look for patterns and trends in customers' behaviour and purchasing and find out what they're 'talking about' online to meet their needs and delight them.

A technique called value chain analysis is another good way to pinpoint customer needs. Working with your customers, you identify and agree the 'critical few' outcomes that really make a difference to them. Once you've done that, you work with your team to examine how you deliver your service to your customers, step by step, to find opportunities to 'delight' your customers and see where you can make improvements.

Once you know what your customers want, set SMART targets (explained on page 327) to focus you and your team on the right actions. After all, if you can't measure it, you can't manage it; and you can't perform it.

● THEORY TO PRACTICE

A lesson on customer expectations

Con's motto is, 'You grow it, I'll mow it'. With his array of specialised tractors of various sizes and a variety of blades, there isn't much in the way of slashing he can't do. His business has grown entirely by word of mouth, and Con's aim is 'Once a customer, always a customer'. He goes out of his way to delight his customers with small extra touches and total reliability.

Con has two types of customers. His industrial customers contract him for big jobs. For example, the electricity company hires him to slash firebreaks under the power lines: 'It doesn't have to be pretty – just cut.' His other customer base is the domestic, semi-rural property owner who wants several hectares at a time slashed. 'Now that *does* have to be pretty. These people don't just want a firebreak, they want a *nice* firebreak. I always spend extra time with the whipper-snipper and blower to make their places look real nice.'

Con's business quickly grew to the point where he needed to take on help. He hired people who were licensed to drive both the tractors and the heavy goods trucks he transported them on. He was careful to select people with a strong work ethic who enjoyed outdoor work and took pride in looking back on a job well done.

John was his star recruit. 'When he started though, boy, did he cost me money,' said Con. 'His first week with me, he spent an entire day hand weeding between the electricity pylons where the machines wouldn't go! I had to explain to him the difference between what our industrial customers consider a "good job" and what our domestic customers want. No point spending time – and time is money – on things the customers don't care about. Well, we have that sorted out now, I'm glad to say. John is going great guns and he now manages his own crew.'

● THE STRATEGIC PERSPECTIVE

Mind the gap

In the largest ever study of chief executives, *The Enterprise of the Future*, conducted by IBM Global Business Services and the Economist Intelligence Unit, business leaders pointed to their own customer base as being the expected source of most of the important changes they would need to address. They identified two new demanding classes of customers that they expected to invest in most: the information omnivore and the socially minded customer.[24]

A difference of opinion ...

Have you ever heard what Henry Ford said about customer surveys at the new Ford Motor Company he founded in the early 20th century? 'If I'd asked customers what they want, they'd have said a faster horse.'[25]

Can you imagine a situation in which your customers think they need one thing and, based on your experience and knowledge, you believe they actually need another? This happens, particularly when you are more expert than your customers (e.g. health professionals, IT service providers, vendors of complex products and equipment).

Don't automatically think or say, 'No, what you want is too hard, too difficult, too time-consuming, too expensive', or give any other excuse for not doing it. Ask questions to make sure you fully understand what your customer is after. Put yourself in their shoes so that you can see the situation from their point of view.

See your role as finding a way to meet your customer's needs. When this proves extremely difficult, seek the assistance of your manager or other specialised staff in finding a way to provide what the customer requires. When your customer is internal, you can meet with them and redesign the workflow between you to overcome or compensate for the constraints you are facing.

When you think you can suggest a better way of meeting your customer's needs, should you keep it to yourself or should you provide them with what they think they need? When you think your customer's expectations are unrealistic, should you help them adjust their expectations? The answer is usually 'Yes' when you are an expert and your customer acknowledges your greater expertise. Share your knowledge tactfully.

How about when you have a hunch that something could be done more effectively another way? Mention it and offer to investigate or test your theory. When you're not more of an expert or more experienced than your customer, think about mentioning your idea anyway. Someone with a fresh approach who isn't bound by convention can sometimes see things that others can't.

● THE STRATEGIC PERSPECTIVE

Customers – who cares?

Professor Stephen Brown, of the University of Ulster in Northern Ireland, says that, while companies clearly can't survive without customers, we're becoming too 'customer-centric'. Forty years ago, when the first few companies began coddling their customers, it gave them a competitive advantage. Now, everyone is doing it and it no longer differentiates one company from another. Customers, he says, often just want to buy a bar of soap. They don't want to be fawned over, pandered to or enter a lifetime relationship.

Citing products like those of Hermès and BMW's Mini Cooper, Professor Brown says people want what they can't have and don't appreciate what they do have. The issue is how best to attract customers and to do that, he suggests, companies should stop pandering to customers and start treating them mean and keeping them keen.[26]

What do you think?

Keep good records

Employees create quality when they interact with customers, so you need to manage and measure those encounters carefully. That's where good customer records come in.

Records showing customers' payment and purchasing history and other behaviours can provide you with important information about structuring and improving your service offering and highlight important trends and risks to take into account. By capturing other information, such as which customers you lose and comparing it with their customer profiles and behaviours, you can spot ways to improve your service and increase customer retention.

You can profile customers to find out which are the most and least profitable and therefore which potential customers to target. You can use your customer data to benchmark important indicators of your ability to provide good service against all organisations and organisations in your industry and to highlight improvement areas.

Keep track of customer compliments, complaints and problems for later study and analysis. Documenting, for example, the nature of compliments and problems, what led to them, how they were dealt with, how long problems took to resolve and how satisfied the customer was with the solution, can provide valuable information regarding where problems are most likely to occur, isolate opportunities to improve your customer care and point to trends to manage before problems worsen. (Page 585 explains how to capture and display this data in a meaningful way.)

When the same type of problem repeatedly occurs, you can work with your team to fix it at its source so it won't happen again (explained on page 529). Look for areas to make improvements, too (explained on page 565). Look for ways to use customers' comments, complaints and suggestions to spot gaps in your service and add value to the way you serve your customers. (Page 505 explains how to monitor the results of your efforts.)

Analytics, or 'big data', will soon be powering consumer products and services in many companies. Every organisation that makes things, moves things, consumes things or works with customers has increasing amounts of data on these activities. Powerful data-gathering and analysis methods means that organisations can gather and analyse those sets of data to find out more about their customers and markets and use the information to predict the future and prescribe optimal actions and decisions.[27] (For more information on analytics, see page 560.)

● THEORY TO PRACTICE

Keeping the customers satisfied

Based in North Carolina in the US, the SAS Institute is the largest private analytics software company in the world. Customer satisfaction is overwhelmingly positive and software renewals are a loyal 98%.

Listening to its customers is key. The SAS Institute gathers and acts on customer complaints and suggestions through its website and over the telephone and solicits feedback once a year through its web-based SASware Ballot, which asks users about additional features they would like. It collects more feedback at an annual users' conference where salespeople build long-term relationships and learn about their clients' needs.

The company prioritises complaints and comments, passes them on to the appropriate experts and tracks problems and suggestions in a database. Through robust pre-market testing from the developer's viewpoint, a salesperson's viewpoint and a customer's viewpoint, it builds quality into its products by fixing errors before they reach the customer.

Customer satisfaction pays off for the SAS Institute. It enjoyed its 38th straight year of revenue growth and profitability in 2013. Customer loyalty is so high that the company saves money on advertising and other sales efforts, allowing it to channel 24% of its revenue directly to research and development, in an industry where the average R&D expenditure is 10%.[28]

3. Building customer relationships

> I told everyone, 'Be afraid of our customers, because those are the folks who have the money. Our competitors are never going to send us money.'
>
> Jeff Bezos (founder, Amazon) 'Institutional Yes', *Harvard Business Review* (October 2007)[29]

Who would you rather buy from, someone you know, like and trust, or someone you hardly know at all? Who would you rather deal with over the counter, however briefly – someone who seems welcoming and friendly, or someone who seems cold and stand-offish?

People deal with people, and most people want to deal with people with whom they feel some sort of connection or bond. Even when that connection is fleeting, people prefer 'feel-good moments' to those that leave them feeling dissatisfied or uncomfortable.

Whether the goal of service providers is to increase sales by helping customers build their businesses, by offering friendly and appreciated advice, or to provide information or assistance, the more quickly and thoroughly they can establish a professional yet cordial relationship, the better their results. Since the key to the success of many businesses is repeat business from loyal customers and word-of-mouth business based on recommendations from loyal customers, everyone in your team needs to know how to, and want to, establish and build strong customer relationships.

This is particularly important in tough economic times, when the pool of potential customers is smaller, making the cost of winning new business more expensive and increasing sales from existing customers very cost-effective. Economic doldrums aside, as discussed above, attracting new customers is expensive.

IN A NUTSHELL

Opportunities to build customer loyalty

You can take care of your customers *before* you provide the product or service, *while* you are providing it and *after* you have provided it. Each of these three opportunities contains six ways to delight your customers and make them feel special. You can:

1. Communicate clearly and honestly.
2. Develop and maintain trust.
3. Meet or exceed your customers' needs and expectations.
4. Recognise their loyalty by offering a privilege they value.
5. Show that you can help your customers achieve their goals.
6. Show that you understand your customers.

Moments of truth

Have you ever noticed that it's the little things that delight people and build goodwill – or do the opposite: alienate them and create ill will? How do the little things that you and your team do build or damage customer goodwill? Examining the moments of truth (MOTs) you and your team provide is a good way to find out.

A moment of truth is any contact a customer has with your organisation. Every contact gives customers information about the quality of service you provide and strengthens (or erodes) their loyalty. MOTs can occur without any contact between a customer and an employee, such as over an automated telephone system or a website, or they can involve direct contact, for example on the telephone or face to face.

Here are some questions you and your team members can ask yourselves to build a picture of what the MOTs with your work team are like:

* Do your internal mechanisms – organisation culture, procedures, systems, training, tools and equipment – support employees to meet customers' needs and even help them delight customers?
* Do the MOTs with your team say 'We care about our customers'?
* Do your team members feel empowered and supported to make on-the-spot decisions to meet customers' needs and make them feel valued and special?
* Does every team member treat every contact they have with customers as an opportunity to grow customer loyalty, win new customers and build the organisation's reputation?
* When team members talk to customers, do they realise they aren't just speaking for themselves – they are representing their department and the entire organisation?

One of the reasons MOTs are so important is that, however fleeting, they firmly establish how highly an organisation values its customers. This goes far deeper than logic. It gets to the heart of the question, 'Who am I as a customer?' The impression is strong and lasting because it involves emotions and, as we see below, emotionally satisfied customers are more loyal than those who are merely satisfied rationally.

Make the most of every customer contact

When MOTs support customers' 'end-to-end' experience with your organisation, you have real customer service strength that's hard to beat. Try mapping the total cycle of dealing with your organisation or team that customers experience.

Similar to the way a flow chart details the way work flows through a department, a *customer service map* identifies each step customers take to accomplish their objective with you. First, list each step of your customers' experience, from when they first decide to deal with you through to the follow-up of the transaction. Next, determine what most influences the customers' perception of value at each step. (Make sure you really know and are not just guessing, as discussed on page 627).

Once you and your team have created the map, look at each step to find opportunities to exceed customers' expectations and make your organisation stand out from the competition. Set some SMART measures of success from your customers' points of view with your team, plan how to improve your performance in each one and track your improvements. Show you're serious by posting a graph of your improvements over time in the kitchen area or some other place where team members regularly gather.

You might be able to benchmark your customers' end-to-end experience with you, too, either within your own organisation or by identifying the organisations that excel at each of these factors, regardless of the industry they're in, and benchmarking your results against theirs.[30]

⦿ IN A NUTSHELL

Are you making the most of the telephone?
The telephone is an important moment of truth. How is it answered in your department? So softly the caller can hardly hear what's said? So quickly the caller can't make out what's said? Are people cut off instead of transferred, sent into a twilight zone of 'Hold please', a black hole of never-ending transfers or a nightmare of irritating recorded messages or music? Are callers ever given incorrect or misleading information? Are the people who answer ever rude or abrupt?

Meet customers' psychological needs

You need to be a bit of a psychologist to be good with customers. And you need to understand that there are two types of satisfied customers: *rationally* satisfied and *emotionally* satisfied. They differ in important factors such as how many take their business elsewhere, how often they take their business elsewhere, how much they spend with you and how frequently they purchase your products or use your services. Emotionally satisfied customers contribute far more to the bottom line than rationally satisfied customers, even though they may both score as satisfied with your offering.

The brains of emotionally satisfied customers actually behave differently: compared with rationally satisfied customers, the brains of emotionally satisfied customers have significantly more activity, measured with an fMRI (functional magnetic resonance imaging) machine, when thinking about a company. Here are the elements of emotional satisfaction in customers:

*   *Confidence*: The company always delivers on its promises.
*   *Integrity*: The company treats customers the way they want to be treated, and when something goes wrong, the company fixes it quickly.
*   *Passion*: The company is irreplaceable in the customer's life and is a 'perfect fit' for their needs.
*   *Pride*: There is a sense of positive identification with the company.[31]

Emotionally satisfied customers are worth their weight in gold.

THE STRATEGIC PERSPECTIVE

What needs do you satisfy?

Look beyond your product or service to identify the emotional need you satisfy for your customers. Is it contentment? Peace of mind? Pride of ownership? Reliability? The relief of a problem easily solved?

That's the strategic perspective to keep in mind when working with your customers.

Moments of truth are one important way to develop productive and emotionally satisfying relationships with your service partners and external customers. Here are four other ways to meet their psychological needs:

1. Make customers feel welcome: What first impression do you present? The way you and your team greet and respond to your customers tells them whether you are glad to see them or think they're a nuisance. No one wants to deal with someone who would clearly rather be elsewhere. Train your team to know and use the visual and vocal elements of friendly service and to 'pass the time of day' with a bit of small talk. Ensure your premises are clean and well lit and that customers can enter easily and find what or whom they want promptly.

2. Make customers feel important: What do you do that makes your customers feel special? Do you and your team show you appreciate and value them and their business? Do your attitudes and actions show you respect your customers and their needs? Do you care enough about them to draw their attention to a product or service you think they might be interested in or suggest ways you can help them?

3. Make customers feel understood: Do you and your team really understand what your customers want and need and pay attention to meeting those needs, or do you just 'go through the motions' or concentrate on what you can easily offer? Do you listen to your customers and respond flexibly? Are you willing to customise for your customers so they get exactly what they want? Do team members have the authority to adjust what they're doing to suit customers' needs or must they blindly follow a prescribed system?

4. Make customers feel comfortable: Do you and your team make your customers feel physically as well as psychologically comfortable? How secure and enjoyable does it feel to do business with you? How confident do you make your customers feel so that you can take care of them properly and meet their needs?

FYI

The price of 'I don't care'

More than two-thirds of customers who stop doing business with a company do so because of perceived indifference towards them.[32]

Are your team members willing to 'think outside the square' and do that little bit extra for customers when they see the need? Or do they fear reprimands for doing something a little bit different or extra? The source of customers' perceived indifference to them can be the result of a lack of training and authority, real or perceived, to identify and meet the customers' needs.

Psychological needs in B2B

Purchasing managers are people too. What their emotional need often boils down to is finding a difference in your offering that would make a noticeable difference to their business. This is known as a *justifier*, and provides a clear-cut reason for selecting one supplier over another. Think of it as the 'tie-breaker'.

The next time another business asks you for 'something else', look for something you can give that, while it would cost your company very little, would add a lot of value to your customer; or while it might involve a bit of extra work on your part, would save the customer much more work. For instance:

* A book publisher might offer to print books with a company's logo on the cover and include a message from the CEO as a foreword for a small minimum order number.
* A company that leases vehicles to corporate customers might allow a customer to cancel contracts up to a specified number of vehicles prematurely without a penalty.
* A project management company might assign someone to manage a project that the client has worked with before and trusts to do a good job.

Once you've found that justifier, purchasing managers can present your offering for approval and show how they are contributing real value to their organisation. Helping them win means you win, too.

Look for justifiers in three areas:

1. How your customer actually uses the offering. Discuss how the customer uses your product or service from arrival to completed use and look for ways to make it easier, faster, more economical, safer and so on. (See page 563 to find out how to do this and page 560 to find out more about trading partnerships.) Your basic question is 'What can we do to be a better supplier?'
2. Form a strategic alliance. You can work with another, non-competitive supplier to combine your offerings in a way that strengthens you both and adds value for your mutual customers. (See page 560 for more information on building strategic alliances.)
3. Cruise the customer's website. Most companies post their values, awards won, key initiatives in the areas of risk management, safety, sustainability, and so on.
   Study these areas to find ways that you can add value. [33]

THEORY TO PRACTICE

Keep tie-breakers fresh

Don't think that once you've found a justifier for a particular customer or industry, you can stop there. As you know from Chapter 19, you need to keep moving to keep your advantage because customers' priorities and concerns change. On top of that, your competitors quickly catch on to what you're offering and offer the same or better.

UPS, one of the world's largest shipment and logistics companies, used to get its ideas for new services and justifiers from its head office product development unit. Today, its industry segment and regional marketing and sales managers offer ideas at annual national meetings and during structured brainstorming at two monthly teleconferences, one at regional level and the other at national level.

The conference calls begin with 'post mortems' of sales won and lost and move on to new business challenges customers face, exploring how UPS could help and how competitors might be helping. The meetings close with ideas for new services and justifiers that might address customers' needs. [34]

Explain in ways your customers can understand

You may have heard the advice 'Sell the sizzle not the sausage'. It highlights the need to stress what matters to customers – their emotional needs – when you communicate with them. Train your team to find out what their customers want and address that, not talk about what *they* – the service providers – think is important, and to use expressions and language customers understand, which usually means leaving out jargon and technical terms.

Often, what customers care most about is what your product or service can do for them, rather than its technical aspects. This means talking about *benefits*, not *features*. For example, imagine you are buying a smartphone and you want to take photos with it when you go bushwalking and sightseeing; you might want to know that it's light (not that it weighs 130 grams) and that it has a long battery life (27 hours, by the way), making it the lightest and longest-lasting smartphone currently on the market so you can rely on it to take lots of photos over a long period. Or perhaps photo quality is more important; that would lead you to a different make and model that would help capture some great memories.

When you know what your customer is looking for, you can advise products that best meet their needs and explain the benefits of those products, helping them to make a decision they will be happy with. (That means teaching your team to gather good information first, as explained on page 156.)

To find the benefit of a feature, keep asking 'So what?' until you have found the core reason that a particular feature of a product or service would be useful to a customer. (The battery life is 27 hours. So what? It will last longer than other smartphone batteries. So what? You don't need to charge it as often. So what? That's really handy when you're bushwalking on or holiday. Ahhhh! I'll take it!)

Some features have several benefits. Which should you mention? Listen as customers talk about what is important to them and note the terms they use to describe what they need and want. This helps you home in on what is most important to the customer, select which benefits to mention and then explain them in terms the customer can readily understand.

> **● ACTION!**
>
> Find out how well you and your team are serving your customers with the interactive self-test: Are you really serving your customers? on  CourseMateExpress.

How are we doing?

Whoever and wherever your customers, service partners and trading partners are, keep the lines of communication open. Talking directly to them can show you what is important to them, what they're thinking and where they're heading.

Thinking about the service you offer before, during and after delivery, ask a few key clients and service partners to tell you what they think you do best and where you could improve. Ask them how easy it is to request your help and how satisfied they are with the promptness, quality and pleasantness of your and your team's responses. Listen for any patterns. Try to spot any trends. Ensure that your measures of success reflect what your customers say is most important to them.

FYI

Superconsumers = 10% of customers, 50% of profits

How many staplers do you have? Would it surprise you that some people own, on average, eight staplers each, even though they don't do more stapling than other people? They are the 'superconsumers', about 10% of the stapler customers, who want just the right stapler for each stapling occasion. Now, wouldn't you think their segment of customers would have no need to buy a 9th or a 10th stapler? You'd be surprised.

Superconsumers are similar to advocates in that they combine big spending with high engagement. Both love to use a product and use it as often as they can but superconsumers also want to find new uses for the product and variations on it.

In many industries, including clothing, consumer durables, consumer packaged goods and financial services, this 10% of customers provide 30–40% of a product's or service's revenue and 50% of the profits. Don't just keep this small valuable segment of your customers happy by treating them like VIPs. Find ways to increase sales to them – they're begging you to.

Fortunately, these superconsumers are easy to reach through social media and direct marketing. Social media is also a way to learn from your superconsumers and advocates how you can satisfy them even more and to pick up new product or service ideas and test them out.[35]

Listen and act on what your customers are saying, particularly your most and least satisfied customers. Observe what they're doing, too. Spotting and responding to trends and patterns can give you an edge in the marketplace and help you refine and improve your service and quality. Get out and about with your customers, trading partners and service partners and see what they're doing and how they're using your products or services.

Informal conversations, monitoring social media and more formal feedback mechanisms such as evaluation forms, face-to-face or virtual meetings, satisfaction surveys and questionnaires can alert you to problems, potential problems and changing needs when you are willing to listen.

THE STRATEGIC PERSPECTIVE

Room for improvement

Australian companies need to pull up their customer service socks, particularly large companies. According to the 2014 American Express Global Customer Service Barometer, Australians hold these opinions about their companies:

- 32% think that our companies generally fail to meet expectations versus 2% who believe our companies generally exceed expectations (down from 40% in the 2012 survey with the 2% constant).
- 38% think that Australian companies are paying less attention to customer service compared to companies in other countries (up from 36% in the 2012 survey and 33% in the 2011 survey).
- 39% prefer speaking with a 'real' person on the phone (up from 37%) and 31% prefer a face-to-face discussion (down from 34 % in the 2012 survey) for more complex queries such as returning a product or getting assistance with a product issue.
- 39% prefer to use a company website or email for simple queries, such as locating a product or checking an account balance (up from 37% in the 2012 survey).

>>

- 41% prefer speaking with a 'real' person on the phone and 38% prefer a face-to-face discussion (up from 40% for each in the 2012 survey) when making a difficult or complicated query, such as disputing a charge or making a complaint.
- 58% of Australians have not completed a transaction or made an intended purchase in the past year because of poor customer service (down from 65% in the 2012 survey).
- 64% of Australians tell an average of 18 other people about poor customer service experiences 'all the time' (in the 2012 survey, 64% of Australians told 22 other people).
- 70% spend more with a company because of its history of positive customer service experiences (down from 72% in the 2012 survey and 75% in the 2011 surveys).

There are many worse things than poor customer service. For example, in 2012, 64% of Australians would rather deal with a customer service representative than spend the holidays with their in-laws, ask their boss for a pay rise, give a public speech or tell someone else's kids to behave in a store. But what about the other 36%?[36]

The ones that get away …

Don't confuse satisfaction with loyalty. Even when you're providing quality service and products, satisfied customers may switch to another supplier when that supplier can do it better.

The truth is, you're always in danger of losing your customers. This makes feedback from lost customers valuable. When you learn why they left, you can often fix the cause before they begin a stampede.

4. Resolving customer difficulties and complaints

Don't make excuses – make good.

Frank Hubbard (pioneer, historical harpsichord building), in *Tongue fu! At school* (2004)[37]

Have you ever complained about a product or service and thought, 'Why did I waste my breath?' Even when complaints are made in the spirit of offering useful information to improve a product or service, they can be brushed aside, brusquely ignored or treated with disdain.

Perhaps you have decided never to deal with a particular organisation again when, had your complaint or feedback been handled differently, you would gladly have kept doing business there. It's a pity when organisations and employees let themselves down by failing to handle complaints courteously, promptly and sensitively, especially since handling complaints properly isn't difficult, often strengthens customer loyalty and helps you improve your product or service for the future.

Yes, some customers are angry and rude. Some are tactless. Some are even abusive. Some lack the communication skills or emotional intelligence to word their complaint well or deliver it properly. Others are just having a bad day or have reached their daily stress threshold.

Whatever the reason, when customers are difficult, guard against allowing the mirror neurons in your brain to 'respond in kind'. Take a deep breath and maintain your professionalism. Tell those difficult customers you need to write down what they're saying to encourage them to think about what they're saying and organise their thoughts; as a bonus, you have a written record to help you deal with the complaint. Then follow the steps described later in the chapter.

However they're delivered, here are three good ways to view complaints, whether they're from service partners or an external customer (or even one of your team members, for that matter):

1. As an opportunity to make amends for a problem.
2. As feedback, or information, intended to help you improve.
3. As a request in disguise.

When you receive a complaint or are alerted to a problem or difficulty by a customer, mentally translate it into a hidden request to provide something the customer wants but did not receive and try to provide it. Then use that information to ensure something similar doesn't occur again.

● THEORY TO PRACTICE

The boomerang principle in action

John Powell, in *Why am I afraid to tell you who I am?*, re-tells a story about the late US syndicated columnist Sydney Harris accompanying his friend to a news stand. The friend greeted the newspaper vendor very courteously but in return received gruff and rude service. Accepting the newspaper shoved in his direction, Harris' friend smiled and politely wished the seller a nice weekend.

As the two friends walked down the street, the columnist asked, 'Does he always treat you so discourteously?' 'Yes, unfortunately he does,' was the reply.

'And are you always so polite and friendly to him?'

'Yes, I am.'

'Why are you so nice to him when he is so unfriendly to you?'

'Because I don't want him to decide how I'm going to act.'

Don't let your customers decide how you're going to act either. [38]

Welcome complaints

Here are four powerful reasons to welcome complaints:

1. It takes time and effort to complain: Why should people bother when it's easier just to shrug and walk away? Unfortunately, that's what most customers do. Very often, you don't even hear what went wrong or have the opportunity to fix it. The customer is lost and, quite likely, other customers are lost for the same reasons.
2. It's often your best and most loyal customers who care enough to complain: After all, they have a vested interest in you 'getting your act together'. Be grateful to the minority of unhappy customers who take the trouble to alert you to a problem. Customers who don't care about your organisation or their relationship with you, those who don't expect to deal with you or work with you again, don't bother to complain. Why should they?
3. When someone complains, it's seldom about an isolated occurrence: Rather, it's usually about something that is symptomatic of the way you and your team operate. Whether customers complain in person, in writing, over the telephone or on social media, appreciate their comments as free information about what it's like to deal with you. Complaints are warnings.
4. Complaints are opportunities: Complainers are more likely than non-complainers to do business with you again. In fact, when you handle a complaint well, the complainer is more loyal to you than when everything goes smoothly.

So be grateful for complaints. Treat them as important information from someone who cares and as opportunities to improve your service and build loyalty.

THE STRATEGIC PERSPECTIVE

Australian complainers

You can take complaints seriously because:

- As many as 90% of dissatisfied customers will not purchase from you again.
- Each dissatisfied complainer is likely to tell 18 others of his or her bad experience.
- Up to 66% of complainers are not satisfied with the way their complaint was handled.

For every 100 dissatisfied customers whose complaints you handle well, 83 become loyal customers and recommend you to five others each. That's a total of 415 valuable recommendations.[39]

Manage complaints

Handling a complaint 'well' does not necessarily mean that every customer gets their way. Handling a complaint well means that the *way* you deal with the complaint satisfies the customer. There is a huge difference.

Nevertheless, even with a mindset that sees complaints as valuable information and as opportunities, dealing with them can be difficult and stressful. Here are three things to do, and to train your staff to do, when dealing with complaints:

1. Manage your own emotions.
2. Manage the customer's emotions.
3. Manage the issue.

Manage your own emotions

However they may come across, complaints aren't generally intended as personal insults. They are seldom directed at a service provider personally, even when the customer's way of wording it makes it sound as though it is. Something has gone wrong and the customer wants it put right. So don't take a complaint personally. Put up a mental 'serene screen' that lets the information through but not the emotions or any personal attacks.

Neurologist and concentration camp survivor, Viktor Frankl, commented on the control you can take of yourself with these wise words, 'The last of the human freedoms – to choose one's attitude.'[40]

In difficult situations, most people's natural tendency is to shallow breathe. Quick, shallow breathing causes panic, confusion and fuzzy thinking. It drains oxygen from your 'thinking brain' and switches on your 'reptilian brain', putting you into fight, flight or freeze mode. Out of breath means out of control – definitely not the way to earn points with unhappy customers.

When you feel yourself tensing up, relax and breathe deeply to increase the flow of oxygen to your brain and heart, calm your nerves and help you think clearly. Remind yourself to keep your cool and make sure your self-talk supports you: 'I can handle this', 'I'll do my best to help this customer' or 'We'll get to the bottom of this and sort it out.'

When you still feel upset after dealing with a complaint, take a few minutes to de-stress and recover your equanimity. Go for a walk somewhere nice or, when that's not possible, close your eyes and spend two minutes visualising yourself in a calm, tranquil place. Breathe deeply, counting slowly to seven on the in breath and 11 on the out breath.

When you often deal with upset customers, adopt some longer term relaxation and stress-management strategies such as yoga, meditation or long walks.

Looking after your team

Service providers can become upset by angry, demanding, rude customers. Some organisations take steps to prevent this by running staff training programs for dealing with problem customers and providing guidelines such as how to respond to abusive customers. Some organisations also warn customers that abusive behaviour is not tolerated. For example, at Guy's and St Thomas' NHS Foundation Trust hospital sites in London there are posters at key locations pointing out that threatening or aggressive behaviour towards staff will not be tolerated.

Manage the customer's emotions

US civil rights advocate and president's wife, Eleanor Roosevelt, said, 'No one can make you feel inferior without your consent.'[41] No one can make you feel angry without your consent, either. Professional service providers guide the conversation by modelling the behaviour they want from the customer. When you remain calm, helpful and polite, you encourage your customer to do the same. That's the boomerang principle. Thanks to the brain's mirror neurons, what a person sends out tends to bounce back. So be courteous, not curt, to customers with a problem.

The more customers feel you aren't listening and are brushing aside their concerns or ignoring their needs, the further to the right on the 'unhappy customer emotions' scale they are likely to move (see Figure 20.2). The further to the right a customer moves on the scale, the more likely he or she is to become upset and even angry and abusive.

Don't make the people who are giving you valuable feedback feel you are pushing against them instead of working with them – that only encourages their emotions to escalate, creating a difficult situation for both of you and losing goodwill for your department or organisation.

Skills for dealing effectively with complaints

Use your skills in the following areas for a successful complaints outcome:

* Communication skills help you ask questions to uncover the real problem and the customer's expectations, and show the customer you're listening and trying to understand the difficulty.
* Empathy helps you see the situation from your customer's point of view, which in turn helps you understand the customer's concerns and needs, and thus take them seriously.
* High self-esteem stops you from taking complaints personally.
* The ability to listen reflectively, or recap both the facts and the customer's feelings, removes the need for the customer to become upset or abusive.
* Strong interpersonal skills help you identify and meet the customer's basic psychological needs.

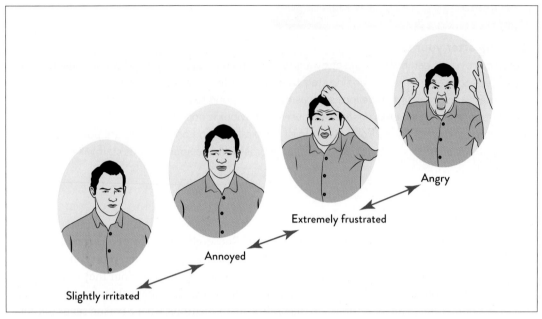

FIGURE 20.2 The complaining customer's scale of emotions

IN A NUTSHELL

Tips for dealing with angry customers

Even your best customers can get upset sometimes and how you handle the situation either strengthens or severs your relationship. It all depends on how and when you respond.

- When a customer sends an email or leaves a voicemail, respond promptly and acknowledge that you know there is a problem.
- When you're on the phone, let your tone of voice reflect your empathy; in person, be cordial and show your concern.
- Listen first. Take notes but don't offer explanations. They can come later.
- Show that you're listening and appreciate the practicalities of the problem as well as how the customer is feeling about it by acknowledging both the problem and the emotion. (See page 159 for more information on acknowledgement listening.)
- Don't ask too many questions. Angry people have trouble thinking clearly and even behaving rationally.
- Agree they have a point (even when they're not totally correct); say you can see why they would be upset. This dislodges a lot of the customer's anger because it's hard to be angry with someone who agrees with you.
- When the customer is right, say so and apologise. An apology is all many angry people want and the last thing they expect. It can knock the fury out of them.
- Let the customer know you care and intend to fix the problem. When appropriate, assure them you are beginning an inquiry into the problem; this makes them less likely to rant and rave and deflects their anger away from you.
- Don't try to solve the problem until the customer has calmed down.

Manage the issue

Show customers that you're on their side in wanting to sort out problems. This means taking a cooperative 'we' approach and seeing the situation as a problem to be resolved, not that the customer needs to be fixed.

Gather any facts you need, time lines, major issues and so on. Take a 'helicopter' or 'strategic perspective' view of what is going on. You know the organisation's situation and you've heard the customer's thoughts. Concentrate on the facts and on what you can do to try to put things right in the customer's eyes.

When you can't resolve the problem on the spot, let customers know you will get back to them by a specific time with a solution, and do so. (Ensure your staff know the company line regarding what's possible and 'do-able'.) Never say 'This will never happen again' because you can't guarantee it; say you will do everything you can to minimise the chances of this happening again.

When something goes wrong, diagnose the cause, develop options and advise your customer, as explained in chapters 18 and 19.

◉ THEORY TO PRACTICE

Customer dis-service

Some customer help lines fail to help and some service centres fail to serve. They seem more concerned with getting the customer off the line to minimise call time than to find the cause of a problem and fix it.

Some organisations insult their customers with clear messages that their time has no value and their frustration is of no concern by making them wait in endless physical or electronic queues or by not having their goods ready when promised or service completed when agreed.

Some organisations make their customers repeat themselves several times to different people until they chance upon someone able or willing to help them.

Some organisations expect their customers to do their work for them – to fill out lengthy reports, track their own orders, install or wire up and dispose of their own equipment.

Do any of these examples of customer dis-service sound familiar?

Three steps to a resolved complaint

It's easy to be helpful and courteous when all is going well. It's when they go wrong that your professionalism is tested. This is when your professionalism counts the most, too.

Since unhappy customers spread bad news more quickly than happy customers spread good news, it's in your interests to deal with complaints properly. As stated above, it's the *way* they are handled – not their outcome – that matters most. Here's how to deal with complaints so that your customers spread good news about you instead of thinking, 'Why did I waste my breath?'

Step 1. Hear the customer out

Respect the customer's experience without jumping to conclusions, prejudging or evaluating. Look for the common ground and work with your customer to resolve the problem. Let the concept of trading partnerships remind you that you and your customer are on the same side.

Use the acronym ALARA to gather good information:

* **A**cknowledge: Make eye contact and use other attentive body language so your customer can see you are listening. As discussed on page 159, acknowledgement listening, or 'nodding

and grunting', shows you're following and helps bring out the full story. When a complaint is made over the telephone, use plenty of 'uh-huhs' and 'I sees'. Saying 'I'm sorry', 'I understand', 'I see', 'I'm going to take care of this for you' allows the customer to continue and shows that you're listening.

- **Listen:** Listen carefully. Really hear what your customers are trying to tell you. When you're tempted to cut them off because you think you know what they're going to say or you have the answer – don't. Letting customers have their say is essential to resolving complaints effectively.
- **Ask the right questions:** Ask questions so you can fully understand the problem. This might be 'How can I best help you now?' or 'Can you explain that a bit more to me, please?' or 'When did that actually happen?' It depends on the situation.
- **Recap:** Summarise what you've understood using objective language, without adding anything or taking anything away. Review both the facts and the customer's feelings (e.g. annoyed, disappointed, inconvenienced). This helps calm down irate customers and gives them an opportunity to clear up anything you haven't fully understood.
- **Act:** Take responsibility for putting matters right or for making sure someone else puts them right. Try to make all your sentences positive and helpful for maximum favourable impact. Say something like 'Thank you for telling me about this. I'm going to sort it out for you as quickly as I can.'

When the customer's facts are wrong, ask yourself whether correcting the customer would serve any purpose. Often, the facts are beside the point. Arguing back and forth about what happened is futile and certainly won't undo what's happened. Even when you can't agree, at least acknowledge how the customer is feeling: 'I can see that this has really inconvenienced you and I'm sorry about that. Let me see what I can do to get things back on track for you.'

Offering condolences when the situation warrants it doesn't mean admitting guilt but, rather, showing empathy and understanding: 'I'm sorry this has happened. I'd like to resolve it for you.' Commiserating means you care.

◉ IN A NUTSHELL

Two more acronyms for hearing the customer out

Here are two other acronyms to help you remember how to hear a customer's complaint:
- **LAST:** Listen – Advise – Solve – Thank. LAST works well with straightforward customer complaints.
- **LEDO:** Listen – Empathise – Depersonalise – Offer. LEDO is good for situations needing conciliation or conflict resolution and with angry customers. Listening to the complaint and empathising with the customer allows them to air their issue and feelings, while depersonalising the situation so you can look at it objectively helps you work together to find a solution that satisfies you both.

Step 2. Put matters right

Find out what the customer wants, or offer a solution (depending on the issue and what you are able to do).

Avoid negative language: not 'I'm sorry your order hasn't arrived; I can't get it for you until Tuesday now', but 'I'm sorry your order hasn't arrived; I can have it here for you Tuesday and once again, I'm so sorry you've been inconvenienced like this'. Don't talk about what you *can't* do but what you *can* do and when. Say, 'There's something ...' not 'There's nothing ...'. Soften 'no' with 'I wish' or 'I hope' to show empathy and not apathy.

Concentrate on the future. Don't blame, deny, excuse or explain – customers aren't interested. They want to know what is going to happen because they bothered to spend their valuable time letting you know that they experienced a problem. Explain what you intend to do to sort it out – right now and, when you can, in the long term to prevent it happening again. 'Here's what I'd like to do now ... And I have made a note that this has happened so we can adjust our system to prevent something similar happening again.' (Page 565 explains how to adjust systems to prevent errors.)

Step 3. Agree and act

To move the conversation on, ask 'Is that a good solution from your point of view?' Once you've settled on what to do, do it.

● IN A NUTSHELL

Dealing with a string of problems

When customers present you with several problems, prioritise them. Say something like, 'I'm sure I can help you with these concerns. Let's work on your biggest one first. Which is that?'

Then respond to it following the three steps to a resolved complaint described above. After that, move onto the customer's next concern. When you run into one you can't answer or deal with straightaway, move it to the bottom of the list and deal with the next one. Say something like, 'I need to check with dispatch to find the answer to that. Before I do, can I help you with another question?'

CourseMateExpress

Go to http://login.cengagebrain.com to access CourseMate Express, your online study tool for *Management Theory & Practice*. CourseMate Express brings chapter concepts to life with interactive learning, and study and exam preparation tools:

- Test your skills in different aspects of management with interactive self-tests and simulations.
- Watch videos that show how real managers operate in real businesses.
- Test your understanding of the changing world of management by taking the revision quiz.

QUICK REVIEW

1. What is the difference between an internal customer and an external customer? Are internal customers just as important as external customers? Why or why not?
2. Explain why increasing the lifetime value of a customer is an inexpensive way to secure the future of an enterprise and the four ways to increase LCV.
3. Explain why it's important to actually ask your customers what they want from your organisation. Does the need to ask them diminish the longer you have known them? Why or why not?
4. Explain the difference between customer satisfaction and customer loyalty.
5. Describe the steps to resolving a customer complaint and explain why the way you do it is so important.

BUILD YOUR SKILLS

1. Do you think customer service is more important to organisations in the private sector than in the not-for-profit and public sectors? Why or why not?
2. Do you think that the threshold of what constitutes good customer service is continually rising? Give some examples from your own experience.
3. How good is your organisation's customer service? How customer-focused are you and your team? After answering these two questions, think about and note down the criteria you used to answer them. What does this tell you about what is important to you as a customer? Would all customers find the same things important? Why or why not? What are some things other people might find important that you don't?
4. For the next organisation you deal with; for example, your insurance company, your local café, a government body or utility provider, list the moments of truth from the initial to the final interaction, and score each on a scale of 1 to 5 for how well they were handled. Overall, how do you rate your satisfaction? Would you use them again? If a convenient competitor organisation opened, would you switch? Why or why not?

WORKPLACE ACTIVITIES

1. Who are your organisation's external customers? Do you and your work team have any direct external customers? If not, how far removed, or 'down the chain', are your external customers? Calculate the lifetime value of a typical external customer of your organisation.
2. Illustrate the internal customer–supplier chain for your own work team.
3. Would you describe your organisation as cost-driven, customer-driven or product-driven? Why? Is it appropriate for its market? How would you describe your organisation's competition?
4. What do your own internal or external customers want and need from you? What data do you collect concerning their problems and concerns? How do you use it?
5. Map the moments of truth your customers have with you and your work team. How well do you think you manage them? What is your evidence for this? In what ways do you meet your customers' psychological needs?
6. What was the last complaint you received from an internal or external customer? Describe how you dealt with it. What constraints did you need to work within? How easy does your organisation or work team make it to complain?

CASE STUDY 20.1

ENGAGED STAFF LEAD TO ENGAGED CUSTOMERS

In 2008, New Zealand's ASB Bank won the accolade of being the country's number one large bank in terms of customer satisfaction for the sixth year in a row. It won the award again in 2011 and 2013. Seven years before its sixth consecutive win, the bank thought its customers were happy – in fact, general customer satisfaction surveys showed they were.

However, another survey the bank conducted in 2002, measuring how 'emotionally' attached to the bank its customers were, painted a very different picture. Most of the bank's customers were prepared to move to the competition at the drop of a hat. They were satisfied, but they weren't loyal. And a changing customer base makes servicing customers expensive and difficult. Lifetime customers are much more lucrative and easier to satisfy.

The bank decided to put a principle from performance management consulting firm Gallup into practice. The motto read, 'Profitability comes from having emotionally engaged customers and emotionally engaged customers come from fully engaged staff.'[42]

The bank devised a plan that included ensuring every employee knew its vision word for word. It gave employees vision statements to carry in their wallets. The vision statement was on every email employees sent and it hung on plaques in every bank. It was a clear, memorable, understandable statement: 'To be New Zealand's best bank and financial services provider, excelling in customer service.'[43]

By 2004, ASB was outperforming 90% of all companies in Gallup's worldwide database of employee engagement. It soon became apparent that engagement translates into profits. For four consecutive years, the bank's operating surplus grew by 20% and its assets increased by more than $7 billion in three years.

ASB didn't stop there. It turned its attention to employees' interactions with customers. The bank had been using mystery shopper surveys, but these didn't delve into customers' emotional engagement. The bank began telephoning customers who had a transaction with the bank during the previous three days and asking questions about their experience based on Gallup's engagement questions. They found out whether customers had a relationship with a personal account manager, what they thought about that relationship, how confident they were in the person serving them, and so on. This showed customers' satisfaction with the bank's service.

To assess customers' emotional engagement, the bank asked customers to respond to statements such as 'ASB always treats me with respect'; 'I feel proud to be an ASB customer'; 'ASB is the perfect bank for people like me'; and 'I can't imagine a world without ASB'. The bank believes that engaged employees are the key to engaged customers. Engaged employees are more committed, more productive and more likely to stay with the organisation, and they give customers a better and more valuable experience.[44] (To find out more about employee engagement, see page 287.)

Questions

1. Do you agree with ASB that engaged employees and satisfied customers are inseparable? Why or why not? Provide examples from your own experience to illustrate your answer.
2. What role do you believe employee engagement plays in earning customer loyalty?
3. What principles of improving customer satisfaction, engagement and retention does this case study illustrate? How can you apply them in your own workplace?

CASE STUDY 20.2

KEEPING THE CUSTOMERS SATISFIED

Shelly Sanders has just been promoted to supervise the home furnishings department of the large department store where she works. The store manager made it clear to her that her first challenge was to turn around the poor showing of the department, particularly in sales, which were below budget, and in customer satisfaction. The department receives more complaints than any other in the store (although it rates about average in the chain).

Reasoning that dissatisfied customers contribute to a poor reputation in the community, which translates into poor sales, Shelly decides she needs to learn about the department's current customers and find out how they feel about purchasing from it. Her first move is to check the department's information on repeat business. There isn't any.

Next, she hunts out the department's customer suggestions and complaints records to analyse and finds a notebook of scrawled customer comments and queries – all negative. Wondering how valid the information is, but realising she probably won't find anything better, she draws up a check sheet to break down complaints and suggestions by frequency and type. Then she transfers the data onto Pareto charts and finds that the most common cause of customer dissatisfaction is problems with the delivery of furniture customers have ordered.

On investigation, she finds that, when furniture is ordered, the manufacturer quotes a lead time, which sales staff pass on to their customers. The manufacturer is often late with delivery. In turn, manufacturers often blame their suppliers for late delivery of raw materials.

However, because the store has no tracking system, the first the staff in the furnishings department hear of a problem is when customers ring up to complain that their order is overdue and to ask when they can expect delivery. The staff then have to search through back orders, check with the supplier to find out the new delivery date and ring the customer back. This is time-consuming and creates ill will between customers and the store. It's also difficult for the staff to find the time to track down late orders, since their priority is meant to be serving customers and ensuring the display area is well presented.

Shelly realises that the problem is too big for her to fix on her own. She gathers her team together to brainstorm all the problems they experience. They then prioritise the problems and plan to resolve each of them in turn. They decide to assign some problems to 'working parties' so that they can work on more than one problem at a time. They're keen to get the ball rolling and see some results. As it happens, the problem that the team decides to work on first is the customer delivery problem.

Questions

1. Referring to Chapter 19 if you need to, discuss what the team's next steps are likely to be as it works on the problem of customer delivery.
2. Should the staff involve their suppliers at any stage? If so, how could they best do this?
3. Do you think Shelly should have involved the staff from the beginning? Why or why not? What can she do to ensure that their motivation remains high as they improve their customers' satisfaction with the furnishings department?

PLANNING AND MANAGING PROJECTS

OVERVIEW

Have you been involved with a project – a temporary venture with a beginning and an end? Projects are an ideal way to find ways to capitalise on core capabilities, create a product or service, develop strategic alliances, increase productivity, reduce costs, refine supply chains, tackle unexpected problems and take advantage of emerging opportunities. Every industry and sector and every type of organisation has people working on projects that vary in duration and range from small and straightforward to large and complex.

Projects can involve a single department or work group, or they can cross an entire organisation, gathering expertise from far-flung divisions. Some projects involve two or more organisations working together in a strategic alliance to produce a joint product or service or develop an integrated value chain.

However, what they have in common is a goal to deliver something that adds value to an organisation and usually, to its customers and other stakeholders, too, and they must do this within identified constraints, particularly cost and time.

1. Do you know how to scope a project and develop a project plan?
2. Are you able lead a project to a successful conclusion?
3. Do you know how to finalise a project and grow into your next project?

Many factors are involved in a successful project: a good project manager, effective project management tools, efficient work practices, experience, good teamwork and hard work, to name a few. In this chapter, you find out how to manage a project to a successful outcome.

SCENARIO

A project is born

Macy and Rosa are sipping a glass of pre-dinner wine as they discuss this afternoon's talk by Zheng Fang, from China's Sichuan University, and Michelle Andrews, from Temple University in the USA. They're attending a conference on sensor networks, finding out how they're going to change the way we shop, talk, work and have fun.

Wireless sensor networks, or WSNs to those in the know, are popping up all over Australia, making gathering all sorts of data cheaper and easier. The sensors, which can be as big as a shoebox or as small as a grain of dust, send information to a central location for analysis. They're a boon for traffic managers, farmers, fire fighters and other emergency services and for businesses such as shops, theatres and restaurants, too, which is why Macy and Rosa are here.

This afternoon's speakers told the audience about their research that combined GPS triangulation with WSN technology to alert customers to special offers. Much as airlines and hotels adjust pricing to fill seats and beds, retailers can use a similar approach to offer customers special deals. The Chinese study examined the best time frames for offering promotions – come and buy today, tomorrow or in two days.

Their research found that immediate offers work best for people within 200 metres of a business, increasing the odds of a purchase by 76% compared to offers with a two-day delay. For customers 500 meters to two kilometres away, promotions for the next day worked best. Two-day delays were the least effective, no matter where customers were.[1]

'If we could find the best time frames for offers here in Australia, imagine how powerful our direct marketing could be! We'd have an edge on our competitors and give our clients real value.' Macy runs through her mental project checklist: Related to an important business issue? Tick. Easily identified start and end points? Tick. Clear and measurable result? Tick. Realistically deliverable? Tick.

'I reckon, Rosa, we've got the makings of a project here. Let's investigate and if it's as promising as I think it is, I'll sponsor you to lead a project putting this technology to use. What do you say?'

1. Planning your project

> You've got to take short-, medium- and long-term horizons and you've got to have options against each one of them.
>
> Ann Sherry in Kwong, 'Future proofing: Planning for tomorrow', *Acuity* (2014)[2]

Someone recognises a need, perhaps to change or improve a process such as invoicing, developing people or improving patient care in hospitals. Or someone sees an opportunity to improve or redesign a function such as purchasing or selling, or to improve or redesign logistics such as storage or distribution.

Perhaps a new strategy is needed, or someone needs to guide and oversee a rescue operation. Or perhaps an organisation decides to develop or enhance its products or services, upgrade or overhaul its IT and communications infrastructure or software, or improve or change its assets (e.g. equipment, plant, premises or vehicles).

That someone – the project sponsor, or 'owner' – writes up a proposal for approval (sometimes called the *project initiation document*) that answers the questions What? When? Where? Who? Why? and How? Once approved and agreed with the project's key stakeholders, this document becomes the *project charter* (sometimes called a *project mandate*). Figure 21.1 shows the project life cycle from beginning to end.

The project charter acknowledges the existence of a project and acts as the project's vision. This is the 'strategic overview' of the project and defines its boundaries and the responsibilities of the project manager, the person who is to guide the project through to its finalisation.

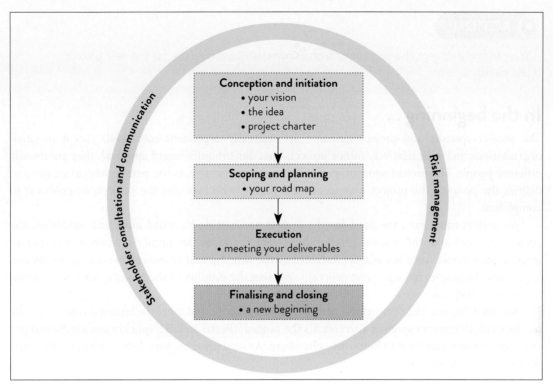

FIGURE 21.1 The project life cycle

IN A NUTSHELL

The project charter

The project charter generally outlines the following information:

- project title
- overall purpose and goals of the project
- background of the project, or what suggested the need for it
- project's main deliverables including a summary of the anticipated schedule, or main phases, of the project
- project's major dependencies that affect the project during its life and interdependencies that exist after the project's implementation
- who will use the results of the project (its customers or clients) and other interested parties, or stakeholders
- business case, or justification for the project, explaining how the organisation benefits and how the project fits into the organisation's strategic plan
- approval requirements: an estimate of the financial and other resources needed and the person responsible for authorising cost and resource use
- main constraints within which the project must operate
- how the project relates to other past or concurrent projects in the organisation
- associated documents such as earlier work, similar projects and other useful information
- success criteria including cost, time, quality and other critical factors, to guide decision making
- prospective project manager.

ACTION!

You can find a Project charter template on **CourseMate**Express to use for the next project you manage.

In the beginning ...

The project sponsor and project manager are mutually dependent roles and, except in small organisations and with relatively minor projects that don't require board approval, they are usually different people. The project sponsor, generally a senior executive, is the person who identifies and defines the project. The project manager is the person who executes the project, or guides it to completion.

As well as conceiving the need for the project and setting its broad aims and outcomes, the project sponsor builds the business case for the project, carries out an initial risk analysis at corporate level, seeks support from key players, establishes the funding and resources needed, appoints and supervises the project manager, and generally oversees the viability of the project, particularly from a financial viewpoint.

Should it become clear the project cannot fulfil its purpose and meet the business case originally put forward, the project sponsor also cancels the project. (Better to kill it quickly and kindly and put the effort, money and time to better use elsewhere. As explained on page 525, don't keep throwing money at a lost cause.)

Finding your feet

Once the project is approved and its charter agreed, the project manager's work – your work – begins. It's mostly mental and iterative work at this stage – scoping, or defining what the project will achieve and won't achieve (its deliverables), identifying and developing broad strategies for how to manage risks and stakeholders, working out the resources you need, planning and scheduling what needs to be done to achieve the project's deliverables and thinking about how you can monitor the project as it unfolds. Work closely with the project sponsor – in effect, your boss – in these initial stages of the project to ensure you are 'working off the same page'.

Begin by thoroughly familiarising yourself with the project charter. Gather any relevant documents it refers to and other useful information you can think of. Then work with your sponsor to clarify the following:

* the project's *assumptions* (factors taken to be true but that could change later)
* the project *constraints* – the operating guidelines you must work within, or the limits on what you can do (including budget, time and other resource limitations)
* delegated limits of your authority and responsibility
* reporting requirements (to whom, how often, in what format(s) and so on)
* resources available and how to obtain them.

List constraints and assumptions

Constraints are the restrictions and resource limitations that you need to work within. Consider them to be unalterable 'givens' and let them guide your project and persuade you to find innovative ways to achieve the project's deliverables despite them.

To identify the project constraints, consider these categories:

* deliverables (scope)
* resources available (including equipment, facilities, financial, funding, and people)
* time frames.

Be specific, because you need to know exactly what you're up against. When you identify a constraint, note its source.

Now list your *assumptions* regarding cost, quality requirements, risk, time and other factors that underlie the project. Assumptions usually include words like 'depends on' and 'relies on' and are not within your control (but could be within someone else's control).

Clear these constraints and assumptions with your sponsor.

THEORY TO PRACTICE

Check out your assumptions

Once upon a time, a project to create a yabby farm was proposed. A key assumption was the ability to sell yabbies into Europe at $25 a kilo. But when that assumption was investigated further, it turned out $25 a kilo was the price for 100 kilo lots, delivered weekly. Alas, the project was not feasible.

Always check out the project's assumptions carefully, particularly cost and quality, to prevent wasted time, effort and money. Otherwise, your project might become what Australian project management coach, Stephen Hartley, calls a 'thought bubble, unencumbered by any reality check.'[3]

ACTION!

Use the Constraints and assumptions template on  to begin your list.

Scoping your project

The project scope develops the information contained in the project charter. It describes the boundaries, or *parameters*, of the project and establishes the work that needs to be done in terms of deliverables and SMART targets. It answers the What? When? Where? Who? Why? and How? questions addressed in the project charter in more detail. Failing to scope a project fully is one of the main causes of unsuccessful projects.

Think of the scope as a box, like the one shown in Figure 21.2: what's inside the box is what the project will deliver; everything outside the box is not part of the project. You might want to generate a list of is/is nots for each deliverable, the 'is' describing what your project will provide and the 'is nots' stating the *exclusions* – what it won't accomplish. (The more detailed project plan, which you draft next, details *how* you'll deliver what's inside the scope box.)

Begin by writing a clear scope statement in 25 words or less along the lines of 'This project will deliver this result by this time in order to … (a clear business benefit).'

This serves as your project purpose, or vision statement.

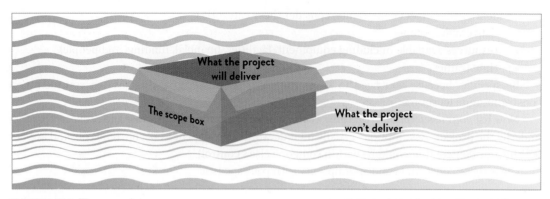

FIGURE 21.2 The scope box

Next, list your deliverables (the product, service or results) and their SMART goals and measures of success (MOS). These are your success criteria, or the conditions that must be met for the deliverables to be approved, as well as the beginnings of your roadmap of milestones for your project schedule, or timetable. Make these deliverables and MOS very clear because you don't want people wondering whether your project met its goals.

Your scope should also include:

* cost
* main risks
* people and other resources needed
* quality requirements
* stakeholder needs and communication arrangements.
  This scope does two things:
1. It helps you and your team stay focused on the task.
2. It provides guidelines for making decisions about any change requests during the project, helping to prevent scope creep.

Review your scope document with the project sponsor and, when agreed, have it formally signed off. Think of this document as your contract, because it spells out what you have committed to achieve, by when and with what resources. You will present this project scope to your team members and stakeholders once the rest of your project plan is complete.

 **ACTION!**

You can find a Scope template on *CourseMateExpress* to help you scope your projects.

Preventing the sin of scope creep

Knowing what's 'inside' the scope box and having clear deliverables and measures of success help prevent the project manager's perennial nightmare – *scope creep*. This is the tendency for deliverables to increase (or occasionally decrease) beyond initial expectations during the life of a project. A team member sees ways to enhance the project's results or clients and stakeholders ask for 'a little bit extra here', a 'small adjustment there'. To keep them happy, you agree and before you know it, you're over budget and over time.

When stakeholders ask for adjustments to the project scope, remember Weiler's Law: Nothing is impossible for the man who doesn't have to do it himself. Keep reinforcing your ultra-clear deliverables and success measures formally and informally (because people tend to forget) so that your scope box doesn't expand beyond reason as stakeholders keep asking for 'More, more, more!'

Unauthorised small changes have an uncanny ability to stall progress through your timelines or in some other way stick a spanner into the works. If you do alter any of the deliverables, clear them with the project sponsor and add them to a *change register* or *change log*, and keep all stakeholders informed about modifications and how they affect them.

◉ ACTION!

Use the Project scope change request form template on *ʃ***CourseMateExpress** to track alterations to the project scope, clear them with the project sponsor and keep stakeholders informed.

Building a stakeholder register

Stakeholder and management engagement needs to be an integral part of the project planning process and continue throughout its execution. Based on the project charter and discussions with your project sponsor, identify and list your project's stakeholders.

Stakeholders are people or groups with a vested interest in the project's success or (sadly) its failure. They are different for each project and each organisation, but include the project sponsor, its clients (or the people who will use the project's results), people with specialist or organisational knowledge you need, people who have control of assets or resources, people who can advocate for the project and people who might oppose your project, as well as your organisation's management.

Stakeholders might also include funding bodies, work teams, the general public, managers of part-time team members – any people, groups or organisations with a perceived direct or indirect *interest in* the project and people or groups directly or indirectly in some way *affected by* the project's outcomes or its various phases or people who can *influence* the project.

The larger the project and the more it crosses organisational boundaries, or operational areas, the more stakeholders you have. (See page 221 to find out more about navigating organisational politics.) Identify the stakeholders methodically and logically so you don't miss anyone.

You can group stakeholders into:

* *Drivers*, who are people who will use your project's results or who stand to benefit from your project
* *Supporters*, who are people who can help your project succeed
* *Opposers*, who are people who believe the project is detrimental to their interests
* *Observers*, who are other interested people who may have a positive or negative influence on the project and its deliverables.

Think of your project's stakeholders as your customers.

◉ ACTION!

Log on to *ʃ***CourseMateExpress** to use the Stakeholder register template to begin your list.

The *stakeholder register* tells you who to consider and who to consult with and how. Begin listing these interested parties by name, title, location and contact information. When a stakeholder is an external body or group or a large group or department in your organisation, identify the person to communicate with and enter their details.

When appropriate, meet with stakeholders formally or informally to get a feel for what is important to them, what problems the project could help them overcome, how a successful project will affect them and so on. Use the opinions of the most powerful stakeholders to shape your project in its early stages; this makes their continuing support more likely (and can also improve your project planning). Work towards developing a matrix like the one shown in Figure 21.3.

Analyse stakeholders

Poor stakeholder management can doom a project. When you understand the 'stakes' of each stakeholder, you can determine the best way to work with them. 'Stakes' might include the usefulness of your project's deliverables to them as well as their psychological stakes (power, prestige, etc).

The stakeholder register is the basis for your *stakeholder analysis* (see Figure 21.3). You will probably complete both with your team soon after it forms, working out stakeholders' interests, whether they're supportive or opposed and the strength and power of their support or opposition. Analyse stakeholders in as much detail as you can so you know what they need and expect from the project, the resources they can provide, and how and how often they want to hear about the project's status from you.

Name	Contact details	Reasons for support/ opposition	Must haves	Desirables	Strongly against	Moderately against	Neutral	Moderately supportive	Strongly supportive	Likely influence – High	Medium	Low	Resources available or potentially available	Preferred mode of communication	Preferred frequency of communication	Last communication date	By (name of team member)

FIGURE 21.3 Stakeholder Analysis

You can distribute the stakeholder register, but keep your analysis separate. You and your team are going to use it to develop a strategy to build effective working relationships with them (as discussed in Chapter 8), manage their changing expectations, maintain their support and win over any stakeholders opposed to your team's work.

 **ACTION!**

How do your stakeholders stack up? Download the Stakeholder analysis template, located on CourseMateExpress to find out.

Develop a stakeholder management strategy

Guided by your stakeholder analysis, you can develop a strategy to begin managing them early in the project life cycle. Your aim is to maintain or increase support from people in favour of your project, winning over those opposed, or at least managing their concerns and mitigating the risks they pose to the project.

Use the guidelines shown in Figure 21.4 to prioritise stakeholders and plan your communication with them. Keep high power/low interest people happy; manage high power/high interest people closely; monitor low power/low interest people; and keep high interest/low power people informed.

As part of scope management, ask the various stakeholders to sign off as milestones (significant events in the schedule/plan) are reached to ensure the project meets everyone's needs. This two-way communication can be critical to the ultimate success of your project.

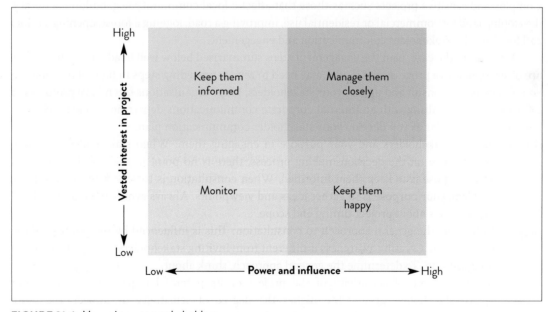

FIGURE 21.4 Managing your stakeholders

Develop a communication plan

Based on your stakeholder analysis, prepare a communication plan showing the when, what, how and to whom of project updates and checking on the effectiveness of these updates. Your goal is to communicate with stakeholders in an organised way, involving them as frequently as needed and providing the information they need in ways that suit them.

Schedule regular review meetings with key stakeholders or stakeholder representatives to keep them up to date. The frequency of these meetings depends on the nature and complexity of the project and the extent to which it affects stakeholders. Some stakeholders will only require one-page status reports at agreed intervals.

⦿ THEORY TO PRACTICE

Stakeholder engagement

Stakeholder engagement is an important part of large government projects, so important, in fact, that communication specialists often develop and manage the communication plans.

Engaging with stakeholders assists in making decisions that better reflect community needs and widens the range of available expertise, knowledge and ideas. It helps identify and explore concerns while plans are being developed, helping to strengthen project plans, address concerns and provide a sense of ownership to the solutions developed.

Government guidelines for consulting with stakeholders ensure that the consultation and decision-making processes are transparent, logical and able to be understood by the stakeholders; that stakeholders are given a fair opportunity to express their views and concerns; and that conflicting requirements are resolved constructively. Good guidelines for any project.

Stakeholder engagement

Complex and sensitive projects such as those that affect a local community (e.g. building a library, developing land for commercial or residential use, improving a road, logging a forest, opening a mine) call for extensive stakeholder communication and engagement.

When that's the case, plan the engagement steps summarised below well in advance. These steps are often an iterative process; that is, you may need to review preceding steps in light of information you obtain as you consult and update your stakeholders. Large organisations often have protocols to follow such as consulting with an internal corporate communications department, public relations department or similar as you develop your stakeholder communication plan.

Step 1.   Identify stakeholders and your purpose in engaging them: When stakeholders can have no influence on the decision-making process, there is no point in seeking their opinion. Your purpose is to keep them informed. When consultation is to seek help in resolving a problem, your purpose is to gather ideas and viewpoints. Always avoid creating unrealistic expectations about project timing and scope.

Step 2.   Determine the general approach to consultation: This is influenced by the purpose of the consultation. Creating awareness is different from inviting stakeholders to participate in the final decision. To determine the general approach, think about:

a.   The degree of sensitivity of the project or its potential impact on a stakeholder or stakeholder group: The higher the degree of sensitivity or impact, the more comprehensive consultation needs to be, which affects timelines and budget; and the higher the degree of sensitivity, the more subject to scrutiny the project is likely to be, so think through your consultation approach carefully and plan it methodically.

b.   The nature of feedback sought: Do stakeholders have an opportunity to significantly affect the outcome or is consultation limited to comment about details?

     c. The degree of technical difficulty: Highly technical projects may limit the number of feasible alternatives and may make communicating the issues more difficult.

Step 3. Identify who, how and how often to consult: You have a variety of options, including brochures and flyers, community displays, community events such as open days, face-to-face and virtual meetings, media releases, newsletters, public meetings and information sessions, public presentations, social media, telephone information lines and surveys and websites. High-impact, complex projects often have a community relations committee or advisory group liaison committee to plan and execute stakeholder engagement.

Step 4. Develop a communication plan: Set out in detail the steps described above: who the stakeholders are, the proposed methods of consultation for each, the resources to be used (e.g. marketing or PR companies), a schedule and the estimated costs.

Step 5. Obtain resources and implement the plan: The plan may call for engaging specialist contractors or consultants or to use in-house experts, depending on the nature and level of the project.

Step 6. Analyse stakeholder feedback: Feed it into the decision-making process for consideration with other information and constraints. Always record statements and promises made by the project team to stakeholders and file these scrupulously. (Stakeholders may be certain a promise has been made regarding, for example, landscaping or noise levels and you need to be able to check your records to determine what was actually agreed to.)

Step 7. Follow up as necessary: Ensure that decisions about the project are readily available to stakeholders.

> **◉ ACTION!**
>
> Begin a Stakeholder communication plan using the template on *CourseMateExpress*. Then use the Joint project review meeting notes template on *CourseMateExpress*, to capture important points raised during your regular review meetings.

Mapping milestones

You are clear about your deliverables. Now you need to plan the action required to achieve them. The more thoroughly you plan the project, the more smoothly you can execute it.

You are going to chart the path of reaching each deliverable as a series of steps that you and your team need to complete. Next you are going to draft a schedule, or time frame, for reaching those milestones. Once your team is in place, they will map the project further by adding the activities, tasks and subtasks needed to reach each milestone and adjusting and firming up your draft schedule.

First, list your deliverables. Then ask a series of questions to drill down to ever-greater detail about what needs to be done to achieve each one, as shown in Figure 21.5. What do we need to do, or what needs to happen, to achieve or produce this deliverable? We need to do A, B and C. What needs to happen to produce A? 1, 2 and 3 needs to happen. What needs to happen to produce 1? And keep going. (Drill down as far as you need to but not to the end, as the team members responsible will finish it off.)

Remember that nothing in this plan is set in concrete but is open for continual revision in order to meet deliverables and timelines and as more information is gathered. Keep the project's assumptions, constraints, deliverables and purpose (your scope statement) in mind as you plan.

Keep your most important stakeholders informed of your progress as you build your project plan and build in their ideas in when you can so they feel more 'ownership' of the project.

Deliverable: _____

Q: What do we need to do to produce this deliverable?
A: We need to do A, B and C.

Q: What do we need to do to produce A?
A: We need to do 1, 2 and 3.

Q: What do we need to do to produce 1?
A: We need to do a, b and c.

Etc

Etc

FIGURE 21.5 Mapping your deliverables

 **IN A NUTSHELL**

Your planning and management tools

You can use a range of planning tools to map and schedule your project. Brainstorming, fishbone diagrams and gap analyses (pages 526 and 60) are good ways to begin structuring your project. You can use Gantt charts and network diagrams (see pages 507 and 508) to show more detail for complex projects and flow charts (see page 593) for less complex projects. Work breakdown structures (see Figure 21.6 on page 661) are useful for scheduling and setting timelines and for identifying and sequencing parallel and interdependent activities. Flow charts, Gantt charts and network diagrams are good monitoring and reporting tools and page 585 explains a number of ways to monitor using statistics, including bar charts, control charts, histograms, Pareto charts, process capability charts, run charts and stratification charts. Financial planning and control mechanisms and administration controls are discussed on page 509.

You can also use specialised software to estimate, plan, schedule, manage budgets, allocate resources, help with making decisions, monitor quality and document progress. At the simple end of the spectrum are word processors and spreadsheets that can create templates for change; risk and stakeholder registers; and that you can use to plan, track and record expenditure. At the other end of the spectrum are dedicated project management tools to guide your project planning, management and closure, matching tasks and resources, scheduling tasks into a project timeline, tracking timesheets and expenses against timelines and so on. They also form the basis for reporting your project's progress.

Some project planning and management software, such as Microsoft Office Project 2013, Gantt Project, MacProject, Planner Suite and Primavera, are PC-based. Some, such as AceProject, Basecamp, Intervals, Mavenlink, and Zoho Projects, are web based. Others, such as Procore, are cloud-based. Some software is free, some generic software is purchased and some is bespoke. Some software includes an array of collaborative features.

Identify milestones

Milestones mark the completion of a major stage or phase of a project. They're important control points that are easy for everyone to recognise. They should be in a clear sequence of events that slowly build to the completion of a deliverable and to the project as a whole. When your team comes on board, review them with your team to identify who they affect and amend your stakeholder register as necessary.

Each milestone needs to be 'owned' by a team member or a sub-team that appoints a convenor from its own ranks; the convenor is ultimately responsible for the sub-team achieving its goals. The team member or sub-team breaks down each milestone into tasks, each with a start date and end date; in sub-teams, these tasks are then assigned to sub-team members. (See Chapter 11 and page 376 to find out more about developing individual and team performance plans.)

⦿ THEORY TO PRACTICE

How many milestones do you need?

You don't want too many milestones or they lose their lustre, but equally, you don't want them so far apart the project loses momentum. Here's a rule of thumb: reach a milestone every two weeks for projects of several months' duration. It's only a rule of thumb because it depends on whether your team members work full time or part time on the project; part-time teams may need more milestones so they can feel a sense of progress, which keeps the momentum going.

Once the milestones are broken down into activities and tasks, a diagram can show what needs to be done; this gives you a visual map of your project based on your deliverables similar to the map shown in Figure 21.6. This *project map* is sometimes called a *work breakdown structure* (WBS).

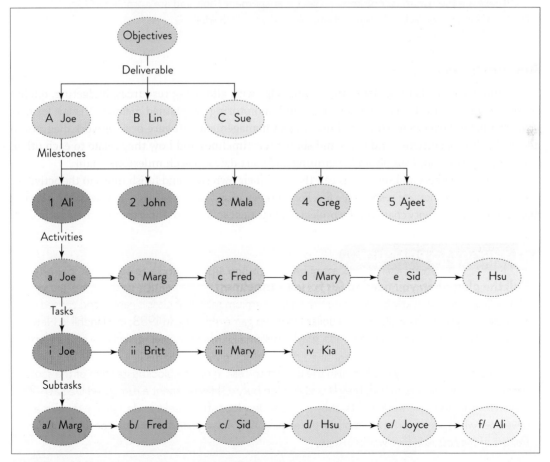

FIGURE 21.6 Your project map, or work breakdown structure

For long or complex projects, give each activity and task an identification number. As a rule of thumb, activities have a maximum duration of 5–10 days, or 40–80 hours, but again, this depends on whether your team is full time or part time.

Make milestones prominent in your project map and track them with a schedule (such as a Gantt chart), a calendar or project tracking software. If a milestone is missed, address it immediately and double check that you have allocated enough resources.

You cannot manage a project successfully without a clear map like this because when you're in uncharted territory, which projects are by their very nature, you are lost without a good roadmap. You can see how all the elements are logically connected and spot any unnecessary or duplicated activities and any important activities that have been left out.

◉ IN A NUTSHELL

PMBOK and Prince2

PMBOK stands for Project Management Body of Knowledge and provides a generic approach you can use in a variety of projects and industries.

Prince2 – PRojects IN Controlled Environments (versions 2)– was developed by the British Government and is now widely used as a project management tool that guides you through the process, or activities, of managing a project.

These are the two most common project management tools and are complementary, PMBOK being knowledge-based and Prince2 being a methodology.

Add timelines

Scheduling what needs to be done, and when, helps with allocating resources, budgeting, quality assurance and control, risk management and monitoring (explained below). Visual formats provide a helpful overview; you could use project management software or a network diagram to depict the flow of activities and tasks and show their timelines and how they relate to each other. Alternatively, you could simply add beginning and start dates to each milestone chain.

The team members and sub-teams can then add their own start and finish times to the activities, tasks and subtasks they are responsible for. For complex projects, sub-teams can also create network diagrams for their activity chains or use project management software to show the milestone's schedule.

◉ THEORY TO PRACTICE

Pull the plug when you need to (or fix your timelines)

Not pulling the plug nearly broke Atari, the once-premium maker of classic games and caused the near collapse of the multi-million dollar US video game industry. In 1983, in a landfill in New Mexico, the company buried thousands, maybe millions, of what has been called one of the worst video games ever: *E.T.*

It seems the company tried to rush the project to cash in on the blockbuster film of the same name and the result was so bad, they literally had to bury it. Having spent a rumoured US$20–25 million for the exclusive world rights, they gave the developer five weeks to design it – the same developer who spent over seven months developing *Yars' Revenge* and six months developing *Raiders of the Lost Ark*. Five weeks? Really?[4]

Estimating the resources required

Although the project charter may have begun to list the resources available, you need to review the project's requirements once you have mapped your project. Think about what the project needs regarding equipment such as office space, supplies and other consumable items, financing, information and people. What technical resources and project management tools do you and the team need?

Review your project scope, work breakdown structure and timelines and think about what you and your team need to achieve them. You can sometimes refer to past projects or discuss potential needs with people who have worked on similar projects. Bearing in mind that projects, by definition, are unique, look for information about the type and quantity of resources used as well as how long tasks take, because these are linked. The number and quality of resources assigned to a task can influence how long the task takes. (Five people can paint a house quicker than two people, and quicker still with high quality equipment.)

So ask yourself what you are going to need. Review your estimates of time taken to reach milestones because of the mutual dependency of resources and the period needed to complete the activity. Identify any assumptions you are making about team members' skills sets and other resources, for example office space. Figure 21.7 illustrates a way to work out the people and other resources your project needs.

As Yale's Professor Sherman Kent says, 'Estimating is what you do when you don't know.'[5] Estimating resources is inherently uncertain. Unless you have a lot of experience estimating resources, have someone experienced in this area review your estimates. Depending on the nature of the project, team members can review and help revise your resource estimates, too.

How long is a piece of string?

The time needed to produce the deliverables to reach a milestone can depend on resources available. Sometimes doubling the resources can halve the time it takes. Sometimes it doesn't. Adding more resources to creative or knowledge work doesn't generally make it produce the deliverable any quicker.

People's skills and experience affect the time it takes to produce deliverables too; generally, the more experienced and skilled team members are, the faster work is completed.

Your own team-building skills in helping the team work well together also affect how long it takes to reach deliverables. High-performing teams have synergy, and work flows smoothly.

Work breakdown sheet	Activity	Resources needed	Dates needed	Time (days/weeks)	Estimated costs	Actual cost

FIGURE 21.7 Resources requirements matrix

ACTION!

How many people and other resources do you need to complete your project successfully? Use the Resources requirements matrix and Who do you need? templates on CourseMateExpress for estimating the human and other resources your project needs.

Refining the project budget

Once you've identified and scheduled the work that needs to be done and the resources needed to do it, you can refine the budget in the project scope. Use the format other projects in your organisation have used or that the finance department may recommend. This may be as simple as a spreadsheet or it may be part of your project planning software.

Figures 21.7 and 21.10 can form the basis of your budget, although you need to include other expenses, such as project finalisation expenses, and perhaps an extra amount for contingencies. When you need to, look at the budgets for similar projects and ask other project managers to get a sense of what funding your project needs.

Building a risk register

Work through your project map and brainstorm the risks the project faces as it progresses. Any issue that can affect the success of your project and its timely completion is a risk.

List the risks you identify in a risk register, or risk log, so that you can be proactive in tracking and managing your project's risks throughout the entire project. Later, you will review and adjust the risk register with your team before analysing the risks and developing risk management plans that detail the best way to respond to each, either to eliminate the chance of a risk happening or to *mitigate*, or lessen, its effects if it does happen. Equally, some risks present opportunities that should be captured (not every risk is negative). Think about involving key stakeholders in identifying risks, too.

Risks may come from a variety of areas including:

- Environmental impacts and issues: What if the project harms the environment or breaches the organisation's sustainability protocols?
- External suppliers: What if they don't deliver on time, go out of business or don't manage their own risks properly?
- Finances: What if your budget blows out due to unforseen circumstances?
- Safety: What if a team member is physically or psychologically injured in the course of their work?
- Security: What if confidential information is inadvertently disclosed?
- Organisational: What if the promised support isn't delivered?
- Stakeholder relations: What if these deteriorate or are managed poorly? What if you lose the support of your supporters and observers join the ranks of the opposers?
- Technical: What if you can't get the right equipment soon enough or it costs more than you estimated?
- The quality of deliverables: What if deliverables fail to meet their success measures?
- Team members: What if you can't bring the right people on board or bring them on board soon enough? What if a key member leaves? What if a team member consistently fails to meet deadlines?
- Timeliness: What if activities along a critical path are delayed, delaying an entire deliverable?

Figure 21.8 summarises the risk management process, which is explained in detail in Chapter 23.

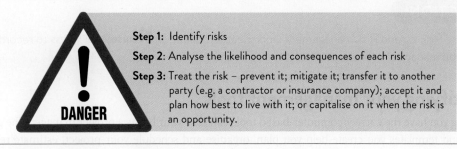

Step 1: Identify risks

Step 2: Analyse the likelihood and consequences of each risk

Step 3: Treat the risk – prevent it; mitigate it; transfer it to another party (e.g. a contractor or insurance company); accept it and plan how best to live with it; or capitalise on it when the risk is an opportunity.

FIGURE 21.8 Identifying and managing risks

Rate the risks you identify from 1 to 5 to assess how *likely* a risk is to occur. Number 1 is a low likelihood and 5 is probable. Rate their *impact* from 1 to 5, too so that 1 is a minimal effect on your project and 5 is catastrophic. To prioritise the risks, multiply likelihood by impact and pay most attention to the risks with the highest number.

As the project progresses, you and your team will identify further risks and some risks might disappear. Update your risk register as necessary and present it in your project status reports to the project sponsor and other stakeholders. Review the risk log regularly throughout the project and stay alert to early warning signs a risk is looming so that you can take timely action.

Highlight identified risks on your work breakdown structure and timeline map so that you know to pay special attention to that activity.

◉ THEORY TO PRACTICE

The Queensland health payroll project fiasco

When Queensland Health (QH) initiated a project to replace its complex and out-of-date payroll system, it never expected it to cost $64.5 million plus $1.2 billion a year to operate. Implemented three years later, in 2010, the new system, which incurred more than $1 billion in cost overruns, has failed to perform adequately with terrible consequences for the employees of QH and serious financial consequences for the state. In fact, when the project went live, thousands of staff went unpaid or underpaid. A 2010 Auditor General's report and a subsequent Commission of Audit report in July 2013 catalogued a long list of classic project management mistakes:

- size, complexity and scope of project significantly underestimated
- lack of planning
- poor tendering process
- unclear roles and responsibilities
- weak governance
- poorly designed, hierarchical team structure
- poor stakeholder engagement
- poorly managed roll-out
- lack of communication and training
- introduced while major problems were unresolved
- problems downgraded during the life of the project so that project could proceed
- lack of risk management and contingency planning.[6]

ACTION!

Use the Risk log and Risk management worksheet templates on **CourseMateExpress** to record and help you manage the risks you identify.

Identifying your management tools

Ensuring you have the correct computer-based tools can ease your life as a project manager. The graphs, charts and templates you create help you plan, organise and schedule your project, estimate resource requirements and allocate resources, identify problems and risks (remember that 'risks' can also be opportunities), and build a dashboard to monitor progress, health and safety, and resource use. (See the 'In a Nutshell: Your planning and management tools', earlier in this chapter.) You can also use the tools discussed on page 421. Follow the guidelines explained on those pages for establishing the ground rules for using your team technology.)

The tools that best suit your project depend on its complexity, duration and nature, and the number and location of team members. Selecting the right tools is important; using a sledgehammer to crack a walnut only bogs projects down with red tape. The tools are there to help you, not rule you. See page 420 for more information in using technology in teams.

Create a dashboard

Now or in the early stages of the project, create a dashboard of indicators that shows whether the project is on track and highlights areas that need attention. (A variety of software is available to help you create the perfect dashboard.) A good dashboard lets you, your team and your stakeholders monitor your project's progress 'at a glance' by consolidating, arranging and summarising key performance measures in visual representations. A dashboard is also the basis for your progress reports, telling you where you are in the project and highlighting any risks, success measures and tasks that need attention.

Dashboards show the actual against planned achievements. They typically include visual indicators such as those shown in Figure 21.9 for various key performance indicators such as milestones started

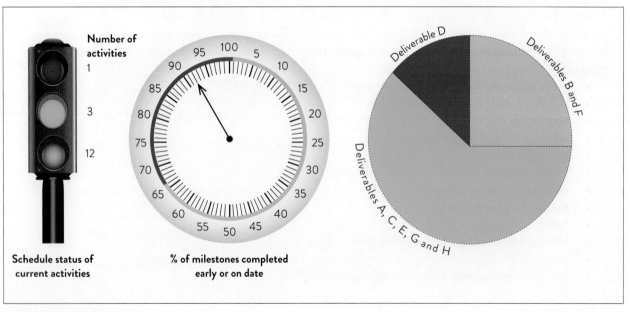

FIGURE 21.9 Dashboard indicators

and completed against planned timelines, progress towards the next milestone for each subsection of the project, an indication of the workload of each team member, performance to resource budgets (e.g. hours worked, money spent) and the current state of risks that could hinder or enhance performance.

Involve your team and key stakeholders in finalising the categories, indicators and their display formats. First decide the categories to monitor. Then select your indicators, or measures of success, for each category. Finally, choose a format for each indicator such as bar charts, pie charts, speedometers and traffic lights (green is going according to plan; yellow for one or more problems; red for one or more serious situations needing attention).

Keep the dashboard front and centre in your team members' minds by posting it in your team room and making it part of the home page of your on-line team room (as described on page 421).

Write up your project plan

Your team is going to spot things you've missed in each of the above areas, and together you will add further levels of detail and continually adjust and fine-tune your roadmap once the project gets underway. Meanwhile, write up your project plan for the project sponsor's and stakeholders' refinement and endorsement.

Once you have the necessary approvals and commitments, you can obtain the management tools and operational resources you need and gather your team, confident that you have the support you need.

◉ ACTION!

Use the Project plan template on  CourseMateExpress when you next write up a project plan.

◉ THEORY TO PRACTICE

Networks of teams

In 1990, Boeing had three layers of more than 200 cross-functional teams, all interlaced, to design the 777 passenger jet. The teams, made up of Boeing's top engineers, worked directly with customers and used new technology. Although it was the most complex project Boeing had undertaken, the project was completed in less than four months and the plane was in the air in less than five years – faster than any other plan previously. There are still 950 Boeing 777s in service.

The jet had fewer than half the number of design problems of earlier projects. The 'flap team', 'tail team' and 'wing team' all communicated with each other through their team leaders, who communicated with the overall cross-functional project management team. Many industry analysts consider the Boeing 777 project the most successful in commercial aviation history.[7]

2. Leading your project

> You're a project manager, not a magician. Magicians have way cooler hats.
>
> Merlin Mann (author, broadcaster), *Task Times* (2008)[8]

Once your project plan is approved, you can gather your team and with them, dot the i's and cross the t's of your project plan, finalise the stakeholder and risk registers and distribute tasks and resources. Then it's a simple (ha!) matter of managing and monitoring the performance of the team and the risks surrounding your project to ensure your plan stays on track and adjusting the plan as needed.

Remember, though, that the project plan describes your intentions and your work breakdown structure visually represents how you expect the project to roll out; the reality might be something quite different.

Remember, too, that the P in Project Management is also about People Management. You may be steering the project but your team are the engine and the wheels, and they ultimately make the project succeed or fail. The way you steer them across different roads, some hectic and some bumpy, some poorly banked and some with blind corners and steep hills, makes all the difference.

When your team members work in the same location, lead them as described in Chapters 9, 10, 11 and 13. When your project team is virtual, lead them as described in Chapters 9, 10, 11, 13 and 14.

Holding a stakeholder alignment meeting

The first major cause of unsuccessful projects we discussed (above) was failing to scope the project fully. The second major cause of unsuccessful projects is that its scope and goals are not understood in the same way by all the stakeholders. This can also lead to scope creep (described above). The stakeholder alignment meeting (or project kick-in meeting) aims to prevent both misunderstandings regarding the project's goals and scope creep. Think of this meeting as your project's success meeting, or safeguard meeting.

The more far-reaching, important and complex the project, the more important it is to present an overview of your project plan to key stakeholders. This one-off meeting, held early on, ensures everyone is clear about the project's outcomes. It needn't be a long meeting and it isn't about the nuts and bolts of the project – it's to ensure that everyone understands the scope and goals of the project and their own role in the project's success. You might also want to let stakeholders air any concerns, although this should all have been covered in advance, in individual stakeholder consultation meetings.

Depending on the project and your organisation's protocols, your team members can participate in the stakeholder alignment meeting or you can lead a kick-off presentation to a joint meeting of team members and stakeholders. This would be your team's introduction to the project. (You will of course hold frequent interim checks with stakeholders as part of your communication plan.)

Putting your team together

Gathering the right people together and leading them so they can meet the project's constraints, timelines, quality standards and other requirements takes thought and skill. Unless you can do that, your project is doomed.

Your team might be virtual or it might bring people with different expertise from the same worksite together. It might include external contractors and advisors and you might bring people in as and when they're needed. Your team might have constantly shifting membership and members might work full-time on the project or remain part of their own work teams and work part-time on your project in addition to their other duties.

Whichever it is, think about the knowledge and skills your team members need to meet your deliverables (see Figure 21.10) and go for a diversity of experience, expertise and personality styles:

* action-oriented people
* creative people who can come up with ideas for others to take forward
* people who are good at implementing and executing
* people who nurture the team and the project along
* people willing to search for information and investigate options.

(See page 802 to find out about determining the attributes, experience and skills you need; page 216 to find out why personality styles are important; and page 846 for more on the importance of diversity in teams.)

When your project is for a specific user group, include one of their number on your team, if not as a full member, at least as someone to regularly liaise with and to review your progress. This person's insights into the user group's culture, informal working relationships, power structures and working styles helps ensure your end product is perfect for its users' needs.

Work breakdown sheet	Activity	Skills and knowledge needed	Skill level needed	Name of team member	Deliverable	Days estimated	Schedule		Days actual	Cost estimated	Cost actual
							Start	Finish			
Activity A Task A 1	Develop research study	Market research design: high-tech and WSN	Expert	Joe	Research ready to trial	3	3/7	6/7		$2000	
A 2	Trial research	Conducting research analytics	Expert	Britt	Results, conclusions and recommend-ations	10	8/7	20/7		$6000	
A 3	Conduct research	Conducting research and applying analytics	Intermediate	Mary	Results and conclusions	35	12/8	23/9		$18 500	

FIGURE 21.10 Who do you need?

Kick-starting your project team

For a project team in which members are able to get together in the same location, set up an actual team room supported by the technology you are using. When your team is virtual, set up a virtual team room (as described on page 421) and ask members to familiarise themselves with it before your launch meeting.

Launch meetings, or kick-off meetings, generally last a half to one day and are your first opportunity to work with the team to gain their buy-in to the project and its objectives. Your agenda should include:

* welcome and opening comments, including a review of the scope statement, which acts as your team purpose statement
* a project overview, describing the project's business case and its sponsor, major deliverables and milestones for each
* self introductions
* agreeing operating guidelines
* a review of the project schedule you have developed
* a review of the stakeholder and risk registers
* a review of the technology your team will use
* reporting requirements.

Post or distribute an agenda for the launch meeting and any pre-meeting documents you want the team to read (such as the project charter, scope and project plan) and advise team members what you want them to cover in their self-introductions to their teammates.

To help make sure peoples' knowledge is used and the team doesn't defer to the person with the loudest voice or to the most articulate person, self-introductions should include members' areas of expertise (which should also be listed in your team room). Ask members to comment on how they believe they can add value to the team, their working style and other projects they've worked on and what they have learned from them that might help this team.

To help team members find out what they have in common and help people bond, which lubricates their working relationships, ask people to say a few words about themselves personally, such as their interests outside work. Figure 21.11 shows why these introductions are so important.

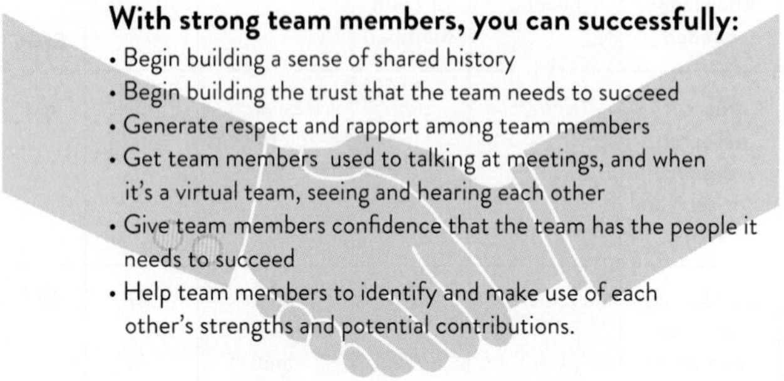

With strong team members, you can successfully:
- Begin building a sense of shared history
- Begin building the trust that the team needs to succeed
- Generate respect and rapport among team members
- Get team members used to talking at meetings, and when it's a virtual team, seeing and hearing each other
- Give team members confidence that the team has the people it needs to succeed
- Help team members to identify and make use of each other's strengths and potential contributions.

FIGURE 21.11   The importance of introductions

After members have introduced themselves, agree how you want to work together and communicate (see 'In a Nutshell: Your team operating agreement'). It's a big mistake to think you can save time by working out your 'rules of engagement' as you go along.

IN A NUTSHELL

Your team operating agreement

Team operating agreements (TOAs) manage team member's assumptions and behaviours about such matters as confidentiality, how to share information and make decisions, what to do if agreement isn't reached, how and when to use which types of communication tools, how quickly to respond to requests and queries, how to air problems and concerns and deal with disagreements and conflict, and where meetings are to be held and who should attend.

TOAs should also cover personal courtesies such as use of mobile phone during meetings and interrupting and overtalking during meetings. (See Figure 28.1 on page 939.)

These are your operating guidelines for working together and become the team's norms after a while. Update them as the need arises and use this information to orient any new members joining the team.

Although your team is probably expected to start producing results quickly, the time you spend laying the groundwork for clear communication and getting to know each other pays off in the long run. However, keep the meeting moving. You don't want to get so bogged down in the 'getting to know you' part that you don't have time to turn to task matters.

Holding your first few meetings

Plan your meetings carefully as described on page 934. You have three initial objectives for your first few meetings (how to lead virtual meetings is explained on page 948):

1. Helping members bond.
2. Agreeing team operating agreements (TOAs).
3. Establishing a team and individual performance plans (see Chapters 11 and page 376) by your third meeting.

Review your work breakdown structure (WBS) and timelines and begin taking them to the next levels of detail; assign individual roles, responsibilities and deliverables so that team members can complete the WBS for their own areas of responsibility and start developing their own performance plans. This forms the basis of the team's work, provides role clarity and gives you a way to assess the team's and individual member's performance and progress. Discuss and agree each team member's performance plan privately, before posting them in the team room.

Also ask team members to review the stakeholder and risk registers, particularly regarding their own areas of responsibility, so you can begin detailing your risk management plan and stakeholder communication plans during your next meeting. Your goal is to have your WBS and risk and stakeholder management plans fleshed out as quickly as you can so the team can get on with their work, while avoiding the omissions and mistakes caused by rushing.

Ask members to keep a learnings log for the post project learnings review and request weekly work updates, or project status reports, from all team members summarising:

* work accomplished
* work planned
* risks identified
* any problems
* any requests.

Working together on the operating protocols, team performance plan, and risk and stakeholder management plans ensures everyone understands the important issues facing the team and feels ownership and accountability for achieving the team's goals.

THEORY TO PRACTICE

Try a project pre-mortem

A project pre-mortem helps you identify what could cause your project to fail and, since forewarned is forearmed, it's a good way to safeguard your project's success.

At your team's second or third meeting, announce that the project has failed spectacularly. Then ask them to spend five or 10 minutes individually listing plausible reasons for the failure on a sheet of paper.

Then go around the team asking for one reason each, listing each on a whiteboard. When all the reasons have been recorded, review the list to find ways to strengthen your plan.

For more complex projects, ask team members to write one reason per index card. Then gather and shuffle the cards and sort them into themes for reviewing and finding ways to strengthen your plan.

Executing and monitoring your project

Now it's time to get to work. As project manager, you're guiding, facilitating, coordinating and controlling the project and managing it from four perspectives:

- *Business*, which covers your organisation's strategic goals and vision and your project's goals
- *Political*, which covers your organisation's and stakeholders' issues and constraints
- *Team*, which ensures team members fully understand their deliverables and timelines and remain focused on, committed to and able to achieve them
- *Technical*, which covers the work that must be done to successfully deliver the project.

As shown in Figure 21.12, your project management activities fall into six areas.

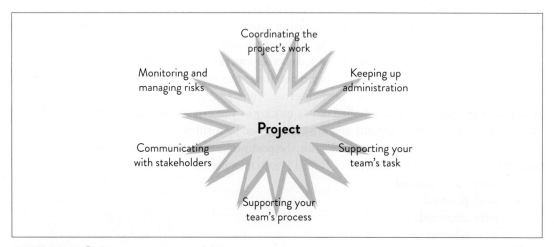

Coordinating the
project's work

Monitoring and
managing risks

Keeping up
administration

Project

Communicating
with stakeholders

Supporting your
team's task

Supporting your
team's process

FIGURE 21.12 Project management activities

Coordinate project work

Tracking milestones and deliverables is essential so you don't fall behind. As Frederick Brooks, the computer scientist who developed IBM's System/360 computers said, 'How does a project get to be a year late? One day at a time.'[9] Neither you nor the project's sponsor or stakeholders should ever be surprised by a project running late, over budget or out of scope.

While team members work on the activities they're responsible for, individually and in subteams, you are monitoring work against timelines, paying particular attention to the critical paths and critical control points so that delays don't hold up other work (see page 421 for more information on critical paths and critical control points.) You're also ensuring needed resources, including information, are reaching team members as they need them. Don't get caught up in day-to-day, unimportant urgent activities (as explained on page 115).

Keep the schedule up-to-date and posted in your team room so everyone knows what's going on. This is also a good way to keep everyone on track and working on the priority tasks, and to remind them of upcoming tasks and milestones.

Monitor the quality of team members' output and provide the support, in terms of equipment, information and resources, that people need to achieve their deliverables. If a milestone is missed, address it immediately, reallocating resources as necessary.

FYI

The best laid plans ...

> But Mousie, thou are no thy-lane [you are not alone], In proving foresight may be vain: The best laid schemes o' Mice an' Men, Gang aft agley [often go awry], An' lea'e us nought but grief an' pain [leave us nothing but grief and pain], For promis'd joy [Instead of joy].
>
> Robert Burns, *To a Mouse*[10]

Should you feel despondent when your best-laid project plan goes awry, remember that it happens to everyone. That's why projects need managers.

The nature of some projects means that testing at various phases is needed. As discussed in Chapter 19, it's generally best to test early and often. To save egg-on-face further down the track, don't take shortcuts with tests, even when budgets and time are tight. You can never know whether something is workable until you try it out.

THEORY TO PRACTICE

Innovations in the ABC

It's good enough for Barack Obama, the Dalai Lama and the Muppets, and it's good enough for Auntie, too. Video Hangouts, that is. One of many innovation projects under the direction of Angela Clark, Director of ABC Innovation, this project was led by Penelope Hogan, Digital Networks Coordinator.

The project charter was based on a low-cost way to broadcast on line using social media engagement. Viewers submit questions on Facebook, Google+ or Twitter to an ABC personality, giving audiences the opportunity to 'get to know' them through a live Q&A.

Using the platform, Hangouts on Air, which allows anyone with an Internet-enabled camera to stream a live discussion via YouTube, the team held a series of tests before the first official hangout, checking everything from the interaction between the cameras to the backdrops, lighting, Internet connection, microphone setup and picture quality.

Once the bugs were removed and the hangout polished to the ABC's high standards, five live trials went to air over six months, attracting a worldwide audience. Dr Karl kicked off the personality Q&As, followed by Todd Sampson, Zan Rowe, Stella Young and Jimmy Giggle. Moderators included triplej's Zan Rowe, Annabel Crabb, and News 24's Kumi Tagutchi. The ABC Hangouts continue to attract plays long after their initial broadcast date.

What's next? One possibility is capturing live 'behind the scenes' footage. But that's for another project.[11]

Keep up with administration

Set time aside for administrative duties, such as updating expenditure records, resource use and time sheets, managing scope change requests, and completing project reports. Track changes to the project scope, cost and schedule variances.

● THEORY TO PRACTICE

When you're heading off course

Alert your project sponsor at the first sign of a timeline or budget overrun. Show you're on top of the problem by leaving the excuses at your desk and arming yourself with options for getting back on track. When you need more time or more money, explain the benefits that can accrue as a result and present your request as an alteration or adjustment to the plan, not a crisis.

Support your team's task

A team's process is the way people interact and conduct themselves and their task is their actual work. You need to attend to both. (Chapters 11, 13 and 14 expand on the information below.)

You ensured that team members know exactly what's expected of them when you mapped the project and assigned deliverables. Train team members to use any of the team's project management tools and techniques they are not familiar with early on; learning as you go is inefficient.

Hold regular status meetings with your team to review progress to date, current status against plans and forecast completion estimates, and discuss any decisions to be made, corrective actions to be taken, looming risks, and the need for additional resources.

Status meetings can range from daily stand-up meetings or 'team huddles' to regular weekly or bi-weekly meetings; try to hold them at the same time on the same day(s). You want to keep everyone up to date without wasting time. If a concern or issue needs to be explored in more detail and not everyone needs to be involved, hold a follow-up meeting with specific team members.

You've probably heard the saying that if everything seems to be going well, you've obviously overlooked something. In project management terms, this means that adjusting the schedule as the project unfolds – adding and removing activities, altering timelines, and so on – is inevitable.

Introduce a 'pause and learn' discussion at the completion of each milestone to identify mishaps and successes and see what you can learn from them and look for ways to work better, faster and smarter (see page 565 for ideas on how to make small improvements). You can use a lessons learned journal or log to capture and distribute these improvements. (Commemorate the achievement of milestones in some way, too, as described below.)

These meetings help pull the project together. As with all meetings, prepare for them in advance and send out a clear agenda with notice of any required reference material and preparation. (See page 951 for more information on how to prepare for and lead actual and virtual meetings.)

Support your team's process

We've considered two main causes of failed projects: partial scoping and stakeholders not being clear on the project's scope and goals. A third major cause of unsuccessful projects is poor working relationships within the team. Hidden agendas, lack of trust, poor interpersonal skills and strong personalities can easily push a project off course.

Building and maintaining a good working environment takes effort but is essential to a project's success. Take particular care to monitor team dynamics and keep morale up when members leave and join the team. (See page 407 for information on what happens when people join and leave teams and page 97 for information on working with group dynamics). Address any concerns, disagreements and disputes early on because minor issues can quickly become full-blown problems.

Don't let peoples' hard work go unrewarded. Recognise accomplishments and small wins and celebrate milestone completions in a fun and energising way.

● THEORY TO PRACTICE

Multiple partners, multiple dangers, multiple benefits

In June 2006, five companies (Connell Wagner – now Aurecon as the result of a merger, Maunsell/AECOM, Queensland Rail (QR), Thiess and United Group) formed a partnership to design and build nine rail projects valued at about $1 billion for QR. They called the consortium TrackStar Alliance. It has hundreds of people, including designers, constructors, rail industry specialists and supporting professionals, and offices on the edge of Brisbane's CBD. And it doesn't exist. It has no ABN and no employees.

With five competing organisations coming together, the potential for conflict – clashing cultures, objectives and working structures – was high. Yet to date, TrackStar has delivered on time and to budget and has won a raft of awards including awards from the Project Management Association, the Environmental Protection Agency and the Queensland Major Contractors Association.

Communication and understanding the needs and wants of the five partners is credited for the success of the alliance. To encourage integration, employees from all five partners work out of the same office. Everyone works around five core words: care, clarity, connection, courage and creativity. Everyone wears special TrackStar clothing, identifying them as members of the same team. Because new team members come on board regularly, management runs a briefing every fortnight for new starts, and once every six months all employees spend a day together working on new project tasks and in different groups. These five strategies have been important in breaking down the usual barriers you would expect in a merged and temporary project team.

To overcome the ever-present risk of coming in late and over budget, TrackStar has 'courageous conversations' once a month. A representative from each partner company and QR meet and are invited to speak out about what they regard is and isn't working. This overcomes the usual reluctance to flag bad news and problems, allowing them to be solved before they fester and irretrievably damage the project.[12]

Communicate

Up to 80% of your time during the project's execution phase should be spent communicating with your team and stakeholders. When team members are part-time and retain responsibilities in their usual roles, check in regularly with their managers to make sure they are aware of the project's progress and their team member's contribution to it.

When you and your team are working in the same location, check in daily with team members individually, however briefly, to see how they're going. When you are in different locations, meet virtually with team members individually at least weekly to discuss progress, concerns, anything that might be holding them back, and so on. When an activity is not on track, work out what corrective action to take.

Remember the small talk, too. Find out what each is enjoying about the project and their contribution to ensure they're motivated and that you know how to keep their motivation high.

Keep in touch with your project sponsor and update stakeholders on the project's progress according to your communication plan. Distribute one-page status reports to stakeholders with a brief overview of accomplishments and successes, key milestones, top five risks and issues, dashboard information and anything else important to the project and stakeholders. Copy the team on these regular formal written communication to stakeholders.

Discuss any risks or decisions you want your sponsor's and stakeholders' input on face-to-face or by telephone rather than email and check in informally to make sure everyone is happy with the way the project is unrolling.

Monitor and manage risks

Keep a constant eye on whatever can endanger or assist your project to remove or mitigate the former and capitalise on the latter. There are lots of ways to manage risk. You can, for example, develop more efficient working methods, redefine or renegotiate project parameters when necessary, reduce costs when this doesn't adversely affect quality, seek further resources to meet deadlines, or multiskill and cross-skill team members.

Diarise reminders so that you don't forget this important activity. The risk management process is explained in detail in Chapter 23.

3. Completing your project

'Begin at the beginning,' the king said gravely, 'and go on till you come to the end; then stop.'

Lewis Carroll, *Alice's adventures in Wonderland* (2010)[13]

Once your team has achieved its deliverables, you still have work to do. It's important to finalise the project correctly – so important that large and long-lived projects often have specialist closure managers.

Begin finalising your project by identifying work that still needs to be completed, and make sure it isn't forgotten. Thank all the team members for their energy, effort and contributions, and formally mark the end of a successful, and hopefully, rewarding, part of your working lives; when appropriate, hold a closing ceremony, silly or serious, and hand out small tokens of appreciation. When the project is lengthy and major, compiling a scrapbook, as described on page 418, can make a nice parting gift from you to team members.

Thank team members' managers, too, and begin releasing those who have completed their assigned deliverables, ensuring they transit to their next role or previous role smoothly. Offer private individual feedback and encouragement to team members and, when appropriate, to the managers whose team members were 'on loan'.

Finish administrative tasks such as finalising your budget and other necessary documentation, writing team member evaluations, organising a formal project closure meeting with your sponsor and stakeholders and preparing a project closure document to send to them after the meeting; this document marks the end of all project activities and the acceptance of the project's deliverables. Store all documents produced during the project in your organisation's knowledge base for future use.

● IN A NUTSHELL

Project closure checklist

Closing a project is as important as its planning. Here is a handy checklist:
- all deliverables delivered
- all invoices paid
- any needed tests completed and finalised
- any needed user group training completed and follow ups scheduled
- lessons learned meeting scheduled with team members and sponsor.

Prepare your project evaluation, or close-out, report. Follow the format used in your organisation or use the following headings:

1. Review the project scope and deliverables.
2. Compare the project's actual achievements in terms of costs, deliverables, timelines and managing risks with the original plan; explain any deviations from the plan; suggest actions to realise or improve benefits.
3. Team member appraisals.
4. Lessons learned (add this after your team learnings meeting).

Here are some questions to consider when writing your report (you can find out more about preparing reports on page 172):

* Is everything in place and working properly?
* Are the users or clients, the project sponsor and stakeholders happy?
* Are there any problems and how will they be addressed?
* How will any areas of dissatisfaction be addressed?
* Does this project lead naturally to other projects to build on its success and extend the benefits delivered?

 **ACTION!**

Use the Close-out report template on **CourseMateExpress** to write your report.

Learning from the project

You and your team want to build on your experiences, growing with each project you undertake. Invite the team to join you once more to celebrate the successful completion of your project and to review it to capture lessons learned. Do this while the project is still fresh in everyone's minds but when you can see whether the organisation has benefited from your project as expected. Consider inviting the project sponsor and key stakeholders to the celebration and project review, too.

The purpose of this kick-out meeting is twofold. You want to officially acknowledge, by way of a celebration, the end of the project to provide closure for team members and thank them for their hard work. And you want to identify lessons that can be applied to other projects. Remember to consider successes as well as shortfalls.

Think about:

* how efficiently and effectively the outcomes were achieved
* how well team members worked together
* what went well in this project
* what to make sure you do again next time
* what didn't go as well as expected and how that can be prevented next time
* what you would do differently next time
* how well you and the team managed the risks and how you could do this better next time
* how well you and the team managed other issues and how you could do better next time
* how well you and the team handled any unforeseen problems and how you could do better next time.

Figure 21.13 shows an example outline for a review meeting. As with any review, focus on the future and keep blame out of all discussions. Document successes and capture the lessons learned to make sure they aren't forgotten. A word of caution: don't go mad on the review process. Its potential benefits need to be worth the time and effort.

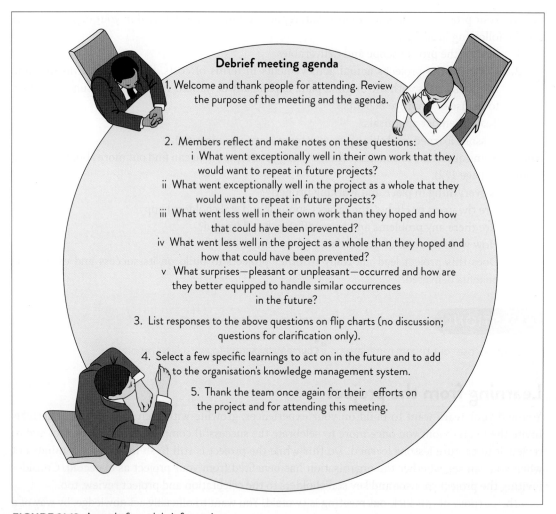

Debrief meeting agenda

1. Welcome and thank people for attending. Review the purpose of the meeting and the agenda.

2. Members reflect and make notes on these questions:
   i What went exceptionally well in their own work that they would want to repeat in future projects?
   ii What went exceptionally well in the project as a whole that they would want to repeat in future projects?
   iii What went less well in their own work than they hoped and how that could have been prevented?
   iv What went less well in the project as a whole than they hoped and how that could have been prevented?
   v What surprises—pleasant or unpleasant—occurred and how are they better equipped to handle similar occurrences in the future?

3. List responses to the above questions on flip charts (no discussion; questions for clarification only).

4. Select a few specific learnings to act on in the future and to add to the organisation's knowledge management system.

5. Thank the team once again for their efforts on the project and for attending this meeting.

FIGURE 21.13 Agenda for a debrief meeting

Think about what you learned as project leader, too: What discoveries did you make? How did people work together at the start of the project? What accounts for that? How well did you work with your sponsor? Did you select team members with the skills and attributes the project needed? What would you do differently next time and what improvements to your leadership could you make?

 **ACTION!**

Are your project management skills as good as you hope they are? Find out with the interactive self-test, How good are you project management skills? on **CourseMate**Express.

CourseMateExpress

Go to http://login.cengagebrain.com to access CourseMate Express, your online study tool for *Management Theory & Practice*. CourseMate Express brings chapter concepts to life with interactive learning, and study and exam preparation tools:

- Test your skills in different aspects of management with interactive self-tests and simulations.
- Watch videos that show how real managers operate in real businesses.
- Test your understanding of the changing world of management by taking the revision quiz.

QUICK REVIEW

1. What is the difference between a project charter and a project scope? Which does the project manager develop?
2. Explain the function of a project scope and list the information it should contain.
3. Explain the uses of a project plan and list the information it should contain. At what point should the project manager stop adjusting it?
4. What is the purpose of stakeholder communication and engagement?
5. What needs to be done to finalise a project?

BUILD YOUR SKILLS

1. Referring to Case Study 19.1 on page 612, use the information in this chapter to develop a plan for bringing the cynics on side. If you have studied Chapter 22, include information from that chapter as well.
2. Referring to Chapter 11's opening Scenario on page 323, draw a flow chart of Damien's approach to setting up his project team and analyse his approach. What advice would you offer him for his next steps in leading the team?
3. Discuss the following statement: Managing projects is mostly about planning, managing risks and managing people.
4. List the three major causes of unsuccessful projects mentioned in this chapter and discuss how each could doom a project. Give specific examples.
5. Referring to Chapter 11's opening Scenario on page 323, how well is Damien going about setting up his project team? Can you offer him any advice for managing the project's initial stages? If Damien's project team were virtual, what additional advice would you offer him?
6. Develop a detailed project scope for building a shed in the back garden.
7. Referring to Chapter 17's opening Scenario on page 491, what might some of the project's deliverables and milestones be? How many sub-teams do you recommend Hamish create and what might their deliverables be? How should these sub-teams communicate? If Hamish does create his own mini-project team, who should be on it?
8. Referring to 'The strategic perspective: Great ideas – but think them through' on page 502, how would a careful project charter and project scope, and proper project execution, have prevented this costly disaster?
9. Develop a project scope for this chapter's opening Scenario.

WORKPLACE ACTIVITIES

1. Find and review two or three examples of project charters in your organisation.
2. Investigate how projects are scoped in your organisation. Is there a template, or a format to follow?
3. What documentation does your organisation require to plan, execute and finalise a project?
4. What information from after action reviews, or project learnings, are held in your organisation's knowledge base? Review the last few documents and summarise the main learnings.

CASE STUDY 21.1

THE EXECUTION BLACK SPOT

Paul sits pondering his close-out report for the traffic black spot improvement project he has just managed. He's noted a few learnings for future projects: Don't use the traffic management contractor I used. They were hopeless. Contact electricity earlier because their timelines are long and complex. That held the project up for a good three weeks, which I could have avoided by earlier liaison. Keep the community better informed and updated more regularly so we're not inundated with complaints and questions.

And what about me personally? I worked hard to get this gig, he thinks. My first as a project manager – putting in my time working on project teams for huge, billion-dollar road projects undertaken by the department, convening sub-teams, networking with the bosses to keep my visibility high, always positive, always 'Can do'. But did I get as big a kick out of managing this project as I expected?

I enjoyed the whole scoping and project planning part. Nice and logical, think it through carefully, just as I learned to do. Get that right and the project flows pretty smoothly, which basically it did, apart from the odd gentle hiccup. The risk assessment was interesting and taught me to be wary of quotes given during a busy period when the contractors have enough work on. They just pull silly numbers out of the air, I reckon. That's something to add to the learnings, too, maybe. But I nailed the bitumen supply – always tricky. I don't know why there's such a shortage of the stuff.

The sponsor was great, a been-there-done-that guy who was happy to give me my head as long as I checked in every week with a progress report. And he was a gentleman and a scholar when I nearly ran over budget (even though we'd built in an extra 10% for contingencies). He knew exactly how to get me back on track. That was a valuable learning experience.

Yeah, loved the scoping and planning. Execution – that's another story. I felt like a pure administrator. No – like an old nag. During execution, my job was hassling people all day. Have you done this? Have you done that? When will this be finished? All that endless following up. Once the project got underway and I handed over work to the Contract Administration Department, their site engineer took over monitoring the contractors and I hardly even got on site to see what was happening.

Perhaps I should go into professional landscaping – then I could plan the project and when it comes to execution, get in there with a shovel and really get my hands dirty. Best of both worlds.

Ah well. Back to the close-out report.

Questions

1. What other learnings might Paul have from scoping and managing the project?
2. How do learnings in a close-out report help organisations and project managers?
3. What sort of attributes do you think a good project manager needs? How would you advise Paul?

THE TEXTBOOK PROJECT

Even though they don't call themselves project managers, many people are. Take a book (known in the publishing trade as a *title*) like this textbook that you're reading now. The person in charge of the book's overall creation isn't called a project manager. She's a publishing editor – meet Margaret. And this book wouldn't exist unless Margaret were a project manager *extraordinaire*. Let's take a look at how projects work inside a publishing house.

A key part of Margaret's role is to develop publishing projects. Acting as the project's sponsor, she writes and presents a detailed proposal to the publishing committee – senior management executives who can authorise the project to move ahead. The proposal contains all of the elements outlined in the 'In a Nutshell: The project charter' on page 651.

Once approved, a development editor picks up the reins – meet John. Poor John actually has to read chapters as the author – meet Sam – sends them in, checking for glaring errors, balderdash and potential law suits, and he looks for ways to enhance the book, for example, by suggesting imaginative illustrations.

John must ensure the project meets its timelines at all costs. Imagine, for example, that author Sam is weeks late in handing over the manuscript, or that John keeps falling asleep while reading the chapters and doesn't get through them all according to schedule? Such delays would trigger a cascade of unpalatable events.

Take the effect on the reviewers, for example. Reviewers are the teachers and practitioners who provide technical checks on the accuracy of the content across the various subject areas covered by a textbook. A delay in the schedule means John needs to put the reviewers on later timelines. Some may not be available at the later date, so John has to find last-minute replacements and persuade them to do some fast (yet comprehensive) night-time reading.

A delay also means the manuscript is late in its handover to the person who is putting together the material for the book's website – meet Allan. Many textbooks have websites, just as this textbook you're reading now has CourseMate Express to extend your experience of the topic you're studying. Allan's deliverables also include writing the learner guides, preparing student-support material and developing the teacher's support manual.

The next important person is the production editor – meet Erin. She picks up the project management reigns from John and coordinates all the activities required before the text is ready to go into print, and also to be turned into an e-book. If the all-important milestone hand-over to Erin is missed, the timelines of the following people are affected: copy editor, internal designers and cover designer, typesetter, printer, proofreader and indexer. The website's designers and IT developers would all need re-negotiated timelines, too.

Most of these people are freelancers or working for other companies and they have already planned their workflow around the original dates agreed. They may well have to move on to their next projects and Erin will need to fill their roles all over again.

Delays in either of the two projects, John's development project or Erin's production project, can hold up the publication date, which means the textbook may miss the new academic cycle, a window that doesn't open again for six months. That means that all the preparatory work of the sales and marketing teams has been for nought and they may lose considerable goodwill with their clients (and that could affect other textbooks they represent). Teachers who have been promised the textbook in time for the next teaching cycle have to find alternative printed and online textbooks for their students. The publisher's internal budgets would have to be revised, too.

In John and Erin's projects, their textbook came off the press on time because they were able to quickly readjust the schedule when some members of the team warned that there was risk of delay.

So, is being in charge of managing a project, whatever you choose to call it, worth it? Ask Margaret, John and Erin and they'll tell you, in unison, that managing projects in the publishing industry is a tricky juggling act, with multiple books on the go at any one time, all at different stages. It's a headache, to be sure. But when a shiny new title rolls off the press, it's all worthwhile.

Questions

1. What specific steps could John take to achieve an on-time handover to production?
2. Erin is coordinating the work of many knowledge workers, most of them external. How would you advise her to build effective working relationships with them? What are some ways she could monitor their work so their deliverables are ready on time?
3. What are the main assumptions and constraints of a book publishing project? What other risks are there besides a timeline blow-out by the author or one of the project managers on their deliverables?

INTRODUCING AND MANAGING CHANGE

Individuals can be misoneists. Work teams and entire organisations can be misoneistic, too. *Misoneism* (mis-o-nee-ism) means hatred or fear of change or innovation. But when you don't change, you don't survive.

Whether we like it or not, today's operating environment is a constantly turning kaleidoscope of change, making change a permanent state in most organisations and something everyone needs to learn to take in their stride. The sudden global financial crisis that began in 2007 demonstrated how quickly external factors can force unexpected change on organisations. (The many factors driving and enabling change in organisations are discussed in Chapter 1.)

Organisations must adapt and transform to live on. They are changing the way they organise and manage their operations and the way they organise and manage employees. They are reinventing themselves – no longer once a generation but once every two or three years.

But the danger of constant change is employee mistrust and burnout. When change comes often and fast, people's tendency is to fight, flee or freeze, which makes leading change both absolutely essential and incredibly difficult. Change management is no longer a specialised skill but one that all leader-managers need.

1. Can you explain the continuing process of change and the six phases of change that continually cycle in all organisations?
2. Can you plan, resource and monitor the introduction of change?
3. Can you promote change with empathy and understanding?
4. Can you overcome people's resistance to change?

This chapter explains how to avoid the curse of misoneism and helps you to develop the highly prized skill of being a leader-manager who can deliver change.

When two become one

Mark stares at the paragraph in an article he's reading that states that mergers and acquisitions continue to be a popular way for organisations to grow, despite that fact that most research indicates that between 50% and 80% of them fail.[1] He grimly contemplates his task of merging two teams from different organisational cultures, introducing some of the team members to different computer and information management systems, and creating new workflows through the department to incorporate the best of each organisation's procedures. His bank and another had recently announced their merger with much fanfare, including a promise that minimal redundancies would result and front-line employees would continue to provide the high-quality service their customers appreciated.

Mark pictures dejected and suspicious faces turning towards him at the first meeting of his newly merged team. The employees know as well as he does that, despite the promises, considerable duplication and overlap of duties are bound to occur as a result of the merger and no organisation can afford to have two people doing one job. He knows his area will be more affected than most in this regard and he also knows how important it will be to find a way to retain the best employees – whichever institution they originate from.

'Maybe I can play the loyalty card,' he thinks. 'Or perhaps the lure of exciting new opportunities can entice the people I need to stay. But that won't work while they're still feeling shocked and abandoned. I'll deal with their emotions first. And I'll acknowledge the strong history of both banks and the contribution everyone in the merged team has already made to both banks' success. I need them to understand that by working together we really can go on to even bigger and better things.

'One thing is certain,' Mark thinks, 'we may have the best strategy, processes and products in the country but unless I can sort out the people issues, my team will take a giant step backwards.'

1. Seeing change as part of life

Nothing endures but change.

Heraclitus (ancient Greek philosopher), *Yale Book of Quotations*, Yale University (2006)[2]

For the past 300 years, a mechanistic view of the world has prevailed. But people and organisations aren't machines, nor are they like machines. And change doesn't occur with the precision of a well-oiled machine, either.

It's probably better to think of people and organisations as living systems, which allows us to see change as a normal part of life, an ever-present cycle that every individual and every organisation goes through. Caterpillars become butterflies; seasons change; babies grow to adulthood.

Jonas Salk, the immunologist and physician who discovered the polio vaccine, describes the natural order of growth that governs living systems as a *sigmoid*, an S-shaped curve of growth, prosperity, stability and decline.[3] The S-curve of change probably applies to families, communities, civilisations and organisations, too. As shown in Figure 22.1, systems need to make great 'leaps' and jump the S-curves in order to escape the decline that is the natural order of life.

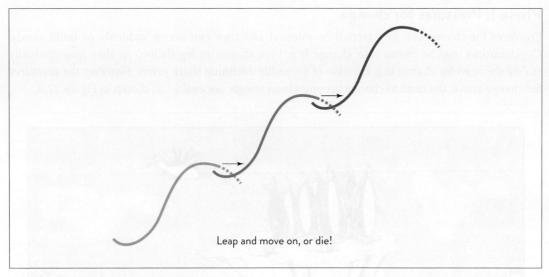

Leap and move on, or die!

FIGURE 22.1 The S-curve of change

The continuous cycle of change

Heraclitus also said, 'All is flux, nothing stays still.'[4] Whether you're thinking about families, organisations or societies, change is a continuing process, not a one-off event. The six phases of change shown in Figure 22.2 continuously cycle around all systems, although the rate at which they cycle differs from one system to another.

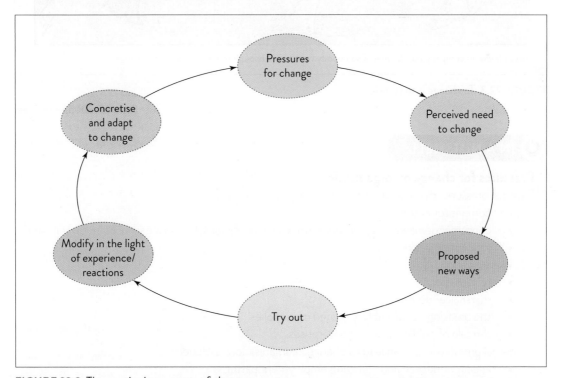

FIGURE 22.2 The continuing process of change

Phase 1: Pressures for change

Pressures for change can be external or internal and they can arrive suddenly or build slowly. Organisations may be forced into change (e.g. by a change in legislation) or they may gradually realise the need for change (e.g. because of a steadily declining share price). However the pressures for change arrive, the need to change becomes increasingly noticeable, as shown in Figure 22.3.

Talbot knew his company was doomed if somebody wasn't bold enough to take a chance on change.

FIGURE 22.3 To change is to survive

Source © 2005 Kevin Pope[5]

IN A NUTSHELL

Pressures for change on organisations

External pressures that can drive change in organisations include:

- competitor activity
- consumer demands (e.g. for more sustainable operations, for better services at lower costs)
- funding cutbacks
- legislation
- privatisation
- shareholder demands
- the breaking-up of publicly owned monopolies
- the sale of publically owned enterprises.

Internal pressures that can lead to change in organisations include:

- ageing workforce and changing employment patterns
- changes resulting from workplace bargaining

>>

- day-to-day quality management activities
- downsizing
- greater demands for employee participation
- increasing labour shortages
- new or revised strategic visions
- outsourcing business operations
- quests for major improvements
- takeovers and mergers
- technological advances
- the need to manage problems (e.g. accident and incident rates, customer dissatisfaction, employee turnover, poor productivity).

THE STRATEGIC PERSPECTIVE

Mind the gap

In the largest ever study of chief executives, 'The Enterprise of the Future', conducted by IBM Global Business Services and the Economist Intelligence Unit, business leaders pointed to their own customer base as being the expected source of most of the important changes they would need to address. They identified two new demanding classes of customers that they expected to invest in most: the 'information omnivore' and the 'socially minded' customer.[6]

Phase 2: The need for change is accepted

As the pressures for change build, a few people begin to accept the need for change and start to rally others to their 'cause'. They often encounter blinkered thinking, confusion, opposition and uneasiness, but eventually the inertia of remaining with the status quo is overcome and a critical mass of people accepts the need for change. Laurence J Peter (co-author of *The Peter Principle*) summed it up like this, 'In spite of warnings, nothing much happens until the status quo becomes more painful than change.'[7]

How quickly this phase gathers speed is a key factor in a smooth transition to the new order. The status quo has a strong pull, though, and doing nothing is generally easier than the effort of action, so pressures for change can build slowly and often need to become quite strong before the need for change is fully accepted.

Phase 3: New ways are proposed

Once the need for change is accepted and people let go of their current beliefs and behaviours, they can think about reorganising themselves into a new way of operating. They discuss the situation, devise alternatives, review them and revise them until enough people are satisfied that a proposal or combination of proposals meets their needs.

The more people that are involved in creating new ways based on the new understandings that grew from the initial pressures to change, the greater the 'buy in' to the change is likely to be. Resistance is often nine parts lack of consultation and one part genuine opposition.

Phase 4: Change is introduced

Walmart founder Sam Walton argued for change this way, 'You can't just keep doing what works one time because everything around you is always changing. To succeed, you have to stay out in front of that change.'[8] Sure Sam, but change can hurt. When an organisation tries a 'new way' of doing something, sometimes with gusto, sometimes gingerly, this can be an uncomfortable time for many people. No one is quite sure whether the changes will work and whether they will work to their advantage.

This makes the try-out phase unpredictable and often difficult to cope with. People can end up working at cross-purposes, there can be a lack of energy in carrying out tasks and resistance can surface. This occurs particularly when key people were not convinced of the need for change in the first place, or not enough people understood the need for change (Phase 2), or not enough people participated in developing the new ways (Phase 3).

 THEORY TO PRACTICE

The price of leaving people out

Perhaps the main reason that change fails in many organisations is that the majority of employees only find out about a change when it's introduced (Phase 4). When the majority of employees have not experienced and understood the pressures for change and grasped the need to change, and have not participated in developing the change (Phases 1–3), it's hardly surprising they don't welcome it and implement it enthusiastically.

That's why simply announcing a change doesn't work. Forcing change on people without their input and with no background information about the whys and wherefores invites resentment and resistance. So, when introducing change:

- Aim for cooperation, not compliance: 'We're all in this together', not 'Do it or else'.
- Build employee feedback into the change process.
- Seek people's ideas and input.
- Share both the good news and the bad news.
- Share the pressures, problems and concerns.

Phase 5: The 'new way' is modified

The changes are monitored and adjustments and refinements made in the light of experience. This is a case of 'many hands make light work'. The more people involved in adjusting and improving the new ways, the faster and better progress is likely to be, both in acceptance and quality.

Phase 6: The 'new way' becomes 'our way'

The change eventually becomes the norm – that is, until pressures for change build again and the continuing cycle of change continues.

 THEORY TO PRACTICE

Why don't people do as they're told?

We can think of change as not only natural, but mandatory. Not to continually change and re-create leads to stagnation and death. Organisations must change to preserve themselves. When an organisation can't change, it eventually dies.

>>

Since change is a natural part of life, people don't just want to participate in it, they need to. Creating, rethinking, redesigning and reorganising keeps people from dying, psychologically as well as physically.

This could explain why people seldom follow directions precisely. They always change a bit here, adjust something there, modify things in some way. This isn't rebellion, resistance, sabotage or stupidity – it's life. People need to be creatively involved in their work. Think about this the next time someone modifies one of your instructions.

2. Introducing change

The reinvent-or-die challenges that used to be rare catastrophes in business have practically become the new normal – but without much direction about how to meet them.

William McComb (CEO, Fifth & Pacific Companies), 'Transformation is an era, not an event', *Harvard Business Review*, April 2014[9]

Change may be a natural and even essential part of life, but it makes most people uneasy. With every change, there are winners and losers, vociferous resisters and indifferent supporters.

That's why the main barrier to genuine change is people. And that's why organisations don't change – people do. While it's true that change management is about goals, new systems and structures, and technical practicalities, it's equally true that change is about peoples' behaviours, hearts and minds. Failing to address the people issues means that the entire change initiative is likely to fail.

To capture people's hearts and minds, you must be personally credible so that people buy into your vision and the reasons for a change. People need to see things in a different way before they can change, so explain why the change is needed and involve them in some way in designing and/or planning it. This allows you to influence people's attitudes and understanding and build their long-term commitment to 'new ways' so that the change 'sticks'.

◉ IN A NUTSHELL

Helping your team understand change
Beginning with the broad goals and moving onto the more detailed and personal aspects of change, here is what your team members most want to hear from you:
- This is the 'strategic perspective' for our organisation.
- This is the change that needs to happen.
- This is why it needs to happen like this – how the change fits into the 'strategic perspective'.
- This is what we think would happen if we didn't make these changes or if we don't make them successfully.
- Here's how our team fits in.
- This is how the change affects each of us individually.
- This is our new operating plan and these are our new systems, processes, policies and procedures.
- This is our transition plan.
- Here is how we plan to monitor progress and measure success.
- Here is how to get more information about the change.

What causes change to fail?

Although most organisational change efforts fail to deliver the hoped-for results, they nearly always result in unexpected and unwanted side effects, including anxious, disheartened and sometimes hostile employees. How does this happen?

Not surprisingly, muddled and half-hearted stabs at change guarantee failure. Change introduced in a climate of poor morale and distrust generally fails. Even when workplace relations are good, mismanagement and poor planning cause change to flounder.

It's tempting to bite off more than you can chew and to expect too much too soon when introducing change, too. You need to be realistic and introduce the change so that it neither proceeds so slowly that people lose heart, nor so quickly that people feel pushed into situations they aren't ready for.

Failing to provide enough information, failing to involve a representative cross-section of employees in planning the changes and trying to railroad a change through despite resistance and misgivings all cause change to fail. Asking people to meet the same or increased goals without providing the resources they need, such as facilities, money, people, time and training, is another clear signal that change efforts are doomed. The following two Nutshells summarise why introducing change is never easy.

 IN A NUTSHELL

Why change succeeds and why it fails
Characteristics of unsuccessful change initiatives include:
* Authoritarian direction, or pushing people into changes they don't understand or feel ready for or are not committed to.
* Failing to integrate the change into the day-to-day operations and the system as a whole.
* Fuzzy, idealistic or grandiose objectives.
* Half-heartedly introducing change due to lack of commitment from managers and other key stakeholders.
* Ignoring or glossing over resistance.
* Inadequate information.
* Insufficient warning or involvement of employees.
* Inappropriate strategies (e.g. inadequate resources or pre-packaged programs).
* Insufficient staff support or other resources.
* Lack of management support (e.g. only a few senior managers understand the change and the reasons for it).
* Lack of support from critical power groups.
* People finding it hard to give up the old ways, or falling back into them, because there is no incentive to keep moving forward with the change.
* People perceiving that the changes impose additional work without removing any work.
* Poor timing (e.g. introducing change too quickly, causing people to feel out of control, or too slowly, inviting cynicism and disillusionment).
* Unrealistic objectives.
* Unclear implementation plans that result in people not knowing precisely how to make the desired changes happen.

>>

Characteristics of successful change initiatives include:

- Adequate rewards for those adopting the change.
- Appropriate strategies to introduce and manage the change.
- Clear and measurable objectives and outcomes.
- Competent staff support.
- Constant, honest and clear communication about the change and its progress.
- Continuing modification and adaptation of the 'new ways' in the light of experience.
- Drawing on support from the existing formal and informal power structures.
- Employee involvement and participation in designing and planning the change.
- Good timing, which means fast enough to give a sense of progress yet not exceeding people's ability to absorb the change and feel in control.
- Integrating the change with the rest of the system and the formal and informal rewards structure.
- Maintaining momentum as the change rolls out.
- Majority support for the change.
- Realistic and limited scale of the change.
- Support from key formal and informal power groups.
- Visible successes throughout the organisation resulting from the change.

IN A NUTSHELL

Difficulties in introducing change

Table 22.1 shows how problems, which emerge with change, can be traced back to their causes.

TABLE 22.1 Reasons for problems that come with change

Problem	Reason
A quick start that fizzles	No clear shared vision
Anxiety and frustration	Insufficient resources allocated to implementing the change
Cynicism and distrust	Leaders not 'showing the way' or 'walking their talk'
Haphazard efforts and false starts	No clear action plan
People go back to the 'old ways'	Changes not reinforced and rewarded
Scepticism	No serious evaluation of the change program's results
No forward movement	No attempts to improve upon the changes.[10]

Source: © Ron Cacioppe, http://www.integral.org.au. Used by permission.

Seven steps to introducing change

Change advances in stages, each building on the previous stage. The bigger the change, the longer this takes. There are no short cuts. Use the seven steps shown in Figure 22.4 and explained below to introduce change effectively. These steps apply whether you are initiating the change or facilitating it on behalf of your organisation.

Step 1: Think it through

Use gap analysis to help you get clear in your own mind precisely what the change is meant to achieve and what support and actions you expect from your team when the change is introduced. Then use force field analysis to explore the forces favouring change and those resisting it. This helps you create a clear, strong and straightforward vision to direct the change effort and develop strategies for realising it. (See pages 60 and 503 to find out how to conduct gap and force field analyses.)

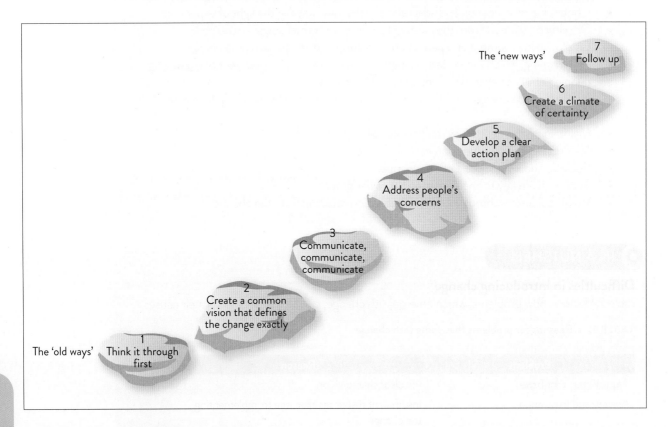

FIGURE 22.4 Seven stepping stones to change

Step 2: Create a common vision

Until you help people accept, adapt and develop new ways of working, they're likely to resent you and your attempts to introduce change. People want to know precisely how the change affects them and how you intend to help them prepare for it. They can probably figure out what they stand to lose as a result of the change so make sure they have a clear understanding of what they stand to gain, too.

Also explain what they stand to lose if change *isn't* made. Why is the change necessary? What is it intended to achieve? Keep it personal – 'you' and 'we'. The more positive and specific you are, the better. The clear common vision you provide helps engage people's hearts as well as their minds. Unless people know the change is important, they won't bother to adopt and adapt to the change.

Provide frequent and enthusiastic communication on these topics:

- The purpose and reason for the change. Why it is necessary?
- An understandable and convincing picture of the desired outcome, including where precisely the organisation and the team are headed. How the change affects employees individually and as a team. And how their working lives will improve as a result of the change.

♦ How the change will take place in clear, small steps. How much effort is required. What you expect each team member to do. And how much support (e.g. training and time to settle in and learn and apply new skills) you plan to provide.

Think about how to frame the change for maximum appeal. You can frame it as an exciting opportunity, a logical transition to the next stage, or a survival mechanism, for example. Use it to get 'fence-sitters' (people who can see both potential benefits and potential losses) on side and ensure the team's informal leader agrees with and supports the vision. The fence-sitters, informal leader and those who have most to gain from the change can become a powerful guiding coalition to help you drive a change.

Step 3: Communicate, communicate, communicate

Telling your employees what they 'need to know' is out. When you don't communicate effectively, employees fill in the blanks themselves – usually in ways that are incorrect. Communicate clearly and often, using every vehicle possible. When it comes to change, you can't over-communicate.

Don't let your team hear things from the grapevine or any other way – make sure you are their primary source of information. Even when you think there's nothing new to communicate, people need to hear from you. Even when you don't yet know the full story, say what you do know, even when you've said it already and even though it may change. You can always give a progress report and reiterate the change goals and vision for the future.

Convey optimism, but don't ignore difficulties and don't sugar-coat the facts – the only way to build the trust you need is through the truth. Even bad news is better than no news. Even when some people will lose out because of the change, you can help them go with the flow of change, not fight it, by helping them understand exactly what is going to happen to them and around them. Help them see where they fit in and find ways to feel good about it in order to maintain their sense of identity and self-esteem.

Consider what you say carefully, because people hear your words as a promise and remember it for a surprisingly long time. They also put their own slant on the information you provide and contribute it to the rumour mill. Everything you say takes on a deep meaning and is repeated, analysed and revised whenever employees gather together.

Everything you don't say takes on a deep meaning, too. Make sure all your messages, verbal and non-verbal, formal and informal, are consistent and that your day-to-day actions support your messages.

Keep talking and keep spreading your message, to team members individually and in team meetings. The more you say, the more you increase the chances that employees hear your words accurately and your message gets through. The less you say, the more likely you are to be misinterpreted.

● THE STRATEGIC PERSPECTIVE

Some channels organisations can use to communicate change
Although people look to their leader-managers to provide most information about impending change, organisations can use other channels to communicate to all employees, too, such as:

* an internal change bulletin website
* corporate breakfast sessions
* informal chats
* newsletters
* other employees who have experienced this or similar change
* posters
* videos.

THEORY TO PRACTICE

Step by step

When the publicly listed IT contracting and recruitment company Peoplebank acquired the privately owned Ambit Recruitment in 2008 to form Australia's largest information technology and telecommunications recruitment company, it faced three key challenges: how to calm staff anxieties, how to merge two very different cultures and how to smoothly blend the operations in a way that would satisfy customers and staff. Ambit had an aggressive sales and marketing arm and strong organic growth, while Peoplebank's strength was efficiently converting sales into operating profits. Ambit was twice Peoplebank's size and its people were, on average, five to 10 years younger than Peoplebank's.

The acquisition was announced in December 2007 for completion in February 2008. This gave management two months to plan how the new organisation could hit the ground running. It also gave the staff of both companies two months' finger-biting time.

The management team knew that people issues, not operational or financial factors, were the key to success. During the two-month gap between the announcement and completion, the management team carefully planned its integration strategy and made operational and personnel decisions, deciding, purely on merit, how to eliminate duplication of middle managers and who would take on what roles. They made addressing people's concerns a priority and communicated quickly and widely, making it clear there would be minimal changes to people. The few redundancies were announced straightaway.

Led by a steering committee, the company rolled out its integration and implementation plan in February. The entire company went to an off-site conference where the common vision was communicated and the staff got to know each other through a 1970's style disco.

Six months later, the functional teams were integrated and not a single client was lost.[11]

Step 4: Address people's concerns

Introducing change can be a delicate balancing act between managing operations and addressing employees' needs. Consider both the 'organisation journey' and the 'employee journey'. The former is logical, procedural and tangible, while the latter involves the emotional impact of change on individuals. Manage both 'journeys'.[12] When you forget about the people, you lose their trust and generate fear and scepticism just when you need loyal, productive and enthusiastic employees.

Change is generally uncomfortable in its early stages. Working out what can go wrong is easy. Visualising a new order is a lot harder. Even with minor change, concerns and questions bubble up and the more people identify personally with what is changing, the more their responses resemble grief over the loss of a loved one. Disregarding people's apprehensions or brushing them aside as 'just being difficult', 'silly' or 'wrong' only strengthens them, so recognise and acknowledge the sadness people hint at or express.

Later in this chapter, under the heading 'The information people need to accept change', you can find out what specific information people need as they progress through Phase 3 through to Phase 6 of the change cycle described earlier in this chapter (see Figure 22.2). Section 4 of this chapter, 'Overcoming resistance to change', explains how to work with employees who resist change.

Show the way
People look to you, their leader-manager, to set the pace and show the way. Do you walk your talk or is it just warm air? Build trust, or your team is likely to sabotage any change efforts. Any hesitation by the leaders, informal leaders or others in positions of influence increases everyone's doubts and therefore their resistance.

Step 5: Develop an action plan

You've explained the need for change and created a common vision. Now gather ideas to make it happen – ignoring people's need to join in is bound to cost you their support. Conversely, inviting participation improves the results. When people work together to create and deal with change, they are also creating the conditions, the new relationships, the ways of thinking and working that make the change succeed. Make sure, though, that employees have the information they need to provide useful input.

Develop clear plans about who is to do what, when and how, in order to achieve your goals: what specifically needs to happen to introduce the change and make it work? Brainstorm all the action steps you can think of that might move you towards the goal. Then review them, sequence them, and assign start and finish dates. Some activities need to be completed before others can begin. Sometimes two things need to be done at the same time. Use a Gantt chart or critical path analysis to create a visual 'path of progress' for yourself and your team.

Make sure your plan shows everyone what they, personally, need to do and empowers people to act on the vision. Remove any obstacles to change and make sure the 'new way' is easier than the 'old way'. Otherwise, people automatically slip back into 'default' – old habits die hard. Put up new standard operating procedures when that would help and post reminders to help break the 'automatic behaviour circuits'. Make your prompts specific and put them close to where and when people are going to do the 'new' (for large-scale change projects, follow the project management procedure explained in Chapter 21).

A sense of progress is heartening and creates its own momentum. Plan for and create short-term wins based on visible performance improvements and build in ways to recognise and reward employees who contribute to the wins. There are plenty of change levers you can build into your change plan to help move change along; for example, incentives, job design and training.

Develop measures of success and a monitoring system that quickly and easily tracks your progress. (For more information on how to develop plans and measures of success and how to monitor plans, see pages 112 and 505.)

Big change takes time
Steve Jobs returned to Apple after John Sculley's 10-year reign and managed to reverse the company's poor performance. People often recall it as a quick turnaround, but it took from 1997 to 2006 and was the result of many changes, not just one.[13]

Step 6: Create a climate of certainty

Our brains are programmed to consider new circumstances in terms of their familiarity. When you've come across a similar situation before, your brain relaxes: 'Ah… I've survived this before, so I probably can again.' Without the comfort of familiarity, you go into full alert: fight, flight or freeze. That's why British consultant Alastair Dryburgh reminds us 'that we experience benefits in the head, but risks in the gut', and advises us to 'speak to the caveman'.[14]

Explain what *will* change and why, by all means; that gives people something specific to focus on. Give them an anchor, too, by saying what *won't* change; this calms the ancient brain program that retreats from the unfamiliar. Build psychological certainty around the 'new ways' at every opportunity, since it's the uncertainty of what change brings that causes the most problems. Do whatever you can to provide a sense of stability and routine.

Here are some other ways to reduce people's anxiety and reassure them about change:

- Celebrate successes whenever progress is made.
- Demonstrate the changes you want.
- Give people a clear path to follow in terms of action steps to help the change move forward.
- Give plenty of individual and team feedback about how the change is progressing and how their efforts and support are helping.
- Involve people through training, discussions, and question and answer sessions, for example, to help them develop new attitudes and knowledge and adapt to the change.
- Maintain as much consistency as you can, including in your leadership; people can tolerate change and uncertainty when their leader is calm and clearheaded.
- Set short-term goals for individuals and groups to work towards and to provide a sense of achievement when they reach them.
- Stay enthusiastic; provide clear direction to overcome any inertia or apathy and to keep up the momentum for change.

Give people a chance to say goodbye to the 'old ways'. Otherwise, they may yearn for 'the good old days' and never fully accept the change. Holding some form of ceremony, however short and simple, that clearly marks the end of the current 'era' and welcomes in the next, helps people to separate, let go and move on.

Step 7: Monitor your progress

Everyone on your team should be able to monitor progress. With widespread organisational change, you may need to hold regular change briefing meetings or change update meetings to keep your team abreast of how the change is progressing across the organisation.

Get feedback from employees about what is working well and what needs improving and work with them to incorporate their improvement ideas. Who is still resisting? Find out why and see what you can do to ease their reservations.

Keep enthusiasm and interest high by making sure your team can see how well the change is progressing and how well it is working. Highlight your team's excellent learning and progress; people feel more confident and secure when they know they are succeeding. Don't wait until the end to celebrate progress. Celebrating achievements as the change progresses helps keep the momentum going.

Express your appreciation of individual and team effort and reward employees who are working with the change. This underscores the benefits of change and helps any remaining resisters see some positive results.

Find ways to consolidate improvements and make them last by integrating them into the system and anchoring them in the team's culture. Eventually, the change becomes the status quo.

Don't rest on your laurels or assume success too soon, though – change needs to sink deeply into people's habitual ways of working. Stay optimistic and keep promoting the change, rewarding people who make it work and celebrating success.

⊙ THEORY TO PRACTICE

A culture reversal

A doom and gloom culture nearly finished off the children's cancer charity Camp Quality in the early 2000s. A decade later, it had transformed its culture into positivity and hope, not just for recipients but also its staff. High employee absenteeism and turnover, low morale and a $1.5 million operating loss due to declining donations morphed into a 40% reduction in sick leave and a 560% increase in income.

Key to the cultural about-face was implementing change in a variety of ways across the organisation, including redefining values, mission and image and instilling a positive culture that extended to activities with parents, children and volunteers – all with the complete commitment of senior management.[15]

⊙ ACTION!

Do you have a change to introduce to your work team? Before doing anything, work through the Planning change template on ⊙**CourseMate**Express.

When the news is mostly bad

Some changes can't be couched in positive terms. A factory, shop or bank branch might close, for example, or people might be subjected to redundancy due to outsourcing or the introduction of new technology.

When announcing such changes, avoid blaming anyone or anything for the bad news. You don't have to pretend to like the change, but make it clear that you support it. Be as open as you can about what's going on and when you know the rationale behind the bad news, share as much of it as you can without breaking confidentiality.

Present the information neutrally and objectively, without trying to make it sound better than it is. Avoid anything that could resemble 'spin' and urging people to see 'the big picture'.

Offer empathy and support as much as possible and offer whatever assistance you can on behalf of the organisation (e.g. outplacement counselling or further training). Acknowledge people's feelings and concerns but avoid giving false hope while doing so. Some venting is normal but don't allow prolonged complaining.

Provide some form of closure to help people say 'goodbye' and move forward at their own pace.

It's all about communication

The merger between Western Australian-based Challenge Bank and Westpac is an example of discontinuous change introduced well and successfully. Their approach to the change included:

- being open about the bad as well as the good, right from the beginning
- communicating informally (person to person) before communicating formally (role to role)
- explaining the reasons for the change and the bridge that would take people to the merged organisation
- explaining the value to the community
- helping people shift their identity, not just their roles or skills
- no-fail first steps
- no sense of crisis
- no spin – helping people make their own decision to buy into the change and foregoing any 'We'll be bigger/better/best' exhortations
- showing care and respect for employees and their families.[16]

ACTION!

Will your change succeed? The interactive self-test on *CourseMateExpress can help you to work out how likely it is that the change you are introducing will be successful.

Predicting resistance to change

Figure 22.5 shows a simple model you can use to predict the success of your change efforts. It considers how deep, or fundamental, the change is and how much it affects the culture of a work group or an organisation. The bigger the change and the more it affects the way people work together, the more resistance you can expect. Conversely, small changes with little cultural impact are relatively easy to implement.

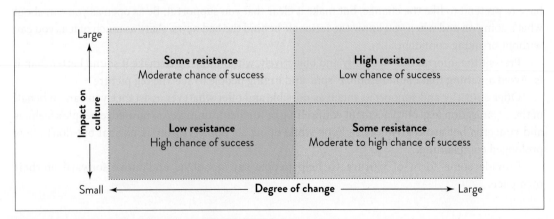

FIGURE 22.5 Predicting resistance to change

3. Promoting change

> Nothing is more difficult to handle, more doubtful of success, nor more dangerous to manage, than to put oneself at the head of introducing new orders. For the introducer has all those who benefit from the old orders as enemies, and he has lukewarm defenders in all those who might benefit from the new order.
>
> Niccoló Machiavelli (Italian renaissance writer), *The Prince* (1998)[17]

As a leader-manager, you sometimes instigate and lead a change; at other times, you respond to and manage a change. The changes may be minor, such as incremental improvements to work methods or workflow, introducing new members to the work group or reallocating duties among team members. Or they may be transformational changes that fundamentally alter the way your organisation operates internally or relates to its external environment. (See 'FYI: Two types of change'.)

Whichever type of change you're promoting, to initiate that new order, you need a well-developed package of skills and personal credibility. Conceptual skills help you to analyse the proposed change to see how it affects your department's operations and your work team. This in turn helps you lead your team to devise a sound action plan for introducing and monitoring the change, one that makes good use of the resources and other supports available to you from the rest of the organisation.

You also need networking and interpersonal skills to promote the change in a way most likely to gain acceptance and cooperation from all stakeholders and resource providers, and conflict-management skills to deal constructively with the conflict that can arise during change.

You need to understand how and why people respond to change as they do, the questions they want you to answer and the order in which they want them answered. Armed with those skills and that information, you can ease people through the three stages of adapting to and adopting change explained below – letting go of the 'old', transitioning to the 'new' and stepping forward into a new beginning.

 FYI

Two types of change

There are two types of change: the *incremental*, step-by-step change, where change builds slowly and is based on current practice; and *discontinuous* change that turns things upside-down.

Incremental change fits nicely into a linear, progressive, predictable world; it's logical. This makes it relatively easy to communicate and to accept. Discontinuous change comes from transformative organisational change, introducing new equipment or technology, major reorganisations such as those resulting from takeovers and mergers, and re-engineering, for example. It breaks with the past, requiring dramatic shifts in habits and beliefs about how things are done, taking people into the unknown and making them uncomfortable (to say the least).[18]

Responses to change

Why is it that when the winds of change blow, some people build walls and others windmills? Is change about loss, misery, uncertainty and vulnerability? Must it lead to anger, anxiety, confusion, doubt and frustration? Or can it be about challenge, growth, innovation and learning? Can change create benefits, better ways, excitement and fun?

FYI

The Semmelweis reflex and why people reject change simply because … it's new

The Semmelweis reflex is named after Dr Ignaz Semmelweis, who came up with a radical idea that could save thousands of lives – only to see his colleagues reject it and patients continue to die. He noticed that women were three times safer having babies in the nurses' maternity ward than in the doctors' maternity ward in the same hospital, even though the mothers going to the doctors' ward were no sicker than the mothers going to the nurses' ward. His radical idea was that instead of coming straight from treating dying people or from the morgue where they were cutting up bodies, in order to deliver babies in their maternity ward doctors should first wash their hands. Not surprisingly, the doctors were highly insulted that Semmelweis should imply that they were killing their patients. Everyone knew that diseases are caused by an 'internal imbalance', not germs.[19]

Ignaz Semmelweis, MD, died impoverished in a mental institution in Vienna General Hospital in 1865. Medical science has since accepted that his theory was correct.

Perhaps the lesson here is to propose new ideas and procedures as 'adjustments' and not to condemn the current practice. Instead of saying 'Hey, doctors, you're killing people!' say 'Hey, with this one small tweak in how we approach delivering babies, I think we might be able to fix our high mortality rate. How about trying washing your hands first?

It's okay to think differently to your peers because you might be right. Just be tactful about it.

People hate change

If change is so natural, why do people build walls of resistance? Perhaps it's because, to coin a phrase, the certainty of misery is better than the misery of uncertainty.

Change is about taking people from the known, predictable and comfortable to the unknown, frightening and threatening. No wonder it can make people uncomfortable. Employees who welcome change with open arms are rarities, even when the change makes their job more challenging and interesting. Consciously or unconsciously, most people think, 'Better the devil we know'.

This is because change, particularly discontinuous change, hits people at core levels. Change to work groups, for example, usually means both formal and informal changes; the unofficial group leadership might change and other internal relationships, including the unofficial 'pecking order' and established networks, may shift.

Change often violates cherished group norms and routines; people may be anxious about having to become used to new routines or work areas, learn new skills or work methods, or work harder. They may fear the loss of their old job, which they liked, or that their new job will be less skilled, less interesting or too demanding. They may resent the implied criticism that the way they have been doing their job is not good enough. They may dislike the thought of outside interference in their job or fear loss of control. As a result, morale, motivation and the working climate suffer.

Not surprisingly, the uncertain future that change creates produces varying degrees of anger, anxiety, apprehension, bewilderment, confusion, dismay and a whole host of other emotions in people. Everyone experiences this discomfort differently and acts in different ways to soothe it. But their aims are the same: to protect themselves and preserve their identity.

> ◉ **IN A NUTSHELL**
>
> **Concerns sparked by change**
> Here are some of the reasons people baulk at change:
> * *Challenges to group norms and culture*: Groups strongly resist any changes to their norms or culture.
> * *Disrupting habits*: Many people prefer their well-known, familiar and predictable routines and don't give them up easily, especially when the routines work for them and they don't know whether the new ways will work.
> * *Disturbing existing social networks*: Change may disband friendships and informal networks. The stronger the group ties being threatened, the greater the resistance.
> * *Losing existing benefits*: Change may bring costs that outweigh its benefits. People resist change that threatens the continuity of their environment, their employment, their career prospects, wages or benefits, or that looks likely to increase job demands.
> * *Threats to position, power and security*: People resist any change that causes them or the group they're part of to lose status, or power prestige. Those with the most to lose resist the most strongly.
> * *Uncertainty about the change and its results*: People try to avoid uncertainty – no one enjoys walking in the dark where unknown dangers may lurk. Lack of understanding or insufficient information about a change leaves a vacuum that attracts anxiety, insecurity, rumour and speculation.

People love change

There is another view of change and it is that people seek the novel – they love to try new fashions, new foods, new restaurants. So why don't people love change at work? Because in organisations, change has been used as a code word for nasty and unpleasant things.[20] Another factor in being open to change is whether it's done *to* you or *by* you. All in all, it isn't surprising that even people who love change outside work may hate it at work.

This doesn't apply to everyone, though. What kind of employees don't mind change at work? Those who:

* are comfortable with uncertainty and willing to step out of their comfort zones and try out new ways of working
* have an open mind
* trust their manager and their organisation to 'do the right thing'
* understand why change is needed and what it entails for them personally, for the organisation and for its stakeholders
* want to learn and develop their skills.

People like this are lifelong learners who work in a climate of trust and support. Is your work team filled with lifelong learners? Have you created a working climate of trust and support?

The information people need to accept change

When you consider all the questions people have at each of the seven stages of adopting a change, it's clear why communication is so important. People need information. More than that, they need certain types of information at certain times – and these certain times may well be different for different individuals.

Drawing on extensive research, Dr Gene Hall developed a seven-level hierarchy (from 0–6 inclusive) that describes the stages people go through in adopting any change (summarised in Figure 22.6 and 'In a Nutshell: Hall's hierarchy for adopting a change'). When a change is introduced, people are at the bottom of the hierarchy. Before they can move up to the next level, their current (and predictable) questions must be answered fully in order to alleviate their concerns and release them to the next stage. The more quickly you help employees move through each successive level, the more quickly and easily the change can progress.

● IN A NUTSHELL

Hall's hierarchy for adopting a change
Figure 22.6 shows how people go through seven levels from 0 to six (inclusive) when adopting change.

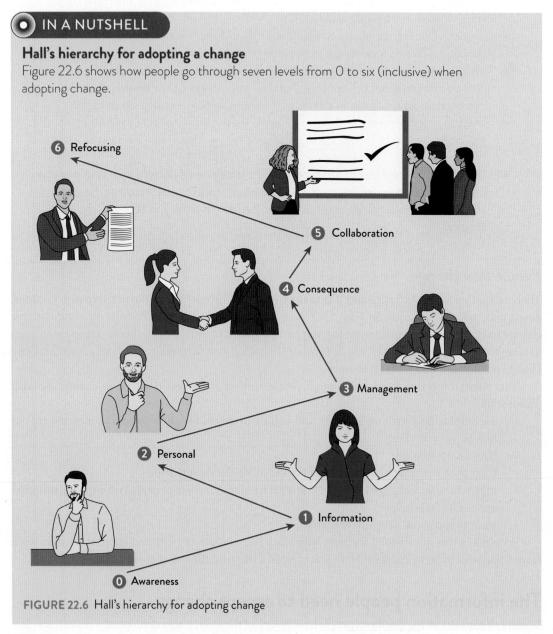

FIGURE 22.6 Hall's hierarchy for adopting change

>>

6 *Refocusing*: 'I have an idea about something that might work even better.' People begin to see ways to refine the change further and extend its benefits. This may include minor or major modifications.

5 *Collaboration*: 'I want to work with others to smooth out the process.' People want to coordinate and cooperate with others to implement the change effectively.

4 *Consequence*: 'How are our customers being affected?' Employees begin to consider the impact of the change on their customers and others in their immediate sphere of influence. They want to make sure the change is benefiting them and achieving what it is supposed to achieve.

3 *Management*: 'I am working hard at doing what this change requires of me.' People turn their attention to implementing the change. They're concerned about building their skills and efficiency, organising and managing themselves and scheduling their time properly in order to efficiently carry out the tasks the change requires.

2 *Personal*: 'How does the change affect me?' 'Will you train me and give me enough time to learn?' 'Will you support me until I master the change?' People want to know how the change affects them and their job, what it requires of them, whether they can meet the demands of the change. They want to know how their existing benefits, formal and informal routines and networks will change.

1 *Information*: 'I would like to know more about the proposed change.' People indicate a general awareness of the change and an interest in learning more about it. They seem not to be worried about themselves in relation to the change and are more interested in the substantive aspects, such as the reasons for the change, its general characteristics or the effects of the change.

0 *Awareness*: 'Change? What change?' 'I'm not aware of any change.' People's behaviour and comments indicate little concern about, or involvement with, the change.[21]

Using Hall's hierarchy to help people through a change speeds its adoption. Understanding where your team members are at any point during the roll-out of a change means you can provide the information they need to move through the hierarchy. This helps them come to terms with the change more quickly and implement it more smoothly.

You can identify where people are on the hierarchy from the questions they ask and from their behaviour. For example, when an employee is at Stage 2 and concerned about how the change affects her personally, it's no good telling her how much the customers will love it. She wants to know things like how much training you plan to provide, how much time she has to learn the new skills required, whether you plan to support her if she has trouble learning them, whether she needs to move her work station and whether you expect her to take on additional duties.

Without pushing too fast, acknowledge which phase team members are in and help them into the next by providing the type of information they need. Remember: people change only when they're ready to believe that the change won't make life worse for them, and that it may even make life better.

THE STRATEGIC PERSPECTIVE

Hang on to your best and brightest through change
When change strikes, it's often your top performers who stand to lose the most. They probably have more options than your other employees and less patience with changes that could jeopardise their success. Give them a good reason to stay by finding them an equally rewarding

>>

role and a chance to shine once the change takes hold. Explain how their role can continue to provide the things they value despite the change.

Think about meeting with them individually to explain the change and why it's needed to show you value them. Give them a role in helping launch the change and involve them in implementing the change as much as you can, too. This increases their buy-in and gives you access to their good ideas.

The three stages of accepting change

As you answer people's questions so they can move up Hall's hierarchy, you're also helping them move through the three stages of accepting change. First, they 'let go' of the 'old', which propels them into the uncomfortable 'transition' phase. Eventually, they reach a point where they can release the past entirely and move into the future, the 'new beginnings' phase.

Stage 1: Letting go

To embark on change, people first need to make a break with the 'old ways'. Letting go of the past can be painful, especially when people have a big investment in what they are losing or strongly identify with it.

Anthropologists have discovered that a ceremony is one of the most powerful and satisfying ways to achieve closure. Closure enables people to let go psychologically of the 'old' and gives them permission to do so, allowing them to begin the 'new'. Find a way to help your team say goodbye to the past. It might be a tea party with silly hats or a solemn ceremony, but whatever you choose, help your team let go.

Steps 2 through 4 of the seven steps to change (described above) help employees let go.

Stage 2: Transition

When important ties are broken, the world can be a confusing and uncomfortable place. People experience a sense of bewilderment, unreality, emptiness and even horror once they let go and enter the in-between phase. They often 'go through the motions' as if in a state of shock, swinging between hopefulness that the change will work out well and worry that it won't. Gradually, a sense of hope begins to emerge.

Use Hall's hierarchy to provide the appropriate information to help your team move through this painful and largely unproductive transition phase and explain your action plan so that people know where they're going and how they'll get there (Steps 5 and 6 of the seven steps to change).

Stage 3: New beginnings

People enter the third and final stage, discovering a new beginning, when they're ready to adopt new goals and start thinking about and planning for the change and the future. The energy they previously spent worrying about and resisting the change is now available for dealing with it constructively.

Remember to follow up to make sure the change is working and that it sticks – Step 7 of the seven steps to change.

Caught in the rip of change

Do you know that rips are the biggest hazard on Australian beaches, and are responsible for at least 21 drownings a year?

Rather than fight a strong current, it's better to swim with it, not against it. Swimming against a rip just exhausts you. Relaxing and 'going with the flow' is better. Strong swimmers should cross the current at 45 degrees swimming parallel to the shore and weak or tired swimmers should just go with the current. Eventually, the rip spits you out and you can swim back to shore or attract a life guard's attention.

You need positive self-talk, too. Keep telling yourself that you'll reach the breaking wave zone where the rip gives up and you'll be fine. That also prevents panic setting in, which paralyses both your body and your mind.[22]

The same advice can work for change. When you're caught in a current of change, don't panic and don't fight it – work with it and think positively.

4. Overcoming resistance to change

> We can never be really prepared for that which is wholly new. We have to adjust ourselves, and every radical adjustment is a crisis in self-esteem; we undergo a test, we have to prove ourselves. It needs inordinate self-confidence to face drastic change without inner trembling.
>
> Eric Hoffer (US longshoreman philosopher), *Between the Devil and the Dragon* (1982)[23]

Some people resist change because their leader-manager hasn't clearly explained why it's needed, what their working life will be like after the change or their own role in making the change a success. Sometimes an individual's make-up or skills incline them towards resistance: they may have negative mindsets about change; they may lack the necessary skills for responding to change and coping with the stress change often produces; or their personality structure might make them wary of change.

Resisting change takes three main forms:

1. *Malicious compliance:* People comply, but in a way they know isn't really what you want and is likely to result in an outcome you don't want.

2. *Passive compliance:* People just 'give up' and go through the motions, without commitment, effort or energy.

3. *Vocal resistance:* People air their concerns openly, either clearly and constructively or negatively and destructively. They may air them to you, making your life easier by giving you the opportunity to deal with their resistance, or behind your back to their workmates, which can seriously undermine your change efforts.

Where there is change, there are health issues

Change is a psychosocial risk factor that, when introduced and managed poorly, can lead to physical and mental health problems (psychosocial risk factors are explained on page 1015). You (and your organisation) have a legal responsibility to be sensitive to the concerns that change can spark and to help team members deal with them effectively.

Feeling unsettled or concerned about change can lead to stress responses such as sleep disturbance, absent-minded behaviour, gloominess and restlessness. When people go into the fight, flight or freeze response, the brain produces the hormones adrenaline and cortisol. Too many of these hormones can lead to long-term health damage.

That's why it's important to make change tolerable at worst and energising at best.

Whatever form resistance takes, ignoring it only strengthens it and delays your change efforts. It's far better to get resisters talking about the change so you can deal with their concerns. Listen carefully, with your heart and your eyes as well as your ears, and use the **SHEER** formula to bring their worries into the open. This way, you can try to allay them so they can accept the change and help make it work:

1. **S**urface: Invite people's thoughts, concerns and questions. They may be reluctant to air them at first, so you may have to ask: 'Here's what we need. Do you see any problems? What concerns do you have?'
2. **H**onour: Listen to people's concerns and feelings.
3. **E**xplore: Find out why people feel the way they do. Ask questions and help them state their misgivings as specifically as possible. This helps you provide the information they need to feel more comfortable with the change and come to terms with it.
4. **E**xplain: Answer people's concerns and questions as fully and honestly as you can, giving both the 'good' and the 'bad' news.
5. **R**echeck: Make sure you have fully addressed people's concerns and questions and satisfied them with your answers. If they still have doubts, go back to the beginning: 'Anything else?' Otherwise, their doubts will fester.

Show resisters you value them and their skills. Involve them as much as you can in designing and building the new ways. Sometimes you can nurse them along; sometimes you need to lay down the law: this is what is changing and you can either play by the new rules or play elsewhere. (See the information on 'the north-bound-bus approach' on page 354.)

● THE STRATEGIC PERSPECTIVE

Forced change wreaks havoc

Consider East Timor, where Indonesian rule was forced upon the people when Portugal moved out. Forced change breeds one of two reactions: people leave; or they form underground resistance, which wreaks havoc. This holds true for organisations as well as for countries.

The two important resistance points to look out for are:

1. *A crisis in energy*: This may result from apathy, which can develop as a stress response and cause the change to lose its momentum, or from accumulated negative energy that stops the change moving forward.
2. *Vested interests*: People who have a lot to lose may increase their efforts to block change or they may combine their efforts to prevent the change going through.

Resistance generally occurs at two points in a change effort. The first is early on, when people are struggling to come to grips with the change and are trying to avoid the real or perceived personal losses that they fear accompany the change. The second is just when everything seems to be going well, often when implementing the change is at about the halfway point or towards the end, when the change is nearly a reality. There are five main causes of stalled change efforts:

1. A leadership vacuum combined with a loss of momentum causes resistance to mushroom.
2. The team gets tired and loses energy and enthusiasm. Change, after all, is hard work. Beginnings are a lot of fun, then reality sets in and spirits lag. Energetic leadership is the antidote.
3. Time and resource shortages. These are often due to poor forecasting and planning and compounded by the fact that it can be difficult to go back and ask for more resources.
4. Trying to move too quickly or moving onto the next project too soon.
5. Unexpected obstacles. When you've never been down this particular track before, naturally you can't foresee all the hurdles.[24]

These snags are godsends to serious resisters, who are most likely to attack when the change is nearly a reality (rather than at the beginning when it may never eventuate).

Using your personal power can help move stalled change along. A personal appeal – 'Just give it a go for me', 'Help me out and try this' – can often be just what's needed. Use the boomerang principle, too: when you can, make a small concession to engage the team's willingness to reciprocate and carry on with the change.

● IN A NUTSHELL

Where change breaks down

Change may be a natural part of life but managers often shoot themselves in the proverbial foot by making it easy for people to baulk at change. Here is what to search out and remove, reduce or help people through:

- Changes are not built into key systems such as performance reviews and operating procedures, making it easy to let them slide and eventually evaporate.
- Conflict and resistance at an individual or group level are poorly managed, resulting in the erosion of group or individual relationships and loss of goodwill towards the change.
- Inertia, or lack of energy to 'get the ball rolling' and keep it moving, holding change back.
- Not enough or not the right equipment, information, money, people, time or other resources are made available to make the change workable.
- People become 'stuck' in the letting go or transition phase of accepting change and can't find a way to move forward.
- People who adopt the change quickly and are not rewarded give up; others, seeing no benefits in adopting the change, don't bother adopting it at all.
- Team leaders or senior management communicate the change incongruently, appearing less than wholehearted in their support of the change.
- There is insufficient monitoring and progress evaluation to ensure the change works and remains in place.

Tips for dealing with persistent resisters

Following the seven steps for introducing change discussed earlier in this chapter helps reduce opposition and makes the change easier for employees to accept. For whatever reason, though, some people seem determined to oppose change. Here are some tips for working with people who insist on resisting:

- *The road-blocker*: This vocal resistance is a nice, clean type of resistance where the employee just says 'No' in one form or another, usually without giving reasons. Help them to be specific about their objection by asking, 'What specifically worries you?' or 'What in particular do you object to?' Their answer tells you what you are dealing with and gives you a starting point for discussion.

  Explore the resistance fully using the SHEER formula outlined on page 706. Or suggest a trial: 'Give it a go for a couple of weeks, just to see'. Before you part, ensure that the employee has clear change-related goals to achieve and that the goals have clear time lines.

- *The passive 'complier'*: This is a hidden form of resistance where the resister says, in effect, 'Tell me exactly what you want me to do'. When you fall for that, the resister can comply with the bare minimum, but not the spirit, of what you want.

  Explaining what you need from the resister and asking, 'Are you quite clear about what I need from you?' or 'Let's talk about how you plan to approach this; what is your first step going to be?' can encourage the resister to accept more responsibility for good performance.

- *The malicious complier*: This is another hidden form of resistance where the resister appears to comply with the changes, but in a way that clearly is going to make the changes fail to work properly.

  Discuss the steps the malicious complier took and together work out how to make the change work more effectively. Then seek commitment to making the agreed changes work.

- *The delayer*: 'I'll get on to it first thing Monday morning' says the delayer. And then, of course, something more important crops up.

  When you think this is a resistance tactic rather than an honest response, try asking, 'Is there anything preventing you from beginning now?'

- *The reverser*: This can be a tricky form of resistance. When you find yourself surprised by someone's enthusiastic response ('Wow! What a great idea!'), followed by a quick delay, you can be fairly sure the employee is telling you what you want to hear but intends to do nothing about it.

  Say something like, 'I'm really glad you think it's a good idea. What in particular do you like about it?'

- *The dodger*: 'Let Jane do it' switches the responsibility to someone else or even another department.

  When your request is reasonable, let dodgers know that it is from them that you are expecting action.

- *The threatener*: These resisters imply that 'the boss' (or someone else) won't approve. This may or may not be true, but don't discuss it now.

  Say something like, 'I appreciate your concern and I'll check it out. Meanwhile, what I'd like you to do is …' or 'I'll bear that in mind. What objections do *you* have?'

- *The sympathy seeker*: Don't let people make you feel guilty for asking them to alter their ways and try something new.

  Empathise with their problem, hear them out and, unless their reasons are sound, repeat your request.

- *The traditionalist*: This resister says, 'But we've always done it the other way'. Sometimes the old way is the best way, but more often the appeal to tradition is straightforward resistance of the 'better the devil we know' variety.

Try saying, 'I understand the old way worked very well; however, we need to adapt to changing customer expectation/market needs' or 'Yes, the old approach worked well – how can we adapt it to this new way?'

Notice that, with all these responses, you clearly communicate the required change, listen to, respect and examine the resistance, and then plan with the employee what action he or she can take to cooperate. Once people state their agreement to trying something out, they're less likely to renege.

● IN A NUTSHELL

How to reduce resistance to change
Lessen people's urge to resist by following these tips:
- Build a 'critical mass' of supporters for the change to help it 'take hold' quickly.
- Commit the necessary resources to the change (e.g. budget, communication, time, training).
- Detail the change clearly in terms of both the 'what' (goals, performance indicators, standards) and the 'how' (vision, behaviours, culture).
- Ensure that key people fully support the change.
- Ensure visible signs of early progress to encourage people and build momentum.
- Explain how the change links with the organisation's values, vision and strategy.
- Explain what successful change will 'look like' and how it benefits people.
- Involve your team in designing and implementing the change as much as you can. Make sure everyone is 'engaged' and has a common understanding of what you're trying to achieve.
- Keep communicating and listening.
- Manage the transition from the old to the new carefully; look after people and help them through the uncomfortable transition zone that bridges 'where we are now' and 'where we want to be'.
- Monitor progress so you know what is and what is not working and where the blockages are that you need to remove.
- Provide training and other opportunities for learning and developing from the change.
- Publicise the successes.
- Thank, support and reward the supporters.

● THE STRATEGIC PERSPECTIVE

Monitor labour turnover
Some people cannot accept a change and choose to leave the organisation. While this is inevitable, don't treat it too lightly. When a person leaves, you lose their experience and knowledge and your investment in their training and development.

CourseMateExpress

Go to http://login.cengagebrain.com to access CourseMate Express, your online study tool for *Management Theory & Practice*. CourseMate Express brings chapter concepts to life with interactive learning, and study and exam preparation tools:

- Test your skills in different aspects of management with interactive self-tests and simulations.
- Watch videos that show how real managers operate in real businesses.
- Test your understanding of the changing world of management by taking the revision quiz.

QUICK REVIEW

1. Summarise the continuous cycle of change that all systems seem to go through.
2. Summarise, or show as a flow chart, the steps to take before introducing a change, listing any key factors to bear in mind at each point in the change planning process.
3. Why is communication such an important part of any successful change effort?
4. Describe the ways leader-managers can handle team members who resist change.

BUILD YOUR SKILLS

1. The organic view asserts that organisations need to change and people need to be involved in change at their workplace. What are the implications of this for leader-managers?
2. Why do you think some people embrace and adapt to change more readily than other people? Discuss the process of adapting to change and illustrate this process with a personal example.
3. Referring to Chapter 17's opening Scenario on page 491, this is a big change for Hamish's section. Develop a plan for informing his team about the changes to come; you may want to use the worksheet: Change planning on CourseMate Express. What resistance and other stumbling blocks to successfully introducing this change to his section might he expect? What questions should he expect? Use the worksheet: Will your change succeed? on CourseMate Express to analyse how well this change is likely to succeed.
4. Briefly explain Hall's hierarchy of adopting a change, and discuss how you can use it to be ready for the questions that your work team will ask and when you should provide certain answers.
5. Read the section in Chapter 10, page 301, on Maslow's ideas about motivation. Relate the three phases of adapting to change discussed in this chapter to Maslow's hierarchy.
6. Referring to Case Study 19.1 on page 612, use the information in this chapter to develop a plan for bringing the cynics on side. If you have studied Chapter 21, include information from that chapter, too.

WORKPLACE ACTIVITIES

1. What changes have you been involved in implementing at your workplace? Select one to review, from beginning to end, using the information from this chapter about the cycle of change, the seven steps to change, predicting and dealing with resistance to change and helping people accept change.

2. Interview someone who has experienced a major change at work. This might have been, for instance, the result of a change in funding, job redesign, a merger or an acquisition, a move to a new location, new management or restructuring. Find out all you can about the impact of this change on the person, the person's work group and the organisation's culture. How was the change introduced and managed? What were the obstacles to this change? What resistance to it occurred? Prepare a report analysing this change in terms of how well the seven steps to introducing change were followed. From your analysis, draw conclusions about how effectively the change was managed. What, if anything, could have been done to help the change take effect more smoothly and quickly?

3. What forms of resistance to change have you encountered and how have you dealt with them? On reflection, could you have dealt with them more effectively and, if so, how?

CASE STUDY 22.1

A MAJOR CHANGE

Chan has been thinking long and hard. As part of the latest workplace agreement, the organisation is about to introduce multiskilling for all non-salaried employees. The goal is to enhance efficiency, flexibility and job satisfaction and help the organisation become an 'employer of choice'.

Section managers are responsible for developing and implementing a learning plan for the employees in their sections. They are to ensure that all employees can benefit, that dignity, equal opportunity and health, safety and welfare issues take top priority, and that a net 3% gain in productivity results in the six months after the training is completed. Measures of each section's success also include attendance rates, labour retention rates, number of grievances registered and output to costs ratios.

As Chan rolls this around in his mind, he can see some obvious benefits to the employees. A greater variety of tasks and increased skills should provide more job satisfaction, and the flexibility resulting from multiskilling should increase efficiencies and productivity. The career opportunities should improve, too. Depending on how the multiskilling takes shape, employees may have the opportunity to undertake complete projects and take on more responsibility and decision-making in their jobs.

And Chan can see plenty of other benefits to the organisation, too, apart from those stated in the workplace agreement: multiskilled staff, improved occupational health and safety, improved and easier recruitment and retention due to increased levels of job satisfaction, more effective use of technology, improved staff morale – it sounds too good to be true!

Then he thinks of Newton's third law: for every action, there is an equal and opposite reaction. What is the downside of all this? he wonders.

Questions
1. How might the move to multiskilling affect individuals in Chan's department? How might this change in the way employees work affect Chan's work team as a whole? What are his team members' concerns likely to be? How would you advise Chan to deal with their concerns?
2. What do you predict will be the major resistance points or obstacles to this change? Discuss how Chan could handle them.
3. If you were to coach Chan on how to plan, introduce and manage this important organisational initiative in his section, what steps would you recommend he follow and why?

CASE STUDY 22.2

WHAT A MESS

Linda can't understand it. Why are people being so difficult? Can't they see that the proposed changes to workflow are to everyone's advantage? Placing responsibility for entire processes with small teams gives people a chance to extend their skills and feel greater satisfaction for a job well done. And yet they are stubbornly digging in their heels and refusing to cooperate.

Linda had held a group meeting and explained how employees would be moved into small teams and how the new workflows would operate. She explained how both their internal and their external customers would benefit and how the organisation as a whole would benefit. But instead of responding positively at the meeting and indicating that they would rise to the challenge and make the most of the new opportunities, everyone sat there sullenly, giving each other sidelong glances and shuffling their feet.

Bruce seems determined not to cooperate. In fact, he simply refuses to accommodate the revised team-based processes, insisting he will continue to perform his tasks as he always has. Just yesterday he stated flatly, 'I'll do what I've been hired to do and what's in my job description and that's all there is to it'.

What now? Does he intend to lead the rest of the group in refusing to cooperate with the required changes? What can she do to prevent this?

Questions

1. Use Hall's hierarchy to explain why Linda's team is resisting. Based on your analysis, develop a plan for Linda to follow to introduce this change.
2. Should Linda invite her team to participate in designing the specific changes? Why or why not?
3. How should Linda deal with Bruce if he continues to resist?

CHAPTER

IDENTIFYING AND MANAGING RISKS

OVERVIEW

Some risks are hard to predict, like the volcanic eruption in Iceland in 2010, but that doesn't mean they don't exist. Some risks are clear but ignored and horrendously mismanaged, like those leading up to the global financial crisis that began in 2007. Some risks are obvious, at least in hindsight, perhaps like the Australian Wheat Board bribery scandal in 2005 or the Fukushima nuclear power plant disaster in 2014. Some risks are unlikely but would be catastrophic should they occur and others are ever present and need to be managed continuously.

When negative risk events strike, business and operational plans go out the window. Organisations can lose customers, income and future business, and can even collapse. People can lose their livelihoods and even their lives. Towns, cities and economies can be ravaged.

And what about the cost of ignoring positive risks – opportunities? That can cost an organisation dearly, too. This makes identifying and managing risks, both positive and negative, and building a strong risk culture, an essential element of sound corporate governance.

Negative risks, and their counterpart, opportunities, can come from outside the organisation, from the marketplace, the political and social environment and from natural hazards. Then there is the array of risks and opportunities that come from inside the organisation that can damage an organisation when managed poorly and strengthen it when managed effectively. And just as organisations are at risk from damage to their reputation and even shareholder value from poor environmental management and sustainability practices, unethical behaviour on the part of employees or unsavoury HR practices, they also stand to benefit when they excel in these areas.

We have moved from a prescriptive model to a principle-based approach to managing risk. This means adopting a set of risk management principles and a continuous improvement framework for managing risk, and developing and implementing sound risk management processes. This also means predicting what could occur, assessing the potential causes and outcomes of those future events and the likelihood of their occurrence, establishing overall priorities for removing or controlling the possible causes of negative risk events and planning how to deal with them should they occur, and planning to capitalise on positive risk events.

1. Do you know what constitutes a risk and what types of risk your organisation is exposed to?
2. Do you understand the principles of risk management and can you develop a cost-effective risk management plan?
3. Can you identify and manage the risks at your workplace and ensure the continuity of operations should the worst occur?

This chapter explains how to second-guess and plan for the future, even for events that are beyond your control. There are a lot of technical terms to come to grips with and many terms have similar meanings. Try keeping a running list of risk management terms (words in bold and italics) showing words that mean the same or link with other terms and their synonyms.

Unforeseen events

Ben goes down to breakfast mulling over the challenges of managing two teams: an offshore team based in Mumbai to whom his company outsources part of the accounts receivable function that he manages, and his local team in Sydney made up of telecommuters, part-timers and casual workers.

He switches on the global TV news while gulping down a quick breakfast. Reports of a major fire overnight in the heart of Mumbai shows the area where his offices are located and images of the ensuing chaos gradually pierce his thoughts and jolt him into action. He grabs his jacket and heads into the Sydney CBD, anxious to find out more details, particularly whether the Mumbai offices have been damaged and, if so, whether any members of his overnight team have been injured.

By the time he's driving into the car park, he's heard from the night team leader that everyone's safe but the area around the Mumbai offices has been closed off. He knows not to expect anyone from the Mumbai team to turn up for work for at least the rest of the week. Since none of them telecommute, the Mumbai centre is effectively closed. How much damage there is from the nearby fire remains to be seen.

Ben makes straight for his desk and logs into an Indian news service to receive continual updates on the situation and then begins telephoning his Sydney staff to arrange for as much overtime as they can manage. It is important that accounts receivable keep up with the workload and therefore the company's cash flow.

Important, but impossible. There is no way his local team can do all their own work as well as all of the Mumbai team's work, even if they all worked double shifts. If the Mumbai centre stays closed for longer than a week, they'll be in serious strife. Who in the world could have foreseen this, he thinks, as he puts his head in his hands. Who indeed?

1. Understanding risk

> I cannot imagine any condition which would cause a ship to founder. I cannot conceive of any vital disaster happening to this vessel. Modern ship building has gone beyond that.
>
> Quotation from Edward John Smith (ship's captain who died in the *Titanic* tragedy), *The New York Times* (16 April 2012 edition)[1]

It may be tempting sometimes to follow the example of Captain Smith of the *Titanic* and pretend risks don't exist. Organisations (and ship's captains) can't afford to think like this. Globalised competition, increasing occurrences of natural disasters, dependence on and vulnerability to communication and information technology, rapidly evolving business models ... the number of risks organisations face increases constantly. Disruptive change is accelerating to the point where there will be no 'new normal' but a continuous series of 'not normal' times.[2] That's why risk management has become progressively more important in safeguarding organisations.

Here are some 'what ifs' to mull over:

- Could your company keep trading should governments and major investors such as superannuation funds dump all their shares and refuse to invest further in your business because it isn't deemed 'green' enough?
- Could work continue should a key external supplier suddenly stop trading or fail to maintain continuity of supplies because of industrial action or political upheaval?
- How would your organisation cope should a major illness strike down 30–75% of its workforce?
- How would your organisation respond if it were suddenly trashed in social media and suffered a major loss of reputation, market share and profits?
- How would your organisation respond should an unexpected competitor suddenly enter the market?

- What would happen if a mouse chewed through the electric wiring at your premises, shutting down operations until the problem could be traced and rectified?
- What would happen to your organisation's operations if your workplace floods or burns down?
- What steps would you take if your team lost all of last week's or even yesterday's work due to a malicious computer virus?
- Would managers and employees in your organisation know how to respond to industrial action, a product recall or another internal event that pushes it into the media spotlight?

What steps would you take should any of these events, or a similar event, occur? How would you look after your employees? How would you protect your organisation's physical assets? How could you and your team keep your work flowing to your internal or external customers?

Here are three more questions to ponder:

1. How could you prevent or reduce the likelihood of adverse events like these occurring?
2. Should your organisation insure for any of these or similar events?
3. What contingency plans does your organisation need to deal with these and similar emergencies should they occur and how should you test those plans?

THE STRATEGIC PERSPECTIVE

The risk event that threatens the global economy

Risk management lagged behind innovation in the financial system as the 21st century began. By 2008, the subprime mortgage debacle in the USA that began in 2007 created severe repercussions throughout the world. In March 2008, Australian broker Opus Prime went into receivership, owing about $1.05 billion to secured creditors including ANZ Bank and Merrill Lynch, and losing hundreds of millions of dollars belonging to its 1200 smaller investors. The ripple effect hit businesses across Australia and led to loss of confidence in some markets.[3]

Major financial institutions wrote off nearly $400 billion in the US alone; global losses stood at $4.2 trillion in October 2008.[4] And central banks around the world instituted emergency measures to restore liquidity. Iceland's financial system collapsed in October 2008 and by November 2008 more than 60% of Australian businesses reported a negative impact from the financial crisis.[5] By 2012, a plethora of countries, including Argentina, Italy, Greece, Latvia, Lithuania, Portugal, South Africa, Spain and the Ukraine, were considered very high risk by a number of international banks. The economies of the Eurozone and the USA continue to struggle.

Savage cuts to slash deficits brought demonstrators to the streets, and capitalism, a victim of its own success, seemed at one point to be in mortal danger as most major economies struggled with overwhelming problems.[6]

There have been other financial crises with worldwide ramifications, such as the Great Depression of 1929–39 when the US stock market crashed and Black Monday, named for Monday 19 October 1987, when share markets around the world crashed. The Asian economic crisis of 1997 sent many companies to the wall. Russia's debt default in 1998 saw a $22.6 billion bail-out by the International Monetary Fund and the World Bank saved the country from financial collapse. Then there was the dot-com bust of 2000 when the speculative investment bubble burst. But this latest risk event has hit organisations around the globe deeper and harder.

What is a risk?

Risks are uncertainties and unknown events that can help or hinder an organisation to achieve its goals. The way organisations think about risk has evolved in the past few decades. Traditionally, risk management was all doom and gloom, concentrating on dangers, hazards, perils and threats. Risk management was called business contingency planning and it was about identifying and minimising negative outcomes for the organisation.

In practice, this meant protecting the organisation's infrastructure against fire, riots and natural disasters such as earthquakes and floods, and having recovery plans detailing what to do should they occur. Until the 1970s, the responsibility for bearing these risks was usually transferred to another party by buying insurance.

Risk management now goes beyond protecting the organisation's infrastructure from isolated occurrences to incorporating unfolding global events such as protecting employees' and the organisation's ability to conduct business during a sustained crisis such as a pandemic and continuing operations in the face of the possible breakdown of the international monetary system.

The modern approach to risk also recognises the upside of risk: opportunity. Take a bank or a credit union, for example. Every new loan is a risk. Every new loan is also an opportunity – in this example, to make a profit. Even though the discipline of predicting and dealing with possible future events is still called risk management, many organisations include identifying and making the most of opportunities to improve product and service delivery in their risk management strategy. (To save repetition, when you read 'risk' in the rest of this chapter, you may also want to think 'and opportunity'.)

An emerging approach to risk is to think about the ways a risk can affect different stakeholders – some win, some lose, and some aren't affected when a risk event occurs. This approach, summarised in Figure 23.1, acknowledges that a risk can be negative, positive or neutral.

Negative risk: Injury, damage or loss measured in degrees of probability

Neutral risk: Risk can be negative, neutral or positive, depending on your perspective

Positive risk: The reward of unexpected gains

FIGURE 23.1 Three faces of risk

Two sources of risk

Risks can result either from an organisation's activities or come from outside the organisation. Those that hail from the environment in which the organisation operates are known as external, or *extrinsic risks*, while those that arise within the organisation itself are known as internal, or *intrinsic risks*. These are summarised in Figure 23.2. Risks from any or all of these areas can affect organisations in a variety of ways.

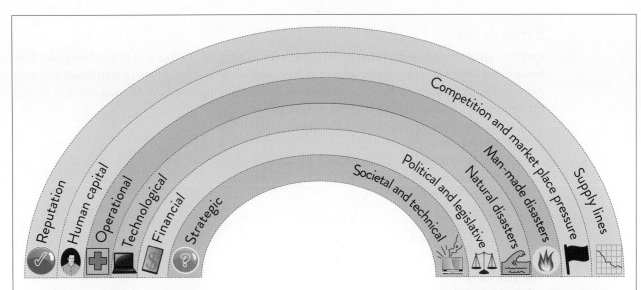

INTERNAL RISKS

Reputation:
Image of responsibility and integrity, brand damage, sabotage

Human capital:
Contract management, culture and values, ethical behaviour, actions and inactions of employees, the departure of key staff, training, performance management and career-pathing systems, human error

Operational:
Equipment control and quality, insurance costs, health, safety and welfare (e.g. asbestos, carcinogens, stress, accidents, environmental pollution, equipment failure, sabotage), product and service quality, recurring problems and near misses

Technological:
Security of information, data and intellectual property, communications and IT systems failure, equipment failure, computer viruses, lost and corrupted data, information, intellectual property, systems and processes

Financial:
Fraud, loss on investment, theft, cash flow, capital management and controls, ability to attract investment

Strategic:
Risk flowing from strategies, plans, projects and policies

EXTERNAL RISKS

Supply lines:
The collapse of a key customer or supplier, variable fuel and raw material availability and costs, a sudden shortage of a key commodity, loss of supplies of energy and other utilities

Competition and marketplace pressure:
Industrial action, national and international economic pressures, rapidly evolving business models, skills shortages, unpredictable capital markets

Man-made disasters:
Fire, nuclear plant power leakage, oil spillage, sabotage, security and supply of energy and utilities, terrorism, transport shutdowns, wars

Natural disasters:
Earthquakes, fires, floods, storms, tsunamis, climate change, epidemics and pandemics

Political and legislative:
Civil unrest, political instability, new legislation and regulations

Societal and technical:
Technical advances, technology-related accidents, changes to demographics, consumer trends, social unrest, social media

FIGURE 23.2 Risks (and opportunities)

Extrinsic risk

Extrinsic risks abound. Some bring opportunities for either profit or loss and others bring only loss. Some bring huge opportunities for some organisations while placing others in significant jeopardy. Advances in technology, for example, can suddenly make an organisation's offering obsolete or offer the opportunity to dramatically improve its operations.

Let's review seven common areas of extrinsic risk:

1. The economy.
2. The government.
3. Information technology (IT).
4. Mother Nature.
5. Pandemics.
6. Social media.
7. Utilities.

The economy

Economies going pear-shaped can lead to election upsets, nationalisation of resources and unpredictable regulation, particularly in countries or regions considered to be unstable. In extreme cases, political regimes can be destabilised, as evidenced by the Arab Spring of 2011 and the resulting regional unrest that followed, carrying consequences for organisations with investments and operations in those countries.[7]

One event often leads to another. The subprime mortgage collapse in the USA in 2008 infected the viability of the global financial system, leading to a global financial meltdown and a sudden reduction of access to credit; the resulting global economic downturn affected the ability of entire nations and their institutions to trade and continue operations. The Australian dollar rose in relation to many trading partners, curtailing the success of many companies that export goods and services.

The state of the Australian economy – boom times, deflation, depression, inflation and recession – affects customers' purchasing power for organisations' products and services and the availability and mobility of the workforce. A period of high market volatility, brought about by, for example, economic uncertainty, natural disasters, pandemics and/or political instability, could increase the number of mergers and acquisitions and make forecasting profits difficult. This in turn could spook investors and affect the value of corporations.[8]

The government

Changes in government and government policy, legislation and regulations are ever-present, with significant repercussions to organisations in all three sectors. The more reforms the government introduces, the bigger the risks.

Banking and financial systems face increased legislation and regulation in the aftermath of the 'subprime meltdown' of the global financial system, for example, and organisations that pollute the environment need to deal with increased legislation and regulation as well as consumer and public demand to operate in more socially responsible and sustainable ways.

Information technology

Information technology (IT) has provided wonderful opportunities as well as dangers. It lets us calculate at the speed of light, design buildings, draw fancy graphs and charts, fly aircraft and rockets, and even perform surgery. Soon, computers will even be parking our cars. Ah, but when they fail or are compromised …

Organisations hold valuable information in a variety of formats and places and it must be protected from increasingly numerous and sophisticated and malicious online attacks that can result in anything from financial or proprietary information loss to a major disruption in business activity. Cyber attacks against Australian organisations are increasing. While many attacks go undetected, more than 20% of 255 major companies surveyed said they had been attacked and 20% of these organisations experienced more than 10 attacks. Slightly more attacks came from external sources (56%) than from within the organisation (44%). Most (44%) chose not to report the event to the police and few (13%) took the matter to court.[9]

Automated attack tools, exploitation of unprotected software and misconfigured operating systems, applications and network devices were the most common attack methods.[10] Because their large storage capacity makes them portable computers, unlocked electronic notebooks and smartphones are other common weak points, as are – wait for it – USB sticks; these little bundles of data are a main cause of infection.[11] Unless employees are careful with their downloads, they also risk trojans, viruses and worms entering their organisation's IT network when connecting them to their computers and the risks heighten with 'bring your own device' policies.

Meanwhile, techniques such as analytics, or 'big data' enabled by rapidly advancing technology, is changing business models and altering logistic possibilities, giving rise to both negative and positive risk. Public cloud computing (as differentiated from the more secure private cloud environment) is emerging as another important risk area.[12]

● THE STRATEGIC PERSPECTIVE

Information, intellectual property and IT security

Since 1997, when IT security was more about making sure the computer room was locked, threats to corporate information security have exploded in volume and the degree of nastiness – email and web threats, denial of service, hacking and other security breaches, hactivism, identity theft, and viruses and worms, to name just a few. Hackers are not looking for bragging rights anymore. They're looking to steal specific intellectual property (IP) to sell for profit.[13]

Cybercrime is soaring and could cost organisations millions of dollars. The year 2013 was dubbed 'the year of mega breach'. More than 522 million identities were exposed. Targeted attack campaigns increased 91%, breaches increased 62% and web-based attacks were up 23% over the previous year. Spear phishing campaigns (emails trying to obtain unauthorised access to sensitive information) increased 91% in 2013 over the previous year, with large, medium and small businesses almost equally the victims of targeted attacks: 30%, 31% and 30% respectively.[14]

Mother Nature

The Fifth Assessment Report of the Intergovernmental Panel on Climate Change makes it clear that the science shows with 95% certainty that human activity has been the main cause of global warming since the middle of the 20th century.[15] This presents huge risks and huge opportunities. Horrific bushfires, earthquakes, floods, hailstorms, tornadoes, torrential rain – they all present huge risks and huge opportunities.

Nearly half the world's disasters occur in our Asia-Pacific region.[16] Natural disasters such as cyclones, tsunamis and volcanoes, and climate change with its associated fires, floods and storms, rising sea levels, shortage of drinkable water, warmer temperatures affecting farmers' ability to grow crops and livestock, and more, affect organisations' ability to obtain resources and to operate effectively. The results of climate change may also require organisations to alter the way they operate and have already presented lucrative new opportunities to some organisations. (Chapter 24 has more information on this aspect of risk management.)

 THEORY TO PRACTICE

Ordinary events pose risk, too

Even ordinary weather patterns can affect organisations. Take Taronga Zoo, Sydney's number one tourist attraction and the largest paid-for attraction in Australia. The number of visitors is a key performance indicator. It can have up to 15 000 visitors a day during the Christmas period but if it rains, daily attendance may drop to 3000. A prolonged wet period during the Christmas holidays can financially devastate that important income stream.[17]

Pandemics

Epidemics (localised outbreaks) and *pandemics* (global outbreaks) such as influenza and ebola outbreaks directly affect staff and their ability to work. Pandemics generally result in more deaths than epidemics and current modelling by the World Health Organization (WHO) suggests that pandemics are likely to come in three waves, or peak periods, each sweeping across the globe in a matter of weeks and lasting as long as three months.

During pandemic waves, organisations could experience absentee rates of between 15% and 30% due to family care responsibilities, fear of contagion, quarantine, sickness and travel restrictions. Because vaccines can't be made in advance, it could be four to eight months after a pandemic begins before the first vaccines are ready for distribution.[18]

The issues arising from a pandemic also apply to chemical, biological, radiological and nuclear events, known by the acronym CBRN, and to major climatic events and all have occupational health and safety implications as well.

 FYI

Deadly viruses

The Antonine Plague of 165–180 AD, possibly smallpox, was the first recorded plague. Since then, the world has experienced the Black Death (1334–50, killing 30 to 50 million people across China and Europe), the bubonic plague (1855–1903, killing 10 million people in China and Hong Kong), five influenza plagues (between 1889 and 2009, killing a total of 54 200 000 people worldwide) and six cholera plagues.

Four times in the 20th century, a new influenza subtype highly infectious to humans emerged, all three resulting from virus mutations. The 1918–19 avian (or Spanish) flu (H1N1) killed 50 million people and the 1956–58 (H2N2) and 1968–69 (H3N3) pandemics killed 3 million people between them. In 2009, swine flu killed about 200 000 people. Since the 1980s, HIV/AIDS has been considered to be an ongoing plague and has killed 40 million people worldwide. Ebola killed 4800 people in the first 11 months of 2014.[19]

The World Health Organization (WHO) uses a series of six phases of pandemic alert, each phase coinciding with a series of recommended actions for WHO, the international community, governments and industry to take. In 2008, WHO judged the threat of bird flu to have been at Phase 3 for more than four years and in April 2009 the threat of swine flu

>>

reached Phase 5. Phase 3 is the point at which organisations should develop and regularly update risk mitigation plans and test them with table-top scenarios and site-level drills. By Phase 4, the time for planning has passed, since the risk management program needs to have been implemented by then. By Phase 5, it's far too late to start planning – it's time for intensive execution of your plans.[20]

Social media

Its reputation is considered a company's biggest strategic risk area.[21] Social media has only been around a few years (e.g. Facebook since 2004, YouTube since 2005 and Twitter since 2006) and has therefore only recently entered risk managers' radars.[22] It is now considered the biggest technology risk to reputation.[23] It's the speed and loss of control that cause the biggest headaches, particularly to an organisation's brand, image and reputation.[24]

Leading companies such as Proctor & Gamble take their risk to reputation from social media so seriously that they constantly scan social media, and top-level management reviews dashboards summarising views on their products and the strength of their various brands.[25]

The chances that your organisation, product or service is being discussed, evaluated, recommended or trashed is high. And people believe what their contacts say. Nielsen research found that 78% of people believe their contacts' negative and positive comments about a company, product or service (versus 16% who believe advertising).[26] Moreover, while until relatively recently organisations could train one or two key people to be their 'face and voice' to the public via the media, every employee now has that ability.

● THEORY TO PRACTICE

The power of social media

Social media can shred a company's reputation in minutes. Take the video posted on YouTube showing two Domino's Pizza employees spitting and urinating in a customer's order for milk and a sandwich, viewed over one million times in less than three days and still being viewed.

Domino's took 48 hours to respond, slow in social media terms, while it debated whether to respond since it didn't want to alert more people to the story. Finally, it decided that a YouTube apology by the company's president was warranted. The words were good but he read from a script and made no eye contact with the camera, making the response seem somewhat half-hearted and the PR disaster lingers.

When well executed, social media can force a company to alter its strategy. Greenpeace's social media campaign against Nestlé, which parodied the 'Have a break, have a Kit Kat' slogan, became a viral hit and exposed Nestlé's use of palm oil in products, including Kit Kat. Apart from its health risks, the palm oil industry is driving the destruction of Indonesian rainforests and pushing orangutans to the brink of extinction. A public 'discussion' ensued on Nestlé's Facebook page, with Nestlé's manager becoming argumentative and rude, badly damaging Nestlé's reputation. Nestle was forced to overhaul its supply chain to exclude companies that owned or managed plantations and farms linked to deforestation.

Utilities

A variety of risks relating to the security and supply of energy and other utilities hover in the background, including broken water mains, electrical blackouts, gas field explosions, power grid failure and telecommunications failure. You may even need to factor in terrorist activities and an interruption of a key supplier's or a major customer's business.

● THE STRATEGIC PERSPECTIVE

Global risk

As the financial crisis that began in 2007–08 shows, global risks arising from interdependent systems of energy, the environment, finance, health, supply chains and telecommunications, have widespread and sometimes long-lasting economic, political and social effects and call for an internationally coordinated response. Here are the top 10 risks the world faces:

1. Fiscal crises in key economies.
2. Structurally high unemployment/underemployment
3. Water crises.
4. Severe income disparity.
5. Failure of climate change mitigation and adaptation.
6. Greater incidence of extreme weather events, such as fires, floods and storms.
7. Global governance failure.
8. Food crises.
9. Failure of a major financial mechanism/institution
10. Profound political and social instability.

These are *systemic risks* that would cause the breakdown of an entire system. The World Economic Forum considers these high impact and high likelihood risks that would have a significant negative impact for several countries and industries for up to 10 years.

Trends to watch include abuse or accidents involving new technologies (e.g. synthetic biology), data mismanagement, the decline of trust in institutions, lack of leadership, persisting gender inequalities and pollution.[28]

Intrinsic risk

There is an element of risk in every activity an organisation undertakes. It is inherent in every strategy an organisation develops, every decision its employees make and every action they take or fail to take. Risk is part of an organisation's commercial, legal and supply chain relationships, management activities and controls, operations, product design and safety, work systems and equipment.

Fortunately, we have more control over internal risks than over external risks. Increasingly important areas to monitor and actively manage include:

- brand, image and reputation management and protection
- compliance requirements
- corporate social responsibility and sustainability
- human capital management, particularly employee engagement, morale and skills development, and workforce planning and retention
- technology and technological issues.

Information governance is growing in importance, too. The need to manage massive amounts of information and store it for ease of access when needed (e.g. for compliance, internal investigations or litigation) is only the beginning. IT data breaches, downtime, equipment failure, theft or loss, recovery from a server failure which can take weeks, means that backing up regularly and installing an antivirus package is no longer enough.

We examine two areas of intrinsic risk below:

1. Employee acts and omissions.
2. Skill shortages and the ageing workforce.

Employee acts and omissions

Over the years, many corporate executives have had to step down following behaviour considered to be 'in a manner unbecoming' of their positions. Many adverse events that have affected companies have had employee acts and omissions at their core, for example:

- breaches of compliance with health and safety legislation
- failure to manage creditors
- fraud (asset misappropriation, corruption, fraudulent statements and misuse of resources)
- lack of vigilance regarding IT security
- reputational damage from internal disputes and legal claims
- theft or poor treatment of key equipment.

Corporate fraud, for example, costs the Australian economy more than $8.5 billion a year and affects half of Australian businesses.[29] Fraud tends to increase in tough economic times and most fraud – 80% – is by employees, 65% of them middle managers. On the face of it, Australian fraud levels are higher than the global average, with 36% of Australian firms reporting fraud costs of more than $1 million in 2014 compared to 17% globally.[30] However, more fraud is detected in Australia because of a higher awareness of and low tolerance for fraud, and strong regulatory and corporate governance.[31]

The intrinsic risks arising from employee misuse of social media alone, magnified by the speed it spreads information and the fact that it's unstoppable, are too great to ignore and include the following:

- cyber bullying, harassment and racial vilification and religious vilification
- defamation
- improper disclosure of confidential information and market-sensitive information
- misrepresentation or breaches of trade practices legislation
- reputation damage.[32]

When identifying internal risks, don't just think about potential crises and disasters; include less visible risks too, such as the ongoing risks discussed later in this chapter. And remember to look for and capitalise on the array of opportunities arising from employee behaviour, too.

◉ THE STRATEGIC PERSPECTIVE

The real cost of cost-cutting

When an organisation cuts costs, the bottom line quickly benefits. But it's important to look further down the track.

BP didn't, when years of cost cutting through reduced maintenance and training at their Texas City refinery, following years of cost cutting by Amoco, the site's previous owners, resulted in an explosion in 2005 that killed 15 and injured 180 people.[33]

The 2013 European horsemeat scandal is similar. Continued price pressure from supermarkets produced small cost savings that included padding out beef, lamb and pork products with (cheaper) horsemeat. Predictably, suppliers were found out and suffered cancelled orders, their food pulled off supermarket shelves, followed by law suits and police raids.[34]

When organisations cut costs, downstream risk may be increased.

Skill shortages and the ageing workforce

Although the Australian population is slowly growing (about 1.2% a year), the workforce is getting smaller. In 2010, for each person over the age of 65, there were 5 working-age people, down from 7.5 in 1975. By 2050, this number is expected to drop to only 2.7 working-age people to every person over 65. The baby boom has become a baby bust.[35] Baby Boomers – people born between 1946 and 1964 – leave the workforce faster than younger people join it.[36]

As with many risks, this is both a positive and a negative. Some organisations will experience difficulties recruiting the skilled employees they need. Others, who introduce flexible working arrangements that both older and younger employees want, will have first choice of available people.

Similarly, older employees present different health and safety risks than younger employees and different age groups need different types of adjustments made to lessen the risks each group of employees presents.

Types of risk

Some risks are risks of *scale* – currency exchange rates fluctuate, but by how much? Others are risks of *timing* – more earthquakes will occur in Japan and New Zealand, but when? Other risks relate to *structure* – computers are bound to be attacked by a virus, but what sort of virus?[37]

What could happen? Where could it happen? When could it happen? Why would it happen? How could it happen? How would you know it was about to happen? These are *future risks* and they can be extrinsic or intrinsic. Former British prime minister, Benjamin Disraeli put it like this, 'What we anticipate seldom occurs; what we least expect generally happens.'[38]

Some risks are *strategic*, others *operational* (discussed later in this chapter, on page 753). Some risks are more *current* or *ongoing*. Some are lurking, or looming, but you don't yet know their precise cause or nature; others arise from current problems and trends that have the potential to worsen, such as:

- abusing stakeholders' goodwill (e.g. by taking short cuts for short-term profits)
- attending to low-priority areas and working on low value-adding tasks instead of important work
- capital availability, credit and liquidity problems
- difficulties in attracting, retaining and engaging staff
- failures and near-failures in routine operations that could be prevented or designed out
- a hostile takeover bid
- letting cumbersome systems that make people's work difficult continue, unimproved
- loss of key personnel
- missed opportunities (e.g. using assets or resources poorly or letting them languish)
- operational exposure to changing regulations
- outsourcing resulting in loss of customer goodwill and reputational damage
- patchy regulatory compliance
- poor organisation culture
- poor product design (e.g. when customers don't understand how to use your product, they may hurt themselves or may not buy it again and tell others of their frustration, harming your organisation's reputation and costing it sales)
- poor relationships with a key business partner or stakeholder
- a public relations disaster
- shareholder activism.

These are often considered 'business as usual risks' and not recorded in registers of potential risks. They should, however, be identified, recorded in a separate risk register, and controlled and reviewed by the *risk owner*. (See the 'In a Nutshell: Risk registers' on page 751.)

Whatever the type of risk, you have the inherent risk, or the risk before treatment, i.e. before controls are established. Residual risk is risk remaining after treatment and needs to be taken into account in your risk management plan. Risk tolerance is the level of residual risk the organisation is willing to bear for a particular risk (see the next section, 'Risk appetite').

And then there are *black swan* events, events with no precedent, such as 9/11, the global financial crisis and the Arab Spring of 2011. Black swan events are extreme events with a low likelihood of occurring, but are hugely catastrophic when they occur.

◉ THEORY TO PRACTICE

The unthinkable does happen

Another recent 'who'd'a'thunk it' (unobvious) risk was the Eyjafjalljökull eruption (otherwise known as the 'volcano with the unpronounceable name') in Iceland in April 2010, which suspended air traffic in Central Europe for five days and stranded thousands of Australian employees trying to return home to work or travelling to attend important business meetings or conferences. Energy giant Rio Tinto, for example, was forced to delay its Melbourne annual general meeting because its board of directors and executives were trapped in London by the volcanic ash covering Europe.

Technology played a starring role in these four hard-to-foresee disasters:

1. A disc bought on eBay revealed details of test launch procedures for the US military Terminal High Altitude Area Defence ground-to-air missile defence system.
2. A failure at an outsourced Danish data centre disrupted the operations of its clients, knocked out a major bank's ATM network and halted milk delivery across the country.
3. A network failure at the London Stock Exchange stopped trading on what would have been one of the busiest days of the year.
4. A UK government employee lost two computer discs containing personal and banking data of approximately 25 million residents, information with an estimated black-market value of $2.5 billion.[39]

That's why you need to go beyond history and plan for a variety of generic disruptions to business.

◉ ACTION!

What extrinsic and intrinsic risks does your organisation face? Use the Extrinsic and intrinsic risks template on **CourseMateExpress** to begin brainstorming them.

Risk appetite

In 1850, the French essayist Marquis de Vauvenargues said of risk, 'There are those who are so scrupulously afraid of doing wrong that they seldom venture to do anything.'[40] How much risk is your organisation willing to take in order to achieve its goals? How much loss is it prepared to accept should an adverse event occur? This is its risk appetite, or *risk tolerance.* You can think of risk appetite as a continuum, as shown in Figure 23.3.

Risk appetite sometimes depends on the industry, but not always. Financial institutions are traditionally very careful but, then again, consider the global financial crisis caused by the finance industry's lack of prudence.

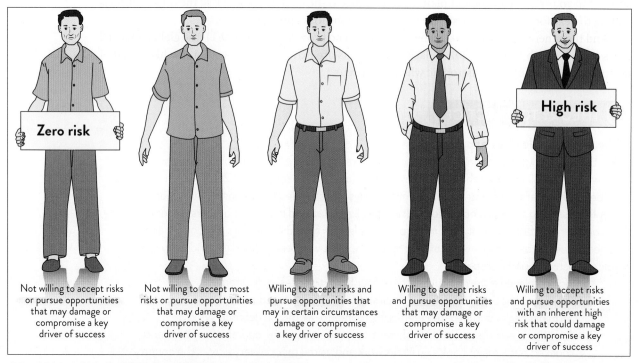

Zero risk				High risk
Not willing to accept risks or pursue opportunities that may damage or compromise a key driver of success	Not willing to accept most risks or pursue opportunities that may damage or compromise a key driver of success	Willing to accept risks and pursue opportunities that may in certain circumstances damage or compromise a key driver of success	Willing to accept risks and pursue opportunities that may damage or compromise a key driver of success	Willing to accept risks and pursue opportunities with an inherent high risk that could damage or compromise a key driver of success

FIGURE 23.3 Risk appetites

● THEORY TO PRACTICE

How risk hungry are you?

You know that stopping at a red light carries less risk of being involved in an adverse risk event (a car accident) than entering an intersection on a yellow light and that going through a red light greatly increases the likelihood of causing an accident. How often do you enter intersections on a yellow light? Under what circumstance, if any, would you take this action? Have you ever gone through a red light? Under what circumstance, if any, would you take this action?

You also know that the faster you drive, the greater your risk exposure. Crowded roads, narrow streets, the presence of pedestrians, rain, fog and winding roads all dramatically increase risk. What steps do you take when driving to mitigate (reduce) these risks?

Do you ever intentionally introduce further risks while driving by, for example, eating, failing to buckle your seatbelt, texting or talking on the telephone, or driving after drinking alcohol? Under what circumstances would you be willing to add further risk to an already dangerous activity by taking these actions?

Let's go back to the example of a bank or credit union making a loan – both a risk and an opportunity. Without taking some risks, such as making a loan, banks and credit unions wouldn't have a business. The key is to manage risks and know how much risk you're willing to accept.

Organisations determine their risk appetites based on their overall strategic objectives. As shown in Figure 23.4, organisations set risk appetite levels for different drivers of success. An organisation might have zero appetite for risks relating to governance, legislative compliance, reputation and brand, and workplace health and safety, and a high risk appetite for research and development of new products and business models where the failure rate might be high but returns great.

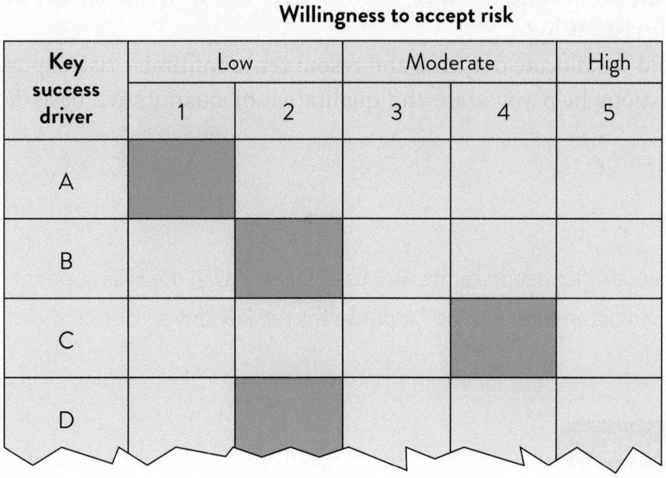

The shaded area shows an organisation's risk appetite for a particular driver of success.

Prepared by: Board risk and audit committee: 11 January 2017
Reviewed by: RMC, 21 September 2016 Approved by: GLK, 9 December 2016

FIGURE 23.4 Risk appetite matrix

⊙ THEORY TO PRACTICE

Risk or opportunity?

A first-year teacher was once offered a six-month contract for teaching in a rural town. No bank would lend him a loan for a reliable car. But a credit union thought that teachers were a good risk and, seeing the loan as an opportunity, lent the young man the money. They also offered him a savings account and a credit or debit card. That young teacher was one happy customer. Some years later, he came back to the credit union for his first home loan. He's still a satisfied customer.

To determine the risk appetite for a particular success driver, weigh up how critical it is to the organisation against what could happen should something compromise it and whether, and to what extent, the organisation is willing to accept those consequences. For opportunities, weigh up how much an opportunity would strengthen a success driver against the effort (e.g. in terms of cost and time) of optimising it.

Answering questions like the following for both operational and strategic risks can help you balance risks against rewards and create an appropriate risk culture:

- Are the risks we pay most attention to consistent with our overall strategy and goals?
- Is the organisation too comfortable with risk, putting itself in excessive danger? Or too risk averse, missing opportunities?
- What level of risk exposure requires a formal strategy to mitigate it? Why?
- What level of risk exposure requires our immediate action? Why?
- What risks are we willing to take? Why? Where is our boundary between acceptable and unacceptable risk? Why?
- Where should we allocate our time and resources to minimise risk exposure? Why?

The 'Why?' questions help you state the qualitative or quantitative basis for the level of risk appetite selected.

● ACTION!

How risk hungry is your organisation for its various activities? Use the Risk appetite template on **₹CourseMateExpress** to determine your risk appetite for the key drivers of success of your work team or organisation.

● IN A NUTSHELL

Risk appetite statement

In many organisations, the Board Risk Management Committee develops a *risk appetite statement* that states how much risk they are prepared to accept in strategically important areas without reference to the board and without compromising good governance. These *boundaries*, or risk limits, can be expressed as averages (e.g. one in five tests successful); frequency of occurrence (e.g. one negative every five years); per cents (e.g. plus or minus % of estimated cost); or time limits (e.g. tolerances checked daily).

Since risk appetite is dynamic and needs to be adjusted as the external and internal environment changes, risk appetite statements are normally reviewed by the board annually and by the Risk Management Committee more frequently.

The organisation's risk appetite forms the basis for establishing its risk culture, risk management policies and risk treatments.

Risk culture

An organisation's risk culture describes how aware of risks and opportunities, and their potential effects on the organisation, employees at all levels and in all parts of the organisation are, and how conscious they are of the role they play in controlling and optimising those risks and opportunities.

Ambiguous or weak risk cultures lead to inappropriate behaviours towards risk. Some serious risks might be treated too lightly some of the time or all of the time, while other far less serious risks consume inordinately large amounts of effort, money and time.

With no risk management processes in place, employees may make their own assessment of how to deal with each risk as it crops up. As a result, the same risk may be dealt with differently in different parts of the organisation, or one area may unintentionally undermine the efforts of another area. Eventually, a sticky end is reached and the organisation's ability to achieve its goals, and probably also its reputation, is damaged.

In a strong risk culture, employees are aware of and manage risks, including the potential risks they may create by their acts and failures to act. Employees are alert to looming risks in their operating and external environments and take appropriate action. Risk management isn't placed in a separate 'silo' of isolated, stand-alone programs. It is an integral part of an organisation's daily routines, processes and practices. From the beginning and through all stages of an activity, asset, operational area, product, project and supply chain, a strong risk management culture and practices protect the organisation.[41]

To build a healthy risk culture in which employees pay attention to all kinds of risks, all the time, and deal with them appropriately, risk analysis and risk management planning needs to be incorporated into strategic, business and operational planning and decision-making and into the organisation's various management systems.

Since people pay attention to what is measured, include risk management measures in business performance measures, performance reporting systems and individual measures of success (see Figure 23.5). This also eliminates the possibility of duplication when measuring and monitoring organisational activities.

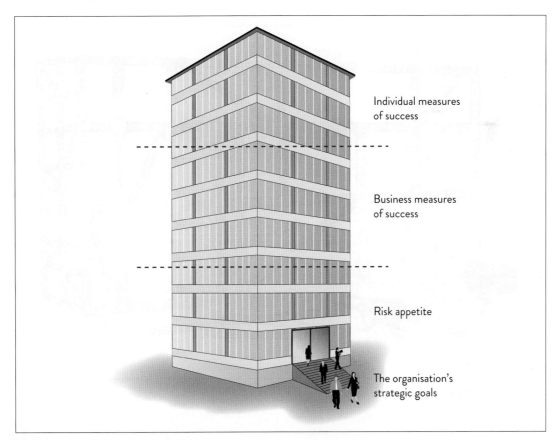

FIGURE 23.5 Elements of a risk culture

2. Understanding the risk management principles and framework

A business is only as good as the sum of its parts, which means you can't afford to have weak parts.

Robert Heller (management author), *The Supermarketers* (1988)[142]

Risk management is part of the overall duty of care and responsibility the organisation's board of directors and senior managers owe to the organisation and its stakeholders and is part of the organisation's larger corporate governance structure. The principles-based approach based on AS/NZS ISO 31000:2009 (which replaces the prescriptive model of the previous guidelines, AS/NZS 4360:2004), state the principles that organisations must follow to achieve effective risk management.

A solid risk management framework (RMF), as shown in Figure 23.6, provides the arrangements needed to identify, prioritise, treat (but not 'over-manage') and monitor the way an organisation identifies and deals with the risks in all aspects of its operations. Stakeholder communication and consultation is an ongoing feature of the RMF, as is continuous improvement. The framework needs to be continually monitored and reviewed so it can evolve and be continually improved as the organisation, its circumstances and its operating environment change.

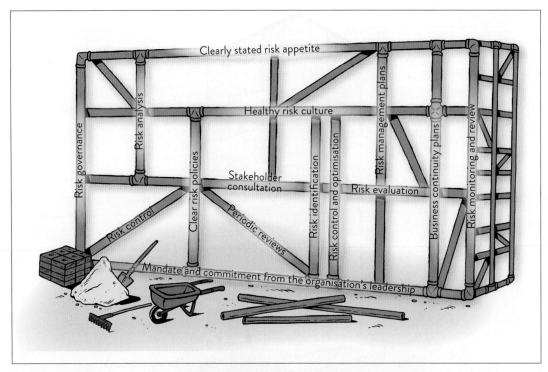

FIGURE 23.6 The risk management framework

● THEORY TO PRACTICE

Empty rhetoric
One of the world's worst man-made risk events was the explosion of BP's Deepwater Horizon oil spill in the Gulf of Mexico in 2010 (see 'Theory to practice: The well from hell and bad apples' on page 522). Investigators blamed the disaster on what amounts to a flimsy risk management framework that prevented 'the ability of individuals involved to identify the risks they faced and to properly evaluate, communicate and address them.'[43]

Why manage risk?

Waiting until you have time to attend to risks or until a negative event threatens operations before deciding how to respond to it may mean you respond too late and your organisation never recovers. Waiting for an opportunity to tap you on the shoulder is more likely to result in it whizzing past you before you've noticed it, leaving you scratching your head and wondering how you could have been so blind.

Identifying and managing risks reduces the chance of serious error, omissions, shocks and unwelcome surprises and helps organisations deal with interruptions to operations and threats to customers, employees, information, intellectual property and public image, as well as identify and grasp opportunities quickly. Paradoxically, effective risk management also allows higher risks to be taken in pursuit of opportunities and goals.

Risk management principles

Adhering to the 11 risk management principles in the 'In a Nutshell: Risk management principles', encourages proactive risk management, improves organisational resilience and increases the likelihood of the organisation achieving its objectives. It helps organisations meet their legal and regulatory responsibilities and international norms, work effectively with stakeholders, and control and allocate resources to treat risks.

● IN A NUTSHELL

Risk management principles
Effective risk management follows 11 standards:
1. It is based on the best available information.
2. It is clear and inclusive.
3. It creates value for the organisation.
4. It is dynamic, ongoing and responsive to change.
5. It encourages continuous improvement.
6. It explicitly addresses uncertainty.
7. It is included in decision-making.
8. It is integral to the organisation's processes.
9. It is systematic, timely and well-thought-out.
10. It is tailored to suit the organisation's needs and goals.
11. It takes human and cultural factors into account.[44]

Who is responsible for managing risk?

Every employee and contractor is responsible for following the organisation's risk management policies and procedures and for remaining aware of the risks they and the organisation might be exposed to and the risks to which they, themselves, might expose the organisation.

However, the ultimate responsibility for identifying and managing risk and establishing a healthy risk culture lies with the board, which establishes the organisation's risk appetite and risk management policies and monitors the effectiveness of the various programs and measures that flow from the policies.

The *board risk management and audit committee* or separate *board risk management* and *board audit committees* oversee the organisation's risk management procedures on behalf of the board. Their role is to satisfy themselves of the adequacy and appropriateness of the organisation's entire risk management framework. At least once a year, sometimes twice a year, committee members audit the organisation's risk management plans to ensure they are up to date and meet the needs of the organisation.

They examine the risk register and the policies and programs for each risk. They may test the effectiveness of risk management arrangements by, for example, asking how a risk assessment was carried out, examining the effectiveness of controls to eliminate or reduce the risk, and identifying improvement areas. They also confirm that 'further actions' identified in the risk management plans (RMPs) by *risk event management teams* or individual managers responsible for a risk have been taken.

At a more strategic level, the board risk management and audit committee monitors the organisation's risk culture, considering the extent to which risk management is built into the organisation's normal decision-making, planning and reporting procedures and identifies areas where it is weak or unhealthy and how it could be improved. It ensures that all key strategic organisational objectives are mapped for risk and that early warning indicators are in place where appropriate.

It also examines the *business impact statements* (periodic monitoring reports) on high level and other significant risks made by risk event management teams (explained below) and examines the processes that identify new or emerging risks, ensuring that positive aspects of risk are also assessed so that the organisation can benefit from opportunities that arise.

Risk management committees (RMCs), made up of a cross-section of employees, stakeholders affected by the risk and experts in the area of the risk, assist the board in carrying out its risk management responsibilities. These committees develop and test risk management plans for individual risks, monitor and report risks, communicate and consult with employees, keep abreast of changing legislative, regulatory and other requirements and monitor project risk registers. *Risk owners*, either risk event management teams or individual managers, are tasked with monitoring individual risks.

Risk management policies

A risk management policy states:

* the organisation's goals and overall approach to identifying and managing risks
* its principles for considering the interests of and communicating with each stakeholder group when managing risk
* how and when risk management plans and programs are trialled, reviewed and updated
* the roles and accountabilities of the board, management, risk committees and any internal risk management specialists.

The international and national benchmarks for risk management
The benchmark, ISO 3100:2009, provides general guidelines on risk management. Covering the principles, framework and process for managing risks, it can be used by associations, groups and individuals, and community, private and public enterprises. The standard applies to a wide range of activities including asset management, functions, operations, processes, products, projects, services, strategies and decisions, and can be applied to any type of risk.

Risk management plans

You need to understand the risks the organisation faces and the impact of those risks on the organisation's operations. You then prioritise those risks and manage them to acceptable levels with risk management plans. As journalist Hunter S Thompson said, 'Call on God, but row away from the rocks.'[45]

A risk management plan (RMP) describes a specific risk and what the organisation is doing to enhance it, remove it or control it (risk management systems), and/or *contingency plans* to deal with it should it occur. RMPs need to reflect and support the organisation's overall strategy and business plans and meet the expectations of its stakeholders. (Section 3 of this chapter explains how to develop an RMP.)

THEORY TO PRACTICE

What if it happens here?
How would the work of your team be affected if the city in which you're located completely shut down for two days and many, if not all, of your team members returned to work traumatised and jittery? It happened in Boston, USA in April 2013 when a bomb went off amid the spectators of the Boston Marathon.

How would your team be affected if a major industrial explosion killed and maimed members of a community near your workplace and left hundreds of others homeless? It happened in Texas when a fertiliser plant exploded in April 2013, two days after the Boston bombing.

Business continuity plans and disaster recovery plans

Business continuity plans detail the steps to take to ensure the organisation's survival after a disruption to its operations. Disaster recovery plans, a subset of business continuity planning, detail the steps to take to recover the organisation's IT systems and infrastructure so that the organisation can continue operating.

These two are often merged under the acronym BC/DR. Both seek to ensure the continuity and survival of the organisation by outlining how, exactly, the organisation is to keep running or resume business after a disruptive event occurs. They state how employees are to communicate, and how and where they are to carry out their work.

The starting point is a *business impact analysis* that identifies the organisation's most essential operations, who performs them, and how losing them would affect the organisation. The more damaging those effects, the higher the priority to develop a business continuity plan.

ACTION!

One of the two measures of risk is consequence (the other is likelihood). What are the consequences of various risks to your organisation? The Business impact analysis template on **CourseMateExpress** can help you work this out.

When developing business continuity plans, it's wise to anticipate interruptions of essential government services and work out how to ensure core business activities can be sustained over months; you don't need to state why, just that this has occurred and take it from there. Factor in the psychological effect of traumatic events such as bushfires and floods on employees, clients and their families, and on the local community, and decide the action you can take to ensure adequate care for the psychological health of employees and to provide assistance to the general community.

BC/DR plans might include, for example:

* alternatives to essential supplier activities (transportation systems to provide essential materials, for example)
* arrangements for regular business continuity exercises with other key parties such as emergency services, firefighters and police
* arrangements to keep contact lists up to date
* arrangements to secure the premises during short or long periods of vacancy
* measures to ensure knowledge and skills are distributed across interstate or geographically dispersed branch offices
* measures to ensure security in the event of multiple demands on the security provider(s)
* multiskilling employees on critical activities and tasks
* nominated off-site crisis meeting points and crisis communication plans for key staff
* off-site storage of copies of all critical information
* providing police and emergency services with a contact and alternative contact in the organisation
* succession/stand-in plans for key personnel
* the procurement of a second IT system to have on stand-by to get your IT systems running immediately after a crippling disruption
* working with emergency services such as firefighters and police to develop your plans.

IN A NUTSHELL

Dealing with a disaster

The more severe the risk, the more detailed your plans need to be. For extreme and high risks, nominate understudies to the risk owner in case the risk owner is unavailable. Make arrangements such as trial runs to ensure that everyone involved in the contingency plan remains familiar with their duties.

Your plan should aim first to stabilise the situation and deal with the immediate consequences of the event, perhaps by making arrangements to work with emergency services and other specialists and nominating a trained person to work with the media. Next, determine which activities and operations are critical and plan how to resume them and in what order, establishing a series of milestones that return the organisation to normal operations. Then you can tackle the underlying cause of the event or figure out how to survive (and thrive) in the new reality.

Once your BC/DR plans are developed, it's critical to test them, perhaps twice a year, to ensure they remain current. You need to act quickly and decisively when a disruptive event or potentially disruptive event occurs. It's easier to pull back from implementing your business continuity plan should a potentially disastrous situation not eventuate than to begin implementation on the backfoot once an emergency situation or disruptive event is underway.

When the time comes, inform employees and customers that your BC/DR plan has been activated, and advise them about what you know and what you don't know about the situation and what they should and should not do. It's better to over-communicate than to under-communicate. A 1800 number, the organisation's Intranet, mobile networks, SMS and social media are all effective ways to reach stakeholders.

 FYI

What makes a good risk manager?
Good risk managers are strategic thinkers who are able to look beyond risks and appreciate broader trends. Yet they're strong on detail, too. They know how to build effective working relationships, communicate clearly and translate risk metrics so management and stakeholders can understand the organisation's risk exposure. They can think outside the box and they've mastered the technical aspects of risk management, especially the models. They're risk takers, too, because when you keep saying 'No', nothing can ever be achieved and you doom the organisation to fail in its mission.

3. Managing risks

> The ordinary rate of profit always rises more or less with risk.
>
> Adam Smith (Scottish philosopher), *The wealth of nations* (1776)[46]

Risk management isn't about avoiding risks but understanding them and dealing with them in a systematic way. Figure 23.7 summarises a continuous process that helps you identify and develop suitable risk management procedures and position your organisation to respond to risks and disruptive events.

We review the process of managing risks below: establishing your organisation's risk management context, or external and internal environments; identifying, analysing and evaluating risks; deciding how best to treat, or deal with each risk; developing and testing a risk management plan for each risk; and consulting and communicating with stakeholders and monitoring the risks and their management plans throughout the process.

Establish the context

Managing risks begins with understanding the external and internal context, or 'givens', in which your organisation operates and manages risks. Defining this context helps you decide whether a risk is acceptable or unacceptable and sets the scene for managing strategic risks.

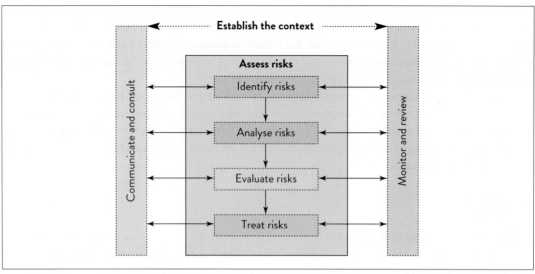

Source: Adapted from ISO 31000 AS4360[47]

FIGURE 23.7 The risk management process

⊙ IN A NUTSHELL

The external and internal contexts

The external context is the organisation's external environment. It includes the:

- cultural, economic, political and social environment
- competitive environment
- external stakeholders
- key trends affecting the organisation
- legal and regulatory environment
- supply quality and reliability
- any other factors that influence the organisation's vision, goals, strategy and operations.

The internal context is the internal factors, guidelines and limitations that influence how an organisation manages risk while working towards achieving its objectives. It includes its:

- capabilities
- contractual relationships
- culture
- decision making processes (both formal and informal)
- governance, standards, guidelines
- internal stakeholders
- organisation policies and structure
- vision, objectives and strategies.

STRATEGIC PERSPECTIVE

Begin with the strategic perspective

Many organisations establish the context at a strategic planning workshop, during which the organisation's vision is reviewed and adjusted as necessary, an environmental scan such as a SWOT analysis is undertaken, and its risk appetite reviewed and agreed. Together, these form the basis for formulating strategy. From there, priorities and targets to achieve the vision and strategy are agreed and incorporated into the strategic plan as *strategic imperatives* or *strategic goals*.

This allows the risk manager to develop a strategic risk and opportunity register to ensure that all uncertainties are addressed so that the organisation can meet its strategic imperatives. The risk management committee reviews the register which then goes to the board of directors for approval. A senior manager or risk management team – the risk owner – is then allocated responsibility for each strategic risk.

Annual reviews and interim progress reports are made against each strategic imperative, risk and opportunity.

Three common frameworks for beginning to understand the context are PEST (Political, Economic, Societal and Technological); STEEP (Social, Technological, Economic, Ecological and Political); and SWOT analyses (Strengths, Weaknesses, Opportunities and Threats). These are explained below. You can also use a cause-and-effect diagram to scan key areas (explained on page 530). This groundwork helps you identify risks and define whether a risk is acceptable, and in this way, sets the scene for managing risks.

Do a PEST analysis

Brainstorm the risks (and opportunities) in the PEST (Political, economic, societal and technological) arenas your organisation operates in. You might begin with an overview of each area and then move on to more specific risks by area. Ask these questions:

- What has happened in this area over the last two to three years?
- What will, or is likely to, happen over the next few years?
- What could happen over the next few years?

ACTION!

You can find PEST analysis and STEEP analysis templates on CourseMateExpress to help you describe your organisation's external operating context.

Do a STEEP analysis

A STEEP analysis considers five perspectives: Social, Technological, Economic, Ecological, Political. Conduct a STEEP analysis as you would a PEST analysis.

● THE STRATEGIC PERSPECTIVE

Climate adaptation

Even if major reductions in fossil fuel emissions occur now, we need to learn to adapt to unavoidable climate change caused by past emissions. The longer the world delays reducing emissions, the greater our adaptation needs to be. Depending on where your organisation is located and the industry you're in, you may need to deal with the economic and human effects of acidifying oceans and rising sea levels, ill health, reduced food and water supplies, water supplies affected by salinity and soil erosion, undermined plant and animal biodiversity, increased frequency and intensity of extreme weather events such as droughts, floods and storms and resulting damage to infrastructure, and even increased conflict and population displacement.

We can expect warmer and drier conditions with more droughts, particularly in southern areas, and wetter conditions in northern Australia, with longer and hotter heat waves striking more often; superimposed on natural variability, wet years are likely to become less frequent and dry years more frequent.[48]

IPCC Chair Rajendra Pachauri said, 'Climate change: It's here. If we don't react, war, pestilence and famine will follow close behind.'[49] Pachauri advised organisations to build climate change into their risk management framework and plans.[50] At the very least, organisations must establish, review and continually improve their risk management plans for various climate change scenarios in their region, marketplaces and through their supply chain, looking at a 10 to 15 year horizon. You might want to check out the Business Adaptation Network established by Green Cross.[51]

● ACTION!

Do you need help in identifying the risks to your organisation arising from climate change? If so, the Risks from Climate Change checklist on ⚡**CourseMate**Express can help you.

Do a SWOT analysis

While PEST and STEEP help you find risks and opportunities in the external environment, SWOT looks both externally and internally for risks and opportunities. It examines the organisation's internal (Strengths and weaknesses, and the opportunities and threats) in its external environment. A SWOT analysis can also be used to develop strategic and business plans.

Internally, and in the context of your organisation's strategies and objectives, key drivers of success, significant organisational issues and the basic parameters in which risks must be managed (e.g. the financial resources available, legislative requirements and the organisation's risk appetite), consider a variety of factors, such as:

* culture (including risk culture) and values
* customer loyalty and unfolding needs
* employee profiles in terms of engagement and flexibility, their ability to meet the organisation's current and future needs in terms of their current skills and potential, and their understanding of risk management principles and their role in risk management
* financial security and stability, security of cash flow, effectiveness of asset distribution, relationships with key creditors, debtors and trading partners

* the growth potential, profitability, range, sustainability and quality of the organisation's products, packaging and services
* the organisation's reputation for quality and reliability
* the quality and reliability of work processes and systems (e.g. administration and information systems, customer service and delivery systems, health, safety and welfare systems, productivity management systems and training systems)
* the quality, soundness and environmental friendliness of buildings, plant, equipment and operating systems, particularly regarding their age and suitability for the future and how they compare with the competition's.

Any of these can be strengths or weaknesses. Also consider the organisation's ability to:

* adapt and respond flexibly to changes in the marketplace and to competitor activity
* build effective working relationships with stakeholders
* empower and develop individuals and teams to meet its goals
* innovate and make continuous improvements
* make sound and timely decisions
* manage costs and information
* nurture a learning environment
* recruit and develop the employees it needs
* think and manage strategically
* reward performance.

In the external environment, ask:

* What do trends in regard to climate, the economy, and politics, society, technology and other key areas, hold in store for the organisation?
* What is likely to happen in the organisation's industry and marketplace, particularly changes and trends in consumer patterns and government regulation, opportunities for expansion, technology and threats from new or existing competitors?
* Is the cost, supply and quality of our raw materials reliable?

Think more broadly, too:

* What is likely to happen in the national economies you operate in and in the global economy?
* What is happening in the world political arena?
* What technological threats and opportunities might develop?

ACTION!

You can find a SWOT analysis template to help you work through your organisation's external opportunities and threats and internal strengths and weaknesses on CourseMateExpress.

FYI

Risk management software

When it comes to risk management software, you're spoiled for choice. Here are three popular types of software packages:

* bespoke, generic or industry specific risk management software with dashboards, remediation strategies, reporting templates, risk registers (with links to incident logs that send out automated emails alerting the appropriate person or committee members of

>>

> a reported incident according to the level of risk), step-by-step planning for a range of risk management plans (e.g. plans targeting business continuity and disaster recovery, operational risks, reputational risks and strategic risks)
> - graphics showing how various risks link to each other
> - tools that can establish whether or not an event reflects an organisation's risk appetite and needs treating.
>
> Automated tools like these are readily available, making your job as a risk manager so much easier.

Identify risks

Based on the context you have established, identify the key risks and opportunities facing the organisation. Begin by preparing a comprehensive list of possible external and internal risk events that could affect the organisation's normal operations. Consider the various types of risk (discussed on page 724) and think widely so that you include even those with a remote likelihood of occurring.

Rather than deal with the organisation as a whole, it's often easier to consider the organisation's strategic goals and functions, operational areas, or, for capabilities-based organisations, its capability streams, and identify risks for each in separate brainstorming workshops. You can also interview key people and use questionnaires and written surveys to replace or supplement the brainstorming workshops. Other ways to identify risks include inspecting accident statistics, safety audits, organisational performance reports (e.g. customer feedback, income and cash flow records), contracts with external organisations and individuals, and other factual documents.

Also consider *risk sources* and *events*, tangible or intangible elements which alone or in combination have inherent potential to give rise to a risk. Risk sources include competitor activity, man-made and natural events (terrorism, floods, etc.), the marketplace, political and legislative changes, the regional, national and international economy and supply lines. In the case of events, remember these can include something not happening as well as happening.

Four other methods for identifying risks are:
- analysing near misses
- identifying risks for critical activities
- scenario planning
- working through your critical resources and supply chain.

Each of these methods can be used alone or in combination.

Verify *every* significant assumption when listing (and later, analysing) a risk. Obtain relevant data whenever possible to analyse and help you spot peaks and troughs, recurring problems and incidents, and trends that could provide valuable insights. (Page 585 explains how to plot and gain useful information from data.)

THE STRATEGIC PERSPECTIVE

Intellectual property – a risky area

Did you know that companies can borrow money against their intellectual property (IP) and license and assign it to others? Knowledge isn't just power – it's also value. Over the last 10 years, intangible assets have contributed more than half of Australia's corporate value and – wait for it – the Apple brand is worth 1.4 times the value of our top 30 brands put together.[52]

>>

IP includes brand names, confidential information (e.g. customer and supplier lists, formulas and tender documents), copyright, designs, images, insider knowledge, know-how (a body of knowledge built up over time), names, patents, symbols and trademarks. How does your organisation protect its IP?

Analyse near misses

Many adverse events are preceded by recurring problems and near misses – close calls that would have been worse if not for chance. As explained on page 522, it's easy to come to see these as 'normal' and brush them aside. But in a healthy risk culture, people are alert to near misses and deviations from the norm. NASA's Edward Rogers said, 'Almost every mishap at NASA can be traced to some series of small signals that went unnoticed at the critical moment.'[53]

A series of small, often seemingly minor mishaps, human errors, technical failures and poor decisions can eventually combine to produce a significant failure. So rather than seeing a near miss as evidence that the system is working well and breathing a sigh of relief, see these incidents as warning signs. Look for the cause and fix it, and review your risk controls (page 523 explains how to spot and analyse deviations, problems and near misses).

● THEORY TO PRACTICE

One 'issue' too many

On 1 February 2003, having completed 27 successful missions, Space Shuttle *Colombia* disintegrated as it returned home, killing all seven crew members. During take off, a piece of foam fell from the external fuel tank and punctured one of Colombia's wings and the intense heat generated when re-entering the earth's atmosphere entered the inside of the shuttle which destroyed its support structure and caused the shuttle to break apart.

'Foam events' had been a problem since the first *Columbia* mission in 1981, but had yet to cause an accident and came to be classified as 'issues' rather than 'near misses'.

Normalisation of deviance (see page 524) is tempting, especially when you're under pressure to complete a mission, a project, or any type of work, and taking time to rectify a known 'issue' would put you behind. So, rather than put the space program behind, *Columbia* was allowed to take off – despite a recent dramatic foam incident and an investigation underway on foam strikes.

It took months to collect the bits of *Columbia* and human remains spread over five states. Where was the risk manager?[54]

Identify risks for critical activities

List the activities, capabilities, operational areas, outcomes, processes, projects and roles critical to the organisation's performance and achieving its strategic imperatives, or main goals. Then work through them one by one, listing the risks, risk sources and events that could affect them, for example through brainstorming or undertaking a SWOT analysis.

● THEORY TO PRACTICE

Conduct a key positions audit

Identify the organisation's most critical job roles and how they may be at risk. For example, if the role-holder left the organisation, how easy or difficult would it be to attract, recruit and train a replacement? What knowledge and information might the role-holder take with him or her and is this information and knowledge captured elsewhere in the organisation? Are internal successors available for key roles? Are role-holders and potential successors kept up to date with technical and other advances in their area?

Use scenario planning to predict the future

Steve Jobs, founder of Apple Inc, said of the future, 'The web will be one more area of significant change and those who don't pay attention will get hurt, while those who see it early enough will get rewarded.'[55] Implausible as this statement sounded at the time, in hindsight it sounds like a case of stating the bleeding obvious.

But imagining a future that isn't an extension of today isn't easy and it's made harder by groupthink and *heuristics*, the brain's unconscious thought processes. (Groupthink and heuristics are explained on pages 523 and 539.) In fact, there are lots of possible futures, some more plausible than others, but each possible. This is where scenario planning can be useful. (Scenario planning was traditionally used to help identify threats, but it's now increasingly used to generate ideas for innovation.)

Scenario planning taps into people's imaginations, intuition and knowledge bases to describe plausible futures and develop 'stories', or scenarios, about how they might unfold three, 10 or even 20 years from now; appropriate responses to each can then be developed. These imagined futures aren't meant to be definitive, but they help organisations anticipate and plan for future risks and opportunities, including the black swan events, that are otherwise difficult to imagine.

To develop possible scenarios, follow these six steps:

1. Work with your organisation's top decision-makers, key stakeholders and thinkers, and gather their views about future developments with questions like: Which decisions are likely to make or break the organisation over the next few years? What trends are most important to our operations and customers now and in the future? Which potential developments in the industry and marketplace excite you the most?
2. Gather and analyse relevant developments and trends and compile a list of external forces that seem most likely to affect your organisation.
3. Weave together the information from Steps 1 and 2 to sketch out plausible future scenarios. Some authorities recommend aiming for three scenarios: your worst nightmare, a different but better world, and a world that is basically an extension of the current world. Give each scenario a name that makes it vivid and memorable.
4. Assess the implications of each scenario for your organisation.
5. Identify the real-life developments and signs that could indicate each scenario is unfolding. These might include competitor activity, demographic changes, environmental trends, regulatory trends and technological trends.
6. Develop appropriate risk management plans and put a risk event management team in place for each scenario.

Work through your critical resources and value chains

Brainstorm risks by key drivers of success and the resources the organisation needs to have working optimally in order to achieve its goals. Think about, for instance:

- *Capabilities:* How the organisation creates value, for example, through design and marketing, delivery and invoicing, the ability to bring new products or services to market quickly, information systems and work flows
- *Cost:* Direct, indirect, economies of scale and scope
- *Culture and values:* For example, customer focus, learning and improvement orientation, problem-solving and communication methods, responsibility and accountability, risk culture, trust, and the way people work together
- *Resource velocity:* The rate at which value is created from applied resources (e.g. asset use, inventory turns, lead times, throughput)
- *Revenue:* Sales, market size, price structure
- *Staff:* For example, the organisation's employer value proposition, the way it attracts and retains staff, employee engagement, motivation and competencies, succession and quality of leadership
- *Structures:* For example, the buildings, finance and budgeting, organisation structure and physical layout
- *Systems:* For example, administration and information systems, customer service and delivery systems, financial and budgetary control systems (e.g. cost and debt control), health, safety and welfare systems, marketing and corporate relations, performance management and productivity systems, training systems, waste and energy management systems.

Work through your organisation's supply chain from beginning to end to identify risks in terms of, for example, reliability, sustainability and flexibility. Risk events may be outside your organisation's control, so you may need to work out how to become aware of and respond to them. Remember that supply chains that are lean and low cost may look good on paper but can be extremely expensive should the unexpected occur.

THEORY TO PRACTICE

Supply chain havoc

Plan for bad things happening even when you don't know the cause. For example, the affected companies probably didn't identify the cause of their supply chain disruption as an earthquake and tsunami that would trigger the Fukushima nuclear disaster in March 2011, but they should have planned for supply chain disruptions and quantified the financial, operational and opportunities-lost impacts of a supply chain disruption for varying lengths of time and developed plans to manage those disruptions.

The combined natural and man-made disaster affected the production and distribution of many of the world's products. It closed Japanese airports, damaged its transport and manufacturing infrastructure and had significant effects on companies such as Fuji, Honda and Toyota. Electronic goods and motor vehicle production fell by up to 60% and distributors around the world experienced major shortages of supplies and products as a result, with flow-on effects including loss of customers and market share, and significant financial and reputational challenges.

Here are some questions to help you think through how at risk your supply chains are:

- How financially stable are companies in your supply chain?
- How prone are they to extreme climatic events because of their location?
- How adversarial/cordial are their industrial relations?
- Are they located in a politically stable area?
- Who do they source their raw materials from? How secure are those sources? What risks might they pose for example, in terms of corporate social responsibility?
- How easily and quickly could your organisation source those supplies elsewhere?
- How dependable is the quality of what they supply?
- Are companies in your supply chain located in the same geographic area, meaning that one event, such as a flood, tsunami or epidemic, would affect the entire chain?
- What would be the cost to your organisation if their operations were disrupted?[57]

Analyse risks

Record the risks and opportunities your organisation faces once you've identified them. You could begin with a simple matrix, adapting the one shown in Figure 23.8 to risk events and risk areas that suit your organisation, grouping risks into categories, or types, and locations. You can also group risks into areas such as brand risk, financial risk, HR risk, IT risk, reputation risk, supply chain risk.

Notice that in Figure 23.8 some risk events are both threats and opportunities. A matrix like this, however, doesn't indicate how various risks interact, which is where good risk management software comes in.

ACTION!

Use the Risk opportunity matrix template on  **CourseMateExpress** to categorise risks and opportunities.

Risk areas	Internal risks				External risks				
INTERNAL AND EXTERNAL RISKS	Accidents and hazards	Information security	Product or service quality	Staff	Competitor activity	Natural disasters	Supply lines	Pandemics	Political and legislative
Buildings	✓		✓	✓O		✓			
Extended supply chain		✓O	✓O	✓O	✓	✓	✓	✓	✓
Financial stability	✓	✓O	✓O	✓O	✓	✓	✓	✓	✓
Image and reputation	✓O	✓	✓O	✓O	✓O	✓O	✓	✓O	
Plant and equipment	✓		✓	✓O		✓			✓
Proprietary information systems, data		✓		✓			✓		
Staff	✓O		✓O		✓	✓O		✓O	

Prepard by: Risk management committee, 26 November 2016; Reviewed by: GHJ, 6 May 2017

✓ = threat

O = opportunity

FIGURE 23.8 Risk/opportunity matrix

Another way to group risks is shown in Table 23.1 (the categories in this table are also useful in reporting and tracking incidents).

TABLE 23.1 Categories of risk

Risks	Risk name/number
Current	'Business as usual' risks such as health and safety of staff and customers
Operational risks	Financial processes, project risk, 'business as usual' risks, unethical conduct
Looming risks	Risks you can see coming in, say, two to three years but are not sure of the precise nature of the risk, for example potential regulatory changes, changing customer patterns
Strategic risks	Fundamental shifts in customer preferences, technology change that affect the organisation's viability, and so on

Define the risk

To analyse each risk, begin by defining it in three parts. The first part defines, or names, the risk event and the second indicates its cause, or source (e.g. 'supply chain breaks due to storm activity', 'IT system crashes due to worm infection'). These are columns 2 and 3 in the Risk Register shown in Table 23.3 on page 751.)

This allows you to determine the initial result of the risk, which is the third part of the risk definition. The result of the risk indicates who and/or what is at risk, for example, life, ongoing operations, people, property, reputation, and why, for example, 'work cannot continue', 'work cannot continue efficiently and some records and data are irretrievable' (see column 4 in the Risk Register shown in Table 23.3).

You then have a risk definition in this format: 'This event could happen due to … and this is what it would mean and why'. For example, 'The supply chain breaks due to violent storm activity, which interrupts our operations and means work cannot continue'. Or another example, 'The IT system crashes due to worm infection, so work cannot continue efficiently and some records and data are irretrievable'.

Determine the risk's consequences

Next, think about the risk's duration and severity of the initial consequences of the risk to the organisation. This is the inherent level of risk. Then think about the longer-term effect and knock-on effects of the risk to the organisation. This is known as its *consequences* or *impact*. Think through possible worst case scenarios. Be thorough in this, as this information allows you to aim *preventive* risk treatments at the sources of risks and reactive or *contingency* treatments at the results of the risks.

Here are two scales for assessing consequences:

Catastrophic – Major – Moderate – Minor – Insignificant
Disastrous – Severe – Moderate – Minimal

You can develop a matrix like the one shown in Table 23.2: Risk consequence table, to assess a risk event's consequence level. Transfer this inherent level of risk to your risk register when you add this risk to it.

● ACTION!

You can find a Risk consequence template on **CourseMateExpress** to help you determine how best to treat each risk.

● IN A NUTSHELL

Which consequences matter most?

Here are some factors to consider when thinking about consequences:
- degree of damage or injury to critical activities, equipment, key capabilities, operations, people, property, stakeholders or systems
- degree of reversibility of harm to the organisation or its stakeholders
- effect on financial stability and systems
- effect on goodwill, image, reputation
- effect on integrated value chain
- financial costs
- legal repercussions (e.g. civil, criminal or industrial lawsuits, legal costs)
- opportunities from, for example, investments, commercial relationships and technology to mitigate (reduce), reverse or even benefit from the consequences
- opportunity-lost costs
- technological consequences (e.g. breakdown, damage to information and communication systems, or theft).

TABLE 23.2 Risk consequence table

Impact area	Catastrophic	Major	Moderate	Minor	Insignificant
Environment	Serious effect. Recovery >10 years	Serious effect. Recovery <10 years	Moderate effect. Recovery in 6–12 months	Minor effect. Recovery in 1–6 months	No damage or residual impact but some clean-up required
Legal	Significant prosecution and fines	Major breach of regulation, major litigation	Serious breach of regulation with investigation or report to authorities and prosecution	Minor legal issues, non-compliances and breaches of regulation	Minor legal issues, non compliance and breaches of regulation
Reputation	Government inquiry	Heavy negative national media coverage	State media coverage	Local press coverage	Incident form filed
Service	1–4 weeks or revenue loss $2 000 000.01	1–7 days or revenue loss $0.5–$2 million	2 hours–1 day or revenue loss $50 000.01 –$0.5m	30–120 minutes or revenue loss $5000–$50 000.01	<30 minutes or revenue loss of <$50 000

Determine your exposure to the risk

You also need to estimate the risk's *probability of occurrence*; this is also known as *exposure* – you have a high exposure to risks with a high probability of occurrence and a low exposure to risks with a low probability of occurrence. Depending on the nature of the risk, this may be in terms of:

- The *frequency of exposure:* Frequently, often, occasionally or seldom.
- The *likelihood of occurrence:* Highly likely, probable, possible or unlikely.

You can assess frequency by how often an event occurs over a particular time period and likelihood by deciding how certain or unlikely it is the event will occur. Figure 23.9 summarises the two dimensions of probability and consequences.

IN A NUTSHELL

How likely?

Here is another scale of likelihood. (This chapter shows several scales for likelihood and consequences. Choose the scale that best suits the risks in your organisation.)

- *Almost certain*: Expected to occur once a year or more frequently in most circumstances.
- *Likely*: Expected to occur in one to three years in most circumstances.
- *Possible*: Expected to occur in one to 10 years.
- *Unlikely*: Expected to occur in one to 30 years.
- *Rare*: Expected to occur in 1 to 100 years in exceptional circumstances.

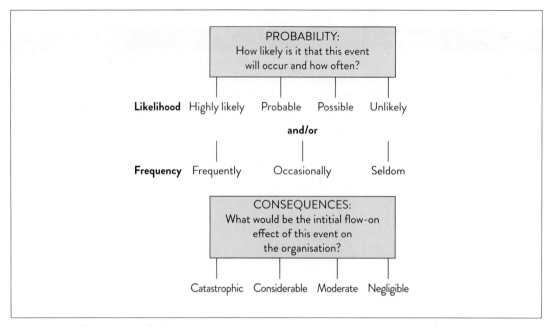

FIGURE 23.9 Dimensions of risk

Evaluate risks

Guided by your organisation's goals, risk appetite and risk management context, weigh up each risk against your *risk criteria* (see 'In a Nutshell: Risk criteria') and decide which risks are acceptable and which are unacceptable and need treatment. When it helps, you can combine a number of risks into one risk to develop a more complete understanding of the overall risk. This is called *risk aggregation*.

 **IN A NUTSHELL**

Risk criteria

Here are some criteria to evaluate risks against. Think about how each risk event would affect your organisation's:

- environmental and social responsibility goals
- financial goals and constraints
- legal and regulatory considerations
- operational goals and constraints
- safety goals and constraints
- staffing goals and constraints
- technical goals and constraints
- timeline goals and constraints
- quality and other outcomes you are aiming for internally.

Also consider whether there are already some controls in place and their effectiveness. Keep your criteria flexible enough to accommodate changing circumstances.

Prioritise the risks

Prioritise the risks by considering their *significance* (also called *level* and *magnitude*). Significance is a function of your *exposure* to each risk (its frequency or likelihood of occurring) and its *consequences* (impact).

When probability is high and consequences low, you might evaluate the risk's significance as moderate. But when consequences are high and probability low, the risk is significant because even a remote chance of a catastrophe warrants more attention than a high chance of a hiccup, so give it a high priority. After all, Qantas has never had a fatal air crash (low probability) but the company still has a major risk to manage due to the enormous consequences of a fatal crash.

To help rank risks according to their significance, you can visually summarise the risks under consideration with a matrix like the one shown in Figure 23.10, writing the risk description, name or number in the appropriate area.

EXPOSURE

CONSEQUENCES

	Frequently	**Occasionally**	**Seldom**
Catastrophic			
Critical			
Moderate			
Negligible			

FIGURE 23.10 Risk significance

A 'heat map', shown in Figure 23.11, is another way to illustrate how risks are prioritised. Risks falling into the hot pink and red zones are the extreme- and high-level risks; give them the highest priority for treatment because their likelihood is high and/or consequences significant. Closely monitor those falling into the yellow zone because either their outcomes are serious or their likelihood

Likelihood	Insignificant 1	Minor 2	Moderate 3	Major 4	Severe 5
A (Almost certain)	M	M	H	VH	VH
B (Likely)	M	M	H	H	VH
C (Possible)	M	M	M	H	VH
D (Unlikely)	L	M	M	H	H
E (Rare)	L	L	M	M	H

FIGURE 23.11 Heat map

is high; treatment is recommended and if you choose not to treat a medium, or yellow-zone risk, you must be able to state your reasons. You probably don't need to treat low, or green-level risks but keep a watchful eye on them, looking particularly for adverse trends.

⦿ THEORY TO PRACTICE

Prioritising IT and IP risk

To manage information and intellectual property risks, identify important information and intellectual property and categorise it according to its value and sensitivity. There are four key questions in this exercise:

1. What 10 pieces of data/information/intellectual property do we rely on most?

For each of the 10 pieces, ask these three questions:

2. What would happen if we lost it entirely?
3. What would happen if we lost it but could only recover it with difficulty?
4. What would happen if the competition acquired it?

The answers indicate priority areas.

Document and file your risk assessment for each risk and the reasons for your evaluation to provide a record of how the decisions were reached. You might want to summarise your evaluation as a heat map as shown in the example in Figure 23.12. Always show when risks were identified, analysed and evaluated and by whom, and when risk analyses and evaluations were reviewed and by whom.

Risk	Probability	Frequency	Consequences	Current risk level
A	Highly likely	Frequently	Catastrophic	Extreme
B	Probable	Often	Critical	High
C	Possible	Occasionally	Moderate	Moderate
D	Unlikely	Seldom	Negligible	Low

Prepared by: Risk Management Committee, 21 December 2017;
Reviewed by: CLM, 6 January 2018

FIGURE 23.12 Summarising risk levels

Build a risk register

Once you've analysed and evaluated the risks you've identified, list them in a risk register and use it to monitor risks. Risk registers take many forms. One form is shown in Table 23.3. Notice that this part of the register has a built in 'heat map' showing each risk's inherent and residual risk level and that it summarises the risk management plan for each risk.

TABLE 23.3 Part of a risk register

Reference No.	Risk	Result	Cause	Risk Owner	Inherent Level*	Residual Level*	Action required
RO-MGTG 00 1317	Loss of market share	Gradual loss of revenue threatens business viability	Outdated products, services and strategies, impacting our ability to archive our financial targets	CEO, marketing diretor	D	S	Invest in R&D; institute service enhancement project; research market trends and drive offerings accordingly; develop more robust measures of customer satisfaction
RO-HR 00 117	Incorrect staffing levels	Loss of productivity (quantity and quality) leading to erosion of customer base	Skill shortage and inability to attract and retain the people we need; inadequate training and succession planning	HR director, general manager	S	Mod	Recruit training manager; undertake gap analysis of skills required versus current skills levels; update recruitment framework, including policies and procedures
RO-OP 00 2217	Critical activities interrupted	Operations interrupted, disrupting supplies to the customers	Extreme weather, terrorism or similar incident	Operations manager	S	Min	RMP to be developed and to include discussions with emergency services and utilities providers. Investigate use of scenario planning.

* Disastrous (D), Severe (S), Moderate (Mod), Minimal (Min)

Risk register prepared by George Hinos, 4 May 2016. Location: Head office.

IN A NUTSHELL

Risk registers

A risk register is a record of information about active risks in the organisation. It may include:

- *risk name, identification number* and *description*
- *risk impact* (consequences)
- *date identified, date reviewed, date updated* and *by whom*
- *cause of risk*
- *risk controls pre-event*: Measures to prevent or mitigate (i.e. lessen by reducing or transferring) the risk, showing where the paperwork is located (e.g. a document file name or number)
- *risk controls post-event*: Contingency plans and business continuity/disaster recovery plans, showing where they are located (e.g. a document file name or number)
- *risk evaluation*, or likelihood of occurrence and the consequences or severity of its effects
- *risk owner*, or the person or team with accountability and authority for managing and monitoring the risk

>>

- *risk score*, or current risk level
- *risk trends*, or performance measures for risk.

Date risk registers and show the name of the person or committee who prepared or updated each one. Also note the date it was examined and by whom, along with any recommendations.

A risk register often takes the form of a matrix summarising identified risks. Risks are listed vertically and identified by name or a phrase describing the risk; sometimes an identifying number is used. The matrix lists information about each risk horizontally.

◉ ACTION!

You can find a Risk register template on ⚡**CourseMateExpress** to use or adapt to summarise your risks.

Treat risks

In large organisations dealing with many risks or when dealing with extreme- and high-level risk events that are costly to remove or mitigate (reduce), it can be very complex to treat, or modify, them. A risk management specialist is often employed to supervise this function.

Risks are normally assigned to an individual or a risk event management team (assisted by a risk management specialist as necessary) to develop (and test, when appropriate) a risk treatment. These individuals and teams are the risk owners who then monitor their risk and respond as necessary. (See 'Theory to practice: A typical communication and consultation process' on page 758.)

In deciding the best way to deal with each risk, follow the problem-solving and decision-making steps outlined on page 526. When the risk is complex, break it down into its component parts, or sub-risks, and deal with each individually.

◉ IN A NUTSHELL

Risk treatments

You can consider a range of responses to various events:

- *Avoid* the risk by removing its source.
- *Reject* unacceptable risks by not starting or continuing with the activity that gives rise to the risk and finding another way to achieve the particular objective.
- *Transfer* the risk to or *share* it with a third party such as an insurance company or contractor (remembering to take into account the consequences of a subcontractor going out of business or performing the work poorly).
- *Reduce* the risk to an acceptable level through controls, or preventive measures to lessen its likelihood or its consequences; these might be devices, policies, practices or other actions to modify the risk; but remember: they don't always succeed.
- *Accept* the risk by informed decision and devise contingency and business continuity/disaster recovery plans to deal with it should it arise. This might be for example, when the effort and expense to mitigate it is not worthwhile or when the risk level is low. Accepting the risk can also include risk financing – setting aside funds to meet or modify the financial consequences should the risk occur.

Operational risks

Some risks are *operational* and arise through the organisation's day-to-day work. These risks can generally be managed by active prevention (e.g. internal control systems such as standard operating procedures), diligent monitoring, establishing clear values and codes of conduct to guide employee behaviour, building strong risk and safety cultures, and effective leadership.[58]

Strategic risks

Strategic risks affect the entire organisation and its ability to meet its vision and overall goals; these are very 'high stake', risks and are managed at board level. Some arise internally and others externally.

Banks take a risk when they loan money; oil companies take a risk when they drill for oil. These are *internal strategic risks* that result as the organisation executes its strategy. Organisations accept these risks because the potential gains outweigh the potential losses from the risk, but they need to manage them well to reduce the likelihood they materialise and to reduce their effects should they occur.

Strategic risks can also arise *externally*. Events such as natural disasters, pandemics and global financial crises are beyond an organisation's control. Organisations can only have contingency plans to mitigate, or lessen, their impact.

Strategic risks need different treatments than operational risks. Think about the worst-case scenario and how your organisation could survive it. Use this information to guide your decisions regarding the extent to which, and how, to manage the risk, aiming to remove it when possible and when that's not possible, to reduce the likelihood it occurs and its consequences if it does.[59]

Follow the risk management hierarchy

The *hierarchy of risk management* is shown as a flow chart in Figure 23.13. (Note that there is a different hierarchy of risk prevention in Chapter 29, which is designed specifically for health, safety and welfare matters.)

First, direct your attention to the source of risks and search for solutions to *prevent* them from occurring. Can you *eliminate* the risk by, for example, altering your extended supply chain, changing suppliers or redesigning a job or process? Or is it better to *avoid* the risk entirely by transferring it to another party through insurance or contracting the job out?

Organisations generally retain low and moderate risks, especially when their risk culture supports ongoing risk management and risk identification, assessment and monitoring as part of its normal reporting procedures. When robust risk management plans are in place, organisations can retain even higher levels of risk. Organisations must retain some risks because insurers do not cover them or make covering them an expensive option; for example, insurance cover for natural disasters like earthquakes, fire and flood, and non-natural disasters such as nuclear accidents, terrorism and war may be available, but it is expensive.

When you can't avoid or prevent a risk from occurring, try to *reduce the likelihood of it occurring*; for example, you might increase the use of virtual meetings, institute working from home or limit business travel to reduce the likelihood of employees contracting a severe virus, or redesign a procedure to reduce the possibility of an accident.

When it is not possible to reduce your exposure to a risk, or when the residual risk (the exposure that remains after treatment) is unacceptable, move on to your third and least preferred option – reducing the consequences of the risk should it occur. Your goal is to *reduce the risk level* from unacceptable to acceptable; this is known as the *target risk level*. An example is shown in Figure 23.14, although target risk levels vary depending on the risk and how much, if any, control over the risk the organisation can take.

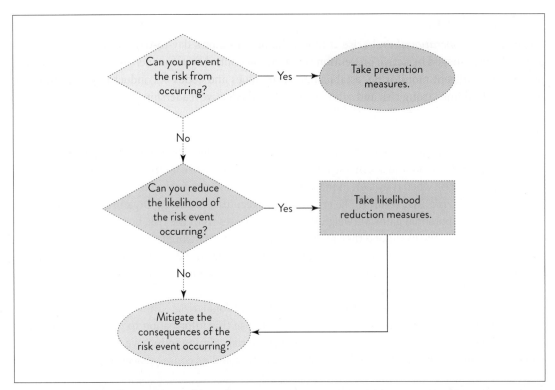

FIGURE 23.13 The risk management hierarchy

Risk	Probability	Frequency	Consequences	Current risk level	Target risk level
A	Possible	n/a	Catastrophic	Extreme	Moderate
B	n/a	Often	Critical	High	Low
C	n/a	Occasionally	Moderate	Moderate	Low
D	Unlikely	Seldom	High	Moderate	Low

Prepared by: Ngaire Ho, 6 September 2016. Location: Main factory.

FIGURE 23.14 Target risk levels

To reach a target risk level, you might accept the risk and develop a contingency plan to *mitigate* its consequences should it occur; for example, you might develop and test a pandemic management program or guard against a loss of power by installing a generator. Or you might *transfer* residual risk (by contracting out that aspect of your operations), *share* the risk (for example through a joint venture) or *spread* the risk across multiple locations. Remember, though, that when you transfer, share or spread a risk, you may still need to develop contingency plans for any remaining risk. Develop several options from which to select based on your goals.

A series of measures is often effective in minimising and managing a risk. For instance, to protect your premises from fire, you might enforce strict housekeeping throughout the premises to reduce the amount of combustible material and install sprinklers that engage automatically in case of fire to make it practically impossible for a fire to cause damage. You would then need to manage the risk of the sprinklers going off unnecessarily and dealing with any water damage; to minimise those risks, you might institute a program of regular testing and maintenance of the sprinklers.

After taking these measures to minimise the risk of fire, you may then decide to transfer the remaining risk to an insurance company, or you may decide you have minimised the risk of fire so effectively that it makes financial sense to retain the risk yourself, saving the expense of fire insurance premiums over a period of years.

Work through your goals, timelines, and so on when selecting risk treatment measures. Consider the cost of their development and implementation (and possibly maintenance) and their ease of execution against their effectiveness. A SWOT analysis or a force field analysis (explained on page 504) can help you choose the most effective treatment plan.

⦿ ACTION!

You can find a template for Target risk levels on **⁂CourseMateExpress**.

⦿ THEORY TO PRACTICE

Planning for and communicating during a pandemic

Risk management plans (RMPs) for pandemics might include instituting mechanisms for communicating with employees; nominating someone to stay abreast of risk levels in locations the organisation operates in and to check the World Health Organization and government websites; and updating absenteeism and travel policies and healthcare support.

Your pandemic RMP should also address operational issues, for example: cross-skilling and multiskilling staff to ensure key work can be carried out in an absentee rate of at least 25–30%; leasing and moving key personnel and their families to remote facilities in safe areas; maintaining a healthy work environment by ensuring adequate air circulation; taking measures to prevent the spread of infection such as providing disinfectant soap, increased disinfectant cleaning of danger spots such as door knobs, lift buttons and light switches, and establishing guidelines for stocking up on disinfectant wipes and disposable gloves and masks (which could become difficult to obtain); minimising the repercussions from interruptions to essential services such as electricity, telecommunications and water; and ensuring the security of premises.

You may also need to develop policies that specifically relate to infectious diseases, for example, to actively prevent infected employees from attending work or not allowing employees who have been exposed to the disease to attend work.

People want and need facts and guidelines that help them behave appropriately and make sensible decisions in such difficult conditions, and the better the information you provide, the more effectively they can act. Collect the resources you need to communicate and provide information on the following:

- *To employees*: The adjusted personal leave policy covering employees who take more than the allowed leave due to illness to discourage employees who have been exposed to risk from coming into work and infecting others (concern about lost wages is the biggest

»

deterrent to self-quarantine); the importance of staying away from the workplace should employees become ill and what to do should they become ill; flexible work practices such as telecommuting to minimise exposure; education regarding the difference between a common cold and influenza; hygiene practices to prevent the spread of infection (e.g. the importance of basic hand and respiratory hygiene and tips on how to stop the spread of germs); mechanisms for employees to raise concerns about exposure; staff movements and evacuation; succession and lines of authority.

- Find out what employees currently believe so that you can best present information. For instance, they may know the importance of hand-washing but not know how or why to correctly wash their hands to kill germs, or they may know the risk of shaking hands but not that the risk multiplies the more hands you shake.
- *To customers and suppliers*: Whether and how you plan to stay open for business; chain and distribution network management.
- *To other stakeholders*: Don't assume you know what they want – consult them using electronic or social media and respond to their concerns and questions.

Document your risk management plan for approval

Document the RMP following your organisation's usual protocol. Begin with the risk definition and its inherent, residual and target risk level that the plan addresses. Outline the treatment(s) selected and explain the rationale behind it. Identify the management and control structures needed to execute the RMP and any other resources the program needs, for example funding to consult with experts, to develop and roll out a communication program to the workforce, to purchase equipment, to train employees or to trial treatment options.

List the action items needed to implement the plan and assign responsibilities for executing each step and overall responsibility for the plan's operation to a risk owner; nominate deputies for each role in case the primary role-holder is not available. Your goal is to practically be able to go on automatic pilot so as not to think your way through each step under extreme pressure and have people running off in different directions.

Finally, establish a review process that involves stakeholders and encourages continuous improvement, innovation and learning.

When the plan is approved, the risk owner takes ongoing responsibility for monitoring, reviewing and improving the RMP. Depending on the risk event, you may need to develop a communication network and a network of cross-functional employees who can coordinate responses, monitor unfolding events and adapt the organisation's responses as the risk unfolds.

◉ ACTION!

Use the Risk management plan template on **CourseMateExpress** to begin developing risk management plans for your high priority risks.

Test your plan

Until you've tested your plan, you have no idea whether it works or will worsen the situation. When your plan is long and complex, test each part separately. (Depending on the risk and your organisation's protocol, testing may be before or after the plan is approved.)

The more serious the risk event, the more important rigorous testing is, so plan the test properly. With large plans or major risk events such as the need to evacuate a building or to have a substantial portion of the workforce work from home, hold a trial run. (Regular trial runs also develop a risk culture and skill level of the participants, which is essential should the plan be needed.)

When an actual trial run is not possible, arrange to test the plan in an environment that reproduces authentic conditions as much as possible. When you can't do that, conduct a round-table theoretical run, or a table-top scenario. Involve a cross-section of the people who would be involved in the actual event, including some devil's advocates. Look for areas in the plan that may fail and for ways to improve the plan. Document and store the test procedures and the results with the RMP.

When you are confident the RMP works, draw up a procedures manual, a checklist of steps to follow or a diagram such as a flow chart or a PERT diagram and incorporate the plan into your organisation's standard operating procedures.

THEORY TO PRACTICE

Honing flexible response skills

Large global firms often find it worthwhile to establish a virtual team with shifting membership that meets virtually for half a day every second month to simulate various crises (e.g. 30% of the workforce is absent for a lengthy period due to a pandemic or the US closes its borders). The goal isn't to create specific contingency plans for these events but to practise problem-solving disastrous scenarios in unpredictable and fast-changing environments.[60]

Consult and communicate with stakeholders

As shown in Figure 23.7, communicating and consulting with stakeholders is an on-going process. Your goal is to obtain, provide or share information about risks and how best to manage them. Identify the stakeholders involved in or affected by the risks facing the organisation and consider how they might be involved in managing those risks.

You might invite stakeholder representatives to join the risk management committee and risk event management teams and consult other stakeholders as you identify and evaluate risks, develop risk management treatments and develop and review the risk management plan. When the risk is organisation-wide, include representatives from all operational areas.

Involving stakeholders is important, but remember that consultation is about informed discussion. Ensure that all decisions are based on factual information, knowledge and experience (page 542 has more information on involving others and page 933 explains how to prepare for and lead meetings.)

Even when the events that would trigger the plan seem remote, communicate the plan to the workforce so that everyone is aware of the plan and its contents and their own related duties and responsibilities. Design and provide any necessary training and education so that people understand the risk and what to do should it occur. Ensure that the plan is readily available and that people know where and how to access it.

Develop and institute rolling communications campaigns to make sure that the RMP's principles and procedures remain fresh in people's minds. Articles in the organisation's newsletters and intranet, periodic drills and trial runs, posters, and training are all good ways to keep people aware of risk management plans and of their own roles in preventing and mitigating risk events. The precise frequency and nature of communication depends on the attrition at your workplace and the nature of the risk event itself.

◉ THEORY TO PRACTICE

A typical communication and consultation process

Here's 'Analice', an experienced Risk and Compliance Manager with a quasi-autonomous government organisation:

'We use a top down and bottom up communication and consultation process. All staff are responsible for identifying and reporting incidents and risks and I provide each department with a *risk log* and an *incident log* to help employees identify risks.

'We analyse risks and controls at the monthly Employee Risk Management Committee (RMC) meetings and discuss ways to improve the risk management process. The RMC members are from key operational areas and sites and consult their internal and external stakeholders to identify emerging risks to present to the RMC for review, along with their current incidents and risks logs. We periodically review contractors' documentation to spot risk exposure, too.

'The workplace health and safety (WHS) coordinator, who reports to me, is responsible for assisting all employees to identify WHS risks and implement controls. WHS risk assessments are tabled at the RMC and WHS Committee meetings.

'The general manager finance and business services chairs the RMC and WHS meetings and escalates extreme and high emerging risks to the senior management team (SMT). Risk management is a permanent agenda item at the monthly SMT meetings. These risks are escalated to the board according to our risk management policy and risk appetite guidelines.

'The board's audit and risk committee reviews all strategic risks as well as extreme and high operational risks at their quarterly meetings and the entire board reviews all risks annually.

'Other consultative committees such as the emergency planning committee and the business continuity management steering committee underpin our risk framework by establishing and reviewing controls against specific risks.

'I keep all employees informed about risks through regular communication mechanisms including awareness posters and Intranet messages. Our whole risk management process is geared to keeping risks and opportunities front-of-mind for all employees. And I think we're doing a really good job.'

Monitor and review your risks and management plans

As shown in Figure 23.7, continual monitoring and review of the risk management process is essential. The risk management committee should periodically review the organisation's risk management framework and risk management process to determine their adequacy, effectiveness and suitability for achieving the organisation's strategic objectives.

The committee should also review extreme- and high-level risks with the risk owner, generally every six months, to ensure the controls remain appropriate and adequate for the level of risk, and review moderate-, low-level, tolerated, mitigated and transferred risks, generally annually. The RMC should also review reported incidents against KPIs for each department monthly.

Regular reviews also allow you to proactively re-examine risks and your evaluation of them, analyse the strengths and weaknesses of the risk management plans, and identify opportunities to improve and update the plans so that they reflect changing circumstances inside and outside the organisation.

While regular reviews are proactive, monitoring is more reactive. The RMC should monitor accident and incident statistics, risk and incident logs, legislative and regulatory updates and project risk registers at its meetings to spot trends and patterns and investigate as necessary. When there is an increasing trend of incidents or a pattern emerges, consider re-assigning the risk(s) to a more severe category.

Risk owners monitor the risks for which they are responsible through continual checks, supervision and observation, and conduct regular reviews (generally annually for low- and moderate-level risks, six-monthly for high-level risks and quarterly or even monthly for extreme-level risks) to ensure the control measures are in place, working and used correctly, and to compare the goals specified in the RMP with the actual results. The review also includes an assessment of the effectiveness of employee and contractor education and training programs and communication strategies, and any communication strategies with the local community and other stakeholders.

Risk owners send or present a report of their findings, often called a *business impact assessment* or a *business impact statement*, to the RMC, which sends reports for extreme and high risks to the board's audit and review committee.

Risk owners also regularly scan the external and internal environments to monitor events and keep abreast of trends that indicate a risk level may be changing and note relevant matters to incorporate in the RMP when it is next reviewed; for instance, any changes to operations, key processes, materials or supply lines reflected in the plan should be fully tested, documented and communicated. When any increased level of risk or a new risk is identified, it should be incorporated into the RMP straightaway and stakeholders notified of the change and the treatment measures.

External reviews help keep the organisation's risk management processes sound, too. Insurance companies and government insurers (for example the Victorian Management Insurance Authority and other state nominated risk insurers and advisors) should periodically review organisations' risk arrangements and recommend improvements. (You can find out how to set up effective monitoring systems and use common monitoring tools on page 503.)

IN A NUTSHELL

Monitoring severe risks

Some risks, such as risks from extreme climatic events, are higher at certain times than at others. When the level of risk is extreme or even high, monitoring might include continual or regular scanning of the environment, opening lines of communication with official sources of information, instituting a communication program with employees and other stakeholders, initiating precautionary measures and participating in local or national strategic response committees.

CourseMateExpress

Go to http://login.cengagebrain.com to access CourseMate Express, your online study tool for *Management Theory & Practice*. CourseMate Express brings chapter concepts to life with interactive learning, and study and exam preparation tools:

- Test your skills in different aspects of management with interactive self-tests and simulations.
- Watch videos that show how real managers operate in real businesses.
- Test your understanding of the changing world of management by taking the revision quiz.

QUICK REVIEW

1. Briefly explain what constitutes a risk and the types of risk that can affect your organisation.
2. Explain the responsibilities of directors, managers and employees in risk management, and the role of board risk and audit management committees, and risk owners.
3. List the information a risk management plan should contain.
4. Prepare a flow chart or a Gantt chart showing the sequence of actions needed to manage risks. (You can find out about flow charts on page 593 and Gantt charts on page 507.)

BUILD YOUR SKILLS

1. Identifying and managing all the possible risks in an organisation or a workplace can be daunting. What measures can you think of to make the process less so?
2. Brainstorm the intrinsic and extrinsic strategic risks and the operational risks at your workplace or another workplace you are familiar with and select two from each group that you estimate to be the most likely to occur. Define each of these risks, identifying their nature and source, and initial and longer term consequences. Then estimate their probability of occurrence.
3. Prepare brief risk management plans for the risk from each group identified in Question 2 with the highest current risk levels.

WORKPLACE ACTIVITIES

1. How would you describe the risk culture of your organisation? What is your evidence for this?
2. What are the main risk factors in your industry? What is their likelihood of occurring and what might be their consequences should they occur? Consider operational and strategic consequences as well as other stakeholder consequences.
3. Describe the risk management frameworks and processes at your workplace.

CASE STUDY 23.1

THE FLOW-ON EFFECTS OF AN ADVERSE EVENT

It's midwinter. A pipeline in a gas plant in Western Australia bursts, sparking a fire. The site is evacuated and, miraculously, no one is hurt.

As a result, though, WA loses one-third of its domestic gas supply. Householders are told to use heat sparingly and industry to save energy. Lights dim and heating systems are turned off.

The business sector is in chaos. Thousands of workers are laid off or asked to take annual leave. The WA Chamber of Commerce says that the crisis will cost about $7 billion.

Gas supplies to iron ore mines and industry in the Pilbara fall by 45%. Gold and mineral sands mines are forced to reduce output, as are nickel smelters and aluminium refineries in the area. Aluminium and nickel prices rise around the world.

Some mines and manufacturers notify customers they are declaring *force majeure*, exempting them from fulfilling their contractual obligations, thereby affecting those customers' businesses and supply lines. A fertiliser manufacturer is forced to delay its float on the share market after its gas suppliers issue it with a *force majeure* notice. WA Brick, the world's largest brickworks, shuts down its kilns. The Great Western Laundry Services closes its doors and the hotel industry struggles to find supplies of clean linen.

The Forestry Industry and Agricultural Industries associations say the state's gas crisis has cost their industries millions of dollars in lost production and both plan to pursue compensation if it is found that the explosion was avoidable and caused by negligence.

Questions

1. The case study mentions a number of flow-on effects of this risk event. What others can you think of? Illustrate the flow-on effects in diagram form.
2. Complete a risk analysis for your workplace for a similar occurrence, either for a major accident on your premises, for a catastrophic event at a key supplier, or for a catastrophic event at a nearby company.

CASE STUDY 23.2

WORST-PRACTICE DATA TRANSFER

The chair calls the meeting of the Social Benefits Department's risk event management team to order. The faces around the table are glum. They are there to review what went wrong with their data security, the risk they are responsible for ensuring doesn't eventuate.

Responsible for paying the full range of government benefits, the department stores a huge amount of personal and confidential data and it has come to light that the previous week, an administrative employee copied the personal data of 20 000 unemployment benefit recipients onto unencrypted discs and popped them in the post to the Canberra office. They never arrived. Upon investigation, they have found the same procedural failure has occurred several times over the last six months.

This particular breach of security, however, was bigger than the others – 'Not that that excuses the others', remarked the chairperson sourly. 'For a start,' he says, 'this amount of information should never have been committed to a single disc or computer. And now, with their addresses, bank and other details in who knows whose hands, these welfare recipients are open to fraud.'

'We need to advise them, then, don't we?' Annette suggests.

'We've already put the part of the risk management plan in place to deal with those immediate issues, thanks Annette. What we need to do now is investigate the causes of these breaches and find out how they could have happened in the first place.'

'It's clearly a staff training issue,' says John. 'I bet we find the assistants responsible for this latest and the other breaches haven't been trained properly.'

'I bet we don't,' says Emily. 'I bet we find that it's because we're so short of people. The latest round of staff cuts and the ban on hiring to replace even key staff who leave voluntarily has really cut deep. Everyone is working their tails off and no one has time to do anything properly any more.'

The chair cuts across them: 'We need to collect the facts and then swing into the problem-solving process to uncover the cause of the breaches of security. Here's what we know: Three weeks ago, someone sent another unencrypted disc containing clients' personal information off to the Adelaide office, again through the post and again unrecorded and unregistered. Again the disc didn't arrive and another was posted – this time by recorded delivery but still against protocol.

'Ten days before that, another disc with personal information of recipients of the aged pension was couriered to our city office. These problems have occurred over the past six weeks and all in our office. But if it's happening here, it could be happening in any of our other offices too, I suspect.

'We've got a critical problem to deal with, so let's put our opinions to one side and start a proper investigation.'

Questions

1. Was this a risk event that could have been predicted and steps taken to lessen the likelihood of occurrence and the consequences should it occur?

2. Where do you think the Social Benefits Department went wrong? Are staff cutbacks an excuse?

3. Describe the information security risks facing the Social Benefits Department. On balance, how foreseeable were they? What protocols, or risk management plans and programs, could have prevented or lessened the likelihood of these risks occurring?

MANAGING FOR SUSTAINABILITY

Businesses (never mind people) cannot survive on a planet that fails. Whether for self-interest or more noble reasons, innovating sustainable operations is in every organisation's interests. A 'green revolution', marked by the rapid reduction in the use of fossil fuels and the introduction of a variety of sustainable management practices, is set to alter the way people live and work — just as the Industrial Revolution of the 19th century, marked by the rapid expansion of the use of fossil fuels, altered the way people lived and worked.

This revolution seems to be unavoidable if the human race and the planet that supports it are to survive. The sad fact is that human beings are using up many of the earth's resources 50% faster than the planet can replace them. By 2030, two planet Earths won't keep us going if we continue on our present course.[1] People are also creating greenhouse gas emissions faster than the earth can absorb them, causing an average global surface temperature increase of 0.8°C between 2000 and 2010[2]. A global surface temperature increase of more than 2°C means the earth's climate system would face catastrophic collapse.[3]

As one of the hottest and driest continents on earth, Australia's economy and environment is set to be hit hard and fast by climate change. Australian agriculture, food production and water supplies, ecosystems like the Great Barrier Reef, the Kakadu wetlands and the Murray–Darling Basin, energy security and all major industries, including tourism, have already been affected and we are experiencing increasing natural disasters associated with climate change. Climate change has the potential to threaten water supplies, intensify salinity and soil erosion, increase the prevalence of weeds, pests and disease, and seriously undermine plant and animal biodiversity and human health.

Many believe the world is teetering on the edge of a crisis and the decisions made today, in a relatively small window of opportunity, can tip the world over the edge or bring it back from the brink.

In Mandarin, the symbol for crisis includes the characters for 'opportunity' and 'danger'. There will be winners and losers. The organisational winners will most likely be those that act early to centre their practices, products and services on sustainability. Organisations that don't will pay a steep price, both financially and socially.

1. Can you help your organisation to develop, communicate and implement a workplace sustainability policy?
2. Can you help your organisation select suitable sustainability programs?
3. Do you know how to monitor and continuously improve your organisation's sustainability policy and programs?

This chapter explains how to make the most of the 'dangerous opportunity' of sustainability. Because sustainability is considered a risk-management issue, you should also read Chapter 23. Other related are chapters 2, 17, 18, 19 and 20. Since there are many specialist terms related to sustainability, you may want to keep a running list of them, with short definitions.

Great strides

Hazza is preparing for the Sustainability Committee's quarterly meeting. Chaired by the operations director, who is a committed environmentalist, working on this committee has become one of the highlights of his job. Although it was formed only 24 months ago, they have already achieved significant savings in energy and materials and its members are seen as 'corporate heroes'.

Hazza has been leading a subcommittee investigating ways to make their premises cleaner and greener and they have been diligently collecting benchmark and other data from their industry association, the UK-based Carbon Disclosure Project (http://www.cdproject.net), IBM's smarter planet website (http://www.ibm.com > smarter planet) and other sources. Although they seem to be in the top quartile in many areas, there is clearly room for improvement. Not only that, his subcommittee has concluded that there is a definite opportunity to process and reuse grey water at a substantial cost saving over a remarkably short period.

As Hazza puts the final touches on his presentation, his thoughts turn to the inbound materials subcommittee's report. Rumour has it they have come up with some substantial and innovative ideas and he's looking forward to hearing them.

1. Developing a workplace sustainability policy and strategies

> The longest and most destructive party ever held is now into its fourth generation and still no one shows any signs of leaving. The problem of when the drink is going to run out is, however, going to have to be faced one day. The planet over which they are floating is no longer the planet it was when they first started floating over it. It is in bad shape.
>
> Douglas Adams (author), *Life, the universe and everything* (1982)[4]

Environment-spoiling activities are set to become increasingly costly liabilities as consumers, employees, governments, investors and other stakeholders exert pressure on organisations to operate more sustainably and responsibly. Corporate responsibility and sustainability are now at the forefront of a new way of organisational thinking, behaving and reporting.

Those organisations going beyond the relatively obvious and simple initiatives in sustainability view it as a path to profit. Enhanced brand value, corporate image, employer brand and employer value proposition result in improved workforce attraction and retention, increased sales and customer loyalty, and more supportive stakeholders.

Once a series of defensive and reactive measures, sustainability, like risk management, has become a key strategic issue for organisations. Turning sustainability into lucrative opportunities rather than expensive burdens means organisations can operate more profitably, more sustainably, and with considerably reduced risk exposure.

Clean operations can create assets and generate income, and designing sustainable processes, products and services as part of or to replace existing product lines, particularly through upcycling, can be more profitable than producing products for obsolescence. As a result, expanded markets, new industries and a new category of jobs, 'green-collar jobs,' are on the horizon.

Best practice is for directors and senior managers to oversee the development of practical and effective sustainability policies and strategies based on the organisation's impact on the environment and its sustainability goals. Like other aspects of risk management, it's important to build sustainability into the organisation's decision-making and planning processes and to fully integrate it into its normal performance reporting. Every investment should automatically be examined for its long-term carbon ramifications and materials use and reuse.

THEORY TO PRACTICE

Plan A (there is no plan B)

Retailer Marks & Spencer (M&S) has shown that becoming sustainable does not need to cost money. In fact, since introducing its comprehensive sustainability programs in 1987, it has added £50 million in additional profits.

M&S set a goal of becoming 'the world's most sustainable major retailer' by 2015. Its sustainability plan is called Plan A, because when it comes to safeguarding the planet, there can be no Plan B. The plan is comprehensive, because it deals with all areas of the company's environmental impact; and holistic, because it recognises the interrelationship between the various aspects of its operations. It embraces the company's culture as well as its external suppliers and customers.

M&S's impressive results include producing zero net worldwide carbon emissions from M&S and joint venture operations in 2014, 34% increased energy efficiency between 2006–07 and 2013–14 and 68% fewer airconditioning emissions compared to 2006–07. The company has received over 140 awards in all areas of sustainability since 2007.[5]

Scope the policy

Policies are statements of intent – commitments that guide an organisation's activities and decisions. They are based on the organisation's vision and mission, set by top-level and senior management. Policies set goals without stating specifically what is to be done – this is left to strategies and strategic, business and operational plans.

The first step in creating a sustainability policy is to define its *scope*. This establishes the framework for developing the policy and ensures stakeholders (those who might be affected by the policy) are identified and consulted.

Find out where you stand by analysing how climate change and resource scarcity are expected to affect your organisation. Then write a purpose statement stating why the organisation is issuing the policy and what the desired effect or outcome of the policy is. Then list the assumptions and constraints the policy should adhere to and state how the policy is to be managed and monitored.

Include the business activities and stakeholders affected by the policy (expressly exclude any actions, operations or people that the organisation does not want the policy to cover if applicable), the date by which the policy should come into force, a responsibilities section – who is to do what in developing and managing the policy – and any definitions for terms and concepts in the policy.

You can base your scope document on the one shown in Figure 24.1 or follow your organisation's preferred format. Formalise its acceptance with the responsible senior manager or sponsor before carrying on.

XZY Pty Ltd

Policy title: -

Date prepared: -

Prepared by: -

1. **Background or reason for policy:** Why have a policy on this subject? What are the goals of the policy? What compliance requirements does the policy address? The purpose of this policy is ...

2. **Responsible persons:** Person or persons responsible for developing the policy for approval and for implementing, managing and monitoring the policy once it is accepted and released.

3. **Policy outline:** An outline of what the policy is to cover, subject to later revision, and the target date for the policy to come into force.

4. **Consistency with other organisational policies:** Set a context for this policy in terms of the organisation's goals and related policies and state what procedures may be required.

5. **Impact on the organisation:** The resources (financial, human, operational, physical, technical etc) expected to be needed to implement and maintain compliance with this policy; the stakeholders and operational activities that the policy may affect, including any systems changes and changes to technical and other procedures anticipated as necessary to comply with the policy.

6. **Assumptions and constraints:** These underline all policies.

7. **Stakeholders:** The interested parties to consult with developing the policy.

FIGURE 24.1 Policy scope statement

Gather information

The more information you have about sustainability and sustainability policies, the easier it is to tailor your policy to the goals and needs of your organisation and its stakeholders. Your first step might be to gather information. Trawl through the Internet and have a look at the policies of organisations with good reputations in this area. You might look, for example, at:

* http://www.brambles.com.au
* http://www.stockland.com.au.

Find out which are the 100 most sustainable corporations in the world by going to http://www.global100.org; to be listed, companies need to show they effectively manage environmental and social factors. Find out how Climate Counts rates various well-known companies at http://www.climatecounts.org > climate scores; Climate Counts is US-based, but most of the organisations rated are international.

Monash University has these pages on its website:

* http://www.monash.edu > policy-bank
* http://fsd.monash.edu.au > environmental-sustainability.

This last point has links to its carbon footprint and its road map to carbon neutrality.

Gather examples and guidelines from your chamber of commerce or relevant government department and your industry association. Reach out to your professional networks for ideas. Explore the website of the World Business Council for Sustainable Development, an association of about 200 major international corporations including 3M, Coca-Cola, DuPont and Sony, at http://www.wbcsd.org.

Build files for the various strategies and programs you come across that may suit your organisation. (Sustainability programs are explored in Section 2 of this chapter.)

Do you know ...

Extreme heat has killed more Australians than any other natural hazard in the past 200 years. And more people died during the 2009 Victorian heatwave than in the Black Saturday bushfires in February 2009.

Increased temperatures aren't the only, or the worst, result of climate change. Changes to rainfall patterns and sea levels may well affect us more.

The world's oceans are warming, and they're warming more quickly than the global average in Australia. Warming oceans contribute to rising sea levels which, around Darwin have risen about 17 cm in the last 20 years, or about seven to 11 mm a year – twice the global average; around the eastern and southern coasts of Australia, rates are around the global average.

Climate change refers to all the effects of 'inadvertent climate modification'. Global warming refers to increasing surface temperatures.[6]

Find out where you are now

Consider your organisation's current impact on the environment. A good place to start is with your carbon and ecological footprints. You can calculate your organisation's various footprints at sites such as http://www.footprintnetwork.org or another that your organisation or industry association may prefer.

Identify the environmental measures that best apply to your organisation, such as usage and trends for energy and water and the use of sustainable and non-sustainable materials, and then find data that can give you meaningful information. Many industry associations provide benchmark information and guidelines on what to measure and how to measure it (page 585 explains how to collect, display and analyse data).

IN A NUTSHELL

Eco-effectiveness and eco-efficiency

Generations of managers have adhered to the principles of *effectiveness* – doing the right things – and *efficiency* – doing things right – to establish and manage their priorities.

The idea has now spread to sustainability circles. *Eco-effectiveness* encompasses the concept of creating processes, products and services with less environmental impact (e.g. by eliminating or reducing the waste and pollution created in the production of goods and services). *Eco-efficiency* encompasses the idea of operating economically (e.g. by buying fewer resources) as well as sustainably (e.g. by reducing pollution and waste and usefully repurposing any waste produced).

You want to look 'inside out' to understand the impact of your organisation's activities on the environment and 'outside in' to see how changing regulations, climate, resource availability and so on may affect your organisation's marketplace and the organisation itself.[7] Include the supply chain when looking inside out and outside in and bear in mind both eco-effectiveness and eco-efficiency.

This approach helps you think broadly when assessing your organisation's overall carbon exposure and sustainability opportunities. Think through the major risk and opportunity areas that affect your organisation and thoroughly explore them both from the inside out and the outside in. 'The Strategic perspective: When outside in is inside out' and the 'Theory to practice: Conduct a risk analysis for climate change', have some examples. They are by no means comprehensive, but they may guide you to develop other questions pertinent to your organisation.

● THE STRATEGIC PERSPECTIVE

When outside in is inside out

What is an inside-out effect to one organisation is an outside-in effect to others. For example, the price of oil and cost of emissions affects industries dependent on oil (e.g. transport industries such as airlines, couriers, road freight and taxis) and may drive down the demand for oil, affecting oil producers, refiners and sellers. The effect on those industries in turn affects others, such as the hospitality industry, which then affects other industries such as laundry services and food and beverage producers and wholesalers.

The price of oil also affects the cost to restaurants for storing food that needs to be kept cold and restaurants may have difficulty sourcing food supplies as the productivity of various regions that have traditionally supplied agricultural and farming products changes and as the cost of transporting food over long distances increases.

The upstream and downstream effects of climate change, increasing legislation and public demand for sustainable operations can reach far.

● ACTION!

How well positioned is your organisation? You can find a Sustainability analysis template to help you think this through on ⚡CourseMateExpress. You can use your findings to begin setting improvement goals and later, for tracking improvements.

● THE STRATEGIC PERSPECTIVE

How climate change affects organisations

Even organisations in industries that are least hit by climate change need to deal with its effects: employee migrations, increases in disease, increases in electricity, fuel and waste disposal prices, shortages of energy, supply-chain breakdowns …

The reputation of multinationals in non-polluting industries may suffer, too, as 'big business' takes flack for climate-related problems.

Conduct a risk analysis for climate change

The current climate change is of a similar magnitude to the change at the end of the last ice age but it is occurring much, much faster. And it's the rate of climate change more than change itself that is so dangerous, since life is flexible when given enough time to adapt.

You can consider the effect of climate change on your organisation from the outside in, in three broad ways. The first two are changing temperature and weather patterns, and regulations and public opinion that increase the financial and image costs of emissions. Both can affect access to traditional trading partners, the availability of supplies, consumer demand, the operations of your integrated value chain and other aspects of your operations.

The third outside-in way to think about how climate change might affect your organisation is to think about how the effects of climate change – for example, more frequent drought, flooding and storms – might affect various aspects of your organisation's operations and the environments it operates in. Pay particular attention to areas that have a limited ability to anticipate and adapt to climate change. For example, countries or areas where the government's ability to respond is limited, where the local ecosystem is fragile and where water supplies are already stretched.

You can also work inside out and consider how much your carbon emissions are costing your organisation now and what they are likely to cost in the future. Think in both financial and corporate image terms. Financially, consider the regulatory regime as well as increasing fuel costs. In image terms, think through the various stakeholders. How does the cleanliness of your organisation's operations attract or repel customers, shareholders and the type of employees your organisation needs now and in the future? How does it strengthen or weaken your public image? Do your suppliers and organisations you supply hesitate or welcome being associated with your organisation because of the sustainability of your operations?

Consult stakeholders

What's important to your stakeholders? When you know this, you can set priorities and begin developing policy and strategy options. Do they want more sustainable products and services? Do they want your existing products and services replaced with new ones with drastically reduced environmental impacts? Do they want you to produce your products or services using much less energy and materials? Maybe they want you to actively protect or even regenerate the earth's natural resources. You don't know until you ask them.

Think through your organisation's operations and identify which roles and processes a sustainability policy could affect. Consult a range of representatives from these areas to obtain their knowledge and opinions so that you can take their experience, ideas and needs into account as you develop the policy.

List and contact as appropriate a range of external stakeholders such as suppliers (who you may require to provide 'green' materials), customers and the wider community, who might appreciate knowing about your sustainability commitments (you can find out about the various stakeholder groups inside and outside the organisation on page 46). Consultation helps enlist their support, gives you ideas and information, and prevents your policies from unintentionally adversely affecting any stakeholders. Consulting and communicating with stakeholders is an ongoing process.

ACTION!

You can find a Stakeholder questions template to fill out on **CourseMateExpress**. This will help you work out the issues that matter most to your stakeholders.

THE STRATEGIC PERSPECTIVE

Shareholder activism

The rapid increase in shareholder activism concerning environmental, social and governance (ESG) issues is now on the radar of most listed companies. Investment funds and institutional investors are becoming increasingly vocal on ESG matters and divesting shares in fossil fuel and other companies seen to be harming the environment. Litigation against listed companies is increasing and not-for-profit organisations are running increasingly sophisticated campaigns targeting not only companies whose operations harm the environment but also institutions that fund those companies.[8]

Speaking at a symposium on risk management in Melbourne, Steven Skala, vice chairman (Australia and New Zealand) of Deutsche Bank had this to say, 'In my view, the objective of the modern corporation is not to make a profit but to live profitably forever. In order to live forever, different considerations must be taken into account apart from the sheer notion of making a profit.'[9]

Set goals and targets

You know where you are. Where do you want to be? Based on stakeholder feedback and the organisation's drivers of success and strategic goals, how much, and how quickly, does the organisation intend to improve its eco-effectiveness and eco-efficiency?

Use the scope of your workplace sustainability policy to guide you to create a 'dashboard' of specific measures of success or key performance indicators (KPIs) for the activities that have the greatest impact on the sustainability of your organisation's operations.

Review these measures quarterly and relay them to stakeholders so that they can track improvements and find further improvement opportunities. These measures should also be reviewed by senior management bi-annually and by the board at least annually. (This is discussed in the final section of this chapter, beginning on page 796.)

Developing resource-efficient supply-chain transport systems, eliminating, reducing or recycling materials, maximising the use of renewable energy and reducing waste and harmful emissions might all be areas in which to set goals and targets.

THE STRATEGIC PERSPECTIVE

Science-based goals

Some companies have set goals based on accounting firm PwC's calculations that the world must reduce *total carbon intensity* (the carbon emitted per dollar of GDP) by 6% until 2100 to prevent temperature increases of 2°C (beyond which the repercussions to the economy and humanity would be devastating). Other companies have based their goals on the international non-government organisation, World Wildlife Fund's recommendation of a 3% annual reduction in *absolute total emissions*.

>>

More than 25 % of the *Fortune* Global 200 companies have targets that meet PwC's or WWF's recommended targets. For example:

- IKEA aims to be powered entirely by renewable energy by 2020 and Lego by 2016.
- GE, Diageo North America, Lloyds Bank and Volkswagen plan to reduce energy intensity in their operations by 25% to 75% depending on the target year; Diageo has already beaten its target and cut operational emissions by 75%.
- Sony plans to cut per-product energy consumption by 30% by 2015.
- Intel aims to make its computer and data centre products 25 times more efficient than its 2010 benchmarks by 2020.

To find the environmental and social goals of the world's largest companies, go to http://www. pivotgoals.com.[10]

● THEORY TO PRACTICE

Audacious goals and lofty ambitions

Office furniture-maker Herman Miller intends to produce no hazardous or landfill waste by 2023, and by 2020 to produce no manufacturing emissions and rely completely on green energy. Challenging goals, but as CEO Brian Walker said: 'If your ambition is lofty enough – and if you measure your progress – you eventually figure out a way to get close to it.'

In 2004, when only 5% of its products met its cradle-to-cradle design standard, Herman Miller set an interim target of 50% of sales meeting that standard by 2010. A big ask, but by 2009 it achieved its target – 12 months ahead of schedule. In 2012, Herman Miller had reduced its operational footprint by 91.8% since its 1994 base year, due largely to reductions of emissions and water use. In 2014, the company had cut waste by over 90% since 1994, well on the track to their zero goal.

The company's 10-year sustainability strategy, Earthright, adopts three principles: positive transparency, products as living things and becoming greener together. It has shaped its goals around being resource-wise, eco-design and becoming community driven.[11]

Four shades of green

How green should the organisation go and how quickly? Should you leave your systems as they are? Should you invest in technologies to reduce pollution? Perhaps you should aim for *carbon neutral* – producing no net contribution to carbon emissions, which requires significant planning and may involve significant expenditure in the short term. Or you may want to aim higher, for *carbon negative* – producing more clean energy than you use and storing and/or selling the surplus to the grid.

Figure 24.2 summarises these options. You can decide how green you want to go on a financial basis, on a philosophical basis, in response to stakeholder demands, or on a combination of these rationales. You may even want to run various scenarios to see which path has the most potential.

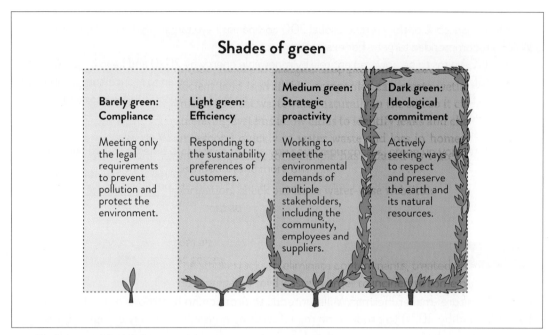

FIGURE 24.2 Shades of green

Being 'barely green' may be cheap and easy in the short term, but for organisations that pollute more than minimally, the costs of mere compliance are likely to increase steeply. Organisations that depend on the goodwill of their customers and repeat business may need to go 'light green' at a minimum to respond to the environmental preference of their customers. Organisations at this level concentrate on efficiency and the cost savings that result.

Many organisations are likely to find it worthwhile to go 'medium green' and meet the environmental demands of multiple stakeholders. Sustainability is part of their core strategy; they might, for example, invest time and effort in re-engineering a function or capability in a way that is difficult for competitors to copy, replace printed product manuals with electronic versions, or develop or purchase virtual meeting technology that allows technicians to troubleshoot problems at a customer's premises remotely, saving on travel costs and the resulting carbon emissions. Cost savings, a significant competitive edge, market leadership, and improved corporate and brand image can all increase the profitability resulting from a smaller ecological footprint and help recoup investments more quickly.

Some organisations may decide to go beyond operational effectiveness and choose the 'dark green' option, actively looking for ways to protect, preserve and restore the earth and its natural resources. For instance, they might make strategic changes that allow them to benefit from climate change and move further towards sustainability, or they might enhance or extend their competitive positioning by creating products such as hybrid cars, water filtering systems or window glass that can capture and store the sun's energy for later use.

FYI

How quickly the world changes

We all depend on the resources that healthy ecosystems provide – clean air, fresh water, productive land, robust biodiversity. In 1961, most countries had enough carrying capacity, i.e. enough biologically productive area, to meet their population's demands and absorb the waste people generate. In 1970, humans reached the earth's biocapacity and ever since we've been in *overshoot*; it now takes the earth 1.5 years to regenerate the renewable resources we use and absorb the CO_2 waste we produce in a year. This allows waste to build up and reduces the planet's ability to support life, and limits the abilities of poor countries to develop and of rich countries to maintain prosperity.[12]

(You can see which regions of the world and which countries have sustainable lifestyles and read about and calculate your organisation's and your own ecological and carbon footprints at http://www.footprintnetwork.org. Find out more about water use and the water footprint at http://www.waterfootprint.org. You can find out about the current state of the planet, biodiversity, climate change impacts and the six priority actions needed to live within Earth's means from the latest Living Planet Report at http://wwf.org.au.)

Knowing how green you want the organisation to be helps you with two other important considerations: whether to adopt the International Organization for Standardization (ISO) 14001:2004 environmental standards and undertake voluntary *sustainability reporting*. (But voluntary for how long? The ASX's draft changes to its governance principles published in 2014 include sustainability reporting.[13])

The input–output–outcome–impact framework

The input–output–outcome–impact framework is a useful way to set goals and measure progress in each of those four areas:

1. *Inputs* could be financial or technological, or they could be initiatives such as a green office program or research and development for new green products, services or systems.
2. *Outputs* consist of what is produced or done with the inputs. They allow you to see the immediate results of your inputs, or how they have been used or applied.
3. *Outcomes* are short-term results from the outputs.
4. *Impacts* are the longer-term results of your efforts.

For example, to reduce the carbon footprint of your organisation's delivery chain, you might decide to spend a specific sum of money (*input*) on installing dual engines in your delivery vehicles (*output*). You would then measure the monthly reduction in vehicle emissions (*outcome*) and, say, 24 months later you would measure the total reduction in vehicle emissions over an annual cycle and find out what portion of your company's total emission reductions it represents. The *impact* of reduced emissions might be improved air quality and a reduction in asthma and other respiratory complaints along your transportation route, a lower carbon footprint and resulting financial savings.

Work with your organisation's finance specialists to calculate the cost-benefit of various inputs.

 **ACTION!**

To analyse your supply chain, log on to **CourseMateExpress** to access an Inputs and outputs template.

Develop strategy options

You know where you are and where you want to be. A gap analysis can help you decide how to get there (explained in the 'FYI: Gap analysis' on page 507). What broad approach to achieving its sustainability goals could your organisation adopt? Large organisations with varied operations, particularly those spread over more than one geographical area, may need different strategies to address different aspects of their operations and/or locations.

Because the road to sustainability may be a long one for many organisations, you may want to identify a range of relatively simple, eco-efficient defensive actions to take now to begin the journey and then move on to offensive strategies:

1. *Do what you've always done – but better.* Go for small, quick wins by reducing costs, risks and waste of resources (e.g. energy, materials, water) by using them more efficiently and showing customers proof of value. (See the heading, 'Identify programs to achieve your objectives' on page 778 for some ideas.) At the same time, begin planning for longer term eco-effectiveness measures and consider the impact of all decisions on eco-efficiency and eco-effectiveness.

2. *Do new tasks in new ways with innovative approaches.* Select functions, operations, products and value chains to redesign for sustainability by optimising their eco-effectiveness and performance, and invest in technologies to make an even greater impact on the sustainability of your organisation's operations.

3. *Build sustainability into the organisation's core activities and supply chains.* This way, sustainability becomes the source of new income and growth, for example, through new products and developing new capabilities (see the heading, 'Collaborate' on page 794 for some ideas).

4. *Build new business models and platforms that use your innovations.* This can enhance your organisation's culture and offerings and secure its future (see page 794).

Look inside out and outside in, think through your organisation's supply chain and the direct and indirect ways its activities affect the environment. Opportunities to make a lighter footprint on the planet can come directly from the activities your organisation controls, and indirectly from the activities of your organisation's suppliers and distribution channels, and from the way customers use and dispose of your products.

THEORY TO PRACTICE

Eco-innovation: Three new green products

Green is here to stay and it comes in more and more different guises.

Green dirt is what you call mixing sewage sludge and green waste. Who would think that could make money and win awards? But it has. Green-Tech, a landscaping firm based in York in the United Kingdom, has developed a green-tree topsoil by blending composted green waste from the local council, processed sewage sludge and silica sand.

As well as being environmentally friendly, the topsoil can be manufactured to a consistent quality (unlike other topsoils) and its density is 1 cubic metre per tonne (compared with 1.6 for most other topsoils), which saves on delivery trips and the attendant traffic congestion and greenhouse gas emissions. In one project alone (the transformation of a former colliery site), its topsoil diverted 20 000 tonnes of organic material from the tip, and thanks to its low density, Green-Tech saved 650 delivery trips on the 30 000 cubic metres of topsoil it supplied.

A green process is what company, Nu-phalt is using to fill the potholes of the UK's roads and car parks more cheaply. And they're doing it more quickly and quietly and with less air pollution, traffic disruption and waste than traditional methods. Its infra-red road-repair system produces a heat-sealed, seamless, ultra-strong repair with limited need for new material and significantly less carbon emissions per square metre – 4.3 kg per pothole versus 51.6 kg with traditional methods, according to an independent study.

Traditional repair methods can last as little as a few months, but Nu-Phalt's infra-red repairs last up to three years. Only one vehicle is needed, reducing traffic disruption. A microprocessor monitors the infra-red pulses, cutting emissions and operating time and increasing productivity. Existing materials are rejuvenated, virtually eliminating waste being dumped. And it's cheaper, costing customers about 40% less than traditional methods. It took four years of R&D, but the results are clearly worth it. (You can find out more about Nu-Phalt's environmental benefits at http://www.nuphalt.com.)[14]

Green insurance attracted more than twice as many customers in its first year than the Green Insurance Company had predicted by making it easy and cost-effective for customers to behave in an environmentally responsible manner. The company offers cheaper premiums to customers with low-emission cars and those who drive less each year, offsets all carbon emissions from customers' vehicles at no extra cost, calculating the amount to offset from customers' actual mileage rather than average mileage, and funds the creation of woodlands all over the UK to capture the CO_2 emitted by the drivers they insure.

Staff attend a six-week training course that combines customer-service skills and environmental awareness and includes field visits to renewable energy sites. The company has expanded into environmentally friendly home insurance, eco-friendly pet insurance and green breakdown cover.[15]

Emissions-intensive activities and low-sustainability activities that add little value are candidates for outsourcing to more eco-efficient and eco-effective organisations. Those that add value are candidates for keeping in-house and re-engineering to reduce their impact on the environment. Finding sustainable ways to perform key activities in ways your competitors can't match gives your organisation a valuable strategic advantage, too.

Improving your resource productivity and reducing waste saves money as well as the environment. Identifying and managing environmentally driven risks is sound risk management and can help you design more sustainable and environmentally friendly operations. Examining and managing your supply chain to reduce your organisation's footprint and finding ways to reduce your organisation's impact on the environment as well as regulatory burdens are other ways to strategically increase your organisation's sustainability.

Here are seven other strategies to achieve more sustainable operations:[16]

1. *Acquire, or buy, someone else's green brand* or a B corporation to gain access to knowledge and sustainable systems. L'Oréal bought The Body Shop, Unilever bought Ben & Jerry's. Beware of culture clash and lack of strategic fit when going for this option. Consider your brand portfolio when adopting this strategy, too. How will the rest of your products look when compared with your wonderful green product? Too big a gulf can undermine your sustainability claims.

2. *Build green offerings from scratch,* as Toyota did with the Prius. This is particularly suited to organisations with a track record of innovation. It can be slower and more costly than the other strategies but the organisation builds valuable, transferable competencies that can

extend to profitable platforms along the way; Toyota produced a hybrid version of Lexus, for example, forcing Mercedes-Benz and BMW to introduce their own hybrid models.

3. *Improve resource productivity and reduce waste* to save money as well as the environment.
4. *Make the most of your organisation's existing or latent green attributes.* Struggling Brita was about to be sold off by Clorox but saved itself by showing how its water filtration systems could keep millions of plastic water bottles out of landfills.
5. *Manage environmentally driven risks* and be sure to find them before they find you.
6. *Manage your integrated value chain* to reduce your organisation's footprint.
7. *Reduce environmental costs and regulatory burdens.*

When selecting strategies, consider which best meet your organisation's mission and goals, taking into account their cost-effectiveness, ongoing expenses, time frames, and social, stakeholder and economic impacts. Consider any underlying capital expenses and the cost of developing any new methodologies, too, weighing them against the cost of polluting and other non-financial costs such as those relating to employer brand and market reputation. When the numbers involved are large, call in the experts and use data-mining, forecasting and optimisation techniques to cost and analyse various options and run simulations on different scenarios to select the strategy.

Carry out a risk analysis (explained on page 744) on any investments; for example, if you invest in a carbon sink forest and it burns down, your investment is lost. Conduct a force field analysis (explained on page 504) on each strategy option. You may also want to do some scenario planning (explained on pages 742) for the strategies that seem most promising.

Use Steps 1–5 of the problem-solving process (described on page 527) to guide you to identify, assess and develop the policy and strategies.

◉ IN A NUTSHELL

Benchmarks for sustainable management practices and corporate social responsibility
The International Organization for Standardization's ISO 14004:2004 provides guidelines on the principles, issues and elements of an environmental management system and how to implement such a system. The ISO 14001:2004 specifies the requirements for an environmental management system and discusses how to provide objective evidence for audits. These standards can help organisations to minimise the effects of their activities on the environment and continually improve their environmental performance. (The ISO's standard on corporate social responsibility is ISO 2600.)

Recommend policy and strategy options

Bearing in mind your organisation's goals and the objectives of its key decision-makers, put forward your policy and strategy recommendations for consideration. Show how each supports your organisation's mission and business strategies and its other policies and reflects the expectations of its stakeholders. Explain the rationale behind each and any downsides, and suggest their likely cost, effectiveness and time frames. (See page 172 for tips on writing and to find out how to be persuasive, and, if you're presenting the options personally, see page 199 to find out how to make great presentations.)

THEORY TO PRACTICE

Stockland – an example of Australian best practice

The Stockland Group is a diversified property group and one of the top 50 listed companies on the Australian Stock Exchange. It is recognised by the Dow Jones Sustainability Index as the world's most sustainable real estate company and remains on the Global 100 list of the world's most sustainable organisations; it has also won various urban development awards for excellence and other green awards and accreditations.

Four policies underpin Stockland's corporate responsibility and sustainability (CR&S) accomplishments: maintaining ethical and responsible marketplace practices, respecting and engaging with employees, strengthening the group's place in the community, and taking care of the environment in which the group operates.

A key strategy is to make CR&S a responsibility of every employee. To this end, CR&S is included in all employees' performance scorecards and employees can be rewarded in this area. An employee CR&S committee meets every month to review risks and opportunities, share knowledge and news, and report on upcoming activities. Committee members are drawn from a range of roles and functions and each member is tasked with improving leadership in an aspect of CR&S. The internal employee survey has registered noticeable improvements in how employees perceive Stockland's performance in the CR&S area.

Stockland has also created a climate change action plan that aims to develop innovative sustainability solutions beyond cutting energy and water consumption. Its retail division conducts workshops that train all shopping centre employees in energy and water management, how to read and understand power and water data and recognise and rectify inefficiencies, and raise their awareness of sustainability issues.[17]

Finalise the policy and strategies and agree introduction methods

Based on the feedback from the decision-makers, write up the policy for final approval. Ensure it reflects the organisation's commitment to sustainability and is written in such a way that it is integral to business planning and decision-making and that it can drive a sustainability culture throughout the organisation. Word the policy in positive terms so that it is seen as a business opportunity and part of the organisation's corporate responsibility measures. State who is to oversee and arrange the policy's implementation, review it and monitor its effectiveness.

Estimate the resources needed to communicate and implement the policy and strategy following the guidelines on planning in Chapter 17 beginning on page 494, implementing plans on page 537 and introducing change on page 689.

Plan to use a range of communication channels to promote the policy and expected outcomes to stakeholders. Aim to create awareness and develop a sense of enthusiasm as well as generate support for the organisation's sustainability commitment. Communication and training should also facilitate compliance so that people know what is expected of them personally. Build in regular communication mechanisms with stakeholders and include ways to keep the resulting policy and the programs fresh and in the minds of employees and other stakeholders.

THEORY TO PRACTICE

Green flooring

With carpeting taking 50 years to begin to decompose and over 5000 truckloads (30 000 tonnes) of commercial carpet going to landfill in Australia and New Zealand every year, carpets are a serious cradle-to-grave problem.

Flooring manufacturer InterfaceFLOR moved towards sustainable operations in 1994 with a philosophy called the Natural Step. Launched by the company's founder and chairperson, it had a bold mission: to become the first company anywhere to be fully sustainable with no negative impacts on the environment from its people, processes or products. Known as Mission Zero™, the timescale for achievement is set at 2020. Post 2020, it intends to become a restorative organisation – giving more to the environment than it takes away.

Mission Zero has three clear goals:

1. To sustain the environment by taking nothing from the earth that we cannot easily and rapidly replace.
2. To sustain society by helping our employees, suppliers, customers and the wider community to understand our impact on the environment and helping them to gain a higher quality of life.
3. To grow our business by creating products that are not only environmentally friendly but profitable as well.

The policy influences every business, design and manufacturing decision and is embedded in the company's approach to people, processes, products and profit – all are designed to move the company towards a zero environmental footprint. Mission Zero has changed the company's business model to make reducing environmental impacts a key business driver and extends to the way it works with its supply chain. The resulting sustainability programs have reached every corner of the company's business and operations.

Results are impressive. Since 1998, the company has reduced energy by 60% per square metre of carpet, reduced non-renewable energy by 75% per square metre of carpet, reduced greenhouse gas emissions by 39%, reduced the use of virgin raw materials by 29%, reduced water use per square metre of carpet by 69% and reduced the amount of waste it sends to landfill per square metre of carpet by 26%. The company accepts compatible competitor products for recycling, has partnered with its yarn supplier to achieve 100% recycled yarn, and has invested in technology that allows it to recycle the nylon as well as the vinyl backing of old carpet tiles, creating 100% carbon neutral carpet tiles with the highest recycled content in the industry.

One project alone, St George Bank's head office refurbishment, was so carbon-neutral it saved the equivalent of 42 passenger cars being taken off the road for a year (at an average of 800 000 kilometres or average car travel, or 700 trips between Sydney and Melbourne). The avoided carbon impact of another refurbishment project, 101 Grenfell St, Adelaide, was the equivalent of 53 cars being off the road for a year. Find out more at <http://www.interfaceflor.com.au>.[18]

2. Developing and implementing sustainability programs

Unless we stop now, we will really doom the lives of our descendants. If we just go on for another forty or fifty years faffing around, they'll have no chance at all, it'll be back to the stone age. There'll be people around still. But civilisation will go.

James Lovelock, in Flannery, *The Weather Makers* (2005)[19]

Naturally, policies alone aren't enough and strategies are empty unless implemented. Your organisation probably needs to adopt a range of sustainability programs to achieve its sustainability goals. In large organisations, save confusion by breaking them down into areas with different teams working on different areas simultaneously, as described under the heading, 'Identify risks' on page 740.

Unfortunately, there isn't a magic formula to follow when developing sustainability programs, since each organisation's approach needs to blend with its overall strategy. However, there are some general guidelines for selecting and implementing suitable sustainability programs.

Begin by identifying a range of categories in which to develop sustainable programs, such as implementing energy- and water-saving initiatives, recycling and upcycling, investing in energy-efficient equipment and production technologies and redesigning processes. Then identify specific programs and select the most suitable

The next step might be to select suppliers with low carbon footprints. After that, you could work with the rest of your organisation's supply chain to look for ways to mitigate sustainability risks and reduce costs while assuring reliable and sustainable supplies. 'Dark green' organisations might investigate ways to create a negative footprint. Ultimately, many organisations will take into their accounting a value for natural capital (e.g. clean air and water, a relatively stable climate, biodiversity that provides animals and plants for food and medicine) and redefine how they measure return on investment.

THEORY TO PRACTICE

Clean cruisers

The Carnival Corporation has been working on sustainability for some time and it's now part of the cruise liner company's culture. An independently certified environmental management system sets a high standard of excellence on board each ship, including:

- a desalination plant that produces fresh water using the waste heat generated by the engines, which reduces the use of boilers to produce fresh water and therefore reduces fuel consumption and greenhouse gas emissions
- an environmental officer who oversees and verifies environmental management and compliance
- dedicated staff who sort all general waste for recycling, or reduce its volume when recycling is not possible
- fuel-efficiency measures, including improved hull coatings to reduce ships' drag, reducing greenhouse gas (GHG) emissions
- low-energy lamps
- recirculation of waste heat
- waste-water management facilities that minimise impact on the oceans.[20]

Identify programs to achieve your objectives

Fortunately, you can employ a wide range of tried, tested and relatively cheap, easy and quick eco-efficiency initiatives while your organisation develops longer-term solutions. Some of these easier, short-term innovations, as well as several more sophisticated initiatives, are reviewed in the following sections. Think of these ideas as 'thought starters' to help you identify practices that suit your own organisation.

The good news is that following eco-effectiveness principles can save more money than it costs; for example, cleaning up pollution after creating it, fines for mismanaging environmental issues, money spent on pollution control equipment, and so on, can be more costly than reducing pollution or not polluting in the first place. (See 'Theory to practice: Stop problems before they start – a smart strategy' below.)

● ACTION!

You can find a Green sourcing checklist to help you source purchases, green up your manufacturing, improve your distribution and more on ⫶CourseMateExpress.

● THEORY TO PRACTICE

Stop problems before they start – a smart strategy

In 1975, 3M placed 'scrubbers' on smokestacks to eliminate contaminants, treated effluents before releasing waste water and segregated solid waste in order to incinerate some of it rather than dump it. Then 3M changed its strategy. It decided that rather than fixing the 'back end' it would be cheaper (and easier) to prevent the pollution entirely and began a program called Pollution Prevention Pays, or 3P. A guiding principle was that any action to reduce pollution should also save money.

The first 20 pollution prevention programs saved many tonnes of pollutants and US$11 million. In its first year, 3P saved the company US$1 billion, prevented 73 000 tons of air emissions and 2800 tons of sludge. Achievements over the past 40 years include cutting GHGs by more than 72% worldwide, contributing US$10 million to keep wild areas wild and reducing water use in India by 5.7 million litres.

DuPont was one of the world's worst polluters in 1980, even though it spent over US$1 billion a year on waste treatment and pollution control. The company estimates the bill would have been over US$2 billion today had it continued with its strategy of 'back end' programs to mitigate pollution after the event.

The chemical company changed its strategy to pollution prevention through re-engineering projects and now spends a fraction of that – $US400 million – a cost–benefit ratio to be proud of.

One of DuPont's strategic imperatives is to not increase its energy use, no matter how quickly the company grows. Between 1990 and 2012, although production increased by 45%, carbon emissions decreased by 59%, energy use by 6%, hazardous waste by 66% and water use by 12%. Between 2004 and 2013, its GHG emissions dropped 25% and water consumption in water-stressed and water-scarce areas dropped 21%.

Du Pont is making money from sustainable products, too. Between 2011 and 2013, the company gained an additional US$2 billion in revenue from products that reduce GHG emissions and US$11 billion from non-depletable resource-based products.[21]

Build-wise

Green buildings with substantially reduced footprints that capture fresh air, cooling breezes and warming sunshine, generate electricity, harvest roof water directly or indirectly (e.g. through roof gardens), treat grey and black water for recycling, provide natural lighting (reducing eye strain when working on computers which increases productivity and saves on energy use which saves money) and use building panels that clean smog, are springing up in most cities. These measures increase productivity while reducing carbon use and energy bills. They're set to become increasingly in demand in workplaces, signalling to visitors and employees that the organisation cares about the environment.

Many workplaces are renovating their existing buildings and hard landscaping to lower their footprints and reduce overall resource consumption. Initiatives include improving glazing and shading, investing in monitoring equipment and control systems to improve a building's energy efficiency, and upgrading office air-conditioning systems, heating, lighting and ventilation. Chilled beams, movement detectors, and solar shading for lighting and heating/cooling to office areas are other ways to create low-energy offices and factories at little cost.

● THEORY TO PRACTICE

Green buildings

The Pixel building in Melbourne has a perfect six-star rating from the Green Building Council of Australia and the world's highest Leadership in Energy and Environmental Design (LEED) rating from the US Green Building Council, scoring 105 points out of a possible 110 – better than the other 44 000 buildings in 120 countries that have used the LEED rating system (the second-best building in the world scores a meagre 95 points).

The building uses 'Pixelcrete', a special concrete with 60% less embodied carbon in the mix, a low water vacuum toilet system, three rooftop vertical wind turbines, fixed and motorised solar panels, multicoloured facade shading panels, a rainwater filtering roof garden, underfloor air vents that deliver fresh air to offices, and lots of other clever eco-innovations.[22]

Meanwhile, the South Australia Health and Medical Research Institute (SAHMRI) building on North Terrace in Adelaide floats above the Riverbank precinct near the University of Adelaide Medical School, University of South Australia Centre for Cancer Biology and the new Royal Adelaide Hospital, creating the largest bio medical precinct in the southern hemisphere and putting Adelaide on a trajectory to becoming an ecologically sustainable city.

SAHMRI minimises energy use through energy-efficient heating, cooling and ventilation and high levels of outdoor air supply coming from the cooler plaza gardens and a sub-labyrinth that cools air naturally. The building also harvests rainwater, re-uses processed water and uses real-time operational measures such as energy and water consumption to monitor and improve energy efficiency. No drinking water is used for toilet flushing or air cooling. Like the Pixel building, a shell of triangular elements wraps around the building to respond to sunlight, heat load, glare and wind while preserving views and natural light.[23]

Buy-wise

Many organisations are moving to green purchasing, purchasing products and services that have minimal or reduced environmental and human health impacts. Purchasing, for example, alternative-fuel vehicles, bio-based products, energy- and water-efficient products, furniture made from products that use recycled or upcycled materials and non-toxic finishes, green cleaning products, locally made and fair-trade products, and recycled paper, is easy, visible and popular with employees.

It also encourages the market for eco-friendly products to grow. Consider your suppliers' suppliers, too – how sustainable are their operations?

When buying green, factors such as longevity and life cycle are important. Think about:

* how equipment and products were manufactured (their environmental and human impact)
* what happens to the product at the end of its life cycle
* whether products contain harmful chemicals or toxins (ingredients that are toxic to life and can leach into waterways when dumped)
* whether recycled or, better still, upcycled materials (which reduce their environmental impact) were used
* whether you really need it, since the best way to conserve is not to consume in the first place.

It can be daunting to track down the greenest products on the market, but there are databases that make buying green at work easier. For example, ECO-Buy http://www.ecobuy.org.au is a not-for-profit company funded by the Victorian government to encourage the purchasing of green products. Its ECO-Find database lists thousands of green products (those that are less damaging for the environment and/or human health) under a variety of categories, such as energy efficient, greenhouse friendly, low toxicity, recycled content, and water saving.

Other useful websites are:

* http://australia.gov.au > Environment friendly products (links to sites that let you compare appliances and check the fuel consumption of passenger cars, four-wheel drives and light commercial vehicles. The site also provides a link to the national GreenPower accreditation program)
* http://www.deh.gov.au (information about the Commonwealth government environmental purchasing guide and checklists)
* http://www.geca.org.au (Good Environmental Choice Australia or GECA)
* http://www.thegreendirectory.com.au.

● THEORY TO PRACTICE

Sustainable sourcing

Unilever launched an ambitious plan in 2011 to double revenue by 2020 while halving the company's environmental impact. One goal is to source 100% of its agricultural resources sustainably by 2020 with an interim goal of 50% by 2015. When the plan began, the company sourced 10% of its agricultural resources sustainably. One year later, it reached 24%. In 2013, it reached 48%, well on the way to meeting its target. Other goals set for 2020 are to cut by half the greenhouse gas impact of their products across their lifecycle, the water associated with the consumer use of their products and the waste associated with the disposal of their products.

The company builds an economic, product and social mission into all its brands and R&D programs and measures the total impact of its activities across its entire supply chain. It's a data driven company that holds people accountable for achieving targets. To overcome the short-term thinking of managers and the market, Unliever has stopped quarterly reporting so employees can concentrate on the long term. Paul Polman, Unilever's CEO put it like this, 'The fact is, it's unsustainable to have 15% of the world's population using 50% of the resources. Companies that don't want to participate in finding a solution risk being isolated by society.' Polman also said, 'Our form of capitalism has brought us far, but it hasn't solved everything. We think that businesses that are responsible and actually make contributing to society a part of their business model will be successful.'[24]

Energy-wise

The cost of energy increased by about 90% between 2007 and 2013, so reducing energy use is a sound investment. There are lots of easy ways to make an organisation's energy use more sustainable. You can save more than 30% of your energy costs through efficiency strategies such as lighting equipment and policy, air-conditioner temperature settings, variable-speed motors and voltage optimisation (VPO) technologies to reduce power use.[25] (See 'The strategic perspective: Making motors more efficient or even redundant'.)

Air-conditioning accounts for 50% of energy consumption in most buildings and lighting for a further 20–39%. That's a lot of greenhouse gas emissions. These can often be simply addressed: for example, fine-tuning existing systems, cleaning air-conditioning ducts, keeping air-conditioning and plumbing systems in good working order, using energy-efficient light bulbs and natural light when possible, can deliver 10–15% improvements in energy consumption. Get people into the habit of turning lights and equipment off at power points when they're not using them and before going home. Think about turning off water coolers and heaters at night, too.

Set thermostats on air-conditioning and heating a couple of degrees higher in summer and lower in winter, and ask people to dress for the season so they adapt to the environment, not the other way around. Use cold water where possible; for example, when rinsing out coffee cups before putting them in the dishwasher.[26]

Set computers to switch off the monitor after 15 minutes, to turn off the hard drive and system standby after 30 minutes, and to hibernate after two hours. Deactivate screensavers and ask people to turn their screen off when they're not using their computers for more than an hour. Measures like these use less electricity and generate less heat.

◉ THE STRATEGIC PERSPECTIVE

Making motors more efficient or even redundant

Power generation accounts for more than 40% of energy-related CO_2 emissions and industry consumes about 42% of all electricity generated,[27] two-thirds of that is used by electric motors. Variable speed drives, which regulate the speed of a motor, can reduce energy consumption by about 50% in many applications. For example, an energy appraisal showed that the heritage-listed State Library of Victoria could save $155 000 a year, with a payback period of 13 months, simply by replacing its system's existing flow control, which uses throttling valves, with variable speed drives.[28]

Voltage Optimisation (VPO) reduces incoming voltage from the grid to 220 volts or whatever is the optimum for a particular piece of equipment. The average incoming volts exceed this and even though equipment designed to operate on 220 volts draws only that amount, you still pay for the extra (unused) volts the grid sends you. VPO prevents that, leaving the extra energy in the grid, available for other users. VPO technology is designed to last for up to 50 years, so it's a sound investment.[29] But maybe we don't even need motors. Thomas Edison reportedly led visitors to his lab through a turnstile that pumped water up to a roof tank.

You can't get much more sustainable than crowd farming: turning energy from people's movements into electricity. (The term crowd farming was coined by MIT graduate students Thaddeus Jusczyk and James Graham who worked out that 84 162 203 people taking one single step could launch the space shuttle.) Today as passengers push through a revolving door at Driebergen-Zeist railway station in the Netherlands, generators capture some of their energy to power ceiling lights. A grocery store in Gloucester, England, has an energy-harvesting car park: cars drive over 'kinetic road plates', spring-loaded pairs of plates that engage a flywheel that turns generators, which in turn power the store's checkouts.[30]

Reducing demand on traditional systems through relatively simple engineering actions is another way to reduce emissions. For example, using hybrid air-treatment systems such as mixed-mode ventilation (combining natural and mechanical ventilation), natural ventilation or cross-ventilation improves indoor air quality and provides an oxygen-rich air supply that improves people's health, boosting both productivity and energy efficiency. Building control technologies and high-efficiency central energy plant and modern lighting systems garner more energy savings.

The next step might be to purchase 100% accredited green electricity or convert to cleaner burning fuels. When your organisation is ready for more sophisticated measures, which also reap higher returns, think about measures such as:

* green manufacturing
* generating renewable energy
* *geosequestration* (injecting greenhouse gases directly into underground geological formations)
* *biosequestration* (harvesting, i.e. capturing and removing, greenhouse gases using biological processes; for example, practices that enhance soil carbon in agriculture and using vegetation to help offset greenhouse gas emissions, such as commercial tree plantations, forests and woodlands, which take up, that is, *sequester*, carbon dioxide from the atmosphere and release oxygen as they grow; vegetation releases that CO_2 again only when it decomposes or is burnt
* *cogeneration* (reducing greenhouse gas emissions by generating electricity on-site, for example, with natural gas-fired generators, and using the recovered heat from in-house electricity generation to provide heat for the building)
* *trigeneration* (which takes cogeneration one stage further by converting waste heat from cogeneration to help cool the building interior using absorption chillers).

 FYI

Turn off the lights

Only Bahrain, Bolivia, Brunei, Kuwait and Qatar emit more CO_2 per person than Australia. Fortunately, we're small, so we generate only about 1.5% of GHGs. Still, our carbon dioxide emissions are nearly twice the OECD average and more than four times the world average, making us among the world's most prolific polluters per person. Every year, we throw away (and there really is no 'away') 106 000 tons of electronic gear, use more than 64 000 gigalitres of water (64 000 times a billion litres) and print out about 773 million pages (or 93 000 trees-worth) of paper.[31] All this waste is expensive.[32]

Office-wise

Green office programs incorporating the more straightforward measures of eco-buying and being energy-, travel-, waste- and water-wise are good ways to involve all employees. Promoting well-being and work–life balance, and teaching staff to make continuous improvements are other common elements of green office programs.

Other quick and easy ways to green up your office include investing in bike racks and showers, promoting car-pooling, recycling bottles, glass and paper and making double-sided printing the default. Small actions accumulate.

You can take green office programs further by setting challenging environmental and carbon-management targets. More sophisticated strategies such as green construction and refurbishment programs and developing or investing in data collection, management and reporting tools to measure your progress are two other ways to ramp up green office programs.

FYI

Living breathing plants

Did you know that green plants can help improve the air quality in offices? For example, kentia palms, peace lilies and dracaenas can remove about 70% of volatile organic compounds, harmful gases emitted by some types of plastic in chairs, furniture and office appliances.[33]

THEORY TO PRACTICE

Green @ Auntie

In September 2006, the ABC committed to cutting its carbon emissions, waste and water without spending any additional public money. In May 2007, it set up a Green Futures Steering Committee and completed an environmental audit on three of its 68 sites: Adelaide, Canberra and Sydney. Based on the findings, the corporation implemented an environmental management system (EMS) and set ambitious targets to cut its emissions by 40% by 2020 and by 60% by 2050. Progress is reviewed annually to keep the corporation on track and Auntie is already two thirds of the way towards reaching its 2020 target, with emissions down 26.5%.

ABC's Property Services and Green Futures Steering Committee developed and introduced a range of programs to help achieve these targets. These included education and awareness programs and energy management such as adjusting the control set points, changing the start and stop times on air conditioning to suit individual areas, installing solar hot water heaters and, where possible, variable speed drives on air conditioning motors, retrofitting buildings with more efficient lighting, and upgrading inefficient air conditioning and lighting. Even though the business is energy intensive and despite switching to digital radio, adding two more TV channels and many new online websites and features, electricity use is down 5%.

The corporation has also reduced air travel, downsized its vehicle fleet and improved waste management and recycling. Making double sided printing the default setting has reduced paper use by 0.3% a year, or 1.2 reams of paper per full-time equivalent employee, and paper is selected based on environmental performance, with 86% being recycled. Water conservation and purchasing are also under the microscope.

You can check out the ABC's goals and progress, find out step by step how they've done it and even play a great game that tests your knowledge about saving energy at http://www.abc.net. au > Green at Work.[34]

Pack-wise

Overpackaging is an environmental insult. Whether it's cardboard, plastic or Styrofoam™, packaging uses up natural resources, damages the environment in its manufacture (e.g. through excessive water use and GHG emissions) and causes disposal problems. Why use huge amounts of materials needlessly?

Take Styrofoam™. Light and durable it may be, but it's an ecological disaster. It's made from petroleum using a carcinogenic chemical called benzene; it's expensive to recycle and when it is, it's downcycled. It doesn't break down; in fact, it takes up to 30% of the landfills around the world and when it's eaten by animals, it can block their digestive tracts and lead to starvation.

Mushroom packaging is an eco-friendly, sustainable alternative. Waste that can't be burned or fed to animals is placed in a mould along with some mushroom roots, which grow and digest the waste. A week later, the resulting 'cushion' is heat treated to stop further growth and voila! A 100% compostable 'foam' packaging material that uses 98% less energy than 'real' foam packaging to produce.[35]

THEORY TO PRACTICE

The 3Cs of sustainable packaging

When you look at packaging, ask yourself these questions:

- *Content*: What is it made of? Could it be made of something more sustainable?
- *Cube*: How big is the box? Could it be smaller?
- *Curb*: Is it easily recycled?

One of Dell's 24 environmental goals for 2020 is to have 100% sustainable packaging. To this end, it uses biodegradable, local, renewable and sustainable bamboo to protect some of its devices and as packaging for shipping. Bamboo grows quickly, so it's highly renewable. It's strong, so it does the job. Its deep roots help promote healthy soil by protecting against land erosion'. It's compostable and because it's grown close to the company's manufacturing facilities, it reduces delivery distances and therefore the company's packaging-related carbon footprint. The recyclable boxes themselves are partially made from upcycled, readily renewable wheat straw (wheat waste that is otherwise burned, contributing to air pollution), which reduces CO_2 emissions by 160 tonnes and takes about 40% less energy and nearly 90% less water to produce than traditional pulped-paper boxes.

Dell also uses sustainable and compostable packaging and cushioning for heavy products made from mushrooms; it looks and acts like Styrofoam but is much kinder to the environment. The plastic protective bags for their products are not made from oil but from carbon pulled out of the air – from industrial carbon emissions. They generate less carbon than they store, making them carbon-negative.[36]

Resource-wise

Did you know that the amount of waste produced in the making of a semiconductor chip is more than 100000 times its weight? Or that the amount of waste in producing a laptop computer is nearly 4000 times its weight? Every product has a history, and too many of these histories harm the environment.

That's why it's important to examine your entire supply chain and analyse your products' life cycles to find ways to reduce your organisation's negative impact on the planet.

Travel-wise

Promoting sustainable transport by encouraging employees to walk or cycle to work (when you have shower facilities!) and to carpool or use public transport to and from work and meetings (when public transport is cost- and time-effective) are two ways to help employees to travel wisely. Flexibility policies, such as increasing the use of telecommuting and staggering shifts to avoid peak traffic periods, reduce time on the roads and also help attract and retain employees, making serious inroads (pardon the pun) to a cleaner, healthier planet.

The organisation can engage in travel-wise activities itself, so that it doesn't place all the responsibility on employees. Fitting more efficient engines on car fleets and delivery and service vehicles, modifying delivery schedules to reduce traffic delays, replacing standard vehicles with hybrid vehicles, travelling less and holding more virtual meetings, are all relatively easy, economical and effective options.

The entire value chain is also a candidate for more efficient travel. Here are some travel-wise websites to browse for more ideas:

- http://www.transport.vic.gov.au/projects > Travel Smart
- http://www.carbonneutral.com.au
- http://www.greenvehicleguide.gov.au.

THEORY TO PRACTICE

Green wine

Tamburlaine Organic Wines in the Hunter Valley is Australia's largest organic wine producer and the country's first carbon neutral winemaker. Its Environment Management System includes sustainable farming using biodynamic practices; water management, including recycling wastewater, collecting and using roof water, filtering and aerobically treating winery drains and using them for irrigation or, after sterilisation, recycling to the winery; composting solid waste; purchasing environmentally friendly products; and a range of energy efficiency measures.

Energy saving measures include energy efficient lighting, building insulation and ventilation, switching off equipment (lights, computers and so on) when not in use, *power factor control technology* (similar to voltage optimisation technology) and predictive and preventative maintenance. Pumping irrigation water during off peak times achieves a cost savings of 30%, replacing the water treatment aerators reduced running and CO_2 costs by 90% and running vehicles on biofuel saves 10 tonnes of CO_2 a year. The re-engineered refrigerator plant saves $100 000 and 450 tonnes of CO_2 a year and the re-engineered the nitrogen generator has reduced running costs by 75% and generates 60% less CO_2. Future plans include generating solar and wind power.[37]

Water-wise

When you look at a photograph of the earth from a certain angle, it looks like the entire surface of the planet is covered by water. In fact, water covers 75% of the earth's surface, but only 2.5% of water on earth is fresh and most of that fresh water is locked up in polar ice caps and glaciers, leaving just 0.075% of the earth's total water available for the world's animals, people and plants. More than 30% of the drinking water produced worldwide never reaches the customer, thanks mostly to leaky pipes.[38]

Saving scarce water doesn't need to be difficult or expensive. Fixing leaks and installing water-efficient fixtures and fittings such as flow restrictors and tap aerators are quick, cheap and easy to do. Infra-red sensors on urinals, replacing conventional taps with spray models and installing water-displacement devices in cisterns are other easy ways to save water.

Many of these programs yield important, if incremental, returns with quick paybacks; and many organisations have already implemented them. Here are a couple of second-tier options that may be more complicated but that can yield even bigger returns and make even bigger inroads towards a sustainable future. These call for strategic changes to an organisations' business philosophy and operations but will make them more resilient, even in the face of extreme events; they can even create new value.

- Site ecology renewal projects take more thought, time and funding but make large impacts. For instance, where sufficient land is available, companies can create wetlands and water run-offs that allow organisms to treat wastewater naturally in the soil so it can be reused.
- On a larger scale, water metering systems allow cities to identify leaks and changes in water-use patterns so they can respond quickly to water waste and loss in homes, offices or the water distribution network. Kalgoorlie, for example has reduced its water loss by 10% by monitoring water flows.[39]

For some more ideas and information, check out these water-wise websites:

- http://www.ourwaterfuture.com.au
- http://www.awa.asn.au
- http://www.savewater.com.au
- http://www.environment.gov.au.

● THE STRATEGIC PERSPECTIVE

Turn on the tap

The NSW communities of Ashfield, Manly and Bundanoon have each made a decision to ban buying bottled water, which costs about 2000 times more than tap water (much of that cost coming from the plastic bottle, lid and label).

It takes a lot of oil to make the plastic bottles, creating GHG emissions in the manufacturing and distribution processes, and even though they can be recycled, 36% end up as landfill, taking 1000 years to break down – a big waste. Drinking bottled water costs as much energy as driving a car.[40]

Make a bigger difference

Since the Industrial Revolution, products have been designed and manufactured by taking raw materials from the earth, making them into a product and then turning these products into waste when their useful life is over, often dumping them and damaging the environment. This is known as cradle-to-grave production. As you know, the world can no longer replace these resources as fast as humans are taking them, using them and throwing them out.

The resource-wise pecking order, summarised in Figure 24.3, can turn our current overshoot situation around. Think through it at every opportunity. Instead of take–make–waste, think:

$$\text{Avoid} \rightarrow \text{upcycle} \rightarrow \text{reduce} \rightarrow \text{reuse} \rightarrow \text{recycle}$$

Visit the following websites for some good ideas for using resources wisely:

- http://www.wastewise.wa.gov.au
- http://www.wmaa.asn.au
- http://www.sustainability.vic.gov.au.

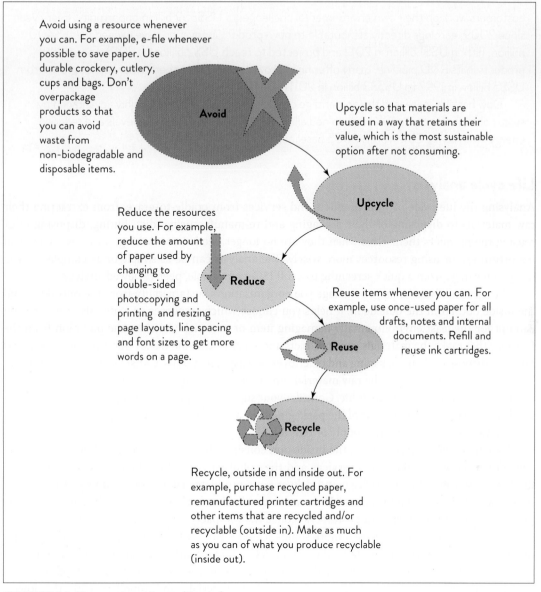

Avoid using a resource whenever you can. For example, e-file whenever possible to save paper. Use durable crockery, cutlery, cups and bags. Don't overpackage products so that you can avoid waste from non-biodegradable and disposable items.

Upcycle so that materials are reused in a way that retains their value, which is the most sustainable option after not consuming.

Avoid

Upcycle

Reduce the resources you use. For example, reduce the amount of paper used by changing to double-sided photocopying and printing and resizing page layouts, line spacing and font sizes to get more words on a page.

Reduce

Reuse items whenever you can. For example, use once-used paper for all drafts, notes and internal documents. Refill and reuse ink cartridges.

Reuse

Recycle

Recycle, outside in and inside out. For example, purchase recycled paper, remanufactured printer cartridges and other items that are recycled and/or recyclable (outside in). Make as much as you can of what you produce recyclable (inside out).

FIGURE 24.3 The resource-wise pecking order

⊙ THEORY TO PRACTICE

From bad to much better

On the wrong side of public opinion for its environmental record, Dow Chemical decided to do something about it in 1992. It began by recruiting a group of leading scientists to help them understand and respond to stakeholder concerns and advise on environmental goals and processes. Among other things, they advised Dow to drop its focus from how to dispose of waste to how to eliminate it completely.

Dow launched 20 years of massive innovation in new products, including solar-cell shingles, and processes, including new health and safety procedures, that together drastically reduced leaks, breaks and spills. As the company improved its sustainability performance, it began helping customers work on their own environmental challenges, a US$359 billion opportunity. Every year since 2009, earnings directly attributable to new-product innovation have exceeded US$400 million, hitting US$1 billion in 2012 and projected to reach US$2 billion by 2015. The value of products in its R&D pipeline, many offering improved sustainability performance, has grown from US$5 billion in 1997 to US$33 billion in 2011.

Dow has also increased the percentage of sales of products that are highly advantaged by sustainable chemistry to 10%, maintained all GHG emissions below 2006 levels and reduced energy intensity by 25% from a 2005 baseline.[41]

Life cycle analysis

Analysing the life cycle of your products and services from cradle-to-grave, from extracting their raw materials to disposing of their packaging and re-manufacturing, distributing, disposing of or reusing the products themselves when they are no longer needed or working, provides an array of opportunities for using resources more wisely. The analysis can be as simple or as complex as you need. You can go from a quick screening to a full ISO-compatible, peer-reviewed analysis.

Life cycle analysis helps you manage your organisation's sustainability from the outside in and the inside out. From the outside in, it helps you choose which resources or materials to use, so you can opt for the least environmentally damaging item or material. Consider the pollution from the factories that make the materials your products and services use, the trucks that transport them and how you dispose of their packaging and of leftover or wasted materials. Consider the incinerator that burns them, or the tip space the raw materials and their packaging that make up your products and services take up at the end of their life. Consider your suppliers' suppliers, too, and how their products measure up. How do you dispose of the packaging they arrive in? Could your suppliers simplify it, or make it more environmentally friendly or reusable?

To manage sustainability from the inside out, consider the pollution from making or providing your organisation's products and services and the pollution created by the products when they're used. How sensibly do you package and deliver your products? How do consumers dispose of or reuse your products and information? How can you make them as low-impact on the environment as possible? How can you help your customers reduce their impact on the environment?

Value chain indices (VCI) are a more sophisticated form of life cycle analysis because they are developed jointly by the integrated value chain. VCIs provide information at brand, factory and individual product level and can be used to compare businesses within a sector to track business performance over time. This helps designers select materials and suppliers with the lowest environmental impact and it helps investment funds select sustainable companies.

● IN A NUTSHELL

What does life cycle analysis involve?

A life cycle analysis includes:

- measuring the energy and other resources associated with materials extraction and the production of goods
- measuring the environmental emissions (acidification, eco-toxicological and human-toxicological pollutants, GHG, smog) that result from the manufacture, assembly, distribution, use and disposal of purchased and produced goods

»

- considering the impact on the environment (e.g. depletion of fossil fuels, desertification and land, minerals and raw materials used in the production, distribution, use and disposal of purchased and produced goods)
- considering all intervening transportation steps needed and resources used for a product or service.

● THE STRATEGIC PERSPECTIVE

The life-cycle cost of paper

The environmental impacts associated with paper at each stage of its life cycle are significant:

- *Producing the raw materials*: To produce 1 tonne of new office paper, 12–24 trees are logged (18 trees for every 10 employees every year), plus 98 tonnes of other resources, are used.
- *Producing the paper itself*: A vast amount of energy is consumed, dangerous chemicals that produce chemical emissions are used, and waste is created as a by-product.
- *Disposing of it*: Each tonne of paper dumped takes up approximately 1 cubic metre of valuable space (a cost to the environment) and as it decomposes it emits large amounts of methane and carbon dioxide, both greenhouse gasses.

The world's forests are its lungs, converting carbon dioxide into oxygen and supplying us with breathable air while helping to maintain a constant global average temperature, anchoring fertile soil, reducing soil salinity and providing a comprehensive wildlife habitat. Paper accounts for 42% of logged trees and cutting down forests accounts for 25% of the annual carbon emissions caused by human activity, speeding up climate change and causing soil erosion.

Making 1 tonne of pulp for paper for most types of printing requires almost 4.5 tonnes of wood to be cut and transported. Recycled pulp requires only 1.4 tonnes of recovered paper, uses less water and results in less pollution discharged in wastewater.[42]

Avoid or upcycle

Traditional manufacturing begins with a chunk of wood or metal and keeps removing it until the desired shape is reached. The 3D printing process does the opposite. It avoids using material by starting from nothing and adding material until the desired shape is reached. Early studies indicate this uses more than 40% less material over a product's life cycle. The other side of producing more with less is accelerating conspicuous consumption, which is the last practice we need.[43]

John Sawhill, President and CEO of the Nature Conservancy, the world's largest private conservation group, noted 'In the end, our society will be defined not only by what we create, but by what we refuse to destroy.'[44] This is where avoiding and upcycling come in.

Although most companies begin their sustainability journey by using less, the logic turns on its head when designing (or redesigning) a product and how to produce it based on upcycling. Upcycling principles include designing methods to recover the materials used to produce the product when it is at the end of its useful life. Ironically, this means you don't have to worry about using less. In fact, it's better to use more, because when you use only small amounts of a material, it's difficult to recover for recycling or upcycling. Using less only makes sense when the product is to be dumped.

Natural products can decompose and be reused in an endless cycle of renewal. Upcycling, or cradle-to-cradle production, achieves the same cycle of renewal. Assessing every material used in a product to determine whether it is safe for the ecosystem and how it can be reused in a way that retains its value creates a 'virtuous cycle' of materials, making upcycling a far better alternative to destroying, downcycling or dumping products.

Companies that take this route find a new meaning to the adage 'stay close to your customer' because their customers also supply their raw materials. This means they need to forecast future demand as well as future returns, which depends in part on the anticipated life cycle of the product; products with long life cycles may require manufacturers to plan for interim material supplies for the first few years.

Cradle-to-cradle producers also need to work out the logistics of getting their used products back to the factory for reprocessing. Depending on the product, customers could, for example, post it back or drop it into a retail outlet; for other products, the company might need to arrange collection of used products and organise routes and timings to use transport efficiently. This is a bit more work, but the good news is that it virtually guarantees repeat sales and dramatically increases an organisation's sustainability (see 'Case study 24.1: Keeping carpets out of the tip' on page 798 to find out more about cradle-to-cradle manufacturing.

● THEORY TO PRACTICE

Earth-friendly printers
French company Markem-Imaje makes industrial printers for marking 'best before' dates on containers for beverages, food, pharmaceuticals and other consumer products. Although it competes with companies manufacturing in countries with much cheaper labour, its high quality printers use solvent-free ink, causing minimal environmental damage, which provides a sustainable solution that its European customers are willing to pay for.[45]

Reduce and simplify

Many companies begin by weeding out toxic materials and/or hazardous chemicals from what they purchase and produce. There are two ways to do this: one is to send a list of prohibited chemicals to suppliers, and the other is to collect detailed information from suppliers about the chemicals in their products and then evaluate the impact of those chemicals on environmental and human health. However, working backwards like this is painstaking and slow.

Redesigning products using *eco-design* principles is often quicker and more effective. The ultimate goal is to design products that can be upcycled and to ensure that any materials that can't be upcycled can be cost-effectively recycled so that it is cheaper to buy those materials reprocessed than new. For instance, up to 75% of steel and more than 50% of aluminium is recycled, mostly because this uses a fraction of the energy needed to produce new metal.[46]

As a producer, when you can't avoid using a material or you can't redesign a product for upcycling, your next best option is to minimise the number and types of materials used. But there is a caveat: reducing resource use should be carried out in a way that doesn't make the product more difficult or impossible to recycle; potato chip bags, for example, are composed of so many ultrathin layers that they are impossible to recycle economically.[47]

Using fewer materials reduces both supply-chain complexity and the number of suppliers you need to deal with. When you reduce the number and types of materials you use, you generally use more of the remaining materials, making it easier to negotiate volume discounts and keep costs down. It also improves the service of suppliers because of the increased volume of business you give them, and it makes the product easier to recycle.

Reuse or recycle

Reusing and recycling are your next best options. Recycling bottles, cans, cardboard, furniture, paper and old equipment is popular. Several national recycling programs have been operating for a number of years, making it relatively straightforward to organise recycling for items such as batteries, computers, mobile phones and printer cartridges. Some offer the choice of using commercial or charity-based recycling programs. In either case, the resources are recycled or reused and saved from the tip.

But here is another caveat: a lot of recycling is actually downcycling. Although it is preferable to dumping or burning these items, recycling is energy-intensive and usually water-intensive, too. That's why upcycling and not using a material at all, thus minimising waste produced at the source by reducing and simplifying, are more effective.

● THE STRATEGIC PERSPECTIVE

The real cost of gadgets and gizmos

Computers, mobile phones, personal digitals assistants, tablets and TVs. We love our gadgets, but not only do they need huge amounts of energy to run, they also emit huge amounts of GHGs, rivalling those of even the aviation industry. When you upgrade and chuck the old ones out, they continue to do damage.

People recycle only 5% of their mobile phones worldwide – a huge waste of resources. Of the three million computers bought in Australia every year, 75% end up in landfill and only 9% are recycled. Arsenic, asbestos, cadmium, chromium, lead, polychlorinated biphenyls and polyvinyl chloride can all seep out of electronic waste in landfills and seriously damage ecosystems. In fact, e-waste is being sent to landfill at three times the rate of general waste and is responsible for 70% of the toxic chemicals found in landfill. Japanese landfill now contains three times the gold, silver and indium (used in coating LCD – liquid crystal display – screens) and six times the platinum the world uses in one year.[48]

The European Community Waste Electrical and Electronic Equipment Directive (WEEE Directive) 2012 sets collection, recycling and recovery targets for electrical goods.[49] It makes electrical and electronic equipment manufacturers responsible for collecting (at no charge to private users) and disposing of their equipment by ecological disposal or reuse/refurbishment; it aims to recycle 85% of electrical and electronic waste. The Australian government introduced a national e-waste recycling scheme in 2011, which also covers other categories of waste. Read about it at http://www.environment.gov.au > National television and computer recycling scheme.

● THEORY TO PRACTICE

Surprising uses for wool

Polystyrene or polyethylene insulation is normally used to keep food chilled during transit. Both are man-made, oil-based products that are not easily disposed of. Angela Morris designed a container that uses sheep's wool, a 'smart fibre' with hygroscopic properties that absorbs and releases moisture from the air to create consistent temperatures. The Wool Packaging Company in the UK, where sheep wool is an abundant and sustainable resource, now markets a system of eco-friendly insulated packaging.

Wool packaging is cost-effective and performs better than the equivalent polystyrene packaging. It has lots of environmental benefits too. For instance, even the coarsest fleeces

>>

require minimal processing. The sludge from washing the fleeces is used for natural fertilisers and slug pellets and the natural lanolin is extracted for use in cosmetics and pharmaceuticals. Big savings are made delivering the fleeces, too. One vehicle can deliver 25 times more wool packaging than it can polystyrene packaging. Wool packaging also removes the need to send polystyrene packaging to landfill. Find out more at http://www.woolcool.com.[50]

Collaborate

Work with your supply chain to ensure they provide clean, green products and find out what your downstream customers want from you regarding sustainability.

Work with your competitors, too. Surprising as this may sound, it's an excellent strategy for sustainability. Coca-Cola, for instance, has teamed with its suppliers, the Consumer Goods Forum, Greenpeace and even its archrival PepsiCo to find substitutes for hydrofluorocarbons, the dangerous greenhouse gas used in refrigeration. What areas of common concern does your organisation have with competitors that you can work on together, even while competing elsewhere? (Coke and Pepsi may compete on taste, distribution networks and marketing, but no one picks their product based on how their vending machines work.)

Collaboration makes sense because new technology can be expensive in the early stages until economies of scale are reached. Collaboration can help spread the development cost and the cost of building the market.[51]

Build platforms

Microsoft Windows and Shaw Industries' sustainable carpet-tile processing technology (described in 'Case study 24.1: Keeping carpets out of the tip' on page 798) are known as platforms. Microsoft leveraged several products off Windows, and Shaw Industries used its knowledge and sustainable carpet-tile technology to move into broadloom carpets. Platforms like these can multiply cost savings and drive up profitability through economies of scale and economies of scope.

Using fewer resources and upcycling can establish sustainable platforms for entire product lines. Patagonia, the US outdoor retailer, follows this strategy via its Worn Wear Program, which produces economies of both scale and scope. Find out more at http://www.patagonia.com/us > Inside Patagonia > Worn Wear and http://www.shawfloors.com/shaw-sustainability/ where you can also read about Shaw's cradle-to-cradle recycling and read its sustainability report.

⊙ THEORY TO PRACTICE

Winning when you're between a rock and a hard place

You have a dilemma when you're in the energy business: on the one hand, investors want to make money and consumers want cheap electricity, making cheap and dirty coal a good option for generating electricity. On the other hand, consumers and the wider community want lower carbon emissions. On top of that, there's the complex regulatory environment that varies from country to country.

The Hong Kong-based CLP Group followed US thinker Buckminster Fuller's advice: 'You never change things by fighting the existing reality. To change something, build a new model that makes the existing model obsolete.'[52]

>>

To this end, the CLP Group developed a new business model that shows how new platforms can help. It can balance renewable and non-renewable sources of energy generation across the Asia-Pacific region to cater for changing regulations and technologies, optimising when and how to use low-carbon energy sources, including hydro-electric, solar and wind power, and understanding how to make emerging technologies for alternative energy sources workable. Investors are happy too. CLP is outperforming on the S&P Index of electric utilities by 20% and its price/earnings ratio rose 41% (compared with a 10% decline for other electric utilities).

Once the company accepted it needed to move away from fossil fuels to generate electricity, it recruited dozens of engineers with green energy competencies. Together, they increased the percentage of electricity coming from renewable sources from less than 1% in 2004 to more than 23.8% in 2012. Sadly, that number dropped to 19.4% in 2013 for the first time since adopting the new business model as a result of acquiring the Mount Piper and Wallerawang power stations in Australia and increasing production from the Jhajjar power station in India.[53]

Implement your sustainability programs

Once you have agreed which programs to adopt, plan their implementation. Assign activities, responsibilities and success measures to those involved in implementing the programs and make sure everyone involved in implementing understands their deliverables.

Think about developing an education program for employees and external customers on sustainability matters and informing your organisation's customers of what you are doing and how they can help you protect the environment; a program like this can be an important marketing tool and another way to increase consumer loyalty (protect your implementation plans as described on page 503.

The process of developing the sustainability policy, identifying, developing and implementing sustainability programs, and consulting and communicating with stakeholders is summarised in Figure 24.4.

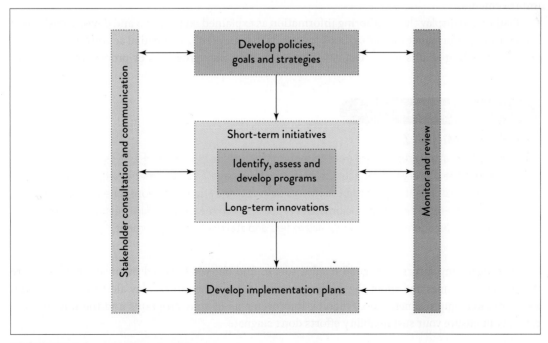

FIGURE 24.4 Increasing sustainability

Myth: We have to save the earth

Nature doesn't give a hoot if human beings are here or not. The planet has survived cataclysmic and catastrophic changes for millions upon millions of years and 99% of all species have come and gone. Saving the environment is really about saving *our* environment – making it safe for ourselves, our children and the world as we know it. If more people saw the issue as saving themselves, we would probably see increased motivation and commitment to actually do so.[54]

3. Monitoring the results of sustainability policies and programs

In my view, people will be increasingly motivated and able to access information about corporate behaviour for a variety of reasons, not least the fact that it is such an important driver of sustainable financial performance.

David Morgan (economist), quoted in Stuart, 'Measuring the immeasurable' (June 2008)[55]

Formally review your sustainability policy and programs at least annually to ensure their ongoing relevance and to incorporate any changes required by legislation, public demand or best practice and make best use of current and emerging technologies and approaches.

Regularly monitor and document the outcomes of the sustainability policy and programs and use the information to provide feedback to stakeholders as part of your ongoing communications on sustainability matters. Follow the four steps to monitoring explained on page 505 and 'Step 7: Monitor and evaluate results' on page 537. You can also use the Plan–Do–Check–Act cycle (monitoring is the 'check' in this cycle) or Ishikawa's expanded six-step cycle (explained on page 587) to ensure your plans achieve the results intended and to find areas in which to make improvements.

Gather and display the monitoring information as explained on page 585 and devise a dashboard showing key performance measures. Look for trends that may require remedial action and investigate any disappointing results so you can act to improve the policy programs or procedures as soon as possible.

Monitoring Mission Zero

Two types of quarterly reports are used to monitor the results of InterfaceFLOR's Mission Zero™ (discussed in the 'Theory to Practice: Green flooring' on page 778). Ecometrics reports, which provide a range of quantitative progress measures including carbon emissions, energy use and water and waste reduction. And sociometrics reports, which measure qualitative improvements in areas such as education, environmental awareness and stakeholder engagement.[56]

Investigate any surprisingly good results, too, to find out what caused them so you can ensure the success continues and adopt the factors promoting it in other areas. Stay alert to opportunities for continuous improvement, too. Ongoing improvements to your programs and the way they are carried out ensure your sustainability efforts don't stagnate.

CourseMateExpress

Go to http://login.cengagebrain.com to access CourseMate Express, your online study tool for *Management Theory & Practice*. CourseMate Express brings chapter concepts to life with interactive learning, and study and exam preparation tools:

- Test your skills in different aspects of management with interactive self-tests and simulations.
- Watch videos that show how real managers operate in real businesses.
- Test your understanding of the changing world of management by taking the revision quiz.

QUICK REVIEW

1. Summarise and explain the steps in developing a sustainability policy and strategies.
2. Explain the resource-wise pecking order and why it is ordered as it is.
3. Discuss the role of monitoring in increasing an organisation's sustainability.

BUILD YOUR SKILLS

1. Dr Goran Carstedt, the former president of Swedish Volvo and former head of IKEA Retail Europe, said in an interview: 'Corporations have a tremendously important role in our future, almost more important than nations in terms of how to create value and wealth and distribute it. If we want to have a future that is financially viable, socially viable and ecologically viable, that has to be part of the corporate agenda.'[57] Do you agree? Why or why not? How do these comments fit in with corporate responsibility and sustainability?
2. Prepare a report summarising your organisation's sustainability initiatives, their results, and recommending improvement opportunities; explain your rationale behind each recommendation in terms of ease of application and estimated costs versus benefits.
3. Develop an electronic file of information on sustainability; use relevant sub-file titles such as 'benchmarks', 'green providers', 'policy development' and 'recyclers'.

WORKPLACE ACTIVITIES

1. Discuss how climate change could affect your organisation over the next 10–15 years; consider its supply chain in your discussion.
2. Describe your organisation's short-term actions and medium- to long-term plans to operate more sustainably. What benefits to the organisation itself and its shareholders and other stakeholders are expected to result?
3. List the key elements and intentions of your organisation's sustainability policy; if your organisation does not have a sustainability policy, list the key elements you believe a sustainability policy should contain and what the organisation's overall strategy and intentions should be regarding the environment.
4. List as many ways as you can think of that your organisation could make money from sustainability.

5. Is your organisation barely green, light green, medium green or dark green? How appropriate do you believe this strategy is, given your organisation's customers, employee profile and shareholder base?

6. List and summarise your organisation's programs for sustainable operations and the goals of each program.

CASE STUDY 24.1

KEEPING CARPETS OUT OF THE TIP

Shaw Industries, a large company based in Georgia, USA, made nylon carpet tiles for commercial customers around the world. When they reached the end of their life, 95% of these carpet tiles went to landfill. When Shaw decided to make virtuous recycling its goal, it went back to the drawing board to rethink its production processes.

The designers searched for a more sustainable solution and eventually chose an eco-friendly polyolefin backing to replace the traditional PVC plastic (a potentially toxic material that is difficult to recycle). Both the backing (which holds the carpet tiles flat) and the nylon face fibre (the walking surface) can be recycled endlessly without losing performance or functionality.

Shaw then developed a production system that can take the carpet back at the end of its life, separate the backing from the walking surface, grind it up and reuse it as backing for new carpet tiles. The company also found a way to upcycle the nylon that used 20% less energy and 50% less water than using brand new nylon, making it cheaper than new nylon.

As well as giving Shaw a fully sustainable product, upcycling also freed the company from price fluctuations and shortages of raw materials. Petroleum, the main input for both the backing and the nylon face fibre of traditionally made carpets, is both non-sustainable and subject to wide price fluctuations.

Radically redesigning its production process wasn't easy and it took courage – the unproven technology required a US$2 million investment and, if it worked, it would make the rest of Shaw's production facilities obsolete. In addition, the company had no concrete evidence that customers would value sustainability in carpeting.

But the gamble paid off. Oil prices rose dramatically after Shaw's move to upcycling and the company has grown its business by leveraging its technology to move into the broadloom carpet market, which accounts for more than 70% of the entire carpeting market.[58]

Questions

1. Summarise the principles of upcycling illustrated in this case study.
2. Shaw's investment seemed like a huge gamble. What five points would you have made to convince Shaw's directors to make the investment? Would these same points persuade your organisation's directors to take such a big risk to move towards virtuous recycling?

CASE STUDY 24.2

CHILD CARE AT THE SEASIDE

Emma sits down feeling slightly overwhelmed. Newly appointed as the director of the Seaside Childcare Centre, she feels she has enough to do without worrying about the welfare of the worm farm. After all, she's responsible for the care of 48 children under the age of six for five days a week, 46 weeks a year, as well as the 17 staff who work across the three care rooms.

Emma is struggling with how to incorporate sustainability into the centre. A key part of the National Quality Assurance Standards under which the centre is accredited, Emma knows that they must not only demonstrate commitment now, but also have policies indicating their plans for improving their sustainability – all to be shown to the assessor who is evaluating the centre next week.

Emma learned about sustainability in her Diploma in Children's Services and believes that it has to be addressed from three angles. First, in the way the centre is managed, making sure they save energy and recycle when possible. Easy, the signs next to each light switch and by the bins solve that. Sure the staff don't always remember, but at least they're trying.

Second, they have to communicate what they are doing to their community, mainly the parents of the children in their care. Well, the monthly newsletter can take care of that, though it doesn't seem as straightforward as Emma imagined. 'If only I could think of something to write' she sniffs. 'I mean, doesn't everyone recycle?'

Third, they have to help the children connect with their environment. The worm farm *was* part of that, but the worms died when no one watered them in the hot weather. The hermit crab had gone the same way as the worms. And we can't have flowers because that would attract bees and that's a WH&S issue. 'Ah, the landscaping!' she thinks. We've got logs and river stones so it looks more natural. There are the plans for the vegetable garden too, though that won't be built for a few months yet. Maybe that's enough. Yeah, right.'

Emma's thoughts drift to the nearby Sandy Bay Childcare Centre which, she happens to know, only achieved 'Working towards National Quality Standard' on their assessment in the sustainability section. Not a good result, and it means that they will be assessed again soon. 'Bodes ill for us,' thinks Emma; 'Sandy Bay has all the same things in place as Seaside. They even have chooks as well as worms – live worms at that. What am I going to do?'

Questions

1. Does Emma have a compliance (barely green), efficiency (light green), strategically proactive (medium green) or ideological commitment (dark green) view of sustainability? What could she do differently?
2. Outline three areas in which Emma could operate the centre under eco-efficiency principles and explain why the areas you select are important.
3. Why is continuous improvement an effective process for implementing sustainability practice in a business environment such as a childcare centre?

PART

5

WORKPLACE PRACTICE

An organisation's workplace practices establish the working environment it provides for its employees. This is more than lighting, work stations and equipment. It relates to the entire package the organisation and individual managers provide in terms of how employees are recruited, managed, trained and developed, and looked after as people.

Do you recruit people carefully, people who are naturally inclined to do the type of work you offer and who can contribute to your organisation in a variety of ways? Do you include a range of people – from different age groups, backgrounds, cultures, experiences and lifestyles – on your team? Do you induct and train employees properly and provide opportunities to continually develop their skills and potential? Do you provide a safe and healthy workplace that affords people dignity? Do you have systems that help employees balance or blend their private lives with their working lives? Do you give them opportunities to get together to develop plans, keep up to date with the organisation's events and results, make improvements and solve problems?

These activities influence how good a job people want to do and are able to do. They influence the type of people organisations are able to attract to work for them and how long organisations are able to retain them. They influence whether organisations are able to make the best use of employees' skills and abilities and draw on their ideas and experience. In short, they influence how successful an organisation is and how well it is positioned for the future.

This part helps you develop a working environment that attracts, develops and retains the employees your organisation needs to succeed.

RECRUITING AND INDUCTING EMPLOYEES

You may have heard the saying that 'one bad apple soon spoils the whole barrel' or the term 'a square peg in a round hole'. Managers who recruit and induct poorly have constant 'rotten apple' and 'square peg' headaches. Everyone who leads and manages people has a critical role to play in attracting and retaining the employees the organisation needs to succeed.

Although it can be difficult to find the right person to fill a vacancy, and sometimes just as difficult to wait patiently until you find that right person, employing an unsuitable person guarantees even bigger headaches, not just in terms of productivity but also in terms of the morale of the rest of the team and in divesting yourself of your mistake. (While it can be hard to find the right person, it's even harder to fire the wrong person.) Worse still is finding the right person and then failing to recruit or induct and manage that person properly.

The process of matching people to positions so that employees can be motivated and engaged begins with a strong employer brand and employer value proposition. Although these are in the purview of the board, senior managers and the organisation's human resource specialists, you need to understand them both. When you don't, you may unwittingly undermine them and cost your organisation a good recruit. You must also understand and support your organisation's career pathing, sustainability, work–life balance and other policies because these are important factors in attracting and retaining employees.

1. Do you know how to use the six tools at your disposal to make the best possible match between candidates, your vacancy and your organisation?
2. Do you know what happens during the recruitment process when a vacancy arises?
3. Are you able to plan and lead an effective behavioural interview in order to make a sound selection decision?
4. Do you know how to induct people who join your team, monitor how well they are doing and help them to reach the required standards of performance quickly?

This chapter explains how to use your organisation's employer brand and employer value proposition to attract the right candidates and select the right person to fill a vacancy. You also find out how to welcome recruits and help them contribute quickly to your team.

The thousand-dollar question

Sesh gazes at her computer screen, considering the people management options on her organisation's Intranet. She clicks on 'recruiting and selecting', muttering 'Where to begin?'

Her most experienced cost accountant has just given four weeks notice and she wants to find a replacement as soon as possible. The information says to begin with a role analysis: What outcomes does she want the role to achieve? What tasks need to be carried out? What are the role's key responsibilities? Can she rearrange duties within her team to eliminate the need to recruit? Or can she reassign duties so she can recruit someone with a different skill set from the person she is replacing? There's a lot to think about.

After completing her role analysis, she can update the role description and develop a person specification describing the 'ideal position-holder'. Then she can meet with one of the organisation's preferred recruitment agencies and use this information to brief them on the vacancy. They will search their database of potential candidates, arrange electronic and print advertising and provide Sesh's IT people with an internal vacancy announcement for their Intranet and corporate website.

The recruitment agency may also undertake a limited search for suitable candidates using their networks, depending on how difficult they expect filling the vacancy to be. According to the website, the agency screens and interviews suitable applicants and then gives Sesh a shortlist of candidates who meet her person specification and the organisation's overall needs to recruit people whose values enable them to bond with the organisation and its goals. Sesh then interviews these candidates and makes the final selection.

A paragraph in bold grabs her attention. It refers to the organisation's employer brand and employer value proposition (EVP) and stresses how important it is that she use these to shape her discussions with the candidates and reinforce them to the candidates when she meets with them. The next paragraph refers her to the organisation's various policies, particularly those on flexible working, corporate social responsibility and sustainability, stressing that she needs to be familiar with these as they form an important part of the organisation's EVP and she needs to be able to discuss them with candidates.

Sesh quickly checks the section on recruitment interviewing and sees some interview guidelines. She diaries to review that section and the key policies more thoroughly to refresh her memory before interviewing the candidates. She fully understands her dual role of genuinely representing the position and the organisation to candidates (almost a selling role, she thinks) and determining how well each candidate would fulfil the role and contribute to the team, and how well the candidates' aspirations fit her job and the culture of her organisation and department (really a buying role).

Sesh figures this is more than a four-week process and decides to arrange for temporary help. 'Better do that first,' she thinks, clicking over to the temporary help section.

1. Making the best match

Hire for attitude. Train for skills.

Herb Kelleher (co-founder, US South West Airlines), 'Hire for attitude, train for skill', Harvard Business Review (1 February 2011)[1]

Google has more than 200 applicants for every vacancy.[2] Few other – if any – organisations can advertise a vacancy and then sit back and wait for eager applicants to beat their doors down. Recruitment is really a 'buying' as well as a 'selling' exercise. On the one hand, you need to find the person best suited to carrying out the work (that's the 'buying' part). On the other hand, you need to attract suitable candidates and then promote the position and the organisation to encourage the most suitable person to accept it (the 'selling' part).

The three 'buying' tools that help you identify and select the person best suited to your vacancy are the *job* or *role analysis,* job or role description and person specification. Together, they help you determine the specific duties and tasks of a vacancy and which candidate would best fill that vacancy.

Two 'selling' tools that help you attract suitable applicants to your organisation are your organisation's employer brand and its employer value proposition (EVP). These are designed to attract candidates who are suited to the organisation and can be energised by its vision and values and engaged by helping to contribute to what it stands for – provided, of course, that the reality of the organisation matches its promises.

Your third 'selling' tool is yourself. No one is more important than you, and the image you present, in encouraging the most suitable candidate to accept the position. Being the sort of person candidates want to work for because you offer what they're looking for in a boss isn't just as easy as 'being yourself' because people from different cultures and different generations look for different qualities in the person they work for.

THE STRATEGIC PERSPECTIVE

Do you really need to recruit?

Maybe training an existing employee would be a better option than recruiting a new employee. Perhaps engaging a contractor or temporary employee would be better.

When deciding, think about costs. It's generally the least expensive to train an existing employee and most expensive to bring in a contractor. But what about the risks? Getting a new hire up to speed often takes a bit less time than training and developing someone from scratch but both take time and the dual risk is that they might leave, or you may not need those skills in five years. On the other hand, most contractors get up to speed quickly – but you pay a premium.

When you're confident in your ability to retain employees and that the skills you're developing are going to meet the medium-term needs of the organisation, training an existing employee or spending time helping a new recruit learn the ropes makes sense. Otherwise it might be better to pay more and reduce your risk by bringing in a contractor. But do that only for special, one-off work rather than for essential on-going work; the latter makes contractors indispensable as well as expensive.

Position analyses

Your first step in successful recruitment is to understand precisely what the position is intended to achieve and the environment in which it is carried out. This is known as a *job analysis* when both the goals and tasks needed to carry them out are clear, and a *role analysis* when the position's goals are clear but the tasks needed to achieve them are less clearly defined. For the sake of simplicity, we'll use the term *position analysis* to cover both. The position analysis involves:

* examining the training document for the position (someone else may have already done the analysis for you)
* observing the position holder(s) while they work
* talking to the position holder(s).

You probably don't need to analyse a position to this extent every time someone leaves your team. However, you should always think about how you might reallocate or recombine duties and responsibilities in order to make better use of the rest of the team's skills and abilities and to accommodate any employee's desire to take on additional or different duties or responsibilities. It's a good idea to check exit interviews for the position, too, as these can highlight important points about the vacancy.

A position analysis also helps you spot where changes to the duties would allow people to work more smoothly or efficiently and where additional resources such as equipment might be needed.

Once you have made the changes you want to make, you can write or update the position description and the person specification. (You can also use position analyses to prepare job breakdowns for training and for developing standard operating procedures.)

ACTION!

You can find a Position analysis template on **CourseMateExpress**. This will guide you as you think through duties and responsibilities of the vacancy.

FYI

Job design

Job design is an important ingredient in employee satisfaction and performance. Boring, monotonous jobs hold people back. Well-designed positions that allow employees as much control as practical over how, when and where tasks are carried out, and offer a variety of tasks, help people perform well. Well-designed positions also have clear goals and measures of success, allow position-holders to complete a whole job or piece of work and stretch their skills. (See page 334 for more information on job design.)

Position descriptions

Position descriptions are clear and concise snapshots of a position. They contain specific language, such as 'able to communicate technical information to non-technical people' rather than 'good communication skills', or 'answering the telephone and taking messages, filing, sorting and distributing correspondence' rather than 'general administrative duties'.

Position descriptions help the organisation and employees in several ways, including:
- acting as reference points for training and developing position-holders
- allowing pay and grading systems to be structured fairly, logically and transparently
- clarifying the organisation's expectations of position-holders
- helping you to match people to positions
- preventing arbitrary interpretation of whether positions are being carried out successfully
- preventing arbitrary interpretation of a position's content and limits
- providing a basis for assessing and reviewing performance.

Position descriptions generally list the internal and external relationships, responsibilities and accountabilities of position-holders and any other information that is relevant to the position. Additional information might include the requirement to work overtime, to lift heavy loads or to travel away from home regularly.

Even a position description only a few years old can be out of date, so always review it and update it as necessary. You can write position descriptions in many formats; choose the format that best suits your needs or follow your organisation's standard format. When you write them up, omit targets, because targets change, and make sure you aren't asking for too much – jobs must be doable. Follow the guidelines on pages 845 and 847 so that your position descriptions are not discriminatory.

Job descriptions

Job descriptions are fairly prescriptive about the the job-holder's tasks and duties. Avoid the temptation to write a laundry list of tasks and responsibilities; instead, aim to provide a sense of the job's priorities (see page 111 for how to write a job purpose statement). Figure 25.1 shows a typical job description form.

XZY Pty Ltd
Job description

Position title:...

Department:...

Reports to:...

Job purpose:..

....

....

Key duties or tasks:..

....

....

Consults with (internal relationships with customers and suppliers):

....

....

Term of employment (if a fixed period):

....

FIGURE 25.1 Common contents of job descriptions

 **ACTION!**

You can find a Job description template on **CourseMateExpress** to use for positions with clear-cut duties.

Competency-based job descriptions

In addition to listing a job's duties, competency-based job descriptions also list the knowledge and skills needed to successfully perform those duties. They are not a 'wish list', so again, limit yourself to the skills and knowledge that are *essential* to carrying out the job successfully.

When a competency-based job description is available, you may not need to prepare a separate person specification, because the job description already contains the knowledge and skills required of the job-holder. However, you may want to add the attributes needed to do the job successfully to the person specification. (You can also use competency-based job descriptions to appraise performance and assess training needs for individual job-holders.)

● ACTION!

You can find a Competency-based job description template on **CourseMate**Express. This helps you list the skills and knowledge required to carry out the position.

● THE STRATEGIC PERSPECTIVE

Think about the long-term, too
Think about the organisation's strategy and vision so the people you hire don't just fill a position for today or tomorrow but help build the organisation for the future.

Role descriptions

Organisations building a performance-focused work culture have moved away from the traditional 'narrow' job descriptions specifying the duties and tasks people are expected to perform, towards broader role descriptions describing value-adding behaviours and functions rather than tasks. Value-adding behaviours might be, for example, continuous improvement of work systems and processes, proactive team work, or problem identification and resolution, while functions might be customer service, policy development or generation of publicity through electronic media.

Role descriptions identify the areas or groups that a position serves and stress end results that are important to the organisation, often in terms of key result areas (KRAs), or areas of responsibility and accountability. In effect, role descriptions say:

* These are our overall goals and this is what we are trying to achieve with this role.
* Here are some ways you can add value (KRAs).

When plenty of feedback on results is provided, role-holders can figure out ways to help the organisation achieve its goals. One framework for developing role descriptions is:

* *Inputs*: This is what you can normally expect to work with.
* *Outputs*: These are some ways you can add value to these inputs.
* *Outcomes*: This is what we want you to achieve in the short term.
* *Impacts*: This is what we want you to help us achieve longer term.

Describing a role this way allows role-holders latitude in how they approach their role and to behave in original ways, and the scope to take on new responsibilities. It also gives organisations the flexibility to adjust employees' roles to respond to operational needs.

● ACTION!

You can find a Role description template on **CourseMate**Express to use with positions with clear goals but when the tasks required to achieve them are less clear-cut.

● IN A NUTSHELL

How to write role descriptions
The key to writing role descriptions is for employees, managers and internal customers and suppliers to work together. There are four approaches:

1. *A pair of employees* who perform similar roles complete a form or questionnaire on their responsibilities and performance expectations, checking with the other employees and managers concerned and modifying as necessary.
2. *A team of three or four employees* complete the role questionnaire. This method is good when lots of people perform similar roles or the same role in several departments. Keep the team numbers relatively small to ensure the process is efficient and consensus can be reached.
3. *A manager and role-holder work together* to complete the role questionnaire. This works well when employees are new to a role, when there are performance or role clarity concerns or when a role is undergoing major changes.
4. *A single employee or manager* completes the role questionnaire. This is fine when only one employee carries out a role or when the position is vacant or new. Because it is the least collaborative, this is the least preferred approach.

Person specifications

Armed with an up-to-date position description, you can ask: What skills, knowledge and attributes does an employee need to do this job successfully? This helps you to pinpoint your *selection criteria* by developing a person specification that describes the person best suited to the work. The person specification describes an imaginary ideal position-holder who would not only enjoy the work and do it well but also engage with the company and its culture and values; this is important for both attracting and retaining employees. Develop it by referring to:

- The position description: What must the position-holder know or be able to do in order to perform well? Think about the abilities, knowledge and skills that would complement those that currently exist in your team. (Remember, though, that it's far easier to train skills and provide information than train attributes and values.)
- The organisation's employer value proposition and employer brand: What sort of person would be most engaged in your organisation? Think about the attributes and values employees need in order to engage with your organisation and flourish from working there – perhaps courtesy, energy, high standards, honesty, integrity, self-discipline, sociability or a strong work ethic. (These attributes and values are difficult to train and then only when candidates have a strong base of them to build on.)

THE STRATEGIC PERSPECTIVE

'We can teach steel but we can't make lazy people productive'

Nucor Corporation is the most successful steel company of the past 30 years. Its efficient 'mini mills' recycle more than 16.3 million tonnes of old steel scrap into a wide range of high-grade steel products using electric arc furnaces rather than blast furnaces, reducing greenhouse gas emissions in excess of its target by 240%.

Nucor builds its 'mini mills' in farming communities because that is where the company believes it can find a strong work ethic. They know they can teach people how to make steel but they can't teach a work ethic.

The moral: Hire people who want to be productive and who share your core vision and values. In the case of Nucor, this is, 'To take care of our customers. We are accomplishing this

>>

> by being the safest, highest quality, lowest cost, most productive and most profitable steel and steel products company in the world ... while being cultural and environmental stewards in our communities where we live and work.'
>
> Nucor's wages are the highest in the industry yet its labour costs are the lowest in the industry. It has created job security and unmatched profitability in an industry ravaged by foreign competition and is proud to have large pools of candidates for every opening.[3]

Make sure the position description and person specification accurately reflect requirements of the vacancy so you don't end up *overrecruiting* (recruiting someone with more skills than needed to do the work well) or *underrecruiting* (recruiting someone without sufficient skills or motivation to do the work properly). When you ask for too much, you are likely to find it difficult to fill your vacancies. You might fill your vacancies with people who are overqualified and become bored and resign, or you might have to pay them more than the position itself merits. The reverse is also true. You don't want a novice in a position calling for an expert.

When you're satisfied with your person specification, you might want to mark with a 'T' any skills and knowledge you can provide through training and are willing to do so. Then mark with an 'M' any knowledge, job and performance skills you believe the employee must come to you with, either because they are not easily 'trainable' or your don't intend to provide training in that particular area. For example, a 'cheerful disposition' would be hard to train into someone naturally sullen; a payroll clerk would need basic numeracy skills and you would not expect to train someone how to add and subtract. Candidates who don't possess those mandatory skills are automatically ruled out. Then you can mark with a 'D' any knowledge, job and performance skills you believe are desirable, although you would not rule out a candidate who didn't possess them.

◉ ACTION!

You can find a Person specification template on ⸜CourseMateExpress to help you think through the type of person who would thrive in the position.

◉ THE STRATEGIC PERSPECTIVE

When 'been there, done that' isn't a good idea

When you are tempted to make prior experience essential in your person specification, think twice. Think first about yourself: If you were looking for a new position, what would you want? Same old, same old, or something a little bit different? Many candidates want to learn and grow into a challenging role.

Second, think about whether you need the position-holder to complete tasks in specific ways. When your 'specific way' of completing a task is different from the way someone already does it, a mechanism called *proactive inhibitory interference*, or PI, kicks in. This is a brain program that protects and preserves existing knowledge and skills by rejecting new knowledge and ways of doing things. This means that when people already know how to do a task and try to learn a

>>

different way of doing it, learning the new way takes a lot longer than when the task is new to them.

Since 'expertise' can slow down people's learning and lengthen the time it takes them to adopt your way of doing things, be wary of making 'similar previous experience' a selection criterion. Look for basic aptitudes and then provide skills training as needed.

Your employer brand and employer value proposition

Why do you think people want to work for your organisation? When you attract people on the basis of 'I need the work' or 'The job is near my house', you don't have a very exciting basis for a lengthy and satisfying employment relationship. But when people actively want to work for you because they've heard such great things about your organisation and want to be associated with those great things, you're starting out on a sound footing.

For this, you need a strong employer brand and employer value proposition. They are the package of the organisation's reputation and practices concerning how it treats its people, its customers and the environment, and how it delivers on its promises. They need to be strong and in harmony with each other.

Just as organisations have cultures and subcultures, roles and departments can have their own 'sub-EVPs'. However, you draft yours to attract people to your vacancy, it must be in tune with the organisation's overall EVP and consistent with its employer brand.

Organisations depend on everyone who leads and manages people to understand and support the package they offer employees, and use it correctly to recruit employees. The EVP must genuinely reflect employees' experience of the organisation and recruits must find the culture they were promised when they join – when that doesn't happen, they leave, and the organisation's investment in attracting them is wasted.

THE STRATEGIC PERSPECTIVE

The strategic importance of the right EVP

You may have heard the phrase 'employer of choice'. Organisations that depend on their employees for their success, particularly those in the knowledge and service industries and those who depend on employees with high degrees of technical skill and experience, strive to become employers of choice. Since they can't afford to be without the right staff, they spend time and energy developing a strong employer brand and employer value proposition package that targets and appeals to the types of employees they need.

Even organisations that don't depend on their employees to the same extent still need the 'presence' in the employment marketplace that an employer brand and EVP provide. For example, McDonald's Australia employs about 75 000 people and has a regular turnover of staff. It recently remodelled its EVP, taking on the tag of beiong an employer of opportunity to encourage applicants of all ages.[4]

> ## ◉ IN A NUTSHELL
>
> ### The employer value proposition
> The EVP is the set of attributes that its employees and the labour market perceive as the value people gain through employment in an organisation. It consists of five dimensions:
> 1. *Characteristics of the organisation*, such as its culture and values, market position, policies and the nature, size, sustainability and locations of its operations.
> 2. *Characteristics of the organisation's people*, such as the degree to which people treat each other with respect and the quality of its managers.
> 3. *Opportunities that the position or organisation offers employees*, such as interesting career paths, mentoring, training and development, work on interesting projects, and the chance to work with and learn from interesting and knowledgeable people.
> 4. *Tangible rewards* that employees receive for their work (compensation and benefits).
> 5. *The work itself*, such as the way positions are designed and the extent to which the work matches employees' interests.
>
> The right EVP benefits an organisation two important ways:
> 1. It attracts the employees it needs, which means it can put the right people in the right positions.
> 2. It attracts more engaged employees who know something about the organisation they are joining and join it for the right reasons, which improves both performance and retention.

Yourself

You are the third selling point in recruitment. Understanding your organisation's employer brand and EVP, and using it to help you recruit, ensures that the people who join your team can feel engaged with the organisation.

Even when the employer brand and EVP help attract the right employees to your vacancy, you cannot retain those 'right people' for long when you fail to live up to the EVP promise or offer employees the management style they want. When you adapt your leadership style in order to lead people from different cultures and generations and with different levels of experience and skill, you can motivate and engage employees, retain them and bring out their best efforts.

2. Understanding the recruitment process

> When I find an employee who turns out to be wrong for the job I feel it is my fault because I made the decision to hire him.
>
> Akio Morita (founder, Sony Corporation), in Heller, *In search of European excellence* (1997)[5]

In smaller organisations, leader-managers are usually involved in the recruitment process from the beginning. In large organisations, the Human Resources (HR) specialist might ask you to do the position analysis, update the position description and prepare the person specification. HR then sources and shortlists candidates for you to interview and you make the final decision.

Some organisations outsource the entire recruitment process to recruitment consultants who manage the recruitment process up to the final interview and appointment stage, including checking references. This is known as *recruitment process outsourcing*. The consultants present a shortlist of candidates (those they consider most suitable) for the leader-manager or a panel to interview and make the selection decision.

Using specialists saves you time and effort in sourcing candidates, conducting the initial interviews, checking references, and so on. In addition, agencies can advise you on the competitiveness of your employer brand, EVP and salary scale. However your organisation handles it, you still need to provide precise information about the nature of the work (a position description) and the type of person required (a person specification).

Opportunities lost

Most candidates say that the application and interview process is very important in shaping their view of the organisation (78%) and see interviews as an opportunity to interview a prospective employer (87%).

Around 40% of candidates have turned down a position because of a bad interview experience and 81% tell up to 10 people about their poor interview experience. Two of the biggest mistakes are not responding to applications and not contacting candidates after an interview.[6]

The entire interviewing process, not just the interview itself, is an opportunity to build a strong employer brand and treat each candidate as a potential customer and potential referee. Return phone calls, electronic applications and emails within 24 hours to show you care enough to respond promptly. Follow up after the interview within 48 hours, thanking candidates for their time; when you haven't made a decision, tell them and say when you expect to make a decision.

Most candidates are excited about the opportunity your vacancy offers. Matching their enthusiasm builds bonds and a good candidate experience, even for those who aren't successful this time.

Reaching potential candidates

Advertising vacancies in print media such as newspapers and specialist journals, and electronically on the organisation's website, Intranet and noticeboards, online job boards, social networking sites and Twitter streams is the most common way to attract applications. E-channels are cheaper than newspapers and especially important in attracting tech-savvy Generation Y, but be careful to use a range of sourcing streams so that you don't unintentionally cut out groups of potential candidates; for instance, exclusive use of social media may not reach older candidates who are suited to the vacancy.

Radio stations popular with candidates you want to target can also be a good way to attract applications. Schools, tertiary education institutions and other training providers can put forward candidates, especially where specialist training is required – brief them clearly on the type of people you are looking for.

Most recruitment agencies, dedicated Internet recruitment sites and large employers have automated interactive websites listing employment opportunities that accept and sort e-applications. When you're looking for a specific skill set, consider designing a targeted campaign to reach the talent pool you're after. Tap into agencies that specialise in mature-age workers, people with disabilities, the long-term unemployed and functional specialisms such as accounting and IT staff and marketing professionals.

You're after a small pool of suitable applicants to select from. When a lot of unsuitable candidates apply, or few suitable candidates apply, you could be advertising your vacancy poorly.

Advertising your vacancy

When advertising or announcing a vacancy, mention only those requirements that are necessary for the performance of a particular position and that do not subtly exclude members of a particular group or sex. Avoid age- and gender-linked position titles; that is, those that describe the position or occupation in terms of one particular age or sex (office junior, salesman, draftsman, waitress and so on). Use titles with no age or gender attachment (office assistant, sales representative, draftsperson, waiter and so on).

When designing the vacancy announcement, cover both the 'selling' and the 'buying'. Keep the people you want to respond to the ad in mind as you write it. Figure 25.2 shows the information to include in your vacancy announcement.

When listing or implying the skills you're after, leave out the obvious. When you want someone who is a 'good communicator', you can figure that out for yourself by reading the applications and listening to the candidates at interview. Similarly, when you're looking for a 'self-starter', someone who's 'detail oriented' or a 'creative thinker', you can get a feel for those attributes from their application and find out more at the interview.

XZY Pty Ltd
Position vacant for floor manager

Title of position (reflecting duties and responsibilities):
....
....

Salary range and benefits:
....
....

Location:
....
....

Relevant EVPs (culture, values, work environment):
....
....

Reason for position and its main duties and responsibilities:
....
....

Applicant's essential skills, knowledge and attributes:
....
....

How to apply:
....
....

FIGURE 25.2 What to include in a vacancy announcement

⊙ THEORY TO PRACTICE

Employee-driven recruitment

Many companies advertise positions internally before advertising them externally or bringing in recruitment consultants. Some give a nominal cash bonus to employees who successfully refer a friend for a vacancy (although the hiring manager and HR staff are not allowed to refer candidates).

Other companies use flexible working arrangements such as home-based work, job-sharing and part-time work, and sponsor overseas professionals through the Federal Government's migrant 457 visa scheme to attract the employees they need. 'Career customisation', health and wellness programs and other HR initiatives help attract employees, too. Employee-friendly strategies like these also assist with staff retention.

⊙ ACTION!

⚡CourseMateExpress has a Job advertisement template to guide you when developing a job ad.

Passive candidates

There are several ways to reach *passive candidates* – people who aren't actively looking for another position. When you have an established, engaged group of employees, you can encourage them to mention the vacancy through their professional networks or recommend people from them for vacancies. Because they're familiar with the nature and requirements of the work and the workplace culture, existing staff generally recommend suitable people, making it more likely that recruits fit in well and engage with the organisation.

People who are, or have been, employed satisfactorily casually or part-time in the organisation can be a good avenue of recruitment, too. They are familiar with the type of work and the organisation, and knowing their work standards and capabilities makes it easier to assess their suitability for the vacancy.

Some organisations maintain close connections with former employees through 'alumni newsletters' and make vacancies known through this network. Former employees may wish to apply or to recommend people from their own networks. (You can maintain contact yourself informally if your organisation doesn't have alumni programs.)

Approaching people known to have the required skills but who are not actively seeking a new position (called *head-hunting*) is becoming more common at all levels. It never hurts to be on the lookout for suitable people, both inside and outside the organisation, to approach directly when a suitable vacancy occurs.

Screening applicants

Application forms are designed to collect a precise and logical summary of applicants' educational and other qualifications, work history and experience, and any other factors relevant to the position. Because the forms present the information in a standardised way, it's easier to compare applicants.

When the task of reading the applications and developing a list of candidates to invite for interview falls to you, read through the application forms to identify which among the applicants meet enough of your selection criteria to merit an interview. Software can do this for you or you can do it manually. Manually is tedious when you have a lot of applicants, so develop a code system to rank applicants. You could, for instance, assign numbers to key skills, knowledge and attributes and note the number on the application form when there seems to be a good match.

Look for skills and experience rather than position titles or length of experience. Look for 'career stories' and the types of work applicants seem drawn to; you're looking for a match between the type of work an applicant enjoys doing and the type of work that you are offering. Have they been given increasing responsibilities in their previous positions? Are any gaps in work history not explained by corresponding entries for volunteer or freelance work or education? From the information provided you may also find some clues that yours is the type of organisation they want to work in.

Take a look at applicants' *résumés or curriculum vitaes (CVs)* and covering email or letter to see what you can glean from them, too. How well laid out are they and how clearly, concisely and logically is the information presented, for instance? When that is relevant to the vacancy, you have more information to help you decide whether to proceed with an applicant.

When you cannot find a 'perfect fit', at least you know which applicants 'best fit' your person specification, which competencies each lacks, and therefore the information and training you would need to provide.

FYI

What's the difference between a curriculum vitae and a résumé?
These two terms are often used synonymously but, strictly speaking, they're different. A *curriculum vitae* contains a detailed and chronological list of work experience and facts. A *résumé* is more of a summary that highlights and interprets key aspects of work experience and facts in reverse chronological order.

Whichever you are examining, here are items to consider:

- How often did the applicant changes jobs? You would want to explore the reasons for the changes or what led to those changes during the interview.
- What were the applicant's relevant achievements in previous jobs? You would want to explore these in more depth during the interview.
- Were there any gaps in employment? You would want to explore the reasons for these gaps during the interview.
- Years of experience can be deceptive; a person can perform poorly after a long time in a job or perform well, and achieve more, after their first few weeks.

THE STRATEGIC PERSPECTIVE

Would you use social media to screen candidates?
Among Australian bosses hiring staff, 28% use social media. Half of those managers have rejected candidates because of what they saw on screen and two-thirds interviewed candidates and ultimately hired them, in part because of their on-screen profile.[7]

Although you can quickly garner an insight into applicants by informally checking them on social networking sites, even a quick peek can be a cauldron of legal hot water. You might become aware of an applicant's age, carer status, marital status, political views, religious beliefs, sexual

>>

orientation – all information that cannot be used to make an employment decision. Should a discrimination claim arise, the burden of proof is on you to show that you did not take that information into account when making a decision to reject the applicant but made your decision on non-discriminatory grounds.

On the other hand, say some, there is a thin line between personal and working lives thanks to technology that lets people work anywhere, anytime. It is up to individuals to ensure the information they make public about themselves is appropriate and to protect themselves, their reputations and their 'personal brand' in their online profiles. As Ray Kroc, the founder of the McDonald's Corporation points out, 'The quality of an individual is reflected in the standards they set for themselves.'[8]

Under the Commonwealth *Privacy Act 1988*, you must inform candidates that you have collected personal information about them and explain why you collected it and who else sees the information you collected. And speaking of the Privacy Act, candidates can also ask to see the notes you made about them during the recruitment process, from checking their social profile to the interview notes themselves. Just as you should only ask questions to bring out vacancy-relevant information, only write down vacancy-relevant information.

An introductory telephone discussion

An initial telephone discussion can sometimes replace the application as the first point of contact, saving wading through written applications and conducting initial interviews. It serves as a 'screening' interview to eliminate clearly unsuitable candidates and encourage the most suitable to continue with their application. You can arrange a time to meet with those who seem suitable and thank those who do not seem suitable for their interest, explaining that you are looking for someone with different skills.

Telephone discussions are particularly useful when recruiting people for work that involves direct contact with the public or telephone work, as they allow you to make an early assessment of the applicant's relevant communication skills.

Selection tests

Pre-employment testing falls into three categories: aptitude and skill tests, medical tests, and psychological tests. And there are a lot to choose from – more than 1500 commercial skills and psychological tests from 90 suppliers are available. Many of them require a qualified person to administer them and some require the supervision of a registered psychologist.

Brief candidates about the purpose of the tests and your organisation's policy for distributing and storing the results, which must be kept confidential. Candidates should also be provided with the test results in a private feedback session.

Find out ahead of time whether the candidates need any special arrangements for the tests (e.g. they may be visually impaired or need an interpreter).

Aptitude and skill tests

Aptitude tests measure abilities such as abstract and verbal reasoning, literacy, mechanical comprehension, numeracy, spatial skills, how quickly a candidate is able to assimilate new information and the ability to check detailed information. These practical tests are usually given at the screening or preliminary interview to help determine whether an applicant has the basic skills or aptitudes to do the work.

Medical tests

Medical tests, conducted by the organisation's nominated medical practitioner, should assess only the applicant's current health status to determine whether an applicant is physically capable of doing specific work. For example, if you were employing a person to work in a boiler room, foundry or glass factory, you would need to ensure that the candidate was medically fit to withstand the high temperatures. Some organisations also carry out drug and alcohol screening.

You cannot refuse to employ a person whose medical examination discloses a disability or an impairment unrelated to their ability to do the work they've applied for. For example, if a person with a disability could do the work despite their disability, you should provide the facilities or services the person would reasonably need, such as wheelchair ramps and suitable toilet facilities. Neither can you use the information to screen out applicants based on their predicted future health or deterioration in health, or for past injuries, unless you can demonstrate that the injury has a direct bearing on the candidate's ability to do the work applied for and that in doing that work, their own or others' health and safety would be at risk. For similar reasons, previous and current workers compensation claims should not be taken into consideration.

Psychological tests

Do you need someone who is self-reliant and self-motivated? Psychological or *psychometric* tests can give you some insight into such matters. Particularly popular when recruiting managers, psychometric tests (literally mental measurement) probe decision-making ability, leadership potential, intelligence, interests, motivation and values, and personality traits such as extroversion/introversion and sociability.

When used correctly these tests can provide useful information to compare with the person specification and, when considered with the candidate's résumé, the interview and comments received from referees, can help ensure a good fit between the candidate and the vacancy.

Interviews

Can you imagine hiring someone without having first met and talked to them? Or accepting a position before meeting your boss-to-be and seeing the workplace? That's why interviews are the most commonly used selection method. They give both parties a chance to learn about each other. The candidate can get a feel for the working environment, climate and culture of the organisation, while the interviewer can gain more detailed information about the candidate's skills and motivational fit.

Some organisations hold three selection interviews:

1. *Screening interview* to eliminate those applicants who are obviously unsuitable (sometimes conducted over the telephone).
2. *Preliminary interview* to select a shortlist of suitable candidates.
3. *Final interview* to decide which candidate to appoint.

When you invite candidates for an interview, you might want to give them clear directions about where to park if they drive, and mention what public transport is available. Say where and what time to report, who to ask for when they arrive and how long you expect the interview to last, and ask whether they have any special needs you should know about (e.g. wheelchair access and facilities) to make sure you accommodate them.

Let candidates know whether you will be interviewing them yourself or whether the interview is to be a panel or group interview. Provide reception with a list of the times and names of people you are interviewing and the position so they can be welcomed and directed appropriately.

ACTION!

You can find a Shortlist template and a Shortlist matrix template on ⫶**CourseMate**Express. You can use either to help you shortlist candidates from whom to make your final selection decision.

You can also find a Letter inviting an applicant for a first interview and a Letter rejecting an applicant at shortlist stage on ⫶**CourseMate**Express.

Employment interviews can be structured or unstructured. People who have never been properly trained in how to conduct an interview favour *unstructured interviews*. They are more like a series of meandering questions aimed at nothing in particular: 'Tell me about yourself', 'What are your strengths and weaknesses?', 'Can you use spreadsheets?'

Structured interviews give you a much better chance of reaching a successful selection decision and are more positively viewed by candidates, who experience them as more relevant and thorough. Behavioural interviews are the most reliable type of structured interview. The next section explains how to conduct a structured behavioural recruitment interview.

FYI

Jack Welch's view on recruitment
Former General Electric CEO Jack Welch saw recruitment interviewing as one of his most important roles. He interviewed all outside candidates for all of the top 500 positions in the company.[9]

Was he looking for technical abilities? No. He was looking for the General Electric mindset on leading and managing people. He was looking for leader-managers who can energise and excite, not enervate, depress and control.

Panel and group interviews

You may find yourself participating in a *panel interview*, in which two or more people conduct the selection interview and make a joint decision about which candidate to appoint. In *group interviews*, several applicants are interviewed together, as a group, usually by several interviewers. This type of interview usually takes the form of candidates interacting with each other as well as with the interviewers. Organisations often use group interviews when the person specification requires 'people skills', such as good communication, poise, tact, resourcefulness, leadership and the ability to cope with stressful situations.

When participating in panel and group interviews, meet first with the other interviewers to determine who will chair the interview and to review the position description and person specification and agree and rank the selection criteria. (See Figure 25.3: A weighted ranking system for candidates, on page 819). You also need to agree on an interview agenda and the approximate time to spend on each area, and then allocate a section of the interview agenda to each interviewer to cover. In other words, one person opens the interview, another explains the position and the EVP, another probes the candidate's work history, and so on. Consider assigning the note-taking role to one person only, since it can be very off-putting to candidates to have several people jotting down notes.

With group and panel interviews, as with one-on-one interviews, aim for a smoothly run, professional interview that proceeds at a steady, orderly pace and covers the desired areas of candidate response. When interviewers jockey for control of the interview, interrupt each other to ask questions, ask questions randomly and hop from one topic to another rather than follow a clear interview outline, they give a poor impression of the organisation and are unlikely to make a sound selection decision. Thorough preparation is time well spent.

● THE STRATEGIC PERSPECTIVE

Public relations in interviewing

Take the opportunity with every interview to spread the word about your employer brand and EVP. Remember that each person you interview is a potential customer or user of your organisation (and so are their family and friends). Also, the candidates you do not select, or people they know, may be suited to another position in the organisation. Make sure, therefore, that each person you interview leaves your workplace feeling that the interview has been fairly and professionally conducted and with a positive impression of your organisation, its EVP and its employer brand.

The drawbacks of interviews

Everyone likes to think they have good 'people sense' and a rare ability to pick the right person. Unfortunately, most people don't. Unless you take great care in the employment interview, research has shown that you could make just as good a selection decision by choosing at random from among the applicants.[10]

This is because everyone has their own biases and prejudices, their own way of sifting and filtering information so that it fits in with what they expect or wish to hear. In addition, the halo/horns effect means that, unless you're careful, one or two positive or negative attributes of candidates can influence you to see them in a generally positive or generally negative light. (To overcome this, assess each set of skills, attributes and characteristics separately.)

Then there is the fact that the first impression, although often incorrect, is a lasting one. This means you can – wrongly – make up your mind about a candidate during the first few minutes of an interview and spend the rest of the interview noticing 'evidence' that confirms your first impression.

Other common interviewing mistakes are not asking each candidate the same questions, not basing questions on the requirements of the position, not knowing what an 'acceptable' answer is, and asking questions in a way that makes the 'correct' answer obvious.

● IN A NUTSHELL

The keys to a successful employment interview

The best way to find a close match between candidates and your person specification is to ask good questions and listen carefully to the answers. You can't find out anything about a candidate while you are talking, so aim to listen for 60–70% of the interview (that's when you do the 'buying') and to talk for only 30–40% (that's when you do the 'selling').

>>

Listen closely to everything the candidate says and consider how well it matches your person specification. While it's tempting to select someone who can 'hit the ground running' because of past experience in similar roles, remember that, long term, the best person is the person who is a good motivational fit with the organisation and the vacancy, even when you need to top up their skills and knowledge with some training. A candidate who relates positively to your organisation based on its EVP, and whose aspirations match your vacancy, is a far better bet than a candidate with all the right skills but without the right attributes.

● THEORY TO PRACTICE

Spread the load

Claudio Fernandez-Araoz, a partner in the executive search firm Egon Zehnder International, believes that a second opinion on a candidate reduces the possibility of hiring error from 50% to 10%, while a third opinion practically guarantees a sound selection decision – provided all interviewers are properly briefed on the ideal candidate profile and are properly trained in behavioural interviewing techniques.[11]

Google agrees. But three interviews is enough. Google has also found that every interview after the fourth adds no extra value in terms of a sound decision. All Google staff take their turn interviewing candidates and are thoroughly trained in interview techniques.[12]

The selection decision

Who best meets your selection criteria? When you find that each candidate matches some parts of the person specification well and doesn't match other parts as well, which candidate do you hire? There is no guaranteed way to tell who best suits the vacancy, but you can increase your chances of hiring the right person by comparing how each candidate meets each of your selection criterion objectively.

You might try a numerical 'scoring' system, like the one shown in Figure 25.3 for this. Give each selection criterion a weighting from 1 (less important) to 5 (very important) and rate each candidate's match to those criteria from 0 (no match) to 1 (poor match) to 5 (excellent match). (Consider the candidates' results in any selection tests used, too.) Multiply the rating by the weights and add up the sums for the candidate's total rating. The candidate with the highest total rating is the best match to your selection criteria.

Selection criterion	A	B	C	D	E	Total
Weight / Candidate	1	3	3	4	5	
Candidate 1	3 / 3	3 / 9	5 / 15	5 / 20	2 / 10	57
Candidate 2	1 / 1	2 / 6	4 / 12	4 / 16	5 / 25	60
Candidate 3	5 / 5	5 / 15	2 / 6	3 / 12	2 / 10	48

FIGURE 25.3 A weighted ranking system for candidates

THE STRATEGIC PERSPECTIVE

Build a strong, diverse team

Recruit a range of people whose personality types, skills, working styles, and so on complement each other. Teams made up of people who are too similar to each other and who all think the same limit your team's ability to innovate and solve problems.

Since it's unlikely that any one candidate can match your person specification perfectly, remember that building skills and providing knowledge is one thing; it is much harder (if not impossible) to teach people values and attributes, so avoid hiring candidates unless there is a good 'fit' or alignment between their values and the organisation's values and their working style and the work requirements. Attributes like these are a 'go' or 'no go' signal – when candidates have the skills and knowledge but not the attributes that allow them to engage with your organisation, move on.

Your aim is to make the best possible match. With this in mind, here are two good rules to follow:

1. *Never settle for the best of a bad bunch.* Review the job or role description and person specification, see whether you can adjust them, and think about starting again when you're not happy with the first group of candidates.
2. *When in doubt, the answer is 'no'.* Your subconscious has probably picked up some evidence that you can't put your finger on. Listen to any 'nagging doubts' – a wrong decision is too costly in terms of time, money and morale.

FYI

The cost of a poor hiring decision

Various formulas are used to calculate the cost of replacing a departing employee. One is to multiply the annual salary by a factor of between 1.54 and 3, depending on the position. It's surprising how expensive recruitment is when you include the cost of advertising and using a recruitment service, the time costs of updating the job or role description and person specification, preparing for the interviews, interviewing, making the decision, checking references and preparing the offer.

Then you need to consider the cost of inducting and training the new employee and lowered productivity as the new employee gets 'up to speed' and reaches the expected performance level. There are also more difficult-to-cost factors such as the disruption to the work team recruits cause and the ruptured relationships with internal and external customers and suppliers. The cost also increases because for many positions, each new hire tends to drive up the wage level for that position with no corresponding increase in productivity.

The impact of poor hiring decisions on the bottom line, although hidden (in that it's seldom formally accounted for) can be huge. So it pays to hire right.

Reference checks

Reference checking protects your organisation's interests by endorsing your selection decision and validating the candidate's main claims. The more damage a poor appointment could do to your team's morale or productivity, the more thorough you need to be in your reference checking. The HR department or employment agency normally carries out the reference check. When there is no HR department or you are not using the services of a recruitment agency, check references yourself.

THE STRATEGIC PERSPECTIVE

Will you be my referee?

Reference checking has become a legal minefield. Remember that candidates are entitled to see all the information given in a reference check.

When someone asks you to act as a referee, agree only when you have directly worked with the person and know their abilities. Do not agree when you have nothing positive or constructive to say about the person.

Some organisations have a policy of confirming only basic factual information such as dates of employment and job title. When this is the case, confirm those details and move on to the next referee. It's best to speak with two or three people who directly managed the candidate. Each reference check usually takes 20–30 minutes and is done over the telephone in the case of external candidates. When the candidate is internal, meet with their current manager (and previous manager when possible) and follow steps three and four.

The procedure is as follows:

1. Telephone the organisation's reception and not to a direct line or mobile phone so that you can verify the person is in the role the candidate said they are.
2. Give the referee your name, position and organisation and explain the reason for your call. Some referees may want to ring you back to ensure that you are who you say you are. (This is good practice and you should do the same when you are approached to act as a referee, again, ringing back through the reception.)
3. Briefly explain the key tasks of the position and your main selection criteria (from the person specification). Ask open questions directly related to the position's requirements and to clarify and substantiate the information you obtained from the candidate during the interview. Pay attention to what referees say and how they say it. Lukewarm comments and half-hearted praise speak volumes.
4. Thank referees for their time and end on a positive note.

In short, reference checks are mostly concerned with:

* Confirming factual information given by the candidate concerning the employer in question such as dates of employment and nature of duties. Don't offer these yourself. Ask the referee
* Probing important areas of the person specification to determine areas of match and mismatch.

THEORY TO PRACTICE

Sample questions for telephone reference checks

Always ask questions based on competencies directly related to the job. For example:

* Are dates of employment, position title and any other important details given correct?
* Did X have any contact with the public (when relevant)?
* Did you form any opinion of the work for which X is best suited?
* How closely did you need to manage X?
* How did X get on with people/team-mates?

>>

- How much potential/initiative did X show?
- How well did X perform the job? How well does X compare with the person currently doing the work?
- How would you rate X's general conduct?
- Was X dependable regarding quality of work? Attendance? Timekeeping?
- What did you/X's manager think of X?
- What were X's main responsibilities?
- What would you say are X's strong points? Weak points?
- X mentioned working on a project with you; how did X contribute to that project?
- Why did X leave?
- Would you re-employ X? Why or why not?

Make an offer

Once you have made your decision, act quickly. Telephone the successful candidate to offer the position and follow up with a written offer. Inform whoever needs to be informed (e.g. HR, salary administration, your boss, your organisation's nurse). Be sure that the letter of offer and contract of employment are sent to the new employee's home and that the recruit knows when, where and to whom to report on their first day.

Include a probationary period, or trial period, of one to three months for new recruits when your organisation's policy allows this.

When your offer has been accepted, tactfully let the unsuccessful candidates know, thanking them once again for their interest and wishing them success in their careers. With the speed and ease of email, there is absolutely no excuse not to do this. Wrapping up loose ends like this is vital to maintaining your organisation's reputation.

● IN A NUTSHELL

Saying, 'No thanks'

How a candidate experiences your recruitment process, including how you say 'No thanks', reflects on your organisation and its corporate brand and it's likely to be shared (and spread) on line and in person.

Don't spoil an opportunity to spread the good word about you and your organisation. Follow the Golden Rule and treat all applicants as you would wish to be treated yourself.

Legal requirements

No discrimination, overt or implied, intended or unintended, against or in favour of candidates, must enter the recruitment process. Attributes such as candidates' age, ethnicity, marital status, physical or mental impairments, religion, sex or sexual preference must not factor into your recruitment decision. (See page 845 for more information about discrimination and anti-discrimination legislation.)

For example, don't ask the following questions:

- Are you married?
- What clubs and organisations do you belong to?

- When do you plan to start a family?
- Where were you born?

Ask the same core questions of each candidate and be certain that these questions relate directly to the position's requirements. Be aware of any underlying assumptions you may be making about people from particular groups. Do not imply unfair or partial attitudes to, for example, race or sex in the questions you ask and give each candidate the same information about the position in the same way.

What can you legally ask an applicant? Here are some guidelines:

- Don't ask questions of applicants from a particular group (e.g. females, minorities or people with disabilities) that you don't ask of all the others. Ask the same position-related questions of all applicants.
- Don't ask about child-care arrangements, family circumstances, family planning, partners' situations or relationships. When you need to know whether the candidate can get into work on time, work overtime or travel away from home for two or three days, ask that question directly.
- Don't state, imply or take into account that certain groups of people have traditionally held or never held particular positions.
- Don't treat candidates from one group differently from candidates from other groups.
- Only ask questions that relate directly to the position's requirements.
- Recognise any biases you may have and guard against letting them cloud your judgement.

Standardise the forms you use during interviews to record questions and answers to help you keep an unbiased record and to impartially compare candidates' skills, knowledge and attributes to the person specification. When a vacancy has special requirements, address these directly. For example:

- This position frequently requires working overtime at short notice. Are you able to do that?
- This position involves working on Saturday mornings from 8 am to noon. Are you able to do that?
- This position requires overtime most Tuesday and Thursday nights until 7.30 pm. Are you able to do that?
- You would need to spend three days a month travelling in this position. Are you able to do that?

Questions such as these should relate specifically to the position's requirements and you should ask them of each candidate.

Keep the details of all applicants and your interview notes on all candidates confidential and in a locked file. You may want to interview a candidate in the future for a different position, or a candidate may complain that you have interviewed them unfairly and your notes can help you dispute this. Don't discuss applicants with anyone other than your manager or the HR department.

ACTION!

You can find an Interview record template and an Interview summary template on CourseMateExpress. The first helps you record your evidence of match and mis-match to the vacancy of each candidate. The second summarises your evidence of all candidates onto one document to help you reach your selection decision.

There is also a Rejection letter template for a candidate who was unsuccessful at the interview. You can use this as a model for your own letter if your organisation doesn't have a set of standard recruitment and selection letters.

> ## ● THEORY TO PRACTICE
>
> ### How the Taj finds stars
> The Taj Group, renowned for its chain of opulent hotels and unrivalled customer service, sets high standards for its employees. It's recruitment system helps it find people it can train to be 'customer-centric'. It hires most of its front-line staff members from smaller towns rather than metropolitan centres because that's where traditional Indian values, such as consideration of others, discipline, honesty, humility, loyalty and respect for elders, are strongest. Once hired, recruits are trained for 18 months, not just the more usual 12 months, at one of six city-based residential Taj Group skill-certification centres.[13]

3. Conducting behavioural interviews

You're only as good as the people you hire.

Ray Kroc (McDonald's executive), in Harris, *Surrender to Win* (2009)[14]

People tend to keep the same basic behaviour patterns they have always had – things like how responsibly they act, how shy or outgoing they are and how thorough or slack they are in the way they do things. Even as people grow older and more mature, their basic personality traits don't change greatly. Similarly, people retain the skills and knowledge they develop. Therefore, the best predictor of future behaviour is past behaviour.

The more you can find out about candidates' position-related personality traits and their skills and knowledge, the better you can predict their ability to do the work well and engage with the organisation. The best way to do this is to ask questions about what candidates have done in the past and questions that give you an insight into their thinking processes. Provided your questions are directly related to the vacancy, the answers indicate how closely a candidate matches your person specification. This is behavioural interviewing.

> ## ● THE STRATEGIC PERSPECTIVE
>
> ### The right person for the position
> Some people spend their working lives frustrated, doing jobs that don't make the best use of their talents and capabilities. This is nothing to do with intelligence or ability and everything to do with preferences for ways of communicating, thinking and working. Behavioural interviewing helps you put the right people in the right positions so they don't spend working lives frustrated – and frustrating you.

Behavioural interviewing has four distinct advantages:
1. Asking about past behaviour and thinking processes helps ensure that candidates base their answers on fact and gives you a reliable insight into their experience, knowledge, motivation, thought processes and values.
2. Asking each candidate the same series of questions helps you compare 'apples with apples'.
3. It helps you assess candidates objectively, based on specifics rather than on 'general impressions', 'gut feelings' or how a candidate 'performs' during an interview.
4. It helps you select and eliminate candidates for vacancy-related reasons only.

The five steps of employment interviewing are described below and summarised in Figure 25.4.

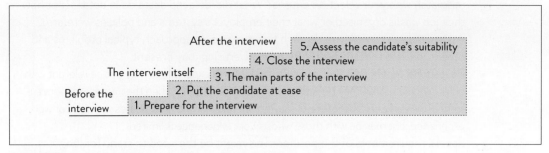

FIGURE 25.4 The five steps to recruitment interviewing

Step 1: Prepare for the interview

Set aside at least 40 minutes for the interview and a further 10 to think about and note down how the candidate matches your selection criteria. When scheduling interviews, leave time between each one to attend to any urgent matters that crop up and to give yourself a break; it's gruelling doing back-to-back interviews!

Make an interview agenda so you can run a smooth and professional interview. Think about your opening remarks to welcome the candidate and how best to briefly describe the position and the opportunities it presents, such as career opportunities and opportunities for learning and developing skills. Then develop a list of questions that target information about the skills, experience and attributes needed to succeed in the position.

Whether you talk a bit about the position and the organisation first and then find out about the candidate, or the other way around, is up to you. Giving information about the position first gives candidates a chance to settle down, collect their thoughts, survey their surroundings and generally relax. Be aware that once you're in 'talking mode', you may find it difficult to stop talking and proceed to the listening part of the interview; you may have trained the candidate into 'listening mode', too.

A good compromise is to ask each candidate which they'd prefer – to hear a bit about the role and the organisation first and then have a chat about themselves, or the other way around.

IN A NUTSHELL

Example of an interview outline
Prepare an interview outline to help you ruin your interview smoothly. Here is a sample outline for you to adapt to your requirements:
1. Welcome: Make the candidate feel comfortable.
2. The sell: Briefly review the EVP and describe the working environment and position, purpose, key duties and responsibilities of the position.
3. The buy: Assess the candidate's skills, experience, attributes.
   - Work background: Assess the candidate's match for aptitude, experience, knowledge, personality traits, skills and abilities, values and workstyle preferences.

Ask for behavioural examples: What did/do candidates actually do that shows match/mismatch with your selection criteria? What did/do candidates do in detail? (not how their job was/is organised or what their employer's systems and policies were/are). Ask candidates to walk you through how they would approach typical problems and other scenarios that the position you're advertising may present.

- Educational experiences and interests: Educational experiences may not be relevant with older candidates, but may be with younger ones, especially when their work experience is limited. Similarly, outside interests may not be relevant with candidates with a lot of work experience, but may be with those whose work experience is limited.
- Special requirements of the position: This might be the need to stand for long periods, to be on 24-hour callout or work overtime at short notice. In these examples, you would ask whether the candidate can stand for long periods, work on 24-hour callout or work overtime, and you should ask every candidate.

4. Thank the candidate and explain the next steps.

The details

Gather any information you need such as pay, conditions and hours of work, and when necessary, book a suitable interview room that gives a favourable but realistic impression of your organisation and is reasonably private and free from distractions. Consider the seating arrangements. You could use a meeting room or your office and sit behind your desk; or you could be less formal and invite candidates to join you at a low coffee table, if you have one in your office.

Make sure that the sun or other harsh light won't blind candidates and that your chairs are the same height. See that telephone calls or visitors will not interrupt you during the interview; put a 'Do not disturb sign on your door when necessary. Inform anyone who needs to know when, where and for what position you are interviewing.

Review each candidate's application, initial letter and completed application form *before* the meeting; never ever, ever read it back to the candidate at the interview. Look for information to follow up and list additional questions to ask and points to cover.

The sell

Consider how you can best present your EVP to interest and enthuse candidates in your vacancy and the organisation. Think about how to describe what your department and organisation are like to work in, your leading and managing style and your expectations of team members. Decide how best to describe the job purpose and key duties and responsibilities of the position.

Be aware that candidates from different generations and different cultures may be interested in different aspects of the organisation's offerings. For example, young people are more likely to ask about work–life balance, sports facilities and your organisation's green credentials than their long-term prospects with the organisation. (Page 855 explains the information that is most likely to interest candidates from different generations and cultures.)

The 'sell' part of recruitment is critical when you're interviewing passive candidates and specialists. Don't waste your moments of truth and even create some positive ones with a follow-up phone call and an email or two to keep in touch; this creates a good impression and signals your continuing interest. Some interviewers ask passive candidates and specialists to discuss, or even to list and weight, their decision criteria in accepting a position. Knowing how candidates assess the position and organisation, means that you can provide information on what they care about most.

When you know, for example, that a candidate is looking for rapid promotion, you could explain how promotions work in your organisation, and talk briefly about the average and quickest time a new hire has been promoted. When it's training that interests a candidate, you can explain the learning and development, both formal and informal, the successful candidate can expect.

Your 'sell' must match reality, so be honest and factual. New employees enter into a psychological contract, or set of mutual expectations, based on the interview process, their position description and a range of discussions that take place as the employment relationship begins. So don't 'oversell' or 'undersell' your organisation or the position; painting an unrealistically rosy picture is likely to result in a dissatisfied employee within a short period, while too gloomy a picture may mean that you lose a potentially excellent employee.

The buy

Write down some questions under various headings based on your selection criteria. Use *open questions*, those that can't be answered by 'yes' or 'no', to encourage candidates to 'open up', for instance:

* 'Tell me about your last position.'
* 'What attracts you to the hospitality industry?'
* 'What made you decide to become an engineer/word processor/operator/trainee accountant?'

These are *general questions* that introduce a topic.

Avoid *leading questions* that flag the answer you're looking for or that lead candidates into answering what they think you want to hear. When you ask a *hypothetical question* such as 'What would you do if a customer were rude to you?', you'd not be surprised to hear: 'Oh, I'd always be pleasant no matter what', would you? So rule those kinds of questions out. Also avoid *multiple questions*, where you lamely ask a string of several questions, leaving the candidate to guess which one you want answered. (To find out more about the art of asking questions, see page 156.)

ACTION!

Just how good are you at developing open interview questions? Find out in the interactive self-test: How are your questioning skills? on  CourseMateExpress.

The Afghanis have a proverb, 'The water will run where it has in the past'. That's why you want to develop these two types of questions:

1. *Behaviour-based questions* target information about candidates' competencies relating to the position's requirements. These seek examples of candidates' past performance and conduct that you can use to predict their behaviour in your vacancy.
2. *Verbal simulation questions* discover the candidate's thinking process and likely future behaviour in a similar situation.

Behaviour-based questions

Behaviour-based questions bring out examples of candidates' experience in various areas of your selection criteria. Their answers build a picture of their competencies that relate to your vacancy.

● IN A NUTSHELL

Examples of behaviour-based questions

Here are some requests, questions and follow-up questions to use as a guide to developing your own to target your specific requirements:

- Adaptability/flexibility: Give me an example of a change in your work that you had to adapt to – how did you feel about it? How did you manage that change? What did you learn from that experience?
- Communication skills: Tell me about a time when, as a team member, you had to use spoken communication skills to get a point across. Were you successful? Did you use any other forms of communication to achieve your desired outcome? Tell me about a time when someone misunderstood something you said or wrote – how did you make your meaning clear? What was the result? Were you able to influence them?
- Customer service orientation: Tell me about a time when you felt you went beyond the call of duty to help a customer. How do you know it was appreciated? Describe a time when a customer requested something that was outside of your organisation's policy or guidelines and how you handled it.
- Innovation: Tell me about a time when you found a way to improve a procedure or the way something was normally done. How do you know your improvement was successful? Describe a problem you faced where the usual solutions wouldn't work and how you dealt with it. What makes you sure your solutions were successful?
- People skills/team working: Describe a situation in which you were able to 'read' another person accurately and deal successfully with them. How did you measure your success in that instance? Describe the most difficult customer/co-worker/manager you have ever encountered and how you handled him/her. What did you learn as a result? How would you do it next time? Give me an example of a time when people were disagreeing about how to proceed and you were able to influence them to work together effectively – what did you say or do? What effect did you have on the group? How do you typically handle conflict? Give me an example.
- Planning/time management: Tell me about a time when you were under pressure to get a lot done, quickly – how did you decide what to do in what order? Was your call correct? How do you know? Describe a lengthy or time-consuming project you have undertaken and how you approached it. Tell me about a time when you were working hard to meet a deadline – how did you manage your time and work with others to finish on time?
- Problem solving: Describe a difficult problem you have recently confronted and how you handled it. What did you learn from that? Describe a time when you needed to identify the cause of a problem in order to resolve it – how did you go about it? How do you know you identified the correct cause?
- Results orientation: Tell me about the most difficult task you have ever tackled. What were those difficulties? How did you deal with them? What was the outcome? Was it successful? How do you know? Tell me about your greatest success/biggest achievement so far. (Probe into reasons.) How did that come about? Which of your achievements make you most proud and why?
- Self-motivated/self-disciplined: What was the most helpful feedback you have received? How did it change your behaviour? Give me an example of a time when you had to 'dig deep' into your personal resources to complete something.

- Work without supervision/self-starter: Describe a time in your last position when you needed to work without supervision. Give me an example of an important goal that you have set in the past and tell me about your success in reaching it. In what areas would you like to expand your skills? How would that help you in your career or personally? What steps have you taken to expand those skills?
- Working style: Describe the most frustrating/enjoyable part of your current position (probe into reasons and get examples). Describe what you liked and disliked about how you were managed in previous positions. Tell me about what you dislike(d) about your current/last position (probe into reasons and get examples). Tell me about the most rewarding position you have held. What in particular made it so rewarding (ask for examples)? What triggered your decision to leave your last position?

Sometimes it is necessary to probe candidates for the specific answers you are looking for. Here are some examples of probing questions you can use in an interview (maintain an expectant silence while maintaining eye contact):

- Exactly what happened?
- Then what did you do?
- What happened next?

Don't let candidates waffle on about matters you are not interested in. Keep questioning to find out exactly what the candidate did and said and what the outcomes were. Here are some questions to draw out results:

- How did you know it was successful?
- How much money/customer loyalty did that make/save for the organisation?
- How much time/effort/money did that save?
- What did you learn as a result that you use in similar situations?

Verbal simulation questions

Since it's unlikely you can literally put candidates into typical work situations to see how they respond, you can give them something close to it with a verbal simulation question. Ask candidates to describe precisely how they would handle a particular situation they are likely to face in your vacancy. For example, you might describe a problem the successful candidate is likely to face during their first month in the position and ask them to walk you through the steps of how they would handle it.

Make sure candidates go into considerable detail in their answers. Listen for what is important in the position as they answer. For example, you might listen for the ability to handle stress; the ability to consult, coordinate or work with others; consideration and tact; problem-solving ability; and whether they included following up to make sure the solution was effective. Ask *follow-up* and *probing questions* as needed to overcome vague or incomplete answers and bring out the information you need ('What would you do next?', 'Then what?').

Although these are, strictly speaking, hypothetical questions, they are competency-based and provide you with considerable detail, giving you a window into candidates' thinking processes and likely future behaviour in a similar situation. Because your verbal simulation questions contain considerable detail, they invite a detailed response, rather than 'flights of fancy' and 'creativity'.

Step 2: Put the candidate at ease

Relaxed candidates are always more forthcoming than nervous ones, so help them relax as quickly as possible. Continuing to write up notes from your last interview, studying the application form or being otherwise 'engaged' is taboo.

Thank the candidate for coming and spend a few minutes building rapport. When you can see the candidate is relaxed and talking, move on to the main part of the interview.

 **IN A NUTSHELL**

Interviewing candidates from other cultures

Here are some tips for interviewing candidates from other cultures:

- Avoid acronyms and abbreviations when explaining the organisation, and avoid jargon, metaphors and expressions that someone from another culture may not understand.
- Be aware of culturally based body language and eye contact (see page 858).
- Don't raise your voice or speak 'baby English' to people with accents or who are hard of hearing.
- Explain the interview process before the candidate arrives and the general topics they can anticipate discussing; you can do this in a letter that also confirms the interview time and details.
- Keep your questions free of culture and value bias.
- When seeking information about candidates' achievements, be aware that some candidates may be more comfortable discussing group achievements.
- With candidates for whom English is a second language, wait patiently while they collect and present their thoughts.
- When you are not sure how to pronounce a name or in which order to use a name, find out before the interview or ask the candidate.
- When you are working with an interview panel, make it culturally diverse to minimise potential bias.
- When you don't understand something the candidate says, ask them to repeat it in a way that accepts responsibility for not understanding rather than places blame on the candidate's speech.

Step 3: The main parts of the interview

Now comes the 'selling' part of the interview, where you explain the position, the organisation and your EVP, and the 'buying' part, where you find out how well the candidate meets your needs. The order of these parts of the interview is a matter of personal preference. The main thing is to avoid going on and on, in far too much detail, about the position or the organisation – the more you talk, the less you learn about the applicant.

Don't rush through interviews. This is an important step for both of you: you want to find out how suitable candidates are for the position, and they want to know whether they want to work with you.

Probing the candidate's suitability

Effective questioning and listening skills develop with practice. Meanwhile, here are two guidelines:

- Question with a purpose: Whether you agree or disagree with the candidate's answers, remain neutral. Get specific evidence of each candidate's ability (or lack of it) to meet your selection criteria.

- Give the applicant enough time to think and respond to your questions: Don't jump in to fill the gap of a thoughtful silence. Show that you are listening with eye contact, periodic summaries, reflective listening responses, and so on (as explained on page 158). Don't jump to conclusions and don't forget to ask some questions whose answers could challenge your assumptions, first impressions and the halo/horns effect.

Find out more about what questions to ask to gather information on page 941.

IN A NUTSHELL

Some Dos and Don'ts when asking questions

If you want the best results from interviewing a candidate, it's important that you do ask some questions and don't ask others. Here are some examples:

Do	Don't
• Aim for a conversational flavour to the interview, not a rigid question-and-answer session.	• Don't allow interruptions or distractions such as telephone calls to spoil your interview.
• Allow candidates enough time to answer.	• Don't ask 'cute' or trick questions such as: 'Tell me about yourself' or 'Why should I give this position to you?' These don't draw out specific behavioural information related to your requirements except by chance.
• Ask neutral questions and use neutral language.	• Don't ask hypothetical questions: 'What would you do if ... ?'
• Ask questions that draw out specific behavioural information that relates to the position's requirements.	• Don't ask illegal or discriminatory questions geared around, for example, age, disabilities, gender, nationality or race.
• Encourage quiet candidates to provide details.	• Don't ask leading questions ('You will be able to work overtime, won't you?').
• Find out whether candidates are *motivated* to do the work as well as whether they *can* do it.	• Don't do all the talking.
• Keep the flow of the interview moving smoothly.	• Don't make snap judgements.
• Keep concentrating and listening.	• Don't unduly pressure candidates or put them under contrived stress to 'test' their tolerance.

As the interview progresses, you probably need to jot down a few brief notes or key words to jog your memory after the interview but keep them short so you can give every candidate your complete attention. It goes without saying that cluttering up an interview with distractions such as shuffling papers, writing or taking telephone calls disrupts your train of thought and is rude – it announces that you don't think the candidate is important enough for your undivided attention.

THEORY TO PRACTICE

Here's how to assess a cultural fit

You can just ask candidates whether they think they would fit into the organisation's culture, but you'd just hear 'Yes, absolutely' to that obvious question. A better way is to give candidates a long list of cultural factors and ask them to select and rank the top five under which they do their best work, and the lowest five – those that they find intolerable. Now you can assess how well a candidate can fit into your organisation and team culture and how well your organisation and team meet their needs.[15]

Step 4: Close the interview

When you have the information you need, find out whether the candidate has any questions. Be ready for questions like 'What's your sustainability policy?' Your response could make the difference between a 'yes' and a 'no' to a job offer.

Before you part, explain the next step (perhaps another interview or that you will make the selection decision after meeting with a few other candidates) and when and how you will be in touch. Thank candidates for coming in and for their interest in the position and your organisation. Check whether they are still interested in the vacancy. Finally, stand up and show them to the door or out of the building; you may want to briefly show them around the work area on the way out.

THEORY TO PRACTICE

Getting the right approach

Imagine you are recruiting an administrator to work in a large open-plan office in a position that requires frequent contact with others both inside and outside the department. You therefore decide that one attribute you need to look for is a friendly, outgoing approach. One candidate spends her spare time reading, listening to music and riding her pony on her own and doesn't belong to any clubs; another applicant regularly plays golf with a group of friends, was president of his school photography club and currently coaches a junior cricket team. Which candidate sounds more promising to you so far?

One of the administrator's duties is filing information accurately for easy retrieval. The cricket coach candidate has had experience filing in other positions and filing information to assist his studies at college. As the interview progresses, though, you find out that, although he has had filing experience, he finds the task mundane and boring. The pony-riding candidate has no previous filing experience but has used her abilities to organise information methodically in other ways. Now which candidate sounds more promising?

Further into the interview, other information or evidence comes to light as you ask questions to find out as much as you can about what each applicant has done, enjoyed and learned in the past and compare it with the position requirements. Gradually, you build up an evidence-based picture of each candidate's skills, knowledge and abilities.

Step 5: Assess the candidate's suitability

No doubt you made a few notes during the interview itself. Nevertheless, take a few minutes after each interview to gather your thoughts. Note down your overall impressions, the strong and weak points of the candidate, and where the candidate matched and didn't match your person specification. You may find it useful to do this point by point, following your person specification. Write down anything you need to help you recall each candidate (remembering they can ask to see your interview notes); it's easy to confuse candidates without clear notes to jog your memory.

Don't overrate the last person you interviewed. That candidate might look better simply because your own interviewing skills have improved with practice. When all the interviews are completed, review the candidates as described on page 819.

As with one-on-one interviews, document the process of group and panel interviews so that, should it be necessary due to a challenge or an appeal, you have an accurate audit trail and can clearly show that the interview was fair.

> **◉ ACTION!**
>
> You can find the checklist: How professionally did you lead the recruitment interview? on  CourseMateExpress. It can help you assess how professionally you led your interview. You can also use it as a pre-interview checklist to make sure you're fully prepared.

4. Helping recruits fit in and do well

> I want all our people to believe they are working for the best agency in the world. A sense of pride works wonders.
>
> David Ogilvy (founder, Ogilvy and Mather advertising agency), *The unpublished David Ogilvy* (2012)[16]

Recruits are usually highly enthusiastic about their new position. Good induction helps ensure they stay enthusiastic, 'find their feet' and begin contributing as soon as possible. It makes people feel welcome and valued.

Induction consists of more than just introducing new employees to their duties and their workmates. It runs the entire gamut of helping them settle in and fit into their new position, work team and organisation as smoothly as possible. It anticipates and answers questions new people might have but don't know who to ask or don't feel sufficiently confident to ask them, and shapes their approach to their new position by establishing clear expectations about their duties and how to carry them out. It also shapes their behaviour in the organisation by reviewing key policies and expectations.

Induction is important for another reason: just as employers often take on a new employee on a probationary basis, employers are also on trial. New employees determine, generally during their first few weeks, whether the position and the organisation live up to their expectations. When induction fails to build engagement and make new employees feel 'this is an organisation I can be proud to be part of', they soon withdraw their efforts and look for other work. Provided you haven't misrepresented your organisation's EVP, when employees leave in the first few months, poor induction rather than poor selection is the likely reason, wasting the time, effort and money spent in recruiting new employees.

A new employee's first few days and weeks are about more than induction, though. Give new team members something useful to do as quickly as possible and give them a goal they can reach in the first few weeks. People need to know they're doing 'real' work and making progress.

◉ IN A NUTSHELL

The advantages of good induction

Here are four good reasons to induct recruits properly:

1. Good induction helps calm the normal nervousness people feel when starting a new position; as you probably remember from your own experience, the first few days in new surroundings can be awkward.

2. Good induction helps show new employees how the EVP works in practice, reinforcing their favourable impression of the organisation and contributing to their overall enthusiasm for their new position. This develops good morale and improves retention.

3. Induction can reduce the time new employees spend ineffectively by providing a carefully planned program to follow during their first few days. Asking too much or too little of new employees can be frustrating and destroy their confidence. An induction program that gently builds employees' skills and knowledge avoids this.

4. Induction lets you launch a good working relationship and begin building trust and rapport with new employees during these early, crucial days. It's an opportunity like no other to establish performance and behavioural guidelines; clearly explaining the rules, regulations, expectations and group norms to minimise misunderstandings. The sooner newcomers are aware of these matters, the more successful and productive their early days can be.

What should induction cover?

Whether an employee is totally new to your organisation or transfers into your department from another part of the organisation, everyone new to your department should receive some sort of induction.

Think of induction as having two parts: induction to the organisation and induction to your department and team. The HR department often carries out induction to the organisation or provides you and new employees with the relevant checklist for accessing information in booklets or electronically. It should be completed soon after employees join the organisation and cover, for example, the organisation's key policies and programs (e.g. corporate social responsibility, risk management and sustainability policies, flexible working and well-being programs) and general items, such as protecting the organisation's intellectual property and maintaining confidentiality, pay arrangements and employee benefits and activities. It should also explain the organisation as a whole: how it is structured, where the recruit fits in, the organisation's history, and its products, services and customers.

If your organisation has no HR function, cover both the organisation and the departmental induction yourself. Think about what you need to cover and how. Develop your own induction checklists and keep them on file so that you can use them with all new employees.

You're in charge of induction to your department. You can do it all yourself, delegate parts of it to a team member or make it a team affair, as described on page 837. The key is to explain the rules and regulations, the safety hazards and procedures, any special duties and responsibilities involved in the position, where to find the necessary equipment and tools, and so on.

Your responsibility for inducting new employees

Induction begins before day one. From the moment you decide which candidate to select, your general approach sets the scene for their future relationship with you, their work team and the organisation. Show interest in new employees and show that you want to help make the transition to their new position smooth and painless.

Email your new team member with information about dress style, security procedures, start time, where to park and where to report on arrival. (File the email in a recruitment e-file so you don't have to reinvent the wheel each time someone joins your team.) Post an information pack that includes the organisation's annual report, employee handbook, terms of employment, a copy of the organisation's latest internal newsletter or magazine, and so on, or email these as links to the organisation's relevant Intranet sites with a temporary password. That way, new employees can begin exploring the organisation and feel more comfortable when they arrive on their first day.

Email internal suppliers and customers, reception, relevant managers and security announcing the new employee's imminent arrival. Give the recruit's name, title and phone extension and a little bit of background information that people can use as conversation starters when they first meet your new team member.

Personally greet and welcome new team members on their first day. Make sure their workspace is cleared and clean for them, including desk drawers and cabinets, and that their IT needs are met; for example, email account up and running, password and security pass issued. Give them a schedule of the briefings you have arranged on different aspects of the organisation and an outline of their induction program.

Use the five keys, particularly the '*what to*' key, to make sure recruits understand their role and responsibilities and how they contribute to the team. Take the opportunity to clearly outline any 'hot-stove', or bottom-line rules. Spend some time getting to know new team members so that you can manage the '*want to*' key effectively. (Chapter 11 explains the five keys to unlocking performance and productivity.)

Think about welcoming new employees with an informal team lunch or morning tea, or invite team members to bring their lunch and adjourn to a nearby park to welcome their new team-mate.

Use the opportunity of a new team member joining to hold a mini team-building meeting during the first week or two. Give team members, including the new team member, a few days to think about the following:

* My special skills and abilities are …
* My working style is …
* The unique knowledge I bring to the team is …
* The benefits my unique knowledge, skills, style and interests bring to the team are …
* Three things I'm most interested in (inside or outside work) are …

Meet over an informal lunch or during a regular team meeting and ask team members to take turns answering the first point, then the second, and so on. In this way, the team and their new colleague quickly learn about each other and how everyone can best contribute to the team's results.

As you go through the induction program, use what you learned during the selection interview to emphasise how the organisation's policies and other arrangements relate to what the new employee values and is interested in.

Setting up an induction program

First, make three lists: a list to remind you of the actions you need to take before a new employee's first day, a list of the topics to cover for organisation induction and a list of topics to cover for department induction. Put the actions and topics into a suitable sequence and add a column for target completion dates and another to sign and date when you've covered the topic. These are your masters – print them off as you need them to use with each new employee, with occasional minor updates.

⦿ ACTION!

If your HR department hasn't developed these lists for you, you can find an Induction checklist on ⦿ CourseMateExpress to help you ensure new team members transition to the team and the organisation smoothly. The checklist also includes things to do before a new team member's first day on the job.

Don't bombard new employees with too much information at once. Information given in one big 'hit' is difficult to remember. Put yourself in the shoes of new employees: What would you want to know first? How much information would you be able to retain? Provide information in 'bite-sized' chunks and stagger it through their first few working weeks (with the emphasis on working, since that's why employees are there).

For example, you might have a 20-day organisation induction plan spread over several weeks, with one activity scheduled for each day, such as meeting the senior manager of your department's function, calling on an internal or external customer, or joining the CEO for an informal lunch (but don't let it drag on so long that both you and the new employee lose interest).

In general, give the information of most direct relevance to new employees first, such as where the toilets are, where they should park and how their pay is calculated. Once they begin to settle in, you can move on to more general information – the overall structure of the organisation, who the senior managers are and what they're responsible for, how superannuation is calculated, and so on. Include the unwritten regulations, rules and taboos of your team and organisation, too, and make sure they know who the power brokers are and how to impress them.

Give new employees some meaningful work to do, too, something where they can score some quick and visible wins if possible – setting up a new database, contributing to the organisation's newsletter, clearing out a backlog of work. Set some short-term deliverables so recruits know what they're shooting for and find out what support they need to achieve them. And remember to provide plenty of positive feedback to boost their confidence.

⦿ THEORY TO PRACTICE

A great place to work

Melbourne-based OBS is an IT services company that stresses work–life balance, health and wellness, a culture that provides empowerment, a sense of family and pride, and staff who stay 'for the long term'. It begins before a new recruit joins, when they're sent a large OBS gift box including OBS shirts, a 'hitchhiker's guide' to OBS, lollies and material relating to their role.

Induction is designed to give recruits the best possible first impression of the organisation and make them feel like part of the family from day one, when they participate in a detailed induction. The rest of their induction, which continues over the next three months, is carefully planned and monitored by their manager.[17]

The 'cobber' system

Sometimes there are so many new hires that if leader-managers were to carry out the entire induction program themselves they would have little time for their other duties. That's when the Australian Army's 'cobber' system comes in. Cobbers, or mates, should be experienced, organisation-minded people who are fully conversant with the organisation's benefits, EVP, procedures, regulations and rules, and who can answer most questions new employees ask.

Try appointing a 'cobber' – an experienced workmate – to assist new employees during their first few days or weeks of employment. This gives them an additional, and appreciated, point of contact and someone to go to with questions, taking some of the load off your shoulders.

A team effort

When you have a cohesive, congenial work group, make induction a team effort. You can welcome the new start to the team and go through their position description, then hand over to various team members, singly and in pairs, to explain other aspects of the induction program. It takes a bit of organising but helps the team and their new colleague get to know each other and develop effective working relationships and helps people feel 'at home' more quickly. An induction like this spread over several weeks becomes more of a dialogue than the traditional 'listen up while I explain this to you'.

E-induction

Some organisations use technology to ease and speed induction. New team members are sent a tablet a few weeks before they start, with downloads on everything from who's who in the workplace to safety procedures and the best places to eat lunch.

With a bit more investment, some organisations develop online induction modules that new employees can access on the organisation's Intranet. Topics such as the organisation's structure and culture, its history, policies, products and services, and messages from the CEO, other leaders and key people such as employee and health and safety representatives are all suited to e-induction. Once these are developed, induction costs are considerably reduced, particularly for organisations that are geographically dispersed.

While technology can never fully replace the personal contact that face-to-face induction provides, it can streamline the induction process, saving money and time and increasing consistency. It can also offer an engaging 'edgy' option that many recruits appreciate and reinforce your organisation's branding, culture and values. And, of course, it's portable – recruits can access e-induction when and where it suits them and digest this important information at their own pace.

THEORY TO PRACTICE

McDuction makes McEfficiency

Part of McDonald's Australia's e-recruitment package is online induction. Every month, an average of 4000 new 'crew' (non-management employees) are paid for two hours at their normal hourly rate to complete their online induction into one of the chain's 780 restaurants around the country. (The system will eventually include e-communication, including a crew portal with social networking, blogging and e-learning.)

McDonald's is a high-volume inductor. Sanofi-Aventis, an ethical pharmaceuticals company, is a low-volume inductor. For Sanofi, online inductions provide a cost-efficient way to deliver timely information to low numbers of recruits scattered around the country. Instead of waiting an average of four months for a critical mass of 30 or 40 new people to build up before running induction centrally, the company can now e-induct new starts on their first day.

>>

In both cases, e-induction supplements, but does not replace, face-to-face orientation. McDonald's franchisees still conduct induction modules face-to-face in the restaurant. However, because of the high numbers of new hires, e-induction saves franchisees a lot of time and, thanks to a more thorough induction, crew turnover is trending downwards. Sanofi continues to run quarterly facilitator-led inductions at head office but still manages to save on airfares, accommodation, materials and time off the road for sales representatives (which alone costs $600 a day).[18]

Employees with special needs

Members of disadvantaged groups are more at risk than others, so identify and take their specific requirements into account when designing or delivering their induction (and other training programs). For example, while you should always pay special attention to health and safety matters and workplace hazards, accident rates are higher and tend to be more serious for young workers, so consider assigning an experienced worker or 'cobber' to ease them into their new position.[19] While young people are not all the same, many lack workplace experience, which can lead to accidents when they don't fully understand the potential dangers and the need for special precautions.

Induction information, safety signs and operating instructions for machinery printed only in English can disadvantage and place at risk people from non-English-speaking backgrounds. To help them, you can obtain health and safety publications printed in a variety of languages from the occupational health and safety authority in your state or territory. Encourage these employees to participate in committees and make sure they have access to all information that affects their employment. Make sure all workers can easily understand the symbols used in the workplace.

Assist people with disabilities. The main goal in inducting and training people with intellectual disabilities is to create independence. Use the 'show me' technique throughout their induction and training to ensure you have explained sufficiently. People with movement problems may have difficulty walking up stairs or reaching or grasping objects. Adjustments to the workplace can assist people with motor impairments and those who are amputees. Work through their individual needs with them carefully.

One in seven workers in Australia do not have the reading and writing skills they need to work efficiently and safely, and in some industries this figure is even higher. This can make it more difficult for them to acquire the needed skills and knowledge, complete forms and understand their workplace rights and responsibilities. They may have difficulty, for example, with written emergency procedures, machine operation manuals, and safety instructions and precautions. Take special care to induct and train them fully (for information on assisting people with visual and hearing impairments, see page 855).

Performance reviews for new team members

Conduct fortnightly or monthly performance discussions with new team members for the first few months and regularly chat with them informally. Let them know how they are progressing and fitting in. Ask whether the position is proving to be what they had expected and whether they are enjoying it. Guided by the five keys, highlight and explain any concerns and analyse with the employee the possible causes and develop an improvement plan. (See pages 437 and 447 for information on how to review performance formally and informally.)

Make certain that there are no misunderstandings at this early stage. Note these discussions in your diary or in the employee's personal file. Should it become clear you've made a mistake and no amount of coaching, cajoling or training can transform the recruit's performance to the required level, terminate the employment before it's too late

CourseMateExpress

Go to http://login.cengagebrain.com to access CourseMate Express, your online study tool for *Management Theory & Practice*. CourseMate Express brings chapter concepts to life with interactive learning, and study and exam preparation tools:

- Test your skills in different aspects of management with interactive self-tests and simulations.
- Watch videos that show how real managers operate in real businesses.
- Test your understanding of the changing world of management by taking the revision quiz.

QUICK REVIEW

1. Briefly explain why recruitment is both a selling and a buying activity and the six tools that help you succeed in these activities.
2. Discuss the sources of information about candidates and the role each plays in building a better understanding of them.
3. Describe the five steps of a recruitment interview. What should interviewers do before and after the interview?
4. What is induction intended to achieve? What are a leader-manager's responsibilities in induction?

BUILD YOUR SKILLS

1. In what way is recruitment a public relations exercise?
2. Develop a short planning agenda for a meeting between members of a panel interview.
3. The next time you are in a fast-food outlet or department store, carefully observe the people who are serving customers. Is anyone particularly good at the job? Is anyone not very good? Based on your observations, develop some criteria for selecting customer service staff for this establishment. Develop six questions you could ask to determine candidates' suitability for a position there.
4. Manager A says she hires only those people who have the experience and competencies she is looking for, because she doesn't have the time to carry out a lot of on-the-job training. Manager B says she would rather hire a person with the right 'approach' and train them herself, so the duties are carried out just the way she wants. Who do you agree with? Why? Which approach would save more time in the long run? Why?

5. Discuss the benefits of thorough induction and training to: (1) the trainee, (2) the manager, (3) the work team and (4) the organisation.

6. Referring to Case Study 9.2 on page 284, discuss how new members are introduced to this team. Would this work at all workplaces? Why or why not?

WORKPLACE ACTIVITIES

1. Which sources of recruitment are best suited for the positions at your workplace? Why?

2. Develop a series of behavioural questions to target key aspects of your own position or a position that reports to you. Refer to the position description and, if there isn't one already, develop a person specification to refer to.

    Next, develop a telephone reference check for this position. Note what you would say at the beginning of the call and list the questions you would ask. Finally, prepare a general outline to use in a monthly performance review with a new employee in this position during their probationary period. Be sure to include key deliverables or measures of success in key result areas.

3. Design an induction program for your department or college and explain how it should be conducted.

CASE STUDY 25.1

SAM'S RECRUITMENT PROBLEM

The business is poised for major growth and discussions with his manager have convinced Sam Tomayko that his success as a team leader depends in part on his recruitment skills. Sam studies his team members to determine what makes them successful. Choosing the best of them, he suggests that they ask their friends to apply for positions he knows will soon be opening up.

This approach seems to work, since a number of prospective applicants contact him. He interviews those who appear to have the necessary experience and personal qualities.

His practice is to fit the interviews into the normal day's activities, with the telephone ringing constantly and people dropping into the office for advice, to leave messages or even to have Sam make one of his 'on-the-spot' decisions. Between these interruptions, Sam carries out the interviews, dominating the time available by talking about the position, the opportunities in the organisation and his own impressions of what makes a successful applicant.

Throughout the interview, he makes notes and symbols on each applicant's form. To save paperwork and time, he likes to make a decision as to whether the applicant has the position before the interview is over and let them know on the spot.

Several weeks later, Sam's manager calls Sam into his office to discuss the people problems developing in his department. It seems that recruits are not suitably qualified for their positions, while applicants known to have the necessary skills were informed at their interviews that they were not the type of employee the organisation was seeking or that the position would not suit them or their background.

Sam's manager wants to work out an action plan to help Sam develop his skills in recruitment and selection. Together, they consider what to include and how it can best be covered.

Questions

1. Is Sam's manager wasting her time? Why, or why not?
2. What are the specific problems with Sam's interviewing technique?
3. Explain a better way to reach a selection decision.
4. What topics should be included in the action plan to develop Sam's skills? How could they be covered (e.g. through reading books, attending evening classes, coaching from the HR manager, role-playing)?

CASE STUDY 25.2

EAST-WEST OIL

The East-West Oil Company is a growing company with a progressive management team. Brian Vawn is in charge of the company's retail outlets (service stations). In general, the company tries to locate a service station in towns with a population of 15 000 or more, but location also depends on business potential, competition and a suitable site.

East-West employs a local manager on a profit-sharing basis in its service stations. The managers operate within broad company guidelines and with minimum direct supervision. Every station is required to sell batteries, oil, tyres and related products as well as petrol and diesel. They can sell additional products at their discretion and many stations carry lines such as confectionery, fast food, grocery items and soft drinks. With company encouragement, most stations operate a service centre that carries out minor car repairs. Most of these centres, for example, balance and align wheels, correct minor electrical troubles, give motor tune-ups and reline brakes.

The manager of the Vancetown station has notified Brian that he intends to retire. Located in an area with a population of 88 000, Vancetown is one of East-West's most profitable and best-equipped stations. Situated at the intersection of two main highways, it attracts a great deal of passing trade as well as local trade.

The station has eight pumps and operates two wash pits, two lubrication bays and a large service centre employing four full-time mechanics. With the exception of the service centre, the station is open 24 hours a day. Turnover has climbed steadily in the last 10 years.

Finding the right person to replace the station manager won't be easy, but Brian is encouraged by the background and record of one applicant, Ralph Lewis. Ralph is a first-rate motor mechanic who has been employed for the past 12 years with a local transport firm. He has a good record with that company and at present is in charge of a fleet of 12 trucks. He has also worked as a front-end specialist, a transmission mechanic and a tune-up specialist.

Questions

1. On the basis of the information presented in the case study, develop a brief role description and person specification for the vacancy.
2. If you were interviewing Ralph Lewis, what would you need to know to make a decision about hiring him?
3. Prepare an interview outline showing several behavioural questions to use at each stage of the interview.

CHAPTER

26

MAKING THE MOST OF DIVERSITY

OVERVIEW

Perhaps a few of your team members look too young to shave while some are old enough to be your parents. Maybe one or two sport a nose ring while another dons a hijab and yet another a turban. Maybe one is an athlete, and another is in a wheelchair, some have parenting responsibilities and others care for elderly relatives.

This shouldn't be too surprising in a country made up of people of varying abilities, ages and responsibilities, and who come from diverse backgrounds and heritages. We vary in age, education, family status, physical and mental abilities, religion, sexual orientation, socioeconomic status and a host of other characteristics. Australia is one of the most diverse nations in the world.

Organisations and work teams that reflect the general population and their customers have a distinct advantage over homogeneous organisations and teams – provided you don't try to apply one set of rules to today's wide range of employees. Leader-managers need to know how to work with, motivate, and bring out the best in a changing and diverse workforce, not just as groups of employees but also as individuals, each with their own unique needs and preferences.

1. Can you explain how diversity benefits organisations, employees, customers and the country and do you know how to promote and make the most of diversity?
2. Can you spot discrimination when it occurs and implement a diversity policy in your work team to encourage a diverse workforce?
3. Do you know how to foster respect for diversity in your work team?

In many ways, strength lies in difference. In this chapter, you find out how to tap the vast Australian reservoir of potential. But a word of warning: don't become so aware of differences that you ignore similarities. What people hold in common provides the basis for building a strong work team. Finding a way to bring everyone's diverse attributes together is what makes diversity – and teams – powerful.

842

I have your back

'The standard you walk past is the standard you accept.' These words were delivered in a speech by Lieutenant General David Morrison as Australia's Chief of Army.[1] The speech was written for him by the former Army Lieutenant Colonel Malcolm McGregor, a cricket-loving, rugby-playing member of the Order of Australia, awarded for exceptional service to the Australian Army.

For some time, Malcolm had felt like an 'out of tune orchestra'. Something was not right. Conflicted about his gender from childhood and on the brink of suicide, he finally stopped fighting his inner feelings and transitioned to Lieutenant Colonel Catherine (Cate) McGregor.

What would her boss, David Morrison, with whom, as Malcolm, she had served as an infantry soldier many years before, make of the transition? Morrison remained true to his word. He said to her, simply, 'I'm with you.' Morrison also remained true to his commitment to stamp out the Army's grim record as a place of bullying and sexual harassment and transform it into a place where respect is a core value.

His support, acceptance and affirmation of Cate's value as a human being and as a soldier became a contributing factor to her life as a woman: 'It's a wonderful feeling to be alive and be me,' she said in an interview in 2014.[2]

1. Promoting the benefits of diversity

We need every human gift and cannot afford to neglect any gift because of artificial barriers of sex or race or class or national origin.

Margaret Mead (anthropologist), in Pipher, *The Middle of Everywhere (2002)*[3]

Can you imagine …

* a woman being forced to resign from a government job because she marries?
* access to superannuation based on your sex?
* the colour of your skin dictating which jobs you are allowed to do?
* your sex determining how much money you earn?

It sounds terrible, but it's far from ancient history. The first three in the list above describe the employment situation in Australia in the 1960s. The fourth situation – your sex determining how much money you earn – continues to apply today (more about that below).

The idea that everyone should have equal access to jobs and opportunities and equal pay for equal work is relatively recent. It wasn't until 1967 that Aboriginal and Torres Strait Islander people were eligible to apply for Federal Government jobs; it wasn't until the 1980s that the Commonwealth outlawed discrimination on the grounds of sex; and it wasn't until the 1990s that it outlawed discrimination on the grounds of a person's disabilities. Of course, outlawing a behaviour doesn't make it stop.

What do you think?

* More women work part time than men. Therefore does it follow that they, and others who work part time, are less committed to their jobs than people who work full-time?
* Are people with disabilities as productive as people without disabilities?
* Are men less patient and intuitive but better with numbers and decision-making than women?
* Do older people learn as quickly as younger people?
* Is it better to try to conform to the **norms** of the workplace than be true to yourself?

It's easy to close doors to people and exclude them from opportunities without meaning to, based on unconsciously held misconceptions.

Australia is a big country, filled with an assortment of people, each with the potential to make meaningful contributions to our economy and to society. Yet there is no doubt that some are members of groups that experience higher levels of unemployment than the population in general, and many face barriers and other disadvantages in their employment throughout their working lives.

The International Labour Organization defines discrimination as 'any distinction, exclusion or preference made based on race, colour, sex, etc. which has the effect of nullifying or impairing equality of opportunity or treatment in employment or occupation'. The groups most at risk of discrimination in Australia have been:

- Aboriginal and Torres Strait Islander people
- migrants
- people with disabilities
- women.

This doesn't mean that every person who belongs to one or more of these groups is disadvantaged, but people who belong to one or more of these groups are more likely to be disadvantaged than those who do not. Statistically, for example, individuals who are members of these groups tend to be:

- concentrated in a limited range of occupations
- concentrated in low-paying, low-status jobs
- excluded from the labour force for reasons not related to their ability to perform a job
- limited in their opportunities for career progression
- more likely to be unemployed
- more likely to face prejudice when applying for a job and throughout their working life.

As a result, organisations aren't making full use of the talent available.

 FYI

Not a pretty picture

Australia has the lowest percentage of women in management and one of the most gender-segregated workforces in the industrialised world.[4] Women are employed in a narrower range of industries and occupations than are men, are clustered lower down the organisational hierarchy and are offered less training than men. For every dollar that men earn, women earn 85.1 cents – a record-high gap.[5] (Gender diversity is discussed on page 867.)

Similar patterns are found in other groups of Australians such as migrants, older workers and people from non-English-speaking backgrounds.

Some of the barriers to career advancement faced by people from disadvantaged groups are:

- a shortage of affordable child care, which particularly affects women
- a conscious or unconscious bias in recruiting and promotion
- exclusion from informal networks
- lack of mentoring opportunities
- lack of role models (few people from disadvantaged groups, for example, are on boards of directors or work at management level)
- perceptions that cultural or religious practices, family responsibilities, and so on interfere with work
- stereotypes and preconceptions based on, for example, sex, race and ethnicity influencing employment-related decisions.

Anti-discrimination legislation

Known collectively as *anti-discrimination legislation,* state and territory legislation closely mirrors the following federal Acts:

- *The Workplace Gender Equality Act 2012* (updating the *Equal Opportunity for Women in the Workplace Act 1999* and renaming the Equal Opportunity for Women in the Workplace Agency the Workplace Gender Equality Agency)
- *The Sex Discrimination Act 1984* with amendments made in 2004
- *The Age Discrimination Act 2004* with amendments made in 2009
- *The Disability Discrimination Act 1992* with amendments made in 2009
- *Fair Work Act 2009*
- *Australian Human Rights Commission Act 2009* (formerly the *Human Rights and Equal Opportunity Commission Act 1986*)
- *The Racial Discrimination Act 1975* with amendments made in 1980.

These Acts are the key legislative mechanisms for achieving diversity and equality in employment and in other areas of life. They prohibit discrimination based on:

- age
- breastfeeding
- carer status
- colour, nationality or national extraction, race and ethnicity
- disability (intellectual, learning, neurological, physical, psychiatric)
- family responsibilities
- gender, gender identity, intersex status and sexual orientation
- irrelevant criminal record
- irrelevant medical record
- marital status
- parental status (including pregnancy)
- political opinion
- religion
- social origin
- the presence of disease-causing illness
- trade union activities.

The Acts are based on common sense and fair play and aim to ensure everyone has a fair go. They cover full-time and part-time employees, temporary employees and contractors. They describe how and to whom people can make complaints concerning discrimination and provide a means to rectify or compensate for acts of discrimination.

Anti-discrimination legislation requires organisations to examine their policies and identify and eliminate differences in employee benefits, conditions of employment, pay, perks, promotions, transfers and a host of other job-related conditions. It requires all managers to make objective decisions relating to hiring, firing, paying, promoting, training and developing, and transferring employees. You can achieve these aims by following these two important principles:

1. Make *merit* – a person's ability to do a job – the sole consideration in employment decisions and ignore irrelevant factors such as age, nationality and sex.
2. Take into account only job-related characteristics, especially skills and abilities.

The diversity dividend

The diversity approach stresses the benefits that organisations can reap from capitalising on all types of individual differences. When organisations manage diversity well, they become more intelligent as people's distinctive strengths and weaknesses combine to make the whole greater than the sum of the parts. Different ways to approach challenges, make suggestions and decisions, and react to problems and think about how to solve them, increase an organisation's creativity, flexibility and innovativeness. Given the right conditions, diverse, or *heterogeneous*, teams can produce better decisions, more robust debate and more and better ideas than *homogeneous* teams, or those made up of people with similar backgrounds.

Workplaces filled with a range of people reflect the customers and communities they serve and provide a greater understanding of the organisation's other stakeholders and its marketplace than homogeneous workplaces. New ways of working and finding new and better ways to serve customers and achieve goals can result, giving culturally complex organisations a competitive advantage and more business opportunities.

Recruitment from the total labour pool and open and fair employment policies and practices enhance an organisation's image and reputation and help it compete for quality employees. An organisation culture that respects diversity means you don't lose good people because they feel marginalised or uncomfortable and you don't spend time and money on diversity-based employee grievances. It also help you to identify and rectify indirect discrimination through appropriately flexible measures that accommodate the differences among the workforce, which builds an environment where everyone is valued, recognised and supported. This increases employee loyalty. When people know they are working for an employer who cares about them as a person, regardless of their sex, race, national origin or anything else, they are more likely to return this respect.

But does diversity make money? Academic research has consistently concluded that it makes good business sense to harness the benefits of cultural diversity and that for the public and private sectors to remain competitive and lead the world in the provision of services, they must adopt cultural diversity.[7]

Diversity can also improve retention. For example, Hewlett-Packard Australia implemented a diversity management strategy that addressed the concerns of minority employees and reduced its workforce turnover from the IT industry average of 25% to about 8% over a three-year period.[8]

Diversity and innovation

Diversity can be *acquired* or *inherent*. Acquired diversity, as the name implies, is gained from experience. You might work with people from different cultures and gain cultural intelligence, for example. Inherent diversity refers to characteristics people are born with, such as gender, ethnicity and some physical and mental impairments.

A large research study found that companies whose leader-managers possess at least three acquired and three inherent diversity traits – *2-D diversity* – out-innovate and out-perform less diverse companies. The researchers concluded that 2-D diversity increases innovation by creating an environment where people feel able to speak up and suggest novel ideas.[9]

2. Implementing a diversity policy

What attracted me [to Infosys] was the company's global perspective. I liked that ... because my natural instincts are to look for people who are different but complimentary.

Jackie Klorhonen (managing director, Infosys), in McManus, *Murthy's Law* (September 2012)[10]

Infosys Australia and New Zealand has a leadership team of approximately one-third Australians, one-third Indians and one-third from a mix of other countries. The aim of diversity is not to assimilate 'outsiders' into a dominant culture but to create a dominant heterogeneous culture in which everyone is valued, has a 'fair go' and has a chance to contribute. This means not letting prejudice or stereotypes influence your judgement about who to recruit, train, coach, promote, reward or assign work and projects to. In short, it means basing all employment-related decisions solely on the requirements of the job and the *merit principle* – a person's ability to do the job.

When you think a factor such as age, criminal record, political opinion, religion or sex is relevant to deciding who to hire, promote or train, or to some other employment-related decision, you need to be able to prove how and why this is the case.

Ways to discriminate

There are five main ways to discriminate:

1. Overt discrimination.
2. Covert discrimination.
3. Direct discrimination.
4. Indirect discrimination.
5. Structural, or systemic, discrimination.

Let's have a look at these in more detail.

Overt and covert discrimination

Have you ever heard someone say, 'We don't want to employ a woman because women can't handle the pressure' or 'Don't employ an Aboriginal – he'll go walkabout on you'? That is *overt discrimination* – clear, direct discrimination on the grounds of race, sex, social origin or one of the other factors listed above.

Covert discrimination is more subtle and therefore more difficult to spot. There are two main types. Have you ever heard someone say, 'I try not to hire newlyweds because they're likely to start a family and come to work to catch up on sleep' or 'It's risky hiring students – they're just here for the beer money'? That type of covert discrimination makes assumptions about people based on characteristics that belong to some members of a group – but not everyone in that group.

For instance, assuming that a woman plans to have a family and intends to leave paid employment to do so can make managers reluctant to promote, train or otherwise invest time, money or effort in her. Or when people return to work after taking a career break to stay at home with young children, their skills may be outdated or rusty, or perceived to be so, and they may lack confidence in their abilities due to their time away from paid employment. Women's child bearing role has placed them at a disadvantage in employment both before and after they have children and in other employment-related matters such as superannuation, which rewards long and continuous periods of employment.

The second type of covert discrimination is based on characteristics that are incorrectly or unfairly associated with people of a particular group. These are normally assumptions based on stereotypes. Saying 'Employing someone with a physical disability would make the rest of the staff feel uncomfortable' is an example of this type of discrimination. People who make assumptions like these, whether they're correctly or incorrectly based on some members of a group, are often unaware that they are discriminating.

Indirect and direct discrimination

Discrimination can also be indirect or direct. *Indirect discrimination* occurs when policies or practices appear on the surface to be neutral but actually adversely affect a particular group of people. Indirect discrimination often results from assumptions that everyone is the same as the policy-makers and these assumptions are embedded into the organisation's policies, practices and procedures. An example of indirect discrimination is providing information about health and safety, leave policies and training opportunities only in English.

There are two types of *direct discrimination*: the subtle *covert* and the clear and open *overt*. An example of *overt direct* discrimination is a clear statement of refusal to hire people from a disadvantaged group. An example of *covert direct* discrimination is a consistent failure to hire suitably qualified and competent applicants from a disadvantaged group.

⦿ THEORY TO PRACTICE

Religious discrimination

You apply for an accountancy position with a small manufacturing company through a recruitment agency. Both the recruitment agency and the company interview you and you are offered the position. The company then withdraws its offer because you need time during the day for prayer.

You register a complaint with the Australian Human Rights Commission, explaining that you advised the recruitment agency that you are Muslim and need to arrange a room at the workplace where you can conduct your daily prayers. You say that you need about three 10-minute prayer breaks during the day and could undertake one set of prayers during your lunch break.

The company says it withdrew its offer of employment for two reasons. First, it has concerns about your honesty because in the interview you did not disclose your need for additional breaks, despite being asked whether anything would prevent you from working normal office hours. Second, despite these concerns, it attempted to find a suitable location for your prayers but, because the office is open plan, the only options available were the meeting room, which has a glass wall, or a nearby park. The company says you rejected these suggestions. Therefore, the company denies it discriminated against you on the ground of your religion.

The Commission holds a conciliation conference. The company agrees to pay you $3500 compensation and provide you with a statement of regret.[11]

Systemic discrimination

Many organisations have gone about as far as they can to remove the more obvious types of discrimination and it is now up to individual leader-managers to identify and remove the nearly invisible *structural,* or *systemic discrimination,* that remains. This is the longstanding direct and indirect discrimination that has been common practice for so long that it seems to be the natural order of things. It is based on established employment practices and unchallenged assumptions about people from particular groups. Because it is entrenched in 'the way we do things', structural discrimination is more difficult to recognise, and potentially of greater sensitivity and difficulty to deal with.

Requirements to work overtime or long hours (paid or unpaid), to travel and work at home on weekends, and so on, assume that someone else can look after home duties, including household management (cooking, cleaning, shopping) and care for children and the elderly; that someone is usually assumed to be a woman. The segregation of occupations is another example of systemic discrimination. So are training only male machine operators to set machines when a vacancy for a setter-operator occurs, recruiting only Asian females to assemble tiny hearing aids because their small hands suit them to this work, or considering only female applicants for personal assistant positions are other examples of systemic discrimination.

Here are three questions to ask to help determine whether systemic discrimination is occurring:

1. *Are people expected to comply with conditions or requirements that put them at a disadvantage?* For example, when a building has no wheelchair access or toilet facilities for people with a disability, people who use a wheelchair would find it extremely difficult to report to work and work normally.

2. *Are people with a particular characteristic expected to comply with a requirement or condition that it is not possible for them to comply with?* For example, continually switching meetings to 5 pm at short notice even though some employees need to leave at 5 pm to pick up children from day care is unreasonable.

3. *Are people with a particular characteristic expected to comply with a requirement or condition that the majority of people without that characteristic can comply with more easily?* For example, employees with child or parental care responsibilities may find it more difficult to attend weekend training workshops or to travel away from home for extended periods on business, things which people from the 'dominant group' find easy to do.

Train your team members to recognise – and avoid – all types of discrimination.

◉ ACTION!

How readily do you spot discrimination? Find out with the interactive self-test: Spot the bias, on
 .

● THEORY TO PRACTICE

When in doubt, ask

A hotel in Ceduna, South Australia, was ordered to pay a female Aboriginal elder $3000 compensation for being refused service at the hotel's drive-through bottle shop. The employee who refused her service assumed she was from Yalata, an Aboriginal community that bans alcohol. He didn't ask whether his thinking was correct. He just refused to serve her.[12]

How easy it would have been to provide some basic diversity training for the hotel's employees. And how much cheaper, too.

Build a diverse work team

Differences can be frightening, puzzling or fascinating. When you have a variety of people on board, it isn't always easy to create a workplace that can rise above the potential friction that people's differences can kindle. For example, diversity can lead to more and different points of view, which can result in longer discussions, misunderstandings and conflict rather than creativity, insight and innovation.

Anne Frank wrote in *The diary of a young girl* that 'We all live with the objective of being happy; our lives are all different and yet the same.'[13] To build a diverse and successful workplace, you may need to help people step out of their comfort zones and accept that 'like me' doesn't have to mean people who look like them, think like them or have a similar background to them. In diverse workplaces, similarity comes from sharing common organisational and team goals, values and visions. In diverse workplaces everyone agrees on the essentials – what they are there to achieve and how to achieve it.

Building a successful, diverse work team means ensuring that behaviours and norms accept and support diversity and respect people's dignity. It means fostering a work climate that values everyone's contributions, that acknowledges, respects and makes the most of individual differences and that builds on the strengths of everyone in the work team.

For example, unnecessarily drawing attention to someone's race, religion or any other characteristic, (the Arab woman, that guy in the turban, the gay guy) highlights distinctions and gives the impression that the person is different from 'us'. Stereotyping people (excitable Italian, whingeing Pom, emotional woman) implies a belief that all individuals from a particular group share that characteristic. Lumping diverse groups together (Asians, Europeans, people with disabilities) denies their many differences. Using language that diminishes people or casts them in a negagive light (oldies, office girls) is disrespectful. Derogatory labels and offensive language are also unacceptable in the workplace.

You don't want to hear comments like these at your workplace because they can easily lead to other forms of discrimination, make people feel uncomfortable, and shatter a culture of dignity, inclusion and respect. Remember: 'The standard you walk past is the standard you accept.'[14]

● IN A NUTSHELL

How to encourage diversity

Like diversity of experience, diversity of culture is a positive contributor in the workplace. Here are some ways you can encourage diversity:

* Create a culture of respect where every team member recognises and values the differences between, and the contributions of, the employees, customers and suppliers they work with.

>>

- Deal quickly and firmly with anyone who does not treat fellow employees, customers or suppliers fairly and respectfully.
- Give everyone equal access to employment opportunities and apply the merit principle to all employment-related decisions and opportunities.
- Investigate any complaints carefully, according to your organisation's policy and provide clear information about where employees can seek assistance.
- Keep refresher training on discrimination issues up to date and record people's attendance.
- Know and adhere to your organisation's policy and programs on diversity-related matters.
- Observe the right of all employees to confidentiality.
- Provide training to help employees work effectively with a range of people and hold them accountable for doing so.
- Recognise that each employee has individual skills and contributions to make.

● ACTION!

How diverse is your team? Take the interactive self-test of the same name on ⚡CourseMateExpress to find out.

● THEORY TO PRACTICE

How IBM makes the most of its diversity

Here's what IBM has to say about diversity: 'IBM believes diversity is a no-brainer. It's the fuel of creativity and innovation, the key to attracting, retaining and motivating talented people, and a critical differentiator in today's business and workplace environment.'[15]

IBM has been a pioneer in diversity programs and a leading organisation in the field of diversity. In fact, there's a little-known people aspect to IBM's impressive turnaround in the 1990s. In 1995, then-CEO Lou Gerstner launched a diversity team to find out how to engage its diverse range of employees and customers more effectively. They established eight task forces, each based on an employee group (Asians, African Americans, Hispanics, Native Americans, people with disabilities, the gay, lesbian, bisexual and transgender community, white males and women) and asked them to research four questions:

1. What does your constituency need to feel welcome and valued at IBM?
2. What can the corporation do, in partnership with your group, to maximise your constituency's productivity?
3. What can the corporation do to influence your constituency's buying decisions so that IBM is seen as a preferred solution provider?
4. With which external organisations should IBM form relationships to better understand the needs of your constituency?

The answers became the basis of IBM's diversity strategy, which had four essential factors going for it: strong support from the organisation's leaders, an employee base fully engaged with the strategy and resulting initiatives, management practices that supported the strategy, and a clear and strong business case for action. Not surprisingly, it got results. In less than 10 years, for example:

- The number of female executives worldwide increased by 370%
- The number of ethnic minority executives born in the US increased by 233%.

>>

- The top 52 executives who determine IBM strategy, known as IBM's Worldwide Management Council, included women, ethnic minorities born in the US and non-US citizens.
- The number of self-identified gay, lesbian, bisexual and transgender executives increased by 733%.
- The number of executives with disabilities more than tripled.

The women's task force led to the establishment of IBM's Market Development Organization, which focuses on multicultural and female-owned businesses, accounting for more than US$300 million in revenue in 2004. Results like this ensured the company quickly realised that diversity helps it achieve business goals, which reduced the need for a big budget to implement diversity programs.

And since then? Diversity Councils in every country, chaired by the country CEO and made up of executive sponsors, diversity program managers and diversity networking group leaders work to heighten employee awareness, increase management sensitivity and encourage IBM's diverse workforce to be used effectively through a range of initiatives and programs.

The company consults with six diversity network groups: Cultural Diversity Networking Group, EAGLE (Employee Alliance for Gay, Lesbian Empowerment), PwD (people with a disability), Diversity Networking Group, WIT (Women in Technology) and Work Life Diversity Networking Group (for flexible workers such as part-time and job-sharing employees).

A network of Diversity Contact Officers – employees trained to handle diversity-related grievances and knowledgeable in equal employment opportunity and anti-discrimination legislation – are conduits of diversity-related information; in addition to their main role, they work as work–life balance coaches and help integrate people with a disability into the IBM workforce. Diversity awards recognise individual employees whose actions encapsulate IBM's diversity principles and communicate success stories, helping to establish cultural diversity as the norm.[16]

Special measures

Sometimes simply modifying the workplace, such as ramp access for wheelchairs, using different languages on signs and in safety information or installing visual alarms for hearing-impaired people, is enough. Sometimes adjusting the conditions of employment, for example, offering flexible working such as job sharing, part-time employment during school hours or working from home in order to accommodate carer, cultural, religious or other personal needs, is enough. (See page 1024 for more information on flexible work practices.)

Sometimes simply ceasing to discriminate isn't enough because equal treatment doesn't always result in fair treatment. Sometimes more is needed to help people from disadvantaged groups catch up quickly so they can compete equally for jobs, training and promotion. This can mean taking steps, known as *special measures* and *affirmative action*, to redress, or put right, barriers faced by specific groups recognised as historically disadvantaged.

The English as a second language (ESL) courses that many TAFE colleges provide for employees whose first language isn't English is an example of a special measure. Mentoring programs, setting a goal of having a specific number of Indigenous or female employees in management positions by a certain year or a quota of 2.6% of all staff with Indigenous backgrounds by a certain year (the same percentage of Indigenous people in the general population) are other examples of actions to overcome the practical effects of disadvantage and discrimination.

THE STRATEGIC PERSPECTIVE

Making poor use and good use of differences

The main barrier to Indigenous employment has been lack of 'job readiness' due to insufficient education and training: 22% of Indigenous Australians complete Year 12, markedly below the national average.

Sean spent two years in a government department as part of its Indigenous cadet program. Not having been given a phone, a computer or even an induction, he felt like his only contribution was filling a quota. He left and went to uni, spending three summers working in Hewlett-Packard's business operations unit as part of HP's internship program. He was given specific goals and objectives to help develop the company's business plan around new international quality standards initiatives. Every 12 weeks, his performance was reviewed and more responsibilities added each time. Sean was also asked to teach HP executives about Aboriginal culture.

Sean worked full-time for HP after graduation before joining KPMG, which has a number of initiatives to improve employment opportunities for Indigenous Australians, including high school and tertiary scholarships, mentoring and work experience programs and cultural awareness training.[17]

The lesson: Don't let your organisation's good intentions go down the drain through lack of follow-through.

Here are some practical steps that organisations have taken to implement a diversity policy, introduce subtle special measures and build diverse work teams:

- Accounting firm Deloitte, an equal opportunity leader for 11 successive years, has run an Inspiring Women program since 2004. The program identifies and supports the firm's talented women with a number of measures including a businesswoman of the year program that identifies talented women early in their careers, a mentoring program that finds mentors for both men and women on request, and structured development programs, including a career-resilience program and networking programs with high-flying females outside the firm.

  The number of female partners in the firm has grown from four in the 1990s to more than 95 in 2013. Deloitte's target is 25% female partners by 2015 and every business unit in the firm is accountable for its progress towards this target. Individual managers are also assessed against performance measures that include women's advancement such as the ratio of voluntary female departures to all voluntary departures. Partners' and directors' pay and performance is evaluated in the context of gender equality.[18]

- Suncorp, the banking, general and life insurance, and superannuation company, tackled the problem with an award-winning three-year diversity strategy. It set a target for 33% females in senior leadership roles, established a Diversity Council chaired by the CEO, introduced flexible working arrangements with Work@Home hubs, flexible leave options and job-sharing, undertook a pay review to redress gender inequities and established a recruitment policy ensuring the final shortlist for senior positions included at least one male and one female candidate.

  The company also identifies high-potential females and provides a number of leadership development programs targeting high potential female business and first-line leader-managers. Workshops for leadership teams explain how unconscious bias can work. The board tracks progress against targets quarterly and so far, Suncorp is ahead of target. Future plans include increasing employment opportunities for people with disability and mature aged workers.[19]

- A Diversity Oversight Committee guides engineering firm Parsons Brinckerhoff's policies on diversity and inclusion. Among other measures, the company makes an effort to recruit female engineers and has introduced flexible start and finish times, telecommuting, phased-in retirements, accrued leave and purchased leave, and has increased maternity leave from six to 16 weeks.

  They have also introduced a mentoring program to develop women and established a PB Women's Network which, in part, provides feedback on the effectiveness of the firm's diversity policies for men and women carers and part-time employees. One female must be present on interview panels for all management roles and one female candidate must be considered for all management vacancies. Fifty-four per cent of external appointments to managerial roles are now women. The managing director meets with all senior women and female managers who leave the firm to hear about their experiences working there.[20]

◉ THEORY TO PRACTICE

What do women want?

Many of World Vision Australia's young female employees who went on parental leave failed to return to work, representing an enormous loss to the organisation of its investment in recruitment, training, knowledge and experience and another big loss to the women's superannuation. Realising it needed to do something to retain them, World Vision introduced a range of family-friendly initiatives on a tiny $10 000 budget. The company arranged:

- a mothers' support group meeting every six weeks
- a nursing mothers' room
- a parents' room to care for sick family members
- optional vaccinations for staff and their families
- the option to bring children to the office if necessary (e.g. during school holidays)
- training courses for staff on parental leave paid for by World Vision
- flexible start and finish times
- use of technology for staff on parental leave so they can stay in touch via email.

Success! In the first three years of these initiatives, 79% of women returned to work after having children, turning the large loss into substantial savings in retained resources. The work environment at World Vision has improved significantly and is more positive, despite its high pressure.

With 90% of its workforce female, Mercy Health, a provider of acute and sub-acute hospital care, mental health services, palliative care, community health and aged care in the eastern states of Australia, faced similar problems: falling retention rates, increasing sick leave and difficulty attracting staff. Its focus groups indicated the importance of flexible work practices, maternity leave and staying in touch with people on maternity leave. Mercy obliged. For example, it let women coming back from maternity leave choose the number of shifts they wanted to work each week and started quarterly luncheons for staff on maternity leave, to which they could bring their babies.

Success! Mercy now has a 98% retention rate and a 97% return rate from maternity leave.[21]

Keep diversity 'on the radar'

Your own day-to-day actions send strong signals about how important a culture of collaboration and respect is to you. You could, for example, put diversity on your team meeting agenda every few meetings, put up diversity posters, make sure everyone in your team knows, understands and follows your organisation's diversity policies, and be a good role model.

Join your team in participating in training that fosters awareness of, and supports, diversity and assists employees to perform in a culturally diverse environment. Training can include:

- the advantages of diversity and how to work effectively in diverse work groups
- cross-cultural training
- the changing work environment and marketplace
- communication skills
- equal employment opportunity and anti-discrimination awareness
- interpersonal skills.

Discuss how to use what you've learned and help everyone to apply the training.

Should a grievance concerning discrimination arise, deal with it fairly, quickly and following your organisation's dispute settlement procedure (see page 1012 to find out how to investigate complaints).

3. Fostering respect for diversity in your work team

> Unity, not uniformity, must be our aim. We attain unity only through variety. Differences must be integrated, not annihilated.
>
> Mary Parker Follett (social worker, author), in Tonn, *Mary P. Follett: Creating Democracy, Transforming Management* (2003)[22]

The Australian workforce of (mostly) white mature males supported by female secretarial staff has become a colourful, heterogeneous mix. In most work groups today, you can find men and women from four generations and from an array of cultural, ethnic and religious backgrounds. They have a range of abilities and many speak English as a second language.

This diversity reflects the country as a whole and means that everyone needs to know how to behave fairly, inclusively and respectfully towards others, taking into account people's different backgrounds, circumstances and needs. In this section, we consider people from four groups that contribute to diversity in most workplaces:

1. People with disabilities
2. People from different cultures and races.
3. People of different sexes, sexual orientations and gender identities.
4. People from different generations.

Legislation and workplace policies alone can't create a diverse work team that works well together. Studies show that concentrating on procedural fairness, while important, ignores the power gulf between those who complain about discrimination and those who deal with those complaints. Similarly, studies show little relationship between mandatory reporting and positive outcomes for people from disadvantaged groups.[23] That means it's up to each and every leader-manager, every day, to set the right example – or it won't happen.

Diversity of abilities

It might surprise you to learn that more than one in five people have a disability and more than half of these people are of working age. It also might surprise you to learn that you have about an 18% chance of becoming disabled at some time during your working life.[24]

FYI

What is disability?

Disability is an umbrella term for activity limitations, impairments and participation restrictions. Disabilities can be caused by accident, disease, genetics or trauma and can be permanent or temporary, partial or total, acquired or lifelong, visible or invisible (almost 90% are invisible).[25]

There are five broad types of disability:

1. Head injury/stroke/brain damage: Long-term effects that restrict everyday activities.
2. Intellectual disabilities: Difficulty in learning or understanding.
3. Physical disabilities: Chronic or recurrent pain, incomplete use of arms or fingers, disfigurement or deformity, and the presence of viruses such as HIV and hepatitis C.
4. Psychological disabilities: A nervous or emotional condition.
5. Sensory and speech: Difficulties seeing, hearing or speaking.

People with disabilities are Australia's largest minority group, made up of both sexes and all age groups, ethnicities, and educational and social backgrounds. Although 15% of the potential workforce has a declared disability, only 53%, compared with 81% for people without a disability, are employed. This is lower than most Organisation for Economic Cooperation and Development (OECD) countries; in fact, Australia ranks 21 out of 29 countries for workforce participation by people with a disability. Perhaps as a result of this low employment rate, 45% of Australians with a disability live in or near poverty – last among the OECD countries.[26] The situation has not improved since 2003.[27] Why is this? Do they not want to work? Or do we not want to hire people with disabilities?

You have probably heard the standard excuses for not employing people with disabilities: 'It costs too much to accommodate their needs', 'They don't fit in', and so on. But these excuses ignore the facts:

- Expensive workplace adjustments are seldom needed and, when they are, 80% cost less than $500 and are paid for by the government.
- People with a disability are as productive or more productive than other employees.
- People with a disability can have lower absenteeism, higher retention rates and take less sick leave than other employees.
- People with a disability can have fewer accidents at work – workers' rehabilitation and compensation costs for people with a disability can be as low as 4% of the compensation costs of other employees.
- People with a disability can build staff morale, raise management awareness of workplace practices and conditions and increase customer and staff loyalty.
- The cost of hiring people with a disability can be as low as 13% of the cost of other employees.[28]

Specialist organisations across Australia work with employers and people with disabilities to match abilities to job requirements. Many also provide ongoing workplace support that helps them remain employed and achieve the outcomes expected of them.

Employing people with disabilities gives them a chance to participate and that chance is often met with commitment, loyalty and a desire to achieve. There really are no excuses. Failing to benefit from the abilities, experience, ideas and skills of over two million working age Australians doesn't make much sense in a country with an ageing population and chronic skills shortages.[29]

Looking beyond disabilities to abilities

Having a disability doesn't mean you don't contribute. Poet and author Henry Lawson and former prime ministers Billy McMahon and Billy Hughes, for example, had hearing impairments. One of the country's first billionaires, media magnate Kerry Packer, had dyslexia. His father thought he was stupid and called him a 'boofhead'. Saint Mary Mackillop had a chronic and painful health condition called dysmenorrhoea, which often left her bedridden for days. She self-medicated with brandy and was accused of being an alcoholic and temporarily was exiled from her religious order.[30]

Employers must make reasonable adjustments for employees with a disability and common sense serves in most situations. For instance, you may need to allow flexibility in weekly hours to allow employees to attend regular medical appointments, provide desks with adjustable heights for people using a wheelchair and provide more regular breaks for people with chronic pain or fatigue. Ask the employee to indicate the assistance you can provide and should something seem too difficult, seek assistance from the Australian Human Rights Commission (http://www.hreoc.gov.au) or Job Access (http://www.jobaccess.gov.au).

Above all, don't think of the people you work with as deaf people, blind people, disabled people or handicapped. Although it's part of who they are, don't let their disability define them – they have families, hobbies, likes and dislikes, trials, tribulations and joys. They are just people who happen to have a disability.

Working with people with hearing impairments

One in six Australians has a hearing loss and for them, communication is the most significant problem.[31] Here are some tips:

- Ask how they prefer to communicate.
- Avoid changing topics abruptly and say when you are changing the topic.
- Check that lighting is adequate so that people with a hearing impairment can see people's faces and what is happening around them.
- Face them when speaking to them, speak clearly at a normal rate and volume (avoid using exaggerated mouth movements and shouting) and keep your hands, food and so on away from your mouth when speaking so they can lip-read.
- Look at people with a hearing loss when they speak to you to show you are interested in what they are saying.
- Provide telephone typewriter (TTY) phone access and other assistive listening devices when necessary.
- Rephrase, rather than repeat, misunderstood comments, explanations or questions.
- Try to reduce background noise because many hearing aids amplify all sounds.
- Use the 'show me' technique to check you have presented the information clearly.
- Use visual clues and, when necessary, write down your message as a backup.
- When necessary, touch their arm gently to gain their attention.

Working with people with visual impairments

One in 63 Australians are blind or visually impaired.[32] There are many easy ways to make the working life of people with visual impairments easier, for example, in the following list.

- Allow them to practise their new job under careful supervision until they are familiar with where everything is located.
- Don't grab their arm when walking with them; they will take your arm if they need to; they'll keep a half step behind to anticipate steps, changes of level and so on.
- Ensure that everyone in the team knows how people with vision impairments are to evacuate the building in an emergency and the role they may play in this.
- Give clear spoken directions indicating surface condition, direction or activity in the room.
- Inform people with limited vision when you rearrange the workspace and take them on a walking tour of the new arrangement, locating new orientation points.
- Provide aids such as closed-circuit television, magnifiers, screen reading software and telescopes.
- Provide touchable orientation points in the working space.
- Read out or mention things you show or do, such as when writing on a flipchart or placing signs on a wall.
- Since people with limited vision concentrate on sounds, avoid holding discussions where there is a lot of background noise or loud music.
- Speak to them directly and do not raise your voice.
- Speak when you enter their work space and tell them who is with you.
- Stay alert to and remove protruding obstructions that could endanger them.
- Until they are familiar with people's voices, identify yourselves when speaking individually with them and in group discussions.
- Use the orientation points the person knows, rather than saying 'here' or 'there' to describe places, or go to these places and say 'here'.

◉ THEORY TO PRACTICE

Blind injustice

Josh, who is blind, has worked in a large government organisation as a desk administrative officer for many years. He performs his duties well. An opportunity for a transfer to another job arises, a job that Josh can do and would enjoy. But he is refused the transfer because, although he can carry out the duties of the position, he is not suitable for promotion to the next job up the line from the transfer position because that position requires a sighted person.

That is discrimination. Failing to transfer Josh is discriminatory and unlawful because more than the required skills and abilities of the job in question have been considered.

Cultural and racial diversity

Nine out of 10 of Australia's fastest-growing export markets are now non-English-speaking countries. By 2010, 16% of people living in Australia spoke a language other than English at home and overseas migrants comprised more than 50% of the country's population growth.[33] Nearly half of the Australian population was either born overseas or had a parent who was born overseas.[34]

Your workplace and work team are likely to be just as culturally diverse. That's handy, because a multicultural workforce can help organisations work effectively in a globalised marketplace, provide access to new markets and help develop internationally successful products and services.

You can expect to report to and supervise people who were born overseas, many in countries where the main language is not English. Many will be from countries with cultures and economies quite different from Australia's culture and economy, with different customs, different behavioural expectations, and even different practices regarding verbal and non-verbal communication. Some will have privileged backgrounds; others will be from poverty-stricken countries and war-torn countries. Your job is to help them feel comfortable in their work surroundings and help their team-mates understand and respect their differences.

To do that, you first need to understand your own cultural background. And that isn't easy – what do fish know about the water in which they swim? But when you can understand other cultures and how yours differs from theirs, then you can work out how to work together effectively.

● THEORY TO PRACTICE

What are your cultural expectations?

In many commonplace situations we behave as we've been brought up to behave, according to the norms of our family and community. How have you been brought up to behave?

- Are you comfortable speaking up in meetings or do you wait until someone asks for your opinion?
- Do you blow your nose or do you sniff when you have a head cold?
- Do you look a senior manager in the eye or do you look down?
- Do you prefer formality or informality?
- Do you shy away from conflict or explore it?
- How close to people are you comfortable standing or sitting?
- How firm or loose is your handshake?
- Is being late for a meeting no big deal or is it a sign of disrespect?
- When you're trying to understand someone's meaning, do you take their words at face value or do you read 'between the lines' and think about what is *not* said?
- Which do you value more: competition or cooperation, the individual or the group?

The behaviours listed in 'Theory to practice: What are your cultural expectations?' are more than personality traits. They're important differentiators between cultures that persist over generations, and they are potential sources of irritation and misunderstanding. How you answer those questions depends on where you grew up, and however you answer them (and there are no 'rights' or 'wrongs'), awareness of how others might answer them is an important skill that makes you a better leader, a better employee and better at working with colleagues, customers and suppliers.

Cultural awareness helps you avoid conflict, miscommunication and misunderstanding. When you're culturally competent, you don't think of the way you do things as 'normal' or view other ways as 'different'. You don't see other cultures and ways of behaving as stereotypes and in a critical light. You don't tend to assume you know the reasons that people from other cultures do something and think you know what they mean or intend based on your own culture rather than the other person's culture.

To increase your cultural competence, try to see situations from other cultural perspectives. This can lead to new understandings and insights and self-awareness. When someone's behaviour puzzles you, discuss it to deepen your understanding. Think ahead about how best to put your message across to someone from another culture.

THEORY TO PRACTICE

Degrees of cultural sensitivity

Which of the ways outlined below most resembles how you respond to people with different backgrounds from yours? How do you think the people in your work team respond?

- *Xenophobia*: Fear – I don't understand you; I don't want to understand you and I want you to go away before you change everything I do, understand and feel comfortable with.
- *Ethnocentrism*: Superiority – my way is best.
- *Forced assimilation*: You should become like us.
- *Segregation*: Remain separate – you can stay, but stay away from me.
- *Acceptance*: Get together, accommodate each other and build relationships.
- *Celebrate*: Make the most of your differences and the fun and new ways of thinking that result.

The skill of being able to work effectively across cultures – cultural intelligence – is not just about nations. All groups have cultures and norms of behaviour – families, generations, neighbourhoods, organisations and teams have cultures, too. This section reviews some important national and regional cultural differences you need to be familiar with as the Australian workforce continues to diversify.

FYI

A snapshot of Anglo-Celtic Aussie culture

People from the Anglo-Celtic section of Australian society give short, firm handshakes, stand at arm's length from people unless they know them very well, look people in the eye and speak up when they have something to say (and sometimes, even when they don't have anything worthwhile to say). Even those who are chronically late know punctuality is important. These Aussies love to enjoy life and have fun. They are independent and informal; they blow their noses when they have a cold, plan their time, respect tradition, love to compete and face up to conflict when they need to (and, sometimes, even when they don't need to).

These characteristics have given rise to a casual, egalitarian, time-focused business culture where results, rather than harmony, count. Communication is clear and direct – 'no' means 'no' and 'yes' means 'yes'; when you want to know something, you ask, and when you want to 'get something off your chest' you 'spit it out' and 'say what you mean and mean what you say'. To people from other cultures, these behaviours can seem aggressive, disrespectful, overbearing, rude and selfish.

Anglo-Celtic Aussie equality assumes everyone is equal, provided they're like 'us', so foreigners are mistrusted when they speak their own language and don't try to fit in. But this way of thinking doesn't lead to working well with people from other cultures.

IN A NUTSHELL

How to communicate with people who don't yet speak English well

Have you ever tried to learn another language and then found you couldn't understand the way people really spoke?

Australians use colloquial slang and abbreviate many words and phrases or leave them out all together. This makes life very hard for someone learning a more formal version of English.

>>

Here's how you can help communicate:
* Avoid complicated and lengthy sentences and explanations.
* Avoid slang.
* Check that you have communicated clearly by asking the employee to repeat your instructions in their own words.
* Don't add unnecessary words or make distracting small talk while giving explanations, instructions or training.
* Explain and reinforce the basic vocabulary of the workplace – often.
* Explain tasks step by step, in the correct order (see page 917 for more information on how to instruct people correctly).
* Make it easy for the employee to ask questions and be aware that they might hesitate to do so from embarrassment or fear of seeming stupid.
* Pause every few sentences to allow them time to process what you've said.
* Speak slowly and clearly, in complete sentences, and don't speak more loudly than usual.
* Use drawings, examples, graphs, hand movements and models to emphasise important points.
* When possible, arrange for others who speak the person's first language to support them.

Although differences within cultures exist, there are greater differences between cultures. Helping your work team to understand and value their cultural differences and build on their similarities and common interests builds a strong work team that can innovate and get results.

Think of the descriptions below as scales, with some cultures lying at one end, other cultures lying at the other end, and some cultures in the middle. Don't use them to stereotype people and ignore what each individual can offer. Rather, use the continuums below as shorthand generalisations to help you work more effectively with people from different cultures by adapting your own style to the people you're working with. Widen your comfort zone so that you can adapt gracefully and quickly to add value and achieve the outcomes you need.

Clarity or ambiguity?

People from some cultures, such as Japanese, Latin American, Middle Eastern, Russian and Southern European cultures, avoid uncertainty and prefer order and agreement. People from these cultures favour strong leadership. They tend to look for one best way to solve a problem or achieve a goal and they expect their leader to know what that one best way is.

When leading people from these cultures, reduce uncertainty for them by providing answers and giving them precise objectives, a clear structure to fit into and rules explaining how to behave and what to do in different situations.

People from Australia and New Zealand, North America, Northern Europe and much of Asia and Africa, on the other hand, tolerate uncertainty and ambiguity more easily. They can 'agree to disagree' and are comfortable with many possible answers, many ways to achieve a goal, and many ways to solve a problem. They are comfortable working flexibly, figuring things out for themselves, taking risks, dealing with change and working with broad goals, and they innovate and experiment more readily. Give them as much freedom as you can to decide how best to achieve their goals.

Hierarchical or egalitarian?

It might not seem that Māoris and people from the Pacific islands, Asia, Brazil, Mexico, the Middle East and Russia have much in common in terms of their culture. But one thing their cultures do have in common is that they are more formal and hierarchical, which makes conformity, procedures and rules important. People from these cultures respect authority, whether it's based on age, caste, gender, job title or race, and their respect for authority dictates a deferential, formal relationship with their boss, regardless of whether or not they like or respect him or her. They assume the boss knows best, so they don't mind taking directions and instructions. Since they're comfortable with hierarchies, they're also comfortable with a 'pecking order' at work.

Contrast these employees with employees from the egalitarian, informal cultures of Australia, New Zealand, North America and Northern Europe, where people are seen not as part of a family, occupation, position or tribe, but as individuals. People from these cultures respect people for their achievements and they don't automatically grant a leader respect and follow orders. Their leaders must earn their respect and the right to tell them what to do. People from these cultures prefer a more informal, even social, relationship with the boss and would rather be consulted than told – and don't even think about pulling rank with any of these employees. Be a coach and a resource and let them get on with their work and achieve their goals in their own way.

This hierarchical–egalitarian continuum can lead to different expectations regarding courtesy. In cultures where status differences are the norm, it's generally not necessary to thank someone for doing their job and receiving compliments can sometimes go against the preference for humility. In cultures that downplay status differences, the expectation is to thank people for their help when they've done their job and to offer praise for good work.

◉ THEORY TO PRACTICE

Diversity: An opportunity, not an obligation, at HSBC Australia

HSBC is a global bank serving more than 125 million customers worldwide, representing almost every nationality and ethnic group. Not surprisingly, the bank aims for a workforce that reflects the diversity of its customers and, when recruiting staff, it actively looks for culturally sensitive people. Males dominate the finance industry as a whole at senior levels and HSBC is actively trying to redress its gender imbalance.

HSBC Australia has a diversity committee chaired by the CEO and made up of employees from around the business who are 'diversity champions'. Diversity initiatives include:

- a flexible work policy with options to work part-time or job-share, work from home, start and finish at flexible times, and work to a compressed working week
- a mentoring program
- childcare placement and support services
- networking groups for women, working parents, and bisexual, gay, intersex, lesbian and intersex employees
- primary and secondary carer leave.

The bank's diversity workshops, which it ran first for the senior management team and is run for all leader-managers, emphasise that diversity is more than just visible attributes such as age, gender and physical ability, and that diversity is about valuing invisible attributes too, including different ways of communicating, thinking and problem-solving. The bank also benchmarks with the Australian Workplace Equality Index and Workplace Gender Equality Agency Employer of Choice to ensure it remains in line with best practice.[35]

Ours or mine?

Is time a limited resource you need to divide, compartmentalise, manage and use carefully? It is to people from Australia and New Zealand, North America, Northern Europe and Singapore, who try to 'save time', avoid 'wasting time' and 'make up for lost time'. Seeing time like this inclines people to do one thing at a time, work in an orderly way and be impatient with interruptions. It predisposes them to think they can plan the future and control events. It gives them a sense of ownership of possessions and space, too: 'my desk', 'my pen', 'my ruler'. Give them a private office and watch their eyes shine! Personal space is important for these people too, so stand – literally – at arm's length from them and make little physical contact.

At the other end of the scale are the people for whom possessions, space and time are less cut and dried. People from Asian, Indian, Latin American and Middle Eastern cultures tend to see time as abundant, so they don't need to distribute and schedule it carefully. This takes the emphasis off punctuality and planning and makes it sensible to work on several things at the same time. Interruptions don't annoy them and privacy and 'mine' aren't sacrosanct – they're happy to share their belongings; in fact, many of these cultures don't even have a word for privacy. When their timekeeping disrupts the work team, point it out to them and explain why it is a problem and what you expect from them instead.

Stand close or stand back?

When it comes to personal space, Latin Americans, Middle Easterners and Southern Europeans are comfortable standing closer, reaching out to touch another person and making more direct eye contact than are most Asians. They gesture more and are more facially expressive than most Asians, too.

In contrast, touching a person – even on the elbow – is taboo in many Asian cultures. In between those two ends of the spectrum are the Northern Europeans and people from English-speaking countries.

We or me?

Some cultures stress the importance of being part of a group. Other cultures emphasise the importance of 'standing on your own two feet'. In *collectivist cultures*, the group takes precedence and takes care of people in exchange for their loyalty. Consensus, group achievement, and group preferences and needs are more important than individual preferences and needs and individual achievement.

People from Arab, Asian, Japanese, Māori and Pacific island cultures tend to be group oriented. 'One for all and all for one' describes the attitude of people from these collectivist cultures; they prefer to be part of a group rather than on their own, whether that group is a community, family or work team. Making a mistake is humiliating and causes them to lose 'face' because they've let their group down and their mistake reflects badly on their group. People from these cultures even use words designed to avoid admitting to mistakes and failures to spare their group dishonour.

Cooperation, not competition, describes the general approach of people from 'we' cultures, so let them work, reach decisions and learn from each other in small groups, and let them coach, support and mentor each other. Make the most of their ability to establish trust and build long-term relationships by letting them do so with customers, suppliers and people in other parts of the organisation.

At the other end of the scale are the 'everyone for themselves' cultures of most English-speaking and Northern European cultures, in which individuals, not relationships, take the front seat. Action and results count more than consensus. Whereas people from 'we' cultures might expect rewards for cooperation, people from 'me' cultures expect rewards for performance. Let those team members work on their own with as little direction as possible.

Direct or indirect?

People from collectivist cultures tend to be modest and are uncomfortable being 'in the spotlight' – presenting to groups, for example. Don't assume they'll speak up when they have something to say in meetings and during one-to-one conversations, either – they prefer not to speak up until they are asked for their thoughts and even then, they keep their comments brief unless they are very senior. When they do speak, they expect not to be interrupted and they leave a pause before speaking when someone finishes to indicate they're listening carefully. They try to avoid raising a dissenting opinion or pointing out a flaw in the team's thinking; in fact, when people from these cultures say 'maybe' or even 'yes', they could mean 'no' and smiles or laughter can conceal a range of negative responses.

The communication of people from collectivist, indirect Arabian, Asian, Māori and Pacific Islands cultures is based on a deep store of shared knowledge and conformity to understood ways of speaking and behaving. Less is put in writing because, to each other, their meaning is clear thanks to their shared understanding and the attention they pay to non-verbal information and the context of each communication. Their communication is layered, nuanced and sophisticated; meanings are implied rather than stated and understanding often depends on reading between the lines.

Cultural feedback

Feedback to people from collectivist cultures is best given in private and peppered with 'downgraders', or words to soften criticism: slightly misguided; nearly on target; could possibly improve. At the opposite end of the scale are the people from most English-speaking and Northern European cultures. These frank and direct communicators need 'upgraders' to make feedback heard: totally inappropriate; absolutely wrong; completely unprofessional. (The English, who are experts at understatement, are the exception. When they say 'We're not quite there yet', they probably mean 'We're nowhere near ready'.)

Remember that people magnify or downgrade your words depending on their cultural background. When you say 'I'm a bit disappointed', a person from Asia might hear, 'You did a terrible job' while an ocker Aussie might think 'I guess I did okay then'.[36]

Direct communicators speak up when they have something to say and spell out what they mean. They can't afford to rely on non-verbal cues, partially due to the heterogeneity of these cultures and the lack of shared understandings this creates. 'Good communication' to people from these cultures is clear, explicit, precise and simple because they take messages at face value – no need to read between the lines. They like their lines though. They love to confirm agreements, arrangements and information in writing.

To people from cooperative, collectivist, indirect cultures, the direct individualists can seem arrogant, offensively blunt, rude, uncaring and lacking in social awareness. To the individualists, the collectivists can seem inscrutable and secretive. When combined with a respect for and an unwillingness to challenge authority, people from more egalitarian cultures can conclude that people from hierarchical cultures lack leadership potential. (See 'The strategic perspective: A cultural tightrope' on page 542.)

Build a team culture where people understand different ways of thinking and communicating. Develop a norm to ask for more information or explanation when you're not sure what someone is saying rather than letting people assume there is more shared understanding than really exists.

IN A NUTSHELL

Listening for the meaning behind the words
To interpret words, think about:
- how those words are spoken
- the background to those words
- the person saying the words
- where you are now
- your relationship to the person speaking the words.

FYI

The bamboo and falafel ceilings
In Australia, an applicant with a Chinese name needs to submit 68% more applications than an applicant with an Anglo-Saxon name and the same qualifications and experience to get as many interviews. People with a Middle Eastern name need to submit 64% more applications. They are far from proportionately represented in Australian political life or the private sector professional workforce.[37] The same holds true for female applicants who also need to apply for more jobs than their male counterparts.[38]

Just why is it that Chinese people, people from the Middle East and women need to demonstrate, beyond a shadow of a doubt, that they are qualified and competent to win a job while white men are assumed to be qualified and competent?

Turning cultural differences into team assets

Don't be surprised to find that many of your team members are not aware of how their team-mates think about basic concepts such as time or whether they are individually or group oriented, competitive or cooperative, and so on. Help them increase their awareness of their teammates' ways of thinking by making them transparent using the team culture wheel shown in Figure 26.1.

Ask team members to think about the aspects shown on the wheel and then use stick-on dots to place themselves on the wheel's continuum spokes. This shows where team member's attitudes differ and highlights where misunderstandings and conflict can occur. You can use this information to discuss which aspects of the culture wheel are central to your team's performance and agree ways to work together.

When team members understand what they do that helps the team work effectively, what they do that disrupts teamwork, what they can do to help the team work more effectively, how others may interpret their behaviour and whether they interpret others' behaviour correctly, their cultural intelligence broadens. They have valuable information they can use to increase their ability to work well in a diverse workplace.

ACTION!

You can find a Team culture wheel template on **Course**MateExpress to help increase your team's cultural competence and agree even better ways of working together.

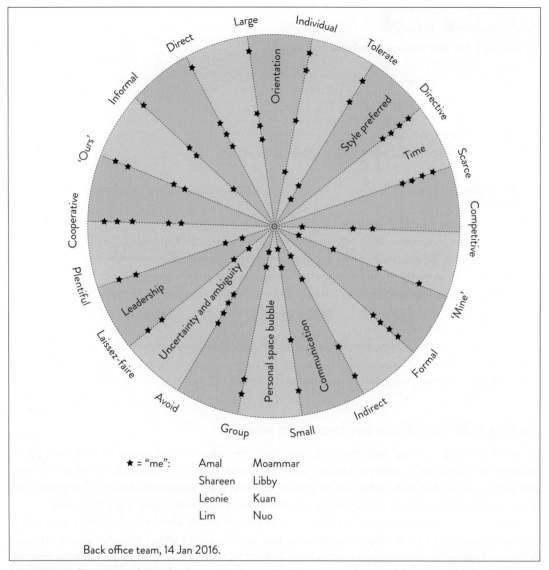

FIGURE 26.1 The team culture wheel

◉ **IN A NUTSHELL**

Managing diverse employees

You can expect to lead employees from many cultures and all age groups, including 'retired' full-time workers. Some will be contract and part-time workers with several contract and part-time jobs. Many will not be with you for more than a year. Yet you need to be able to encourage each one to share your vision and the organisation's vision and help them feel like important, contributing members of the organisation. Here are some ways to bring out the best from everyone in a diverse team:

>>

- Accommodate differences and create choices. Learn about team members and accommodate their personal needs when you can.
- Be aware of the characteristics of different cultures and generations, but think in terms of individuals and skills.
- Concentrate on output, meeting customers' needs and teamwork.
- Facilitate mentoring inside your team; for example, make it easy for older, more experienced employees to show younger employees 'the ropes', for younger, techno-savvy employees to help Baby Boomers improve their skills, for people from the same or similar cultures to support each other and for people from different cultures to learn from each other.
- Help everyone learn and develop their skills.
- Stress people's similarities, not their differences.
- Tailor your leadership approach to suit different individuals with different needs, expectations and task-readiness levels.
- When managing older employees, think about what it would be like to manage your mother or father and what it would be like for your parents to be managed by someone your age.

Gender diversity

Here are some stark facts:

- Women make up about 51% of the Australian population.
- They have similar educational levels to men.
- Of professionals in Australia, 49% are women.
- Women run 35% of the country's small businesses.
- Women start up businesses three times faster than men.

Sir John Bond, retired chair of HSBC, one of the world's largest banks, noted, 'Mao Zedong had the good sense to say women hold up half the sky, but you wouldn't think so if you looked at the FTSE-100 boards.'[39] Here, in fact, is how Australia's 200 largest companies, representing about 80% of the total value of all shares traded, perform in terms of diversity:[40]

- 4.5% have a female CEO
- 12.76% of corporate board directors are women
- 60.6% have no female executives
- 10% of senior managers are women.

  Here's how Australia's 500 largest companies perform in terms of diversity:

- 2.4% have a female CEO
- 9% of board directors are women
- 63.1% have no female executives
- 10% of senior managers are women.

This is about the same as it was in 2004. Is it because the people who can work long hours and put work first are men, so they are rewarded with the top jobs? Or because there aren't enough talented women to fill the top jobs? Perhaps it's because women are less ambitious and don't want the top jobs? Or as former director of the Equal Opportunity for Women in the Workplace agency Anna McPhee, noted, 'When your workplace is a boys' club, you are going to employ those who are going to fit into that boys' club culture and you are going to mainly recruit boys. This culture continues to impact on women's ability to take on more responsibility.'[41]

Those women who do manage to break through the glass ceiling don't shatter it. While it's expected that men benefit from the 'old-boy' network to 'rise through the ranks', women who benefit from special measures are seen as 'rising through the ranks' as a result of special treatment, not because they qualify for their positions.[42] This is the same culture of thinking that has men 'networking' but women 'gossiping', that sees men as 'independent thinkers' but women as 'difficult' executives whose comments reduce collegiality.

Is the gender wage gap mentioned in 'FYI: Not a pretty picture', on page 844, because women take time out to have children and can't catch up? It seems not, since that gap begins early. Male graduates, for example, earn $5000 a year more, on average, than female graduates. An analysis of the gap tells us that 60% of the gender wage gap is a penalty for 'being female'.[43]

A 'motherhood penalty' multiplies the 'female penalty'. For every child a woman has, her salary decreases between $2000 to $7000 a year. Female managers with three children earn an average of $77 000 a year compared to female managers with equivalent work experience and no children, who earn an average of $95 000 a year. A female manager with 30 years of work experience and three children earns $53 000 a year less than a male manager with 30 years experience and three children.[44] It literally doesn't pay to be female.

Yet gender diversity in the boardroom and in senior management is a strong indicator of a well-governed, well-performing organisation.[45] Noting the strong links between board gender diversity on the one hand and financial performance and quality governance on the other, the Australian Council of Superannuation Investors (ASCI) set a three-year target to reach 30% female board membership of ASX200 companies by 2018. The ASCI believes this will improve the value of their investments in these companies.[46]

● THEORY TO PRACTICE

Deep-seated beliefs

People often assume that Cancer Council's chief executive Susan Rooney works *for* her male colleagues.

At an industry function, Southern Cross Austereo general manager Linda Wayman's male date was introduced as the event sponsor by the host, who wrongly assumed he was the boss.[47]

Bridging the gender gap isn't just about women, though. It's also illegal to discriminate against someone because of their sexual orientation, gender identity (the way people express their gender) or intersex status (having physical, hormonal or genetic features that are a combination of male and female). Not discriminating – against anyone – isn't only about fairness, it's also about performance.

More than one third of gay and lesbian staff conceal their sexual orientation from their co-workers and employers.[48] It's a shame they feel they need to. When you feel marginalised enough to 'cover', for example avoiding using 'her' or 'him' when discussing your partner to avoid the 'gay penalty' (or not mentioning day care or other family responsibilities to avoid the 'motherhood penalty'), how can you possibly feel fully engaged at work and perform at your best? An important part of engagement and 'giving your all' is trusting your organisation and co-workers to value you and your capabilities as an individual, without looking through the lenses of sexual orientation or gender.

Is it perceptions, not chromosomes, that determine earning capacity?

Why is it that women continue to earn over 17 % less than men?[49] Maybe they're less motivated by money than men are. Maybe.

Someone once said of US neurobiologist Ben Barres that his work was much better than his sister's. The 'sister' was Barbara Barres, Ben's name prior to his gender affirmation surgery.

Two researchers, Kristen Schilt and Matthew Wiswall, examined what happens to the salaries of people who switch gender mid-career. Would men who became women earn less than they did before, and would women who became men earn more than they did before? It seems so. The women who became men earned slightly more and the men who became women earned nearly one-third less than their previous wage after their sex change.[50]

Of course, the sample size was small – 14 male-to-females and 24 female-to-males, and they weren't necessarily representative of people who switch genders. But food for thought nevertheless.

Gender transition and gender identity

The same laws, policies and procedures that apply to other forms of discrimination and harassment apply to people whose gender identity and gender expression are different from that on their birth certificate, as well as to people whose sexual orientation is towards the same or both sexes. Every employee is entitled to be treated with respect, to enjoy their workplace and use its facilities.

THEORY TO PRACTICE

But what about the dunny?

This is often a hot issue when a team member transitions from male to female or vice versa. You can always take some interim (up to three months) steps until the team feels more comfortable with 'The Dunny Dilemma'. For example:

- When there is more than one bathroom, the transitioning employee could use the one closest to their workstation and others who are not comfortable can use another one.
- When there is only one bathroom, the transitioning employee might agree to use it during the first 30 minutes of every hour.
- Switch to unisex bathrooms.[51]

When an employee affirms a different gender, make sure you use the correct pronouns and use the employee's new name. This reinforces that you and the organisation fully support the employee. Make clear to the gender-affirmed or intersex employee that your policy is zero tolerance for harassment or any actions creating loss of dignity and to notify you immediately of any problems. Promptly deal with any misconduct, reminding the offender that crude conduct and harassment of any kind is not tolerated (as explained in Chapter 30).

As US author and gender transitioner Kate Bornstein said, 'It's a difficult place to live, being neither/nor in an either/or world.'[52] Educate your team so that they understand the struggle their colleague has gone through. Instruct team members to direct any concerns they have to you, not to their teammate. Remember, your team are watching you for clues as to how to behave and what to say. The key is for everyone to be able to live openly as their true selves.

Should concerns be raised about a front-line employee dealing with customers, remember that 'What will the customers say?' concerns were also expressed when racial minorities, people with disabilities and even people sporting nose rings joined the workforce, and those concerns didn't last long.

 FYI

Language is important
Rather than using the 'trans' prefex of the terms 'transgender' and 'transexual', which suggest the person has changed, rather than accepted, their true gender identity, the term 'gender affirmation' is currently preferred. This is seen as affirming the gender the person has always had, rather than transitioning from one gender identity to another. However, rather than making assumptions, ask the employee which term they prefer.

Generational diversity

The workforce is ageing rapidly and low birth rates mean that there aren't enough younger workers to replace those retiring. Many organisations are finding it increasingly difficult to employ the skilled and qualified people they need. As a result, they must hire, train, and retrain people regardless of their age, and actively seek to attract and retain older workers to fill the void. Older workers will be working alongside and reporting to employees young enough to be their children and even grandchildren as the youngest generation of employees, Generation Z, continues to join the workforce. This means we can expect four and even five generations in the workplace.[53]

Different generations have different ways of working, different expectations, different skill sets, and different motivators and personality profiles.[54] And those generational differences have the potential to lead to misunderstandings and conflict. Some believe that attitudinal differences between older and younger workers are so marked that workplace tensions are likely to increase. Turning potential intergenerational misunderstandings and conflict into a creative, energising, positive, competitive advantage is a challenge that leader-managers are increasingly grappling with.

As with any diversity, making the most of people from different age groups is not about assimilation but about adaptability, for employees as well as for organisations. It's about valuing the abilities and talents of all generations, from the energy and enthusiasm of young people entering the workforce to the experience and thoroughness of mature-age workers. And it's about understanding the needs and goals of employees at different phases in their life cycle and careers.

Generational differences

What is the 'generation gap'? It's more than just tensions between teenagers and their parents and it's more than muscle tone and wrinkles that distinguish the generations.

How could those born and raised in the industrial age *not* be different to those born and raised in the information age? How could growing up in the cultural milieu of the dippie hippie 1960s, with the Cold War, building the Berlin Wall, the Vietnam war, the first people in space and on the moon, the assassinations of John and Robert Kennedy and the disappearance of Prime Minister Harold Holt, Nelson Mandela's imprisonment for life, the Chinese Cultural Revolution, mechanical typewriters, *Doctor Who* and *Star Trek*, the Beatles, Rolling Stones, Johnny Farnham and Johnny O'Keefe, *not* produce different people than those growing up in the cultural milieu of the 1990s. They had the end of the Cold War and collapse of the Soviet Union, terrorism, the repeal of Apartheid and release of Nelson Mandela, the birth of the Internet, mad cow disease, HIV/AIDS, *Baywatch*, Kylie Minogue, Madonna, the Spice Girls and Savage Garden.

People born in the same era tend to share similar attitudes, cultural references, motivations, outlooks on life, values and work ethics, and these are different from people born in other eras. While there are obviously differences between the individuals in each generation, there are more differences between the generations themselves – people from the same generation usually have more in common with each other than they have with people from other generations. Cultural events, politics and technology that people grow up with can affect how they view and live in the world for the rest of their lives. Generational culture gives people a sense of solidarity. People of the same generation feel comfortable with each other. They are on similar wavelengths and they can think and speak in the same 'shorthand'.

Not surprisingly, marked differences between the generations have been found in their attitudes towards work, too. Surveys of employees across Australia, China, Germany, Singapore and the USA found that work has a much greater focus for older staff than it does for younger people, for whom it's just one part of their life. This supports the widespread notion of a weaker work ethic in younger generations, with Baby Boomers valuing 'hard work', Generation X valuing self-discipline and self-improvement, Generation Y valuing leisure.[55]

Slowly climbing the organisational ladder no longer has the pull it once had and loyalty to employers has followed loyalty to employees into the distant past. Understanding each generation's distinguishing characteristics helps you manage and work with people from different generations in ways that work for them. And be warned: what's good for the goose (one generation) may not be good for the gander (another generation). Your insight into the combination of factors that motivates and drives each generation helps you lead them more effectively.

However, the usual precautions apply. In the same way that seeing other cultures through your own cultural lenses is dangerous, so is seeing other generations through your own generational lenses. And just as putting everyone from the same culture in the same box is dangerous, so is putting people from the same generation in the one box.

Not everyone fits the profile. Use the generalisations below as a framework, remembering that just as people are shaped by the times they live in and by their peers, they are also shaped by the values and beliefs of their cultures and personal experiences.

● IN A NUTSHELL

The working generations

If you aren't already, you will soon be leading, managing and working with up to five generations at the same time, including people older than yourself, and each will be expecting different things from you and their jobs. The handles for each generation as well as the range of birth dates varies slightly from source to source, but here's the gist:

1. *Generation Z*: Many of the oldest of this 'Digital Native' generation – those born between 1996 and 2009 and the first to have not experienced 'life before the Internet' – are well ensconced in the workforce.

2. *Generation Y*: Many of this generation of techno-savvy, highly confident, mobile employees born between 1981 and 1995 are in leader-manager roles; all need to be managed carefully to harness their innovation and creativity and to benefit from their enthusiasm and energy.

3. *Generation X*: Some of those born between 1965 and 1980 are already planning their retirement and others are now the 'leader-manager' class, managing Baby Boomers, Generation Y-ers, Generation Z-ers and even Traditionalists.

>>

4. *Baby Boomers*: Born between 1946 and 1964, the largest generation in history and a quarter of the Australian population, Boomers are retiring in large numbers and many are taking sabbaticals and choosing to switch to part-time and contract work before they fully retire.

5. *Traditionalists*: There are still a few people in the workforce born between 1920 and 1945 in the workplace. Some love to work; some need to work because their superannuation hasn't worked for them as they'd hoped.

Did you notice the span of years of generations is shrinking? That's mostly because of the rapid rise and development of technology.

Generation Z

Many of the 4.6 million Australians born between 1996 and 2009 are already working and, over the next decade, will become a growing proportion of the workforce. Typically the children of Gen X (born after the fall of the Soviet Union into a fast-moving, complex world shaped by recession and 9/11), Generation Z grew up with information and media technology at their fingertips – all reflected in their attitudes, aptitudes, expectations, attention spans and learning styles. Idealistic and aware of the environmental, human rights and socio-economic challenges their generation inherits, they are creative, open to change, philanthropic and keen on social justice.

This mobile, highly connected, social networking generation is adaptable, confident, contrarian, curious, independent, innovative and intelligent. Gen Z-ers place a high priority on speed as they quickly shift their attention from one project to another, and can consume and process information from multiple media sources at the same time. They can process information quickly, and they are suited to complex projects. They work fast, taking little time to reflect, which tends to result in a lack of attention to detail, lack of depth in their research, and thin critical-thinking skills.

Thanks to their wide range of experience and opportunities (e.g. free, instant real-time access to entertainment, information and global communities, greater educational opportunites and more travel during their formative years than other generations) Gen Z-ers are less similar to each other than are other generations. Most are natural networkers and good collaborators; some love to work in teams – virtual or actual, it makes no difference – although others prefer to work independently. So (as with all employees) take the time to get to know them, their motivations and aspirations and lead them accordingly.

Generation Z employees tend to be results-driven and self-motivated, so give them a job and let them get on with it. Check in frequently for chats about their progress and manage them by output, not time. Since they tend to see the big picture rather than the details, monitor their accuracy and explain why it's important. Keep them engaged and let them learn by doing and helping others. Thanks to their large, global social networks, they are highly attuned to social trends, so let them help identify and meet customer needs and use their networks to contribute to your organisation.

Generation Y

The 4.2 million Australians born between 1981 and 1995 are an important segment of the workforce. Raised in child-focused households by dual-career or single parents, these Gen Y-ers are the coddled, confident, sociable and socially conservative offspring of the most age-diverse group of parents ever. As a result, they see adults, including managers, as people who work in their best interests and help them solve their problems. Having been praised for the most meagre of accomplishments, Gen Y-ers have huge faith in themselves and their abilities and expect a stream of positive feedback.

Many Gen Y-ers live at home for years longer than previous generations and don't see themselves as adults until their late 20s. Carrying no baggage of 'hard times', they are more ambitions, demanding, hedonistic, materialistic, optimistic, self-absorbed, self-indulgent and more into instant gratification than other generations, spending money they don't have on clothes, entertainment and travel.

The first generation raised on the Internet, computers and interactive technology, most Gen Y-ers have a complete grasp of technology. They are more highly educated than previous generations and can synthesise information and establish what is important to them. They are comfortable with change, which makes them valuable innovators. They want to work in teams, work well in teams and want to know they're an important member of their team. Although they're used to intense peer pressure, acceptance is critical for them, which makes recognition from their peers important.

Employees from Generation Y tend to be more team-oriented and less self-motivated and solution-focused than their younger colleagues. Their personal learning and development is important to them and they expect (often unrealistically) rapid career progress. Gen Y-ers are used to doing what it takes to get what they want, making them good negotiators but tricky employees. It's been said that Gen Y-ers want all the money and all the perks, but on their own terms. They're aready transforming workplaces to suit their needs.

 IN A NUTSHELL

Gen Y-ers as leaders

Many Gen Y-ers are already leader-managers. As the last of the Baby Boomers retire from the workplace over the next 15 years, you can expect to see even more Gen Y-ers in leadership roles, and many more of them women than in previous generations of leader-managers.

Gen Y-ers are egalitarians who are both people and productivity focused. As leaders, they're likely to be less authoritarian and structured, and more collaborative, consultative, communicative and open than previous generations of leaders. Their self-confidence makes them entrepreneurially inclined, and their technological competence and the fact that they value flexibility and meaningful work, and understand the power of teamwork, distinguishes them from older leaders, too.

This means that you can expect to see those cushy corner offices going and more open-spaced working environments that encourage collaboration between everyone – regardless of their seniority. Y-ers are unlikely to assign meaningless 'busy work' and are more likely to let people work when they want and where they want, reducing the need for expensive office space and making 'hot-desking', or temporary work stations for 'visiting' employees to use more common. (As a bonus, the smaller premises that result will lower rental, heating and other costs.) They'll manage by results and evaluate on performance, not presence.

Work-life balance, so craved by Boomers to separate work from home life, becomes work–life blending for Gen Y-ers since they tend to prefer to work anywhere, everywhere and at any time of day or night to being 'chained' to a desk nine-to-five, five days a week – so 20th century. The trade-off is being able to leave work to care for aging parents and pick the kids up from school and plug in again when it's quiet.

Gen Y-ers are also more likely to forsake email and use more advanced technologies to foster collaboration than older leaders. They'll communicate and spread their message by phone calls and instant messaging rather than email, and one-to-one, face-to-face discussions rather than meetings help them do more work in real time.

Managing this high-maintenance 'diva' generation is something of an art form. They want a boss they respect, who provides an egalitarian, fun, happy, informal and social work environment and who puts them in a diverse team. Meet often with them to discuss what they have achieved and what they need to do to keep moving forward. Provide plenty of support and lots of attention, informal reviews, positive feedback and 'chats' (think 'microfeedback' for Twitterholics) as they build experience. Recognise the results they achieve and offer plenty of appreciation for a job well done. Listen to their opinions and give them a say – their egos are hurt when you don't.

Remember that Gen Y-ers are drawn to workplaces with a fast, stimulating pace. Assign them work that gives them variety and allows frequent interaction with others, and let them work in teams whenever you can – but guard against work becoming a solely social occasion. Keep them focused on their own job purpose and the team's purpose and goals as well as the organisation's vision and strategic direction, and keep them enthused. They thrive on feeling tested and are easily bored, so give the Y-ers on your team responsibility as a mark of your trust and faith in their abilities. Remember their need to enjoy life as well as work, so think about providing extended leave for study or travel as well as flexible work schedules.

Most Gen Y-ers see jobs as stepping stones across organisations to progress their careers and they change jobs readily, especially when they aren't getting the challenge and recognition they want from work. Because of this, some leader-managers are reluctant to performance manage Gen Y-ers, fearing that when they tell them their work isn't up to scratch, they'll leave. That's a mistake. When their performance isn't as good as it should be, discuss it with them and coach them. Find ways to help them improve their performance and make sure they understand that achieving their goals can help them build their careers. Remember, too, Y-ers are into learning and expect you to help them solve their problems (see Chapter 16 to find out more about managing underperformance and page 905 for more about coaching).

● THEORY TO PRACTICE

Leading Millennials

You've probably noticed that Gen Z-ers and Y-ers share many characteristics and respond to similar leadership and management styles. In fact, they're sometimes grouped together as 'Millennials'.

Both generations view work–life balance and job interest as important as, or even more important, than money and seek opportunities rather than jobs. Let them telecommute at least some of the time and work to flexible schedules so they can blend work and home life. In fact, particularly for the Z-ers, work may never be the centre of their lives, so be a boss who understands the importance of work–life balance.

Millennials switch off when they're bored but will work long hours when they enjoy a job, expecting flexibility in return. They want to work at jobs they enjoy and can learn from and that provide the opportunity to do a variety of demanding tasks that give them a sense of purpose and achievement and the freedom to try things out. Let them know how they can benefit from working in the organisation, and keep challenging them – or they're likely to move on. Danny Gorog, co-founder of Outwear, one of Australia's biggest and most successful app companies, puts it like this, 'It's not just paying people the right amount. It's about providing them with a place they're happy to come to every day, because sometimes the work is tough.'[56]

They are averse to working through a chain of command, preferring to communicate directly with the person in charge of a project, and they expect to be taken seriously and given state-of-the-art technology. Although most Millennials don't want to be told how, when and where to work, praise them frequently and reward them often as they produce their deliverables. Make sure your feedback is regular and acknowledges the difference they make to the organisation.

Guide and mentor them, rather than manage them. Meet with them frequently, face-to-face or online. Help them with workplace etiquette. Explain how to write reports and emails; and help them fine-tune the way they present ideas and information. Give them guidelines for using social media at work.

Ensure the Millennials in your team feel included and 'in' on what's happening in the organisation. Provide more attention, structure and supervision than you would with older employees.

Generation X

Born between 1965 and 1980 into a more dangerous, uncertain and unfriendly world than their parents, Gen X-ers are the first generation to grow up with both parents working or in single-parent families as children of divorce. These 'latchkey kids' of downsized and overworked parents are apt to be slightly cynical. They've seen their parents work hard and for long hours with little thanks in return and don't want the same for themselves.

Consequently, Gen X-ers aren't as interested in long-term careers as their parents and don't expect lifelong employment with any one company or one lifelong career path. Currently the largest generation in the workforce, they see themselves as free agents and many are happy with a lateral career approach rather than a promotion or specialism path. In common with their younger co-workers, they're comfortable with the idea of several careers in one lifetime. They are willing to put in long hours provided they receive top salaries and working conditions in return – and they won't do it forever.

Gen X-ers want flexibility in all aspects of their lives. They focus on relationships, outcomes, their rights and their skills. They expect choices, control and independence on the job, and they dislike routine – things done in the same way on the same day at the same time. Like Gen Y-ers and Z-ers, their orientation to time and space is non-traditional: where and when a job is done is irrelevant as long as it's done.

Although benefits and perks are important to them, job satisfaction motivates Gen X-ers more. Resourceful, individualistic and self-reliant, and casual in their dress and communication style, they believe in working smarter, not harder. They're more sophisticated about technology than Baby Boomers and comfortable with using computers to produce more work in less time. Gen X-ers are also comfortable with women in leadership roles and they're a little more caring and a little less command and control than the previous generation of Baby Boomer leaders.

To bring out Gen X-ers' best work, don't micromanage them. Give them the goal, explain the constraints and let them reach it in a way that suits them. Give them multiple tasks and let them set the priorities. Take time to get to know them, to thank them and to ask for their reactions and opinions. Listen to what they have to say and show your respect for their subject-matter expertise.

THE STRATEGIC PERSPECTIVE

Generational similarities and differences

Gen X-ers and Gen Y-ers have many differences; for example, rather than try to change things they don't like at work, Gen Y-ers just leave, whereas Gen X-ers first try to change them. Whereas Gen Y-ers like to work in teams, older Gen X-ers are more into 'me'. In fact, they're often called the 'me generation'. Yet X-ers and Y-ers are more like each other than they are like Baby Boomers:

- Unlike the workaholic Boomers who seemed willing to accept poor management practices and to bend to fit the organisation, Gen X-ers and Gen Y-ers don't tolerate poor management practices and expect the organisation to bend to fit them.
- Gen X-ers and Y-ers insist on informality, fun, flexibility and feedback at work, and the opportunity to learn on the job and keep extending their skills is essential. The expectations of Boomers aren't as high.
- Gen X-ers and Gen Y-ers are from questioning generations. They're inclined to examine processes and look for ways to improve them, while Boomers tend to accept the status quo and follow directions.
- Gen X-ers aren't as techno-savvy as Gen Y-ers but are light-years ahead of most Boomers.
- Baby Boomers are less formally educated than Gen X-ers and Y-ers and, unlike them, have no tradition of undertaking extra training.

Baby Boomers

The generation born in the peaceful years after World War II, between 1946 and 1964, is the largest generation in history. Although they grew up in the 'electronic age' of television, they are not 'naturally' electronically skilled and often have technological-access problems. Most entered the workforce before computers were common and had to learn how to use them, and many are still not comfortable with technology in general.

Open-minded, idealistic and rebellious in their youth and heavily into the civil rights and women's movements, Baby Boomers became conservative in their 30s and 40s, going from making love to making money, many sacrificing family life in favour of career advancement. Their high divorce rate was partly responsible for women of this generation entering the workforce in large numbers.

Unlike the Y-ers who were raised on competitions where there were no losers and everyone was a winner, for Boomers there are clear winners and losers in life just as in sports and war. Although drawn to the values of congenial, consensual, inclusive leadership and teamworking, many Boomers lack the skills required to implement it. They may know it, but they probably don't do it. In fact, they're often called the 'know-it-all generation'. They know things intellectually but are often unaware of how to put their knowledge into practice.

Ambitious, competitive, loyal, optimistic and single-minded about their careers, Boomers expected to work for only one or two organisations during their careers. Thinking that loyalty to their employer would reap loyalty in return, they became a generation of workaholics – until they were hit by downsizing and discovered the importance of life outside work.

Trained in 'job for life' thinking, Boomers don't understand what they view as the 'job-hopping' mentality of Millennials. And tensions arise when Boomers are confronted with the self-assuredness and lack of automatic deference of Millennials.

From baby boom to baby bust

In 1970, only 8% of Australia's population was aged 65 and over. By 2013, that figure was 14% and is projected to reach about 23% by 2050. There are now almost twice as many people aged 55 and over in the workforce as there were in the 1980s.

The shrinking, greying workforce means organisations face increasing competition for employees. This is one reason that retaining the participation of older workers and of women in the workforce have been identified as the two top reforms needed to ensure the supply of employees needed to keep the Australian economy healthy. Boomers and women also comprise huge consumer and user markets, too, and as employees, are able to help organisations relate to those two groups of customers better.[57]

Boomers like to think of themselves as the stars of the show and are proud of the skills they've acquired (to the point of sometimes being stuck in their ways), so acknowledge them, their contributions and their dedicated work ethic with public recognition. They're highly individualistic (to the point of being self-obsessed), which makes them less consultative, so let them work independently. Tap into the large networks they are likely to have built for two reasons: to learn from them and to take advantage of them to help spread your messages. Draw on their experience and ability to see the strategic perspective to help solve problems and mentor others.

Give Boomers the respect they think they deserve but be aware that because they grew up questioning authority, you need to earn their respect. Approach them as an equal, develop a friendly relationship with them and keep the communication channels open. Use your persuasion skills and 'prove yourself' by quietly demonstrating the value you bring to the team.

While Gen X-ers and Y-ers vastly outnumber them in the workforce, Boomers still outrank them in seniority and management. Over the next decade, this will change and, as Boomers continue to retire in droves leaving gaping holes in their wake, do what you can to keep them on your team. Ensure that they know they can avail themselves of your organisation's flexible working arrangements because quality of life is important to the semi-retired and considering-retirement Boomers.

Traditionalists

Born between 1920 and 1945, the values of hard work and respect for authority were instilled into this generation. They grew up under the influence of the Roaring 20s, the Great Depression, World Wars I and II and the injunctions to be 'seen and not heard' and to 'waste not, want not'. For them, work is a privilege and the way to earn your way in the world. Theirs was the generation that shaped our world, creating the vaccines that wiped out many killer diseases, developing the space program and building big corporations.

Most are now retired but a few remain, some because they love to work, others because their retirement plans haven't materialised as expected due to their superannuation turning to dust as a result of the global financial crisis. Whatever their reasons for working, you can expect them to be loyal and non-confrontational conformists who don't 'rock the boat', but 'do the right thing'.

You may have one or two of these Traditionalists in your team, working as casuals, consultants, contractors or part-timers, or brought in for mentoring programs. Whatever their role, treat them respectfully. Draw on their wealth of accumulated knowledge and understanding when you can.

Correct, consistent conformers, the Traditionalists are self-disciplined, logical thinkers who are happy in hierarchies. Give them their deliverables, explain what you want and why, and check in with them occasionally to make sure they're settling in, to see if they need anything and to assure yourself they're on track. When you want something done in a particular way, say so – traditionalists are adept at following directions and attending to detail, and they're fine with leaders telling them what they want done and how.

Traditionalists are good team players, too, so take the time to integrate them into the team. And don't pester them to Tweet.

THE STRATEGIC PERSPECTIVE

Some reasons to hang onto mature-aged workers

Living gives people, at least those who pay attention, deeper and wider life skills. The longer you live and learn, the more your emotional intelligence grows, helping you to put matters into perspective. Living and learning increases your patience and ability to think problems and decisions through. Experience and practice guide you to achieve goals in ways that work for you. In many ways, older people can hold their own against younger people and even surpass them.

One reason for this is that as people age, the two hemispheres of the brain work better together, meaning that older people have a fuller access to all their mental power. Another reason is that the brain never stops growing and re-shaping itself in response to its environment and what it learns.

As time passes, people become more emotionally stable and satisfied with their lives. Their people skills and ability to avoid conflict improve. Priorities become clearer, and job-related knowledge and vocabularies grow. So does people's ability to see the strategic perspective.

Maybe that's why older employees are often called 'Wisdom Workers'. Why is it, then, that there are two million unemployed Australians over the age of 55 who are interested in working? Their inability to find employment could be costing the economy $10.8 billion a year?[58]

CourseMateExpress

Go to http://login.cengagebrain.com to access CourseMate Express, your online study tool for *Management Theory & Practice*. CourseMate Express brings chapter concepts to life with interactive learning, and study and exam preparation tools:

- Test your skills in different aspects of management with interactive self-tests and simulations.
- Watch videos that show how real managers operate in real businesses.
- Test your understanding of the changing world of management by taking the revision quiz.

QUICK REVIEW

1. Which groups of people are most likely to be discriminated against in Australian society and what effect is this likely to have on their employment? How does discrimination affect organisations?
2. Review some of the ways organisations encourage diversity and discuss the steps you can take as a leader-manager to build a diverse work team. In what ways do organisations benefit from being inclusive?
3. Review the cultural differences you can expect to find in Australian workplaces and give some examples from your own experience to illustrate your explanation.
4. Review the generational differences found in Australian workplaces and explain the tensions that can arise as a result. How can these tensions be overcome by good team leadership?

BUILD YOUR SKILLS

1. Provide an example of each of the three following forms of discrimination in terms of opportunity or treatment in employment: *exclusion*, *preference* and *distinction*. State whether the example you have given is of overt or covert discrimination and whether it is direct or indirect and explain whether the examples you have given might be systemic in nature.
2. Do you think there is a difference between not discriminating and encouraging diversity at work? How important is senior management's support of diversity? Explain your reasoning using examples if possible.
3. How would you handle the three situations below in a way that would strengthen your team's ability to work together and value each other's differences?
   a. One team member freely uses the desks of other team members and when she needs a ruler or a stapler she rummages through her teammates' drawers to find one. She's naturally friendly and can't understand why her teammates give her the 'cold shoulder'. Her teammates can't stand it any more and complain to you.
   b. You value punctuality and one of your team members consistently turns up late for work and for meetings. When you point out his tardiness, he responds, 'Hey, what's a few minutes here or there? I was doing something else and it was important!'
   c. A new team member, fresh from university, often texts, checks messages and seems to consulte various apps on her smartphone during meetings. Some of the other team members roll their eyes when she does this, but haven't said anything either to you or to their new colleague.
4. Referring to Case Study 9.2 on page 284, how do you think the team would be different in terms of creativity, innovation and productivity were it not made up of a diverse group of people?
5. Referring to the Scenario at the beginning of this chapter, what message would have been sent to the troops had Lieutenant General Morrison transferred Lieutenant Colonel McGregor to another post?
6. Read Case Study 16.2 on page 354 and complete the questions. (You can find out about 'I' messages on page 469.)

WORKPLACE ACTIVITIES

1. Analyse the diversity of your organisation's workforce or your workplace. For example, does it employ members of all groups in the full range of jobs or are people from some groups concentrated into a few types of jobs? Are some groups of people concentrated in a few levels

of the organisational structure? Are any groups or individuals disadvantaged or excluded? If so, how? Do the requirements of the jobs involved justify these disadvantages or exclusions? Assess how your workplace measures up in terms of diversity and discrimination and develop a plan for increasing diversity in your work team that targets specific benefits that align with your organisation's strategy, vision and values.

2. Interview someone from a disadvantaged group. Find out whether they have ever felt discriminated against. If they have, find out how they may have been disadvantaged and how they believe their treatment might have affected the organisation in which they worked at the time.

3. Describe the steps you have taken to establish common goals and create a collective team culture to bind a diverse work team together in your work team. What diversity policies and programs does your organisation have in place and how have they aided you in building a diverse work team? Based on qualitative and quantitative measures, how successful have your own and your organisation's inclusivity measures been?

CASE STUDY 26.1

KNOW-IT-ALLS OR WISDOM WORKERS?

'Thank you for being such a good listener, Jan. It's really helpful to be able to talk things through like this.'

'No worries. It's interesting for me to hear about the real world. A good break from nappies. Although you're making me wonder whether I should go back to work. Never mind. Tell me more about Greg and this project he's managing.'

'Do you know what really gets me? He constantly goes over my head to the director. I discussed that with him and all I got was. "I think he understands where I'm coming from better than you do." Can you believe that? On Monday, the three of us went for a meeting – myself, the director and Greg, just a little way outside the city. We're standing outside waiting for our taxi to get back to work and Greg says, "You'd hate working here, Claire. Not enough shopping." They're forming a boy's club and I'm excluded.'

'Is he the one who comes to meetings, no pen, no paper and just sits with his arms behind his head, leaning back and looking down his nose at you?'

'Ah, that would be Rolf, who was in the team I led last year. We'd meet and he'd agree to make a couple of changes to a project he managed for me. I asked him once how he remembered what we agree without taking any notes and and you know what he said? "Oh, I've done it all before so if there's anything you can tell me now, I'd be very surprised."'

'How rude! How old was this Rolf?'

'Old enough to know better. He was 50-something, late 50s, I think. About the same as Greg, a couple of years younger than the director.'

'These men don't think a female should be in charge of them.'

'Worse than that. A *young* female. *They* should be in charge of *me,* is what they think. I'm 37 years old. I'm a mother; I have years of solid experience in leading projects and managing teams and they think I'm a kid.'

'What about the women on your team?'

'Clara is great. She's younger than me and we bounce ideas off one another all the time. But the Boomers – you assign them work, they go off and do it, bring it back, done. It's fine. They do the job fine. But there's no bouncing ideas back and forth, which I find very valuable for everyone. I'd asked Maria – she was one of the older women on my last team – about chatting through what she was working on and she'd just say, "No, I don't need to."'

'The older ones just think differently. Uncle Ed says it's because the Boomers – he prefers the term 'Wisdom Workers' – think bouncing ideas around makes it seem like they don't know what they're doing. They expect to just get on with the work. Younger people, he says, like to do the team thing and chat and let ideas evolve. He should know – he's a Boomer – sorry, a 'Wisdom Worker' – who manages quite a few Gen Ys like Clara.

'The younger ones on the team like to try new things, too. But Ann, she's another Boomer on my current team – you say, "I'd like to try this and see how it goes", and all you get is "Won't work. Didn't work then. Won't work now." Drives me mad. She's been there for 20-odd years, though. I guess that makes it kind of hard to adapt.

'But her length of service is great in other ways. You say, "Hey, I think I saw some information about such and such" and she says, "Oh, yes, I know where it is. I'll pull it out for you."

'Just this last little grizzle and then I'm done. I was going through some applications for a vacancy on the team and there are a couple of applicants who are not only Boomers, but Boomers applying for roles well below their last roles. I've had that before. Sometimes they've been made redundant. Sometimes they retired and and then they missed working. Sometimes they just want a stop-gap job until they can get something better (which is a disaster waiting to happen). Sometimes it's a work–life balance need. Tricky, but at least it tests my interviewing skills.

'That's what I did. I dropped down a level when I had my son because I wanted regular hours. You know, Jan, I still wonder whether that was the right choice and whether I'll ever catch up to myself again.

'Okay, your turn. What's up with you?'

Questions

1. List Claire's specific challenges with her present and past 'Wisdom Workers'.
2. What role does the director play in Claire's current difficulties? How should Claire handle this?
3. What could Claire do or have done to make the most of her older employees' experience while still adding her own value to their projects based on her own experience, training and perhaps her different perspective?
4. Claire mentioned that she herself dropped back a level, in her case for work–life balance reasons. How might that affect her career?

CASE STUDY 26.2

DAMLA'S DILEMMA

Newly arrived in Australia with limited English skills, Damla finds a casual job preparing packaged sandwiches for the retail lunch trade. Her hours are generally 3 am to 8 am, which allows her just enough time to get home before her husband leaves for work and to care for her children, aged two, three and five years.

Damla understood that those were to be her usual hours and that she would be employed with reasonable regularity, and all goes well for eight or nine weeks. Then her boss begins asking her to stay late to help complete orders. She explains as best she can that she cannot stay because she needs to get home to her children. There are always several other workers willing to stay and Damla believes they can easily complete the work.

Then Damla's boss begins making remarks about people who aren't committed to their jobs and just there for the money. These comments soon escalate into thinly veiled remarks about people from Damla's homeland, the number of children 'they' have, 'their' lack of a 'real work ethic' and so on. Before long, several of the other workers join in, commenting on the way she dresses, asking her pointed questions about her religion and smirking when she enters the room.

This upsets Damla but she needs her job to help pay the bills. She gets on with her duties and remains silent. Her boss continues to press her to work beyond 8 am but Damla cannot. She doesn't feel able to explain her concern that her husband would be angry with her if she came home late as he has clear expectations about her role as a wife and mother.

Five weeks later, her boss fires her, saying he needs someone who is flexible enough to stay until all the work is finished. Damla is devastated. How can she face her husband now that she has lost her job? The family depends on the money she brings home to make ends meet.

Questions

1. Is it reasonable for Damla's boss to insist she stay longer than the agreed hours?
2. Assess the way Damla's boss handled the situation.
3. Does Damla have any recourse that would allow her to keep her job?

CHAPTER

27

ENCOURAGING A LEARNING ENVIRONMENT AND DEVELOPING EMPLOYEES

OVERVIEW

An ancient Chinese proverb seems more relevant than ever in today's fast-changing world: 'Learning is like rowing upstream. Not to advance is to drop back.'[1]

The world is constantly changing and the only way to survive and thrive is to move with, or better still, ahead of the changes. To do this, organisations need to keep developing their capabilities and teams and individuals need to keep learning and developing their skills. That can't happen without a learning culture.

In learning cultures, building skills and knowledge is part of the way individuals and teams work. People are willing to get out of their comfort zones and try things out, and they use mistakes as feedback. They do this formally and informally, learning from each other, from their leader-managers, from working on special assignments, projects and delegated duties, and in all sorts of other ways.

This is the 21st-century way of running organisations: People continually extending their own competencies and their organsation's capabilities. Establishing a workplace climate that encourages and facilitates learning is an important part of every leader-manager's job. Why? Because in a fiercely competitive global economy, the skills and knowledge of the workforce are an important resource and a worthwhile investment – as worthwhile an investment as machinery and equipment. And unlike other resources, the value of knowledge doesn't lessen when it's used – it increases.

1. Do you know how to facilitate and promote learning, create learning opportunities and encourage a learning culture that creates and supports meaningful learning and development opportunities for employees?
2. Can you identify your own and your team members' training needs, and develop and gain approval for learning plans?
3. Do you understand how people learn and are you able to help learners improve their learning effectiveness and assess the effectiveness of learning activities?
4. Do you know how to plan and conduct one-on-one and small-group skills training?

This chapter explains how to build a working environment that keeps people effective and up to date to meet your organisation's needs now and in the future. You should also read the section, 'Providing informal feedback on performance' on page 447.

SCENARIO

Cutting-edge learning

Gina is stoked! The company is launching an extensive series of in-house, just-in-time learning packages this week. Employees can access state-of-the-art training, covering technical as well as interpersonal and customer service skills, on the company's Intranet and on their tablets and smartphones. Learning – anywhere, any time. When employees successfully complete a learning module that is part of their approved development plan, they receive a specified number of hours' pay, depending on the training package.

As the leader of a team of front-line customer support staff, Gina knows this is a huge help. No more down time during slow periods – just learning time. When it suits them, employees can log onto the Intranet on their home computers and learn or sit on the bus and learn – great for the contractors and part-timers and great for the company because now they'll be as well trained as the full-time staff.

When a new or modified product is introduced, which on average is once a month, everyone can plug into the training system and learn the product details at their own pace, whenever it suits them. Or they can brush up on their soft skills. Gina has already worked out personal development agreements with most team members, targeting the packages to work on first.

This training is more than just self-paced learning on a computer screen. It is high-tech and interactive. Each time a learner uses a program, it is different from the last time, so learners can use each learning package many times without becoming bored. Along with core scenarios and examples, the programs randomly deliver a range of additional examples and scenarios each time a learner logs on. Best of all, the software monitors each learner's strengths and areas needing further development, and selects examples and scenarios targeted to provide practice on areas they need most. Learning is automatically tailored to each person's needs – a dream come true!

This makes learning by doing safe. When people make a mistake, there are no red faces or adverse customer consequences – learners can just try again and keep trying until they are competent and confident.

Gina and her team members can also request a summary of their strengths and development needs from the system whenever they want to, and when learners successfully complete a module they and Gina both receive a print-out summarising the learner's scores and suggesting areas for further development. This gives Gina information about individual coaching and other development opportunities she should provide for each team member. And she can quickly spot who might be having problems in which areas, who is up to date with their learning and who might need a gentle reminder. Gina can also print out a summary for her entire team to get an idea of other training she should plan for them as a group.

Gina's mind is buzzing. Because she can see who is strongest in which areas, she can pair up team members to coach each other. She can use the software to help her select people and place them in jobs that suit them best. People can learn by themselves or in small discussion groups – great for the interpersonal skills programs. Best of all, these interactive training packages put people in charge of their own learning. Isn't technology glorious?

1. Encouraging a learning culture

In a time of drastic change it is the learners who inherit the future. The learned usually find themselves equipped to live in a world that no longer exists.

Eric Hoffer (writer and philosopher), *Reflection on the Human Condition* (1973)[2]

Few companies survived the Industrial Revolution of the 1800s. Few even survived electrification. Why? Because they failed to grasp the need to change the way they made and sold things in a changing world. As we saw in Chapter 1, we're in the midst of another revolution, the information revolution. How many of today's companies can live to tell the tale?

The central challenge of industrial-age work was efficiency; for knowledge-age work, it's learning. In today's knowledge and service economy, you're not just trying to do the same things you've always done, but better, cheaper or faster; you're also trying to find ways to operate that are completely different and to innovate completely different offerings.

Encouraging and supporting learning, capturing what people learn and making it widely and easily available to others is essential in order to avoid organisational (and career) extinction. In fact, without a skilled and adaptable workforce, organisations' competitiveness and Australia's economic future erodes. We need to be able to learn, unlearn and relearn in order to innovate, recognise risks and take the right risks, and make the most of our changing environment (See page 10 for more information on the knowledge economy, page 407 to find out how to manage knowledge workers and page 872 to find out how important learning and development are to younger employees).

Do you know that every dollar's worth of plastic in Lego bricks sells to the customer for $75?[3] That's the value of knowledge. With knowledge such an important asset, it doesn't make sense to leave its development to chance. The more your team or your organisation depends on knowledge and cooperative, innovative, smart employees, the more you need to nurture and manage their learning and experience methodically and deliberately and help them put what they've learned into practice.

◉ THEORY TO PRACTICE

How Google expands knowledge

Google excels at analytical decision-making, experimentation, improvisation, participative product development and other relatively unusual forms of innovation. Hardly a day goes by without the company announcing a new product or feature that moves it further along the road to fulfilling its mission 'to organise the world's information and make it universally accessible and useful'.

New ideas are often generated by employees from the bottom up. Technical employees spend 80% of their time on the company's core search and advertising businesses and 20% on technical projects of their own choosing. A new engineer might blog, 'This isn't a matter of doing something in your spare time, but more of actively making time for it. Heck, I don't have a good 20% project yet and I need one. If I don't come up with something I'm sure it could negatively impact my [performance] review.'

Managers are also required to spend some of their time on innovation: 70% on the core business, 20% on related but different projects and 10% on entirely new business and products. Google even has a 'director of other' position to help manage the 10% time requirement. This explicit investment in innovation has produced streams of new products and features. During one six-month period, more than 50 new products resulted from Google engineers' 20% time investments, including Gmail, AdSense and Google News.[4]

Create learning opportunities

One of the most valuable things you can do as a leader is build learning into your team's culture. When you do that, gaining knowledge and skills is something that occurs all the time.

Opportunities for learning are everywhere. For example, you can extend employees' skills and experience through additional responsibilities, empowerment, multiskilling, upskilling, participation in multifunctional teams or job redesign. You can second people to other functions or divisions and give them projects and special assignments. You can mentor people and coach them (and you can find a list of the many ways to learn in the 'In a nutshell: Lots of ways to learn' on page 139, and later in this chapter on page 894).

Make time for yourself and your team, alone and together, to reflect, diagnose problems, and learn from experience. Review how the team is working and its procedures to find ways to improve. Help people learn from mistakes and listen to minority viewpoints. Encourage team members to stay open to new ideas and opinions and see them as valuable for developing novel approaches and solutions. Airing ideas, asking questions, seeking out dissenting views and paying attention to them, and looking for underlying assumptions that may be holding back improvements or acting as a flawed basis for decision-making and problem-solving are other ways to encourage people to keep thinking and learning.

Gather information on best practice, customer wants and needs, and economic, social and technological trends and make it readily available to people to assist their creative and continuous improvement thinking. Promote learning from employees' own experience and from their external and internal customers, external and internal suppliers, contractors and networks, and help them to cultivate and nurture these knowledge bases.

Encourage and reward information sharing among your team – for example, by holding regular 'learning meetings' during which team members take turns briefing the rest of the team on a course they've attended or a book they've read. The learning cycle, shown in Figure 27.1, is a great way to help individuals and the team as a whole identify what they learn as they go about their jobs and put it to good use. As they say: 'Experience is the greatest teacher, but only when you learn from it'

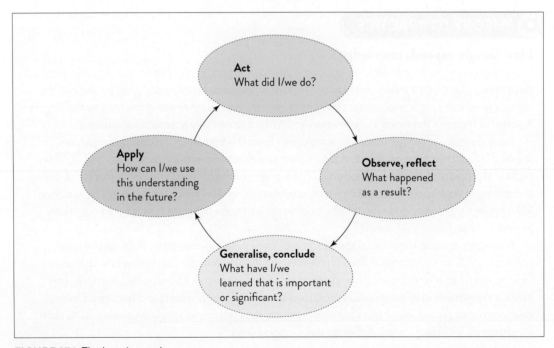

FIGURE 27.1 The learning cycle

(see page 575 to fine-tune the way the team works together and the systems and procedures they follow during your learning meetings).

Individual work and individual rewards can pit people against each other, so encourage and reward teamwork. Encourage adaptability, continuous improvement, curiosity, innovation, learning and sharing learning, willingness to explore different points of view and other behaviours consistent with a learning environment. Build a team whose members trust each other and their organisation and make sure everyone knows what everyone else is working to achieve.

Think about meeting with other teams and with your external and internal customers and suppliers over a structured lunch to learn about what they do, how it affects your team and your customers, and how your teams might be able to help each other more. Find out how they approach making innovations, find and solve problems, and make continuous improvements. See what you and your team can learn from their specialism and expertise.

Work with employees to produce individual learning and development (L&D) goals and discuss how to achieve them. During the normal performance review cycle is a good time for this and any time in between is fine, too (see page 443 for more information on this aspect of encouraging learning).

◉ THEORY TO PRACTICE

End-of-year team performance review

Before the summer break, take some time out with your team to reflect on the past year. Ask team members to consider the following questions before you meet. Set aside two to three hours to meet and discuss:

- What are you and we as a team proud of?
- What worked well last year for you? For the team?
- What are the three biggest lessons you learned this past year?
- What are the three biggest lessons we, as a team, learned this past year?
- How would you describe the team's energy at this point?
- What projects or processes do we need to improve?
- Who are three people you should thank for their help in making the past year successful for you? (Call them or send a card, or similar, over the next couple of weeks or early in the new year.)
- Who are three people or other teams the team should thank for their help in making the past year successful for us? How can we thank them?

Congratulate yourselves on what went well, and plan what the team and its members can do to make the next year an even better one. Ask each team member to write down one 'To do' idea along the lines of 'From now on I intend to ...' and share his or her commitment with the others. Then, as a team, brainstorm ideas for working better as a team next year. Select the top five ideas, print them up and post them on the noticeboard. Review them when the team meets in the new year.

In virtual teams, post the questions in the virtual team room and set up a threaded discussion, conference call or videoconference.

Using mistakes to learn

Here's what former Procter & Gamble CEO Alan 'A.G.' Lafley, said about mistakes, 'Failure is in my view, all about learning. It's about learning what you can do better.'[5] Lafley also had this to say: 'It isn't enough to take responsibility for your failures. It's important to create a culture that turns failures into learning and leads to continual improvement.'[6] Like many successful people, he views mistakes as part of growth and improvement, not just for individiuals but also for organisations. That attitude helps people and organisations to learn from mistakes and keep getting better.

It must be said that while mistakes can be learning opportunities, success is better. We learn more from success than failure because success that leads to a reward strengthens the relevant neural pathway. This means that the successful behaviour is repeated more efficiently the next time.

The problem with mistakes is that, unless there is a clear and direct negative consequence, or unless we carefully examine the mistake to learn from it, the brain isn't sure what to store or how to rewire itself, so it does nothing. So you need to 'force' your brain to learn from mistakes.

Here is another important reason to think through failures to work out what went wrong and how to prevent the same thing happening next time: when your mind looks for precedents among past actions when deciding what to do (*pattern recognition* is explained on page 527) it doesn't take into account whether an action was successful or not. This means you can end up repeating your mistakes unless you've thought through what went wrong and what to do instead.

The only stupid mistakes, then, are those you keep making because you failed to learn the lesson they hold. When you take the time to learn from your mistakes, you don't make the same mistake twice, and that makes them smart mistakes. That's why some of your more important and insightful learning is more likely to come from failures than successes – provided you worked out what went wrong.

That's a good reason not to ignore mistakes, cover them up, make excuses or find someone else to blame. A much better way to go is to fix them – analyse what went wrong and decide what corrective action to take and take it. When it's appropriate, explain (not excuse) where you went wrong, how you've rectified it and most important of all, what you intend to do to make sure it doesn't happen again. The more you try out new things, the more mistakes you're bound to make; and the more successes you're bound to have, too. The old cliché, 'Out on a limb is where the fruit is', is a useful one. People who score a lot of goals also kick a lot of misses. People who shoot a lot of baskets also throw a lot of duds. People who achieve anything worthwhile make more mistakes than most because they try out more things than most.

 FYI

Valuable mistakes

Thomas Alva Edison is reputed to have said, 'I have not failed 10 000 times. I have not failed once. I have succeeded in proving that those 10 000 ways will not work.'[7] That prolific inventor also knew that mistakes can give you valuable information and golden opportunities when you let them.

Here are some other worthwhile mistakes:

- In 1894, the Kellogg brothers developed Corn Flakes after leaving out a sticky, doughy mess of wheat, which then went stale. Rather than throw it out, they processed the mess and baked it. Their customers loved the cooked flakes that were the result.
- In 1961, meteorologist Edward Lorenz' weather simulation was going terribly wrong. When he looked for the reason, he discovered that rounding off his figures by dropping the last three decimal places had a spectacular impact on complex systems. He had discovered chaos theory.
- Paying attention to mistakes was how the cholera vaccine, dynamite, penicillin, photography, Post-it notes, radium, Scotchguard, shatterproof glass, silly putty, vulcanised rubber and X-rays were discovered.

THEORY TO PRACTICE

How to more than double your success rate

One way for organisations to grow and learn is through acquisitions – buy another company, their customers, their products, their processes, their employees, and so on. But acquisitions have a meagre 30% success rate. Under A.G. Lafley's guidance, a Procter & Gamble (P&G) team studied the company's acquisitions between 1970 and 2000 in detail in order to pinpoint the problems and discover patterns in the failures. They found five main causes of failed acquisitions:

1. The absence of a winning strategy to take the combined companies forward.
2. Not integrating the companies well enough or quickly enough.
3. Not achieving the expected synergies.
4. Incompatible cultures.
5. Internal leadership infighting.

Once they knew the problems, they knew what had to change. They could work out how best to organise for each phase of an acquisition, the processes they needed to introduce and the interim measures they could monitor to ensure the acquisition was progressing as expected.

Identifying their mistakes and planning how to overcome them meant P&G improved their acquisition success rate from below 30% to above 60% over the following 10 years.

For example, when P&G acquired Gillette in 2005, one of the 10 largest acquisitions ever, they achieved more than 150% of the estimated cost synergies. That alone created enough value to make the Gillette acquisition a success. Yet P&G still managed to identify and learn from mistakes during that acquisition to apply to their next acquisition.[8]

2. Identifying learning needs and planning to meet them

> In a world that is constantly changing, there is no one subject or set of subjects that will serve for the foreseeable future, let alone for the rest of your life. The most important skill to acquire now is learning how to learn.
>
> John Naisbitt (US author and futurist), *Megatrends*, 1984[9]

Effective L&D is an important part of many organisations' employer value proposition, essential to attracting and retaining the people they need. L&D makes sense as an investment in other ways, too. As well as boosting productivity, learning can boost morale because it helps to meet people's needs for recognition and development. It is generally reflected in indicators of employee satisfaction such as absenteeism, engagement, retention and timekeeping.

You can find out how to provide induction training to people who are new to your department and the organisation on page 833. Experienced workers need periodic training to add to, extend or update their skills and knowledge, to lift their current job performance and to become familiar with new policies, products and initiatives.

THE STRATEGIC PERSPECTIVE

Three poor reasons not to train

In economic downturns, 'expenses' like training, marketing, and research and development are usually the first to be cut. This quickly improves the bottom line and may not damage the organisation in the short term, but it can do long-term damage. In fact, so important is a skilled workforce that many business experts believe that training should be regarded as a core business expense or even an investment, not something to do only in the 'good times' and to cut when times get tough.

The higher an organisation's or a department's attrition and the more part-timers and casuals it employs, the easier it is to question whether L&D is even a sensible investment. After all, employees may not remain in the organisation for long, so training may be a waste of money and, to add insult to injury, the employees' productivity will be lost while they are training. Yet, with part-timers and casuals making up an increasing proportion of the workforce, their skills have make-or-break implications for the success of the organisations they work for.

Similarly, once employees hit their 40s, many organisations stop spending money on training them. Not smart – especially given the worsening shortage of skilled and experienced workers.

Whether they're full-time, part-time or casual employees, whether or not they speak English as a first language, whether or not they have disabilities or wrinkles, whether the economy is boom, bust or in between, all employees need ongoing support, coaching and training to keep pace with the changes inside organisations, changing customer expectations and changing technology. Otherwise, how can an organisation ensure that all of its employees develop the skills, knowledge and attitudes it needs now and in the future?

Learning isn't just about providing, updating or upgrading technical skills; there are also the all-important people skills. Training and coaching in people skills improves employees' abilities to work cooperatively with others, to communicate clearly and to be part of high performance, high productivity teams.

So the question is not whether to train, but how to train. Planned, systematic training can help people work together better and show them how to do their jobs more efficiently. Training can also reduce accidents, minimise customer complaints, contribute to a positive employer brand and employer value proposition, and enhance an organisation's global competitiveness. It reduces the length of time it takes new employees to reach what is known as *experienced worker standard*, saving time and money, cutting down on waste and increasing quality. Training targeted to meet the strategic needs of the organisation can also increase employees' skills and ability to take on other jobs, positioning the organisation to meet its future challenges. When combined with a learning culture, managing employees' learning properly greatly strengthens an organisation.

● THE STRATEGIC PERSPECTIVE

Intellectual capital

An organisation's competitive advantage increasingly depends on its intellectual capital. Intellectual capital is about knowledge, but not just any knowledge. When everyone knows something, it's a commodity.

Knowledge that generates substantial cash flow is valuable, as is knowledge that is critical for products and services and for which customers are willing to pay. This includes *technical knowledge* that is transferable to others in the company, *industry knowledge* about competitors, customers and suppliers, and *organisational knowledge* about the corporate culture, its politics and values, how to access information, and so on. These are the types of knowledge on which to concentrate.

>>

To reap the benefits of intellectual capital, you don't necessarily need to employ really smart people or people with a lot of qualifications. You need to employ people with the ability to learn and to share and use what they've learned, people with creativity, good networks, and the desire and drive to do a good job. And you need to capture and retrieve their built-up knowledge, insights and experience, build an organisation of committed and dedicated people and support them with the culture, equipment, facilities, tools, training and other resources they need to do their jobs well.

Identify learning and development needs

Organisational changes, job changes and individual and team performance shortfalls can all indicate a need for training. Learning needs aren't just about plugging gaps, though. They are also about strengthening existing skills, identifying development opportunities and developing employees for the future.

There are two main ways to identify learning needs. The first is by discussing them with each employee either informally or formally (as discussed on page 443). The second way is through a *learning needs analysis* (LNA). Both approaches can identify clear knowledge or performance gaps, for example, by comparing the current with desired competencies or current with desired results. Any shortfall points to a learning or development need relating to attitudes, knowledge or skills. These approaches can also identify opportunities to extend or improve already strong skills and add new skills.

There are other ways to identify learning needs, too, including:

* analysing business records, employee profiles, exit interviews and performance reviews
* analysing customer feedback and data such as accident and incident statistics and quality measures
* comparing performance against industry or in-house benchmarks
* considering your organisation's future plans (e.g. for expansion or the introduction of new technology)
* having employees complete specially designed questionnaires and competency checklists
* holding group meetings where the team brainstorms its training needs
* observing staff as they carry out their duties.

The more you involve employees in identifying their own learning needs, the more readily they accept the need for and look forward to extending their knowledge and skills.

Whenever you identify a learning need, ensure that it links back to the organisation's strategy and plans and key organisation objectives.

● IN A NUTSHELL

Indicators of learning needs

Training isn't the answer to every problem, but whenever any of the following symptoms appear, check whether additional or refresher training would help.

Indicators of individual employee and team training needs include:

* continually asking the team leader to make routine decisions
* excessive absences
* excessive customer complaints

>>

- high accident and/or incident rates
- high need for rework, high error rates
- inefficient use of time
- lack of teamwork and team support
- low productivity
- need for excessive overtime
- repeatedly coming to the team leader with problems.
     Indicators of leader-manager training needs include:
- above-average resignations or dismissals
- excessive overtime
- lack of teamwork and team support
- poor employee morale
- poor productivity and/or performance of the team or individuals
- repeatedly asking for help with problems and decisions
- unusual lateness or absenteeism of team members.

Learning needs analysis

A thorough learning needs analysis ensures training and learning activities aren't 'plug-in' solutions that don't work but are targeted to the precise needs of your team and organisation. When L&D specialists are involved, a clear and specific needs analysis also helps them develop the best training and learning intervention possible. The specialists may be experts in their field but they don't know the precise learning needs or learning styles of your team members, their past training experiences or their current skill levels. You can provide valuable information in these areas. You can also brief them on the type of learning activities your team has enjoyed most and least in the past, and what training and learning interventions have been most and least successful in terms of content, style and timing.

A learning needs analysis identifies gaps between between job knowledge and skills required now or in the future and the current knowledge and skills of an employee or a group of employees. A *learning plan* shows which individuals or groups of employees in a department (or an organisation) are to be trained in which task or skill, by when and by whom.

You can quickly and easily develop both for your team with a matrix. List the key tasks and duties of your team across the top of a spreadsheet and the names of the employees down the left-hand side. You can also include any tasks or duties that are not done now but will be in the near future. At the bottom, show the ideal number of people that should be available at all times to carry out each task (see Figure 27.2).

Place a tick (✔) where employees carry out a task or duty competently and a cross (✘) against any tasks or duties that employees don't need to know how to do. Then compare the number of people who can do each task with the ideal number of people who should be able to do it. This shows you how many people you need to train and in which tasks. You can also take into account any jobs that employees would like to learn. You now know the degree of urgency and priority you should give to individual training needs.

For instance, you can see in Figure 27.2 that all jobs except 1, 4, 6 and 7 have adequate job cover and that, of these, 4 and 6 can be covered with a minimum amount of training, so you should probably give special attention to training for jobs 1 and 7. In addition, you can see that Morgan, a very able employee, can do all the required jobs. Perhaps you should think about additional training and development for her so that she does not become bored and her performance level drop as a result. You can also see that jobs 2 and 3 are potentially overstaffed, which may lead you to wonder whether the milk bar itself is overstaffed. One possible place to make a cutback or to allow natural attrition would be Alf's position, where few skills are required.

To turn your learning needs analysis into a learning plan, add target dates to each person's square showing when you intend to begin or complete training for that job. For instance, to have Jean fully trained in job 7 by 4 September, you would write 4/9 in that box.

	A	B	C	D	E	F	G	H	I
1					TASK DUTIES				
2							Operate	Answer	Resolve
3		Stock	Price	Order	Take	Make	cash	customer	customer
4		shelves	goods	goods	inventory	change	register	queries	complaints
5		1	2	3	4	5	6	7	8
6	Jean	✓	✓	+	+	✓	✓	+	✓
7	Yunhua	–	–	✓	✓	✓	✓	✓	✓
8	Alf	+	✓	×	×	+	+	–	+
9	Morgan	✓	✓	✓	✓	✓	✓	✓	✓
10	Terry	✓	+	+	+	✓	+	+	✓
11	Actual number able to perform task	3	3	2	2	4	3	2	4
12	Ideal number able to perform task	5	3	2	3	4	4	5	4

Key
✓ can do well
+ can do but needs more training/experience
× cannot do and does not need to do
– cannot do and should be trained to do

Prepared by Melanie, 19/6/16

FIGURE 27.2 Learning needs analysis and a learning plan for a milk bar

THEORY TO PRACTICE

How many people are 'ideal'?

What is the 'ideal number' of people able to do a job? Probably more than just one. Don't forget to allow cover for busy work periods, holidays, personal and sick leave, time taken off for training and even lunch breaks.

The 'FYI: Estimating staffing requirements' on page 499 explains this in more detail.

Your own learning needs

In a Boyer Lecture, Rupert Murdoch pointed out, 'The most important skills you will need in your careers is the ability to acquire new skills.'[10] Einstein said, 'Life is like riding a bicycle. In order to keep your balance, you must keep moving.'[11]

You probably agree that your own L&D is a never-ending investment in your future. It isn't just children who need to learn – we all have something to learn, our whole lives long. Learning keeps us young, fresh and interesting, it keeps our brains healthy and it keeps us employable.

Think about your strongest skills and how you can develop them further. Think about the path your industry and your organisation are on and what skills you need to develop for the future. Some of your skills may have grown rusty or obsolete and you need to update or upgrade them. Decide what you want to learn over the next six months, plan how to do it and set time aside to ensure you complete your plan (see page 133, 'Work to your strengths' and page 137 'Plan your professional development' to find out more about planning your own L&D).

Employees take their cues from you – your attitudes and the way you approach your work and the people you work with. To encourage the people in your team to see learning as a lifelong journey and to take responsibility for their own L&D, you need to do the same. As a bonus, acting as a positive role model also makes you a more valuable employee, because as organisations continue to develop and change, people are valued as much for what they can learn tomorrow as for what they can do today.

ACTION!

Don't get too comfortable with the status quo, because it's going to change. Use the interactive self-test: How do you rate as a role model for learning? on *CourseMateExpress to assess how well you act as a role model for learning.

ACTION!

On *CourseMateExpress in Chapter 5, you can identify your strengths with the Strengths audit, then summarise them with the What do I value most? checklist in chapter 7. You can also work out the ways in which you're smart with the How are you smart? interactive self-test and your career preferences with the Career preferences template in chapter 5. These will help you design your own learning plan.

Decide the learning method

Once you have identified your own and your team's learning needs, your next step is to determine the precise outcomes you want by answering these two questions:

1. How do you want your own and your team members' behaviour – what they say and do on the job – to be different?
2. What specific outcomes do you want to achieve as a result?

For example, I would like the people who attend the spreadsheet workshop to be able to design and maintain spreadsheets so that we can track our sales by customer and type of sale, order size, order frequency and payment status.

Then you can decide whether to provide formal or informal training or whether there is a better alternative to training. For example, when the learning is to improve job performance, work through the five keys (explained in Chapter 11) to see whether improving systems, procedures, tools or equipment, providing more time or information, or improving teamwork would be a better solution (see 'The strategic perspective: Is training really the answer?' on page 895).

IN A NUTSHELL

Types of training and development

Here are the main types of training organisations provide:

- *Awareness training*: For example, equal employment opportunity and workplace diversity, risk management, sexual harassment and bullying, sustainability.
- *Basic skills training*: For example, business writing, English as a second language, remedial training in literacy, maths, reading comprehension.

- *IT training*: For example, how to use computer software and groupware, spreadsheets, databases and graphics (both off-the-shelf and company-specific), how to use sophisticated aspects of your devices to manage time, information security.
- *Customer service training*: For example, call centre operations, dealing with and learning from customer complaints, maintaining and improving customer relations.
- *Executive development*: For example, creativity, due diligence, global marketing, leadership, strategic planning.
- *Induction training:* For example, information about the organisation and its operations, functions, mission and policies, compensation and benefits, work requirements, standards and rules.
- *Job-specific technical skills training*: For example, equipment, procedures, products, service delivery, technology.
- *Leader-manager development*: For example, budgeting, conducting performance reviews, implementing regulations and policies, managing projects and processes, performance management, planning.
- *Occupational safety and compliance training*: For example, safety hazards, procedures, regulations.
- *Product knowledge training*: For example, product specifications, repair, upgrading, maintenance for sales and service professionals.
- *Professional skills training*: For example, specialised knowledge and applications in accounting, consulting, computer science, engineering, information systems management, law, project management.
- *Quality, competition and business practices*: For example, benchmarking, business fundamentals, process re-engineering, quality management and continuous improvement.
- *Sales training*: For example, the attitudes, skills and habits needed to influence the purchasing decisions of prospects and customers for franchisees, dealers and salespeople.
- *Teamworking skills and team building*: Individual and group training to improve, for example, communication, collaboration and teamwork, conflict resolution, decision-making.

● THE STRATEGIC PERSPECTIVE

Is training really the answer?

Providing learning opportunities is a good solution when learners don't *know*, when they don't know *how*, or when they need to improve at something. It's also great when people need to learn specific pieces of information (programmed knowledge) and when there is one correct answer.

Training is not the answer when people lack motivation, when inefficient systems are causing poor performance, or when it's the tools, equipment and other resources, not the people, that aren't up to the job. Training is not the answer when you're short-staffed and there aren't enough hours in the day to do everything that needs to be done, when people aren't clear about what you expect of them, or when the organisation's leadership or the team's leader-manager is setting such a poor example that people are completely cynical about their jobs and their organisation. Nor can training 'fix' people who are temperamentally unsuited to the job or who are in the wrong job to begin with.

● THEORY TO PRACTICE

Peer assistance programs

Why not bring a group of people doing the same jobs in different locations together to share ideas and success stories? This happens naturally at corporate training sessions or you can formalise it with, for example, monthly knowledge-sharing meetings. Each meeting could address a specific topic such as cost control, customer relations or managing stock. Someone who excels in that area could describe how they approach it and answer questions. A facilitator could help the rest of the group figure out how to apply what they've heard in their own teams.

You could set up a peer assistance program that allows job holders, project teams or cross-functional teams to request assistance from a similar team. Teams could meet virtually or face to face.

To prove the organisation is serious about sharing knowledge and using learning, it could introduce a bonus to members of the knowledge-sharing group based on the the group's joint performance. Of course, you don't need financial incentives to encourage knowledge sharing. Pride and people's natural willingness to share also work.

When you need to update, extend or develop business, interpersonal or technical skills, formal training, on-the-job or off-the-job, is one of many possible solutions. Here are some others:

* acting in higher positions
* additional responsibilities to those of the current job (upskilling, cross-skilling or multiskilling)
* coaching in specific skills
* committee work
* delegated duties
* job rotation
* mentoring
* observation
* on-the-job experience
* peer assistance programs (discussions with other work areas or employees with expertise in the relevant area)
* personal study (e.g. day-release courses, part-time study, reading, self-paced and e-learning)
* physical and virtual learning communities and knowledge exchanges
* project work and temporary and special assignments
* shadowing a more experienced or expert employee
* short-term secondments (e.g. with clients or suppliers).

The learning method or methods you choose depend on how much time and money you have, the nature of the training needed and the number of people you want to train. Consider employees' varying abilities and take special needs into account. You may need to be quite creative in the way you design and offer L&D so that it appeals to the various people in your work team.

Some employees like hands-on training and to learn by doing, others are fine with lectures, some want a podcast or Intranet video, and still others like to learn from games. Discuss possible strategies with the learners and choose those that suit them best and are the most cost-effective. The more you involve learners in identifying their learning needs and planning to meet them, the more effective their learning is likely to be. After all, they are the customers in the process.

Whatever method you select, agree clear learning objectives with the learner(s) and debrief the learner(s) during and after the learning process to ensure the learning objectives have been met. The following sections review the main types of training and other learning methods to choose from.

> **● IN A NUTSHELL**
>
> **The three domains of learning: The heart, the head and the hands**
> There are three types of learning: *affective*, *cognitive* and *psychomotor*, or attitudes and emotions, or knowledge and skills. These are known as *domains*, or categories, of learning and include how people approach learning as well as the subject matter.
>
> The *affective domain* includes the way people learn emotionally (e.g. with enthusiasm or apprehension) and covers topics like dealing with difficult customers, emotional intelligence and offering feedback.
>
> The *cognitive domain* involves awareness of how you think and covers the development of conceptual skills and knowledge including recognising and recalling specific concepts, facts and procedures and being able to apply them.
>
> The *psychomotor domain* includes physical movement, coordination, and manual or physical skills. Developing psychomotor skills requires practice and is measured in terms of distance, precision or accuracy, and speed, and correct execution of procedures and techniques.[12]

Off-the-job learning

Parts of induction programs, product training and other conceptual and physical skills training often take place off the job, particularly when the training takes longer than two or three weeks and a number of employees need to be trained. Training for technical aspects of a job generally takes place in a training room that duplicates work conditions as much as possible; for instance, it might be equipped with machines, telephones and other job tools. Machine operators, bank tellers, technical salespeople and some customer service personnel (e.g. retail salespeople and telephone support staff) are often trained away from the workplace.

Off-the-job training can also include elements such as plant visits, secondments to other organisations and study tours. Plant visits can open trainees' eyes to other ways of doing things and extend their general knowledge. Secondments and study tours can be time-consuming and expensive, so they need to target learning needs carefully, and the participants need to be thoroughly briefed and debriefed.

Off-the-job training allows people to learn and make mistakes in a safe environment. Winston Churchill once said: 'Personally, I am always ready to learn although I do not always like being taught.'[13] This applies to many learners, which is why experienced trainers use a variety of techniques to engage learners and develop their skills and understanding.

These include *experiential learning* activities where people learn by doing rather than 'talking about' something. This can make learning quicker and more enjoyable and help learners retain the knowledge more easily. Experiential techniques include simulations and other high-tech training, specially designed 'games' and case studies, and role-playing based on trainees' real-life job issues. Off-the-job training also includes practising the techniques and concepts being taught, short lectures and group discussions. To ensure learning occurs, the learning cycle needs to be used to help learners reflect on their actions and the consequences of their actions so that learnings are captured and insights applied in the future.

Well-designed and facilitated off-the-job training workshops can effectively provide in-depth knowledge and an understanding of principles and how to apply them in practice. They can:

- Develop conceptual skills in areas such as decision-making, planning, problem-solving and time management.
- Develop 'soft' skills in areas such as communication, leadership, performance management and teamwork.
- Extend technical understanding of aspects of employees' jobs in areas such as business writing, computer applications, health and safety training, sales, and negotiation skills.

IN A NUTSHELL

A range of off-the-job learning options

The wide range of off-the-job learning options includes:

- corporate, or *in-house*, seminars and workshops on specific topics
- distance learning such as satellite or video conferences and virtual seminars (useful for reaching large numbers of people dispersed geographically)
- evening classes on various work-related topics
- external courses, conferences, lectures and training programs organised for the public or by professional bodies and industry associations for their members and guests
- formal study such as day-release for tertiary studies and updating qualifications such as post-trade training
- self-paced online learning, or e-learning
- team-building workshops.

The main advantages of in-house training programs are that they are generally less costly per person and can be designed specifically to meet the organisation's learning goals and support its culture, strategy and values. Participants can extend their knowledge of how the organisation operates and their networks within it, which is motivating. Public courses, although generally more costly, can expose participants to a range of experiences, opinions and thinking. Both allow participants to share and learn from each other's experiences as well as from their course leader.

When lasting longer than one day, off-the-job programs can be residential, which allows the learners to work on into the evening, study in the evening, or strengthen their working relationships over a meal and a relaxing get-together. The choice depends on the nature and the objectives of the program.

The HR or L&D department, if there is one, often arranges off-the-job training. It may organise it only for the organisation's own employees (in-house programs) held on site or at an external venue, or it may recommend a public course when only one or a few employees need training.

THEORY TO PRACTICE

Infosys University

Consulting and IT services company Infosys has built the largest private university in the world in Mysore in India. A collection of majestically classical and ultra-modern buildings is set on 140 hectares among gardens with 60 000 trees. Students' residence blocks are designed in the shape of each of the letters in the company's name and can be read from the sky.

>>

Recreation facilities include swimming pools, soccer fields, athletics tracks, a bowling alley, a 12-table billiard room, and squash and badminton courts. Daily recreational classes such as dance, guitar and aerobics also keep the annual intake of about 15 000 students, including many graduates from international universities, occupied when they aren't studying.

Infosys also invests heavily in developing future leaders and nurturing existing leaders. The Infosys Leadership Institute is charged with developing about 750 people at the top of the company. It adopts a scientific approach to assessing people's strengths and development needs and providing one-on-one mentoring with some of the world's foremost experts in the particular development area.[14]

Games and simulations

Games are active learning experiences that extend learners' skills, knowledge and experience. On the surface, some may seem to have nothing to do with the learners' jobs. However, with skillfully guided discussions afterwards, participants can learn about themselves and each other, how to more effectively work in groups to achieve goals, how to improve their own work style, and how to develop useful working procedures. Many indoor and outdoor team-building activities use such games and learning experiences and e-learning is moving towards using games to provide learning experiences.

Simulations allow trainees to perform a task under virtual conditions. For example, a machine that simulates driving conditions can test and improve a trainee's driving reflexes and skills through lifelike practice. Some sophisticated training packages use fuzzy logic and realistic scenarios to provide hands-on virtual practice in a range of technical and interpersonal skills and allow learners to build their skills in a situation that is nearly live without their mistakes having serious repercussions. You can experience an example of this type of simulation on CourseMate Express.

Business games are another example of a simulation. A computer imitates market conditions while trainees operate a business and make key decisions about establishing advertising and research and development budgets, setting a selling price and purchasing raw materials.

Self-paced, e-learning and blended learning

When it's difficult to release employees for blocks of training, perhaps because staffing levels are lean or because the organisation is geographically spread out or has small numbers needing training at any one time, or when taking people off their usual shift times would be inconvenient, bringing training to employees, rather than the other way around, through self-paced and e-learning, is a possible solution. When large numbers of learners are involved, organisations save money in travel and accommodation costs and employees spend less time away from their jobs.

Self-paced workbooks with study guides and e-learning modules are transportable and flexible, so people can learn wherever and whenever suits them best. They can accommodate different rates of learning, and learners can review and repeat learning points in a way that is not possible with traditional conferences, seminars and training workshops. Well-designed self-paced and e-learning involves learners and stimulates thinking throughout the learning process, as well as after it, and the best e-learning products are fully interactive.

A variety of media can be used for e-learning, including audio and video podcasts, blogs, chat rooms and discussion boards, online learning programs, web-based courses and wikis. An increasing number of tools are being used to access e-learning media, including tablets, smartphones and other portable media players, VoIP services such as Skype, the Extranet (private, secure networks that use Internet technology to link organisations with their customers, suppliers or other organisations with shared goals or common learning needs) and CD-ROM. Many of these platforms take advantage of interactive capabilities for learning and assessment, with some providing dedicated chat rooms with a tutor available at specified times.

With so many options, the only way to make the right choice is to establish your objectives, consider your learners and your budget and see whether self-paced or e-learning can meet your needs. Sometimes the answer is no for cost reasons or because only good, old-fashioned learning through human interaction will do.

● IN A NUTSHELL

Encouraging e-learning
Here are five ways to encourage e-learning:
1. Let people know how well it's worked for other individuals and teams.
2. Explain how the training links with their job and personal goals.
3. Discuss what will be covered before the training begins and ask trainees to think about real work problems the training could help with so they can relate what they're learning to the job.
4. Check in regularly as the training progresses to discuss how it's going and how the learner is using it.
5. Encourage trainees to complete the e-program, and when they have, discuss how they have used it and plan to continue using it on the job.

The downside is that high-tech e-training and some self-paced training can be expensive and the products can become outdated quickly, resulting in a high cost per use. And this type of training is not for people who want spoon-feeding. These learning methods require more dedication and discipline from the learner than traditional workshop-type training (although, even when well-designed, it's easy to lean back, get comfortable and mentally 'switch off' in traditional training, too.) In addition, self-paced learning and e-learning generally fails to deliver the interaction and collaboration that traditional training offers.

You can have the best of both with guided online learning, or *blended learning*. It combines the convenience of online learning with the benefits of traditional face-to-face learning with an expert facilitator. Hands-on practice to build skills, discussion and interaction, ideas and knowledge sharing with other learners and the facilitator, the opportunity to ask questions, reflect, share experiences, develop networks and get feedback from others, all enhance learning and make blended learning more challenging and engaging than self-paced and e-training.

● THE STRATEGIC PERSPECTIVE

Not a cheap, easy or lazy option
Merely sending around a list of available self-paced learning and e-learning programs and hoping employees will train themselves doesn't work. Self-paced learning, e-learning and blended learning needs to be integrated into the organisation's broader learning and performance support

>>

activities. You also need a strong learning culture, extensive, ongoing publicity such as brochures, e-reminders and posters to let people know what is available, and effective administrative and monitoring systems to ensure that they are used effectively.

The latter can be achieved through learning management systems (LMS), software that helps administer e-learning by registering learners, tracking their progress and measuring results for later cost–benefit analysis. Many can also analyse skill gaps, develop curricula, manage courses from multiple sources and publish course catalogues for learners to choose from.

Informal learning with technology

People have always learned opportunistically, by osmosis – the gradual, often unconscious assimilation of ideas, knowledge and understanding. Leaning over someone's shoulder to watch as they do something, listening to workmates think out loud, observing how others manage their time and difficult situations, chatting problems through over lunch break – it all builds people's competencies.

Technology can now make that natural learning mobile and 'just-in-time', too. People can easily and quickly find the information they need and capture, retrieve and share experience, information and insights – regardless of geography and hierarchy.

Smartphones can access information as employees need it for a specific project or task. Social media can engage younger generations of learners through micro blogs, shared workspaces, social networks and wikis, supplementing traditional training with collaboration and co-creation, and bringing distant employees together into communities of learning. Networking sites can also support employee development programs and help employees coach each other remotely. Some organisations set up communities of interest on their Intranets.

Wiki software is being used increasingly. Organisations are setting up wikis on their Intranets to allow employees to add or edit content ranging from product specifications to explanations of complicated acronyms and procedures, saving hours unearthing or re-creating information, and to brainstorm new products and processes, document best practice and plan meetings. Some organisations invite their customers and suppliers to contribute to and use their wikis, too.

◉ THEORY TO PRACTICE

One person with the knowledge of thousands

How would you like to have someone in a similar role to yourself to mull over problems, inspirations, dilemmas, 'Aha!' and 'Oh, no!' moments with? Or better still, a group of people? That's what two young US army officers began doing in 1995. They were neighbours at an army base in Hawaii, both first-time company commanders responsible for three platoons – about 120 soldiers – each. In the evenings, they'd get together and talk through the challenges of their assignments.

This grew into CompanyCommand, an army Intranet chat site through which junior officers could seek advice from others who had been in similar situations. This virtual community of practice develops new leaders and helps them learn from their peers, receive emotional as well as practical support, and get advice specific to their situation (rather than the general advice provided by, for example, a structured training program). CompanyCommand now has a website filled with resources for its members. It has saved lives and money and helped its members avoid mistakes and overcome problems.[15]

In a changing world, the accumulated wisdom of expert elders doesn't always hit the mark. And people are often more receptive to advice from someone in their own situation. Would a peer-mentoring group like this work in your organisation or industry?

Learning by doing

Acting in higher positions, becoming a committee member (e.g. of a health and safety committee or a risk management event team), rotating jobs, secondments (temporarily transferring to another role in the organisation), shadowing a more experienced employee, and undertaking delegated duties and special assignments and projects, are all ways for employees to develop skills and knowledge on the job and add value to the organisation at the same time. Learning by doing can be an effective, enjoyable and inexpensive way to build knowledge, skills, attitudes and experience.

The following sections review two of these methods: action learning and undertaking special assignments and projects. (Delegation is explained in Chapter 12.)

THEORY TO PRACTICE

The mayor's community leadership program

For several years, a city council in South Australia funded a leadership and management course that culminated in dozens of successfully executed community projects that participants planned, tendered for the funding and carried out, as well as Cert IV qualifications in leadership and community services for the participants. Projects included setting up a centre that provided a swag and canopy to homeless people, training young netball club umpires to replace a surge of retiring umpires and providing a drop-in centre for long-term unemployed to teach them basic computing skills and provide assistance with résumé writing, interviewing techniques and other skills aimed at securing employment.

Selected participants spent one or two days a month for a year studying management and project management and devising, planning and implementing their projects. A formal mentoring program with community leaders was an important aspect of the program.

Learning by doing at its best, with a bonus of worthwhile outcomes for the community.[16]

Action learning

With problems and challenges that are complex or have many possible answers, people need to think critically, explore issues and reflect on possibilities. Action learning encourages such reflection and insight by helping people learn from each other and from a process of open questioning and exploring based on the learning cycle (shown in Figure 27.1). Learners then transfer the process they learn to use to other situations.

Action learning brings a group of people together in an action-learning team, or set, of four to six members who meet with a facilitator or adviser who supports them, particularly in the early meetings. Team members are selected based on both the skills and the knowledge they can bring to the team and their learning needs. (This dual focus makes action-learning sets different from quality teams, which focus only on improvements, and project teams, which work on their project.)

Sets can work on either an organisational problem – a project that addresses a significant organisational issue – or a member's work problem, with members taking turns to present a work challenge they are currently grappling with. These projects or current work problems provide learning opportunities and, at the same time, improve the organisation's performance when resolved.

Sets usually meet once a fortnight for several months, with meetings generally lasting a half day or a full day. Advisers begin by establishing the ground rules for working well and productively together. They help set members replace bad habits – such as jumping in to give advice too quickly or not exploring and analysing a problem sufficiently – with skills such as effective listening and questioning. They model the questioning process, help set members to develop their own questioning skills, and promote other 'learning to learn' behaviours. Facilitators also create a safe space for open discussion, advise on resources and models, act as timekeepers, and provide training in problem-solving and decision-making as required. The result is *double-loop learning*, a deeper form of learning than, for example, trial and error, or *single-loop learning*.

In single-loop learning, people learn from their mistakes and change their day-to-day behaviour as a tactical response, without questioning or altering their underlying assumptions and beliefs. In double-loop learning, people think over and adjust their assumptions, beliefs and/or guiding principles based on their results; this gives them a profound grasp of what happens in a situation and lets them rethink their entire strategy. The difference between these two types of learning is illustrated in Figure 27.3.

Figure 27.4 summarises the process used when action-learning sets work on an individual member's issue or problem. (The process is similar when sets work on an organisational problem.)

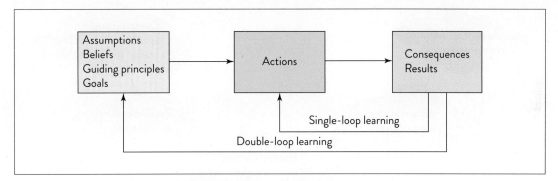

FIGURE 27.3 Single- and double-loop learning

A set member is allocated five to 10 minutes of uninterrupted time to outline a challenge, issue or problem the member is facing or a question or decision the member is wrestling with. Set members then ask clarification and exploratory questions, followed by questions to challenge assumptions, opinions, perceptions and views. Reflective and analytical questions are asked next and, finally, questions are directed towards future action. The facilitator intervenes if the questioning becomes adversarial or advisory.

When the issue has been explored and possible actions clarified, the set member with the issue provides feedback on how he or she experienced the process and what he or she learned. Other set members then offer their observations and learning on both process and content; these steps usually take about two hours. Double-loop learning occurs in two ways: set members examine their underlying assumptions and mental models from the questions other members ask, and they receive feedback on their actions during the meeting.

Finally, the set member outlines an action plan for dealing with the issue until the next meeting. After the meeting, the set member trials the plan and reports the results back to the set when it next meets – what worked, what didn't work and possible explanations. The set learns from the implementation and discusses any corrections or refinements needed, draws conclusions, notes what has been learnt, and discusses how to put its learnings and new knowledge into practice.

Special assignments and projects

Projects, secondments and special assignments allow employees to broaden their perspectives and expand their skills, knowledge and experience while contributing their own experience and knowledge. They also let employees extend their networks and develop their teamworking skills.

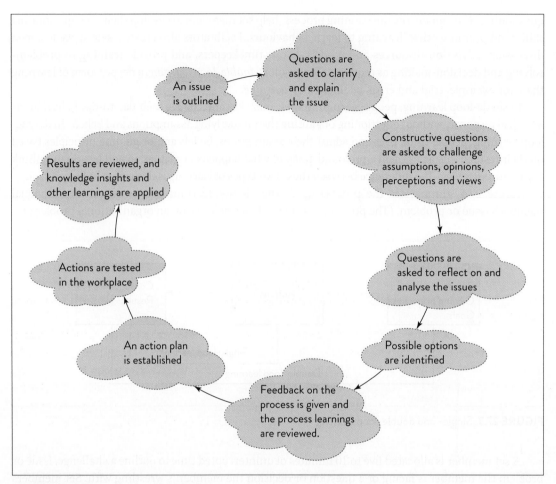

FIGURE 27.4 The action learning process

When teams are cross-cultural, they strengthen employees' cultural intelligence. When teams are virtual, they build valuable technological expertise.

Like action-learning projects, special assignments and projects should be directed at improving the organisation's performance. Equally, they should meet the following important criteria:

- Allow employees to build important networks throughout the organisation, encouraging a learning culture.
- Allow employees to work with a variety of people in a variety of disciplines, further improving their interpersonal skills and extending their knowledge.
- Challenge and extend employees' technical and interpersonal skills.
- Help employees learn more about the organisation in a holistic sense, making them more valuable to the organisation
- Provide lateral career paths.

Projects like these go a long way towards offering the L&D, teamworking and networking opportunities that younger employees, especially, want. They also allow mature-aged employees, whether as full- or part-time employees or contractors, to share their knowledge and coach and mentor younger employees.

When you get these assignments, projects and secondments right, they increase employees' motivation, performance and productivity, as well as organisational flexibility, knowledge and responsiveness. As organisations become more efficient and competitive in this way, everyone wins.

Coaching

The Chinese have a proverb that says, 'A single conversation with a wise man is better than 10 years of study.'[17] This is the aim of coaching and mentoring. Coaches and mentors are more experienced or skilled people who strengthen the skills and understanding of the employees they are working with. They also share their experience and ways of thinking to extend employees' job skills and personal and professional development. Both are personalised, one-on-one ways to develop employees. Although the terms are often used interchangeably, there is a difference, as you're about to see.

There are two types of coaches: *expert coaches* and *generalist coaches*. Expert coaches are usually from inside the organisation, but sometimes from outside it, and they help employees hone and polish a specific job skill. Leader-managers and selected professionals or specialists such as accountants or computer experts are the most common expert coaches. Some organisations have introduced 'upward coaching', which involves a younger employee teaming with an older employee to develop the older person's skills, for example in IT.

The second type of coach is not necessarily an expert, but uses a process to meet a specific learning or development need and improve performance. They can be employees, often from the L&D or HR departments who have been trained in coaching, or corporate coaches who work independently.

Some generalist coaches are well trained in coaching techniques, others less so or not trained at all. Some independent coaches have purchased a franchise and trained in that franchise's methods; others have paid for training in a particular coaching system from one of many coach training schools worldwide. Unfortunately, there is little consistency in standards and, since people pay for their training, the franchise or school is unlikely to fail them. This means it's important to choose a generalist coach carefully, because no matter how good the coaching model they follow and how well they follow it, a system can't compensate for life and organisational experience.

Generalist coaches might use tools such as the 360-degree review and psychological tests to identify employees' strengths and weaknesses, pinpoint L&D needs, and help the people they're coaching uncover underlying mindsets that may limit their effectiveness.

Coaching sessions usually take place over several meetings. Whether the coach is an expert or a generalist, they should encourage winning behaviours and confront negative attitudes and beliefs, and the best coaches have the knack of finding people's potential and honing it (find out more about coaching techniques on page 912).

 **ACTION!**

Can you effectively coach your team members day-to-day to help them polish their performance? Find out in the self-test: Are you a coach or a critic? on **CourseMateExpress**.

Mentoring

Mentors are usually experienced and respected people who take their protégés' longer-term personal as well as professional goals into account, making mentoring a more extended relationship than coaching. Whether they come from inside or outside the organisation, mentors take a more junior person under their wing and help them to build their career and expertise. Opportunities for people to mingle, such as company-sponsored conferences, seminars and social events, can help people forge their own mentoring and networking relationships.

By offering advice, guidance, information and support, and acting as a sounding board, wise guide and devil's advocate, mentors can open doors to new information and the organisational and strategic perspectives, and further mentees' personal and professional growth. Approachable and empathic, mentors can explain how the organisation works and help mentees navigate the informal organisation. Mentors assist in networking and help mentees deal with difficult or negative experiences and feedback. They also offer feedback to the people they mentor. They can listen to personal challenges and offer encouragement, different viewpoints and ideas, and provide support in times of crisis and change. Most of all, mentors share valuable experience, knowledge and accumulated wisdom, and teach by example.

Although mentoring is generally an informal, voluntary process, some organisations have formalised it as part of the career planning and performance review process. Employees complete personal development plans, stating their development goals, and then either select a mentor or a mentor is assigned to them. The mentor and the mentee meet informally or semi-formally at agreed intervals, for example once a month, to discuss progress, difficulties, plans, and so on. Formal mentoring programs have mixed results, possibly because successful mentoring is based on positive chemistry between people and you can't predict the affinity people will have for one another.[18] (Find out more about mentoring techniques on page 912.)

● IN A NUTSHELL

What's the difference between instructing, coaching and mentoring?

Instructing works best for straightforward cognitive and psychomotor skills and activities. Mentoring works best in complex situations, for affective and complex cognitive thinking and reasoning – for example, in situations where many answers are possible and when the skills to be learned involve interpersonal relations. Coaching falls somewhere in between. Table 27.1 examines the differences in the three activities.

TABLE 27.1 Instructing, coaching and mentoring compared

Instructing	Coaching	Mentoring
Teaching	Supporting	Enabling
Showing	Guiding	Encouraging self-development
Telling	Explaining	Listening, questioning, sharing, advising

Prepare a learning and development plan

Who is to receive *what* learning support, and *when*, *where*, *how* and *why*? These are the questions a learning plan answers. It generally contains the following information:

- A summary of an individual's or a team's learning needs and an indication of any priority areas. What (the specific skills, knowledge or attitudes to be taught or developed)? Why (the learning objectives)?
- The learning method and when and where the learning is to occur.
- How you will assess the effectiveness of the learning.
- The links with the organisation's vision, mission and business plan.

When establishing timelines and learning methods, think about constraints, such as the availability of any resources the L&D plan needs and your team's busy periods and peak holiday periods. Ensure that learners agree with the learning needs and objectives or you will be wasting your time.

Prepare a business case when needed

You probably need to make a sound business case for any off-the-job training you want to provide, following your organisation's usual procedures. You might want to begin by stating the objectives of the training and the benefits to the organisation in a clear sentence. Here are two examples:

1. The goals of this learning support are to … so that …
2. This learning will result in … which will help us to …

Show that the training you propose is relevant, timely and targeted to meet identified learning needs that can lead to performance improvements that benefit the individual, team and organisation.

The key is to identify strategic benefits and convert them into hard numbers. How can you calculate the *return on investment* (ROI)? How can you demonstrate, preferably in measurable terms, how the training can positively affect the organisation's vision, mission and business plan, how it can contribute to the overall improvement of the organisation, to your organisation's key measures of effectiveness, and to other matters the decision-makers care most about?

When training addresses an identified problem, you can measure the cost of the current situation against the cost of the expected situation after the training. The difference shows you how much the training, assuming it works, can save the organisation, quantifying your return on investment. Provided you can make a case for ongoing savings, you can also calculate the *payback period* for the training. This is the time it takes for the training to cover its costs through increased performance and productivity. The point at which the training has covered its costs is known as the *break-even point*. After that point, the training is saving the organisation money. Naturally, the sooner the training pays for itself, the more likely senior management is to agree to it.

Similarly, when training is intended to result in a general improvement in something – for instance customer satisfaction, leadership or teamwork – you can develop a range of measures to track its effectiveness. For example, to measure the value of leadership training, you could measure absenteeism, attrition and productivity before the training and track them for a period after the training. When training relates to compliance to government regulations, you can compare the cost of the training to the penalties for non-compliance.

THEORY TO PRACTICE

Two ways to work out the numbers
The more persuasively you can show, in factual and objective terms, that your department and the organisation is likely to benefit from the training you propose, the more likely it is that scarce funds can be made available to pay for it.

Here is a commonly used equation:[19]

$$ROI\% = \frac{\text{Total benefit in } \$ \times 100}{\text{Total training cost}}$$

Remember that L&D can do more than improve work performance in the short term. Although it can be difficult to quantify, regular, high-quality training and learning interventions can make your organisation a more attractive place to work, improve people's ability to innovate, reduce overheads through greater flexibility and multiskilling, and reduce costly staff turnover.

3. Helping people learn

The illiterate of the 21st century will not be those who cannot read and write, but those who cannot learn, unlearn, and relearn.

Herbert Gerjuoy (psychologist), in *Future Shock* (1984)[20]

Understanding the basic principles of how people learn makes it much easier to establish a learning environment in which people learn and, better still, put what they've learned to good use. People of all ages and intellectual capacities can learn new skills and behaviours – provided they *want* to. The motivation, or desire to learn, can take many forms, including financial incentives, increased promotional prospects, personal development, personal satisfaction or the respect of teammates. Find out what motivates each of your team members best.

Some tricks of the trade

The more you can involve learners to make learning active, rather than passive, the better. And particularly with conceptual skills and understanding, the more you help people reach their own conclusions, the better. As Confucius said, 'Tell me, and I will forget. Show me, and I may remember. Involve me, and I will understand.'[21]

But don't just leave learners to it. People learn more rapidly under guidance – trial and error is frustrating, time-consuming and sometimes unsafe. It too easily results in inefficient and unsafe work habits, and only partial understanding or even reaching incorrect conclusions. Provide clear instructions when necessary and set clear learning goals and measures of success that trainees can work towards and use to measure their progress. Monitor their progress along with them, so you can provide enough feedback and show you're interested and are there to help when needed. Remember to positively reinforce correct behaviours to cement them in.

Good training materials and teaching aids are always important. Use job breakdowns (as described in Section 4 of this chapter), examples, diagrams, Socratic questions (explained later in this chapter) and other techniques appropriate to the skill and knowledge you're teaching, and try to use a variety of techniques (also explained later) to stave off boredom. Learning requires attention and concentration, so when people are learning and practising new tasks, provide a quiet area as free as possible from distractions. Snatched minutes of practice between normal job tasks seldom works.

When you need to repeat an instruction or explanation, try something different. The next way might work when the first one didn't. Take into account each trainee's motivations and remember to allow for individual differences in learning.

● THEORY TO PRACTICE

Don't say, 'Just give it a go'

Even when you think a job is simple, don't tell an employee who has never been shown how to do it to 'give it a go' because it may not be as easy as you think and it could result in injury.

That's exactly what happened at a bakery where an employee worked as a pastry cook. Her team leader instructed her to reassemble a doughnut machine without providing instruction, telling her to 'just give it a go'. She injured her finger and arm and the NSW District Court found the employer negligent and awarded the employee substantial damages.[22]

Always make sure employees understand how to carry out a task safely. When an employee requests instruction or guidance, provide it – no matter how 'simple' the task seems to you.

Actual learning represents a change in behaviour and all changes require adjustment, so give people time to adjust, internalise and assimilate what they've learned. Give them plenty of time to practise and build their experience, because with experience comes confidence and long-term retention.

Provide variety

People have different levels of ability in different areas, different interests, different levels of motivation to learn and different background knowledge. You need to take them all into account when deciding the best way to help people learn. For example, you wouldn't teach someone advanced accounting methods before they had a sound grasp of basic arithmetic or put someone in charge of an organisation before they had a sound grasp of strategic thinking, leadership, communication and other core management skills.

People may also have preferences about how they learn, known as *learning styles*, possibly based on what they're used to and feel most comfortable with. There are more than 100 accredited learning style models, although research has shown that, while people may have preferences about how to learn, they can learn just as well whether information is presented in their preferred learning style or another.[23] Nevertheless, it's a good idea to tweak the way you coach and train people to their preferred learning style when you can. And there is no doubt that presenting information in a variety of ways helps engage learners, if for no other reason than variety holds people's attention.

The Honey and Mumford learning style model, shown in Figure 27.5, describes four learning styles.[24]

1. *Activists* like to roll up their sleeves and get 'stuck in', learning as they go. They enjoy trying new things and having new experiences and prefer relatively short learning activities and competitive team exercises. Say 'Explain what you're doing as you try out this procedure.'
2. *Pragmatists* want to know how to apply the techniques and processes they are learning 'in the real world' and to their current job. Make the immediate relevance of your training clear to them. Ask 'How can you use this to improve your productivity and make your job easier?'
3. *Reflectors* prefer to listen and observe others before having a go themselves. Give them a chance to collect information and time to review and think about what they are learning before trying it out. Ask 'What did you find easy/difficult in using this procedure?'
4. *Theorists* learn well from concepts, models and theories, and prefer to think about what they are learning in abstract and systems terms. Stretch them and let them work in structured situations with a clear purpose. Give them time to explore associations and interrelationships, question assumptions and logic, analyse and generalise. Ask 'What conclusions can you draw from . . .?'

Here is a summary of other ways you can present information to learners based on three other learning styles models: David Kolb's learning styles, the Felder-Silverman model and the Herrmann brain dominance. Become familiar with the various ways you can help people learn so that you can add some spice and variety to instructions, coaching and mentoring.

*   *Expressive and symbolic*: Present information in a creative, expressive, interesting, personal, symbolic way. Try to incorporate as many senses as you can: seeing, hearing, touching/ feeling/doing, are easy; smell and taste take a bit more thought and aren't always possible.
*   *Holistic, big picture*: Present information from the strategic perspective; explain the entire system and how what you're explaining fits in.
*   *Logical, analytical*: Present information factually, logically, analytically and quantitatively, in an ordered fashion and in small steps. Zoom in on the details. Provide evidence.

Source: Adapted from Honey and Mumford, Learning styles[25]

FIGURE 27.5 Honey and Mumford's learning styles

- *Pragmatic*: Provide concrete, practical learning activities concentrating on facts and procedures. Move from the specific to the general as you present information.
- *Relevance*: Provide plenty of reasons to learn what you're explaining and the benefits derived from learning it.
- *Sequential*: Present information chronologically or step-by-step, in an organised, structured manner.
- *Show*: Demonstrate or model the skill or behaviour and give the learner time to think it through on their own and work out how they can apply it or become comfortable with applying it.
- *Theory to practice*: Explain the theory or concept and how it applies to what you're explaining. Move from the general to the specific as you present information.
- *Try it for yourself*: Provide guidance on how to do a task and let learners practice or let people learn by doing or even by discovery (within health and safety constraints).
- *Verbal*: Provide written and spoken explanations.
- *Visual*: Use bar charts, diagrams, maps, pictures and so on to make your points.

The learning generations

You found out about different generational characteristics stem from the era that people were born into and grew up in on page 870. These lead to differences in the way people from different generations tend to prefer to work and be managed and also differences in the ways they prefer to learn.

Don't ignore the development needs of your Baby Boomer and Traditionalist team members (roughly, people over the age of 50). Training shows you and the organisation are interested in them and their future. While Baby Boomers and Traditionalists can learn from the time-honoured classroom and lecture-style methods, your young Gen Z team members are likely to be strong visual learners with short attention spans. They like to learn in short, sharp bursts that provide specific job skills. When appropriate, let them learn by discovery (under supervision) rather than simply telling them what to do or how to do it.

Those in between, Gen Y-ers and Gen X-ers also demand exciting, fast-paced learning with the bells and whistles of graphics, bullet lists and hands-on activities. They understand that knowledge and skills increase their marketability, which makes them motivated learners.

Many from Gen X appreciate small bits of information and lots of graphics to convey key points. Most Boomers aren't as open to continual learning and they dislike the role-plays that Gen Y-ers and Gen X-ers like, but they do enjoy interactive discussion.

Most Gen Y-ers (aged in their 20s to mid-30s) appreciate coaching, guidance and mentoring support (rather than 'teaching') and expect continuous L&D. Help them develop their skills and show them what they need to work effectively in your team with an entertaining, active and interactive approach. You may find that difficult customers and authority figures intimidate them, so show them how to overcome objections and to deal with difficult people.

They may be aces at instant messaging, but you may need to help the Y-ers and the Z-ers, your youngest team members, with more traditional forms of communication such as writing business documents properly (in full sentences and using vowels and correct punctuation), how to organise and present evidence that supports their ideas, and with verbal presentations. You may also need to teach them basic corporate manners (turn off the tablet and silence the smartphone at meetings, for instance).

Keep your younger team members involved as they learn. Many Gen Y-ers and Z-ers grew up with gaming and are active as well as pragmatic learners (see Figure 27.5 on page 910). They are interested in learning conceptual and physical skills that are immediately relevant and increase their job opportunities, so ensure they can use the skills you help them learn straight away. Forget the theory, facts and figures (which they can Google when the need arises) and concentrate on the practical 'how tos' they need to succeed in their jobs.

Teaching old dogs new tricks

The notion about not being able to teach old dogs new tricks is a furphy. Older workers not only learn as well as younger workers but, once they've acquired skills, they can apply them more effectively. This is partly due to their experience and partly to their brainpower. Inductive reasoning (moving from the specific to the general) and spatial orientation (awareness of the space around you and where your body is in relation to it) peak around 50 years of age, and verbal abilities and verbal memory peak around 60 years of age. In terms of performance, research shows that, until people reach their 80s, age accounts for less difference in performance than individual differences.

Coaching and mentoring techniques

Ron Dennis of the McLaren Formula One car-racing team clearly states his view of the leader-manager's role when he says 'The role of management is always to identify the weakest links, support them and strengthen them.'[26] Very true. To perform that role well, you can develop your coaching and mentoring skills so you can share your experience, expertise and insights with others. The more effectively you can do this, the more easily you can build a learning environment and attract quality people to work with and remain in your team.

You can use role-play and guided practice to fill skill gaps and you can develop knowledge and understanding through conversation and asking questions to help people think issues, problems and situations through. You can use 'I' messages and the Describe–Explain–Suggest model, explained on page 469 to build skills. You can pass on rules of thumb and relate illustrative personal stories or examples from which to generalise and analyse events, creating mental scaffolds for people to hang and make sense of experience. You can help people learn by doing while you observe and offer feedback.

Five other techniques to use when coaching and mentoring are reviewed on the following pages. Remember to take people's preferred learning methods and task-readiness level (prior knowledge, experience and confidence level, explained on page 268) into account when you're mentoring and coaching.

1. Gap analysis: This is a good way to begin a coaching session. Ask the person you're coaching three questions: 'Where are you now (in this skill) out of 10?'; 'Where would you like to be?'; and 'How can you get there?'

2. Flag–example–benefit model: Specific positive feedback encourages behaviours you want to continue. By flagging what you're about to comment on, giving an example of it and explaining why it works, your feedback becomes very powerful. For example, if you were coaching an industrial sales representative, you might say:
   - Flag: I liked your use of open questions with that customer
   - Example: and I thought it was great when you asked about his goals for the business
   - Benefit: because that gave you a lot of useful information to build on.

This model also works with constructive feedback. For example, you might say:
   - Flag: I thought you began well by asking the customer how business was going.
   - Example: I think you could learn even more useful information by following up with some probing questions. For instance, when she said business was going well, you could ask where she sees the business in two or three years' time.
   - Benefit: That would give you further information about her needs so that you could select the best products for her and explain them to her in the light of her goals; that would make you more persuasive and increase your chances of closing the sale.

(To find out more about the types of feedback and their uses, see page 447.)

3. Intent–outcome model: When helping people understand the effects of their behaviour on other people or situations, ask what they intend their behaviour or action to achieve. Then ask what actual outcome they are getting. When the two don't match, help the learner develop alternative strategies, making suggestions when necessary, to bring their intention and outcome closer together. When appropriate, you can explore their *espoused theory* and their *theory-in-use* (explained on page 211).

4. Overuse–appropriate use–underuse model: Strengths can be double-edged swords. When you're highly skilled at something – for instance, at asking Socratic questions (discussed next) when coaching – you might use that skill even when using another skill would provide a better outcome. As a result, you underuse other skills; in this example, you might keep asking questions when you should tactfully put forward your experience, knowledge or opinion for consideration.

No matter how useful a skill is, overusing it leads to an unwanted outcome. When coaching people who overuse one skill, help them discover when to use it appropriately and when a different skill would work better. When coaching a salesperson who excels at listening, for example, you might help her pinpoint when to stop listening to the customer's needs and begin explaining what she recommends; when a salesperson provides clear and compelling explanations of a product's features and benefits, you would help him understand when to stop explaining and ask for the order.

5. Socratic questioning: Asking questions and suggesting points to consider, to guide people to work out the answers and ideas for themselves, is known as the Socratic method. Skilful questioning, based on the 'tell me more' approach, invites people to consider the accuracy and completeness of their thinking and explore the implications of their positions; it draws out new ideas and perspectives and helps people think matters through.

Helping people find their own insights and solutions is a powerful way to help them increase their effectiveness. When you do that, they're less likely to feel threatened and more likely to follow through. Linking an important value of the person you're helping to learn with the skill you're helping them strengthen makes your support even more effective because when values lead, behaviour follows.

> ### ● IN A NUTSHELL
>
> **Top tips for coaching and mentoring**
> Coaches and mentors need to be the best. Here are six tips to put you among the best:
> 1. Find remedies, not faults.
> 2. Highlight the positive, so people feel good about themselves and can do their best work.
> 3. Include everyone, not just your best people – everyone has unique talents and contributions to make.
> 4. Talk about subtly shifting or adjusting, rather than changing, behaviour – it's much less daunting and it doesn't take a complete overhaul to boost someone's performance.
> 5. Use phrases like 'I've noticed that …', 'I realise that …', 'Would you be interested to hear what I observed?' or 'I'd like to suggest something that can make this easier/that can get you an even better result' to take the sting out of constructive feedback.
> 6. Work on one area at a time to avoid overwhelming the learner; when someone needs coaching in more than one area, set up separate meetings for each area.

Learning plateaus

People learn at different rates and almost everyone has periods when their performance doesn't improve, regardless of how much effort they are putting into the job or the quality of the training. This is called a *learning plateau*. It is as though the learner is saturated with new skills and knowledge and subconsciously 'switches off' in order to consolidate what they have recently learned.

Most people experience plateaus when learning something new. The difficulty lies in identifying them, because they occur at different times and last for varying lengths of time for different people and different tasks.

Try to recognise this difficult part of learning when you're coaching, mentoring or training people. Slow down and stop pushing when you suspect a learner has 'hit the wall' and reassure them that it is only temporary.

Three types of learners
Here are three types of learners:
1. *Surface learners*, who do as little as possible to get by.
2. *Strategic learners*, who go for top marks rather than true understanding.
3. *Deep learners*, who go for deep and genuine understanding.[27]
    Which one are you?

Ensure learning is used

The best training in the world is useless unless you support it and it's applied in practice. This applies to both on-the-job and off-the-job learning and development as well as to the various structured and unstructured learning activities you organise.

When your team or any team members undertake any type of learning activity, you want to make sure it is effective. The two things that most influence the effectiveness of any learning are what you (the learner's leader-manager) do *before* and *after* the learning activity. Both are critical. And both are up to you.

Before the training takes place, discuss it with the employee(s). Develop three to five clear learning goals and discuss how meeting those learning goals can assist them on the job. This helps them concentrate on the learning content. (When training is on-the-job, monitor learners while they're learning to determine any additional support they may need and any workplace health and safety issues.)

After the training, discuss how it went, what they learned and how they plan to use it. Identify any barriers in the work and team environment that may prevent them from applying what they've learned and discuss how they can be removed. Then remove them.

Whether they are technical skills or people skills, support and encourage people to use them. Show employees that you notice them using their newly acquired skills. When you fail to do this, employees think that using their new skills is not important and go back to their old ways, wasting the time and effort they spent on learning and the organisation's investment. Don't ignore this essential support for training.

Helping people learn
People learn better when they expect to share their learnings with others or teach it to others. They need to reflect on what they've learned, look for the key points, think about how to explain them and organise them in a logical way – all vital elements of learning.[28]

Why not make it part of your team learning culture that when people attend an off-the-job learning event such as a lecture, training program, seminar or workshop, or even a meeting on a topic that affects the rest of the team, they provide a summary of what they've learned, how they plan to use it and how others might use it, too?

Here are some other ways to protect your investment in employees' learning and assist them to become better learners when they attend off-the-job training programs or courses of study:

- Advise them to arrive early, introduce themselves to the trainer and express their interest in the program.
- Advise them to sit near the front in order to be more involved and hear and see better, and to take notes of the main points for later reference; writing information down also helps reinforce learning.
- Work out who is to cover their critical duties while they attend the training program so they are free to concentrate on the training without worrying about how things are going at work.
- Explain that reviewing the training materials within 72 hours after the session improves retention by 50% and ask them to set aside some review time during that period.
- After the learning activity, or periodically during it when the learning is over an extended period, set some time aside to discuss it:
    ◊ What did they learn or what are they learning?
    ◊ How do they plan to use it or how are they using it?
    ◊ How can they share what they have learned or are learning with the rest of the team?
- Create a team training notebook – electronically or on paper – in which everyone who attends a training session enters a one-page summary of what they've learned, how they can use it and how it can help the team.

Don't forget the all-important administrative functions. Follow your organisation's systems for keeping records of training and learning activities undertaken by people in your work team and for logging any certificates of competency they earn. This important information helps you at performance review time when you undertake further learning needs analyses, and when you update learning plans.

Evaluate learning effectiveness

How do you know whether an L&D activity has effectively met the learners' needs? Training and learning activities need to be more than 'enjoyable' to be worth the effort. Learners need to put what they've learned to use and the organisation needs to benefit in some way, even when it's only from the positive employer brand and improved employee retention that result.

One way to find out is to ask learners how they are applying what they have learned and what results they have achieved. Put some hard numbers on their achievements whenever you can. Don't just ask once – the more often you ask people how they're applying what they've learned, the more clear your message: 'I expect you to put your training to good use.' You can also use learners' feedback to introduce improvements in future L&D activities.

Another way to assess effectiveness is to measure learners' performance after the training and compare it with their performance before the training. You can directly measure whatever results the training is targeting or you can measure a range of generic results, such as absenteeism, employee turnover, output, overtime, quality, timekeeping and waste. You can easily convert most of these measures into dollars to assess the cost–benefit of the training.

That isn't a truly scientific way to evaluate a training program, because you cannot always be sure that improved performance is due to learning. For example:

- When sales people sell more after a sales training program, is this because of the training or would sales have increased anyway? Or when they sell less after sales training, does this mean that the training failed? Maybe the competition ran a special offer during the period for which you measured sales.

- You might train leader-managers to run induction courses for new employees with a goal of reducing their staff turnover. When turnover drops after training, how can you prove that your training was responsible? It could also have been due to altered employment practices, a downturn in the local economy, improved recruitment practices, recent wage increases or the time of year.

One way to find out is to compare the group of employees who were trained with another group who were not trained (a *control group*). This might show, for example, that the group who received training increased their sales by an average of 12%, while the average sales of the control group declined by 8%. This would strongly indicate that the training was worthwhile.

The many variables, or factors, that can affect results make it difficult to isolate the precise benefits of training. This means that you often can't get incontestable *proof* that learning has been effective and must go for *evidence* instead. Objective observation and self-reports plus any objective measures you can apply are generally considered sufficient evidence.

● IN A NUTSHELL

Five levels of evaluation

Here are five levels to evaluate training, which are used all over the world:

- Level 1, Reaction: How satisfied are the learners with the content, trainer and facilities?
- Level 2, Learning: Can learners prove that they have learned, for example, by pre-training and post-training skill tests or skill assessments, or by their action plans?
- Level 3, Behaviour: Even when learning occurs, transferring it to the workplace can be prevented or avoided for many reasons, so it's important to determine whether learners are using what they've learned. You can assess this through observation, self-reports, surveys, action plan monitoring and discussion.
- Level 4, Results: Are the new behaviours leading to the expected improved results? There are many ways to measure this, depending on the learning content and objectives.
- Level 5, Return on investment: What was the return on investment, particularly in terms of performance measures and business results?[29]

Here are some tips for measuring the effectiveness of training:

- Allow time for changes in behaviour to occur and the results to be realised.
- Compare the costs against the benefits of the training.
- Look for evidence when proof is not possible.
- Measure before and after results when possible.
- Seek either a 100% response or use a large enough sample so that the results are meaningful.
- Use a control group not receiving the training when you can.

It is easier to measure the effectiveness of manual skills training. For example, you can measure keyboarding speed and accuracy before and after keyboarding training. When competency-based training methods are used, assessors can determine whether and how well each trainee was able to apply the skills learned on a training program.

It's usually more difficult to assess the effectiveness of training in topic areas such as communication, decision-making, leadership or teamwork. Tests might show that employees have learned something, or they may say that they enjoyed a workshop and benefited from it, but that doesn't guarantee they can effectively put what they've learned to use in their job. (But as discussed earlier, you can help to ensure that employees put their learning to use on the job by discussing it with them beforehand and afterwards, by asking how they are using it.)

Be sure that the cost of evaluating the results of training is justified. When a training program is to be run only once or twice, or when small numbers of learners are involved in various learning activities, it might not be worth spending much time and effort on evaluation. Nor is it always practical to implement a full-blown evaluation effort.

Imagine a company pursuing a level 3 evaluation, asking learners to complete a survey reporting how they used the training. Say the total hourly pay of the 50 respondents is worth $1500 (at $30 an hour each) and it takes 30 minutes to complete the survey. The cost of the survey would be $750. But have you learned anything worthwhile, such as how to improve the transfer of knowledge gained on the training program back to the job? Would that evaluation be worth the time and money involved? Or could the leader-managers of the participants judge the effectiveness of the training through observation and discussion equally well, and strengthen working relationships at the same time as a bonus?

4. Delivering training

Get over the idea that only children should spend their time in study. Be a student so long as you still have something to learn, and this will mean all your life.

Henry L Doherty (entrepreneur), *Forbes* (1963)[30]

Training is far, far more than lectures, lessons and lifting weights! You can expect to train individual employees and small groups of employees for many reasons, including cross-skilling, multiskilling and upskilling team members, training people for job rotations, secondments, acting in higher positions and undertaking delegated duties, and for equipping them to adapt to organisational change.

When less than two or three weeks' training in skills or procedures is needed, it is usually provided on the job by the employee's leader-manager, at the employee's workplace or work station. To train properly, you need to be able to develop a job breakdown and apply the four steps to systematic instruction described in this chapter. In large departments where there might be several trainees, you might delegate this training to another experienced worker who should also be trained to break a job down and teach it following the four-step instruction method.

Prepare job breakdowns

Job breakdowns help you instruct correctly and thoroughly by ensuring that you teach the job in the most logical sequence (*stages*) and that you include all the important considerations (*key points*). They discipline your training and speed up learning by making sure you don't give too much information for the learner to master but only cover what is important. This reduces training time by helping trainees easily remember how to do the job correctly and safely.

Always develop a job breakdown and follow it whenever you give on-the-job training. Once developed, you can file it and use it over and over again. This makes sure you continue to present all – and only – relevant information.

Job breakdowns help you divide a job into its major components and teach it in the most logical sequence. There are two steps to preparing a job breakdown: the first is determining the stages and the second is determining the key points. The acid test of a good job breakdown is being able to do the job using only the stages you have written in the job breakdown.

First, go through the job and break it down into stages. Physically do the job so that you don't miss anything important. In other words, do the job and make notes as you go; don't just think about how you would do it or how you have done it in the past. Stages are usually natural breaks in the action, activity or process of the job. A job breakdown should have a maximum of seven stages; more than this is too much for most learners to remember all at once. When a job has more than seven stages, break it down into separate units and teach each unit separately.

Once you've determined the stages, do the job again to establish the key points for each stage. Key points are actions that make each stage easier for the learners to remember and carry out correctly, efficiently and safely. Key points are anything about a stage that might:

* affect safety
* affect quality
* cause injury
* make the work easier
* provide any special information (e.g. special knacks or know-how).

Safety factors are always key points. When a stage contains more than five key points, break it down into two stages.

At the top of the job breakdown, list any tools or materials needed to do the task. List the measures of success, or results learners are aiming for, at the bottom. When necessary, add a series of 'if/then' instructions: 'If this happens, then do this.' When there are a lot of 'ifs' and 'thens' or several choice points, develop a flow chart from the job breakdown stages.

⦿ IN A NUTSHELL

Job breakdown: Cooking scrambled eggs

A good way to practice breaking a job down into its essential parts is to apply it to a job you do almost daily. Your breakdown could look like Table 27.2.

TABLE 27.2 Job breakdown: Preparing and cooking scrambled eggs

Tools and materials required	
Tablespoon	Bowl
Oil	Organic waste bin
Pan	Fork
Stove	Spatula
3 eggs	Plate

Stages	Key points
1. Grease pan	• One tablespoon of oil per egg • Swirl oil around to cover bottom of pan
2. Place pan on stove	• Temperature to high • Safety warning: Point pan handle away from you
3. Crack eggs into bowl	• Short, sharp crack across the middle of each egg • Grasp gently between fingers and thumb and break with thumbs along crack • Contents into bowl • Shells in organic waste bin

>>

4. Beat eggs	• Rapid, upward circular stirring movements with fork • Uniform colour • Paste-like consistency
5. Add eggs to pan	• Pour quickly
6. Cook eggs	• Approximately 4 minutes • Turn with spatula every 8 seconds • Eggs cooked when mix begins to dry and colour lightens • Transfer to plate.

Measures of success:
- light, fluffy eggs
- pan not burned.

Two other uses for job breakdowns

You can easily adapt job breakdowns into standard operating procedures (SOPs). These step-by-step guides are handy references for employees to turn to when they need to confirm how to do a task. When turning your job breakdowns into SOPs, make sure you use the active voice (e.g. 'Grease the pan', not 'The pan should be greased') and use the same terms throughout the SOP (e.g. don't say 'pan' in one place and 'saucepan' in another).

You can also give a copy of the job breakdown to the learners to refer to while their confidence builds.

In long and complex jobs that you break into several training units with a job breakdown for each unit, some units will be easier than others. Sometimes, you can teach the easiest units first, gradually moving on to the more difficult ones. Sometimes this won't be possible, for example, the job may need to be completed in a particular sequence, in which case, complete the job in its correct sequence: teach the trainee the easiest units as you come to them and complete the more difficult ones yourself. As the trainee masters the easier units, begin teaching the more difficult ones. This allows trainees to build their skills gradually until they can complete the entire job.

Instruct systematically

Once you have your job breakdown, all you need do is use it to follow these four steps to good training:

1. *Prepare for the training*: Before beginning, tidy the workspace so there are no distractions and to present a professional, welcoming area to the trainee. Remove any equipment or materials you don't need and lay out the equipment and materials you need. Place the job breakdown where you can see it clearly.

2. *Present the training*: Explain what you are going to show the learner how to do, why it's important and how it fits into the team's or department's work. State what you expect the learner to be able to do after your training.

   When you begin training, complete the job with slow and deliberate movements, stating the name of each stage as you come to it and stressing each key point with examples, exaggerated movements, repetition or changes in voice tone or speed (louder, slower, softer, quicker). Don't make the mistake of instructing too fast – let the trainee digest each stage before moving on to the next one. Look at the trainee when you finish demonstrating each stage and watch for a nod or some other sign of understanding before moving on.

3. *Confirm understanding of the training*: After slowly demonstrating how to do the job, it's time to make sure that the learner has understood what to do. Ask the trainee to go through the job, naming each stage as he or she comes to it and stating each key point. Let the learner concentrate – this is not the time to make small talk to fill a silence. Provided you have written a clear and complete job breakdown of seven or fewer stages, with no more than five key points per stage, trainees probably need to perform the job for you only once, twice or three times. When you are satisfied that the trainee can continue practising the job without your supervision, ask something like 'What else can I tell you?' to make sure there are no questions.

4. *Put the trainee to work*: Added to a desire to learn, repetition builds competence. Keep in touch while trainees practise on their own. Learning a new skill or mastering a new task takes time – the more complex the skill or task, the more time it takes to become proficient. Allow time between practice sessions to let the brain consolidate the new information and actions. Implement a regular follow-up program to ensure that the trainee continues to do the job in the required manner and to the required standard – you don't want any bad habits to creep in. Your follow-ups can become less frequent as the trainee gains experience.

These four instruction steps are written as a job breakdown in Table 27.3. Although it is written with sentences under key points for clarity, strictly speaking, you need only key words rather than sentences as key points because your job breakdown is your 'memory jogger'.

TABLE 27.3 A typical job breakdown training process

Step 1 Prepare for the training	
Stage	**Key points**
Gather materials	• Job breakdown guide, other training aids. • Ensure workspace is clean, tidy and free of tools and equipment that are not required.
Relax the learner	• A nervous person cannot learn effectively.
Explain	• Explain what you are going to show the learner how to do and explain your aim – what you expect the learner to be able to do after your training.
Can they do it?	• Ask the learner what they know about the job. Have they ever done anything like this? • If yes, build on existing knowledge and make associations with the learner's past experience to make learning easier. • If learners say they can do the job, ask them to demonstrate their method. (You may not need to teach it, or you may find gaps in skills and knowledge that need filling.)
Motivate the learner	• Give the learner a good reason to learn. People who want to learn are the easiest to teach. • Explain why the job is important, how it fits into the overall purpose of the organisation and the benefits the learner will gain from learning it.
Ensure correct position	• The learner must be able to hear what you are saying and have a clear view of the job you are about to demonstrate.

>>

Step 2 Present the training	
Stage	**Key points**
Create understanding.	• Use your job breakdown as a guide. • Carry out the job yourself stage by stage, emphasising the key points. • Instruct patiently, clearly and slowly, not too fast.

Step 3 Confirm understanding of the training	
Stage	**Key points**
Ask the learner to do the job.	• Have them do the job exactly the way you have just demonstrated.
Ask the learner to tell you, out loud, what they are doing.	• Listen to make sure the learner repeats the key points back to you. • If any key points are missed, ask the learner what they have just done, in order to draw out all the key points.
Stop learners if they make a mistake, or if you can see that a mistake is about to be made.	• Tell the learner they did something that was not quite right and ask if they can identify it. It is better for learners to work out their mistakes than for you to tell them.
Continue until satisfied.	• Have the learner continue doing the job for you, explaining to you what they are doing, until you are satisfied they have learned it correctly.

Step 4 Put the trainee to work	
Stage	**Key points**
Application.	• Leave the learner to practise their newly acquired skills and gain experience and confidence. • Indicate precise measures of success by explaining what you expect the learner to do. For example, to complete 12 forms over the next 2½ hours. • Always provide a job goal for learners to aim for to help them assess their own performance.
Problem-solving	• Indicate to whom the learner can go should a problem arise and you are unavailable.
Check back.	• Go back and check as often as necessary to ensure that the job is being done as you have taught it: safely, efficiently and correctly.

Avoid teaching too much at once

The most common error in instructing is trying to teach too much at once. Distinguishing between *must know*, *should know* and *could know* stops you from giving learners too much information to absorb and allows you to target only the most important information (see Figure 27.6.)

'*Must know*' refers to the stages and essential key points of a job, all the basics that learners must know in order to do the job correctly. Your job breakdowns should contain only '*must knows*'.

Once the learner has mastered the basics of the job, after Step 4 of the training process, you can explain the '*should knows*'. This is information that learners really should have but which is not essential in the early stages of learning.

When the learner has become proficient in the job, it is time to add the icing on the cake, to explain the '*could knows*' or '*nice to knows*'. These details add job interest and round out a person's job knowledge.

With the example of cooking scrambled eggs used earlier, the '*must knows*' are all contained in the job breakdown. '*Should knows*' might include egg sizes, various egg-beating techniques and how to test eggs for freshness. '*Could knows*' might include pan sizes, materials and thickness, additional flavourings and optional ingredients, how to store eggs correctly and why the eggs are cooked at a high temperature.

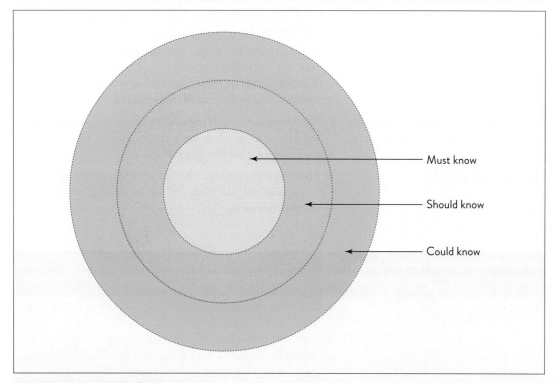

FIGURE 27.6 Levels of information

● THEORY TO PRACTICE

Some practical tips for training
Training sometimes means less is more. You guide rather than lead. Try these tips to help you along the way:
- Assess learners regularly and keep a record of how they are doing against their learning goals; review their results with them from time to time.
- Build learners' confidence with lots of specific positive and constructive feedback related to the learning goals and measures of success.
- Don't step in and take over when learners make a mistake. Help them figure out what they did wrong and how to correct it.
- Explain and reinforce basic workplace terms as you train.

>>

- Follow your job breakdown strictly.
- Frequently review what you've covered; since people tend to recall what they've heard first and last, pay special attention to emphasising, reinforcing and reviewing the middle bits.
- Have frequent breaks so learners can refresh themselves and you can check your messages and deal with any urgent matters that have arisen.
- Keep learners involved and active, not just sitting there watching you. Learning takes place by *doing*, not watching.
- Make it clear what learners should do once they've finished the task that you've set them, so they don't just sit there. For example, should they come and ask you to check what they've done, ask for another task or read a product manual?
- Relate the training to the learners' prior experience and knowledge.
- Smile, use a friendly voice and watch for signs of understanding or confusion.

Instructing small groups

Group instruction is broadly similar to individual instruction. You still use your job breakdown and instruct following the four steps described earlier. However, when you come to the third step (show me), give each learner a turn at doing a stage of the job. Ask them to say out loud what they are doing while you and the other trainees watch and listen for key points.

The other important point with group instruction is to ensure that the whole group can hear and see what you are doing in Step 2. This isn't always as easy as ensuring that just one trainee can see you.

> **○ FYI**
>
> ### Systematic, planned training
> Systematic job training was first introduced during World War II when large numbers of new factory workers needed to be trained to replace the experienced tradespeople who had gone off to war. Many factories reduced the length of the training period from four years to 12–18 months with no loss to quality or speed.

 CourseMateExpress

Go to http://login.cengagebrain.com to access CourseMate Express, your online study tool for *Management Theory & Practice*. CourseMate Express brings chapter concepts to life with interactive learning, and study and exam preparation tools:

- Test your skills in different aspects of management with interactive self-tests and simulations.
- Watch videos that show how real managers operate in real businesses.
- Test your understanding of the changing world of management by taking the revision quiz.

QUICK REVIEW

1. Explain the various ways that employees can learn as they work and how you can encourage and reinforce people's learning.
2. What are the two most important things managers can do to support off-the-job training?
3. Describe some ways to assess the effectiveness of training and learning activities.
4. Discuss the benefits of systematic on-the-job training to a team, the learner(s), a department and the organisation. Which, if any, of these benefits overlap?

BUILD YOUR SKILLS

1. Why does the shift to the knowledge economy make effective employee learning and development critical to an organisation's success? (See page 10 to find out more about the knowledge and service economy.)
2. Describe the steps you would take to assess a new employee's L&D needs.
3. Explain your role as a leader-manager in terms of the coaching, mentoring and feedback you need to provide.
4. Prepare a job breakdown for a task you do regularly following the layout shown in this chapter and use it to instruct someone who doesn't know how to do that task. Then ask for feedback on how clear your instructions were and what you could do to improve.
5. What are your own top three priority learning and development goals for the next 12 months?

WORKPLACE ACTIVITIES

1. List 10 actions you can take to build or strengthen a learning environment in your work team.
2. Develop a learning plan for your work team to meet its current and anticipated needs, indicating priority areas.
3. Prepare a job breakdown and use it to instruct someone in your team to meet a learning need identified in the learning plan developed in Question 2. Then ask for feedback on how clear your instructions were and what you could do to improve.

CASE STUDY 27.1

CUTTING-EDGE LEARNING

Referring to the Scenario at the start of this chapter, answer the following questions:

Questions
1. Gina is very clear about the benefits her company's new learning packages offer her work team. How important do you think her enthusiasm and support for the packages is to encouraging her team to make the best use of them?
2. How would you advise Gina to maintain the momentum once the learning packages have been up and operating for several months?
3. How could Gina monitor and evaluate the packages' effectiveness and ensure training doesn't become 'hit or miss' but is targeted at individual learning needs and the needs of her team?

CASE STUDY 27.2

TRAINING THE BOSS

Giam Swiegers joined the accounting firm Deloitte in South Africa after completing university. Two decades later, he was posted to Australia to run the Brisbane office. He knew he'd have some adjustments to make. He had done all his schooling in Afrikaans and had a heavy accent, and was used to a more authoritarian leadership style than Australians accept. He gathered a team of mentors and coaches, including an elocution coach, internal consultants, a psychologist and a public relations specialist to help him adapt to Australian ways. He even had coaching in hosting dinners, learned to make Australian-appropriate speech references and analogies, learned to become comfortable with Australian free-floating conversation and debate and found out that 'you don't have to put your hand up to make a point around the board table'.

A few years later, Swiegers won the top Deloitte job in Australia, taking over a demoralised firm upset over the sudden resignation of his predecessor, Domenic Martino, in controversial circumstances. The firm was also struggling with a large slump in revenue. Swiegers had always considered mentoring essential to the business and, shortly after his appointment, he decided that bold action was needed before the partners would sit up and take notice of its importance. He sent an email to all 2800 employees asking them to vote on the partners' mentoring abilities and left a voicemail explaining that people and their performance were his number one issue. There was a 75% employee participation rate in the vote.

Based on their scores, only 50% of the partners had 'acceptable' levels of mentoring. Swiegers announced the firm's top 25 mentors at the annual partners' conference later that month, making a big fuss of the winners. He also wrote to congratulate those who scored well but didn't make the top 25. To those who scored very low – zero to one vote – he wrote asking, 'How can it be possible for you to have 10 people working for you and not a single person regards you as a good mentor? And please, tell me what you are going to do about this.' To fuel the peer pressure fire, he also sent all 272 partners (and only partners) the full list of scores from top to bottom, letting it be known that the exercise would be repeated the following year.

According to Swiegers, everyone in the firm, including the partners, knew who was good at mentoring and who wasn't, so the list offered no surprises in that regard. But it did offer personal surprises and, in Johari Window terms, punched holes in quite a few partners' blind spots (see page 210 for more information on the Johari Window).

As expected, mentoring became the hot topic at the water cooler. Some partners met with their teams, told them their personal scores, expressed their disappointment in them, and asked, 'Would you mind telling me what I am doing wrong?' Many partners attended Deloitte's internal mentoring and coaching programs.

Swiegers also took the executive team to a one-week course at the Kellogg Business School at Northwestern University in Chicago, where the focus was on motivating teams and people and a lot of attention was paid to the benefits of mentoring. In the following months, that group worked with their teams to develop and retain talent, with mentoring central to that process.

When Swiegers repeated the survey the next year, most of the partners had improved their scores, some spectacularly. The list of poor performers had shrunk dramatically and there was a greater spread of votes among the partners; and 80% of the partners had 'acceptable' levels of mentoring. The participation rate in the survey also went up.[31]

Questions

1. What characteristics of a lifelong learner does Giam Swiegers seem to exhibit?
2. Swiegers wanted to make mentoring a 'water cooler topic'. How effective was his strategy? What were the risks in his strategy?
3. What did the greater spread of votes among the partners and the other results from the second survey indicate? Why do you think the participation rate in the survey went up?

CHAPTER

28

LEADING AND ATTENDING MEETINGS

OVERVIEW

People are social animals. Since we first walked the earth, we have come together in small groups to plan, make decisions, learn from and help each other, and have fun. Meetings are part of the Australian culture, both Indigenous and migrant. Modern technology allows people in different cities, states and countries to meet in real time. In fact, meeting has never been easier.

Yet many leader-managers claim that they meet too much. They complain that too many meetings achieve little, waste time and run on without a purpose. It is true that meetings can give an illusion of progress where, in truth, none exists.

Despite all the complaints about meetings, though, what alternative is there? Meetings are a way to share and work with information and help people do their jobs better. They also help people work together and build a sense of belonging, shared responsibility, shared goals and team spirit.

1. Are you familiar with the types of meetings and when to call them?
2. Do you know what you are responsible for when you lead a meeting and how to avoid the common mistakes that meeting leaders make?
3. Do you know how to lead virtual meetings?
4. Do you know how to participate effectively in meetings?
5. Do you understand the different requirements of formal and informal meetings?

This chapter takes you through the ins and outs of meetings and explains how to make meetings – actual and virtual – work.

The stand-in

Grace's boss has asked her to chair the quarterly team leaders' meeting in four weeks' time. He has delegated everything to her – the choice of venue, the time and duration of the meeting, the agenda, the whole works. This is a major event in the team leaders' calendar and an opportunity for her to show her organising and leadership skills. She wants to make sure she gets everything right.

Where should she begin? What should she do first? What should she say when she opens the meeting? How can she keep order and stop babbling Ben from talking too much and get Anh Qui, who is really smart, creative – and quiet – to contribute? How can she make sure people don't interrupt each other and prevent a cacophony of voices with no one able to listen?

When he handed her the assignment, Grace's manager gave her a few words of advice. 'Grace,' he said, 'do your preparation for the meeting well in advance. Once you have everything planned and thought through, everything falls into place.'

'Preparation?' thought Grace. 'What should I prepare first? How should I prepare? What should I prepare?

1. Calling the right type of meeting at the right time

Meetings are a great trap... They are indispensable when you don't want to do anything.

John Kenneth Galbraith (economist), *Ambassador's journal* (1969) [1]

When properly planned and run, meetings can make a significant contribution to an organisation's effectiveness. They can be a good way to give people information on a more personal basis than, say, an official notice. They can help you identify and solve problems, gather information, opinions and ideas, allow full and open discussion on important matters and reach agreement.

In addition to these task functions, meetings have other, more subtle, purposes called maintenance functions. They can define the team and make people feel part of it: those who attend a work group meeting are part of the team, while those who do not attend are not. Everyone can look around and clearly see the group of which they are a part. This can help make a group more *cohesive*, or unified, and build people's attachment to it. In fact, the only time many work groups exist as a team and work together as a team is during a meeting.

Meetings also show who the official team leader is; in many work groups, a meeting is the only time the leader is clearly seen as the leader of the group, rather than as a person doing a job or the person to whom people report to individually. Meetings can clarify the aims of the group as a whole, helping members to understand where their own work fits in. Well-run meetings create commitment to decisions and objectives, especially when consensus methods are used.

When everyone contributes, meetings can create a pool of shared knowledge and experience and an opportunity for a group to revise, refresh and add to its collective understanding. This helps a group grow and develop, increases the speed and efficiency of communication between members, enhances their work performance and helps the team achieve its goals.

IN A NUTSHELL

Meetings succeed when ...

It's true that meetings can be the biggest time wasters in business. So make your meetings matter. Here are some tips:

- Decisions are made thoughtfully, without compromising anyone's feelings or opinions or applying pressure to agree, and next steps made clear.
- Everyone at the meeting feels comfortable exchanging information, regardless of alliances or status differences.
- Everyone at the meeting has good reason to be there.
- Everyone takes responsibility for what goes on in the meeting.
- Good records are kept, so ideas, information and action plans are not lost.
- No one dominates the meeting or prevents others from airing their views.
- People feel free to express their ideas and know they will be considered.
- Real agreement, not just an easy way out, is reached.
- The people attending the meeting are genuinely involved in the decisions made.
- The results achieved outweigh their cost in terms of money and time.
- There is no bickering, resentment or power plays.
- They are held only when necessary.
- They have clear objectives and a tight agenda.
- They start on time and finish on time.
- Time is not wasted on irrelevant side issues, hobbyhorses or going over old ground.

Types of meetings

Meetings can serve a variety of purposes. Know why you're calling a meeting so that you don't confuse participants by blending two or more types of meeting together.

The following sections introduce you to four main types of meetings that you can expect to attend or to lead.

General update meetings

Many leader-managers find that monthly team meetings interspersed with fortnightly individual meetings with each of their direct reports keep the channels of communication open, strengthen working relationships and keep people's attention on goals and results.

Time your meetings

It generally takes about 30 minutes of team time to bring everyone 'up to speed' with team results, review progress on goals and long-term projects and generally check in with team members.

To prevent team meetings from rambling, give each team member two minutes to update the others on what they're working on, what problems they've resolved or are facing, any improvement suggestions, and so on. Then allow up to three minutes of questions from the others.

The week before the team meeting, post an agenda on a noticeboard and ask people to add any topics to it they want to discuss or questions they would like answered. With sensitive or ambiguous topics, clarify with the person who suggested the agenda item just what he or she wishes to discuss.

Try mini-meetings

Mini-meetings are also useful for work groups in which people work more as individuals but still want to be aware of what others are up to. You can stand up to keep them short and give everyone 60 seconds to say how they're doing and what is urgent or important for them that day or week.

Leader-managers who need to direct team activities, discuss changes or make announcements related to the day's or week's work often begin each day or week with a quick team meeting, or 'huddle', that lasts only five or 10 minutes.

Information-giving meetings

Call an information-giving meeting when you need to pass on information to a group of people. Use demonstrations, slides, videos or other aids to reinforce your verbal message. Allow some discussion and questions, but keep the focus on providing information.

Do you need a meeting?

Before calling an information meeting, be sure you cannot get the information across more cheaply and effectively in other ways, such as one-to-one, over the telephone or in writing. Information-giving meetings are useful when the information to be shared:

* has major implications for the meeting attendees
* has symbolic value in being given personally
* is complex or controversial
* needs to be heard from a particular person
* requires clarification or comments to help people make sense of it
* requires some discussion or information exchange.

Meetings to introduce change

These meetings allow you to introduce and explain fully changes that will be made in order to help your team to understand the reasons for the changes and to gain their support. This is the type of meeting to hold to announce and explain an organisation restructure or merger, for example, or a change to procedures or a policy.

Since change is unsettling to most people, it is important to explain the change fully and clearly and allow time for questions, discussion and dissent. When there is a great deal of opposition, it is tempting (but a mistake) to close the meeting with 'Well, that's the way it is.' Instead, explore people's concerns fully. The bigger the change, the more unrealistic it is to expect people to accept it quickly. Be prepared to discuss the issues involved and allow people time to air their thoughts and opinions (for more on this, see page 689.)

Information-seeking and information-exchange meetings

When you want to gather opinions, facts and other information or give people the opportunity to discuss and exchange information and ideas, information-seeking and information-exchange meetings are the answer. Aim to achieve a full and open discussion with all participating members.

Innovation meetings

When you want to generate ideas or develop new offerings or ways of working, call an innovation meeting. Questions like 'What are our options?' and 'How could we …?' help people exchange information and ideas.

Brainstorming sessions are the best known type of new-ideas meeting. Brainstorming helps to generate ideas quickly. Later, the participants explore, refine and develop those ideas (brainstorming is explained further on pages 534 and 937).

Information-seeking and innovation meetings combine the knowledge, skills, ideas and experience of several people at once. Hold them when something new, such as a way to cut costs or develop a new procedure, needs to be developed. With everyone contributing, creative solutions are more easily conceived (see Case Study 9.1 on page 283 for examples of weekly informal information-exchange and innovation meetings.)

Planning meetings

When you want people to help plan something, perhaps because they'll be involved in executing the plan or to draw on their expertise, call a planning meeting. Members can decide or offer suggestions on what is to be done, who is to do it and where, and when and how it is to be done.

Guide participants to decide or suggest action steps, distribute responsibilities and tasks and set priorities. Begin with a clear outcome or goal to be accomplished and aim to finish with a clear action plan to achieve it.

Problem-solving and decision-making meetings

Call this type of meeting when you need to discuss, consider and agree solutions, and make or recommend a decision. Explain how the final decision is to be made. For example, by you after consultation with the meeting participants or by consensus among the participants. Aim for a free and lively discussion that builds on the diverse talents, backgrounds and experiences of all the participants.

Before reaching the decision, ask, 'What information are we missing?' and 'Does anyone have any information we need that we haven't discussed?' Once the decision is reached, discuss possible signals that the decision is working and possible signals that it is going wrong; this alerts everyone to pay attention to those areas.

In problem-solving meetings, you are looking for solutions. What may seem at first to be wild ideas can turn out to be excellent ones after a little polishing and refining. Problem-solving meetings typically go through the steps shown in Figure 18.2: The problem-solving and decision-making process, on page 527. When the problem is complex, this may take several meetings.

Quality improvement meetings

Originally called *quality circles,* quality improvement meetings now go by various names, but they all share the goal of identifying and solving problems, gathering ideas, deciding and planning how to improve work systems and provide better service to internal and external customers.

● THEORY TO PRACTICE

Sit or stand?

Should you sit or stand when leading meetings? Sitting usually looks more informal and less rehearsed and 'prepared'. It conveys that you are open to discussion and questions and puts you on a more equal footing with team members. More feedback, opinions and discussion usually result when the leader is seated.

Standing shows you 'have the floor' and seems more formal and prepared. It is also more authoritative, saying 'this is important'. People grant you more control when you stand, but it may look as though you don't want feedback or discussion. This means that team members might save any negative comments until after the session, for the corridors and cafe bars.

You can have it both ways. Stand for the information-giving part and then sit for the discussion, for example.

Team-briefing meetings

The purpose of team briefings is to:

- allow questions and suggestions to be fed back from all staff to senior management
- create a culture of open communication, clearing information blockages, reducing misunderstandings and increasing commitment
- develop a shared sense of mission, vision, collective aims and reasons why things are being done as they are
- develop greater awareness and understanding of key organisational and workplace issues and results and encourage involvement at all levels
- enable and improve downward, upward and lateral (sideways) communication through the organisation
- explain financial, commercial and strategic issues
- prevent guesswork, rumour and 'the grapevine' from gaining credibility
- strengthen clarity of direction and information from senior management.

Because the briefings are face to face, team leaders can ensure that people understand what is happening, and why, and can ask questions and explore issues that affect them. The briefings give team leaders an opportunity to reinforce their 'management message' and keep lines of communication open.

Here's how they work: The managing director, chief executive officer or board of directors issues a *core management brief* or *core brief*, covering the main commercial, financial, people, policy and strategic issues. This information is cascaded through the organisation as every manager and team leader incorporates the core brief points into their own *local brief*, which contains issues relevant to their team, generally working through these headings:

- *People*: Matters concerning people in the company and the team, new appointments and visitors.
- *Progress:* How the organisation/division/team has performed overall in relation to key measures in areas such as customer satisfaction, finance, safety and quality.
- *Policy*: Any new policies or procedures or changes to corporate or workplace policy or procedures that need to be explained or reinforced.
- *Points for action*: Priorities over the next month for the team and the organisation; what's coming up and the team's or organisation's response.
- *Any general information*.

Team briefings can be weekly or monthly, depending on the organisation's needs, with dates set well in advance. People meet in teams of four to 15 people, and meetings, led by the team's leader-manager, usually last around 30 minutes. A feedback form captures questions that arise at briefings and questions the team leader can't answer are passed upwards so that they can be answered at the next briefing meeting.

 IN A NUTSHELL

Preparing and presenting a local brief

Know exactly what information you want to relay and then present it clearly and concisely. Here are some pointers for preparing and presenting information:

- Avoid long words, rambling repetition, jargon and any technical terms that may be unfamiliar to the team members.
- Avoid tired clichés like 'Let's go for it!'
- Deliver difficult messages in a tactful, non-threatening way.

>>

- Make your key points clearly to minimise misunderstanding.
- Emphasise key points by drawing an analogy or a word picture, by slowing down or saying them more softly or loudly, or by using descriptive adjectives and action verbs.
- Ensure key messages 'stick' by making important points three times, in three different ways.
- Remember, it isn't just what you say, but how you say it, that gets results. Look and sound confident and use positive words and phrases.
- Use praise to motivate, but don't indulge in empty praise.
- Use short sentences that you can say in one breath.
- Leave a short, three- to five-second pause after each important point to let it sink in.

Clarify any questions you don't understand and, when you can, answer them immediately. Otherwise, write them on the feedback form and answer them at the next briefing meeting.

When to call a meeting

The question is not whether to have meetings – you will. But think twice before calling a meeting because the number of hours in a day is limited. When travel is involved, think about replacing a face-to-face meeting with a less expensive and less time-consuming alternative such as a conference call or virtual meeting (discussed in Section 3 of this chapter).

How can you predict a meeting is worth the time and trouble? Call a meeting when there is no better or less expensive way, such as email, telephone, virtual meeting or word of mouth, to get the job done and when you:

- need other people's help to solve problems or implement solutions or decisions
- need to gain commitment
- need to generate discussion or ideas
- need to present information to a group of people quickly and communicating in writing would not be appropriate (e.g. to deliver 'bad news')
- want to motivate people and create energy about an idea.

Skip the meeting when:

- involving others would only complicate matters
- it's a power trip
- it's just a substitute for real work or a stalling device
- it's only to rubber-stamp a decision
- there is nothing specific to discuss
- you don't need others' input.

2. Planning and leading meetings

In meetings, I try to be sure that everybody has an opportunity to speak.

John D deButts (former chair, AT&T), in Fletcher 'On the way up: How to keep cool in the hot seat', Management Today (1999)[2]

Any meeting worth holding is worth planning. And even the best-planned meetings need to be led effectively. Planning and leading meetings are both important skill sets for leader-managers and they each require a different set of competencies. Planning a meeting involves establishing objectives, planning the agenda, selecting participants, choosing a time and place, and distributing the agenda.

Establish objectives

Ask yourself these three questions:

1. What do I need this meeting to achieve?
2. How can I know whether it has succeeded?
3. What do I want the atmosphere of the meeting to be like?

The answers should form a clear picture in your mind and provide the explicit objectives that every successful meeting works towards.

Here are some other questions to think through beforehand:

- How can I best convey my objectives to the meeting participants?
- Do we need to make any decisions at the meeting? If so, what information do we need?
- What topics do we need to cover?
- What issues or concerns are likely to come up?
- What needs to happen before the meeting can take place?

Plan the agenda

Some meetings have only one objective – for example, to give information or to reach a decision. Others have several objectives and cover several topics. When this is the case, list the topics in writing; this forms the basis of your agenda.

When listing the topics, keep them results-oriented by using a verb to begin each item: Decide … Plan for … Generate ideas about … Gather opinions on … and so on. This emphasises the intended outcome.

It's also a good idea to indicate the time you've allocated each topic. Don't make the agenda so rigid that it can't be adjusted, though. Some topics can take more or less time to discuss than expected and others may arise that were not anticipated.

Even small informal meetings benefit from agendas like this because they provide a sense of direction. They also clarify and speed up meetings by highlighting the purpose of a discussion and indicating what is (and isn't) relevant to discuss.

> **◉ ACTION!**
>
> Planning a meeting? You can find a simple Agenda for team meetings template on .

Start with an item that is brief and easy to deal with and that you expect participants to receive positively. Even when you have some information to pass on, put items requiring discussion and active input first, because once people have sat quietly in listening mode it's hard to make the switch to contributing mode. Put routine matters, 'FYI' items and items you want to deal with briefly towards the end and make the final topic one that gives members a sense of unity or achieves a positive outcome.

Here are some other ideas for ordering agendas:

- Put the most important item second on the agenda and use the first item to warm participants up.
- Schedule items of great interest to everyone for the lull in the meeting that seems to come 15–20 minutes after its start.

- Sequence the topics logically so that they build on each other, or from the easiest to the most difficult or controversial, or the most to the least urgent.
- Since people tend to be more lively and creative and have a longer attention span during the early part of a meeting, put items that require a lot of mental work first.

Be aware of your options and consciously choose between them. At the top of the agenda, indicate where and when the meeting will be held.

Try to keep meetings to less than an hour to avoid people becoming restless. When a meeting must go on for longer than one hour, schedule a short break every 50 to 75 minutes and encourage people to stand up and walk around to rev up their blood flow.

Distribute the agenda to participants, giving them enough time to prepare for the meeting. Two or three days before the meeting is usually enough for informal team meetings; formal meetings often specify how many days or weeks prior to the meeting the agenda should be sent out. Ask participants to suggest any changes to the agenda before the meeting.

 FYI

The importance of breaks
A study at Wellington Hospital in New Zealand found that employees who sit for several hours without getting up (e.g. at a meeting or even at their desks) are more likely to develop deep-vein thrombosis (DVT) than those who move about more often.[3]

IN A NUTSHELL

Guidelines for writing an agenda
Your agenda can make or break your meeting. Get the agenda right and your meeting will flow and, equally important, stop on time.
- Avoid topics best handled by individuals or subgroups.
- Consider your opening remarks and how best to introduce each topic on the agenda.
- Don't try to cover too much. Keep the number of items within reasonable limits.
- Make the intended outcomes of discussions clear and indicate how long you expect to spend on each topic.
- Separate information exchange and problem analysis from problem-solving.
- State start and finish times for the meeting.

Select participants

More is not merrier. More than 12 participants makes a meeting difficult to control and to hold everyone's attention, and harder for each participant to contribute fully. Large numbers also mean that the meeting is likely to last longer. Four to seven participants is ideal, 10 is tolerable.

When you can't limit the numbers, try holding two smaller meetings. Or form subgroups to discuss topics in advance. Each group can then send a representative to the main meeting. Failing that, structure the agenda so that some members join at half-time and others leave, or invite people in for the specific sections of the agenda that they are concerned with or can contribute to.

Sometimes the decision of who to invite is made for you – it might automatically be your whole team, for example. At other times, you need to think through who should attend. Invite people who can best contribute to the discussion – people with the relevant knowledge, skills or experience. You probably want to invite people affected by the outcome of the meeting and leave the decision of whether to attend up to them.

You might want to include people who you can count on to support you, people whose commitment you need or people who have resources that you need such as budget, influence, other staff or time. You might want to include specialists from different areas of the organisation in order to get broad representation and a balanced group.

 THE STRATEGIC PERSPECTIVE

What makes a team smarter?

Women make a team smarter. Researchers in the USA found that while there is little correlation between a group's collective intelligence and the individual IQs of its members, when a group includes more women, its collective intelligence rises.

This can be explained in part, the researchers think, by differences in social sensitivity, which is also important to group performance: listening to each other, keeping an open mind, sharing criticism constructively, and so on, are all factors that help people work well together.[4]

When you're not sure whether to invite someone, think about how much they're paid and whether your meeting is worth their pay. Consider too what they may have been doing were they not attending your meeting. When people need to be kept 'in the loop' but don't need to attend, make the minutes available to them and pass on any essential information.

Try to select participants who are about equal in rank to avoid inhibiting some participants. When it is necessary for people from different levels or interest groups in the organisation to attend, try to obtain a rough balance of status and power among them.

Use your intra-office communications to invite people to meetings and take RSVPs. State the main meeting objective in the title and attach the agenda. Or try http//www.doodle.com, which is a free meeting scheduler.

FYI

The two-thirds rule

The *two-thirds rule* is a good rule of thumb to follow when deciding who should attend: each person attending a meeting should be directly concerned with two out of three, or two-thirds, of the agenda items. This prevents the meeting from wasting anyone's time.

Decide when and where to hold the meeting

Select a time during working hours convenient to everyone. Meetings held outside working hours work in some organisations, but when a meeting isn't held during working hours, people may reason that the topics can't be too important and may resent having their personal time taken up by what is essentially company business, even when the outcome affects them. Out-of-hours meetings also disadvantage people who have home responsibilities and other personal commitments. When you schedule a meeting over lunch, provide food.

What time of day is best? People are generally fresher early in the day and have less on their minds. They may also be more eager to get on with the meeting so they can get on with the rest of their work. A meeting may take on a more leisurely tone late in the afternoon.

When you think a meeting may drag on too long, arrange for it to finish at lunchtime or going-home time; finish on time as people may have personal errands to attend to at lunchtime or carer commitments at the end of the day.

Your choice of where to hold the meeting has a subtle but significant impact on its success and sends out messages about its importance, style, and so on. Think about your objectives for the meeting as you select the location.

Conference rooms are neutral but can be bland. Your office gives you 'home turf' advantage and is generally more comfortable for small meetings, especially when people sit informally around a coffee table. You might hold a brief informal meeting in the main work area or in your office. However, when you need to tackle difficult problems and the meeting may take more than 20 minutes, opt for a conference room or a quiet, well-lit, temperature-controlled room arranged so that everyone can see and hear each other. Look for comfortable seating, temperature and ventilation, freedom from distractions and relative quiet.

Seating arrangements

Seating arrangements affect the way people participate. For example:

- When you want to encourage collaboration, cross-talk and ideas sharing, arrange seating in a *circle*, *hollow square* or *U-shape*.
- When you want people's attention to be on the meeting leader, use a *semi-circle*.
- For information-giving meetings, seat people in chairs in rows, 'theatre style'; add tables so that people can take notes when you provide technical or procedural information.
- When you want to send a message that the meeting is serious and important, try *boardroom style* and seat people around a conference table.
- When time is tight and for short, sharp meetings, don't sit – *stand up* and meet.

Meeting roles

The leader-manager usually leads team meetings although you may occasionally rotate the chair among team members to give everyone valuable experience in leading meetings. You may also act as *recorder*, or secretary, jotting down important points raised by meeting members. Again, this role can be rotated among meeting members.

Traditionally, the recorder kept individual notes for later posting or distribution. A useful variation is for the recorder to take the notes on an electronic whiteboard or a laptop projected onto a screen or the wall, or as a shared document in virtual meetings. This way, meeting members can see what is being recorded and no one has to worry that their point has been missed. Visible minutes also help meeting members keep to the topic at hand.

Another useful role is that of *meeting facilitator*. This is a different role from the leader's role. The meeting leader is formally in charge of the meeting, whereas the facilitator's job is to lead the *process* of the meeting, staying away from *content* (i.e. meeting facilitators don't normally contribute any ideas themselves). For example, in a brainstorming session, the facilitator ensures that everyone is contributing and no one is criticising. The meeting facilitator also points out when meeting members are not following the agreed meeting ground rules (see Figure 28.1). Again, the role of facilitator can be usefully rotated among group members.

Lead an effective meeting

Leading meetings requires six important skills:

1. Assertiveness.
2. Sensitivity to group dynamics.
3. The ability to guide and maintain a balanced discussion that stays on track and moves towards the desired outcomes.
4. The ability to listen carefully and summarise accurately and clearly.
5. The ability to open and close the meeting well.
6. The ability to engage participants' attention and energy.

Of course, meetings are about more than listening and talking. They are called to achieve specific goals: the task. The way meeting members go about achieving their task is called the process and reflects the dynamics of the group, or the way people are working together. Pay careful attention to the task by following the agenda. Here are some ideas for monitoring a meeting's process.

Some meetings are cooperative, cordial and relaxed while still being 'business-like'. Other meetings are stiff and awkward, filled with embarrassment, game playing, ill will and undercurrents. Which better describes the meetings you lead and attend? These dynamics can make or break a meeting's success.

Notice the communication patterns between participants: who talks to whom, for how long and how often? What style of communication is used? Aggressive? Assertive? Passive? What tone of voice do people use? What sort of questions do they ask and how do they ask them? Is the language formal and stilted or friendly and informal? What does the body language of the meeting participants tell you? Answers to these questions provide important information about how well meeting members are working together, how involved they are and how committed they are to achieving the meeting's objectives.

Who supports who? Are cliques or factions developing? This indicates internal tension in the group, which prevents it from working optimally.

Who do people look at when they talk? This can show you who the informal leader is. That is, the person who wields the most influence in the group. Who is often interrupted? This can show you who wields the least influence in the group – yet this does not make their contributions or opinions any less useful.

● IN A NUTSHELL

Achieving the meeting's task

Keep participants on track and prevent misunderstandings and confusion by:

- clarifying any points participants make that are not clear
- following the agenda
- gathering facts and opinions, ensuring that opinions are not disguised as facts
- helping participants build on each others' experience and knowledge
- helping participants explore issues fully before reaching a decision
- making the objectives of the meeting clear
- making sure all meeting participants understand the issues and why they are being discussed
- recording decisions, agreements and action points
- restricting the discussion to the topic at hand
- summarising often.

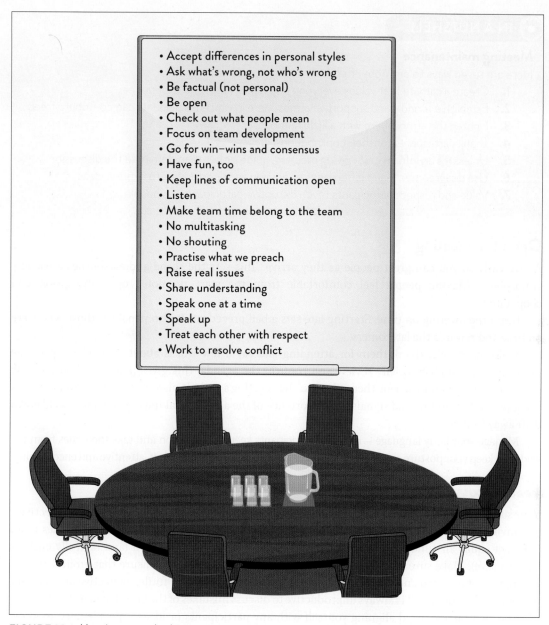

- Accept differences in personal styles
- Ask what's wrong, not who's wrong
- Be factual (not personal)
- Be open
- Check out what people mean
- Focus on team development
- Go for win–wins and consensus
- Have fun, too
- Keep lines of communication open
- Listen
- Make team time belong to the team
- No multitasking
- No shouting
- Practise what we preach
- Raise real issues
- Share understanding
- Speak one at a time
- Speak up
- Treat each other with respect
- Work to resolve conflict

FIGURE 28.1 Meeting ground rules

What group norms are apparent? For example, do people arrive early, on time or late? Prepared or unprepared? Do they hold side conversations or text during the meeting or does everyone pay full attention to whoever holds the floor? The group norms can give you an insight into the priorities of the group.

When you're paying attention to the meeting group's norms and dynamics, you can address behaviours that seem to be harming the meeting's effectiveness. In fact, you can prevent any harmful norms and processes from developing by asking participants at the start of the meeting to develop or refer to previously developed ground rules for the meeting. Figure 28.1 shows an example of the ground rules one team agreed to. (Find out more about these aspects of people working together on pages 93 and 379.)

> ### ● IN A NUTSHELL
>
> **Meeting maintenance**
> Here are seven ways to promote effective meeting processes:
> 1. Create a climate that values everyone's opinions, ideas and experience.
> 2. Establish a friendly and supportive atmosphere in which participants can contribute freely.
> 3. Lighten the atmosphere with a little humour.
> 4. Thank participants for their contributions.
> 5. Unless it's an information-giving meeting, guide rather than dominate the discussion.
> 6. Use disagreements and differences of opinion as opportunities to explore ideas.
> 7. Value and respect participants (even disruptive participants) as people.

Open the meeting

Arrive early so you can greet people as they arrive. This sets the scene and establishes a friendly atmosphere. Making people feel comfortable from the start promotes open discussion and cooperation.

Begin the meeting on time. Starting late sets a bad precedent. It also penalises those who were on time and rewards the latecomers.

Welcome people, thank them for attending and say a few words about what you expect the meeting to accomplish. Briefly review and confirm the agenda; this gives people a chance to ask questions and generally orient themselves to the meeting's task. It also ensures that everyone has the same understanding and signals the importance of the agenda, making participants less likely to drift away from it.

Manage your body language – meeting participants keep their eyes on and take their cues from the leader, so keep your posture erect and positive and your facial expressions alert, attentive and encouraging.

Lead discussions

Your success in gathering information and ideas or in reaching a decision depends on how effectively you invite free and open participation. Keep discussions balanced by ensuring that all sides of an issue get equal 'air time' and that all participants have a say and are heard (and tactfully curbing the talkative). Make sure comments are on topic and listen carefully to ensure that ground already covered is not repeated and that discussions don't drag on. Don't allow futile, ineffective or irrelevant discussion; for example, it is always unproductive to discuss mistakes of the past that can't be changed.

Stay neutral and avoid aligning yourself with any participants or ideas – people need to know you're not taking sides. Treat everyone equally; for example, don't say 'good idea' to some but not others – respond to ideas and contributions, not individuals.

Explore issues fully, clarifying and asking the right questions so that discussions don't disintegrate into confusion or become aimless. Summarise often, to help people keep on track and on the 'same page'. Make sure that people discuss what they know (not what they don't know). Don't ask for input on matters participants know nothing about, have no expertise in or have no solid information about.

Asking the right question of the right person at the right time isn't hard, but it does require careful listening and practice. When you get it right, everyone's views and information is aired, discussions flow and people stay on topic. Here is an overview of the main types of questions to use when leading discussions.

- *Closed*: Use closed questions when you want direct and specific information or facts. Follow with a probing question when you need to.
- *Clarifying*: Ask a clarifying question to make sure you have understood someone's comment or to summarise in the form of a question.
- *Consensus-seeking*: These ask for the meeting's confirmation that everyone is in agreement and you can move on.
- *Consequences*: These ask participants to consider the consequences or implications of their decision, solution or suggestions.
- *Direct*: These are questions aimed at a specific meeting member. Take care not to make people feel like you're putting them 'on the spot'. Use them mostly to direct a question to someone about their particular expertise or when you see a non-verbal cue that someone has something to say.
- *General*: These are questions you ask to everyone at the meeting, leaving it up to individuals to respond or not. They can be open or closed questions, consensus-seeking questions or consequences questions.
- *Open*: Because they allow so much latitude in the way people respond, open questions are the best for finding out what people think and know and for drawing out ideas.
- *Probing*: Ask a probing question when you want more information or detail, an example or the reasoning behind what someone has stated.
- *Redirected*: When someone asks you or another meeting member a question, you may want to direct it to the entire meeting or a particular person to keep meeting members participating and to prevent a discussion between only two people.

Hold your own ideas until last to encourage more open contributions since your team may not want to openly disagree with you or challenge your opinions. This also helps to avoid anchoring your opinion in people's minds, groupthink and rubber-stamping. When meeting members reach a decision, summarise it clearly and, when appropriate, discuss how to implement it (pages 523 and 539 explain anchoring and groupthink.)

◉ IN A NUTSHELL

Five ways to encourage participation

Swipple's Rule of Order states that 'He who shouts loudest has the floor.'[5] Here are five ways to encourage participation so that this rule doesn't take over:

1. Address quiet members by name: 'Pat, we haven't heard from you on this. What are your thoughts?'
2. Ask an open-ended question.
3. Ask for a show of hands when the topic is non-confrontational and doing so won't set up a win–lose climate.
4. Go around the group, asking each person for their thoughts, one at a time.
5. Put the question or topic in writing. Give all members a copy and ask them to quickly jot down their responses. Collect the responses and read them to the group or ask people to share what they've written.

Don't announce a consensus when you feel people have unspoken reservations. Encourage people to air their genuine concerns (but stay alert for any 'hidden agendas' – ulterior motives – and self-interest). Don't stifle disharmony when participants are exploring an issue; make sure debate is respectful so it doesn't collapse into poisonous conflict. Make sure that all participants respect every speaker's right to be heard so that only one person speaks at a time and people keep their voices down. (You can find more information on consensus and participation in meetings on page 543, and how to achieve it on page 544. Page 539 has more information on ways to reach decisions in meetings.)

When you're not able to reach agreement, ask:

- What do the experts say? People listen to topic experts.
- What does the informal leader say? People listen to them, too.
- What do you think? People listen to the official leader, too.

Close a discussion only when it is clear that:

- consensus has been reached
- events are changing rapidly and are likely to alter the basis of discussion quite soon
- more facts are required before further progress can be made
- participants need more time to think about an issue or discuss it with colleagues not present
- the meeting needs the views of people not present
- there is not enough time to discuss the issues fully
- two or three members can settle the topic being discussed outside the meeting without taking up the time of everyone present.

When all the points have been covered or agreement has been reached, summarise once more and move on to the next agenda item. Draw participants' attention to it, briefly explain the background to the item and confirm the purpose of the discussion.

◉ THEORY TO PRACTICE

What to do when a meeting strays or gets stuck

When energy wanes and enthusiasm wilts, it's up to you to get the meeting back on track.

Ask your meeting participants:

- Are there any further thoughts or more information on this?
- Have we covered this sufficiently?
- Is that it or do we have more?
- We have 10 minutes left on this before we need to move on to our next item – or are we ready to move on now?
- What are our options?
- What's the solution?
- Where do we go from here?
- Which way do we want to proceed?

Or take these actions:

- Back up and redefine the problem.
- Promise a quick finish in return for progress; for example, 'We can wrap up in 15 minutes if we can finish off this plan' or 'Let's come up with just a few more ideas to take forward before we stop'.
- Review what you've achieved and what you've yet to achieve: 'We seem to agree on A, B and C so far but we need to reach consensus on D and E.'
- Review your objectives.
- Take a short break.

Close the meeting

Clarify the next steps, particularly who is responsible for doing what and by when. Double check that all decisions and actions to be taken have been recorded and confirm that these will be distributed to all meeting members. When you're tempted to ask lamely, 'What else do we need to discuss?', change the question to 'What do we need to put on the agenda for the next meeting?' When appropriate, agree on the time and place of the next meeting.

Finally, thank everyone for their participation and spend a few minutes talking about how well the meeting went. Always try to end a meeting on a positive note and with a sense of accomplishment. You can do this, for example, by summarising a major achievement of the meeting.

● IN A NUTSHELL

Avoiding the most common mistakes meeting leaders make

Poor leadership can ruin any meeting. Here are the top 10 mistakes that meeting leaders make and ways to avoid them:

1. Arriving late and starting late: Yes, you're busy, but when the meeting leader is late it encourages everyone to turn up late next time. Similarly, delaying starting a meeting until everyone is present sets a bad precedent. Starting on time encourages everyone to arrive on time.

2. Being too controlling or too relaxed: Chairing a meeting doesn't give you a licence to do all the talking yourself and force your ideas on everyone else. Learn to lead discussions and reach consensus. The opposite mistake is being too laissez-faire and letting everyone talk at once, whether or not their comments relate to the agenda, and paying more attention to making the meeting 'enjoyable' than to the meeting's goals. Keep the main purpose of your meeting in mind and balance maintenance and task issues.

3. Failing to inform others in plenty of time: Meeting participants need to prepare too, even when it's only to study the agenda and do a bit of thinking about it beforehand. Give participants the agenda early enough to allow them to prepare for the meeting, but don't schedule the meeting so far in advance that people misplace the agenda or forget about the meeting.

4. Failing to prepare: Remember the adage 'prior planning prevents poor performance'. Think through your objectives and the issues that the meeting needs to address, and gather the information you need beforehand.

5. Failing to record decisions and agreements: Keep a note of all action items, responsibilities assigned and decisions reached; then diarise to follow them up.

6. Inhibiting free discussion: This happens when you ask leading questions, state your opinion before hearing others' opinions, and defend rather than explore. Don't fall into the trap of cutting off anyone who disagrees with your conclusions, ideas and opinions. Instead, use different points of view as opportunities to explore issues more deeply. See yourself as the gatekeeper, coordinator and compromiser.

7. Launching straight into the agenda without attending to maintenance issues: Establish the right climate and help people orient themselves to the meeting before moving on to your first agenda item. Open the meeting on a pleasant note; welcome people and thank them for coming. Say a few words about what you intend the meeting to achieve and, when you have meeting guidelines, draw people's attention to them.

>>

8. Permitting the group to wander from the point and failing to finish on time: Allowing digressions and rambling shoptalk kills any meeting. Keep discussions on track and to the point and don't let the meeting drag on.

9. Poor sequencing of the agenda: A good agenda is important because it anchors the meeting. Follow the guidelines for preparing an agenda outlined earlier.

10. Rushing: Don't speed through the meeting without providing time for members to develop their own solution or approach. See that everyone has a chance to air their thoughts and hear everyone else's so they can develop a joint resolution.

ACTION!

You can assess your meeting skills on **CourseMateExpress** with the interactive self-test: How well do you lead meetings? You will also find a Leading meetings competencies checklist to help you prepare a development plan to improve your skills.

After the meeting

Gourd's axiom states that meetings are events where minutes are kept and hours lost.[6] When you lead the meeting well, the time isn't lost and you have something worthwhile to write up in your minutes.

Minutes are a record of the major points discussed and the conclusions reached. Even when your brief summary is only a handwritten note in your diary or journal notes in Outlook or a similar system, it's a useful memory aid. When appropriate, write up a short set of minutes to distribute to the meeting participants or post on your team's noticeboard or Intranet team room in the meetings section.

Head the minutes with the date, time and place of the meeting and who attended. You can set out the minutes in one of these ways:

* Show each agenda item in order, with a brief summary of the discussion, conclusions and decisions reached, tasks assigned and timelines for any action or follow-up action agreed, and those responsible for taking action.

* Organise the minutes into 'information shared', 'items discussed', 'decisions made', 'actions to be taken', 'pending issues', and so on, to make it easy for people to scan them.

You don't need to include every detail, just the facts, key points, important decisions, and actions to be taken by whom and by when. They should accurately reflect the meeting's tone and main themes. Show the time the meeting ended and the date, time and place of the next meeting. Transfer actions to be taken and responsibilities to the agenda for the next meeting so you can follow through on them.

ACTION!

You can find a Writing minutes template on **CourseMateExpress**.

Keep control

A clear agenda, experience and self-confidence are your best tools for making sure your meetings stay on track. Observe other good meeting leaders to see what tips you can pick up from them. You may notice that they use more direct control than usual when strong and potentially disruptive feelings are present, when the group is moving towards a decision or when time is tight.

Short of formal parliamentary procedures (described at the end of this chapter), two of the more common, less intrusive techniques for keeping control are making a short summary after each contribution and using an electronic whiteboard, flip chart or groupware to record these summaries (this is handy for writing up the minutes afterwards, too.) Non-verbally, a glance at the clock can help keep the meeting focused and moving forward.

Don't use control techniques to smother differences of opinion and strong feelings – this would probably strengthen them and increase tension or lead to groupthink.

Disruptive behaviours

What do you do when someone argues over every point, holds whispered side conversations, dominates the discussion, moves away from the topic under discussion, sits in silence or talks over everyone else? Behaviours like these present problems for meeting leaders.

The following sections examine some common disruptive behaviours with suggestions for dealing with them during the meeting. After the meeting and in private, calmly, assertively and politely speak with the participant concerned, using an 'I' message (explained on page 469). Name the behaviour you want to stop and say what you would like instead. For example, you might say to someone who held side conversations, 'Alex, when you talk while someone else is addressing the meeting, I get quite distracted. I need to have just one person speaking at a time. Can you help me out with that?'

Arriving unprepared

When a meeting participant repeatedly turns up to meetings unprepared and without the information that the rest of the meeting participants need to get on with the agenda, address the behaviour sooner rather than later. Remind the participant to prepare before the meeting and make it clear that you don't intend to make a habit of always reminding them. Discuss what steps they will take to ensure they arrive prepared in future.

Constantly criticising

Some people seem to criticise every idea, every point of view, every helpful suggestion, pointing out the downsides but seldom offering alternatives or positive suggestions in return. This behaviour saps a meeting's creativity, energy and goodwill. Don't allow it.

You could gently point out that unconstructive criticism doesn't move the meeting forward, ask what they do like about a suggestion, or ask for their thoughts on how to improve it. This might refocus them on the positive.

You could try treating comments and criticisms as though they were normal and routine by rephrasing and restating them so they appear to be conforming to the approach you want, and then asking for a response from other members. For example: 'Terry isn't convinced this approach is feasible. What could we do to make it work?'

You may decide not to invite them to your next meeting, but bear in mind that with a bit of 'retraining' they may have a useful role as devil's advocate.

Day-dreaming and hesitating

Some people let their minds wander and others may be shy or become self-conscious when speaking before a group and even when they have a good point to make, they just can't seem to find the words; others prefer to wait to be invited to contribute. Be patient and supportive to help their thoughts and ideas to see the light of day.

Encourage them to speak when you think they have a contribution to make, but don't embarrass them by asking a difficult, direct question. Instead, invite them to respond to questions you know they can answer or let them know in advance that you'll be directing a specific question to them. For example, 'Sonya, I'd like to ask you for your thoughts on this in a minute, after we've heard from Stan.' (When Stan is a bit of a digresser or a dominator, this serves the dual purpose of warning him to limit his comments.)

Summarise when the day-dreamer or hesitator is finished and thank them for their contribution. Your want to encourage them to speak so that the rest of the group can hear their worthwhile contributions.

Digressing

Questions and comments that lead the group astray are sometimes referred to as 'red herrings'. They retard progress, sidetrack meetings, and test the skill and tact of even the best meeting leader. There are several useful techniques to keep the meeting on track.

Try to link the off-point comments to the topic at hand. If that doesn't work, try summarising what has been said so far to return to the topic under discussion. Failing that, you can say, 'That's an interesting observation. How does it fit into our topic?' to highlight the digression and encourage the digresser to return to the topic. You may have to be even more direct: 'This discussion is interesting, but I suggest we postpone it until next month's meeting when I can put that topic on the agenda.' As a last resort, you may simply have to rule the discussion out of order and move on with the agenda.

Dominating

Some people just talk too much. Others keep pushing their point of view until everyone folds and sees it their way. Monopolising discussions wastes the meeting's time and destroys its sense of purpose.

When you know in advance that someone is likely to dominate a discussion, try seating them to your extreme left (or right if you are left-handed); this makes it easier to avoid seeing their attempts to get the floor. When they do get the floor, let them have a reasonable amount of time, then interrupt by saying something like, 'You've got some good points there. Now let's hear what others think and then you're welcome to respond.'

Interrupting

Some people interrupt so much that other participants just give up and yield the floor. Help them out by signalling to the chronic interrupter that talking over people is not acceptable. You could say something like, 'Hang on, Ian, let's hear the idea Kim is explaining', or 'Kim, you were starting to suggest something. Could you finish please?' Put your hand up to the interrupter as a 'stop' signal when necessary.

Failing to follow-through or speak frankly

When you suspect someone may not complete an assignment, after the meeting or informally over coffee during a break (to avoid taking up the meeting's time) ask them what might prevent them from completing the accepted assignment on time; then ask how they can prevent that and confirm that they can take the action they've agreed to.

You may occasionally sense that someone isn't expressing their true opinion or is holding back from providing information. Bring any concerns to the surface by directly asking for their opinion or what information they can add to the discussion.

Reiterating

Someone may continually repeat the same point, even when the subject has moved on. Gently remind them that their views have been heard. When you're making summaries on a whiteboard or groupware, point to the chart as visual evidence that their point has been noted.

A good general technique, especially when a meeting member is inclined to dominate a discussion, veer off point or repeat a point unnecessarily, is to nominate three or four people at a time, selecting the speakers who need to be restrained to speak first: 'John, let's hear from you first, then Jane, then Jacob, and after that Jenny.' This puts pressure on the earlier speakers to be succinct, since the people after them are waiting their turn. Should someone hog the floor anyway, remind them that there are others the meeting needs to hear from.

Side conversations

Side conversations are distracting. You can ignore them for a while but not to the point where people whispering together irritate those near them. Here are three ways to deal with the problem:

1. Break in and say, 'Excuse me. I want to have one discussion at a time. (Whisperers), are you ready to join us now?'
2. Look at the speaker (not the chatterboxes) and say, 'Excuse me, (Speaker), let's wait until we have everyone's attention'. When everyone is silent, invite the speaker to continue.
3. Look at the whisperers and ask them whether they have any comments they would like to share with the rest of the meeting.

When you don't allow side conversations, you soon won't have to worry about them at all.

⊙ IN A NUTSHELL

Four important meeting roles

Different meetings sometimes require different role-playing by the leader. Here are four roles that leaders may choose in order to produce the smoothest meeting:

1. *Gatekeeper*: ensuring everyone has the opportunity to speak
2. *Coordinator*: summarises progress and leads to the next step
3. *Compromiser*: helps people who disagree to build on their viewpoints and reach agreement
4. *Clown*: relieves tension and provides a quick mental break through humour.

⊙ ACTION!

You can find a template listing Helpful and unhelpful meeting behaviours on ⫶**CourseMate**Express. You can use it to record the type of comments people make in order to consider how best to deal with them (e.g. positive specific reinforcement for helpful meeting behaviours and 'I' messages for unhelpful behaviours).

Completing this template also highlights the strengths of different meeting members and any gaps in positive meeting behaviours, so you know which ones to encourage. You can also distribute these templates to the participants and together, identify behaviours that need to be strengthened to help your meetings succeed.

3. Leading virtual meetings

Few things tend more to alienate friendship than a want of punctuality in our engagements.

William Hazlitt (writer), *Liber amoris: Or, the new Pygmalion* (1823)[7]

People need to meet, but the further away they are from each other and the meeting location, the more costly meetings are in time, money and pollution. Hotel and meal costs may enter the equation, raising the costs further.

Virtual meetings minimise these problems. The meetings themselves are often quicker, too: first, because people are less inclined to ramble and more inclined to articulate their views concisely; and secondly, because the leader and attendees tend to plan and prepare more carefully for them (you can ensure this is the case by developing a clear meeting protocol when you first meet virtually as described on page 669. See also Figure 28.1.)

Virtual meetings – particularly web meetings – are cheaper and easier to organise than traditional meetings, giving team members, customers and suppliers greater access to each other in subgroups or the entire team or supply chain. You can meet more often, speeding communication, decision-making, discussion and information sharing. Members of virtual teams can even meet quickly every morning (time zones allowing), at critical stages of a project or just for the psychological satisfaction a quick 'hello' provides.

Although it is not the same as meeting in person, virtual meetings allow for interaction and immediate feedback. However, because they are not (yet) completely 'natural', people need to get used to asking questions like 'What do you think?' more often than usual and speaking more slowly than they otherwise might.

⊙ IN A NUTSHELL

Types of virtual meetings

Here is a run-down on the most widely used and increasingly popular alternatives to meeting face to face.

- *Instant messaging* or *texting*: This is a quick and efficient way to communicate short messages or ask quick questions, but written words are all you have, so misunderstandings can occur.
- *Teleconferencing* or *conference calls*: Although easy to arrange and cost-effective, your voice and words are all you have to communicate with, which can lead to misunderstandings, and interactions can be a bit unnatural.

>>

- *Videoconferencing*: This is not a cheap option and some videoconferencing equipment is somewhat 'jerky' and artificial. The latest telepresence or 'halo rooms' let people meet around a virtual conference room and participants feel as though they're in the same room, which improves visibility and interaction and smooths communications; although still expensive, payback is quick when compared with air fares.
- *Webconferencing*: Real-time conversations between people at multiple locations using the Internet or Intranet are a cost-effective way to achieve real-time meetings, even though interactions can be delayed or stilted.

One-off virtual meetings

When you're organising a one-off webconference, videoconference or teleconference, be considerate of those in other time zones when deciding the time. Send out the agenda and supporting documents in plenty of time to allow people to prepare. Include a list of participants by location, balancing the number of participants from each location when possible. Attach any other pertinent information, such as the start and finish times of the meeting in local times (and emphasise that the meeting will start and finish on time), locations and contact details of participants, and their job titles and phone numbers. (PDFs display and print more predictably than other document formats.)

Detail any information or material that participants need to have at the meeting. For example, when participants don't know each other, ask them to be ready to give a 30-second general background introduction of themselves. This helps participants know how the other members can contribute and gets everyone used to speaking and to hearing the sound of others' voices and, when it's a video or webconference, seeing them. For videoconferences and webconferences, you can ask people to bring large tent-type name cards and to write their names on them using a marker pen. Confirm that everyone can hear (and see, when it's a videoconference or webconference) clearly. This groundwork helps people settle in comfortably and sets up good dynamics for the rest of the meeting.

When a video director isn't assigned to you for a videoconference, familiarise yourself and the participants with the equipment when you need to. Know where the controls are, how to zoom in, pan out and sweep from side to side, where to position your documents or diagrams for participants to refer to, and so on. Ask someone to operate cameras, microphones and lights, as it is difficult to lead the meeting and act as technician at the same time.

Depending on your organisation's protocol, you may decide to email a reminder to participants a few days before the conference, confirming the details.

 FYI

Virtual meeting etiquette
Etiquette in meetings produces a common level of courtesy, which is essential when people come together for any reason. You can apply these basic courtesies to your meeting:
- Avoid unnecessary extraneous noise (e.g. such as shuffling feet, tapping pencils), which the microphone picks up.
- Be courteous and tactful so your comments aren't taken the wrong way in the absence of body language cues.

>>

- Don't hold side conversations. When you need to speak to someone in the room, mute your microphone.
- Don't interrupt someone who is speaking.
- Speak slowly and clearly, and avoid jargon and expressions that may not be familiar to everyone.
- When you didn't hear a comment, ask the speaker to repeat it.

Teleconferences

When a teleconference lasts more than 30 minutes, assess the mood of the participants occasionally. Hear from each site ('Location A, how are you going?' or 'Location B, do you have any questions?'). If someone hasn't said anything for a while, ask them to contribute: 'Sam, we haven't heard from you for a while. Can you add something at this point?'

Until people get to know each other and can recognise each other's voices, ask them to say their name when they speak and the name of anyone they may be addressing a question to; for example, 'This is Graham. I'd like to ask Pat …'

Lengthy teleconferences that cover several agenda items can be trying. Because people avoid making distracting 'uh huh' sounds that could replace non-verbal nods and eye contact, it can sometimes feel like you're speaking into empty space. And without the visual element to anchor people's attention, minds can wander.

● THEORY TO PRACTICE

Tips for teleconferences and audio-only web meetings

All you need to have for a webconference are an Internet connection, microphone, speakers and software to facilitate the conference. Some software allows you to include 'live' video (which needs a webcam, or digital video camera) and real-time collaboration.

Here are some 'To dos' for basic, audio-only meetings:

- Let people know if you leave the room so they don't address comments to you and get no response.
- Sit up straight and wear a pleasant expression on your face. Your expression is reflected in your voice.
- When some people are face to face and others virtual, the virtual people can fade out as the face-to-face people start talking to each other and the virtual participants find it difficult to follow them. So when some meeting members work at the same site, ask them to sit in different rooms rather than cluster around a speaker. This 'levels the playing field' and encourages equal attention from everyone.
- When you can't see everyone, it's easy to forget who is actually 'present'. Draw your own 'map' to keep fully tuned in. Write the names of those present on a piece of paper and put it in front of you. If it helps, draw it as you would if people were sitting around a conference table.

Videoconferences and webconferences

Videoconferences and webconferences let you bring far-flung people together in real time, where they can see each other as they work their way through the agenda. They can see slides and videos together and work on documents together using interactive features such as screen-sharing.

There are several videoconference options to select from:

- *Chair controlled*: One site is designated as the 'chair' site and all sites see the chair.
- *Continuous presence video*: The video is segmented into four quadrants, each displaying a different site simultaneously.
- *Leader controlled*: The team leader can see, and be seen by, all team members.
- *Telephone-only participation*: When someone can't get to a site with the necessary equipment or is delayed in transit, they can still participate using audio-only capability. That is, they can hear and be heard but cannot see or be seen by the other participants.
- *Voice-switched video*: Everyone sees the current speaker and the current speaker sees the image of the last speaker.

The ultimate is webconferencing using collaborative technology. This allows you to have a totally interactive meeting in which meeting participants can share documents online, simultaneously exchanging, viewing and working on them. For example, team members can collaboratively edit a document or spreadsheet of any file type and receive emails or Really Simple Syndication (RSS) alerts when changes or comments are made on documents or a project. An additional window displays the data file, which can be moved around when it obstructs the view of any of the other quadrants showing other conference participants. Collaboration tools also let you:

- create a virtual team room where you can conduct real-time brainstorming and problem-solving sessions, meetings and training
- make 10 to 15 participants at a time visible during team meetings (depending on the software)
- record a meeting or a presentation
- share files
- share software applications
- take live minutes 'on screen'
- use a 'whiteboard' interactively to diagram, capture and share ideas
- use audio controls to mute or 'unmute' participants and control their volume levels.

You can even gauge the mood of meeting members with mood indicators!

Your organisation might own its own equipment and software or it might go through a web-conference hosting company or videoconferencing provider.

THEORY TO PRACTICE

Secure meetings, even at a distance

Some organisations use webconferencing for online project team meetings between, for example, an engineering head office and its engineers in the field, speeding up problem-solving, troubleshooting and decision-making. Teams can meet securely to discuss sensitive documents and can view and revise complex technical drawings and plans.

Webconference security

During a webconference, data is stored temporarily on an Internet server that belongs either to the organisation or to the company providing hosting services in the cloud. It is at this time that the data is most vulnerable to hackers. Even when your organisation uses its own in-house network that doesn't use the Internet, all conferencing and collaboration tools should defend the traffic that flows between the participants through encryption (data scrambling) with Secure Socket Layer (SSL) technology to make the data unreadable.

Ideally, each computer involved in the conference should have a digital security certificate that is used to authenticate the computer to the conference host computer. You can assign longer term security certificates to permanent team members, provide contractors with security certificates that last the length of their contract and give temporary team members (e.g. external consultants or specialists) certificates of a shorter duration that you specify.

THEORY TO PRACTICE

Tips for videoconferences and webconferences

Cameras and their speakers are turned on all the time in videoconferencing and webconferencing so be aware of what you're doing and how you can make your colleagues comfortable in this environment. Here are some tips:

- Avoid side conversations because the voice-activated microphones pick them up and the camera refocuses on you.
- When your facility has a third monitor that allows you to preview your image, use it.
- Keep in mind that there can be a lag between the spoken word and when it's heard.
- Keep reasonably still and refrain from hand gestures to avoid creating distractions. Use slower and smaller movements than you would in a face-to-face meeting and avoid jerky movements, which the video exaggerates.
- Mind your body language. People may be able to see you even when you aren't the one talking.
- Sit face-on to the camera rather than at an angle, and when you have a choice, go for full- or wide-angle shots rather than close-ups.
- Smile and maintain 'eye' (camera) contact. Use the monitor to see others and the camera to make eye contact with them.
- Stay two to three metres away from the camera and don't lean into it or toward the listeners because that looks aggressive.
- Watch your wardrobe. Go for plain, solid colours except for white (which is 'too hot' for the camera), red (which 'bleeds') and black. Avoid small designs, patterns, plaids or stripes (which the camera distorts, making them 'bleed' and 'move').

Run effective virtual meetings

Leading virtual meetings is the same as leading actual meetings, only with complications. People are social and it's normal to want to feel connected with each other; chatting about what's going on in their lives, sharing stories and so on, before a meeting begins is a good way to do that. When people are in the same place, it's easy. It's also good for productivity because people are more willing to help each other out when they know and like each other as people. A group of independent workers can never achieve the results or innovate as much as a team that pulls together.

The informal chitchat and banter is more difficult in virtual meetings and the lack of personal connection can hamper productivity. So it's a good idea to begin the meeting by checking in with everyone in turn and asking them to share something that's happened in their lives since the last meeting, either personal or work related. This makes people feel part of the team and helps them get to know each other and build bonds.

Take particular care when some members are not native English speakers. They need to feel comfortable so they are willing to contribute when they have something to say. Going around the room so people can speak helps in three ways:

1. It helps the non-native English speakers tune in their 'English ears'.
2. It reminds everyone to take care with how they speak and to listen sharply, as accents can be tricky.
3. It reminds people to tune in their cultural sensitivities.

As with any meeting, prepare and post the agenda. At the beginning of the first meeting, agree meeting protocols like those shown in Figure 28.1 on page 939. It is particularly important participants agree not to multitask, as this is often common in virtual meetings, especially conference calls. People need to be fully mentally present and engaged and not working on another task or checking emails. Set that as an expectation from the beginning and involve everyone in contributing to the meeting frequently to reduce the multitasking temptation. Also agree how meeting members should gain the floor when someone has something to contribute.

Open by welcoming everyone and confirming what the meeting is intended to achieve. Include something unexpected or some interesting news in your opening comments to make your virtual meetings special, so no one wants to miss them. Then move on to your first agenda item. Make it a topic that gets people talking.

Keep to the agenda and for meetings that run longer than an hour, remember to schedule short breaks. End the meeting as you would any meeting: summarise the key points and confirm decisions and action items. Acknowledge what the meeting has achieved. Thank participants for their time and attention. And confirm when you will post the minutes (when you don't put up live minutes on screen).

Follow up as you would with any meeting, too. Post the minutes showing key information such as actions and responsibilities that team members can check off as they complete, discussion points and issues, decisions and next steps. Make a checklist of action items to follow up on before the next meeting.

4. Attending meetings

Meetings ... are rather like cocktail parties. You don't want to go but you're cross not to be asked.

Jilly Cooper (British author), *How To Survive from Nine to Five*, 1970[8]

Meetings can eat up your day when you let them. So before agreeing to attend, find out specifically what the meeting is intended to achieve ('just talking through' something isn't good enough). Then you can decide whether you could achieve the same goal differently or whether someone else could or should attend in your place.

Negotiate the length of short informal meetings in advance so they don't devour all of your time. Ask people how much time they think they'll need and agree when the meeting will begin and end. Open-ended meetings can go on forever; prevent this by asking the person to send you a short, specific agenda estimating how long to spend on each topic.

When a meeting has several agenda items and will take considerable time, you may be able to arrange with the chairperson to drop in and out so that you're present only for the items that directly concern you.

Participate professionally

Even when you are participating in a meeting rather than leading it, you still have some work to do. How effectively you participate is an important factor in how you are perceived in the organisation (and hence in your career success). Here's how to be an effective meeting participant.

Before the meeting, think about the items on the agenda and do any research that would help you make a worthwhile contribution. Bring any information and paperwork you might need with you, along with copies for others when this would be helpful.

Arrive fully prepared and on time – tardiness is disrespectful to others. Bring some work to do while you wait for a meeting to start to give you a choice between networking or getting on with other work rather than killing time until the meeting begins. Unless you're expecting an important call or message, turn off your mobile phone, or switch it to silent and explain to the meeting leader why you need to leave it on; should you need to take an urgent call, leave the room.

Speak up when you can contribute and take care to use only your share of the speaking time. To project a professional impression and avoid rambling, organise your thoughts in your head or on paper before speaking.

Except in formal meetings where you address the chair, speak to the entire meeting. Keep your contributions relevant to the subject under discussion. Make your point succinctly; you can pull out some of your detailed information when people have questions. Omit personal stories unless they make a point and avoid 'inside jokes'. Make all your comments clear and loud enough to be heard and make eye contact with everyone, not just one or two other meeting participants.

Encourage good ideas suggested by others and don't play devil's advocate for the sake of it. To disagree without being disagreeable, paraphrase the other person's point before expressing your reservations, concern or confusion in a way that shows you're open to alternatives, and offer an alternative or a way to make the idea work better. Don't set a pattern of always disagreeing or seeing the negative side; offer solutions and encouragement too.

 FYI

Different strokes

The concept of 'men are from Mars, women are from Venus' has grown from research beginning over 40 years ago. Women's speech, for example, typically displays a range of features that mark it as inferior and project uncertainty and lack of authority.[9] Here are some examples:

- *Apologising more*: 'Sorry, but I think ...'
- *Avoiding coarse language*
- *Emphasising words through voice tone*: 'I'm *very* annoyed with you.'
- *Empty adjectives*: divine, gorgeous
- *Hedging*: 'sort of', 'it seems like'
- *Hyper-correct grammar and pronunciation*
- *Indirect questions*: 'Gee, it's hot in here' rather than 'Does anyone object if I open a window?'
- *Fewer jokes*
- *Speaking less often*
- *Super polite*: 'Would you mind...', 'Is it ok if ...?'
- *Tag questions*: 'I don't think that will work, do you?'

Other research shows that men more often nominate topics, interrupt more often, hold the floor for longer and display other dominant behaviours.[10]

>>

Does this reflect differences between male and female behaviour of two generations ago, or is male conversational style naturally more competitive and female conversational style naturally more cooperative? Do Generation X, Y and Z males continue to dominate meetings and speak even when they have nothing of value to contribute and do women of those generations still wait their turn (permission) and contribute only when they're sure they have something useful to add? And if so, is this a gender issue or does culture come into play? For example, are only Western Anglo-Saxon men and women like this?

Margaret Byrne, researching behavioural differences between the sexes during meetings, found that personalities, culture and generational differences also play a part. For example, Phuc Dung, a migrant from Vietnam, felt forgotten in meetings, which made him feel he was unfairly treated. Even after 14 years in Australia, he was not willing to interrupt a speaker, preferring to wait to be addressed. Other meeting participants saw him as 'a good bloke' and didn't call on him because they didn't want to embarrass him or put him on the spot when he had nothing to say.[11]

When you're asked to contribute and you don't have anything to say, it's fine to say, 'I can't add anything to what's been said' or 'I don't know anything about that and I don't want to confuse the issue.'

Don't explain other people's remarks: 'I think what Bill is trying to say is ...' When someone interprets your comments incorrectly, correct them: 'Actually, Bill, that isn't quite what I meant. What I meant was ...'

When you let people interrupt you, they will continue to do so. Keep the floor by saying: 'I have three points I'd like to make. First ...' Keep numbering as you go so that people know you haven't finished when you pause to draw breath. Keep your points brief, though!

Follow through on any promises you make, tasks assigned to you or actions you agree to take. Unless you have a good reason, avoid accepting tasks that do not properly belong to you or your work group. Otherwise, you could end up being too snowed-under to get your own work done.

5. Understanding meeting protocol

Robert's Rules provides for constructive and democratic meetings, to help, not hinder, the business of the assembly. Under no circumstances should 'undue strictness' be allowed to intimidate members or limit full participation.

Henry M Roberts, *Robert's Rules of Order* (1915)[12]

Meetings can vary greatly in their degree of formality. Some meetings are very informal and seem more like a conversation among colleagues. Don't let the relaxed and casual atmosphere fool you. People discuss some very significant matters and make important decisions in informal meetings. Most work team meetings and many other meetings that managers attend are run informally. This is particularly so with smaller groups and people who meet together regularly.

At the other extreme are formal meetings that follow parliamentary protocol. The meeting's *constitution* is the list of written rules that guide how the meeting is conducted and how many members must be present before the meeting can take place. This is called a *quorum*.

Official meetings between employer and employee representatives (e.g. workplace bargaining) and many health and safety committees and teams, and committees made up of people who don't know each other well and are brought together temporarily for special purposes, often use formal procedures. So do professional bodies and associations, local councils and boards of directors.

Formal meeting roles and protocol

When you first join a committee or an organisation that follows formal meeting protocol, find out the rules, the terms of reference they follow, and a bit about the other members, the informal power structure and 'pecking order' of members. Try to gain an understanding of the 'politics', or informal alliances between members, too. How do people dress for the meetings? Follow their lead. Aim to observe the way the meetings work for your first two or three meetings so that you don't make any unintentional blunders.

People are elected or appointed to carry out certain important duties on behalf of the meeting. The *chairperson* develops the agenda before the meeting, often inviting participants to submit agenda items for it and including them when they are appropriate for that particular meeting. The chairperson also sees that everyone who is necessary to the meeting is invited to attend.

A chairperson leads the meeting, ensures that the constitution of the meeting is followed, maintains a sense of order and direction, opens and closes the meeting, introduces each topic on the agenda, calls on members to speak and calls for votes. The person in the chair should deal impartially and objectively with all sides of the issues being discussed.

Like any good meeting leader, a good chairperson gives each participant the opportunity to speak and ensures that no one dominates or in any other way disrupts the meeting. Participants of formal meetings make remarks only when invited to do so by the chairperson and these remarks are usually made 'through the chair' – that is, they are directed to the chairperson.

The *secretary* is responsible for arranging a suitable venue for the meeting, preparing and distributing the agenda before each meeting along with any necessary background information or paperwork for members to refer to, carrying out any correspondence or other written communication as instructed by the meeting, and preparing and distributing the minutes of each meeting as directed by the chairperson.

The official meeting secretary lists *attendance* (who attends the meeting), *apologies* received (advance notification from any members not able to attend the meeting) and *absences* (people who didn't turn up and omitted to put in an apology). These are included in the minutes.

The first item on the agenda of most formal meetings is a call by the chairperson for members to approve the minutes of the previous meeting. This means they agree that the minutes accurately reflect the previous meeting. The chairperson then signs the minutes and places them in a special minutes file for storage and future reference.

Before members can discuss or vote on a topic, someone must *propose* it as a *motion*. Another member must then *second* it. This ensures that two people (at least) agree that the matter is worth discussing. In very formal meetings, the chairperson gives the floor alternately to people speaking for the motion and people speaking against it.

A meeting member can propose an *amendment* to the wording of a motion before it is voted on. Another meeting member then needs to second the amendment. After the discussion and before the group votes on a motion, the chairperson gives the original proposer the right of reply to say a few final words about it.

Meeting members then vote *for* or *against* the motion or they can *abstain* (refrain) from voting. Voting can be by ballot, verbally or by a show of hands. When a majority of meeting participants vote in favour of a motion, it is *carried* and becomes a *resolution*. The secretary records this, as well as the key points of the discussion (who said what), in the minutes.

CourseMateExpress

Go to http://login.cengagebrain.com to access CourseMate Express, your online study tool for *Management Theory & Practice*. CourseMate Express brings chapter concepts to life with interactive learning, and study and exam preparation tools:

- Test your skills in different aspects of management with interactive self-tests and simulations.
- Watch videos that show how real managers operate in real businesses.
- Test your understanding of the changing world of management by taking the revision quiz.

QUICK REVIEW

1. Review the useful task and maintenance functions meetings can serve and discuss whether these apply to actual and virtual meetings alike. Which task and maintenance issues do meeting leaders need to be most alert to in actual meetings? In virtual meetings?
2. List seven things you can do to lead a productive meeting, whether actual or virtual, and explain why they're important.
3. Briefly explain the purpose of agendas and minutes and what they should include, and discuss whether it is preferable to have them for all meetings, however informal.
4. What are the main responsibilities of people attending a meeting? How does honouring these responsibilities help a meeting succeed and how does failing to honour them hamper a meeting's success?

BUILD YOUR SKILLS

1. What types of meetings have you participated in? Consider meetings with your family, friends and fellow students, clubs and organisations to which you belong, as well as work meetings. Describe four of these meetings, commenting on their degree of formality and their effectiveness. Discuss the skills needed by the leader and the participants in each. In retrospect, what could the meeting leader and the participants have done to make the meetings more effective?
2. Thinking about both the task and the maintenance needs of a meeting, discuss the steps that leader-managers can take to ensure that their work group reaches consensus at a meeting.
3. Attend a formal meeting at your college or local council and observe the protocol followed. What helpful and unhelpful meeting behaviours did you observe? What was their effect? How did the chairperson respond to those behaviours? Prepare a short report summarising it.

WORKPLACE ACTIVITIES

1. Referring to Case study 9.2 on page 284, discuss the types of meetings this team has and how they contribute to the culture and productivity of the team.
2. Develop and distribute an agenda for a meeting at your workplace.
3. Take and prepare minutes for a meeting at your workplace.
4. Lead an informal meeting at your workplace using the skills and approaches described in this chapter.

CASE STUDY 28.1

GATHERING GOOD IDEAS

You manage a department with 26 employees divided into three work groups, each with a team leader. As Australia Day approaches and the general workload eases up a bit, you think it might be a good idea for your department to show its appreciation to its internal and external suppliers and customers in a fun way. You don't want this to involve great expense but you do want to do something a bit different that will have an impact. You decide to canvass your staff to see what ideas they can come up with.

Questions

1. What type of meeting (or meetings) would you hold for this purpose and how would you organise it (or them)?
2. Would you ask all employees to one big meeting, or would you hold two or three small meetings? What would your cut-off point be in terms of numbers?
3. What would you say to open the meeting? How would you proceed from there?

CASE STUDY 28.2

ELECTRIC COMPONENTS COMPANY

As his first assignment with the Electric Components Company, Frank Romanowski was placed in charge of the company's central store. The company is a large, nationally known business engaged in the design, manufacture and sale of a wide range of electronic products. Amplifiers, recorders, speakers and transmitters are just a few of its products. Commonly used parts in these products are stocked and issued to factory sub-stores from one centralised store. More than 10 000 different parts are stocked, including various sizes and types of bolts, circuit boards, nuts and panel screws.

As a recent graduate, Frank is eager to put his studies to use and make a good impression. To this end, he is keen to introduce improvements. One of the problem areas he identifies is maintaining a sufficient stock of 72 different sizes and lengths of screws and nuts. He wonders about the necessity of the various sizes and decides to see what can be done to reduce the number.

On checking product specifications, he finds that the design engineers have specified for each product that a screw must extend beyond the nut exactly two threads. This, he discovers, accounts in part for the large variety of screw lengths he is required to stock. Furthermore, he finds that each design engineer chooses whatever diameter screw he or she feels is appropriate for the product at the time. This accounts in part for the variety in the diameter of the screws. In general, the number of threads per millimetre is fairly standard.

After talking to several of the design and product engineers, Frank believes that the company can reduce the variety of screws stocked. Accordingly, he prepares a report for management showing the excess dollars tied up in the allegedly needless varieties of screws. The plant manager is impressed with the report and decides to call a meeting to discuss the subject further, asking Frank to chair the meeting.

Questions

1. Around what theme should Frank organise the meeting?
2. Who should he invite to attend?
3. Draft a possible agenda for the meeting. What, if any, background information should accompany the agenda when Frank sends it out?
4. Should this meeting be formal or informal? Why?
5. What can Frank do before the meeting to help ensure that his ideas are accepted? (Refer to the section 'Promote your ideas' in Chapter 8 if you need some ideas.)

CHAPTER

29

ENSURING A SAFE AND HEALTHY WORKPLACE

OVERVIEW

Of the 12.5 million Australians who were employed during 2013–14, 537 500 people were injured at work – this equates to 4.3%, or 43 out of every 1000 workers – and 61% of those injured people were men. Most work-related injuries come from sprains, strains, cuts and chronic joint and muscle conditions. About 56% of injured employees receive workers compensation.[1]

In 2011–12, 120 155 serious workers compensation claims (11.4 per 1000 employees) and 169 workers compensation fatality claims were accepted; 89.2% of the fatality claims were due to injury and 10.8% to disease, such as occupational cancers and cardiovascular disease. (The figure for fatality claims is underestimated because some fatalities involved no dependents to lodge a claim and others were self-employed workers.)[2]

The typical workers compensation claim involves four weeks off work, although 25% involve more than 12 weeks off work. One in four compensation claims involve the use of non-powered hand tools or equipment and one in five involve an injury to the back.[3]

Workplace accidents affect individuals, the community and organisations. Their social and economic costs are immense, with employers bearing 3% of the costs, employees 49% of the costs and the community 47% of the costs. The average cost to a worker affected by work-related disease (e.g. contact dermatitis, infectious parasitic diseases, mental disorders, musculoskeletal disorders, respiratory diseases and noise-induced hearing loss) is $87 800, and the average cost due to an injury is $52 400. The cost to the community is $65 200 for a disease and $57 100 per incident or injury, while the overall cost to the Australian economy is estimated at $57.5 billion a year, or 5.9% of the gross domestic product.[4]

1. Are you familiar with the recent nationally harmonised workplace health and safety legislation?
2. Are you aware of the consultative arrangements required by workplace health and safety legislation and can you explain how consultation can assist in promoting a safe and healthy workplace?
3. Do you understand the causes and effects of accidents and how to investigate accidents?
4. Can you identify and control hazards to foster a safe workplace?

This chapter concentrates on workplace health and safety legislation and your day-to-day responsibilities for protecting employees' physical safety. Chapter 30 examines your responsibilities for protecting employees' dignity and well-being – the psychological aspect of workplace health and safety.

Workplace health and safety in the office

After thanking everyone for their time, Michael opens the monthly staff meeting. 'As you know, I've spoken with most of you, as well as our cleaning contractors, and studied our accident and incident books. I've now completed my risks assessment. I'll give each of you a copy in a minute and I'll also post one on our notice board. First, I'd like to say that we're doing a great job and we've reduced our injuries by 40%, which I think is fantastic, although it's stating the obvious to say that I know we'd all like to have zero injuries. Let me go over the hazards I think we need to pay a bit more attention to.

'Slips and trips are still on the agenda, even though our housekeeping is generally excellent and Ben has done a terrific job making sure there aren't any trailing cables or leads and everyone is doing their bit keeping work areas clear. The key thing we still need to improve is our housekeeping in the kitchen, like wiping up spills immediately so no one can slip and fall. That's up to everyone so let me thank you in advance for doing the right thing there. And let me now unveil the safety poster I bought us as a reminder: 'A spill ... a slip ... a hospital trip.'

'And one more reminder: the trolley is there to be used, so please use it whenever you're moving boxes of paper and other heavy items. Back injuries hurt and they just aren't worth the risk.

'The next item on my checklist is work stations. Everyone seems happy with our ergonomic campaign and I'm pleased to say, since we've been paying more attention to posture, glare and so on, the injury book is satisfyingly empty of those type of injuries. So keep it up, keep taking regular breaks and keep changing your activities regularly – standing up and moving every 30 minutes or so – maybe walk up and down the stairs rather than take the lift. I'll hand over to Amy now so she can brief us on the ergonomics checklist for the induction program that she's prepared. Amy?'

1. Understanding the legislative framework

> Creating a safe work environment is critical to the success of your business, and is one of the best ways to retain staff and maximise productivity.
>
> Australian Government, 'Workplace health and safety (WHS)'[5]

How would you feel if someone on your work team was badly injured or killed? How would you like to be the one to take the bad news to the family? No one wants this.

The Commonwealth *Work Health and Safety Act 2011*[6] came into force on 1 January 2012. Administered by Comcare (http://www.comcare.gov.au), the Act seeks to protect Australian workers from workplace death, disease and injury. It covers people at any workplace, including state and local government premises, private offices and home offices, mobile worksites, workshops and factories. That is, everywhere people work and anywhere people go while at work. When employees leave their employer's premises in the course of their duties, their workplace goes with them.

The Act places a duty of care on employers to ensure, so far as is reasonably practicable (i.e. realistically possible), the health, safety and welfare of employees and other people on their premises, including self-employed people, contractors, voluntary workers and visitors. Employers must also protect the workplace health and safety of people in the vicinity of their premises from risks arising from their activities. They must also consult with employees to determine how best to reduce risks arising from work activities and comply with their other workplace health and safety (WHS) responsibilities.

Detailed *regulations* and *codes of practice* and a system of advice, compliance activities, education, inspection and, where appropriate, fines and prosecution, support the Act. Figure 29.1 shows the relationship between the Act and its supporting regulations and codes.

Acts: Set principles and philosophy – the general duties of care applying to employees, self-employed persons, employees, etc. It enables codes of practice to be approved.

Regulations: Pick up particular issues of the Act.

Codes of practice: Give practical guidelines for complying with a general duty under the Act or putting a specific duty under the relevant regulation into effect to eliminate or reduce risks to health, safety and welfare. Although codes are not mandatory, because you can comply with the Act or a regulation in some other way, if you comply with the code, you are probably complying with the provisions of the Act or relevant regulation.

Australian standards: Provide details of how to comply with Regulations and Codes of practice. Safe Work Australia develops Standards (e.g. for atmospheric contaminants in the occupational environment, classifying hazardous substances, manual handling, manual tasks, noise, safe working in a confined space, the storage and handling of workplace dangerous goods, and for construction work). They are intended to guide organisations in their operations and are non-prescriptive models that detail not what to do but focus on the desired outcome or standard to be achieved.

FIGURE 29.1 Workplace health and safety legislation in Australia

Serious stuff

The Commonwealth *Work Health and Safety Act 2011* imposes penalties on individuals and organisations who, by their acts or omissions, put others at risk. Companies and individuals found to be negligent in WHS matters can be fined and/or prosecuted. For example, an employee engaging in reckless conduct can be fined $300 000 or given five years imprisonment, or both. A person conducting a business who acts recklessly can be fined $600 000 or given five years imprisonment, or both; a body corporate acting recklessly can be fined $3 million. Failing to comply with a WHS duty that exposes someone to a risk of death, serious injury or illness brings fines of $150 000 for employees, $300 000 for persons conducting a business or $1.5 million for a body corporate.[7]

Employers cannot discriminate against employees who exercise their rights under the Act. For example, for acting as, having acted or proposing to act as a WHS representative or a member of a WHS committee or for raising a concern about workplace health and safety with management, an inspector, a WHS representative, a WHS committee member or another employee. Discriminatory conduct includes dismissal or termination of employment or a contract for services, altering the duties or position of an employee to the employee's detriment, refusing or failing to offer to engage someone, or treating someone less favourably due to their WHS activities.

It is also unlawful for employers to assist, authorise, encourage, induce, instruct or request another person to engage in discriminatory conduct. To do so carries an individual penalty of $100 000 and a penalty to a body corporate of $500 000.

As with any legislation, WHS legislation can make a workplace only as safe as its safety culture dictates. Every leader-manager is important in setting a good example in upholding not only the law but also the spirit of the law. As the safety slogan goes, 'Safety is about doing the right thing – even when no one is looking'. And that's what a safety culture is all about.

Inspectors and notices

Inspectors can enter any workplace, with or without notice and with or without permission, to assess compliance with the legislation and all employees are required to provide reasonable assistance. Hindering or obstructing an inspector or inducing someone else to do so is an offence carrying a penalty of $10 000 for an individual and $50 000 for a body corporate. Assaulting, threatening or intimidating an inspector carries penalties of $50 000 and/or two years imprisonment for an individual and a fine of $250 000 for a body corporate.

When inspectors believe a provision of the Act is contravened or likely to be contravened, they issue a written *improvement notice* to remedy the contravention or prevent it from occurring, stating the date by which this must be done. Inspectors can verbally issue a *prohibition notice* for activities they believe involve a serious risk to health or safety with later confirmation in writing. *Non-disturbance notices* are given to preserve a site at which a notifiable incident has occurred for up to seven days. Notifiable incidents are those involving:

- a death
- serious injury or illness (one that could be considered to require treatment as an in-patient in a hospital or medical treatment within 48 hours of exposure to a substance)
- a dangerous incident (one that exposes someone to a serious risk to workplace health and safety, such as an uncontrolled escape, spillage or leakage of a substance; an uncontrolled implosion, explosion or fire; or an electric shock).

Employers are required to notify Comcare of notifiable incidents as soon as reasonably possible.

Inspectors can also issue an *infringement notice* based on reasonable belief that a person has contravened the Act. The notice explains the contravention, the maximum penalty, when and where the contravention occurred, the amount payable under the notice and an explanation of how the payment is to be made. When an infringement notice is paid within 28 days, there is no admission of guilt or liability and no prosecution is made.

Inspectors can also mediate between employees and management on WHS matters; for example, concerning disagreements about membership of WHS committees and paying for WHS training.

Employers' responsibilities

Safety begins at the top. The ultimate responsibility for the health, safety and welfare of employees and others at the workplace ultimately rests with employers. As Figure 29.2 shows, employers' responsibilities for providing safe systems of work can be grouped into eight interconnected areas. (Apart from employee welfare, which is explained in Chapter 30, these areas are reviewed in this chapter.)

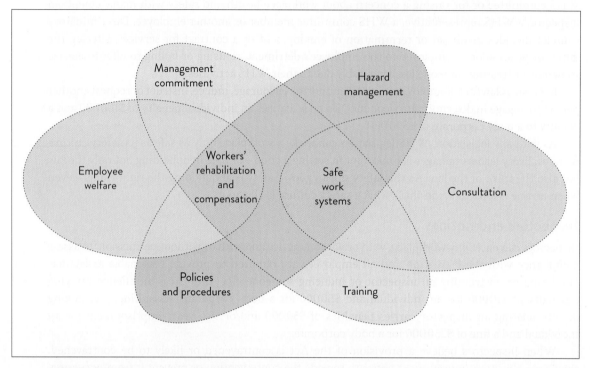

FIGURE 29.2 Employers' responsibilities for providing safe systems of work

Management commitment

Senior management must understand the philosophy and principles of managing the organisation with regard to WHS matters. The CEO or another senior person must be fully conversant with the relevant legislation and ensure that the organisation takes all possible steps to comply with it. That person must understand the hazards and risks associated with the organisation's operations and ensure that appropriate resources and processes are available, and used, to eliminate or minimise those hazards and risks.

Senior managers must assess the effectiveness of WHS measures, ensure that employees adhere to them and ensure that information about accidents is properly recorded, considered and acted on. They should give safety matters the same degree of attention as functional areas such as finance, production and supply. This is known as *due diligence*.

Employers must provide a sufficient number of employees to do a job safely and not expect people to work beyond the bounds of reasonable human effort. They must also provide appropriate WHS consultative mechanisms.

When employers cannot assess remote or offsite workplaces for risk, they should train their employees to assess the risks themselves and keep them aware of the need for vigilance in safety matters with regular updates and reminders. Home offices and mobile worksites of employees who work from a vehicle should be equipped with the same safety and emergency equipment, such as fire extinguishers, first aid kits and personal protective equipment, that is found at the employees' main workplace or base. In short, employer responsibility extends to wherever they have the capacity to act or control matters related to workplace health and safety.

◉ THEORY TO PRACTICE

NAB's starsafety initiative

NAB's WHS strategy management framework, called starsafety, is part of the bank's commitment to employee health, safety and wellbeing. The slogan 'Injuries are no accident and all injuries are preventable' aims to establish an internal mindset that injuries are not unfortunate accidents and are unacceptable.

The framework is built on five pillars: consultation and communication, effective risk management, employee well-being, increased knowledge and skills, and leadership and commitment. A consultation forum, committed leadership, improved management systems, and training programs support the five pillars.

Starsafety has had measurable success. In two years, workers compensation claims dropped 30% and lost-time injuries (those resulting in time off work of one or more days or shifts or a fatality or a permanent injury) dropped by more than 40%, resulting in improved community perceptions of the bank as a socially responsible employer, improved customer experience with employee interactions, increased employee morale and productivity, increased levels of employee engagement and retention, and tangible cost savings.[8]

Middle management should act in the same way with regard to their departments as the chief executive acts on behalf of the entire organisation. They should organise processes and workflows safely and efficiently, plan safe procedures and work systems, set up WHS systems of education and training and see that they are carried out. Middle managers should become more directly involved in the detailed activities of WHS programs than senior managers. This includes, for example, ensuring that chairs are ergonomically suitable, dangerous machines and equipment are guarded, photocopy rooms are properly ventilated and workplace temperatures are comfortable.

◉ THE STRATEGIC PERSPECTIVE

Looking after home workers

Lots of people work from home all or some of the time. This has significant WHS implications for the organisations employing them. Although, in practice, they have little control over these workers, the employers' legal duty of care, which includes providing WHS training and information, safe work systems and a safe workplace, extends to home offices.

Here are some steps you can take to look after teleworkers:

* Encourage homeworkers to create a separate work area at home.
* Ensure that home offices are set up in an ergonomically correct way, have adequate heating, lighting and ventilation, that there are sufficient power points to avoid overload and the resulting fire hazard, and are made safe by, for example, removing lifting and tripping hazards.
* Ensure teleworkers understand to report WHS concerns and incidents to you.
* Ensure emergency plans for medical treatment are in line with those for employees in the office and home workers are aware of them.
* Install smoke detectors.
* Provide a first aid kit and ask the teleworkers to keep it readily available.
* Provide a self-assessment checklist for home workers to use to check for hazards periodically or conduct periodic safety audits with them when practical.

Consultation and hazard management

Consultation and hazard management and their role in providing a safe workplace are discussed in Sections 2 and 4 in this chapter.

Policies and procedures

Senior management must develop written WHS policies, programs and procedures, make them available to all concerned and monitor their effectiveness. They should contain considerable detail about how the organisation ensures a healthy and safe working environment and describe its overall arrangements for health, safety and welfare. For example:

- how accidents are prevented and investigated
- how employees and others on the employer's premises, including members of the public, are protected from, for example, electricity, explosions, exposure to harmful substances such as asbestos and lead, falling objects, fire, noise and radiation
- how the buildings and land, and the equipment, operations and processes carried out at the workplace, are made safe
- improvement targets in key WHS areas
- the mechanisms to review the effectiveness of policies, programs and procedures
- the procedures to remove or reduce specific hazards in the organisation
- the resources available to put the policies into action
- the safety reporting and recording procedures followed
- the type of safety training and education provided.

As the safety slogan says, 'Safety rules are your best tools'. But like all policies and procedures, those relating to WHS apply to every employee, at every level and function, equally. They need to clearly state what is and is not acceptable behaviour and the consequences of unacceptable behaviour.

Where common law fits in

Common law is not written in statutes but built up over time through judges' rulings. It reflects the way judges have interpreted legislation and is based on, and sets, precedents. When common law isn't enough, or is outdated or inequitable, an Act of Parliament makes a new law and the process of interpretation and precedent setting begins again.

Employers have four basic duties under common law. They must do everything practicable to provide and maintain:

1. A safe system of work.
2. A safe workplace.
3. Competent staff.
4. Safe plant and equipment.

Safe work systems and training

Following safe and correct procedures shouldn't be an added burden or create additional steps. Rather, doing tasks safely and correctly should be part of the normal systems of work and integrated into all aspects of operational planning.

Employers must provide adequate safety training and instruction and ensure that employees understand and follow safe and correct procedures. Training needs to be ongoing and consistent to be effective.

Workers' rehabilitation and compensation

Employers are required to insure their employees against workplace disease and injury so that employees injured at work can receive weekly payments to cover loss of earnings, medical and rehabilitation expenses, and, when an injured person has to establish a new career, retraining costs. These payments are made regardless of whether the injury was the fault of the employee or the employer. When it is not possible for an injured worker to return to work because of death or disablement, lump-sum compensation payments can be made.

Employers must have a rehabilitation and return-to-work program for employees injured on the job. The aim is to get them back into the workforce as quickly as possible after suffering a work-related injury.

Workers' rehabilitation and compensation covers employees at work in any workplace, including home offices. Employers can self insure or insure through an approved insurer. Premiums are calculated according to two factors:

1. The industry category of the employer: The more dangerous the industry, the higher the premiums.
2. The individual employer's safety record: The better the organisation's safety record, the lower its premiums.

 FYI

Why don't people apply for workers comp?

The main reasons people don't apply for or receive compensation include not being aware of their right to claim a workers compensation benefit, thinking they were not eligible for compensation, and concerns about the impact of a claim on their future employment. Thirty-six per cent of employees who take five or more days off work do not apply for workers' compensation; many use personal leave instead.[9]

 THE STRATEGIC PERSPECTIVE

Environmental hazards

Pandemics and biological, chemical, nuclear and radiological incidents have WHS implications as well as the business continuity implications discussed in Chapter 23. You must not expose employees to disease-causing agents such as asbestos or radiation and you must take reasonable steps to ensure employees' work activities do not expose them to the risk of contamination from infection such as swine flu. If you know or even think an employee has been exposed to a serious virus and continue to allow that employee to come to work and come into contact with other employees or customers, you are potentially breaching your duty of care.

Your responsibilities

Leader-managers are the key people in WHS programs and represent the organisation in health, safety and welfare matters to non-management employees. They set the safety climate, make sure people work safely and are held accountable for the safe work practices of their work areas.

Your WHS responsibilities begin with inducting new employees when you explain the organisation's WHS policy and the role of others in the organisation regarding WHS matters, and show new employees the emergency procedures, safety procedures (e.g. incident reporting) and safety requirements of the work area. You must ensure all employees understand their own WHS responsibilities, identify the WHS training needs of those in your work group, and develop suitable training plans to meet those needs, both in a formal, systematic way, as well as through formal and informal on-the-job training.

It's also important to keep communicating about WHS matters so they remain in the forefront of people's minds. You also want to act as a positive role model, because your team members derive their impressions of the meaning of 'safety' from what you say and, more importantly, what you do. Safe working practices are only as good as you insist they be.

⊙ THEORY TO PRACTICE

Good housekeeping saves money and reduces injuries

Housekeeping refers to the standard of cleanliness and tidiness of a workplace. Good housekeeping is a reliable indicator of how well managed a workplace is and how safety conscious the people working there are. Creating and maintaining a clean, safe working environment is a good way to save money and boost morale and productivity as well as reduce accidents.

Consider, for instance, the large aluminium foundry in the United Kingdom where there were too many slips and trips, mostly due to poor housekeeping and poorly maintained machinery leaking oil onto the floor. The company implemented the '5S Philosophy': Sort, Set in order, Shine, Standardise and Sustain to keep up the good work.

The result:

- obvious improvements to housekeeping by marking pedestrian routes and introducing non-slip surfaces, keeping walkways clear and removing trailing floor cables, and removing clutter (by giving all items and tools a 'home' and putting them 'home' when not in use), which reduced slipping and tripping hazards and lost-time injuries and meant fewer lost items thanks to improved, more 'visible' storage
- avoiding duplication of work and purchasing unnecessary equipment by making each team responsible for its own equipment
- keeping plant and equipment clean and identifying maintenance problems at an earlier stage, which reduced production downtime and saved money
- positioning tools and equipment ergonomically which reduced strains and fatigue.

Now that everything looks under control, impressing customers, visitors and employees alike, morale has improved, as has productivity.[10] (See 'In a Nutshell: The five' S's of lean Six Sigma' on page 568 for more on the '5S Philosophy'.)

⊙ ACTION!

Do you know the actions you should be taking as a leader-manager regarding workplace health and safety? You can find a Leader-manager's WHS actions checklist on ⫶**CourseMate**Express to guide you.

Employees' responsibilities

Employees have a legal duty to cooperate with their employers in ensuring the workplace health and safety of their workplaces. This involves taking reasonable care to protect themselves and others around them: employees must not, through their acts or omissions, endanger themselves, their colleagues or members of the public.

This means, for example, that employees must ensure that they are not affected by alcohol or other drugs while at work, they must follow safety procedures and use the equipment provided for WHS purposes, and follow reasonable instructions concerning workplace health and safety. Employees should not carry out or continue with work when they have a reasonable concern that doing so would expose them to a serious risk to their health or safety; in such situations, they must notify management and remain available to carry out suitable alternative work.

2. Consulting with employees

Employers must ... Consult with all employees, including youth workers, about decisions that will affect safety in the workplace.

'Talking safety with young workers', Employee and employer WHS rights and responsibilities[11]

The Commonwealth *Work Health and Safety Act 2011* requires employers and employees to agree procedures for ongoing consultation on WHS matters. This gives employees an opportunity to influence matters affecting their health, safety and welfare, and gives organisations access to the detailed knowledge that employees have of the risks related to the work they perform. This is valuable for identifying and assessing risks and in working out effective and economical control measures.

Consultation is not one party making a decision and limiting discussion to when and how to implement it. Employees and their representatives must have access to relevant information on, for example, hazards and potential hazards, work conditions, work organisation, and plant, equipment and materials used in the workplace, and they must contribute to the decision-making process relating to WHS matters.

Consultation should begin when workplace changes are contemplated and continue as they are introduced so that employees' experience and expertise can be taken into account when it can most effectively be used. Employees should be given a reasonable opportunity to express their views and raise workplace WHS issues and should be advised of the outcome of consultations in a timely manner.

Consultation can take place directly with employees, with workplace health and safety representatives or with workplace health and safety committees. The penalty for failing to consult employees is $20 000 for an individual and $100 000 for a body corporate.

Consultation should also occur with other interested stakeholders such as suppliers, contractors, and the owner of the building where work is carried out.

> **⊙ THEORY TO PRACTICE**
>
> **When to consult employees on WHS matters**
> The Act requires consultation when:
> - assessing the risk of new processes
> - deciding how to consult with employees
> - deciding how to eliminate or minimise risk
> - deciding how to implement regulations
> - deciding how to monitor the health of employees
> - deciding how to monitor working conditions
> - deciding how to provide information and training for employees
> - deciding how to resolve workplace health or safety issues
> - identifying hazards and assessing their risk
> - making decisions about the adequacy of welfare facilities for employees
> - proposing or planning to change work or work processes that may affect the health or safety of workers
> - reviewing the effectiveness of control measures.

Workplace health and safety officers

Many medium-sized and large organisations employ a specialist workplace health and safety officer to advise on and oversee WHS matters and to take responsibility for safety and accident prevention programs. WHS officers are knowledgeable about the *Work Health and Safety Act 2011*, regulations and codes of practice, methods of investigating and preventing accidents, and the best ways to protect the organisation's workforce. Smaller organisations that don't need a full-time safety officer may appoint an existing manager to take on the responsibility of managing the safety program.

Safety officers usually report to a senior and influential person in the organisation who can help achieve its WHS goals. Although safety officers act in a support role, when they discover an imminent and serious danger during a routine hazard inspection they usually have the authority to stop the work until the problem is rectified.

Other common duties of safety officers include:
- advising and guiding line staff
- conducting safety audits
- examining plant, equipment, processes and working methods
- helping leader-managers to develop safety plans for their areas
- investigating accidents and incidents
- keeping and monitoring accident and incident records and statistics
- organising the circulation of safety information
- preparing safety instructions and advising on safe working practices
- reporting to and advising management and individual leader-managers on all safety matters
- serving on the safety committee as technical advisers
- testing fire and other emergency protection activities through drills and exercises
- training management and employees in safety matters.

Workplace health and safety representatives

An employee can request the organisation's assistance in conducting an election for one or more WHS representatives and deputy representatives to represent employees in WHS matters. Elections are carried out in work groups and representatives and deputy representatives must be from that work group. The term of office is three years, at which time representatives and deputy representatives can stand for re-election.

Deputy WHS representatives carry out the duties of WHS representatives when they are not available or are no longer able to carry out their duties. This might be because they resign in writing before the end of their period of office, leave their work group, are disqualified by a court because of improper use of their power as a representative or have disclosed information acquired as a representative for reasons other than in connection with their role as a representative, or are removed from their position by a majority of the members of the work group.

The powers and functions of WHS representatives are generally limited to their work group. An exception is when, for instance, a member of another work group asks for the representative's assistance or there is a serious risk to workplace health and safety from an immediate or imminent exposure to a hazard that affects or may affect a member of another work group.

● IN A NUTSHELL

Duties of workplace health and safety representatives

WHS representatives represent the employees in their work group in matters relating to work workplace health and safety. They:

- inquire into anything that appears to be a risk to the health or safety of workers in the work group
- investigate complaints from members of the work group relating to workplace health and safety
- monitor the effectiveness of measures taken by the organisation to comply with the WHS legislation in relation to their work group.

In order to carry out these duties, WHS representatives may:

- accompany inspectors during workplace inspections
- assist in investigating accidents and near misses (incidents)
- attend interviews concerning workplace health and safety between leader-managers or inspectors and one or more employees they represent with the consent of those employees
- inspect the workplace for hazards and compliance with WHS regulations
- receive information concerning the workplace health and safety of employees in the work group in a form that does not identify or lead to the identification of the employees (they can access personal or medical information concerning an employee with that employee's consent)
- request the establishment of a WHS committee.

When WHS representatives identify unsafe work, they should consult with management to remove the hazard or protect the employee. Only when consultative attempts fail and when representatives have completed their initial training may they direct employees to cease the unsafe work. However, when the risk is so serious and immediate or imminent that it is not reasonable to consult or attempt to remove it, they may direct the unsafe work to cease and consult with management as soon as practicable afterwards.

WHS representatives can issue a written provisional improvement notice (similar to the improvement notices inspectors issue) after consultation with management and display it as soon as possible in a prominent place near the work area affected by the notice. An inspector then reviews the notice and confirms it, confirms it with changes or cancels it.

Employers have a number of responsibilities regarding working with WHS representatives. They must:

- allow representatives access to discussions with inspectors on WHS matters
- consult them on WHS matters
- give them access to information relating to hazards and associated risks
- give them access to information relating to the workplace health and safety of employees in the work group
- give them time off work to attend approved WHS courses with their normal pay and pay the course fees and other reasonable costs associated with attending the training
- let them accompany an inspector during an inspection of their work group's workplace
- provide resources and facilities to help them perform their role as a WHS representative.

Employers must also make a list of WHS representatives and deputy representatives for each work group. They must keep it up to date and display it at the workplace where it is readily accessible to workers in the relevant work groups.

WHS representatives are key players in workplace consultation and are valuable allies for leader-managers. They should be your first point of contact in sounding out employees on WHS issues. Think of them as an extra pair of hands, ears and eyes to help you identify and control hazards, and consult them on any changes to the workplace that might affect the health, safety or welfare of the employees they represent.

FYI

What's the difference between practical and practicable?
Practical means usable. Practicable is a more specific term. It means do-able, feasible or possible.

Workplace health and safety committees

Organisations that don't already have one or more WHS committees must establish a committee within two months of being requested to do so by a WHS representative or five or more employees, or when the regulations require them to do so. Membership of the committee is agreed between employees and management, aiming to ensure that members represent a cross-section of employees from all levels and areas of the organisation.

Although there is no ideal number of committee members, at least half must be employees who are not nominated by the organisation. Elected employee members, elected WHS representatives, a WHS officer and nominated members of the management team (including leader-managers) generally participate on WHS committees. Because these committees can be an effective way to involve people in WHS matters, many organisations rotate committee membership every year or two so that as many people as possible have a chance to learn and serve in this capacity.

The number of WHS committees should be kept to the minimum required to provide the necessary coverage of the workplace and work performed. WHS committees should meet at least every three months and at any reasonable time at the request of at least half the members of the committee.

The main aim of WHS committees is to help management and non-management employees work cooperatively towards common safety goals. They tend to consider strategic health, safety and welfare issues that relate to the organisation as a whole and consider policy matters that have an organisation-wide impact rather than becoming involved in departmental or work group matters. This means they may instigate, develop and carry out measures designed to ensure workplace health and safety at work and assist in developing WHS standards, rules and procedures for the workplace. More specifically, they:

- assist employees who have suffered work-related injuries to return to work and find suitable employment for employees who suffer from any form of disability
- assist in formulating, reviewing and distributing (in appropriate languages) WHS policies and procedures
- assist in resolving WHS concerns that arise
- consult on any proposed changes to WHS policies and changes to workplace practices and procedures that may affect workplace health, safety or welfare
- develop purchasing policies for new plant, equipment and substances that address WHS issues
- develop and monitor an injury reporting system
- develop and monitor methods for conducting regular safety audits of the workplace
- develop procedures to ensure compliance with new and existing regulations and approved codes of practice
- establish a priority list of WHS issues to address
- encourage effective cooperation between management and employees when initiating, developing, carrying out and monitoring measures designed to ensure workplace health, safety and welfare
- review the availability of resources for health, safety and welfare
- review progress in rehabilitating employees who have suffered work-related injuries.

Employers must let committee members spend the time that is reasonably necessary to attend meetings and carry out their duties as a member of the committee and pay them at their normal rate of pay. They must also provide information relating to hazards and their associated risks and the workplace health and safety of employees (but not personal or medical information without the employee's consent unless it doesn't identify or lead to the identification of the employee).

IN A NUTSHELL

Effective safety committees

A number of practices contribute to the effectiveness of safety committees:

- carefully preparing an agenda for every meeting to ensure that discussions don't ramble or become confused
- encouraging a climate of openness and trust so that members feel free to express their opinions
- holding regular meetings – many organisations have found that once a month is suitable
- providing the safety committee with necessary information (e.g. accident statistics) so that it can base its recommendations on full knowledge of a situation
- receiving the full support of senior management by, for instance, allowing members time off work to attend meetings and safety training seminars, and providing a comfortable, well-furnished meeting room and secretarial assistance
- selecting members based on a genuine interest in WHS matters
- training in WHS matters for committee members.

3. Understanding accidents

The model Work Health and Safety (WHS) Act sets out certain types of workplace incidents that need to be notified to regulators. Only the most serious safety incidents are intended to be notifiable and they trigger requirements to preserve the incident site pending further direction from the regulator.

Safe Work Australia, 'Workplace incident reporting'[12]

Accidents are costly. They destroy efficiency, interfere with people's work and make everyone's job harder. Accidents are symptoms that something is wrong. They signal a lack of control over people, materials and/or processes and point to inefficient operations. It isn't just serious accidents that cause trouble; a series of minor accidents indicates inefficiency and can drive a workplace into a state of uncertainty.

But a safe workplace is more than just the absence of major and minor accidents. It's an attitude of mind and a way of approaching jobs, day in and day out.

⦿ IN A NUTSHELL

Who is most at risk for serious injury, and where?

Men lodge 64% of all serious workers compensation claims, sustaining nearly twice as many serious injuries as female employees. Workers in the agriculture, forestry and fishing industries are injured at nearly twice the national rate of employees in other industries; industries with the next three highest injury rates are transport and storage, personal and other services, and manufacturing.

Sprains and strains of joints and adjacent muscles account for 59% of serious compensation claims, lifting for 33% and falls for 22%. The most common disease claims involve disorders of muscle, tendons and other soft tissues (7%), disorders of spinal vertebrae (6%) and mental disorders (6%). The back is most often injured (22% of serious claims) followed by hands, fingers and thumbs (12%), shoulders (10%) and knees (9%).[13]

The high price of accidents

There's a safety slogan that says, 'Slip, trip and fall are four-letter words'. Accident isn't a four-letter word but it may as well be. Here's why.

Suppose an employee is injured at your workplace. Work is likely to be held up. Property, machinery or equipment may be damaged and you will probably need to arrange to have it replaced or repaired. Other employees are affected; people rushing to assist and sympathetic onlookers mean further lost output. You will be called away from whatever you are doing, for minutes or maybe hours. You may need to reorganise staff and their work, and find, and possibly train, a replacement to take on the injured worker's job. You will spend time investigating the cause of the accident and preparing an accident report. Medical expenses (e.g. for hospitalisation, doctor's visits and rehabilitation), legal costs and the cost of hiring a replacement worker may be high.

Apart from the obvious costs, there are hidden costs, such as lowered morale. There are also human costs. Pain and suffering, loss of enjoyment, permanent disability or death, loss of earnings, the psychological effects of an accident and its consequences, and disruption to the victim's private life are only some of them.

There are costs to the community, too, which must, for example, provide hospitals in which to treat the injuries and support facilities for permanently injured workers. And there are costs to society. Not only could millions of dollars be wiped off the national debt through improved WHS practices, but the number of productive working days in Australia could be increased.

In 2009, the methods of assessing the cost of work-related injuries and illnesses in Australia was reviewed. The starting cost under the new measures was $60.6 billion, 4.8% of GDP for that financial year. This will form the basis for comparison when further figures are released for the post-2009 decade and post 2019 decade.[14]

The total cost of a particular accident is difficult to measure precisely, but Figure 29.3 shows the 'iceberg effect' of some of these financial costs; it includes both direct and indirect costs.

As Figure 29.4 shows, the costs of poor workplace health and safety are like a pebble dropping into a still pool of water – the repercussions can go on and on.

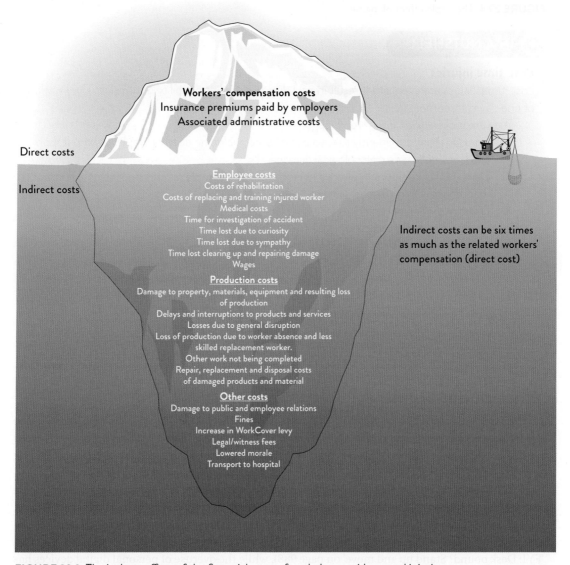

Workers' compensation costs
Insurance premiums paid by employers
Associated administrative costs

Direct costs

Indirect costs

<u>Employee costs</u>
Costs of rehabilitation
Costs of replacing and training injured worker
Medical costs
Time for investigation of accident
Time lost due to curiosity
Time lost due to sympathy
Time lost clearing up and repairing damage
Wages

<u>Production costs</u>
Damage to property, materials, equipment and resulting loss of production
Delays and interruptions to products and services
Losses due to general disruption
Loss of production due to worker absence and less skilled replacement worker.
Other work not being completed
Repair, replacement and disposal costs of damaged products and material

<u>Other costs</u>
Damage to public and employee relations
Fines
Increase in WorkCover levy
Legal/witness fees
Lowered morale
Transport to hospital

Indirect costs can be six times as much as the related workers' compensation (direct cost)

FIGURE 29.3 The iceberg effect of the financial costs of workplace accidents and injuries

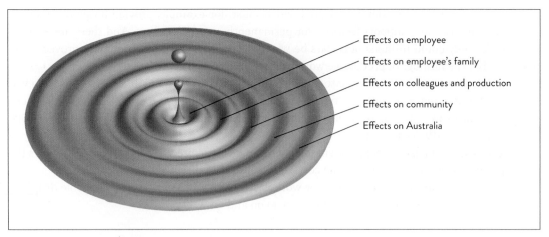

FIGURE 29.4 The ripple effect of injuries

IN A NUTSHELL

Lost-time injuries

Lost-time injuries are events that result in a fatality, permanent disability or time lost from work of one day/shift or more.[15]

They are broken down into three categories:

1. Damage that permanently alters a person's life, including death, paraplegia, amputation of a limb and severe psychological damage.
2. Damage that temporarily alters a person's life, for example, a fractured leg or a deep cut that repairs with no lasting damage.
3. Damage that inconveniences a person's life.

The *Lost-Time Injury Frequency Rate* (LTIFR) is the number of lost-time injuries within a given accounting period relative to the number of hours worked in that same period. To calculate the number of lost-time injuries per hour worked during a period, divide the number of lost time injuries by the total hours worked in a period. That always results in a tiny number, so it's multiplied by one million and reported as the number of lost-time injuries per million hours worked. (Because of the difficulties of collecting nationally consistent workers' compensation data for time lost, Safe Work Australia uses only workers' compensation claims of one or more weeks of lost time to calculate LTIFRs.)[16]

What causes accidents?

As the nature of work has changed in Australia, so has the pattern of work-related injuries. The expanding service sector and changing workplace technology, combined with high workloads, poor job design and tight deadlines, have resulted in an increase in stress and stress-related issues leading to *psychosocial problems*, such as bullying and workplace violence, as well as physical injuries.

Health concerns related to computer use include *musculoskeletal disorders* (injuries affecting the soft tissues of the body – tendons, ligaments, muscles and nerves) such as carpal tunnel syndrome, tension or motion strain from mouse usage, and eye fatigue, blurred vision and headaches from glare and poor lighting. Prolonged sitting can result in back and neck pain from poor seating posture (see 'FYI: Desk bound? Stand up and move' on page 988), while the overuse of personal digital devices has led to an increase in sprained thumbs. New and emerging technologies, for example, nanotechnology (see page 8 for more on nanotechnology), also have WHS implications.

Whatever the nature of the work, however, the fact remains that accidents don't happen by themselves. They are not 'acts of God' or bad luck. All accidents have a cause and at the root of every accident is a failure in a system of work, a machine or a piece of equipment.

This is why you should treat all accidents and near misses, or incidents, seriously and investigate them, whether or not someone has been injured. You need to determine the chain of events that led to the accident or incident and take steps to eliminate or minimise the hazards, acts or omissions that contributed to it. (See, for example, 'Theory to practice: One 'issue' too many' on page 741 and 'Theory to practice: Seven avoidable deaths, an avoidable war and more' on page 540 to find out how near misses can lead to major accidents when not attended to.)

The most common factors contributing to accidents are:
* faulty planning of work processes
* inadequate supervision
* inadequate training
* incorrect work practices
* miscellaneous conditions such as weather (for instance, excessive heat) or time of day (for instance, at the end of a shift)
* output goals set too high, forcing people to hurry and cut corners
* personal factors such as stress, error or inappropriate behaviour
* poor housekeeping
* poor job design
* poor machinery and equipment maintenance
* poor safety culture.

● IN A NUTSHELL

Negligent or not?

In deciding whether an organisation or a person has been negligent or failed to meet their duty of care, several factors are considered:
* Was the accident foreseeable?
* Was it preventable?
* Was it reasonably practicable to provide methods to prevent it?
* Was there causality, or a direct link between the negligence and the injury?

When the answers to these questions are 'yes', the person or the organisation is legally accountable and penalties are imposed.

Systems failure or poorly designed work systems, including faulty machinery and equipment, cause many accidents. You and your work team should be in the habit of regularly checking the condition of equipment, machinery and tools and fix any defects promptly. The same applies to regularly checking methods, procedures and systems of work, and looking for ways to improve them (see Chapter 19 for more information on making continuous improvements.)

Human error also causes accidents but there should, in most cases, be no attachment of blame. An error is generally an act that is inappropriate and which the system of work allowed to be taken; after all, people don't injure themselves intentionally. Human error includes unsafe or inappropriate behaviour by an employee, such as absent-mindedness, forgetfulness, ignorance of risk or tiredness, which can often be traced back to poor job design, supervision or training.

Accident-prone employees

Partly due to genes, partly to experience, high-risk people exist. These are people who have 'problematic personalities'; for example, risk-takers, stress addicts and closet thugs. These are the 20% of people who have 80% of the accidents and who, even when placed in safe, low-risk environments, keep having accidents. When you look at the accident and incident statistics, you see patterns. The same few people with multiple entries, year after year.

Some employees have attitudes, beliefs and habits that lead to taking risks – even with their own safety. They may have an external locus of control and believe that chance, fate or luck have more to do with injuring themselves than their own behaviour or lack of caution, so why pay attention to safety? As a result, they may behave unsafely and suffer more injuries. Some employees may seek sensation and be willing to place themselves in the path of risk for the thrill they experience. Others may have trouble paying attention. They, too, are likely to suffer more accidents and injury at work.

◉ IN A NUTSHELL

Level of employee risk and possible causes
Table 29.1 has a summary of circumstances that might place so-called accident-prone employees at risk and the contributing factors.

TABLE 29.1 Risk circumstances and contributing factors

Cause of accident	Contributing factors
Carelessness and lack of concentration	Lack of mindfulness; poor training; poor supervision
Dislike of the job or the leader-manager	Poor job placement; poor job design; poor supervision
Existence of hazards	Unsafe work systems; poor supervision
Failure to follow safe work practices	Poor training; poor supervision
Insufficient manual skills to perform the job correctly	Poor job placement; poor training; poor supervision
Level of intelligence too low for the job they are required to do	Poor job placement; poor training; poor supervision
Poor sight, poor hearing or lack of stamina	Poor job placement
Poor use of plant and equipment	Poor training; poor supervision
Stress, fatigue	Poor supervision; poor work systems allowing for long or double shifts

Labelling people as 'accident-prone' doesn't help them or the organisation and simply blaming accidents on employees is clearly no answer. Any control or measure that depends solely on individual behaviour for its success is guaranteed to fail sooner or later and, in the 'In a Nutshell: Level of employee risk and possible causes' you can see how few accidents are solely the employee's fault.

The safety records of some 'accident-prone' employees are often symptoms of a system failure that you can correct. Your first step is to investigate whether unsafe behaviour is easier or faster than safe behaviour; when it is, rectify it (refer to the *'chance to'* key on page 339). Then assess your safety culture and work towards improving it when necessary. Make the safety slogan 'No safety, know pain; know safety, no pain' top of everyone's mind.

Design jobs properly, place employees in jobs that suit them, train them correctly and supervise them adequately (see the five keys – *'what to'*, *'want to'*, *'how to'*, *'chance to'* and *'led to'* in Chapter 11.) For more information on how to identify learning needs and provide job training, see pages 891 and 917. Establish clear, safe and efficient work systems and procedures and see that employees consistently follow them and use equipment properly. Improve work systems as necessary so that the possibility of unsafe behaviours is less likely or removed altogether.

Ensure that carelessness is not seen as acceptable practice and work targets are realistic. Conduct a job safety analysis and develop a critical behaviour checklist, then use it to observe employees and give feedback and remedial training as necessary. Teach people to practise mindfulness (explained on page 194) as a way to improve their concentration.

When employees don't respond to training or your other interventions and continue to engage in risky behaviour, they are more liable to injury than are other workers. Placing them under hazardous conditions is a menace to themselves and to others and contravenes your duty of care. When you can, place at-risk employees in jobs where their efforts are more likely to be safe and effective. Should they continually disregard safe working procedures or behave inappropriately, manage their performance as explained in Chapter 16.

● THEORY TO PRACTICE

Protect employees who can't protect themselves

Many organisations have a zero tolerance policy regarding illicit substances in the workplace. If yours doesn't and you suspect that an employee is under the influence of drugs or alcohol and you do not take steps to protect him or her, you could be failing in your duty of care.

Treat drug and alcohol misuse as a WHS risk and support the employee as far as possible, for example through employee assistance programs (EAPs), as explained on page 1030.

What to do in the event of accident, incident or injury

You can learn something from every accident, incident and injury. Investigate each one as soon as possible after it occurs, while the event is still fresh in people's minds. Reconstruct the chain of events leading up to it so you can pinpoint the factors that contributed to it. Once you know why your policies, procedures or practices failed, you can take measures to prevent a recurrence.

While several factors may contribute to an accident or near miss, concentrate on those you can actually do something about. When appropriate, involve others, such as the safety officer or WHS representative, in your investigation and in taking steps to ensure that the event never happens again.

 **IN A NUTSHELL**

Should a serious accident occur …

If a serious accident occurs, executives of the organisation may need to deal with the media and to minimise any adverse market and community responses that may adversely affect the company in the longer term. Efficient organisations have crisis management policies in place to deal with this. It's important that only appointed representatives speak to the media. (Leader-managers should remind their team members not to discuss any organisation matters that arise on social media because this can cause problems for the organisation and also for those affected by the serious accident and their families.)

As a leader-manager, you are perfectly positioned to keep employees, who are likely to be feeling vulnerable and looking to you for information and reassurance, aware of what is happening and how they may be affected. Keep people posted. Set a schedule to update employees and stick to it. Even when there's nothing new to report, meet anyhow and say so. Set a good example because your team members take their cues from your attitude and behaviour.

The object of your investigation is to:

- find the facts, particularly which system failure led to the accident or incident
- identify and analyse the circumstances involved
- select remedies to eliminate the hazard or, when this is not possible, to reduce and manage the risk it presents.

Interview any witnesses to the event and the person involved to gather facts and hear their views on what led up to the event and any contributing factors. Carry out these interviews in a friendly, informal atmosphere. They are not cross-examinations. You're not looking to find fault, just reasons, so that you can identify why policies and procedures failed in order to prevent a similar accident.

Conduct your investigation at the site of the accident or incident. Leave everything exactly as it was when the event took place, especially in the case of serious injury. When necessary, take steps to prevent further injury to people or damage to equipment (e.g. by switching off the power supply to an unguarded or dangerous machine).

Afterwards, record the incident or accident and injury, write a report summarising your investigation and findings, and file it according to your organisation's protocol. When someone was injured, inform your team what occurred and what is happening to the injured person. Explain what action is being taken to ensure that a similar accident does not occur and discuss how best to make interim workplace arrangements and adjustments. Periodically analyse accident, incident and injury information as described on page 585 to alert you to patterns and trends that need special attention.

 **IN A NUTSHELL**

What to do when an employee has a lost-time injury

While injured employees are at home, phone to ask how they are and update them on workplace news. Find out what you can do to help them get better and back to work.

When injured employees return to work, make every effort to accommodate any restrictions caused by the injury, aiming to provide ongoing employment where reasonably practical.

Minor accidents and near misses

Employees should report all accidents and near misses, however minor, to you. This ensures you can take remedial action before an incident ultimately causes injury or ill health. It is a good idea to have a special form to complete to give to the safety committee, safety officer or another nominated person.

⊙ ACTION!

To help you keep track of accidents or other incidents and assess their frequency patterns, you can use the Accident/incident log template on .

In the case of minor accidents in larger organisations, the injured person would report to the first aid centre for treatment and be asked to take a report form back to you. In other organisations, you should ensure the employee's injury is treated appropriately and then complete your report after discussing the circumstances of the accident with the injured employee and conducting any necessary investigations. The form normally then goes to the safety officer or another nominated person, who may decide to investigate further or simply file the form and record the details for statistical purposes and later analysis.

Near misses are lucky escapes, so always investigate them as well as actual accidents, no matter how minor. Both can damage morale and are symptoms that something is wrong. As shown in Figure 29.5, a near miss and several near misses are generally a precursor to an accident involving injury. Investigating and analysing them helps you to catch and prevent injuries before they happen.

For every major injury or fatality, there are:	
10 minor injuries	⊬⊬ ⊬⊬
30 lost-time accidents	⊬⊬ ⊬⊬ ⊬⊬ ⊬⊬ ⊬⊬ ⊬⊬
100 minor accidents	⊬⊬ ⊬⊬ ⊬⊬ ⊬⊬ ⊬⊬ ⊬⊬ ⊬⊬ ⊬⊬ ⊬⊬ ⊬⊬ ⊬⊬ ⊬⊬ ⊬⊬ ⊬⊬ ⊬⊬ ⊬⊬ ⊬⊬ ⊬⊬ ⊬⊬ ⊬⊬
600 near misses	⊬⊬ ⊬⊬ ⊬⊬ ⊬⊬ ⊬⊬ ⊬⊬ ⊬⊬ ⊬⊬ ⊬⊬ ⊬⊬ ⊬⊬ ⊬⊬ ⊬⊬ ⊬⊬ ⊬⊬ ⊬⊬ ⊬⊬ ⊬⊬ ⊬⊬ ⊬⊬
	⊬⊬ ⊬⊬ ⊬⊬ ⊬⊬ ⊬⊬ ⊬⊬ ⊬⊬ ⊬⊬ ⊬⊬ ⊬⊬ ⊬⊬ ⊬⊬ ⊬⊬ ⊬⊬ ⊬⊬ ⊬⊬ ⊬⊬ ⊬⊬ ⊬⊬ ⊬⊬
	⊬⊬ ⊬⊬ ⊬⊬ ⊬⊬ ⊬⊬ ⊬⊬ ⊬⊬ ⊬⊬ ⊬⊬ ⊬⊬ ⊬⊬ ⊬⊬ ⊬⊬ ⊬⊬ ⊬⊬ ⊬⊬ ⊬⊬ ⊬⊬ ⊬⊬ ⊬⊬
	⊬⊬ ⊬⊬ ⊬⊬ ⊬⊬ ⊬⊬ ⊬⊬ ⊬⊬ ⊬⊬ ⊬⊬ ⊬⊬ ⊬⊬ ⊬⊬ ⊬⊬ ⊬⊬ ⊬⊬ ⊬⊬ ⊬⊬ ⊬⊬ ⊬⊬ ⊬⊬
	⊬⊬ ⊬⊬ ⊬⊬ ⊬⊬ ⊬⊬ ⊬⊬ ⊬⊬ ⊬⊬ ⊬⊬ ⊬⊬ ⊬⊬ ⊬⊬ ⊬⊬ ⊬⊬ ⊬⊬ ⊬⊬ ⊬⊬ ⊬⊬ ⊬⊬ ⊬⊬
	⊬⊬ ⊬⊬ ⊬⊬ ⊬⊬ ⊬⊬ ⊬⊬ ⊬⊬ ⊬⊬ ⊬⊬ ⊬⊬ ⊬⊬ ⊬⊬ ⊬⊬ ⊬⊬ ⊬⊬ ⊬⊬ ⊬⊬ ⊬⊬ ⊬⊬ ⊬⊬

FIGURE 29.5 Types of accidents

⊙ THEORY TO PRACTICE

Uncover incidents

Employees don't always report incidents. This could be because of embarrassment in admitting a mistake, fear of criticism, habituation (*normalisation bias*), not realising its significance, not wanting to spoil a good safety record or peer pressure. (See 'Theory to practice: The well from hell and bad apples' on page 522 for more information on normalisation and outcome biases and how near misses precede and foreshadow accidents, injuries and deaths and business crises.)

To uncover near misses and prevent them from becoming serious injuries, ask employees to recall how many incidents with potential for serious injury they have been aware of over a certain period, say six months. Assure them that you intend to keep all statements confidential. Use the information to develop specifically targeted programs to manage the hazards uncovered.

4. Preventing accidents

A hazard is anything that could hurt you or someone else.

'Hazard identification, risk assessment and risk control', Government of Victoria, Department of Education & Training[17]

To prevent workplace death, disease and injury, you need to find hazards and remove or minimise their risk. Known by the acronym HIRAC: Hazard Identification, Risk Assessment and Control, this is a proactive approach. You *prevent* problems, rather than react to them after they occur. Two organisations in a similar business may prevent accidents in different ways and this is fine as long as each approach works.

Identifying and controlling hazards is your main occupational WHS obligation. Work with employees, safety representatives and committee members to identify and manage hazards and make the workplace safer. Follow these three steps:

1. *Identify hazards*: that is, things that, by their very nature, could cause an accident or injury, or harm health or property.
2. *Assess their associated risks*: That is, the likelihood of the hazard causing harm and the severity of its potential illness or injury to people or damage to the environment or property.
3. *Control hazards*: Follow the information in Figure 29.6: How to control hazards.

Begin with the most serious hazards and eliminate them. When you can't eliminate them, minimise the risks they present using the hierarchy of prevention.

For instance, it is hazardous to cross a road – a passing vehicle might hit you. Before crossing a road, you probably assess the risk of being hit. The risk is higher at peak hour, in the dark, the more slowly you cross and/or the faster the traffic moves. The greater you assess the risk to be, the more important it is that you take steps to eliminate it by, for example, using a pedestrian bridge or tunnel. When you can't eliminate the risk, you might minimise it by crossing the road at a brisk pace and only when the traffic lights indicate you can do so, looking carefully in both directions before crossing and wearing light-coloured clothing after dark.

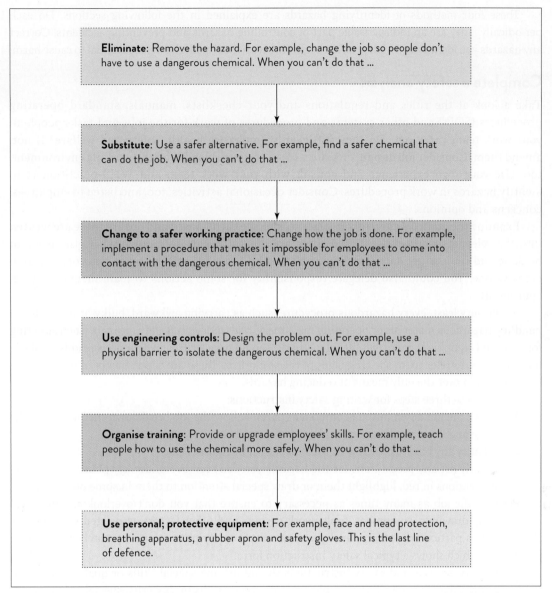

Eliminate: Remove the hazard. For example, change the job so people don't have to use a dangerous chemical. When you can't do that ...

Substitute: Use a safer alternative. For example, find a safer chemical that can do the job. When you can't do that ...

Change to a safer working practice: Change how the job is done. For example, implement a procedure that makes it impossible for employees to come into contact with the dangerous chemical. When you can't do that ...

Use engineering controls: Design the problem out. For example, use a physical barrier to isolate the dangerous chemical. When you can't do that ...

Organise training: Provide or upgrade employees' skills. For example, teach people how to use the chemical more safely. When you can't do that ...

Use personal; protective equipment: For example, face and head protection, breathing apparatus, a rubber apron and safety gloves. This is the last line of defence.

FIGURE 29.6 How to control hazards

Step 1: Identify hazards

A hazard is anything with the potential to harm life, health or property. There are four ways to identify hazards:

1. Complete a safety analysis.
2. Conduct a safety audit (or hazard inspection).
3. Observe the way jobs and procedures are carried out to make sure they are completed following safe work practices.
4. Study the accident and incident statistics to understand what the previous problems have been, who could be harmed by the hazards, and how.

These four methods of identifying hazards are explained in the following sections. Do each periodically. They are an indispensable part of controlling hazards and preventing accidents. Correct any hazards you identify as a high priority, beginning with those with the most potential to cause harm.

Complete a safety analysis

Take a look at the rules and regulations and your checklists, manuals, standard operating procedures (SOPs) and other systems and procedures of work for the jobs and tasks people in your work team carry out. Do they sufficiently emphasise health, safety and welfare? If not, amend them. Consider job design, measures of success, workloads and the working environment, too. Use your own experience and consult with your work team and WHS practitioners to identify hazards in work procedures. Consider occasional activities, too, and listen to employees' concerns and opinions.

Examine the controls currently in place to manage each hazard and ensure these are written into the relevant document(s). When these are not sufficient, note down what else needs to be done and set a target date; check your plans with the safety officer when your organisation employs one. You could also delegate responsibility for some actions to team members, when appropriate.

At the very least, every hazardous procedure (such as carrying awkward, bulky or heavy items, handling hazardous materials or operating machinery) and important safety measure (such as caring for tools and equipment or correct lifting methods) should have written instructions readily available for employees to refer to, in the languages of the workforce. These are supplements to safe working methods, and never the only means of reducing hazards.

Follow these three steps for writing safety instructions:

1. Break the job down into its component parts. Follow the job breakdown method using the stage and key-point headings explained on page 803.
2. Identify any hazards. Deal with them as shown in Figure 29.6.
3. Clearly list any precautions for the hazards you can't remove under key points. Print these precautions in red, highlight them or draw special attention to them in some other way.

Perform the job as many times as necessary to ensure that you don't overlook anything and examine any drawings, equipment, tools, work permits and other factors associated with the job. When a job is particularly hazardous, list any necessary safety precautions separately as shown in Figure 29.7, which shows a typical safety instruction form.

Your safety analysis and safety instructions should list any special skills or qualifications that someone doing the job needs. For example, certain manual skills or dexterity, special coordination, special training or a licence to perform high-risk work. You should also incorporate these requirements into the person specification, discussed on page 807, to avoid putting the wrong person in a job, since a poorly selected or placed employee is more at risk of injury than one whose capacities match the job requirements.

Preparing safety instructions is neither difficult nor time-consuming. The challenge lies in keeping them up to date and ensuring that people always follow them. One way to do this is to involve the people who use the instructions in writing them. Make your safety instructions part of the induction process for new staff and diarise to review your safety analysis at least annually, or immediately when there are major changes in the workplace.

Safety instruction form

Job				
Prepared by .... Approved .... Date				
Stage	Key point	Hazards	Safety precautions	Skills/training/ licence/other requirements

FIGURE 29.7 Safety instruction form

Conduct a safety audit

It's amazing how many hazards surround us. To spot them, walk around with a safety audit form, such as the form on CourseMate Express (the precise items on these lists vary, depending on the workplace.) When you identify a hazard, tick the box and note the location so you can follow up later with appropriate action.

Two pairs of eyes are generally better than one, so think about inviting one of your team members or a safety representative or safety officer to accompany you when you go hazard spotting. When you see the same hazards every day, you often stop seeing them, so fresh eyes are a bonus.

Sign and date your safety audit or summarise it in a report like the one shown in Figure 29.8, discuss your findings with your team and post the audit in a prominent place. Sign and date identified actions to be taken as they are completed.

Diarise to review and update your safety audit at least annually, or immediately when there are major changes in the workplace.

Safety inspection report

| Date of inspection .... |
| Department/section .... |
| Inspector/s .... |

Hazard found	Location	Person notified	Action taken	Date	Initials

FIGURE 29.8 Safety inspection report

⦿ ACTION!

To summarise and track the hazards that you identify, download the office or factory/warehouse Safety audit template from ⦿CourseMateExpress.

Before inspecting your own workplace, have a practice session by going to https://www. comcare.gov.au and click on Virtual Office. Here you can explore the many hazards lurking in an office environment and discover some effective ways to control them.

⦿ IN A NUTSHELL

Common hazards

Here are seven common workplace hazards to look out for all the time, not just when you undertake a safety audit:

1. *Accidents waiting to happen*: Sadly, most accidents are preventable, with some of the most common being slips, trips and falls, which may not lead to major health problems but can cause broken bones and worse.
2. *Air quality*: Stay alert to the quality of air in your workplace. It is affected by air movement and changes, temperature and humidity, and contaminants such as chemical fumes, dust and other particles.
3. *Dangerous chemicals* (e.g. adhesives, cleaning products, fuels, heavy metals, paints and paint thinners, pesticides, petroleum products, photocopier toner): Label

>>

all dangerous substances with a warning for users and attach a *material safety data sheet* (MSDS) that explains the health effects, instructions for safe use and emergency instructions.

4. *Drugs and alcohol*: You don't want any accidents or incidents involving or caused by employees under the influence of alcohol or prescription or illicit drugs.

5. *Manual handling*: Up to one-third of work injuries are from activities involving effort such as carrying, holding, lifting, lowering, pulling, pushing or moving. Particularly hazardous are bending, reaching or twisting; heavy work requiring forceful movements; poor posture; repetitive movements; and sudden, jerky or hard-to-control movements. The three largest areas of injuries are back and muscle injuries due to manual handling and overuse injuries due to repetitive movements. Workers in the cleaning, hospitality and manufacturing industries are most at risk.[18]

6. *Needlestick injuries*: Every year, thousands of Australian healthcare professionals suffer needlestick injuries from, for example, discarded needless and sharp or pointed objects used to treat patents. These are a major, and growing, occupational hazard, especially for health and community service employees.

7. *Stress*: Stress at work is a very serious issue and can potentially lead to burnout, depression and even addiction and suicide. An Australian Council of Trade Unions (ACTU) study found that one in four employees regularly takes time off work due to stress.[19] Common causes of stress are excessive workloads, insufficient training, long work hours, poor job design and poor-quality supervision.

 **ACTION!**

To summarise the results of your safety audit, you can print off a Safety inspection report template from **CourseMateExpress**.

Observe people as they work

You can spot accidents and incidents waiting to happen and flaws in working procedures and methods by noticing how people work, particularly in high-risk areas and on high-risk tasks, and when new equipment or work is introduced. When you notice, for example, corners being cut, safety procedures not being followed or unsafe habits developing (e.g. sitting incorrectly or carrying heavy items rather than using the trolley), you can step in and take appropriate measures. As they say, 'Alert today; alive tomorrow.'

You might provide training or coaching to respond to gaps in knowledge, give a gentle reminder or have a chat with someone to adjust their perception of risk. You might find out why someone isn't following safe working procedure and work with them to make it easy to do so — easier than working unsafely. Should someone continually breach safety protocols that could lead to dangerous incidents or accidents despite your interventions, use the hot-stove principle to begin managing their performance. Now is *not* the time to turn a blind eye.

FYI

Desk bound? Stand up and move

Sitting, compared to even just standing, makes the body 'go to sleep'. There's nothing for the muscles to do, which slows down metabolism. But the problem is worse than that.

People who work at computers for long periods, whether as secretaries, data entry and call centre workers, or professionals and managers, experience high levels of arm, back, neck and shoulder pain, despite ergonomics education and better workstation and seating design. The long-term results of prolonged sitting and lack of physical activity can include blood clots, cardiovascular disease, diabetes and obesity. It can even reduce life expectancy by three years.[20]

There are measures you can take to prevent this. They include performing some work while standing, walking to a colleague's desk rather than sending an email, holding standing and walking meetings and placing telephones and in-trays away from people's desks. Organisations can encourage healthy lifestyles that include exercise (but even exercise can't mitigate the problems of sitting for hours on end at work).[21]

Study the stats

The fourth way to identify hazards is to collect accident, incident and injury information, present it in a useable way (see for example, Figures 19.19 and 19.21 on pages 604 and 606) and periodically analyse the numbers to see what they can tell you. You can use graphs of lost-time injuries, medical treatments, positive performance indicators and workers compensation claims to facilitate continual improvements and identify looming problems.

Look at lost-time injuries (explained in the 'In the Nutshell: Lost-time injuries' on page 976) and look for patterns and trends, such as:

* *What types* of accidents, injuries and incidents occur most often? For example, are they mostly falls, back injuries, or cuts and abrasions?
* *Where* do most occur? Does one location stand out among all others as having a higher rate of accidents, injuries or near misses?
* *When* do accidents, injuries and near misses occur? Is there a particular time of day – for example, the beginning or end of a shift – during which they tend to happen?
* *Who* is involved? Is it mostly new employees, old hands, people under training or some other identifiable group who seem to be most at risk?
* *What types* of equipment, machinery or processes are involved?
* *Which hazards* and incidents are the most likely to result in an accident or injury? Which would be the most serious?

Answers to questions like these can give you good information about particular areas and jobs to monitor or investigate for the cause in order to correct it. (You can find out how to analyse and present data beginning on page 585.)

> ⬤ **THEORY TO PRACTICE**
>
> **Keep good files**
> Build a work, heath and safety (WHS) file with the following information:
> - a list of chemicals used at your workplace
> - a list of WHS and related training courses that employees have attended
> - a list of identified hazards
> - accident and incident records
> - accident report forms
> - first aid record book
> - hazardous substances register
> - licences/competency to safely operate equipment or carry out procedures
> - maintenance and service records for equipment
> - plant and equipment safety information
> - workers' compensation insurance claim file
> - workplace safety rules
> - written job instructions that include safety instructions.

Where are most hazards found?

A popular safety slogan says, 'Safety never takes a break'. That's because hazards are everywhere, particularly:
- around machinery, especially machines run by operators and those with moving parts
- wherever people lift or move items, especially heavy or awkward items (or people in the case of carers), regardless of whether cranes, forklift trucks and hoists are used or the lifting is done manually
- wherever people stand or sit for long periods
- wherever people use hand tools
- wherever people use hazardous substances and chemicals
- wherever people walk: on aisles, ladders, ramps, scaffolds and stairs.

Once you know what the hazards in your work area are, you can set priorities and concentrate first on those with the highest risk.

Step 2: Assess risks

Risk estimates the likelihood and severity of potential illness or injury, or damage to the environment or property, resulting from a hazard. You can attach a degree of risk, such as high, medium or low, to all hazards. Chapter 23 explains some other ways of assessing risk levels.

When assessing a hazard's degree of risk, consider these factors:
- *Frequency*: How often is a person exposed to the hazard? You would deal with frequent, say daily or weekly, exposure differently from infrequent, say once-a-year, exposure.
- *Probability*: How likely is the hazard to result in an accident? The higher the probability, the more urgent it is to eliminate or minimise it.

- *Severity*: How potentially serious would an accident caused by this hazard be? You would deal with the risk of a paper cut differently from the risk of death.
- *How the above factors combine*: For example, when a hazard has a very low chance of occurring (frequency) you would treat it as a high priority if it had a catastrophic outcome (severity). Draw up a matrix, as explained on page 744, to see whether the way the factors combine changes a hazard's priority.

Based on your risk assessment, determine priorities for dealing with hazards, beginning with those with the highest risk.

⦿ THE STRATEGIC PERSPECTIVE

Stop that noise!

Workers (and customers) in clubs, gyms and pubs are at risk. Gardeners are at risk. Maintenance staff are at risk. In fact, the risk of hearing damage is present in a surprising number of workplaces, not just the obvious heavy engineering workplaces. Between July 2002 and June 2007, there were about 15 500 successful workers' compensation claims for industrial deafness in Australia.[22]

Providing ear protection isn't enough. Codes of practice for noise management and hearing protection at work promote:

- developing a noise policy covering noise goals
- funding a noise-control program
- implementing a program of action, which should include a noise assessment, hearing tests, a plan to replace noisy plant, ongoing training for employees and reducing exposure time to noise
- purchasing plant and equipment that is as quiet as practicable.

Hearing protection for individual workers is the last resort.

Step 3: Control hazards

Use the flow chart for risk control shown in Figure 29.9 (which is based on the six tiers of prevention shown in Figure 29.6) or follow Figure 29.6 to manage hazards. Select and implement appropriate control measures in consultation with employees, engineers (when appropriate) and WHS specialists.

Think of the possible actions to control risks as a series of preferred steps. The best remedy is to *eliminate* the hazard. When you can't, then *reduce* the risk it poses by substitution or isolation. When neither of those options is possible, introduce *administrative* (or engineering) *controls*.

Personal protection is your last resort because it is usually the least effective. Personal protection devices include aprons and overalls, earmuffs and earplugs, gloves, hairnets, hard hats, hoods and shields, safety goggles and glasses, safety shoes and boots, and self-contained air breathing apparatus and filter respirators.

The main drawback of personal safety devices like these is that they don't eliminate, reduce (provide a safer alternative or safer working practice) or isolate (through engineering) the hazard. Personal protection is only a thin line of defence between the employee and the unsafe condition.

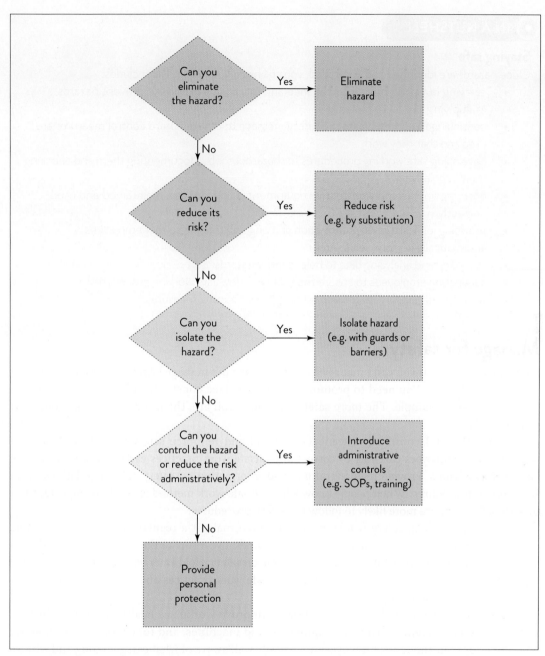

FIGURE 29.9 Flow chart for hazard control

That's why it's far better to remove the need for personal safety equipment by eliminating, minimising or segregating hazards.

The other drawback to personal safety devices is that they can be unsightly, restrictive or cumbersome to use and employees often prefer not to use them, despite the danger of not doing so. People can also become so familiar with a job that they become careless in their use of safety equipment, which increases the risk of an accident. When personal protection is the only option, though, you must ensure that employees use them. When it comes to safety, there is no excuse for lenient management. Think 'tough love' instead.

> ### ● IN A NUTSHELL
>
> **Staying safe**
> Once hazards are identified and controlled, you still have work to do. This includes:
> - carrying out preventive maintenance and corrective actions to prevent hazards multiplying
> - continuing to communicate the safety message to ensure hazard control measures are used and that they work
> - developing safe working procedures for hazardous jobs, documenting them and checking them regularly
> - ensuring any personal protective equipment is appropriate, maintained and used correctly
> - providing job instruction, information and ongoing training so that employees automatically perform work safely
> - recording and analysing data to help identify hazards
> - supervising employees to ensure they always follow safe working procedures
> - working with employees to keep refining hazard control measures.

Manage for safety

Someone once said, 'If you can't manage for safety, you can't manage.' And it's certainly true that safety is no accident. You need to promote a safe workplace constantly and consistently. Begin by setting a good example. The more safety conscious you are, the more safety conscious your work team is.

Use positive and constructive feedback to build and reinforce safe work habits. Train and supervise new employees carefully to correct any unsafe work practices early before they become hard-to-break habits. Provide regular training and information on safety rules, regulations, work systems and procedures. When people know what the safe work method is and how important it is to work safely, they are more likely to follow the safety procedures.

Communicate about safety regularly; you can even make it a regular item on team meeting agendas. Hold mini training sessions three or four times a year; invite the safety officer in, show a safety video or ask a team member to give a short talk on safety. Hold emergency drills for evacuating the work area and for giving first aid, and include safe work practices and safety consciousness in your regular performance appraisals.

Consult employees for their ideas on how to improve workplace health and safety. Inspect new items (such as chairs, chemicals, equipment and machines, and tools) for hazards and ask employees for their thoughts. Employees are usually well aware of what can go wrong and why, so listening to them is an easy and effective way to identify workplace hazards. Their observations and suggestions are likely to be good, since they are involved in the day-to-day operations and work processes.

Respond to employees' concerns and questions on workplace health and safety, whether they make them directly to you or through their WHS representative. Act on, and provide prompt feedback on, the issues they raise. This encourages employees to report hazards and incidents and to remain safety conscious.

CourseMateExpress

Go to http://login.cengagebrain.com to access CourseMate Express, your online study tool for *Management Theory & Practice*. CourseMate Express brings chapter concepts to life with interactive learning, and study and exam preparation tools:

- Test your skills in different aspects of management with interactive self-tests and simulations.
- Watch videos that show how real managers operate in real businesses.
- Test your understanding of the changing world of management by taking the revision quiz.

QUICK REVIEW

1. Employers, managers and employees all have responsibilities under the Commonwealth *Work Health and Safety Act 2011*. Outline the senior and middle managers' responsibilities, leader-managers' responsibilities and employees' responsibilities.
2. What are safety committees and who are safety representatives? How do they differ from safety officers?
3. Describe the steps to take should an accident or incident occur in the work area you are responsible for. Draw this as a flow chart if you prefer.
4. What is the difference between a hazard and a risk? Refer to Figure 29.9 to explain what to do when you become aware of a hazard.

BUILD YOUR SKILLS

1. Obtain information on your state's workers' compensation and rehabilitation program and requirements, and prepare a short report summarising how the system works.
2. Are some people accident prone? Discuss what leader-managers should do about employees who seem to have more accidents than others.
3. Explain how accidents and injuries are prevented in your work area or college and give two examples of the steps to take to prevent a physical injury. Explain how you would assess the risk in the examples you give and how you recommend managing each.
4. Write safety instructions for a task you are familiar with that contains one or more hazards, such as changing a bicycle tyre or lighting a campfire. Refer to the information on preparing a job breakdown on page 917 if you need to.

WORKPLACE ACTIVITIES

1. Develop a plan for keeping employees abreast of safety procedures and regulations in your organisation.

2. If possible, attend a safety committee meeting as an observer and report on the proceedings and what the meeting achieved. If that's not possible, interview a safety officer or a safety representative. What are their duties in relation to health, safety and welfare matters? What support does their organisation provide them in carrying out their duties? What are their main sources of information? Their main challenges?

3. Join a leader-manager, a safety officer or a safety committee member in a safety audit. Learn as much as you can about the potential hazards in the area being inspected and how they can be spotted. How is the inspection documented and acted on?

4. Find out what WHS records your organisation or college keeps, where it keeps them and for how long it keeps them. Prepare a report summarising these records and how they are used.

5. Draw Pareto charts, as described on page 597, for the main categories of accidents and injuries based on the WHS records you collected in the previous activity. Draw another Pareto chart showing the groups of workers injured (e.g. males, females, employees in various age groups, employees by area and by occupation). Break this down further by charting specific injuries by groups of workers. What do your charts tell you about who is most at risk in your organisation, where and from what? Establish priorities and a target for improving the situation.

CASE STUDY 29.1

DANGEROUS COMPUTERS

Gina Marina manages several shops retailing computers and associated hardware, software and accessories in the metropolitan area. Each shop has a small core of permanent staff and several casual staff who come in as required. In general, the employees at the outlets are friendly, responsible and work well together. Gina personally trains them in their duties and pays special attention to ensuring that they understand and apply the safety procedures she covers as part of the standard operating procedures. Since she only hires technically competent 'geeks', technical and product training looks after itself.

While safety isn't a major issue, it nevertheless remains in the back of Gina's mind. She doesn't want anyone getting hurt; apart from the personal consequences, she has her staffing levels finely tuned and really can't afford people to be off work due to injuries.

Gina's accident, near-miss and injury statistics are similar to other groups of stores in the chain. The company uses Pareto charts to benchmark the lost-time injury frequency rate (LTIFR) figures for each group of stores. The main injury reported is back injury caused by incorrect lifting; this is most likely to occur when fresh stock arrives and the staff help off-load the boxes into the back room before sorting, coding and shelving the merchandise. The second biggest cause of injury is strain, followed by over-reaching, which can occur when staff are stocking the highest and lowest shelves. Falls account for the third main category of injuries, usually a result of overbalancing when putting up display materials such as posters and stocking the high shelves.

Gina's stores normally benchmark in the best 75% of stores in the chain and, as the accident and incident figures are reasonably low anyway, she is content.

That is, she was content until this quarter's figures came out. These show a marked increase in falls in all but one of the stores she manages. The resulting lost time due to injuries also weakened her staff utilisation performance figures for the period. She feels her own personal efficiency has decreased, too, because dealing with the injuries diverts her attention from other important matters. Clearly, she needs to manage this outbreak of accidents before it becomes an epidemic.

Questions

1. How seriously do you believe Gina and her company take workplace health and safety? What is your evidence?
2. Outline what Gina's next steps should be.
3. If Gina decides that the cause of the increase in injuries is failure to follow safety procedures, especially when lifting and stocking shelves, how could she ensure that staff follow the safety procedures? What contingency plans would you advise regarding employees who do not follow safety procedures after Gina reminds them of their importance?
4. Since Gina manages several stores and cannot be everywhere at once, how could she go about monitoring employees' observance of safety procedures?

CASE STUDY 29.2

BROWNE (ESTATE OF) VERSUS ACE BUILDING CONTRACTORS

Ace Building Contractors is a small, owner-operated company that mostly builds and remodels private homes. It employs two permanent full-time and two part-time employees in the office who look after invoicing and materials ordering. Ace subcontracts specific projects to self-employed tradespeople such as bricklayers, carpenters, electricians, painters and plumbers. It also employs a few casual labourers as needed. Because it is reasonably efficient in the way it manages and supervises its building projects, and because it tries to employ only tried and tested tradespeople, Ace has a sound reputation in the community for good-quality work at reasonable prices.

Last spring, Ace sent a crew to erect the frame for a new home. An inspector paid an on-site visit and found a ladder with a broken rung and a lean that could easily (and often did) cause the ladder to slip sideways. On the advice of the inspector, the site manager immediately cut off the rung and asked one of the carpenters, Al Browne, to throw the ladder on the rubbish heap for later removal.

One month later, Browne and a colleague are weatherboarding the house. Browne is up a ladder nailing the boards, and the colleague is holding the base of the ladder. Browne runs out of nails and sends his colleague to get him a new box. Meanwhile, he climbs the ladder again to check on some previous work. As he is doing this, the ladder falls sideways, bringing him down onto the cement driveway. Browne is fatally injured.

Subsequent investigation reveals that Browne was not wearing a hardhat or safety boots. The site manager states that he has 'nagged Browne for ages' about wearing safety gear but had recently given up. It is also discovered that the ladder used that day was the one found by the inspector to be unsafe. The only repair made to it was a jammed wooden rung to replace the one that had been cut off.

Browne's colleague states that there was no other ladder available on the site, and that they were keen to get the job completed in order to meet their contractual obligations with the home owner.

Questions

1. What could the site manager have done to prevent the accident?
2. What could Ace Building Contractors have done to prevent the accident?
3. Is Ace liable for prosecution?
4. Is the site manager liable for prosecution?

CHAPTER

30

MANAGING FOR PSYCHOLOGICAL SAFETY AND WELL-BEING

OVERVIEW

Have you ever felt uncomfortable or fearful? It's hard to do your best when you're always looking over your shoulder, protecting yourself physically or psychologically, or tuning out unpleasant or cruel comments and remarks. It's hard to do your best when you feel like an 'outsider' and your contributions and potential aren't appreciated or even understood, or when your mind continually returns to events in your personal life.

Psychological safety is part of the workplace health and safety domain. Employers have a legal and moral responsibility to ensure their employees, customers and others on their premises are treated with dignity and respect. Many organisations have grasped the benefits of helping their employees, and often their families, to maintain physical and mental fitness. As a result, they have extended their efforts beyond merely preventing harm to employees' physical and psychological safety to actively encouraging their physical and psychological health. This is known as employee wellness, or well-being.

1. Can you recognise harassment in its various forms and other assaults to people's dignity and create a culture that appreciates and respects everyone?
2. Do you know how to investigate complaints concerning dignity violations?
3. Are you able to encourage employee welfare and well-being?

This chapter deals with psychological health and safety, explaining how to protect employees' psychological health and encourage their well-being (Chapter 29 explains the health and safety legislative framework and how to identify and manage hazards).

Procedural fairness

Paula walks into the HR department and from the expression on her face everyone immediately knows the hospital has lost the case.

'Come on into my office,' says Paula, 'and I'll "share",' she says glumly.

It takes only seconds for the team to silently perch in Paula's office to hear the details. 'It seems our investigation into Grey's complaint was so "unprofessional" that Landry's dismissal was "unfair".' Eyes widen. 'It gets worse. The judge ruled Landry was the victim of assault, not Grey.' Mouths drop open. 'We have to reinstate Landry and pay her compensation for lost earnings.' Now there are audible gasps.

They all recall when Grey ventured into the department to lodge a formal complaint that Landry had assaulted her during a rostering dispute.

'It seems I didn't handle the investigation properly. I should have given Landry a copy of our findings from our interviews and copies of the allegations against her when she asked for them. That's part of the "full disclosure" that we should be following in our DSP [dispute settlement procedure]. People are entitled to a full disclosure of everything that is going to be used against them. Well, that's not exactly what the judge said. What he said was that we should give the accused person all the information we intend to consider when reaching our decision, or something like that.

'Okay. That's it. Thanks everybody. Isn't it wonderful? You're never too old to learn and to get a right royal telling off. Maram, would you mind updating the file on Grey and our stats and then making a few notes on our grievance handling procedure indicating where we need to clarify requirements, please? I just don't have the energy.

'I think we should all meet properly next week and review the case from beginning to end so we all know precisely where we went wrong and what to do next time. Cherie, would you organise a time for that and book a meeting room for us, please? Let's call it "the procedural fairness meeting",' Paula says wryly.

She stands up. 'Now I have to go and tell the boss. That'll be fun. Not.'

1. Managing for psychological safety and employee dignity

Everyone has a right not to be bullied or harassed at work.

'Bullying & harassment', Fair Work Ombudsman[1]

Organisations have a clear duty of care to ensure that employees are psychologically safe. Harassment, racial and religious vilification and occupational violence are significant workplace hazards and should be measured, monitored and treated in the same way as physical hazards.

It's important that you (and every leader-manager) understand your organisation's policies on psychological safety and know how to deal quickly with any instances of unacceptable behaviour. It's also critical that you model appropriate behaviour and set clear expectations of others regarding acceptable and unacceptable behaviour.

Harassment, vilification and workplace violence undermine the victim's work performance, psychological health and well-being, career and enjoyment at work. Harassment and violence make their victims miserable and can cause physical illness from the stress they cause. The emotional and psychological costs to victims include depression, headaches, lowered creativity, poor concentration, sleep disruption, and feelings of anxiety, insecurity and shame.

Although the financial costs are often hidden, organisations pay in terms of morale, productivity and reputation. Victims may take sick days or stress leave, or leave the job altogether, particularly when they feel they have no other recourse. For example, a study from the University of South Australia found that 60% of employees who made complaints of sexual harassment either resigned or were dismissed as a consequence.[2]

The majority of victims do not come forward. Since many bullies show a charming face to others, especially those higher up the hierarchy, their victims are often reluctant to speak up for fear they won't be believed. Or victims may not come forward because of fear of reprisals, of sounding weak, of affecting their future employment or promotion prospects, or even because they don't believe anything will change when they complain. A safety culture with clear policies, training, and open communication and support can lessen victims' concerns about making a complaint. (You can find more information on organisation culture on page 93.)

 FYI

When time off is reportable
Absences due to psychological stress can easily last for more than 30 consecutive days. These absences are regarded as notifiable incidents and must be reported to Comcare.

Who is most at risk?

Although harassment, vilification and violence can be directed at anyone, some groups of workers are more at risk than others. Casual employees, juniors, trainees and young employees are most at risk. Others might become victims because they lack social skills or because of a disability, their appearance, gender, personality style, physical characteristics, race or nationality, or sexual orientation. A person can even become a victim because they are more competent than their persecutors.

However, the most sensible and realistic view to take, known as the *universal precautions approach*, is that harassment, vilification and violence can happen to anyone in any workplace. It can also occur away from the workplace for example, at off-site business-related functions (business trips, conferences, social events, trade shows etc.), in clients' workplaces, and even over the telephone and electronically. Wherever it takes place, employers have a duty of care to take the initiative in identifying the risks their employees and people who come into contact with their employees face and to remove or reduce those risks. When they don't, the costs can be steep – to the victims as well as to the organisation.

Create a safety culture

Do you recall that wonderful quote from Lieutenant General David Morrison that opened the Chapter 26 Scenario? He said, 'The standard you walk past is the standard you accept.'[3]

To ignore harassment or violence is to condone it. In organisations with weak safety cultures, abusive behaviour is tolerated; infringements of people's dignity are brushed aside, ignored or joked about. These organisations are typified by aggressive behaviour and overly competitive organisation cultures of fear and insecurity. They often have different conditions of employment for different groups of workers, poor job training, and lack clear and transparent grievance procedures.

Uncompromising performance-related pay schemes, poor performance management systems, unclear or unreasonable performance measures, targets and timeframes combined with pressure to get the job done – regardless – and toxic, often authoritarian leadership styles are common in organisations in which harassment and violence – verbal and/or physical – are allowed to occur.

In organisations like these, position and power are misused, and demanding customers or clients, personality clashes and personal prejudice are allowed to dictate the work climate to the detriment of dignity and productivity.

In contrast, organisations with strong safety cultures do not tolerate attacks on peoples' dignity or damage people's feeling of well-being. It is clearly understood that it is every employee's responsibility to treat other employees, customers and suppliers with respect, and respect is a core organisational value. What constitutes unacceptable behaviour is clear and everyone knows how unacceptable behaviour is dealt with should it occur.

In strong safety cultures, induction programs explain the organisation's policies and this information is informally reviewed throughout the working year, for example at team meetings. Ongoing communication, regular workforce awareness training and other training (e.g. in assertiveness, communication, conflict resolution and other interpersonal skills) are part of the organisation's normal routines. Literature on the various aspects of a dignified workplace, such as government pamphlets in English and in the languages of people from non-English-speaking backgrounds, and the organisation's policies covering dignity, diversity, safety and stress management) is readily available and understood.

Everyone knows what harassment, vilification and violence mean in practice, how to make a complaint and where to go for advice and support. Everyone knows the procedure is to keep a record of the dates and times of incidents and what was said and done so that it can be used should they need to make a formal complaint. They also know what to do should they become stressed in the course of their work and how the organisation can help.

Clear policies

A formal policy or policies on bullying, sexual harassment, occupational violence, and racial and religious vilification is the first step in proactively creating an organisation culture that values and respects people's dignity. When the nature of the work performed is itself stressful, the organisation's measures to reduce stress and programs to help employees suffering from stress should be explained in its health and safety or welfare policies.

Policies should explain how complaints are to be addressed confidentially, fairly, impartially and quickly. The policies should be administered by a trained person and widely circulated, and all managers should be trained in implementing them.

Dignity policies and the procedures that support them are part of the organisation's health and safety package. They should be available and explained to all employees and reviewed regularly for effectiveness. Best practice is for an initial round of training for all staff, followed by quarterly updates and annual refresher training. Some ways to ensure that the policies are visible are to post them where people meet, for example in kitchen areas, meeting rooms and rest rooms; display them on computer screen pop-ups or tabs; and make them easily accessible on the organisation's Intranet.

Clearly documented policies show the organisation takes these issues seriously and can ensure that trouble is addressed quickly and effectively. They should serve to alert the organisation to patterns of unacceptable conduct and the need for training and other prevention measures in particular areas.

From a purely practical standpoint, this makes it less likely that complaints escalate to government authorities, which can be costly, time-consuming and damaging to the organisation's public image. From a morale and productivity standpoint, they help maintain a positive working climate and positive working relationships, and reassure victims and minimise their stress. When widely promoted, understood and supported, these policies are the foundation for a culture that values everyone's contributions and respects individual differences in styles and abilities.

THE STRATEGIC PERSPECTIVE

What should a dignity policy include?

Dignity policies must follow the principles of procedural justice (see 'In a Nutshell: Procedural justice' on page 1012) and be understood and supported by all employees at all levels. They must include:

- a definition of bullying, sexual harassment, workplace violence and racial and religious vilification
- a statement that these behaviours are unlawful
- the complaints process, including how to make a complaint and how investigations and resolutions are to be conducted
- the consequences for any employee who engages in these unlawful behaviours.

Other common ingredients of dignity policies are:

- a clear range of responses to deal with offenders, beginning with performance counselling and ending with termination of employment
- a clear undertaking that people who make complaints will not be disadvantaged or victimised and that complaints and discussions are confidential
- a commitment to a workplace environment that values people's safety, dignity, welfare and well-being
- a commitment to prompt action, generally within three days
- a list of people to approach to discuss the problem (including union representatives, when appropriate)
- accessible supporters who are from all levels of the organisation and who have been trained to give confidential emotional support to people considering taking action and to the alleged offender(s)
- an outline of the responsibilities of all executives, managers and employees in applying the organisation's dignity principles
- champions of the policies at senior level throughout the organisation, to promote and give credibility to the policies
- clear guidance on internal investigation procedures and record-keeping
- clear standards regarding acceptable behaviour, with the stated objective of ensuring dignity for everyone and creating a positive working environment
- formal and informal internal complaints procedures and access to an independent external investigator – with no requirement that the informal complaints path should be followed first or that internal procedures be followed before approaching the relevant government authority – and a clear statement that employees may at any time pursue a formal approach with the Australian Human Rights Commission or, if it appears to be a criminal matter, the police
- incorporation of dignity-at-work issues into training programs.

Stay alert and observant

Merely dealing appropriately with a complaint is not enough. You must also take steps to prevent harassment. Be alert to your own unexamined assumptions and actions based on these assumptions and to the actions of others that may cause unnecessary discomfort, embarrassment or unpleasantness. Create a climate in which people's beliefs and feelings are respected and that rejects offensive behaviour and language. Make it possible for employees to raise concerns informally with you.

Train yourself to recognise early signals of harassment, vilification and violence so you can step in quickly. Early signs include:

- a change in demeanour or mood, for example an employee becoming withdrawn and isolated or looking tired
- an employee experiencing a number of minor workplace injuries
- higher than usual, unexplained absenteeism
- new employees, particularly those most at risk, resigning suddenly and without explanation
- reduced productivity
- regularly damaged personal effects or work tools
- regularly torn clothing or uniforms.

When employees take stress leave, think about the possibility that workplace abuse might be the cause; medical certificates are unlikely to mention harassment, but merely state that the employee is unwell due to emotional stress at work.

 THE STRATEGIC PERSPECTIVE

Find it and fix it

Organisations should use statistics to help spot problem areas and potential problem areas. They should also proactively monitor patterns in key indicators for signs of harassment and violence; for example, high levels of attrition or absenteeism associated with particular shifts, departments or teams. Other indicators and patterns to monitor are accident and incident statistics, use of employee assistance programs, employee satisfaction surveys, exit interviews, grievances, lost productivity, personal leave, reported incidents of bullying, harassment, racial or religious vilification and workplace violence, as well as workers' compensation claims.

These types of indicators of employee satisfaction and productivity help organisations to identify problems early on, investigate them and respond quickly with appropriate support and assistance.

Train people not to put up with assaults on their dignity. If they are assaulted, they should report it immediately. Generally, the targets of harassment, vilification and violence are best not trying to sort out the situation by themselves because responding could make the situation worse.

At the first sign of threatened or actual violence, employees should inform their leader-manager or the appropriate person at the workplace (e.g. an employee relations manager) and use the organisation's grievance procedure. They should avoid being alone with the alleged perpetrator, get witnesses to the incidents whenever possible and begin a written record of all incidents.

THE STRATEGIC PERSPECTIVE

A selection of people's responsibilities

Everyone has a responsibility to:

- allow others to hold opinions different from their own
- allow others to refuse requests
- consider the needs and wishes of others as well as themselves
- not cause others to feel in danger or uneasy
- treat others with dignity and respect.

Harassment

Harassment is unwelcome and uninvited physical or verbal conduct that is offensive to its recipient. Whether it's based on ability, age, gender, marital status, pregnancy, race, religion or sexuality, it leaves the harassed person feeling angry, frightened, humiliated, intimidated, offended, resentful or trapped.

Harassment has to do with dominance and the exercise of power, real or perceived, in the workplace. This is why the most common (but not the only) victims of harassment are young people and women employed in positions lower down the organisational hierarchy. These people generally find it awkward, difficult or embarrassing to make complaints about the treatment they are receiving. Leader-managers of young people need to be particularly alert to the possibilities of harassment taking place.

Some harassing behaviour may be based on unexamined assumptions and be unthinking rather than malicious. Whether or not harm is intended, however, harassment creates an unpleasant working environment and reduces the victim's job satisfaction and their ability to complete their duties effectively.

 FYI

Harassment isn't just down the line

Harassment claims are generally more costly than physical injury claims because employees typically need more time off work. Like physical injury, the impact of harassment stretches beyond the victim to their family and colleagues through damaged morale and lowered productivity.

- An employee must not harass another employee in the same organisation. For example, a manager must not harass an employee; a group of employees must not harass another employee; one employee must not harass another employee.
- An employee of one organisation must not harass an employee of another organisation during the course of his or her work. For example, a technician servicing a client's equipment on the client's premises must not harass that client's employees.
- An employee or a group of employees of an organisation must not harass an employee of another organisation who visits to provide goods or services. For example, the employees at the client company must not harass the technician in the previous example.
- A person must not harass another person when providing goods or a service. For example, a hairdresser must not harass a customer.
- Employees must not be harassed by the people to whom they are providing goods or services. For example, a customer must not harass a hairdresser.

Should any of these types of harassment take place, employers have a responsibility to protect the victim from harassment and to prevent their employees from harassing others.

Bullying

Bullying is a form of harassment. It is repeated inappropriate, unreasonable and potentially aggressive behaviour directed towards a person or group of persons at a workplace and creates a risk to health and safety. It includes threats and abusive language, or the opposite – shunning – and it degrades, embarrasses, humiliates, intimidates or undermines the victim(s).

No one knows precisely how much bullying goes on in Australian workplaces because it is very under-reported. Some experts say that between one in four and one in two employees are bullied at least once during their career; it is estimated that between 400000 and two million Australians are bullied at work every year and 2.5 to 5 million will experience bullying at some time during their career.[4] Bullying and harassment are growing as a proportion of psychological injury workers' compensation claims and tend to be more costly on average than claims for less serious physical injuries, both in terms of direct costs and time taken off work, costing employers an average of $17000 to $24000 per claim.[5] And it costs the Australian economy as much as $36 billion a year when you consider hidden and lost opportunity costs (e.g. costs associated with increased attrition or the associated recruitment and retraining costs, the cost of time spent dealing with internal complaints, and intangible costs associated with lowered loyalty, staff morale and trust).[6]

Bullies invalidate and demean their victims, gradually wearing them down and eroding their self-esteem with a constant stream of hostility, ridicule and petty fault finding. Unlike physical abuse, bullying doesn't leave marks that you can see, but it's just as painful. It is intended to make the victim feel miserable. It drains the victim's self-confidence and leaves them unable to perform effectively; meanwhile, the perpetrator feels superior and dominant.

Here is how some victims have described being bullied:
* 'She would time me when I went to the toilet.'
* 'He would tear strips off me at meetings, in front of my peers.'
* 'People used to cower when he entered the room. Some people literally jumped.'
* 'My work was never good enough, no matter how hard I tried. And I know I was doing what I was expected to do, and as well as everyone else.'
* 'She'd set an impossible deadline and then say something like: "Just remember. Jobs are no longer for life."'

Some bullies repeatedly target one individual. Others spread their aggression and intimidation around. Some offend, demean or put people down in private, others in front of colleagues, clients or customers. Some bully openly (*overt bullying*), others in subtle and not easily observed ways (*covert bullying*). Some bullying is done electronically (*cyber bullying*) and some is done by groups (*mobbing*). Some bullying is through exclusion or *ostracism*. Some people even harass their manager (*upwards bullying*) by spreading rumours, skipping meetings and ignoring the manager's opinions and views.[7]

◉ THEORY TO PRACTICE

The high cost of bad behaviour

For the five years she worked at the Monash University bookstore, sales assistant Wendy Swan was bullied by her manager Kristen Cowell, who, among other behaviours, made her memorise booklists and complete other meaningless tasks, verbally abused her with tirades that sometimes left her in tears, and flung a book and calculator at her for the way she answered the phone.

Wendy wrote letters to the directors about the sarcasm, hostility, rudeness and violent behaviour that she was subjected to and even complained to the chairman of the board, Paul Somers. Wendy only stuck it out so long because she refused to be pushed out by a bully.

But her health suffered and she eventually experienced significant psychological injury. When she made a formal complaint, the court held that she was unnecessarily and unreasonably exposed to stress at work.

Wendy was awarded nearly $600000 compensation: $292544.38 for loss of income (past and future) and $300000 for pain and suffering and loss of enjoyment of life.[8]

Bullying can take two forms:

1 Unreasonable and inappropriate acts of *commission* – a pattern of repeatedly doing or saying something,

2 Acts of *omission* – a pattern of repeatedly failing to do something that should reasonably expected to be done.

Table 30.1 shows examples of the two forms of bullying.

TABLE 30.1 Bullying in the workplace: Acts of commission and omission

Acts of commission	Acts of omission
Adjusting rosters and work allocation so the victim is near the leader-manager/bully and isolated from the team	Deliberately withholding information, support or access to needed information, resources or training
Approving leave for the victim only when the manager has leave scheduled	Denying opportunities (e.g. for promotion, secondments, training)
Belittling the employee through derogatory comments, graffiti, personally offensive remarks, sarcasm or teasing	Exclusion from social events
Blocking promotion	Failure to pass on messages or supply the correct or necessary information
Constant fault finding and put-downs	Pointedly ignoring the victim while speaking to others
Constantly changing targets or guidelines	Regularly delegating interesting work and assignments to everyone but the victim
Intimidating the employee (e.g. invading their personal space)	Unfairly allocating work benefits
Making threats (e.g. about job security)	
Making unwelcome remarks (e.g. about a person's dress or appearance, or more subtle embarrassing comments)	
Micromanaging or supervising in an overbearing fashion	
Persistently questioning a person's beliefs, customs, racial or ethnic origin or religion	
Sabotaging the victim's work (e.g. by hiding important documents or supplying incorrect information)	
Setting impossible assignments, deadlines or unreasonable workloads	
Shouting and screaming at employees	
Spreading malicious rumours	
Telling jokes and stories of a humiliating nature	
Verbally abusing people	
Undermining by constant public criticism, ridiculing the victim's opinion and work contribution in front of the team	

THEORY TO PRACTICE

Some euphemisms for bullying

Have you heard any of these 'spins' to excuse bullying?

- 'It's a personality clash.'
- 'There's nothing wrong – she just needs to adjust her attitude.'
- 'That's just old Brucie complaining again.'
- 'We have a robust management style in this company.'
- 'We're tough here – but it works.'
- 'Yes, she can be a bit abrasive at times. But she gets results.'

Identifying bullies

Bullies use strength of personality or power to coerce and dominate others by fear. Some bullies are socially inept oafs whose lack of interpersonal skills is revealed in menacing and unprofessional behaviour. However, many bullies are clever, competent, sophisticated manipulators who delight in making others uncomfortable. Because they have had so much practice at it, they are masters of using verbal hostility to wield power over others and even terrorise them.

Bullies may be people with low self-esteem who try to enhance their self-worth by demeaning others. Their desire to dominate and humiliate leads them to deny or ignore the accomplishments, experiences, feelings, opinions, plans and values of those around them. While many bullies attack people with less power who are likely to feel powerless to complain, other bullies target competent, successful people who make them feel inadequate or threatened in some way.

While some bullies are their victim's peers – often the most unproductive of peers – studies in Australia and overseas show that it's mostly leader-managers, both male and female, who are the bullies.

Many bullies began their careers as bullies in childhood and carry the behaviour over into adulthood and into their working lives. Other people become bullies when they feel under pressure. Intense work pressure leaves less time to develop the healthy working relationships that reduce both bullying and the perception of bullying.

Overloaded bullies may be becoming more common due to stress resulting from restructuring and downsizing and the need for fewer people to achieve more with less. These bullies may not have a deep-seated need to humiliate others but lack the skills to deal more effectively with the stress job demands put on them; bullying is how they cope.

Don't confuse strong, directive management with bullying. Most managers occasionally need to put pressure on people to achieve results but bullies can be relied on to pile on the pressure.

Table 30.2 shows the difference between professional leader-managers' behaviour and the way bullies behave.

TABLE 30.2 Bullying: Professional behaviour versus bullying

Professional leader-manager	Destructive bully
Constructive criticism	Personal attack
Build employee's self-esteem and confidence	Tear down self-esteem and confidence
Use their influence	Abuse their power
Find ways to draw on people's talent and treat everyone the same	Single people out
Deal productively with under-performing employees	Attack even high-performing employees

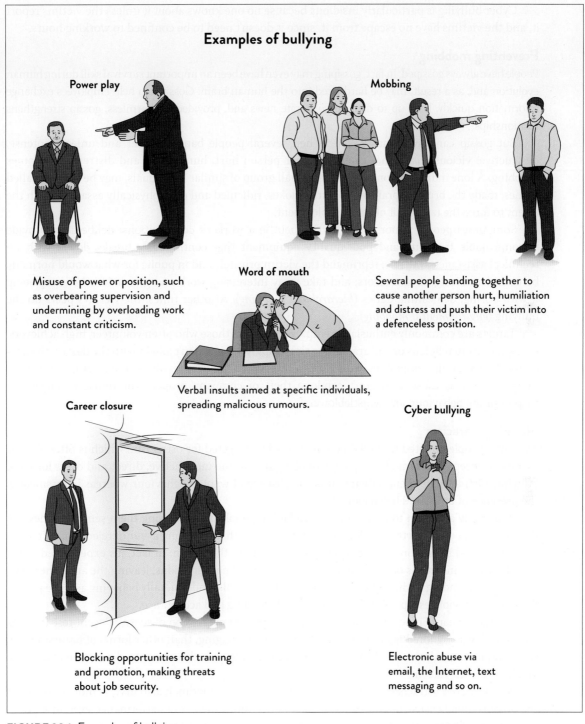

Examples of bullying

Power play
Misuse of power or position, such as overbearing supervision and undermining by overloading work and constant criticism.

Word of mouth
Verbal insults aimed at specific individuals, spreading malicious rumours.

Mobbing
Several people banding together to cause another person hurt, humiliation and distress and push their victim into a defenceless position.

Career closure
Blocking opportunities for training and promotion, making threats about job security.

Cyber bullying
Electronic abuse via email, the Internet, text messaging and so on.

FIGURE 30.1 Examples of bullying

Dealing with cyber bullying

Enabled by the explosion of smartphones and the growth of social networking sites, cyber bullying in the workplace can cause major problems. These technologies may also allow cyber bullies to be even more aggressive than people who bully face to face due to the anonymity they offer.

Cyber bullying is particularly insidious because no one knows about it unless the victims report it, and the victims have no escape from it, since it doesn't need to be confined to working hours.

Preventing mobbing

People have always gossiped. In fact, gossiping may even have been an important survival skill during human evolution and, as a result, may be hardwired into the human brain. Gossip can help employees exchange information quickly, keep up to date on corporate news and, provided it's harmless, gossip strengthens relationships.

But gossip can have a nasty side. When several people band together and unleash intense, destructive, vicious gossip that causes another person hurt, humiliation and distress, it becomes mobbing. A lone individual, or sometimes a small group of similar individuals, may be bullied, called names, made the brunt of pranks or practical jokes, ridiculed and even physically assaulted with the intent to force the target out of their employment.

Sometimes people senior to the victim belittle a worker's contributions; deliberately provide uncomfortable furniture and poor-quality equipment that continuously breaks down, with no technical assistance available; reprimand the victim privately and in public for what would normally be considered insignificant errors; and take away interesting work and give it to others, replacing it with boring, demeaning duties (*hierarchical mobbing*). At other times, the victim's peers do the bullying (*environmental mobbing*).

Targets are commonly enthusiastic employees such as those who often volunteer, high achievers, employees from religious or cultural minorities, employees who don't join in with the destructiveness of the larger group, employees with family responsibilities (especially women), employees with integrity such as those who don't condone theft of company property or refuse to engage in inappropriate behaviour, and whistleblowers.

Stopping ostracism

The same people targeted for bullying may instead be targeted for ostracism, which is often viewed as a more acceptable form of social control compared to the more active, direct and overt forms of bullying. Ostracism is silent bullying. It is the absence of wanted behaviour whereas harassment is the presence of unwanted behaviour.

Bullies pay attention to their victims. Excluding people by ostracising them sends the message that they're not even worth the effort of bullying. Rather than instilling a *fear* of rejection, ostracism *is* rejection and so is more psychologically devastating to the victim; in fact, it's experienced much like physical pain. This is because shutting a person out of conversations, leaving the area when they enter, not responding to their questions, comments or emails, and generally behaving as if the person does not exist, violates a person's basic needs for belonging and acceptance.

George Bernard Shaw said, 'Silence is the most perfect expression of scorn'.[9] Recent research has found that being ignored is more common, and more damaging, than other forms of harassment in the workplace. It's also more likely to lead to health problems such as anxiety, depression and stress, and lowered self-esteem.

Not only does ostracism seem to be more harmful to the victim, it also may be more harmful to the organisation because it reduces job satisfaction, commitment and performance even more than other forms of harassment and causes more resignations than harassment.[10]

Thwarting a bully

Never ignore bullying of any sort or turn a blind eye – bullies continue to bully as long as people let them. When bullying is reported to you or hinted at, or when you suspect it is occurring, tackle it quickly. Don't force the victim to address the bullying themselves, resign, suffer in silence or take stress leave. Tactfully find out whether others are being bullied and are willing to speak up.

As a leader-manager, you are the most likely person to spot the isolation of a team member. Treat the situation seriously and intervene quickly. Explain the deep pain it can cause and make it clear that ostracising a co-worker is not professional behaviour, is not harmless and is not acceptable, and that you will deal with behaviour that excludes teammates as you would with any other underperformance issue.

When bullying behaviour is more overt and direct, make it clear that it is not tolerated. Because bullying is generally a long-established habit, one discussion is usually not enough. Address the bullying behaviour each time it occurs. Use the hot-stove principle and begin managing the behaviour as described in on page 332. Since many bullies lack the interpersonal skills to deal with people differently, name the bullying behaviour and tell the bully what to do instead.

To counteract a culture of bullying of any sort, build a diverse team in which people are respected as individuals and for the roles they carry out. Make sure everyone is aware of your organisation's dignity policies through regular discussions and team meetings.

Sexual harassment

The Commonwealth *Sex and Age Discrimination Legislation Amendment Act 2011* defines sexual harassment as a person making a sexual advance, requesting sexual favours or engaging in other conduct of a sexual nature that is unwelcome and takes place in circumstances that a reasonable person would have anticipated *the possibility* that the person harassed would be humiliated, intimidated or offended (see Figure 30.2).[11] It expands the definition of sexual harassment to cover areas outside of the workplace or educational institutions.

Is it sexual in nature?

Is it unwelcome?

Would a reasonable person, in the circumstances, anticipate the possibility that the victim would be offended? Humiliated? Intimidated?

When the answer to any of these questions is 'yes', then it is sexual harassment.

FIGURE 30.2 Is it sexual harassment?

Any unwelcome or unwanted sexual advance, request for sexual favours or unwelcome sexual conduct is sexual harassment. It includes the tacky 'grab and grope' as well as less overt but unwelcome touches and pats, and verbal and non-verbal behaviour and innuendo; it can even be electronic.

Here are some examples of sexually harassing behaviour:

- displaying or distributing offensive messages or material (including cartoons, 'girlie' posters and lewd jokes) either on hard copy or electronically
- irrelevant and unnecessary references to sex
- leering or staring
- persistent unwelcome emails, instant messages, social invitations, telephone calls, text messages, and so on, at work or at home
- physical contact ranging from, for example, unwanted and unwarranted 'patting', pinching and touching to criminal assault
- remarks or jokes about a person's alleged sexual activities or private life
- sexually explicit communications through emails, text messages, and so on
- sexually suggestive comments, jokes or remarks
- unwelcome sexual advances.

Just over one in five people (21%) over the age of 15 have experienced one or more of these unwanted behaviours in the past five years; most of these people are women, although male harassment of other men is increasing. The Australian Human Rights Commission national survey on sexual harassment revealed that sexual harassment was still a problem and concluded that progress in purging workplace sexual harassment had 'stalled'. The survey showed:

- Women, mostly under the age of 40, were the largest harassed group, with one in four (25%) having experienced sexual harassment; men, either a co-worker (52%), boss or employer (22%), constituted 90% of the harassers.
- One in six men (15%) also experienced sexual harassment.
- Understanding and reporting sexual harassment had not increased noticeably, despite stronger legal protections. Only one in five (20%) people who were harassed made a complaint and one in three (29%) sought support or advice.
- Few people witnessed sexual harassment first hand (13%) and 51% of witnesses had taken action to prevent and reduce the harm of sexual harassment.
- The number of people experiencing negative consequences (e.g. demotion, victimisation) from making a complaint had increased significantly, to nearly one third (29%).

The survey also found that when people made a formal complaint of harassment, usually to their manager or boss, the harassment stopped in 45% of the cases. The majority of complainants were satisfied or extremely satisfied with the complaint process and 78% of complaints were finalised in less than a month.

Male and female employees and managers in professional, office and service work, and males in skilled trades are the most likely groups to be harassed. The majority of sexual harassment continues to be experienced in the workplace (68%) and occurs in workplaces of all sizes: large (41%), medium (24%) and small (33%) organisations.[12]

Occupational violence

Occupational violence is defined as any incident during which an employee is physically attacked or threatened in the workplace. It need not be repeated – once is enough. Violence includes both physical and psychological harm. Physical violence in the workplace can result in bruising, fractures and even death. It includes the direct or indirect application of force to the victim's body, to equipment or to clothing worn by the victim that places their health and safety at risk. Grabbing, indecent physical contact, kicking, pushing, striking, spitting, throwing objects, tripping and use of weapons are all included.

Psychological violence includes ostracism (discussed earlier), verbal abuse, stalking and other forms of unwanted communications and intrusions into a person's private life, whether in person or electronically. Sexual harassment, racial and religious harassment and all forms of bullying are forms of workplace violence, as is physical action directed at inanimate objects (banging a table, throwing objects), vandalism and destruction of another employee's or the organisation's property, and rude or offensive gesturing.[13]

A threat means a statement or behaviour that causes someone to believe he or she is in danger of being physically attacked, regardless of the attacker's intent. For example, a customer may become so verbally abusive towards a sales assistant that it seems likely he or she will become physically violent. Or perhaps a colleague threatens 'I'll see you in the car park', or an employee repeatedly draws a finger across his throat while looking menacingly at another employee. These acts are considered workplace violence, and when behaviours like these occur they must be stopped and prevented from recurring.

'But I didn't mean it', 'I was only trying to scare her' or 'I was just joking' is no defence. Neither is mental incapacity an excuse when violence is a predictable outcome. For example, employers must take steps to protect employees and others from people with brain injuries or mental illness who are inconsistent in taking anti-psychosis or other suitable medication or who have a history of violence.

Workplace violence: Who is most at risk?

Workplace violence occurs in all industries and occupations although it's more common in some workplaces than others. Employees who face a greater risk of violence are those who:

- carry out inspection or enforcement duties such as government employees, police officers and prison officers
- handle money, prescription drugs or valuables such as doctors' surgery staff and retail staff
- have a mobile workplace, for example a taxi
- provide advice, care, education or services such as healthcare workers, social services employees and teachers
- work alone or in small numbers such as meter readers, petrol station cashiers and real estate agents, or in isolated or low-traffic areas such as storage areas, utility rooms and washrooms
- work during periods of intense organisational change or conflict for example, during downsizing or industrial action
- work in community-based settings such as nurses, social workers and other home visitors
- work in premises where alcohol is served (e.g. food and beverage staff)
- work near businesses at risk of violent crime, such as pubs and banks
- work with the public, for example, Centrelink employees and insolvency and trustee officers
- work with unstable or volatile persons such as social services or criminal justice system employees.

Racial and religious vilification

Racial and religious vilification is behaviour that incites or encourages hatred, revulsion, serious contempt or severe ridicule against a person or group of people because of their race or religion. It includes drawings, gestures, graffiti, images, spoken words and written material. People who are subject to vilification feel harassed, humiliated, intimidated or physically threatened.

No self-respecting organisation or leader-manager allows that to happen to any of its employees. Again, an organisation needs to respond with clear policies supported by senior executives and leader-managers and ongoing awareness training and communication, well-known and easily accessed complaints procedures, regular monitoring of key measures and a zero-tolerance approach.

The Commonwealth *Racial Discrimination Act 1975* and the Commonwealth *Racial Discrimination Amendment Act 1980* make any behaviour that belittles, denigrates, humiliates, insults or maligns a person or group in public based on their colour, national or ethnic origin, or race illegal.

2. Investigating complaints

> If you have made a complaint to your manager or others in your workplace and there have not been adequate steps taken to stop the bullying there are a number of options that you can take to get help.
>
> 'Workplace bullying: Violence, harassment and bullying fact sheet', Australian Human Rights Commission[14]

The way complaints are treated as they move up the levels of the legal process are taken into account by investigating authorities as much or more than the details of the complaint itself.[15] This makes it essential to follow your organisation's policies and procedures. People who are upset by unwelcome conduct normally complain to their leader-manager first. Never attempt to skirt around a complaint or pressure complainants to drop their claim.

Early intervention is the key. All complaints concerning harassment, violence or vilification require a prompt (within three days) formal investigation by discussing the incident(s) with the complainer and the subject of the complaint.

● THEORY TO PRACTICE

The price of poor advice
Susan Spiteri's claim of bullying and harassment against IBM escalated to the Federal Court. After making her allegations, she was told to go away and think about whether she really wanted to pursue a complaint. This became a central part of her case and she was awarded $1.1 million compensation.[16]

Take immediate steps to prevent any further occurrence of the illegal behaviour, offer any necessary assistance and, when allegations are serious, suspend the alleged perpetrator. Report allegations and incidents of workplace violence to the police for investigation. Harassment and vilification allegations can be investigated and dealt with in-house unless the complainant prefers to go to an external authority.

Equally, deal quickly with any behaviour that puts others at physical or psychological risk, even when you only suspect that harassing or bullying behaviour or violence or vilification may be taking place in your work group.

Conducting an investigation yourself

If your organisation hasn't nominated someone to investigate complaints, do so yourself – promptly. Determine whether the complaint is serious enough to bring in an external independent mediator. When you investigate the complaint yourself, interview the people concerned. Advise everyone you interview of the need for total confidentiality and that breaches are a disciplinary issue. This is to prevent gossip and claims of defamation. Either or both the complainant and the person accused can have a support person attend the interviews with them. Make full notes of your investigation, including the dates of interviews and of writing your notes.

Use the communication skills described in Chapter 6. Speak with the victim and document the allegations fully, including dates and any witnesses. Then put the allegations to the alleged offender and hear their version of the events. Let both the complainer and the alleged offender know about any support systems available to them, such as employee assistance programs (EAPs), harassment or violence contact officers, and peer support systems.

When there is a dispute over facts, interview any first-hand witnesses and gather any relevant information or evidence. Evidence might be a lack of evidence where you would logically expect it to exist, complaints or information provided by other employees about the behaviour of the alleged perpetrator, records kept by the victim and personnel records that may show, for example, unexplained requests for transfer or a sudden increase in sick leave, and the complainant having discussed the matter with a counsellor, friend, medical practitioner or relative.

Try to keep the two sides apart until the issue is resolved because it can distress victims to have to carry on working with someone they feel is harassing, threatening or vilifying them. Don't move either party into a less important or less senior role, however. You may need to supervise the work group more closely while you are investigating the complaint to make sure that the behaviour does not continue, and you need to maintain the confidentiality of both the victim and the alleged offender while doing this.

Remain neutral as you look for what is actually happening. The fact that there are no witnesses is not sufficient to dismiss a complaint on the grounds that it can't be substantiated. Remember that, because of the nature of workplace violence and harassment, the matter is unlikely to be clear-cut and you may have to form an opinion based on probabilities.

⦿ IN A NUTSHELL

Procedural justice

Procedural justice (known as *due process* in the USA and *fundamental justice* in Canada) is about the fairness with which decisions concerning disputes are reached. Employers should observe the following principles when developing complaints procedures:
- Explain to both parties how the matter is to be dealt with.
- Fully inform the alleged offender of the complaint and give them an opportunity to respond.
- Fully inform the victim of the response and give the victim an opportunity to respond.
- Make a full inquiry into the matter.
- Seek evidence to support a decision.
- You must act honestly, impartially and without bias and you must be seen to do so by both parties.

⦿ THE STRATEGIC PERSPECTIVE

Dealing with complaints

Depending on the severity of a complaint, it can be handled in three ways:
1. *Mild*: A trained manager can handle the complaint by facilitating a discussion between the employees involved.
2. *More complex and serious*: An independent mediator such as a professional dispute manager handles the complaint.
3. *Severe*: The accused person should be suspended during the investigations.

Substantiated complaints

When you believe the complaint is substantiated, meet formally with the offender to discuss the misconduct, then meet with other relevant staff, for example your manager, to discuss the next steps. Inform the victim of your finding and the options for addressing the matter. Do not require the victim to 'negotiate' an outcome or enter into a dispute-resolution process with the perpetrator.

Take disciplinary action with the offender in line with the seriousness of the matter so that the 'punishment' fits the 'crime'. Never excuse the behaviour or overlook it, but take into account factors such as disciplinary history, such as any prior similar incidents or complaints, the desired outcome of the victim and the severity and frequency of the proscribed (illegal) behaviour.

The outcome is often, but not always, termination of employment; other resolution measures might be a formal apology from the offender and the commitment not to repeat the behaviour, an official warning, recrediting leave taken by the victim because of the illegal behaviour, and training and counselling for one or both parties.

Unsubstantiated complaints

When the complaint is not substantiated, possibly for lack of evidence or witnesses or on the balance of probabilities, notify both parties of the outcome. The fact that the complaint cannot be proven does not mean that harassment or violence has not occurred or that the complainer has lied. Your finding may be that the harassment, threats of violence or vilification may or may not have occurred and that it is impossible to make a conclusive finding. When that is the case, consider whether to provide further training to the work team and monitor the situation closely.

Let the complainant know about avenues for support. Employees who are dissatisfied with the outcome can complain to an independent body, for example the Australian Human Rights Commission.

Officially appointed investigators

Most organisations nominate a senior person formally trained in workplace investigations, such as the equal employment opportunity manager, health and safety manager, HR manager or workplace diversity manager, or an external expert consultant, to receive and investigate dignity complaints. In addition to being formally trained, these people need to possess the interpersonal skills, emotional intelligence and experience to handle an investigation that is likely to be emotive and fraught with legal issues. They also need to be able to deal with the stress and pressure of the investigation and handle cross-examination should the complaint progress to an outside tribunal or court.

The investigation must be clearly impartial and independent in order to avoid allegations of cover-up or favouritism. Investigators begin by agreeing specific terms of reference with senior management and asking for the complaint to be put in writing. They then review all relevant awards, workplace agreements, legislation, policies, procedures and personal files, prepare interview questions and arrange for a quiet, private room to meet separately with the parties concerned.

Generally, the complainant is interviewed first to obtain full details of the allegation, including the names of witnesses, if any. The subject of the complaint is then interviewed, told the exact nature of the complaint and provided with full details. The investigator obtains the alleged perpetrator's response, concentrating on the facts (not rumour or hearsay), and provides an opportunity to respond in writing. When necessary, any witnesses are then interviewed (this is not normally required when there is no dispute between the parties concerning the facts) and the investigator reinterviews the complainant, the accused person and witnesses.

The next step is usually mediation. The mediator should ask what the complainant's desired outcome is and advise the parties of the process and its likely duration. When the complainant is not satisfied with the outcome, a conciliation phase generally begins. A representative from the appropriate government body or another independent conciliator listens to both sides and then tries to help the parties reach an agreement or a compromise that is satisfactory to both parties.

When agreement is not reached, or if either party is unhappy with the outcome, arbitration is the next step. This involves tribunals and then courts, which, in most cases, have powers to enforce their decisions. Findings in favour of the complainant may include paying compensation, reinstating the complainant (when the complainant has resigned or been transferred) or other action that is felt appropriate. Hearings by a government body are in private and are relatively informal. Tribunals and courts tend to be public and more formal.

An alternative to mediation, conciliation and arbitration is to move, in effect, straight to arbitration and ask the investigator to make findings of facts as to whether or not the complaint has been substantiated and recommend the action to take (e.g. an apology and counselling, demotion, discipline, termination of employment, training or transfer). These actions are directed at the perpetrator when the complaint is substantiated or at the complainant when there is clear evidence that the complaint was vexatious or malicious. Management generally makes the final decision about the action to take.

◉ IN A NUTSHELL

Two points to bear in mind

It takes courage to lodge a complaint and you don't want to make it any tougher than it already is. That's why it's illegal to:

1. Disadvantage someone who has threatened to take, or is in the process of taking, action under the legislation (e.g. you cannot terminate their employment or make working life so difficult for them that they resign).
2. Disadvantage the complainant with the way the complaint is resolved (unless there is strong evidence that the complaint was vexatious or malicious, in which case disciplinary action may be recommended against the complainant).

---

3. Managing for employee welfare and wellness

By investing in strategies and programs that support the health and well-being of employees, business can work towards minimising the impact of presenteeism and improving productivity in the workplace.

'Sick at work: The cost of presenteeism to your business and the economy', Medibank Private[17]

Since 1984, employers have been required to prevent psychological as well as physical harm to employees and provide not just a safe, but also a healthy, working environment. The latest move in the health and safety arena, summarised in Figure 30.3, is to actively encourage physical and psychological health and well-being.

The organisations at the forefront of managing for employee welfare and wellness are those keenest to attract and retain a high-quality, engaged and productive workforce. The working environment they provide isn't just neutral, but actively seeks to promote employees' physical and psychological health. The best programs continuously improve their health promotion activities.[18]

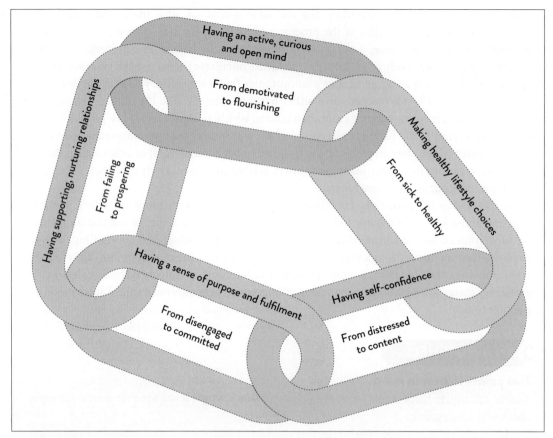

FIGURE 30.3 From preventing to encouraging

Although organisations are still learning how to quantify the benefits of employee welfare and wellness programs precisely, those that have introduced them have both quantitative and qualitative evidence that well-targeted programs work. They can help to counteract the skills shortage and boost the bottom line by:

- increasing return on learning and development investment
- improving employee engagement
- improving employee morale, satisfaction and motivation
- improving employee retention
- improving employer brand and employer value proposition
- improving work performance and productivity
- improving workplace relationships
- reducing absenteeism and sick leave
- reducing the cost of workers' rehabilitation and compensation
- reducing presenteeism.[19]

Employees benefit too. Apart from living longer, they gain:

- a greater capacity to enjoy life both at work and away from work
- increased health awareness and knowledge
- increased physical health and mental well-being
- improved morale, job satisfaction and motivation
- improved opportunities for a healthier lifestyle.[20]

The cost of presenteeism

On average, every employee loses 6.5 working days a year through presenteeism – coming to work but not being fully productive. Presenteeism costs the Australian economy $34.1 billion per year, or 2.7% of GDP, which is far greater than the cost of absenteeism. (The cost to the economy takes into account factors such as reduction in exports and investments.)

Employees who come to work when they're ill are more prone to injury, make more mistakes and need to repeat tasks, work more slowly than usual and, when contagious, can pass on their illness to other employees, beginning a vicious cycle of presenteeism that costs organisations far more than would the absence through illness of the employee who was originally sick.

The most common cause of presenteeism is depression (21%), followed by allergies (17%), hypertension (13%) and diabetes (12%).[21]

Employee welfare

Providing a working environment that is healthy encompasses a range of measures, including ensuring the workplace is well lit and ventilated and providing amenities and facilities such as adequate drinking water, hot water, space for eating meals and toilet facilities. But this is just the beginning.

Better lighting or the Hawthorne effect?

The artificial lighting in most offices may not be the most effective in terms of maintaining employees' alertness. Research involving 104 office workers, carried out at the Surrey Sleep Centre at the University of Surrey in the United Kingdom in partnership with Philips Lighting, found that replacing traditional white-light with blue-enriched lighting helped the workers stay more alert and feel less sleepy during the day. The workers also subjectively reported improvements in concentration, mood and work performance, less eye strain, irritability and fatigue in the evening, and improved sleep quality.[22]

The Hawthorne Effect, named after the Hawthorne plant of the Western Electric Company in Illinois, explains why experiments can have falsely positive results. A research team led by Professor Elton Mayo of Harvard University found that even minute changes in illumination levels in a factory, which at one point were as low as bright moonlight, resulted in improved productivity.

During five years of experimentation between 1927 and 1932, the researchers made other refinements to the work environment, such as clearing floors of obstacles, maintaining clean work stations and relocating work stations. Each small change was followed by increased productivity.

The researchers finally realised the actual source of the improved productivity: the relationship they had developed with the workers – one of respect and camaraderie. This type of relationship was certainly not a part of standard worker–management relations in the early 1900s.

The researchers concluded that people produce more when they feel appreciated, when people pay attention to them and seek their opinions, and when their expertise is being studied. It may sound like a no-brainer today, but it was revolutionary at the time.

Psychosocial factors

Psychosocial factors, the interaction of psychological and social factors with the environment, can harm or help employees' physical and psychological health, thereby affecting an organisation's effectiveness. When you look through the 'In a Nutshell: Psychosocial risk factors' you can see just how much there is to be aware of, as a leader-manager, in looking after the welfare of your team members. Any and all of these factors can cause stress and weaken the immune system, opening the door to physical illness and stress-related disorders. As discussed, they can lead to bullying and stress, reduce productivity and increase the organisation's costs through increased attrition, compensation and time off. Good employers aim to limit or reduce all of these factors.

◉ IN A NUTSHELL

Psychosocial risk factors

Here are the main groups of risk to employee welfare and well-being:

- Career development, pay, status: Insufficient recognition and rewards, job insecurity, lack of opportunities for growth and development, lack of promotion prospects, unclear or unfair performance evaluation systems, work of low 'social value'.
- Interpersonal relationships: Bullying, harassment and violence; customer aggression, inadequate supervision, high staff turnover, inconsiderate or unsupportive supervision; isolated or solitary work; no agreed procedures for dealing with complaints or problems; poor relationships with colleagues.
- Job content: Lack of clarity of roles and responsibilities, lack of control of the work and working methods, lack of variety, monotonous and meaningless tasks, unpleasant tasks all caused by poor job design.
- Organisational culture: Excessive competition, incivility and lack of respect; not feeling able to ask questions, report mistakes and problems; organisational change, organisational politics, poor communication; poor leadership; unclear organisational objectives and structure.
- Organisational role: Suitability to job, conflicting roles within the same job, continuously dealing with other people and their problems, responsibility for people, unclear role and responsibilities, job insecurity.
- Participation and control: Lack of control over, for example, work environment, working hours, work methods and work pace, lack of involvement in decision-making, not feeling involved and able to influence decisions and events.
- Working hours: Badly designed shift systems, excessive work hours, inflexible work schedules, long and unsocial hours, and shift work, unpredictable working hours.
- Work–life balance: Conflicting demands of work and home life, lack of support for domestic problems at work, lack of support for work problems at home.
- Workload and work pace: Having too much or too little to do, excessive time pressure such as tight deadlines, unreasonable performance demands.

The impact of these factors depends on personality attributes, such as the ability to cope with pressure, as well as factors in the work environment.[23] (Did you notice how many of these factors leader-managers can directly influence?)

So it isn't just physical risk factors, such as noise, poor seating and lighting, poor posture or repetitive movements that disrupt concentration, harm the body and lead to physical and mental problems. People's work environment, working relationships and the work itself can cause harm, too.

This means you need to identify and control both physical and psychosocial risk factors in order to provide a healthy workplace. Providing well-designed jobs and placing the right person in the right job, building strong teams and engaging employees with your leadership style and organisation culture are not just good management but part of your duty of care as a leader-manager.

Mental health

According to the Department of Health and Ageing, mental health issues 'are the largest cause of non-fatal disability of any disease in the country. It is a bigger barrier to workforce participation than any other illness in the country'.[24] Mental illness is a common problem in Australia and people experience it in a range of ways, from mild or moderate conditions to severe and debilitating disorders.[25] Work and the workplace affect people's mental health for better or for worse and an employee's health problems affect the workplace.

Organisations have a duty of care to employees suffering from mental illness under the Commonwealth *Disability Discrimination and Other Human Rights Legislation Amendment Act 2009* and the *Commonwealth Privacy Act 1988*.[26] The Commonwealth *Disability Discrimination Act 1992* places the burden of proof on employers to show they have taken all necessary and reasonable steps to adjust their workplaces so that employees suffering from any form of disability can work safely.

Many biological, environmental and psychosocial factors affect people's mental health. With positive mental health, or psychological well-being, you can interact with others and the environment in ways that you feel good about. Without it, you can develop behaviours and symptoms that distress yourself or others and interfere with your social functioning, productivity and ability to negotiate daily life.

While many organisations manage for physical safety and support employees with physical disabilities and injuries, mental health issues are not yet as widely dealt with. Employees may hesitate to speak up for fear of being stigmatised and it can be difficult for their leader-managers to identify problems and, when they do, to address them and offer support.

Organisations and leader-managers can help meet employees' mental health needs by creating a culture in which mental health issues are not unmentionable and by raising awareness of how people can look after their own and others' mental well-being. Many organisations also offer confidential assistance and support through employee assistance programs.

Depression and stress are the two biggest mental health issues in organisations. You should also be aware of the possibility of other psychological problems such as grief and loss, obsessive-compulsive disorders, pathological bullying, personal trauma, poor anger management and self-esteem issues, and know your organisation's procedures for offering assistance with these.

What is mental illness?
Mental illness, or *mental disorder*, is a general term that refers to a group of illnesses in the same way that heart disease refers to a group of illnesses and disorders affecting the heart. About 32% of the Australian population, or one in three people, experience one of the more common mental disorders or mood disorders, such as depression, anxiety disorders or substance-use disorders.[27]

>>

A *mental health problem* is less severe but can develop into a mental illness when not effectively dealt with. Most people experience a mental health problem at some time in their lives. Mental illnesses and mental health problems both interfere with how a person behaves, feels, thinks and interacts with others, but to different degrees.

Depression

Depression and anxiety disorders are the second largest cause of disability and death in Australia.[28] Depression is a mood disorder characterised by feelings of loss of interest or pleasure in most activities, hopelessness and sadness, and suicidal thoughts or self-blame. It is a condition that generally comes and goes and is driven by biological or genetic factors or is a response to a major life event. Depression is linked with a range of health risk behaviours including alcohol misuse and dependence, eating disorders, tobacco use and illicit drug use.

● IN A NUTSHELL

Signs of mental health needs

When an underperforming employee raises a psychological reason to justify poor performance or misconduct, or is repeatedly absent from work and exhibits one or more of the signs listed below, draw on your organisation's wellness programs to assist the employee and manage the underperformance (only) through counselling, as described in Chapter 16:

- aggression, bullying, boundary issues
- attendance problems (constantly arriving late, frequent absenteeism or presenteesim)
- breaks with reality, confused thoughts, odd behaviours
- difficulties following directions or following through on tasks and projects
- increased anxiety
- increased interpersonal conflict
- injuries that may be self-inflicted
- lack of emotional control
- lethargy
- poor concentration
- signs of intoxication or hangover
- social withdrawal
- tearfulness.

The World Health Organization has predicted that by 2020 depression will be the world's second biggest health problem behind heart disease. That's already the case in Australia where 45% of Australians are expected to experience depression at least once in their lives and 20% of Australians suffer from depression every year. Rates of depression decline with age, with people aged 16–24 experiencing the highest rates of depression.[29]

Every year, six million working days, or three to four days a month, are lost through depression, costing the Australian economy $14.9 billion and the community over $600 million in treatment expenses. When untreated, depression costs Australian organisations $642 000 for every 100 000 employees.[30] Although it is the leading cause of non-fatal disability and despite effective treatments, less than 50% of sufferers seek professional help.[31]

Stress

While a manageable level of stress is motivating, too much stress can cause productivity to deteriorate and is a growing concern for employers and employees alike. According to the World Health Organization, 'Workers who are stressed are also more likely to be unhealthy, poorly motivated, less productive and less safe at work. Their organizations are less likely to be successful in a competitive market'.[32]

Stress-related disorders are among the leading causes of early retirement from work, high absence rates, low organisational productivity and overall health impairment.[33] Symptoms include anxiety, cynicism, depression, excessive distrust, fatigue, headaches, loss of concentration and memory, mood swings and tiredness. The Commonwealth *Work Health and Safety Act 2011* requires organisations to manage stress-related illnesses and disorders and the return to work of employees suffering from such illnesses.

Psychosocial factors can lead not only to stress, a hazard in its own right, but also to musculoskeletal disorders. For example, stress-related changes in the body such as increased muscle tension can make people more susceptible to injuries, arthritis and back problems.[34] As well as physical problems, stress, when not addressed, can lead to ill mental health as problems such as burnout syndrome or more serious disorders like depression. There is significant evidence that people under stress are also more vulnerable to illness. And although many employees who suffer from stress keep quiet about it, their work and morale suffer.

The first step is identifying the original cause of the stress or, when the source of the stress is outside of work, determining the conditions at work that worsen the stress. When you or the organisation can control any of the contributors to the employee's stress, you should do so. There are a range of options available to manage these situations.

⊙ ACTION!

Do you suffer from stress? Find out with the interactive self-test: Are you stressed? on
CourseMateExpress.

⊙ IN A NUTSHELL

How workplace stress affects the workplace

Workplace stress can result in serious problems, including:
- damaged organisational image both internally and externally
- decreased commitment to work
- difficulties in attracting staff
- increased absenteeism
- increased complaints from clients and customers
- increased liability to legal claims and actions by stressed workers
- increased unsafe work practices and accident rates
- increased employee turnover
- reduced job performance and productivity.[35]

⊙ THEORY TO PRACTICE

Managing ambos' stress

Every year, more than 1100 career and 1600 volunteer staff of the South Australian Ambulance Service provide over 260 000 emergency, non-emergency, rescue and retrieval services across nearly one million square kilometres. Peer support officers work with professional psychologists to provide confidential psychological assistance and support as part of the South Australian Ambulance Service's staff wellness and assistance programs. The system helps mitigate the often difficult, stressful and traumatic events that occur on the job as well as stressful events at home and is also available to immediate family members.

Peer support officers receive ongoing training and development in 'psychological first aid', such as conducting debriefings and one-on-one critical-incident stress management. The South Australian Ambulance Service helps all staff prepare for stressful situations with pre-incident education known as 'psychological immunisation' as well as other professional development programs that assist in stress management.[36]

● THEORY TO PRACTICE

Conduct a stress audit

Is stress a problem for you or your team members? Conduct a stress audit to find out:

- Ask team members to list their main problems and sources of frustration at work and ask whether they feel they may be adversely affecting their health.
- Ask team members to list their three 'best' and three 'worst' aspects of their job and ask whether they think any of them place them under too much pressure.
- Ask more detailed questions, based on the causes of stress, asking whether any of those possible problems apply to your team member's own jobs.
- Regularly monitor absenteeism, accidents and mistakes, attrition and performance levels and look for changes, excesses and patterns.

For organisation-wide audits, ask a representative sample of employees. This information can alert you to 'at-risk' work and work groups.

Then analyse the results. Are employees who feel stressed clustered in a particular area or at a particular level? Are the numbers higher than you would expect? If so, your organisation has a duty of care to take measures to control stress. (You can find how to analyse the results of your audit on page 585.)

Based on the results, decide the best approach for your work group. Record what you decide to do and your reasons for choosing that approach.

Work–life harmony

Australia rates above average in all but one of 11 dimensions of quality of life. What's the out-of-kilter one? Work–life balance; we're in the bottom 20%. That's a concern, because, as George Eastman (inventor of roll film and founder of the Eastman Kodak Company) pointed out, 'What we do during our working hours determines what we have; what we do in our leisure hours determines what we are'.[37] (The remaining 10 dimensions of quality of life are civic engagement, education and skills, environmental quality and health, governance, housing, income and wealth, jobs and earnings, personal security, social connections and subjective well-being.)[38]

To add insult to injury, so to speak, many of us are 'donating' more than our annual leave entitlement back to our employers in the form of unpaid overtime. International comparisons show that Australians work some of the longest hours in the developed world. Australian employees work more than they are paid to work, ranging from an average of an extra three hours a week for part-time employees and six hours a week for full-time employees. This equates to 1.13 million unpaid hours or a donation of $2.1 billion unpaid overtime a week across the workforce.[39]

Why do we do it? Some say that if they didn't put in the extra time the work wouldn't get done, suggesting that organisations are placing excessive demands on employees. Then there's the organisation culture, whereby unpaid overtime is often 'compulsory', 'expected' or 'not discouraged'. In some workplaces, taking advantage of work–life balance and work–life blending measures is still very much a career-limiting option, despite the fact that we know that people work better and more productively when they lead balanced lives, as shown in Figure 30.4: The results of work–life imbalance.

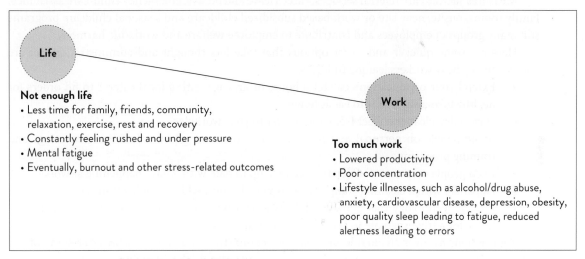

FIGURE 30.4 The results of work–life imbalance

● THE STRATEGIC PERSPECTIVE

Take a break

Knocking-off time no longer means the end of work – not with tablets, smartphones and laptops keeping people constantly hooked up to their jobs. In response to the growing awareness that psychological detachment from work during non-work time is important for employee health, some companies are flipping the 'Off' switch. Volkswagen in Germany stops its BlackBerry servers sending emails to employees from half an hour after leaving work to half an hour before starting work. Brazil has legislation entitling workers to overtime pay for answering work emails while off duty. Deutsch Telekom and Google have scheduled breaks from the Internet. French IT company Atos plans to ban internal email completely.

Studies also suggest that constant connectivity wreaks havoc with people's ability to concentrate and that regular downtime leads to greater productivity. To this end, some companies insist employees take breaks. Lloyd's Bank banned all employees from travelling during the third week of every month, not only improving employees' work–life balance but also significantly reducing costs – 70 000 fewer trips were taken during the first six months after the ban. Google's well-being program includes 'energy pods' – recharging spaces for 20- or 30-minute breaks.[40]

US President Thomas Jefferson said, 'The happiest moments of my life have been the few which I have passed at home in the bosom of my family.'[41] Nothing has changed really. Why should work interfere with personal responsibilities or prevent the active enjoyment of family life when we can find ways to get the best of both worlds – fulfil job responsibilities as well as out-of-work responsibilities? Similarly, why should home responsibilities, for example looking after a sick child, interfere with getting our work done when we can find ways to do both?

A rich life is a rounded life. Maybe that's why the adage 'All work and no play makes Jack a dull boy' has stuck around for so long. And generally speaking, employees with well-rounded lives are more productive employees. Yet achieving harmony in all areas of their lives is a struggle for many Australians.

Measures such as care referral services, carer's leave and breaks, emergency child-care assistance, family rooms, onsite, near-site or work-based subsidised childcare and seasonal childcare programs suit many groups of employees and contribute to employee welfare and work–life harmony.

Here are some quicker and easier options that take less thought and administration, yet are appreciated by busy workers leading full lives:

- Extend your organisation's cafeteria hours or arrange with a local caterer to fill orders for healthy take-away meals to eat at home.
- Have a dry-cleaner collect from and deliver to your workplace.
- Invite people on personal and parental leave to attend relevant functions, meetings and training programs.
- Keep people on personal and parental leave up to date with what's happening at work.
- Negotiate with a cleaning company to provide discounted household cleaning.
- Provide technology that allows people to work from home when children are sick, to stay home for a tradesperson, to accept a delivery, and so on.

Your actions as an individual leader-manager count, too. You can probably offer some of the options on the previous list to your work team. You could also do the following:

- Allow make-up time so employees can make up hours when they need time off to attend needed medical procedures, court hearings or a partner or a child's university graduation.
- Allow team members to take annual leave in single days.
- Allow team members to use work mobile phones for emergency family reasons.
- Consult staff on rostering arrangements.
- Discourage regular weekend working and staying back late.
- Include your organisation's welfare and wellness policies in letters of offer to new employees.
- Introduce 'keep in touch' arrangements for staff on parental or extended sick leave.
- Negotiate flexible start and finish times.
- Schedule meetings within normal working hours.

Provide support like this to everyone equally and encourage everyone to make use of it.

Flexible working

Technology lets people work any time, any where, so rather than fight it, why not make the most of it? For many employees of all ages, work–life balance has morphed into work–life blending, made possible by flexible working arrangements and communications technology.

Flexible working arrangements are becoming increasingly important and virtually mandatory for employers depending on a capable, engaged and productive workforce and those wanting to retain knowledgeable older employees and other valuable employees. They are also an important way for organisations to reduce work-related stress and, along with cross-skilling and multiskilling, to respond rapidly to changing market conditions. They multiply the other benefits of looking after employee welfare, too: reduced absenteeism, attrition and presenteeism, and increased motivation and productivity.

Flexible working reflects the reality of modern Australian society by acknowledging the non-work responsibilities and outside interests of all employees. Flexible working isn't just for women with young families. In fact, offering flexible working only to women or allowing it to be seen as supporting only female employees backfires because it results in women being seen as different and more costly to employ.

Flexible working benefits everyone, male and female, employees without families and employees with families – whether those families are traditional nuclear families or extended families and whether the family members are young, old or in between. They benefit people who want to combine work with study or community service and people who want to downshift towards phased or permanent retirement.

Different forms of flexible working suit different people and meet different organisational needs. For example, older workers (those born before the mid 1960s) are retiring in large numbers and organisations wanting to retain their expertise and experience need to offer them working hours that allow a life outside work. Career break schemes, part-time work, phased retirement, project work and sabbaticals are some ways organisations are keeping these employees at work longer while accommodating a life outside work as well.

The generations born after the mid 1960s aren't as prepared as were their elders to work long hours, at least not for long periods of time and not without significant psychological and material rewards. These employees want a life outside work; they want to enjoy it; and they're willing – even wanting – to work when and where it suits them provided they can arrange their working days and weeks to fit in with the rest of their lives. Organisations that allow flexible working practices and don't demand long hours tied to the workplace can attract and retain those employees more easily.

Fortunately, a wide range of flexible working measures exists to accommodate individual needs and improve job satisfaction and family lives. Here are some flexible working options:

- *Annualised hours*: Specifying working hours for 12 months and agreeing how best to fill the yearly quota allows employees to work flexibly and organisations to organise work around an annual cycle to meet peak demand periods as well as cover for unforeseen events such as short-term surges in demand or abnormal absenteeism.
- *Banked time*: Allowing employees to save accumulated worked time up to an agreed total of hours or weeks to 'cash in' later for time off in single days or as part of another form of leave, gives them more control over the way they blend their working and private lives and allows them increased flexibility to deal with planned or unexpected events in their private lives.
- *Career break opportunities and sabbaticals*: Extended leave from work from two to 12 months lets employees rejuvenate, study, travel, undertake carer responsibilities – whatever they want, knowing their jobs is waiting for them when they return.
- *Compressed working weeks*: Condensing the standard 40-hour week into fewer days, for example nine-day fortnights or four-day weeks, lets employees work fewer days for the same pay and retains their productivity levels.
- *Flexitime*: Staggered start and finish times and a wider spread of ordinary hours, generally with mandatory attendance during specified core hours, can help employees avoid stressful and time-consuming rush hours and arrange their working day to suit their personal needs.
- *Job-sharing*: Splitting a full-time job between two or more part-time workers, each receiving the relevant proportion of pay and leave and other benefits gets the job done and allows employees to contribute part-time.
- *Part-time working*: Offering people the option to work shorter weeks extends the employment pool you can tap into.

- *Phased retirement*: Allows employees to prepare for retirement while continuing to contribute by working successively shorter days or hours over an agreed period.
- *Purchased leave*: Also called reduced work time, flexible working years and 48/52, this allows employees to have periods of up to, for example, four weeks of unpaid leave in addition to their paid leave.
- *Telecommuting* or *teleworking*: Working from home, from a satellite office or workplace hub near home or from a mobile office, such as a vehicle, for all, most or some of the time, linked to the employer's office through information and communications technology offers many employees the flexibility they crave.
- *Term-time working*: Sometimes combined with temporary or on-call contractors to cover for employees needing to take time off during school holidays.

Sadly, many employees fail to take advantage of flexible working arrangements because the culture of their workplace doesn't encourage it – you're not 'serious' about your job when you take the afternoon off to watch your child play footy.

This is despite, and due to, the intensification of work in all sectors, which has had a negative impact on employee health and stress and makes flexible working arrangements all the more sensible. Employees often feel that to take advantage of flexible working arrangements is career suicide and that it lets their teammates down by putting more pressure on them. Yet when organisations don't accommodate employees' lives outside work, employees can come to a sudden realisation that they're giving everything to their job and are drained to the point where there's nothing left to give. No one wins.

⊚ THE STRATEGIC PERSPECTIVE

Some myths to overcome

Before flexible working can really work, we need to quash a few myths:

- Being 'present' equals being productive and hours at work equals results.
- Flexible working is for non-management employees.
- Flexible working is for women.
- Flexible working means management loses control.
- Flexible working means productivity suffers.
- Flexible working is unfair to employees without children.
- People should leave their personal lives at home.
- People who take up flexible working options aren't serious about their jobs.

Employee well-being

Not causing physical or psychological ill health is one side of the coin; the other is actively promoting physical and psychological health. There's a big difference.

The UK Chartered Institute of Personnel Development defines employee well-being like this: 'Creating an environment to promote a state of contentment that allows employees to flourish and achieve their full potential for the benefit of themselves and their organisations'.[42] This goes beyond making sure employees aren't injured or their health damaged on the job. That's risk management. Well-being is about finding ways to make work more engaging and enjoyable and help employees manage their physical, mental and social health, as shown in Figure 30.5. This is in the organisation's best interests as well as the employees' best interests.

Happy employees produce more. They average higher productivity and higher sales and are much more creative than their less happy colleagues.[43] They have lower absenteeism and illness (saving their

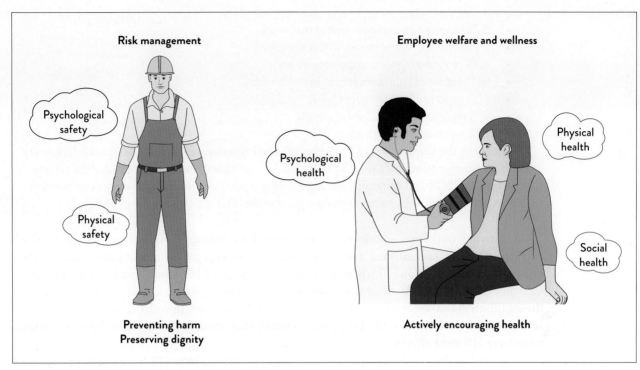

FIGURE 30.5 Components of wellness

organisations lost time) and lower attrition; they go above and beyond the call of duty and attract other people's commitment to the job.[44]

THE STRATEGIC PERSPECTIVE

The workplace benefits of health

The Global Corporate Challenge (GCC) is a 16-week event in which participants undertake a virtual walking journey around the world by using pedometers to record the number of steps they take each day and translating this into their progression around the walking course.

At the beginning of the 2012 GCC, 58% of participating employees rated their health as either good or excellent. By the end of the challenge, this number increased to 83%. The 9% of participating employees who rated themselves as having poor health at the start fell to less than 2% by the end.

According to the Foundation for Chronic Disease Prevention, participation in the Global Corporate Challenge resulted in:

- 41% fewer sick days than non-participants
- an average weight loss of 4.5kgs by participants
- 62% of participating employees reduced their waist circumference by an average of 5.2cm
- 5% of participating employees with high-risk blood pressure at the beginning of the challenge were categorised as low risk by the end
- 37% of participating employees improved the quality of their nutrition.

Participating employees were pleased with the results, too:

- 33% reported increased productivity
- 54% were more satisfied in their jobs

- 57% reported an improvement in teamwork
- 75% reported higher morale in the workplace
- 52% reported higher engagement at work
- 90% reported improvements in overall health
- 65% reported lowered stress levels
- 71% reported increased energy levels
- 51% reported sleeping better.

A study by the Department of Epidemiology and Preventative Medicine at Monash University found the positive effects of the GCC to be lasting: participants increased their physical activity levels by over 350% and demonstrated significant and sustained improvements in blood pressure, body mass index and waist circumference eight months after completing the challenge.[45]

A 'thriving' workforce – those whose employees have feelings of well-being – is one in which employees are not just satisfied and productive but also engaged in creating the future – their organisation's and their own. Thriving employees are energised but know how to avoid burnout; in fact, they have 125% less burnout than their peers. Thriving employees are 32% more committed to the organisation and 46% more satisfied with their jobs. Thriving white-collar employees demonstrate 16% better job performance and perform 27% better than their non-thriving colleagues. Thriving leaders are 21% more effective, too.[46]

A happy, healthy workforce is productive. Healthy employees have 42% higher work performance than employees with a high-risk health status and take over 97% less time off work because of illness. There is also a clear relationship between health and job satisfaction: employees with high-risk health status are 8.5 times more likely to have poor job satisfaction than employees with good health.[47]

Physically fit people typically respond better to stress, sidestepping a basketful of stress-related health issues such as depression and high blood pressure. Fit people have a higher quality of life, live longer, recover from illness faster and rest more effectively. Wellness policies and programs don't just improve employees' health and well-being, they can bolster the organisation's bottom-line; fit, healthy, happy people are more attentive, creative, innovative, productive and service-oriented than their out-of-sorts counterparts.

◉ THEORY TO PRACTICE

Health is a good investment

Unisys Australia was losing 27 593 work days through its employees' poor health. Just over half – 54% – had below-average health while 31% were in the 'at-risk' category. (The two key drivers of high-risk status are insufficient physical activity and nutritional imbalance.) An intervention was needed.

Unisys launched a program to help employees improve their health and well-being called Living Well @ Unisys. Targeted at the employees' needs over 12 months, it included a hydration campaign (4 weeks), physical activity education and interactive team challenges (12 weeks), a nutrition program (8 weeks) and a strength and resilience program that taught stress management (8 weeks).

After 12 months, employees' health and well-being score improved 5.7%; stress reduced by 11%, risk behaviour reduced by 8.8% and nutrition improved by 4.2%. This resulted in a $4.9 million saving to the business, a positive return on investment of $4.13 for every $1 spent in reducing absenteeism and a return of $17.50 for every $1 spent in improving workplace effectiveness.[48]

To begin employee wellness efforts, identify the particular health issues affecting your employees and design a campaign and programs to target them. Educate employees so that illnesses don't go undiagnosed and provide information on lifestyle management to prevent and manage illness.

THEORY TO PRACTICE

A fun environment and enjoyable work

You may have read about Melbourne-based OBS' induction program in 'Theory to practice: A great place to work' on page 836. The IT company also considers work–life balance and health and wellness to be essential to employees doing their jobs effectively. Its office has a purpose-built games room with a large screen TV and Xbox, lounges, beanbags and tables to encourage staff to take breaks. It offers weekly training programs in a range of sports and sponsors teams of employees to participate in events such as Ride Around the Bay, the BRW triathlon and the Oxfam Trailwalker. Social events known as 'funsters' get staff together for activities like go-karting and trivia nights, and birthdays are celebrated with a company-wide email and birthday cake.

Central to the company's modus operandi is a strong team culture that is non-bureaucratic and empowering and encourages people to be curious and to question.[49]

Wellness programs

Employee wellness is more a management approach than a checklist of benefits. A fair balance between effort and reward goes beyond money. It includes a good boss, good relationships with colleagues, interesting jobs, knowing how you fit into and contribute to the organisation, and procedural justice so you know you're being treated fairly. With these elements in place, you can start looking at more specific wellness programs. These might include:

* an on-site visiting nurse
* corporate gymnasium
* fitness and lifestyle packages
* flu injection subsidy
* fruit in the tearoom
* gym membership subsidy
* health and well-being education and promotions
* health assessments
* massage rooms
* posture improvement and ergonomics coaching
* prayer rooms.

Wellness programs don't have to cost a lot. When you want people to increase their fitness, give a trophy to the team or department that improves the most. Articles in the newsletter, short emails with tips for healthy eating, brain-boosting activities and fitness, a list of health and lifestyle smartphone apps and so on are all free and need minimal time to organise.

Health education and prevention programs promoting employee health and well-being aren't expensive either. Personal development sessions help employees feel more confident and develop healthy relationships. Wellness programs easily combine with the organisation's other learning and development programs to encourage an intellectually, physically, mentally and socially healthy life.

Most people know that measures, such as blood pressure, cholesterol levels, glucose levels and height:weight ratios are indicators of risk factors but few people actually know their personal measures and risk levels. Personal health assessments can make it easy for employees to act effectively to improve their health and the aggregate data can help organisations identify health and well-being risks across their workforce and develop suitable programs to address the risks. This can be done with a mixture of face-to-face checks for some of these health measures and online programs that let employees self-assess other measures. Online programs can also provide a range of follow-up tools such as diet plans, exercise programs and a health information library.

Employee assistance programs

Few people go through life without a personal crisis, difficulty or problem. Perhaps that's why 80% of Australia's top 500 companies have employee assistance programs (EAPs) that offer external counselling services.[50] A large Australian study found that about twice as many women as men avail themselves of EAPs (66% and 34%, respectively) and nearly half of them are from Generation X (perhaps not surprising as this age group also has the highest divorce rate and highest levels of personal debt). Personal issues, mostly concerning family/relationship (35.4%) or psychological difficulties (29.4%), are the most common reasons for taking up the counselling, with work-related issues making up a much smaller percentage.[51]

What are the signs that someone needs support? Any change in an employee's usual performance or behaviour signals that the employee may be having personal difficulties. The most obvious is a slip in work performance, although any behaviour change is worthy of note; for example, a normally cheerful person becoming quiet and glum or a normally shy and reserved employee becoming unusually boisterous or talkative. There are also some obvious signs to look for when you suspect drug or alcohol abuse. When you take an interest in your team members, you are likely to notice when something is wrong.

● IN A NUTSHELL

Signs of drug misuse

Common signs of drug abuse include:
- a tendency to become confused
- abnormal fluctuations in concentration and energy
- deteriorating work relationships
- dishonesty and theft (in order to maintain an expensive habit)
- impaired job performance
- increased short-term absenteeism
- poor timekeeping
- sudden mood changes
- unusual irritability or aggression.

Stress and other factors can also cause these symptoms. When you suspect an employee may have a drug problem, follow your organisation's drug and alcohol policy and other health and safety policies.

Employee assistance programs offer confidential, short-term counselling to employees (and often their immediate families) with personal problems that affect their work performance, regardless of whether these problems are caused by workplace issues. The aim is to restore their well-being and return the employees to previous levels of performance (see 'FYI: Employee assistance programs' on page 483).

Most organisations refer employees to professionals or agencies or subcontract EAPs to provider organisations that can deal with a range of issues such as aged care and parenting difficulties, balancing work and family, depression, eating disorders, family violence, financial difficulties, gambling, grief, legal problems, retirement planning, separation, stress and substance abuse – areas where leader-managers should rarely venture (see page 482 to find out what leader-managers can reasonably do to support a team member with personal problems). Some EAP providers can provide crisis counselling and work with employees on disability issues and long-term illnesses.

Contact details of EAP providers should be readily available to employees. Some organisations allow employees to approach EAP services directly and receive an annual or biannual statement showing only numbers of employees counselled and the areas worked on. Other organisations request employees to approach a nominated person in the organisation, such as the HR manager or a health professional in the medical department, for referral to the appropriate professional or agency.

Using EAPs is generally voluntary, although leader-managers can refer or request employees in difficulty to obtain assistance when they believe it could prevent their performance from deteriorating significantly. These are considered informal referrals and generally no record appears on the employee's file. When performance has deteriorated and you believe that assistance could sufficiently improve the employee's difficulties so that performance could return to previous levels, you can make a formal referral, based on job performance. This referral may or may not appear in the employee's file, depending on your organisation's policy. What is discussed during counselling sessions of EAPs is not reported to the employer in any of these situations.

Without this strict confidentiality, employees may not avail themselves of assistance. As with any health and safety program, it is important to have senior management support, management and employee training in how the EAPs work, promotion of the EAPs and encouragement to use them, and periodic evaluation to ensure the needs of employees and the organisation are being met.

Steps you can take

Do you want to increase your team's performance and productivity, your customers' satisfaction and your team members' creativity so they can find ways to solve sticky problems and work more effectively? Pay attention to easing the psychosocial risks to employee welfare and well-being listed in the 'In a Nutshell: Psychosocial risk factors' on page 1018. How to manage to reduce or remove these risks is discussed throughout this text. The following sections look at four other ways to look after your team members' well-being.

Help people concentrate

Have you ever noticed how often your mind wanders? In fact, we concentrate about 50% of the workday and our minds wander – almost always to personal concerns – the other 50%. But mind-wandering lowers people's spirits and productivity. People are much happier when they are *mindful* – fully engaged in what they're doing (see page 194 for more information on mindfulness). To optimise employees' emotional well-being, find ways to help them concentrate. As a bonus, selective attention drives up your intelligence. The more you concentrate, the more you *can concentrate*.[52] For example:

- Encourage people to set a goal for the task they're engaged on; working aimlessly pulls you in different directions.
- Greasy, heavy meals overload your digestive system, robbing your mind of energy; light fresh food helps you concentrate. Be a good role model and have a healthy, light lunch at work to encourage team members to do the same.

- Make sure people understand *why* their work is important; when you don't know how tasks fit into the bigger picture, it's hard to concentrate on them.
- Multitasking and distractions kill your concentration – encourage people to clear their desks, silence email and other electronic alerts and work on their high priorities.
- Pent up energy makes you mentally distracted; exercise, particularly first thing in the morning when you can sweat out impurities and reflect on the day ahead, clears your mind and uses up distracting energy.
- Regular breaks clear your mind, too, which helps you concentrate.
- When you haven't had enough rest, it's hard to concentrate. Discuss how important getting enough – but not too much – sleep is.[53]

Keep in touch

Have regular, informal conversations with each team member on how they're performing. Every day, send a quick email or verbally praise one team member on their work, their contribution to a larger effort or to the team, or something they did that put the organisation's values into action. When people work with a positive mindset and know their contributions are valued, their creativity, engagement, work quality and productivity improve.

Develop effective working relationships in your team

Happiness is more related to moment-to-moment experiences, routine interactions with colleagues and daily contributions to projects than to job title or salary.[54] This highlights the importance of providing meaningful work and establishing a strong, respectful, high-performance team culture. Make it a pleasant work culture too – people work best when they're enjoying themselves.

Create opportunities for people to work collaboratively together on projects that use their skills and talents and to share their ideas and experience. Employees who provide lots of support to other employees, by developing good working relationships, helping out a teammate who is overloaded with work, and so on, are 10 times more likely to be engaged at work than people who provide little support to colleagues.[55] Should you witness behaviour or a conversation that disrespects someone, intervene promptly.

How healthy is your lifestyle?

A popular sport saying sums up a healthy lifestyle: '*Mens sana in corpore sano*' (A sound mind in a sound body).[56]

According to the Australian Government's National Physical Activity Guidelines, you should participate in at least 150 minutes of moderately intense physical activity (brisk walking, dancing, social tennis, swimming, etc.) at least five times a week if you want to be considered 'physically active'. The minimum required for good health is 30 minutes of moderately intense physical activity most days of the week. You should also do muscle strengthening activities at least twice a week and break up long periods of sitting.

Three healthy meals a day made up of 50% vegetables or salad, 25% low GI carbohydrates (e.g. wholegrain breads and cereals) and 25% lean protein, plus healthy snacks, improve concentration and digestion and assist weight management.[57]

Build a balanced and healthy culture in your team

Make sure people have meaningful targets to work towards, so they have a sense of progress at work, but remember: work isn't everything. Don't make being contactable at any time, day or night, weekends and on holiday, part of your team's culture. You and your team members don't need the over-engagement and burnout that results.

Teach your team individual wellness strategies. For example, taking short active breaks is energising; putting your hand up for projects that engage you expands your experience, knowledge and skills, job interest and networks. Hold walking meetings with team members and short standing meeting with your team. Get team members into the habit of walking to another team member's work area to discuss something or pass on information and taking the stairs instead of the lift. Make a pact to walk to the *next* bus stop instead of the closest one at the beginning and end of the day to get some fresh air and gather your thoughts.

Interesting how dignity, welfare and wellness boils down to good management, isn't it?

CourseMateExpress

Go to http://login.cengagebrain.com to access CourseMate Express, your online study tool for *Management Theory & Practice*. CourseMate Express brings chapter concepts to life with interactive learning, and study and exam preparation tools:

- Test your skills in different aspects of management with interactive self-tests and simulations.
- Watch videos that show how real managers operate in real businesses.
- Test your understanding of the changing world of management by taking the revision quiz.

QUICK REVIEW

1. In your own words, define 'bullying', 'sexual harassment', 'occupational violence' and 'racial and religious vilification'. Then check your definitions with the definitions in the glossary.
2. What are some steps leader-managers can take to prevent bullying, sexual harassment, occupational violence, and racial and religious vilification? What responsibility does the organisation have to protect employees?
3. List or flow chart the steps you would take to conduct an investigation into harassment, occupational violence, and racial and religious vilification and explain the purpose of each.
4. Discuss the concepts of employee welfare and wellness and why they are becoming increasingly important.

BUILD YOUR SKILLS

1. Review several cases of bullying, sexual harassment, occupational violence, and racial and religious vilification on the Internet and develop guidelines based on the judges' findings.
2. Based on one of the cases you reviewed, discuss the difficulties the victim may have faced in coming forward with a complaint.
3. Explain the steps to controlling hazards in Figure 29.6 or Figure 29.9 on pages 983 and 991 for preventing accidents and injuries in your work area or college and give two examples of using them to prevent a psychological injury. Explain how you would assess the risk in the examples you give and how you would manage each.
4. Discuss how the work environment can affect people's physical and psychological health and welfare and feeling of well-being, and the measures organisations and leader-managers can take to promote employee well-being.

WORKPLACE ACTIVITIES

1. What do your workplace statistics on harassment, occupational violence and vilification indicate about its dignity culture?
2. Develop a plan for keeping your team members abreast of employee welfare and wellness initiatives in your organisation.
3. Who in your organisation is most at risk of dignity violations and why?
4. Develop a flow chart, as described on page 593, of your organisation's complaints procedures.
5. What employee welfare and well-being measures does your organisation take? Build a case for increasing programs in these areas. List the actions you have taken as an individual leader-manager to enhance the welfare and well-being of the people who report to you.
6. Draw a Pareto chart, as described on page 597, for the main categories of dignity injuries (harassment, violence and vilification, and mental illness). Draw another Pareto chart showing the groups of workers affected in your organisation (e.g. males, females, employees in various age groups, employees by area and by occupation). Break this down further by charting specific dignity injuries by groups of workers. What do your charts tell you about who is most at risk in your organisation, where and from what? Establish priorities and a target for improving the situation.

CASE STUDY 30.1

CARMEN'S PROBLEM?

'Come in, Carmen, and sit down. I want to talk to you about how you're getting on here. You seem a bit nervous and edgy lately and I'm worried that it seems to be affecting your work performance. Is anything wrong?'

'No, everything's fine ... (pause) ... It's just, well – oh, it's nothing, really. Not important.'

'I'd like to hear what it is, Carmen, although of course I'll understand if it's personal and you'd rather not tell me.'

'It's stupid – you'll think I'm just being silly ...'

'It seems to be bothering you, whatever it is. Why don't you tell me about it?'

'Well, you know how the men fool around and make jokes and things.'

'Yes, I know they all get along well together. What is it you mean, Carmen?'

'Well, they tease us a lot. It doesn't seem to bother the other girls much, but it makes me upset. I'm not used to that sort of thing. I don't know what to do about it.'

● ● ●

'What do you mean, they "tease" you?'

'For instance, when we have to climb up those ladders to get at the things stored up there, they make remarks. I don't always understand what they say, but they always laugh loudly and I get embarrassed. I sometimes drop things and they laugh even louder.'

'Is this only with you, or does this happen with the other women too?'

'Oh, no, it isn't just me – they tease them, too. I don't think they really like it much either, but they pretend to laugh back.'

'I see ...'

Questions

1. If you were Carmen's manager, what would you say now?
2. What action would you take?
3. How difficult do you think it was for Carmen to talk about this?

JOE WINS OUT

CASE STUDY 30.2

Joe moved to Australia to find work to help support his family back in Fiji. He quickly found a job with a building company as a casual labourer and then became a permanent employee. Over the 10 months Joe worked for the company, the racial taunts aimed at him became more frequent, louder and nastier. Many of his colleagues used offensive race-based names and insults in his presence and spoke to him aggressively.

Finally, Joe had enough and complained to the company director who spoke to the employees to find out whether Joe's claims were true. They admitted to making some of the comments but said they were only jokes and not meant personally. The director told the workers their behaviour was unacceptable.

After that, Joe's colleagues refused to speak to him at all and refused to work with him. A week after the director's discussion with the crew, Joe was placed back on casual status and was gradually offered less and less work and, eventually, no more work. Joe was at a loss to know what to do, because he and his family back home depended on the money he earned. Surfing the Internet one evening to look for an answer to his dilemma, he found the Australian Human Rights Commission's website and read its information.

'Maybe I should make a claim. What can I lose? Maybe I'll get my job back.'

Joe did complain. The company agreed to mediation, which failed, and then to conciliation. In the end, Joe was paid $7000 compensation, provided with a written reference and the company agreed to provide anti-discrimination training for its staff.

Questions

1. Did the company director do all that the law required?
2. How do you assess the treatment Joe received at the hands of his colleagues?
3. How should the situation have been handled?

GLOSSARY

360-degree feedback
A type of performance review whereby a selection of people dealing with a job-holder (peers, reports, managers, external and internal customers and suppliers) comment on the job-holder's performance. The intention is to build up a full picture of how a person does their job so that they can improve their performance and productivity; also known as a multi-rater feedback.

3D manufacturing
Additive manufacturing using plastic.

80:20 principle
See Pareto principle.

85:15 rule
Provided people know precisely what is expected of them and are trained to do it properly, 85% of the causes of poor performance and low productivity can be found in the work environment (information, job design, systems and processes, teamwork, time, and tools and equipment) and are not the direct fault of the employee. 'Acts of God' and personal problems account for the remaining 15%.

absenteeism
Unplanned non-attendance of employees when they are expected to attend, which can reflect conflict between personal and work-related responsibilities, genuine illness, low motivation or a poor work culture. *See* presenteeism.

accident
An unexpected event that results in injury or damage to health or property and points to inefficient operations and lack of control over materials, people and processes. *See* incident.

accountability
Being held answerable for the work for which one is assigned.

acknowledgement listening
Responding to a speaker with eye contact, nods, 'uh-huhs' and other minimal encouragers.

action-centred leadership
See functional leadership.

action learning
Facilitated learning by a group (an action-learning set) that works on current problems and issues relevant to the organisation, simultaneously solving problems and providing learning opportunities that set members can transfer to other situations.

active listening
See reflective listening.

additive manufacturing
As distinct from the traditional manufacturing that removes and re-shapes materials, additive manufacturing makes complex goods by adding layer upon layer of various materials, which reduces waste; also known as digital manufacturing. (*See* 3D manufacturing.)

after-action review
See learning cycle.

agenda
A list of the topics to be covered during a meeting and the order in which they are to be covered. The most effective agendas are written with verbs to indicate the purpose of each discussion (agree X, decide Y, explore Z).

aggressive behaviour
Putting your own wants and needs ahead of others, often ignoring the wants and needs of others. *See* assertive behaviour and passive behaviour.

analytics
The systematic analysis of large amounts of data from sources such as digital images, mobile phone GPS signals, posts to social-networking sites, sensors, transaction records of online purchases, and videos posted online in order to find meaningful patterns and trends to analyse risks, capitalise on opportunities, inform decision-making and generate insights to increase competitiveness and predict events; also known as big data.

arbitration
When agreement is not reached through conciliation, a neutral third party, having heard and considered both sides, makes a ruling by which both parties must abide; the ruling can be enforced as if it were a court order.

ask 'Why?' five times
A technique used to uncover the main cause of a problem.

assertive behaviour
A learned style of communicating and relating to others based on mutual respect that results in clear, open communication; the ability to state and work

towards realising your own wants and needs while at the same time respecting the wants and needs of others. *See* aggressive behaviour and passive behaviour.

attrition
Employee turnover; also known as churn. The frequency with which employees leave an organisation, usually expressed as a percentage of the total workforce; below-average turnover is generally a sign of high morale and employee engagement, while above-average turnover is generally a sign of low morale and engagement. The opposite measure is retention.

authoritarian leaders
Task-centred leaders who exercise strong control, offer followers little opportunity to participate in decision-making and provide minimal information; also known as autocratic leaders.

authority
The right to decide what is to be done and who is to do it; also known as legitimate power.

autocratic leaders
See authoritarian leaders.

award
A legally enforceable order made by the Full Bench of the Fair Work Commission providing additional minimum terms and conditions supplementing the National Employment Standards for those employees in a particular industry or group of occupations to whom it applies; unique to Australia.

B Corporation
Companies that have stated their commitment to environmental and social goals, as well as profit; also known as B corps.

balance sheet
One of three statements required in a financial report, it is a 'snapshot' of the financial health of a business, showing what it owns (assets and reserves) and what it owes (liabilities) on a specific date, comparing this period to the last period's position and showing the change as a percentage. *See* cash flow statement, income statement, intangible assets and tangible assets.

balanced scorecard
Measuring customer satisfaction, internal business process efficiencies and effectiveness, and organisational learning and growth (including training and workplace culture) in addition to (and in order to 'balance') financial measures (which

measure only past performance); designed to help organisations continuously improve their strategic performance and results. Also a method of reviewing performance.

bar chart
A visual display of quantities using bars, or lines, whose lengths are in proportion to those quantities.

behavioural approach to leadership
Examines what effective leaders say and do.

behavioural interviewing
A method of interviewing that probes what candidates have done and been motivated by in the past and that uses this information to predict what they will do and be motivated by in the future; it allows interviewers to compare the candidates with the person specification to reach sound-selection decisions.

benchmarking
Using meaningful standard measures of performance to gauge an organisation's performance, either internally or across other similar and/ or nearby organisations. *See* best practice benchmarking.

best practice benchmarking
Comparing measures of an organisation's performance with those of leading organisations in the same or different industries.

big data
See analytics.

biocapacity
See carrying capacity.

biodiversity (or biological diversity)
The variety of life forms in an ecosystem (biome) or on the entire planet; a measure of the health of biological systems, measured by the Living Planet Index and the ecological footprint.

board of directors
The policy- and strategy-establishing body of a company, which represents its shareholders and which guides the organisation's operations.

body language
The unspoken messages people send with their bodies – the ways they sit and stand, move and change position, and the pitches, speeds, tones and volumes of their voices.

boomerang principle
The concept that what people 'send out' to others returns to them, for example, when you are polite to someone, that person is likely to be polite in return.

brainstorming
A technique that helps produce a large number of ideas for later evaluation.

budget
A summary of expected income and expenses for a given period or project.

bullying
Aggressive remarks and/or behaviours that repeatedly demean, humiliate and/or undermine the recipient, carried out in person or electronically (cyber bulling) and committed by one person or several (mobbing); illegal behaviour. Ostracism, or repeated exclusion, is silent bullying.

bureaucracy
An organisation characterised by a formal chain of command, a rigid or semi-rigid hierarchy, specialisation of tasks and strict rules and procedures.

burnout
The result of unalleviated stress.

business collaboration
See strategic alliance.

business complexity
Having numerous diverse and interdependent parts.

business contingency planning
See risk management.

business continuity plans
The steps an organisation intends to take to ensure its survival in the event of a disruption to its operations. *See* disaster recovery plans.

business ethics
The way an organisation conducts its affairs according to the morals and principles accepted by society and the organisation's stated values. *See* corporate citizenship.

business model
How a business makes its offering distinctive by creating value for its customers and obtaining value from the value it creates.

capabilities-based competition
Creating value and competitive advantage through capabilities in processes, such as design and marketing, delivery and invoicing, the ability to enter emerging markets successfully, to bring new products to market quickly, to respond promptly to customer complaints; also known as competency-based competition.

capabilities-based organisation
One structured around its core capabilities, or business processes, executed in a way that is difficult to copy; based on cross-functional teamwork and strategic investment in support systems that span business units and functions.

capability
What an organisation excels at – information systems and work flows, logistics, marketing, people, processes, technology, and so on; usually built over time and difficult to copy; a set of processes that require cross-functional teamwork and strategic investment in support systems. *See* intangible assets and organisational capabilities.

carbon footprint (CF)
A measure of the greenhouse gases released by using fossil fuels. There are several ways to calculate CF although many simply calculate the tonnes of carbon rather than demand on bioproductive area; also known as CO_2 footprint. *See* ecological footprint.

carbon sinks
Natural or man-made systems that absorb carbon dioxide from the atmosphere and store it, including trees, plants and oceans; also known as carbon reservoirs.

carrying capacity
The number of humans, animals and plants an environment can support, given its climate, food, habitat, living space, water and other necessities available, without significant negative impacts; also known as biocapacity and ecological reserve.

cash flow statement
One of three statements required in a financial report, it indicates the liquidity (cash and assets converting easily into cash,) of an organisation by showing how much working capital (money) is available; it summarises an organisation's cash flow from its operating, investing and financing activities, showing a net increase or decrease in cash, the source (money received) and application (money paid out) of funds. *See* balance sheet, income statement, intangible assets and tangible assets.

casual employees
Those who have no expectation of ongoing work from the employer and who do not receive paid holiday or sick leave entitlements. They are called in on a day-to-day basis when needed by the employer and paid only for the hours worked at a higher pay rate called casualloading. *See* temporary employees.

casualisation (of the workforce)
The increasing use of casual and temporary employees (contractors) who have less stability and security of employment but who provide employers with greater flexibility at reduced employment costs.

cause-and-effect diagram
A pictorial representation that helps to identify problems, isolate the main cause of a problem or clarify a problem by allowing you to view it in its entirety; also known as Ishikawa diagrams and fishbone diagrams.

centralised organisation
One in which decision-making authority resides with management.

chain of command
The formal reporting relationships in an organisation, as shown in an organisation chart.

charismatic leadership
Leadership based on personal magnetism and other qualities.

check sheet
A method of gathering data, based on sample observations, that helps detect and isolate patterns of non-conformance and variation.

checkerboard analysis
A matrix used to analyse a problem by comparing various elements of the problem with each other.

circling
A technique to break a complex issue into its elements by circling key words to arrive at a succinct problem definition.

climate change
The human-amplified long-term (decades to centuries) alteration in global weather patterns, particularly increases in average temperature and storm activity (as opposed to natural climate variability, which is years to decades fluctuations in climate; e.g. El Niño).

closed question
One that can be answered with 'yes', 'no' or a short statement of fact.

coach
A colleague or manager who helps develop another's talents, skills and understanding; or selected professionals or specialists such as accountants, computer experts or professional coaches who develop another's skills and understanding.

coaching
Passing on one's experienceor skills, or using a particular process to help people develop someone's talents, skills and understanding.

collaborative systems technology
Software that helps people work together, such as chat systems, email and Lotus Notes ('low-end' technology), Voice-over Internet Protocol and videoconferencing systems ('mid-level' technology), and software that allows people to work remotely together, in real time, on documents, spreadsheets and so on; these are underpinned by base-level technologies such as the Internet, encryption (to protect data while it travels across the Internet) and compression (to make the data smaller so it travels quickly, taking less time to transmit); also known as groupware, application sharing and collaborative software.

common law
Principles and rules based on judicial decisions, custom and precedent; judge-made law built up over time; not written in statutes.

competency
Knowledge and skills needed to carry out a task successfully; discrete, observable behaviours that enable a person to perform an activity to the standard expected under normal working conditions.

competency-based job description
A position description showing the knowledge and skills (i.e. competencies) required by the jobholder. *See* job description and role description.

conciliation
A neutral third party helping two disagreeing parties, (e.g. an employer and a group of employees or a manager and a direct report) reach agreement.

conciliator
Conciliators take a more direct role than mediators and may even suggest a way or ways to resolve a dispute.

conscious capitalism
A business philosophy based on organisations working to benefit all stakeholders, not just shareholders, as the preferred path to long-term competitive advantage; it differentiates itself from corporate social responsibility, which it sees as a response to external pressure.

consensus
Exploring, analysing and discussing an issue until a group reaches widespread, or near-unanimous, agreement.

consideration
A dimension of leadership concern that includes behaviour indicating mutual trust, rapport and respect between the leader and followers. *See* structure.

constructive dismissal
When an employer's actions leave an employee no option but to resign; illegal behaviour. *See* instant dismissal, unfair dismissal and unlawful dismissal.

constructive feedback
Information that helps people further improve their performance and productivity, polish their skills and build on their strengths. *See* corrective feedback, feedback, negative feedback and positive feedback.

consultation
Seeking the informed ideas and opinions of employees (and, when appropriate, other stakeholders) about the organisation's operations and important decisions; influencing a decision; not joint decision-making.

contingency approach to leadership
A situational approach to leadership that identifies three factors determining the most appropriate leadership style: leader–member relations, task structure and the leader's position power.

continuous improvement
Frequent small enhancements, or incremental improvements, to a process, product or service; also known as kaizen.

continuum of leadership styles
A model of leadership based on the amount of authority the leader retains and the corresponding amount of freedom allowed to followers, resulting in a range of leadership behaviours labelled telling, selling, consulting, sharing and delegating.

contract of employment
A binding (legally enforceable) agreement between an organisation and an employee covering duties, hours of work, location of work, remuneration, and so on; these matters are specified in the award or workplace agreement and role description.

contractor
A business or an individual engaged by an organisation to perform work; for example, a company may call in a building or painting contractor to paint its offices or contract a trucking company to deliver its products rather than employ its own drivers and purchase and maintain its own fleet of delivery vehicles. Dependent contractors are sometimes called 'false self-employed' because the contractor's income is dependent on one client, making the contractor an 'in fact' employee, yet not entitled to the protections of an employment relationship; independent contractors contract to perform work for another person or organisation (the client) but are not employed by the client and are paid for results, the client having minimal control over when, where and how the work is performed.

control chart
A type of run chart showing the upper and lower acceptable limits of variation in the results of a process on either side of the average; used for quality control purposes.

core process redesign
See re-engineering.

corporate citizenship
An organisation's legal and moral obligations to its community and society, including support of charities and local initiatives, and care for the environment. *See* business ethics and conscious capitalism.

corporate governance
Managing a company and its processes according to legal requirements and regulations; the way an organisation is governed and controlled, particularly by its board of directors. It includes the organisation's code of conduct for ethical behaviour, its policies and programs on corporate social responsibility, risk management and sustainability, and its human resource policies, programs and management systems; it is often considered to be concerned not only with compliance with the law but also with the way an organisation is run as a whole, balancing economic and social goals, and communal and individual goals.

corporate responsibility (CR)
The next iteration of corporate social responsibility, which is considered to be prescriptive, 'one-size-fits-all', while CR seeks to identify the needs and expectations of stakeholders and meet the most important. Most major companies now have a CR, sustainability, corporate citizenship or similar department and publish a CR report. *See* conscious capitalism.

corporate social responsibility (CSR)
Doing the right thing economically, environmentally,ethically and socially. *See* business ethics, conscious capitalism, corporate citizenship and corporate responsibility.

corporate strategy
A plan, method or some consistently intended course of action to achieve a desired outcome; how an organisation intends to achieve value for its stakeholders. Strategy is about choice: who to target as customers, what products and services to offer them at what quality, how to deliver those products and services, what financial targets to aim for, how to manage the organisation's human resources and other key assets; decisions like these guide an organisation's operations and differentiate it from its competitors.

corporation
A business that exists independently of its owners and employees; a legal entity in its own right.

corrective feedback
Information given to employees who are underperforming or whose behaviour is unacceptable in some way. It describes what to do to improve performance, productivity or behaviour. *See* constructive feedback, feedback, negative feedback, positive feedback and performance counselling.

cost–benefit analysis
Weighing up the cost of introducing an initiative or making a purchase against the benefits to be gained, by quantifying and then adding all the positive factors (the benefits) and quantifying and subtracting the negatives (the costs); the difference indicates whether the course of action or purchase is advisable.

cost of employment
The total cost to an organisation of employing a person, including pay plus contribution to overheads (e.g. infrastructure costs such as cost of equipment, office space, support staff) and other employment costs such as superannuation and workers' compensation contributions; often considered to be double the remuneration.

covert discrimination
Unequal treatment based on characteristics that belong to, or are connected with, some members of a group of people; often subtle and unconscious. *See* overt discrimination and systemic discrimination.

cradle-to-cradle
Taking raw materials from the earth, making them into a product and, at the end of the product's life, upcycling it to reuse the materials to make the same product again, or another product that retains the value of those raw materials (rather than downcycling them, destroying them or dumping them in landfills). *See* cradle-to-grave, downcycling, upcycling.

cradle-to-grave
The conventional way of manufacturing that takes raw materials from the earth, makes them into a product and, at the end of the product's life, it is downcycled, dumped or destroyed, generating greenhouse gases in the process. *See* cradle-to-cradle.

critical control points
The most important aspects of a plan or project to monitor.

critical path
The path, or series of tasks that must start and finish on time so that a project or plan finishes on time; any delay on the critical path delays the project.

critical path analysis (CPA)
A type of network diagram that shows the various activities of a plan or project as they relate to each other and when each activity should begin and finish; also known as critical path method (CPM). *See* PERT diagram.

critical path diagram
See critical path analysis.

cross-functional team
See multifunctional team.

cross-skilling
Increasing the ability of employees to carry out a wider range of tasks at the same or similar levels of responsibility; also known as cross-training, in the sense that employees can do each other's tasks and therefore can cover for each other. *See* job enlargement, job enrichment, multiskilling and upskilling.

culture
The beliefs, customs, habits and practices of a country, a group, an organisation or a team; the collection of unwritten codes of behaviour and rules by which people operate.

cultural intelligence
The ability to operate across cultures, and not just internationally, because all groups have cultures – communities, families, generations, neighbourhoods, organisations, work teams, and so on.

customer
A person who benefits from your efforts, whether inside or outside the organisation. *See* external customers and internal customers.

customer–supplier chain
A systems view of an organisation that sees the internal relationships in the organisation (departments or activities) as one continuous process of supplying and receiving products, services or information and adding value at each step.

decentralised organisation
An organisation in which decision-making authority is located as close as possible to the area affected by the decision.

delegation
Assigning work to a team member.

deliverable
A tangible or intangible, but quantifiable, end result of mental or physical effort such as a design, document, innovation or report; a building block of a job or project.

democratic leaders
People-centred leaders who encourage participation and involve people.

demotion
Reassignment to a job of lower rank and pay.

deregulation
For the private sector: removing protection from overseas competition by reducing tariff and non-tariff barriers on trade in goods and services, floating currencies and opening financial markets by reducing barriers to direct foreign investment and other international capital flows, resulting in freer trade between countries; a major driver of globalisation. For the public sector: allowing private providers to enter markets traditionally served by the public bodies.

dictatorial leaders
Negative, task-centred leaders who rule through force and threats of punishment.

digital manufacturing
See additive manufacturing.

direct discrimination
Refusal or consistent failure to treat people from disadvantaged groups equally in employment matters. *See* indirect discrimination.

disability
A physical or mental impairment or restriction in activities.

disaster recovery plans
The steps an organisation plans to take to recover its IT systems and infrastructure after a disruptive event. *See* business continuity plans.

discipline
Addressing employee behaviour or work performance or productivity that is below the expected standard of conduct or output.

discrimination
Unequal treatment before, during or after employment on the grounds of age, breastfeeding, carer status, colour, ethnicity or race, irrelevant criminal record, family responsibilities, marital status, irrelevant medical record, national extraction, national origin, nationality, parental status (including pregnancy), physical or intellectual disability, political opinion, religion, sex, sexual preference, social origin, the presence of disease-causing illness, trade union activities, political opinion or social origin; a distinction, exclusion or preference based on one or more of the above grounds that has the effect of impairing equality of opportunity or treatment in employment or occupation.

dismissal
When an employer ends a contract of employment; this should be done with notice and the employee paid any leave owing. *See* constructive dismissal, instant dismissal, unfair dismissal and unlawful dismissal.

dispute settlement procedure (DSP)
A clear procedure detailing the steps for dealing with conflict, disagreements and grievances between employers and employees, either in groups (e.g. concerning the application of an award or workplace agreement) or individually (e.g. concerning a performance review or unfair treatment by a line manager) that should be clearly set out in all workplace agreements and preferably confirmed in a separate policy; also known as grievance-handling procedure.

distress
See stress.

diversity
A general term indicating that people with a variety of differences (e.g. ability, age, cultural, ethnicity, gender, language, race, religion, sexual orientation) are present, welcome and productive in an organisation.

downcycling
Reuse, but in a way that lessens the item's original value; for example, melting a computer casing into a speed bump. *See* cradle-to-cradle, cradle-to-grave and upcycling.

downsizing
Reducing the number of employees in an organisation in an effort to lower costs, increase profitability and be more responsive in the marketplace by streamlining internal operations.

drivers of success
The factors that work together to propel an organisation forward towards achieving its strategic goals; these are different for each organisation but may include, for example, organisation culture, growth, human capital, information capital and innovation.

duty of care
The legal obligation to avoid causing harm to others. In health, safety and welfare, the legal obligation of employers to ensure that their business, so far as is practicable, does not harm employees or the general public. In risk management, understanding the organisation's risk profile and developing plans to manage risks for the continuity and survival of the organisation.

dynamics
See group dynamics.

e-learning
Training delivered over the Internet, Intranet, smartphones or other electronic technology.

ecological footprint (EF)
Expressed in global hectares (gha) and widely used as a measure of environmental sustainability and the extent of human demand, or impact, on the planet's ecosystems, the EF estimates how many planet earths are needed to support humanity if everyone lived a given lifestyle. It measures the amount of biologically productive land and water area required to produce the resources an individual, a population or an activity consumes and to absorb the waste generated, given prevailing technology and resource management; therefore, small is better.

economies of scale
Efficiencies associated with the quantity produced— the more products or services an organisation produces, the cheaper each becomes.

economies of scope
Reducing the average total cost of production by increasing the number of different products produced or by using the outputs of one business as the inputs of another. For example, a fast-food outlet can produce both hamburgers and chips at a lower average cost than two separate organisations could because it can spread the costs of food storage, preparation facilities, and so on; cosmetic and healthcare products manufacturers can share expensive graphic designers, marketers and salespeople who work across product lines, lowering the average total cost for each product. This leads to product bundling, product linking and family branding.

ecosystem
A localised and interdependent dynamic community of plants, animals, insects and micro-organisms that interact and depend on each other as well as on the non-living aspects of the environment (e.g. air, climate, sunlight and water) to function as a unit (lakes and even some suburban gardens are ecosystems). (A biome is a large ecosystem. The Great Barrier Reef, deserts, oceans and rainforests, are examples of biomes.)

elements of leadership approach
A situational approach to leadership that uses the task, the followers and the leader's own inclinations to select the most appropriate leadership style.

emotional intelligence (EI or EQ)
The (largely learned) ability to monitor your own and other people's emotions and use that information to guide your thinking and actions.

empathic leadership
A way of leading that considers followers' perspectives and uses empathy when giving advice, directions and support.

empathy
The ability to see problems and situations from another person's point of view.

employee assistance programs (EAPs)
Programs that help employees, and often members of their immediate families as well, through difficult or traumatic events, incidents or issues; some programs concentrate on events in employees' working lives while others also deal with issues in employees'

private lives to help create a generally healthier, happier, more productive workforce.

employee engagement
The psychological commitment employees feel towards their employer, based on identifying with the organisation's values and vision and ways of operating.

employer brand
An organisation's image that attracts potential employees and retains current employees, made up of factors such as its practices, products and services, reputation for quality and customer service, how it treats its employees, how it delivers its promises and corporate social responsibility.

employer value proposition (EVP)
The total package of an organisation's offering to employees that attracts and helps retain the employees it needs at all levels; it includes its career- and performance-management systems, culture, values, vision and mission, employer brand, health and wellness policies, reputation for corporate social responsibility, management practices, technologies, learning and development processes, and working benefits and arrangements (e.g. for flexible working).

employment contract
See contract of employment.

empowerment
See job empowerment.

engagement
See employee engagement.

enrichment
See job enrichment.

enterprise agreement
See workplace agreement.

enterprise bargaining
See workplace bargaining.

eustress
See stress.

executive board
See inside board.

executive directors
Members of the board who also work in the company. *See* non-executive directors.

exit interview
A discussion, usually held between a neutral party, such as an HR officer, and an employee who has resigned, to discover the reason for the resignation. The information is used to improve the organisation's ability to retain valued employees.

expectancy theory
The idea that the strength of a person's motivation depends on how much they believe they can succeed (expectancy), how likely they believe they are to receive a reward they value in return for their efforts (instrumentality), and how much they believe that the reward is worth their effort (valence).

external board
A board of directors made up entirely of directors not employed by the company in another capacity; also known as a non-executive board. *See* inside board and mixed board.

external customers
The people or organisations who purchase or use an organisation's products or services. *See* internal customers.

external suppliers
People and organisations outside the organisation who supply information, materials or services. *See* internal suppliers.

feedback
Information about performance, productivity or behaviour used to make improvements. *See* constructive feedback, corrective feedback, negative feedback and positive feedback.

fight, flight or freeze response
An instinctive reaction to a dangerous or an unpleasant situation: to stay and fight, to turn and flee from it or to freeze when there is no hope, when fight or flight is impossible.

first-line management
The level of management between the non-management workforce and the rest of management. (Note: the terms leader-manager and first-line manager are used interchangeably in this text.)

fishbone diagram
See cause-and-effect diagram.

five keys
The five keys to, or components of, performance excellence and high productivity: *'what to'*, *'want to'*, *'how to'*, *'chance to'* and *'led to'*.

flexible working
Measures, such as annualised hours, banked time, compressed working weeks, flexitime and purchased leave, intended to help balance work and personal responsibilities and increase workforce flexibility and organisational effectiveness.

flow chart
A pictorial representation showing all the steps of a process or an activity.

force field analysis
A technique that helps to ensure the smooth implementation of a plan or decision by highlighting factors working against you (resisting forces), to diminish or remove them, and factors in your favour (driving forces), to capitalise on in order to move from the current to the desired situation.

formal leader
The official leader of a group or team. *See* informal leader.

framing statement
A short sentence used to nominate and introduce a topic for discussionor to describe a problem or decision to be made.

free-rein leadership
See laissez-faire leaders.

functional leadership
Satisfying three areas of need in order to be an effective leader: the task, the team and the individual.

Gantt chart
A planning and monitoring aid that lists planned activities vertically and time periods horizontally, showing what needs to be done and when.

gap analysis
Answering the questions: 'Where are we now?' (current situation), 'Where do we want to be?' (desired situation) and 'How will we get there?' (the plan or strategy)in order to establish how to bridge the gap, or move from the current to the desired situation.

global warming
Increasing temperatures on the Earth's surface. *See* greenhouse gases and climate change.

globalisation
Treating the world as one marketplace; the integration of the world's economic, financial, trade and communications systems. Driven by national and international deregulation of trade and investment and enabled by the IT-related revolution, the central feature of which is the ability to manipulate, store and transmit large quantities of information at very low cost.

goal
An overall or longer-term aim providing direction for day-to-day activities and acting as reference points for decision-making and assessing performance and productivity.

green electricity
See renewable energy.

greenhouse gases (GHG)
Gases that contribute to the warming of the earth's atmosphere by trapping and reflecting heat back to the earth's surface; they include carbon dioxide (CO_2), which is of the greatest concern because it generates just over 55% of human-induced greenhouse gases and remains in the atmosphere for about 100 years, halocarbons (compressed gas) and chlorofluorocarbons (CFCs), methane (CH_4), nitrous oxide (N_2O), ozone (O_3), sulphur hexafluoride (SF_6) and water vapour. Greenhouse gases are released by human activities, including cutting down forests, driving cars and flying aircraft, growing crops and keeping livestock (animal waste gives off methane), industrial processes, and power plants that use fossil fuels for electricity.

grievance
A complaint or an objection that employees, either singly or collectively, have formally registered with a trade union or a management official according to the organisation's agreed dispute-settlement procedure.

group dynamics
The unique pattern of forces operating in a group that affects particularly the interactions between members and their relationships with each other; the way people work together and their behaviour towards each other, which influences how they go about achieving their goals.

groupthink
A phenomenon of highly cohesive groups that occurs when group members would rather maintain a group's equanimity than cause friction by challenging ideas, stating an opposing point of view or putting forward contrary evidence; this inhibits constructive criticism, disagreement and a full assessment of alternatives, and filters out contraindications to a decision or chosen course of action.

groupware
See collaborative systems technology.

halo/horns effect
Allowing a positive or a negative characteristic of a person or situation to 'spread' and influence your perception of other characteristics, even though they are not connected, causing you to see the person or situation in an artificially positive or negative light.

harassment
Unwanted or unwelcome behaviour, including verbal as well as non-verbal behaviour and innuendo; illegal behaviour.

hazard
Anything with the potential to harm life, health or property.

hazard identification survey
See safety audit.

hierarchy of needs
Six levels of basic human needs that people are motivated to fulfil; also known as Maslow's hierarchy of needs.

histogram
A bar chart that displays the distribution of measurement data in graph form, illustrating how often these events occur, to show the amount of variation in a process and help people to identify and describe a problem and monitor its solution.

horizontal integration
Horizontally integrated organisations seek complementary products or uses for their products and facilities. *See* vertical integration.

hot-stove principle
Providing advanced warning about the need to comply with important rules and regulations, followed by immediate, consistent and impartial discipline when they are not followed.

hub working
See workplace hub.

human capital
The health, knowledge, skills, motivation and productivity of an organisation's employees, measured by, for example, attrition rate, employee engagement and innovation. *See* intellectual capital, relationship capital and structural capital.

human capital management (HCM)
The way an organisation attracts, engages and retains the employees it needs to succeed and helps them perform optimally through career management, coaching, developing their skills and abilities, mentoring, talent and performance management, reward and recognition schemes, and so on; also known as human resources management (HRM).

hygiene factors
Factors in the job environment which, when satisfactory, put people in 'neutral' so that they can be motivated; poor hygiene factors dishearten and 'demotivate' workers. *See* motivation factors.

'I' language
An assertive style of communication that involves taking responsibility for and communicating your own feelings, thoughts and opinions.

'I' message
A clear, succinct and blame-free statement of how someone's actions affect you and/or the team, and the behaviour you want instead.

incident
An event which, on this occasion, did not result in injury or damage to property; also known as a near miss. *See* notifiable incident.

income statement
One of three statements required in a financial report, it shows a company's trading result (profit or loss) from sales and other income minus direct costs and overheads) over a weekly, monthly, quarterly or yearly period, incurred to the date of preparing the statement; commonly called the profit and loss (P&L) account. *See* balance sheet, cash flow statement, intangible assets and tangible assets.

indirect discrimination
Policies and practices that appear on the surface to be neutral but which act to disadvantage members of some disadvantaged groups. *See* direct discrimination.

induction
Welcoming and introducing new employees to, and familiarising them with, the organisation, their departments and their workmates to help them fit in smoothly and reach the expected performance and productivity levels as quickly as possible.

influence
The informal power a person holds.

informal leader
The person with the most influence in a group or team. *See* formal leader.

inherent risk
The risk with no controls in place.

input–output–outcome–impact framework
A measuring system that sets goals and measures progress in each of these four areas, tracking the short-term (outcomes) and long-term benefits (impacts) of inputs (e.g. funds, new technology, initiatives) and outputs (what was done with the inputs).

inside board
A board of directors made up entirely of executive directors; also known as an executive board. *See* external board and mixed board.

instant dismissal
Termination of employment without warning or pay in lieu of notice for a serious offence such as theft, wilful damage to company or customer property or workplace violence; also known as summary dismissal. *See* constructive dismissal, unfair dismissal and unlawful dismissal.

intangible assets
Items such as brand and image in the marketplace, capabilities, customer and supplier relationships, intellectual capital, organisation structure and strategies, all of which can increase competitiveness because they are difficult for competitors to replicate; considered to account for up to 75% of a company's value even though they are difficult to measure in dollars; also known as organisational capabilities. *See* balance sheet, cash flow statement, income statement and tangible assets.

integrated value chain
See supply chain.

intellectual capital
How much an organisation knows and is able to use; its knowledge, made up of human capital, relationship capital and structural capital.

internal customers
People inside an organisation who benefit from other employees' efforts in the organisation. *See* external customers.

internal suppliers
People and organisations inside the organisation who provide information, materials and services. *See* external suppliers.

International Organization for Standardization (ISO)
The world's largest developer and publisher of international quality standards that are used around the world to assure product and service quality; there are currently more than 19 500 standards covering most aspects of technology and business. The ISO's Central Secretariat in Geneva in Switzerland coordinates the network of 157 national standards institutes of its member countries.

is/is not comparison
A technique that helps identify and analyse problems by comparing the what, where, when, who, extent, frequency and so on, of something that is a problem with something similar that is not a problem.

Ishikawa diagram
See cause-and-effect diagram.

ISO
See International Organization for Standardization.

job breakdown
An instruction tool that divides a job or task into its stages and key points.

job description
A document outlining the activities, duties, key objectives, relationships, responsibilities and tasks of a job and any special conditions such as requirements to work overtime or travel away from home. *See* competency-based job description and role description.

job design
The way a position is structured in terms of its specific duties, responsibilities and tasks; an important source of job satisfaction and an enabler of high performance and productivity. *See* job redesign.

job empowerment
The training and workplace conditions that enable employees or work teams to increase their range of decision-making authority and responsibility.

job enlargement
Expanding a job horizontally, at the same or similar level of authority and responsibility. *See* cross-skilling.

job enrichment
Expanding a job vertically, to a higher level of authority and responsibility. *See* upskilling.

job placement
Assigning duties to suit an employee's aptitudes, interests, knowledge, skills, temperament and work-style preferences.

job purpose
A succinct, motivational statement that expresses the main reason a job exists.

job redesign
Altering the way a job is structured. *See* job design.

Johari Window
A model for self-awareness based on two dimensions: aspects of yourself known or not known to yourself and aspects of yourself known or not known to others, resulting in four 'windows' or areas of knowledge about yourself.

kaizen
See continuous improvement.

key performance indicators (KPIs)
Measures of success in reaching goals for activities, processes or projects; a series of KPIs helps manage, monitor and assess the effectiveness of activities and employees; also known as key success indicators.

key result areas (KRAs)
The main areas of accountability and responsibility of a job.

knowledge economy
An economy based not on what people make but on what people know.

knowledge workers
People who develop or use information and knowledge in their work, such as academics, people in information technology, professional workers, researchers, scientists, systems analysts and technical writers.

labour costs
A measure of how productive employees are; a function of labour rates (how much the organisation pays employees per hour or other unit of time and productivity).

labour turnover
See attrition.

lag indicators
Measures of results after a process is completed; historical measures. *See* lead indicators.

laissez-faire leader
A non-directive, delegative leader who provides information and leaves employees to do their jobs, with little or no directions or other input.

lead indicators
Measures taken during a process; current measures of what is happening as the process occurs. *See* lag indicators.

leader-manager
First-line manager; also known as supervisor.

lean
A methodology for innovating and making improvements to existing processes.

learning culture
The value an organisation and its employees place on learning; a strong learning culture is one in which employees at all levels continually learn and share their learning, building their competencies and their organsation's capabilities at the same time.

learning cycle
A way to improve individual or team performance by reviewing what was done, which actions worked well and what could have been done better and how, and planning to apply this insight to improve subsequent performance; also known as after-action review.

levels of management
The traditional categorisation of management into four levels: top-level, senior, middle and first-line or supervisory management.

life cycle analysis
Investigating and assessing the environmental impacts of a product or service throughout its life in order to choose the least burdensome one; also known as cradle-to-grave analysis, ecobalance and lifecycle assessment. *See* upcycling.

line positions
Those whose activities are directly associated with the production of the goods or provision of the services of an organisation. *See* staff positions.

loading
An amount of money paid on top of normal wages for a specific purpose, such as annual leave loading, casual loading (to compensate casual employees for not receiving normal employee entitlements such as holiday pay and superannuation contributions) and working on a public holiday.

locus of control, external
An inability to control one's emotions, actions and reactions to people and events; as a result, other people and events dictate a person's behaviour and actions; thought to result from seeing the cause of events as outside oneself, resulting from, for example, luck, chance or fate.

locus of control, internal
The ability to control one's emotions, actions and reactions to people and events.

lose–lose position
The 'I lose and you lose' mindset that characterises passive behaviour. *See* lose–win, win–lose and win–win positions.

lose–win position
The 'I lose and you win' mindset that characterises passive behaviour. *See* lose–lose, win–lose and win–win positions.

lost-time injury
An event resulting in a fatality, permanent disability or time lost from work of one day or a shift or more.

maintenance functions
Daily actions and interactions that assist a team to work together effectively such as establishing a friendly and supportive working climate, morale-building activities, nurturing feelings of belonging and team cohesion, and taking time out for a bit of fun or humour. *See* task functions.

management by exception
Asking people to report only important deviations; when nothing is reported, work is going according to plan and agreed targets are being reached.

management by objectives (MBO)
A performance management system whereby employees and managers agree specific performance objectives and targets, aligned with corporate goals and strategy, to be accomplished within a given time period.

managerial grid
A system that describes five possible leadership styles based on how much attention a leader pays to output and to people.

matrix organisation
An organisation in which relationships and activities are arranged so that individuals report to different managers for different activities.

matrix teams
Teams whose members belong to two or more teams.

MBO
See management by objectives.

measures of success (MOS)
Also called key performance indicators, objectives and targets, they quantify and measure important aspects of a job, task or project to track how well it is being performed.

mediation
The process of assisting disputing parties to clarify the disputed issue(s) and develop and agree ways to reach agreement.

mediator
A neutral person trained to lead parties of a grievance or dispute through a mediation process to reach a mutually acceptable agreement without advising on or determining the outcome.

mentor
A person (usually older, more senior or experienced) who takes an interest in someone's career and provides advice, encouragement, help and support.

mentoring
Helping a less experienced person build their career by offering advice, assistance, support, and so on.

middle management
The level of management between senior management and first-line management.

milestones
Clear, specific measuring posts, or interim objectives, indicating progress towards achieving a goal; significant events or major stages in a project schedule or plan.

mindset
The views a person holds about themselves, others and the world around them; also known as mental model and paradigm.

minutes
A record of what has been discussed and agreed during a meeting, also indicating the attendees, date, time and place of the meeting.

mission
The overriding or overall strategic goal set by senior managers and directors of an organisation, answering the questions, 'What business are we in?' and 'How will we achieve our vision?'

mixed board
One in which the board of directors is made up of both executive and non-executive directors. *See* inside board and external board.

moments of truth (MOTs)
Any contact a person has with an organisation, personally or electronically.

monitoring
Regularly checking actual performance and productivity against desired output of employees or processes.

morale
Inclination to perform tasks well and willingly, which can be high or low; also known as esprit de corps.

motivation
How willing a person is to expend energy and effort in doing a job or task.

motivation factors
Factors in the job itself that provide job satisfaction and encourage people to perform enthusiastically. *See* hygiene factors.

multifunctional team
A team responsible for delivering an entire product or service, including design, marketing, manufacture, after-sales service and delivery. Also, a temporary team made up of people from several operational areas of the organisation; also known as a cross-functional team.

multi-rater feedback
See 360-degree review.

multiskilling
Training across a broad range of skills, enabling employees to carry out a wider range of tasks. *See* cross-skilling, job enlargement, job enrichment and upskilling.

narcissistic leaders
Strong leaders with personal dynamism and magnetism who can become convinced of their invincibility, distrustful of others and emotionally isolated.

near miss
See incident.

negative feedback
Unspecific criticism that makes people feel unimportant and unappreciated, lowering morale and self-esteem. When specific, it is constructive feedback or corrective feedback and can reduce or eliminate the behaviour in question or improve results. *See* feedback and positive feedback.

network diagram
A chart or schematic representation showing the sequence and relationships of the steps in an activity or a process (e.g. critical path analysis, flow charts and PERT diagrams); used for scheduling and monitoring plans and projects.

networking
Building a range of mutually supportive, informal relationships with others inside and outside the organisation in order to advise, help and support each other.

non-executive board
See external board.

non-executive directors
Members of the board of directors who are not involved in the business in any other capacity. *See* executive directors.

norms
The collection of unwritten rules or codes of behaviour by which people in an organisation or a team operate ('It's how we do things around here').

not-for-profit (NFP) sector
Non-government organisations whose purpose is to fulfil a mission other than make a profit.

notifiable incident
An incident involving death, serious injury or illness (one that results in treatment as an in-patient in a hospital or medical treatment within 48 hours of exposure to a substance) or a dangerous incident (one that exposes someone to a serious risk to their physical or psychological health and safety, such as an uncontrolled escape, spillage or leakage of a substance; an uncontrolled implosion, explosion or fire; an electric shock; psychological abuse). These must be reported to Comcare as soon as reasonably possible.

objective
A short-term goal.

occupational violence
Any incident in which an employee is physically attacked or threatened with violence in the workplace, including the direct or indirect application of force to their body, equipment or clothing; illegal behaviour.

open question
One that encourages a full response, not just 'yes', 'no' or a short statement of fact.

organisation chart
A diagram that shows the deployment of people into capabilities or functions and how they relate to each other; depicts the formal organisation structure or framework, showing direct and indirect reporting arrangements and spans of management.

organisation design
Creating or developing the most suitable organisation structure.

organisation structure
The way an organisation links its employees and capabilities or functions together, depicted in an organisation chart.

organisational capabilities
See intangible assets.

organisational politics
Building alliances to help achieve the organisation's goals.

outsourcing
Contracting out non-essential or non-core functions and operations to independent providers; contracting work to, or purchasing parts from, outside the organisation that are not integral to

the organisation's operations, usually to cut costs or benefit from efficiencies and expertise not available within, or not worth keeping within, the organisation; also known as contracting out.

overt discrimination
Direct, clear discrimination on the grounds of, for example, national origin, race or sex. *See* covert discrimination and systemic discrimination.

paradigm
People's often unconscious and unquestioned beliefs about the world and how it operates that guide their behaviour; also known as mindset, world view and mental model.

Pareto chart
A vertical bar chart that displays the relative importance of problems or events, showing attribute data in descending order of quantity.

Pareto principle
The 80:20 rule of Vilfredo Pareto that says that 20% of people's efforts gain 80% of their results, and vice versa.

participation
Involving employees in the operations and decisions of an organisation.

participative leaders
See democratic leaders.

participative management
See participation.

partnership
An enterprise in which two or more people share the ownership of a business and have unlimited liability.

passive behaviour
Putting other people's wants and needs ahead of your own. *See* aggressive behaviour and assertive behaviour.

path-goal approach to leadership
Leading by showing the way and helping followers along the path.

P–D–C–A cycle
The Plan–Do–Check–Act system for making and maintaining improvements to a process; also known as the PDSA (for Plan–Do–Study–Act) cycle and the Shewhart Learning and Improvement Cycle, after the person who developed it, Walter Shewhart.

performance
How well work is done; a measure of quality. *See* productivity.

performance appraisal
See performance review.

performance counselling
Discussing an employee's performance with a view to improving it so that performance expectations are met. *See* corrective feedback.

performance gap
The difference between expected performance and actual performance, preferably measurable, although it can be behavioural (i.e. something you see or hear).

performance management
Part of an organisation's human capital management systems to align the organisation's strategic and business plans with individual employees' performance plans, and assisting and enabling employees to attain them by managing the five keys to peak performance and productivity.

performance measure
A clear, quantifiable standard of performance and productivity. *See* measures of success.

performance plan
Agreed goals and SMART targets.

performance review
A formal, systematic assessment and discussion of an employee's past performance and productivity, agreeing goals and success measures for future output and planning for future development and training; also known as performance appraisal and formal performance discussion.

person specification
A description of the abilities, knowledge and skills, or competencies, required by an ideal job-holder.

personal counselling
Helping a person to explore, understand and sometimes solve or resolve problems of a personal, non-work-related nature.

personal power
Authority derived from personal attributes.

personality types
Systematic methods of categorising people's key personality traits; Jung's model of personality types, for example, sees introversion and extroversion as two basic ways of relating to the world, and identifies four ways of receiving and dealing with information: thinking, intuiting, feeling and sensing.

PERT diagram
A type of network diagram that shows a plan's or project's various activities as they relate to each other and when each activity should begin and

finish; used to schedule, organise and coordinate plans and projects. *See* critical path analysis.

pie chart
A circular graph showing percentages of the data being studied displayed like slices of a pie.

Plan–Do–Check–Act
See P–D–C–A cycle.

politics, organisational
See organisational politics.

position description
See competency-based job description, job description and role description.

position power
Formal authority derived from a person's job.

positive feedback
When specific, provides information about actions and outcomes that you appreciate, which makes it more likely they will continue. When general, helps build a positive working climate and raises self-confidence.

power
A person's ability to 'make things happen', which comes from their formal position and/or their informal power, or influence, which comes from their personal attributes.

presenteeism
Being unproductive while at work, physically present but psychologically absent; can reflect a lack of work–life balance, low motivation, longer-term health problems such as arthritis, asthma or depression, short-term health problems such as an allergy or a cold, an unhealthy lifestyle, underemployment or a poor work culture. *See* absenteeism.

prevention hierarchy
The preferred order of control for workplace hazards and risks.

private company
The term for a proprietary company in Queensland.

private sector
Corporations, firms and partnerships whose primary goal is to make money for their owners through the provision of goods or services.

probation
A 'getting to know you' period of a few weeks to a few months; a recruit's employment can be terminated during this period if he or she is found to be unsuited to the job; the period should be written into the employment agreement.

procedural justice
The right to be given a fair hearing with the opportunity to present one's case and to have a logic-based decision made by an unbiased decision-maker; called due process in the USA and fundamental justice in Canada.

process
The methods by which inputs are converted to outputs.

process (team)
How a group of people work together, including absence or presence of tension, communication patterns and style, group norms, and level of participation. *See* group dynamics and task.

process capability chart
A graph used to show whether a process, or the way work is carried out, is capable of meeting the specifications and to monitor the performance of a system.

process re-engineering
See re-engineering.

productivity
A ratio of the output of goods and services to the cost of the various resources used to achieve that output; when an organisation produces more with the same resources or produces the same with fewer resources, its productivity has improved. *See* performance.

profit and loss account (P&L)
See income statement.

program evaluation and review technique
See PERT diagram.

programmed decisions
Routine decisions for which one answer consistently applies; also known as standing plans. *See* standard operating procedure.

project
A temporary undertaking with a defined beginning and end, aimed at creating a product, a service or some other result, such as tackling a problem, identifying and capitalising on an emerging opportunityor redesigning or improving a process.

project management
A systematic approach to planning and guiding a project from beginning to end.

project manager
The person who guides a project from conception to finalisation.

project sponsor
A senior manager with overall 'ownership' of a project.

project teams
Temporary teams brought together to undertake a specific assignment.

proprietary limited company
A corporation with limited liability that has up to 50 owners; signified by the abbreviation Pty Ltd after its name.

psychological contract
The unwritten and often unstated expectations and norms about what employers and employees expect from each other, for example, 'the organisation offers stable employment and training in return for faithful and loyal service'.

public company
A corporation with limited liability that has any number of owners and is quoted on the Australian Securities Exchange (ASX); signified by the abbreviation Ltd or the word Limited after its name.

public sector
Organisations involved either directly or indirectly in the business of governing the country.

Pygmalion effect
See self-fulfilling prophecy.

quality certification
Recognition by an auditing body that an organisation is capable of reliably producing a product or service that meets requirements, based on its quality management systems and conformance to the relevant Australian or international quality standards; such organisations are known as 'certified' or 'registered'.

quality culture
The value and importance an organisation and its employees place on quality; a strong quality culture is one in which employees at all levels, in all areas of the organisation, pay attention to the small details that add up to providing a quality product or service and continually seek to improve their offering.

quality management
See total quality management.

quality standard
A document that provides guidelines, requirements or specifications that can be used to ensure that processes, products and services consistently meet **requirements**.

quality systems
The internal procedures and processes an organisation has in place to formally control its activities to manage and ensure the quality of its products and services.

racial vilification
Illegal behaviour that humiliates, insults, intimidates or offends a person or group of people because of their colour, national or ethnic origin, or race.

rapport
The feeling of being 'in sync' or in harmony with another person; a feeling of comfortable affinity.

redundancy
Termination of employment because the position has been eliminated, usually due to job redesign, outsourcing or restructuring.

re-engineering
Using technology and systematic analytical methods to radically redesign processes and operating procedures from top to bottom to achieve dramatic improvements in productivity; essentially, reorganising around core capabilities; also known as process re-engineering, business process re-engineering and core process redesign.

reflective listening
Briefly stating your understanding of the speaker's feelings and/or meaning; also known as active listening.

relationship capital
The value of an organisation's relationships with its customers, suppliers, outsourcing and financing partners that are built over time and reflected in loyalty to the organisation; measured by, for example, brand value, customer retention rate and customer satisfaction. *See* human capital, intellectual capital and structural capital.

religious vilification
Illegal behaviour that humiliates, insults, intimidates or offends a person or group of people because of their religion.

remuneration
An employee's total reward package including, for example, base pay (or compensation), plus fringe benefits, such as allowances, bonuses, loadings, penalty rates and provision of a motor vehicle.

renewable energy
One hundred per cent 'clean' energy, or power generation, sourced from the sun, wind, waste or water; also known as green electricity and green power.

residual risk
The risk remaining after the original risk (inherent risk) has been treated.

resilience
The (largely learned) ability to recover swiftly from problems and setbacks.

responsibility
The obligation employees have to their managers to do a job that has been assigned.

restructuring
The process of altering the organisational design.

retention
The opposite of attrition. The ability to keep employees; an important measure of organisational culture, employee engagement and morale. Strategies for retention include career management, training and development programs, flexible working, job design and monitoring staff concerns.

retrenchment
Lay-offs caused by lack of work to keep people fully occupied.

risk
In health and safety: the measure of the likelihood and severity of potential illness or injury (psychological or physical) to people or damage to the environment or property resulting from a hazard. In risk management, an adverse or favourable event resulting from an organisation's operations or its operating environment that could advantage or jeopardise the organisation's ability to achieve its goals.

risk analysis
Deciding what could go wrong with (or enhance the outcome of) a plan, project, potential event or strategy; considering the likelihood, or probability, of the event occurring; and examining the consequences of the negative (or positive) event to determine how best to deal with it.

risk appetite
The number and type of risks an organisation is prepared to take in pursuit of its goals; generally articulated in a risk appetite statement.

risk culture
How an organisation and its employees approach risk; a strong risk culture is one in which employees at all levels, in all areas of the organisation, are aware of potential risks and opportunities and their role in controlling or optimising them.

risk log
See risk register.

risk management
Systematically applying policies, practices and procedures to identify, analyse, evaluate, prioritise, treat, monitor and report on both positive and negative risks, or potential events, in order to minimise or optimise them.

risk management framework
The way an organisation designs, implements, monitors, reviews and continually improves its risk management processes.

risk management plan (RMP)
The organisation's intended approach and the resources to be applied to dealing with a risk by enhancing, removing or controlling it before the event (risk management systems) and/or dealing with it should it occur (contingency plans) and, in the case of extreme negative risk events, to ensure the continuity and survival of the organisation; ideally, critical operations and services can continue and should they be disrupted, they are resumed as rapidly as required. The RMP can be applied to a process, product, or project, and part of or all of the organisation.

risk management process
The systematic application of management policies, procedures and practices to communicate, consult, establish the context, identify, analyse, evaluate, treat, monitor and review risk.

risk register
A master document listing identified risks, showing an analysis of the risk severity and possible mitigations (i.e. preventions) for each risk; generally presented in a spreadsheet; also known as risk log and risk and opportunity register.

risk tolerance
The level of residual risk the organisation is willing to bear. *See* risk appetite.

role clarity
Knowing what is expected of you in terms of clear standards of behaviour, performance and productivity.

role conflict
When the various roles a person plays require different and incompatible behaviour, beliefs or attitudes.

role description
A document outlining the value-adding behaviours expected of a job-holder and the key functions, goals, relationships and responsibilities of a position without prescribing how to achieve them; used for more open-ended positions. *See* competency-based job description and job description.

role expectations
The expectations that others hold about a role.

role model
A person whose behaviour and actions others emulate in order to develop those skills and attributes in themselves.

role perception
A person's idea of what their role demands regarding behaviour, attitudes, behaviours, dress, and so on.

roles
The personas that people play in different situations such as colleague, employee, friend, learner, manager, mentor, parent, sibling and student.

run chart
A simple way to graph trends in a process.

S-curve of change
The natural order of growth, prosperity, plateauing and fading that governs living systems.

safety analysis
Examining a task or job to pinpoint its hazards and safety requirements; also known as job safety analysis.

safety audit
An examination of the workplace to identify specific health, safety and welfare hazards present and check the effectiveness of existing controls; also known as hazard identification survey and hazard inspection.

safety culture
The value and importance an organisation and its employees place on safety; a strong safety culture is one in which employees at all levels, in all areas of the organisation, are aware of physical and psychological hazards and consistently follow safe working procedures.

scatter diagram
A way of displaying what happens to one variable when you change another variable, revealing any relationships, or correlations, between those variables.

scenario planning
A technique that helps strategic planners and risk managers envision different ways the future might unfold and plan appropriate responses to each.

self-awareness
The degree to which a person understands their own attitudes, beliefs, feelings, motivations, perceptions of the world and values as the underlying causes of their actions.

self-esteem
A person's feelings of self-respect and self-worth.

self-fulfilling prophecy
The way people's beliefs and paradigms influence the way they perceive the world and others and drive their behaviour; people tend to see what they expect, which reinforces their beliefs and in turn, people tend to respond by living up (or down) to other's expectations; also known as Pygmalion effect.

self-managed teams
Work teams that are empowered to make their own decisions.

self-paced learning
Employees learn by themselves using purpose-designed learning modules or study guides, as and when time permits, either during or after working hours.

self-talk
The often unconscious thoughts or messages people give themselves, which direct their behaviour.

senior management
The level of management in an organisation that falls between middle management and top-level management; also known as executives.

servant leadership
Leadership based on an unselfish and genuine desire to help people achieve their potential.

service economy
An economy based on services such as accounting and finance, aged care, banking, entertainment, home services, hospitality, insurance, law, media, technology and tourism rather than, for example, agriculture, knowledge or manufacturing.

service partners
Internal customers and internal suppliers.

service-profit chain
The roll-on effect of high-quality internal service, raising employee satisfaction, which fuels employee loyalty and productivity, which boosts external service value, which increases customer satisfaction and loyalty.

sexual harassment
Illegal behaviour that includes unwanted or unwelcome sexual advances, comments or conduct of a sexual nature, including verbal and non-verbal behaviour and innuendo, or requests for sexual favours that are embarrassing, humiliating, intimidating or offensive; unrelated to mutual attraction or friendship.

shareholder
A person (natural or corporate) who owns a share (portion) of a company, having 'lent' the company money in return for a share of its profits.

sigma
A statistical measure of variation used to measure defects per million. The greater the sigma number, the fewer the defects. *See* Six Sigma.

situational leadership
Modifying the style of leadership to suit the circumstances.

Six Sigma
3.4 defects per million— virtually error-free.

SMART targets
Objectives that are Specific (which usually means measurable and time-framed), Motivating, Ambitious, Related to the organisation's vision and goals, and Trackable.

sole trader
A person who is the single owner of a business with unlimited liability.

span of control
See span of management.

span of management
The number of people a manager supervises.

staff positions
Employees whose activities are indirectly associated with the production of goods or the provision of services, such as advisory and internal service positions. *See* line positions.

stakeholders
Those people and groups affected by, or who perceive themselves to be affected by, the operations of the organisation; they are considered to be customers/clients, employees, owners, suppliers, the wider society and the closer community; in project management, the people and groups affected by, or who perceive themselves to be affected by, the outcome of a project.

standard operating procedure (SOP)
A document listing the step-by-step method for carrying out a task or procedure, to be followed at all times.

statement of financial position
See balance sheet.

strategic alliance
Collaborating with non-competitor organisations to combine strengths to each produce a better service or product.

strategy
A plan, method or some consistently intended course of action to achieve a desired outcome; how an organisation intends to achieve value for its stakeholders. Strategy is about choice: who to target as customers, what products and services to offer them at what quality, how to deliver those products and services, what financial targets to aim for, how to manage the organisation's human resources and other key assets; decisions like these guide an organisation's operations and differentiate it from its competitors.

stratification chart
A way to graph and analyse data by breaking it down into meaningful categories, helping to isolate a problem.

stress
The pressures, demands and constraints (stressors) people place on themselves and that are placed on them by their environment and by others, resulting in physical or psychological tension; can be positive and energising (eustress) or negative and debilitating (distress).

structural capital
An organisation's competitive intelligence, copyrights, customer files, databases, information systems, processes and so on created over time; measures include how often and how quickly new products and services are offered to the market, the quality of processes and the value of databases. *See* human capital, intellectual capital and relationship capital.

structural discrimination
See systemic discrimination.

structure
A dimension of leadership concern that focuses on the task at hand. *See* consideration.

subculture
The culture of subgroups that form part of a larger group.

subtractive manufacturing
See additive manufacturing.

summary dismissal
See instant dismissal.

suppliers
People and organisations, whether inside or outside the organisation, who provide information, materials and services. *See* external suppliers and internal suppliers.

supply chain
The network of organisations, people, information, resources and technology that contribute to the creation of a product or service, beginning with and including external suppliers and ending with and including external customers; also known as integrated value chain. *See* supply-chain management, trading partnerships and value chain analysis.

supply-chain management
Working with suppliers and customers to create a smooth and efficient supply chain, or integrated value chain, that offers value to all parties.

sustainability
Using natural resources without destroying the ecological balance, enabling their continued use; a subset of corporate social responsibility.

SWOT analysis
A systematic way to identify an organisation's internal Strengths and Weaknesses and external Opportunities and Threats.

synergy
The ability of the whole team to achieve more than its individual members could achieve singly.

systemic discrimination
The result of longstanding direct and indirect discrimination that seems to be the 'natural order of things'. *See* covert discrimination and overt discrimination.

tangible assets
Physical assets such as buildings, equipment and money in the bank.

target
A specific, measurable and trackable performance indicator, or measure of success.

task
The work an individual or a team carries out to achieve its goals and objectives. *See* process (team).

task functions
Actions that move a group towards achieving the job at hand. *See* maintenance functions.

task-readiness level
An employee's ability and willingness to carry out a particular task; used to determine the most appropriate leadership style.

task-readiness approach to leadership
A situational approach to leadership that uses task-readiness levels to determine the most appropriate leadership style.

team building
Assisting a team to clarify its overall team purpose and goals (its task) and agree ways to work better together (its process) to achieve its purpose and goals.

team life cycle
A model that describes the five predictable stages through which teams mature: forming, storming, norming, performing and adjourning.

team maintenance
See maintenance functions.

team purpose
A succinct statement that expresses why a team exists; a team mission statement.

telecommuters
See teleworkers.

telecommuting
Working from home, from a satellite office near home or from a mobile office, such as a vehicle, for all, most or some of the time, linked to the employer's office through information and communications technology; also known as teleworking.

teleworkers
People who work from home, a satellite office near home or a mobile office such as a vehicle.

temporary employees
People employed for a specific number of weeks on a fixed-term contract. *See* casual employees.

termination of employment
A permanent separation from the organisation, usually a result of poor job performance or a serious offence by the employee.

termination of employment, unfair
See unfair dismissal.

termination of employment, unlawful
See unlawful dismissal.

Theory X
A type of leadership style: Theory X leaders believe that employees are lazy and work only for money and therefore need to be managed with coercion and threats of punishment. *See* Theory Y.

Theory Y
A type of leadership style: Theory Y leaders believe that employees want to do their jobs well and seek responsibility and challenge; they therefore have high expectations of them, set challenging targets and coach followers to achieve them. *See* Theory X.

top-level management
The most senior level of management in an organisation, consisting of the chief executive officer or managing director, and the members of the board of directors.

total quality management (TQM)
The culture, mindsets and methods that drive quality in an organisation in order to improve customer satisfaction, performance, productivity and profitability; finding ways to work that are cheaper, easier, faster and more reliable.

trading partnerships
Organisations working with their external customers and suppliers in mutually beneficial relationships.

trait approach to leadership
Examines the personal qualities a leader possesses, such as intelligence, height and self-assurance.

transactional approach to leadership
A way of thinking about leadership that relies on rewards and punishments to elicit good performance and productivity.

transformational leadership
Leadership that takes an organisation in new directions, largely through the leader's personal dynamism and drive.

triple bottom line
A framework for measuring and reporting the value a company adds to (or subtracts from) the economy, the environment and society.

turnover (employee)
See attrition.

unfair dismissal
Dismissing an employee in a manner that is harsh, unjust or unreasonable (e.g. without giving notice about unsatisfactory behaviour, performance or productivity and without giving the employee an opportunity to respond) or not consistent with the Small Business Fair Dismissal Code. *See* constructive dismissal, instant dismissal and unlawful dismissal.

unity of command
A principle that states that each employee should receive instructions from only one person about a task, job or project.

unlawful dismissal
Dismissal for reasons that are discriminatory; for temporary absence from work because of illness, injury, maternity or parental leave or for engaging in a voluntary emergency management activity;

for trade union membership or non-membership; or for filing a complaint or participating in proceedings against an employer. *See* constructive dismissal, instant dismissal and unfair dismissal.

upcycling
Planning beyond the end of a product's life to use its constituent materials in a way that maintains their value, without loss of quality or performance; also known as virtuous cycle and cradle-to-cradle. *See* downcycling and life cycle analysis.

upskilling
Increasing employees' skills to enable them to take on increased responsibility and/or work at a higher level. *See* cross-skilling, job enrichment and multiskilling.

value chain
See supply chain.

value chain analysis
Working with customers to identify and agree on the critical few outcomes that make a difference to them and then examining the organisation's service delivery in this light, step by step, with a view to improving it.

variation
The normal ups and downs in a process; the challenge is to minimise variability to attain reliable product or service quality.

vertical integration
Vertically integrated organisations attempt to secure control of critical suppliers and customers of their products and services. *See* horizontal integration.

virtual meeting
A meeting between remote participants run electronically, such as a webconference, videoconference or teleconference, or a simultaneous text-messaging meeting using the Internet or an organisation's Intranet.

virtual organisation
One in which people work together but are based in different locations, seldom or never meeting face-to-face but using sophisticated communications and information technologies to communicate and collaborate.

virtual teams
Teams made up of members based in different geographical locations.

virtual working
Working at locations different from the rest of one's team and manager and using advanced

communications, collaborative systems and information technologies to facilitate team working.

vision
A statement describing the beliefs, culture and operating philosophy an organisation, team or project aspires to, answering the questions, 'Who are we?' and 'How do we operate?'

well-being
Encouraging employees' physical, mental and social health; also known as wellness.

wiki
Server software that allows users to create and edit contributions as well as the original web page content.

win–lose position
'I win and you lose'; a mindset that characterises aggressive behaviour. *See* lose–lose, lose–win and win–win positions.

win–win position
'I win and you win too': both parties can be satisfied; a mindset that characterises assertive behaviour. *See* lose–lose, lose–win and win–lose positions.

workers' compensation
See workers' rehabilitation and compensation.

workers' rehabilitation and compensation
Insurance for occupational injury designed to cover lost income resulting from an industrial accident or disease, the associated medical expenses and, when necessary, retraining costs; aimed at no-fault compensation and getting people back into the workforce as quickly as possible.

work–life balance
The ability to honour both work and home commitments.

work–life blending
Integrating work and private life, made possible by technology, so that, for example, an employee might take the afternoon off to care for a child or parent or attend a child's school play, and make up the time working at home after hours. The idea is that where you work is fluid and shifting and need not be just from the office or cubicle; also known as 'bleisure' (business and leisure).

workplace agreement
An employment agreement negotiated between an employer and representatives of a group of employees, or an employer directly with a group of employees under Fair Work legislation; also known as collective agreement, industrial agreement and enterprise agreement.

workplace bargaining
Negotiating rules, pay and employment conditions at a workplace, resulting in a workplace agreement; also known as enterprise bargaining.

workplace hub
Independent or company-provided informal, shared workspaces for telecommuters, freelancers and corporate remote workers, often based around 'communities' of workers engaged in similar work, to come together; also known as co-working centre, co-working space.

INDEX